IMPORTANT

✓ W9-BOM-165

HERE IS YOUR REGISTRATION CODE TO ACCESS MCGRAW-HILL PREMIUM CONTENT AND MCGRAW-HILL ONLINE RESOURCES

For key premium online resources you need THIS CODE to gain access. Once the code is entered, you will be able to use the web resources for the length of your course.

Access is provided only if you have purchased a new book.

If the registration code is missing from this book, the registration screen on our website, and within your WebCT or Blackboard course will tell you how to obtain your new code. Your registration code can be used only once to establish access. It is not transferable.

To gain access to these online resources

1. **USE** your web browser to go to: **http://www.mhhe.com/santrockc9**

2. **CLICK** on "First Time User"

3. **ENTER** the Registration Code printed on the tear-off bookmark on the right

4. After you have entered your registration code, click on "Register"

5. **FOLLOW** the instructions to setup your personal UserID and Password

6. **WRITE** your UserID and Password down for future reference. Keep it in a safe place.

If your course is using WebCT or Blackboard, you'll be able to use this code to access the McGraw-Hill content within your instructor's online course.

To gain access to the McGraw-Hill content in your instructor's WebCT or Blackboard course simply log into the course with the user ID and Password provided by your instructor. Enter the registration code exactly as it appears to the right when prompted by the system. You will only need to use this code the first time you click on McGraw-Hill content.

These instructions are specifically for student access. Instructors are not required to register via the above instructions.

The McGraw-Hill Companies

Mc Graw Hill | **Higher Education**

Thank you, and welcome to your McGraw-Hill Online Resources.

13 Digit: 978-0-07-310735-6
10 Digit: 0-07-310735-2 t/a
Santrock
Children, 9/e

9CAP-YVMT-77G7-PDJ9-JVUK

REGISTRATION CODE
REGISTRATION CODE

The McGraw-Hill Companies

Mc Graw Hill | Higher Education

CHILDREN

CHILDREN

Ninth Edition

JOHN W. SANTROCK

University of Texas at Dallas

Boston   Burr Ridge, IL   Dubuque, IA   Madison, WI   New York   San Francisco   St. Louis
Bangkok   Bogotá   Caracas   Kuala Lumpur   Lisbon   London   Madrid   Mexico City
Milan   Montreal   New Delhi   Santiago   Seoul   Singapore   Sydney   Taipei   Toronto

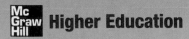

Higher Education

CHILDREN, NINTH EDITION

Published by McGraw-Hill, a business unit of The McGraw-Hill Companies, Inc., 1221
Avenue of the Americas, New York, NY, 10020. Copyright © 2007, 2005, 2003, 2001,
1998 by The McGraw-Hill Companies, Inc. All rights reserved. No part of this publication
may be reproduced or distributed in any form or by any means, or stored in a database
or retrieval system, without the prior written consent of The McGraw-Hill Companies, Inc.,
including, but not limited to, in any network or other electronic storage or transmission,
or broadcast for distance learning.

Some ancillaries, including electronic and print components, may not be available to
customers outside the United States.

This book is printed on acid-free paper.

1 2 3 4 5 6 7 8 9 0 QPD/QPD 0 9 8 7 6 5

ISBN-13: 978-0-07-310730-1
ISBN-10: 0-07-310730-1

Editor in Chief: *Emily Barrosse*
Publisher: *Beth Mejia*
Executive Editor: *Michael J. Sugarman*
Senior Developmental Editor: *Judith Kromm*
Freelance Development Editor: *Marilyn Rothenberger*
Marketing Manager: *Melissa S. Caughlin*
Permissions Editor: *Marty Granahan*
Managing Editor: *Jean Dal Porto*
Project Manager: *Rick Hecker*
Art Director: *Jeanne Schreiber*
Senior Designer: *Kim Menning*
Interior Design: *Caroline McGowan*
Cover Design: *Linda Robertson*
Media Producer: *Stephanie George*
Art Manager: *Robin Mouat*
Illustrators: *Rennie Evans; John* and *Judy Waller*
Senior Photo Research Coordinator: *Alexandra Ambrose*
Cover Credit: © *John Henley Photography/CORBIS*
Media Project Manager: *Kate Boylan*
Production Supervisor: *Janean A. Utley*
Senior Supplement Producer: *Louis Swaim*
Composition: *9.5/12 Meridian, by Cenveo*
Printing: *45 # Pub Matte Recycle, Quebecor World Dubuque*

Credits: The credits section for this book begins on page C-1 and is considered
an extension of the copyright page.

Library of Congress Cataloging-in-Publication Data

Santrock, John W.
    Children / John W. Santrock.— 9th ed.
      p. cm.
    Includes bibliographical references and indexes.
    ISBN-13: 978-0-07-310730-1 (softcover : alk. paper)
    ISBN-10: 0-07-310730-1 (softcover : alk. paper)
    1. Child development. 2. Adolescence. I. Title.
  HQ767.9.S268 2007
  305.23—dc22

2005054321

The Internet addresses listed in the text were accurate at the time of publication. The inclusion of
a Web site does not indicate an endorsement by the authors of McGraw-Hill, and McGraw-Hill does not
guarantee the accuracy of the information presented at these sites.

wwww.mhhe.com

With special appreciation to my grandchildren,
Jordan and Alex

ABOUT THE AUTHOR

JOHN W. SANTROCK

received his Ph.D. from the University of Minnesota in 1973. He taught at the University of Charleston and the University of Georgia before joining the psychology department at the University of Texas at Dallas. He has been a member of the editorial boards of *Developmental Psychology* and *Child Development*. His research on father custody is widely cited and used in expert witness testimony to promote flexibility and alternative considerations in custody disputes. John has also authored these exceptional McGraw-Hill texts: *Child Development*, Eleventh Edition; *Adolescence*, Eleventh Edition; *Life-Span Development*, Tenth Edition; *Psychology*, Seventh Edition; *A Topical Approach to Life-Span Development*, Third Edition; *Human Adjustment* and *Educational Psychology*, Second Edition.

For many years, John was involved in tennis as a player, teaching professional, and coach of professional tennis players. He has been married for more than 35 years to his wife, Mary Jo, who is a realtor. He has two daughters—Tracy, who is studying to become a financial planner at Duke University, and Jennifer who is a medical sales specialist at Medtronic. He has one granddaughter, Jordan, age 14, and one grandson, Alex, age 1. Tracy recently completed the New York Marathon, and Jennifer was in the top 100 ranked players on the Women's Professional Tennis Tour. In the last decade, John also has spent time painting expressionist art.

John Santrock, teaching an undergraduate course at the University of Texas at Dallas.

BRIEF CONTENTS

CONTENTS

Preface xix

Section 1
THE NATURE OF CHILDREN'S DEVELOPMENT 2

Section 2

BEGINNINGS 76

Chapter 3
BIOLOGICAL BEGINNINGS 78

Section 4
EARLY CHILDHOOD 270

Chapter 11

SOCIOEMOTIONAL DEVELOPMENT IN EARLY CHILDHOOD 336

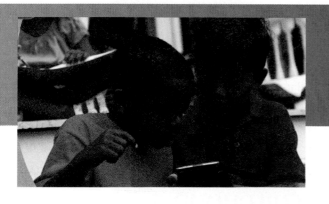

Section 5

MIDDLE AND LATE CHILDHOOD 378

Chapter 12

PHYSICAL DEVELOPMENT IN MIDDLE AND LATE CHILDHOOD 380

Chapter 13

COGNITIVE DEVELOPMENT IN MIDDLE AND LATE CHILDHOOD 412

Chapter 14

SOCIOEMOTIONAL DEVELOPMENT IN MIDDLE AND LATE CHILDHOOD 456

Section 6

ADOLESCENCE 494

Chapter 17

SOCIOEMOTIONAL DEVELOPMENT IN ADOLESCENCE 568

Children have a very special place in every society because they are every society's future. The study of development gives those who care for children many tools for improving the lives of children throughout the world and, therefore, contributing to a better future for humankind. This is an ambitious goal, but not an impossible one. As research in child development has progressed and the information applied to family, educational, health, child care, and a variety of other contexts, it has become clear that developmentalists can make a difference in children's lives.

In a broad sense, this text seeks to convey a clear understanding of what we know about child development, how we arrived at this level of understanding, and how research in child development can be applied in the various settings in which children develop. To achieve this goal, I have continued to emphasize and update *Children* in three main areas:

- Research and content
- Applications
- Accessibility and interest

First, I will generally describe the thrust of the changes in the ninth edition of *Children*. Then I will specify the key changes in each chapter.

RESEARCH AND CONTENT

Above all, a text on child development must include a solid research foundation. This edition of *Children* presents the latest, most contemporary research. *Children,* ninth edition, has more than 1,600 citations from 2000 through 2006, making it truly a twenty-first-century rendition of the field of child development.

Coverage has been updated and expanded throughout the book. Notably, I have incorporated information from the sixth edition of the *Handbook of Child Psychology* (Damon & Lerner, 2006). In addition, although this text has always emphasized diversity and culture, in this edition this coverage of these important contexts of development has been significantly increased and updated. For example, a new section on socioeconomic status has been added in chapter 1, chapter 11 includes a new section on parenting styles and ethnicity, and chapter 17 discusses new research on the positive aspects of ethnic identity (Bracy, Bamaca, & Umana-Taylor, 2004; Umana-Taylor, 2004). Additional content changes in each chapter will be highlighted shortly.

APPLICATIONS

It is important not only to present the scientific foundation of child development to students, but also to demonstrate that research has real-world applications, to include many applied examples of concepts, and to give students a sense that the field of child development has personal meaning for them. For example, chapter 4 includes new recommendations by the U.S. Food and Drug Administration (2004) regarding the types and amount of fish to avoid during pregnancy, and chapter 10 has a new discussion of what caregivers can do to ensure children's readiness for school (Ramey & Ramey, 2004).

Applications of research in child development to health, parenting, and education receive special attention throughout the text. Among these applications are:

- *Caring for Children* interludes in every chapter that outline important ways to improve the lives of children.
- Strategies for effectively interacting with children to enhance their development. For example, chapter 14 includes a number of strategies for interacting with ethnically diverse children, and chapter 17 discusses a number of parenting strategies for interacting effectively with adolescents.
- Every chapter also has at least one *Careers in Child Development* insert that profiles an individual whose career relates to the chapter's content. For example, chapter 1 has two new *Careers* inserts, one on Valerie Pang, a college professor, and one on Katherine Duchen Smith, a pediatric nurse. Most of the *Careers* inserts include a photograph of the person at work. In addition, the section titled "What Are the Main Careers in Child Development?" in chapter 1 describes a number of careers in the education/research, clinical/counseling, medical/nursing/physical, and family/relationship categories. Numerous Web links provide students with opportunities to read about these careers in depth.
- At the end of each chapter, two features—*Making a Difference* and *Children Resources*—provide valuable information about ways to improve children's lives.
- On the book's website, students can hone their decision-making skills by completing exercises related to children's health and well-being, parenting, and education.

ACCESSIBILITY AND INTEREST

Many students today juggle numerous responsibilities in addition to their coursework. To help them make the most of their study time, I have made this book as accessible as possible without watering down the content. The writing, organization, and learning system of *Children* will engage students and provide a clear foundation in child development.

Writing and Organization

For each new edition of *Children*, every sentence, every paragraph, and every section of every chapter is carefully considered and, if appropriate, moved, streamlined, expanded, or eliminated in order to integrate new research and to make the book more accessible. Positive feedback on previous editions from instructors and students has affirmed the value of this effort.

The Learning System

I strongly believe that students not only should be challenged to study hard and think more deeply and productively about child development, but also should be provided with an effective way to learn the content. Instructors and students continue to provide extremely positive feedback about the book's learning system and student-friendly presentation.

Students often struggle to find the main ideas in their courses, especially in child development, which includes so much material. This book's learning system centers on learning goals that, together with the main text headings, keep the key ideas in front of the reader from the beginning to the end of the chapter. Each chapter has no more than five main headings and corresponding learning goals, which are presented side-by-side in the chapter-opening spread. At the end of each main section of a chapter, the learning goal is repeated in a feature called "Review and Reflect," which prompts students to review the key topics in the section and poses a question to encourage them to think critically about what they have read. At the end of the chapter, under the heading, "Reach Your Learning Goals," the learning goals guide students through the bulleted chapter review.

In addition to the verbal tools just described, visual organizers, or maps, that link up with the learning goals are presented at the beginning of each major section in the chapter. At the end of each chapter, the section maps are assembled into a complete map of the chapter that provides a visual review guide. The complete learning system, including many additional features not mentioned here, is illustrated in a section titled "To the Student," which follows this Preface on p. xxxi.

CHAPTER-BY-CHAPTER CHANGES

I made a number of changes in all 17 chapters of *Children*, ninth edition. Highlights of these changes follow.

Chapter 1
INTRODUCTION

New discussion of research on language delay in maltreated children (Eigsti & Cicchetti, 2004).

New section on socioeconomic status (SES) in the discussion of culture, including discussion of poverty and children's development.

Updated statistics on children living in low-income families (Federal Register, 2004; National Center for Children in Poverty, 2004).

Two new Careers in Child Development inserts—one on Valerie Pang, a college professor, and one on Katherine Duchen Smith, a pediatric nurse.

Chapter 2
THE SCIENCE OF CHILD DEVELOPMENT

Extensively revised and updated Caring for Children interlude on family and school connections.

Chapter 3
BIOLOGICAL BEGINNINGS

Extensive rewriting and reorganization of chapter, including a number of new introductions to topics and transitions between topics for improved clarity and understanding.

Updating and revision of genetic discussions based on input from leading experts Gilbert Gottlieb and David Moore.

Update on Human Genome Project with revised new estimate of the number of human genes now down to 20,000 to 25,000 (International Human Genome Sequencing Consortium, 2004).

New discussion of pregnancy sickness as an adaptation in evolution (Schmitt & Pilcher, 2004).

Coverage of recent twin study on conduct problems (Scourfield & others, 2004).

Chapter 4
PRENATAL DEVELOPMENT

New chapter opening story about "Mr. Littles."

Description of recent recommendations by the U.S. Food and Drug Administration (2004) regarding the type and amount of fish to avoid during pregnancy.

Coverage of recent study on fetal death and maternal age (Canterino & others, 2004).

Discussion of recent study linking alcohol consumption during the week of conception to early pregnancy loss (Henriksen & others, 2004).

Coverage of recent study linking binge drinking during pregnancy to lower IQ and greater incidence of acting out behavior at age seven (Bailey & others, 2004).

Discussion of longitudinal study on maternal cigarette smoking during pregnancy and later cigarette smoking by adolescent offspring (Porath & Fried, 2005).

Description of recent research review on marijuana use by pregnant women and developmental outcomes in their offspring (Kalant, 2004).

Recent analysis of trends in smoking during pregnancy in the United States (Centers for Disease Control and Prevention, 2004).

Coverage of recent study on multivitamin use prior to conception and incidence of preterm delivery (Vahratian & others, 2004).

Description of recent study on a link between maternal use of folic acid and iron and a lower risk of Down syndrome in offspring (Czeizel & Puho, 2005).

Inclusion of recent research on maternal obesity and central nervous system birth defects in offspring (Anderson & others, 2005).

Chapter 5
BIRTH

Expanded coverage of reasons for the increase in Cesarean delivery and recent data on trends in Cesarean delivery (Coleman & others, 2005; Martin & others, 2005; Sarsam, Elliott, & Lam, 2005).

Expanded information about preterm births in the United States, including factors that are likely responsible for their substantial increase in recent years; new Figure 5.2 showing a 27 percent increase since 1982 (National Center for Health Statistics, 2004; Petrini, 2004).

New coverage of the recently constructed Neonatal Intensive Care Unit Network Neurobehavioral Scale (NNBS) (Lester, Tronick, & Brazelton, 2004).

Updated discussion of Tiffany Field's research on massage therapy with preterm infants (Field, Hernandez-Reif, & Freedman, 2004).

Coverage of recent study on death rates in small for date infants (Regev & others, 2003).

Updated statistics on percentage of low birth weight infants in the United States (National Center for Health Statistics, 2004).

Discussion of recent study on the reading and academic achievement of low birth weight individuals at age 17 (Breslau, Paneth, & Lucia, 2004).

Coverage of recent study documenting the positive effects of exercise on maternal well-being in the postpartum period (Blum, Beaudoin, & Caton-Lemos, 2005).

Chapter 6
PHYSICAL DEVELOPMENT IN INFANCY

Revision of material on motor and perceptual development based on input from leading expert, Rachel Keen (2005a).

New discussion of "shaken baby syndrome" (Minns & Busuttil, 2004; Newton & Vandeven, 2005).

Inclusion of recent study showing that infants reach for their toys with their feet weeks before using their hands, indicating that early leg movements can be precisely controlled and that early motor behaviors don't always follow a cephalocaudal pattern (Galloway & Thelen, 2004).

Revised and updated interpretation of variations in developmental motor milestones in infancy, including description of the increasing number of babies who do not crawl (likely linked to parents increasingly placing the babies on their backs when sleeping to reduce the risk of SIDS) (Adolph & Berger, 2005, 2006).

Description of recent research study showing the importance of experience in reaching and grasping (Needham, Barrett, & Peterman, 2002), including new figure 6.16.

Description of recent study involving the Hawaii Health Start program and its effect on maternal alcohol use, partner abuse, and child abuse (Duggan & others, 2004).

Inclusion of recent review of 61 studies on the link between breast feeding and lower incidence of obesity in childhood and adulthood (Owen & others, 2005).

New description of applications of Karen Adolph's research involving little transfer between crawling and walking (Keen, 2005a).

Expanded and updated coverage of reaching and grasping in the first two years of life (Keen, 2005a; Oztop, Bradley, & Arbib, 2004).

New coverage of the importance of exercising fine motor skills (Keen, 2005a).

Expanded and updated description of techniques used to study infant perception that now includes the orienting response and tracking, and high-amplitude sucking (Keen, 2005a; Menn & Stoel-Gammon, 2005).

Inclusion of information about whether experience is necessary for the vision of infants to develop normally (Sugita, 2004).

Discussion of recent study on the ability of human fetuses to recognize their mother's own voice (Kisilevsky & others, 2003).

Chapter 7
COGNITIVE DEVELOPMENT IN INFANCY

New section on concept formation and categorization (Mandler, 2004).

New coverage of attention, including recent research on distractibilty in infants and links between attention and memory in infancy (Courage, Howe, & Squires, 2004; Ruff & Capozzoli, 2003), and discussion of a recent study on sustained attention in 4-month-old infants (Shaddy & Colombo, 2004).

Coverage of comprehensive longitudinal study on links between important dimensions of poverty (timing, chronic nature) and children's cognitive development (NICHD Early Child Care Research Network, 2005).

Editing and revision of infant language discussion based on input by leading experts Jean Berko Gleason and John Bonvillian.

Chapter 8
SOCIOEMOTIONAL DEVELOPMENT IN INFANCY

Revised and updated discussion of what emotion is (Campos, 2004; Saarni & others, 2006).

Expanded and updated description of the distinction between primary and self-conscious emotions.

New material on strategies for calming crying infants, including the effectiveness of swaddling (Ohgi & others, 2004).

Coverage of recent study on links between maternal separation anxiety and maternal characteristics (Hsu, 2004).

Inclusion of the contemporary view of the developmentally evolving nature of temperament (Thompson & Goodvin, 2005).

Expanded and updated discussion of temperament, including Mary Rothbart's (2004) recent view of the main dimensions of temperament.

Description of recent research on goodness of fit in temperament involving a combination of high infant fearlessness and harsh parenting, as well as the type of temperament most likely to reduce the effects of negative environments (Rothbart & Bates, 2006; Shaw & others, 2003).

Expanded and updated description of self-understanding in infancy (Thompson, 2006).

Expanded coverage of the nature of attachment and how the infant's and young child's social cognitive advances contribute to attachment (Thompson, 2006).

Coverage of recent research on child care for children from low-income families (Votruba-Drzal & others, 2004).

Description of the outcomes of early attachment security and later outcomes in childhood and adolescence by Alan Sroufe and his colleagues (2005) and updated conclusions about the importance of early secure attachment *and* later positive social experiences in predicting development (Thompson, 2006).

Updated coverage of the NICHD Early Child Care Research Network Study, including recent findings on amount of time spent in child care and child outcomes (Vandell, 2004).

New coverage of links between long hours spent in center-based care and negative outcomes for children with certain types of temperament (Crockenberg & Leerkes, 2005).

New book recommendation: *The Happiest Baby on the Block* by Harvey Kopp (2002).

Chapter 9
PHYSICAL DEVELOPMENT IN EARLY CHILDHOOD

Coverage of recent fMRI study showing low levels of myelination in young Children with developmental delays in cognitive and motor development (Pujol & others, 2004).

Expanded emphasis on the importance of the maturation of the prefrontal cortex in cognitive and socioemotional development (Espy & others, 2004; Levesque & others, 2004).

Discussion of recent research review on the motor skills, intelligence, and achievement of children with short stature (Wheeler & others, 2004).

Description of recent study on the activity levels of 3- to 5-year-old children (Pate & others, 2004).

Discussion of recent study that compared childhood obesity rates in 34 countries (Janssen & others, 2005).

Coverage of longitudinal study on malnutrition at age 3 and behavioral problems at ages 8, 11, and 17 (Liu & others, 2004).

Discussion of recent research studies linking participating in the WIC program with positive nutritional outcomes in young children from low-income families (Melgar-Quinonez & Kaiser, 2004; Siega-Riz & others, 2004).

New section on ethnicity and children's health, including recent research (Andrulis, 2005; Malat, Oh, & Hamilton, 2005; Shi & Stevens, 2005).

Chapter 10
COGNITIVE DEVELOPMENT IN EARLY CHILDHOOD

Discussion of recent study on how children's early experiences at home can influence their attention and memory later in childhood (NICHD Early Child Care Research Network, 2005).

New coverage of the limitations of young children's theory of mind and comparison with advances in middle and late childhood (Wellman, 2004).

New discussion of how the toddler, who is relatively stimulus-driven, changes into a child who is more flexible and goal-directed in solving problems in early childhood (Zelazo & others, 2003).

Description of recent research review on factors linked to children's suggestibility (Bruck & Melnyk, 2004; Clarke-Stewart, Malloy, & Allhusen, 2004; Crossman, Scullin, & Melnyk, 2004) and coverage of a recent study showing that older children are more likely to reject the occurrence of false events than younger children (Ghetti & Alexander, 2004).

Description of recent data on the positive outcomes of the Perry Preschool program at age 40 (High/Scope Resource, 2005).

Coverage of Ramey and Ramey's (1999, 2004) recent analysis of research on what caregivers need to do to ensure children's school readiness.

Description of recent study on the role of developmental changes and socioeconomic status in children's ability to focus their attention and resist interfering demands (Mezzacappa, 2004).

Coverage of recent study showing that older children are more likely to reject the occurrence of false events than younger children (Ghetti & Alexander, 2004).

Discussion of longitudinal study linking language skills in kindergarten with reading success in the first and second grades (Schatttschneider & others, 2004).

Description of number of states that now have learning standards for young children and what dimensions of children's development may be slighted in these standards (Jacobson, 2004; Kagan & Scott-Little, 2004).

Coverage of current consideration by the U.S. Congress of infusing Project Head Start with a stronger academic focus and commentary by early childhood experts about some concerns with this academic emphasis (Stipek, 2004).

Chapter 11
SOCIOEMOTIONAL DEVELOPMENT IN EARLY CHILDHOOD

New section on parenting styles and ethnicity, including Ruth Chao's recent research on Asian American parenting styles.

New discussion of effects of video game playing on children's development and recent conclusions about media violence and children's development (Anderson & others, 2003; Van Mierlo & Van den Bulck, 2004).

Revised organization of emotional development, including new section on emotion and peer relations.

Coverage of recent study showing a link between secure attachment and infancy and adaptive parenting and promotion of the child's conscience in early childhood (Kochanska & others, 2004).

Description of recent review of the use of nonabusive physical punishment by parents in African American families and child outcomes (Horn, Joseph, & Cheng, 2004).

Discussion of recent national U.S. study of the percentage of parents with preschool children who spank and yell at them frequently (Regalado & others, 2004).

Coverage of longitudinal study showing a link between spanking in infancy and later behavioral problems (Slade & Wissow, 2004).

Much expanded coverage of child maltreatment, including more in-depth discussion of types of abuse, recent research, and an effective prevention (Cicchetti & Toth, 2005, 2006; Cicchetti, Toth, & Rogosch, 2005). Inclusion of recent material on sibling relations (Bank, Burraston, & Snyder, 2004; Brody, 2004).

Discussion of recent research on the importance of secure attachment in divorced children's lives (Brockmeyer, Treboux, & Crowell, 2005).

New description of developmental changes in peer relations during early childhood based on a recent review (Rubin, Bukowski, & Parker, 2006).

Expanded and updated coverage of how television is linked to school achievement based on a recent research review (Comstock & Scharrer, 2006).

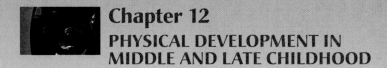

Chapter 12
PHYSICAL DEVELOPMENT IN MIDDLE AND LATE CHILDHOOD

Much expanded and updated discussion of nutrition, obesity, and exercise (Botero & Wolfsdorf, 2005; Fitzgibbon & others, 2005).

Expanded and updated research discussion of links between low activity levels and TV viewing in children (Fox, 2004; Hancox, Milne, & Poulton, 2004).

Discussion of recent study on amount of time in physical education in the first grade and the weight of girls (Datar & Sturm, 2004).

Description of recent study on number of hours spent in sports by 9-year-old boys and links to physical fitness and fat mass (Ara & others, 2004).

Inclusion of recent research on a link between obesity and bullying behavior (Janssen & others, 2004).

Coverage of recent educational intervention that lowered the consumption of carbonated drinks and was related to a lower incidence of being overweight (James & others, 2004).

Discussion of recent intervention study involving diet and exercise on the cardiovascular functioning of children (Woo & others, 2004).

Inclusion of recent study on high blood pressure in children from different ethnic groups (Sorof & others, 2004).

Research update and expanded coverage of the Bogalusa Heart Study that reveals links between childhood risk factors and cardiovascular disease in adulthood (Berensen & others, 2005; Lee & others, 2005; Freedman & others, 2005).

Description of recent research review on risk factors for the development of asthma in children (King, Mannino, & Holguin, 2004).

Updated information about the percentage of students who receive special education services for a range of disabilities (Figure 12.6).

New sections on the identification of learning disabilities and causes and intervention strategies with children who have a learning disability (Berninger, 2006; Francis & others, 2005; Litt & others, 2005).

Expanded and updated coverage of the autism spectrum disorders, including new key term definitions for autism spectrum disorders and autistic disorder, and discussion of brain functioning and heredity (Baron-Cohen, 2004; Muhle, Trentacoste, & Rapin, 2004).

Revised and updated discussion of how stimulants work in the treatment of ADHD (Reeves & Schweitzer, 2004).

New description of the 2004 reauthorization of IDEA and its link with No Child Left Behind legislation (Hallahan & Kauffman, 2006).

New discussion of James Kauffman and his colleagues' (Kauffman & Hallahan, 2005; Kauffman, McGee, & Brigham, 2004) views that in some cases inclusion has become too extreme and that too often children with disabilities are not challenged to become all they can be.

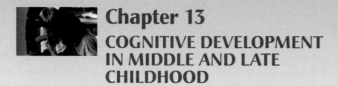

Chapter 13
COGNITIVE DEVELOPMENT IN MIDDLE AND LATE CHILDHOOD

New section on the fuzzy trace theory of memory (Reyna, 2004).

Expanded coverage of expertise, including the role of heredity and practice.

Revised and updated coverage of critical thinking (Winn, 2004).

Revision of section on reconstructive memories and added definitions of schema theory and schemas as key terms.

Updated research on creativity, including brainstorming versus working alone (Rickards & deCock, 2003; Runco, 2004).

New description of teaching strategies in guiding children's scientific thinking (Bransford & Donovan, 2005; Lehrer & Schauble, 2006).

New coverage of Pressley and his colleagues' observations of how extensively and intensely teachers in elementary and secondary school classrooms use strategy instruction (Pressley & Hilden, 2006; Pressley & others, 2001, 2003, 2004).

New Caring of Children interlude, Strategies for Improving the Education of Children Who Are Gifted (Davidson & Davidson, 2004; Winner, 2006).

New discussion of Phyllis Blumenfeld and her colleagues (2006) view of how to incorporate intrinsic motivation into classrooms.

Inclusion of recent study linking mastery motivation to higher math and reading grades in elementary school students (Broussard, 2004).

Updated and expanded coverage of changes in vocabulary and grammar (Berko Gleason, 2005).

New section on metalinguistic awareness (Berko Gleason, 2005; Ely, 2005).

New coverage of the importance of vocabulary in reading comprehension (Berninger, 2006; Snow & Kang, 2006).

Updated and expanded discussion of bilingual education (Hakuta, 2005; Snow & Kang, 2006).

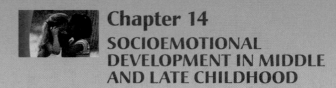

Chapter 14
SOCIOEMOTIONAL DEVELOPMENT IN MIDDLE AND LATE CHILDHOOD

New chapter opening story about children's perception of what world on a make-believe planet might be like.

Revision and improved flow of material on self-esteem.

Coverage of recent concern that too many children grow up receiving empty praise, which can harm their school achievement (Graham, 2005; Stipek, 2005).

New overview of main changes in emotional development during middle and late childhood (Thompson & Goodvin, 2005).

Discussion of recent research on Gilligan's care perspective (Eisenberg & Morris, 2004; Wark & Krebs, in press).

New section on the moral exemplar approach, including recent research by Lawrence Walker and his colleagues (Walker, 2002; Matsuba & Walker, 2004; Walker & Henning, 2004).

Updated coverage of gender differences in the brain (Luders & others, 2004).

Updated information about gender differences in visual-spatial skills (Blakemore, Berenbaum, & Liben, 2005; Ruble, Martin, & Berenbaum, 2006).

Updated and expanded discussion of gender differences in aggression, emotion, and self-regulation (Ruble, Martin, & Berenbaum, 2006).

Criticism of Tannen's ideas on gender differences in communication (Edwards & Hamilton, 2004), including recent research documenting more similarities than differences in men and women in their talk about relationship problems (MacGeorge & others, 2004) and a meta-analytic review of research documenting the importance of context in gender differences (Leaper & Smith, 2004).

Updated coverage of gender similarities based on a recent meta-analysis by Janet Shibley Hyde (2005, in press).

Recent research on gender-role classification and academic self-efficacy (Choi, 2004).

Updated coverage of stepfamily problems and strategies for coping in a stepfamily (O'Neil & Brown, 2005).

New discussion of the recent NICHD Early Childcare Research Care Network Study (2004) of five types of before- and after-school care and other recent research on self-care/latchkey children (Coley, Morris, & Hernandez, 2004).

New coverage of custody issues involving gay and lesbian parents (Peplau & Beals, 2004).

New discussion of recent longitudinal research on the outcomes of not having a friend (Wentzel, Barry, & Caldwell, 2004).

New main section on developmental changes in peer relations (Rubin, Bukowski, & Parker, 2006).

New material on the reasons peer rejected aggressive boys have problems in social functioning and may engage in antisocial behavior over time (Coie, 2004).

Discussion of a recent successful intervention with peer rejected children (DeRosier & Marcus, 2005).

Expanded and updated coverage of research on bullying and recommendations for teachers and parents in regard to reducing bullying (Fekkes, Pijpers, & Verlove-Vanhorick, 2004; Limber, 2004).

Significantly revised section on accountability in education with new discussion of the No Child Left Behind legislation (Goldberg, 2005; Lewis, 2005).

Chapter 15
PHYSICAL DEVELOPMENT IN ADOLESCENCE

New section on developmental changes in the brain during adolescence (Dahl, 2004; Spear, 2004; Steinberg, 2004, 2006).

New coverage of Peter Benson's (2004) recent views on what is needed to improve U.S. social policy regarding adolescents.

Discussion of recent research that found a link between watching sex on television and sexual activity by adolescents (Collins & others, 2004).

Updated figures for the continued decline in adolescent pregnancy rates (Centers for Disease Control and Prevention, 2003).

Updated coverage of AIDS in Sub-Saharan Africa (Singh & others, 2004).

New section on risk factors, youth assets, and sexual problems, including discussion of a recent study on the sexual debuts of early maturing girls from different ethnic groups (Cavanaugh, 2004), coverage of recent study on the psychosocial risk factors related to initiating sexual intercourse in early adolescence (Santelli & others, 2004b), and discussion of recent study on youth assets that are associated with not having had sexual intercourse at the age of 15 (Vesely & others, 2004b).

Expanded and updated section on same-sex attraction in adolescence (Diamond, 2004).

Description of recent longitudinal study on changes in the initiation of sexual intercourse and contraceptive use in U.S. 15- to 17-year-olds from 1991 to 2001 (Santelli & others, 2004a).

Updated description of very recent trends in adolescent drug use (Johnston & others, 2005).

New discussion of the recent increase in the use of painkillers by adolescents (Partnership for a Drug Free America, 2005; Sung & others, 2005).

Coverage of recent study indicating a relation between parental control and monitoring and lower drug use by adolescents (Fletcher, Steinberg, & Williams-Wheeler, 2004).

New section on risk-taking behavior (Dahl, 2004; Masten, 2004; Steinberg, 2004).

Substantial updating and revision of material on obesity in adolescence, including a recent research review on what type of intervention strategy is most likely to help overweight adolescents lose weight (Fowler-Brown & Kahwati, 2004).

Updated coverage of adolescents' use of health services (Cohall & others, 2004).

Discussion of recent study indicating a link between early maturation in girls and mental disorders in early adulthood (Graber & others, 2004).

Chapter 16
COGNITIVE DEVELOPMENT IN ADOLESCENCE

New chapter opening Images of Children that focuses on the variations in the cultural adaptation of Asian American children and immigrants.

New section on executive functioning in adolescence, including much expanded and updated discussion of decision making in adolescence (Klaczynski, 2005, in press; Kuhn, 2005, in press; Kuhn & Franklin, 2006).

Expanded coverage of adolescents living in low-income contexts and career development (Chaves & others, 2004).

Expanded and updated information about service learning and its benefits to adolescents (Benson & others, 2006; Metz & Youniss, 2005).

Updated and expanded discussion of religion and adolescent development, including recent research (Kerestes, Youniss, & Metz, 2004; King & Benson, 2005; Ozer, Scarlett, & Bucher, 2006).

Coverage of recent research on adolescents' perceptions of the most important values they can possess (Steen, Kachorek, & Peterson, 2004).

New discussion of gender differences in school dropout rates and revised estimates of the dropout rate for Native American youth.

Description of recent review of research on effective school dropout programs (Lehr & others, 2003).

Updated and expanded coverage of the "I Have a Dream Program" and movement of its discussion to be the topic of the Caring for Children interlude ("I Have a Dream" Foundation, 2005).

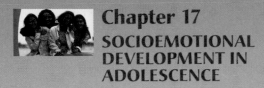

Chapter 17
SOCIOEMOTIONAL DEVELOPMENT IN ADOLESCENCE

Coverage of recent research on a link between ethnic identity and positive outcomes in adolescence (Bracy, Bamaca, & Umana-Taylor, 2004; Fuligni, Witkow, & Garcia, 2005; Umana-Taylor, 2004).

Discussion of recent research on the role of mothers and friends in identity development (Reis & Youniss, 2004).

Expanded and updated coverage of the sequence of relationships in sexual minority youth (Savin-Williams & Diamond, 2004).

New discussion of gender and friendship in adolescence (Ruble, Bukowski, & Berenbaum, 2006).

Description of recent research dating and social anxiety in adolescence (La Greca & Harrison, 2005).

Description of recent research on the role of mixed-gender peer groups in romantic relationships (Connolly & others, 2004).

Coverage of recent research on romantic relationships and adjustment during adolescence (Furman, Ho, & Low, 2005).

Description of the varied cultural backgrounds of immigrant families with adolescents and their family obligations (Parke & Buriel, 2006).

New discussion of the Federal Drug Administration's (2004) recent review of a link between antidepressant use and an increase in suicidal thoughts in adolescents.

Description of recent study indicating an association between being overly self-critical and having a sense of hopelessness with increased suicidal behavior (Cox, Enns, & Clara, 2004).

Coverage of recent study linking illegal drug use by adolescents with an increase in suicidal ideation and attempts (Hallfors & others, 2004).

Research on developmental aspects of suicide ideation in adolescence (Rueter & Kwon, 2005).

Discussion of recent study linking father absence and incarceration of youth (Harper & McLanahan, 2004).

Description of recent research on peers and delinquency (Heinze, Toro, & Urberg, 2004).

ACKNOWLEDGMENTS

I very much appreciate the support and guidance provided to me by many people at McGraw-Hill. Mike Sugarman, Executive Editor, has brought a wealth of publishing knowledge and vision to bear on improving my texts. Judith Kromm, Senior Developmental Editor, has done a superb job of organizing and monitoring the many tasks necessary to move this book through the editorial and production process. Kate Russillo, Editorial Coordinator, skillfully coordinated the reviews and juggled many editorial duties related to the book's develop-

ment. Melissa Caughlin, Marketing Manager, has contributed in numerous positive ways to this book. Jeanne Schreiber provided a beautiful design. Bea Sussman was excellent in her first assignment as my developmental editor, as was Pat Steele as the book's copy editor.

I would like to welcome home two individuals who played important roles in my books in the past and once again are providing valuable support for my books. Marilyn Rothenberger did a terrific job in coordinating the book's production and Marcie Melia is a superb field publisher.

I also want to thank my wife, Mary Jo, our children, Tracy and Jennifer, and our grandchildren, Jordan and Alex, for their wonderful contributions to my life and for helping me to better understand the marvels and mysteries of children's development.

REVIEWERS

I owe a great deal of thanks to the instructors who teach child development and who have provided feedback about the book. Many of the changes in *Children*, ninth edition, are based on their input. For their help and encouragement, I thank these individuals:

NINTH EDITION REVIEWERS

Bonnie Wright, *Gardner Webb University*
Teion Wells, *Florida State University–Tallahassee*
Naomi Wagner, *San Jose State University*
Pamela Schuetze-Pizarro, *Buffalo State College*
Beverly Edmondson, *Buena Vista University*
Sara Lawrence, *California State University–Northridge*
Linda Anderson, *Northwestern Michigan College*
Lynne Rompelman, *Concordia University–Wisconsin*
Art Gonchar, *University of La Verne*
Anita Thomas, *Northeastern Illinois University*

REVIEWERS OF PREVIOUS EDITIONS

I also remain indebted to the individuals who reviewed previous editions and whose recommendations have been carried forward into the present edition.

John A. Addleman, *Messiah College*
Harry H. Avis, *Sierra College*
Diana Baumrind, *University of California–Berkeley*
Lori A. Beasley, *University of Central Oklahoma*
Patricia J. Bence, *Tompkins Cortland Community College*
Michael Bergmire, *Jefferson College*
Belinda Blevins-Knabe, *University of Arkansas–Little Rock*
Ruth Brinkman, *St. Louis Community College, Florissant Valley*
Eileen Donahue Brittain, *City College of Harry S Truman*
Urie Bronfenbrenner, *Cornell University*
Phyllis Bronstein, *University of Vermont*

Dan W. Brunworth, *Kishwaukee College*
Carole Burke-Braxton, *Austin Community College*
Alison S. Carson, *Hofstra University*
Rosalind Charlesworth, *Weber State University*
Nancy Coghill, *University of Southwest Louisiana*
Malinda Jo Colwell, *Texas Tech University*
Jennifer Cousins, *University of Houston*
Dixie R. Crase, *Memphis State University*
Kathleen Crowley-Long, *The College of Saint Rose*
Florence Denmark, *Pace University*
Sheridan DeWolf, *Grossmont Community College*
Swen H. Digranes, *Northeastern State University*
Ruth H. Doyle, N.C.C., L.P.C., *Casper College*
Laura Duvall, *Heartland Community College*
Celina V. Echols, *Southeastern Louisiana State University*
Beverly Edmonson, *Buena Vista University*
Timothy P. Eicher, *Dixie Community College*
Sarah Erikson, *University of New Mexico*
Jennifer Fager, *Western Michigan University*
JoAnn Farver, *Oklahoma State University*
Greta Fein, *University of Maryland*
Tiffany Field, *University of Miami (FL)*
Johanna Filp, *Sonoma State University*
Cheryl Fortner-Wood, *Winthrop College*
Janet Fuller, *Mansfield University*
Thomas Gerry, *Columbia Greene Community College*
Sam Givhan, *Minnesota State University*
Sandra Graham, *UCLA*
Susan Hale, *Holyoke Community College*
Barbara Springer Hammons, *Palomar College*
Cory Anne Hansen, *Arizona State University*
Barbara H. Harkness, *San Bernardino Valley College*
Algea Harrison, *Oakland University*
Susan Heidrich, *University of Wisconsin*
Ashleigh Hillier, *Ohio University*
Alice S. Hoenig, *Syracuse University*
Sally Hoppstetter, *Palo Alto College*
Robert J. Ivy, *George Mason University*
Diane Carlson Jones, *Texas A&M University*
Ellen Junn, *Indiana University*
Marcia Karwas, *California State University–Monterey*
Melvyn B. King, *State College of New York at Cortland*
Kathleen Kleissler, *Kutztown University*
Dene G. Klinzing, *University of Delaware*
Claire B. Kopp, *UCLA*
Cally Beth Kostakis, *Rockland Community College*
Tara L. Kuther, *Western Connecticut State University*
Linda Lavine, *State University of New York–Cortland*
Sara Lawrence, *California State University at Northridge*
Gloria Lopez, *Sacramento City College*
James E. Marcia, *Simon Fraser University*
Deborah N. Margolis, *Boston College*
Julie Ann McIntyre, *Russell Sage College*
Mary Ann McLaughlin, *Clarion University*
Chloe Merrill, *Weber State College*
Karla Miley, *Black Hawk College*

Jody Miller, *Los Angeles Pierce College*
Carrie L. Mori, *Boise State University*
Joyce Munsch, *California State University at Northridge*
Barbara J. Myers, *Virginia Commonwealth University*
Jeffrey Nagelbush, *Ferris State University*
Sonia Nieves, *Broward Community College*
Caroline Olko, *Nassau Community College*
Sandy Osborne, *Montana State University*
William H. Overman, *University of North Carolina at Wilmington*
Michelle Paludi, *Michelle Paludi & Affiliates*
Susan Peet, *Bowling Green State University*
Pete Peterson, *Johnson County Community College*
Pamela Schuetze Pizarro, *Buffalo State College*
Joe Price, *San Diego State University*
Charles L. Reid, *Essex County College*
Barbara Reynolds, *College of the Sequoias*
Richard Riggle, *Coe College*
Lynne Rompelman, *Concordia University, Wisconsin*
James A. Rysberg, *California State University, Chico*
Marcia Rysztak, *Lansing Community College*
David Sadker, *The American University, Washington DC*
Peter C. Scales, *Search Institute*
Pamela A. Schulze, *University of Akron*
Diane Scott-Jones, *University of Illinois*
Clyde Shepherd, *Keene State College*
Carol S. Soule, *Appalachian State University*
Dorothy D. Sweeney, *Bristol Community College*
Ross A. Thompson, *University of Nebraska, Lincoln*
Naomi Wagner, *San Jose State University*
Richard L. Wagner, *Mount Senario College*
Patricia J. Wall, *Northern Arizona University*
Dorothy A. Wedge, *Fairmont State College*
Carla Graham Wells, *Odessa College*
Becky G. West, *Coahoma Community College*
Alida Westman, *Eastern Michigan University*
Allan Wigfield, *University of Maryland, College Park*
Marilyn E. Willis, *Indiana University of Pennsylvania*
Mary E. Wilson, *Northern Essex Community College*
Susan D. Witt, *University of Akron*
Sarah Young, *Longwood College*
William H. Zachry, *University of Tennessee, Martin*

SUPPLEMENTS

The supplements listed here may accompany *Children,* ninth edition. Please contact your McGraw-Hill representative for details concerning policies, prices, and availability as some restrictions may apply.

FOR THE INSTRUCTOR
Instructor's Manual

by Andrea Rosati, Elmira College

Each chapter of the *Instructor's Manual* contains a Total Teaching Package Outline, a fully integrated tool to help instructors better use the many resources for the course. This outline shows instructors which supplementary materials can be used in the teaching of a particular chapter topic. In addition, there is a chapter outline, suggested lecture topics, classroom activities and demonstrations, suggested student research projects, essay questions, critical thinking questions, and implications for guidance.

Test Bank and Dual-Platform Computerized Test Bank on CD-ROM

by John Addleman, Messiah College

This comprehensive test bank includes more than 2000 factual, conceptual, and applied multiple-choice questions, as well as approximately 75 essay questions per chapter. Available on the Instructor's Resource CD-ROM as Word files and in computerized EZ Test format, the test bank is compatible with Macintosh and Windows platforms. McGraw-Hill's EZ Test is a flexible and easy-to-use electronic testing program. The program enables instructors to create tests from book-specific items. It accommodates a wide range of question types and instructors may add their own questions. Multiple versions of the test can be created and any test can be exported for use with course management systems such as WebCT, BlackBoard or PageOut. EZ Test Online is a new service that gives you a place to easily administer your EZ Test created exams and quizzes online. The program is available for Windows and Macintosh environments.

PowerPoint Slide Presentations

by L. Ann Butzin, Owens Community College

This resource offers the instructor an array of PowerPoint slides for each chapter of *Children*. The slides can be downloaded from the instructor's side of the Online Learning Center or from the Instructor's Resource CD-ROM.

Instructor's Resource CD-ROM (IRCD)

This CD-ROM offers instructors a convenient tool for customizing the McGraw-Hill materials to prepare for and create lecture presentations. Included on the IRCD are the instructor's manual, test bank, and PowerPoint slides.

McGraw-Hill's Visual Assets Database (VAD) for Lifespan Development

by Jasna Jovanovic, University of Illinois– Urbana-Champaign

McGraw-Hill's Visual Assets Database is a password-protected online database of hundreds of multimedia resources for use in classroom presentations, including original video clips, audi clips, photographs, and illustrations—all designed to bring to life concepts in human development. In addition to offering

multimedia presentations for every stage of the lifespan, the VAD's search engine and unique "My Modules" program enables instructors to select from the database's resources to create customized presentations, or "modules." These customized presentations are saved in an instructor's folder on the McGraw-Hill site, and the presentation is then run directly from the VAD to the Internet-equipped classroom. For information about this unique resource, contact your McGraw-Hill representative.

McGraw-Hill Contemporary Learning Series

Taking Sides: Clashing Views on Controversial Issues in Childhood and Society presents current controversial issues in a debate-style format designed to stimulate student interest and develop critical thinking skills. Each issue is thoughtfully framed with an issue summary, an issue introduction, and a postscript. An instructor's manual with testing material is available for each volume. *Using Taking Sides In The Classroom* is also an excellent instructor resource with practical suggestions on incorporating this effective approach in the classroom. Each *Taking Sides* reader features an annotated listing of selected World Wide Web sites and is supported by our student website, **www.mhcls.com.**

Annual Editions: Child Growth and Development is a collection of articles on topics related to the latest research and thinking in human development. These editions are updated regularly and contain useful features, including a topic guide, an annotated table of contents, unit overviews, and a topical index. An instructor's guide, containing testing materials, is also available.

Online Learning Center (OLC)

This extensive website, designed specifically to accompany this edition of *Children,* offers a wide variety of resources for instructors and students. The password-protected instructor's side of the site includes the instructor's manual, PowerPoint lecture slides, images, and a link to McGraw-Hill's Visual Asset Database of brief film clips, audio clips, and photographs. These resources and more can be found by logging on to the text website (www.mhhe.com/santrockc9).

FOR THE STUDENT
Study Guide

by Anita Rosenfield, Yavapai College

This comprehensive study guide integrates the learning system found in the textbook. Designed to promote active learning, it includes chapter outlines, flashcards of key terms and concepts, multiple-choice questions with answer key, matching exercises with answer key, and essay questions with answer key. The Study Guide also includes research projects and Internet projects, as well as a listing of relevant websites. Designed to help students make the most of their time, this resource also integrates the learning goals found in the textbook.

Online Learning Center (OLC)

This companion website for this edition of *Children* offers a wide variety of resources for students, including a Career Appendix, learning goals, chapter outlines, and multiple-choice and true-false quizzes. In addition, it offers interactive scenarios and short video clips from McGraw-Hill's Visual Assets Database for Lifespan Development, as well as Web links to additional sources of information about the topics discussed in the book. These resources and more can be found by logging on to the website (www.mhhe.com/santrockc9).

Multimedia Courseware for Child Development

by Charlotte J. Patterson, University of Virginia

This interactive CD-ROM includes video footage of classic and contemporary experiments, detailed viewing guides, challenging preview, follow-up and interactive feedback, graphics, graduated developmental charts, a variety of hands on projects, related websites, and navigation aids. The CD-ROM is programmed in a modular format. Its content focuses on integrating digital media to better explain physical, cognitive, social, and emotional development throughout childhood and adolescence. It is compatible with both MacIntosh and Windows computers.

TO THE STUDENT

This book provides important study tools to help you learn effectively about life-span development. Especially important is the learning system that is integrated in each chapter. In this visual walk-through of features, pay special attention to how the learning system works.

THE LEARNING SYSTEM

Using the learning goals and related study tools in this book will help you learn and retain the course material more easily. Key aspects of the learning system are the learning goals, chapter maps, review and reflect, and reach your learning goals sections, which are all linked together.

At the beginning of each chapter, you will see both a chapter outline and three to six learning goals that preview the chapter's main themes and underscore the most important ideas in the chapter. Then, at the beginning of each major section of a chapter, you will see a section map of the key topics to be discussed in that section. At the end of each section in a Review and Reflect box, the learning goal for the section is restated, a series of review questions related to the key topics are asked, and a question appears that encourages you to think critically about a topic related to the section. At the end of the chapter, you will come to a section titled: Reach Your Learning Goals. This includes a map of the chapter that visually organizes all of the main headings, a restatement of the chapter's learning goals, and a summary of the chapter's content that is directly linked to the chapter outline at the beginning of the chapter and the questions asked in the Review part of Review and Reflect within the chapter. The summary essentially answers the questions asked in the within-chapter Review sections.

CHAPTER OUTLINE AND
LEARNING GOALS

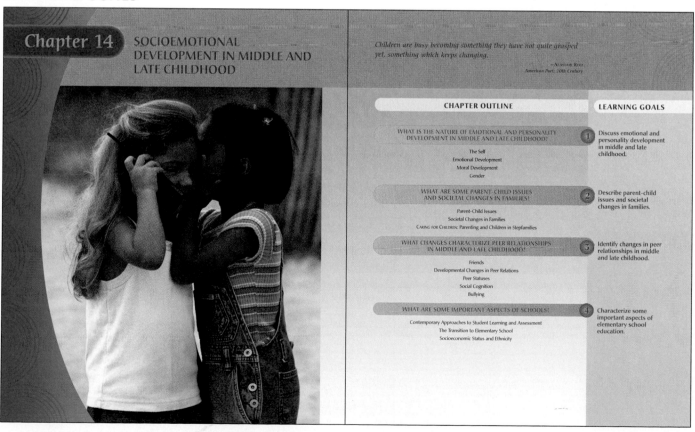

WITHIN-CHAPTER MAPS

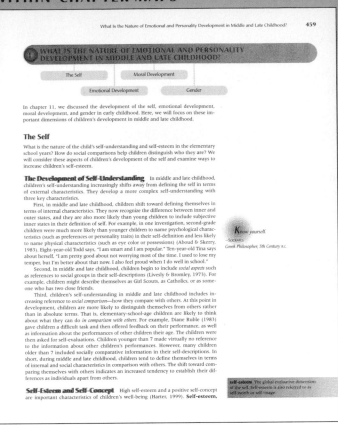

REVIEW AND REFLECT

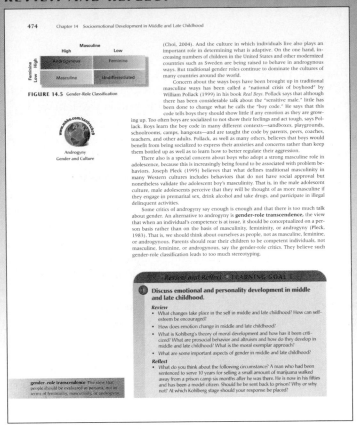

REACH YOUR LEARNING GOALS

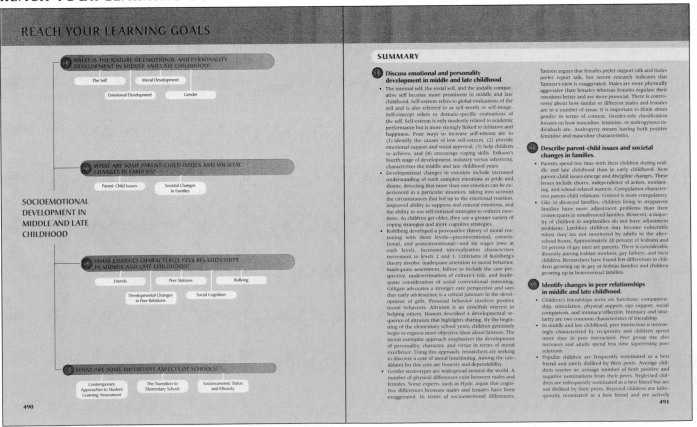

OTHER LEARNING SYSTEM FEATURES

IMAGES OF CHILDREN

Each chapter opens with a high-interest story that is linked to the chapter's content.

Images of Children
The Story of Pax, the Make-Believe-Planet

Can children understand such concepts as discrimination, economic inequality, affirmative action, and comparable worth? Probably not, if we use those terms, but might we be able to construct circumstances involving those concepts that they are able to understand? Phyllis Katz (1987) asked elementary-school-age children to pretend that they had taken a long ride on a spaceship to a make-believe planet called Pax. She asked for their opinions about various situations in which they found themselves. The situations involved conflict, socioeconomic inequality, and civil-political rights. For example, regarding conflict she asked them what a teacher should do when two students were tied for a prize or when they have been fighting. The economic equality dilemmas included a proposed field trip that not all students could afford, a comparable-worth situation in which janitors were paid more than teachers, and an employment situation that discriminated against those with dots on their noses instead of stripes. The rights items dealt with minority rights and freedom of the press.

The elementary school children did indeed recognize injustice and often came up with interesting solutions to problems. For example, all but two children believed that teachers should earn as much as janitors—the holdouts said teachers should make less because they stay in one room or because cleaning toilets is more disgusting and therefore deserves higher wages. Children were especially responsive to the economic inequality items. All but one thought that not giving a job to a qualified applicant who had different physical characteristics (a dotted rather than a striped nose) was unfair. The majority recommended an affirmative action solution—giving the job to the one from the discriminated-against minority. None of the children verbalized the concept of freedom of the press or seemed to understand that a newspaper has the right to criticize a mayor in print without being punished. What are our schools teaching children about democracy? Some of the courses of action suggested were intriguing. Several argued that the reporters should be jailed. One child said that, if she were the mayor being criticized, she would worry, make speeches, and say, "I didn't do anything wrong," not unlike what American presidents have done in recent years. Another said that the mayor should not put the newspaper people out of work, because that might make them print more bad things. "Make them write comics instead," he said. The children believed that poverty exists on Earth but mainly in Africa, big cities, or Vietnam. War was mentioned as the biggest problem on Earth, although children were not certain whether it is presently occurring. Other problems mentioned were crime, hatred, school, smog, and meanness. Overall, the types of rules the children believed a society should abide by were quite sensible—almost all included the need for equitable sharing of resources and work and prohibitions against aggression.

PREVIEW

Children's socioemotional development in middle and late childhood changes in many ways. Transformations in their relationships with parents and their peers occur, and schooling takes on a more academic flavor. Their self-conceptions, moral development, and gender development also undergo significant changes.

458

CAREERS IN CHILD DEVELOPMENT PROFILE

Every chapter has one or more Careers in Child Development profiles, which feature a person working in a child development field related to the chapter's content.

488 Chapter 14 Socioemotional Development in Middle and Late Childhood

CAREERS in CHILD DEVELOPMENT

James Comer
Child Psychiatrist

James Comer grew up in a low-income neighborhood in East Chicago, Indiana, and credits his parents with leaving no doubt about the importance of education. He obtained a BA degree from Indiana University. He went on to obtain a medical degree from Howard University College of Medicine, a Master of Public Health degree from the University of Michigan School of Public Health, and psychiatry training at the Yale University School of Medicine's Child Study Center. He currently is the Maurice Falk Professor of Child Psychiatry at the Yale University Child Study Center and an associate dean at the Yale University Medical School. During his years at Yale, Comer has concentrated his career on promoting a focus on child development as a way of improving schools. His efforts in support of healthy development of young people are known internationally.

Dr. Comer, perhaps, is best known for the founding of the School Development Program in 1968, which promotes the collaboration of parents, educators, and community to improve social, emotional, and academic outcomes for children. His concept of teamwork is currently improving the educational environment in more than 500 schools throughout America.

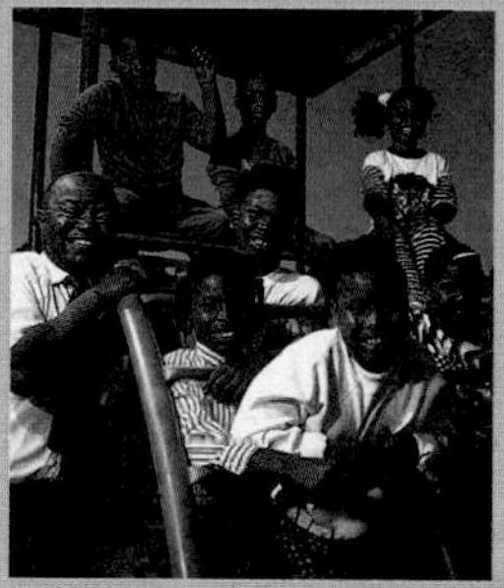

James Comer (*left*) is shown with some of the inner-city African American children who attend a school that became a better learning environment because of Comer's intervention. Comer is convinced that a strong, familylike atmosphere is a key to improving the quality of inner-city schools.

School segregation is still a factor in U.S. education (Spring, 2005; Tozer, Senese, & Violas, 2005). Almost one-third of all African American and Latino students attend schools in which 90 percent or more of the students are from minority groups (Banks, 2002, 2003, 2006).

The school experiences of students from different ethnic groups vary considerably (Diaz, Pelletier, & Provenzo, 2006; Pang, 2005; Powell & Caseau, 2004; Spencer, 2006). African American and Latino students are much less likely than non-Latino White or Asian American students to be enrolled in academic, college preparatory programs and are much more likely to be enrolled in remedial and special education programs. Asian American students are far more likely than other ethnic minority groups to take advanced math and science courses in high school. African American students are twice as likely as Latinos, Native Americans, or Whites to be suspended from school. In one study of middle schools in predominantly Latino areas of Miami, Latino and White teachers rated African American students as having more behavioral problems than African American teachers rated the same students as having (Zimmerman & others, 1995).

Some experts say that a form of institutional racism permeates many American schools by which teachers accept a low level of performance from children of color (Ogbu, 2003; Ogbu & Stern, 2001). American anthropologist John Ogbu (1989) proposed the view that ethnic minority students are placed in a position of subordination and exploitation in the American educational system. He believes that students of color, especially African Americans and Latinos, have inferior educational opportunities, are exposed to teachers and school administrators who have low academic expectations for them, and encounter negative stereotypes (Ogbu & Stern, 2001).

Here are some strategies for improving relationships among ethnically diverse students (Santrock, 2006):

- *Turn the class into a jigsaw classroom.* When Eliot Aronson was a professor at the University of Texas at Austin, the school system contacted him for ideas on how to reduce the increasing racial tension in classrooms. Aronson (1986) developed the concept of "jigsaw classroom," in which students from different cultural backgrounds are placed in a cooperative group in which they have to construct different parts of a project to reach a common goal. Aronson used the term *jigsaw* because he saw the technique as much like a group of students cooperating to put different pieces together to complete a jigsaw puzzle. How might this work? Team sports, drama productions, and music performances are examples of contexts in which students cooperatively participate to reach a common goal.
- *Use technology to foster cooperation with students from around the world.*

CARING FOR CHILDREN INTERLUDE

One Caring for Children interlude appears in every chapter. These interludes focus on applications for improving the lives of children.

476 Chapter 14 Socioemotional Development in Middle and Late Childhood

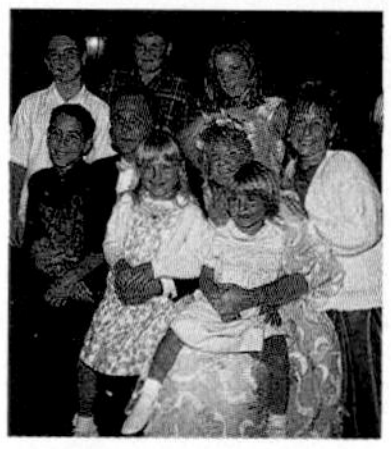

How does living in a stepfamily influence a child's development?

www.mhhe.com/santrockc9

School-Family Linkages
Stepfamilies
Stepfamily Resources
Stepfamily Support

Societal Changes in Families

As we discussed in chapter 11, increasing numbers of children are growing up in divorced families and families in which both parents work outside the home. But there are several other major shifts in the composition of family life that especially affect children in middle and late childhood. Parents are divorcing in greater numbers than ever before and are also getting remarried more (Dunn & others, 2001; Stewart, 2005). It takes time for parents to marry, have children, get divorced, and then remarry. Consequently, there are far more elementary and secondary school children than infant or preschool children living in stepfamilies.

Stepfamilies The number of remarriages involving children has grown steadily in recent years (Ganong, Coleman, & Haas, 2005). Also, divorces occur at a 10 percent higher rate in remarriages than in first marriages (Cherlin & Furstenberg, 1994). As a result of their parents' successive marital transitions, about half of all children whose parents divorce will have a stepparent within four years of parental separation.

In some cases, the creation of a stepfamily may have been preceded by the death of a spouse. However, the formation of most stepfamilies is preceded by divorce rather than death (Pasley & Moorefield, 2004).

Three common types of stepfamily structure are (1) stepfather, (2) stepmother, and (3) blended or complex. In stepfather families, the mother typically had custody of the children and remarried, introducing a stepfather into her children's lives. In stepmother families, the father usually had custody and remarried, introducing a stepmother into his children's lives. In a blended or complex stepfamily, both parents bring children from previous marriages to live in the newly formed stepfamily.

Researchers have found that children's relationships with custodial parents (mothers in stepfather families, fathers in stepmother families) are often better than with stepparents (Santrock, Sitterle, & Warshak, 1988). Also, children in simple families (stepmother, stepfather) often show better adjustment than their counterparts in complex (blended) families (Anderson & others, 1999; Hetherington & Kelly, 2002).

As in divorced families, children in stepfamilies show more adjustment problems than children in nondivorced families (Hetherington, Bridges, & Isabella, 1998). The adjustment problems are similar to those in divorced children—academic problems and lower self-esteem, for example (Anderson & others, 1999). However, as with divorced children, it is important to recognize that a majority of children in stepfamilies do not have problems. In one recent study, 20 percent of children from stepfamilies showed adjustment problems compared with 10 percent in intact, never-divorced families (Hetherington & Kelly, 2002; Hetherington & Stanley-Hagan, 2002).

In terms of the age of the child, researchers have found that early adolescence is an especially difficult time for the formation of a stepfamily (Anderson & others, 1999). This may occur because the stepfamily circumstances exacerbate normal adolescent concerns about identity, sexuality, and autonomy. In the Caring for Children interlude that follows, you can read further about parenting and stepfamilies.

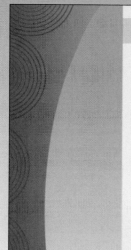

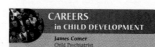

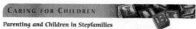

CARING FOR CHILDREN

Parenting and Children in Stepfamilies

What are some problems frequently encountered by stepfamilies? What are some ways to build a strong, positive stepfamily? The following guidelines address these questions (O'Neil & Brown, 2005, pp. 12, 15).

Frequently Encountered Problems in Stepfamilies

- "Adapting to multiple viewpoints, attitudes, and personalities

What Are Some Parent-Child Issues and Societal Changes in Families? 477

- Arranging to comply with the visitation and other custodial rights granted by a court to the absent natural parent (holidays and vacations can pose special problems)
- Conflicting ideas concerning discipline expectations of the children
- Continuing legal battles over child custody issues
- Disagreements over expenses and how family finances are to be used
- Feelings of anger, hurt, mistrust, or guilt regarding ex-spouses that may be unduly transferred to the new mate
- Financial constraints related to feeding, clothing, housing, health care, and providing for the many economic needs and desires of children
- Interference by in-laws (especially grandparents) who may have an interest in the children
- Reduced space, privacy, and personal time
- Refusal of the children to follow the rules and wishes of the stepparent
- Reluctance of the children to accept the stepparent, with outright rejection a possibility
- Rivalry between children for attention and affection, especially when two sets of children are involved
- Unresolved emotional problems of the children arising from the great changes in their lives
- Unresolved personal problems of the parents, which may accompany individuals into the new union (alcoholism, drug use, psychological or behavioral problems) . . .

Strategies for Building a Strong, Positive Stepfamily

- "Agree upon and follow set rules of conduct.
- Attempt to develop and maintain a cooperative relationship with the absent natural parent who still has legal rights to the children.
- Create and maintain a stable home environment in which all family members feel physically and emotionally safe and secure.
- Develop good communication between family members and communicate clearly.
- Give the children age-appropriate responsibilities.
- Make a commitment to talk about and resolve disagreements based on mutual respect and kindness.
- Master those personal problems that may adversely affect the family.
- Openly express love and affection.
- Plan at least one sit-down meal per day that includes all family members.
- Plan family group entertainment and recreation.
- Respect individual privacy rights.
- Support one anothers' member's interests, hobbies, and goals.
- Talk with and listen to one another.
- Try not to react defensively to criticism; instead put it to constructive use.
- When family conflicts seem irreconcilable, or if the behavior of a child poses serious problems, seek professional help."

Self-Care/Latchkey Children We concluded in chapter 9 that when both parents work outside the home it does not necessarily have negative outcomes for their children. However, a certain subset of children from dual-earner families deserves further scrutiny. These children typically do not see their parents from the time they leave for school in the morning until about 6 or 7 P.M. They are sometimes called "latchkey" children because they are given the key to their home, take the key to school, and then use it to let themselves into the home while their parents are still at

KEY TERMS AND GLOSSARY

Key terms appear in boldface. Their definitions appear in the margin near where they are introduced.

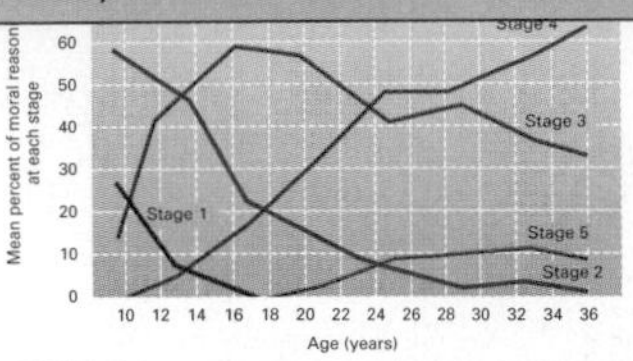
Mean percent of moral reason at each stage
60
50
40
30
20
10
0
10 12 14 16 18 20 22 24 26 28 30 32 34 36
Age (years)
Stage 4
Stage 3
Stage 1
Stage 5
Stage 2

FIGURE 14.3 **Age and the Percentage of Individuals at Each Kohlberg Stage** In one longitudinal study of males from 10 to 36 years of age, at age 10 most moral reasoning was at stage 2 (Colby & others, 1983). At 16 to 18 years of age, stage 3 became the most frequent type of moral reasoning, and it was not until the mid-twenties that stage 4 became the most frequent. Stage 5 did not appear until 20 to 22 years of age and it never characterized more than 10 percent of the individuals. In this study, the moral stages appeared somewhat later than Kohlberg envisioned and stage 6 was absent.

purposes or even as doing God's will. Bandura provides the example of Islamic extremists who mount jihad (holy war) as self-defense against tyrannical, decadent people who they see as seeking to enslave the Islamic world.

Culture and Moral Development Yet another criticism of Kohlberg's view is that it is culturally biased (Miller, 2005; Tappan, 2005; Wainryb, 2005). A review of research on moral development in 27 countries concluded that moral reasoning is more culture-specific than Kohlberg envisioned and that Kohlberg's scoring system does not recognize higher-level moral reasoning in certain cultural groups (Snarey, 1987). Examples of higher-level moral reasoning that would not be scored as such by Kohlberg's system are values related to communal equity and collective happiness in Israel, the unity and sacredness of all life-forms in India, and the relation of the individual to the community in New Guinea. These examples of moral reasoning would not be scored at the highest level in Kohlberg's system because they do not emphasize the individual's rights and abstract principles of justice.

Family Processes and Moral Development Kohlberg believed that family processes are essentially unimportant in children's moral development. He argued that parent-child relationships are usually power-oriented and provide children with little opportunity for mutual give and take or perspective taking. Rather, Kohlberg said that such opportunities are more likely to be provided by children's peer relations (Brabeck, 2000).

Kohlberg likely underestimated the contribution of family relationships to moral development (White & Matawie, 2004). Inductive discipline, which involves the use of reasoning and focuses children's attention on the consequences of their actions for others, positively influences moral development (Hoffman, 1970). Parents' moral values influence children's developing moral thoughts (Gibbs, 2003).

www.mhhe.com/santrock9

Gilligan's Care Perspective

Gender and the Care Perspective Carol Gilligan (1982, 1992, 1996) believes that Kohlberg's theory of moral development does not adequately reflect relationships and concern for others. The **justice perspective** is a moral perspective that is built on the rights of the individual; individuals stand alone and make moral decisions independently. Kohlberg's theory is a justice perspective. By contrast, the **care perspective** is a moral perspective that views people in terms of their connectedness with others and emphasizes interpersonal communication, relationships with others, and concern for others. Gilligan's theory is a care perspective.

According to Gilligan, Kohlberg greatly underplayed the care perspective in moral development. She believes that this may have happened because he was a male, because most of his research was with males rather than females, and because he used male responses as a model for his theory.

Gilligan believes that girls reach a critical juncture in their development when they reach adolescence. Usually around 11 to 12 years of age, girls become aware that their intense interest in intimacy is not prized by the male-dominated culture, even though society values women as caring and altruistic. The dilemma is that girls are presented with a choice that makes them look either selfish or selfless. Gilligan believes that, as adolescent girls experience this dilemma, they increasingly silence their "distinctive voice."

justice perspective A moral perspective that focuses on the rights of the individual; individuals independently make moral decisions. Kohlberg's theory is a justice perspective.

care perspective The moral perspective that views people in terms of their connectedness with others and emphasizes interpersonal communication, relationships with others, and concern for others. Carol Gilligan's perspective is a care perspective.

CRITICAL THINKING AND CONTENT QUESTIONS IN PHOTOGRAPH CAPTIONS

Most photographs have a caption that ends with a critical thinking or knowledge question in italics to stimulate further thought about a topic.

What Are Some Important Aspects of Schools? 487

The Education of Students from Low-Socioeconomic Backgrounds Many children in poverty face problems at home that present barriers to their learning (Bradley & Corwyn, 2002). They might have parents who don't set high educational standards for them, who are incapable of reading to them, and who don't have enough money to pay for educational materials and experiences, such as books and trips to zoos and museums. They might be malnourished and live in areas where crime and violence are a way of life.

Children from a low-SES background face another obstacle: their schools (Bradley & Corwyn, 2002; Cooter, 2004). Compared with schools in higher-income areas, schools in low-income areas are more likely to have more students with low achievement test scores, low graduation rates, and small percentages of students going to college; they are more likely to have young teachers with less experience; and they are more likely to encourage rote learning (Spring, 2005). Too few schools in low-income neighborhoods provide students with environments that are conducive to learning. Many of the schools' buildings and classrooms are old and crumbling.

Jonathan Kozol (1991) vividly described some of the problems that children of poverty face in their neighborhood and at school in *Savage Inequalities*. Following are some of his observations in one inner-city area, East St. Louis, Illinois, which has no obstetric services, no regular trash collection, and few jobs. Nearly one-third of the families live on less than $7,500 a year, and 75 percent of its population lives on welfare of some form. Blocks upon blocks of housing consist of dilapidated, skeletal buildings. Residents breathe the chemical pollution of nearby Monsanto Chemical Company. Raw sewage repeatedly backs up into homes. Lead from nearby smelters poisons the soil. Child malnutrition and fear of violence are common. The problems of the streets spill over into the schools, where sewage also backs up from time to time. Classrooms and hallways are old and unattractive, athletic facilities inadequate. Teachers run out of chalk and paper, the science labs are 30 to 50 years out of date, and the school's heating system has never worked correctly. A history teacher has 110 students but only 26 books. Anyone who visits places like East St. Louis, says Kozol, comes away profoundly shaken.

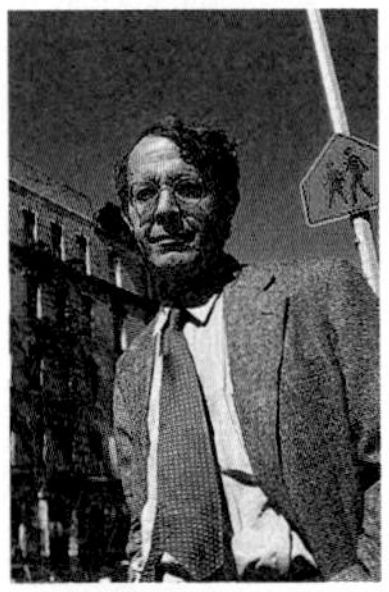

In his book *Savage Inequalities*, Jonathan Kozol (*above*) vividly portrayed the problems that children of poverty face in their neighborhood and at school. *What are some of these problems?*

Ethnicity in Schools East St. Louis is 98 percent African American. Kozol's interest was in describing what life is like in the nation's inner-city neighborhoods and schools, which are predominantly African American and Latino. More than one-third of all African American and almost one-third of all Latino students attend schools in the 47 largest city school districts in the United States, compared with only 5 percent of all White and 22 percent of all Asian American students. Many of these inner-city schools are still segregated, are grossly underfunded, and do not provide adequate opportunities for children to learn effectively. Thus, the effects of SES and the effects of ethnicity are often intertwined.

www.mhhe.com/santrock9

Interview with Jonathan Kozol
Diversity and Education

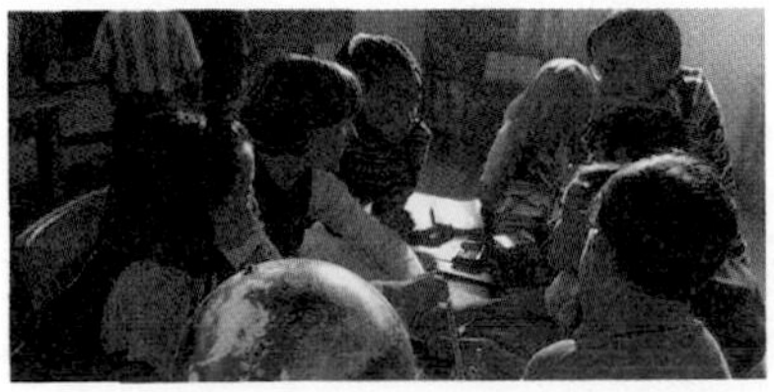

What are some positive strategies for improving interethnic relations among students in schools?

KEY TERMS AND GLOSSARY

Key terms also are listed and page-referenced at the end of each chapter.

KEY TERMS

self-esteem 459
self-concept 460
industry versus inferiority 461
internalization 463
preconventional reasoning 463
conventional reasoning 463
postconventional reasoning 464
justice perspective 466
care perspective 466
altruism 467
moral exemplar approach 467
gender stereotypes 468
rapport talk 470
report talk 470
androgyny 473
gender-role transcendence 474
popular children 480
average children 481
neglected children 481
rejected children 481
controversial children 481
direct instruction approach 484
cognitive constructivist approach 484
social constructivist approach 484

KEY TERMS AND GLOSSARY

Key terms are alphabetically listed, defined, and page-referenced in a Glossary at the end of the book.

G-6 Glossary

shifts from a purely sensorimotor plane to a symbolic plane, and the infant develops the ability to use primitive symbols. 212

intrinsic motivation Internal factors such as self-determination, curiosity, challenge, and effort. 440

intuitive thought substage Piaget's second substage of preoperational thought, in which children begin to use primitive reasoning and want to know the answers to all sorts of questions (between 4 and 7 years of age). 304

involution The process by which the uterus returns to its prepregnant size. 155

J

justice perspective A moral perspective that focuses on the rights of the individual; individuals independently make moral decisions. Kohlberg's theory is a justice perspective. 466

juvenile delinquent An adolescent who breaks the law or engages in behavior that is considered illegal. 593

K

kangaroo care A way of holding an infant so that there is skin-to-skin contact. 152

Klinefelter syndrome A chromosomal disorder in which males have an extra X chromosome, making them XXY instead of XY. 89

kwashiorkor A condition caused by a deficiency in protein in which the child's abdomen and feet become swollen with water. 179

L

labeling Identifying the names of objects. 233

laboratory A controlled setting in which many of the complex factors of the "real world" are removed. 57

language A form of communication, whether spoken, written, or signed, that is based on a system of symbols. 224

language acquisition device (LAD) Chomsky's term that describes a biological endowment that enables the child to detect the features and rules of language, including phonology, syntax, and semantics. 230

lateralization Specialization of function in one hemisphere of the cerebral cortex or the other. 173

learning disability Includes three components: (1) a minimum IQ level, (2) a significant difficulty in a school-related area (especially reading or mathematics), and (3) exclusion of only severe emotional disorders, second-language background, sensory disabilities, and/or specific neurological deficits. 397

least restrictive environment (LRE) The concept that a child with a disability must be educated in a setting that is as similar as possible to the one in which children who do not have a disability are educated. 405

longitudinal approach A research strategy in which the same individuals are studied over a period of time, usually several years or more. 62

long-term memory A relatively permanent type of memory that holds huge amounts of information for a long period of time. 419

low birth weight infant Weighs less than 5½ pounds at birth. 148

low vision Visual acuity between 20/70 and 20/2000. 402

M

manual approaches Educational approaches to help hearing-impaired children; they include sign language and finger spelling. 402

marasmus A wasting away of body tissues in the infant's first year, caused by severe protein-calorie deficiency. 179

mastery orientation An orientation in which one is task-oriented and, instead of focusing on one's ability, is concerned with learning strategies. 441

meiosis A specialized form of cell division that occurs to form eggs and sperm (or gametes). 86

memory A central feature of cognitive development, pertaining to all situations in which an individual retains information over time. 217

menarche A girl's first menstrual period. 502

mental age (MA) Binet's measure of an individual's level of mental development, compared with that of others. 426

mental retardation A condition of limited mental ability in which an individual has a low IQ, usually below 70 on a traditional test of intelligence, and has difficulty adapting to everyday life. 437

mesoderm The middle layer of cells, which becomes the circulatory system, bones, muscles, excretory system, and reproductive system. 109

metacognition Cognition about cognition or knowing about knowing. 424

middle and late childhood The developmental period that extends from about 6 to 11 years of age, sometimes called the elementary school years. 19

mitosis Cellular reproduction in which the cell's nucleus duplicates itself with two new cells being formed, each containing the same DNA as the parent cell, arranged in the same 23 pairs of chromosomes. 86

Montessori approach An educational philosophy in which children are given considerable freedom and spontaneity in choosing activities and are allowed to move from one activity to another as they desire. 318

moral development Development regarding rules and conventions about what people should do in their interactions with other people. 342

moral exemplar approach Emphasizes the development of personality, character, and virtue in terms of moral excellence. 467

Moro reflex A neonatal startle response that occurs in reaction to a sudden, intense noise or movement. When startled, the newborn arches its back, throws its head back, and flings out its arms and legs. Then the newborn rapidly closes its arms and legs to the center of the body. 184

morphology Units of meaning involved in word formation. 225

multiple-factor theory L. L. Thurstone's theory that intelligence consists of seven primary mental abilities: verbal comprehension, number ability, word fluency, spatial visualization, associative memory, reasoning, and perceptual speed. 428

myelination The process in which the nerve cells are covered and insulated with a layer of fat cells, which increases the speed at which information travels through the nervous system. 277

N

natural childbirth Developed in 1914 by Dick-Read, it attempts to reduce the mother's pain by decreasing her fear through education about childbirth and relaxation techniques during delivery. 145

naturalistic observation Observing behavior in real-world settings. 58

QUOTATIONS

These appear occasionally in the margins to stimulate further thought about a topic.

reasoning development, further along in forming an adult identity, and more willing to enter into close relationships" (Matsuba & Walker, 2004, p. 413).

Gender

In chapter 11, we discussed the biological, cognitive, and social influences on gender development. Gender is such a pervasive aspect of a individual's identity that we will further consider its role in children's development here. Among the gender-related topics we will examine are gender stereotypes, similarities, and differences; and gender-role classification.

Gender Stereotyping **Gender stereotypes** are general impressions and beliefs about females and males. For example, men are powerful; women are weak. Men make good mechanics; women make good nurses. Men are good with numbers; women are good with words. Women are emotional; men are not. All of these are stereotypes. They are generalizations about a group that reflect widely held beliefs.

What are little boys made of?
Frogs and snails
And puppy dogs' tails.
What are little girls made of?
Sugar and spice
And all that's nice

—J. O. Halliwell
English Author, 19th Century

Traditional Masculinity and Femininity A classic study in the early 1970s assessed which traits and behaviors college students believed were characteristic of females and which they believed were characteristic of males (Broverman & others, 1972). The traits associated with males were labeled *instrumental*—they included characteristics such as being independent, aggressive, and power-oriented. The traits associated with females were labeled *expressive*—they included characteristics such as being warm and sensitive.

Thus, the instrumental traits associated with males suited them for the traditional masculine role of going out into the world as the breadwinner. The expressive traits associated with females paralleled the traditional feminine role of being the sensitive, nurturing caregiver in the home.

These roles and traits, however, are not just different; they also are unequal in terms of social status and power. The traditional feminine characteristics are childlike, suitable for someone who is dependent and subordinate to others. The traditional masculine characteristics suit one to deal competently with the wider world and to

Web icons appear a number of times in each chapter. They signal you to go to the book's website, where you will find connecting links that provide additional information on the topic discussed in the text. The labels under the Web icon appear as Web links at the Santrock *Children,* ninth edition, website, under that chapter for easy access.

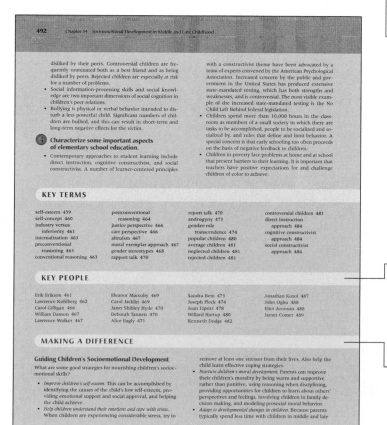

CHILDREN'S RESOURCES

At the end of each chapter, this feature highlights recommended reading and resources for learning more about children and improving their lives.

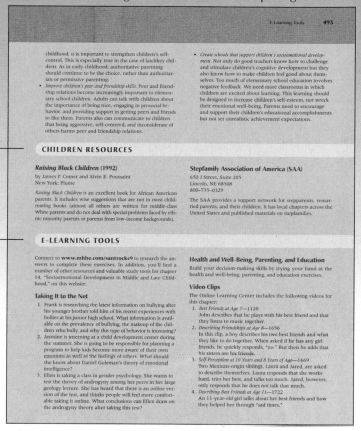

E-LEARNING TOOLS

This end-of-chapter feature includes *Taking It To the Net* exercises; Health and Well-Being, Parenting, and Education scenarios; and Video Clips.

KEY PEOPLE

The most important theorists and researchers discussed in the chapter are listed and page-referenced at the end of the chapter.

MAKING A DIFFERENCE

At the end of each chapter, this feature provides practical information that individuals can use to improve children's lives.

Images of Children
The Stories of Jeffrey Dahmer and Alice Walker

Jeffrey Dahmer
What are some possible causes of the brutal acts of violence that he committed?

Alice Walker
What might be some reasons that she overcame trauma in her childhood to develop in positive ways?

Jeffrey Dahmer had a troubled childhood. His parents constantly bickered before they divorced, his mother had emotional problems and doted on his younger brother, and he felt that his father neglected him. When he was 8 years old, Jeffrey was sexually abused by an older boy. But most individuals who suffer through such childhood pains never go on to commit Dahmer's grisly crimes.

In 1991, a man in handcuffs dashed out of Dahmer's bizarrely cluttered apartment in a tough Milwaukee neighborhood, called the police, and stammered that Dahmer had tried to kill him. At least 17 other victims did not get away.

Alice Walker was born in 1944. She was the eighth child of Georgia sharecroppers who earned $300 a year. When Walker was 8, her brother accidentally shot her in the left eye with a BB gun. By the time her parents got her to the hospital a week later (they had no car), she was blind in that eye and it had developed a disfiguring layer of scar tissue.

Despite the counts against her, Alice Walker went on to become an essayist, a poet, and an award-winning novelist. She won the Pulitzer Prize for her book *The Color Purple*. Like her characters, especially the women, Alice Walker overcame pain and anger to celebrate the human spirit. Walker writes about people who "make it, who come out of nothing. People who triumph."

What leads one child to grow up and commit brutal acts of violence and another to turn poverty and trauma into a rich literary harvest? How can we explain how one child picks up the pieces of a life shattered by tragedy, while another becomes unhinged by life's stress? Why is it that some children are whirlwinds—full of energy, successful in school, and able to get along well with their peers—while others stay on the sidelines, mere spectators of life? If you ever have wondered about why children turn out the way they do, you have asked yourself the central questions we will explore in this book.

Why study children? Perhaps you are or will be a parent or teacher, and responsibility for children is or will be a part of your everyday life. The more you learn about children, the better you can guide them. Perhaps you hope to gain an understanding of your own history—as an infant, as a child, and as an adolescent. Perhaps you accidentally came across the course description and found it intriguing. Whatever your reasons, you will discover that the study of child development is provocative, intriguing, and informative.

PREVIEW

This book is about development, a pattern of movement or change that begins at conception and continues through the human life span. Most development involves growth, although it also includes decline (as in death and dying). This chapter previews the themes and issues that we will explore throughout our study of children's development. First, we look at how children's lives can be improved. Next, we familiarize ourselves with how children were thought of and studied in the past and how they are perceived and studied today. Second we will examine the processes and periods that characterize children's development. Third, we will study the primary issues that developmentalists debate, issues that will come up repeatedly in the text. Finally, a special feature toward the end of the chapter identifies the career paths that you can follow if you have an interest in working with children.

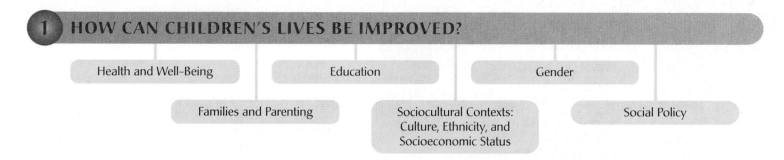

1 HOW CAN CHILDREN'S LIVES BE IMPROVED?

Health and Well-Being

Education

Gender

Families and Parenting

Sociocultural Contexts: Culture, Ethnicity, and Socioeconomic Status

Social Policy

Consider some of the topics you read about every day in newspaper and magazines: health and well-being, families and parenting, education, culture and ethnicity, and socioeconomic status; gender; and social policy. What child development researchers are discovering in each of these areas has direct and significant consequences for understanding children and for improving their lives (Cooper & others, 2005; Eccles & Roesser, 2005; Parke & Buriel, 2006; Ramey, Ramey, & Lanzi, 2006; Spencer, 2006). In this book, we will discuss the latest research on these topics. Let's now take a closer look at each of these topics.

development The pattern of movement or change that begins at conception and continues through the human life span.

Health and Well-Being

Although we have become a nation obsessed with health and well-being, the health and well-being of our nation's children and children in many countries around the world are jeopardized by many factors, including

- poverty
- the AIDS epidemic
- starvation
- poor-quality health care
- inadequate nutrition and exercise
- alcohol and drug abuse in adolescence
- sexual abuse of children

Children are the legacy we leave for the time we will not live to see.

—ARISTOTLE
Greek Philosopher, 4th Century B.C.

Asian physicians around 2600 B.C.E. and Greek physicians around 500 B.C.E. recognized that good habits are essential for good health. They did not blame the gods for illness and think that magic would cure it. They realized that people have some control over their health and well-being. A physician's role was as guide, assisting patients in restoring a natural and emotional balance.

In the beginning of the twenty-first century, we again recognize the power of lifestyles and psychological states in promoting health and well-being (Compas, 2004; Hahn, Payne, & Mauer, 2005). We are returning to the ancient view that the ultimate responsibility for our health and well-being, both ours and our children's, rests in our hands. Parents, teachers, nurses, physicians, and other adults serve as important models of health and well-being for children. They also can communicate effective strategies for health and well-being to children and monitor how effectively children are following these strategies. The importance of promoting health and well-being in children can be seen in the work of clinical child psychologist Luis Vargas, which is described in the Careers in Child Development insert.

www.mhhe.com/santrockc9

Prevention Programs

Research on Premature Infants   One researcher whose work focuses on the health and well-being of children is Tiffany Field, whose research focuses on how massage therapy can facilitate weight gain in preterm infants (Field 2001, 2003; Field, Hernandez-Reif, & Freedman, 2004). In their initial research, Field and her colleagues (1986) found that massage therapy conducted three times per day for 15 minutes with preterm infants led to 47 percent greater weight gain than standard medical treatment. The massaged infants also showed improved social and motor skills. The same positive results for massage therapy has been found in the Philippines and in Israel

CAREERS in CHILD DEVELOPMENT

Luis Vargas
Clinical Child Psychologist

Luis Vargas is Director of the Clinical Child Psychology Internship Program and a professor in child and adolescent psychiatry at the University of New Mexico School of Medicine. Vargas obtained an undergraduate degree in psychology from Trinity University in Texas and a Ph.D. in clinical psychology at the University of Nebraska–Lincoln.

Vargas' work includes assessing and treating children, adolescents, and their families, especially when a child or adolescent has a serious mental disorder. He also trains mental health professionals to provide culturally responsive and developmentally appropriate mental health services. In addition, he is interested in cultural and assessment issues with children, adolescents, and their families. He co-authored (with Joan Koss-Chiono, a medical anthropologist) (1999) *Working with Latino Youth: Culture, Context, and Development.*

Vargas' clinical work is heavily influenced by contextual and ecological theories of development (which we will discuss in chapter 2, "The Science of Child Development"). His first undergraduate course in human development, and subsequent courses in development, contributed to his decision to pursue a career in clinical child psychology.

Toward the end of this chapter you can read about many careers in child development, including more about the field of child clinical psychology. Also, to provide you with a better sense of the breadth of careers in child development, throughout the book at appropriate places in various chapters we will provide profiles of individuals in various child development careers.

Luis Vargas (left) conducting a child therapy session.

(Goldstein-Ferber, 1997; Jinon, 1996). We will discuss Field's massage therapy in chapter 5, "Birth."

Families and Parenting

Relationships with family members and parenting are important influences on children's development. Experts increasingly describe the pressures on contemporary families (Garbarino, Bradshaw, & Kostelny, 2005; Harvey & Fine, 2004; Luster & Okaghi, 2005). The number of families in which both parents work is increasing; at the same time, the number of one-parent families has risen over the past two decades as a result of a climbing divorce rate. With more children being raised by single parents or by two working parents, the time parents have to spend with their children is being squeezed and the quality of child care is of concern to many (Crouter & Booth, 2004; Zaslow, 2004). Are working parents more effectively using the decreased time with their children? Do child-care arrangements provide high-quality alternatives for parents? How concerned should we be about the increasing number of latchkey children—those at home alone after school, waiting for their parents to return from work? Answering these questions requires several types of information obtained by experts in child development. For example, information comes from studies of the way working parents use time with their children, studies of the ways various child-care arrangements influence children's social and intellectual growth in relation to home-care arrangements, and examination of the consequences of a child being without adult supervision for hours every day after school (Mahoney, Larson, & Eccles, 2004).

Making a positive difference in the lives of children is a major theme of this book. The poster at the top of the next page that states "Children learn to love when they are loved" reflects this theme.

Twentieth-century Irish playwright George Bernard Shaw once commented that, although parenting is a very important profession, no test of fitness for it is ever imposed. If a test were imposed, some parents would turn out to be more fit than others. Parents want their children to grow into socially mature individuals, but they often are not sure how to help their children reach this goal. One reason for parents' frustration is that they often receive conflicting messages about child rearing. One "expert" might urge them to be more permissive with their children. Another might tell them to place stricter controls on them or they will grow up to be spoiled brats.

You might be a parent someday or might already be one. You should take seriously the importance of rearing your children, because they are the future of our society. Good parenting takes considerable time. If you plan to become a parent, commit yourself day after day, week after week, month after month, and year after year to providing your children with a warm, supportive, safe, and stimulating environment that will make them feel secure and allow them to reach their full potential as human beings.

Understanding the nature of children's development can help you become a better parent (Cowan & others, 2005; Lamb & Lewis, 2005; Luster & Okagki, 2005; Parke & Buriel, 2006; Powell, 2005, 2006). Many parents learn parenting practices from their parents. Unfortunately, when parenting practices and child-care strategies are passed from one generation to the next, both desirable and undesirable ones are usually perpetuated. This book and your instructor's lectures in this course can help you become more knowledgeable about children's development and sort through which practices in your own upbringing you should continue with your own children and which you should abandon.

Research on Child Maltreatment   One topic that is of great concern is child maltreatment (Cicchetti & Toth, 2006; Higgins, 2004; Pittman & Lee, 2004). One recent study compared the language development of maltreated children (children who have been abused) and nonmaltreated children (Eigsti & Cicchetti, 2004). Observations of the children's speech during play sessions with their mothers indicated that the maltreated children experienced language delay in both vocabulary and syntax. Observations of mother-child interaction provided one indication of why these children might experience language delay: mothers of the maltreated children produced fewer utterances than mothers of non-maltreated children. Also the trauma involved in maltreatment may produce emotional difficulties for children that can interfere with learning language.

We will have more to say about maltreated children in chapter 11, "Socioemotional Development in Early Childhood."

Children learn to love when they are loved

Education

Children learn from their parents, but they also learn from their siblings, from their peers, from books, from watching television, from computers, and from formal schooling. All of this learning is part of a child's education, an extremely important dimension of children's lives (Driscoll, 2005; Eccles & Roeser, 2005; Schunk, 2004).

What can we do to make the education of children more effective? There is widespread agreement that something needs to be done to improve the education of our nation's children (Blumenfeld, Krajcik, & Kempler, 2006; Sadker & Sadker, 2005; Santrock, 2006a; Wigfield & others, 2006). There are many views in contemporary education, which involve such questions as:

- Should the school day be longer or shorter, the school year longer or shorter, or should they stay the same and the focus be more on changing the curriculum itself?
- Should there be more accountability in schools with accountability of student learning and teaching assessed by formal tests?
- Should schooling involve less memorization and more attention to the development of children's ability to process information more efficiently?
- Have schools become too soft and watered down? Should they make more demands on and have higher expectations of children?
- Should schools focus only on developing the child's knowledge and cognitive skills, or should they pay more attention to the whole child and consider the child's socioemotional and physical development as well? For example, should schools be dramatically changed so that they serve as a locus for a wide range of services, such as primary health care, child care, preschool education, parent

www.mhhe.com/santrockc9

Education Resources
Diversity
Children's Rights
Children Now
Children and Advocacy

education, recreation, and family counseling, as well as the traditional educational activities, such as learning in the classroom?

- Should more tax dollars be spent on schools, and should teachers be paid more to educate our nation's children?

Research on Mentoring   Mentoring programs are increasingly being advocated as a strategy for improving the achievement of children and adolescents who are at risk for failure (Black, Suarez, & Medina, 2004; Dopp & Block, 2004; Hamilton & Hamilton, 2004). One study focused on 959 adolescents who had applied to the Big Brothers/Big Sisters program (Rhodes, Grossman, & Resch, 2000). Half of the adolescents were mentored through extensive discussions about school, careers, and life, as well as participation in leisure activities with other adolescents. The other half were not mentored. Mentoring led to reduced unexcused absences from school, improvements in classroom performance, and better relationships with parents.

Sociocultural Contexts: Culture, Ethnicity, and Socioeconomic Status

Sociocultural contexts of development involve these important concepts: contexts, culture, ethnicity, and socioeconomic status. The concepts are central to our discussion of children's development in this book, so we need to define them clearly. **Context** refers to the setting in which development occurs, a setting that is influenced by historical, economic, social, and cultural factors. To sense how important context is in understanding children's development, consider a researcher who wants to discover whether children today are more racially tolerant than children were a decade ago. Without reference to the historical, economic, social, and cultural aspects of race relations, students' racial tolerance cannot be fully understood. Every child's development occurs in numerous contexts (Luster & Okagaki, 2005; Secada, 2005). Contexts include homes, schools, peer groups, churches, cities, neighborhoods, communities, and countries—each with meaningful historical, economic, social, and cultural legacies (Leventhal & Brooks-Gunn, 2003; Pang, 2005).

Culture   **Culture** encompasses the behavior patterns, beliefs, and all other products of a particular group of people that are passed on from generation to generation. The products result from the interaction between groups of people and their environment over many years. A cultural group can be as large as the United States or as small as an African hunter-gatherer group. Whatever its size, the group's culture influences the identity, learning, and social behavior of its members (Cole, 2005, 2006; Shweder & others, 2006).

   Cross-cultural studies are comparisons of one culture with one or more other cultures. They provide information about the degree to which children's development is similar, or universal, across cultures and to what degree it is culture-specific. For example, the United States is an achievement-oriented culture with a strong work ethic. However, cross-cultural studies of American and Japanese children revealed that the Japanese children were better at math, spend more time working on math in school, and spend more time doing homework than the American children (Stevenson, 1995, 2000). Among the explanations for the higher math achievement in Japanese children are higher expectations for achievement and more time and effort spent in learning.

Ethnicity   **Ethnicity** (the word *ethnic* comes from the Greek word for "nation") is rooted in cultural heritage, nationality characteristics, race, religion, and language. Ethnicity is central to the development of an **ethnic identity,** which is a sense of membership in an ethnic group, based on shared language, religion, customs, values, history, and race. You are a member of one or more ethnic groups. Your ethnic identity reflects your deliberate decision to identify with an ancestor or ancestral group

context The settings, influenced by historical, economic, social, and cultural factors, in which development occurs.

culture The behavior patterns, beliefs, and all other products of a group that are passed on from generation to generation.

cross-cultural studies Comparisons of one culture with one or more other cultures. These provide information about the degree to which children's development is similar, or universal, across cultures, and to the degree to which it is culture-specific.

ethnicity A characteristic based on cultural heritage, nationality, race, religion, and language.

ethnic identity A sense of membership in an ethnic group, based on shared language, religion, customs, values, history, and race.

(Phinney, 2003; Quintana, 2004; Umana-Taylor & Fine, 2004). If you are of Native American and African slave ancestry, you might choose to align yourself with the traditions and history of Native Americans, although an outsider might believe that your identity is African American.

The tapestry of American culture has changed dramatically in recent years. Nowhere is the change more noticeable than in the increasing ethnic diversity of America's citizens. Non-White ethnic minority groups—African American, Latino, Native American (American Indian), and Asian American, for example—made up 20 percent of all children and adolescents under the age of 17 in 1989. As we begin the twenty-first century, one-third of all school-age children fall into this category. By the end of the twenty-first century, if current trends continue, projections indicate that there will be more Latino children and adolescents in the United States than non-Latino White children and adolescents (U.S. Bureau of the Census, 2002). This changing demography promises not only the richness that diversity produces but also difficult challenges in extending the American dream to individuals of all ethnic groups (Diaz, Pelletier, & Provenzo, 2006; Garcia Coll, Szalacha, & Palacios, 2005; Matsumoto, 2004; McLoyd, 2005; Spencer, 2006).

Historically, immigrant and non-White ethnic minorities have found themselves at the bottom of the economic and social order. They have been disproportionately represented among the poor and the inadequately educated (Leyendecker & others, 2005). Half of all African American children and one-third of all Latino children live in poverty. School dropout rates for minority youth reach the alarming rate of 60 percent in some urban areas. These population trends and our nation's inability to prepare minority individuals for full participation in American life have produced an imperative for the social institutions that serve minorities (Diaz, 2003). Schools, social services, health and mental health agencies, juvenile probation services, and other programs need to become more sensitive to ethnic issues and to provide improved services to ethnic minority and low-income individuals (Farr, 2005; Koppelman, 2005; Sheets, 2005).

Not only is there ethnic diversity within a culture such as the United States, but there is also considerable diversity within each ethnic group (Parrillo, 2004). Not all African American children come from low-income families. Not all Latino children are members of the Catholic church. Not all Asian American children are academically gifted. Not all Native American children drop out of school. It is easy to make the mistake of stereotyping the members of an ethnic minority group as all being the same. Keep in mind, as we describe children from ethnic groups, that each group is heterogeneous.

Shown here are two Korean–born children on the day they became U.S. citizens. Asian American children are the fastest-growing group of ethnic minority children in the United States.

Socioeconomic Status (SES)

Socioeconomic status (SES) refers to the grouping of people with similar occupational, educational, and economic characteristics. Socioeconomic status implies certain inequalities. Generally, members of a society have (1) occupations that vary in prestige, and some individuals have more access than others to higher-status occupations; (2) different levels of educational attainment, and some individuals have more access than others to better education; (3) different economic resources; and (4) different levels of power to influence a community's institutions. These differences in the ability to control resources and to participate in society's rewards produce unequal opportunities for children.

There is a special concern about children who grow up in poverty (Bernstein, 2004; Blumenfeld & others, 2005; Evans, 2004). In a review of research, Jeanne Brooks-Gunn and her colleagues (2003) concluded that poverty in the first few years of life is a better predictor of school completion and achievement at 18 than poverty in the adolescent years. However, she also revealed that early intervention for two or three years doesn't permanently reduce socioeconomic disparities in children's achievement because poor children are likely to continue facing obstacles to success, such as schools that are not conducive to learning and neighborhoods with high levels of violence and unsafe play areas. Thus, intervention may need to continue beyond the early child years into the elementary school years and even adolescent years to improve the lives of children living in poverty. Other researchers are seeking to find

socioeconomic status (SES) The grouping of people with similar occupational, educational, and economic characteristics.

ways to help families living in poverty improve their well-being (Clampet-Lundquist & others, 2004; Perry-Jenkins, 2004).

Research on Children's Ethnicity, Poverty, and Type of Home Environment
One study recently examined the home environments of four ethnic groups: European American, African American, Latino, and Asian American (Bradley & others, 2001). The home environments were assessed by a combination of observations and maternal interviews at five points in children's lives from infancy through early adolescence. There were some ethnic differences but the most consistent results involved poverty, which was a much more powerful indicator of the type of home environment children experienced than ethnicity.

Gender

Gender involves the psychological and sociocultural dimensions of being female or male. *Sex* refers to the biological dimension of being female or male. Few aspects of our development are more central to our identity and social relationships than gender (Galambos, 2004; Hyde, 2004; Lippa, 2005; Poelmans, 2005; Ruble, Martin, & Berenbaum, 2006). Our society's attitudes about gender are changing, but how much?

Research on Gender
One cross-cultural study of more than 2,000 second- to sixth-graders from a number of European countries, Russia, Japan, and the United States found that girls consistently earned higher grades in school than boys (Stetsenko & others, 2000). However, even though they were aware that they made better grades than boys, the girls did not report stronger beliefs in their own ability. Why might girls have less confidence in their academic ability than their performance warrants? One concern is gender stereotyping of boys as being smarter than girls, which can result in parent, teachers, and other adults providing negative feedback to girls about their academic ability.

Social Policy

Social policy refers to the laws, regulations, and government programs that influence the welfare of its citizens. The shape and scope of social policy related to children are tied to the political system. The values held by individual lawmakers, the nation's economic strengths and weaknesses, and partisan politics all influence the policy agenda. Comprehensive social policy often grows out of concern over broad social issues. Child labor laws were established in the early twentieth century to protect children and jobs for adults as well; federal child-care funding during World War II was justified by the need for women laborers in factories; and the Head Start program in the 1960s was implemented to decrease intergenerational poverty.

Among the groups that have worked to improve the lives of children are UNICEF in New York and the Children's Defense Fund in Washington, D.C. Marian Wright Edelman, president of the Children's Defense Fund, has been a leading advocate of children's rights. Especially troubling to Edelman (2004) are the indicators that rank the United States as one of the worst industrialized nations in terms of social neglect of its children. To improve conditions for children, Edelman says that we need a better health-care system for families, safer schools and neighborhoods, better parent education, and improved family support systems.

The large majority of children in the United States live in prosperous circumstances. However, far too many U.S. children live in poverty (Children's Defense Fund, 2004; National Center for Health Statistics, 2004). In the positive economic times of the 1990s, the poverty rate of families declined. However, as the economy declined at the beginning of the twenty-first century, the poverty rate of families began to increase. In 2005, the average poverty threshold for a family of four was $19,350 and $16,092 for a family of three (Federal Register, 2005). In 2004, approximately 17 percent of U.S. children lived in poor families and about 4.6 million

If our American way of life fails the child, it fails us all.

—PEARL BUCK
American Author, 20th Century

www.mhhe.com/santrockc9

Social Policy
UNICEF

gender The psychological and sociocultural dimension of being female or male.

social policy The laws, regulations, and government programs that influence the welfare of its citizens.

Marian Wright Edelman, president of the Children's Defense Fund (shown here interacting with some young children), has been a tireless advocate of children's rights and has been instrumental in calling attention to the needs of children. *What are some of these needs?*

children lived in families that do not have an employed parent (National Center for Children in Poverty, 2004).

Out of concern that policymakers are doing too little to protect the well-being of children, researchers increasingly are undertaking studies that they hope will lead to wise and effective decision making in the area of social policy (Benson & others, 2005; Groark & McCall, 2005; Renninger & Sigel, 2006; Waldfogel, 2004). When more than 15 percent of all children and almost half of all ethnic minority children are being raised in poverty, when children and young adolescents are giving birth, when the use and abuse of drugs are widespread, and when the specter of AIDS is present, our nation needs revised social policy. Revising social policy includes creating government provisions for helping children when ordinary family support systems fail or when families seriously endanger their children's well-being. To read further about improving the lives of children, see the Caring for Children interlude that follows.

CARING FOR CHILDREN

Improving Family Policy

In the United States, the national government, state governments, and city governments affect the well-being of children (Linver & others, 2004; Yeung, Linver, & Brooks-Gunn, 2002). At the national and state level, controversy has focused on whether the government can promote children's well-being by giving money to parents who are very poor so that they can feed and house their children. If the government gives money to the parents, what should it expect in return? Should the government help parents living in poverty pay for someone to take care of their children so that the parents can work? If parents are homeless, what if anything should he government do for the parents or their children?

Answers to these questions are part of a government's family policy. Some experts argue that an effective family policy will not come from legislators in Washington, D.C., but rather from parents themselves, when they realize the importance of positive links between families, schools, and communities (Louv, 1990).

The family policies of the United States are overwhelmingly treatment-oriented: only those families and individuals who already have problems are eligible. Few preventive programs are available on any widespread basis. For example, families in which the children are on the verge of being placed in foster care are eligible, and

(continued on next page)

Source	Characteristic
Individual	Good intellectual functioning Appealing, sociable, easygoing disposition Self-confidence, high self-esteem Talents Faith
Family	Close relationship to caring parent figure Authoritative parenting: warmth, structure, high expectations Socioeconomic advantages Connections to extended supportive family networks
Extrafamilial context	Bonds to caring adults outside the family Connections to positive organizations Attending effective schools

FIGURE 1.1 Characteristics of Resilient Children and Their Contexts

often required, to receive counseling; families in which problems are brewing but are not yet full-blown usually cannot qualify for public services. Most experts on family policy believe that more attention should be given to preventing family problems (Hawkins & Whiteman, 2004; Kalil & DeLeire, 2004).

One recent study examined influence of the Minnesota Family Investment Program (MFIP) on children (Gennetian & Miller, 2002). The MFIP was designed to primarily affect the employment behavior and economic self-sufficiency of adults. An important positive outcome of the study was that increased income for working poor parents was linked with their children's improved achievement in school and a reduction in behavioral problems.

Some children do triumph over life's adversities. These children are resilient—that is, they are able to succeed and thrive despite experiencing negative conditions or events (for example, parental abuse or neglect or the death of a parent). Ann Masten and her colleagues (2001, 2004; Masten & Coatsworth, 1998; Roisman & others, 2004) analyzed the research literature on resilience and concluded that a number of individual factors (such as good intellectual functioning), family factors (close relationship to a caring parent figure), and extrafamilial factors (bonds to prosocial adults outside the family) characterize resilient children and adolescents (see figure 1.1).

Norman Garmezy (1993) described a setting in a Harlem neighborhood of New York City to illustrate resilience: In the foyer of the walk-up apartment building is a large frame on a wall in the entranceway. It displays the photographs of children who live in the apartment building, with a written request that if anyone sees any of the children endangered on the street, they bring them back to the apartment house. Garmezy commented that this is an excellent example of adult competence and concern for the safety and well-being of children.

At the beginning of the twenty-first century, the well-being of children is one of America's foremost concerns. We all cherish the future of our children because they are the future of any society. Children who not reach their potential, who are unable to contribute effectively to society, and who do not take their place as productive adults diminish the power of society's future (Horowitz & O'Brien, 1989).

Review and Reflect • LEARNING GOAL 1

1 Identify six areas in which children's lives can be improved.

Review

- How do health and well-being affect children's development?
- What are some current concerns about families and parenting?
- What are some issues involved in the education of today's children?
- How do sociocultural contexts influence children's development?
- What is gender and how might it affect children's development?
- What is social policy and what is its status in regard to America's children? What characterizes resilient children?

Reflect

- Imagine what your development as a child would have been like in a culture that offered fewer or distinctly different choices than your own. How might your development have been different if your family was significantly richer or poorer than it was?

2 WHAT ARE SOME HISTORICAL VIEWS OF CHILD DEVELOPMENT?

Early Views of Children   The Modern Study of Child Development   Early Modern Theorists

Today the media describe new policies or research in child development almost daily. Historically, though, interest in the development of children has been uneven.

Early Views of Children

Childhood has become such a distinct period that it is hard to imagine that it was not always thought of in that way. However, in medieval times, laws generally did not distinguish between child and adult offenses. After analyzing samples of art along with available publications, historian Philippe Ariès (1962) concluded that European societies did not accord any special status to children prior to 1600. In paintings, children were often dressed in adult-like clothing (see figure 1.2).

Were children actually treated as adults in medieval Europe? Ariès primarily sampled aristocratic, idealized subjects, which might have been misleading. In medieval times, children often worked, and their emotional bond with parents might not have been as strong as it is for many children today. However, childhood probably was recognized as a distinct phase of life more than Ariès believed. Also, we know that the ancient Egyptians, Greeks, and Romans held rich conceptions of children's development.

Throughout history, philosophers have speculated at length about the nature of children and how they should be reared. Three influential philosophical views portray children in terms of original sin, tabula rasa, and innate goodness:

FIGURE 1.2 Historical Perception of Children This artistic impression shows how some children were viewed as miniature adults earlier in history. Many artists' renditions of children as miniature adults may have been too stereotypical.

- In the **original sin view,** especially advocated during the Middle Ages, children were perceived as being basically bad, born into the world as evil beings. The goal of child rearing was to provide salvation, to remove sin from the child's life.
- Toward the end of the seventeenth century, the **tabula rasa view** was proposed by English philosopher John Locke. He argued that children are not innately bad but, instead, are like a "blank tablet." Locke believed that childhood experiences are important in determining adult characteristics. He advised parents to spend time with their children and to help them become contributing members of society.
- In the eighteenth century, the **innate goodness view** was presented by Swiss-born French philosopher Jean-Jacques Rousseau. He stressed that children are inherently good. Because children are basically good, said Rousseau, they should be permitted to grow naturally, with little parental monitoring or constraint.

In the past century and a half, our view of children has changed dramatically. We now conceive of childhood as a highly eventful and unique period of life that lays an important foundation for the adult years and is highly differentiated from them. Most approaches to childhood identify distinct periods in which children master special skills and confront new life tasks. Childhood is no longer seen as an inconvenient "waiting" period during which adults must suffer the incompetencies of the young. We now value childhood as a special time of growth and change, and we invest great resources in caring for and educating our children. We protect them from the stresses and responsibilities of adult work through strict child labor laws. We treat their crimes against society under a special system of juvenile justice. We also have governmental

original sin view Advocated during the Middle Ages, the belief that children were born into the world as evil beings and were basically bad.

tabula rasa view The idea, proposed by John Locke, that children are like a "blank tablet."

innate goodness view The idea, presented by Swiss-born French philosopher Jean-Jacques Rousseau, that children are inherently good.

provisions for helping children when ordinary family support systems fail or when families seriously interfere with children's well-being.

The Modern Study of Child Development

The modern era of studying children has a history that spans only a little more than a century (Cairns, 1983, 2006). Since it began in the late 1800s, the study of child development has evolved into a sophisticated science. A number of major theories, along with elegant techniques and methods of study, help organize our thinking about children's development. New knowledge about children—based on direct observation and testing—is accumulating at a breathtaking pace.

During the late 1800s, a major shift took place—from a strictly philosophical perspective on human psychology to a perspective that includes direct observation and experimentation. Most of the influential early psychologists were trained either in the natural sciences (such as biology or medicine) or in philosophy. In the field of child development, this was true of such influential thinkers as Charles Darwin, G. Stanley Hall, James Mark Baldwin, and Sigmund Freud. Natural scientists underscored the importance of conducting experiments and collecting reliable observations. This approach had advanced the state of knowledge in physics, chemistry, and biology; however, these scientists were not at all sure that people, much less children or infants, could be studied in this way. Their hesitation was due, in part, to a lack of examples to follow in studying children. Philosophers of the time also debated, on both intellectual and ethical grounds, whether the methods of science were appropriate for studying people.

The deadlock was broken when some daring thinkers began to try out new ways of studying infants, children, and adolescents. For example, near the turn of the twentieth century, French psychologist Alfred Binet invented many tasks to study attention and memory. He used them to study his own daughters, other normal children, children with mental retardation, extremely gifted children, and adults. Eventually, he collaborated in the development of the first modern test of intelligence, which is named after him (the Binet test). At about the same time, G. Stanley Hall pioneered the use of questionnaires with large groups of children. In one investigation, Hall tested 400 children in the Boston schools to find out how much they "knew" about themselves and the world, asking them such questions as "Where are your ribs?"

Later, during the 1920s, a large number of child development research centers were created (White, 1995), and their professional staffs began to observe and chart a myriad of behaviors in infants and children. The centers at the Universities of Minnesota, Iowa, California at Berkeley, Columbia, and Toronto became famous for their investigations of children's play, friendship patterns, fears, aggression and conflict, and sociability. This work became closely associated with the so-called child study movement, and a new organization, the Society for Research in Child Development, was formed at about the same time.

Early Modern Theorists

In the first half of the twentieth century, a number of theorists influenced prevailing views of children's development. These early modern theorists included Arnold Gesell, G. Stanley Hall, Sigmund Freud, John Watson, James Mark Baldwin, and Jean Piaget.

Arnold Gesell   Arnold Gesell (1928) theorized that certain characteristics of children simply "bloom" with age because of a biological, maturational blueprint. Gesell strove for precision in charting what a child is like at a specific age. To systematically observe children's behavior without interrupting them, he created a photographic dome (see figure 1.3).

G. Stanley Hall Gesell's views, as well as G. Stanley Hall's, were strongly influenced by Charles Darwin's evolutionary theory (Darwin had made the scientific study of children respectable when he developed a baby journal for recording systematic observations of children). Hall (1904) believed that child development follows a natural evolutionary course that can be revealed by child study. He also theorized that child development unfolds in stages, with distinct motives and capabilities at each stage. Hall had much to say about adolescence, arguing that it is full of "storm and stress."

Sigmund Freud Sigmund Freud's psychoanalytic theory was prominent in the early part of the twentieth century. Freud reasoned that children are rarely aware of the motives and reasons for their behavior and that the bulk of their mental life is largely unconscious. His ideas were compatible with Hall's, emphasizing conflict and biological influences on development, although Freud stressed that a child's experiences with parents in the first five years of life are important determinants of later personality development. Freud envisioned the child moving through a series of psychosexual stages filled with conflict between biological urges and societal demands. Freud's theory has had a profound influence on the study of children's personality development and socialization, especially in the areas of gender, morality, family processes, and problems and disturbances.

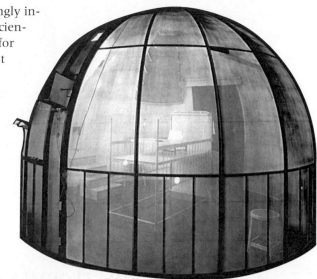

FIGURE 1.3 **Gesell's Photographic Dome** Cameras rode on metal tracks at the top of the dome and were moved as needed to record the child's activities. Others could observe from outside the dome without being seen by the child.

John Watson During the 1920s and 1930s, John Watson's (1928) theory of behaviorism included a view of children that was very different from Freud's. Watson argued that children's development can be shaped by examining and changing their environment. One element of Watson's view, and of behaviorism in general, was a strong belief in the systematic observation of behavior under controlled conditions. Watson had some provocative views about child rearing as well. He claimed that parents are too soft on children; quit cuddling and smiling at babies so much, he told parents.

James Mark Baldwin Whereas John Watson was observing the environment's influence on children's behavior and Sigmund Freud was probing the depths of the unconscious mind to discover clues about our early experiences with our parents, others were more interested in the development of children's conscious thoughts—that is, the thoughts of which they are aware. James Mark Baldwin was a pioneer in the study of children's thought (Cairns, 2006). **Genetic epistemology** was the term that Baldwin gave to the study of how children's knowledge changes over the course of their development. (The term *genetic* at that time was a synonym for "developmental," and the term *epistemology* means "the nature or study of knowledge"). An example of genetic epistemology is young children thinking in more symbolic ways than they did as infants. Baldwin's ideas initially were proposed in the 1880s.

Jean Piaget Twentieth-century Swiss psychologist Jean Piaget adopted and elaborated on many of Baldwin's themes, keenly observing the development of thoughts in his own children and devising clever experiments to investigate how children think. Piaget became a giant in developmental psychology. Some of you, perhaps, are already familiar with his view that children pass through a series of cognitive, or thought, stages from infancy through adolescence. According to Piaget, children think in a qualitatively different manner than adults do.

Our brief introduction to several influential and diverse theories of children's development provided you a glimpse of the different ways children have been viewed as the study of child development unfolded. You will read more about theoretical perspectives later in the text.

genetic epistemology The study of how children's knowledge changes over the course of their development.

Review and Reflect • LEARNING GOAL 2

2 **Characterize how children were viewed historically and by early theorists.**

Review
- How has childhood been discussed through history?
- What is the early modern study of child development like?
- Who were the early modern theorists and what were their views?

Reflect
- Which of the three philosophical views of children—original sin, tabula rasa, or innate goodness—appeals to you? Why?

---

3   WHAT ARE THE DEVELOPMENTAL PROCESSES AND PERIODS?

| Biological, Cognitive, and Socioemotional Processes | Periods of Development |

Each of us develops in certain ways like all other individuals, like some other individuals, and like no other individuals. Most of the time, our attention is directed to a person's uniqueness, but psychologists who study development are drawn to our shared characteristics as well as what makes us unique. As humans, we all have traveled some common paths. Each of us—Leonardo da Vinci, Joan of Arc, George Washington, Martin Luther King, Jr., and you—walked at about the age of 1, engaged in fantasy play as a young child, and became more independent as a youth.

As we saw at the beginning of the chapter, *development* is the pattern of change that begins at conception and continues through the life span. The patterns of development are complex because they are the product of several processes—biological, cognitive, and socioemotional.

Biological, Cognitive, and Socioemotional Processes

Biological processes produce changes in an individual's body. Genes inherited from parents, the development of the brain, height and weight gains, motor skills, and the hormonal changes of puberty all reflect the role of biological processes in development.

biological processes Changes in an individual's body.

PEANUTS reprinted by permission of Newspaper Enterprise Association, Inc.

Cognitive processes refer to changes in an individual's thought, intelligence, and language. Watching a colorful mobile swinging above a crib, putting together a two-word sentence, memorizing a poem, solving a math problem, and imagining what it would be like to be a movie star all involve cognitive processes.

Socioemotional processes involve changes in an individual's relationships with other people, changes in emotions, and changes in personality. An infant's smile in response to her mother's touch, a young boy's aggressive attack on a playmate, a girl's development of assertiveness, and an adolescent's joy at the senior prom all reflect socioemotional development.

Biological, cognitive, and socioemotional processes are intricately intertwined. For example, consider a baby smiling in response to its mother's touch. This response depends on biological processes (the physical nature of the touch and responsiveness to it), cognitive processes (the ability to understand intentional acts), and socioemotional processes (the act of smiling often reflects a positive emotional feeling and smiling helps to connect infants in positive ways with other human beings).

We typically will study the various processes involved in children's development in separate sections of the book. However, keep in mind that these processees are interrelated. It is through their interactions that an integrated human child with only one body and mind develops (see figure 1.4).

FIGURE 1.4 Biological, Cognitive, and Socioemotional Processes Changes in development are the result of biological, cognitive, and socioemotional processes. These processes interact as individuals develop.

Periods of Development

For the purposes of organization and understanding, development is commonly described in terms of periods. The most widely used classification of developmental periods involves the following sequence: the prenatal period, infancy, early childhood, middle and late childhood, and adolescence. Approximate age ranges are placed on the periods to provide a general idea of when a period starts and when it ends.

The **prenatal period** is the time from conception to birth, roughly a nine-month period. It is a time of tremendous growth—from a single cell to a human organism, complete with a brain and behavioral capabilities.

Infancy is the developmental period that extends from birth to 18 to 24 months. Infancy is a time of extreme dependence on adults. Many psychological activities are just beginning—language, symbolic thought, sensorimotor coordination, and social learning, for example.

Early childhood is the developmental period that extends from the end of infancy to about 5 to 6 years of age; sometimes this period is called the preschool years. During this time, young children learn to become more self-sufficient and to care for themselves, they develop school readiness skills (following instructions, identifying letters), and they spend many hours in play and with peers. First grade typically marks the end of this period.

Middle and late childhood is the developmental period that extends from about 6 to 11 years of age; sometimes this period is referred to as the elementary school years. Children master the fundamental skills of reading, writing, and arithmetic, and they are formally exposed to the larger world and its culture. Achievement becomes a more central theme of the child's world, and self-control increases.

Adolescence is the developmental period of transition from childhood to early adulthood, entered at approximately 10 to 12 years of age and ending at 18 to 22 years of age. Adolescence begins with rapid physical changes—dramatic gains in height and weight; changes in body contour; and the development of sexual characteristics such as enlargement of the breasts, development of pubic and facial hair, and deepening of the voice. At this point in development, the pursuit of independence and an identity are prominent. Thought is more logical, abstract, and idealistic. More and more time is spent outside of the family during this period.

cognitive processes Changes in an individual's thought, intelligence, and language.

socioemotional processes Changes in an individual's relationships with other people, emotions, and personality.

prenatal period The time from conception to birth.

infancy The developmental period that extends from birth to 18 to 24 months.

early childhood The developmental period that extends from the end of infancy to about 5 to 6 years, sometimes called the preschool years.

middle and late childhood The developmental period that extends from about 6 to 11 years of age, sometimes called the elementary school years.

adolescence The developmental period of transition from childhood to early adulthood, entered at approximately 10 to 12 years of age and ending at 18 to 22 years of age.

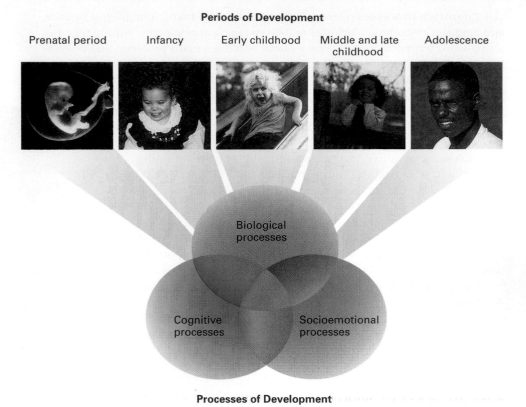

FIGURE 1.5 Processes and Periods of Development Development moves through the prenatal, infancy, early childhood, middle and late childhood, and adolescence periods. These periods of development are the result of biological, cognitive, and socioemotional processes. Development is the creation of increasingly complex forms.

Today, developmentalists do not believe that change ends with adolescence (Baltes, 2003; Baltes, Lindenberger, & Staudinger, 2006; Elder & Shanahan, 2006; Santrock, 2006b). They describe development as a lifelong process. However, the purpose of this text is to describe the changes in development that take place from conception through adolescence.

The periods of development from conception through adolescence are shown in figure 1.5, along with the processes of development—biological, cognitive, and socioemotional. The interplay of biological, cognitive, and socioemotional processes produces the periods of development.

Review and Reflect ● **LEARNING GOAL 3**

 Discuss the most important developmental processes and periods.

Review
- What are three key developmental processes?
- What are five main developmental periods?

Reflect
- At what age did you become an adolescent? Were you physically, cognitively, and socioemotionally different when you became an adolescent? If so, how?

4 WHAT ARE THE CORE ISSUES IN CHILD DEVELOPMENT?

Nature and Nurture

Early and Later Experience

Continuity and Discontinuity

Evaluating the Developmental Issues

There are some overriding main issues that characterize children's development at all periods of development. Three of these are nature and nurture, continuity and discontinuity, and early and later experience.

Nature and Nurture

The **nature-nurture issue** involves the debate about whether development is primarily influenced by nature or by nurture (Coll, Bearer, & Lerner, 2004; Kagan & Herschkowitz, 2005; Lippa, 2005; Tomasello & Slobin, 2005). *Nature* refers to an organism's biological inheritance, *nurture* to its environmental experiences. "Nature" proponents claim that the most important influence on development is biological inheritance. "Nurture" proponents claim that environmental experiences are the most important influence.

According to the nature advocates, just as a sunflower grows in an orderly way—unless defeated by an unfriendly environment—so does the human grow in an orderly way. The range of environments can be vast, but the nature approach argues that a genetic blueprint produces commonalities in growth and development. We walk before we talk, speak one word before two words, grow rapidly in infancy and less so in early childhood, and experience a rush of sexual hormones in puberty. The nature proponents acknowledge that extreme environments—those that are psychologically barren or hostile—can depress development. However, they believe that basic growth tendencies are genetically wired into humans.

By contrast, other psychologists emphasize the importance of nurture, or environmental experiences, in development. Experiences run the gamut from the individual's biological environment (nutrition, medical care, drugs, and physical accidents) to the social environment (family, peers, schools, community, media, and culture). For example, researchers have found that caring adults who provide a supportive, nurturing environment have a substantial positive influence on children's development (Bornstein, 2006; Parke & Buriel, 2006; Parke & others, 2005; Powell, 2005, 2006; Thompson, 2006).

Continuity and Discontinuity

Think about your own development for a moment. Did you become the person you are gradually, like the seedling that slowly, cumulatively grows into a giant oak? Or did you experience sudden, distinct changes in your growth, like the caterpillar that changes into a butterfly (see figure 1.6)? For the most part, developmentalists who emphasize nurture usually describe development as a gradual, continuous process. Those who emphasize nature often describe development as a series of distinct stages.

The **continuity-discontinuity issue** focuses on the extent to which development involves gradual, cumulative change (continuity) or distinct stages (discontinuity). In terms of continuity, as the oak grows from seedling to giant oak, it becomes *more* oak—its development is continuous. Similarly, a child's first word, though seemingly an abrupt, discontinuous event, is actually the result of weeks and months of growth and practice. Puberty, another seemingly abrupt, discontinuous occurrence, is actually a gradual process occurring over several years.

Continuity

Discontinuity

FIGURE 1.6 **Continuity and Discontinuity in Development** Is our development like that of a seedling gradually growing into a giant oak? Or is it more like that of a caterpillar suddenly becoming a butterfly?

nature-nurture issue Nature refers to an organism's biological inheritance, nurture to environmental influences. The "nature" proponents claim biological inheritance is the most important influence on development; the "nurture" proponents claim that environmental experiences are the most important.

continuity-discontinuity issue The issue regarding whether development involves gradual, cumulative change (continuity) or distinct stages (discontinuity).

What characterizes the early and later experience issue?

In terms of discontinuity, each person is described as passing through a sequence of stages in which change is qualitatively rather than quantitatively different. As the caterpillar changes to a butterfly, it is not just more caterpillar, it is a *different kind* of organism—its development is discontinuous. Similarly, at some point a child moves from not being able to think abstractly about the world to being able to. This is a qualitative, discontinuous change in development, not a quantitative, continuous change.

Early and Later Experience

Another important developmental topic is the **early-later experience issue,** which focuses on the degree to which early experiences (especially in infancy) or later experiences are the key determinants of the child's development. That is, if infants experience negative, stressful circumstances in their lives, can those experiences be overcome by later, more-positive experiences? Or are the early experiences so critical—possibly because they are the infant's first, prototypical experiences—that they cannot be overridden by a later, better environment?

The early-later experience issue has a long history and continues to be hotly debated among developmentalists (Gottlieb, 2004). Some believe that, unless infants experience warm, nurturant caregiving in the first year or so of life, their development will never be optimal (Carlson, Sroufe, & Egelund, 2004; Sroufe & others, 2005). The Greek philospher Plato (427–347 B.C.E.) was sure that infants who were held and rocked frequently would become better athletes. Nineteenth-century New England ministers told parents in Sunday sermons that the way they handled their infants would determine their children's future character. The emphasis on the importance of early experience rests on the belief that each life is an unbroken trail on which a psychological quality can be traced back to its origin (Kagan, 1992, 2002; Kagan & Herschkowitz, 2005).

The early-experience doctrine contrasts with the later-experience view that development, like a river, ebbs and flows continuously. The later-experience advocates argue that children are malleable throughout development and that later sensitive caregiving is just as important as earlier sensitive caregiving. A number of life-span developmentalists, who focus on the entire life span rather than only on child development, stress that too little attention has been given to later experiences in development (Baltes, 2003; Baltes, Lindenberger, & Staudinger, 2006). They accept that early experiences are important contributors to development, but no more important than later experiences. Jerome Kagan (2000; Kagan & Herschkowitz, 2005) points out that even children who show the qualities of an inhibited temperament, which is linked to heredity, have the capacity to change their behavior. In his research, almost one-third of a group of children who had an inhibited temperament at 2 years of age were not unusually shy or fearful when they were 4 years of age (Kagan & Snidman, 1991).

People in Western cultures, especially those steeped in the Freudian belief that the key experiences in development are children's relationships with their parents in the first five years of life, have tended to support the idea that early experiences are more important than later experiences (Chan, 1963; Lamb & Sternberg, 1992). By contrast, the majority of people in the world do not share this belief. For example, people in many Asian countries believe that experiences occurring after about 6 to 7 years of age are more important to development than are earlier experiences. This stance stems from the long-standing belief in Eastern cultures that children's reasoning skills begin to develop in important ways in the middle childhood years.

Evaluating the Developmental Issues

Most developmentalists recognize that it is unwise to take an extreme position on the issues of nature and nurture, continuity and discontinuity, and early and later experiences. Development is not all nature or all nurture, not all continuity or all discontinuity, and not all early or later experiences (Overton, 2004). Nature and nurture,

early-later experience issue The issue of the degree to which early experiences (especially infancy) or later experiences are the key determinants of the child's development.

continuity and discontinuity, and early and later experiences all characterize development through the human life span. With respect to the nature-nurture issue then, the key to development is the *interaction* of nature and nurture rather than either factor alone (Gottlieb, 2004). Thus, an individual's cognitive development is the result of heredity-environment interaction, not heredity or environment alone. Heredity-environment interaction is covered in more depth in chapter 3.

Although most developmentalists do not take extreme positions on these three important issues, this consensus has not meant the absence of spirited debate about how strongly development is influenced by each of these factors (Caspi, 2006; Coll, Bearer, & Lerner, 2004; Kagan & Fox, 2006; Lippa, 2005; Sroufe & others, 2005). Are girls less likely to do well in math because of their "feminine" nature or because of society's masculine bias? Can enriched experiences in adolescence remove the "deficits" resulting from childhood experiences of poverty, neglect by parents, and poor schooling? The answers given by developmentalists to such questions depend on their stances on the issues of nature and nurture, continuity and discontinuity, and early and later experience. The answers to these questions also have a bearing on social policy decisions about children and adolescents, and consequently on each of our lives.

Review and Reflect • LEARNING GOAL 4

4 **Describe three key developmental issues.**

Review
- What is the nature and nurture issue?
- What is the continuity and discontinuity issue?
- What is the early and later experience issue?
- What is a good strategy for evaluating the developmental issues?

Reflect
- Can you identify an early experience that you believe contributed significantly to your development? Can you identify a recent or current (later) experience that you think had (is having) a strong influence on your development?

5 WHAT ARE THE MAIN CAREERS IN CHILD DEVELOPMENT?

| Education and Research | Medical, Nursing, and Physical Development | Website Connections for Careers in Child Development |

| Clinical and Counseling | Families and Relationships |

Some of you may be quite sure about what you plan to make your life's work. Others of you may not have decided on a major yet and are uncertain about which career path you want to follow. Each of us wants to find a rewarding career and enjoy the work we do. The field of child development offers an amazing breadth of career options that can provide extremely satisfying work.

If you decide to pursue a career in child development, what options are available to you? There are many. College and university professors teach courses in many different areas of child development, education, family development, nursing, and medicine. Teachers impart knowledge, understanding, and skills to children and adolescents. Counselors, clinical psychologists, nurses, and physicians help parents and children of different ages to cope more effectively with their lives and well-being. Various professionals work with families to improve the quality of family functioning.

Although an advanced degree is not absolutely necessary in some areas of child development, you usually can expand your opportunities (and income) considerably by obtaining a graduate degree. Many careers in child development pay reasonably well. For example, psychologists earn well above the median salary in the United States. Also, by working in the field of child development you can guide people in improving their lives, understand yourself and others better, possibly advance the state of knowledge in the field, and have an enjoyable time while you are doing these things.

If you are considering a career in child development, would you prefer to work with infants? Children? Adolescents? Parents? As you go through this term, try to spend some time with children of different ages. Observe their behavior. Talk with them about their lives. Think about whether you would like to work with children of this age.

Another important aspect of exploring careers is talking with people who work in various settings. For example, if you have some interest in becoming a school counselor, call a school, ask to speak with a counselor, and set up an appointment to discuss the counselor's career and work. If you have an interest in becoming a nurse, think about whether you would rather work with babies, children, or adolescents. Call a hospital, ask to speak with the nursing department, and set up an appointment to talk with the nursing coordinator about a nursing career.

Something else that should benefit you is to work in one or more jobs related to your career interests while you are in college. Many colleges and universities have internships or work experiences for students who major in child development. In some instances, these opportunities are for course credit or pay; in others, they are strictly on a volunteer basis. Take advantage of these opportunities. They can provide valuable experiences to help you decide if this is the right career area for you and they can help you get into graduate school, if you decide you want to go.

In the upcoming sections, we will profile a number of careers in four areas: education and research; clinical and counseling; medical, nursing, and physical development; and families and relationships. These are not the only career options in child development, but they are representative. In profiling these careers, we will address the amount of education required, the nature of the training, and a description of the work.

Education and Research

There are numerous career opportunities in education or research that involve children. These range from college professor to child-care director to school psychologist.

College/University Professor
Courses in child development are taught in many different programs and schools in college and universities, including psychology, education, nursing, child and family studies, social work, and medicine. A Ph.D. or master's degree almost always is required to teach in some area of child development in a college or university. Obtaining a doctoral degree usually takes four to six years of graduate work. A master's degree requires approximately two years of graduate work. The professorial job might be at a research university with one or more master's or Ph.D. programs in child development, at a four-year college with no graduate programs, or at a community college.

The training involves taking graduate courses, learning to conduct research, and attending and presenting papers at professional meetings. Many graduate students work as teaching or research assistants for professors in an apprenticeship relationship that helps them to become competent teachers and researchers. The work that college professors do includes teaching courses either at the undergraduate or graduate level (or both), conducting research in a specific area, advising students and/or directing their research, and serving on college or university committees. Some college instructors do not conduct research as part of their job but instead focus mainly on teaching. In many instances, research is most likely to be part of the job description at universities with master's and Ph.D. programs.

If you are interested in becoming a college or university professor, you might want to make an appointment with your instructor in this class on child development to learn more about his or her profession and work. To read about the work of one college professor, see the Careers in Child Development insert.

Researcher

Some individuals in the field of child development work in research positions. In most instances, they will have a Ph.D. in some area of child development. The researchers might work at a university, in government at such agencies as the National Institute of Mental Health, or in private industry. Individuals who have full-time research positions in child development generate innovative research ideas, plan studies, carry out the research by collecting data, analyze the data, and then interpret it. Then, they will usually attempt to publish the research in a scientific journal. A researcher often works in a collaborative manner with other researchers on a project and may present the research at scientific meetings, where she or he also learns about other research. One researcher might spend much of his or her time in a laboratory while another researcher might work in the field, that is, in schools, hospitals, and other settings.

Elementary or Secondary School Teacher

Becoming an elementary or secondary school teacher requires a minimum of an undergraduate degree. The training involves taking a wide range of courses with a major or concentration in education as well as completing a supervised practice-teaching internship. Elementary or secondary school teachers teach one or more subject areas, prepare the curriculum, give tests, assign grades, monitor students' progress, conduct parent-teacher conferences, and attend in-service workshops.

Exceptional Children (Special Education) Teacher

Becoming a teacher of exceptional children requires a minimum of an undergraduate degree. The training consists of taking a wide range of courses in education and a concentration of courses in educating children with disabilities or children who are gifted. The work of a teacher of exceptional children involves spending concentrated time with individual children who have a disability or are gifted. A teacher of exceptional children might work with children with learning disabilities, ADHD (attention deficit hyperactivity disorder), mental retardation, or a physical disability such as cerebral palsy. Some of this work will usually be done outside of the student's regular classroom, some of it will be carried out when the student is in the regular classroom. A teacher of exceptional children works closely with the student's regular classroom teacher and parents to create the best educational program for the student. Teachers of exceptional

CAREERS in CHILD DEVELOPMENT

Valerie Pang,
Professor of Teacher Education

Valerie Pang is a professor of teacher education at San Diego State University and formerly was an elementary school teacher. Like Dr. Pang, many professors of teacher education have a doctorate and have experience in teaching at the elementary or secondary school level.

Pang earned a doctorate at the University of Washington. She has received a Multicultural Educator Award from the National Association of Multicultural Education for her work on culture and equity. She also was given the Distinguished Scholar Award from the American Educational Research Association's Committee on the Role and Status of Minorities in Education.

Pang (2005) believes that competant teachers need to:

- Recognize the power and complexity of cultural influences on students.

- Be sensitive to whether their expectations for students are culturally biased.
- Evaluate whether they are doing a good job of seeing life from the perspective of students who come from different cultures.

Valerie Pang is a professor in the School of Education of San Diego State University and formerly an elementary school teacher. Valerie believes it is important for teachers to create a caring classroom that affirms all students.

children often continue their education after obtaining their undergraduate degree and attain a master's degree.

Early Childhood Educator   Early childhood educators work on college faculties and have a minimum of a master's degree in their field. In graduate school, they take courses in early childhood education and receive supervisory training in childcare or early childhood programs. Early childhood educators usually teach in community colleges that award an associate degree in early childhood education.

Preschool/Kindergarten Teacher   Preschool teachers teach mainly 4-year-old children and kindergarten teachers primarily teach 5-year-old children. They usually have an undergraduate degree in education, specializing in early childhood education. State certification to become a preschool or kindergarten teacher usually is required. These teachers direct the educational activities of young children.

Family and Consumer Science Educator   Family and consumer science educators may specialize in early childhood education or instruct middle and high school students about such matters as nutrition, interpersonal relationships, human sexuality, parenting, and human development. Hundreds of colleges and universities throughout the United States offer two- and four-year degree programs in family and consumer science. These programs usually include an internship requirement. Additional education courses may be needed to obtain a teaching certificate. Some family and consumer educators go on to graduate school for further training, which provides a background for possible jobs in college teaching or research.

Educational Psychologist   An educational psychologist most often teaches in a college or university and conducts research in such areas of educational psychology as learning, motivation, classroom management, and assessment. Most educational psychologists have a doctorate in education, which takes four to six years of graduate work. They help to train students who will take various positions in education, including educational psychology, school psychology, and teaching.

School Psychologist   School psychologists focus on improving the psychological and intellectual well-being of elementary and secondary school students. They usually have a master's or doctoral degree in school psychology. In graduate school, they take courses in counseling, assessment, learning, and other areas of education and psychology. School psychologists may work in a centralized office in a school district or in one or more schools. They give psychological tests, interview students and their parents, consult with teachers, and may provide counseling to students and their families.

Clinical Practice and Counseling

There are a wide variety of clinical and counseling jobs that are linked with child development. These range from child clinical psychologist to social worker to adolescent drug counselor.

Clinical Psychologist   Clinical psychologists seek to help people with psychological problems. They work in a variety of settings, including colleges and universities, clinics, medical schools, and private practice. Clinical psychologists have either a Ph.D. (which involves clinical and research training) or a Psy.D. degree (which involves clinical training). This graduate training usually takes five to seven years and only includes courses in clinical psychology and a one-year supervised internship in an accredited setting toward the end of the training. Most states have licensing requirements for a clinical psychologist. Some clinical psychologists only conduct psychotherapy, others do psychological assessment and psychotherapy, and some also do research. Clinical psychologists may specialize in a particular age group, such as children (child clinical psychologist).

Psychiatrist   Psychiatrists obtain a medical degree and then do a residency in psychiatry. Medical school takes approximately four years and the psychiatry residency another three to four years. Unlike psychologists (who do not go to medical school) in most states, psychiatrists can administer drugs to clients. Like clinical psychologists, psychiatrists might specialize in working with children (child psychiatry) or adolescents (adolescent psychiatry). Psychiatrists might work in medical schools in teaching and research roles, in a medical clinic, or in private practice. In addition to administering drugs to help improve the lives of people with psychological problems, psychiatrists also may conduct psychotherapy.

Counseling Psychologist   Counseling psychologists go through much of the same training as clinical psychologists, although in a graduate program in counseling rather than clinical psychology. Counseling psychologists have either a master's degree or a doctoral degree. They also must go through a licensing procedure. One type of master's degree in counseling leads to the designation of licensed professional counselor. They work in the same settings as clinical psychologists, and may do psychotherapy, teach, or conduct research. In many instances, counseling psychologists do not do therapy with individuals who have a severe mental disorder. A counseling psychologist might specialize in working with children, adolescents, and/or families.

School Counselor   School counselors help to identify students' abilities and interests, guide students in developing academic plans, and explore career options with students. They may help students cope with adjustment problems. They may work with students individually, in small groups, or even in a classroom. They often consult with parents, teachers, and school administrators when trying to help students with their problems. School counselors usually have a master's degree in counseling. High school counselors advise students on choosing a major, admissions requirements for college, taking entrance exams, applying for financial aid, and on appropriate vocational and technical training. Elementary school counselors primarily counsel students about social and personal problems. They may observe children in the classroom and at play as part of their work.

Career Counselor   Career counselors help individuals to identify what the best career options are for them and guide them in applying for jobs. They may work in private industry or at a college or university. They usually interview individuals and give them vocational and/or psychological tests to help their clients choose careers that fit their interests and abilities. Sometimes they help individuals to create professional resumes or conduct mock interviews to help them feel comfortable in a job interview. They may create and promote job fairs or other recruiting events to help individuals obtain jobs.

Social Worker   Social workers often are involved in helping people with social or economic problems. They may investigate, evaluate, and attempt to rectify reported cases of abuse, neglect, endangerment, or domestic disputes. They can intervene in families if necessary and provide counseling and referral services to individuals and families. They have a minimum of an undergraduate degree from a school of social work that includes course work in various areas of sociology and psychology. Some social workers also have a master's or doctoral degree. They often work for publicly funded agencies at the city, state, or national level, although increasingly they work in the private sector in areas such as drug rehabilitation and family counseling.

In some cases, social workers specialize in a certain area, as is true of a medical social worker, who has a master's degree in social work (M.S.W.). This involves graduate course work and supervised clinical experiences in medical settings. A medical social worker might coordinate a variety of support services to people with a severe or long-term disability. Family care social workers often work with families who need support services.

Drug Counselor   Drug counselors provide counseling to individuals with drug abuse problems. They may work on an individual basis with a substance abuser or conduct group therapy sessions. At a minimum, drug counselors go through an associate-degree or certificate program. Many have an undergraduate degree in substance-abuse counseling, and some have master's and doctoral degrees. They may work in private practice, with a state or federal government agency, with a company, or in a hospital setting. Some drug counselors specialize in working with adolescents or families. Most states provide a licensing procedure for individuals who want to practice drug counseling.

Medicine, Nursing, and Physical Development

This third main area of careers in child development includes a wide range of careers in the medical and nursing areas, as well as jobs pertaining to improving some aspect of the child's physical development. These range from pediatrician to speech therapist to genetic counselor.

Obstetrician/Gynecologist   An obstetrician/gynecologist prescribes prenatal and postnatal care and performs deliveries in maternity cases, and treats diseases and injuries of the female reproductive system. Becoming an obstetrician/gynecologist requires a medical degree plus three to five years of residency in obstetrics/gynecology. They may work in private practice, in a medical clinic, a hospital, or in a medical school.

Pediatrician   A pediatrician monitors infants' and children's health, works to prevent disease or injury, helps children attain optimal health, and treats children with health problems. Pediatricians have attained a medical degree and then go on to do a three- to five-year residency in pediatrics. Pediatricians may work in private practice, in a medical clinic, in a hospital, or in a medical school. As medical doctors, they can administer drugs to children and may counsel parents and children on ways to improve the children's health. Many pediatricians on the faculty of medical schools also teach and conduct research on children's health and diseases.

Neonatal Nurse   A neonatal nurse cares for newborn infants. The neonatal nurse may work to improve the health and well-being of infants born under normal circumstances or be involved in the delivery of and care of the premature and critically ill neonates. A minimum of an undergraduate degree in nursing with a specialization in the newborn is required. This training involves course work in nursing and the biological sciences, as well as supervisory clinical experiences.

Nurse-Midwife   A nurse-midwife formulates and provides comprehensive care to selected maternity patients, cares for the expectant mother as she prepares to give birth and guides her through the birth process, and cares for the postpartum patient. The nurse-midwife also may provide care to the newborn, counsel parents on the infant's development and parenting, and provide guidance about health practices. Becoming a nurse-midwife generally requires an undergraduate degree from a school of nursing. A nurse-midwife most often works in a hospital setting.

Pediatric Nurse
Pediatric nurses have a degree in nursing that takes from two to five years to complete. Some also may go on to obtain a master's or doctoral degree in pediatric nursing. Pediatric nurses take courses in biological sciences, nursing care, and pediatrics, usually in a school of nursing. They also undergo supervised clinical experiences in medical settings. They monitor infants' and children's health, work to prevent disease or injury, and help children attain optimal health. They may work in hospitals, schools of nursing, or with pediatricians in private practice or at a medical clinic. To read about the work of one pediatric nurse, see the Careers in Child Development insert.

Audiologist
An audiologist has a minimum of an undergraduate degree in hearing science. This includes courses and supervisory training. Audiologists assess and identify the presence and severity of hearing loss, as well as problems in balance. Some audiologists also go on to obtain a master's and/or doctoral degree. They may work in a medical clinic, with a physician in private practice, in a hospital, or in a medical school.

Speech Therapist
Speech therapists are health-care professionals who are trained to identify, assess, and treat speech and language problems. They may work with physicians, psychologists, social workers, and other health-care professionals in a team approach to help individuals with physical or psychological problems in which speech and language are involved. Speech therapists have a minimum of an undergraduate degree in the speech and hearing science or communications disorders. They may work in private practice, in hospitals and medical schools, and in government agencies with individuals of any age. Some may specialize in working with children or in a particular type of speech disorder.

Genetic Counselor
Genetic counselors are health professionals with specialized graduate degrees and experience in the areas of medical genetics and counseling. Most enter the field after majoring in undergraduate school in such disciplines as biology, genetics, psychology, nursing, public health, and social work. Genetic counselors work as members of a health-care team, providing information and support to families who have members with birth defects or genetic disorders and to families who may be at risk for a variety of inherited conditions. They identify families at risk and provide supportive counseling. They serve as educators and resource people for other health-care professionals and the public. Almost half work in university medical centers and another one-fourth work in private hospital settings.

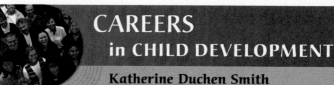

CAREERS in CHILD DEVELOPMENT

Katherine Duchen Smith
Nurse and Child-Care Health Consultant

Katherine Duchen Smith has a master's degree in nursing and works as a child-care health consultant. She lives in Ft. Collins, Colorado, and in 2004 was appointed as the public relations chair of the National Association of Pediatric Nurse Practitioners (NAPNAP), which has more than 6,000 members.

Smith provides health consultation and educational services to child-care centers, private schools, and hospitals. She also teaches in the Regis University Family Nurse Practitioner Program. Smith developed an interest in outreach and public relations activities during her five-year term as a board member for the Fort Collins Poudre Valley Hospital System. Later, she became the organization's outreach consultant.

As child-care health consultants, nurses might provide telephone consultation and link children, families, or staff with primary care providers. In underserved areas, they might also be asked to administer immunizations, help chronically ill children access specialty care, or develop a comprehensive health promotion or injury prevention program for caregivers and families.

Katherine Duchen Smith (left), nurse and child-care health consultant, at a child-care center where she is a consultant.

Families and Relationships

A number of careers and jobs are available for individuals interested in working with families and relationship problems. These range from being a child welfare worker to a marriage and family therapist.

Child Welfare Worker   A child welfare worker is employed by the Child Protective Services Unit of each state. The child welfare worker protects the child's rights, evaluates any maltreatment the child might experience, and may have the child removed from the home if necessary. A child welfare worker has a minimum of an undergraduate degree in social work.

Child Life Specialist   Child life specialists work with children and their families when the child needs to be hospitalized. They monitor the child patient's activities, seek to reduce the child's stress, help the child cope effectively, and assist the child in enjoying the hospital experience as much as possible. Child life specialists may provide parent education and develop individualized treatment plans based on an assessment of the child's development, temperament, medical plan, and available social supports. Child life specialists have an undergraduate degree and they take courses in child development and education, as well as courses in a child life program.

Marriage and Family Therapist   Marriage and family therapists work on the principle that many individuals who have psychological problems benefit when psychotherapy is provided in the context of a marital or family relationship. Marriage and family therapists may provide marital therapy, couple therapy to individuals in a relationship who are not married, and family therapy to two or more members of a family.

Marriage and family therapists have a master's and/or doctoral degree. They go through a training program in graduate school similar to a clinical psychologist but with the focus on marital and family relationships. Most states require a license to practice marital and family therapy.

Website Connections for Careers in Child Development

By going to the website for this book **(www.mhhe.com/santrockc9)** you can obtain more detailed career information about the various careers in child development described here. Go to the Web connections for chapter 1, where you will see a description of the websites. Then click on the title and you will be able to go directly to the website described. Here are the website connections:

Education and Research
  Careers in Psychology
  Elementary and Secondary School Teaching
  Exceptional Children Teachers
  Early Childhood Education
  Family and Consumer Science Education
  Educational Psychology
  School Psychology
Clinical and Counseling
  Clinical Psychology
  Psychiatry
  Counseling Psychology
  School Counseling
  Social Work
  Drug Counseling

Medical, Nursing, and Physical Development
    Obstetrics and Gynecology
    Pediatrics
    Nurse-Midwife
    Neonatal Nursing
    Pediatric Nursing
    Audiology and Speech Pathology
    Genetic Counseling
Families and Relationships
    Child Welfare Worker
    Child Life Specialist
    Marriage and Family Therapist

Review and Reflect • LEARNING GOAL 5

Summarize the career paths for working with children.

Review

- What are some education and research careers that involve working with children?

- What are some clinical and counseling careers that involve working with children?

- What are some medical, nursing, and physical development careers that involve working with children?

- What are some family and relationship-oriented careers that involve working with children?

Reflect

- Which of the careers that were described are the most interesting to you? Choose three of these careers and go to the related websites to learn more about them.

REACH YOUR LEARNING GOALS

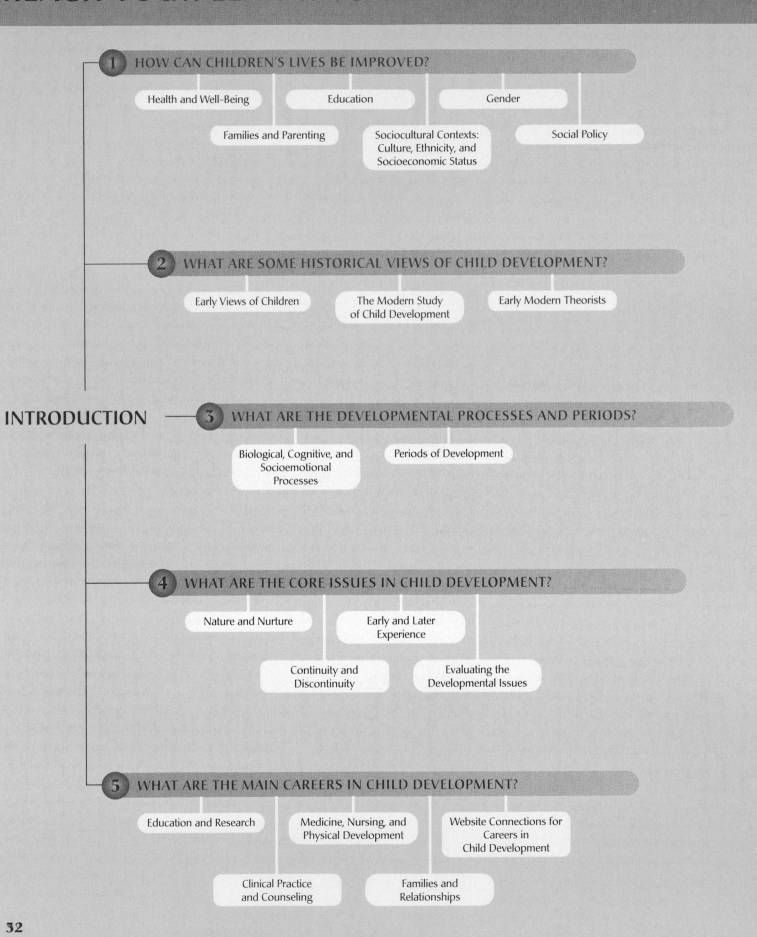

INTRODUCTION

1 HOW CAN CHILDREN'S LIVES BE IMPROVED?

Health and Well-Being

Education

Gender

Families and Parenting

Sociocultural Contexts: Culture, Ethnicity, and Socioeconomic Status

Social Policy

2 WHAT ARE SOME HISTORICAL VIEWS OF CHILD DEVELOPMENT?

Early Views of Children

The Modern Study of Child Development

Early Modern Theorists

3 WHAT ARE THE DEVELOPMENTAL PROCESSES AND PERIODS?

Biological, Cognitive, and Socioemotional Processes

Periods of Development

4 WHAT ARE THE CORE ISSUES IN CHILD DEVELOPMENT?

Nature and Nurture

Early and Later Experience

Continuity and Discontinuity

Evaluating the Developmental Issues

5 WHAT ARE THE MAIN CAREERS IN CHILD DEVELOPMENT?

Education and Research

Medicine, Nursing, and Physical Development

Website Connections for Careers in Child Development

Clinical Practice and Counseling

Families and Relationships

SUMMARY

 Identify six areas in which children's lives can be improved.

- Health and well-being is an important area in which children's lives can be improved. Today, many children in the United States and around the world need improved health care. We now recognize the importance of lifestyles and psychological states in promoting health and well-being.
- Families and parenting are important influences on children's development. One-parent families, working parents, and child care are among the family issues that influence children's well-being.
- Education can also contribute to children's health and well-being. There is widespread concern that the education of children needs to be more effective and there are many views in contemporary education about ways to improve schools.
- Sociocultural contexts are important influences on children's development. Contexts, culture, ethnicity, and socioeconomic status are four key aspects of sociocultural contexts. Context refers to the setting in which development occurs. Culture encompasses the behavior patterns, beliefs, and all other products of a particular group of people that are passed on from generation to generation. Cross-cultural studies are comparisons of one culture with one or more other cultures. Ethnicity is rooted in cultural heritage, nationality characteristics, race, religion, and language. Ethnicity is central to an ethnic identity, which is a sense of membership in an ethnic group based on shared language, religion, customs, values, history, and race. The tapestry of American culture has changed dramatically in recent years, becoming more ethnically diverse. Socioeconomic status (SES) refers to the grouping of people with similar occupational, educational, and economic characteristics. SES implies certain inequalities with differences in the ability to control social resources and participation in society's rewards producing unequal opportunities for children.
- Gender involves the psychological and sociocultural dimensions of being female or male. Few aspects of our development are more central to our identity and social relationships than gender.
- Social policy is a national government's course of action designed to influence the welfare of its citizens. Researchers increasingly are conducting studies that are related to social policy. A number of groups, including the Children's Defense Fund, work to improve social policy related to children. Family policy is an especially important aspect of social policy. Studying resilient children can provide information about how to help children re-

sist the negative effects of adverse conditions. Individual factors, family factors, and extrafamilial factors characterize resilient children.

 Characterize how children were viewed historically and by early theorists.

- The history of interest in children is long and rich. Prior to the nineteenth century, philosophical views of childhood were prominent, including the notions of original sin (children are basically bad, born into the world as evil beings), tabula rasa (children are not innately bad or good but rather like a "blank tablet"), and innate goodness (children are inherently good). Today, we conceive of childhood as an important time of development.
- The modern era of studying children spans a little more than a century, an era in which the study of child development has become a sophisticated science. During the late 1800s, a major shift took place—from a strictly philosophical perspective to one that focuses on direct observation and experimentation. During the 1920s, a number of child development research centers were created.
- Early modern theorists included Arnold Gesell, who believed that certain characteristics of children simply "bloom" with age because of a biological, maturational blueprint; G. Stanley Hall, who theorized that child development follows an evolutionary course and that adolescence is filled with "storm and stress"; Sigmund Freud, who thought that children were rarely aware of the motives and reasons for their behaviors as they moved through a series of psychosexual stages; John Watson, who argued that children can be shaped into whatever society wishes by examining and changing the environment; James Mark Baldwin, who was a pioneer in the study of children's thought; and Jean Piaget, who proposed a sequence of cognitive stages that children pass through.

Discuss the most important developmental processes and periods.

- Three key processes of development are biological, cognitive, and socioemotional. Biological processes (such as genes inherited from parents) involve changes in an individual's physical nature. Cognitive processes (such as thinking) consist of changes in an individual's thought, intelligence, and language. Socioemotional processes (such as smiling) include changes in an individual's relationships with others, in emotions, and in personality.
- Childhood's five main developmental periods are (1) prenatal—conception to birth, (2) infancy—birth to 18 to 24 months, (3) early childhood—end of infancy to

about 5 to 6 years of age, (4) middle and late child-hood—6 to about 11 years of age, and (5) adolescence—begins at about 10 to 12 and ends at about 18 to 22 years of age.

4 Describe three key developmental issues.

- The nature-nurture issue focuses on the extent to which development is mainly influenced by nature (biological inheritance) or nurture (environmental experience).
- Some developmentalists describe development as continuous (gradual, cumulative change), others describe it as discontinuous (a sequence of abrupt stages).
- The early-later experience issue focuses on whether early experiences (especially in infancy) are more important in development than later experiences.
- Most developmentalists recognize that extreme positions on the nature-nurture, continuity-discontinuity, and early-later experience issues are not supported by research. Despite this consensus, they continue to debate the degree to which each position influences children's development.

5 Summarize the career paths for working with children.

- Education and research careers include college/university professor, researcher, elementary or secondary teacher, exceptional children teacher, early childhood educator, preschool/kindergarten teacher, family and consumer science educator, educational psychologist, and school psychologist.
- Clinical and counseling careers include clinical psychologist, psychiatrist, counseling psychologist, school counselor, career counselor, social worker, and drug counselor.
- Medical, nursing, and physical development careers include obstetrician/gynecologist, pediatrician, neonatal nurse, nurse-midwife, pediatric nurse, audiologist, speech therapist, and genetic counselor.
- Families and relationships careers include child welfare worker, child life specialist, and marriage and family therapist.

KEY TERMS

development 7	gender 12	cognitive processes 19	nature-nurture issue 21
context 10	social policy 12	socioemotional processes 19	continuity-discontinuity issue 21
culture 10	original sin view 15	prenatal period 19	early-later experience issue 22
cross-cultural studies 10	tabula rasa view 15	infancy 19	
ethnicity 10	innate goodness view 15	early childhood 19	
ethnic identity 10	genetic epistemology 17	middle and late childhood 19	
socioeconomic status (SES) 10	biological processes 18	adolescence 19	

KEY PEOPLE

Jeanne Brooks-Gunn 11	John Locke 15	Charles Darwin 17	Jean Piaget 17
Marian Wright Edelman 12	Jean-Jacques Rousseau 15	Sigmund Freud 17	Jerome Kagan 22
Ann Masten 14	Arnold Gesell 16	John Watson 17	
Philippe Ariès 15	G. Stanley Hall 17	James Mark Baldwin 17	

MAKING A DIFFERENCE

Lessons for Life

Marian Wright Edelman (1992, 2000, 2004) is one of America's foremost crusaders in the quest for improving the lives of children. Here are some of the main strategies she advocates for improving not only children's lives but our own as well (Edelman, 1992, pp. xxi, 42, 60).

- *"Don't feel as if you are entitled to anything that you don't sweat and struggle for."* Take the initiative to create opportunities.

Don't wait around for people to give you favors. A door never has to stay closed. Push on it until it opens.

- *"Don't be afraid of taking risks or of being criticized."* We all make mistakes. It is only through making mistakes that we learn how to do things right. "It doesn't matter how many times you fall down. What matters is how many times we get up." We need "more courageous shepherds and fewer sheep."
- *"Don't ever stop learning and improving your mind or you're going to get left behind."* College is a great investment but

don't think you can park your mind there and everything you need to know will somehow be magically poured into it. Be an active learner. Be curious and ask questions. Explore new horizons.

- *Stand up for children.* According to Edelman, this is the most important mission in the world. Parenting and nurturing the next generation of children are our society's most important functions and we need to take them more seriously than we have in the past.

CHILDREN RESOURCES

Child Development and Social Policy (2000)

by Edward Zigler and Nancy Hall. New York: McGraw-Hill.

An analysis of what needs to be done to improve America's social policy for children.

Children's Defense Fund

25 E Street
Washington, DC 20001
800–424–9602
www.childrensdefense.org

The Children's Defense Fund exists to provide a strong and effective voice for children and adolescents who cannot vote, lobby, or speak for themselves. The Children's Defense Fund is

especially interested in the needs of poor, minority, and handicapped children and adolescents. The fund provides information, technical assistance, and support to a network of state and local child and youth advocates. The Children's Defense Fund publishes a number of excellent books and pamphlets related to children's needs.

Handbook of Child Psychology (6th Ed., Vols, 1–4) (2006)

Edited by William Damon and Richard Lerner. New York: John Wiley

The *Handbook of Child Psychology* is the standard reference work for overviews of theory and research in this field. It has in-depth discussions of many topics that we will explore in this book.

E-LEARNING TOOLS

Connect to **www.mhhe.com/santrockc9** to research the answers to and complete the following exercises. In addition, you'll find a number of other resources and valuable study tools for chapter 1, "Introduction," on this website.

Taking It to the Net

1. George is teaching fourth grade. He wants his students to learn about the difficulties and challenges of being a child in colonial America. What was life like for children in the early history of our country?
2. Janice thinks that better and stricter gun control laws will help decrease violent crime among children. Her husband, Elliott, disagrees. Janice found a March 2000 Department of Justice study that provides support for her argument. What facts in the report can she point to in order to convince Elliott?
3. For his political science class, Darren has to track federal funding appropriations in the most recent Congress for any issue of his choice. He has chosen children's issues. How

did children and families fare in terms of congressional appropriations in the first half of the 106th Congress?

Health and Well-Being, Parenting, and Education Exercises

Build your decision-making skills by trying your hand at the health and well-being, parenting, and education exercises.

Video Clips

The Online Learning Center includes the following videos for this chapter:

1. *Career in Child Development*–905
   Dr. Richard Lerner gives a very humorous account of decision to major in psychology in college.
2. *Career in Developmental Psychology*–245
   Dr. Weinraub, one of the leading researchers on the NICHD Early Childcare Study, describes how she became interested in developmental psychology.

There is nothing quite so practical as a good theory.

—KURT LEWIN
American Social Psychologist, 20th Century

Images of Children
The Stories of Jean Piaget and Erik Erikson

What motivates someone to construct a theory of child development? A person interested in developing a theory usually goes through a long university training program that culminates in a doctoral degree. As part of the training, the future theorist is exposed to many ideas about a particular area of development, such as biological, cognitive, or socioemotional development. Another factor that could explain why someone develops a particular theory is that person's life experiences. Let's look at the lives of two important developmental theorists, Erik Erikson and Jean Piaget, as they were growing up to discover how their experiences might have contributed to the theories they developed.

Erik Homberger Erikson (1902–1994) was born near Frankfurt, Germany, to Danish parents. Before Erik was born, his parents separated, and his mother left Denmark to live in Germany. At age 3, Erik became ill, and his mother took him to see a pediatrician named Homberger. Young Erik's mother fell in love with the pediatrician, married him, and renamed Erik after his new stepfather.

Erik attended primary school from the ages of 6 to 10 and then the gymnasium (high school) from 11 to 18. He studied art and a number of languages. Erik did not like the atmosphere of formal schooling, and this attitude was reflected in his grades. Rather than going to college at age 18, the adolescent Erikson wandered around Europe, keeping a diary about his experiences. After a year of travel, he returned to Germany and enrolled in art school, became dissatisfied, and enrolled in another. Later he traveled to Florence, Italy. Psychiatrist Robert Coles described Erikson at this time:

> To the Italians he was the young, tall, thin Nordic expatriate with long, blond hair. He wore a corduroy suit and was seen by his family and friends as not odd or "sick" but as a wandering artist who was trying to come to grips with himself, a not unnatural or unusual struggle. (Coles, 1970, p. 15)

Contrast Erikson's experiences that led to develop a theory of identity development with the experiences of Jean Piaget. Piaget (1896–1980) was born in Neuchâtel, Switzerland. Jean's father was an intellectual who taught young Jean to think systematically. Jean's mother was also very bright. His father had an air of detachment from his mother, whom Piaget described as prone to frequent outbursts of neurotic behavior.

In his autobiography, Piaget detailed why he chose to study cognitive development rather than social or abnormal development:

> I started to forego playing for serious work very early. Indeed, I have always detested any departure from reality, an attitude which I relate to . . . my mother's poor health. It was this disturbing factor which at the beginning of my studies in psychology made me keenly interested in psychoanalytic and pathological psychology. Though this interest helped me to achieve independence and widen my cultural background, I have never since felt any desire to involve myself deeper in that particular direction, always much preferring the study of normalcy and of the workings of the intellect to that of the tricks of the unconscious. (Piaget, 1952a, p. 238)

These snapshots of Erikson and Piaget illustrate how personal experiences might influence the direction in which a particular theorist goes. Erikson's wanderings and search for self contributed to his theory of identity development, and Piaget's intellectual experiences with his parents and schooling contributed to his emphasis on cognitive development.

PREVIEW

This chapter introduces the theories and methods that are the foundation of the science of child development.

We will describe and evaluate these theories: psychoanalytic, cognitive, behavioral and social cognitive, ethological, and ecological. At the end of the chapter we will explore some of the ethical challenges and biases that researchers must guard against to protect the *integrity of their results and respect the rights of the participants in their studies.*

HOW IS CHILD DEVELOPMENT A SCIENCE?

| The Importance of Research in Child Development | The Scientific Research Approach |

Is child development really a science? Theories are part of the science of child development. When a person comes up with a theory, it must be tested scientifically to determine if it is accurate. Some individuals have difficulty thinking of child development as a science like physics, chemistry, and biology. Can a discipline that studies how parents nurture children, how peers interact, the developmental changes in children's thinking, and whether watching TV hour after hour is linked with being overweight be equated with disciplines that study the molecular structure of a compound and how gravity works? The answer is yes. Science is defined not by *what* it investigates, but by *how* it investigates. Whether you're studying photosynthesis, butterflies, Saturn's moons, or children's development, it is the way you study that makes the approach scientific or not.

The Importance of Research in Child Development

It sometimes is said that experience is the most important teacher. We get a great deal of knowledge from personal experience, generalize from what we observe, and frequently turn memorable encounters into lifetime "truths." But how valid are these conclusions? At times we err in making these personal observations or misinterpret what we see and hear. Chances are, you can think of many situations in which you thought other people read you the wrong way, just as they may have felt that you misread them. When we base information only on personal experiences, we aren't always completely objective, because sometimes we make judgments that protect our ego and self-esteem (McMillan, 2004; Reynolds, Livingston, & Wilson, 2006).

We get information not only from personal experiences but also from authorities and experts. You may hear experts spell out a "best way" to parent children or educate them, but the authorities and experts don't always agree. One expert may proclaim that one particular strategy for interacting with children is the best and, the next week, another expert may tout a very different strategy as the best. How can you tell which one to believe? One way to clarify the situation is to carefully examine research on the topic.

The Scientific Research Approach

Researchers take a skeptical, scientific attitude toward knowledge. When they hear someone claim that a particular method is effective in helping children cope with stress, they want to know if the claim is based on *good* research. The science part of child development seeks to sort fact from fancy by using particular strategies for obtaining information (Gronlund, 2006; Salkind, 2003; Wiertsma & Jurs, 2005).

Scientific research is objective, systematic, and testable. It reduces the likelihood that information will be based on personal beliefs, opinions, and feelings (McMillan & Wergin, 2002; Mertler & Charles, 2005). Scientific research is based on the **scientific method,** an approach that can be used to discover accurate information. It includes

*S*cience *refines everyday thinking.*
—ALBERT EINSTEIN
German-born American Physicist, 20th Century

scientific method An approach that can be used to obtain accurate information. It includes these steps: (1) conceptualize the problem, (2) collect data, (3) draw conclusions, and (4) revise research conclusions and theory.

these steps: conceptualize the problem, collect data, draw conclusions, and revise research conclusions and theory.

The first step, *conceptualizing a problem,* involves identifying the problem. At a general level, this may not seem like a difficult task. However, researchers must go beyond a general description of the problem by isolating, analyzing, narrowing, and focusing more specifically on what they want to study. For example, a team of researchers decide to study ways to improve the achievement of children from impoverished backgrounds. Perhaps they choose to examine whether mentoring that involves sustained support, guidance, and concrete assistance can improve the children's academic performance. At this point, even more narrowing and focusing takes place. For instance, what specific strategies should the mentors use? How often will they see the children? How long will the mentoring program last? What aspects of the children's achievement will be assessed?

As part of the first step in formulating a problem to study, researchers often draw on *theories* and *develop hypothesis.* A **theory** is an interrelated, coherent set of ideas that helps to explain and to make predictions. For example, a theory on mentoring might attempt to explain and predict why sustained support, guidance, and concrete experience make a difference in the lives of children from impoverished backgrounds. The theory might focus on children's opportunities to model the behavior and strategies of mentors, or it might focus on the effects of individual attention, which might be missing in the children's lives. A **hypothesis** is a specific testable assumption or prediction. A hypothesis is often written as an *if-then* statement. In our example, a sample hypothesis might be: If children from impoverished backgrounds are given individual attention by mentors, the children will spend more time studying and make higher grades. Testing a hypothesis can inform researchers whether or not a theory may be accurate.

The second step in the scientific method is to *collect information (data).* In the study of mentoring, the researchers might decide to conduct the mentoring program for six months. Their data might consist of classroom observations, teachers' ratings, and achievement tests given to the mentored children before the mentoring began and at the end of six months of mentoring.

Once data have been collected, child development researchers use *statistical procedures* to understand the meaning of the data (Hurlburt, 2006). Then they try to *draw conclusions.* In this third step, statistics help to determine whether or not the researchers' observations are due to chance.

After data have been collected and analyzed, researchers compare their findings with those of other researchers on the same topic. The final step in the scientific method is *revising research conclusions and theory.* Figure 2.1 illustrates the steps in the scientific method applied to the study of mentoring we have been discussing. We will introduce the main theories of child development shortly and you will also read about theories throughout the text.

Review and Reflect ● LEARNING GOAL 1

 Discuss the importance of research in child development and the scientific method.

Review
- Why is research on child development important?
- What is the scientific method? What are its four main steps?

Reflect
- Imagine that a friend says she saw an ad on TV claiming a particular toy is something all parents need to buy to ensure their child is getting adequate learning opportunities. Based on what you have read in this section, why might you be skeptical of this claim?

theory An interrelated, coherent set of ideas that helps to explain and to make predictions.

hypothesis Specific assumption and prediction that can be tested to determine accuracy.

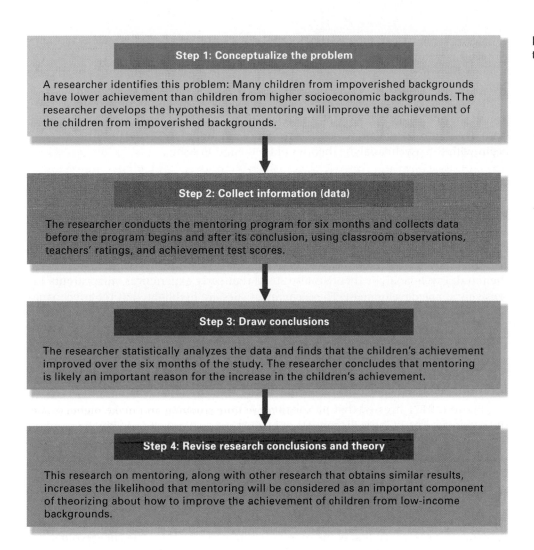

FIGURE 2.1 The Scientific Method Applied to a Study of Mentoring

Step 1: Conceptualize the problem

A researcher identifies this problem: Many children from impoverished backgrounds have lower achievement than children from higher socioeconomic backgrounds. The researcher develops the hypothesis that mentoring will improve the achievement of the children from impoverished backgrounds.

Step 2: Collect information (data)

The researcher conducts the mentoring program for six months and collects data before the program begins and after its conclusion, using classroom observations, teachers' ratings, and achievement test scores.

Step 3: Draw conclusions

The researcher statistically analyzes the data and finds that the children's achievement improved over the six months of the study. The researcher concludes that mentoring is likely an important reason for the increase in the children's achievement.

Step 4: Revise research conclusions and theory

This research on mentoring, along with other research that obtains similar results, increases the likelihood that mentoring will be considered as an important component of theorizing about how to improve the achievement of children from low-income backgrounds.

2 WHAT ARE THE MAIN THEORIES OF CHILD DEVELOPMENT?

Psychoanalytic Theories

Behavioral and Social Cognitive Theories

Ecological Theory

Cognitive Theories

Ethological Theory

An Eclectic Theoretical Orientation

The diversity of theories makes understanding children's development a challenging undertaking (Lerner, Theokas, & Bobeck, 2005; Thomas, 2005). Just when you think one theory is the best explanation of children's development, another theory crops up and makes you rethink your earlier conclusion. To keep from getting frustrated, remember that child development is a complex, multifaceted topic. No single theory has been able to account for all aspects of child development. Each theory contributes an important piece to the child development puzzle. Although the theories sometimes disagree, much of their information is complementary rather than contradictory. Together they let us see the total landscape of life-span development in all its richness.

We will briefly explore five major theoretical perspectives on development: psychoanalytic, cognitive, behavioral and social cognitive, ethological, and ecological. In

Sigmund Freud, the pioneering architect of psychoanalytic theory. *How did Freud believe each individual's personality is organized?*

www.mhhe.com/santrockc9

Freud's Theory

chapter 1, we described the three major processes involved in children's development: biological, cognitive, and socioemotional. The theoretical approaches that we will describe reflect these processes. Biological processes are important in Freud's psychoanalytic and ethological theory. Cognitive processes are important in Piaget's, Vygotsky's, information-processing, and social cognitive theories. Socioemotional processes are important in Freud's and Erikson's psychoanalytic theories, Vygotsky's sociocultural cognitive theory, behavioral and social cognitive theories, and ecological theory. Let's begin with the psychoanalytic theories of Freud and Erikson.

Psychoanalytic Theories

Psychoanalytic theories describe development as primarily unconscious (beyond awareness) and heavily colored by emotion. Psychoanalytic theorists argue that behavior is merely a surface characteristic and that a true understanding of development requires analyzing the symbolic meanings of behavior and the deep inner workings of the mind. Psychoanalytic theorists also stress that early experiences with parents extensively shape development. These characteristics are highlighted in the psychoanalytic theory of Sigmund Freud.

Freud's Psychosexual Theory   Freud (1856–1939) developed his ideas about psychoanalytic theory while working with mental patients. He was a medical doctor who specialized in neurology. He spent most of his years in Vienna, though he moved to London near the end of his career because of Nazi anti-Semitism.

Freud (1917) stressed that personality has three structures: the id, the ego, and the superego. The *id*, he said, consists of instincts, which are an individual's reservoir of psychic energy. In Freud's view, the id is totally unconscious; it has no contact with reality. As children experience the demands and constraints of reality, a new part of personality emerges—the *ego*, the Freudian personality structure that deals with the demands of reality. The ego is called the executive branch of personality because it uses reasoning to make decisions. The id and the ego have no morality. They do not take into account whether something is right or wrong. The *superego* is the Freudian structure of personality that is the moral branch of personality. The superego decides whether something is right or wrong. Think of the superego as what we often refer to as our "conscience." You probably are beginning to sense that both the id and the superego make life rough for the ego. Your ego might say, "I will have sex only occasionally and be sure to take the proper precautions because I don't want the intrusion of a child in the development of my career." However, your id is saying, "I want to be satisfied; sex is pleasurable." Your superego is at work, too: "I feel guilty about having sex."

As Freud listened to, probed, and analyzed his patients, he became convinced that their problems were the result of experiences early in life. Freud proposed that we go through five stages of psychosexual development, and that at each stage of development, we experience pleasure in one part of the body more than in others.

Freud thought that our adult personality is determined by the way we resolve conflicts between these early sources of pleasure—the mouth, the anus, and then the genitals—and the demands of reality. When these conflicts are not resolved, the individual may become fixated at a particular stage of development. Fixation occurs when the individual remains locked in an earlier developmental stage because needs are undergratified or overgratified. For example, a parent might wean a child too early, be too strict in toilet training the child, punish the child for masturbation, or "smother" the child with too much attention. Figure 2.2 summarizes the five Freudian psychosexual stages: oral, anal, phallic, latency, and genital.

The *oral stage* is the first Freudian stage of development, occurring during the first 18 months of life, in which the infant's pleasure centers around the mouth. Chewing, sucking, and biting are the chief sources of pleasure. These actions reduce tension in the infant.

psychoanalytic theories Describe development as primarily unconscious and heavily colored by emotion. Behavior is merely a surface characteristic and the symbolic workings of the mind have to be analyzed to understand behavior. Early experiences with parents are emphasized.

Oral Stage	Anal Stage	Phallic Stage	Latency Stage	Genital Stage
Infant's pleasure centers on the mouth.	Child's pleasure focuses on the anus.	Child's pleasure focuses on the genitals.	Child represses sexual interest and develops social and intellectual skills.	A time of sexual reawakening; source of sexual pleasure becomes someone outside the family.
Birth to 1½ Years	**1½ to 3 Years**	**3 to 6 Years**	**6 Years to Puberty**	**Puberty Onward**

FIGURE 2.2 Freudian Stages

The *anal stage* is the second Freudian stage of development, occurring between 1½ and 3 years of age, in which the child's greatest pleasure involves the anus or the eliminative functions associated with it. In Freud's view, the exercise of anal muscles reduces tension.

The *phallic stage* is the third Freudian stage of development. The phallic stage occurs between the ages of 3 and 6; its name comes from the Latin word *phallus,* which means "penis." During the phallic stage, pleasure focuses on the genitals as both boys and girls discover that self-manipulation is enjoyable.

In Freud's view, the phallic stage has a special importance in personality development because it is during this period that the Oedipus complex appears. This name comes from Greek mythology, in which Oedipus, the son of the King of Thebes, unwittingly kills his father and marries his mother. The *Oedipus complex,* according to Freudian theory, is the young child's development of an intense desire to replace the same-sex parent and enjoy the affections of the opposite-sex parent.

How is the Oedipus complex resolved? At about 5 to 6 years of age, children recognize that their same-sex parent might punish them for their incestuous wishes. To reduce this conflict, the child identifies with the same-sex parent, striving to be like that parent. If the conflict is not resolved, though, the individual may become fixated at the phallic stage.

The *latency stage* is the fourth Freudian stage of development, which occurs between approximately 6 years of age and puberty. During this period, the child represses all interest in sexuality and develops social and intellectual skills. This activity channels much of the child's energy into emotionally safe areas and helps the child forget the highly stressful conflicts of the phallic stage.

The *genital stage* is the fifth and final Freudian stage of development, occurring from puberty on. The genital stage is a time of sexual reawakening; the source of sexual pleasure now becomes someone outside of the family. Freud believed that unresolved conflicts with parents reemerge during adolescence. When these conflicts have been resolved, the individual is capable of developing a mature love relationship and functioning independently as an adult.

Freud's theory has undergone significant revisions by a number of psychoanalytic theorists (Eagle, 2000). Many contemporary psychoanalytic theorists place less emphasis on sexual instincts and more emphasis on cultural experiences as determinants of an individual's development. Unconscious thought remains a central theme, but most contemporary psychoanalysts believe that conscious thought makes up more of the mind than Freud envisioned.

Erikson's Psychosocial Theory   Erik Erikson recognized Freud's contributions but believed that Freud misjudged some important dimensions of human development. Erikson (1950, 1968) said we develop in *psychosocial* stages, rather than in *psychosexual* stages. For Freud, the primary motivation for human behavior was sexual in nature, for Erikson it was social and reflected a desire to affiliate with other people. Erikson emphasized developmental change throughout the human life span, whereas

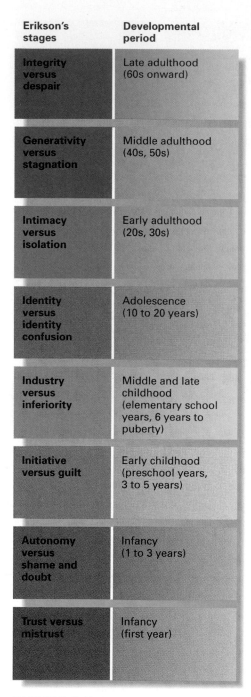

Erikson's stages	Developmental period
Integrity versus despair	Late adulthood (60s onward)
Generativity versus stagnation	Middle adulthood (40s, 50s)
Intimacy versus isolation	Early adulthood (20s, 30s)
Identity versus identity confusion	Adolescence (10 to 20 years)
Industry versus inferiority	Middle and late childhood (elementary school years, 6 years to puberty)
Initiative versus guilt	Early childhood (preschool years, 3 to 5 years)
Autonomy versus shame and doubt	Infancy (1 to 3 years)
Trust versus mistrust	Infancy (first year)

FIGURE 2.3 Erikson's Eight Life-Span Stages

Erikson's Theory

Erikson's theory Includes eight stages of human development. Each stage consists of a unique developmental task that confronts individuals with a crisis that must be faced.

Freud argued that our basic personality is shaped in the first five years of life. In **Erikson's theory,** eight stages of development unfold through the life span (see figure 2.3). Each stage consists of a unique developmental task that confronts individuals with a crisis that must be resolved. According to Erikson, this crisis is not a catastrophe but a turning point of increased vulnerability and enhanced potential. The more successfully an individual resolves the crises, the healthier development will be (Hopkins, 2000).

Trust versus mistrust is Erikson's first psychosocial stage, which is experienced in the first year of life. A sense of trust requires a feeling of physical comfort and a minimal amount of fear and apprehension about the future. Trust in infancy sets the stage for a lifelong expectation that the world will be a good and pleasant place in which to live.

Autonomy versus shame and doubt is Erikson's second stage of development. This stage occurs in late infancy and toddlerhood (1 to 3 years of age). After gaining trust in their caregivers, infants begin to discover that their behavior is their own. They start to assert their sense of independence, or autonomy. They realize their *will*. If infants are restrained too much or punished too harshly, they are likely to develop a sense of shame and doubt.

Initiative versus guilt, Erikson's third stage of development, occurs during the preschool years. As preschool children encounter a widening social world, they are challenged more than when they were infants. Active, purposeful behavior is needed to cope with these challenges. Children are asked to assume responsibility for their bodies, their behavior, their toys, and their pets. Developing a sense of responsibility increases initiative. Uncomfortable guilt feelings may arise, though, if the child is irresponsible and is made to feel too anxious. Erikson has a positive outlook on this stage. He believes that most guilt is quickly compensated for by a sense of accomplishment.

Industry versus inferiority is Erikson's fourth developmental stage, which occurs during the elementary school years. Children's initiative brings them in contact with a wealth of new experiences. As they move into middle and late childhood, they direct their energy toward mastering knowledge and intellectual skills. At no other time is the child more enthusiastic about learning than at the end of early childhood's period of expansive imagination. The danger during the elementary school years is that the child can develop a sense of inferiority—feeling incompetent and unproductive. Erikson believed that teachers have a special responsibility for children's development of industry. Teachers should "mildly but firmly coerce children into the adventure of finding out that one can learn to accomplish things which one would never have thought of by oneself" (Erikson, 1968, p. 127).

Identity versus identity confusion is Erikson's fifth developmental stage, which individuals experience during the adolescent years. At this time, individuals are faced with finding out who they are, what they are all about, and where they are going in life. Adolescents are confronted with many new roles and adult statuses—vocational and romantic, for example. Parents need to allow adolescents to explore many different roles and different paths within a particular role. If the adolescent explores such roles in a healthy manner and arrives at a positive path to follow in life, then a positive identity will be achieved. If an identity is pushed on the adolescent by parents, if the adolescent does not adequately explore many roles, and if a positive future path is not defined, then identity confusion reigns.

Intimacy versus isolation is Erikson's sixth developmental stage, which individuals experience during the early adulthood years. At this time, individuals face the developmental task of forming intimate relationships with others. Erikson describes intimacy as finding oneself yet losing oneself in another. If the young adult forms healthy friendships and an intimate relationship with another individual, intimacy will be achieved; if not, isolation will result.

Generativity versus stagnation is Erikson's seventh developmental stage, which individuals experience during middle adulthood. A chief concern is to assist the younger generation in developing and leading useful lives—this is what Erikson means by generativity. The feeling of having done nothing to help the next generation is stagnation.

Integrity versus despair is Erikson's eighth and final stage of development, which individuals experience in late adulthood. During this stage, a person reflects on the past and either pieces together a positive review or concludes that life has not been spent well. Through many different routes, the older person may have developed a positive outlook in most or all of the previous stages of development. If so, the retrospective glances will reveal a picture of a life well spent, and the person will feel a sense of satisfaction—integrity will be achieved. If the older adult resolved many of the earlier stages negatively, the retrospective glances likely will yield doubt or gloom—the despair Erikson talks about.

Erikson did not hold that the proper solution to a stage crisis is always completely positive. Some exposure or commitment to the negative side of the person's crisis is sometimes inevitable—you cannot trust all people under all circumstances and survive, for example. Nonetheless, in the healthy solution to a stage crisis, the positive resolution dominates. We will discuss Erikson's theory again on a number of occasions in the chapters on socioemotional development.

Erik Erikson with his wife, Joan, an artist. Erikson generated one of the most important developmental theories of the twentieth century. *Which stage of Erikson's theory are you in? Does Erikson's description of this stage characterize you?*

Evaluating the Psychoanalytic Theories
Here are some contributions of psychoanalytic theories:

- Early experiences play an important part in development.
- Family relationships are a central aspect of development.
- Personality can be better understood if it is examined developmentally.
- The mind is not all conscious; unconscious aspects of the mind need to be considered.
- Changes take place in adulthood as well as in childhood (Erikson).

Here are some criticisms of psychoanalytic theories:

- The main concepts of psychoanalytic theories have been difficult to test scientifically.
- Much of the data used to support psychoanalytic theories come from individuals' reconstruction of the past, often the distant past, and are of unknown accuracy.
- The sexual underpinnings of development are given too much importance (especially in Freud's theory).
- The unconscious mind is given too much credit for influencing development.
- Psychoanalytic theories, especially Freud's, present an image of humans that is too negative.
- Psychoanalytic theories are culture- and gender-biased.

Cognitive Theories

Whereas psychoanalytic theories stress the importance of children's unconscious thoughts, cognitive theories emphasize their conscious thoughts. Three important cognitive theories are Piaget's cognitive developmental theory, Vygotsky's sociocultural cognitive theory, and information-processing theory.

Piaget's theory will be covered in detail later in this book, when we discuss cognitive development in infancy, early childhood, middle and late childhood, and adolescence. Here we briefly present the main ideas of his theory.

Piaget's Cognitive Developmental Theory
Piaget's theory states that children actively construct their understanding of the world and go through four stages of cognitive development. Two processes underlie this cognitive construction of the world: organization and adaptation. To make sense of our world, we organize our experiences. For example, we separate important ideas from less important ideas. We connect one idea to another. In addition to organizing our observations and experiences, we *adapt* our thinking to include new ideas because additional information furthers understanding.

www.mhhe.com/santrockc9

Horney's Theory

Piaget's theory States that children actively construct their understanding of the world and go through four stages of cognitive development.

Jean Piaget, the famous Swiss developmental psychologist, changed the way we think about the development of children's minds. *What are some key ideas in Piaget's theory?*

www.mhhe.com/santrockc9

Piaget's Theory

assimilation Occurs when children incorporate new information into their existing knowledge.

accommodation Occurs when children adjust their knowledge to fit new information and experience.

Piaget (1954) believed that we adapt in two ways: assimilation and accommodation. **Assimilation** occurs when children incorporate new information into their existing knowledge. **Accommodation** occurs when children adjust their knowledge to fit new information and experiences. Consider an 8-year-old girl who is given a hammer and nails to hang a picture on the wall. She has never used a hammer, but from experience and observation she realizes that a hammer is an object to be held, that it is swung by the handle to hit the nail, and that it is usually swung a number of times. Recognizing each of these things, she fits the current task into her existing knowledge (assimilation). However, the hammer is heavy, so she holds it near the top. She swings too hard and the nail bends, so she adjusts the pressure of her strikes. These adjustments reveal her ability to alter her knowledge (accommodation).

Piaget also believed that we go through four stages in understanding the world (see figure 2.4). Each of the stages is age-related and consists of distinct ways of thinking. Remember, it is the *different* way of understanding the world that makes one stage more advanced than another; knowing *more* information does not make the child's thinking more advanced, in the Piagetian view. This is what Piaget meant when he said the child's cognition is *qualitatively* different in one stage compared with another (Mooney, 2006; Vidal, 2000). What are Piaget's four stages of cognitive development like?

The *sensorimotor stage,* which lasts from birth to about 2 years of age, is the first Piagetian stage. In this stage, infants construct an understanding of the world by coordinating sensory experiences (such as seeing and hearing) with physical, motoric actions—hence the term *sensorimotor.* At the beginning of this stage, newborns have little more than reflexive patterns with which to work. At the end of the stage, 2-year-olds have complex sensorimotor patterns and are beginning to operate with primitive symbols.

The *preoperational stage,* which lasts from approximately 2 to 7 years of age, is the second Piagetian stage. In this stage, children begin to represent the world with words, images, and drawings. Symbolic thought goes beyond simple connections of sensory information and physical action. However, although preschool children can symbolically represent the world, according to Piaget, they still lack the ability to perform *operations,* the Piagetian term for internalized mental actions that allow children to do mentally what they previously did physically.

The *concrete operational stage,* which lasts from approximately 7 to 11 years of age, is the third Piagetian stage. In this stage, children can perform operations, and logical reasoning replaces intuitive thought as long as reasoning can be applied to specific or concrete examples. For instance, concrete operational thinkers cannot imagine the steps necessary to complete an algebraic equation, which is too abstract for thinking at this stage of development.

The *formal operational stage,* which appears between the ages of 11 and 15, is the fourth and final Piagetian stage. In this stage, individuals move beyond concrete experiences and think in abstract and more logical terms. As part of thinking more abstractly, adolescents develop images of ideal circumstances. They might think about what an ideal parent is like and compare their parents with this ideal standard. They begin to entertain possibilities for the future and are fascinated with what they can be. In solving problems, formal operational thinkers are more systematic, developing hypothesis about why something is happening the way it is, then testing these hypothesis in a deductive manner. We will examine Piaget's cognitive developmental theory further in chapters 7, 10, 13, and 16.

At this point, we have discussed three major stage theories of human development—Freud's, Erikson's, and Piaget's. Figure 2.5 compares these stage theories. Notice that Erikson's theory involves far greater change in the adult years than Freud's or Piaget's theory.

Vygotsky's Sociocultural Theory Like Piaget, the Russian developmentalist Lev Vygotsky (1896–1934) also stressed that children actively construct their knowledge. However, Vygotsky gave social interaction and culture far more important

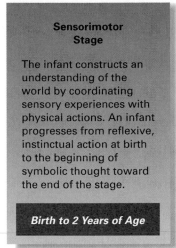
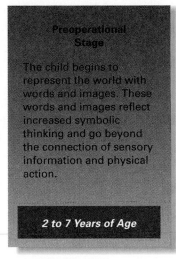
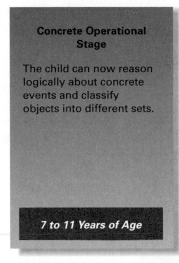
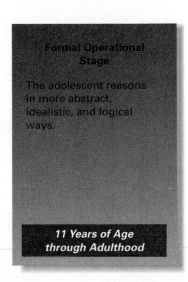

Sensorimotor Stage

The infant constructs an understanding of the world by coordinating sensory experiences with physical actions. An infant progresses from reflexive, instinctual action at birth to the beginning of symbolic thought toward the end of the stage.

Birth to 2 Years of Age

Preoperational Stage

The child begins to represent the world with words and images. These words and images reflect increased symbolic thinking and go beyond the connection of sensory information and physical action.

2 to 7 Years of Age

Concrete Operational Stage

The child can now reason logically about concrete events and classify objects into different sets.

7 to 11 Years of Age

Formal Operational Stage

The adolescent reasons in more abstract, idealistic, and logical ways.

11 Years of Age through Adulthood

FIGURE 2.4 Piaget's Four Stages of Cognitive Development

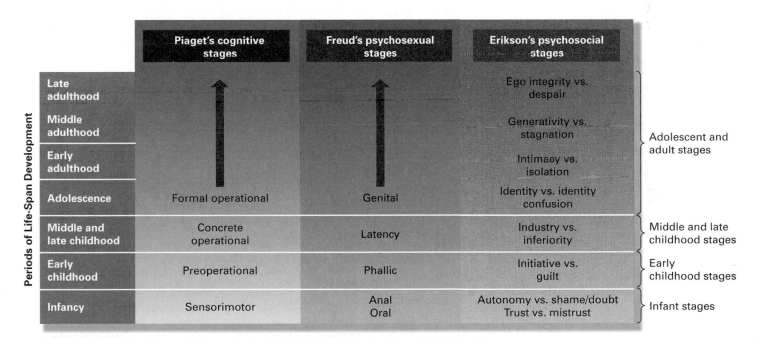

FIGURE 2.5 Comparison of Piaget's, Freud's, and Erikson's Stages

roles in cognitive development than Piaget did. **Vygotsky's theory** is a sociocultural cognitive theory that emphasizes how culture and social interaction guide cognitive development. Vygotsky was born the same year as Piaget, but he died much earlier, at the age of 37. Both Piaget's and Vygotsky's ideas remained virtually unknown to American scholars until the 1960s. In the past several decades, American psychologists and educators have shown increased interest in Vygotsky's (1962) views.

Vygotsky portrayed the child's development as inseparable from social and cultural activities (Mooney, 2006). He believed that the development of memory, attention, and reasoning involves learning to use the inventions of society, such as language, mathematical systems, and memory strategies. In one culture, this might consist of learning to count with the help of a computer. In another, it might consist of counting on one's fingers or using beads.

www.mhhe.com/santrockc9

Vygotsky's Theory

Vygotsky's theory A sociocultural cognitive theory that emphasizes how culture and social interaction guide cognitive development.

There is considerable interest today in Lev Vygotsky's sociocultural cognitive theory of child development. *What were Vygotsky's basic ideas about children's development?*

Vygotsky's theory has stimulated considerable interest in the view that knowledge is *situated* and *collaborative* (John-Steiner & Mahn, 2003; Rogoff, 2003; Rowe & Wertsch, 2004). In this view, knowledge is not generated from within the individual but rather is constructed through interaction with other people and objects in the culture, such as books. This suggests that knowing can best be advanced through interaction with others in cooperative activities.

Vygotsky believed that children's social interaction with more-skilled adults and peers is indispensable in advancing cognitive development. It is through this interaction that less-skilled members of the culture learn to use the tools that will help them adapt and be successful in the culture. For example, when a skilled reader regularly helps a child learn how to read, this not only advances a child's reading skills but also communicates to the child that reading is an important activity in the culture.

Vygotsky articulated unique and influential ideas about cognitive development. In chapter 10, "Cognitive Development in Early Childhood," we will further explore Vygotsky's contributions to our understanding of children's development.

Information-Processing Theory

Machines may be the best candidate for the title of "founding father" of information-processing theory. Although a number of factors stimulated the growth of this theory, none was more important than the computer. Psychologists began to wonder if the logical operations carried out by computers might tell us something about how the human mind works. They drew analogies between a computer's hardware and the brain and between computer software and cognition. The physical brain is said to be analogous to the computer's hardware, cognition is said to be analogous to its software.

This line of thinking helped to generate **information-processing theory,** which emphasizes that individuals manipulate information, monitor it, and strategize about it. According to this theory, individuals develop a gradually increasing capacity for processing information, which allows them to acquire increasingly complex knowledge and skills (Birney & others, 2005; Mayer, 2003; Munakata, 2006; Siegler, 2006; Siegler & Alibali, 2005). Unlike Piaget's theory, but like Vygotsky's theory, information-processing theory does not describe development as stagelike.

Robert Siegler (1998, 2006), a leading expert on children's information processing, believes that thinking is information processing. He says that when individuals perceive, encode, represent, store, and retrieve information, they are thinking. Siegler suggests that learning good strategies for processing information is especially important to cognitive development. For example, becoming a better reader might involve learning to monitor the key themes of the material being read (McCormick, 2003).

Evaluating the Cognitive Theories

Here are some contributions of cognitive theories:

- The cognitive theories present a positive view of development, emphasizing conscious thinking.
- The cognitive theories (especially Piaget's and Vygotsky's) emphasize the individual's active construction of understanding.
- Piaget's and Vygotsky's theories underscore the importance of examining developmental changes in children's thinking.
- Information-processing theory offers detailed descriptions of cognitive processes.

Here are some criticisms of cognitive theories:

- There is skepticism about the pureness of Piaget's stages.
- The cognitive theories do not give adequate attention to individual variations in cognitive development.
- Information-processing theory does not provide an adequate description of developmental changes in cognition.

information-processing theory A theory that emphasizes that individuals manipulate information, monitor it, and strategize about it. The processes of memory and thinking are central.

- Psychoanalytic theorists argue that the cognitive theories do not give enough credit to unconscious thought.

Behavioral and Social Cognitive Theories

At about the same time as Freud was interpreting patients' unconscious minds through their early childhood experiences, Ivan Pavlov and John B. Watson were conducting detailed observations of behavior in controlled laboratory settings. Out of the behavioral tradition grew the belief that development is observable behavior that can be learned through experience with the environment (Bugenthal & Grusec, 2006). Behavioralists essentially believe that scientifically we can study only what can be directly observed and measured. The three versions of the behavioral approach that we will explore are Pavlov's classical conditioning, Skinner's operant conditioning, and Bandura's social cognitive theory.

B. F. Skinner was a tinkerer who liked to make new gadgets. The younger of his two daughters, Deborah, was raised in Skinner's enclosed Air-Crib, which he invented because he wanted to control her environment completely. The Air-Crib was sound-proofed and temperature-controlled. Debbie, shown here as a child with her parents, is currently a successful artist, is married, and lives in London. *What do you think about Skinner's Air-Crib?*

Pavlov's Classical Conditioning   In the early 1900s, Russian physiologist Ivan Pavlov (1927) knew that dogs innately salivate when they taste food. He became curious when he observed that dogs salivate to various sights and sounds before eating their food. For example, if a bell rang when the dog was given food, the dog subsequently salivated whenever the bell rang. Pavlov had discovered the principle of *classical conditioning:* After a neutral stimulus (in our example, ringing a bell) has been paired with a stimulus (in our example, food) that automatically produces a response, that response will be elicited by the previously neutral stimulus on its own.

In the 1920s, John Watson applied classical conditioning to human beings. He showed a little boy named Albert a white rat to see if he was afraid of it. He was not. As Albert played with the rat, Watson sounded a loud nose behind Albert's head. As you might imagine, the noise caused little Albert to cry. After only several pairings of the loud noise and the white rat, Albert began to fear the rat even when the noise was not sounded (Watson & Rayner, 1920).

Similarly, many of our fears can be learned through classical conditioning. For instance, we might learn fear of the dentist from a painful dental experience, fear of driving from being in an automobile incident, fear of heights from falling off a highchair when we were infants, and fear of dogs from being bitten. Classical conditioning explains how we develop many involuntary responses, such as these fears, but B. F. Skinner showed how many of our actions might be explained by a different type of learning known as operant conditioning.

Skinner's Operant Conditioning   In Skinner's (1938) *operant conditioning,* the consequences of a behavior produce changes in the probability of the behavior's occurrence. A behavior that is followed by a rewarding stimulus is more likely to recur, but a behavior that is followed by a punishing stimulus is less likely to recur. For example, a child is more likely to repeat a behavior if it is greeted with a smile than if it is met with a nasty look.

For Skinner, such rewards and punishments shape individuals' development. For example, according to Skinner, a child learns to be shy as a result of environment experiences; rearranging the environment can help a child to become more socially oriented.

Bandura's Social Cognitive Theory   Some psychologists found that although classical and operant conditioning could explain some aspects of behavior, their failure to consider how people think required a different type of behavioral theory (Mischel, 2004). **Social cognitive theory** holds that behavior, environment, and person/cognition are important factors in development. Cognitive factors (for example, thinking and planning) and person factors (for example, being introverted or extraverted and believing that one can effectively control one's experiences) mediate connections between environment and behavior.

social cognitive theory The view of psychologists who emphasize that behavior, environment, and person/cognition are the key factors in development.

Albert Bandura has been one of the leading architects of social cognitive theory. *What is the nature of his theory?*

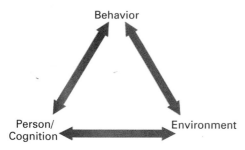

FIGURE 2.6 **Bandura's Social Cognitive Model** The arrows illustrate how relations between behavior, person/cognition, and environment are reciprocal rather than unidirectional.

Behavioral and Social Cognitive Theories
Albert Bandura

ethological theory of development Stresses that behavior is strongly influenced by biology, is tied to evolution, and is characterized by critical or sensitive periods.

Albert Bandura (1986, 2001, 2004) is the leading architect of contemporary social cognitive theory. Bandura's early research focused heavily on *observational learning*—learning that occurs through observing what others do. Observational learning is also referred to as imitation or modeling. In observational learning, people cognitively represent the behavior of others and then sometimes adopt this behavior themselves. For example, a young boy who regularly observes his father's aggressive outbursts and hostile interchanges with people might also be very aggressive with his peers. A girl who adopts the dominating, sarcastic style of her teacher might say to her younger brother, "You are so slow! How can you do this work so slowly?" People acquire a wide range of such behaviors, thoughts, and feelings through observing others' behavior.

In his recent work, Bandura (2001, 2004) emphasizes interactions among behavior, the person/cognition, and the environment, as shown in figure 2.6. Behavior can influence person/cognitive factors and vice versa. The person's cognitive activities can influence the environment, the environment can change the person's cognition, and so on.

Let's consider how Bandura's model might work in the case of a college student's achievement behavior. As the student diligently studies and gets good grades, her behavior produces positive thoughts about her abilities. As part of her effort to make good grades, she plans and develops strategies to make her studying more efficient. In these ways, her behavior has influenced her thought and her thought has influenced her behavior. At the beginning of the term, her college made a special effort to involve students in a study skills program. She decided to join. Because of her success, along with that of other students in the program, the college is expanding the program next semester. In these ways, environment influenced behavior, and behavior changed the environment. And the college administrators' expectations that the study skills program would work made it possible in the first place. The program's success has spurred expectations that this type of program could work in other colleges. In these ways, cognition changed the environment and the environment changed cognition.

Evaluating the Behavioral and Social Cognitive Theories   Here are some contributions of the behavioral and social cognitive theories:

- They emphasize the importance of scientific research.
- They focus on the environmental determinants of behavior.
- Bandura's theory underscores the importance of observational learning.
- Social cognitive theory emphasizes person and cognitive factors.

Here are some criticisms of the behavioral and social cognitive theories:

- Skinner's theory places too little emphasis on cognition.
- They overemphasize environmental determinants.
- They pay inadequate attention to developmental changes.
- Their consideration of human spontaneity and creativity is mechanical and inadequate.

Ethological Theory

In striking contrast to the behavioral and social cognitive theories, another approach to development grew out of ethology, a scientific discipline that studies animal behavior. The **ethological theory of development** holds that behavior is strongly influenced by biology and evolution (Hinde, 1992; Rosenzweig, 2000). It also emphasizes that our sensitivity to different kinds of experience varies during our life span. In other words, there are critical or sensitive periods for some experiences. If we fail to have these experiences during this sensitive period, ethological theory argues that our development is not likely to be optimal.

Konrad Lorenz, a pioneering student of animal behavior, is followed through the water by three imprinted greylag geese. Describe Lorenz's experiment with the geese. *Do you think his experiment would have the same results with human babies? Explain.*

Ethology emerged as an important contributor to theories of human development because of the work of European zoologists, especially Konrad Lorenz (1903–1989). Working mostly with greylag geese, Lorenz (1965) studied a behavior pattern that was thought to be programmed by the birds' genes. A newly hatched gosling seemed to be born with the instinct to follow its mother. Observations showed that the gosling was capable of such behavior as soon as it hatched. Lorenz proved that it was incorrect to assume that such behavior was programmed in the animal. In a remarkable set of experiments, Lorenz separated the eggs laid by one goose into two groups. One group he returned to the goose to be hatched by her. The other group was hatched in an incubator. The goslings in the first group performed as predicted. They followed their mother as soon as they hatched. However, those in the second group, which saw Lorenz when they first hatched, followed him everywhere, as though he were their mother.

Lorenz marked the goslings and then placed both groups under a box. Mother goose and "mother" Lorenz stood aside as the box lifted. Each group of goslings went directly to its "mother." Lorenz called this process *imprinting:* the rapid, innate learning within a limited critical period of time that involves attachment to the first moving object seen.

The ethological view of Lorenz and other European zoologists forced American developmental psychologists to recognize the importance of the biological basis of behavior. However, the research and theorizing of ethology still lacked some ingredients that would elevate it to the ranks of the other theories discussed so far in this chapter. In particular, there was little or nothing in the classical ethological view about the nature of social relationships across the human life span, something that any major theory of development must explain. Also, its concept of *critical period,* a fixed time period very early in development during which certain behaviors optimally emerge, seemed to be overdrawn. Classical ethological theory was weak in simulating studies with humans.

Recent expansion of the ethological view has improved its status as a viable developmental perspective. One way ethological theory has become more viable with humans is that rather than relying on a rigid, very narrow critical period, more emphasis has been given to a longer *sensitive period.*

One of the most important applications of ethological theory to human development involves John Bowlby's (1969, 1989) theory of attachment. Bowlby argues that attachment to a caregiver over the first year of life has important consequences throughout the life span. In his view, if this attachment is positive and secure, the individual will likely develop more positively in childhood and adulthood. If it is negative and insecure, life-span development will likely not be optimal. In chapter 8, "Socioemotional Development in Infancy," we will explore the concept of infant attachment in much greater detail.

www.mhhe.com/santrockc9

Exploring Ethology

FIGURE 2.7 Bronfenbrenner's Ecological Theory of Development Bronfenbrenner's ecological theory consists of five environmental systems: microsystem, mesosystem, exosystem, macrosystem, and chronosystem.

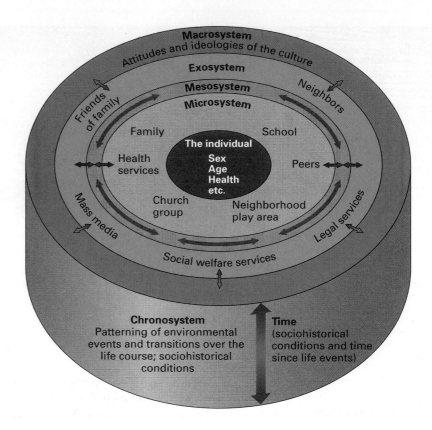

Evaluating Ethological Theory

Here are some contributions of ethological theory:

- It increased the focus on the biological and evolutionary basis of development.
- It uses careful observations in naturalistic settings.
- It emphasizes sensitive periods of development.

Here are some criticisms of ethological theory:

- The concepts of critical period and sensitive period may still be too rigid.
- It places too much emphasis on biological foundations.
- It gives inadequate attention to cognition.
- The theory has been better at generating research with animals than with humans.

Ecological Theory

Unlike ethological theory, which stresses biological factors, ecological theory emphasizes environmental contexts. One ecological theory that has important implications for understanding life-span development was created by Urie Bronfenbrenner (1917–   ).

Ecological theory is Bronfenbrenner's view that development is influenced by five environmental systems, ranging from the fine-grained contexts of direct interactions with people to the broad-based contexts of culture. The five systems in Bronfenbrenner's (1986, 1995, 2000, 2004; Bronfenbrenner & Morris, 1998, 2006) ecological theory are the microsystem, mesosystem, exosystem, macrosystem, and chronosystem (see figure 2.7):

- The *microsystem* is the setting in which the individual lives. These contexts include the person's family, peers, school, and neighborhood. It is in the

ecological theory Bronfenbrenner's environmental systems theory that focuses on five environmental systems: microsystem, mesosystem, exosystem, macrosystem, and chronosystem.

microsystem that the most direct interactions with social agents take place—with parents, peers, and teachers, for example.

- The *mesosystem* involves relationships between microsystems, or connections between contexts. Examples are the relation of family experiences to school experiences, school experiences to church experiences, and family experiences to peer experiences.

- The *exosystem* is involved when experiences in another social setting—in which the individual does not have an active role—influence what the individual experiences in an immediate context. For example, work experiences can affect a woman's relationship with her husband and their child. The mother might receive a promotion that requires more travel, which could increase marital conflict and change patterns of parent-child interaction.

- The *macrosystem* involves the culture in which individuals live. *Culture* refers to the behavior patterns, beliefs, and all other products of a group of people that are passed on from generation to generation (Cole, 2006). For example, many Asian American parents have higher expectations for their children's achievement than parents from other cultural groups in the United States (Stevenson, 2000).

- The *chronosystem* involves the patterning of environmental events and transitions over the life course, as well as sociohistorical circumstances. For example, in studying the effects of divorce on children, researchers have found that the negative effects often peak in the first year after the divorce (Hetherington, 1993, 2000). By two years after the divorce, family interaction is less chaotic and more stable. With regard to sociocultural circumstances, women today are much more likely to be encouraged to pursue a career than they were 20 or 30 years ago.

Bronfenbrenner (2000, 2004; Bronfenbrenner & Morris, 1998, 2006) recently added biological influences to his theory and now describes it as a *bioecological* theory. Nonetheless, ecological, environmental contexts still predominate in Bronfenbrenner's theory (Ceci, 2000).

Bronfenbrenner described the mesosystem as one of the five key environmental systems. To read about the important mesosystem connection between family and school, see the Caring for Children interlude.

Urie Bronfenbrenner developed ecological theory, a perspective that is receiving increased attention. *What is the nature of ecological theory?*

Bronfenbrenner's Theory
Bronfenbrenner and a
Multicultural Framework

CARING FOR CHILDREN

Mesosystem Connection: Family and School Communication

Researchers have consistently found that successful students benefit from having both competent teachers in school and supportive parents at home (Cowan & others, 2005; Hyson, Copple, & Jones, 2005; Mattanah, 2005; Pressley & others, 2003). An important aspect of students receiving support for school at home is creating and maintaining channels of communication between schools and families (Epstein, 2001; Epstein & Sanders, 2002; Epstein & others, 2002).

A recent review of research on links between schools and families revealed that programs and special efforts to engage families can often make a difference in children's achievement (Henderson & Mapp, 2002). Parental involvement in their children's education is related to higher grade point averages, better attendance, and improved behavior at school and home. Successful strategies include teachers meeting face-to-face with parents and keeping in touch with parents on a regular basis about students' progress.

Joyce Epstein (2001; Epstein & others, 2002) stresses that these areas can be especially helpful to target in improving school-family connections:

(continued on next page)

- *Provide assistance to families.* For example, schools can provide parents with information about child-rearing skills, family support, and child and adolescent development.
- *Encourage parents to be volunteers.* In some schools, parents are extensively involved in educational planning and assisting teachers.
- *Involve families with their children in learning activities at home.* This can include homework and curriculum-linked activities.
- *Include families as participants in school decisions.* Parents can be invited to be on PTA/PTO boards, various committees, councils, and other parent organizations.
- *Coordinate community collaboration.* Schools can interconnect the work and resources of community businesses, agencies, colleges, and other groups to strengthen school programs, family practices, and student learning. Schools can alert families to community programs and services that may benefit them.

Let's look at two programs that have been developed to enhance communication between schools and families. The first program involves the school system of Lima, Ohio, where the main goal is for each school to establish a personal relationship with every parent. At an initial parent-teacher conference, parents are given a packet that is designed to increase their likelihood of engaging in learning activities with their children at home. Conferences, regular phone calls, and home visits establish an atmosphere of mutual understanding that makes other types of communication (progress reports, report cards, activity calendars, and discussions about problems that arise during the year) more welcome and successful. The second program is at Hanshaw Middle School in California's Stanislaus County. The program created a resource center for students' families where parents can take classes in many subjects including parenting and computers. They can also take courses toward earning a high school equivalency degree. Latino parents find assistance in communicating with the school's teachers and administrators. The center also features a case management team and referral service that is available for students and their families.

Evaluating Ecological Theory   Here are some contributions of ecological theory:

- It systematically examines macro and micro dimensions of environmental systems.

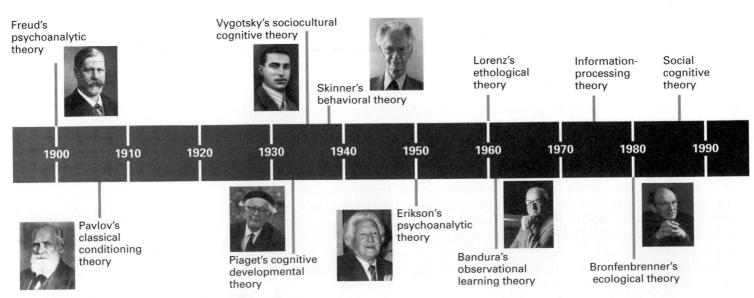

FIGURE 2.8 Time Line for Major Developmental Theories

- It pays attention to connections between environmental settings (mesosystem).
- It considers the sociohistorical influences on development (chronosystem).

Here are some criticisms of ecological theory:

- Even with the added discussion of biological influences in recent years, it still gives too little attention to biological foundations of development.
- It does not pay enough attention to cognitive processes.

In addition to ecological theory, the theories that we have discussed—psychoanalytic, cognitive, behavioral and social cognitive, and ethological—were conceived at different points in the twentieth century. For a chronology of when these theories were proposed, see figure 2.8. Figure 2.9 compares the main theoretical perspectives in terms of the three main issues discussed in chapter 1—nature and nurture, continuity and discontinuity, and early versus later experience—plus the importance of cognition.

Theory	Issues			
	Nature and nurture	**Early and later experience**	**Continuity and discontinuity**	**Importance of cognition**
Psychoanalytic	Freud's biological determinism interacting with early family experiences; Erikson's more balanced biological/cultural interaction perspective	Early experiences in the family very important influences	Emphasis on discontinuity between stages	Emphasized, but in the forms of unconcious thought
Cognitive	Piaget's emphasis on interaction and adaptation; environment provides the setting for cognitive structures to develop. Vygotsky's theory involves interaction of nature and nurture with strong emphasis on culture. The information-processing approach has not addressed this issue extensively; mainly emphasizes biological-environment interaction.	Childhood experiences important influences	Discontinuity between stages in Piaget's theory; no stages in Vygotsky's theory or the information-processing approach	The primary determinant of behavior
Behavioral and social cognitive	Environment viewed as the main influence on development	Experiences important at all points in development	Continuity with no stages	Strongly deemphasized in the behavioral approach but an important mediator in social cognitive theory
Ethological	Strong biological view	Early experience very important, which can contribute to change early in development; after early critical or sensitive period has passed, stability likely to occur	Discontinuity because of early critical or sensitive period; no stages	Not emphasized
Ecological	Strong environmental view	Experiences involving the five environmental systems important at all points in the development	No stages but little attention to the issue	Not emphasized

FIGURE 2.9 A Comparison of Theories and Issues in Child Development

An Eclectic Theoretical Orientation

No single theory described in this chapter can entirely explain the rich complexity of children's development. Each of the theories, however, has made important contributions to our understanding of development. Psychoanalytic theory best explains the unconscious mind and Erikson's theory best describes the changes that occur throughout the human life span. Piaget's, Vygotsky's, and the information-processing views provide the most complete descriptions of cognitive development. The behavioral and social cognitive and ecological theories have been the most adept at examining the environmental determinants of development. The ethological theories have made us aware of biology's role and the importance of sensitive periods in development.

It is important to recognize that, although theories are helpful guides, it would probably be a mistake to rely on a single theory to explain development. An **eclectic theoretical orientation** does not follow any theoretical approach but rather selects and uses what is considered the best in each theory. This is the approach that will be maintained throughout the book. In this way, you can view the study of development as it exists—with different theorists making different assumptions, stressing different empirical problems, and using different strategies to discover information.

Review and Reflect • LEARNING GOAL 2

2 Describe the main theories of child development.

Review

- How can the psychoanalytic theories be defined? What characterizes Freud's and Erikson's theories? What are some contributions and criticisms of psychoanalytic theories?
- What are the three main cognitive theories? What are some contributions and criticisms of the cognitive theories?
- What are the three main behavioral and social cognitive theories? What are some of the contributions and criticisms of these theories?
- What is ethological theory? What are some contributions and criticisms of the theory?
- What is ecological theory? What are contributions and criticisms of the theory?
- What is an eclectic theoretical orientation?

Reflect

- Which of the theories do you think best explains your own development? Why?

3 WHAT ARE THE MAIN RESEARCH METHODS IN CHILD DEVELOPMENT?

Methods for Collecting Data

Time Span of Research

Research Designs

Research Journals

If you take an eclectic approach, how do you decide what is "best" in different theories? Scientific research is the answer. All scientific knowledge stems from a rigorous, systematic method of research. Through research, theories are modified to reflect new data.

How are data about children's development collected? What types of research designs are used to study children's development? If researchers want to study children

eclectic theoretical orientation An orientation that does follow any one theoretical approach, but rather, selects from each theory whatever is considered the best in it.

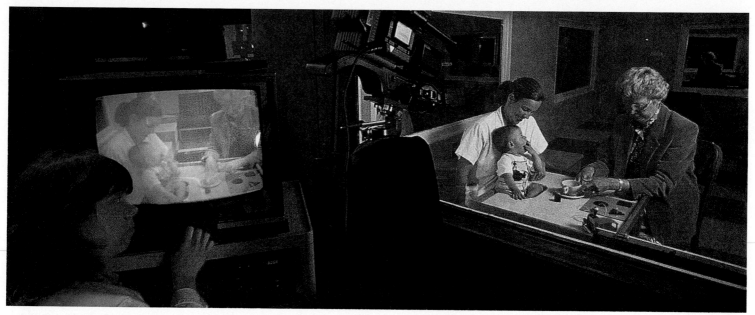

In this research study, mother–child interaction is being videotaped. Later, researchers will code the interaction using precise categories.

of different ages, what research designs can they use? These are the questions that we will examine next.

Methods for Collecting Data

Whether we are interested in studying attachment in infants, children's cognitive skills, or pubertal change in adolescents, we can choose from several ways of collecting data. Here we discuss the measures most often used, including their advantages and disadvantages, beginning with observation. We then describe surveys and interviews, standardized tests, and the case study.

Observation   Scientific observation requires an important set of skills (McMillan & Schumacher, 2006; McMillan & Wergin, 2002). Unless we are trained observers and practice our skills regularly, we might not know what to look for, we might not remember what we saw, we might not realize that what we are looking for is changing from one moment to the next, and we might not communicate our observations effectively.

For observations to be effective, they have to be systematic (Gall, Gall, & Borg, 2005; Kantowitz, Roedinger, & Elmes, 2005). We have to have some idea of what we are looking for. We have to know whom we are observing, when and where we will observe, and how the observations will be made. In what form will they be recorded: In writing? Tape recording? Video?

Where should we make our observations? We have two choices: (1) a **laboratory,** which is a controlled setting with many of the complex factors of the "real world" removed, and (2) the everyday world.

Making observations in a laboratory allows us to control certain factors that influence behavior but are not the focus of our inquiry (Crano & Brewer, 2002; Hoyle & Judd, 2002). For this reason, some research in child development is conducted in a laboratory.

However, laboratory research does have some drawbacks (Beins, 2004). First, it is almost impossible to conduct research without the participants' knowing they are being studied. Second, the laboratory setting is unnatural and therefore can cause the participants to behave unnaturally. Third, parents and children who are willing and

laboratory A controlled setting in which many of the complex factors of the "real world" are removed.

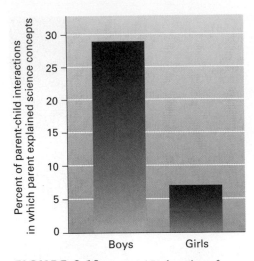

FIGURE 2.10 Parents' Explanation of Science to Sons and Daughters at a Science Museum In a naturalistic observation study at a children's science museum, parents were three times more likely to explain science to boys than girls (Crowley & others, 2001). The gender difference occurred regardless of whether the father, the mother, or both parents were with the child, although the gender difference was greatest for fathers' science explanations to sons and daughters.

able to come to a university laboratory may not fairly represent the population we are interested in studying. Those who are unfamiliar with university settings, and with the idea of "helping science," may be intimidated by the setting. Finally, some aspects of child development are difficult if not impossible to examine in the laboratory.

Naturalistic observation provides insights that we sometimes cannot achieve in the laboratory (Billman, 2003; Langston, 2002). **Naturalistic observation** means observing behavior in real-world settings, making no effort to manipulate or control the situation. Child development researchers conduct naturalistic observations at homes, child-care centers, schools, playgrounds, malls, and other places children live in and frequent.

Figure 2.10 shows the results of a study using naturalistic observation. In this case, researchers observed how mothers and fathers interacted with their sons and daughters in a children's science museum (Crowley & others, 2001). Parents were three times as likely to engage boys as girls in explanatory talk while visiting different exhibits at the science museum, suggesting a gender bias that encourages boys more than girls in science.

Survey and Interview

Sometimes the best and quickest way to get information about people is to ask them for it. One technique is to *interview* them directly. A related method that is especially useful when information from many people is needed is the *survey*, sometimes referred to as a questionnaire. A standard set of questions is used to obtain peoples' self-reported attitudes or beliefs about a particular topic. In a good survey, the questions are clear and unbiased, allowing respondents to answer unambiguously (Tourangeau, 2004).

Surveys and interviews can be used to study a wide range of topics from parenting attitudes to perceptions of friends to whether or not individuals use drugs. Surveys and interviews can be conducted in person or over the telephone. In addition, a growing number of surveys are now being conducted on computers over the Internet.

Some survey and interview questions are unstructured and open-ended, such as "Tell me about your relationship with your child?" or "What is your school like?" They allow for unique responses from each person surveyed. Other survey and interview questions are more structured and specific. For example, one national poll on beliefs about what needs to be done to improve U.S. schools asked: "Of the following four possibilities, which one do you think offers the most promise for improving public schools in the community: a qualified, competent teacher in every classroom; free choice for parents among a number of private, church-related, and public schools; rigorous academic standards; the elimination of social promotion; or don't know?" (Rose & Gallup, 2000). More than half of the respondents said that the most important way to improve schools is to have a qualified, competent teacher in every classroom.

One problem with surveys and interviews is the tendency of participants to answer questions in a way that they think is socially acceptable or desirable rather than telling what they truly think or feel (Babbie, 2005; Best & Kahn, 2003). For example, on a survey or in an interview some adolescents might say that they do not take drugs even though they do.

Standardized Test

A **standardized test** has uniform procedures for administration and scoring. Many standardized tests allow a person's performance to be compared with the performance of other individuals (Aiken, 2003; Fraenkel & Wallen, 2006; Gregory, 2004). One example is the Stanford-Binet intelligence test, which is described in chapter 13, "Cognitive Development in Middle and Late Childhood."

Scores on standardized tests are often stated in *percentiles*, which indicate how much higher or lower one person's score is than the scores of people who previously took the test. If you scored in the 92nd percentile on the SAT, 92 percent of a large group of individuals who previously took the test received scores lower than yours.

naturalistic observation Observing behavior in real-world settings.

standardized test A test with uniform procedures for administration and scoring. Many standardized tests allow a person's performance to be compared with the performance of other individuals.

The main advantage of standardized tests is that they provide information about individual differences among people (Best & Kahn, 2006; Osterlind, 2006; Walsh & Betz, 2001). One problem with standardized tests is that they do not always predict behavior in nontest situations. Another problem is that standardized tests are based on the belief that a person's behavior is consistent and stable, yet personality and intelligence—two primary targets of standardized testing—can vary with the situation. For example, a child may perform poorly on a standardized intelligence test in a school psychologist's office but score much higher at home, where the child is less anxious. This criticism is especially relevant for members of minority groups, some of whom have been inaccurately classified as mentally retarded on the basis of their scores on intelligence tests (Valencia & Suzuki, 2001).

In addition, cross-cultural psychologists caution that many psychological tests developed in Western cultures might not be appropriate in other cultures (Cushner, 2003). People in other cultures may have had experiences that cause them to interpret and respond to questions much differently from the people on whom the test was standardized.

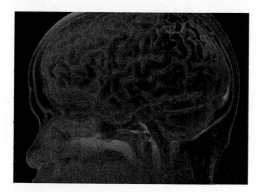

FIGURE 2.11 Magnetic Resonance Imaging

Psychophysiological Measures
Psychophysiological measures have been used to assess the functioning of the central nervous system (CNS), the autonomic nervous system (ANS), and the endocrine system.

The central nervous system consists of the brain and spinal cord. Both neuroimaging techniques and the electroencephalograph have been used to assess the brain's functioning. Especially useful is *magnetic resonance imaging (MRI),* which involves creating a magnetic field around a person's body and using radio waves to construct images of the person's tissues and biochemical activities. MRI provides very clear pictures of the brain's interior (see figure 2.11).

The *electroencephalogram (EEG)* records the brain's electrical activity. Electrodes placed on the scalp detect brainwave activity, which is recorded on a chart known as an *electroencephalograph*. This device has been used to assess the brain's functioning during performance on memory tasks and to measure brain damage (Nelson, 2003; Nelson, Thomas, & de Haan, 2006).

The autonomic nervous system takes messages to and from the body's internal organs, monitoring such processes as heart rate, breathing, and digestion. Heart rate and breathing can be measured even in very young infants, and they can give useful indicators of an infant's capacities. For example, "Heart rate has proved to be an especially sensitive and productive index of infant capacity. For example, heart rate indicates whether an infant is simply staring blankly at a stimulus (heart rate is stable) or is actually attending to and processing the stimulus (heart rate slows during periods of concentration)" (Lamb, Bornstein, & Teti, 2002, p. 81).

The endocrine system consists of a set of glands that regulate the activities of certain organs by producing and releasing the chemical products known as *hormones* into the bloodstream. Measuring hormone concentrations in the blood can provide information about many aspects of a person's emotional and physical status, such as stress levels and pubertal change (Gunnar & Davis, 2003; Susman & Rogol, 2004). For example, the hormone cortisol is secreted in times of stress, such as when an infant is awakened by a loud noise. And levels of estrogens and androgens change as girls and boys go through puberty.

Caution needs to be exercised in interpreting data obtained using psychophysical measures. "Many factors determine responses, and thus there is never an exact one-to-one correspondence between a physiological index (such as heart rate acceleration or cortisol level) and a psychological state (such as fear)" (Lamb, Bornstein, & Teti, 2002, p. 84).

Case Study
A **case study** is an in-depth look at a single individual. Case studies are performed mainly by mental health professionals when, for either practical or

case study An in-depth look at a single individual.

Mahatma Gandhi was the spiritual leader of India in the middle of the twentieth century. Erik Erikson conducted an extensive case study of his life to determine what contributed to his identity development. *What are some limitations of the case study approach?*

ethical reasons, the unique aspects of an individual's life cannot be duplicated and tested in other individuals (Dattilio, 2001). A case study provides information about one person's fears, hopes, fantasies, traumatic experiences, upbringing, family relationships, health, or anything that helps the psychologist understand the person's mind and behavior.

An example of a case study is Erik Erikson's (1969) analysis of India's spiritual leader Mahatma Gandhi. Erikson studied Gandhi's life in great depth to discover insights about how his positive spiritual identity developed, especially during Gandhi's youth. In putting the pieces of Gandhi's identity development together, Erikson described the contributions of culture, history, family, and various other factors that might affect the way other people develop an identity.

Case histories provide dramatic, in-depth portrayals of people's lives, but remember that we must be cautious when generalizing from this information (Leary, 2004). The subject of a case study is unique, with a genetic makeup and personal history that no one else shares. In addition, case studies involve judgments of unknown reliability. Psychologists who conduct case studies rarely check to see if other psychologists agree with their observations.

Research Designs

Suppose you want to find out whether the children of permissive parents are more likely than other children to be rude and unruly. The data-collection method that researchers choose often depends on the goal of their research. The goal may be simply to describe a phenomenon, or it may be to describe relationships between phenomena, or to determine the causes or effects of a certain phenomenon.

Perhaps you decide that you need to observe both permissive and strict parents with their children and compare them. How would you do that? In addition to a method for collecting data, you would need a research design. There are three main types of research designs: descriptive, correlational, and experimental.

Descriptive Research   All of the data-collection methods that we have discussed can be used in **descriptive research,** which aims to observe and record behavior. For example, a researcher might observe the extent to which children are altruistic or aggressive toward each other. By itself, descriptive research cannot prove what causes some phenomenon, but it can reveal important information about people's behavior.

Correlational Research   In contrast to descriptive research, correlational research goes beyond describing phenomena to provide information that will help us to predict how people will behave. In **correlational research,** the goal is to describe the strength of the relationship between two or more events or characteristics. The more strongly the two events are correlated (or related or associated), the more effectively we can predict one event from the other (Whitley, 2002).

For example, to study if children of permissive parents have less self-control than other children, you would need to carefully record observations of parents' permissiveness and their children's self-control. The data could then be analyzed statistically to yield a numerical measure, called a **correlation coefficient,** which is a number based on a statistical analysis that is used to describe the degree of association between two variables. The correlation coefficient ranges from −1.00 to +1.00. A negative number means an inverse relation. For example, researchers often find a *negative* correlation between permissive parenting and children's self-control. By contrast, they often find a *positive* correlation between parental monitoring of children and children's self-control. The higher the correlation coefficient (whether positive or negative), the stronger the association between the two variables. A correlation of 0 means that there is no association between the variables. A correlation of −.40 is stronger than a

descriptive research Research that aims to observe and record behavior.

correlational research Research in which the goal is to describe the strength of the relation between two or more events or characteristics.

correlation coefficient A number based on a statistical analysis that is used to describe the degree of association between two variables.

Observed correlation   **Possible explanations for this correlation**

As permissive parenting increases, children's self-control decreases.

Permissive parenting — causes → Children's lack of self-control

Children's lack of self-control — causes → Permissive parenting

Other factors, such as genetic tendencies, poverty, and sociohistorical circumstances — cause both → Permissive parenting and Children's lack of self-control

FIGURE 2.12 Possible Explanations for Correlational Data An observed correlation between two events cannot be used to conclude that one event caused the other. Some possibilities are that the second event caused the first event or that a third, unknown event caused the correlation between the first two events.

correlation of −.20 because we disregard whether the correlation is positive or negative in determining the strength of the correlation.

A caution is in order, however. Correlation does not equal causation (Rosnow & Rosenthal, 2005). The correlational finding just mentioned does not mean that permissive parenting necessarily causes low self-control in children. It could mean that, but it also could mean that a child's lack of self-control caused the parents to simply throw up their arms in despair and give up trying to control the child. It also could mean that other factors, such as heredity or poverty, caused the correlation between permissive parenting and low self-control in children. Figure 2.12 illustrates these possible interpretations of correlational data.

Throughout this book you will read about numerous correlational research studies. Keep in mind how easy it is to assume causality when two events or characteristics merely are correlated (Christensen, 2004).

Experimental Research   To study causality, researchers turn to experimental research. An **experiment** is a carefully regulated procedure in which one or more factors believed to influence the behavior being studied are manipulated while all other factors are held constant. If the behavior under study changes when a factor is manipulated, we say that the manipulated factor has caused the behavior to change. In other words, the experiment has demonstrated cause and effect. The cause is the factor that was manipulated. The effect is the behavior that changed because of the manipulation. Nonexperimental research methods (descriptive and correlational research) cannot establish cause and effect because they do not involve manipulating factors in a controlled way (Martin, 2004).

Independent and Dependent Variables   Experiments include two types of changeable factors, or variables: independent and dependent. An *independent variable* is a manipulated, influential, experimental factor. It is a potential cause. The label *independent* is used because this variable can be manipulated independently of other factors to determine its effect. One experiment may include several independent variables.

A *dependent variable* is a factor that can change in an experiment, in response to changes in the independent variable. As researchers manipulate the independent variable, they measure the dependent variable for any resulting effect.

For example, suppose that you conducted a study to determine whether aerobic exercise by pregnant women changes the breathing and sleeping patterns of newborn babies. You might require one group of pregnant women to engage in a certain amount of exercise each week; the amount of exercise is thus the independent

Correlational Research
Experimental Research

experiment A carefully regulated procedure in which one or more of the factors believed to influence the behavior being studied is manipulated and all other factors are held constant.

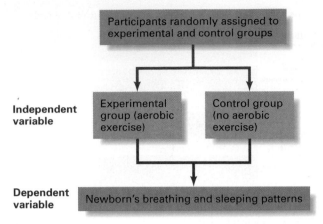

Participants randomly assigned to experimental and control groups

Independent variable

Experimental group (aerobic exercise)

Control group (no aerobic exercise)

Dependent variable

Newborn's breathing and sleeping patterns

FIGURE 2.13   Principles of Experimental Research Imagine that you decide to conduct an experimental study of the effects of aerobic exercise by pregnant women on their newborns' breathing and sleeping patterns. You would randomly assign pregnant women to experimental and control groups. The experimental-group women would engage in aerobic exercise over a specified number of sessions and weeks. The control group would not. Then, when the infants are born, you would assess their breathing and sleeping patterns. If the breathing and sleeping patterns of newborns whose mothers were in the experimental group arc more positive than those of the control group, you would conclude that aerobic exercise caused the positive effects.

variable. When the infants are born, you would observe and measure their breathing and sleeping patterns. These patterns are the dependent variable, the factor that changes as the result of your manipulation.

Experimental and Control Groups   Experiments can involve one or more experimental groups and one or more control groups. An *experimental group* is a group whose experience is manipulated. A *control group* is a comparison group that is as much like the experimental group as possible and that is treated in every way like the experimental group except for the manipulated factor (independent variable). The control group serves as a baseline against which the effects of the manipulated condition can be compared.

Random assignment is an important principle for deciding whether each participant will be placed in the experimental group or in the control group. *Random assignment* means that researchers assign participants to experimental and control groups by chance (Kantowitz, Roediger, & Elmes, 2005). It reduces the likelihood that the experiment's results will be due to any preexisting differences between groups. In the example of the effects of aerobic exercise by pregnant women on the breathing and sleeping patterns of their newborns, you would randomly assign half of the pregnant women to engage in aerobic exercise over a period of weeks (the experimental group) and the other half to not exercise over the same number of weeks (the control group). Figure 2.13 illustrates the nature of experimental research.

Time Span of Research

Developmentalists must deal with some additional issues when they design research. Often, they want to focus on the relation of age to some other variable. The time span of a research investigation is a special concern to them (Hartmann & Pelzel, 2005). Researchers can study different individuals of different ages and compare them or they can study the same individuals as they age over time.

Cross-Sectional Approach   The **cross-sectional approach** is a research strategy in which individuals of different ages are compared at one time. A typical cross-sectional study might include a group of 5-year-olds, 8-year-olds, and 11-year-olds. The different groups can be compared with respect to a variety of dependent variables: IQ, memory, peer relations, attachment to parents, hormonal changes, and so on. All of this can be accomplished in a short time. In some studies data are collected in a single day. Even in large-scale cross-sectional studies with hundreds of subjects, data collection does not usually take longer than several months to complete.

The main advantage of the cross-sectional study is that the researcher does not have to wait for the individuals to grow up or become older. Despite its time efficiency, the cross-sectional approach has its drawbacks. It gives no information about how individuals change or about the stability of their characteristics. The increases and decreases of development—the hills and valleys of growth and development—can become obscured in the cross-sectional approach. For example, in a cross-sectional study of self-esteem, average increases and decreases might be revealed. But the study would not show how the self-esteem of individual adults waxed and waned over the years.

Longitudinal Approach   The **longitudinal approach** is a research strategy in which the same individuals are studied over a period of time, usually several years or more. For example, if a study of self-esteem were conducted longitudinally, the same children might be assessed three times—at 5, 8, and 11 years of age, for example. Some longitudinal studies take place over shorter time frames, even just a year or so.

cross-sectional approach A research strategy in which individuals of different ages are compared at one time.

longitudinal approach A research strategy in which the same individuals are studied over a period of time, usually several years or more.

Research Method	Theory
Observation	• All theories emphasize some form of observation. • Behavioral and social cognitive theories place the strongest emphasis on laboratory observation. • Ethological theory places the strongest emphasis on naturalistic observation.
Interview/survey	• Psychoanalytic and cognitive studies (Piaget, Vygotsky) often use interviews. • Behavioral, social cognitive, and ethological theories are the least likely to use surveys or interviews.
Standardized test	• None of the theories discussed emphasize the use of this method.
Physiological measures	• None of the theories discussed address psychophysiological measures to any significant degree.
Case study	• Psychoanalytic theories (Freud, Erikson) are the most likely to use this method.
Correlational research	• All of the theories use this research method, although psychoanalytic theories are the least likely to use it.
Experimental research	• The behavioral and social cognitive theories and the information-processing theories are the most likely to use the experimental method. • Psychoanalytic theories are the least likely to use it.
Cross-sectional/ longitudinal methods	• No theory described uses these methods more than any other.

FIGURE 2.14 Connections of Research Methods to Theories

Although longitudinal studies provide a wealth of information about such important issues as stability and change in development and the importance of early experience for later development, they are not without their problems (Hartmann & Pelzel, 2005; Raudenbush, 2001). They are expensive and time-consuming. The longer the study lasts, the more participants drop out. For example, children's families may move, get sick, lose interest, and so forth. Participants can bias the outcome of a study, because those who remain may be dissimilar to those who drop out. Those individuals who remain in a longitudinal study over a number of years may be more compulsive and conformity-oriented, for example, or they might have more stable lives.

An important point is that theories often are linked with a particular research method or methods. Thus, method(s) researchers use are associated with their particular theoretical approach. Figure 2.14 illustrates the connections between research methods and theories.

Research Journals

Regardless of whether you pursue a career in child development, education, psychology, nursing, or a related field, you can benefit by learning about research journals. Possibly as a student you will be required to look up original research in journals as part of writing a term paper. As a parent, teacher, or nurse you might want to consult journals to obtain information that will help you understand and work more effectively with children. And, as an inquiring person, you might want to look up information in journals after you have heard or read something that piqued your curiosity.

www.mhhe.com/santrockc9

Developmental Psychology
Child Development

Research journals are the core of information in virtually every academic discipline. Those shown here are among the increasing number of research journals that publish information about child development. *What are the main parts of a research article that presents findings from original research?*

A *journal* publishes scholarly and academic information, usually in a specific domain, such as physics, math, sociology, or, in the case of our interest, child development. Scholars in these fields publish most of their research in journals, which are the core information source in virtually every academic discipline.

Journal articles are usually written for other professionals in the same field as the journal's focus—such as geology, anthropology, or child development. Because the articles are written for other professionals, they often contain technical language and specialized terms related to a specific discipline that are difficult for nonprofessionals to understand. You have probably already had one or more courses in psychology, and you will be learning a great deal more about the specialized field of child development in this course, which should improve your ability to understand journal articles in this field.

An increasing number of journals publish information about children's development. Among the leading journals of child development are *Child Development, Developmental Psychology, Infant Behavior and Development, Pediatric Nursing, Pediatrics, Early Childhood Research Quarterly*, and *Journal of Research on Adolescence*. Also, a number of journals that do not focus solely on development include articles on children's development, such as *Journal of Educational Psychology, Sex Roles, Journal of Cross-Cultural Psychology, Journal of Marriage and the Family*, and *Journal of Consulting and Clinical Psychology*.

In psychology and the field of child development, most journal articles are reports of original research. Many journals also include review articles that present an overview of different studies on a particular topic, such as a review of child care, a review of the transition to elementary school, or a review of adolescent depression.

Many journals are highly selective about what they publish. Every journal has a board of experts that evaluates articles submitted for publication. One or more of the experts carefully examine the submitted paper and accept or reject it on such factors as its contribution to the field, its theoretical relevance, its methodological excellence, and its clarity of writing. Some of the most prestigious journals reject as many as 80 to 90 percent of the articles that are submitted because they fail to meet the journal's standards.

Where can you find research journals? Your college or university library likely has one or more of the journals listed. Some public libraries also carry journals. An increasing number of research journals can be accessed on the Internet.

An *abstract* is a brief summary that appears at the beginning of a journal article. The abstract lets readers quickly determine whether the article is relevant to their interests and if they want to read the entire article. The *introduction*, as its title suggests, introduces the problem or issue that is being studied. It includes a concise review of research relevant to the topic, theoretical ties, and one or more hypothesis to be tested. The *method* section consists of a clear description of the subjects evaluated in the study, the measures used, and the procedures followed. The method section should be sufficiently clear and detailed so that, by reading it, another researcher could repeat, or replicate, the study. The *results* section reports the analysis of the data collected. In most cases, the results section includes statistical analyses that are difficult for nonprofessionals to understand. The *discussion* section describes the author's conclusions, inferences, and interpretation of the findings. Statements are usually made about whether the hypotheses presented in the introduction were supported, the limitations of the study, and suggestions for future research. The last part of a journal article is called *references*, which lists bibliographic information for every source cited in the article. The references section is often a good source for finding other articles relevant to the topic you are interested in.

3 Explain how research on child development is conducted.

Review

- How are data on children's development collected?
- What are the main research designs used in studying development?
- What are some ways that researchers study the time span of peoples' lives?
- What are research journals like? What are the main sections of a research journal article?

Reflect

- You have learned that correlation does not equal causation. Develop an example of two variables (two sets of observations) that are correlated but that you believe certainly have no causal relationship.

4 WHAT ARE SOME CHALLENGES IN CHILD DEVELOPMENT RESEARCH?

| Conducting Ethical Research | Minimizing Bias | Thinking Critically About Research on Children's Development |

The scientific foundation of research in child development helps to minimize the effect of individual researchers' biases and to maximize the objectivity of the results. Still, some subtle challenges remain. One is to ensure that research is conducted in an ethical way; another is to recognize, and try to overcome, researchers' deeply buried personal biases.

Conducting Ethical Research

Ethics is an important part of understanding the science of child development. Even if you have no formal exposure to child development beyond this course, you will find that scientific research in this field and related disciplines affects your everyday life. For one thing, decision makers in government, schools, and many other institutions use the results of research in child development to help children and the adults who care for them lead happier, healthier, more productive lives.

The explosion in technology has forced society to grapple with looming ethics questions that were unimaginable only a few decades ago. The same line of research that enables previously sterile couples to have children might also let prospective parents "call up and order" the characteristics they prefer in their children and someday tip the balance of males and females in the world. Should embryos left over from procedures for increasing fertility be saved or discarded? Research that enables previously sterile couples to have children has also led to the spectacle of frozen embryos being passed about in the courts as a part of divorce settlements.

Ethics in research may affect you more personally if you serve at some point as a participant in a study. In that event, you need to know about your rights as a participant and about the responsibilities researchers have in assuring that these rights are safeguarded. The failure to consider participants' well-being can have life-altering consequences for them. For example, one investigation of young dating couples asked them to complete a questionnaire that coincidentally stimulated some of the participants to think about potentially troublesome issues (Rubin & Mitchell, 1976). One year later, when the researchers followed up with the original sample, 9 of 10 participants said they had discussed their answers with their dating partner. In most instances, the discussions helped to strengthen the relationships. In some cases, though, the participants used the questionnaire as a springboard to discuss previously hidden problems or concerns. One participant said, "The study definitely played a role in ending my relationship with Larry." In this case, the couple had different views about how long they expected to be together. She was thinking of a short-term dating relationship only, while he was thinking in terms of a lifetime. Their answers to the questions brought the disparity in their views to the surface and led to the end of their relationship. Researchers have a responsibility to anticipate the personal problems their study might cause and to at least inform the participants of the possible fallout.

If you become a researcher in child development, you will need an even deeper understanding of ethics. Even if you conduct one or more studies in this or other courses, you must consider the rights of the participants who serve in the experiments. A student might think, "I volunteer in a home several hours a week for individuals who are mentally retarded. I can use the residents of the home in my study to see if a particular treatment helps improve their memory for everyday tasks." But without proper permissions the most well-meaning, kind, and considerate studies still violate the rights of the participants.

Safeguarding the rights of research participants is a challenge because the potential harm is not always obvious. At first glance, you might not imagine that a questionnaire on dating relationships would have any substantial impact. However, researchers increasingly recognize that lasting harm might come to the participants in a study of children's development.

Today colleges and universities have review boards that evaluate the ethical nature of research conducted at their institutions. Proposed research plans must pass the scrutiny of a research ethics committee before the research can be initiated.

In addition, the American Psychological Association (APA) has developed ethics guidelines for its members. The code of ethics instructs psychologists to protect their participants from mental and physical harm. The participants' best interests need to be kept foremost in the researcher's mind (Rosnow, 1995). APA's guidelines address four important issues:

www.mhhe.com/santrockc9

Psychologists' Ethical Principles

- *Informed consent.* All participants, if they are old enough (typically 7 years or older), must give their consent to participate. If they are not old enough, their parents' or guardians' consent must be attained. Informed consent means that the participants (and/or their parents or legal guardians) have been told what their participation will entail and any risks that might be involved. For example, if researchers want to study the effects of conflict in divorced families on children's self-esteem, the participants should be informed that in some instances discussion of a family's experiences might improve family relationships, but in other cases might raise unwanted stress. After informed consent is given, participants have the right to withdraw at any time.
- *Confidentiality.* Researchers are responsible for keeping all of the data they gather on individuals completely confidential and when possible, completely anonymous.
- *Debriefing.* After the study has been completed, participants should be informed of its purpose and the methods that were used. In most cases, the experimenter also can inform participants in a general manner beforehand about the purpose of the research without leading participants to behave in a way they think that the experimenter is expecting. When preliminary information about the study is likely to affect the results, participants at least can be debriefed after the study has been completed.
- *Deception.* This is an ethical issue that psychologists debate extensively (Hoyle & Judd, 2002; Whitley, 2002). In some circumstances, telling the participant beforehand what the research study is about substantially alters the participant's

(a)

(b)

Look at these two photogrphs, (*a*) one of all non–Latino White boys, the other (*b*) of boys and girls from diverse ethnic backgrounds. Consider a topic in child development such as independence seeking, cultural values, parenting education, or health care. *If you were conducting research on this topic, might the results of the study be different depending on whether the participants in your study were the children in the photo on the left or the photo on the right?*

behavior and invalidates the researcher's data. In all cases of deception, however, the researcher must ensure that the deception will not harm the participant and that the participant will be told the complete nature of the study (debriefed) as soon as possible after the study is completed.

Minimizing Bias

Research on children's development also creates another concern—conducting research without bias or prejudice toward any group of people. Of special concern is bias based on gender and bias based on culture or ethnicity.

Gender Bias

For decades, society has had a strong gender bias, a preconceived notion about the abilities of females and males that prevented individuals from pursuing their own interests and achieving their potential. But gender bias also has had a less obvious effect within the field of child development (Paludi, 2002). For example, it is not unusual for conclusions to be drawn about females' attitudes and behaviors from research conducted with males as the only participants.

Florence Denmark and her colleagues (1988) argue as well that when gender differences are found, they sometimes are unduly magnified. For example, a researcher might report in a study that 74 percent of the boys had high achievement expectations versus only 67 percent of the girls and go on to talk about the differences in some detail. In reality, this might be a rather small difference. It also might disappear if the study were repeated or the study might have methodological problems that don't allow such strong interpretations.

Cultural and Ethnic Bias

Research on child development needs to include more people from diverse ethnic groups (Banks, 2006; Garcia Coll, Szalacha, & Palacios, 2005; Graham, 1992; Parke & Clarke-Stewart, 2003). Historically, people from ethnic minority groups (African American, Latino, Asian American, and Native American) have been discounted from most research in the United States and simply thought of as variations from the norm or average. Because their scores don't always fit neatly into measures of central tendency (such as a mean score to reflect the average performance of a group of participants), minority individuals have been viewed as confounds or "noise" in data. Consequently, researchers have deliberately excluded them from the samples they have selected (Ryan-Finn, Cauce, & Grove,

CAREERS in CHILD DEVELOPMENT

Pam Reid
Educational and Development Psychologist

When she was a child, Pam Reid liked to play with chemistry sets. She majored in chemistry during college and wanted to become doctor. However, when some of her friends signed up for a psychology class as an elective, she also decided to take the course. She was intrigued by learning about how people think, behave, and develop—so much so that she changed her major to psychology. Reid went on to obtain her Ph.D. in psychology (American Psychological Association, 2003, p. 16).

For a number of years, Reid was professor of education and psychology at the University of Michigan, where she also was a research scientist at the Institute for Research on Women and Gender. Her main focus has been on how children and adolescents develop social skills with a special interest in the development of African American girls (Reid & Zalk, 2001). In 2004, Reid became Provost and Executive Vice-President at Roosevelt University in Chicago.

Pam Reid (center, back row) with some of the graduate students she mentored at the University of Michigan.

ethnic gloss Using an ethnic label such as African American or Latino is a superficial way that portrays an ethnic group as being more homogeneous than it really is.

1995). Because individuals from diverse ethnic groups were excluded from research on child development for so long, we might reasonably conclude that children's real lives are perhaps more varied than earlier research data have indicated (Ponterotto & others, 2001).

Researchers also have tended to overgeneralize about ethnic groups (Banks, 2006; Diaz, Pelletier, & Provenzo, 2006; Trimble, 1989). **Ethnic gloss** is using an ethnic label such as African American or Latino in a superficial way that portrays an ethnic group as being more homogeneous than it really is. For example, a researcher might describe a research sample like this: "The participants were 20 Latinos and 20 Anglo-Americans." A more complete description of the Latino group might be something like this: "The 20 Latino participants were Mexican Americans from low-income neighborhoods in the southwestern area of Los Angeles. Twelve were from homes in which Spanish is the dominant language spoken, eight from homes in which English is the main language spoken. Ten were born in the United States, ten in Mexico. Ten described themselves as Mexican American, five as Mexican, three as American, two as Chicano, and one as Latino." Ethnic gloss can cause researchers to obtain samples of ethnic groups that are not representative of the group's diversity, which can lead to overgeneralization and stereotyping.

Pam Reid is a leading researcher who studies gender and ethnic bias in development. To read about Pam's interests, see the Careers in Child Development insert.

Thinking Critically About Research on Children's Development

We live in a society that generates a vast amount of information about children in various media ranging from research journals to newspaper and television accounts. The information varies greatly in quality. How can you evaluate this information?

Be Cautious About What Is Reported in the Media
Television, radio, newspapers, and magazines frequently report research on child development. Many researchers regularly supply the media with information about children. In some cases, this research has been published in professional journals or presented at national meetings and then is picked up by the popular media. And most colleges have a media relations department that contacts the press about current faculty research.

However, not all research on children that appears in the media comes from professionals with excellent credentials and reputations. Journalists, television reporters, and other media personnel generally are not scientifically trained. It is not an easy task for them to sort through the avalanche of material they receive and to make sound decisions about which information to report.

Unfortunately, the media often tend to focus on sensational, dramatic findings. They want you to stay tuned or buy their publication. When the information they gather from research journals is not sensational, they may embellish it and sensationalize it, going beyond what the researcher intended.

Another problem with research reported in the media is a lack of time or space to go into important details about a study. They often have only a few lines or a few minutes to summarize as best they can what may be complex findings. Too often this means that what is reported is overgeneralized and stereotyped (Stanovich, 2004).

Don't Assume Group Research Applies to an Individual   Most research focuses on groups, yet it often is the case that people want to know how it applies to one individual. Individual variations about how participants respond are usually not the focus of research. For example, if researchers are interested in the effects of divorce on a child's ability to cope with stress, they might conduct a study with 50 children from divorced families and 50 children from intact, never-divorced families. They might find that the children from divorced families, as a group, had lower self-esteem than did the children from intact families. That is a group finding that applies to children from divorced families as a group, and that is what is commonly reported in the media and in research journals. In this study, it is likely that some of the children from divorced families had higher school achievement than did the children from intact families—not as many, but some. Indeed, it is entirely possible that, of the 100 children in the study, the 2 or 3 children with the highest school achievement were from divorced families, but that was never reported.

Group research provides valuable information about the characteristics of a group of children, revealing strengths and weaknesses of the group. However, in many instances, parents, teachers, and others want to know about how to help one particular child cope and learn more effectively. Unfortunately, although group research can point to problems for certain groups of children, it does not always apply to an individual child.

Don't Overgeneralize About a Small or Clinical Sample   There often isn't space or time in media presentations to go into detail about the nature of the sample of the children on which a study was based. In many cases, samples are too small to generalize to a larger population. For example, if a study of children from divorced families is based on only 10 to 20 children, what is found in the study cannot be generalized to all children from divorced families. Perhaps the sample was drawn from families who have substantial economic resources, are Anglo-American, live in a small southern town, and are undergoing therapy. From this study, we clearly would be making unwarranted generalizations if we thought the findings also characterize children from low- to moderate-income families, other ethnic backgrounds, different geographic regions, and those not undergoing therapy.

Don't Generally Take a Single Study as the Defining Word   The media might identify a single interesting research study and claim that it is a phenomenal breakthrough with far-reaching implications. Should you accept this claim at face value? Remember that it is extremely rare for a single study to have earth-shattering, conclusive answers that apply to all children. In fact, where large numbers of studies focus on a particular issue, it is not unusual to find conflicting results from one study to the next. Reliable answers about children's development usually emerge only after many researchers have conducted similar studies and have drawn similar conclusions. In the case of divorce, if one study reports that a counseling program for children from divorced families improved their self-esteem, we cannot conclude that the counseling program will work as effectively with all children from divorced families until many more studies have been conducted.

Don't Accept Causal Conclusions from Correlational Studies
Drawing causal conclusions from correlational studies is one of the most common mistakes made by the media. In nonexperimental studies (remember that, in an experiment, participants are randomly assigned to treatments or experiences), two variables or factors may be related to each other. However, causal conclusions cannot be drawn

when two or more factors simply are correlated; we cannot say that one causes the other. In the case of divorce, the headline might read "Divorce Causes Children to Have Low Self-Esteem." We read the story and find out that the information is based on the results of a research study. Because obviously we cannot, for ethical and practical reasons, randomly assign children to families that either will become divorced or will remain intact, this headline is based on a correlational study, and the causal statements are unproved. It might well be, for example, that another factor, such as family conflict or economic problems, is typically responsible for both children's poor school performance and parents' divorce.

Always Consider the Source of Information and Evaluate Its Credibility   Finally, be aware that studies are not automatically accepted by the research community. As discussed earlier in the chapter, researchers usually have to submit their findings to a research journal, where it is reviewed by their colleagues, who decide whether or not to publish the paper. Though the quality of research in journals is far from uniform, in most cases the quality of the research has undergone far more scrutiny and careful consideration than has research or other information that has not gone through the journal process. Within the media, we can distinguish between what is presented in respected newspapers and magazines, such as the *New York Times* and *Newsweek,* and what appears in much less respected tabloids, such as the *National Enquirer.*

As you continue your study of children's development, remember to think critically about the research information you read about, hear about, and see in the media.

Review and Reflect • LEARNING GOAL 4

4 **Summarize challenges in child development research.**

Review
- What are researchers' ethical responsibilities to the people they study?
- What research cautions need to be exercised regarding gender, cultural, and ethnic bias?
- What are some good strategies for thinking critically about research on children's development?

Reflect
- Choose one of the topics in this book and course—such as child care, parenting, or adolescent problems. Find an article in a research journal (for example, *Child Development* or *Developmental Psychology*) and an article in a newspaper or magazine on the same topic. How did the research article on the topic differ from the newspaper or magazine article? What did you learn from this comparison?

In this chapter we examined how children's development is studied from a scientific research perspective. In chapter 3, we will begin the journey of childhood by exploring biological beginnings.

REACH YOUR LEARNING GOALS

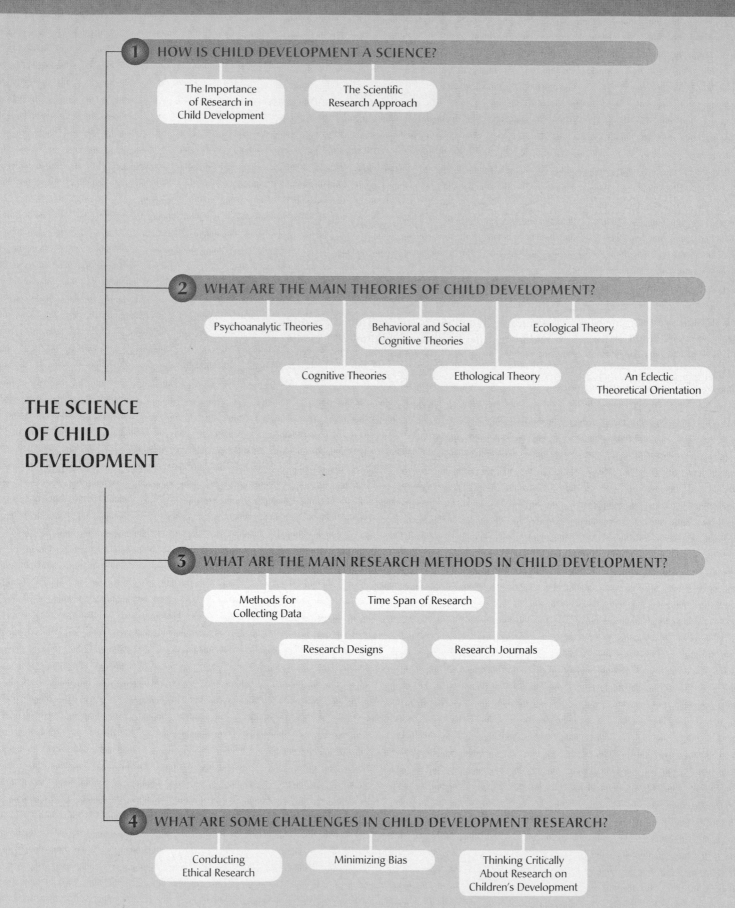

THE SCIENCE OF CHILD DEVELOPMENT

1 HOW IS CHILD DEVELOPMENT A SCIENCE?

The Importance of Research in Child Development

The Scientific Research Approach

2 WHAT ARE THE MAIN THEORIES OF CHILD DEVELOPMENT?

Psychoanalytic Theories

Behavioral and Social Cognitive Theories

Ecological Theory

Cognitive Theories

Ethological Theory

An Eclectic Theoretical Orientation

3 WHAT ARE THE MAIN RESEARCH METHODS IN CHILD DEVELOPMENT?

Methods for Collecting Data

Time Span of Research

Research Designs

Research Journals

4 WHAT ARE SOME CHALLENGES IN CHILD DEVELOPMENT RESEARCH?

Conducting Ethical Research

Minimizing Bias

Thinking Critically About Research on Children's Development

SUMMARY

1 Discuss the importance of research in child development and the scientific method.

- When we base information on personal experience, we aren't always objective. Research provides a vehicle for evaluating the accuracy of what experts and authorities say.
- Scientific research is objective, systematic, and testable. Scientific research is based on the scientific method, which includes these steps: conceptualize the problem, collect data, draw conclusions, and revise theory.

2 Describe the main theories of child development.

- Psychoanalytic theories describe development as primarily unconscious and as heavily colored by emotion. Psychoanalytic theorists believe that behavior is merely a surface characteristic and that early experiences with parents shape development. Freud said that personality is made up of three structures—id, ego, and superego. The conflicting demands of these structures produce anxiety. Freud also believed that individuals go through five psychosexual stages—oral, anal, phallic, latency, and genital. Erikson's theory emphasizes these eight psychosocial stages of development: trust versus mistrust, autonomy versus shame and doubt, initiative versus guilt, industry versus inferiority, identity versus identity confusion, intimacy versus isolation, generativity versus stagnation, and integrity versus despair. Contributions of psychoanalytic theories include an emphasis on early experiences and family relationships. Criticisms include difficulty in scientifically testing the main concepts and too much emphasis on sexual underpinnings.
- The three main cognitive theories are Piaget's cognitive developmental theory, Vygotsky's sociocultural cognitive theory, and information-processing theory. Cognitive theories emphasize conscious thoughts. Piaget proposed a cognitive developmental theory in which children use the processes of organization and adaptation (assimilation and accommodation) to understand their world. In Piaget's theory, children go through four cognitive stages: sensorimotor, preoperational, concrete operational, and formal operational. Vygotsky's sociocultural cognitive theory emphasizes how culture and social interaction guide cognitive development. Information-processing theory emphasizes that individuals manipulate information, monitor it, and strategize about it. Contributions of cognitive theories include a positive view of development and an emphasis on the active construction of understanding. Criticisms include giving too

little attention to individual variations and not enough emphasis to unconscious thought.
- Three versions of the behavioral approach are (1) Pavlov's classical conditioning, (2) Skinner's operant conditioning, and (3) Bandura's social cognitive theory. In Pavlov's classical conditioning, a neutral stimulus acquires the ability to produce a response originally produced by another stimulus. In Skinner's operant conditioning, the consequences of a behavior produce changes in the probability of the behavior's occurrence. In Bandura's social cognitive theory, observational learning is a key aspect of life-span development. Bandura emphasizes reciprocal interactions among the person/cognition, behavior, and the environment. Contributions of the behavioral and social cognitive theories include an emphasis on scientific research and environmental influences. Criticisms include giving inadequate attention to developmental changes and emphasizing environmental influences too strongly.
- Ethological theory stresses that behavior is strongly influenced by biology, is tied to evolution, and is characterized by critical or sensitive periods. Ethological theory emerged as an important contributor to developmental theories because of the work of European zoologists, especially Konrad Lorenz, whose research with greylag geese demonstrated the process of imprinting. Contributions of ethological theory include a focus on the biological and evolutionary basis of development, as well as careful observations in naturalistic settings. Criticisms include a belief that the critical and sensitive period concepts are too rigid and place too much emphasis on biological foundations.
- Ecological theory is Bronfenbrenner's environmental systems view of development. It consists of five environmental systems: microsystem, mesosystem, exosystem, macrosystem, and chronosystem. Contributions of the theory include a systematic examination of macro and micro dimensions of environmental systems, as well as paying attention to connections between settings. Criticisms include giving inadequate attention to biological factors and cognitive factors.
- An eclectic theoretical orientation does not follow any one theoretical approach, but rather selects from each theory whatever is considered the best in it.

3 Explain how research on child development is conducted.

- Methods for collecting data include observation, interview and survey, standardized test, psychophysiological measures, and case study.

- Three main research designs are descriptive, correlational, and experimental. Descriptive research aims to observe and record behavior. In correlational research, the goal is to describe the strength of the relationship between two or more events or characteristics. Experimental research involves conducting an experiment, which can determine cause and effect. An independent variable is the manipulated, influential, experimental factor. A dependent variable is a factor that can change in an experiment, in response to changes in the independent variable. Experiments can involve one or more experimental groups and control groups. In random assignment, researchers assign participants to experimental and control groups by chance.
- When researchers decide about the time span of their research, they can conduct cross-sectional or longitudinal studies.
- A research journal publishes scholarly and academic information, and an increasing number of journals publish information about child development. Most journal articles are reports of original research. Most research journal articles follow this format: abstract, introduction, methods, results, discussion, and references.

 Summarize challenges in child development research.

- Researchers' ethical responsibilities include seeking participants' informed consent, ensuring their confidentiality, debriefing them about the purpose and potential personal consequences of participating, and avoiding unnecessary deception of participants.
- Researchers need to guard against gender, cultural, and ethnic bias in research. Every effort should be made to make research equitable for both females and males. More children from ethnic minority backgrounds need to be included in child development research.
- Thinking critically about child development research includes being cautious about what is reported in the media, not automatically applying results from group research to one individual, not overgeneralizing about a small or clinical sample, not taking a single study as the defining word, not accepting causal interpretations from correlational studies, and always considering the source of the information and evaluating its credibility.

KEY TERMS

KEY PEOPLE

MAKING A DIFFERENCE

Developing Children's Self-Efficacy

Earlier in the chapter, we discussed Albert Bandura's social cognitive theory and Albert Bandura's belief that self-efficacy is one of the most important aspects of children's development. Here are Bandura's (1997) recommendations for how adults can make a difference in children's lives by guiding their development of self-efficacy:

- *Young children require extensive monitoring by competent adults.* Very young children lack knowledge of their own capabilities and the hazards of their world. Adult monitoring gets children through this early formative time until they become aware of what they can do and what situations require in the way of skills.
- *Recognize "that actions produce outcomes"* (p.164). Infants need a stimulating environment that encourages them to

sense that they can make things happen and to regard themselves as the doers.

- *Parental sources of self-efficacy.* Parental enabling activities increase infants' and children's exploratory and cognitive competence. Overprotective parents constrain children's mastery capabilities. By contrast, secure parents are more likely to encourage children's exploratory efforts and to give them an opportunity to experience a feeling of mastery.
- *The school's role.* "As children master cognitive skills, they develop a growing sense of intellectual self-efficacy. . . . A fundamental goal of education is to equip children with the self-regulatory skills that enable them to educate themselves" (p. 174). This self-regulation includes learning how to develop plans, be organized, become motivated, and use resources. Schools play an important role not only in children's intellectual self-efficacy but also in their health self-efficacy. The effectiveness of health education programs hinges on their ability to impart a sense of self-efficacy to manage one's health habits effectively.
- *The transition to adolescence.* As children move into adolescence, they have to assume increasing responsibility for their behavior. The way in which adolescents develop and exercise their self-efficacy can be critical in setting the courses that their life paths take. Being around competent parents, peers, and teachers who model self-efficacy increases adolescents' self-efficacy.

CHILDREN RESOURCES

Identity: Youth and Crisis (1968)

by Erik H. Erikson
New York: W. W. Norton

Erik Erikson was one of the leading theorists in the field of life-span development. In *Identity: Youth and Crisis,* he outlines his eight stages of life-span development and provides numerous examples from his clinical practice to illustrate the stages. Special attention is given to the fifth stage in Erikson's theory, identity versus identity confusion. Especially worthwhile are Erikson's commentaries about identity development in different cultures.

Observational Strategies of Child Study (1990)

by D. M. Irwin and M. M. Bushnell
Fort Worth, TX: Harcourt Brace

Being a good observer can benefit you a great deal in helping children reach their full potential. Observational skills can be learned. This practical book gives you a rich set of observational strategies that will help you become a more sensitive observer of children's behavior.

E-LEARNING TOOLS

Connect to **www.mhhe.com/santrockc9** to research the answers to complete the following exercises. In addition, you'll find a number of other resources and valuable study tools for chapter 2, "The Science of Child Development," on this website.

Taking It to the Net

1. Erika has never put much faith in Freud's theories, especially the one about the "Oedipus complex" and how it accounts for differences in male and female moral development. Her child development teacher challenged her to find out if there is any empirical evidence to back up Freud's claims. Is there empirical evidence to back up Freud's claims?
2. Sean has to do a presentation in his psychology class on how ethological theories can be utilized to understand some aspects of child development. How can Sean find information to compare and contrast how and why nonhuman primates and human beings imitate others of their species?
3. For her senior psychology project, Doris wants to study the effect on self-esteem of mandatory school uniforms.

She wants to limit her study to fourth-graders. She has located a school with a mandatory uniform policy and one without such a policy. What type of research design should she use?

Health and Well-Being, Parenting, and Education

Build your decision-making skills by trying your hand at the health and well-being, parenting, and education exercises.

Video Clips

The Online Learning Center includes the following videos for this chapter:

1. *Ethical Issues in Studying Infants*—274
   Renowned infant researcher Albert Yonas discusses the ethical issues he faces when studying infants.
2. *Schools and Public Policy*—931
   Dr. Jacquelynne Eccles describes how her research on gender and school transitions has influenced public policy.

are higher in toxins and may harm the fetus. Thus, pregnancy sickness may have been favored as an evolutionary adaptation because it enhances the mother's ability to produce a healthy baby, helping to ensure the survival of the species.

Evolutionary Psychology

Although Darwin introduced the theory of evolution by natural selection in 1859, his ideas only recently have become a popular framework for explaining behavior. Psychology's newest approach, **evolutionary psychology,** emphasizes the importance of adaptation, reproduction, and "survival of the fittest" in shaping behavior. "Fit" in this sense refers to the ability to bear offspring that survive long enough to bear offspring of their own. In this view, the evolutionary process of natural selection has favored behaviors that increase our reproductive success, our ability to pass our genes to the next generation.

David Buss (1995, 2000, 2004) has been especially influential in stimulating new interest in how evolution can explain human behavior. He believes that just as evolution shapes our physical features, such as body shape and height, it also pervasively influences how we make decisions, how aggressive we are, our fears, and our mating patterns. For example, assume that our ancestors were hunterers and gatherers on the plains and that men did most of the hunting and women stayed close to home gathering seeds and plants for food. If you have to travel some distance from your home in an effort to find and slay a fleeing animal, you need not only certain physical traits but also the ability for certain types of spatial thinking. Men born with these traits would be more likely than men without them to survive, to bring home lots of food, and to be considered attractive mates—and thus to reproduce and pass on these characteristics to their children. In other words, some traits would provide a reproductive advantage for males and, over many generations, men with good spatial thinking skills might become more numerous in the population. Critics point out that this example based on evolutionary theory may or may not have actually happened.

Evolutionary Developmental Psychology Much of the thinking about evolutionary psychology has not had a developmental focus. Recently, however, interest has grown in applying the concepts of evolutionary psychology to the changes that take place as people develop (Barnhill, 2004). Here are a few ideas proposed by evolutionary developmental psychologists (Bjorklund & Pellegrini, 2002, pp. 336–340):

- *An extended "'juvenile"' period evolved because humans require time to develop a large brain and learn the complexity of human social communities.* Humans take longer to become reproductively mature than any other mammal (see figure 3.1). During this time they develop a large brain and the experiences required for mastering the complexities of human society.
- *"Many aspects of childhood function as preparations for adulthood and were selected over the course of evolution"* (p. 337). Play is one possible example. Beginning in the preschool years, boys in all cultures engage in more rough-and-tumble play than girls. Perhaps rough-and-tumble play prepares boys for fighting and hunting as adults. In contrast to boys, girls engage in play that involves more imitation of parents, such as caring for dolls, and less physical dominance. This, according to evolutionary psychologists, is an evolved tendency that prepares females for becoming the primary caregivers for their offspring.
- *Some characteristics of childhood were selected because they are adaptive at specific points in development, not because they prepare children for adulthood.* For example, some aspects of play may function, not to prepare us for adulthood, but to help children adapt to their immediate circumstances, perhaps to learn about their current environment.

Evolution
Evolution and Behavior
Evolutionary Psychology
Handbook of Evolutionary Psychology

evolutionary psychology Emphasizes the importance of adaptation, reproduction, and "survival of the fittest" in shaping behavior.

- *Many evolved psychological mechanisms are domain-specific.* That is, the mechanisms apply only to a specific aspect of a person's psychological makeup (Atkinson & Wheeler, 2004; Kanazawa, 2004; Rubenstein, 2004). According to evolutionary psychology, information processing is one example. In this view, the mind is not a general-purpose device that can be applied equally to a vast array of problems. Instead, as our ancestors dealt with certain recurring problems, specialized modules evolved that process information related to those problems, such as a module for physical knowledge, a module for mathematical knowledge, and a module for language. Also in this view, "infants enter the world 'prepared' to process and learn some information more readily than others, and these preparations serve as the foundation for social and cognitive development" (p. 338).

- *Evolved mechanisms are not always adaptive in contemporary society.* Some behaviors that were adaptive for our prehistoric ancestors may not serve us well today. For example, the food-scarce environment of our ancestors likely led to humans' propensity to gorge when food is available and to crave high-caloric foods, a trait that might lead to an epidemic of obesity when food is plentiful.

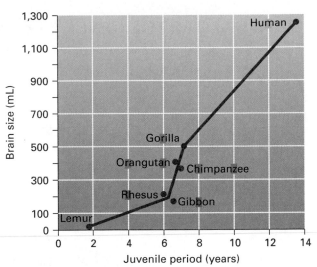

FIGURE 3.1 The Brain Sizes of Various Primates and Humans in Relation to the Length of the Juvenile Period

Evaluating Evolutionary Psychology   Although the popular press gives a lot of attention to the ideas of evolutionary psychology, it remains just one theoretical approach. Like the theories described in chapter 2, it has limitations, weaknesses, and critics. Albert Bandura (1998), whose social cognitive theory was described in chapter 1, acknowledges the important influence of evolution on human adaptation. However, he rejects what he calls "one-sided evolutionism," which sees social behavior as the product of evolved biology. An alternative is a *bidirectional view*, in which environmental and biological conditions influence each other. For example, evolutionary pressures created changes in biological structures that allowed the use of tools, which enabled organisms to manipulate the environment, constructing new environmental conditions. In turn, environmental innovations produced new selection pressures that led to the evolution of specialized biological systems for consciousness, thought, and language.

In other words, evolution gave us bodily structures and biological potentialities; it does not dictate behavior. People have used their biological capacities to produce diverse cultures—aggressive and pacific, egalitarian and autocratic. As American scientist Steven Jay Gould (1981) concluded, in most domains of human functioning, biology allows a broad range of cultural possibilities.

Review and Reflect • LEARNING GOAL 1

 Discuss the evolutionary perspective on development.

Review
- How can natural selection and adaptive behavior be defined?
- What is evolutionary psychology? What are some basic ideas about human development proposed by evolutionary psychologists? How can evolutionary psychology be evaluated?

Reflect
- Which is more persuasive to you: the views of evolutionary psychologists or their critics? Why?

2   WHAT ARE THE GENETIC FOUNDATIONS OF DEVELOPMENT?

| The Genetic Process | Genetic Principles | Chromosomal and Gene-Linked Abnormalities |

Every species has a mechanism for transmitting characteristics from one generation to the next. This mechanism is explained by the principles of genetics. Each of us carries a "genetic code" that we inherited from our parents, and it is a distinctly human code. Because a fertilized egg carries this human code, a fertilized human egg cannot grow into an egret, eagle, or elephant.

The Genetic Process

Each of us began life as a single cell weighing about one twenty-millionth of an ounce! This tiny piece of matter housed our entire genetic code—instructions that orchestrated growth from that single cell to a person made of trillions of cells, each containing a replica of the original code. That code is carried by our genes. What are genes and what do they do? For the answer, we need to look into our cells.

chromosomes Threadlike structures that come in 23 pairs, one member of each pair coming from each parent. Chromosomes contain the genetic substance DNA.

DNA A complex molecule that contains genetic information.

genes Units of hereditary information composed of DNA. Genes direct cells to reproduce themselves and manufacture the proteins that maintain life.

DNA and the Collaborative Gene   The nucleus of each human cell contains **chromosomes,** which are threadlike structures that contain the remark chemical substance deoxyribonucleic acid, or DNA. **DNA** is a complex molecule that has a double helix shape, like a spiral staircase, and contains genetic information. **Genes,** the units of hereditary information, are short segments composed of DNA, as you can see in figure 3.2. They direct cells to reproduce themselves and to assemble proteins. Proteins, in turn, are the building blocks of cells as well as the regulators that direct the body's processes (Cummings, 2006; Hartwell & others, 2004).

Each gene has its own function and each gene has its own location, its own designated place on a particular chromosome. Today, there is a great deal of enthusiasm about efforts to discover the specific locations of genes that are linked to certain func-

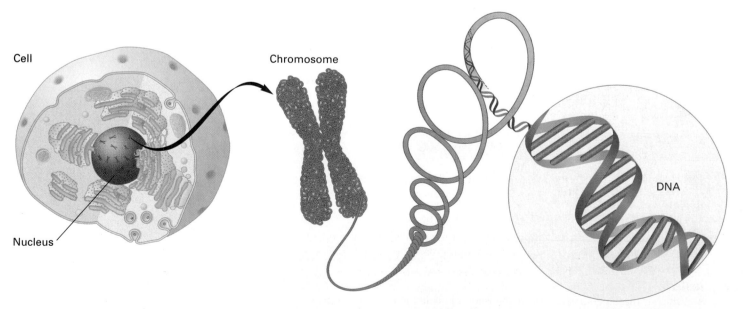

FIGURE 3.2   Cells, Chromosomes, Genes, and DNA (*Left*) The body contains billions of cells, which are the basic structural units of life. Each cell contains a central structure, the nucleus. (*Middle*) Chromosomes and genes are located in the cell's nucleus. Chromosomes are threadlike structures composed mainly of DNA molecules. (*Right*) A gene, which is a segment of DNA that contains the hereditary code. The structure of DNA is a spiraled double chain of molecules.

Calvin and Hobbes   by Bill Watterson

tions (Benfey, 2005; Brooker, 2005; Lewin, 2006; Lewis, 2007). An important step in this direction was accomplished when the Human Genome Project and the Celera Corporation completed a preliminary map of the human *genome*—the complete set of developmental instructions for creating proteins that initiate the making of a human organism (U.S. Department of Energy, 2001).

One of the big surprises of the Human Genome Project was a report indicating that humans have only about 30,000 genes (U.S. Department of Energy, 2001). More recently, the number of human genes has been revised further downward to 20,000 to 25,000 (International Human Genome Sequencing Consortium, 2004). Scientists had thought that humans had as many as 100,000 or more genes. They had also believed that each gene programmed just one protein. In fact, humans appear to have far more proteins than they have genes, so there cannot be a one-to-one correspondence between genes and proteins (Commoner, 2002; Moore, 2001). Each gene of DNA is not translated, in automation-like fashion, into one and only one protein. It does not act independently, as developmental psychologist David Moore (2001) emphasized by titling his recent book *The Dependent Gene.*

In short, a single gene is rarely the source of a protein's genetic information, much less of an inherited trait (Gottlieb, 2003, 2004; Gottlieb, Wahlsten, & Lickliter, 2006; Moore, 2001). Rather than being a group of independent genes, the human genome consists of many collaborative genes. Rather than being an independent source of developmental information, DNA collaborates with other sources of information to specify our characteristics. The collaboration operates at many points. For example, the cellular machinery mixes, matches, and links small pieces of DNA to reproduce the genes and that machinery is influenced by what is going on around it. Whether a gene is turned "on," working to assemble proteins, is also a matter of collaboration. The activity of genes (*genetic expression*) is affected by their environment (Gottlieb, 2003, 2004; Gottlieb, Wahlsten, & Lickliter, 2006). For example, hormones that circulate in the blood make their way into the cell where they can turn genes "on" and "off." And the flow of hormones can be affected by environmental conditions, such as light, day length, nutrition, and behavior. Numerous studies have shown that external events outside of the cell and the person, as well as events inside the cell, can excite or inhibit gene expression (Gottlieb, Wahlsten, & Lickliter, 1998, 2006; Mauro & others, 1994; Rusak & others, 1990).

Genes and Chromosomes   Genes not only are collaborative; they are enduring. How do the genes manage to get passed from generation to generation and end up in all of the trillion cells in the body? Three processes explain the heart of the story: mitosis, meiosis, and fertilization.

Mitosis, Meiosis, and Fertilization   All cells in your body (except the sperm and egg) have 46 chromosomes arranged in 23 pairs. Why pairs? Because you inherited one

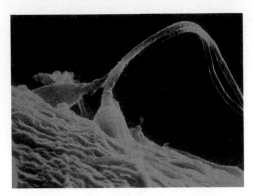

FIGURE 3.3 Union of Sperm and Egg

Landmarks in the History of Genetics
Human Genome Project

mitosis Cellular reproduction in which the cell's nucleus duplicates itself with two new cells being formed, each containing the same DNA as the parent cell, arranged in the same 23 pairs of chromosomes.

meiosis A specialized form of cell division that occurs to form eggs and sperm (or gametes).

fertilization A stage in reproduction whereby an egg and a sperm fuse to create a single cell, called a zygote.

zygote A single cell formed through fertilization.

genotype A person's genetic heritage; the actual genetic material.

phenotype The way an individual's genotype is expressed in observed and measurable characteristics.

chromosome from your mother and one from your father. These cells reproduce by a process called **mitosis.** During mitosis, the cell's nucleus—including the chromosomes—duplicates itself and the cell divides. Two new cells are formed, each containing the same DNA as the parent cell, arranged in the same 23 pairs of chromosomes.

However, a different type of cell division—**meiosis**—forms eggs and sperm (or *gametes*). During meiosis, a cell produced by a man's testes or by a woman's ovaries duplicates its chromosomes just as in mitosis, but then divides *twice*, thus forming four cells, each of which has only half of the genetic material of the parent cell. By the end of meiosis, each egg or sperm has 23 *unpaired* chromosomes.

The next stage in the process of reproduction is **fertilization,** whereby an egg and a sperm fuse to create a single cell, called a **zygote** (see figure 3.3). In the zygote, the unpaired chromosomes from the egg and the unpaired chromosomes from the sperm combine to form one set of paired chromosomes—one member of each pair from the mother's egg and the other member from the father's sperm. In this manner, each parent contributes half of the offspring's genetic material.

Sources of Variability Combining the genes of two parents in offspring increases the population's genetic variability, which is valuable for a species because it provides more characteristics for natural selection to operate on (Klug & Cummings, 2005; Klug, Cummings, & Spencer, 2006; Krogh, 2005). However, the zygote's chromosomes are not exact copies of either parent's chromosomes. During the formation of the sperm and egg in meiosis, the members of each pair of chromosomes are separated, but which chromosome in the pair goes to the gamete is a matter of chance. In addition, before the pairs separate, pieces of the two chromosomes in each pair are exchanged, creating a new combination of genes on each chromosome. Thus, when chromosomes from the mother's egg and the father's sperm are brought together in the zygote, the result is a truly unique combination of genes.

Figure 3.4 shows 23 paired chromosomes of a male and a female. The members of each pair of chromosomes are both similar and different: Each chromosome in the pair contains varying forms of the same genes, at the same location on the chromosome. A gene for hair color, for example, is located on both members of one pair of chromosomes, in the same location on each. However, one of those chromosomes might carry the gene for blonde hair; the other chromosome in the pair might carry the gene for brown hair.

Do you notice any obvious differences between the chromosomes of the male and the chromosomes of the female in figure 3.4? The difference lies in the 23rd pair. Ordinarily, in females this pair consists of two chromosomes called *X chromosomes*; in males the 23rd pair consists of an X and a *Y chromosome*. The presence of a Y chromosome is what makes an individual male.

All of a person's genetic material makes up his or her **genotype.** However, not all of the genetic material is apparent in our observed and measurable characteristics (Wong, Gottesman, & Petronis, 2005). A **phenotype** consists of observable characteristics. Phenotypes include physical characteristics (such as height, weight, and hair color) and psychological characteristics (such as personality and intelligence). For each genotype, a range of phenotypes can be expressed, providing another source of variability (Gottlieb, Wahlsten, & Lickliter, 2006; Loos & Rankinen, 2005). An individual can inherit the genetic potential to grow very large, for example, but nutrition will influence how much of that potential is achieved. This principle is so widely applicable, it has a name—heredity-environment interaction—and later in the chapter we will devote considerable attention to it. The giggle sisters introduced in the chapter opening might have inherited the same genetic potential to be very tall, but if Daphne had grown up malnourished, she might have ended up noticeably shorter than Barbara.

Yet another source of variability comes from DNA. Chance, a mistake by cellular machinery, or damage from an environmental agent such as radiation may produce a *mutated gene*, which is a permanently altered segment of DNA.

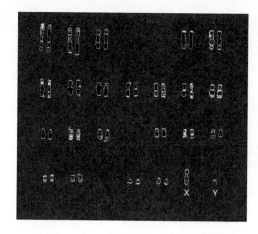 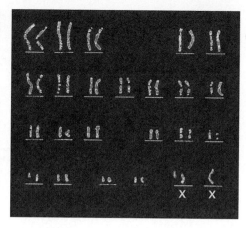

FIGURE 3.4 **The Genetic Difference Between Males and Females** The chromosome structure of a male (*left*) and female (*right*). The 23rd pair is shown at bottom right. Notice that the male's Y chromosome is smaller than his X chromosome. To obtain pictures of chromosomes, a cell is removed from a person's body, usually a cheek cell. Cheek cells are found in saliva so a special procedure is not required to obtain them. The chromosomes are photographed under magnification.

Genetic Principles

What determines how a phenotype is expressed to create a particular phenotype? Much is unknown about the answer to this question (Klug, Cummings, & Spencer, 2006; Lewis, 2005; Tobin & Dusheck, 2005). However, a number of genetic principles have been discovered, including dominant-recessive genes, sex-linked genes, genetic imprinting, and polygenically determined characteristics.

Dominant-Recessive Genes Principle
In some cases, one gene of a pair always exerts its effects; it is *dominant,* overriding the potential influence of the other gene, called the *recessive* gene. This is the *dominant-recessive genes principle.* A recessive gene exerts its influence only if the two genes of a pair are both recessive. If you inherit a recessive gene for a trait from each of your parents, you will show the trait. If you inherit a recessive gene from only one parent, you may never know you carry the gene. Brown hair, farsightedness, and dimples rule over blonde hair, nearsightedness, and freckles in the world of dominant-recessive genes. Can two brown-haired parents have a blonde-haired child? Yes, they can. Suppose that in each parent the gene pair that governs hair color includes a dominant gene for brown hair and a recessive gene for blonde hair. Since dominant genes override recessive genes, the parents have brown hair, but both are carriers of blondeness and pass on their recessive genes for blonde hair. With no dominant gene to override them, the recessive genes can make the child's hair blonde. Figure 3.5 illustrates the dominant-recessive genes principle.

Sex-Linked Genes
X-linked inheritance is the term used to describe the inheritance of an altered (*mutated*) gene that is carried on the X chromosome (Trappe & others, 2001). Most such mutated genes are recessive, but remember that males have only one X chromosome. When there is an alteration of the X chromosome, males have no "backup" copy and therefore may carry an X-linked disease. However, females have a second X chromosome, which is likely to be unchanged. As a result, they are not likely to have the X-linked disease. Thus, most individuals who have X-linked diseases are males. Females who have one changed copy of the X gene are known as "carriers," and they usually do not show any signs of the X-linked disease. Hemophilia and fragile-X syndrome, which we will discuss later in the chapter, are examples of X-linked inheritance (Gonzales-del Angel & others, 2000).

Genetic Imprinting
Genetic imprinting occurs when genes have differing effects depending on whether they are inherited from the mother or the father (Beaudet, 2004; Curley & others, 2004). In most instances, a gene inherited from the father and a gene inherited from the mother will both be active. However, in some cases only one will be active and that gene is marked or "imprinted" during meiosis. An imprinted

FIGURE 3.5 **How Brown-Haired Parents Can Have a Blonde-Haired Child** Although both parents have brown hair, each parent can have a recessive gene for blonde hair. In this example, both parents have brown hair, but each parent carries the recessive gene for blonde hair. Therefore, the odds of their child having blonde hair is one in four—the probability the child will receive a recessive gene (*b*) from each parent.

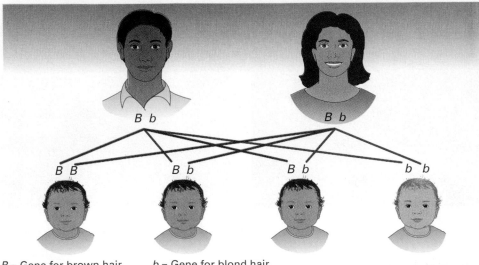

B = Gene for brown hair   *b* = Gene for blond hair

gene dominates one that has not been imprinted. Genetic imprinting may explain why individuals who inherit Turner syndrome (which is characterized by underdeveloped sex organs) from their fathers tend to show better cognitive and social skills than when they inherit the disorder from their mothers (Martinez-Pasarell & others, 1999). We will further discuss Turner syndrome later in the chapter.

Polygenic Inheritance   Genetic transmission is usually more complex than the simple examples we have examined thus far (Lewis, 2005; Starr, 2005). Few psychological characteristics are the result of a single gene or pair of genes. Most are determined by the interaction of many different genes; they are said to be *polygenically determined. Polygenic inheritance* occurs when many genes interact to influence a characteristic. There are about 20,000 to 25,000 human genes, so you can imagine that possible combinations are staggering in number.

Chromosomal and Gene-Linked Abnormalities

In some cases, abnormalities characterize the genetic process (Lewis, 2007; Starr, 2006). Some of these abnormalities can involve whole chromosomes that do not separate properly during meiosis or parts of a chromosome that split off. Other abnormalities are produced by inheriting harmful mutated genes (genes with an abrupt, permanent changes in their material).

Chromosomal Abnormalities   Sometimes, when a gamete is formed, the male's sperm and the female's ovum do not have their normal set of 23 chromosomes. The most notable examples involve Down syndrome and abnormalities of the sex chromosomes (see figure 3.6).

Down Syndrome   An individual with **Down syndrome** has a round face, a flattened skull, an extra fold of skin over the eyelids, a protruding tongue, short limbs, and retardation of motor and mental abilities (Alfirevic & Neilson, 2004; Egan & others, 2004; Matias, Montenegro, & Blickstein, 2005). The syndrome is caused by the presence of an extra copy of chromosome 21. It is not known why the extra chromosome is present, but the health of the parent's sperm or ovum may be involved (Antonarakis & others, 2004; Liou & others, 2004). Down syndrome appears approximately once in every 700 live births. Women between the ages of 18 and 38 are less likely to give

www.mhhe.com/santrockc9

Genetic Disorders
Prenatal Testing

Down syndrome A chromosomally transmitted form of mental retardation, caused by the presence of an extra copy of chromosome 21.

Name	Description	Treatment	Incidence
Down syndrome	An extra chromosome causes mild to severe retardation and physical abnormalities.	Surgery, early intervention, infant stimulation, and special learning programs	1 in 1,900 births at age 20 1 in 300 births at age 35 1 in 30 births at age 45
Klinefelter syndrome	An extra X chromosome causes physical abnormalities.	Hormone therapy can be effective	1 in 800 males
Fragile X syndrome	An abnormality in the X chromosome can cause mental retardation, learning disabilities, or short attention span.	Special education, speech and language therapy	More common in males than in females
Turner syndrome	A missing X chromosome in females can cause mental retardation and sexual underdevelopment.	Hormone therapy in childhood and puberty	1 in 2,500 female births
XYY syndrome	An extra Y chromosome can cause above-average height.	No special treatment required	1 in 1,000 male births

FIGURE 3.6 **Some Chromosomal Abnormalities** *Note:* Treatment does not necessarily erase the problem but may improve the individual's adaptive behavior and quality of life.

birth to a child with Down syndrome than are younger or older women. African American children are rarely born with Down syndrome.

Sex-Linked Chromosomal Abnormalities   Recall that a newborn normally has either an X and a Y chromosome, or two X chromosomes. Human embryos must possess at least one X chromosome to be viable. The most common sex-linked chromosome abnormalities involve the presence of an extra chromosome (either an X or Y) or the absence of one X chromosome in females.

Klinefelter syndrome is a genetic disorder in which males have an extra X chromosome, making them XXY instead of XY (Denschlag & others, 2004; Tyler & Edman, 2004). Males with this disorder have undeveloped testes, and they usually have enlarged breasts and become tall. Klinefelter syndrome occurs approximately once in every 800 live male births.

Fragile X syndrome is a genetic disorder that results from an abnormality in the X chromosome, which becomes constricted and often breaks. Mental deficiency often is an outcome but it may take the form of mental retardation, a learning disability, or a short attention span (Irwin & others, 2005; Lewis, 2005, 2007). This disorder occurs more frequently in males than in females, possibly because the second X chromosome in females negates the disorder's negative effects (Chiurazzi, Neri, & Oostra, 2003).

Turner syndrome is a chromosomal disorder in females in which either an X chromosome is missing, making the person XO instead of XX, or the second chromosome is partially deleted (Frias & Davenport, 2003). These females are short in stature and have a webbed neck. They might be infertile and have difficulty in mathematics, but their verbal ability is often quite good. Turner syndrome occurs in approximately 1 of every 2,500 live females births.

The **XYY syndrome** is a chromosomal disorder in which the male has an extra Y chromosome (Monastirli & others, 2005). Early interest in this syndrome focused on the belief that the extra Y chromosome found in some males contributed to aggression and violence. However, researchers subsequently found that XYY males are no more likely to commit crimes than are XY males (Witkin & others, 1976).

Gene-Linked Abnormalities   Abnormalities can be produced by an uneven number of chromosomes; they also can result from harmful genes. More than 7,000 such genetic disorders have been identified, although most of them are rare.

These athletes, many of whom have Down syndrome, are participating in a Special Olympics competition. Notice the distinctive facial features of the individuals with Down syndrome, such as a round face and a flattened skull. *What causes Down syndrome?*

Klinefelter syndrome A chromosomal disorder in which males have an extra X chromosome, making them XXY instead of XY.

fragile X syndrome A genetic disorder involving an abnormality in the X chromosome, which becomes constricted and often breaks.

Turner syndrome A chromosome disorder in females in which either an X chromosome is missing, making the person XO instead of XX, or the second X chromosome is partially deleted.

XYY syndrome A chromosomal disorder in which males have an extra Y chromosome.

Name	Description	Treatment	Incidence
Cystic fibrosis	Glandular dysfunction that interferes with mucus production; breathing and digestion are hampered, resulting in a shortened life span.	Physical and oxygen therapy, synthetic enzymes, and antibiotics; most individuals live to middle age.	1 in 2,000 births
Diabetes	Body does not produce enough insulin, which causes abnormal metabolism of sugar.	Early onset can be fatal unless treated with insulin.	1 in 2,500 births
Hemophilia	Delayed blood clotting causes internal and external bleeding.	Blood transfusions/injections can reduce or prevent damage due to internal bleeding.	1 in 10,000 males
Phenylketonuria (PKU)	Metabolic disorder that, left untreated, causes mental retardation.	Special diet can result in average intelligence and normal life span.	1 in 15,000 births
Sickle-cell anemia	Blood disorder that limits the body's oxygen supply; it can cause joint swelling, as well as heart and kidney failure.	Penicillin, medication for pain, antibiotics, and blood transfusions.	1 in 400 African American children (lower among other groups)
Spina bifida	Neural tube disorder that causes brain and spine abnormalities.	Corrective surgery at birth, orthopedic devices, and physical/medical therapy.	2 in 1,000 births
Tay-Sachs disease	Deceleration of mental and physical development caused by an accumulation of lipids in the nervous system.	Medication and special diet are used, but death is likely by 5 years of age.	One in 30 American Jews is a carrier.

FIGURE 3.7 Some Gene-Linked Abnormalities

Phenylketonuria (PKU) is a genetic disorder in which the individual cannot properly metabolize phenylalanine, an amino acid (Brumm & others, 2004; Channon & others, 2004; Zaffanelo, Maffeis, & Zamboni, 2005). It results from a recessive gene and occurs about once in every 15,000 live births. If phenylketonuria is left untreated, mental retardation and hyperactivity result. Phenylketonuria accounts for approximately 1 percent of institutionalized individuals who are mentally retarded, and it occurs primarily in Whites. Today, phenylketonuria is easily detected and it is treated by diet that prevents an excess accumulation of phenylalanine.

phenylketonuria (PKU) A genetic disorder in which an individual cannot properly metabolize phenylalanine, an amino acid. PKU is now easily detected but, if left untreated, results in mental retardation and hyperactivity.

During a physical examination for a college football tryout, Jerry Hubbard, 32, learned that he carried the gene for sickle-cell anemia. Daughter Sara is healthy but daughter Avery (in the print dress) has sickle-cell anemia. *If you were a genetic counselor, would you recommend that this family have more children? Explain.*

The story of phenylketonuria has important implications for the nature-nurture issue. Although phenylketonuria is a genetic disorder (nature), how or whether a gene's influence in phenylketonuria is played out can depend on environmental influences since the disorder can be treated (nurture) (Merrick, Aspler, & Schwartz, 2001). That is, the presence of a genetic defect *does not* inevitably lead to the development of the disorder *if* the individual develops in the right environment (one free of phenylalanine). This is one example of the important principle of heredity-environment interaction that was mentioned earlier. Under one environmental condition (phenylalanine in the diet), mental retardation occurs but when other nutrients replace phenylalanine, intelligence develops in the normal range. The same genotype can give rise to different outcomes.

Sickle-cell anemia, which occurs most often in African Americans, is a genetic disorder that impairs the body's red blood cells. A red blood cell is usually shaped like a disk, but in sickle-cell anemia, a recessive gene causes the cell to become a hook-shaped "sickle." These cells die quickly, causing anemia and early death of the individual because of their failure to carry oxygen to the body's cells (Benz, 2004; De, 2005; Persons & Tisdale, 2004). About 1 in 400 African American babies is affected. One in 10 African Americans is a carrier, as is 1 in 20 Latin Americans.

Other diseases resulting from genetic abnormalities include cystic fibrosis, diabetes, hemophilia, spina bifida, and Tay-Sachs disease (Mayeux, 2005). Figure 3.7 provides further information about the genetic abnormalities we have discussed. The work of the Human Genome Project and similar research holds out the promise that someday scientists may identify why these and other genetic abnormalities occur and discover how to cure them. The Human Genome Project has already linked specific DNA variations with increased risk of a number of diseases and conditions (Armstrong & others, 2004; Norremolle & others, 2004).

Dealing with Genetic Abnormalities
Genetic disorders can sometimes be compensated for by other genes or developmental events (Gottlieb, 2004; Gottlieb, Wahlsten, & Lickliter, 2006). As a result, it often is the case that not all of the affected individuals show the disorder. Thus, genes are not destiny. However, when they are missing, nonfunctional, or mutated, they can be associated with disorders because the normal gene is not functioning.

Every individual carries DNA variations that might predispose that person to serious physical disease or mental disorder. Identifying the flaws could enable doctors to predict an individual's disease risks, recommend healthy lifestyle regimens, and prescribe the safest and most effective drugs. A decade or two from now, parents of a newborn baby may be able to leave the hospital with a full genome analysis of their offspring that reveals disease risks.

CAREERS in CHILD DEVELOPMENT

Holly Ishmael
Genetic Counselor

Holly Ishmael is a genetic counselor at Children's Mercy Hospital in Kansas City. She obtained an undergraduate degree in psychology from Sarah Lawrence College and then a master's degree in genetic counseling from the same college.

Genetic counselors have specialized graduate degrees in the areas of medical genetics and counseling. They enter graduate school in these areas with undergraduate backgrounds from a variety of disciplines, including biology, genetics, psychology, public health, and social work. Genetic counselors, like Ishmael, work as members of a health-care team, providing information and support to families with birth defects or genetic disorders. They identify families at risk by analyzing inheritance patterns and explore options with the family. Genetic counselors may serve as educators and resource people for other health-care professionals and the public. Some genetic counselors also work in administrative positions or conduct research. Some genetic counselors, like Ishmael, become specialists in prenatal and pediatric genetics; others might specialize in cancer genetics or psychiatric genetic disorders.

Ishmael says, "Genetic counseling is a perfect combination for people who want to do something science-oriented, but need human contact and don't want to spend all of their time in a lab or have their nose in a book."

There are approximately 30 graduate genetic counseling programs in the United States. If you are interested in this profession, you can obtain further information from the National Society of Genetic Counselors at this website: *http://www.nsgc.org*.

Holly Ishmael (*left*) conducting genetic counseling.

sickle-cell anemia A genetic disorder that affects the red blood cells and occurs most often in people of African descent.

However, this knowledge might bring important costs as well as benefits. Who would have access to a person's genetic profile? An individual's ability to land and hold jobs or obtain insurance might be threatened if it is known that a person is considered at risk for some disease. For example, should an airline pilot or a neurosurgeon who is predisposed to develop a disorder that makes one's hands shake be required to leave that job early? To think further about such issues, see figure 3.7.

Genetic counselors, usually physicians or biologists who are well versed in the field of medical genetics, are familiar with the kinds of problems just described, the odds of encountering them, and helpful strategies for offsetting some of their effects (Kollicker, 2005; Mao & others, 2005; Watson & others, 2005). To read about the career and work of a genetic counselor, see the Careers in Child Development profile.

Review and Reflect • LEARNING GOAL 2

 Describe what genes are and how they influence human development.

Review
- How does the genetic process work?
- How can the genetic principles of dominant-recessive genes, sex-linked genes, genetic imprinting, and polygenic inheritance, be characterized?
- What are some chromosomal and gene-linked abnormalities?

Reflect
- What are some possible ethical issues regarding genetics and development that might arise in the future?

---

3 WHAT ARE SOME REPRODUCTIVE CHALLENGES AND CHOICES?

| Prenatal Diagnostic Tests | Infertility and Reproductive Technology | Adoption |

Earlier in this chapter we discussed several principles of genetics, including the role of meiosis in reproduction. Having also examined a number of genetic abnormalities that can occur, we now have some background to consider challenges and choices facing prospective parents.

Prenatal Diagnostic Tests

One choice open to prospective mothers is the extent to which they should undergo prenatal testing. Scientists have developed a number of tests to determine whether a fetus is developing normally (Murphy, Fowlie, & McGuire, 2004; Robinson & others, 2005). These tests include: ultrasound sonography, chorionic villi sampling, amniocentesis, and maternal blood screening.

An ultrasound test is often conducted 7 weeks into a pregnancy and at various times later in pregnancy. *Ultrasound sonography* is a prenatal medical procedure in which high-frequency sound waves are directed into the pregnant woman's abdomen. The echo from the sounds is transformed into a visual representation of the fetus. This technique can detect many structural abnormalities in the fetus, including microencephaly, which is a form of mental retardation involving an abnormally small brain, determine the number of fetuses, and give clues to the baby's sex (Filkins & Koos, 2005; Sepulveda, Dezerega, & Be, 2004).

At some point between the 8th and 11th weeks of pregnancy, chorionic villi sampling may be used to detect genetic defects and chromosome abnormalities (Jenkins & others, 2004). Diagnosis takes approximately 10 days. *Chorionic villi sampling* is a prenatal medical procedure in which a small sample of the placenta (the vascular organ that links the fetus to the mother's uterus) is removed.

Between the 15th and 18th weeks of pregnancy, amniocentesis may be performed. *Amniocentesis* is a prenatal medical procedure in which a sample of amniotic fluid is withdrawn by syringe and tested for any chromosomal or metabolic disorders (Ramsey & others, 2004). The amnionic fluid is found within the amnion, a thin sac in which the embryo is suspended. Ultrasound sonography is often used during amniocentesis so that the syringe can be placed at the precise location of the fetus in the mother's abdomen (Leitner & others, 2004). The later amniocentesis is performed, the better its diagnostic potential (Seeds, 2004). The earlier it is performed, the more useful it is in deciding how to handle a pregnancy.

Both amniocentesis and chorionic villi sampling provide valuable information about the presence of birth defects, but they also raise difficult issues for parents about whether an abortion should be obtained if birth defects are present (Papp & Papp, 2003). Chorionic villi sampling allows a decision to be made sooner, near the end of the first 12 weeks of pregnancy, when abortion is safer and less traumatic than later, but chorionic villi sampling carries greater risks than amniocentesis. Amniocentesis brings a small risk of miscarriage: about 1 woman in every 200 to 300 miscarries after amniocentesis. Chorionic villi sampling brings a slightly higher risk of miscarriage than amniocentesis and is linked with a slight risk of limb deformities.

During the 16th to 18th weeks of pregnancy, maternal blood screening may be performed. *Maternal blood screening* identifies pregnancies that have an elevated risk for birth defects such as spina bifida (a typically fatal defect in the spinal cord) and Down syndrome (Bassett & others, 2004; Benn, Fang, & Egan, 2005; Summers & others, 2004). The current blood test is called the *triple screen* because it measures three substances in the mother's blood: alpha-fetoprotein (AFP), estriol, and human chorionic gonadotropin. After an abnormal triple screen result, the next step is usually an ultrasound examination. If an ultrasound does not explain the abnormal triple screen results, amniocentesis is typically used.

Infertility and Reproductive Technology

Recent advances in biological knowledge have also opened up many choices for infertile people. Approximately 10 to 15 percent of couples in the United States experience infertility, which is defined as the inability to conceive a child after 12 months of regular intercourse without contraception. The cause of infertility can rest with the woman or the man (Said & others, 2004). The woman may not be ovulating (releasing eggs to be fertilized), she may be producing abnormal ova, her fallopian tubes by which ova normally reach the womb may be blocked, or she may have a disease that prevents implantation of the embryo into the uterus. The man may produce too few sperm, the sperm may lack motility (the ability to move adequately), or he may have a blocked passageway.

In the United States, more than 2 million couples seek help for infertility every year. Some cases of infertility may be corrected by surgery; for others, hormone-based drugs may improve the probability of having a child. Of those seeking help to fulfill their desire to become parents each year, about 40,000 try high-tech assisted reproduction. The three most common techniques are:

- *In vitro fertilization (IVF).* Eggs and sperm are combined in a laboratory dish. If any eggs are successfully fertilized, one or more of the resulting embryos is transferred into the woman's uterus or womb.

A 6-month old infant poses with the ultrasound sonography record taken four months into the baby's prenatal development. *What is ultrasound sonography?*

www.mhhe.com/santrockc9

Amniocentesis
Obstetric Ultrasound
Chorionic Villi Sampling

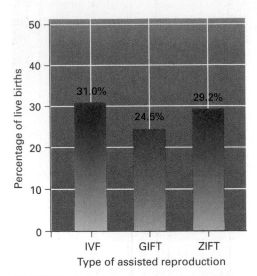

FIGURE 3.8 **Success Rates of Three Different Assisted Reproduction Techniques** *Note:* The results were combined across the ages of the couples because there was little variation in success rates based on age.

- *Gamete intrafallopian transfer (GIFT).* A doctor inserts eggs and sperm directly into a woman's fallopian tube.
- *Zygote intrafallopian transfer (ZIFT).* This is a two-step procedure. First, eggs are fertilized in the laboratory. Then, any resulting zygotes are transferred to a fallopian tube.

The success rates for these three assisted reproduction techniques, based on a national study in the United States in 2000 by the Centers for Disease Control and Prevention, is shown in figure 3.8. IVF is by far the most common technique used (98 percent of all cases in the national study) and had the highest success rate in the national study of slightly more than 30 percent.

One consequence of fertility treatments is an increase in multiple births (Appleman & Furman, 2005). Twenty-five to 30 percent of pregnancies achieved by fertility treatments—including in vitro fertilization—now result in multiple births. Any multiple birth increases the likelihood that the babies will have life-threatening and costly problems, such as extremely low birth weight.

Creating families through the new reproductive technologies raises important questions about the psychological consequences for children. A longitudinal study examined 34 in vitro fertilization families, 49 adoptive families, and 38 families with a naturally conceived child (Golombok, MacCallum, & Goodman, 2001). Each family type had a similar portion of boys and girls. Also, the age of the young adolescents did not differ according to family type (mean age of 11 years, 11 months). No significant differences were found among the children from the in vitro fertilization, adoptive, and naturally conceiving families. The results from the Social Adjustment Inventory for Children and Adolescents are shown in figure 3.9. Thus, this study, as well as others (Hahn & DiPietro, 2001), support the idea that "test-tube" babies function well.

Adoption

Although surgery and fertility drugs can sometimes solve the infertility problem, another choice open to individuals is to adopt a child (Burrow, Tubman, & Finley, 2004; Haugaard & Hazan, 2004). Adoption is the social and legal process by which a parent-child relationship is established between persons unrelated at birth. It is estimated that approximately 2 to 4 percent of children in the United States are adopted (Stolley, 1993).

Several changes occurred during the last several decades of the twentieth century in the characteristics both of adopted children and of adoptive parents (Brodzinsky & Pinderhughes, 2002, pp. 280–282). Until the 1960s, most U.S. adopted children were healthy, European American infants, who were adopted within a few days or weeks after birth. However, in recent decades, an increasing number of unmarried U.S. mothers decided to keep their babies, and the number of unwanted births decreased as contraception became readily available and abortion was legalized. As a result, the number of healthy European American infants available for adoption dropped dramatically. Increasingly, U.S. couples adopted children who were not European Americans, children from other countries, and children in foster care whose characteristics—such as age, minority status, exposure to neglect or abuse, or physical and mental health problems—"were once thought to be barriers to adoption" (p. 281).

Changes also have characterized adoptive parents. Until the last several decades of the twentieth century, most adoptive parents had a middle- or upper-socioeconomic status and were "married, infertile, European American couples, usually in their 30s and 40s, and free of any disability. Adoption agencies *screened out* couples who did not have these characteristics" (p. 281). Today, however, many adoption agencies *screen in* as many applicants as possible and have no income requirements for

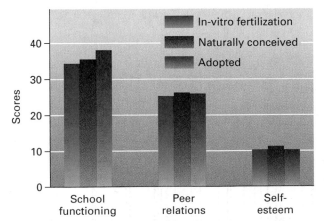

FIGURE 3.9 **Socioemotional Development at Adolescence of Children in Three Family Types: In Vitro Fertilization, Naturally Conceived, and Adopted** In this study, there were no significant differences in socioemotional development at the beginning of adolescence in terms of school functioning, peer relations, and self-esteem (Golombok, MacCallum, & Goodman). The mean scores shown for the different measures are all in the normal range of functioning.

adoptive parents. Many agencies now permit single adults, older adults, and gay and lesbian adults to adopt children (Rampage & others, 2003).

The changes in adoption practice over the last several decades make it difficult to generalize about the average adopted child or average adoptive parent. But many researchers have provided useful comparisons between adopted children and non-adopted children and their families. How do adopted children fare after they are adopted?

Children who are adopted very early in their lives are more likely to have positive outcomes than children adopted later in life. In one study, the later adoption occurred, the more problems the adoptees had. Infant adoptees had the fewest adjustment difficulties; those adopted after they were 10 years of age had the most problems (Sharma, McGue, & Benson, 1996).

In general, adopted children and adolescents often show more psychological and school-related problems than nonadopted children (Brozinsky & others, 1984; Brodzinsky, Lang, & Smith, 1995; Brodzinsky & Pinderhughes, 2002). For example, adopted adolescents are referred to psychological treatment two to five times as often as their nonadopted peers (Grotevant & McRoy, 1990). In one study of 1,587 adopted and 87,165 nonadopted adolescents, the adopted adolescents were at higher risk for all problems examined, including problems with school, substance abuse, psychological well-being, and physical health (Miller & others, 2000). Also, the adolescents with the most problems were far more likely to be adopted than nonadopted. In this study, adopted adolescents were more likely to have problems if the adoptive parents had low levels of education.

Research that contrasts adopted and nonadopted adolescents has found positive as well as negative characteristics among the adopted adolescents. In one study, adopted adolescents had more school adjustment problems, were more likely to use illicit drugs, and were more likely to engage in delinquent behavior (Sharma, McGue, & Benson, 1998). However, compared with nonadopted siblings, adopted siblings were also less withdrawn and engaged in more prosocial behavior, such as being altruistic, caring, and supportive of others.

Although adoption is associated with increased academic and psychological difficulties, the vast majority of adopted children (including those adopted at older ages, transracially, and across national borders) adjust effectively, and their parents report considerable satisfaction with their decision to adopt (Brodzinsky & Pinderhughes, 2002). Furthermore, adopted children fare much better than children in long-term foster care or in an institutional environment (Brodzinsky & Pinderhughes, 2002).

Children whose biological parents could not or would not provide adequate care for them benefit from adoption. To read further about adoption, see the Caring for Children interlude in which we discuss effective parenting strategies with adopted children.

What changes have taken place in adoption in recent years?

CARING FOR CHILDREN

Parenting Adopted Children

Many keys to effectively parenting adopted children are no different than those for effectively parenting biological children: Be supportive and caring, be involved and monitor the child's behavior and whereabouts, be a good communicator, and help the child to learn to develop self-control. However, parents of adopted children face some unique circumstances. These include recognizing the differences involved in adoptive family life, communicating about these differences, showing respect for the birth family, and supporting the child's search for self and identity.

David Brodzinsky and Ellen Pinderhughes (2002, pp. 288–292) recently discussed how to handle some of the challenges that adoptive parents face when their children are at different points in development:

(continued on next page)

- *Infancy.* Researchers have found few differences in the attachment that adopted and nonadopted infants form with their parents, but attachment can be compromised "when parents have difficulty in claiming the child as their own either because of unresolved fertility issues, lack of support from family and friends, and/or when their expectations about the child have not been met" (p. 288). Competent adoption agencies or counselors can help prospective adoptive parents develop realistic expectations, especially if the child has special needs.
- *Early childhood.* During infancy, adoptive parents' focus is often on integrating the child into the family and developing a strong bond with the child. In early childhood the focus shifts. Early childhood is when most parents begin to talk with their child about adoption. Because many children begin to ask where they came from when they are about 4 to 6 years old, this is a natural time to begin to talk in simple ways to children about their adoption status (Warshak, 2004). Some parents (although not as many as in the past) decide not to tell their children about the adoption, this secrecy may create psychological risks for the child if he or she later finds out about the adoption.
- *Middle and late childhood.* During the elementary school years, children begin to express "much more curiosity about their origins: *Where did I come from? What did my birthmother and birthfather look like? Why didn't they keep me? Where are they now? Can I meet them?*" (p. 290). As they grow older, children may become more ambivalent about being adopted and question their adoptive parents' explanations. It is important for adoptive parents to recognize that this ambivalence is normal. Also, clinical psychologists report that problems may come from the desire of adoptive parents to make life too perfect for the adoptive child and to present a perfect image of themselves to the child. The result too often is that adopted children feel that they cannot release any angry feelings and openly discuss problems (Warshak, 2004).
- *Adolescence.* Adolescents are likely to develop more abstract and logical thinking, to focus their attention on their bodies, and to search for an identity. These characteristics provide the foundation for adopted adolescents to reflect on their adoption status in more complex ways, to become "preoccupied with the lack of physical resemblance between themselves and others in the family" (p. 291), and explore how the fact that they were adopted fits into their identity. Adoptive parents "need to be aware of these many complexities and provide teenagers with the support they need to cope with these adoption-related tasks" (p. 292).

Review and Reflect • LEARNING GOAL 3

3 **Identify some important reproductive challenges and choices.**

Review
- What are some common prenatal diagnostic tests?
- What are some causes of infertility? What types of reproductive technology are used to improve the success rates of having children for infertile couples?
- How does adoption affect children's development?

Reflect
- We discussed a number of studies indicating that adoption is linked with negative outcomes for children? Does that mean that all adopted children have more negative outcomes than all nonadopted children? Explain.

4 HOW DO HEREDITY AND ENVIRONMENT INTERACT? THE NATURE-NURTURE DEBATE

Behavior Genetics

Shared and Nonshared Environmental Experiences

Conclusions About Heredity-Environment Interaction

Heredity-Environment Correlations

The Epigenetic View

In each section of this chapter so far we have examined parts of the nature-nurture debate. We have seen how the environment exerts selective pressures on the characteristics of species over generations, examined how genes are passed from parents to children, and discussed how reproductive technologies and adoption influence the course of children's lives. But in all of these situations, heredity and environment interact to produce environment. After all, Jim and Jim (and each of the other pairs of identical twins discussed in the opening of the chapter) have the same genotype, but they are not the same person, each is unique. What made them different? Whether we are studying how genes produce proteins, their influence on how tall a person is, or how PKU might affect an individual, we end up discussing heredity-environment interactions. Is it possible to untangle the influence of heredity from that of environment and discover the role of each in producing individual differences in development? When heredity and environment interact, how does heredity influence the environment, and vice versa?

Behavior Genetics

Behavior genetics is the field that seeks to discover the influence of heredity and environment on individual differences in human traits and development (Kuo & others, 2004). What behavior geneticists try to do is to figure out what is responsible for those differences—that is, to what extent do people differ because of differences in genes, environment, or a combination of these (Haig, 2003)?

To study the influence of heredity on behavior, behavior geneticists often use either twins or adoption situations. In the most common **twin study,** the behavioral similarity of identical twins is compared with the behavioral similarity of fraternal twins. *Identical twins* (called monozygotic twins) develop from a single fertilized egg that splits into two genetically identical replicas, each of which becomes a person. *Fraternal twins* (called dizygotic twins) develop from separate eggs and separate sperm, making them genetically no more similar than ordinary siblings. Although fraternal twins share the same womb, they are no more alike genetically than are nontwin brothers and sisters, and they may be of different sexes.

By comparing groups of identical and fraternal twins, behavior geneticists capitalize on the basic knowledge that identical twins are more similar genetically than are fraternal twins (Harvald & others, 2004; Rietveld & others, 2003; Wadsworth & others, 2004). A recent study found that conduct problems were more prevalent in identical twins than fraternal twins; the researchers concluded that the study demonstrated an important role for heredity in conduct problems (Scourfield & others, 2004).

However, several issues complicate interpretation of twin studies. For example, perhaps the environments of identical twins are more similar than the environments of fraternal twins. Adults might stress the similarities of identical twins more than those of fraternal twins, and identical twins might perceive themselves as a "set" and play together more than fraternal twins do. If so, the influence of the environment

Identical twins develop from a single fertilized egg that splits into two genetically identical organisms. Twin studies compare identical twins with fraternal twins. Fraternal twins develop from separate eggs, making them genetically no more similar than nontwin siblings. *What is the nature of the twin study method?*

www.mhhe.com/santrockc9

Behavior Genetics

behavior genetics The field that seeks to discover the influence of heredity and environment on individual differences in human traits and development.

twin study A study in which the behavioral similarity of identical twins is compared with the behavioral similarity of fraternal twins.

Heredity-Environment Correlation	Description	Examples
Passive	Children inherit genetic tendencies from their parents and parents also provide an environment that matches their own genetic tendencies.	Musically inclined parents usually have musically inclined children and they are likely to provide an environment rich in music for their children.
Evocative	The child's genetic tendencies elicit stimulation from the environment that supports a particular trait. Thus genes evoke environmental support.	A happy, outgoing child elicits smiles and friendly responses from others.
Active (niche-picking)	Children actively seek out "niches" in their environment that reflect their own interests and talents and are thus in accord with their genotype.	Libraries, sports fields, and a store with musical instruments are examples of environmental niches children might seek out if they have intellectual interests in books, talent in sports, or musical talents, respectively.

FIGURE 3.10 Exploring Heredity-Environment Correlations

on the observed similarities between identical and fraternal twins might be very significant.

In an **adoption study,** investigators seek to discover whether the behavior and psychological characteristics of adopted children are more like those of their adoptive parents, who have provided a home environment, or more like those of their biological parents, who have contributed their heredity (Haugaard & Hazan, 2004). Another form of the adoption study compares adoptive and biological siblings.

Heredity-Environment Correlations

The difficulties that researchers encounter when they interpret the results of twin studies and adoption studies reflect the complexities of heredity-environment interaction. Some of these interactions are *heredity-environment correlations*, which means that individuals' genes influence the types of environments to which they are exposed. In a sense, individuals "inherit" environments that are related or linked to genetic propensities (Plomin & others, 2001). Behavior geneticist Sandra Scarr (1993) described three ways that heredity and environment are correlated (see figure 3.10):

- **Passive genotype-environment correlations** occur because biological parents, who are genetically related to the child, provide a rearing environment for the child. For example, the parents might have a genetic predisposition to be intelligent and read skillfully. Because they read well and enjoy reading, they provide their children with books to read. The likely outcome is that their children, given their own inherited predispositions from their parents and their book-filled environment, will become skilled readers.
- **Evocative genotype-environment correlations** occur because a child's characteristics elicit certain types of environments. For example, active, smiling children receive more social stimulation than passive, quiet children do. Cooperative, attentive children evoke more pleasant and instructional responses from the adults around them than uncooperative, distractible children do.
- **Active (niche-picking) genotype-environment correlations** occur when children seek out environments that they find compatible and stimulating. *Niche-picking* refers to finding a setting that is suited to one's abilities. Children select from their surrounding environment some aspect that they respond to, learn about, or ignore. Their active selections of environments are related to their particular genotype. For example, outgoing children tend to seek out social contexts in which to interact with people, whereas shy children don't. Children who are musically inclined are likely to select musical environments in which they can successfully perform their skills.

adoption study A study in which investigators seek to discover whether, in behavior and psychological characteristics, adopted children are more like their adoptive parents, who provided a home environment, or more like their biological parents, who contributed their heredity. Another form of the adoption study is to compare adoptive and biological siblings.

passive genotype-environment correlations Correlations that exist when the biological parents, who are genetically related to the child, provide a rearing environment for the child.

evocative genotype-environment correlations Correlations that exist when the child's genotype elicits certain types of physical and social environments.

active (niche-picking) genotype-environment correlations Correlations that exist when children seek out environments they find compatible and stimulating.

Scarr believes that the relative importance of the three genotype-environment correlations changes as children develop from infancy through adolescence. In infancy, much of the environment that children experience is provided by adults. Thus, passive genotype-environment correlations are more common in the lives of infants and young children than they are for older children and adolescents who can extend their experiences beyond the family's influence and create their environments to a greater degree.

Critics argue that the concept of heredity-environment correlation gives heredity too much of a one-sided influence in determining development because it does not consider the role of prior environmental influences in shaping the correlation itself (Gottlieb, 2003, 2004; Gottlieb, Wahlsten, & Lickliter, 2006). Heredity-environment correlation stresses that heredity may influence the types of environments children's experience but does not address *how* the correlation comes about developmentally in the first place. How correlation comes about will be described shortly in the discussion of epigenetic view. Before turning to the epigenetic view, we will examine a view that emphasizes the importance of the nonshared environment of siblings and their heredity as important influences on their development.

Shared and Nonshared Environmental Experiences

Does the concept of heredity-environment correlation downplay the importance of environment in our development? Behavior geneticists have argued that to understand the environment's role in differences between people, we should distinguish between shared and nonshared environments. That is, we should consider experiences that children share in common with other children living in the same home, and experiences that are not shared (Becker-Blease & others, 2004; Feinberg & Hetherington, 2001; Petrill & Deater-Deckard, 2004; Plomin, Asbury, & Dunn, 2001).

Shared environmental experiences are siblings' common experiences, such as their parents' personalities or intellectual orientation, the family's socioeconomic status, and the neighborhood in which they live. By contrast, **nonshared environmental experiences** are a child's unique experiences, both within the family and outside the family, that are not shared with a sibling. Even experiences occurring within the family can be part of the "nonshared environment." For example, parents often interact differently with each sibling, and siblings interact differently with parents (Hetherington, Reiss, & Plomin, 1994). Siblings often have different peer groups, different friends, and different teachers at school.

Behavior geneticist Robert Plomin (1993) has found that shared environment accounts for little of the variation in children's personality or interests. In other words, even though two children live under the same roof with the same parents, their personalities are often very different. Further, Plomin argues that heredity influences the nonshared environments of siblings through the heredity-environment correlations we described earlier. For example, a child who has inherited a genetic tendency to be athletic is likely to spend more time in environments related to sports, while a child who has inherited a tendency to be musically inclined is more likely to spend time in environments related to music.

What are the implications of Plomin's interpretation of the role of shared and nonshared environments in development? In the *Nurture Assumption,* Judith Harris (1998) argued that what parents do does not make a difference in their children's and adolescents' behavior. Yell at them. Hug them. Read to them. Ignore them. Harris says it won't influence how they turn out. She argues that genes and peers are far more important than parents in children's and adolescents' development.

Genes and peers do matter, but Harris' descriptions of peer influences do not take into account the complexity of peer contexts and developmental trajectories (Hartup, 1999). In addition, Harris is wrong in saying that parents don't matter. For example, in the early childhood years parents play an important role in selecting children's peers and indirectly influencing children's development (Baumrind, 1999). A huge

shared environmental experiences Siblings' common environmental experiences, such as their parents' personalities and intellectual orientation, the family's socioeconomic status, and the neighborhood in which they live.

nonshared environmental experiences The child's own unique experiences, both within the family and outside the family, that are not shared by another sibling. Thus, experiences occurring within the family can be part of the "nonshared environment."

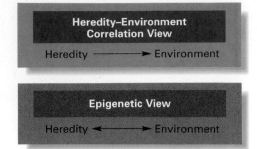

FIGURE 3.11 Comparison of the Heredity-Environment Correlation and Epigenetic Views

parenting literature with many research studies documents the importance of parents in children's development (Collins & others, 2000, 2001; Maccoby, 2002). We will discuss parents' important roles throughout this book.

The Epigenetic View

The heredity-environment correlation view emphasizes how heredity directs the kind of environmental experiences individuals have. However, earlier in the chapter we discussed how genes are collaborative, not determining an individual's traits in an independent manner, but rather in an interactive manner with the environment. In line with the concept of a collaborative gene, Gilbert Gottlieb (1998, 2003, 2004; Gottlieb, Wahlsten, & Lickliter, 2006) emphasizes the **epigenetic view,** which states that development is the result of an ongoing, bidirectional interchange between heredity and the environment (Gottlieb, 1998, 2003, 2004; Gottlieb, Wahlsten, & Lickliter, 2006). Figure 3.11 compares the heredity-environment correlation and epigenetic views of development.

Let's look at an example that reflects the epigenetic view. A baby inherits genes from both parents at conception. During prenatal development, toxins, nutrition, and stress can influence some genes to stop functioning while others become stronger or weaker. During infancy, environmental experiences such as toxins, nutrition, stress, learning, and encouragement continue to modify genetic activity and the activity of the nervous system that directly underlies behavior.

Conclusions About Heredity-Environment Interaction

Heredity and environment operate together—or collaborate—to produce a person's intelligence, temperament, height, weight, ability to pitch a baseball, ability to read, and so on (Coll, Bearer, & Lerner, 2004; Gottlieb, 2004; Gottlieb, Wahlsten, & Lickliter, 1998, 2006; McClearn, 2004). If an attractive, popular, intelligent girl is elected president of her senior class in high school, is her success due to heredity or to environment? Of course, the answer is both.

The relative contributions of heredity and environment are not additive. That is, we can't say that such-and-such a percentage of nature and such-and-such a percentage of experience make us who we are. Nor is it accurate to say that full genetic expression happens once, around conception or birth, after which we carry our genetic legacy into the world to see how far it takes us. Genes produce proteins throughout the life span, in many different environments. Or they don't produce these proteins, depending in part on how harsh or nourishing those environments are.

The emerging view is that many complex behaviors likely have some *genetic loading* that gives people a propensity for a particular developmental trajectory (Knafo, Iervolino & Plomin, 2005; Plomin & others, 2001; Tholin & others, 2005; Walker, Petrill, & Plomin, 2005). However, the actual development requires more: an environment. And that environment is complex, just like the mixture of genes we inherit (Bronfenbrenner & Morris, 2006; Sternberg & Grigorenko, 2001; Overton, 2004; Spencer, 2006; Spencer & Harpalani, 2004). Environmental influences range from the things we lump together under "nurture" (such as parenting, family dynamics, schooling, and neighborhood quality) to biological encounters (such as viruses, birth complications, and even biological events in cells) (Greenough, 1997, 1999; Greenough & others, 2001).

Imagine for a moment that there is a cluster of genes somehow associated with youth violence (this example is hypothetical because we don't know of any such combination). The adolescent who carries this genetic mixture might experience a world of loving parents, regular nutritious meals, lots of books, and a series of masterful teachers. Or the adolescent's world might include parental neglect, a neighborhood in which gunshots and crime are everyday occurrences, and inadequate schooling. In which of these environments are the adolescent's genes likely to manufacture the biological underpinnings of criminality?

epigenetic view Emphasizes that development is the result of an ongoing, bidirectional interchange between heredity and environment.

mother's abdomen enlarge
pectant mother and her pa

Preparation for the I

the expectant mother's pro
The expectant mother may
easier to breathe and eat. F
pectant mother's bladder, s

Toward the end of the
Braxton Hicks contractions
curred intermittently throu
expectant mother, help inc
not directly associated with
labor. As the pregnancy co
pectant mother's pelvis, he
of readiness for labor and b

Awkwardness and fatig
nancy to end. She may fee
same time, the expectant n
energy that often results in
its her physician or midwife
is preparing for labor and b

The Expectant Motl and Exercise

The mother's nutrition can
Here we will discuss the mo
nancy, as well as the role of

Nutrition and Weight

during pregnancy is a satisf
optimal weight gain depenc
prepregnant nutritional star
to 35 pounds are associated

Approximately one-thir
amount (Cogswell & other:
outcomes through increased
and infections in the mothe
in obese women are charact
deliveries, and late fetal de
Dereure & Bringer, 2002).

The pattern of weight ga
ing pregnancy is 2 to 4.4 pou
of 1 pound per week during
the weight gain is due to inc
and associated tissue and flu
weight gain mainly involve
weight gain during pregnanc

- 11 pounds: fetus, placen
- 5 pounds: maternal stor
- 4 pounds: increased bloc
- 3 pounds: tissue fluid
- 2 pounds: uterus and br

Review and Reflect ● LEARNING GOAL 4

4 **Characterize some of the ways that heredity and environment interact to produce individual differences in development.**

Review
- What is behavior genetics?
- What are three types of heredity-environment correlations, according to Scarr?
- What is meant by the concepts of shared and nonshared environmental experiences?
- What is the epigenetic view of development?
- What conclusions can be reached about heredity-environment interaction?

Reflect
- Someone tells you that he or she has analyzed his or her genetic background and environmental experiences and reached the conclusion that environment definitely has had little influence on his or her intelligence. What would you say to this person about his or her ability to make this self-diagnosis?

In the third trimester of pregnan
couple may feel protective of th
*What are some good communica
between the expectant mother an
about their needs?*

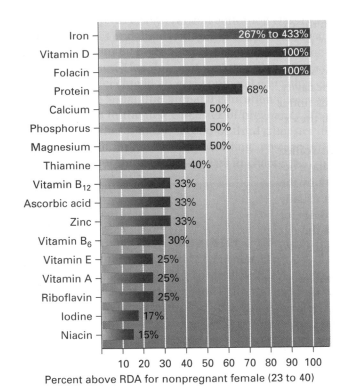

FIGURE 4.5 Recommended Nutrient Increases for Expectant Mothers

www.mhhe.com/santrockc9

Nutrition and Pregnancy
Exercise in Pregnancy

During the second and third trimesters, inadequate gains of less than 2.2 pounds per month or excessive gains of more than 6.6 pounds per month should be evaluated and the need for nutritional counseling considered. Inadequate weight gain has been associated with low birth weight infants. Sudden sharp increases in weight of 3 to 5 pounds in a week may result from fluid retention and may require evaluation.

The recommended daily allowance (RDA) for all nutrients increases during pregnancy. The expectant mother should eat three meals a day, with nutritious snacks of fruits, cheese, milk, or other foods between meals if desired. More frequent, smaller meals also are recommended. Water is an essential nutrient. Four to six 8-ounce glasses of water and a total of 8 to 10 cups (64 to 80 ounces) of total fluid should be consumed daily. The need for protein, iron, vitamin D, calcium, phosphorus, and magnesium increases by 50 percent or more. Recommended increases for other nutrients range from 15 to 50 percent (see figure 4.5). Researchers have recently found that women who take a multivitamin prior to pregnancy may be at a reduced risk for delivering a preterm infant (Vahratian & others, 2004).

Exercise   How much and what type of exercise is best during pregnancy depends to some degree on the course of the pregnancy, the expectant mother's fitness, and her customary activity level. Normal participation in exercise can continue throughout an uncomplicated pregnancy. In general, the skilled sportswoman is no longer discouraged from participating in sports she participated in prior to her pregnancy. However, pregnancy is not the appropriate time to begin strenuous activity.

Because of the increased emphasis on physical fitness in our society, more women routinely jog as part of a physical fitness program prior to pregnancy. There are few concerns about continuing to jog during the early part of pregnancy, but in the latter part of pregnancy there is some concern about the jarring effect of jogging on the breasts and abdomen. As pregnancy progresses, low-impact activities, such as walking, swimming, and bicycling, are safer and provide fitness as well as greater comfort, eliminating the bouncing associated with jogging.

These guidelines for exercise are recommended for expectant mothers (Olds, London, & Ladewig, 1988, pp. 387–388):

- "*Exercise for shorter intervals.* By exercising for 10 to 15 minutes, resting for a few minutes, and then exercising for an additional 10 to 15 minutes, the woman decreases potential problems associated with the shunting of blood to the musculoskeletal system and away from organs, such as the uterus."
- "*As pregnancy progresses, decrease the intensity of exercise.* This helps compensate for the decreased cardiac reserve, increased respiratory effort, and increased weight of the pregnant woman."
- "*Avoid prolonged overheating.* Strenuous exercise, especially in a humid environment, can raise the core body temperature" and increase the risk of fetal problems. Remember to avoid overheating in saunas and hot tubs.
- "*As pregnancy increases, avoid high-risk activities such as skydiving, mountain climbing, racquetball, and surfing.*" An expectant mother's changed center of gravity and softened joints may decrease her coordination and increase the risk of falls and injuries in such sports.
- "*Warm up and stretch to help prepare the joints for activity, and cool down with a period of mild activity to help restore circulation. . . .*"
- "*After exercising, lie on the left side for ten minutes to rest.* This improves return of circulation from the extremities. . . ."

- *"Wear supportive shoes and a supportive bra."*
- *"Stop exercising and contact the caregiver if dizziness, shortness of breath, tingling, numbness, vaginal bleeding, or abdominal pain occur."*
- *"Reduce exercise significantly during the last four weeks of pregnancy.* Some evidence suggests that strenuous exercise near term increases the risk of low birth weight, stillbirth, and infant death. . . ."

Exercise during pregnancy helps prevent constipation, conditions the body, and is associated with a more positive mental state (Ezmerli, 2000; Paisley, Joy, & Price, 2003). However, it is important to remember to not overdo it. Pregnant women should always consult their physician before starting any exercise program.

Might the mother's exercise during pregnancy be related to the development of the fetus and the birth of the child? Few studies have been conducted on this topic, but recently several studies indicated that moderate exercise three to four times a week was linked to healthy weight gain in the fetus and a normal birth weight, whereas the risk of low birth weight increased for women who exercised intensely most days of the week and for women who exercised less than twice a week or not at all (Campbell & Mottola, 2001; Clapp & others, 2000).

Elizabeth Noble is a physical therapist and childbirth educator who has influenced many women to engage in prenatal and postnatal exercise. To read about her work, see the Careers in Child Development profile.

Culture and Prenatal Care

What is prenatal care in the United States like compared with that of other countries? What are some cultural beliefs about pregnancy?

Prenatal Care in the United States and Around the World

CAREERS in CHILD DEVELOPMENT

Elizabeth Noble
Physical Therapist and Childbirth Educator

Elizabeth Noble grew up in Australia where she obtained undergraduate degrees in physiotherapy, philosophy, and anthropology. She moved to the United States in the 1970s and founded the Women's Health section of the American Physical Therapy Association.

Dr. Noble has authored numerous books such as *Essential Exercises for the Childbearing Years.* She also is a consultant, lecturer, and workshop leader. More than 2,000 instructors in prenatal and postpartum exercise have been trained by Dr. Noble. Currently, she is the director of Women's Health Resources in Harwich, Massachusetts.

Elizabeth Noble, demonstrating an effective postpartum exercise.

Prenatal care varies enormously, but usually involves a package of medical care services in a defined schedule of visits (McCormick, 2001). In addition to medical care, prenatal care programs often include comprehensive educational, social, and nutritional services (Nichols & Humenick, 2000; Shiono & Behrman, 1995). A recent study revealed that low birth weight and delivering preterm were common in U.S. women who received no prenatal care (Maupin & others, 2004).

Prenatal care usually includes screening for manageable conditions and/or treatable diseases that can affect the baby or the mother. The education an expectant woman receives about pregnancy, labor and delivery, and caring for the newborn can be extremely valuable, especially for first-time mothers (Chang & others, 2003; Cosey & Bechtel, 2001). Prenatal care is also very important for women in poverty—it links them with other social services (Lewallen, 2004). The legacy of prenatal care continues after birth, because women who receive this type of care are more likely to seek preventive care for their infants (Bates & others, 1994).

Inadequate prenatal care can occur for a variety of reasons, including the health-care system, provider practices, and individual and social characteristics (Howell,

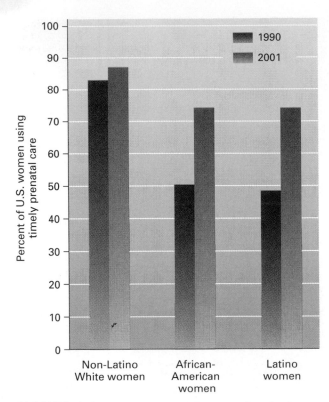

FIGURE 4.6 Percentage of U.S. Women Using Timely Prenatal Care: 1990 to 2001 From 1990 to 2001, the use of timely prenatal care increased by 6 percent (to 88.5) for non–Latino White women, by 23 percent (to 74.5) for African American women, and by 26 percent to (75.7) for Latino women in the United States (MacDorman & others, 2002).

2001; Maulik, 2003; Parmet, Lynn, & Glass, 2004; Thompson & others, 2003). In one national study, 71 percent of low-income women experienced problems obtaining prenatal care (U.S. General Accounting Office, 1987). Lack of transportation and child care, as well as financial difficulties, were commonly cited as barriers to getting prenatal care. One recent study found that U.S. women with no prenatal care were far more likely to have infants who were low birth weight, had increased mortality, and had more physical problems than their counterparts who received prenatal care (Herbst & others, 2003).

Although the United States is economically and technologically advanced, it still has more low birth weight infants than a number of other countries (Grant, 1996; Smulian & others, 2002). Only 4 percent of the infants born in Sweden, Finland, the Netherlands, and Norway are low birth weight, and only 5 percent of those born in New Zealand, Australia, France, and Japan are low birth weight. In the United States, 7 percent of all infants are low birth weight. In some developing countries, such as Bangladesh, where poverty is rampant and the health and nutrition of mothers is poor, the percentage of low birth weight infants reaches as high as 50 percent.

In many countries with a lower percentage of low birth weight infants than the United States, either free or very low cost prenatal and postnatal care is available to mothers. This care includes paid maternity leave from work that ranges from 9 to 40 weeks. In Norway and the Netherlands, prenatal care is coordinated with a general practitioner, an obstetrician, and a midwife. One recent national study found that in the United States, the absence of prenatal care increased the risk for preterm birth by almost threefold for both non-Latino White and African American women (Vintzileos & others, 2002). Another recent study found that the later prenatal care begins, the greater the risk of congenital malformations (Carmichael, Shaw, & Nelson, 2002).

Pregnant women in the United States do not receive the uniform prenatal care that women in many Scandinavian and Western European countries receive (Burnes Bolton, Giger, & Georges, 2004; McCormick, 2001). The United States does not have a national policy of health care that assures high-quality assistance for pregnant women. The cost of giving birth is approximately $4,000 in the United States (more than $5,000 for a cesarean birth). Over 25 percent of all American women of prime childbearing age do not have health-care insurance that covers these hospital costs.

For many years, there was a discrepancy in the prenatal care obtained by non-Latino White and African American expectant mothers. For example, in the 1980s, more than one-fifth of all non-Latino White mothers and one-third of all African American mothers did not receive prenatal care in the first trimester of their pregnancy, and 5 percent of non-Latino White mothers and 10 percent of African American mothers received no prenatal care at all. However, from 1990 to 2001, the use of timely prenatal care increased for women from a variety of ethnic backgrounds in the United States, although this care still characterized non-Latino White women more than African American and Latino women (MacDorman & others, 2002) (see figure 4.6). Other researchers also have found that the discrepancy in prenatal care for non-Latino White and African American women is decreasing (Alexander, Kogan, & Nabukera, 2002).

Many infant-development researchers argue that the United States needs more comprehensive medical and educational services to improve the quality of prenatal care and to reduce the percentage of low birth weight infants (Bloom & others, 2004; Grady & Bloom, 2004; Maulik, 2003; Sheppard, Zambrana, & O'Malley, 2004).

In India, a midwife checks on the size, position, and heartbeat of a fetus. Midwives deliver babies in many cultures around the world. *What are some cultural variations in prenatal care?*

Cultural Beliefs About Pregnancy and Development

Specific actions in pregnancy are often determined by cultural beliefs. Certain behaviors are expected if a culture views pregnancy as a medical condition, whereas other behaviors are expected if pregnancy is viewed as a natural occurrence. Prenatal care may not be a priority for expectant mothers who view pregnancy as a natural occurrence. It is important for health-care providers to become aware of the health practices of various cultural groups, including health beliefs about pregnancy and prenatal development (Mathole & others, 2004; Paredes & others, 2005). Cultural assessment is an important dimension of providing adequate health care for expectant mothers from all cultural groups (Laditka & others, 2005; McCray, 2004; Wong, Korenbrot, & Stewart, 2004). Cultural assessment includes identifying the beliefs, values, and behaviors related to pregnancy and childbearing. Among the important cultural dimensions are ethnic background, degree of affiliation with the ethnic group, patterns of decision making, religious preference, language, communication style, and common etiquette practices.

Health-care practices during pregnancy are influenced by numerous factors, including the prevalence of traditional home care remedies and folk beliefs, the importance of indigenous healers, religious beliefs, and the influence of professional health-care workers (Ativeh & El-Mohandes, 2005; Browne-Krimsley, 2004; Cioffi, 2004; Fullerton & others, 2004; Holder, 2004; Willis & others, 2004). Many Mexican American mothers are strongly influenced by their mothers and older women in their culture, often seeking and following their advice during pregnancy. In Mexican American culture, the indigenous healer is called a *curandero*. In some Native American tribes, the medicine woman or man fulfills the healing role. Herbalists are often found in Asian cultures, and faith healers, root doctors, and spiritualists are sometimes found in African American culture. Health-care providers need to assess whether such cultural practices pose a threat to the expectant mother and the fetus. If they pose no threat, there is no reason to try to change them. On the other hand, if certain cultural practices do pose a threat to the health of the expectant mother or the fetus, the health-care provider should consider a culturally sensitive way to handle the problem. For example, some Filipinos will not take any medication during pregnancy.

Characterize expectant parents' experiences during prenatal development.

Review
- How can the pregnancy be confirmed and the due date calculated?
- What are some positive strategies for expectant parents in the three trimesters of prenatal development and preparation for the birth?
- What are some recommendations for the expectant mother's nutrition, weight gain, and exercise?
- How is culture linked with prenatal care?

Reflect
- What are some beliefs about pregnancy and prenatal development in your culture?

3 WHAT ARE SOME POTENTIAL HAZARDS TO PRENATAL DEVELOPMENT?

Some General Principles

Prescription and Nonprescription Drugs

Psychoactive Drugs

Environmental Hazards

Infectious Diseases

Incompatible Blood Types

Other Parental Factors

Although living in a protected, comfortable environment, the fetus is not totally immune to the larger world surrounding the mother. The environment can affect the child in many well-documented ways (Brent, 2004). Thousands of babies are born deformed or mentally retarded every year as the result of events in the mother's life. Factors related to the father also can influence the health of the fetus.

Some General Principles

Any agent that causes a birth defect is known as a **teratogen.** (The word comes from the Greek word *tera* meaning "monster.") The field of study that investigates the causes of birth defects is called *teratology.* So many teratogens exist that practically every fetus is exposed to at least some teratogens. For this reason, it is difficult to determine which teratogen causes which birth defect. In addition, it may take a long time for the effects of a teratogen to show up (Iannucci, 2000). Only about half of all potential effects appear at birth. A specific teratogen (such as a drug) usually does not cause a specific birth defect (such as malformation of the legs). The dose, genetic susceptibility, and the time of exposure to a particular agent influence the severity of the damage and the type of defect that occurs:

- *Dose.* The greater the dose of an agent, such as a drug, the greater the effect.
- *Genetic susceptibility.* The type and severity of abnormalities caused by a teratogen are linked to the genotype of the pregnant woman and the genotype of the fetus (Lidral & Murray, 2005). For example, the pregnant woman's genotype may create variations in metabolism, placental membranes, and placental transport that can influence the degree to which a drug's effects are transmitted to the fetus. The genotype of the fetus may also influence vulnerability to a particular teratogen.

teratogen From the Greek word *tera*, meaning "monster," any agent that causes a birth defect. The field of study that investigates the causes of birth defects is called teratology.

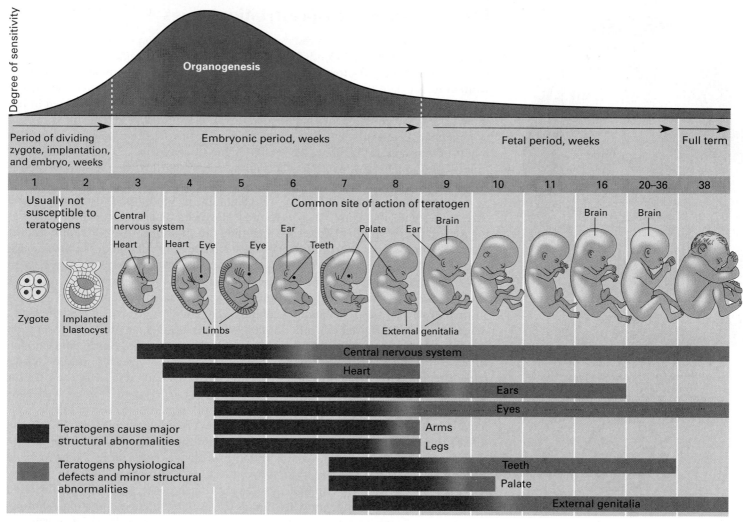

FIGURE 4.7 **Teratogens and the Timing of Their Effects on Prenatal Development** The danger of structural defects caused by teratogens is greatest early in embryonic development. The period of organogenesis (red color) lasts for about six weeks. Later assaults by teratogens (blue color) mainly occur in the fetal period and instead of causing structural damage are more likely to stunt growth or cause problems of organ function.

- *Time of exposure.* Teratogens do more damage when they occur at some points in development than at others. In general, the embryonic period of the first trimester is a more vulnerable time than the second and third trimesters.

Figure 4.7 summarizes additional information about teratogens and the effects of the time of exposure. The probability of a structural defect is greatest earliest in the embryonic period because this is when organs are being formed. The vulnerability of the brain is greatest at 15 to 25 days after conception, the eyes at 24 to 40 days, the heart at 20 to 40 days, and the legs at 24 to 36 days. Each body structure has its own critical period of formation, as shown in figure 4.7.

Recall from chapter 2 that a critical period is a fixed time period very early in development during which certain experiences or events can have a long-lasting effect on development. After organogenesis is complete, teratogens are less likely to cause anatomical defects. Exposure later, during the fetal period, is more likely to stunt growth or to create problems in the way organs function.

What kinds of agents can harm the unborn child? Major types of teratogens include certain medicines and other drugs, radiation and various pollutants, and infectious diseases in the mother.

Exploring Teratology
High-Risk Situations

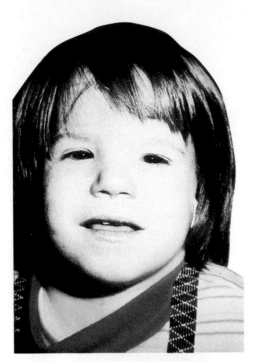

A child with fetal alcohol syndrome. Notice the wide-set eyes, flat bones, and thin upper lip.

www.mhhe.com/santrocke9

Fetal Alcohol Syndrome

Prescription and Nonprescription Drugs

Occasionally, the damage that prescription and nonprescription drugs can create is discovered only after a cluster of deformed babies is born. This tragic example occurred in 1961 after many doctors prescribed the tranquilizer thalidomide for pregnant women to alleviate their morning sickness. In adults, the effects of thalidomide are mild; in embryos, however, they are devastating. Not all infants were affected in the same way. If the mother took thalidomide on day 26 (probably before she knew she was pregnant), an arm might not grow. If she took the drug two days later, the arm might not grow past the elbow. The thalidomide tragedy shocked the medical community and taught a valuable lesson: taking the wrong drug at the wrong time is enough to physically handicap the offspring for life.

Because of the devastating effects of thalidomide on embryos, its use in the United States and some other countries was banned. However, thalidomide is once again being used to treat a number of diseases, including cancer and leprosy (Chaudhry & others, 2002; Jin & others, 2002). The renewed availability of thalidomide is controversial because of the fear that it may be misused and once again harm embryos.

Prescription drugs that can function as teratogens include antibiotics, such as streptomycin and tetracycline; some antidepressants; certain hormones, such as progestin and synthetic estrogen; and Accutane (which often is prescribed for acne) (Andrade & others, 2004; Malm & others, 2004; Webster & Freeman, 2003).

Nonprescription drugs that can be harmful include diet pills, aspirin, and caffeine (Black & Hill, 2003). Let's explore the research on caffeine. A review of studies on caffeine consumption during pregnancy concluded that a small increase in the risks for spontaneous abortion and low birth weight occurs for pregnant women who consumed more than 150 milligrams of caffeine (approximately two cups of brewed coffee or two to three 12-ounce cans of cola) per day (Fernandes & others, 1998). We will discuss the implications of low birth weight later in the chapter. For example, in one study, pregnant women who drank caffeinated coffee were more likely to have preterm deliveries and newborns with a lower birth weight compared with their counterparts who did not drink caffeinated coffee (Eskenazi & others, 1999). Decaffeinated coffee had no effects. Taking into account such results, the Food and Drug Administration recommends that pregnant women either not consume caffeine or consume it only sparingly.

Psychoactive Drugs

Psychoactive drugs are drugs that act on the nervous system to alter states of consciousness, modify perceptions, and change moods. A number of legal and illegal psychoactive drugs—including alcohol, nicotine, cocaine, marijuana, and heroin—have been studied to determine their links to prenatal and child development (Noland & others, 2005; Stanwood & Levitt, 2004). We'll also take a look at the growing use of methamphetamine.

Alcohol   Heavy drinking by pregnant women can be devastating to offspring (Barr & Streissguth, 2001; Caley, Kramer, & Robinson, 2005; Committee on Substance Abuse, 2000; Enoch & Goldman, 2002). **Fetal alcohol syndrome (FAS)** is a cluster of abnormalities that appears in the offspring of mothers who drink alcohol heavily during pregnancy (Archibald & others, 2001). The abnormalities include facial deformities and defective limbs, face, and heart. Most of these children are below average in intelligence, and some are mentally retarded (Lee & others, 2004; Sokol, Delaney-Black, & Nordstrom, 2003; West & Blake, 2005). One recent study found that prenatal exposure to binge drinking was linked to a greater likelihood of having IQ scores in the mentally retarded range and a higher incidence of acting out behavior at 7 years of age (Bailey & others, 2004). According to another study, adults with FAS are at increased risk for mental disorders, such as depression or anxiety (Famy, Streissguth, &

fetal alcohol syndrome (FAS) A cluster of abnormalities that appears in the offspring of mothers who drink alcohol heavily during pregnancy.

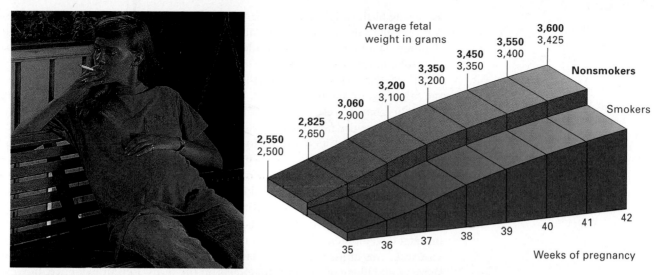

FIGURE 4.8 The Effects of Smoking by Expectant Mothers on Fetal Weight Throughout prenatal development, the fetuses of expectant mothers who smoke weigh less than the fetuses of expectant mothers who do not smoke.

Unis, 1998). Although many mothers of FAS infants are heavy drinkers, many mothers who are heavy drinkers do not have children with FAS or have one child with FAS and other children who do not have it.

Researchers have found that even moderate drinking by pregnant women also can be harmful (Burden & others, 2005; Howell & others, 2005, in press; Willford & others, 2004). In one study, children whose mothers drank one to two drinks a day during pregnancy were less attentive and alert at 4 years of age (Streissguth & others, 1984). A recent study found that when pregnant women had three or more drinks a day, risk of preterm birth increased (Parazzini & others, 2003). Also, in a longitudinal study, the more alcohol mothers drank in the first trimester of pregnancy, the more their 14-year-olds fell behind on growth markers such as weight, height, and head size (Day & others, 2002).

What are some guidelines for alcohol use during pregnancy? Drinking one or two servings of beer or wine or one serving of hard liquor a few days a week can have negative effects on the fetus, although it is generally agreed that this level of alcohol use will not cause fetal alcohol syndrome. The U.S. Surgeon General recommends that *no* alcohol be consumed during pregnancy. And recent research suggests that it may not be wise to consume alcohol at the time of conception. One study revealed that "both male and female alcohol intakes during the week of conception increased the risk of early pregnancy loss" (Henriksen & others, 2004, p. 661).

Nicotine   Cigarette smoking by pregnant women can also adversely influence prenatal development, birth, and postnatal development (Pringle & others, 2005; Vaglenova & others, 2004; Zdravkovic & others, 2005). Fetal and neonatal deaths, preterm births, low birth weights, respiratory problems, and sudden infant death syndrome (also known as crib death) are all more common among the offspring of smoking than nonsmoking mothers (Godding & others, 2004; Moore & Davies, 2005; Sawnani & others, 2004) (see figure 4.8). One study also linked prenatal exposure to cigarette smoking to poorer language and cognitive skills at 4 years of age (Fried & Watkinson, 1990). And a recent study revealed a link between maternal smoking during pregnancy and increased incidence of attention deficit hyperactivity disorder in almost 3,000 children 5 to 16 years of age (Thapar & others, 2003). A longitudinal study found that maternal cigarette smoking during pregnancy was a risk factor for later cigarette smoking by adolescent offspring (Porath & Fried, 2005). Intervention programs to help pregnant women stop smoking can reduce some of smoking's effects, especially by raising birth weights (Klesges & others, 2001; Lightwood, Phibbs, & Glantz, 1999). A recent analysis indicated a decline in smoking during pregnancy from 1990 to 2002, although smoking by pregnant adolescents still remained high (Centers for Disease Control and Prevention, 2004).

The father's smoking during the mother's pregnancy also can cause problems for the offspring. In one investigation, the newborns of fathers who smoked during their wives' pregnancy were 4 ounces lighter at birth for each pack of cigarettes smoked per day than were the newborns whose fathers did not smoke during their wives' pregnancy (Rubin & others, 1986). In another study, in China, the longer the fathers smoked, the stronger the risk was for their children to develop cancer (Ji & others, 1997). Also, in an analysis of seven studies, it was recently concluded that an association exists between paternal smoking and the development of brain tumors in children (Huncharek, Kupelnick, & Klassen, 2002). In such studies, it is difficult to tease apart prenatal and postnatal effects. Also, the negative influence of paternal smoking on fetal development was likely due to environmental tobacco smoke exposure. Previously it was argued that if the father did not smoke around the pregnant woman, there would likely be no harmful effects on the fetus. Recent evidence, however, suggests that men who smoke have a lower density of sperm, a higher percentage of sperm defects, and an increased risk of producing sperm that lack the correct number of chromosomes (Ong, Shen, & Chia, 2002).

Cocaine   Does cocaine use during pregnancy harm the developing embryo and fetus? The most consistent finding is that cocaine exposure during prenatal development is associated with reduced birth weight, length, and head circumference (Smith & others, 2001). Also, in one study, prenatal cocaine exposure was associated with impaired motor development at 2 years of age (Arendt & others, 1999). In a recent study that was controlled for the use of other drugs, at 1 month of age cocaine exposure during pregnancy was related to lower arousal, less effective self-regulation, higher excitability, and lower quality of reflexes (Lester & others, 2002). Other studies link cocaine use with impaired information processing (Harvey, 2004; Morrow & others, 2003; Singer & others, 1999), poor attentional skills through 5 years of age (Bandstra & others, 2000), and impaired processing of auditory information after birth (Potter & others, 2000).

A cautious interpretation of these findings has been emphasized (Arendt & others, 2004; Chavkin, 2001; Vidaeff & Mastrobattista, 2003). Why? Because other factors (such as poverty, malnutrition, and other substance abuse) in the lives of pregnant women who use cocaine often cannot be ruled out as possible contributors to the problems found in their children (Hurt & others, 2005; Kaugers, Russ, & Singer, 2000). For example, cocaine users are more likely than nonusers to smoke cigarettes, use marijuana, drink alcohol, and take amphetamines.

However, despite these cautions in interpretation, the weight of recent research evidence indicates that children born to cocaine-using mothers are likely to have neurological and cognitive deficits (Bandstra & others, 2004; Estelles & others, 2005; Lewis & others, 2004; Mayes, 2003). Because of the potential harmful effect of cocaine to the pregnant mother, and to the fetus, its use is not recommended.

Methamphetamine   Although babies born to cocaine users are at risk for problems, babies born to mothers who use methamphetamine, or "meth," during pregnancy also are at significant risk for various problems, including high infant mortality, low birth weight, and developmental and behavioral difficulties (Chang & others, 2005). Meth use during pregnancy is increasing. Some prenatal experts conclude that methamphetamine now has become as widespread a problem, or an even greater problem, than cocaine for pregnant women (Elliott, 2004).

Meth (also called crystal, crank, or speed) is often "cooked up" in dangerous, clandestine home-based labs, exposing babies before and after birth to toxic chemicals and fumes. These children are at increased risk for a number of problems, including respiratory difficulties and neurological abnormalities, poor cognitive functioning, and abuse and neglect by their meth-addicted parents (Swetlow, 2003).

Marijuana   Despite marijuana being used by a number of women of reproductive age, there has not been extensive research investigation of its effects on their offspring. A recent research review concluded that marijuana use by pregnant women is related to negative outcomes in memory and information processing in their offspring (Kalant, 2004). For example, in a longitudinal study, prenatal marijuana exposure was related to learning and memory difficulties at age 11 (Richardson & others, 2002). Another research review concluded that marijuana use during pregnancy may be related to impairment of a child's attention (Fried & Smith, 2001). Also, a National Institute of Drug Abuse's (2001) review of marijuana effects concluded that babies born to mothers who used marijuana during pregnancy are smaller than babies born to mothers who did not use the drug. However, because of the small numbers of studies, it is difficult to reach conclusions about effects on the child's development resulting from the expectant mother's marijuana use. Nonetheless, marijuana use is not recommended for use by pregnant women.

Heroin   It is well documented that infants whose mothers are addicted to heroin show behavioral difficulties (Hulse & others, 2001; Johnson, Gerada, & Greenough, 2003). These infants have tremors and display irritability, abnormal crying, disturbed sleep, and impaired motor control—all heroin withdrawal symptoms. Many still have behavioral problems at 1 year of age and some show attention deficits later in development. Newborns whose mothers received methadone, the most common treatment for heroin addiction, may also display severe withdrawal symptoms.

The effects of various drugs—the main ones we have discussed as well as others—on the offspring and guidelines for safe use of these drugs is presented in figure 4.9.

Environmental Hazards

The medicines and other drugs discussed so far are teratogens that a pregnant woman can avoid in order to protect her offspring. But many other teratogens come from the environment and are beyond a mother's or a father's control (Bellinger, 2005; Brent, 2004; Rodier, 2004). For example, men's exposure to lead, radiation, certain pesticides, and petrochemicals may cause abnormalities in sperm that can lead to miscarriage or diseases, such as childhood cancer (Trasler, 2000). Radiation, many chemicals, and other features of our modern world are potential hazards to the embryo or fetus (Grigorenko, 2001; McKinney & others, 2003).

Exposure to radiation of various sorts can cause gene mutations. Chromosomal abnormalities are higher among the offspring of fathers exposed to high levels of radiation in their occupations (Schrag & Dixon, 1985). Radiation from X rays also can affect the developing embryo and fetus, with the most dangerous time being the first several weeks after conception, when women do not yet know they are pregnant (Barnett & Maulik, 2001; Urbano & Tait, 2004). It is important for women and their physicians to weigh the risk of an X ray when an actual or potential pregnancy is involved (Shaw, 2001). Computer monitors also emit radiation but researchers have not found exposure to computer monitors to be related to miscarriage (Schnorr & others, 1991).

Environmental pollutants and toxic wastes are also sources of danger to unborn children. Among the dangerous pollutants are carbon monoxide, mercury, and lead. People may be exposed to lead because they live in houses in which lead-based paint flakes off the walls or near busy highways, where there are heavy automobile emissions from leaded gasoline. Researchers believe that early exposure to lead affects children's mental development (Markowitz, 2000; Yang & others, 2003). For example, in

An explosion at the Chernobyl nuclear power plant in the Ukraine produced radioactive contamination that spread to surrounding areas. Thousands of infants were born with health problems and deformities as a result of the nuclear contamination, including this boy whose arm did not form. *Other than radioactive contamination, what are some other types of environmental hazards to prenatal development?*

Drug	Effects on fetus and offspring	Safe use of the drug
Alcohol	Three or more drinks a day on a regular basis or binge drinking early in pregnancy can cause fetal alcohol syndrome. Moderate drinking (1 or 2 servings of beer or wine or 1 serving of hard liquor a few days a week) can have negative effects on the fetus, but this level of alcohol exposure does not cause fetal alcohol syndrome.	Avoid use.
Nicotine	Heavy smoking is associated with low birth weight babies, which means the babies may have more health problems than other infants. Smoking may be especially harmful in the second half of pregnancy. Smoking may damage a man's sperm and reduce semen quality.	Avoid use.
Tranquilizers	Taken during the first three months of pregnancy, they may cause cleft palate or other congenital malformations.	Avoid use if you might become pregnant and during early pregnancy. Use only under a doctor's supervision.
Barbiturates	Mothers who take large doses may have babies who are addicted. Babies may have tremors, restlessness, and irritability.	Use only under a doctor's supervision.
Amphetamines	They may cause birth defects.	Use only under a doctor's supervision.
Cocaine	Cocaine may cause drug dependency and withdrawal symptoms at birth, as well as physical and mental problems, especially if the mother uses cocaine in the first three months of pregnancy. There is a higher risk of hypertension, heart problems, developmental retardation, and learning difficulties. Cocaine's independent effects are still controversial.	Avoid use.
Methamphetamine	"Meth" use is linked with infant mortality, respiratory and neurological abnormalities, and low birth weight.	Avoid use
Marijuana	It may be linked with babies being smaller and impaired attention information processing.	Avoid use.

FIGURE 4.9 Drug Use During Pregnancy

one study, 2-year-olds who prenatally had high levels of lead in their umbilical-cord blood performed poorly on a test of mental development (Bellinger & others, 1987).

Some fish contain high levels of mercury, which is released into the air both naturally and by industrial pollution. When mercury falls into the water it can become toxic and accumulates in large fish, such as shark, swordfish, kin mackerel, and some species of large tuna. Because mercury is easily transferred across the placenta, the embryo is highly sensitive to birth defects involving the developing brain and nervous system (Castoldi, Coccini, & Manzo, 2003; Patterson, Ryan, & Dickey, 2004; Stephenson, 2004). The U.S. Food and Drug Administration (2004) recently provided the following recommendations for women of childbearing age and young children: Don't eat shark, swordfish, king mackerel, or tilefish; eat up to 12 ounces (2 average meals) a week of fish and shellfish that are lower in mercury, such as shrimp, canned light tuna, salmon, pollock, and catfish.

Manufacturing chemicals known as PCBs (polychlorinated biphenyls) are also harmful to prenatal development (Fitzgerald & others, 2004; ten Tusscher & Koppe, 2004; Vreugdenhil & others, 2004). Although banned in the 1970s in the United States, PCBs continue to be present in landfills, sediments, and wildlife. One study kept track of the extent to which pregnant women ate PCB-polluted fish from Lake Michigan; subsequently the researchers observed their children as newborns, young children, and at 11 years of age (Jacobson & others, 1984; Jacobson & Jacobson, 2002, 2003). The women who had eaten more PCB-polluted fish were more likely to have smaller, preterm infants who were more likely to react slowly to stimuli. As preschool children, their exposure to PCBs was linked with less effective short-term memory, and at age 11 with lower verbal intelligence and reading comprehension.

Infectious Diseases

Some maternal diseases and infections can produce defects in the mother's offspring by crossing the placental barrier, or they can cause damage during the birth process itself (Iannucci, 2000; Kirkham, Harris, & Grzbowski, 2005). Rubella and certain sexually transmitted infections are the most common examples. Rubella (German measles) is a maternal disease that can cause prenatal defects (Kobayashi & others, 2005). A rubella outbreak in 1964–1965 resulted in 30,000 prenatal and neonatal (newborn) deaths, and more than 20,000 affected infants were born with problems, including mental retardation, blindness, deafness, and heart defects. The greatest damage occurs when mothers contract rubella in the third and fourth weeks of pregnancy, although infection during the second month is also damaging. Elaborate preventive efforts ensure that rubella will never again have the disastrous effects it had in the mid 1960s. A vaccine that prevents German measles is now routinely administered to children, and women who plan to have children should have a blood test before they become pregnant to determine if they are immune to the disease (Bar-Oz & others, 2004).

Syphilis, a sexually transmitted infection, is more damaging later in prenatal development—4 months or more after conception. Rather than affecting organogenesis, as rubella does, syphilis damages organs after they have formed. Damage includes eye lesions, which can cause blindness, and skin lesions. When syphilis is present at birth, other problems, involving the central nervous system and gastrointestinal tract, can develop (Hollier & others, 2001; Mullick, Beksinksa, & Msomi, 2005). Most states require that pregnant women be given a blood test to detect the presence of syphilis.

Another infection that has received widespread attention recently is genital herpes (Rupp, Rosenthal, & Stanberry, 2005). Newborns contract this virus when they are delivered through the birth canal of a mother with genital herpes (Qutub & others, 2001; Thung & Grobman, 2005). About one-third of babies delivered through an infected birth canal die; another one-fourth become brain damaged. If an active case of genital herpes is detected in a pregnant woman close to her delivery date, a cesarean section can be performed (in which the infant is delivered through an incision in the mother's abdomen) to keep the virus from infecting the newborn.

AIDS is a sexually transmitted infection that is caused by the human immunodeficiency virus (HIV), which destroys the body's immune system. Mothers infected with HIV may transmit the virus to their offspring in three ways: (1) during gestation across the placenta, (2) during delivery through contact with maternal blood or fluids, and (3) postpartum (after birth) through breast feeding. Babies born to HIV-infected mothers can be (1) infected and symptomatic (show AIDS symptoms), (2) infected but *asymptomatic* (not show AIDS symptoms), or (3) not infected at all. An infant who is infected and asymptomatic may still develop HIV symptoms up until 15 months of age.

Pregnancy and HIV

In the early 1990s, before preventive treatments were available, 1,000 to 2,000 infants were born with HIV infection each year in the United States. This number has been dramatically reduced by giving zidovudine (AZT) to infected women during pregnancy and delivery and to the infants after birth (Mohlala & others, 2005; Sullivan, 2003; Thorne & Newell, 2003). In many poor countries, however, treatment with AZT is limited and HIV infection of infants remains a major problem (Chama, Audu & Kyari, 2004; Iliyasu & others, 2005; Sobieszczyk & others, 2005).

Incompatible Blood Types

Incompatibility between the mother's and the father's blood types is a risk to prenatal development. In addition to the blood group (A, B, O, AB), the *Rh factor* is either

Because the fetus depends entirely on its mother for nutrition, it is important for the pregnant woman to have good nutritional habits. In Kenya, this government clinic provides pregnant women with information about how their diet can influence the health of their fetus and offspring. *What might the information about diet be like?*

positive or negative. A woman is at risk during pregnancy when she has a negative Rh factor and her partner has a positive Rh factor (Harty-Golder, 2005; Reid, 2002; Weiss, 2001). This combination can produce a fetus whose blood has a positive Rh factor. When the fetus' blood is Rh positive and the mother's is Rh negative, antibodies in the mother may attack the fetus. This can result in any number of problems, including miscarriage or stillbirth, anemia, jaundice, heart defects, brain damage, or death soon after birth (Moise, 2005; Narang & Jain, 2001).

In most instances, the first Rh-positive baby of an Rh-negative mother is not affected, but with each pregnancy the risk becomes greater. A vaccine (RhoGAM) may be given to the mother within three days after the child's birth that will prevent her body from making antibodies that will attack future Rh-positive fetuses. Also, babies affected by Rh incompatibility can be given blood transfusions, in some cases before birth (Mannessier & others, 2000).

Other Parental Factors

So far we have discussed a number of drugs, environmental hazards, maternal diseases, and incompatible blood types that can harm the embryo or fetus. Here we will explore other characteristics of the mother and father that can affect prenatal and child development: nutrition, age, and emotional states and stress.

Nutrition   A developing fetus depends completely on its mother for nutrition, which comes from the mother's blood (Matthews, Youngman, & Neil, 2004). The nutritional status of the fetus is determined by the mother's total caloric intake, and also by appropriate levels of proteins, vitamins, and minerals. Children born to malnourished mothers are more likely to be malformed or be low in birth weight (Ramakrishnan, 2004; Wong & others, 2003).

One aspect of maternal nutrition of particular interest is folic acid (Bailey & Berry, 2005; Callender, Rickard, & Rinsky-Eng, 2001; Stepanuk & others, 2002; Wen & Walker, 2005). The U.S. Public Health Service recommends that pregnant women consume a minimum of 400 micrograms of folic acid per day (that is about twice the amount the average woman gets in one day). What is important about folic acid? A lack of folic acid is linked with neural-tube defects in offspring, such as spina bifida, which is an incomplete closure in the spinal column ranging from mild to severe (Felkner & others, 2005; Honein & others, 2001). Researchers have found that neural-tube defects are more likely to be prevented through the consumption of natural folic-acid-rich foods, such as orange juice and spinach, than through supplements (Langley-Evans & Langley-Evans, 2002). One recent study also found that maternal use of folic acid and iron during the first month of pregnancy was associated with a lower risk of Down syndrome in offspring (Czeizel & Puho, 2005).

Being overweight before and during pregnancy can also affect the fetus (Dietl, 2005; Elwig, 2005; Martinez-Frias & others, 2005). In two studies, obese women had a significant risk of late fetal death although the risk of preterm delivery was reduced in these women (Cnattinugius & others, 1998; Kumari, 2001). A recent study also found that maternal obesity was associated with central nervous system birth defects in offspring (Anderson & others, 2005).

Maternal Age   When possible harmful effects on the fetus and infant are considered, two maternal ages are of special interest: adolescence and the thirties and beyond (Aliyu & others, 2004; Callaghan & Berg, 2003; Spandorfer & others, 2004). Approximately one of every five births in the United States is to an adolescent; in some urban areas, the figure reaches as high as one in every two births. Infants born to adolescents are often preterm (Ekwo & Moawad, 2000). The mortality rate of infants born to adolescent mothers is double that of infants born to mothers in their twenties. Although this high rate probably reflects the immaturity of the mother's reproductive system, poor nutrition, lack of prenatal care, and low socioeconomic status may also play a role (Lenders, McElrath, & Scholl, 2000). Prenatal care decreases the probability that a child born to an adolescent girl will have physical problems. However, adolescents are the least likely of women in all age groups to obtain prenatal assistance from clinics, pediatricians, and health services.

Key dangers to the fetus when the mother is older than 35 include an increased risk for low birth weight and for Down syndrome (Cleary-Goldman & others, 2005; Mirowsky, 2005). The risk for Down syndrome is related to the mother's age (Holding, 2002). One recent study found that low birth weight delivery increased 11 percent and preterm delivery increased 14 percent in women 35 years and older (Tough & others, 2002). A baby with Down syndrome rarely is born to a mother under the age of 30, but the risk increases after the mother reaches 30. By age 40, the probability is slightly over 1 in 100, and by age 50 it is almost 1 in 10. The risk also is higher before age 18.

Fetal death is also more likely to occur in older women. Fetal death was low for women 30 to 34 years of age but increased progressively for women 35 to 39 and 40 to 44 years of age in one recent study (Canterino & others, 2004).

The father's age also makes a difference (Klonoff-Cohen & Natarajan, 2004; Slama & others, 2005). When fathers are older, their offspring face increased risk for certain birth defects, including Down syndrome (about 5 percent of these children have older fathers), dwarfism, and Marfan syndrome, which involves head and limb deformities.

There are also risks to offspring when both the mother and father are older (Dunson, Baird, & Colombo, 2004). In one recent study, the risk of an adverse pregnancy outcome, such as miscarriage, was much greater when the woman was 35 years or older and the man was 40 years of age or older (de la Rocheborchard & Thonneau, 2002).

We still have much to learn about the role of the mother's age in pregnancy and childbirth. As women remain active, exercise regularly, and are careful about their nutrition, their reproductive systems may remain healthier at older ages than was thought possible in the past.

Emotional States and Stress   Tales abound about how a pregnant woman's emotional state affects the fetus. For centuries it was thought that frightening experiences—such as a severe thunderstorm or a family member's death—leave birthmarks on the child or affect the child in more serious ways. In fact, a mother's stress can be transmitted to the fetus, but we now have a better grasp of how this takes place (Federenko & Wadhwa, 2004; Niederhofer & Reiter, 2004; Van den Bergh & others, 2005). When a pregnant woman experiences intense fears, anxieties, and other emotions, physiological changes occur that may also affect her fetus. For example, producing adrenaline in response to fear restricts blood flow to the uterine area and can deprive the fetus of adequate oxygen.

Researchers have been uncovering links between fetal health and various states in the mother, although the mechanisms that link the two are still far from certain. In studies by Christine Dunkel-Schetter and her colleagues (1998, 2001), women under high levels of stress were about four times more likely than their low-stress counterparts to deliver babies prematurely. Why? Maternal stress may increase the level of corticotropin-releasing hormone (CRH) early in pregnancy (Hobel & others, 1999; Wadhwa, 2005; Weinstock, 2005). CRH, in turn, has been linked to premature delivery. A mother's stress may also influence the fetus indirectly by increasing the likelihood that the mother will engage in unhealthy behaviors, such as taking drugs and engaging in poor prenatal care.

The possibility that hormonal treatments can decrease the number of preterm births has recently been investigated. In one recent study, weekly injections of the hormone progesterone, which is naturally produced by the ovaries, lowered the rate of preterm births by one-third (Meis, 2003). High-risk women could receive the hormone treatment now, but researchers are recommending that further research first be conducted to determine the safest and most effective way to administer the drug.

What are some of the risks for infants born to adolescent mothers?

www.mhhe.com/santrockc9

Later Life Pregnancy
Reproductive Health Links

The mother's emotional state during pregnancy can influence the birth process, too. An emotionally distraught mother might have irregular contractions and a more difficult labor, which can cause irregularities in the supply of oxygen to the fetus or other problems after birth. Babies born after extended labor also may adjust more slowly to their world and be more irritable.

Positive emotional states also appear to make a difference to the fetus. Pregnant women who are optimistic thinkers have less adverse outcomes than pregnant women who are pessimistic thinkers (Lobel & Yalli, 1999). Optimists are more likely to believe that they have control over the outcomes of their pregnancies (Lobel & others, 2002). In fact, although our discussion in this section has focused on what can go wrong with prenatal development, most pregnancies do not go awry. In most pregnancies, development follows along the positive path we described earlier in the chapter (Lester, 2000).

Review and Reflect • LEARNING GOAL 3

Describe potential hazards during prenatal development.

Review

- What is teratology? What are some general principles regarding teratogens?
- Which prescription and nonprescription drugs can influence prenatal development?
- How do different psychoactive drugs affect prenatal development?
- What are some environmental hazards that can influence prenatal development?
- Which infectious diseases can affect prenatal development?
- How do incompatible blood types influence prenatal development?
- What other parental factors affect prenatal development?

Reflect

- What can be done to convince women who are pregnant not to smoke or drink? Consider the role of health-care providers, the role of insurance companies, and specific programs targeted at women who are pregnant.

KEY TERMS

germinal period 109
blastocyst 109
trophoblast 109
embryonic period 109

endoderm 109
ectoderm 109
mesoderm 109
amnion 110

organogenesis 110
fetal period 111
teratogen 122

fetal alcohol syndrome
(FAS) 124

KEY PEOPLE

Christine Dunkel-Schetter 131

MAKING A DIFFERENCE

Maximizing Positive Prenatal Outcomes

What are some good strategies during pregnancy that are likely to maximize positive outcomes for prenatal development?

- *Eat nutritiously and monitor weight gain.* The recommended daily allowances for all nutrients increase during pregnancy. The pregnant woman should eat three balanced meals a day and nutritious snacks between meals if desired. Weight gains that average 25 to 35 pounds are associated with the best reproductive outcomes.
- *Engage in safe exercise.* How much and what type of exercise is best during pregnancy depends to some degree on the course of the pregnancy, the expectant mother's fitness, and her customary activity level. Normal participation in exercise can continue throughout an uncomplicated pregnancy. It is important to remember not to overdo exercise. Exercising for shorter intervals and decreasing the intensity of exercise as pregnancy proceeds are good strategies. Pregnant women should always consult a physician before starting an exercise program.
- *Don't drink alcohol or take other potentially harmful drugs.* An important strategy for pregnancy is to totally abstain from alcohol and other drugs, such as nicotine and cocaine. In this chapter, we described the harmful effects that these drugs can have on the developing fetus. Fathers also need to be aware of potentially harmful effects they can have on prenatal development.
- *Have a support system of family and friends.* The pregnant woman benefits from a support system of family members and friends. A positive relationship with a spouse helps keep stress levels down, as does a close relationship with one or more friends.
- *Reduce stress and stay calm.* Try to maintain an even, calm emotional state during pregnancy. High stress levels can harm the fetus. Pregnant women who are feeling a lot of anxiety can reduce their anxiety through a relaxation or stress management program.
- *Stay away from environmental hazards.* We saw in this chapter that some environmental hazards, such as pollutants and toxic wastes, can harm prenatal development. Be aware of these hazards and stay away from them.
- *Get excellent prenatal care.* The quality of prenatal care varies extensively. The education the mother receives about pregnancy, labor and delivery, and care of the newborn can be valuable, especially for first-time mothers.
- *Read a good book for expectant mothers.* An excellent one is *What to Expect When You Are Expecting.*

CHILDREN RESOURCES

National Center for Education in Maternal and Child Health (NCEMCH)

2115 Wisconsin Avenue, NW
Suite 601
Washington, DC 20007
202–784–9770

NCEMCH answers questions about pregnancy and childbirth, high-risk infants, and maternal and child health programs. It also publishes a free guide, *Maternal and Child Health Publications.*

Prenatal Care Tips

Pregnant women can call this federal government toll-free number for prenatal care advice and referral to local health-care providers: 800–311–2229.

E-LEARNING TOOLS

Connect to **www.mhhe.com/santrockc9** to research the answers to complete the following exercises. In addition, you'll find a number of other resources and valuable study tools for chapter 4, "Prenatal Development," on this website.

Taking It to the Net

1. Margaret's best friend, Sarah, suffered a miscarriage after several years of trying to become pregnant. Before Margaret goes to visit Sarah, how can she find out more about the psychological trauma that Sarah may be experiencing as a result of the miscarriage?
2. Candice, age 28, has just learned that she is pregnant. She is proud of the fact that she weighs the same as she did in high school. She is terrified of getting fat and not being able to lose the weight after the baby is born. How can Candice eat properly to keep her and her baby healthy while minimizing unnecessary and unhealthy weight gain?
3. Jackson and Diana have made an application with a foreign adoption agency to adopt a child from a former Soviet Union state. The agency told them the boy they have chosen may be suffering from a mild version of fetal alcohol syndrome. How can Jackson and Diane find out more about FAS before their application is approved?

Health and Well-Being, Parenting, and Education

Build your decision-making skills by trying your hand at the health and well-being, parenting, and education exercises.

Video Clips

The Online Learning Center includes the following videos for this chapter:

1. *Childbirth Education Alternatives*—1936
   A childbirth educator describes the types of childbirth classes that are available to expectant parents and the benefits of childbirth education.
2. *Teen Pregnancy and Families*—553
   Dr. Gunn describes the risk factors that are related to teen pregnancy. All involve the context in which these young girls are raised (e.g., poverty, poor schools).

Images of Children
Tanner Roberts' Birth: A Fantastic Voyage

Tanner Roberts was born in a suite at St. Joseph's Medical Center in Burbank, California (Warrick, 1992, pp. E1, E11, E12). Let's examine what took place in the hours leading up to his birth. It is day 266 of his mother Cindy's pregnancy. She is in the frozen-food aisle of a convenience store and feels a sharp pain, starting in the small of her back and reaching around her middle, which causes her to gasp. For weeks, painless Braxton Hicks spasms (named for the gynecologist who discovered them) have been flexing her uterine muscles. But these practice contractions were not nearly as intense and painful as the one she just experienced. After six hours of irregular spasms, her uterus settles into a more predictable rhythm.

At 3 A.M., Cindy and her husband, Tom, are wide awake. They time Cindy's contractions with a stopwatch. The contractions are now only six minutes apart. It's time to call the hospital. A short time later, Tom and Cindy arrive at the hospital's labor-delivery suite. A nurse puts a webbed belt and fetal monitor around Cindy's middle to measure her labor. The monitor picks up the fetal heart rate. With each contraction of the uterine wall, Tanner's heartbeat jumps from its resting state of about 140 beats to 160 to 170 beats per minute. When the cervix is dilated to more than 4 centimeters, or almost half open, Cindy receives her first medication. As Demerol begins to drip in her veins, the pain of her contractions is less intense. Tanner's heart rate dips to 130 and then 120.

Contractions are now coming every three to four minutes, each one lasting about 25 seconds. The Demerol does not completely obliterate Cindy's pain. She hugs her husband as the nurse urges her to "relax those muscles. Breathe deep. Relax. You're almost there."

Each contraction briefly cuts off Tanner's source of oxygen, his mother's blood. However, in the minutes of rest between contractions, Cindy's deep breathing helps rush fresh blood to the baby's heart and brain.

At 8 A.M., Cindy's cervix is almost completely dilated and the obstetrician arrives. Using a tool made for the purpose, he reaches into the birth canal and tears the membranes of the amniotic sac, and about half a liter of clear fluid flows out. Contractions are now coming every two minutes, and each one is lasting a full minute.

By 9 A.M., the labor suite has been transformed into a delivery room. Tanner's body is compressed by his mother's contractions and pushes. As he nears his entrance into the world, the compressions help press the fluid from his lungs in preparation for his first breath. Squeezed tightly in the birth canal, the top of Tanner's head emerges. His face is puffy and scrunched. Although fiercely squinting because of the sudden light, Tanner's eyes are open. Tiny bubbles of clear mucus are on his lips. Before any more of his body emerges, the nurse cradles Tanner's head and suctions his nose and mouth. Tanner takes his first breath, a large gasp followed by whimpering, and then a loud cry. Tanner's body is wet but only slightly bloody as the doctor lifts him onto his mother's abdomen. The umbilical cord, still connecting Tanner with his mother, slows and stops pulsating. The obstetrician cuts it, severing Tanner's connection to his mother's womb. Now Tanner's blood flows not to his mother's body for nourishment, but to his own lungs, intestines, and other organs.

PREVIEW

As the story of Tanner Roberts' birth reveals, many changes take place during the birth of a baby. In this chapter, we will further explore what happens during the birth process, the development of low birth weight infants, widely used measures of neonatal health and responsiveness, and characteristics of the postpartum period.

1   WHAT HAPPENS DURING THE BIRTH PROCESS?

| Stages of the Birth Process | The Fetus/Newborn Transition | Childbirth Strategies and Decisions |

Our coverage of the birth process focuses on its stages, what the experience of birth is like for the fetus and newborn, and the range of childbirth strategies and decisions. We also will examine three measures of neonatal health and explore the parents' physical and psychological adjustments to their new baby.

Stages of the Birth Process

The birth process occurs in three stages. The first stage is the longest of the three stages. Uterine contractions are 15 to 20 minutes apart at the beginning and last up to a minute. These contractions cause the woman's cervix to stretch and open. As the first stage progresses, the contractions come closer together, appearing every two to five minutes. Their intensity increases. By the end of the first birth stage, contractions dilate the cervix to an opening of about 4 inches, so that the baby can move from the uterus to the birth canal. For a woman having her first child, the first stage lasts an average of 12 to 14 hours; for subsequent children, this stage may be shorter.

The second birth stage begins when the baby's head starts to move through the cervix and the birth canal. It terminates when the baby completely emerges from the mother's body. With each contraction, the mother bears down hard to push the baby out of her body. By the time the baby's head is out of the mother's body, the contractions come almost every minute and last for about a minute. This stage typically lasts approximately 45 minutes to an hour.

Afterbirth is the third stage, at which time the placenta, umbilical cord, and other membranes are detached and expelled. This final stage is the shortest of the three birth stages, lasting only minutes (see figure 5.1).

The Fetus/Newborn Transition

Being born involves considerable stress for the baby. During each contraction, when the placenta and umbilical cord are compressed as the uterine muscles draw together, the supply of oxygen to the fetus is decreased. **Anoxia** is the term used to describe the condition in which the fetus/newborn has an insufficient supply of oxygen. Anoxia can cause brain damage (Bukowski & others, 2003; Kendall & Peebles, 2005). Although the supply of oxygen is briefly decreased with each contraction, the term *anoxia* usually refers to longer-lasting, more chronic oxygen deprivation. If the delivery takes too long, anoxia can develop.

The baby has considerable capacity to withstand the stress of birth. Large quantities of adrenaline and noradrenaline, hormones that are important in protecting the fetus in the event of oxygen deficiency, are secreted in stressful circumstances (Jankov, Asztolos, & Skidmore, 2000). These hormones increase the heart's pumping activity, speed up heart rate, channel blood flow to the brain, and raise the blood sugar level. Never again in life will such large amounts of these hormones be secreted. This circumstance underscores how stressful it is to be born but also how prepared and adapted the fetus is for birth (Miller & others, 2005; VanBeveren, 2004).

As we saw in the case of Tanner Roberts, the umbilical cord is cut immediately after birth, and the baby is on its own. Now 25 million little air sacs in the lungs must be filled with air. Until now, these air sacs have held fluid, but this fluid is rapidly expelled in blood and lymph. The first breaths may be the hardest ones at any point in the life span. Before birth, oxygen came from the mother via the umbilical cord, but now the

afterbirth The third stage of birth, when the placenta, umbilical cord, and other membranes are detached and expelled.

anoxia The insufficient availability of oxygen to the fetus/newborn.

FIGURE 5.1 **The Stages of Birth** (a) First stage: cervix is dilating; (b) late first stage (transition stage): cervix is fully dilated, and the amniotic sac has ruptured, releasing amniotic fluid; (c) second stage: birth of the infant; (d) third stage: delivery of the placenta (afterbirth).

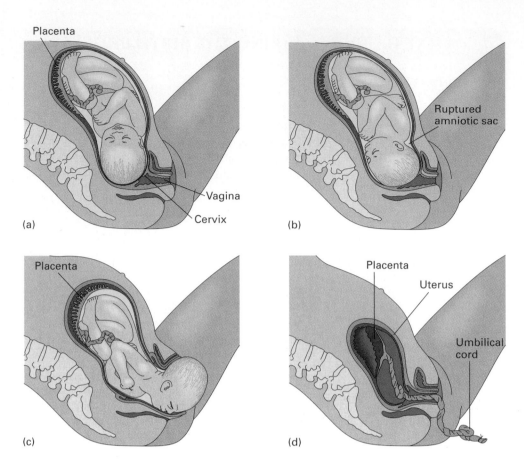

Birth Mailing Lists and Newsgroups
Newborn Care
Preparing for Birth

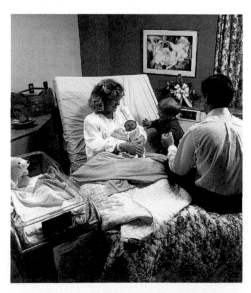

What are some characteristics of the childbirth setting in the United States?

baby has to be self-sufficient and breathe on its own. The newborn's bloodstream is redirected through the lungs and to all parts of the body.

At the time of birth, the baby is covered with what is called *vernix caseosa,* a protective skin grease. This vernix consists of fatty secretions and dead cells, thought to function in protecting the baby's skin against heat loss before and during birth. After the baby and mother have met and become acquainted with each other, the baby is taken to be cleaned, examined, weighed, and evaluated. Later in the chapter, we will discuss three widely used measures for evaluating the newborn's health and responsiveness.

Childbirth Strategies and Decisions

Now that we have studied the stages of birth and fetus/newborn transition, let's turn our attention to some important childbirth strategies and decisions. For example, is it better to deliver a baby in a hospital or at home? Who will attend the birth? Which childbirth technique will be used? What are the roles of the father and siblings?

Childbirth Setting and Attendants   In the United States, 99 percent of births take place in hospitals, and more than 90 percent are attended by physicians (Ventura & others, 1997). Hospital stays are typically two days for a vaginal delivery and three days for a cesarean delivery.

Many hospitals now have birthing centers, where fathers or birth coaches may be with the mother during labor and delivery. Birthing centers offer a good compromise between a technological, depersonalized hospital birth (which cannot offer the emotional experience of a home birth) and a birth at home (which cannot offer the medical backup of a hospital). A birthing room approximates a home setting as much as possible and allows for a full range of birth experiences, from a totally unmedicated, natural birth to complex, medically intensive care. Some women with good medical histories and low risk for problem delivery choose a home delivery or a delivery in a birthing center that is not in a hospital, which is usually staffed by nurse-midwives (Wong, Perry, & Hockenberry, 2001). Regardless of the childbirth setting, there is increasing research evidence that supportive care improves the outcomes for both the mother and the baby (Sauls, 2002).

To read about an obstetrician/gynecologist whose focus is on providing supportive health-care services, see the Careers in Child Development profile about Rachel Thompson.

Approximately 6 percent of women who deliver a baby in the United States are attended by a midwife (Tritten, 2004; Ventura & others, 1997). In the United States, most midwives are nurses who are specially trained in delivering babies (Hyde & Roche-Reid, 2004; Kerr, 2005; Mansfield, 2005; O'Dowd, 2004). Midwives are mainly used for uncomplicated, vaginal deliveries, and physicians are used for more complicated deliveries.

One study found that the risk of neonatal mortality (an infant death occurring in the first 28 days of life) was 33 percent lower and the risk of a low birth weight baby was 31 percent lower for births attended by a certified midwife than for births attended to by a physician (MacDorman & Singh, 1998). Compared with physicians, certified midwives generally spend more time with women during prenatal visits, place more emphasis on counseling and education, provide more emotional support, and are more likely to be with the woman one-on-one during the entire labor and delivery process, which may explain the more positive outcomes for babies delivered by a certified midwife (Davis, 2005). Other reasons that more positive outcomes characterize babies delivered by midwives include: they don't attend complicated births and the women who select midwives as their attendants may be more motivated to take care of themselves during pregnancy.

In many countries, babies are more likely to be delivered at home than they are in the United States. For example, in Holland, 35 percent of the babies are born at home, and more than 40 percent are delivered by midwives rather than doctors (Treffers & others, 1990).

In many countries, a doula attends a childbearing woman. *Doula* is a Greek word that means "a woman who helps." A **doula** is a professional trained in childbirth who provides continuous physical, emotional, and educational support for the mother before, during, and after childbirth. Doulas remain with the mother throughout labor, assessing and responding to her needs (Stein, Kennell, & Fulcher, 2004). They are not responsible for the delivery itself but rather to provide support for the mother. The doula's role includes providing specific labor support skills; offering guidance and encouragement; assisting others to cover gaps in their care; building a team relationship; and encouraging communication between the patient, nursing staff, and medical caregivers (Lantz & others, 2005; Pascali-Bonaro & Kroeger, 2004).

Recent reviews of research found that doula-supported mothers experience less pain during labor, have lower anxiety about birth before the birth and more positive feelings about birth after the birth, and decreased symptoms of depression and

CAREERS in CHILD DEVELOPMENT

Rachel Thompson
Obstetrician/Gynecologist

Rachel Thompson is the senior member of Houston Women's Care Associates, which specializes in health care for women. She has one of Houston's most popular obstetrics/gynecology (OB/GYN) practices. Thompson's medical degree is from Baylor College of Medicine, where she also completed her internship and residency. Thompson's work focuses on many of the topics we discuss in this chapter on prenatal development, birth, and the postpartum period.

In addition to her clinical practice, Thompson also is a clinical instructor in the Department of Obstetrics and Gynecology at Baylor College of Medicine. Thompson says that one of the unique features of their health-care group is that the staff is comprised only of women who are full-time practitioners.

Rachel Thompson *(right)* talking with one of her patients at Houston Women's Care Associates.

doula A professional trained in childbirth who provides continuous physical, emotional, and educational support to the mother before, during, and just after childbirth.

A woman in the African !Kung culture giving birth in a sitting position. Notice the help and support being given by another woman. *What are some cultural variations in childbirth?*

www.mhhe.com/santrockc9

Childbirth Setting and Attendants
Doula
Labor Induction
Lamaze
Cesarean Childbirth

analgesia Drugs used to alleviate pain, such as tranquilizers, barbiturates, and narcotics.

anesthesia Drugs used in late first-stage labor and during expulsion of the baby to block sensation in an area of the body or to block consciousness.

oxytocics Drugs that are synthetic hormones designed to stimulate contractions.

increased sensitivity to the child's needs in the postpartum period (Scott, Klaus, & Klaus, 1999; Stein, Kennell, & Fulcher, 2004). Doulas typically function as part of a birthing team, serving as an adjunct to the midwife or the hospital obstetric staff (McGrath & others, 1999; Pascali-Bonaro, 2002).

In many cultures, several people attend the mother during labor and delivery. Which persons attend the mother may vary across cultures. In the East African Nigoni culture, men are completely excluded from the childbirth process. In this culture, women even conceal their pregnancy from their husbands as long as possible. In the Nigoni culture, when a woman is ready to give birth, female relatives move into the woman's hut and the husband leaves, taking his belongings (clothes, tools, weapons, and so on) with him. He is not permitted to return to the hut until after the baby is born.

A common characteristic in nonindustrialized cultures is for one of the female helpers to hold the woman from behind while she gives birth. In the Mayan culture in Mexico, a head helper breathes with her during each contraction (Jordan, 1993). In some cultures, childbirth is much more of an open, community affair than in the United States. For example, in the Pukapukan culture in the Pacific Islands, women give birth in a shelter that is open for villagers to observe.

Methods of Delivery
As we have just seen, birth may take place in a hospital, a freestanding birth center, or at home. Attendants may include a midwife or doula. Now let's examine a woman's choice of which method of delivery will be used.

Medicated   The American Academy of Pediatrics recommends the least possible medication during delivery (Hotchner, 1997). Three basic kinds of drugs are used for labor: analgesia, anesthesia, and oxytocics:

- **Analgesia** is used to relieve pain. Analgesics include tranquilizers, barbiturates, and narcotics. Potential side effects for the mother can include nausea, vomiting, and low blood pressure. Narcotics such as Demerol can cross the placenta during labor and affect the baby by causing such problems as central nervous system depression and impaired early breast feeding (American Pregnancy Association, 2004).
- **Anesthesia** is used in late first-stage labor and during expulsion of the baby to block sensation in an area of the body or to block consciousness. There is a trend toward not using general anesthesia in normal births because it can be transmitted through the placenta to the fetus. However, an epidural anesthetic does not cross the placenta (Lieberman & others, 2005; Villevielle & others, 2003). An *epidural block* is regional anesthesia that numbs the woman's body from the waist down (Howell & others, 2002). Even this technique, thought to be relatively safe, has come under recent criticism because it is associated with fever, extended labor, and increased risk for cesarean delivery (Glant, 2005; Ransjo-Arvidson & others, 2001).
- **Oxytocics** are synthetic hormones that are used to stimulate contractions (Durodola & others, 2005, in press; Khan & El-Refaey, 2003). Pitocin is the most commonly used oxytocic (Gard & others, 2002).

Predicting how a particular drug will affect an individual pregnant woman and the fetus is difficult. While we have many commonalities as human beings, we also vary a great deal. Thus, a particular drug may have only a minimal effect on one fetus yet have a much stronger effect on another fetus. The drug's dosage also is a factor, with stronger doses of tranquilizers and narcotics given to decrease the mother's pain having a potentially more negative effect on the fetus than mild doses.

It is important for the mother to assess her level of pain and be an important voice in the decision of whether she should receive medication or not. To read about Linda Pugh, a perinatal nurse whose work has included efforts to improve the childbearing experience of women, see the Careers in Child Development profile.

Although the trend at one time was toward a natural childbirth without any medication, today the emphasis is on using some medication but keeping it to a minimum when possible. Today, a pregnant woman is encouraged to learn about the process of childbirth so that she can be reassured and confident. Next, we will consider natural and prepared childbirth, which reflect this emphasis on education.

Natural and Prepared Childbirth **Natural childbirth** was developed in 1914 by an English obstetrician, Grantley Dick-Read. It attempts to reduce the mother's pain by decreasing her fear through education about childbirth and by teaching her to use breathing methods and relaxation techniques during delivery (Day-Stirk, 2005; Moscucci, 2003). Dick-Read also believed that the doctor's relationship with the mother is an important dimension of reducing her perception of pain. He said the doctor should be present during her active labor prior to delivery and should provide reassurance.

Prepared childbirth was developed by French obstetrician Ferdinand Lamaze. This childbirth strategy is similar to natural childbirth but includes a special breathing technique to control pushing in the final stages of labor and a more detailed anatomy and physiology course. The Lamaze method has become very popular in the United States. The pregnant woman's husband, partner, or friend usually serves as a coach, who attends childbirth classes with her and helps her with her breathing and relaxation during delivery.

Many other prepared childbirth techniques also have been developed. They usually include elements of Dick-Read's natural childbirth or Lamaze's method, plus one or more new components (Harper, 2000; McCracken, 2000). For instance, the Bradley method places special emphasis on the father's role as a labor coach (Signore, 2004). Virtually all of the prepared childbirth methods emphasize some degree of education, relaxation and breathing exercises, and support. In recent years, new ways of teaching relaxation have been offered, including guided mental imagery, massage, and meditation. In sum, the current belief in prepared childbirth is that, when information and support are provided, women *know* how to give birth.

Cesarean Delivery In a **cesarean delivery,** the baby is removed from the mother's uterus through an incision made in her abdomen. This also is sometimes called a cesarean section. A cesarean section is usually performed if the baby is in a **breech position,** which causes the baby's buttocks to be the first part to emerge from the vagina (Hauth & Cunningham, 2002). Normally, the crown of the baby's head comes through the vagina first, but in 1 of every 25 babies, the head does not come through first. Breech babies' heads are still in the uterus while the rest of their bodies are out, which can cause respiratory problems (Hannah, 2005; Krebs & Langhoff-Roos, 2003; Levy & others, 2005).

Cesarean deliveries also are performed if the baby is lying crosswise in the uterus, if the baby's head is too large to pass through the mother's pelvis, if the baby develops complications, or if the mother is bleeding vaginally. The benefits and risks of cesarean sections continue to be debated (Ben-Meir, Schenker & Ezra, 2005; Lee & others,

CAREERS
in CHILD DEVELOPMENT

Linda Pugh
Perinatal Nurse

Perinatal nurses work with childbearing women to support health and growth during the childbearing experience. Linda Pugh (Ph.D., R.N.C.) is a perinatal nurse on the faculty at the Johns Hopkins University School of Nursing. She is certified as an inpatient obstetric nurse and specializes in the care of women during labor and delivery. Pugh teaches nursing to both undergraduate and graduate students. In addition to educating professional nurses and conducting research, Pugh consults with hospitals and organizations about women's health issues.

Pugh's research interests include nursing interventions with low-income breast-feeding women, discovering ways to prevent and ameliorate fatigue during childbearing, and using effective breathing exercises during labor.

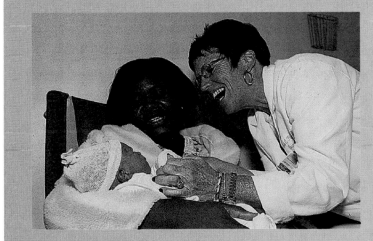

Linda Pugh *(right)* with a mother and her newborn.

natural childbirth Developed in 1914 by Dick-Read, it attempts to reduce the mother's pain by decreasing her fear through education about childbirth and relaxation techniques during delivery.

prepared childbirth Developed by French obstetrician Ferdinand Lamaze, this childbirth strategy is similar to natural childbirth but includes a special breathing technique to control pushing in the final stages of labor and a more detailed anatomy and physiology course.

cesarean delivery The baby is removed from the mother's uterus through an incision made in her abdomen. This also is sometimes referred to as cesarean section.

breech position The baby's position in the uterus that causes the buttocks to be the first part to emerge from the vagina.

2005; Sarsam, Elliott, & Lam, 2005; Sheiner & others, 2005). Cesarean deliveries are safer than breech deliveries, but they involve a higher infection rate, longer hospital stay, and greater expense and stress that accompany any surgery.

Some critics believe that too many babies are delivered by cesarean section in the United States . The cesarean delivery rate jumped 6 percent from 2002 to 2003 in the United States to 27.6 percent of all births, the highest level reported since these data began being reported on birth certificates in 1989 (Martin & others, 2005). Indeed, more cesarean sections are performed in the United States than in any other country in the world. Higher rates may be due to a better ability to identify infants in distress during birth and the increase in overweight and obese pregnant women (Coleman & others, 2005; Sarsam, Elliott, & Lam, 2005). Also, some doctors may be overly cautious and recommend a cesarean delivery to defend against a potential lawsuit.

Family Involvement   In the past several decades, fathers increasingly have participated in childbirth. Siblings often attend the birth or visit the mother shortly afterward.

Fathers   Fathers-to-be are now more likely to go to at least one meeting with the obstetrician or caregiver during the pregnancy, attend childbirth preparation classes, learn about labor and birth, and be more involved in the care of the young infant. The change is consistent with our culture's movement toward less rigid concepts of "masculine" and "feminine" (Draper, 2003).

For many expectant couples today, the father is trained to be the expectant mother's coach during labor, helping her learn relaxation methods and special breathing techniques for labor and birth. Most health professionals now believe that, just as with pregnancy, childbirth should be an intimate, shared moment between two people who are creating a new life together. Nonetheless, some men do not want to participate in prepared childbirth, and some women also still prefer that they not have a very active role (Johnson, 2002). In such cases, other people can provide support for childbirth—mother, sister, friend, midwife, or physician, for example.

Husbands or partners who are motivated to participate in childbirth have an important role at their wife's side. In the long stretches when there is no staff attendant present, a husband or partner can provide companionship, support, and encouragement. In difficult moments of examination or medication, he can be comforting. Initially, he may feel embarrassed to use the breathing techniques he has learned in preparation classes, but he usually begins to feel more at home when he realizes he is performing a necessary function for his wife during each contraction.

Some individuals question whether the father is the best coach during labor. He may be nervous and feel uncomfortable in the hospital. Never having gone through labor himself, he might not understand the expectant mother's needs as well as another woman. There is no universal answer to this issue. Some laboring women want to depend on another woman, someone who has been through labor herself. Others want their husband to intimately share the childbirth experience. Many cultures exclude men from births, just as the American culture did until the past several decades. In some cultures, the woman's mother, or occasionally a daughter, serves as her assistant.

Siblings   If a couple has a child and is expecting another, it is important for them to prepare the older child for the birth of a sibling. Sibling preparation includes providing the child with information about pregnancy, birth, and life with a newborn that is realistic and appropriate for the child's age.

Parents can prepare their older child for the approaching birth at any time during pregnancy. The expectant mother might announce the pregnancy early to explain her fatigue and vomiting. If the child is young and unable to understand the concept of waiting, parents may want to delay announcing the pregnancy until later, when the expectant mother's pregnancy becomes obvious to the child.

Many husbands, or coaches, take childbirth classes with their wives or friends as part of prepared or natural childbirth. This is a Lamaze training session. *What is the nature of the Lamaze method? Who devised it?*

www.mhhe.com/santrockc9

Fathers and Childbirth
Siblings and Childbirth

Parents may want to consider having the child present at the birth. Many family-centered hospitals, birth centers, and home births make this option available. Some parents wish to minimize or avoid separation from the older child, so they choose to give birth where sibling involvement is possible. These parents feel that, if there is no separation, the child will not develop separation anxiety and will not see the new baby as someone who took the mother away. Sibling involvement in the birth may enhance the attachment between the older child and the new baby. On the other hand, some children may not want to participate in the birthing process and should not be forced into it. Some preschool children may be overwhelmed by the whole process, and older children may feel embarrassed.

If the birth will be in a hospital with a typical stay of two to three days, parents need to consider the possibility that the child may feel separation anxiety by being separated from one or both parents. To ease the child's separation anxiety, the expectant mother should let the child know approximately when she will be going to the hospital, should tour the hospital with the child if possible, and, when labor begins, should tell the child where she is going. Before birth, the expectant mother can increase the father's role as a caregiver, if he is not already responsible for much of the child's daily care. Parents can ask about the regulations at the hospital or birth setting and, if possible, have the child visit the mother there. As sibling visitation has become recognized as a positive emotional experience for the entire family, hospitals are increasingly allowing children to visit their mothers after the birth of the baby. Some hospitals even allow siblings in the recovery room to see both the mother and the newborn.

In addition to being separated from the mother, the child now has to cope with another emotionally taxing experience: the permanent presence of a crying newborn who requires extensive care and attention from the mother. Life is never the same for the older child after the newborn arrives. Parents who once might have given complete attention to the child now suddenly have less time available for the child—all because of the new sibling. It is not unusual for a child to ask a parent, "When are you going to take it back to the hospital?" Many children engage in regressive and attention-seeking behaviors after a new sibling arrives, such as sucking their thumb, directing anger at their parents or the baby (hitting, biting, or throwing things), wanting a bottle or the mother's breasts for themselves, or bed-wetting. These behaviors are natural and represent the child's way of coping with stress. Parents don't need to worry about these behaviors unless they persist after the child has had a reasonable amount of time to adjust to the new baby. To help the child cope with the arrival of a new baby, parents can (Simkin, Whalley, & Keppler, 2001):

- Read books to the child about living with a new baby before and after the birth.
- Plan for time alone with the older child and do what he or she wants to do.
- Use the time when the baby is asleep and the parent is rested to give special attention to the older child.
- Give a gift to the older child in the hospital or at home.
- Tell the baby about his or her special older brother or sister when the older sibling is listening.

How can parents prepare a child for the birth of a sibling?

Review and Reflect ● LEARNING GOAL 1

1 **Discuss the stages, transitions, and decisions involved in birth.**

Review
- What are the three stages involved in the birth process?
- What is the fetus/newborn transition like?
- What are some childbirth strategies and decisions?

Reflect
- Which childbirth strategies do you plan to follow if you have a child? Why?

2   HOW DO LOW BIRTH WEIGHT INFANTS DEVELOP?

| Preterm and Small for Date Infants | Long-Term Outcomes for Low Birth Weight Infants | Nurturing Preterm Infants |

A **low birth weight infant** weighs less than 5½ pounds at birth. *Very low birth weight infants* weigh less than 3 pounds and *extremely low birth weight infants* weigh less than 2 pounds (Tang and others, 2004). In 2000, 66 percent of all infant deaths in the United States occurred among the 7.6 percent of infants born with low birth weight (Mac-Dorman & others, 2002).

During the last two decades, the number of low birth weight infants in the United States has increased (Cuevas & others, 2005; National Center for Health Statistics, 2004). This may be due to the rising number of adolescents having babies (especially in the 1980s), drug abuse, poor nutrition, more preterm deliveries, and induction of labor.

Equal opportunity for life is an American ideal that is not fulfilled at birth. In 2001, 12.9 percent of African American babies were born with low birth weight compared with 6.7 percent of non-Latino White babies and 6.5 percent of Latino babies (National Center for Health Statistics, 2002). A similar disparity for African Americans occurs in the number of infants born that are alive but who die in the first year of life.

In the developing world, low birth weight stems mainly from the mother's poor health and nutrition (Lasker & others, 2005). Diseases such as diarrhea and malaria, which are common in developing countries, can impair fetal growth if the mother becomes infected while she is pregnant. In developed countries, cigarette smoking during pregnancy is the leading cause of low birth weight (Ashdown-Lambert, 2005; Okah, Cai, & Hoff, 2005; UNICEF, 2001). In both developed and developing countries, adolescents who give birth when their bodies have yet to fully mature are at risk for having low birth weight babies (Ashdown-Lambert, 2005; Bacak & others, 2005).

Preterm and Small for Date Infants

Low birth weight babies may be preterm or simply small for their date of birth. **Preterm infants** are those born three weeks or more before the pregnancy has reached its full term. This means that the term "preterm" is given to an infant who is born at 35 weeks or less after conception. Most preterm babies are also low birth weight babies. The preterm birth rate in the United States increased 27 percent from 1982 to 2002 (National Center for Health Statistics, 2004). As shown in figure 5.2, approximately 12 percent of U.S. births are now preterm. The increase in preterm birth is likely to such factors as the increasing number of births to women 35 years and older, increasing rates of multiple births, increased management of maternal and fetal conditions, substance abuse (tobacco, alcohol), and increased stress (Ananth & others, 2005; Petrini, 2004).

A short gestation period does not necessarily harm an infant. It is distinguished from retarded prenatal growth, in which the fetus has been damaged (Jordan & others, 2005; Kopp, 1992). The neurological development of a preterm baby continues after birth on approximately the same timetable as if the infant still were in the womb. For example, consider a preterm baby born 30 weeks after conception. At 38 weeks, approximately two months after birth, this infant shows the same level of brain development as a 38-week fetus who is yet to be born.

Small for date infants (also called **small for gestational age infants**) are those whose birth weight is below normal when the length of pregnancy is considered. Small for date infants may be preterm or full term. They weigh less than 90 percent of all babies of the same gestational age. Inadequate nutrition and smoking by the pregnant woman are among the main factors in producing small for date infants

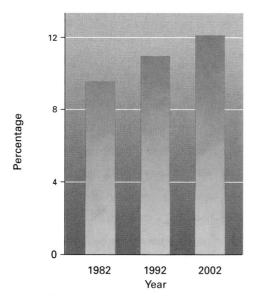

FIGURE 5.2 **Preterm births in the United States: 1982–2002.** *Source: National Center for Health Statistics (2004).*

low birth weight infant Weighs less than 5½ pounds at birth.

preterm infants Babies born three weeks or more before the pregnancy has reached its full term.

small for date (small for gestational age) infants Babies whose birth weight is below normal when the length of pregnancy is considered.

(England & others, 2001; Hayakawa & others, 2003; Ventura & others, 2003). One recent study found that small for date infants had more than a fourfold risk for death (Regev & others, 2004).

Long-Term Outcomes for Low Birth Weight Infants

Although most low birth weight infants are normal and healthy, as a group they have more health and developmental problems than normal birth weight infants (Drake & Walker, 2004; Gale & Martin, 2004; Hintz & others, 2005; Litt & others, 2005; Pietz & others, 2004). The number and severity of these problems increase as birth weight decreases (Kilbride, Thorstad, & Daily, 2004). With the improved survival rates for infants who are born very early and very small come increases in severe brain damage. Cerebral palsy and other forms of brain injury are highly correlated with brain weight—the lower the brain weight, the greater the likelihood of brain injury (Watemberg & others, 2002). Approximately 7 percent of moderately low birth weight infants (3 pounds 5 ounces to 5 pounds 8 ounces) have brain injuries. This figure increases to 20 percent for the smallest newborns (1 pound 2 ounces to 3 pounds 5 ounces). Low birth weight infants are also more likely than normal birth weight infants to have lung or liver diseases.

At school age, children who were born low in birth weight are more likely than their normal birth weight counterparts to have a learning disability, attention deficit hyperactivity disorder, or breathing problems such as asthma (Taylor, Klein, & Hack, 1994). Very low birth weight children have more learning problems and lower levels of achievement in reading and math than moderately low birth weight children (Litt & others, 2005). Approximately 50 percent of all low birth weight children are enrolled in special education programs. One recent study of extremely low birth weight infants in four locations (New Jersey, Ontario, Bavaria, and Holland) found that when they were 8 to 11 years old more than half required special education and/or repeated a grade (Saigal & others, 2003).

Do these negative outcomes of low birth weight continue into adolescence? In one study, the outcomes at middle school age of being very low birth weight (under 750 grams) were examined (Taylor & others, 2000). When compared with a control group that was born at full term, the low birth weight adolescents had lower cognitive skills, weaker academic records, and showed more behavioral problems (see figure 5.3). In another recent study, 17-year-olds who were born with low birth weight were 50 percent more likely than normal birth weight individuals to have reading and mathematics deficits (Breslau, Paneth, & Lucia, 2004). However, the majority of very low birth weight infants in another study, who weighed just over 2 pounds at birth on average, had improved IQ test scores from 3 years of age (average IQ = 90) to 8 (average IQ = 95) years of age (Ment & others, 2003). Despite the improvement, the IQ scores of the very low birth weight infants were still in the low average range. The very low birth weight infants who improved the most had received early speech therapy and had highly educated mothers. Note that not all of the adverse consequences can be attributed solely to being born low in birth weight. Some of the less severe but more common developmental and physical delays occur because many low birth weight children come from disadvantaged environments.

Some of the devastating effects of being born low in birth weight can be reversed (Strathearn, 2003). Intensive enrichment programs that provide medical and educational services for both the parents and the child have been shown to improve short-term developmental outcomes for low birth weight children (Kleberg, Westrup, & Stjernqvist, 2000). Federal laws mandate that services for school-age children with disabilities (which include medical, educational, psychological, occupational, and physical care) be expanded to include family-based care for infants. At present, these services are aimed at children born with severe congenital disabilities. The availability of services for moderately low birth weight children who do not have severe physical problems varies from state to state, but generally these services are not available.

A "kilogram kid," weighing less than 2.3 pounds at birth. *What are some possible outcomes for low birth weight infants?*

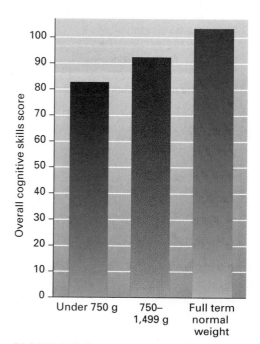

FIGURE 5.3 **Comparison of the Overall Cognitive Processing Skills of Middle School Students Who Were Born Low Birth Weight or Normal Birth Weight** *The overall cognitive skills score was a composite score arrived at by combining students' scores on several cognitive measures such as the Kaufman Assessment Battery for Children (an intelligence test), analogies (a task that requires individuals to understand how concepts are similar), and other tests.*

The possibility that hormonal treatments can decrease the number of preterm births has recently been investigated. In one recent study, weekly injections of the hormone progesterone, which is naturally produced by the ovaries, lowered the rate of preterm births by one-third (Meis, 2003). High-risk women could now receive the hormone treatment but researchers are recommending that further research first be conducted to determine the safest and most effective way to administer the drug. Let's now further explore some ways to improve the outcomes for preterm infants.

Nurturing Preterm Infants

Just three decades ago, preterm infants were perceived to be too fragile to cope well with environmental stimulation, and the recommendation was to handle such infants as little as possible. The climate of opinion changed when the adverse effects of *maternal deprivation* (mothers' neglect of their infants) became known and was interpreted to include a lack of stimulation. A number of research studies followed that indicated a "more is better" approach in the stimulation of preterm infants. Today, however, experts on infant development argue that preterm infant care is far too complex to be described only in terms of amount of stimulation (Liaw, 2000).

Appropriate stimulation of preterm infants may vary with infants' conceptual age, illness, and individual makeup (Lester & Tronick, 1990). A preterm infant's immature brain is less likely to be able to handle excessive, inappropriate, or mistimed stimulation than the full-term infant's brain. Infants born very early should probably be protected from stimulation that could destabilize their condition. As preterm infants becomes less fragile and approach term, their behavioral cues help to determine appropriate interventions. If the infant responds to stimulation in a stressful or avoidant manner, the stimulation probably should be terminated, whereas positive responses suggest that stimulation likely is appropriate.

Massage   Throughout history and in many cultures, infant massage has been used by caregivers (Spencer, 2004). In India, Africa, and Asia, infants are routinely massaged by parents or other family members for several months after birth.

Many preterm infants experience less touch than full-term infants because they are isolated in temperature-controlled incubators (Beachy, 2003). However, the research of Tiffany Field (1998, 2001, 2002, 2003; Field, Hernandez-Reif, & Freedman, 2004) has led to a surge of interest in the role that massage might play in improving the developmental outcomes of preterm infants. To read about her research, see the Caring for Children interlude.

www.mhhe.com/santrock9

Touch Research Institute

CARING FOR CHILDREN

The Power of Touch and Massage in Development

Picture Sarah, a preterm tiny infant lying in an incubator. Her breathing is erratic, she is unable to breast or bottle feed on her own, and she cannot regulate her body temperature. Sarah lies in a sea of wires and tubes, has very little close human contact, and lacks warm nurturing stimulation.

Babies like Sarah stimulated Tiffany Field to investigate the benefits of massage therapy for preterm infants. In Field's first study in this area, the infants were firmly stroked with the palms of the hands, three times daily, for 15-minute periods (Field & others, 1986). Did the study have positive results? The answer is yes. Massage therapy led to a 47 percent greater weight gain than standard medical treatment (see figure 5.4). The massaged infants were also more active and alert than preterm infants who were not massaged, and they performed better on developmental tests.

In later studies, Field demonstrated the benefits of massage therapy for infants with a variety of problems. For example, in one study, Field (1992) massaged preterm

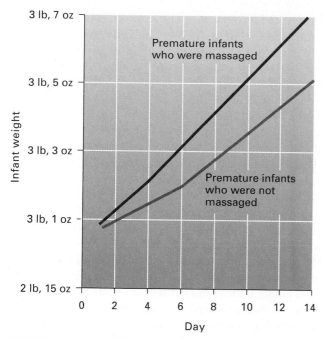

FIGURE 5.4 Weight Gain Comparison of Premature Infants Who Were Massaged or Not Massaged The graph shows that the mean daily weight gain of premature infants who were massaged was greater than for premature infants who were not massaged.

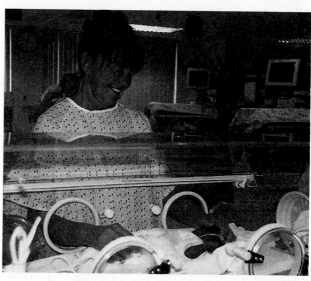

Shown here is Dr. Tiffany Field massaging a newborn infant. *What types of infants has massage therapy been shown to help?*

infants exposed to cocaine in utero. These infants gained weight and improved their scores on developmental tests. In another investigation, newborns born to HIV-positive mothers were randomly assigned to a massage therapy group or to a control group that did not receive the therapy (Scafidi & Field, 1996). Infants in the massage therapy group received three 15-minute massages daily for 10 days. The massaged infants showed superior performance on a wide range of assessments, including daily weight gain. Another study investigated 1- to 3-month-old infants born to depressed adolescent mothers (Field & others, 1996). The infants of depressed mothers who received massage therapy had lower stress—as well as improved emotionality, sociability, and soothability—compared with the nonmassaged infants of depressed mothers.

In a recent review of massage therapy with preterm infants, Field and her colleagues (2004) concluded that the most consistent findings involve (1) increased weight gain and (2) earlier discharge from the hospital that ranges from three to six days.

Why might massage improve the developmental outcomes of preterm infants? The precise mechanism behind the positive effects of massaging preterm infants is not completely known. However, massage directly stimulates the musculoskeletal, nervous, and circulatory systems. Further, massage promotes weight gain, moderates infants' stress hormones (such as cortisol), and improves immune system functioning.

In other studies by Field and her colleagues, infants are not the only ones who may benefit from massage therapy. They have demonstrated the benefits of massage therapy for reducing women's labor pain (Field, Hernandez-Rief, Taylor, & others, 1997), for children with arthritis (Field, Hernandez-Rief, Seligman, & others, 1997), for asthmatic children (Field, Henteleff, & others, 1998), for autistic children (Field, Lasko, & others, 1997), and for adolescents with attention deficit hyperactivity disorder (Field, Quintino, & others, 1998).

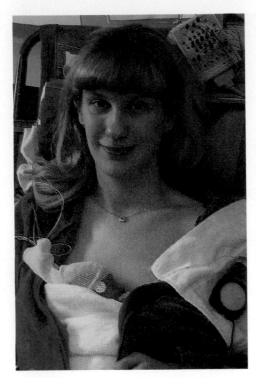

A new mother practicing kangaroo care. *What is kangaroo care?*

Kangaroo Care   **Kangaroo care** is a way of holding an infant so that there is skin-to-skin contact (Ludington-Hoe & Golant, 1993). The baby, wearing only a diaper, is held upright against the parent's bare chest. Kangaroo care is typically practiced for two to three hours per day, skin-to-skin over an extended time period in early infancy (Feldman & others, 2003).

The label *kangaroo care* was chosen to describe this strategy because the method is similar to how a kangaroo is carried by its mother. It is estimated that more than 200 neonatal intensive-care units practice kangaroo care today compared with less than 70 in the early 1990s. One recent survey found that 82 percent of neonatal intensive-care units use kangaroo care in the United States today (Engler & others, 2002).

Why use kangaroo care with preterm infants? Researchers have found that the close physical contact with the parent can help to stabilize the preterm infant's heartbeat, temperature, and breathing (Dodd, 2005; Feldman & Eidelman, 2003; Ferber & Makhoul, 2004). Preterm infants often have difficulty coordinating their breathing and heart rate. Researchers also have found that mothers who use kangaroo care often have more success with breast feeding and improve their milk supply. Further, preterm infants who experience kangaroo care have longer periods of sleep, gain more weight, decrease their crying, have longer periods of alertness, and earlier hospital discharge (Lehtonen & Martin, 2004; Ludington-Hoe & others, 2004; Worku & Kassir, 2005). One recent study compared 26 low birth weight infants who received kangaroo care with 27 low birth weight infants who received standard medical/nursing care (Ohgi & others, 2002). At both 6 and 12 months of age, the kangaroo care infants were able to better regulate their body states, had better orientation, and had a more positive mood. Another recent study found that kangaroo care preterm infants had better control of their arousal, more effectively attended to stimuli, and showed sustained exploration in a toy session than a control group of preterm infants who did not receive kangaroo care (Feldman & others, 2002). Increasingly kangaroo care is being recommended for full-term infants as well (Johnson, 2005).

Review and Reflect • LEARNING GOAL 2

 Characterize the development of low birth weight infants.

Review
- What is a low birth weight infant? How can preterm and small for date infants be distinguished?
- What are the long-term outcomes for low birth weight infants?
- What is known about the roles of stimulation, massage, and contact with preterm infants?

Reflect
- What can be done to reduce the United States' high rates of low birth weight babies?

---

3   WHAT ARE THREE MEASURES OF NEONATAL HEALTH AND RESPONSIVENESS?

kangaroo care A way of holding an infant so that there is skin-to-skin contact.

Apgar Scale A widely used method to assess the health of newborns at one and five minutes after birth. The Apgar Scale evaluates infants' heart rate, respiratory effort, muscle tone, body color, and reflex irritability.

Now that we have studied a number of ideas about preterm infants and ways that they can be helped, let's turn our attention to the way that the newborn's health and responsiveness are assessed. The **Apgar Scale** is a method widely used to assess the health of newborns at one and five minutes after birth. The Apgar Scale evaluates infants' heart rate, respiratory effort, muscle tone, body color, and reflex irritability. An obstetrician or a nurse does the evaluation and gives the newborn a score, or reading, of 0, 1, or 2 on each of these five health signs (see figure 5.5). A total score of 7 to

Score	0	1	2	
Heart rate	Absent	Slow—less than 100 beats per minute	Fast—100 to 140 beats per minute	
Respiratory effort	No breathing for more than one minute	Irregular and slow	Good breathing with normal crying	
Muscle tone	Limp and flaccid	Weak, inactive, but some flexion of extremities	Strong, active motion	
Body color	Blue and pale	Body pink, but extremities blue	Entire body pink	
Reflex irritability	No response	Grimace	Coughing, sneezing, and crying	

FIGURE 5.5 The Apgar Scale

10 indicates that the newborn's condition is good. A score of 5 indicates there may be developmental difficulties. A score of 3 or below signals an emergency and indicates that the baby might not survive. The Apgar Scale is especially good at assessing the newborn's ability to respond to the stress of delivery, labor, and the new environment (Decca & others, 2004; Gojnic & others, 2004; Waltman & others, 2004). The Apgar Scale also identifies high-risk infants who need immediate medical intervention.

In one recent study, Apgar results from more than 145,000 babies born across a decade were analyzed (Casey, McIntire, & Leveno, 2001). Based on scores obtained five minutes after birth, the Apgar was an excellent predictor of which infants would survive or die in the first month of life.

To evaluate the newborn more thoroughly, the **Brazelton Neonatal Behavioral Assessment Scale (NBAS)** is performed within 24 to 36 hours after birth to evaluate the newborn's neurological development, reflexes, and reactions to people. The Brazelton scale assesses what a newborn can do in a number of areas of development (Field & others, 2003; Keenan, Gunthorpe, & Young, 2002). The Brazelton is not routinely done and is often not available (since it requires a trained assessor) even if requested. It is primarily used for research purposes although there is a movement to use it as a clinical tool for parent education.

When the Brazelton is given, the newborn is treated as an active participant, and the score attained is based on the newborn's best performance. Sixteen reflexes, such as sneezing, blinking, and rooting, are assessed, along with reactions to circumstances, such as the infant's reaction to a rattle. (We will have more to say about reflexes in chapter 6, when we discuss physical development in infancy.) The examiner rates the newborn on each of 27 categories (see figure 5.6). As an indication of how detailed the ratings are, consider item 15: "cuddliness." Nine categories are involved in assessing this item, with infant behavior scored on a continuum that ranges from the infant's being very resistant to being held to the infant's being extremely cuddly and clinging. The Brazelton scale not only is used as a sensitive index of neurological competence in the week after birth, but it also is used widely as a measure in many research studies on infant development (Feldman & Eidelman, 2003; Myers & others, 2003; Nakai & others, 2004; Ohgi, Akiyama, & Fukuda, 2005). In scoring the Brazelton scale, T. Berry Brazelton and his colleagues (Brazelton, Nugent, & Lester, 1987) categorize the 27 items into four categories—physiological, motoric, state, and interaction. They also classify the baby in global terms, such as "worrisome," "normal," or "superior," based on these categories (Nugent & Brazelton, 2000).

Brazelton Neonatal Behavioral Assessment Scale (NBAS) A test performed within 24 to 36 hours after birth to assess newborns' neurological development, reflexes, and reactions to people.

1. Response decrement to repeated visual stimuli
2. Response decrement to rattle
3. Response decrement to bell

4. Response decrement to pinprick
5. Orienting response to inanimate visual stimuli
6. Orienting response to inanimate auditory stimuli

7. Orienting response to inanimate visual and auditory stimuli
8. Orienting response to animate visual stimuli—examiner's face
9. Orienting response to animate auditory stimuli—examiner's voice
10. Orienting response to animate visual and auditory stimuli
11. Quality and duration of alert periods
12. General muscle tone—in resting and in response to being handled, passive, and active

13. Motor activity
14. Traction responses as the infant is pulled to sit
15. Cuddliness—responses to being cuddled by examiner

16. Defensive movements—reactions to a cloth over the infant's face
17. Consolability with intervention by examiner
18. Peak of excitement and capacity to control self
19. Rapidity of buildup to crying state
20. Irritability during examination
21. General assessment of kind and degree of activity

22. Tremulousness
23. Amount of startling
24. Lability of skin color—measuring autonomic lability

25. Lability of states during entire examination
26. Self-quieting activity—attempts to console self and control state
27. Hand-to-mouth activity

FIGURE 5.6 The 27 Categories on the Brazelton Neonatal Behavioral Assessment Scale (NBAS)

A very low Brazelton score can indicate brain damage, or it can reflect stress to the brain that may heal in time. However, if an infant merely seems sluggish in responding to social circumstances, parents are encouraged to give the infant attention and become more sensitive to the infant's needs. Parents are shown how the newborn can respond to people and how to stimulate such responses. Researchers have found that the social interaction skills of both high-risk infants and healthy, responsive infants can be improved through such communication with parents (Worobey & Belsky, 1982).

Recently, Brazelton, along with Barry Lester and Edward Tronick, developed a new neonatal assessment, the **Neonatal Intensive Care Unit Network Neurobehavioral Scale (NNNS)** (Lester, Tronick, & Brazelton, 2004). Described as an "offspring" of the NBAS, the NNNS provides a more comprehensive analysis of the newborn's behavior, neurological and stress responses, and regulatory capacities (Brazelton, 2004). The NNNS was created to assess the at-risk infant, especially those who are preterm (although it may not be appropriate for those less than 30 weeks' gestational age) and/or substance-exposed whereas the NBAS was developed to assess the behavior of normal, healthy, term infants (Miller-Loncar & others, 2005). According to Brazelton (2004), although initially created to evaluate at-risk infants, the NNNS is appropriate for assessing normal, healthy, full-term infants.

For clinical purposes in assessing high-risk infants, contributions of the NBAS include (Boukydis, Bigsby, & Lester, 2004, p. 680):

- Items to assess the infant's capacity for regulating arousal, "responsiveness to stimulation, self-soothing, and tolerance of handling."

- The Stress/Abstinence Scale, which provides information about the physiological and "behavioral manifestations of drug dependence or environment-related stress."

Neonatal Intensive Care Unit Network Neurobehavioral Scale (NNNS) An "offspring" of the NBAS, the NNNS provides a more comprehensive analysis of the newborn's behavior, neurological and stress responses, and regulatory capacities.

Review and Reflect • LEARNING GOAL 3

3 **Describe three measures of neonatal health and responsiveness.**

Review
- How can the Apgar Scale, the Brazelton Neonatal Behavioral Assessment Scale, and the Neonatal Intensive Care Unit Network Neurobehavioral Scale be characterized?

Reflect
- What information does the Brazelton assessment provide that the Apgar does not? If you had a newborn child, would you want it to be assessed with both of these measures? Explain.

4 WHAT HAPPENS DURING THE POSTPARTUM PERIOD?

| Physical Adjustments | Emotional and Psychological Adjustments | Bonding |

Many health professionals believe that the best postpartum care is family centered, using the family's resources to support an early and smooth adjustment to the newborn by all family members. What is the postpartum period?

The **postpartum period** is the period after childbirth, or delivery. It is a time when the woman's body adjusts, both physically and psychologically, to the process of childbearing. It lasts for about six weeks or until the body has completed its adjustment and has nearly returned to its prepregnant state. Some health professionals refer to the postpartum period as the "fourth trimester." Although the postpartum period does not necessarily cover three months, the "fourth trimester" demonstrates the idea of continuity and the importance of the first several months after birth for the mother.

The postpartum period is influenced by what preceded it. During pregnancy, the woman's body gradually adjusted to physical changes, but now it is forced to respond quickly. The method of delivery and circumstances surrounding the delivery affect the speed with which the woman's body readjusts during the postpartum period.

The postpartum period involves a great deal of adjustment and adaptation. The baby must be cared for; the mother needs to recover from childbirth; the mother has to learn how to take care of the baby; the mother needs to learn to feel good about herself as a mother; the father needs to learn how to take care of his recovering wife; the father needs to learn how to take care of the baby; and the father needs to learn how to feel good about himself as a father.

The postpartum period is a time of considerable adjustment and adaptation for both the mother and the father. *What are some of these adjustments?*

Physical Adjustments

The woman's body makes numerous physical adjustments in the first days and weeks after childbirth. For example, during the birth process she may have received an *episiotomy*, a surgical incision used to enlarge the vaginal opening and help accommodate the emerging baby's head. Stitches are used to close the cut and her body will need special care to effectively heal.

The new mother may have a great deal of energy or feel exhausted and let down. Most new mothers feel tired and need rest. Though these changes are normal, fatigue can undermine her sense of well-being and confidence in her ability to cope with a new baby and a new family life.

Involution is the process by which the uterus returns to its prepregnant size five or six weeks after birth. Immediately following birth, the uterus weighs 2 to 3 pounds, and the fundus can be felt midway between the naval and the pubic bone. By the end of five or six weeks, the uterus weighs 2 to 3½ ounces and it has returned to its prepregnancy size. Nursing the baby helps contract the uterus at a rapid rate.

After delivery, a woman's body undergoes sudden and dramatic changes in hormone production. When the placenta is delivered, estrogen and progesterone levels drop steeply and remain low until the ovaries start producing hormones again. The woman will probably begin menstruating again in four to eight weeks if she is not breast feeding. If she is breast feeding, she might not menstruate for several months, though ovulation can occur during this time. The first several menstrual periods following delivery may be heavier than usual, but periods soon return to normal.

Some women and men want to resume sexual intercourse as soon as possible after the birth. Others feel constrained or afraid. A sore perineum (the area between the anus and vagina in the female), a demanding baby, lack of help, and extreme fatigue affect a woman's ability to relax and to enjoy making love. Physicians often

postpartum period The period after childbirth when the mother adjusts, both physically and psychologically, to the process of childbearing. This period lasts for about six weeks, or until her body has completed its adjustment and has returned to a near-prepregnant state.

involution The process by which the uterus returns to its prepregnant size.

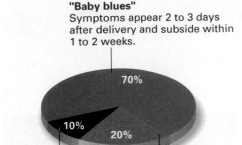

"Baby blues"
Symptoms appear 2 to 3 days after delivery and subside within 1 to 2 weeks.

70%

10%

20%

Postpartum depression
Symptoms linger for weeks or months and interfere with daily functioning.

No symptoms

FIGURE 5.7 Percentage of U.S. Women Who Experience "Baby Blues" and Postpartum Depression

www.mhhe.com/santrockc9

Postpartum Adjustment
Mothers, Fathers, and Newborns
Postpartum Resources

postpartum depression Strong feelings of sadness, anxiety, or despair in new mothers that make it difficult for them to carry out daily tasks.

recommend that women refrain from having sexual intercourse for approximately six weeks following the birth of the baby. However, it is probably safe to have sexual intercourse when the stitches heal, vaginal discharge stops, and the woman feels like it.

If the woman regularly engaged in conditioning exercises during pregnancy, exercise will help her recover her former body contour and strength during the postpartum period. With a caregiver's approval, she can begin some exercises as soon as one hour after delivery. A recent study found that women who maintained or increased their exercise from prepregnancy to postpartum had better maternal well-being than women who engaged in no exercise or decreased their exercise from prepregnancy to postpartum (Blum, Beaudoin, & Caton-Lemos, 2005). In addition to recommending exercise in the postpartum period for women, health professionals also increasingly recommend that women practice the relaxation techniques they used during pregnancy and childbirth. Five minutes of slow breathing on a stressful day in the postpartum period can relax and refresh the new mother, as well as the new baby.

Emotional and Psychological Adjustments

Emotional fluctuations are common on the part of the mother in the postpartum period. These emotional fluctuations may be due to any of a number of factors: hormonal changes, fatigue, inexperience or lack of confidence with newborn babies, or the extensive time and demands involved in caring for a newborn. For some women, the emotional fluctuations decrease within several weeks after the delivery and are a minor aspect of their motherhood. For others, they are more long-lasting and may produce feelings of anxiety, depression, and difficulty in coping with stress (Bloch & others, 2005, in press; Cooper & others, 2003; Goodman, 2004; Hall, 2005). Mothers who have such feelings, even when they are getting adequate rest, may benefit from professional help in dealing with their problems (Horowitz & Goodman, 2005; Marks, Siddle, & Warwick, 2003; Seehusen & others, 2005).

Postpartum Depression   As shown in figure 5.7, about 70 percent of new mothers have what are called "baby blues." About two to three days after birth, they begin to feel depressed, anxious, and upset. These feelings may come and go for several days after the birth, often peaking about three to five days after the birth, but they usually go away after one or two weeks without treatment. Women with **postpartum depression,** however, have such strong feelings of sadness, anxiety, or despair that they have trouble coping with their daily tasks. Postpartum depression involves a major depressive episode that typically occurs about four weeks after delivery. Without treatment, postpartum depression may become worse and last for many months (Bonari & others, 2004; Clay & Seehusen, 2004; Dennis, 2004; Thoppil, Riutcel, & Nalesnik, 2005). Postpartum depression occurs in approximately 10 percent of new mothers. Between 25 and 50 percent of these depressed new mothers have episodes that last six months or longer (Beck, 2002). If untreated, approximately 25 percent of these women are still depressed a year later.

Here are some of the signs that may indicate a need for professional help in treating postpartum adaptation:

- Excessive worrying
- Depression
- Extreme changes in appetite
- Crying spells
- Inability to sleep

Though the hormonal changes occurring after childbirth are believed to play a role in postpartum depression, the precise nature of this hormonal role has not been identified (Dennis & Stewart, 2004). Estrogen has been shown to have positive effects in treating postpartum depression for some women, but the possible negative side effects of estrogen are problematic (Grigoriadis & Kennedy, 2002; Tsigos & Chrousos,

2002). Several antidepressant drugs are effective in treating postpartum depression and appear to be safe for breast-feeding women (Sharma, 2002). Psychotherapy, especially cognitive therapy, has also been found to be an effective treatment of postpartum depression (Beck, 2002; Kennedy, Beck, & Driscoll, 2002; Lasiuk & Ferguson, 2005).

Postpartum depression can affect not only the new mother but also her child (Stanley, Murray, & Stein, 2004). For example, in one recent study, a sample of 570 women and their infants were assessed three months after delivery (Rightti-Veltema & others, 2002). Ten percent of the mothers were classified as experiencing postpartum depression on the basis of their responses to the Edinburgh Postnatal Depression Scale (Cox, Holden, & Sagovsky, 1987). The depressed mothers had less vocal and visual communication with their infant, touched the infant less, and smiled less at the infant than did nondepressed mothers. The negative effects on the infant involved eating or sleeping problems.

Staying at Home or Working   A special concern of many new mothers is whether they should stay home with the baby or go back to work. Some mothers want to return to work as soon as possible after the infant is born; others want to stay home with the infant for several months, then return to work; others want to stay home for a year before they return to work; and yet others did not work outside the home prior to the baby's arrival and do not plan to do so in the future.

Many women, because of a variety of pressures—societal, career, financial—do not have the option of staying at home after their babies are born. However, for women who have to make the choice, the decision-making process is often very difficult (Delmore-Ko & others, 2000).

The Father's Adjustment   The father also undergoes considerable adjustment in the postpartum period, although in many cases he will be away at work all day, whereas the mother will be at home, at least in the first few weeks (de Montigny & Lacharite, 2004; Goodman, 2004; Johnson & Baker, 2004). One of the most common reactions of the husband is the feeling that the baby comes first and gets all of the attention. In some marriages, the man may have had that relationship with his wife and now feels that he has been replaced by the baby. Some reports have surfaced that men can experience postpartum depression, especially when their partners have postpartum depression (Goodman, 2004).

One strategy to help the man's postpartum reaction is for the parents to set aside some special time to be together with each other. The father's postpartum reaction also likely will be improved if he has taken childbirth classes with his wife and is an active participant in caring for the baby.

Important factors for both the mother and the father are the time and thought that go into being a competent parent of a young infant (Cowan & Cowan, 2000; Hipwell & others, 2005; McVeigh, Baafi & Williamson, 2002). Both the mother and the father need to become aware of the young infant's developmental needs—physical, psychological, and emotional. The new parents need to develop a sensitive, comfortable relationship with the baby. We will have more to say about the transition to parenting and the mother's and father's role in infant development in chapter 8.

Bonding

A special component of the parent-infant relationship is **bonding,** the formation of connection, especially a physical bond between parents and newborn in the period shortly after birth. Some physicians believe that this period shortly after birth is critical in development. During this time, the parents and child need to form an important emotional attachment that provides a foundation for optimal development in years to come (Kennell & McGrath, 1999). Special interest in bonding stems from concern by pediatricians that the circumstances surrounding delivery often separate mothers and

bonding A close connection, especially a physical bond between parents and their newborn in the period shortly after birth.

A mother bonds with her infant moments after it is born. *How critical is bonding for the development of social competence later in childhood?*

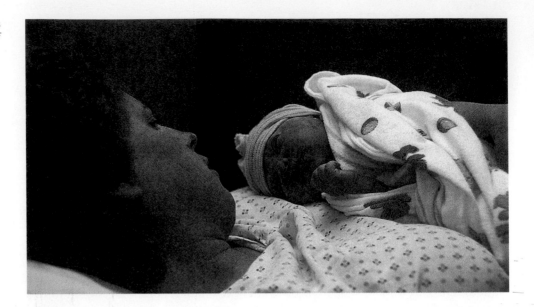

their infants, preventing or making difficult the development of a bond. The pediatricians further argued that giving the mother drugs to make her delivery less painful may contribute to the lack of bonding. The drugs may make the mother drowsy, thus interfering with her ability to respond to and stimulate the newborn. Advocates of bonding also assert that preterm infants are isolated from their mothers to an even greater degree than are full-term infants, thereby increasing their difficulty in bonding.

Is close contact between mothers and newborns critical for optimal development later in life? Although some research supports the bonding hypothesis (Klaus & Kennell, 1976), a body of research challenges the significance of the first few days of life as a critical period (Bakeman & Brown, 1980; Rode & others, 1981). Indeed, the extreme form of the bonding hypothesis—that the newborn must have close contact with the mother in the first few days of life to develop optimally—simply is not true.

Nonetheless, the weakness of the maternal-infant bonding research should not be used as an excuse to keep motivated mothers from interacting with their infants in the postpartum period. Such contact brings pleasure to many mothers. In some mother-infant pairs—including preterm infants, adolescent mothers, or mothers from disadvantaged circumstances—the practice of bonding may set in motion a climate for improved interaction after the mother and infant leave the hospital. For example, earlier in the chapter, we described an extensive form of skin-to-skin contact—kangaroo care—that is increasingly being used with preterm infants and has very positive outcomes.

In recognition of the belief that bonding may have a positive effect on getting the parental-infant relationship off to a good start, many hospitals now offer a *rooming-in* arrangement, in which the baby remains in the mother's room most of the time during its hospital stay. However, if parents choose not to use this rooming-in arrangement, the weight of the research evidence suggests that it will not harm the infant emotionally (Lamb, 1994).

4 **Explain the physical and psychological aspects of the postpartum period.**

Review
- What is the postpartum period? What physical adjustments on the part of the mother characterize the postpartum period?
- What emotional and psychological adjustments are involved on the part of the mother and the father in the postpartum period?
- What is bonding? Is it critical for optimal human development?

Reflect
- Should the mother stay home with the baby or go back to work if she has had a job outside of the home? If you think she should stay home, how long should she stay home with the baby before returning to work?

REACH YOUR LEARNING GOALS

BIRTH

1 WHAT HAPPENS DURING THE BIRTH PROCESS?

Stages of the Birth Process

The Fetus/Newborn Transition

Childbirth Strategies and Decisions

2 HOW DO LOW BIRTH WEIGHT INFANTS DEVELOP?

Preterm and Small for Date Infants

Long-Term Outcomes for Low Birth Weight Infants

Nurturing Preterm Infants

3 WHAT ARE THREE MEASURES OF NEONATAL HEALTH AND RESPONSIVENESS?

4 WHAT HAPPENS DURING THE POSTPARTUM PERIOD?

Physical Adjustments

Emotional and Psychological Adjustments

Bonding

SUMMARY

1 Discuss the stages, transitions, and decisions involved in birth.

- The first stage of birth lasts about 12 to 14 hours for a woman having her first child. The cervix dilates to about 4 inches. The second stage begins when the baby's head starts to move through the cervix and ends with the baby's complete emergence. The third stage is afterbirth.

- In some cases, anoxia occurs. Anoxia involves an insufficient supply of oxygen in the fetus/newborn condition. Being born involves considerable stress but the baby is well prepared and adapted to handle the stress. Huge quantities of stress-related hormones (adrenaline and noradrenaline) are secreted during the fetus/newborn transition.

- In the United States, the vast majority of births occur in hospitals and are attended by physicians. Many hospitals now have birthing centers. Some women with good medical histories and who are at low risk for problem deliveries have babies at home. In many countries, such as Holland, much higher percentages of babies are born at home. Some births are attended by a midwife, and in many countries a doula attends. Among the methods of delivery are medicated, natural and prepared, and cesarean. The three basic kinds of drugs used in delivering a baby are analgesics, anesthesia, and oxytocics. Predicting how a particular drug will affect an individual pregnant woman and the fetus is difficult. Today the trend is toward using some medication during childbirth but keeping it to a minimum, if possible. The Lamaze method of childbirth is widely used in the United States. In the past several decades, fathers increasingly have participated in childbirth. In some cultures, the father is excluded from childbirth, as was the case in the United States until recently. Sibling preparation includes providing the child with information about the pregnancy, birth, and life with a newborn that is realistic and appropriate for the child's age.

2 Characterize the development of low birth weight infants.

- Low birth weight infants weigh less than 5½ pounds at birth. Low birth weight babies may be preterm (born 3 weeks or more before the pregnancy has reached full term) or small for date (also called small for gestational age, which refers to infants whose birth weight is below normal when the length of pregnancy is considered). Small for date infants may be preterm or full term.

- Although most low birth weight babies are normal and healthy, as a group they have more health and developmental problems than full-term babies. The number and severity of the problems increases as birth weight decreases.

- Preterm infant care is much too complex to only be described only in terms of amount of stimulation. Preterm infants' responses vary according to their conceptual age, illness, and individual makeup. Intervention should be organized in the form of an individualized developmental plan. Massage therapy is increasingly being used with preterm infants and has positive outcomes. Kangaroo care, a way of holding a preterm infant so that there is skin-to-skin contact, has positive effects on preterm infants.

3 Describe three measures of neonatal health and responsiveness.

- For many years, the Apgar Scale has been used to assess the newborn's health. It is used one and five minutes after birth and assesses heart rate, respiratory effort, muscle tone, body color, and reflex irritability. The Brazelton Neonatal Behavioral Assessment is performed within 24 to 36 hours after birth to examine the newborn's neurological development, reflexes, and reactions to people. Recently, the Neonatal Intensive Care Unit Network Neurobehavioral Scale (NNNS) was constructed; it provides a more comprehensive analysis of the newborn's behavior, neurological and stress responses, and regulatory capacities.

4 Explain the physical and psychological aspects of the postpartum period.

- The postpartum period is the period after childbirth or delivery. It is a time when the woman adjusts, both physically and psychologically, to the process of childbearing. It lasts for about six weeks or until the body has completed its adjustment. Physical adjustments include fatigue, involution, hormonal changes that include a dramatic drop in estrogen and progesterone, deciding when to resume sexual intercourse, and exercises to recover former body contour and strength.

- The mother's emotional fluctuations are common in the postpartum period. These fluctuations may be due to hormonal changes, fatigue, inexperience or lack of confidence in caring for a newborn, or the extensive demands involved in caring for a newborn. For some, these emotional fluctuations are minimal and disappear in several weeks, but for others they can be more long-lasting. Postpartum depression involves such strong feelings of sadness, anxiety, or despair that new mothers have difficulty carrying out daily tasks. Postpartum depression affects approximately 10 percent of U.S.

women. The father also goes through a postpartum adjustment. He may feel that the baby now receives all his wife's attention. Some new fathers also may experience postpartum depression, especially if his partner has postpartum depression. Another adjustment for both the mother and the father is the time and thought that go into being a competent parent of a young infant.

- Bonding refers to the occurrence of a connection, especially a physical bond between parents and the newborn shortly after birth. Bonding has not been found to be critical in the development of a competent infant or child, although it may stimulate positive interaction between some mother-infant pairs.

KEY TERMS

afterbirth 141
anoxia 141
doula 143
analgesia 144
anesthesia 144
oxytocics 144
natural childbirth 145

prepared childbirth 145
cesarean delivery 145
breech position 145
low birth weight infant 148
preterm infants 148
small for date (small for
   gestational age) infants 148

kangaroo care 152
Apgar Scale 152
Brazelton Neonatal
   Behavioral Assessment
   Scale (NBAS) 153
Neonatal Intensive Care
   Unit Network

Neurobehavioral Scale
   (NNNS) 154
postpartum period 155
involution 155
postpartum depression 156
bonding 157

KEY PEOPLE

Grantley Dick-Read 145
Ferdinand Lamaze 145
Tiffany Field 150

T. Berry Brazelton, Barry
   Lester, and Edward
   Tronick 154

MAKING A DIFFERENCE

Effective Birth Strategies

Here are some birth strategies that may benefit the baby and the mother:

- *Take a childbirth class.* These classes provide information about the childbirth experience.
- *Become knowledgeable about different childbirth techniques.* We described a number of different childbirth techniques in this chapter, including Lamaze and using doulas. Obtain more detailed information about such techniques by reading a good book, such as *Pregnancy & Childbirth* (1997) by Tracie Hotchner.
- *At-risk infants can benefit from positive intervention.* Massage can improve the developmental outcome of at-risk infants. Intensive enrichment programs that include medical, educational, psychological, occupational, and physical domains can benefit low birth weight infants. Intervention with low birth weight infants should involve an individualized plan.
- *Involve the family in the birth process.* If they are motivated to participate, the husband and siblings can benefit from being involved in the birth process. A mother, sister, or friend can also provide support.
- *Know about the adaptation required in the postpartum period.* The postpartum period involves considerable adaptation and adjustment by the mother. This adjustment is both physical and emotional. Exercise and relaxation techniques can benefit mothers in the postpartum period. So can an understanding, supportive husband.

CHILDREN RESOURCES

ASPO/Lamaze

1840 Wilson Boulevard, Suite 204
Arlington, VA 22201
800–368–4404

ASPO/Lamaze provides information about the Lamaze method and taking or teaching Lamaze classes.

Birth: Issues in Perinatal Care

This multidisciplinary journal on perinatal care is written for health professionals and contains articles on research and clinical practice, review articles, and commentary.

Cesareans/Support, Education, and Concern (C/SEC)

22 Forest Road
Framingham, MA 01701
508–877–8266

C/SEC provides information and advice about cesarean birth.

Postpartum Support International (PSI)

927 North Kellogg Avenue
Santa Barbara, CA 93111
805–967–7636

PSI provides information about postpartum depression.

La Leche League International (LLLI)

9616 Minneapolis Avenue
Franklin Park, IL 60131
800–LA–LECHE

LLLI provides information about the benefits of breast feeding. It also publishes the very thorough book *The Womanly Art of Breastfeeding* (New York: Plume, 1991).

E-LEARNING TOOLS

Connect to **www.mhhe.com/santrockc9** to research the answers to complete these exercises. In addition, you'll find a number of other resources and valuable study tools for chapter 5, "Birth," on this website.

Taking It to the Net

1. Jessica and Eric have just given birth to their first child. Eric has noticed that since the birth three months ago, Jessica has seemed a bit withdrawn and sad. He remembers from their Lamaze classes that there is a condition called "Postpartum Depression." What can Eric do to help Jessica through this difficult time period?
2. The author of your text provides a summary of the most widely used birthing methods in the United States. What other birthing methods might a woman consider?
3. You have just given birth, and the nurse has informed you that tomorrow your baby will be assessed using the Brazelton Neonatal Behavioral Assessment Scale. What will your baby's experience be like during this assessment?

Health and Well-Being, Parenting, and Education

Build your decision-making skills by trying your hand at the health and well-being, parenting, and education exercises.

Video Clips

The Online Learning Center includes the following videos for this chapter:

1. *Midwifery*—1524
   A certified midwife discusses midwives and how they differ from obstetricians.
2. *Breast vs. Bottle Feeding*—1931
   A discussion of the numerous benefits of breast feeding over bottle feeding.
3. *Sudden Infant Death Syndrome*—1074
   Dr. Toby Milgrome describes Sudden Infant Death Syndrome (SIDS), the risk factors, and its suspected causes. As she describes the recommended sleep position for infants, we watch a newborn asleep on his back.

Section 3
INFANCY

Babies are such a nice way to start people.

—DON HEROLD
American Writer, 20th Century

As newborns, we were not empty-headed organisms. We had some basic reflexes, among them crying, kicking, and coughing. We slept a lot, and occasionally we smiled, although the meaning of our first smiles was not entirely clear. We ate and we grew. We crawled and then we walked, a journey of a thousand miles beginning with a single step. Sometimes we conformed; sometimes others conformed to us. Our development was a continuous creation of more complex forms. Our helpless kind demanded the meeting eyes of love. We juggled the necessity of curbing our will with becoming what we could will freely. Section 3 contains three chapters: "Physical Development in Infancy" (chapter 6), "Cognitive Development in Infancy" (chapter 7), and "Socioemotional Development in Infancy" (chapter 8).

Chapter 6

PHYSICAL DEVELOPMENT IN INFANCY

A baby is the most complicated object made by unskilled labor.

—ANONYMOUS

Images of Children
The Stories of Latonya and Ramona: Breast and Bottle Feeding in Africa

Latonya is a newborn baby in the African country of Ghana. The culture into which she was born discourages breast feeding. She has been kept apart from her mother and bottle fed in her first days of infancy. Manufacturers of infant formula provide the hospital where she was born with free or subsidized milk powder. Her mother has been persuaded to bottle feed rather than breast feed her. When her mother bottle feeds Latonya, she overdilutes the milk formula with unclean water. Latonya's feeding bottles also have not been sterilized. Latonya becomes very sick. She dies before her first birthday.

By contrast, Ramona's mother is breast feeding her. Ramona was born at a Nigerian hospital where a "baby-friendly" program has been initiated. In this program, babies are not separated from their mothers at birth, and the mothers are encouraged to breast feed them. The mothers are told of the perils of bottle feeding that involve unsafe water and unsterilized bottles. They also are informed about the advantages of breast milk, including its nutritious and hygienic qualities, its ability to immunize babies against common illnesses, and its role in reducing the mother's risk of breast and ovarian cancer. At 1 year of age, Ramona is very healthy.

In recent years, the World Health Organization and UNICEF have tried to reverse the trend of bottle feeding infants, which has emerged in many impoverished countries. Together, both organizations have instituted the "baby-friendly" program in many countries (Grant, 1997). They have also persuaded the International Association of Infant Formula Manufacturers to stop marketing their baby formulas to hospitals in countries where the governments support the baby-friendly initiatives.

Hospitals play a vital role in convincing mothers to breast feed their babies. For many years, maternity units favored bottle feeding and did not give mothers adequate information about the benefits of breast feeding. With the initiatives of the World Health Organization and UNICEF, practices are changing, but many places in the world still have not implemented the baby-friendly initiatives (UNICEF, 2004).

The advantages of breast feeding—especially in impoverished countries—are substantial. However, these advantages are now counterbalanced by the risk of passing HIV to the baby through breast milk because many mothers don't know that they are infected (Chama, Audu, & Kyari, 2004; Henderson, Martines, & de Zoysa, 2004; Thorne & Newell, 2004). In some areas of Africa more than 30 percent of mothers carry HIV. Another risk factor for passing HIV to babies is shared breast feeding. A recent study in the Central African country of Gabon found that 40 percent of nursing mothers breast fed other babies in addition to their own babies, increasing the chances of more babies being exposed to HIV through breast milk (Ramharter & others, 2004).

PREVIEW

It is very important for infants to get a healthy start. In this chapter, we will explore the following aspects of infants' development: physical growth, motor development, and sensory and perceptual development.

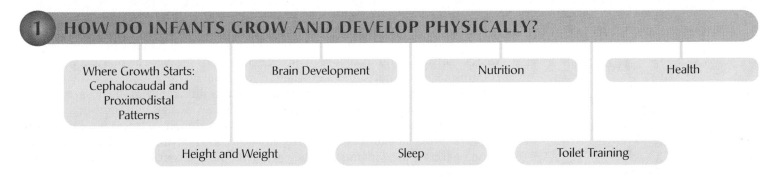

1 HOW DO INFANTS GROW AND DEVELOP PHYSICALLY?

> Where Growth Starts: Cephalocaudal and Proximodistal Patterns
>
> Brain Development
>
> Nutrition
>
> Health
>
> Height and Weight
>
> Sleep
>
> Toilet Training

Infants' physical development in the first two years of life is extensive. At birth, neonates have a gigantic head (relative to the rest of the body), which flops around uncontrollably. They also possess reflexes that are dominated by evolutionary movements. In the span of 12 months, infants become capable of sitting anywhere, standing, stooping, climbing, and usually walking. During the second year, growth decelerates, but rapid increases in activities such as running and climbing take place. Let's now examine the sequence of physical development in infancy in more detail.

International Society on Infant Studies
Development of the Brain

Where Growth Starts: Cephalocaudal and Proximodistal Patterns

The **cephalocaudal pattern** is the sequence in which the greatest growth always occurs at the top—the head—with physical growth in size, weight, and feature differentiation gradually working its way down from top to bottom (for example, shoulders, middle trunk, and so on). This same pattern occurs in the head area, because the top parts of the head—the eyes and brain—grow faster than the lower parts, such as the jaw. An extraordinary proportion of the total body is occupied by the head during prenatal development and early infancy (see figure 6.1). Later in the chapter you will see that sensory and motor development proceed according to the cephalocaudal principle. For example, infants see objects before they can control their trunk and they can use their hands long before they can crawl or walk.

> **cephalocaudal pattern** The sequence in which the greatest growth occurs at the top—the head—with physical growth in size, weight, and feature differentiation gradually working from top to bottom.

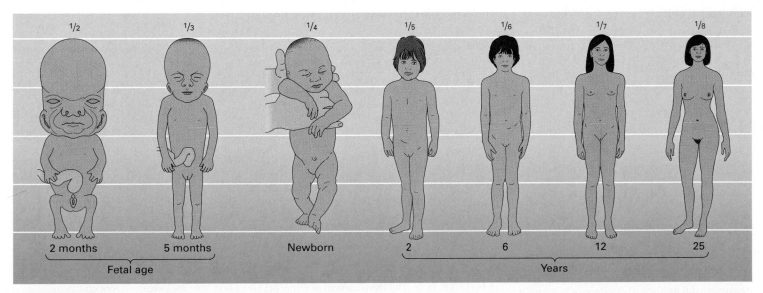

FIGURE 6.1 **Changes in Proportions of the Human Body During Growth** As individuals develop from infancy through adulthood, one of the most noticeable physical changes is that the head becomes smaller in relation to the rest of the body. The fractions listed refer to head size as a proportion of total body length at different ages.

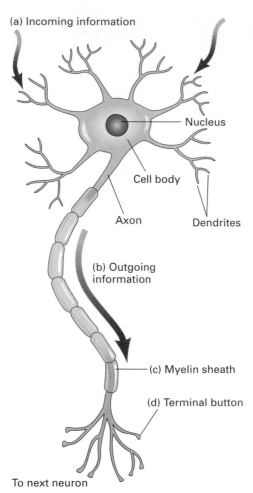

(a) Incoming information

Nucleus

Cell body

Axon

Dendrites

(b) Outgoing information

(c) Myelin sheath

(d) Terminal button

To next neuron

FIGURE 6.2 The Neuron (*a*) The dendrites of the cell body receive information from other neurons, muscles, or glands through the axon. (*b*) Axons transmit information away from the cell body. (*c*) A myelin sheath covers most axons and speeds information transmission. (*d*) As the axon ends, it branches out into terminal buttons.

proximodistal pattern The sequence in which growth starts at the center of the body and moves toward the extremities.

However, one recent study found that infants reached for toys with their feet before using their hands (Galloway & Thelen, 2004). On average, infants first contacted the toy with their feet when they were 12 weeks old and with their hands when they were 16 weeks old. Thus, contrary to long-standing beliefs, early leg movements can be precisely controlled, some aspects of development of reaching do not involve lengthy practice, and early motor behaviors don't always develop in a strict cephalocaudal pattern.

The **proximodistal pattern** is the sequence in which growth starts at the center of the body and moves toward the extremities. An example of this is the early maturation of muscular control of the trunk and arms, as compared with that of the hands and fingers. Further, infants use their whole hand as a unit before they can control several fingers.

Height and Weight

The average North American newborn is 20 inches long and weighs 7½ pounds. Ninety-five percent of full-term newborns are 18 to 22 inches long and weigh between 5½ and 10 pounds.

Most newborns lose 5 to 7 percent of their body weight in the first several days of life before they learn to adjust to neonatal feeding. Once infants adjust to sucking, swallowing, and digesting, they grow rapidly, gaining an average of 5 to 6 ounces per week during the first month. They double their birth weight by 4 months of age and nearly triple it by their first birthday. Infants grow about 1 inch per month during the first year, reaching approximately 1½ times their birth length by their first birthday.

Infants' rate of growth is considerably slower in the second year of life. By 2 years of age, infants weigh approximately 26 to 32 pounds, having gained a quarter to a half pound per month during the second year; now they have reached about one-fifth of their adult weight. At 2 years of age, the average infant is 32 to 35 inches tall, which is nearly half their adult height.

Brain Development

Brain development occurs extensively *in utero* and continues through infancy and later. Because the brain develops extensively in infancy, the infant's head should be protected from falls or other injuries and the baby should never be shaken. *Shaken baby syndrome,* which includes brain swelling and hemorrhaging, affects hundreds of babies in the United States each year (Harding, Risdon, & Krous, 2004; Minns & Busuttil, 2004; Newton & Vandeven, 2005) .

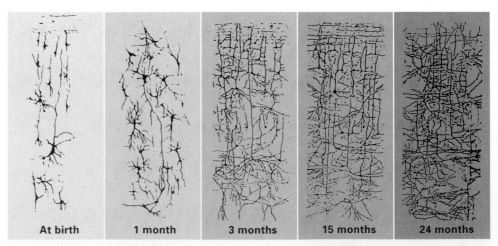

At birth   **1 month**   **3 months**   **15 months**   **24 months**

FIGURE 6.3 The Development of Dendritic Spreading Note the increase in connectedness between neurons over the course of the first two years of life. Reprinted by permission of the publisher from *The Postnatal Development of the Human Cerebral Cortex, Vols. I-VIII* by Jesse LeRoy Conel, Cambridge, Mass.: Harvard University Press. Copyright © 1939, 1975 by the President and Fellows of Harvard College.

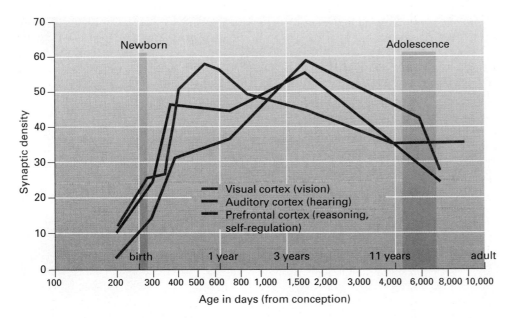

FIGURE 6.4 Synaptic Density in the Human Brain from Infancy to Adulthood The graph shows the dramatic increase and then pruning in synaptic density for three regions of the brain: visual cortex, auditory cortex, and prefrontal cortex. Synaptic density is believed to be an important indication of the extent of connectivity between neurons.

From Huttenlocher and Dabholkar, "Regional Differences in the Synaptogenesis in the Human Cerebral Cortex," Journal of Comparative Neurology, 387 (2), 1997, 167–168. Copyright © 1997.

As an infant walks, talks, runs, shakes a rattle, smiles, and frowns, changes are occurring in its brain. Consider that the infant began life as a single cell and nine months later was born with a brain and nervous system that contained approximately 100 billion nerve cells, or neurons. A **neuron** is a nerve cell that handles information processing at the cellular level (see figure 6.2). Indeed, at birth the infant probably has all of the neurons it will ever have.

In addition to dendritic spreading and the encasement of axons through myelination, another important aspect of the brain's development at the cellular level is the dramatic increase in connections between neurons (Ramey & Ramey, 2000). *Synapses* are tiny gaps between neurons where connections between axons and dendrites take place. As the infant develops, synaptic connections between axons and dendrites proliferate (Neville & Bavelier, 2002).

Among the most dramatic changes in the brain in the first two years of life are the spreading connections of dendrites (which receive information from other neurons) to each other. Figure 6.3 illustrates these changes.

A myelin sheath, which is a layer of fat cells, encases most axons (review figure 6.2). The myelin sheath insulates nerve cells and also helps nerve impulses travel faster. Myelination, the process of encasing axons with fat cells, begins prenatally and continues after birth. Myelination for visual pathways occurs rapidly after birth, being completed in the first 6 months. Auditory myelination is not completed until 4 or 5 years of age. Some aspects of myelination continue into adolescence.

Researchers have discovered that nearly twice as many synaptic connections are made as will ever be needed (Huttenlocher & others, 1991; Huttenlocher & Dabholkar, 1997). The connections that are used become strengthened and survive while the unused ones are replaced by other pathways or disappear (Casey, Durston, & Fossella, 2001). That is, these connections will be "pruned," in the language of neuroscience. Figure 6.4 vividly illustrates the dramatic growth and later pruning of synapses in the visual, auditory, and prefrontal cortex areas of the brain (Huttenlocher & Dabholkar, 1997). These areas are critical for higher-level cognitive functioning such as learning, memory, and reasoning.

As shown in figure 6.4, "blooming and pruning" vary considerably by brain region in humans (Thompson & Nelson, 2001). For example, the peak of synaptic overproduction in the visual cortex occurs at about the fourth postnatal month, followed by a gradual retraction until the middle to end of the preschool years (Huttenlocher & Dabhoker, 1997). In areas of the brain involved in hearing and language, a similar, though somewhat later, course is detected. However, in the prefrontal cortex (the area of the

neuron Nerve cell that handles information processing at the cellular level.

FIGURE 6.5 Measuring the Brain's Activity in Research on Infant Memory In Charles Nelson's research, electrodes are attached to a baby's scalp to measure the brain's activity to determine its role in the development of an infant's memory.

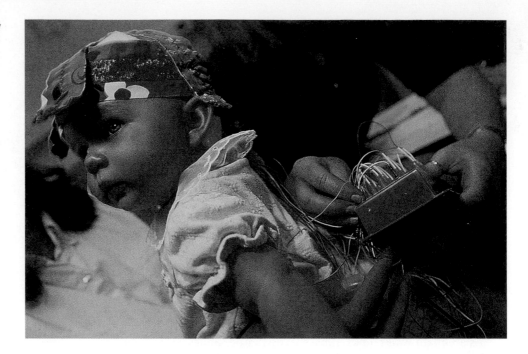

www.mhhe.com/santrockc9

Neural Processes
Charles Nelson's Research
Development of the Brain
Early Experience and the Brain

brain where higher-level thinking and self-regulation occur), the peak of overproduction takes place at about 1 year of age and it is not until middle to late adolescence that the adult density of synapses is achieved. Both heredity and environment are thought to influence the timing and course of synaptic overproduction and subsequent retraction (Greenough, 2000).

Using the electroencephalogram (EEG), which measures the brain's electrical activity, researchers have found that a spurt in EEG activity occurs from about 1½ to 2 years of age (Fischer & Bidell, 1998; Fischer & Rose, 1995). Other spurts seem to take place at about 9, 12, 15, and 18 to 20 years of age. Researchers believe that these spurts of brain activity may coincide with important changes in cognitive development. For example, the increase in EEG brain activity at 1½ to 2 years of age is likely associated with an increase in conceptual and language growth.

At birth, the newborn's brain is about 25 percent of its adult weight. By the second birthday, the brain is about 75 percent of its adult weight. However, the brain's areas do not mature uniformly. Some areas, such as the primary motor areas, develop earlier than others, such as the primary sensory areas.

Studying the brain's development in infancy is not as easy as it might seem, because even the latest brain-imaging technologies can't make out fine details and therefore can't be used on infants. PET (positron emission tomography) scans pose a radiation risk, and infants wriggle too much for magnetic resonance imaging, or an MRI (Marcus, Mulrine, & Wong, 1999). However, one researcher who is making strides in finding out more about the brain's development in infancy is Charles Nelson (1999, 2003; Nelson, Thomas, & de Haan, 2006); some of his research involves attaching up to 128 electrodes to a baby's scalp (see figure 6.5). He has found that even newborns produce distinctive brain waves that reveal they can distinguish their mother's voices from another woman's, even while they are asleep. In other research, Nelson has found that by 8 months of age babies can distinguish the picture of a wooden toy they were allowed to feel, but not see, from pictures of other toys. This achievement coincides with the development of neurons in the brain's hippocampus (an important structure in memory), allowing the infant to remember specific items and events.

The Brain's Lobes and Hemispheres   The brain is divided into four lobes and two hemispheres. Let's take a look at the function of each of these areas of the brain. The forebrain is the highest level of the brain. It consists of a number of structures, including the *cerebral cortex,* which covers the lower portions of the brain like a cap. The cerebral cortex plays a critical role in many important human functions, such as perception, language, and thinking. The cerebral cortex is divided into four main areas called lobes (see figure 6.6):

- The *frontal lobe* is involved in voluntary movement and thinking.
- The *occipital lobe* is involved in vision.
- The *temporal lobe* is involved in hearing.
- The *parietal lobe* is involved in processing information about body sensations.

The frontal lobe is immature in the newborn. However, as neurons in the frontal lobe become myelinated and interconnected during the first year of life, infants develop an ability to regulate their physiological states (such as sleep) and gain more control over their reflexes. Cognitive skills that require deliberate thinking don't emerge until later (Bell & Fox, 1992). Indeed, as we saw earlier, the prefrontal region of the frontal lobe has the most prolonged development of any brain region with changes detectable at least into the adolescent years (Johnson, 2001, 2005).

The cerebral cortex is divided into two halves, or hemispheres (see figure 6.7). **Lateralization** is the specialization of function in one hemisphere of the cerebral cortex or the other. There continues to be considerable interest in the degree to which each is involved in various aspects of thinking, feeling, and behavior (Jansen & others, 2004; Rilea, Roskos-Ewoldsen, & Boles, 2004; Sininger & Cone-Wesson, 2004).

The most extensive research on the brain's hemispheres has focused on language (Coney, 2004; Wood & others, 2004). At birth, the hemispheres already have started to specialize: Newborns show greater electrical brain activity in the left hemisphere than the right hemisphere when they are listening to speech sounds (Hahn, 1987). A common misconception is that virtually all language processing is carried out in the left hemisphere. Speech and grammar are localized to the left hemisphere in most people; however, some aspects of language such as appropriate language use in different contexts and the use of metaphor and humor involve the right hemisphere (Jabbour & others, 2005; Sakai & others, 2005). Thus, language does not occur exclusively in the brain's left hemisphere (Johnson, 2000, 2005; Tremblay, Monetta, & Joanette, 2004).

Early Experience and the Brain

Until the middle of the twentieth century, scientists believed that the brain's development was determined almost exclusively by genetic factors. Researcher Mark Rosenzweig (1969) was curious about whether early experiences change the brain's development. He conducted a number of experiments with rats and other animals to investigate this possibility. Animals were randomly assigned to grow up in different environments. Animals in an enriched early environment lived in cages with stimulating features, such as wheels to rotate, steps to climb, levers to press, and toys to manipulate. In contrast, other animals had the early experience of growing up in standard cages or in barren, isolated conditions.

The results were stunning. The brains of the animals growing up in the enriched environment developed better than the brains of the animals reared in standard or isolated conditions. The brains of the "enriched" animals weighed more, had thicker layers, had more neuronal connections, and had higher levels of neurochemical activity.

Similar findings occurred when older animals were reared in vastly different environments, although the results were not as strong as for the younger animals. Such results give hope that enriching the lives of infants and young children who live in impoverished environments can produce positive changes in their development.

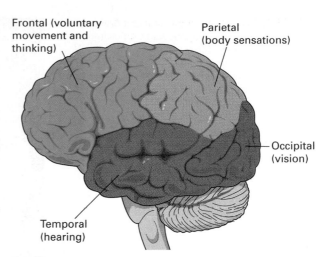

FIGURE 6.6 **The Brain's Four Lobes** Shown here are the locations of the brain's four lobes: frontal, occipital, temporal, and parietal.

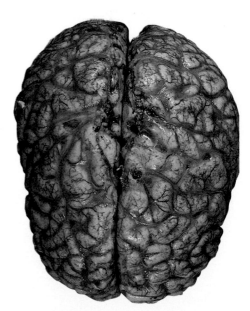

FIGURE 6.7 **The Human Brain's Hemispheres** The two halves (hemispheres) of the human brain are clearly seen in this photograph.

lateralization Specialization of function in one hemisphere of the cerebral cortex or the other.

FIGURE 6.8 **Early Deprivation and Brain Activity** These two photographs are PET (positron emission tomography) scans—which use radioactive tracers to image and analyze blood flow and metabolic activity in the body's organs—of the brains of (*a*) a normal child and (*b*) an institutionalized Romanian orphan who experienced substantial deprivation since birth. In PET scans, the highest to lowest brain activity is reflected in the colors of red, yellow, green, blue, and black, respectively. As can be seen, red and yellow show up to a much greater degree in the PET scan of the normal child than the deprived Romanian orphan.

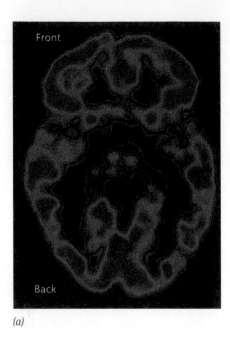

(a)

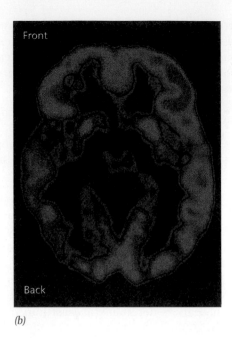

(b)

Depressed brain activity has recently been found in children who grow up in a deprived environment (Cicchetti, 2001). As shown in figure 6.8, a child who grew up in the unresponsive and unstimulating environment of a Romanian orphanage showed considerably depressed brain activity compared with a normal child (Begley, 1997).

The profusion of connections provides the growing brain with plasticity and resilience. Consider 14-year-old Michael Rehbein. At age 7, he began to experience uncontrollable seizures—as many as 400 a day. Doctors said the only solution was to remove the left hemisphere of his brain where the seizures were occurring. Recovery was slow but his right hemisphere began to reorganize and take over functions that normally occur in the brain's left hemisphere. One of these functions was speech (see figure 6.9).

Neuroscientists believe that what wires the brain—or rewires it, in the case of Michael Rehbein—is repeated experience (Nash, 1997). Each time a baby tries to touch an attractive object or gazes intently at a face, tiny bursts of electricity shoot through the brain, knitting together neurons into circuits. The results are some of the behavioral milestones we discuss in this and other chapters. For example, at about 2 months of age, the motor-control centers of the brain develop to the point at which infants can suddenly reach out and grab a nearby object. At about 4 months, the neural connections necessary for depth perception begin to form. And at about 12 months the brain's speech centers are poised to produce one of infancy's magical moments: when the infant utters its first word.

In sum, neural connections are formed early in life (Ito, 2004). The infant's brain literally is waiting for experiences to determine how connections are made (Greenough, 2001; Johnson, 2000, 2005). Before birth, it appears that genes mainly direct how the brain establishes basic wiring patterns. Neurons grow and travel to distant places awaiting further instructions. After birth, environmental experiences are important in the brain's development (Als & others, 2004; Komitova & others, 2005). The inflowing stream of sights, sounds, smells, touches, language, and eye contact help shape the brain's neural connections (Black, 2001; Graven, 2004).

Sleep

The organization of the sleep-wake cycle reflects neurological maturation and the developing ability of infants to regulate their own states (Lamb, Bornstein, & Teti, 2001).

When we were infants, sleep consumed more of our time than it does now. Newborns sleep 16 to 17 hours a day, although some sleep more and others less. The range is from a low of about 10 hours to a high of about 21 hours, although the longest period of sleep is not always between 11 P.M. and 7 A.M. Although total sleep remains somewhat consistent for young infants, their sleep during the day does not always follow a rhythmic pattern. An infant might change from sleeping several long bouts of 7 or 8 hours to three or four shorter sessions only a few hours in duration. By about 1 month of age, most infants have begun to sleep longer at night, and, by about 4 months of age, they usually have moved closer to adult-like sleep patterns, spending the most time sleeping at night and the most time awake during the day (Daws, 2000).

There are cultural variations in infant sleeping patterns. For example, in the Kipsigis culture in the African country of Kenya, infants sleep next to their mothers at night and are permitted to nurse on demand when they awaken in the night (Super & Harkness, 1997). As a result, the Kipsigis infants do not sleep through the night until much later than American infants. During the day, Kipsigis infants are frequently awake, strapped to their mothers' backs, accompanying them on their daily rounds of chores and social activities. In the first 8 months of postnatal life, these infants rarely sleep longer than 3 hours at a stretch, even at night. This contrasts with American infants, many of whom begin to sleep up to 8 hours a night by 8 months of age.

REM Sleep   Researchers are especially interested in *REM (rapid eye movement) sleep.* Most adults spend about one-fifth of their night in REM sleep, and REM sleep usually appears about 1 hour after non-REM sleep. However, about half of an infant's sleep is REM sleep, and infants often begin their sleep cycle with REM sleep rather than non-REM sleep. By the time infants reach 3 months of age, the percentage of time they spend in REM sleep falls to about 40 percent, and REM sleep no longer begins their sleep cycle. The large amount of REM sleep may provide infants with added self-stimulation, since they spend less time awake than do older children. REM sleep also might promote the brain's development in infancy. Figure 6.10 illustrates the average number of total hours spent in sleep, and the amount of time spent in REM sleep, across the human life span. As can be seen, infants sleep far more than children and adults, and a much greater amount of time is taken up by REM sleep in infancy than at any other point in the life span.

Shared Sleep: A Cultural Choice   There is considerable variation across cultures in newborns' sleeping arrangements (Berkowitz, 2004). Sharing a bed with a mother is common in many cultures, whereas in other cultures newborns sleep in a crib, either in the same room as the parents or in a separate room (Cortesi & others, 2004). In the United States, sleeping in a crib in a separate room is the most frequent sleeping arrangement for an infant. In one cross-cultural study, American mothers said they have their infants sleep in a separate room to promote the infant's self-reliance and independence (Morelli & others, 1992). By contrast, Mayan mothers in rural Guatemala had infants sleep in their bed until the birth of a new sibling, at which time the infant would sleep with another family member or in a separate bed in the mother's room. The Mayan mothers believed that the co-sleeping arrangement with their infants enhances the closeness of their relationship with the infants, and the mothers were shocked when told that American mothers have their baby sleep alone.

Some child experts believe there are benefits to shared sleeping, such as promoting breast feeding, responding more quickly to the baby's cries, and detecting potentially dangerous breathing pauses in the baby (McKenna, Mosko, & Richard, 1997). However, one recent study found physiological responses indicative of greater stress in co-sleeping (shared sleeping) infants than non-co-sleeping infants (Hunsley & Thoman, 2002). The American Academy of Pediatrics Task Force on Infant Positioning and SIDS (2000; Cohen, 2000) discourages shared sleeping. The Task Force concluded that in some instances bed sharing might lead to sudden infant death syndrome (SIDS), as could be the case if a sleeping mother rolls over on her baby.

(a)

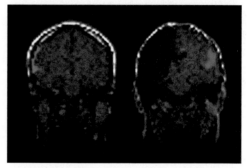

(b)

FIGURE 6.9   **Phasticity in the Brain's Hemispheres** *(a)* Michael Rehbein at 14 years of age. *(b)* Michael's right hemisphere *(right)* has reorganized to take over the language functions normally carried out by corresponding areas in the left hemisphere of an intact brain *(left)*. However, the right hemisphere is not as efficient as the left, and more areas of the brain are recruited to process speech.

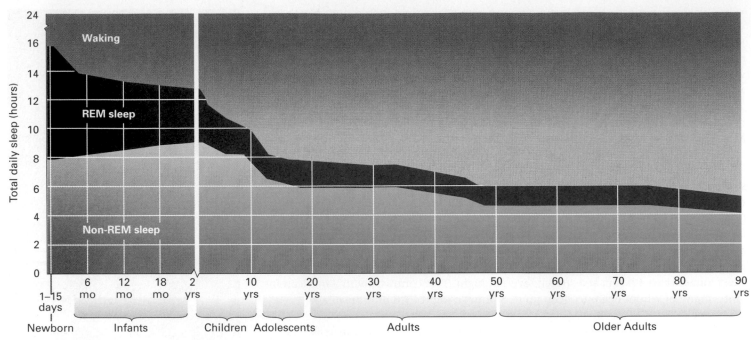

FIGURE 6.10 Sleep Across the Human Life Span

Sudden Infant Death Syndrome

One of the most devastating tragedies new parents can experience is the sudden death of their seemingly healthy baby. **Sudden infant death syndrome (SIDS),** also called *crib death,* occurs when infants stop breathing, usually during the night, and abruptly die without an apparent cause and without warning. SIDS remains the highest cause of infant death in the United States with nearly 3,000 infant deaths annually due to SIDS. Risk of SIDS is highest at 4 to 6 weeks of age (Mathews, Menacker, & MacDorman, 2003).

What can be done to help decrease the incidence of SIDS? Researchers have found that SIDS decreases when infants sleep on their backs rather than on their stomachs or sides (Alexander & Radisch, 2005; Hunt & others, 2003; Moon, Oden, & Grady, 2004: Rusen & others, 2004). Among the reasons given for prone sleeping being a high risk factor for SIDS are that it impairs arousal from sleep and restricts the ability to swallow effectively (Horne, Parslow, & Harding, 2004; Kahn & others, 2004: Tuladhar & others, 2003).

The American Academy of Pediatrics recommends that infants be placed to sleep on their backs to reduce the risk of SIDS. Since 1992, when the recommendation was made, the frequency of prone sleeping has decreased from 70 percent to 20 percent of U.S. infants (American Academy of Pediatrics Task Force on Infant Sleep Position and SIDS, 2000).

In addition to sleeping in a prone position, researchers have also found these risk factors for SIDS (American Academy of Pediatrics Task Force on Infant Sleep Position and SIDS, 2000; Goldwater, 2001):

- Low birth weight infants are 5 to 10 times more likely to die of SIDS than are their normal-weight counterparts (Horne & others, 2002; Sowter & others, 1999).
- Infants whose siblings have died of SIDS are two to four times as likely to die of it (Getahun & others, 2004; Lenoir, Mallet, & Calenda, 2000).
- Six percent of infants with *sleep apnea,* a temporary cessation of breathing in which the airway is completely blocked, usually 10 seconds or longer, die of SIDS (McNamara & Sullivan, 2000).
- African American and Eskimo infants are two to six times as likely as all others to die of SIDS (Ige & Shelton, 2004; Unger & others, 2003). One recent study

SIDS

sudden infant death syndrome (SIDS) Occurs when an infant stops breathing, usually during the night, and suddenly dies without an apparent cause; also called crib death.

found that prone sleeping was linked to SIDS in African American infants, suggesting the importance of educational outreach to African American families regarding the importance of placing infants on their backs while sleeping (Hauck & others, 2002).

- SIDS is more common in lower socioeconomic groups (Mitchell & others, 2000).
- SIDS is more common in infants who are passively exposed to cigarette smoke (Chan-Yeung & Dimich-Ward, 2003; Horne & others, 2004; Spitzer, 2005; Tong, England, & Glantz, 2005; Tutka, Wielosz, & Zatonski, 2003).
- Soft bedding is not recommended (Flick & others, 2001).

Nutrition

To develop healthily, infants not only need adequate sleep but also appropriate nutrition (Brown, 2006; Crocetti, Dudas, & Krugman, 2004; Morin, 2004; Wardlaw, 2006). The importance of adequate energy and nutrient intake consumed in a loving and supportive environment during the infant years cannot be overstated (Samour, Helm, & Lang, 2000; Sizer & Whitney, 2006). From birth to 1 year of age, infants triple their weight and increase their length by 50 percent. Individual differences among infants in terms of their nutrient reserves, body composition, growth rates, and activity patterns make defining actual nutrient needs difficult. However, because parents need guidelines, nutritionists recommend that infants consume approximately 50 calories per day for each pound they weigh—more than twice an adult's requirement per pound.

Today, Americans are extremely nutrition-conscious. Does the same type of nutrition that makes us healthy adults also make young infants healthy? Some affluent, well-educated parents almost starve their babies by feeding them the low-fat, low-calorie diet they eat themselves. Diets designed for adult weight loss and prevention of heart disease may actually retard growth and development in babies. Fat is very important for babies. Nature's food—breast milk—is not low in fat or calories. No child under the age of 2 should be consuming skim milk.

In one investigation, seven babies 7 to 22 months of age were found to be undernourished by their unwitting health-conscious parents (Lifshitz & others, 1987). In some instances, the parents had been fat themselves and were determined that their child was not going to be. The well-meaning parents substituted vegetables, skim milk, and other low-fat foods for what they called junk food. However, for growing infants, high-calorie, high-energy foods are part of a balanced diet.

Some years ago, controversy surrounded the issue of whether a baby should be fed on demand or on a regular schedule. Behaviorist John Watson (1928) argued that scheduled feeding is superior because it increases the child's orderliness. An example of a recommended schedule for newborns was 4 ounces of formula every six hours. In recent years, demand feeding—in which the timing and amount of feeding are determined by the infant—has become more popular.

Breast Feeding Versus Bottle Feeding Another controversy focuses on whether it is better to breast feed or bottle feed an infant. Human milk, or alternative formula, is the baby's source of nutrients and energy for the first four to six months of life. In the United States, "formula" became the conventional choice for a while, but breast feeding is increasing and is better for the infant's and the mother's health (Chapman & others, 2004; DiGiorgio, 2005; Marild & others, 2004; Mezzacappa, 2004; Thompson, 2005). As shown in figure 6.11, the prevalence of initiating breast feeding in the hospital and breast feeding at six months after birth in the United States reached an all-time high of 69.5 percent and 32.5 percent, respectively, in 2001 (Ryan, Wenjun, & Acosta, 2002).

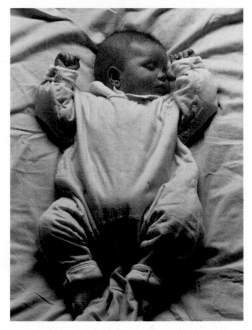

Is this a good sleep position for infants? Why or why not?

www.mhhe.com/santrockc9

Breastfeeding

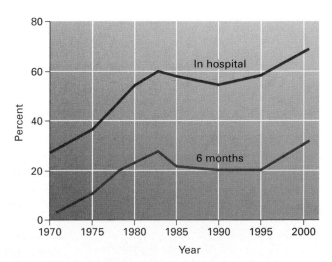

FIGURE 6.11 Trends in Breast Feeding in the United States: 1970–2001.

Human milk, or an alternative formula is a baby's source of nutrients for the first 4 to 6 months. The growing consensus is that breast feeding is better for the baby's health, although controversy still swirls about the issue of breast feeding versus bottlefeeding. *Why is breast feeding strongly recommended by pediatricians?*

The American Pediatric Association and the American Dietetic Association strongly endorse breast feeding throughout the first year of life (AAP Work Group on Breastfeeding, 1997; James & Dobson, 2005). Increasingly, mothers who return to work during the infant's first year use a breast pump to extract breast milk that can be stored and later fed to the infant in a bottle when the mother is not present. What are some of the benefits of breast feeding? During the first two years of life and later, they include (AAP Work Group on Breastfeeding, 1997; Eiger & Olds, 1999; Hanson & others, 2002; Kramer, 2003):

- Appropriate weight gain and lowered risk of childhood obesity (Grummer-Strawn & Mei, 2004). A recent review of 11 studies found that breast feeding reduces the risk of childhood obesity to a moderate extent (Dewey, 2003). Another recent review of 61 studies concluded that breast feeding protects against obesity in childhood and adulthood (Owen & others, 2005). One candidate for explaining this lowered risk is early metabolic programming.
- Fewer allergies (Becker, 2004; Friedman & Zeiger, 2005; Host & Halken, 2005)
- Prevention or reduction of diarrhea, respiratory infections (such as pneumonia and bronchitis), bacterial and urinary tract infections, and otitis media (a middle ear infection) (Isaacs, 2005; Kuiper & others, 2005; Morrow & Rangel, 2004; Wills-Karp, Brandt, & Morrow, 2004)
- Denser bones in childhood and adulthood (Gibson & others, 2000)
- Reduced childhood cancer and reduced incidence of breast cancer in mothers and their female offspring (Eisinger & Burke, 2003; Kwan & others, 2004)
- Lower incidence of sudden infant death syndrome (SIDS) (Horne & others, 2004). In one study, for every month of exclusive breast feeding, the rate of SIDS was cut in half (Fredrickson, 1993)
- More advanced neurological and cognitive development (Brody, 1994; Eidelman & Feldman, 2004; Gustaffson & others, 2004)
- Better visual acuity (Makrides & others, 1995)

Does breast feeding also bring psychological benefits? Some researchers have found no psychological differences between breast fed and bottle fed infants (Ferguson, Harwood, & Shannon, 1987; Young, 1990).

Are there circumstances when mothers should not breast feed? Yes, they are (1) if the mother is infected with AIDS, which can be transmitted through her milk, or if she has another infectious disease; (2) if she has active tuberculosis; or (3) if she is taking any drug that might not be safe for the infant (AAP Work Group on Breastfeeding, 1997; Jain & Lacy, 2005; Kiare & others, 2004; Merchant & Lala, 2005).

Some women cannot breast feed their infants because of physical difficulties. Also, if they are not constantly at home, some women may be deterred from breast feeding because they are uncomfortable breast feeding in public places. Yet other women may feel guilty if they terminate breast feeding early (Mozingo & others, 2000).

Which women are least likely to breast feed? They include mothers who work full time outside of the home, mothers under age 25, mothers without a high school education, African American mothers, and mothers in low-income circumstances (DiGiorgio, 2005; Ryan, 1997). In one study of low-income mothers in Georgia, interventions (such as counseling focused on the benefits of breast feeding and the free loan of a breast pump) increased the incidence of breast feeding (Ahluwalia & others, 2000).

In poor countries in particular, breast feeding may be the only way a mother can feed her infant adequately. In many of the world's developing countries, mothers used to breast feed their infants for at least two years. To become more modern, some stopped breast feeding or abandoned it earlier in the infant's life. Sometimes the substitute for breast-fed milk is an unsuitable and unsanitary cow's milk formula;

sometimes it is a form of tapioca or rice. The result may be malnutrition. Studies in countries such as Afghanistan, Haiti, Ghana, and Chile found that the death rate of bottle-fed infants is as much as five times that of breast-fed infants (Grant, 1997). However, as indicated at the beginning of this chapter, a special concern is the dramatic increase in mothers infected with the HIV virus and the risk of passing the virus to the baby through breast milk (Henderson, Martines, & de Zoysa, 2004; Pinoz & Ross, 2005; Shanker & others, 2005).

Malnutrition in Infancy Two conditions that can result from malnutrition in infancy are marasmus and kwashiorkor. **Marasmus** is a wasting away of body tissues in the infant's first year, caused by severe protein-calorie deficiency. The infant becomes grossly underweight, and its muscles atrophy. **Kwashiorkor** is a condition caused by a deficiency in protein in which the child's abdomen and feet swell with water. This disease usually appears between 1 to 3 years of age. Kwashiorkor makes children sometimes appear to be well-fed even though they are not. Kwashiorkor causes a child's vital organs to collect available nutrients and deprive other parts of the body of them. The child's hair also becomes thin, brittle, and colorless. And the child's behavior often becomes listless.

In the United States, there is concern about the energy and nutrient intakes of infants from low-income families. One recent study found low intakes of vitamin D, zinc, and iron, especially at 12 and 18 months (Nolan & others, 2002). In this study, high protein intake was noted at all of the ages the infants were assessed: 3, 6, 9, 12, 18, and 24 months.

Even if not fatal, severe and lengthy malnutrition is detrimental to physical, cognitive, and social development (Gonzales-Barranco & Rios-Torres, 2004; Grantham-McGregor, Ani, & Fernald, 2001). In some cases, even moderate malnutrition can produce subtle difficulties in development. In one investigation, two groups of extremely malnourished 1-year-old South African infants were studied (Bayley, 1970). The children in one group were given adequate nourishment during the next six years; no intervention took place in the lives of the other group. After the seventh year, the poorly nourished group performed much worse on tests of intelligence than did the adequately nourished group. Another study indicated that the diets of rural Guatemalan infants were associated with their social development at the time they entered elementary school (Barrett, Radke-Yarrow, & Klein, 1982). Children whose mothers had been given nutritious supplements during pregnancy and who themselves had been given more nutritious, high-calorie foods in their first two years of life were more active, more involved, more helpful with their peers, less anxious, and happier than their counterparts who had not been given nutritional supplements. The results suggest how important it is for parents to be attentive to the nutritional needs of their infants.

In further research on early supplementary feeding and children's cognitive development, Ernesto Pollitt and his colleagues (1993) conducted a longitudinal investigation over two decades in rural Guatemala. They found that early nutritional supplements in the form of protein and increased calories can have positive long-term effects on cognitive development. The researchers also found that the relation of nutrition to cognitive performance is moderated both by the time period during which the supplement is given and by the sociodemographic context. For example, the children in the lowest socioeconomic groups benefited more than did the children in higher socioeconomic groups. Although there still was a positive nutritional influence when supplementation began after 2 years of age, the effect on cognitive development was less powerful.

To adequately develop physically, as well as cognitively and socioemotionally, caregivers need to provide a nurturant, supportive environment. One individual who has stood out as an advocate of caring for children is T. Berry Brazelton, who is featured in the Careers in Child Development profile.

This Honduran child has kwashiorkor. Notice the telltale sign of kwashiorkor—a greatly expanded abdomen without the appearance of such expansion in other body areas, such as arms and legs. *What are some other characteristics of kwashiorkor?*

marasmus A wasting away of body tissues in the infant's first year, caused by severe protein-calorie deficiency.

kwashiorkor A condition caused by a deficiency in protein in which the child's abdomen and feet become swollen with water.

CAREERS
in CHILD DEVELOPMENT

T. Berry Brazelton
Pediatrician

T. Berry Brazelton is America's best-known pediatrician as a result of his numerous books, television appearances, and newspaper and magazine articles about parenting and children's health. He takes a family-centered approach to child development issues and communicates with parents in easy-to-understand ways.

Brazelton founded the Child Development Unit at Boston Children's Hospital and created the Brazelton Neonatal Behavioral Assessment Scale, a widely used measure of the newborn's health and well-being (which you read about in chapter 5). He also has conducted a number of research studies on infants and children and has been President of the Society for Research in Child Development, a leading research organization.

T. Berry Brazelton, pediatrician, with a young child.

www.mhhe.com/santrockc9

Toilet Training
Immunization
Injury Prevention

Toilet Training

The ability to control elimination depends on both muscular maturation and motivation. Children must be able to control their muscles to eliminate at the appropriate time, and they must want to eliminate in the toilet or potty, rather than in their pants. Many toddlers are physically able to do this by the time they are about 2 years of age (Maizels, Rosenbaum, & Keating, 1999). When toilet training is initiated, it should be accomplished in a warm, relaxed, supportive manner (Michel, 2000; Weaver & Dobson, 2004).

Many parents today are being encouraged to use a "readiness" approach to toilet training—that is, wait until children show signs that they are ready for toilet training. One recent survey of 103 U.S. pediatricians found that a majority endorsed a gradual, passive rather than intensive, active approach to toilet training (Polaha, Warzak, & Dittmer-Memahon, 2002). However, almost 30 percent advocated the more intense approach.

Pediatricians note that toilet training is being delayed until an older age today more than in earlier generations (American Academy of Pediatrics, 2001; Blum, Taubman, & Nemeth, 2004). One recent study of almost 500 U.S. children found that 50 percent of the girls were toilet trained by 35 months and 50 percent of the boys by 39 months (Schum & others, 2001).

Some developmentalists argue that delaying toilet training until the twos and threes can make it a battleground because many children at these ages are pushing so strongly for autonomy. Another argument is that late toilet training can be difficult for children who go to child care, because older children in diapers or training pants can be stigmatized by peers. Also, one study found that the later toilet training began the more it was associated with daytime and nighttime wetting in the elementary school years (Bakker & others, 2002). In sum, there still is controversy about when to initiate toilet training and more research is needed in this area.

Health

Among the important aspects of infant health are immunization and accident prevention. Immunization has greatly improved children's health.

Immunization One of the most dramatic advances in infant health has been the decline of infectious diseases over the past four decades because of widespread immunization for preventable diseases. Though many presently available immunizations can be given to individuals of any age, the recommended schedule is to begin in infancy (American Academy of Pediatrics, 2004; Bardenheier & others, 2004). The recommended age for various immunizations is shown in figure 6.12.

Accident Prevention Accidents are a major cause of death in infancy, especially from 6 to 12 months of age (Currie & Hotz, 2004). Infants need to be closely monitored as they gain increased locomotor and manipulative skills, along with a strong curiosity to explore the environment (Rivara, 2004). Aspiration of foreign objects, suffocation, falls, poisoning, burns, and motor vehicle accidents are among the most common accidents in infancy.

Asphyxiation by foreign material in the respiratory tract is the leading cause of fatal injury in infants under 1 year of age. Toys need to be carefully inspected for potential danger. An active infant can grab a low-hanging mobile and rapidly chew off a piece. Balloons, whether partially inflated, uninflated, or popped, cause more infant choking deaths than any other kind of small object and should be kept away from infants and young children. Other choking hazards include foods such as whole grapes, nuts, hard candy, popcorn, and any uncooked hard vegetables (for example, green beans). In addition, caregivers need to mash chunky cooked foods and cut meats such as hot dogs into tiny narrow pieces to avoid choking accidents.

Burns are often not perceived to be a particular danger to infants, but several hazards exist, such as scalding water, excessive sunburn, and burns from electrical wires, sockets, and space heaters. One of the best burn safety devices is a smoke detector; parents are advised to have at least one in every level of their homes.

Automobile accidents are the leading cause of accidental deaths in children over 1 year of age. The major danger for the infant is improper restraint within the motor vehicle (Agran, Anderson, & Winn, 2004). All infants, newborns included, should be secured in special infant car seats, rather than being held on an adult's lap or placed on the seat of the car. Infant car seats should be positioned in the backseat of the car to avoid injury from air bags.

Accidents can also harm infants in other ways. For example, sharp, jagged objects can cause skin wounds and long, pointed objects can be poked in the eye. Thus, a fork should not be given for self-feeding until the child has mastered the spoon, which usually happens by 18 months of age. Another often unrecognized danger to infants is attacks by young siblings and pets, especially dogs and cats.

We have discussed many aspects of the infant's health in this chapter. In the following Caring for Children interlude, we will further explore aspects of getting infants off to a healthy start in life.

Age	Immunization
Birth	Hepatitis B
2 months	Diphtheria, tetanus, pertussis Polio Influenza Pneumococcal
4 months	Hepatitis B Diphtheria, tetanus, pertussis Polio Influenza Pneumococcal
6 months	Diphtheria, tetanus, pertussis Influenza Pneumococcal
1 year	Influenza Pneumococcal
15 months	Measles, mumps, rubella Influenza Varicella
18 months	Hepatitis B Diphtheria, tetanus, pertussis Polio
4 to 6 years	Diphtheria, tetanus, pertussis Polio Measles, mumps, rubella
11 to 12 years	Measles, mumps, rubella
14 to 16 years	Tetanus-diphtheria

FIGURE 6.12 Recommended Immunization Schedule of Infants and Children

CARING FOR CHILDREN

A Healthy Start

The Hawaii Family Support/Healthy Start Program began in 1985 (Allen, Brown, & Finlay, 1992). It was designed by the Hawaii Family Stress Center in Honolulu, which already had been using home-visitor services to improve family functioning and reduce child abuse for more than a decade. Participation is voluntary. Families of newborns are screened for family risk factors, including unstable housing, histories of substance abuse, depression, parents' abuse as children, late or no prenatal care, fewer than 12 years of schooling, poverty, and unemployment. Early identification workers screen and interview new mothers in the hospital. They also screen families referred by physicians, nurses, and others. Because the demand for services outstrips available resources, only families with a substantial number of risk factors can participate.

(continued on next page)

The Hawaii Family Support/Healthy Start Program provides overburdened families of newborns and young children many home-visitor services. This program has been very successful in reducing abuse and neglect in families.

Newly participating families receive a weekly visit from a family support worker. Each of the program's eight home visitors works with approximately 25 families at a time. The worker helps the family cope with any immediate crises, such as unemployment or substance abuse. The family also is linked directly with a pediatrician to ensure that the children receive regular health care. Infants are screened for developmental delays and are immunized on schedule. Pediatricians have been educated about the program. They are notified when a child is enrolled in Healthy Start and when a family at risk stops participating.

The Family Support/Healthy Start Program recently hired a child development specialist to work with families of children with special needs. And, in some instances, the program's male family support worker also visits a father to talk specifically about his role in the family. The support workers encourage parents to participate in group activities held each week at the program center located in a neighborhood shopping center.

Over time, parents are encouraged to assume more responsibility for their family's health and well-being. Families can participate in Healthy Start until the child is 5 and enters public school. One recent study found that the Hawaiian Healthy Start program produced a lower incidence of maternal alcohol abuse and partner violence but did not reduce child abuse (Duggan & others, 2004).

Review and Reflect • LEARNING GOAL 1

1 Discuss physical growth and development in infancy.

- What are cephalocaudal and proximodistal patterns?
- What changes in height and weight take place in infancy?
- What are some key features of the brain and its development in infancy?
- What changes occur in sleep during infancy? What is SIDS?
- What are infants' nutritional needs? What characterizes malnutrition in infancy?
- When should toilet training be attained?
- How are immunization and accidents involved in infant health?

Reflect
- What three pieces of advice about the infant's physical development would you want to give a friend who has just had a baby? Why those three?

2 HOW DO INFANTS DEVELOP MOTOR SKILLS?

The Dynamic Systems View   Gross Motor Skills

Reflexes   Fine Motor Skills

New insights are being made into the ways in which infants acquire motor skills. We will begin our exploration of motor development by examining a theory that captures these new insights: the dynamic systems view. Then we will discuss infants' reflexes and subsequently turn our attention to the development of gross and fine motor skills.

The Dynamic Systems View

Developmentalist Arnold Gesell (1934) thought his painstaking observations had revealed how people develop their motor skills. He discovered that infants and children develop rolling, sitting, standing, and other motor skills in a fixed order and within specific time frames. These observations, said Gesell, show that motor development comes about through the unfolding of a genetic plan, or *maturation.*

Later studies, however, demonstrated that the sequence of developmental milestones is not as fixed as Gesell indicated and not due as strongly to heredity as Gesell argued (Adolph & Berger, 2005, 2006). In the 1990s, the study of motor development experienced a renaissance as psychologists developed new insights about *how* motor skills develop (Thelen & Smith, 1998, 2006). One increasingly influential theory is the dynamic systems theory proposed by Esther Thelen.

According to **dynamic systems theory,** infants assemble motor skills for perceiving and acting. Notice that perception and action are coupled according to this theory (Thelen, 1995, 2000, 2001; Thelen & Smith, 1998, 2006; Thelen & Whitmeyer, 2005). In order to develop motor skills, infants must perceive something in the environment that motivates them to act and use their perceptions to fine-tune their movements. Motor skills represent solutions to the infant's goals.

How is a motor skill developed according to this theory? When infants are motivated to do something, they might create a new motor behavior. The new behavior is the result of many converging factors: the development of the nervous system, the body's physical properties and its possibilities for movement, the goal the child is motivated to reach, and the environmental support for the skill. For example, babies learn to walk only when maturation of the nervous system allows them to control certain leg muscles, when their legs have grown enough to support their weight, and when they want to move (Hallemans & others, 2005).

Mastering a motor skill requires the infant's active efforts to coordinate several components of the skill. Infants explore and select possible solutions to the demands of a new task; they assemble adaptive patterns by modifying their current movement patterns. The first step occurs when the infant is motivated by a new challenge—such as the desire to cross a room—and gets into the "ball park" of the task demands by taking a couple of stumbling steps. Then, the infant "tunes" these movements to make them smoother and more effective. The tuning is achieved through repeated cycles of action and perception of the consequences of that action. According to the dynamic systems view, even universal milestones, such as crawling, reaching, and walking, are learned through this process of adaptation: Infants modulate their movement patterns to fit a new task by exploring and selecting possible configurations (Adolph & Berger, 2005, 2006).

To see how dynamic systems theory explains motor behavior, imagine that you offer a new toy to a boy named Gabriel (Thelen & others, 1993). There is no exact program that can tell Gabriel ahead of time how to move his arm and hand and fingers to grasp the toy. Gabriel must adapt to his goal—grasping the toy—and the context. From his sitting position, he must make split-second adjustments to extend his arm, holding his body steady so that his arm and torso don't plow into the toy. Muscles in his arm and shoulder contract and stretch in a host of combinations, exerting a variety of forces. He improvises a way to reach out with one arm and wrap his fingers around the toy.

Thus, according to dynamic systems theory, motor development is not a passive process in which genes dictate the unfolding of a sequence of skills over time. Rather, the infant actively puts together a skill in order to achieve a goal within the constraints set by the infant's body and environment. Nature and nurture, the infant and the environment, are all working together as part of an ever-changing system (Thelen & Smith, 2005).

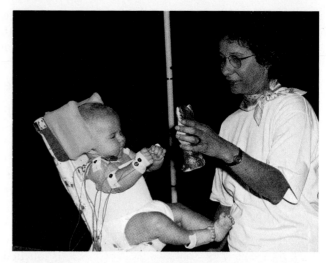

Esther Thelen is shown conducting an experiment to discover how infants learn to control their arms to reach and grasp for objects. A computer device is used to monitor the infant's arm movements and to track muscle patterns. Thelen's research is conducted from a dynamic systems perspective. *What is the nature of this perspective?*

www.mhhe.com/santrockc9

Esther Thelen's Research

dynamic systems theory A theory, proposed by Esther Thelen, that seeks to explain how motor behaviors are assembled for perceiving and acting.

The infant is by no means as helpless as it looks and is quite capable of some very complex and important actions.

—HERB PICK
Contemporary Developmental Psychologist, University of Minnesota

As we examine the course of motor development, we will describe how dynamic systems theory applies to some specific skills. First, though, let's examine how the story of motor development begins with reflexes.

Reflexes

The newborn is not completely helpless. Among other things, it has some basic reflexes. For example, the newborn automatically holds its breath and contracts its throat to keep water out. Reflexes are built-in reactions to stimuli; they govern the newborn's movements, which are automatic and beyond the newborn's control. Reflexes are genetically carried survival mechanisms. They allow infants to respond adaptively to their environment before they have had the opportunity to learn.

The rooting and sucking reflexes are important examples. Both have survival value for newborn mammals, who must find a mother's breast to obtain nourishment. The **rooting reflex** occurs when the infant's cheek is stroked or the side of the mouth is touched. In response, the infant turns its head toward the side that was touched in an apparent effort to find something to suck. The **sucking reflex** occurs when newborns automatically suck an object placed in their mouth. This reflex enables newborns to get nourishment before they have associated a nipple with food.

Another example is the **Moro reflex,** which occurs in response to a sudden, intense noise or movement. When startled, the newborn arches its back, throws back its head, and flings out its arms and legs. Then the newborn rapidly closes its arms and legs. The Moro reflex is believed to be a way of grabbing for support while falling; it would have had survival value for our primate ancestors.

Some reflexes—coughing, blinking, and yawning, for example—persist throughout life. They are as important for the adult as they are for the infant. Other reflexes, though, disappear several months following birth, as the infant's brain matures, and voluntary control over many behaviors develops. The rooting, sucking, and Moro reflexes, for example, all tend to disappear when the infant is 3 to 4 months old.

The movements of some reflexes eventually become incorporated into more complex, voluntary actions. One important example is the **grasping reflex,** which occurs when something touches the infant's palms. The infant responds by grasping tightly. By the end of the third month, the grasping reflex diminishes, and the infant shows a more voluntary grasp. For example, when an infant sees a mobile turning slowly above a crib, it may reach out and try to grasp it. As its motor development becomes smoother, the infant will grasp objects, carefully manipulate them, and explore their qualities. An overview of several reflexes we have discussed, along with others, is given in figure 6.13.

Although reflexes are automatic and inborn, differences in reflexive behavior are soon apparent. For example, the sucking capabilities of newborns vary considerably. Some newborns are efficient at forceful sucking and obtaining milk; others are not as adept and get tired before they are full. Most infants take several weeks to establish a sucking style that is coordinated with the way the mother is holding the infant, the way milk is coming out of the bottle or breast, and the infant's temperament.

Pediatrician T. Berry Brazelton (1956) observed how infants' sucking changed as they grew older. Over 85 percent of the infants engaged in considerable sucking behavior unrelated to feeding. They sucked their finger, their fists, and pacifiers. By the age of 1 year, most had stopped the sucking behavior, but as many as 40 percent of children continue to suck their thumbs after they have started school (Kessen, Haith, & Salapatek, 1970). Most developmentalists do not attach a great deal of significance to this behavior.

Gross Motor Skills

Ask any parents about their baby, and sooner or later you are likely to hear about one or more motor milestone, such as "Cassandra just learned to crawl," "Jesse is finally

rooting reflex A newborn's built-in reaction that occurs when the infant's cheek is stroked or the side of the mouth is touched. In response, the infant turns its head toward the side that was touched, in an apparent effort to find something to suck.

sucking reflex A newborn's built-in reaction of automatically sucking an object placed in its mouth. The sucking reflex enables the infant to get nourishment before it has associated a nipple with food.

Moro reflex A neonatal startle response that occurs in reaction to a sudden, intense noise or movement. When startled, the newborn arches its back, throws its head back, and flings out its arms and legs. Then the newborn rapidly closes its arms and legs to the center of the body.

grasping reflex A neonatal reflex that occurs when something touches the infant's palms. The infant responds by grasping tightly.

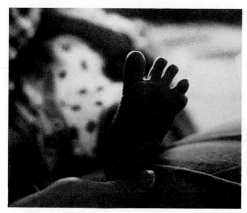
Babinski reflex

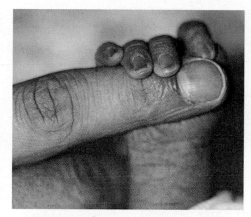
Grasping reflex

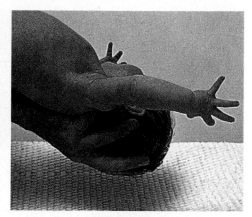
Moro reflex

Reflex	Stimulation	Infant's Response	Developmental Pattern
Blinking	Flash of light, puff of air	Closes both eyes	Permanent
Babinski	Sole of foot stroked	Fans out toes, twists foot in	Disappears after 9 months to 1 year
Grasping	Palms touched	Grasps tightly	Weakens after 3 months, disappears after 1 year
Moro (startle)	Sudden stimulation, such as hearing loud noise or being dropped	Startles, arches back, throws head back, flings out arms and legs and then rapidly closes them to center of body	Disappears after 3 to 4 months
Rooting	Cheek stroked or side of mouth touched	Turns head, opens mouth, begins sucking	Disappears after 3 to 4 months
Stepping	Infant held above surface and feet lowered to touch surface	Moves feet as if to walk	Disappears after 3 to 4 months
Sucking	Object touching mouth	Sucks automatically	Disappears after 3 to 4 months
Swimming	Infant put face down in water	Makes coordinated swimming movements	Disappears after 6 to 7 months
Tonic neck	Infant placed on back	Forms fists with both hands and usually turns head to the right (sometimes called the "fencer's pose" because the infant looks like it is assuming a fencer's position)	Disappears after 2 months

FIGURE 6.13 Infant Reflexes

sitting alone," or "Angela took her first step last week." Parents proudly announce such milestones as their children transform themselves from babies unable to lift their heads to toddlers who grab things off the grocery store shelf, chase a cat, and participate actively in the family's social life (Thelen, 1995, 2000). These milestones are examples of **gross motor skills,** which are skills that involve large-muscle activities, such as moving one's arms and walking.

The Development of Posture　How do gross motor skills develop? As a foundation, these skills, like many other activities, require postural control (Thelen, 1995, 2000). For example, to track moving objects, you must be able to control your head in order to stabilize your gaze; before you can walk, you must be able to balance on one leg.

Posture is more than just holding still and straight. In Thelen's (1995, 2000) view, posture is a dynamic process that is linked with sensory information from proprioceptive cues in the skin, joints, and muscles, which tell us where we are in space; from

gross motor skills Motor skills that involve large-muscle activities, such as walking.

Newly crawling infant

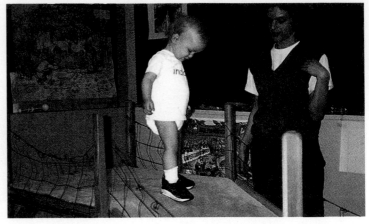

Experienced walker

FIGURE 6.14   The Role of Experience in Crawling and Walking Infants' Judgments of Whether to Go Down a Slope Karen Adolph (1997) found that locomotor experience rather than age was the primary predictor of adaptive responding on slopes of varying steepness. Newly crawling and walking infants could not judge the safety of the various slopes. With experience, they learned to avoid slopes where they would fall. When expert crawlers began to walk, they again made mistakes and fell, even though they had judged the same slope accurately when crawling. Adolph referred to this as the *specificity of learning* because it does not transfer across crawling and walking.

vestibular organs in the inner ear that regulate balance and equilibrium; and from vision and hearing (Spencer & others, 2000).

Newborn infants cannot voluntarily control their posture. Within a few weeks, though, they can hold their heads erect, and soon they can lift their heads while prone. By 2 months of age, babies can sit while supported on a lap or an infant seat, but they cannot sit independently until they are 6 or 7 months of age. Standing also develops gradually during the first year of life. By about 8 months of age, infants usually learn to pull themselves up and hold onto a chair, and they often can stand alone by about 10 to 12 months of age.

Learning to Walk   Locomotion and postural control are closely linked, especially in walking upright (Adolph & Berger, 2005). To walking upright, the baby must be able both to balance on one leg as the other is swung forward and to shift the weight from one leg to the other (Thelen, 2000).

Even young infants can make alternating leg movements that are needed for walking. The neural pathways that control leg alternation are in place from a very early age, possibly even at birth or before. Infants engage in frequent alternating kicking movements throughout the first six months of life when they are lying on their backs. Also when 1- to 2-month-olds are given support with their feet in contact with a motorized treadmill, they show well-coordinated, alternating steps. Despite these early abilities, most infants do not learn to walk until about the time of their first birthday.

If infants can produce forward stepping movements so early, why does it take them so long to learn to walk? The key skills in learning to walk appear to be stabilizing balance on one leg long enough to swing the other forward and shifting the weight without falling. This is a difficult biomechanical problem to solve, and it takes infants about a year to do it.

In learning to locomote, infants learn what kinds of places and surfaces afford safe locomotion (Adoph & Berger, 2005). Karen Adolph (1997) investigated how experienced and inexperienced crawling infants and walking infants go down steep slopes (see figure 6.14). Newly crawling infants, who averaged about 8½ months in age, rather indiscriminately went down the steep slopes, often falling in the process (with their mothers next to the slope to catch them). After weeks of practice, the crawling babies became more adept at judging which slopes were too steep to crawl down and

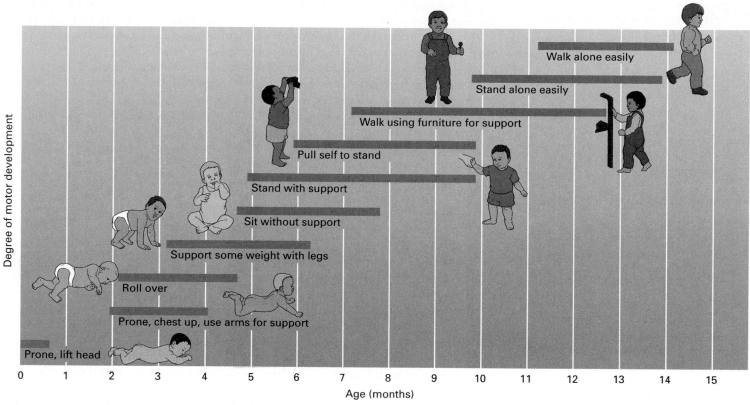

FIGURE 6.15 Milestones in Gross Motor Development

which ones they could navigate safely. Newly walking infants also could not judge the safety of the slopes, but infants who were experienced walkers accurately matched their skills with the steepness of the slopes. They rarely fell downhill, either refusing to go down the steep slopes or going down backward in a cautious manner. Experienced walkers perceptually assessed the situation—looking, swaying, touching, and thinking before they moved down the slope. With experience both the crawlers and the walkers learned to avoid the risky slopes where they would fall, integrating perceptual information with the development of a new motor behavior. In this research, we again see the importance of perceptual-motor coupling in the development of motor skills.

There are practical applications of Adolph's research in that there is little transfer in moving from crawling to walking (Keen, 2005a). Parents should realize how accident-prone children are at this early stage of locomotion. They seem very competent motorically, but cognitively they don't realize potential dangers they might encounter. It takes many weeks of walking before children learn that drop-offs, steps, and slopes are dangerous. Falls and other accidents are common when infants begin to walk and caregivers need to be constantly on guard.

Indeed, practice is especially important in learning to walk (Adolph & Berger, 2005, 2006). "Thousands of daily walking steps, each step slightly different from the last because of variations in terrain and the continually varying biomechanical constraints on the body, may help infants to identify the relevant combination of strength and balance required to improve their walking skill" (Adolph, Vereijkeni, & Shrout, 2003, p. 495).

Figure 6.15 summarizes important accomplishments in gross motor skills during the first year, culminating in the ability to walk easily. The timing of these milestones especially the later ones, may vary by as much as two to four months, and experiences can modify the onset of these accomplishments. For example, since 1992, when

www.mhhe.com/santrockc9

**Developmental Milestones
Karen Adolph's Research**

A baby is an angel whose wings decrease as his legs increase.

FRENCH PROVERBS

pediatricians began recommending that parents keep their infants supine at night, fewer babies crawl and the age of onset of crawling is later (Davis & others, 1998). Also, some infants do not follow the standard sequence of motor accomplishments. For example, many American infants never crawl on their belly or on their hands and knees. They may discover an idiosyncratic form of locomotion before walking such as rolling, or they might never locomote until they get upright (Adolph, 2002). In the African Mali tribe, most infants do not crawl (Bril, 1999).

According to Karen Adolph and Sarah Berger (2005, p. 273), "the old-fashioned view that growth and motor development reflect merely the age-related output of maturation is, at best, incomplete. Rather, infants acquire new skills with the help of their caregivers in a real-world environment of objects, surfaces, and places."

Development in the Second Year   The motor accomplishments of the first year bring increasing independence, allowing infants to explore their environment more extensively and to initiate interaction with others more readily. In the second year of life, toddlers become more motorically skilled and mobile. They are no longer content in a playpen and want to move all over the place. Child development experts believe that motor activity during the second year is vital to the child's competent development and that few restrictions, except for safety, should be placed on their adventures (Fraiberg, 1959).

By 13 to 18 months, toddlers can pull a toy attached to a string and use their hands and legs to climb up a number of steps. By 18 to 24 months, toddlers can walk quickly or run stiffly for a short distance, balance on their feet in a squat position while playing with objects on the floor, walk backward without losing their balance, stand and kick a ball without falling, stand and throw a ball, and jump in place.

Can parents give their babies a head start on becoming physically fit and physically talented through structured exercise classes? Physical fitness classes for babies range from passive fare—with adults putting infants through the paces—to programs called "aerobic" because they demand crawling, tumbling, and ball skills. Pediatricians point out that when an adult is stretching and moving an infant's limbs, it is easy for them to go beyond the infant's physical limits without knowing. Pediatricians also recommend that exercise for infants should not be of the intense, aerobic variety. Babies cannot adequately stretch their bodies to achieve aerobic benefits.

In short, most infancy experts recommend against structured exercise classes for babies. But there are other ways of guiding infants' motor development. Caregivers in some cultures do handle babies vigorously, and this might advance motor development, as we discuss in the next section.

Cultural Variations in Guiding Infants' Motor Development
Mothers in developing cultures tend to stimulate their infants' motor skills more than mothers in more advanced cultures (Hopkins, 1991). Also, Jamaican mothers regularly massage their infants and stretch their arms and legs, and this is linked with advanced motor development (Hopkins, 1991). Mothers in the Gusii culture of Kenya also encourage vigorous movement in their babies (Hopkins & Westra, 1988). We can only speculate about the reasons for this cultural difference. Perhaps this stimulation in developing countries improves the infants' chances of survival or perhaps caregivers recognize that motor skills are required for important jobs in the culture.

Do these cultural variations make a difference in the infant's motor development? When caregivers provide babies with physical guidance by physically handling them in special ways (such as stroking, massaging, or stretching) or by giving them opportunities for exercise, the infants often attain motor milestones earlier than infants whose caregivers have not provided these physical activities. For example, Jamaican mothers expect their infants to sit and walk alone two to three months earlier than English mothers do (Hopkins & Westra, 1990).

Nonetheless, regardless of how much practice and stretching takes place, infants around the world still reach these motor milestones within a close age range. For

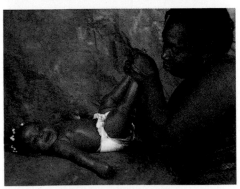

(*Top*) In the Algonquin culture in Quebec, Canada, babies are strapped to a cradle board for much of their infancy. (*Bottom*) In Jamaica, mothers massage and stretch their infants' arms and legs. *To what extent do cultural variations in the activity infants engage in influence the time at which they reach motor milestones?*

example, Algonquin infants in Quebec, Canada, spend much of their first year strapped to a cradle board. Despite their inactivity, these infants still sit up, crawl, and walk within an age range similar to infants in cultures who have had much greater opportunity for activity.

In sum, there are variations in the ages at which infants reach motor milestones in different cultures that likely depend on their activity opportunities. However, the variations are not large and milestones are reached within normal age ranges.

Fine Motor Skills

Whereas gross motor skills involve large-muscle activity, **fine motor skills** involve finely tuned movements. Buttoning a shirt, typing, or anything that requires finger dexterity demonstrates fine motor skills.

Infants have hardly any control over fine motor skills at birth, but they have many components of what will become finely coordinated arm, hand, and finger movements (Rosenblith, 1992). A significant achievement in their interactions with their surroundings comes with the onset of reaching and grasping (McCarty & Ashmead, 1999; Oztop, Bradley, & Arbib, 2004).

The infant's grasping system is very flexible. Infants vary their grip on an object depending on its size and shape, as well as the size of their own hands relative to the object's size. Infants grip small objects with their thumb and forefinger (and sometimes their middle finger too), whereas they grip large objects with all of the fingers of one hand or both hands.

Perceptual-motor coupling is necessary for the infant to coordinate grasping. In studies of grasping, age differences have been found in regard to which perceptual system is most likely to be used in coordinating grasping. Four-month-old infants rely greatly on touch to determine how they will grip an object; 8-month-olds are more likely to use vision as a guide (Newell & others, 1989). This developmental change is efficient because vision lets infants preshape their hands as they reach for an object.

For many years it was believed that when infants reach for an object, they must continuously have sight of the hand and the target (White, Castle, & Held, 1964). However, Rachel Clifton and her colleagues (1993) demonstrated that infants do not have to see their own hands in order to reach for an object. They concluded that proprioceptive cues from muscles, tendons, and joints, not sight of the limb, guide reaching by 4-month-old infants.

The development of reaching and grasping becomes more refined during the first two years of life (Keen, 2005a; Oztop, Bradley, & Arbib, 2004). Initially, infants move their shoulders and elbows crudely, but later they move their wrists, rotate their hands, and coordinate their thumb and forefinger. The developmental sequence of grasping involves the palmer and pincer grasps. Initially infants grasp with the whole hand, which is called a *palmer grasp*. Later, toward the end of the first year, infants grasp small objects with their thumb and forefinger, which is called the *pincer grasp*.

Experience plays a role in reaching and grasping. In one recent study, three-month old infants were given 10 to 14 10-minute play sessions wearing "sticky mittens" ("mittens with palms that stuck to the edges of toys and allowed the infants to pick up the toys") (Needham, Barrett, & Peterman, 2002) (see Figure 6.16). Following the mitten sessions, these infants grasped and manipulated objects earlier in their development than a control group of infants who did not receive the "mitten" experience. The experienced infants looked at the objects longer, swatted at them more during visual contact, and were more likely to mouth the objects.

fine motor skills Motor skills that involve more finely tuned movements, such as finger dexterity.

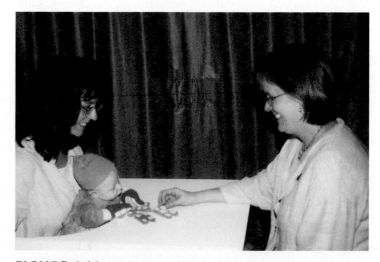

FIGURE 6.16 Infants' Use of "Sticky Mittens" to Explore Objects
Amy Needham and her colleagues (2002) found that "sticky mittens" enhanced young infants' object exploration skills.

Just as infants need to exercise their gross motor skills, they also need to exercise their fine motor skills (Keen, 2005a). Especially when they can manage using a pincer grip, they delight in picking up small objects. The pincer grip often emerges at about the same time as crawling, and infants at this point pick up virtually every object in sight, especially on the floor, and put them in their mouth. Thus, parents need to be vigilant in regularly monitoring what objects are within the infant's reach.

Review and Reflect • LEARNING GOAL 2

 2 **Describe infants' motor development.**

Review
- What is dynamic systems theory?
- What are reflexes? What are some reflexes that infants have?
- What are gross motor skills and how do they develop in infancy?
- What are fine motor skills and how do they develop in infancy?

Reflect
- Which view of infant motor development do you prefer—the traditional maturational view or the dynamic systems view? Why?

---

3 HOW CAN INFANTS' SENSORY AND PERCEPTUAL DEVELOPMENT BE CHARACTERIZED?

Defining Sensation and Perception	Studying Infant Perception	Other Senses	Perceptual–Motor Coupling

The Ecological View	Visual Perception	Intermodal Perception

Right now, I am looking at my computer screen to make sure the words are being printed accurately as I am typing them. My perceptual and motor skills are working together. Recall that even control of posture uses information from the senses. And when people grasp an object, they use perceptual information about the object to adjust their motions.

How do these sensations and perceptions develop? Can a newborn see? If so, what can it perceive? What about the other senses—hearing, smell, taste, touch, and pain? What are they like in the newborn, and how do they develop? Can an infant put together information from two modalities, such as sight and sound? These are among the intriguing questions that we will explore in this section.

Defining Sensation and Perception

How does a newborn know that her mother's skin is soft rather than rough? How does a 5-year-old know what color his hair is? How does a 10-year-old know that a firecracker is louder than a cat's meow? Infants and children "know" these things because information comes through the senses. Without vision, hearing, touch, taste, smell, and other senses, we would be isolated from the world; we would live in dark silence, a tasteless, colorless, feelingless void.

Sensation occurs when information interacts with sensory *receptors*—the eyes, ears, tongue, nostrils, and skin. The sensation of hearing occurs when waves of pulsating air are collected by the outer ear and transmitted through the bones of the inner ear to the auditory nerve. The sensation of vision occurs as rays of light contact the eyes, become focused on the retina, and are transmitted by the optic nerve to the visual centers of the brain.

Perception is the interpretation of what is sensed. The air waves that contact the ears might be interpreted as noise or musical sounds, for example. The physical energy transmitted to the retina of the eye might be interpreted as a particular color, pattern, or shape.

The Ecological View

For the past several decades, much of the research on perceptual development in infancy has been guided by the ecological view of Eleanor and James J. Gibson (E. Gibson, 1969, 1989, 2001; J. Gibson, 1966, 1979). They argue that we do not have to take bits and pieces of data from sensations and build up representations of the world in our minds. The environment itself is rich with information; our perceptual system selects from that rich output.

According to the Gibsons' **ecological view,** we directly perceive information that exists in the world around us. Perception brings us into contact with the environment in order to interact with and adapt to it. Perception is designed for action. Perception gives people such information as when to duck, when to turn their bodies through a narrow passageway, and when to put their hands up to catch something.

In the Gibsons' view, all objects have **affordances,** which are opportunities for interaction offered by objects that fit within our capabilities to perform activities. A pot may afford you something to cook with, and may afford a toddler something to bang. Adults immediately know when a chair is appropriate for sitting, when a surface is safe for walking, or when an object is within reach. We directly and accurately perceive these affordances by sensing information from the environment —the light or sound reflecting from the surfaces of the world—and from our own bodies through muscle receptors, joint receptors, and skin receptors, for example.

Through perceptual development, children become more efficient at discovering and using affordances. An important developmental question is, What affordances can infants or children detect and use? In one study, for example, when babies who could walk were faced with a squishy waterbed, they stopped and explored it, then chose to crawl rather than walk across it (Gibson & others, 1987). They combined perception and action to adapt to the demands of the task.

Similarly, as we described earlier in the section on motor development, infants who were just learning to crawl or just learning to walk were less cautious when confronted with a steep slope than experienced crawlers or walkers were (Adolph, 1997; Adolph & Avolio, 2000). The more experienced crawlers and walkers perceived that a slope *affords* the possibility not only for faster locomotion but also for falling. Again, infants coupled perception and action to make a decision about what do in their environment.

Studying Infant Perception

The creature has poor motor coordination and can move itself only with great difficulty. Although it cries when uncomfortable, it uses few other vocalizations. In fact, it sleeps most of the time, about 16 to 17 hours a day. You are curious about this creature and want to know more about what it can do. You think to yourself, "I wonder if it can see. How could I find out?"

You obviously have a communication problem with the creature. You must devise a way that will allow the creature to "tell" you that it can see. While examining the creature one day, you make an interesting discovery. When you move an object

sensation Reaction that occurs when information contacts sensory receptors—the eyes, ears, tongue, nostrils, and skin.

perception The interpretation of sensation.

ecological view The view, proposed by the Gibsons, that people directly perceive information in the world around them. Perception brings people in contact with the environment in order to interact with it and adapt to it.

affordances Opportunities for interaction offered by objects that fit within our capabilities to perform activities.

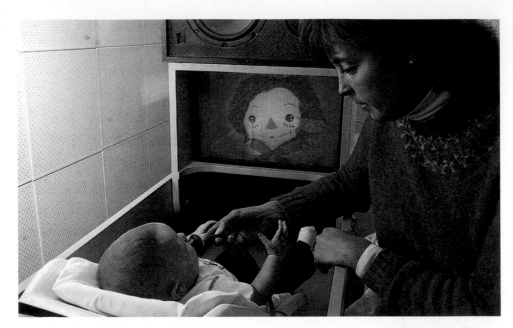

Researchers have developed ingenious techniques to assess how the infant perceives the world. This researcher is studying whether the infant can distinguish between Raggedy Ann and Raggedy Andy. If the infant stops sucking on the nipple when a new face appears, this indicates that the infant can tell the difference.

horizontally in front of the creature, its eyes follow the object's movement. The creature's head movement suggests that it has at least some vision.

In case you haven't already guessed, the creature you have been reading about is the human infant, and the role you played is that of a researcher interested in devising techniques to learn about the infant's visual perception. After years of work, scientists have developed research methods and tools sophisticated enough to examine the subtle abilities of infants and to interpret their complex actions (Bendersky & Sullivan, 2002; Kellman & Arterberry, 2006; Kellman & Banks, 1998; Slater, 2004).

Visual Preference Method
Robert Fantz (1963) was a pioneer in this effort. Fantz made an important discovery that advanced the ability of researchers to investigate infants' visual perception: Infants look at different things for different lengths of time. Fantz placed infants in a "looking chamber," which had two visual displays on the ceiling above the infant's head. An experimenter viewed the infant's eyes by looking through a peephole. If the infant was fixating on one of the displays, the experimenter could see the display's reflection in the infant's eyes. This allowed the experimenter to determine how long the infant looked at each display. Fantz (1963) found that infants only 2 days old look longer at patterned stimuli, such as faces and concentric circles, than at red, white, or yellow discs. Infants 2 to 3 weeks old preferred to look at patterns—a face, a piece of printed matter, or a bull's-eye—longer than at red, yellow, or white discs (see Figure 6.17). Fantz' research method—studying whether infants can distinguish one stimulus from another by measuring the length of time they attend to different stimuli—is referred to as the **visual preference method.**

Habituation and Dishabituation
Another way that researchers have studied infant perception is to present a stimulus (such as a sight or a sound) a number of times. If the infant reduces its attention to the stimulus after a number of presentations, it indicates that the infant is no longer interested in the stimulus (Sirois & Mareschal, 2004). This research method is referred to as **habituation**—decreased

visual preference method A method developed by Fantz to determine whether infants can distinguish one stimulus from another by measuring the length of time they attend to different stimuli.

habituation Decreased responsiveness to a stimulus after repeated presentations of the stimulus.

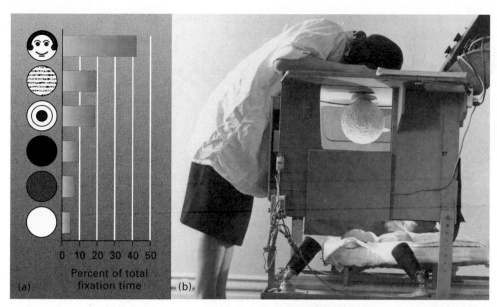

FIGURE 6.17 **Fantz's Experiment on Infants' Visual Perception** (*a*) Infants 2 to 3 weeks old preferred to look at some stimuli more than others. In Fantz's experiment, infants preferred to look at patterns rather than at color or brightness. For example, they looked longer at a face, a piece of printed matter, or a bull's-eye than at red, yellow, or white discs. (*b*) Fantz used a "looking chamber" to study infants' perception of stimuli.

responsiveness to a stimulus after repeated presentations of the stimulus. **Dishabituation** is the recovery of an habituated response after a change in stimulation. Among the measures researchers use to study whether habituation is occurring are sucking behavior (sucking behavior stops when the young infant attends to a novel object), heart and respiration rates, and the length of time the infant looks at an object. Newborn infants can habituate to repeated sights, sounds, smells, or touches (Rovee-Collier, 2004). Figure 6.18 shows the results of one study of habituation and dishabituation with newborns (Slater, Morison, & Somers, 1988).

High-Amplitude Sucking   To assess an infant's attention to sound, researchers often use a method called *high-amplitude sucking*. In this method, infants are given a non-nutritive nipple to suck, and the nipple is connected to "a sound generating system. Each suck causes a noise to be generated and the infant learns quickly that sucking brings about this noise. At first, babies suck frequently, so the noise occurs often. Then, gradually, they lose interest in hearing repetitions of the same noise and begin to suck less frequently. At this point, the experimenter changes the sound that is being generated. If the babies renew vigorous sucking, we infer that they have discriminated the sound change and are sucking more because they want to hear the interesting new sound" (Menn & Stoel-Gammon, 2005, p. 71).

The Orienting Response and Tracking   A technique that can be used to determine if an infant can see or hear is the *orienting response*, which involves turning one's head toward a sight or sound (Keen, 2005a). Another technique, *tracking*, consists of eye movements that follow (*track*) a moving object and can be used to determine if an infant can see.

Equipment   New technology is expanding researchers' ability to record and compare infants' actions and reactions. Videotape equipment allows us to investigate even elusive behaviors, and computers make it possible to quickly perform complex data analysis. Other equipment records respiration, heart rate, body movement, visual

dishabituation The recovery of a habituated response after a change in stimulation.

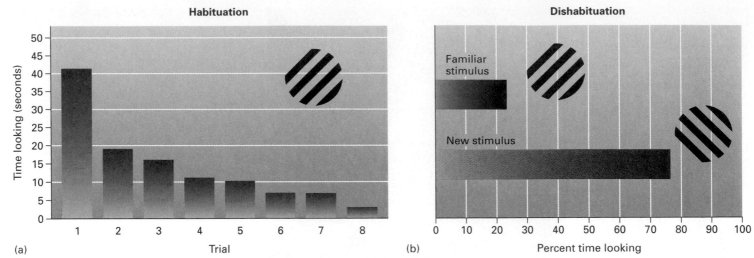

FIGURE 6.18 **Habituation and Dishabituation** In the first part of one study, 7-hour-old newborns were shown the stimulus in (*a*). As indicated, the newborns looked at it an average of 41 seconds when it was first presented to them (Slater, Morison, & Somers, 1988). Over seven more presentations of the stimulus, they looked at it less and less. In the second part of the study, infants were presented with both the familiar stimulus to which they had just become habituated to (*a*) and a new stimulus (shown in *b*, which was rotated 90 degrees). The newborns looked at the new stimulus three times as much as the familiar stimulus.

fixation, and sucking behavior, which provide clues to what the infant is perceiving. For example, some researchers use equipment that detects if a change in infants' respiration follows a change in the pitch of a sound. If so, it suggests that the infants heard the pitch change. Thus, scientists have become ingenious at assessing infant development, discovering ways to "interview" them even though they cannot yet talk.

Visual Perception

Some important changes in visual perception with age can be traced to differences in how the eye itself functions over time. These changes in the eye's functioning influence, for example, how clearly we can see an object, whether we can differentiate its colors, at what distance, and in what light.

Visual Acuity and Color Psychologist William James (1890–1950) called the newborn's perceptual world a "blooming, buzzing confusion." A century later, we can safely say that he was wrong (Slater, 2004). Even the newborn perceives a world with some order. That world, however, is far different from the one perceived by the toddler or the adult.

Just how well can infants see? Newborns cannot see small things that are far away. The newborn's vision is estimated to be 20/600 on the well-known Snellen chart, with which you are tested when you have your eyes examined (Banks & Salapatek, 1983). In other words, an object 20 feet away is only as clear to the newborn as it would be if it were 600 feet away from an adult with normal vision (20/20). By 6 months of age, though, vision is 20/100 or better, and by about the first birthday, the infant's vision approximates that of an adult (Banks & Salapatek, 1983). Figure 6.19 shows a computer estimation of what a picture of a face looks like to an infant at different ages from a distance of about 6 inches.

The infant's color vision also improves. At birth, babies can distinguish between green and red (Adams, 1989). Adultlike functioning of all of the eye's color-sensitive receptors (*cones*) is present by 2 months of age.

An important question focuses on whether experience is necessary for the vision of infants to develop normally. Researchers have found that deprivation of vision in

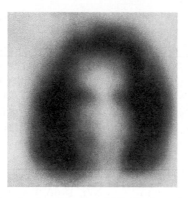

FIGURE 6.19 **Visual Acuity During the First Months of Life** The four photographs represent a computer estimation of what a picture of a face looks like to a 1-month-old, 2-month-old, 3-month-old, and 1-year-old (which approximates that of an adult).

one eye (called monocular deprivation) during infancy produces a loss of binocular depth perception (Billson, Fitzgerald, and Provis, 1985). A recent study also found that early experience with color is necessary for normal color vision (Sugita, 2004).

Perceiving Patterns

What does the world look like to infants? Do they recognize patterns? As we saw earlier, using his "looking chamber," Robert Fantz (1963) revealed that infants look at different things for different lengths of time. Even 2- to 3-month-old infants prefer to look at patterned displays than nonpatterned displays. For example, they prefer to look at a normal human face rather than one with scrambled features, and prefer to look at a bull's-eye target or black and white stripes rather than a plain circle.

Even very young infants soon change the way they gather information from the visual world. By using a special mirror arrangement, researchers projected an image of human faces in front of infants' eyes so that the infants' eye movements could be photographed (Maurer & Salapatek, 1976). Figure 6.20 shows the plotting of eye fixations of a 1-month-old and a 2-month-old infant. Notice that the 2-month-old scanned a much wider area of the face than the 1-month-old. The older infant also spent more time examining the internal details of the face, whereas the younger infant concentrated on the outer contours of the face.

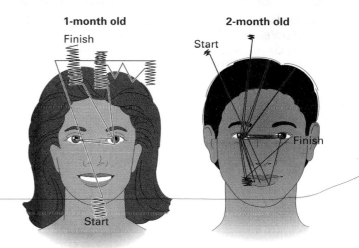

FIGURE 6.20 **How 1- and 2-Month-Old Infants Scan the Human Face**

Perceptual Constancy

Some perceptual accomplishments are especially intriguing because they indicate that the infant's perception is better than it should be based on sensory information (Bower, 2002; Slater, Field, & Hernandez-Reif, 2002). This is the case in *perceptual constancy,* in which sensory stimulation is changing but perception of the physical world remains constant. Two types of perceptual constancy are size constancy and shape constancy.

Size constancy is the recognition that an object remains the same even though the retinal image of the object changes. The size of an object on the retina is not sufficient to determine its actual size. The farther away from us an object is, the smaller its image is on our eyes. For example, a bicycle standing right in front of a child appears smaller than the car parked across the street, even though the bicycle casts a larger image on the child's eyes than the car does.

But what about babies? Do they have size constancy? Researchers have found that babies as young as 3 months of age show size constancy (Bower, 1966; Day & McKenzie, 1973). However, at 3 months of age, this ability is not full-blown and continues to develop. As infants' binocular vision develops between 4 and 5 months of age, their ability to perceive size constancy improves (Aslin, 1987). Further progress in

size constancy Recognition that an object remains the same even though the retinal image of the object changes.

FIGURE 6.21 **Examining Infants' Depth Perception on the Visual Cliff** Eleanor Gibson and Richard Walk (1960) found that most infants would not crawl out on the glass, which indicated that they had depth perception.

perceiving size constancy continues until 10 or 11 years of age (Kellman & Banks, 1998).

Shape constancy is the recognition that an object remains the same shape even though its orientation to us changes. Look around the room you are in right now. You likely see objects of varying shapes, such as tables and chairs. If you get up and walk around the room, you will see these objects from different sides and angles. Even though your retinal image of the objects changes as you walk and look, you will still perceive the objects as the same shape.

Do babies have shape constancy? As with size constancy, researchers have found that babies as young as 3 months of age have shape constancy (Bower, 1966; Day & McKenzie, 1973). Three-month-old infants, however, do not have shape constancy for irregularly-shaped objects, such as tilted planes (Cook & Birch, 1984).

Why is it important for infants to develop perceptual constancy early in their lives? If infants did not develop perceptual constancy, each time they saw an object at a different distance or in a different orientation, they would perceive it as a different object. Thus, the development of perceptual constancy allows the infant to perceive its world as stable.

Depth Perception   Decades ago, the inspiration for what would become a classic experiment came to Eleanor Gibson as she was eating a picnic lunch on the edge of the Grand Canyon. She wondered whether an infant looking over the canyon's rim would perceive the dangerous dropoff and back up. She also was worried that her own two young children would play too close to the canyon's edge and fall off. Do even young children perceive depth?

To investigate this question, Eleanor Gibson and Richard Walk (1960) constructed a miniature cliff with a drop-off covered by glass in their laboratory. They placed infants on the edge of this visual cliff and had their mothers coax them to crawl onto the glass (see figure 6.21). Most infants would not crawl out on the glass, choosing instead to remain on the shallow side, indicating that they could perceive depth.

Exactly how early in life does depth perception develop? The 6- to 12-month-old infants in the visual cliff experiment had extensive visual experience. Do younger infants without this experience still perceive depth? Since younger infants do not crawl, this question is difficult to answer. As we noted earlier, infants develop the ability to use binocular cues to depth by about 3 to 4 months of age. Two- to 4-month-old infants show differences in heart rate when they are placed directly on the deep side of the visual cliff instead of on the shallow side (Campos, Langer, & Krowitz, 1970). However, these differences might mean that young infants respond to differences in some visual characteristics of the deep and shallow cliffs, with no actual knowledge of depth.

Visual Expectations   Infants not only see forms and figures at an early age but also develop expectations about future events in their world by the time they are 3 months of age (Adler & Haith, 2003). Marshall Haith and his colleagues (Canfield & Haith, 1991; Haith, Hazen, & Goodman, 1988) studied whether babies would form expectations about where an interesting picture would appear. The pictures were presented to the infants in either a regular alternating (such as left, right, left, right) or an unpredictable sequence (such as right, right, left, right). When the sequence was predictable, the 3-month-old infants began to anticipate the location of the picture, looking at the side on which it was expected to appear. The young infants formed this visual expectation in less than 1 minute. However, younger infants did not develop expectations about where a picture would be presented.

Elizabeth Spelke (1991, 2000; Spelke & Hespos, 2001) also has demonstrated that young infants form visual expectations. She placed babies before a puppet stage and

shape constancy Recognition that an object remains the same even though its orientation to us changes.

(a)

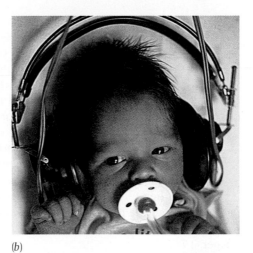
(b)

FIGURE 6.22 **Hearing in the Womb** (a) Pregnant mothers read *The Cat in the Hat* to their fetuses during the last few months of pregnancy. (b) When they were born, the babies preferred listening to a recording of their mothers reading *The Cat in the Hat*, as evidenced by their sucking on a nipple that produced this recording, rather than another story, *The King, the Mice and the Cheese.*

showed them a series of unexpected actions—for example, one ball seemed to roll through a solid barrier, another seemed to leap between two platforms, and a third appeared to hang in midair (Spelke, 1979). Spelke measured the babies' looking times and recorded longer intervals for unexpected than expected actions. She concluded that, by 4 months of age, even though infants do not yet have the ability to talk about objects, move around objects, manipulate objects, or even see objects with high resolution, they can recognize the solidity of objects and the continuity of objects. However, she has found that at 4 months of age, infants do not expect an object to obey gravitational constraints (Spelke & others, 1992).

By 6 to 8 months, infants have learned to perceive gravity and support—that an object hanging on the end of a table should fall, that ball-bearings will travel farther when rolled down a longer rather than a shorter ramp, and that cup handles will not fall when attached to a cup (Slater, Field, & Hernandez-Reif, 2002). As infants develop, their experiences and actions on objects help them to understand physical laws.

Other Senses

As infants develop, they not only obtain information about the world from their eyes. They also gather information about the world through sensory receptors in their ears, skin, nose, and tongue.

Hearing   Can the fetus hear? What kind of changes in hearing take place in infancy? During the last months of pregnancy, the fetus can hear sounds as it nestles in its mother's womb: It hears the mother's voice, music, and so on (Kisilevsky, 1995; Kisilevsky & others, 2005; Smith, Muir, & Kisilevsky, 2001). Two psychologists wanted to find out if a fetus that heard Dr. Seuss' classic story *The Cat in the Hat* while still in the mother's womb would prefer hearing the story after birth (DeCasper & Spence, 1986). During the last months of pregnancy, sixteen women read *The Cat in the Hat* to their fetuses. Then shortly after they were born, the mothers read to them either *The Cat in the Hat* or a story with a different rhyme and pace, *The King, the Mice and the Cheese* (which was not read to them during prenatal development). The infants sucked on a nipple in a different way when the mothers read the two stories, suggesting that the infants recognized its pattern and tone of *The Cat in the Hat* (see figure 6.22). This study illustrates that an infant's brain has a remarkable ability to learn even before birth and reflects the ingenuity of researchers in assessing development.

A recent study examined the ability of human fetuses to recognize their own mother's voice (Kisilevsky & others, 2003). Sixty term fetuses (mean gestational age: 38.4 weeks) were assigned to one of two conditions in which they were exposed to a tape recording of their mother or a female stranger reading a passage. Voice stimuli were delivered through a loudspeaker held just above the mother's abdomen. Fetal heart rate was monitored and increased in response to the mother's voice but decreased in response to the stranger's voice. This finding indicates that experience influences fetal voice processing.

Newborns are especially sensitive to the sounds of human speech (Saffran, Werker, & Werner, 2006). They will suck more rapidly on a nipple in order to listen to some sounds rather than others. Their sucking behavior indicates that they prefer a recording of their mother's voice to the voice of an unfamiliar woman, their mother's native language to a foreign language, and the classical music of Beethoven to the rock music of Aerosmith (Flohr & others, 2001; Mehler & others, 1988; Spence & De-Casper, 1987).

Hearing changes in infancy involve a sound's loudness, pitch, and localization. Immediately after birth, infants cannot hear soft sounds quite as well as adults can; a stimulus must be louder to be heard by a newborn than by an adult (Trehub & others, 1991). For example, an adult can hear a whisper from about 4 to 5 feet away but a newborn requires that sounds be closer to a normal conversational level to be heard at that distance. Infants are also less sensitive to the pitch of a sound than adults are. *Pitch* is the perception of the frequency of a sound. A soprano voice sounds high pitched, a bass voice low pitched. Infants are less sensitive to low-pitched sounds and are more likely to hear high-pitched sounds (Aslin, Jusczyk, & Pisoni, 1998). By 2 years of age, infants have considerably improved their ability to distinguish sounds with different pitches. It is important to be able *localize* sounds, detecting their origins. Even newborns can determine the general location from where a sound is coming but by 6 months of age, they are more proficient at localizing sounds and this ability continues to improve in the second year (Litovsky & Ashmead, 1997; Morrongiello, Fenwick, & Chance, 1990).

Our sensory-perceptual system seems built to give a special place to the sounds of language. Babies are born into the world prepared to respond to the sounds of any human language. Even young infants can discriminate subtle phonetic differences, such as those between the speech sounds of *ba* and *ga*. Experience with the native language, however, has an effect on speech perception. In the second half of the first year of life, infants become "native listeners," especially attuned to the sounds of their native language (Jusczyk, 2002). In chapter 7, "Cognitive Development in Infancy," we will further discuss development of infants' ability to distinguish the sounds they need for speech.

Touch and Pain   Do newborns respond to touch? Can they feel pain? Newborns do respond to touch. A touch to the cheek produces a turning of the head; a touch to the lips produces sucking movements.

An important ability that develops in infancy is to connect information about vision with information about touch. Coordination of vision and touch has been well-documented in 6-month-olds (Rose, 1990) and in one study was demonstrated in 2- to 3-year-olds (Steri, 1987).

If and when you have a son and need to consider whether he should be circumcised, the issue of an infant's pain perception probably will become important to you. Circumcision is usually performed on young boys during the first several days after birth. Will your young son experience pain if he is circumcised when he is a few days old? An investigation by Megan Gunnar and her colleagues (1987) found that newborn infant males cried intensely during circumcision. The circumcised infant also displays amazing resiliency. Within several minutes after the surgery, they can nurse and interact in a normal manner with their mothers. And, if allowed to, the newly circumcised newborn drifts into a deep sleep, which seems to serve as a coping mechanism.

For many years, doctors performed operations on newborns without anesthesia. This practice was accepted because of the dangers of anesthesia and because of the supposition that newborns do not feel pain. As researchers demonstrated that newborns can feel pain, the practice of operating on newborns without anesthesia is being challenged. Anesthesia now is used in some circumcisions.

Smell   As with the other senses, most research on developmental changes in smell focuses on early infancy and aging. Newborns can differentiate odors. The expressions on their faces seem to indicate that they like the way vanilla and strawberry smell but do not like the way rotten eggs and fish smell (Steiner, 1979). In one investigation, 6-day-old infants who were breast fed showed a clear preference for smelling their mother's breast pad (MacFarlane, 1975) (see figure 6.23). However, when they were 2 days old, they did not show this preference (compared with a clean breast pad), indicating that they require several days of experience to recognize this odor.

Taste   Sensitivity to taste might be present even before birth. When saccharin was added to the amniotic fluid of a near-term fetus, swallowing increased (Windle, 1940). In one study, even at only 2 hours of age, babies made different facial expressions when they tasted sweet, sour, and bitter solutions (Rosenstein & Oster, 1988) (see figure 6.24). At about 4 months of age, infants begin to prefer salty tastes, which as newborns they had found to be aversive (Harris, Thomas, & Booth, 1990).

FIGURE 6.23 Newborns' Preference for the Smell of Their Mother's Breast Pad In the experiment by MacFarlane (1975), 6-day-old infants preferred to smell their mother's breast pad over a clean one that had never been used, but 2-day-old infants did not show this preference, indicating that this odor preference requires several days of experience to develop.

Intermodal Perception

Imagine yourself playing basketball or tennis. You are experiencing many visual inputs: the ball coming and going, other players moving around, and so on. However, you are experiencing many auditory inputs as well: the sound of the ball bouncing or being hit, the grunts and groans, and so on. There is good correspondence between much of the visual and auditory information: When you see the ball bounce, you hear a bouncing sound; when a player stretches to hit a ball, you hear a groan.

We live in a world of objects and events that can be seen, heard, and felt. When mature observers simultaneously look at and listen to an event, they experience a unitary episode. All of this is so commonplace that it scarcely seems worth mentioning. But consider the task of very young infants with little practice at perceiving. Can they put vision and sound together as precisely as adults do?

Intermodal perception involves integrating information from two or more sensory modalities, such as vision and hearing. To test intermodal perception, Elizabeth Spelke (1979) showed 4-month-old infants two films simultaneously. In each film, a puppet jumped up and down, but in one of the films the soundtrack matched the puppet's dancing movements; in the other film, it did not. By measuring the infant's gaze, Spelke found that the infants looked more at the puppet whose actions were synchronized with the sound track, suggesting that they recognized the visual-sound correspondence. Young infants can also coordinate visual-auditory information involving people. In one study, as early as at 3½ months old, infants looked more at their mother when they also heard her voice and longer at their father when they also heard his voice (Spelke & Owsley, 1979).

Might auditory-visual relations be coordinated even in newborns? Newborns do turn their eyes and their head toward the sound of a voice or rattle when the sound is maintained for several seconds (Clifton & others, 1981), but the newborn can localize a sound and look at an object only in a crude way (Bechtold, Bushnell, & Salapatek, 1979). Improved accuracy at auditory-visual coordination likely requires a sharpening through experience with visual and auditory stimuli.

In sum, crude exploratory forms of intermodal perception exist in newborns (Chen, Striano, & Rakoczy, 2004). These exploratory forms of intermodal perception become sharpened with experience in the first year of life (Hollich, Newman, & Jusczyk, 2005). In the first six months, infants have difficulty connecting sensory

intermodal perception The ability to relate and integrate information about two or more sensory modalities, such as vision and hearing.

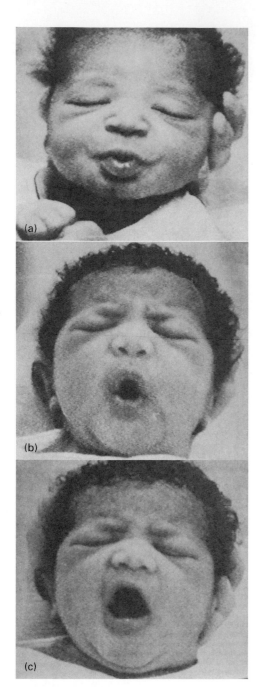

FIGURE 6.24 Newborns' Facial Responses to Basic Tastes Facial expressions elicited by (*a*) a sweet solution, (*b*) a sour solution, and (*c*) a bitter solution.

input from different modes, but in the second half of the first year they show an increased ability to make this connection mentally. Thus, babies are born into the world with some innate abilities to perceive relations among sensory modalities, but their intermodal abilities improve considerably through experience. As with all aspects of development, in perceptual development, nature and nurture interact and cooperate (Condry, Smith, & Spelke, 2001; Lickliter & Bahrick, 2000).

Perceptual-Motor Coupling

As we come to end of this chapter, we return to the important theme of perceptual-motor coupling. The distinction between perceiving and doing has been a time-honored tradition in psychology. However, a number of experts on perceptual and motor development question whether this distinction makes sense (Gibson, 2001; Lochman, 2000; Thelen & Whitmeyer, 2005). The main thrust of research in Esther Thelen's dynamic systems approach is to explore how people assemble motor behaviors for perceiving and acting. The main theme of the ecological approach of Eleanor and James J. Gibson is to discover how perception guides action. Action can guide perception and perception can guide action. Only by moving one's eyes, head, hands, and arms and by moving from one location to another can an individual fully experience his or her environment and learn how to adapt to it. Perception and action are coupled.

Babies, for example, continually coordinate their movements with perceptual information to learn how to maintain balance, reach for objects in space, and move across various surfaces and terrains (Adolph & Berger, 2006; Thelen, 2000; Thelen & Smith, 2006; Thelen & Whitmeyer, 2005). They are motivated to move by what they perceive. Consider the sight of an attractive toy across the room. In this situation, infants must perceive the current state of their bodies and learn how to use their limbs to reach the toy. Although their movements at first are awkward and uncoordinated, babies soon learn to select patterns that are appropriate for reaching their goals.

Equally important is the other part of the perception-action coupling. That is, action educates perception. For example, watching an object while exploring it manually helps infants to discriminate its properties of texture, size, and hardness. Locomoting in the environment teaches babies about how objects and people look from different perspectives, or whether surfaces will support their weight. Individuals perceive in order to move and move in order to perceive. Perceptual and motor development do not occur in isolation from one another but instead are coupled (Adolph & Berger, 2006; Bornstein, Arterberry, & Mash, 2005; Kellman & Arterberry, 2006; Thelen, 1995, 2000; Thelen & Smith, 2006; Thelen & Whitmeyer, 2005).

Review and Reflect • LEARNING GOAL 3

 Outline the course of sensory and perceptual development.

Review

- What are sensation and perception?
- What is the ecological view of perception?
- What are some research methods used to study infant perception?
- How does vision develop?
- How does hearing develop? How do touch and pain develop? How does smell develop? How does taste develop?
- What is intermodal perception and how does it develop?
- How are perception and motor actions coupled in the development of infants?

Reflect

- What would you do to effectively stimulate the hearing of a 1-year-old infant?

REACH YOUR LEARNING GOALS

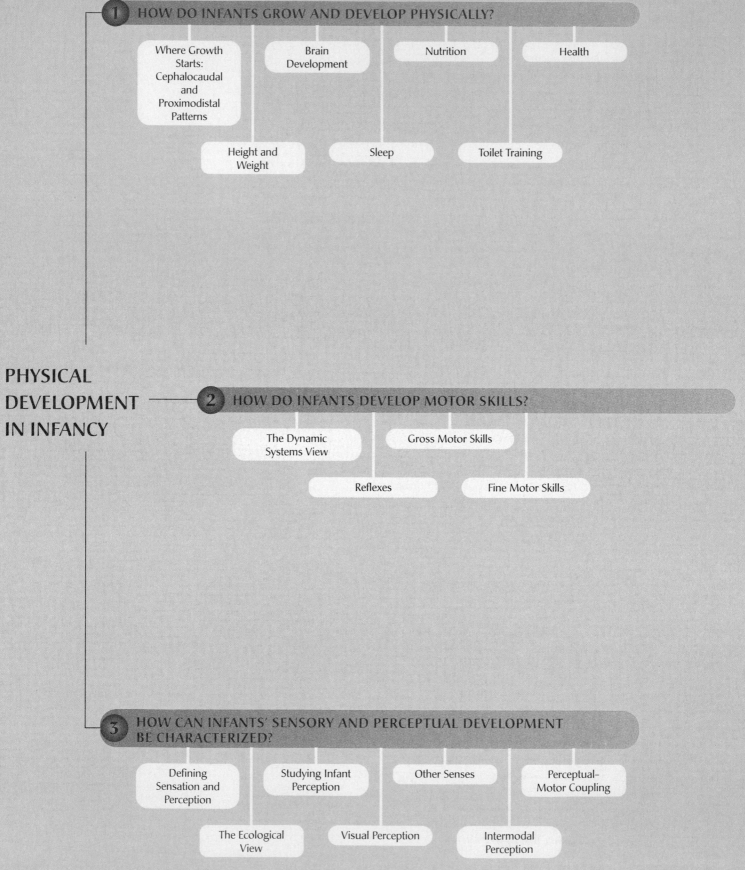

PHYSICAL DEVELOPMENT IN INFANCY

1 HOW DO INFANTS GROW AND DEVELOP PHYSICALLY?

- Where Growth Starts: Cephalocaudal and Proximodistal Patterns
- Height and Weight
- Brain Development
- Sleep
- Nutrition
- Toilet Training
- Health

2 HOW DO INFANTS DEVELOP MOTOR SKILLS?

- The Dynamic Systems View
- Reflexes
- Gross Motor Skills
- Fine Motor Skills

3 HOW CAN INFANTS' SENSORY AND PERCEPTUAL DEVELOPMENT BE CHARACTERIZED?

- Defining Sensation and Perception
- The Ecological View
- Studying Infant Perception
- Visual Perception
- Other Senses
- Intermodal Perception
- Perceptual–Motor Coupling

SUMMARY

 Discuss physical growth and development in infancy.

- The cephalocaudal pattern is the sequence in which the greatest growth proceeds from top to bottom. The proximodistal pattern is the sequence in which growth starts at the center of the body and moves toward the extremities.
- Infants grow about 1 inch per month in the first year and nearly triple their weight by their first birthday. The rate of growth slows in the second year.
- One of the most dramatic changes in the brain in the first two years of life is dendritic spreading. Myelination continues through infancy and into childhood. The cerebral cortex has two hemispheres (left and right). Lateralization refers to the specialization of function in one hemisphere or the other. Research with animals suggests that the environment plays a key role in early brain development. Neural connections are formed early in an infant's life. Before birth, genes mainly direct neurons to different locations. After birth, the inflowing stream of sights, sounds, smells, touches, language, and eye contact help shape the brain's neural connections.
- Newborns usually sleep 16 to 17 hours a day. By 4 months of age, many American infants approach adult-like sleeping patterns. REM sleep—during which dreaming occurs—is present more in early infancy than in childhood and adulthood. Sleeping arrangements for infants vary across cultures. In America, infants are more likely to sleep alone than in many other cultures. Some experts believe shared sleeping can lead to sudden infant death syndrome (SIDS), also called crib death, which occurs when a sleeping infant suddenly stops breathing and dies without an apparent cause.
- Infants need to consume about 50 calories per day for each pound they weigh. The growing consensus is that breast feeding is superior to bottle feeding. However, a special concern is the increase in HIV-infected mothers, in poor countries in particular, who risk passing the virus to the baby through breast milk. Severe infant malnutrition is still prevalent in many parts of the world. A concern in impoverished countries is early weaning from breast milk, which can result in marasmus or kwashiorkor.
- Toilet training is expected to be attained by about 3 years of age in North America. Toilet training should be carried out in a relaxed, supportive manner.
- Widespread immunization of infants has led to a significant decline in infectious diseases. Accidents are a major cause of death in infancy. These accidents include the aspiration of foreign objects, suffocation, and falls.

 Describe infants' motor development.

- The study of motor development has experienced a renaissance in recent years. Much of this renaissance is captured by Thelen's dynamic systems theory, which seeks to explain how motor behaviors are assembled for perceiving and acting. Perception and action are coupled. According to this theory, motor skills are the result of many converging factors, such as the development of the nervous system, the body's physical properties and its movement possibilities, the goal the child is motivated to reach, and environmental support for the skill. In the dynamic systems view, motor development is far more complex than the result of a genetic blueprint.
- Reflexes—automatic movements—govern the newborn's behavior. They include the sucking, rooting, and Moro reflexes—all of which typically disappear after three to four months. Other reflexes present in newborns, such as blinking and yawning, persist throughout life.
- Gross motor skills involve large-muscle activities, such as moving one's arms and walking. In Thelen's view, postural control is critical for engaging in adaptive activities. Locomotion and postural control are closely linked, especially in walking upright. A number of gross motor milestones occur in infancy but the timing of the milestones may vary as much as two to four months. What remains fairly uniform is the sequence of motor accomplishments. There are some cultural variations in reaching motor milestones in infancy, but overall, infants reach these milestones within similar age ranges.
- Fine motor skills involve movements that are more finely tuned than gross motor skills. A number of fine motor milestones occur in infancy. The development of reaching and grasping become more refined over the first two years of life.

 Outline the course of sensory and perceptual development.

- Sensation occurs when information interacts with sensory receptors. Perception is the interpretation of sensation.
- Created by the Gibsons, the ecological view states that people directly perceive information that exists in the world around them. Perception brings people in contact with the environment in order to interact and adapt to it. Affordances provide opportunities for interaction offered by objects that fit within our capabilities to perform activities.
- Researchers have developed a number of methods to assess the infant's perception, including the visual preference method (which Fantz used to determine young

infants' interest in looking at patterned over nonpatterned displays), habituation and dishabituation, and tracking.

- The infant's visual acuity increases dramatically in the first year of life. In color vision, newborns can distinguish green and red. All the color-sensitive receptors (cones) function in adult-like ways by 2 months of age. Young infants systematically scan human faces. By 3 months of age, infants show size and shape constancy. As visual perception develops, infants develop visual expectations. In Gibson and Walk's classic study, infants as young as 6 months of age had depth perception. Crawling is linked with decisions infants make on the visual cliff.
- The fetus can hear several months prior to birth. Immediately after birth, newborns can hear, but their sensory threshold is higher than that of adults. Developmental changes in the perception of loudness, pitch, and localization of sound occur during infancy. Newborns can respond to touch and feel pain. Newborns can differentiate odors, and sensitivity to taste may be present before birth.
- Infants as young as 2 months of age have intermodal perception—the ability to relate and integrate information from two or more sensory modalities. Crude, exploratory forms of intermodal perception are present in newborns and become sharpened over the first year of life.
- Perception and action are often not isolated but rather are coupled. Individuals perceive in order to move and move in order to perceive.

KEY TERMS

cephalocaudal pattern 169
proximodistal pattern 170
neuron 171
lateralization 173
sudden infant death
   syndrome (SIDS) 176
marasmus 179

kwashiorkor 179
dynamic systems theory 183
rooting reflex 184
sucking reflex 184
Moro reflex 184
grasping reflex 184
gross motor skills 185

fine motor skills 189
sensation 191
perception 191
ecological view 191
affordances 191
visual preference method 192
habituation 192

dishabituation 193
size constancy 195
shape constancy 196
intermodal perception 199

KEY PEOPLE

Charles Nelson 172
Mark Rosenzweig 173
Ernesto Pollitt 179
T. Berry Brazelton 179

Esther Thelen 183
Karen Adolph 186
Rachel Clifton 189

Eleanor and James J.
   Gibson 191
Robert Fantz 192
William James 194

Richard Walk 196
Marshall Haith 196
Elizabeth Spelke 196
Megan Gunnar 198

MAKING A DIFFERENCE

Supporting the Infant's Physical Development

What are some good strategies for helping the infant develop in physically competent ways?

- *Be flexible about the infant's sleep patterns.* Don't try to put the infant on a rigid sleep schedule. By about 4 months of age, most infants have moved closer to adultlike sleep patterns.
- *Provide the infant with good nutrition.* Make sure the infant has adequate energy and nutrient intake. Provide this in a loving and supportive environment. Don't put an infant on a diet. Weaning should be gradual, not abrupt.

- *Breast feed the infant, if possible.* Breast feeding provides more ideal nutrition than bottle feeding. If because of work demands the mother cannot breastfeed the infant, she should consider "pumping."
- *Toilet train the infant in a warm, relaxed, supportive manner.* Twenty months to 2 years of age is a recommended time to begin toilet training, so that it is accomplished before the "terrible twos." Like good strategies for the infant's sleep and nutrition, toilet training should not be done in a harsh, rigid way.
- *Give the infant extensive opportunities to explore safe environments.* Infants don't need exercise classes. What they

should be provided are many opportunities to actively explore safe environments. Infants should not be constricted to small, confined environments for any length of time.

- *Don't push the infant's physical development or get uptight about physical norms.* In American culture, we tend to want

our child to grow faster than other children. Remember that there is wide individual variation in normal physical development. Just because an infant is not at the top of a physical chart doesn't mean parents should start pushing the infant's physical skills. Infants develop at different paces. Respect and nurture the infant's individuality.

CHILDREN RESOURCES

Baby Steps (1994)

by Claire Kopp
New York: W. H. Freeman

Baby Steps is a guide to physical, cognitive, and socioemotional development in the first two years of life. The book is organized developmentally, with major sections divided into birth through 3 months, 4 through 7 months, 8 through 12 months, and the second year.

Infancy (1990)

by Tiffany Field
Cambridge, MA: Harvard University Press

Infancy is an outstanding book on infant development, written by one of the world's leading researchers on the topic. The book accurately captures the flavor of the young infant as an active learner and one far more competent than once was believed.

Solve Your Child's Sleep Problems (1985)

by Richard Ferber
New York: Simon & Schuster

Solve Your Child's Sleep Problems helps parents recognize when their infant or child has a sleep problem and tells them what to do about it.

E-LEARNING TOOLS

Connect to **www.mhhe.com/santrockc9** to research the answers to complete the following exercises. In addition, you'll find a number of other resources and valuable study tools for chapter 6, "Physical Development in Infancy," on this website.

Taking It to the Net

1. Angie and Dennis are first time parents. Angie insists that their 2-month-old daughter, LeAnn, can tell the difference between her mother and father's face, voice, and touch. Dennis says that is ridiculous. Who is correct?
2. Mary's mother, Robin, has just arrived from out of town and has seen her 3-month-old grandson, Troy, for the first time. Robin exclaims, "What are you feeding this roly-poly hunk? He looks overweight to me." Mary is shocked. She didn't think a baby could be overweight. Should she cut back on Troy's feedings?
3. Nicole, who has had three children, volunteers to babysit for her friend Nick's 5-month-old boy so that Nick can go on a job interview. As Nicole is undressing Justin, she thinks it's odd that he doesn't seem to be able to turn over in his crib. When she cradles him in her arm to bathe him, he feels "floppy" and appears to lack muscle strength. Is Justin evidencing any motor development delays?

Health and Well-Being, Parenting, and Education

Build your decision-making skills by trying your hand at the health and well-being, parenting, and education exercises.

Video Clips

The Online Learning Center includes the following videos for this chapter:

1. *Babinski Reflex at 2 weeks*—261
   The distinct Babinski reflex is demonstrated on this 2-week-old boy.
2. *Startle Reflex at 2 weeks*—263
   Here we see the newborn startle reflex as a 2-week-old boy reacts to a sudden bang of a tambourine.
3. *Crying at 10 Weeks*—697
   Here a 10-week-old baby boy cries and waves his arms and legs around as his mother attempts to soothe him.
4. *Auditory Tracking at 4 Months*—178
   A 4-month-old girl demonstrates auditory perception when she looks up at her mother, after hearing her mother call her name.

Chapter 7

COGNITIVE DEVELOPMENT IN INFANCY

I wish I could travel by the road that crosses baby's mind
Where Reason makes kites of her laws and flies them. . . .

—RABINDRANATH TAGORE
Bengali Poet, Essayist, 20th Century

CHAPTER OUTLINE

LEARNING GOALS

WHAT IS PIAGET'S THEORY OF INFANT DEVELOPMENT?

1 Summarize Piaget's theory of infant development.

Processes of Development

The Sensorimotor Stage

Evaluating Piaget's Sensorimotor Stage

HOW DO INFANTS LEARN AND REMEMBER?

2 Describe how infants learn and remember.

Conditioning

Attention

Imitation

Memory

Concept Formation and Categorization

HOW ARE INDIVIDUAL DIFFERENCES IN INFANT INTELLIGENCE ASSESSED?

3 Discuss the assessment of intelligence in infancy.

WHAT ARE SOME EARLY ENVIRONMENTAL INFLUENCES ON COGNITIVE DEVELOPMENT?

4 Characterize early environmental influences on cognitive development.

Nutrition

Poverty

WHAT IS THE NATURE OF LANGUAGE AND HOW DOES IT DEVELOP IN INFANCY?

5 Describe the nature of language and how it develops in infancy.

What Language Is

Language's Rule Systems

How Language Develops in Infancy

Biological and Environmental Influences

CARING FOR CHILDREN: How Parents Can Facilitate Infants'
and Toddlers' Language Development

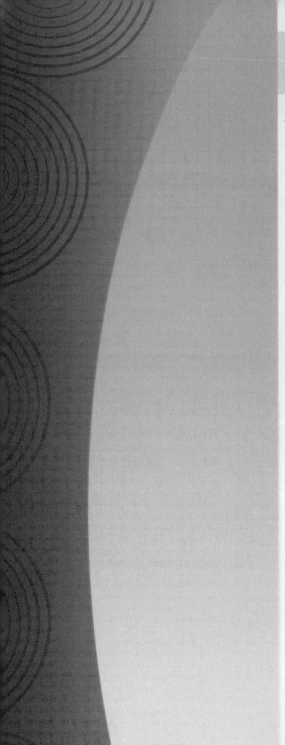

Images of Children
The Stories of Laurent, Lucienne, and Jacqueline

Jean Piaget, the famous Swiss psychologist, was a meticulous observer of his three children—Laurent, Lucienne, and Jacqueline. His books on cognitive development are filled with these observations. Here are a few of Piaget's observations of his children's cognitive development in infancy (Piaget, 1952):

- At 21 days of age, "Laurent found his thumb after three attempts: prolonged sucking begins each time. But, once he has been placed on his back, he does not know how to coordinate the movement of the arms with that of the mouth and his hands draw back even when his lips are seeking them" (p. 27).
- During the third month, thumb sucking becomes less important to Laurent because of new visual and auditory interests. But, when he cries, his thumb goes to the rescue.
- Toward the end of Lucienne's fourth month, while she is lying in her crib, Piaget hangs a doll above her feet. Lucienne thrusts her feet at the doll and makes it move. "Afterward, she looks at her motionless foot for a second, then recommences. There is no visual control of her foot, for the movements are the same when Lucienne only looks at the doll or when I place the doll over her head. On the other hand, the tactile control of the foot is apparent: after the first shakes, Lucienne makes slow foot movements as though to grasp and explore" (p. 159).
- At 11 months, "Jacqueline is seated and shakes a little bell. She then pauses abruptly in order to delicately place the bell in front of her right foot; then she kicks hard. Unable to recapture it, she grasps a ball which she then places at the same spot in order to give it another kick" (p. 225).
- At 1 year, 2 months, "Jacqueline holds in her hands an object which is new to her: a round, flat box which she turns all over, shakes, (and) rubs against the bassinet. . . . She lets it go and tries to pick it up. But she only succeeds in touching it with her index finger, without grasping it. She nevertheless makes an attempt and presses on the edge. The box then tilts up and falls again" (p. 273). Jacqueline shows an interest in this result and studies the fallen box.
- At 1 year, 8 months, "Jacqueline arrives at a closed door with a blade of grass in each hand. She stretches out her right hand toward the [door] knob but sees that she cannot turn it without letting go of the grass. She puts the grass on the floor, opens the door, picks up the grass again, and enters. But when she wants to leave the room, things become complicated. She puts the grass on the floor and grasps the doorknob. But then she perceives that in pulling the door toward her she will simultaneously chase away the grass which she placed between the door and the threshold. She therefore picks it up in order to put it outside the door's zone of movement" (p. 339).

For Piaget, these observations reflect important changes in the infant's cognitive development. Later in the chapter, you will learn that Piaget believed that infants go through six substages of development and that the behaviors you have just read about characterize those substages.

The excitement and enthusiasm about infant cognition has been fueled by interest in what an infant knows at birth and soon after, by continued fascination about innate and learned factors in the infant's cognitive development, and by controversies about whether infants construct their knowledge (as Piaget stressed) or whether they know their world more directly. In this chapter, we will study Piaget's theory of infant development, learning and remembering, individual differences in intelligence, some early environmental *influences on cognitive development, and language development.*

---

1 WHAT IS PIAGET'S THEORY OF INFANT DEVELOPMENT?

| Processes of Development | The Sensorimotor Stage | Evaluating Piaget's Sensorimotor Stage |

Piaget thought that, just as our physical bodies have structures that enable us to adapt to the world, we build mental structures that help us to adapt to the world. *Adaptation* involves adjusting to new environmental demands. Piaget also stressed that children actively construct their own cognitive worlds; information is not just poured into their minds from the environment. He sought to discover how children at different points in their development think about the world and how these systematic changes occur.

Processes of Development

Poet Nora Perry asked, "Who knows the thoughts of the child?" As much as anyone, Piaget knew. Through careful observations of his own three children—Laurent, Lucienne, and Jacqueline—and inquisitive interviews of other children, Piaget changed our perceptions of the way children think about the world. What processes do children use as they construct their knowledge of the world? Piaget believed that these processes are especially important in this regard: schemes, assimilation, and accommodation.

Schemes Piaget (1952) said that as the child seeks to construct an understanding of the world, the developing brain creates **schemes.** These are actions or mental representations that organize knowledge. In Piaget's theory, behavioral schemes (physical activities) characterize infancy and mental schemes (cognitive activities) develop in childhood (Lamb, Bornstein, & Teti, 2002).

A baby's schemes are structured by simple actions—such as sucking, looking, and grasping that can be performed on objects. Older children's schemes include strategies and plans for solving problems. For example, a 5-year-old might have a scheme that involves the strategy of classifying objects by size, shape, or color. By the time we have reached adulthood, we have constructed an enormous number of diverse schemes, ranging from how to drive a car to balancing a budget to the concept of fairness.

Assimilation and Accommodation To explain how children use and adapt their schemes, Piaget offered two concepts: assimilation and accommodation. (Recall that we initially described these concepts in chapter 2; here we review these concepts and provide further examples of them.) **Assimilation** occurs when children incorporate new information into their existing knowledge (schemes). **Accommodation** occurs when children adjust their schemes to fit new information and experiences. Consider a toddler who has learned the word *car* to identify the family's car. The toddler might call all moving vehicles on roads "cars," including motorcycles and trucks; the toddler has assimilated these objects into his or her existing scheme. But the child soon learns that motorcycles and trucks are not cars and fine-tunes the category to exclude motorcycles and trucks, accommodating the scheme.

Even in very young infants assimilation and accommodation operate. Newborns reflexively suck everything that touches their lips; they assimilate all sorts of objects

schemes In Piaget's theory, actions or mental representations that organize knowledge.

assimilation Piagetian concept of the incorporation of new information into existing knowledge (schemes).

accommodation Piagetian concept of adjusting schemes to fit new information and experiences.

into their sucking scheme. By sucking different objects, they learn about their taste, texture, shape, and so on. After several months of experience, though, they construct their understanding of the world differently. Some objects, such as fingers and the mother's breast, can be sucked, and others, such as fuzzy blankets, should not be sucked. In other words, they accommodate their sucking scheme.

Piaget's theory is a general, unifying story of how biology and experience sculpt the infant's cognitive development. Assimilation and accommodation always take the child to a higher ground. For Piaget, the motivation for change is an internal search for equilibrium. As a result of this change toward becoming more cognitively competent, Piaget theorized that individuals go through four stages of development. A different way of understanding the world makes one stage more advanced than another. Cognition is *qualitatively* different in one stage compared with another. In other words, the way children reason at one stage is different from the way they reason at another stage. This contrasts with the *quantitative* assessments of intelligence made through the use of standardized intelligence tests, which we will discuss in chapter 13. In these tests, the focus is on *what* the child knows, or how many questions the child can answer correctly.

Each of Piaget's stages is age-related and consists of distinct ways of thinking. Recall from our discussion of Piaget's theory in chapter 2 that Piaget argued there are four stages of cognitive development: sensorimotor, preoperational, concrete operational, and formal operational. In this chapter on cognitive development in infancy, we will examine the sensorimotor stage.

Piaget's Stages

The Sensorimotor Stage

The **sensorimotor stage** lasts from birth to about 2 years of age and is nonsymbolic throughout. In this stage, infants construct an understanding of the world by coordinating sensory experiences (such as seeing and hearing) with physical, motoric actions—hence the term "sensorimotor." At the beginning of this stage, newborns have little more than reflexive patterns with which to work. At the end of the stage, 2-year-olds have complex sensorimotor patterns and are beginning to operate with primitive symbols. We first will summarize Piaget's descriptions of how infants develop. Later we will consider criticisms of his view.

Substages of Sensorimotor Development
Piaget divided the sensorimotor stage into six substages: (1) simple reflexes; (2) first habits and primary circular reactions; (3) secondary circular reactions; (4) coordination of secondary circular reactions; (5) tertiary circular reactions, novelty, and curiosity; and (6) internalization of schemes (see figure 7.1).

Simple reflexes, the first sensorimotor substage, corresponds to the first month after birth. In this substage, sensation and action are coordinated primarily through reflexive behaviors. These include the rooting and sucking reflexes, which the infant has at birth. In this substage, the infant develops an ability to produce behaviors that resemble reflexes in the absence of the usual stimulus for the reflex. For example, when the baby was just born, a bottle or nipple would produce sucking only when it was placed directly in the baby's mouth or touched to the lips. But soon the infant might suck when a bottle or nipple is only nearby. Reflexlike actions in the absence of a triggering stimulus demonstrate that the infant is initiating action and is actively structuring experiences in the first month of life.

First habits and primary circular reactions is the second sensorimotor substage, which develops between 1 and 4 months of age. In this substage, the infant learns to coordinate sensation and two types of schemes: habits and primary circular reactions. A *habit* is a scheme based on a reflex that has become completely separated from its eliciting stimulus. For example, infants in substage 1 might suck when bottles are put to their lips or when they see a bottle. Infants in substage 2 might suck even when no bottle is present. A *circular reaction* is a repetitive or stereotyped action.

sensorimotor stage The first of Piaget's stages, which lasts from birth to about 2 years of age and is nonsymbolic throughout; infants construct an understanding of the world by coordinating sensory experiences (such as seeing and hearing) with motoric actions.

simple reflexes Piaget's first sensorimotor substage, which corresponds to the first month after birth. In this substage, the basic means of coordinating sensation and action is through reflexive behaviors, such as rooting and sucking, which the infant has at birth.

first habits and primary circular reactions Piaget's second sensorimotor substage, which develops between 1 and 4 months of age. In this substage, infants' reflexes evolve into adaptive schemes that are more refined and coordinated.

Simple reflexes

Infants are limited to exercising simple reflexes, such as rooting and sucking.

0 to 1 month of age

First habits and primary circular reactions

Infants' reflexes evolve into adaptive schemes that are more refined and coordinated.

1 to 4 months of age

Secondary circular reactions

Infants become more outwardly oriented, moving beyond self-preoccupation. They discover procedures for producing interesting events.

4 to 8 months of age

Coordination of secondary circular reactions

Infants combine and recombine earlier schemes and engage for the first time in truly intentional behavior. Infants can now separate means and end in trying to reach a goal.

8 to 12 months of age

Tertiary circular reactions, novelty, and curiosity

Infants start to vary schemes to produce new effects.

12 to 18 months of age

Internalization of schemes

Infants' capacity for symbolic thought emerges.

18 to 24 months of age

A **primary circular reaction** is a scheme based on the attempt to reproduce an event that initially occurred by chance. For example, suppose an infant accidentally sucks his fingers when they are placed near his mouth. Later, he searches for his fingers to suck them again, but the fingers do not cooperate because the infant cannot coordinate visual and manual actions.

primary circular reaction A scheme based on the infant's attempt to reproduce an interesting or a pleasurable event that initially occurred by chance.

Habits and circular reactions are stereotyped: That is, the infant repeats them the same way each time. During this substage, the infant's own body remains the infant's center of attention. There is no outward pull by environmental events.

Secondary circular reactions is the third sensorimotor substage, which develops between 4 and 8 months of age. In this substage, the infant becomes more object-oriented, moving beyond preoccupation with the self. By chance, an infant might shake a rattle. The infant repeats this action for the sake of experiencing fascination. The infant also imitates some simple actions, such as the baby talk or burbling of adults, and some physical gestures. However, the baby imitates only actions that he or she is already able to produce. Although directed toward objects in the world, the infant's schemes lack an intentional, goal-directed quality.

Coordination of secondary circular reactions is Piaget's fourth sensorimotor substage, which develops between 8 and 12 months of age. The critical requirement for the infant to progress into this substage is the coordination of vision and the sense of touch, or hand-eye coordination. Actions become more outwardly directed. Significant changes in this substage involve the coordination of schemes and intentionality. Infants readily combine and recombine previously learned schemes in a coordinated way. They might look at an object and grasp it simultaneously, or they might visually inspect a toy, such as a rattle, and finger it simultaneously, in obvious tactile exploration. Actions are even more outwardly directed than before. Related to this coordination is the second achievement—the presence of intentionality. For example, infants might manipulate a stick in order to bring a desired toy within reach or they might knock over one block to reach and play with another one.

Tertiary circular reactions, novelty, and curiosity is Piaget's fifth sensorimotor substage, which develops between 12 and 18 months of age. In this substage, infants become intrigued by the many properties of objects and by the many things that they can make happen to objects. A block can be made to fall, spin, hit another object, and slide across the ground. *Tertiary circular reactions* are schemes in which the infant purposely explores new possibilities with objects, continually doing new things to them and exploring the results. Piaget says that this stage marks the starting point for human curiosity and interest in novelty.

Internalization of schemes is Piaget's sixth and final sensorimotor substage, which develops between 18 and 24 months of age. In this substage, the infant develops the ability to use primitive symbols. For Piaget, a *symbol* is an internalized sensory image or word that represents an event. Primitive symbols permit the infant to think about concrete events without directly acting them out or perceiving them. Moreover, symbols allow the infant to manipulate and transform the represented events in simple ways. In a favorite Piagetian example, Piaget's young daughter saw a matchbox being opened and closed. Later, she mimicked the event by opening and closing her mouth. This was an obvious expression of her image of the event.

Understanding Physical Reality

Piaget thought that children, even infants, are much like little scientists, examining the world to find out how it works. Developmentalists are interested in how infants' knowledge of the physical world develops (Bremner, 2004). Key aspects of infants' understanding of physical reality are object permanence and cause and effect.

Object Permanence

Imagine what your life would be like if you could not distinguish between yourself and your world. It would be chaotic and unpredictable. This is what the life of a newborn must be like, according to Piaget. There is no differentiation between the self and world; objects have no separate, permanent existence.

By the end of the sensorimotor period, however, both are present. **Object permanence** is the understanding that objects and events continue to exist even when they cannot be seen, heard, or touched. Acquiring the sense of object permanence is one of the infant's most important accomplishments.

---

secondary circular reactions Piaget's third sensorimotor substage, which develops between 4 and 8 months of age. In this substage, the infant becomes more object-oriented, or focused on the world, moving beyond preoccupation with the self in sensorimotor interactions.

coordination of secondary circular reactions Piaget's fourth sensorimotor substage, which develops between 8 and 12 months of age. In this substage, several significant changes take place involving the coordination of schemes and intentionality.

tertiary circular reactions, novelty, and curiosity Piaget's fifth sensorimotor substage, which develops between 12 and 18 months of age. In this substage, infants become intrigued by the variety of properties that objects possess and by the multiplicity of things they can make happen to objects.

internalization of schemes Piaget's sixth and final sensorimotor substage, which develops between 18 and 24 months of age. In this substage, the infant's mental functioning shifts from a purely sensorimotor plane to a symbolic plane, and the infant develops the ability to use primitive symbols.

object permanence The Piagetian term for one of an infant's most important accomplishments: understanding that objects and events continue to exist even when they cannot directly be seen, heard, or touched.

How could Piaget or other developmentalists know whether or not an infant had a sense of object permanence? One way that object permanence is studied is by watching an infant's reaction when an interesting object disappears (see figure 7.2). If infants search for the object, it is assumed that they believe it continues to exist.

A research method that Renée Baillargeon and her colleagues use to assess object permanence is *violation of expectations.* In this method, infants see an event happen as it normally would. Then, the event is changed in a way that violates what the infant expects to see. When infants look longer at the event that violates their expectations it indicates they are surprised by it (Baillargeon, 2004). In one study focused on object permanence, researchers showed infants a toy car that moved down an inclined track, disappeared behind a screen, and then reemerged at the other end, still on the track (Baillargeon & DeVos, 1991) (see figure 7.3*a*). After this sequence was repeated several times, the infants then saw something different take place. In a "possible event" a toy mouse was placed *behind* the tracks but was hidden by the screen while the car rolled by (*b*). Then, in an "impossible event," the toy mouse was placed *on* the tracks but was secretly removed after the screen was lowered so that the car seemed to go through the mouse (*c*). In this study, infants as young as 3½ months of age looked longer at the impossible event than at the possible event, indicating that they were surprised by it. Their surprised look suggested they remembered not only that the toy mouse still existed (object permanence) but its location.

Understanding of Causality Another study using the violation of expectations method focused on the infant's understanding of causality. Researchers found that even young infants comprehend that the size of a moving object determines how far it will move a stationary object that it collides with (Kotovsky & Baillargeon, 1994) (see figure 7.4). In this research, a cylinder rolls down a ramp and hits a toy bug at the bottom of the ramp. By 5½ and 6½ months of age, infants understand that the bug will roll farther if it is hit by a large cylinder than if it is hit by a small cylinder after they have observed how far it will be pushed by a medium-sized cylinder. Thus, by the middle of the first year of life these infants understood that the size of the cylinder was a causal factor in determining how far the bug would move if it was hit by the cylinder.

(a)

(b)

FIGURE 7.2 Object Permanence Piaget thought that object permanence was one of infancy's landmark cognitive accomplishments. For this 5-month-old boy, out of sight is literally out of mind. The infant looks at the toy dog (*top*), but when his view of the toy is blocked (*bottom*), he does not search for it. In a few more months, he will search for hidden toys, reflecting the presence of object permanence.

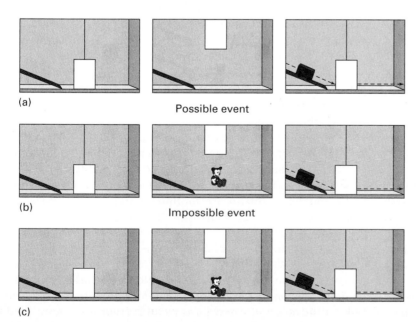

(a)

Possible event

(b)

Impossible event

(c)

FIGURE 7.3 Using the Violation of Expectations Method to Study Object Permanence in Infants

FIGURE 7.4 **The Infants' Understanding of Causality** After young infants saw how far the medium-sized cylinder (*a*) pushed a toy bug, they showed more surprise at the event in (*c*) that showed a very small cylinder pushing the toy bug as far as the large cylinder (*b*). Their surprise, indicated by looking at (*c*) longer than (*b*), indicated that they understood the size of a cylinder was a causal factor in determining how far the toy bug would be pushed when it was hit by the cylinder.

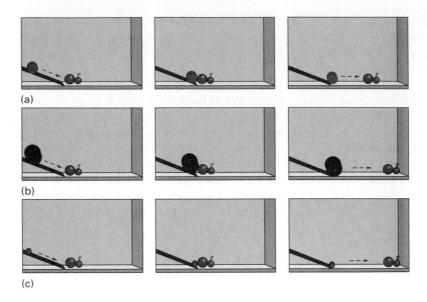

(a)

(b)

(c)

www.mhhe.com/santrockc9

Challenges to Piaget

Evaluating Piaget's Sensorimotor Stage

Piaget opened up a new way of looking at infants with his view that their main task is to coordinate their sensory impressions with their motor activity. However, the infant's cognitive world is not as neatly packaged as Piaget portrayed it, and some of Piaget's explanations for the cause of change are debated (Cohen & Cashon, 2006).

Piaget constructed his view of infancy mainly by observing the development of his own three children. In the past several decades, sophisticated experimental techniques have been devised to study infants, and there have been a large number of research studies on infant development (Kellman & Arterberry, 2006). Much of the new research suggests that Piaget's view of sensorimotor development needs to be modified.

A number of theorists, such as Eleanor Gibson (2001) and Elizabeth Spelke (1991; Spelke & Newport, 1998), believe that infants' perceptual abilities are highly developed very early in development. For example, in chapter 6 we discussed Spelke's research demonstrating the presence of intermodal perception—the ability to coordinate information from two more sensory modalities, such as vision and hearing. Research by Renée Baillargeon (1995, 2002, 2004) and her colleagues (Aguiar & Baillargeon, 2002; Luo & Baillargeon, 2005; Wang, Baillargeon, & Paterson, 2005) documents that infants as young as 3 to 4 months expect objects to be *substantial* (in the sense that other objects cannot move through them) and *permanent* (in the sense that objects continue to exist when they are hidden).

Researchers stress that infants see objects as bounded, unitary, solid, and separate from their background, possibly at birth or shortly thereafter, but definitely by 3 to 4 months of age, much earlier than Piaget envisioned. Young infants still have much to learn about objects, but the world appears both stable and orderly to them and, thus, capable of being conceptualized. Infants are continually trying to structure and make sense of their world (Meltzoff, 2002; Meltzoff & Decety, 2003; Meltzoff & Gopnik, 1997.)

Piaget claimed that certain processes are crucial in stage transitions, but the data do not always support his explanations. For example, in Piaget's theory, an important feature in the progression into substage 4, coordination of secondary circular reactions, is an infant's inclination to search for a hidden object in a familiar location rather than to look for the object in a new location. **AB error** is the term used to describe infants who make the mistake of selecting the familiar hiding place (A) rather than the new hiding place (B̄) as they progress into substage 4. Researchers have found, however, that the AB̄ error does not show up consistently (Corrigan, 1981; Sophian, 1985). The evidence indicates that AB̄ errors are sensitive to the delay

AB̄ error The Piagetian object-permanence concept in which an infant progressing into substage 4 makes frequent mistakes, selecting the familiar hiding place (A) rather than the new hiding place (B̄).

between hiding the object at $\overline{B}$ and the infant's attempt to find it (Diamond, 1985). Thus, the A$\overline{B}$ error might be due to a failure in memory.

Many of today's researchers argue that Piaget wasn't specific enough about how infants learn about their world and that infants are more competent than Piaget thought (Cohen & Cashon, 2006; Mandler, 2000, 2003, 2004). As they have examined the specific ways that infants learn, the field of infant cognition has become very specialized. Many researchers are working on different questions, with no general theory emerging that can connect all of the different findings (Nelson, 1999). Their theories are local theories, focused on specific research questions, rather than grand theories like Piaget's (Kuhn, 1998). Investigators in infant development continue to struggle with how developmental changes in cognition take place and the big issue of nature and nurture.

> *Infants know that objects are substantial and permanent at an earlier age than Piaget envisioned.*
>
> —RENÉE BAILLARGEON
> *Contemporary Psychologist, University of Illinois*

 Review and Reflect • LEARNING GOAL 1

1 Summarize Piaget's theory of infant development.

Review
- What are some key processes in Piaget's theory of cognitive development?
- How can Piaget's stage of sensorimotor development be described?
- What are some contributions and criticisms of Piaget's sensorimotor stage?

Reflect
- What are some implications of Piaget's theory of infant development for parenting?

---

2 HOW DO INFANTS LEARN AND REMEMBER?

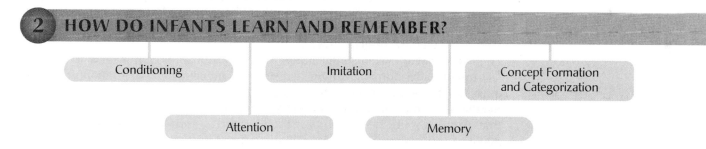

Conditioning   Imitation   Concept Formation and Categorization

Attention   Memory

In this section, we will explore the following aspects of how infants learn and remember: conditioning, attention, imitation, memory, and concept formation and categorization. In contrast to Piaget's theory, the approaches we will look at here do not describe infant development in terms of stages.

Conditioning

In chapter 2, "The Science of Child Development," we described Pavlov's classical conditioning and Skinner's operant conditioning. Both types of conditioning have been demonstrated in infants.

Through classical conditioning, an infant may develop a lifelong fear of heights from falling from a high chair. In contrast, in operant conditioning, the consequences of the infant's behavior produce changes in the probability of the behavior's occurrence. For instance, if an infant's behavior is followed by a rewarding stimulus, the behavior is likely to recur.

Operant conditioning has especially been helpful in researchers' efforts to determine what infants perceive. For example, infants will suck faster on a nipple when the sucking behavior is followed by a visual display, music, or a human voice (Rovee-Collier, 1987).

FIGURE 7.5 The Technique Used in Rovee-Collier's Investigation of Infant Memory In Rovee-Collier's experiment, operant conditioning was used to demonstrate that infants as young as 2½ months of age can retain information from the experience of being conditioned.

Carolyn Rovee-Collier (1987) has also demonstrated how infants can retain information from the experience of being conditioned. In a characteristic experiment, she places a 2½-month-old baby in a crib under an elaborate mobile. She then ties one end of a ribbon to the baby's ankle and the other end to the mobile. Subsequently, she observes that the baby kicks and makes the mobile move. The movement of the mobile is the reinforcing stimulus (which increases the baby's kicking behavior) in this experiment. Weeks later, the baby is returned to the crib, but its foot is not tied to the mobile. The baby kicks, which suggests it has retained the information that if it kicks a leg, the mobile will move (see figure 7.5).

Attention

Attention is the focusing of mental resources. Attention improves cognitive processing on many tasks. Even newborns can detect a contour and fixate on it. Older infants scan patterns more thoroughly. Infants as young as 4 months can selectively attend to an object and sustain their attention. In a recent study, 4-month-old infants were more likely to look longer at a dynamic stimulus with an audio track than at a static stimulus that was mute (Shaddy & Columbo, 2004).

Closely linked with attention are the processes of habituation and dishabituation that we discussed in chapter 6, "Physical Development in Infancy." Recall that if a stimulus—a sight or sound—is presented to infants several times in a row, they usually pay less attention to it each time. This suggests they are bored with it. This is the process of *habituation*— decreased responsiveness to a stimulus after repeated presentations of the stimulus. *Dishabituation* is the recovery of a habituated response after a change in stimulation.

Researchers study habituation to determine the extent to which infants can see, hear, smell, taste, and experience touch (Slater, 2004). Studies of habituation can also indicate whether infants recognize something they have previously experienced.

The extensive assessment of habituation in recent years has resulted in its use as a measure of an infant's maturity and well-being. Infants with brain damage or who have suffered birth traumas, such as insufficient oxygen, do not habituate well and might later have developmental and learning problems.

Infants' attention is so strongly governed by novelty and habituation that when an object becomes familiar, attention becomes shorter, making infants more vulnerable to distraction (Oakes, Kannass, & Shaddy, 2002). One recent study found that 10-month-olds were more distractible than 26-month-olds (Ruff & Capozzoli, 2003). Another recent study revealed that infants who were labeled "short lookers" because of the brief time they focused attention had better memory at 1 year of age than were "long lookers," who had more sustained attention (Courage, Howe, & Squires, 2004).

A knowledge of habituation and dishabituation can benefit parent-infant interaction. Infants respond to changes in stimulation. If stimulation is repeated often, the infant's response will decrease to the point that the infant no longer responds to the parent. In parent-infant interaction, it is important for parents to do novel things and to repeat them often until the infant stops responding. The wise parent senses when the infant shows an interest and that many repetitions of the stimulus may be necessary for the infant to process the information. The parent stops or changes behaviors when the infant redirects her attention (Rosenblith, 1992).

Imitation

Can infants imitate someone else's emotional expressions? If an adult smiles, will the baby follow with a smile? If an adult protrudes her lower lip, wrinkles her forehead, and frowns, will the baby show a sad face? If an adult opens his mouth, widens his eyes, and raises his eyebrows, will the baby follow suit? Can infants only a few days old do these things?

attention The focusing of mental resources.

Infant development researcher Andrew Meltzoff (2002; Meltzoff & Decety, 2003; Meltzoff & Moore, 1999) has conducted numerous studies of infants' imitative abilities. He believes infants' imitative abilities are biologically based, because infants can imitate a facial expression within the first few days after birth. This occurs before they have had the opportunity to observe social agents in their environment protruding their tongues and engaging in other behaviors. He also emphasizes that the infant's imitative abilities do not resemble what ethologists conceptualize as a hardwired, reflexive, innate releasing mechanism but rather involve flexibility, adaptability, and intermodal perception. In Meltzoff's observations of infants in the first 72 hours of life, the infants gradually displayed a full imitative response of an adult's facial expression, such as protruding the tongue or opening the mouth wide (see figure 7.6).

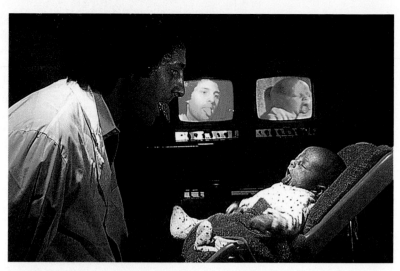

FIGURE 7.6 **Infant Imitation** Infant development researcher Andrew Meltzoff protrudes his tongue in an attempt to get the infant to imitate his behavior.

Not all experts on infant development accept Meltzoff's conclusions that newborns are capable of imitation. Some say that these babies were engaging in little more than automatic responses to a stimulus. Others argue that these studies cannot be consistently replicated.

Meltzoff also has studied **deferred imitation,** which occurs after a time delay of hours or days. In one study, Meltzoff (1988) demonstrated that 9-month-old infants could imitate actions that they had seen performed 24 hours earlier. Each action consisted of an unusual gesture—such as pushing a recessed button in a box (which produced a beeping sound). Piaget believed that deferred imitation doesn't occur until about 18 months of age. Meltzoff's research suggested that it occurs much earlier.

Andrew Meltzoff's Research
Infant Cognition
Patricia Bauer's Research

Memory

Memory is a central feature of cognitive development that involves the retention of information over time. Sometimes information is retained only for a few seconds, and at other times it is retained for a lifetime.

Popular child-rearing expert Penelope Leach (1990) told parents that 6- to 8-month-old babies cannot hold in their mind a picture of their mother or father. And historically psychologists believed that infants cannot store memories until they have language skills. What does the research evidence say about infant memory?

First Memories
Some infant researchers, such as Carolyn Rovee-Collier, argue that infants as young as 2 to 6 months of age can remember some experiences through 1½ to 2 years of age (Rovee-Collier, 2004). However, critics such as Jean Mandler (2000, 2004), a leading expert on infant cognition, argue that Rovee-Collier fails to distinguish between retention of a perceptual-motor variety that is involved in conditioning tasks (like that involved in kicking a mobile), often referred to as *implicit memory,* and the ability to consciously recall the past, often referred to as *explicit memory.* When people think about what memory is, they are referring to the latter, which most researchers find does not occur until the second half of the first year (Mandler & McDonough, 1995).

By 9 months of age, infants' explicit memory is readily apparent (Bauer, 2004, 2005, 2006). For example, in one study, 9-month-old infants displayed long-term recall of a two-step sequence (such as "Make Big Bird turn on the light") (Carver & Bauer, 1999). Five weeks after experiencing such two-step sequences, 45 percent of the infants demonstrated their long-term memory by producing the two actions in the sequence. The other 55 percent did not show evidence of remembering the sequence of actions, reflecting individual differences in infant memory. Also, in a related

deferred imitation Imitation that occurs after a time delay of hours or days.

memory A central feature of cognitive development, pertaining to all situations in which an individual retains information over time.

assessment of infants, researchers demonstrated changes in the brain activity of the infants as they engaged in recall of the sequences they had experienced five weeks earlier (Bauer & others, 2003).

Although explicit memory merges in the second half of the first year, the results of other research reveal that it undergoes substantial development and consolidation over the course of the second year of life (Carver & Bauer, 2001). In one longitudinal study, infants were assessed several times during the second year of life (Bauer & others, 2000). The older infants showed more accurate memory and required fewer prompts to demonstrate their memory than infants under the age of 1.

Infantile Amnesia Do you remember your third birthday party? Probably not. Most adults can remember little if anything from the first three years of their life. This is called *infantile* or *childhood amnesia.* The few reported adult memories of life at age 2 or 3 are at best very sketchy (Hayne, 2004; Neisser, 2004; Newcombe & others, 2000). Elementary school children also do not remember much of their early child years. In one study, about three years after leaving preschool, children were much poorer at remembering their former classmates than their teacher was (Lie & Newcombe, 1999). In another study, 10-year-olds were shown pictures of their preschool classmates and they recognized only about 20 percent of them (Newcombe & Fox, 1994).

What is the cause of infantile amnesia? One reason for the difficulty older children and adults have in recalling events from their infant and early child years is the immaturity of the prefrontal lobes of the brain, which are believed to play an important role in memory for events (Boyer & Diamond, 1992).

Concept Formation and Categorization

Concepts group objects, events, and characteristics on the basis of common properties. Concepts help us to simplify and summarize information. Imagine a world in which we had no concepts: We would see each object as unique and would not be able to make any generalizations.

Do infants have concepts? Yes they do and they form concepts very early in their development (Horst, Oakes, & Madole, 2005; Nelson, 2004; Quinn, 2004). Infants as young as 3 months of age begin to form categories on the basis of perceptual features. How can researchers determine that infants so young can do this? They use the habituation technique discussed earlier in the chapter. For example, in one study 3- and 4-month-olds were shown paired photographs of animals, such as dogs and cats (Quinn & Eimas, 1996). When the infants were presented with paired photographs of dogs across several trials, they habituated to them (that is, over time they looked at them less). However, when the infants were subsequently shown photographs of a dog paired with a cat, the infants looked longer at the cat, indicating they recognized it as being different from the dogs they had previously seen. Infants less than 6 months of age have also shown the ability to categorize geometric patterns, men's and women's voices, and chairs and tables (Haith & Benson, 1998).

Jean Mandler (2000, 2004) argues that these early categorizations are best described as *perceptual categorization.* That is, the categorizations are based on similar perceptual features of objects, such as size, color, and movement, as well as parts of objects, such as legs for animals. She concludes that it is not until about 7 to 9 months of age that infants form *conceptual* categories characterized by perceptual variability. For example, in one study of 7- to 11-month-olds, infants classified birds as animals and airplanes as vehicles even though the objects were perceptually similar—airplanes and birds with their wings spread (Mandler & McDonough, 1993).

Further advances in categorization occur in the second year of life. In Mandler's (2005) analysis, many of infants' "first concepts are broad and global in nature, such as 'animal' or 'indoor thing.' Gradually, over the first two years these broad concepts become more differentiated into concepts such as 'land animal,' then 'dog,' or to 'furniture,' then 'chair'" (p. 1).

concepts Categories that group objects, events, and characteristics on the basis of common properties.

2 Describe how infants learn and remember.

- How do infants learn through conditioning?
- What is attention and how is it linked with habituation and dishabituation?
- How is imitation involved in infant learning?
- What is memory? To what extent can infants remember? To what extent can older children and adults remember their infant experiences?
- What are concepts? Do infants have concepts?

Reflect

- If someone said that they remember being abused by their parents when they were 2 years old, would you believe them? Explain your answer.

3 HOW ARE INDIVIDUAL DIFFERENCES IN INFANT INTELLIGENCE ASSESSED?

So far, we have discussed how the cognitive development of infants generally progresses. We have emphasized what is typical of the largest number of infants or the average infant, but the results obtained for most infants do not apply to all infants. It is advantageous to know whether an infant is developing at a slow, normal, or advanced pace during the course of infancy. If an infant advances at an especially slow rate, then some form of enrichment may be necessary. If an infant develops at an advanced pace, parents may be advised to provide toys that stimulate cognitive growth in slightly older infants. Individual differences in infant cognitive development have been studied primarily through the use of developmental scales, or infant intelligence tests.

The infant testing movement grew out of the tradition of IQ testing of older children. However, the measures for assessing infants are necessarily less verbal than IQ tests that assess the intelligence of older children. The infant developmental scales contain far more perceptual-motor items. They also include measures of social interaction.

The most important early contributor to the developmental testing of infants was Arnold Gesell (1934). He developed a measure used as a clinical tool to help distinguish potentially normal babies from abnormal ones. This was especially useful to adoption agencies, which had large numbers of babies awaiting placement. Gesell's examination was used widely for many years and is still frequently used by pediatricians to assess infants. The current version of the Gesell test has four categories of behavior: motor, language, adaptive, and personal-social. The **developmental quotient (DQ)** is an overall developmental score that combines subscores in motor, language, adaptive, and personal-social domains in the Gesell assessment of infants.

The **Bayley Scales of Infant Development,** developed by Nancy Bayley, are widely used in the assessment of infant development. The current version has three components: a mental scale, a motor scale, and an infant behavior profile. Unlike Gesell, whose scales were clinically motivated, Bayley (1969) wanted to develop scales to assess infant behavior and predict later development. The early version of the Bayley scales covered only the first year of development. In the 1950s, the scales were extended to assess older infants. In 1993, the Bayley-II was published, with updated norms for diagnostic assessment at a younger age.

Because our discussion in this chapter centers on the infant's cognitive development, our primary interest is in Bayley's mental scale. It includes assessment of the following:

- Auditory and visual attention to stimuli

developmental quotient (DQ) An overall developmental score that combines subscores in motor, language, adaptive, and personal-social domains in the Gesell assessment of infants.

Bayley Scales of Infant Development Scales developed by Nancy Bayley, which are widely used in the assessment of infant development. The current version has three components: a mental scale, a motor scale, and an infant behavior profile.

CAREERS in CHILD DEVELOPMENT

Toosje Thyssen VanBeveren
Infant Assessment Specialist

Toosje Thyssen VanBeveren is a developmental psychologist at the University of Texas Medical Center in Dallas. She has a master's degree in chid clinical psychology and a Ph.D. in human development.

Her main current work is in a program called New Connections. This 12-week program is a comprehensive intervention for young children (0 to 6 years of age) who were affected by substance abuse prenatally and for their caregivers.

In the New Connections program, VanBeveren conducts assessments of infants' developmental status and progress, identifying delays and deficits. She might refer the infants to a speech, physical, or occupational therapist and monitor the infants' therapeutic services and developmental progress. VanBeveren trains the program staff and encourages them to use the exercises she recommends. She also discusses the child's problems with the primary caregivers, suggests activities they can carry out with their children, and assists them in enrolling their infants in appropriate programs.

During her graduate work at the University of Texas at Dallas, VanBeveren was author John Santrock's teaching assistant for four years in his undergraduate course on development. As a teaching assistant, she attended classes, graded exams, counseled students, and occasionally gave lectures. Each semester, VanBeveren returns to give a lecture on prenatal development and infancy. VanBeveren also teaches part-time in the psychology department at UT-Dallas. She teaches an undergraduate course, "The Child in Society" and a graduate course, "Infant Development."

In VanBeveren's words, "My days are busy and full. The work is often challenging. There are some disappointments but mostly the work is enormously gratifying."

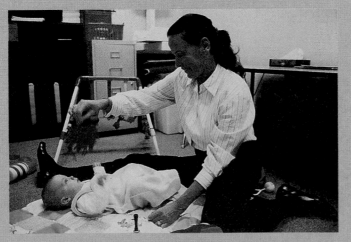

Toosje Thyssen VanBeveren conducting an infant assessment.

- Manipulation, such as combining objects or shaking a rattle
- Examiner interaction, such as babbling and imitation
- Relation with toys, such as banging spoons together
- Memory involved in object permanence, as when the infant finds a hidden toy
- Goal-directed behavior that involves persistence, such as putting pegs in a board
- Ability to follow directions and knowledge of objects' names, such as understanding the concept of "one"

How well should a 6-month-old perform on the Bayley mental scale? The 6-month-old infant should be able to vocalize pleasure and displeasure, persistently search for objects that are just out of immediate reach, and approach a mirror placed in front of the infant by the examiner. How well should a 12-month-old perform? By 12 months of age, the infant should be able to inhibit behavior when directed to do so, imitate words the examiner says (such as *Mama*), and respond to simple requests (such as "Take a drink").

Another assessment tool, the Fagan Test of Infant Intelligence, is increasingly being used (Fagan, 1992). This test focuses on the infant's ability to process information, including encoding the attributes of objects, detecting similarities and differences between objects, forming mental representations, and retrieving these representations. The Fagan Test of Infant Intelligence estimates babies' intelligence by comparing the amount of time they look at a new object with the amount of time they spend looking at a familiar object. This test elicits similar performances from infants in different cultures and is correlated with measures of intelligence in older children.

Tests of infant intelligence have been valuable in assessing the effects of malnutrition, drugs, maternal deprivation, and environmental stimulation on the development of infants. However, they do not correlate highly with IQ scores obtained later in childhood. This shortcoming is not surprising because the test items are considerably less verbal than the items on intelligence tests given to older children. Yet specific aspects of infant intelligence are related to specific aspects of childhood intelligence. For example, in one study, infant language abilities assessed by the Bayley test predicted language, reading, and spelling ability at 6 to 8 years of age (Siegel, 1989). Infant perceptual-motor skills predicted visuospatial, arithmetic, and fine motor skills at 6 to 8 years of age. These results indicate that an item analysis of infant scales like Bayley's can provide information about the development of specific intellectual functions.

Toosje Thyssen VanBeveren is an infant assessment specialist who administers tests like the Bayley scales and the Fagan Test of Infant Intelligence. To read about her work with infants, see the Careers in Child Development profile.

The explosion of interest in infant development has produced many new measures, especially using tasks to evaluate how infants process information (Colombo & others, 2004). Evidence is accumulating that measures of habituation and dishabituation in infancy are related to intelligence in childhood (McCall & Carriger, 1993). Less cumulative attention by an infant in the habituation situation and greater amounts of attention in the dishabituation situation reflect more efficient information processing. Both types of attention—a decrease and a recovery—when measured in the first six months of infancy, are related to higher IQ scores on standardized intelligence tests given at various times between infancy and adolescence. In sum, more precise assessments of the infant's cognition with information-processing tasks involving attention have led to the conclusion that continuity between infant and childhood intelligence is greater than was previously believed.

It is important, however, not to go too far and think that the connections between early infant cognitive development and later childhood cognitive development are so strong that no discontinuity takes place. Rather than asking whether cognitive development is continuous *or* discontinuous, perhaps we should be examining the ways cognitive development is both continuous and discontinuous. Some important changes in cognitive development take place after infancy, changes that underscore the discontinuity of cognitive development. We will describe these changes in cognitive development in subsequent chapters, which focus on later periods of development.

Review and Reflect ● LEARNING GOAL 3

3 **Describe the assessment of intelligence in infancy.**

Review
- How is infant intelligence measured?

Reflect
- Parents have their 1-year-old infant assessed with a developmental scale and the infant does very well on it. How confident should they be that the infant is going to be a genius when she grows up?

4 WHAT ARE SOME EARLY ENVIRONMENTAL INFLUENCES ON COGNITIVE DEVELOPMENT?

| Nutrition | Poverty |

So far, we have discussed a number of approaches to infants' cognitive development, but important aspects of this development remain to be examined. What are some early environmental experiences that might influence this cognitive development? Two areas in which researchers have investigated this question are nutrition and poverty.

Nutrition

When we think about how nutrition affects development, we usually think of physical development, such as skeletal growth, body shape, and susceptibility to disease—all of which can be adversely affected by malnutrition. In addition, malnutrition also can restrict an infant's cognitive development (Grantham- McGregor, Ani, & Fernald, 2001).

In one study, two groups of extremely malnourished 1-year-old South African infants were examined (Bayley, 1970). The children in one group were given adequate nourishment during the next six years. No intervention took place in the lives of the other group of children. After the seventh year, the poorly nourished group of children performed worse on intelligence tests than did the adequately nourished group.

In another study, George Gutherie and his co-workers (1976) evaluated a group of severely underweight, malnourished infants in a rural area of the Philippines. They found that a combination of malnutrition, infection, and inadequate social stimulation from caregivers was associated with very low scores on the Bayley Scales of Infant Development.

In more recent research on nutrition and cognitive development, which we initially discussed in chapter 6, "Physical Development in Infancy," Ernesto Pollitt and his colleagues (1993) conducted a longitudinal study over two decades in rural Guatemala. They found that early nutritional supplements in the form of protein and increased calories can have positive long-term consequences for cognitive development. In the study, the link between nutrition and cognitive development was moderated by the time period in which the supplements were given and by the social context. For example, the children in the lowest socioeconomic groups benefited more than did the children in the higher socioeconomic groups. And, although there still was a positive nutritional influence when the supplements were given after 2 years of age, the effect was more powerful before the age of 2. In sum, good nutrition in infancy is important, not only for the child's physical development but also for the child's cognitive development.

Children and Poverty
National Center for Children in Poverty
Zero to Three

The highest-risk children often benefit the most cognitively when they experience early interventions.

—CRAIG RAMEY
Contemporary Psychologist, University of Alabama–Birmingham

Poverty

Poverty is a key environmental factor in children's cognitive development (Powell, 2006; Ramey, Ramey, & Lanzi, 2006). A comprehensive longitudinal study of children from birth to 9 years of age compared the cognitive performance of children from families who were never poor, poor only early in development (birth to 3 years of age), poor in early and middle childhood (4 to 9 years of age), and chronically poor (NICHD Early Child Care Research Network, 2005). Measures of cognitive performance included school-readiness skills and language development. Children in chronically poor families showed the lowest level of cognitive performance, which was linked to lower quality childrearing environments that included less home enrichment and a lower level of maternal sensitivity. Experiencing poverty later was related to lower cognitive performance than experiencing it earlier, although living in chronic poverty was more strongly linked to negative child outcomes than the timing of poverty.

Researchers are increasingly interested in manipulating the early environment in children's lives when they are living in poverty, in hope that the changes will have a positive effect on their cognitive development (McLoyd, 1998; Seifer, 2001). Two ways this can be carried out are (1) to change parents' adaptive and responsive functioning and (2) to provide competent educational day care.

The emphasis on children at risk for low intelligence is on prevention rather than remediation (Powell, 2004, 2006; Ramey & Ramey, 2000; Ramey, Ramey, & Lanzi, 2006). Many low-income parents have difficulty providing an intellectually stimulating environment for their children. Programs that educate parents to be more sensitive caregivers and train them to be better teachers, as well as support services, such as high-quality Head Start programs, can make a difference in a child's intellectual

What are the characteristics of effective early intervention programs for infants in poverty conditions?

development. The current trend is to conduct two-generation poverty interventions by working to improve the quality of life and skills of parents, as well as providing the child with an enriched environment (McLoyd, 1998).

The Abecedarian Intervention program at the University of North Carolina at Chapel Hill is conducted by Craig Ramey and his associates (Ramey & Campbell, 1984; Ramey & Ramey, 1998; Ramey, Ramey, & Lanzi, 2006). They randomly assigned 111 young children from low-income, poorly educated families to either an intervention group, which experienced full-time, year-round child care along with medical and social work services, or a control group, which got medical and social benefits but no child care. The child-care program included gamelike learning activities aimed at improving language, motor, social, and cognitive skills. The success of the program in improving IQ was evident by the time the children were 3 years old, at which time the children in the experimental group showed normal IQs averaging 101, a 17-point advantage over the control group. Recent follow-up results suggest that the effects are long-lasting. More than a decade later, at age 15, children from the intervention group still maintained an IQ advantage of 5 points over the control group children (97.7 to 92.6) (Ramey, Ramey, & Lanzi, 2001). They also did better on standardized tests of reading and math, and were less likely to be held back a year in school (see figure 7.7). Also the greatest IQ gains were by the children whose mothers had especially low IQs—below 70. At age 15, these children showed a 10-point IQ advantage over a group of children whose mothers had IQs below 70 but did not experience the child-care intervention.

Early Intervention programs for infants in poverty vary (Powell, 2006; Ramey, Ramey, & Lanzi, 2006). Some are center-based, like the North Carolina program just described, others are home-based. Some are brief interventions; others are long-term. Some are time-intensive (such as all-day educational child care), others less intensive (such as one-hour-a-day or once-a-week sessions). In general, researchers have found that early intervention programs for infants living in poverty have the most positive developmental outcomes when (1) the program is long-lasting; (2) the program is time-intensive; (3) the program provides direct educational benefits, often in educational contexts, and does not rely on parental training alone; and (4) the program is comprehensive and multidimensional, including educational, health, and counseling services for parents, in addition to working directly with infants. We will further explore intervention in the lives of children in poverty by discussing Project Head Start in chapter 10, "Cognitive Development in Early Childhood," and by examining many factors in poverty interventions in chapter 12, "Physical Development in Middle and Late Childhood."

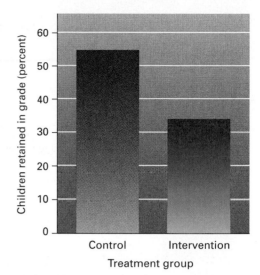

FIGURE 7.7 Early Intervention and Retention in School When the children in the Abecedarian program were 15 years of age, those who experienced the preschool intervention were less likely to have been retained in a grade than the children in the control group.

Review and Reflect ● LEARNING GOAL 4

4 **Characterize early environmental influences on cognitive development.**

Review
- How is nutrition linked with infants' cognitive development?
- What role does poverty play in infants' cognitive development?

Reflect
- If you were going to conduct an intervention to improve the cognitive skills of infants living in poverty, what would the intervention involve? Write down a minimum of five components in the intervention.

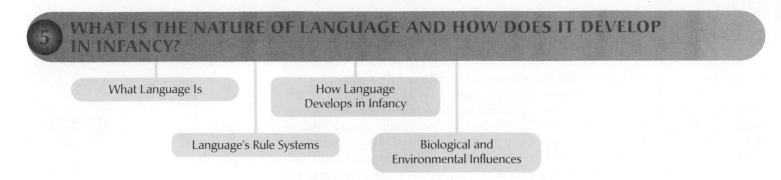

5 WHAT IS THE NATURE OF LANGUAGE AND HOW DOES IT DEVELOP IN INFANCY?

What Language Is

How Language Develops in Infancy

Language's Rule Systems

Biological and Environmental Influences

In 1799, a nude boy was observed running through the woods in France. The boy was captured when he was 11 years old. He was called the Wild Boy of Aveyron and was believed to have lived in the woods alone for six years. When found, he made no effort to communicate. Even after a number of years, he never learned to communicate effectively. Sadly, a modern-day wild child named Genie was discovered in Los Angeles in 1970. Despite intensive intervention, Genie never acquired more than a primitive form of language. Both cases—the Wild Boy of Aveyron and Genie—raise questions about the biological and environmental determinants of language, topics that we will examine in greater detail later in this chapter. First, though, we need to explore what language is.

What Language Is

Language is a form of communication—whether spoken, written, or signed—that is based on a system of symbols. Language consists of the words used by a community and the rules for varying and combining them.

Think how important language is in our everyday lives. We need language to speak with others, listen to others, read, and write. Our language enables us to describe past events in detail and to plan for the future. Language lets us pass down information from one generation to the next and create a rich cultural heritage.

All human languages have some common characteristics. These include infinite generativity and organizational rules. **Infinite generativity** is the ability to produce an endless number of meaningful sentences using a finite set of words and rules. Let's further explore what these rules involve.

Language's Rule Systems

Language is highly ordered and organized. The organization involves five systems of rules: phonology, morphology, syntax, semantics, and pragmatics. When we say "rules" we mean that language is orderly and the rules describe the way language works (Berko Gleason, 2005).

Phonology   Every language is made up of basic sounds. **Phonology** is the sound system of the language, including the sounds that are used and how they may be combined (Menn & Stoel-Gammon, 2005). For example, English has the initial consonant cluster *spr* as in *spring*, but no words begin with the cluster *rsp*. Phonology provides a basis for constructing a large and expandable set of words out of two or three dozen phonemes.

The basic unit of sound in a language is a *phoneme*; it is the smallest unit of sound that affects meaning. A good example of phonemes in English is /k/, the sound represented by the letter *k* in the word *ski* and the letter *c* in the word *cat*. The /k/ sound is slightly different in the two words. However, this variation is not distinguished in English, and the /k/ sound is therefore a single phoneme. In some languages, such as Arabic, this variation represents separate phonemes.

language A form of communication, whether spoken, written, or signed, that is based on a system of symbols.

infinite generativity The ability to produce an endless number of meaningful sentences using a finite set of words and rules.

phonology Rules regarding how sounds are perceived as different and which sound sequences may occur in the language.

FRANK & ERNEST: © Thaves/Dist. by Newspaper Enterprise Association, Inc.

Morphology

Morphology refers to the units of meaning involved in word formation. A *morpheme* is a minimal unit of meaning; it is a word or a part of a word that cannot be broken into smaller meaningful parts. Every word in the English language is made up of one or more morphemes.

Some words consist of a single morpheme (for example, *help*), whereas others are made up of more than one morpheme (for example, *helper,* which has two morphemes, *help* + *er,* with the morpheme *-er* meaning "one who," in this case "one who helps"). Thus, not all morphemes are words by themselves (for example, *-pre, -tion,* and *-ing*).

Just as the rules that govern phonology describe the sound sequences that can occur in a language, the rules of morphology describe the way meaningful units (morphemes) can be combined in words (Ravid, Levi, & Ben-Zvi, 2004; Tager-Flusberg, 2005). Morphemes have many jobs in grammar, such as marking tense (for example, she walks versus she walked) and number (she walks versus they walk).

Syntax

Syntax involves the way words are combined to form acceptable phrases and sentences. If someone says to you, "Bob slugged Tom" or "Bob was slugged by Tom," you know who did the slugging and who was slugged in each case because you have a syntactic understanding of these sentence structures. You also understand that the sentence, "You didn't stay, did you?" is a grammatical sentence but that "You didn't stay, didn't you?" is unacceptable and ambiguous.

If you learn another language, English syntax will not get you very far. For example, in English an adjective usually precedes a noun (as in *blue sky*), whereas in Spanish the adjective usually follows the noun *(cielo azul).* Despite the differences in their syntactic structures, however, the world's languages have much in common. For example, consider the following short sentences:

The cat killed the mouse.
The mouse ate the cheese.
The farmer chased the cat.

In many languages it is possible to combine these sentences into more complex sentences. For example:

The farmer chased the cat that killed the mouse.
The mouse the cat killed ate the cheese.

However, no language we know of permits sentences like the following one:

The mouse the cat the farmer chased killed ate the cheese.

Can you make sense of this sentence? If you can, you probably can do it only after wrestling with it for several minutes. You likely could not understand it at all if someone uttered it during a conversation. It appears that language users cannot process subjects and objects arranged in too complex a fashion in a sentence. That is good news for language learners, because it means that all syntactic systems adhere

morphology Units of meaning involved in word formation.

syntax The ways words are combined to form acceptable phrases and sentences.

Rule System	Description	Examples
Phonology	The sound system of a language. A phoneme is the smallest sound unit in a language.	The word *chat* has three phonemes or sounds: /ch/ /a/ /t/. An example of phonological rule in the English language is while the phoneme /r/ can follow the phonemes /t/ or /d/ in an English consonant cluster (such as *track* or *drab*), the phoneme /l/ cannot follow these letters.
Morphology	The system of meaningful units involved in word formation.	The smallest sound units that have a meaning are called morphemes, or meaning units. The word *girl* is one morpheme, or meaning unit; it cannot be broken down any further and still have meaning. When the suffix *s* is added, the word becomes *girls* and has two morphemes because the *s* changed the meaning of the word, indicating that there is more than one girl.
Syntax	The system that involves the way words are combined to form acceptable phrases and sentences.	Word order is very important in determining meaning in the English language. For example, the sentence, "Sebastian pushed the bike" has a different meaning than "The bike pushed Sebastian."
Semantics	The system that involves the meaning of words and sentences.	Knowing the meaning of individual words—that is, vocabulary. For example, semantics includes knowing the meaning of such words as *orange*, *transportation*, and *intelligent*.
Pragmatics	The system of using appropriate conversation and knowledge of how to effectively use language in context.	An example is using polite language in appropriate situations, such as being mannerly when talking with one's teacher. Taking turns in a conversation involves pragmatics.

FIGURE 7.8 The Rule Systems of Language

to some common ground. Such findings are also considered important by researchers who are interested in the universal properties of syntax (de Jong, 2004).

Semantics

Semantics refers to the meaning of words and sentences. Every word has a set of semantic features, or required attributes related to meaning. *Girl* and *woman*, for example, share many semantic features but they differ semantically in regard to age.

Words have semantic restrictions on how they can be used in sentences (Pan, 2005). The sentence *The bicycle talked the boy into buying a candy bar* is syntactically correct but semantically incorrect. The sentence violates our semantic knowledge that bicycles don't talk.

Pragmatics

A final set of language rules involves **pragmatics,** the appropriate use of language in different contexts (Bryant, 2005). The domain of language is broad. When you take turns speaking in a discussion or use a question to convey a command ("Why is it so noisy in here?" "What is this, Grand Central Station?"), you are demonstrating knowledge of pragmatics. You also apply the pragmatics of English when you use polite language in appropriate situations (for example, when talking to one's teacher) or tell stories that are interesting, jokes that are funny, and lies that convince.

Pragmatic rules can be complex and differ from one culture to another (Bryant, 2005). If you were to study the Japanese language, you would come face-to-face with countless pragmatic rules about conversing with individuals of various social levels and with various relationships to you. Some of these pragmatic rules concern the ways of saying thank you. Indeed, the pragmatics of saying thank you are complex even in our own culture. Preschoolers' use of the phrase *thank you* varies with sex, socioeconomic status, and the age of the individual they are addressing.

At this point, we have discussed five important rule systems involved in language. An overview of these rule systems is presented in figure 7.8.

semantics The meanings of words and sentences.

pragmatics The appropriate use of language in context.

How Language Develops in Infancy

According to an ancient historian, in the thirteenth century, Frederick II, Emperor of Germany, had a cruel idea. He wanted to know what language children would speak if no one talked to them. He selected several newborns and threatened their caregivers with death if they ever talked to the infants. Frederick never found out what language the children spoke because they all died. As we move forward in the twenty-first century, we are still curious about infants' development of language, although our experiments and observations are, to say the least, far more humane than the evil Frederick's.

Whatever language they learn, infants all over the world follow a similar path in language development. What are some key milestones in this development?

Babbling and Other Vocalizations
Babies actively produce sounds from birth onward (Lock, 2004; Volterra & others, 2005). The purpose of these early communications is to attract attention from caregivers and others in the environment. Babies sounds and gestures go through this sequence during the first year:

- *Crying.* Babies cry even at birth and crying can signal distress. However, as we will discuss in chapter 8, there are different types of cries that signal different things.
- *Cooing.* Babies first coo at about 1 to 2 months. These are pleasure sounds made in the back of the throat and usually occur during interaction with the caregiver.
- *Babbling.* This first occurs in the middle of the first year and includes strings of consonant-vowel combinations, such as "ba, ba, ba, ba."
- *Gestures.* Infants start using gestures, such as showing and pointing, at about 8 to 12 months of age. They may wave bye-bye, nod to mean "yes," show an empty cup to get more milk, and point to a dog to draw attention to it.

Deaf infants, born to deaf parents who use sign language, babble with their hands and fingers at about the same age as hearing children babble vocally (Bloom, 1998). Such similarities in timing and structure between manual and vocal babbling indicate the presence of a unified language capacity that underlies signed and spoken language.

Recognizing Language Sounds and Word Boundaries
Long before they begin to learn words, infants can make fine distinctions among the sounds of the language (Balem & Plunkett, 2005; Lock, 2004; Menn and Stoel-Gammon, 2005). Patricia Kuhl (1993, 2000) explored how infants perceive the sounds of speech by piping through a speaker phonemes from languages all over the world for infants to hear (see figure 7.9). A string of identical syllables is played and the sound changes. A box with a toy bear in it is placed where the infant can see it. If the infant turns its head when the sounds of the syllables change, the darkened box lights up and the bear briefly dances and drums. That is, if the infant turns its head to look at the box as soon as it notices the sound changing, the infant is rewarded by getting to see the bear's performance.

Kuhl's research has demonstrated that from birth up to about 6 months of age, infants are "citizens of the world": they recognize when sounds change most of the time no matter what language the syllables come from. But over the next six months, infants get even better at perceiving the changes in sounds from their "own" language, the one their parents speak, and gradually lose the ability to recognize changes in sounds that don't exist in their native tongue.

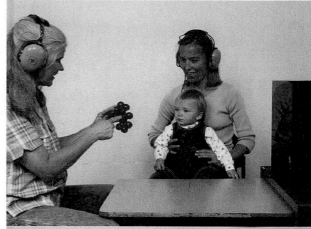

FIGURE 7.9 From Universal Linguist to Language-Specific Listener A baby is shown in Patricia Kuhl's research laboratory. In this research, babies listen to tape-recorded voices that repeat syllables. When the sounds of the syllables change, the babies quickly learn to look at the bear. Using this technique, Kuhl has demonstrated that babies are universal linguists until about 6 months of age, but in the next six months become language-specific listeners.

www.mhhe.com/santrockc9

Patricia Kuhl's Research
Language Milestones
Babbling

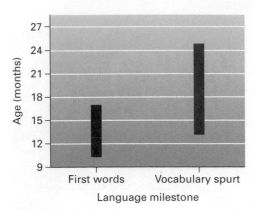

FIGURE 7.10 Variation in Language Milestones

An example involves the English "r" and "l" sounds, which distinguish words such as "rake" and "lake" (Iverson & Kuhl, 1996; Iverson & others, 2003). In the United States, infants from English-speaking homes detect the changes from "ra" to "la" when they are 6 months old and get better at detecting the change by 12 months of age. However, in Japanese there is no such "r" or "l" distinction. In Japan, 6-month-old infants perform as well as their American counterparts in recognizing the "r" and "l" distinction, but by 12 months of age they lose this ability.

Infants must fish out individual words from the nonstop stream of sound that makes up ordinary speech (Brownlee, 1998; Jusczyk, 2000). To do so, they must find the boundaries between words, which is very difficult for infants because adults don't pause between words when they speak. Still, infants begin to detect word boundaries by 8 months of age. For example, in one study, 8-month-old infants listened to recorded stories that contained unusual words, such as *hornbill* and *python* (Jusczyk & Hohne, 1997). Two weeks later, the researchers tested the infants with two lists of words, one made up of words in the stories, the other of new, unusual words that did not appear in the stories. The infants listened to the familiar words for a second longer, on average, than to new words.

First Words   The infant's first word is a milestone eagerly anticipated by every parent. This event usually occurs between 10 to 15 months of age and at an average of about 13 months. However, as we have seen, long before babies say their first words, they have been communicating with their parents, often by gesturing and using their own special sounds. The appearance of first words is a continuation of this communication process (Berko Gleason, 2002).

A child's first words include those that name important people (*dada*), familiar animals (*kitty*), vehicles (*car*), toys (*ball*), food (*milk*), body parts (*eye*), clothes (*hat*), household items (*clock*), and greeting terms (*bye*). These were the first words of babies 50 years ago. They are the first words of babies today. Children often express various intentions with their single words, so that "cookie" might mean, "That's a cookie" or "I want a cookie."

Between about 8 to 12 months of age, infants often indicate their first understanding of words. On the average, infants understand about 50 words at about 13 months but they can't say this many words until about 18 months (Menyuk, Liebergott, & Schultz, 1995). Thus, in infancy *receptive vocabulary* (words the child understands) considerably exceeds *spoken vocabulary* (words the child uses).

The infant's spoken vocabulary rapidly increases once the first word is spoken (Camaioni, 2004; Houston-Price, Plunkett, & Harris, 2005; Waxman, 2004; Waxman & Lidz, 2006). The average 18-month-old can speak about 50 words, but by the age of 2 years can speak about 200 words. This rapid increase in vocabulary that begins at approximately 18 months is called the *vocabulary spurt* (Bloom, Lifter, & Broughton, 1985).

The timing of a child's first word and vocabulary spurt varies (Bloom, 1998; Dale & Goodman, 2005; Marchman & Thal, 2005). Figure 7.10 shows the range for these two language milestones in 14 children. On average, these children said their first word at 13 months and had a vocabulary spurt at 19 months. However, the ages for the first word of individual children varied from 10 to 17 months and for their vocabulary spurt from 13 to 25 months.

Children sometimes overextend or underextend the meanings of the words they use (Woodward & Markman, 1998). *Overextension* is the tendency to apply a word to objects that are not related to, or are inappropriate for, the word's meaning. For example, when children say "*dada*" for "father," they often also apply the word to other men, strangers, or boys. With time, overextensions decrease and eventually disappear. *Underextension* is the tendency to apply a word too narrowly; it occurs when children fail to name a relevant event or object. For example, a child might use the word *boy* to describe a 5-year-old neighbor but not apply the word to a male infant or to a nine-year-old male.

Around the world, young children learn to speak in two-word utterances at 18 to 24 months of age. *What implications does this have for the biological basis of language?*

Two-Word Utterances   By the time children are 18 to 24 months of age, they usually utter two-word utterances. To convey meaning with just two words, the child relies heavily on gesture, tone, and context. The wealth of meaning children can communicate with a two-word utterance includes the following (Slobin, 1972):

- Identification: "See doggie."
- Location: "Book there."
- Repetition: "More milk."
- Nonexistence: "All gone thing."
- Negation: "Not wolf."
- Possession: "My candy."
- Attribution: "Big car."
- Agent-action: "Mama walk."
- Action-direct object: "Hit you."
- Action-indirect object: "Give Papa."
- Action-instrument: "Cut knife."
- Question: "Where ball?"

Age	Language milestones
Birth	Crying
1 to 2 months	Cooing begins
6 months	Babbling begins
6 to 12 months	Change from universal linguist to language-specific listener
8 to 12 months	Use gestures, such as showing and pointing Comprehension of words appears
13 months	First word spoken
18 months	Vocabulary spurt starts
18 to 24 months	Uses two-word utterances Rapid expansion of understanding of words

FIGURE 7.11   Some Language Milestones in Infancy

These examples are from children whose first language is English, German, Russian, Finnish, Turkish, or Samoan.

Notice that the two-word utterances omit many parts of speech and are remarkably succinct. In fact, in every language, a child's first combinations of words have this economical quality; they are telegraphic. **Telegraphic speech** is the use of short and precise words without grammatical markers such as articles, auxiliary verbs, and other connectives. Telegraphic speech is not limited to two words. "Mommy give ice cream" and "Mommy give Tommy ice cream" also are examples of telegraphic speech.

We have discussed a number of language milestones in infancy. Figure 7.11 summarizes the time at which infants typically reach these milestones.

Biological and Environmental Influences

We have described how language develops, but we have not explained what makes this amazing development possible. Everyone who uses language in some way "knows" its rules and has the ability to create an infinite number of words and sentences. Where does this knowledge come from? Is it the product of biology? Or is language learned and influenced by experiences?

Biological Influences   Some language scholars view the remarkable similarities in how children acquire language all over the world, despite the vast variation in language input they receive, as strong evidence that language has a biological basis. What role did evolution play in the biological foundations of language?

Evolution and the Brain's Role in Language Development   The ability to speak and understand language requires a certain vocal apparatus as well as a nervous system with certain capabilities. The nervous system and vocal apparatus of humanity's predecessors changed over hundreds of thousands or millions of years. With advances in the nervous system and vocal structures, *Homo sapiens* went beyond gestures and signs to develop spoken language. Although estimates vary, many experts believe that humans acquired spoken language about 100,000 years ago, which in evolutionary time, represents a very recent acquisition. It clearly gave humans an enormous edge over other animals and increased the chances of human survival (Pinker, 1994).

There is evidence that particular regions of the brain are predisposed to be used for language (Dick & others, 2005). Two regions involved in language were first discovered in studies of brain-damaged individuals. In 1861, a patient of Paul Broca, a French surgeon and anthropologist, received an injury to the left side of his brain. The

In the wild, chimps communicate through calls, gestures, and expressions, which evolutionary psychologists believe might be the roots of true language. *How strong is biology's role in language?*

telegraphic speech   The use of short and precise words without grammatical markers such as articles, auxiliary verbs, and other connectives.

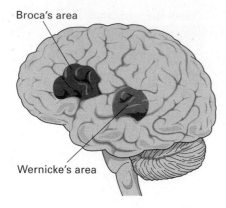

Broca's area

Wernicke's area

FIGURE 7.12 Broca's Area and Wernicke's Area Broca's area is located in the brain's left hemisphere, and it is involved in the control of speech. Individuals with damage to Broca's area have problems saying words correctly. Also shown is Wernicke's area, a portion of the left hemisphere that is involved in understanding language. Individuals with damage to this area cannot comprehend words; that is, they hear the words but don't know what they mean.

www.mhhe.com/santrock9

Brain and Language Development

aphasia A language disorder resulting from brain damage that involves a loss of the ability to use words.

Broca's area An area of the brain's left frontal lobe that directs the muscle movements involved in speech production.

Wernicke's area An area of the brain's left hemisphere that is involved in language comprehension.

language acquisition device (LAD) Chomsky's term that describes a biological endowment that enables the child to detect the features and rules of language, including phonology, syntax, and semantics.

patient became known as Tan, because that was the only word he could speak after his brain injury. Tan suffered from **aphasia,** a language disorder resulting from brain damage that involves a loss of the ability to use words. Tan died several days after Broca evaluated him, and an autopsy revealed the location of the injury. Today, we refer to the part of the brain in which Broca's patient was injured as **Broca's area,** an area of the left frontal lobe of the brain that directs the muscle movements involved in speech production (see figure 7.12).

Another place in the brain where an injury can seriously impair language is **Wernicke's area,** a region of the brain's left hemisphere involved in language comprehension (see figure 7.12). Individuals with damage to Wernicke's area often babble words in a meaningless way.

Note that both Broca's area and Wernicke's area are in the brain's left hemisphere. Evidence suggests that language processing primarily occurs in the left hemisphere (Gazzaniga, 1986; Gazzaniga, Ivy, and Magnum, 2002). But keep in mind that in most activities there is an interplay between the brain's two hemispheres (Grodzinsky, 2001; Nocentini & others, 2001). For example, in reading, most people rely on activity in areas of the left hemisphere for comprehending syntax, but most people rely on activity in the right hemisphere to understand intonation and emotion.

Language Acquisition Device Linguist Noam Chomsky (1957) believes that humans are biologically prewired to learn language at a certain time and in a certain way. He said that children are born into the world with a **language acquisition device (LAD),** a biological endowment that enables the child to detect the features and rules of language, including phonology, syntax, and semantics. Children are prepared by nature with the ability to detect the sounds of language, for example, and to detect and follow rules such as how to form plurals and ask questions.

Chomsky's LAD is a theoretical construct, not a physical part of the brain. Is there evidence for the existence of a LAD? Supporters of the LAD concept cite the uniformity of language milestones across languages and cultures, evidence that children create language even in the absence of well-formed input, and biological substrates of language.

Is There a Critical Period for Learning Language? Most babies learn a language by a certain age if they are to learn to speak at all. Recall from chapter 2 that a *critical period* is a fixed time period in which certain experiences can have a long-lasting effect on development. It is a time of readiness for learning, after which learning is difficult or impossible. For example, baby white-crowned sparrows learn their song quite well if they are exposed to it during a specific time as a chick. After this time, they can never develop a fully formed song pattern; thus, for these sparrows there seems to be a critical period for learning their song.

Whether the notion of a critical period can be extended to human learning is much less certain. Almost all children learn one or more languages during their early years, so it is difficult to determine whether there is a critical period for language development (Obler, 1993). In the 1960s, Eric Lenneberg (1967) proposed that language depends on maturation and that there is a critical period between about 18 months and puberty, during which a first language must be acquired. Lenneberg especially thought that the preschool years were an important time frame because this is when language develops rapidly and with ease.

The case study of Genie, a modern-day "wild child" with stunted language development, addresses the issue of a critical period in language development. In 1970, a California social worker made a routine visit to the home of a partially blind woman who had applied for public assistance. The social worker discovered that the woman and her husband had kept their 13-year-old daughter, Genie, locked away in almost total isolation during her childhood. Genie could not speak or stand erect. She had spent every day bound naked to a child's potty seat. She could move only her hands and feet. At night she was placed in a kind of straightjacket and caged in a crib with wire mesh sides and a cover. Whenever Genie made a noise, her father beat her. He never communicated with her in words; he growled and barked at her instead (Rymer, 1992).

After she was rescued from her parents, Genie spent a number of years in extensive rehabilitation programs, including speech and physical therapy (Curtiss, 1977). She eventually learned to walk, although with a jerky motion, and to use the toilet. Genie also learned to recognize many words and to speak in rudimentary sentences. Eventually, she was able to string together two-word combinations, such as "Big teeth," "Little marble," and "Two hand," then three-word combinations such as "Small two cup." As far as we know, unlike normal children, Genie did not learn to ask questions and did not develop a language system that allowed her to understand English grammar. Four years after she began stringing words together, Genie's speech still sounded like a garbled telegram. As an adult, she speaks in short, mangled sentences, such as "Father hit leg," "Big wood," and "Genie hurt."

Children like Genie, who are abandoned, abused, and not exposed to language for many years, rarely speak normally. Although some language experts have argued that cases such as Genie support the existence of a critical period for language development, because these children also suffer severe emotional trauma and possible neurological deficits, the issue is still far from clear.

Are the preschool years a critical period for language acquisition? Evidence for this notion comes from studies of brain development in young children, and from the amount of language learned by preschool children. However, other evidence suggests that we do not have a critical period for language learning. First of all, although much language learning takes place during the preschool years, learning continues well into the later school years and adulthood (Hakuta, Bialystok, & Wiley, 2003). In other words, young children's proficiency in language does not seem to involve a biologically critical period that older children and adults have passed.

Behavioral and Environmental Influences

As we said earlier, some language scholars view the similarities in children's language acquisition all over the world as strong evidence that language has a biological foundation. However, other language experts argue that experiences of the child, the particular language to be learned, and the context in which learning takes place can strongly influence language acquisition (Snow & Yang, 2006; Tomasello, 2006).

The Behavioral View   According to behaviorists, language is a complex learned skill, much like playing the piano or dancing. Behaviorists argued that language represents chains of responses acquired through reinforcement (Skinner, 1957). A baby happens to babble "Ma-ma"; Mama rewards the baby with hugs and smiles; the baby says "Mama" more and more. Bit by bit, the baby's language is built up. This view of language acquisition has several problems.

First, the behaviorist view does not explain how people create novel sentences—sentences that people have never heard or spoken before. For example, the child hears the sentence, "The plate fell on the floor" and then after dropping a mirror on a blanket says, "My mirror fell on the blanket."

Second, the evidence indicates that children learn the syntax of their native language even if they are not reinforced for doing so. Social psychologist Roger Brown (1973) spent long hours observing parents and their young children. He found that parents did not directly or explicitly reward or correct the syntax of most children's utterances. That is, parents did not say "good," "correct," "right," "wrong," and so on. Also, there was not direct correction along the lines of saying something like, "You should say, two shoes, not two shoe." However, as we will see shortly many parents do expand on their young children's grammatically incorrect utterance and recast many of those that have grammatical errors (Bonvillian, 2005).

A third problem with the behavioral view is that it fails to explain the extensive orderliness of language. Because each child has a unique history of reinforcement, behaviorists predict that vast individual differences should appear in children's speech

MIT linguist Noam Chomsky was one of the early architects of the view that children's language development cannot be explained by environmental input. In Chomsky's view, language has strong biological underpinnings, with children biologically prewired to learn language at a certain time and in a certain way.

Genie. *What were Genie's experiences like? What implications do they have for language acquisition?*

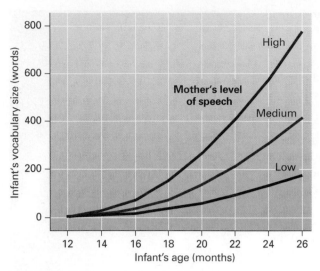

FIGURE 7.13 Level of Maternal Speech and Infant Vocabulary

development. When children learn a certain aspect of a language, according to the behaviorist view, should depend on whether their parents or someone else has rewarded or punished them for something they have said. But as we have seen, a compelling fact about language is its orderly development. For example, all toddlers produce one-word utterances before two-word utterances.

Environmental Influences Although the behavioral view is no longer considered to be a viable explanation of language, the environment contributes in important ways to the development of children's language skills (Mazur, Flynn, & Eichorst, 2005; Pan & others, 2005; Tomasello, 2006). In one study, Janellen Huttenlocher and her colleagues (1991) observed mothers' speech when interacting with their infants. As indicated in figure 7.13, mothers who used a higher level of language (more talkative and used far more words) when interacting with their infants had infants with markedly larger vocabularies. By the second birthday, vocabulary differences were substantial and linked to the level of language input provided by the mother.

Researchers have also found that the quantity of talk that parents direct to their children is linked with the children's vocabulary growth and the socioeconomic status of families. In another study, extensive conversations between 22 toddlers and their mothers were taped during the children's typical daily activities (Huttenlocher, Levine, & Vevea, 1998). Tapings were carried out every two to four months when the children were 16 to 26 months of age. The researchers found a strong link between the size of children's vocabularies and the talkativeness of their mothers. The mothers varied as much as tenfold in how much they talked. The toddlers of the most talkative mothers had a vocabulary more than four times the size of the vocabulary of the child with the quietest mother. This link might be due at least partly to genetics. However, Huttenlocher believes that is not the case, because the mothers did not vary much in their verbal IQs. Also, the children clearly were picking up what their mothers were saying, because the words each child used the most often mirrored those favored by the mother.

Young children's vocabularies are linked to the socioeconomic status of their families. Betty Hart and Todd Risley (1995) observed the language environments of children whose parents were professionals and children whose parents were on welfare. Compared with the professional parents, the welfare parents talked much less to their young children, talked less about past events, and provided less elaboration. All of the children learned to talk and acquired all of the forms of English. However, as indicated in figure 7.14, the children of the professional parents had a much larger vocabulary at 36 months of age than the children of the welfare parents.

One intriguing component of the young child's linguistic environment is **child-directed speech,** language spoken in a higher pitch than normal with simple words and sentences (Thiessen, Hill, & Saffran, 2005; Wong, 2004). Child-directed speech has the important function of capturing the infant's attention and maintaining communication. It is hard to use child-directed speech when not in the presence of a baby. As soon as you start talking to a baby, though, you shift into child-directed speech. Much of this is automatic and something most parents are not aware they are doing. Older children also modify their speech when talking to babies and younger children who are learning language. Even 4-year-olds speak in simpler ways to 2-year-olds than to their 4-year-old friends.

Are there strategies other than child-directed speech that adults use to enhance the child's acquisition of language? Three candidates are recasting, expanding, and labeling:

- **Recasting** is rephrasing something the child has said, perhaps turning it into a question or restating the child's immature utterance in the form of a fully

child-directed speech Language spoken in a higher pitch than normal with simple words and sentences.

recasting Rephrasing a statement that a child has said, perhaps turning it into a question or restating the child's utterance in the form of a fully grammatical sentence.

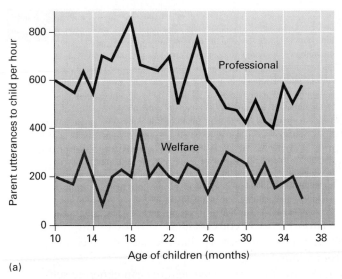

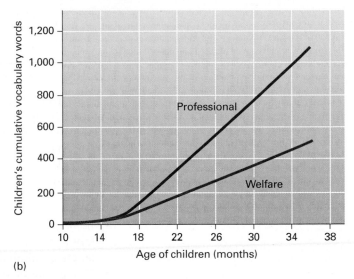

(a)   (b)

FIGURE 7.14 Language Input in Professional and Welfare Families and Young Children's Vocabulary Development *(a)* Parents from professional families talked with their young children more than parents from welfare families. *(b)* Children from professional families developed vocabularies twice as large as those from welfare families. Thus, by the time children go to preschool, they already have experienced considerable differences in language input in their families and developed different levels of vocabulary linked to the socioeconomic context in which they have lived.

grammatical sentence. For example, if the child says, "The dog was barking," the adult can respond by asking, "When was the dog barking?" Effective use of recasting involves letting the child indicate an interest and then elaborating on that interest.

- **Expanding** is restating, in a linguistically sophisticated form, what a child has said.
- **Labeling** is identifying the names of objects. Young children are forever being asked to identify the names of objects. Roger Brown (1986) called this "the great word game" and claimed that much of a child's early vocabulary is motivated by this adult pressure to identify the words associated with objects.

These strategies are used naturally and in meaningful conversations. Parents do not (and should not) use any deliberate method to teach their children to talk, even for children who are slow in learning language. Children usually benefit when parents guide their children's discovery of language rather than overloading them with language; "following in order to lead" helps a child learn language. If children are not ready to take in some information, they are likely to tell you (as by turning away). Thus, giving the child more information is not always better.

Children vary in their ability to acquire language and this variation cannot be readily explained by differences in environmental input alone. For children who are slow in developing language skills, however, opportunities to talk and be talked with are important. Children whose parents provide them with a rich verbal environment show many positive benefits. Parents who pay attention to what their children are trying to say, expand their children's utterances, read to them, and label things in the environment, are providing valuable, if unintentional, benefits (Berko Gleason, 2002, 2005).

Remember, though, that the encouragement of language development, not drill and practice, is the key. Language development is not a simple matter of imitation and reinforcement. To read further about ways that parents can facilitate children's language development, see the following Caring for Children interlude.

expanding Restating, in a linguistically sophisticated form, what a child has said.

labeling Identifying the names of objects.

CARING FOR CHILDREN

How Parents Can Facilitate Infants' and Toddlers' Language Development

Naomi Baron is a specialist in language acquisition, English linguistics, and written language. In her book, *Growing Up with Language: How Children Learn to Talk* (1992), Baron explores the way children learn to talk from birth to 6 years of age. Her book provides parents with techniques to promote their child's language development, illustrates language learning milestones, and discusses babytalk. Here is a summary of her ideas to help facilitate infants' and toddlers' language development:

Infants

- *Be an active conversational partner.* Initiate conversation with the infant. If the infant is in a daylong child-care program, ensure that the baby receives adequate language stimulation from adults.
- *Talk as if the infant understands what you are saying.* Parents can generate self-fulfilling prophecies by addressing their young children as if they understand what is being said. The process may take four to five years, but children gradually rise to match the language model presented to them.
- *Use a language style with which you feel comfortable.* Don't worry about how you sound to other adults when you talk with your child. Your affect, not your content, is more important when talking with an infant. Use whatever type of baby talk with which you feel comfortable.

Toddlers

- *Continue to be an active conversational partner.* Engaging toddlers in conversation, even one-sided conversation, is the most important thing a parent can do to nourish a child linguistically.
- *Remember to listen.* Since toddlers' speech is often slow and laborious, parents are often tempted to supply words and thoughts for them. Be patient and let toddlers express themselves, no matter how painstaking the process is or how great a hurry you are in.
- *Use a language style with which you are comfortable, but consider ways of expanding your child's language abilities and horizons.* For example, using long sentences need not be problematic. Don't be afraid to use ungrammatical language to imitate the toddler's novel forms (such as "No eat"). Use rhymes. Ask questions that encourage answers other than "Yes" and "No." Actively repeat, expand, and recast the child's utterances. Introduce new topics. And use humor in your conversation.
- *Adjust to your child's idiosyncrasies instead of working against them.* Many toddlers have difficulty pronouncing words and making themselves understood. Whenever possible, make toddlers feel that they are being understood.
- *Avoid sexual stereotypes.* Don't let the toddler's sex determine your amount or style of conversation. Many American mothers are more linguistically supportive of girls than of boys, and many fathers talk less with their children than mothers do. Cognitively enriching initiatives from both mothers and fathers benefit both boys and girls.
- *Resist making normative comparisons.* Be aware of the ages at which your child reaches specific milestones (first word, first 50 words, first grammatical combination). However, be careful not to measure this development rigidly against children of neighbors or friends. Such social comparisons can bring about unnecessary anxiety.

It is a good idea for parents to begin talking to their babies at the start. The best language teaching occurs when the talking is begun before the infant becomes capable of its first intelligible speech. *What are some other guidelines for parents to follow in helping their infants and toddlers develop their language?*

An Interactionist View of Language   If language acquisition depended only on biology, then Genie and the Wild Boy of Aveyron (discussed in the chapter's opening) should have talked without difficulty. Children do not learn language in a social vacuum. The child's experiences influence language acquisition. But we have seen that language does have strong biological foundations (MacWhinney, 2005). No matter how much you converse with a dog, it won't learn to talk. In contrast, children are biologically prepared to learn language. Children all over the world acquire language milestones at about the same time and in about the same order. An interactionist view emphasizes that both biology and experience contribute to language development.

American psychologist Jerome Bruner (1983, 1996) proposed that the sociocultural context is extremely important in understanding children's language development. His view has some similarities with the ideas of Lev Vygotsky that were described in chapter 2. Bruner stresses the role of parents and teachers in constructing what he called *language acquisition support system (LASS)*. The LASS resembles Vygotsky's concept of a zone of proximal development, which will be discussed in chapter 10, "Cognitive Development in Early Childhood."

Today, most language acquisition researchers believe that children from a wide variety of cultural contexts acquire their native language without explicit teaching. In some cases, they do so even without encouragement. Thus, very few aids are necessary for learning language. However, caregivers greatly facilitate a child's language learning (Berko Gleason, 2005).

Review and Reflect ● LEARNING GOAL 5

 Describe the nature of language and how it develops in infancy.

Review
- What is language?
- What are language's rule systems?
- How does language develop in infancy?
- What are the biological and environmental aspects of language?

Reflect
- Would it be a good idea for parents to hold large flash cards of words in front of their infant to help the infant learn language? Why or why not? What do you think Piaget would say about this activity?

REACH YOUR LEARNING GOALS

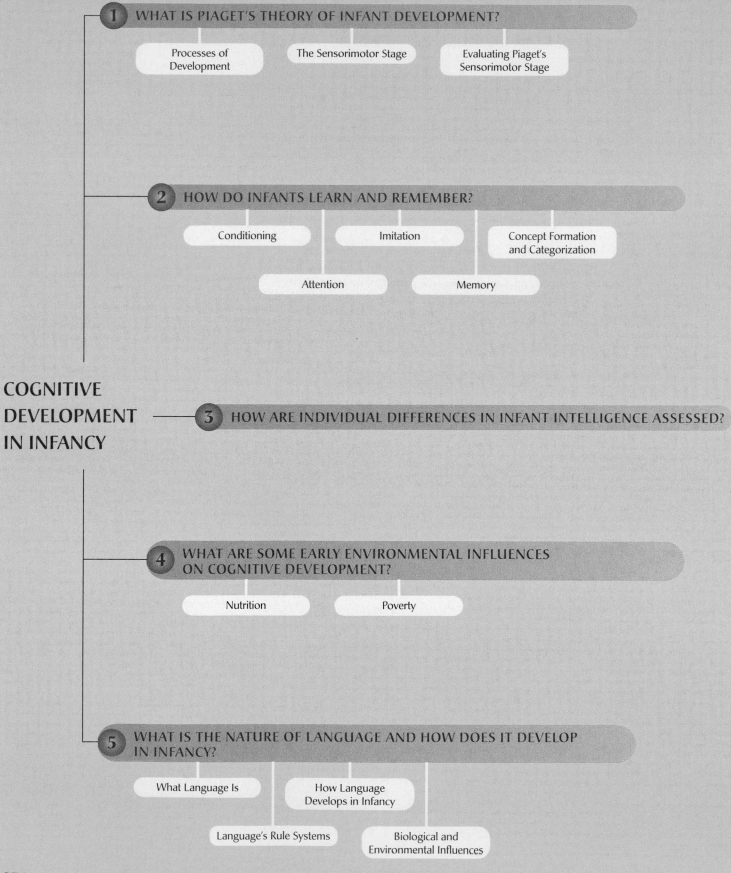

1 WHAT IS PIAGET'S THEORY OF INFANT DEVELOPMENT?

Processes of Development

The Sensorimotor Stage

Evaluating Piaget's Sensorimotor Stage

2 HOW DO INFANTS LEARN AND REMEMBER?

Conditioning

Imitation

Concept Formation and Categorization

Attention

Memory

COGNITIVE DEVELOPMENT IN INFANCY

3 HOW ARE INDIVIDUAL DIFFERENCES IN INFANT INTELLIGENCE ASSESSED?

4 WHAT ARE SOME EARLY ENVIRONMENTAL INFLUENCES ON COGNITIVE DEVELOPMENT?

Nutrition

Poverty

5 WHAT IS THE NATURE OF LANGUAGE AND HOW DOES IT DEVELOP IN INFANCY?

What Language Is

How Language Develops in Infancy

Language's Rule Systems

Biological and Environmental Influences

SUMMARY

1 Summarize Piaget's theory of infant development.

- In Piaget's theory, children construct their own cognitive worlds, building mental structures to adapt to their world. Schemes are actions or mental representations that organize knowledge. Behavioral schemes (physical activities) characterize infancy, whereas mental schemes (cognitive activities) develop in childhood. Adaptation involves assimilation and accommodation. Assimilation occurs when children incorporate new information into existing knowledge. Accommodation refers to children's adjustment to new information. According to Piaget, there are four qualitatively different stages of thought: sensorimotor, preoperational, concrete operational, and formal operational.
- In sensorimotor thought, the first of Piaget's four stages, the infant organizes and coordinates sensations with physical movements. The stage lasts from birth to about 2 years of age and is nonsymbolic throughout, according to Piaget. Sensorimotor thought has six substages: simple reflexes; first habits and primary circular reactions; secondary circular reactions; coordination of secondary circular reactions; tertiary circular reactions, novelty, and curiosity; and internalization of schemes. One key aspect of this stage is object permanence, the ability to understand that objects continue to exist even though the infant is no longer observing them. Another aspect involves infants' understanding of cause and effect.
- Piaget opened up a whole new way of looking at infant development in terms of coordinating sensory input with motoric actions. In the past several decades, revisions of Piaget's view have been proposed based on research. For example, researchers have found that a stable and differentiated perceptual world is established earlier than Piaget envisioned. They also believe young infants conceptualize the world much earlier than Piaget thought.

2 Describe how infants learn and remember.

- Both classical and operant conditioning occur in infants. Operant conditioning techniques have especially been useful to researchers in demonstrating infants' perception and retention of information about perceptual-motor actions.
- Attention is the focusing of mental resources and in infancy attention is closely linked with habituation. Habituation is the repeated presentation of the same stimulus, causing reduced attention to the stimulus. If a different stimulus is presented and the infant pays increased attention to it, dishabituation is occurring. Newborn infants can habituate to repetitive stimulation.
- Meltzoff has shown that newborns can match their behaviors (such as protruding their tongue) to a model. His research also shows that deferred imitation occurs as early as 9 months of age.
- Memory is the retention of information over time. Infants as young as 2 to 6 months of age display implicit memory, which is memory without conscious recollection as in memory of perceptual-motor skills. However, many experts believe that explicit memory, which is the conscious memory of facts and experiences, does not emerge until the second half of the first year of life. Older children and adults remember little if anything from the first three years of their lives.
- Concepts group objects, events, and characteristics on the basis of common properties. Infants form concepts early in their development with perceptual categorization appearing as early as 3 months of age. Mandler argues that it is not until about 7 to 9 months of age that infants form conceptual categories. Infants' first concepts are broad. Over the first two years of life, these broad concepts gradually become more differentiated.

3 Discuss the assessment of intelligence in infancy.

- Developmental scales for infants grew out of the tradition of IQ testing of older children. These scales are less verbal than IQ tests. Gesell was an early developer of an infant test. His scale is still widely used by pediatricians; it provides a developmental quotient (DQ). The Bayley scales are the developmental scales most widely used today; developed by Nancy Bayley, they consist of a motor scale, a mental scale, and an infant behavior profile. Increasingly used, the Fagan test assesses how effectively the infant processes information. Global infant intelligence measures are not good predictors of childhood intelligence. However, specific aspects of infant intelligence, such as information-processing tasks involving attention, have been better predictors of childhood intelligence, especially in a specific area. There is both continuity and discontinuity between infant cognitive development and cognitive development later in childhood.

4 Characterize early environmental influences on cognitive development.

- Nutritional supplements given to malnourished infants improve their cognitive development.
- Early intervention programs that target infants living in poverty are often more effective when they are (1) long-term, (2) time-intensive, (3) able to provide direct

What are some developmental changes in emotion during infancy? What are some different types of crying that infants display?

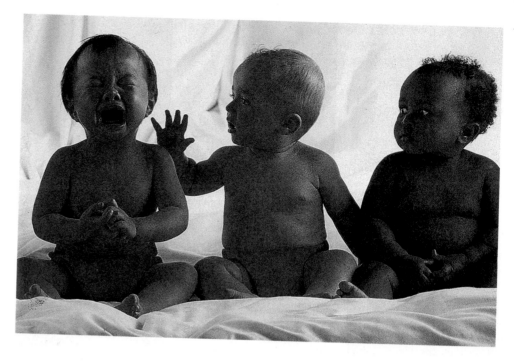

Infant Crying
Exploring Infant Crying

Controversy, however, still characterizes the question of whether or how parents should respond to an infant's cries (Alvarez, 2004; Hiscock & Jordan, 2004; Lewis & Ramsay, 1999). Developmentalists increasingly argue that an infant cannot be spoiled in the first year of life, which suggests that parents should soothe a crying infant rather than be unresponsive. This reaction should help infants develop a sense of trust and secure attachment to the caregiver.

Smiling Smiling is another important communicative emotion-linked behavior of the infant. Two types of smiling can be distinguished in infants:

- **Reflexive smile:** a smile that does not occur in response to external stimuli and appears during the first month after birth, usually during sleep
- **Social smile:** a smile that occurs in response to an external stimulus, typically a face in the case of the young infant

Social smiling does not occur until 2 months of age (Emde, Gaensbauer, & Harmon, 1976; Lewis, Hitchcock, & Sullivan, 2004), although some researchers believe that infants grin in response to voices as early as 3 weeks of age (Sroufe & Waters, 1976). The power of the infant's smiles was appropriately captured by British theorist John Bowlby (1969): "Can we doubt that the more and better an infant smiles the better he is loved and cared for? It is fortunate for their survival that babies are so designed by nature that they beguile and enslave mothers."

Fear As indicated in figure 8.1, fear typically first appears at about 6 months of age and peaks at about 18 months. The most frequent expression of an infant's fear involves **stranger anxiety,** in which an infant shows a fear and wariness of strangers. Not all infants show distress when they encounter a stranger. Besides individual variations, whether an infant shows stranger anxiety also depends on the social context and the stranger's characteristics.

Stranger anxiety usually emerges gradually. It first appears at about 6 months of age in the form of wary reactions. By age 9 months, the fear of strangers is often more intense, and it continues to escalate through the infant's first birthday (Emde, Gaensbauer, & Harmon, 1976).

Infants show less stranger anxiety when they are in familiar settings. In one study, 10-month-olds showed little stranger anxiety when they met a stranger in their own

reflexive smile A smile that does not occur in response to external stimuli. It happens during the month after birth, usually during sleep.

social smile A smile in response to an external stimulus, which, early in development, typically is in response to a face.

stranger anxiety An infant's fear and wariness of strangers that typically appears in the second half of the first year of life.

home but much greater fear when they encountered a stranger in a research laboratory (Sroufe, Waters, & Matas, 1974). Also, infants show less stranger anxiety when they are sitting on their mother's laps than when placed in an infant seat several feet away from their mothers (Bohlin & Hagekull, 1993). Thus, it appears that, when infants have a sense of security, they are less likely to show stranger anxiety.

Who the stranger is and how the stranger behaves also influence stranger anxiety in infants. Infants are less fearful of child strangers than adult strangers. They also are less fearful of friendly, outgoing, smiling strangers than of passive, unsmiling strangers (Bretherton, Stolberg, & Kreye, 1981).

In addition to stranger anxiety, infants experience fear of being separated from their caregivers. The result is **separation protest**—crying when the caregiver leaves. Separation protest tends to peak at about 15 months among U.S. infants. In fact, in one study, separation protest peaked at about 13 to 15 months in four different cultures (Kagan, Kearsley, & Zelazo, 1978). As indicated in figure 8.3, the percentage of infants who engaged in separation protest varied across cultures, but the infants reached a peak of protest at about the same age—just before the middle of the second year of life. Also, one recent study found that mothers with high separation anxiety were oversensitive to infants' negative signals but undersensitive to infants' positive signals (Hsu, 2004).

Social Referencing
Social referencing involves "reading" emotional cues in others to help determine how to act in a particular situation. The development of social referencing helps infants to interpret ambiguous situations more accurately, as when they encounter a stranger and need to know whether to fear the person (Mumme, Fernald, & Herrera, 1996; Thompson, 2006).

Infants become better at social referencing in the second year of life. At this age, they tend to "check" with their mother before they act; they look at her to see if she is happy, angry, or fearful. For example, in one study, 14- to 22-month-old infants were more likely to look at their mother's face as a source of information for how to act in a situation than were 6- to 9-month-old infants (Walden, 1991).

Emotional Regulation and Coping
Emotional regulation is the effective management of arousal to adapt and reach a goal. During the first year of life, infants have a limited ability to control their emotional states but gradually are able to develop an ability to inhibit, or minimize, the intensity and duration of their emotional reactions (Eisenberg, 2001; Eisenberg, Spinrad, & Smith, 2004). From early in infancy, babies put their thumbs in their mouths as a self-soothing strategy. At first, infants mainly depend on caregivers to help them soothe their emotions, as when a caregiver rocks an infant to sleep, sings lullabies to the infant, gently strokes the infant, and so on. Many developmentalists argue it is a good strategy for a caregiver to soothe an infant before the infant gets into an intense, agitated, uncontrolled state (Thompson, 1994).

Later in infancy, when they become aroused, infants sometimes redirect their attention or distract themselves in order to reduce their arousal (Grolnick, Bridges, & Connell, 1996). By 2 years of age, toddlers can use language to define their feeling states and the context that is upsetting them (Kopp & Neufeld, 2002). A toddler might say, "Feel bad. Dog scare." This type of communication may help caregivers to help the child in regulating emotion.

Contexts can influence emotional regulation (Kopp & Neufeld, 2002; Saarni, 1999; Saarni & others, 2006). Infants are often affected by fatigue, hunger, time of day, which people are around them, and where they are. Infants must learn to adapt to

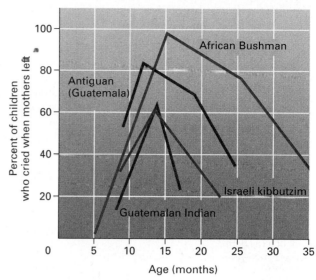

FIGURE 8.3 **Separation Protest in Four Cultures** Note that separation protest peaked at about the same time in all four cultures in this study (13 to 15 months of age). However, a higher percentage (100 percent) of infants in an African Bushman culture engaged in separation protest compared to only about 60 percent of infants in Guatemalan Indian and Israeli kibbutzim cultures. *Reprinted by permission of the publisher from Infancy: Its Place in Human Development by Jerome Kagan, Richard B. Kearsley, and Philip R. Zelazo, p. 107, Cambridge, Mass.: Harvard University Press. Copyright 1978 by the President and Fellows of Harvard College.*

separation protest Infants' distress to being separated from their caregivers.

social referencing "Reading" emotional cues in others to help determine how to act in a particular situation.

emotional regulation Effectively managing arousal to adapt and reach a goal.

"Oh, he's cute, all right, but he's got the temperament of a car alarm."

www.mhhe.com/santrockc9

Infant Temperament

different contexts that require emotional regulation. Further, new demands appear as the infant becomes older and parents modify their expectations. For example, a parent may take it in stride if a 6-month-old infant screams in a restaurant but may react very differently if a 1½-year-old starts screaming.

Later in the book, when we discuss early childhood and middle and late childhood in chapters 11 and 14, we will further discuss emotional regulation. Now that we have examined some basic ideas about emotional development in infancy, let's turn our attention to the concept of temperament and see how it often is linked with emotional responding.

Temperament

Do you get upset a lot? Does it take much to get you angry, or to make you laugh? Even at birth, babies seem to have different emotional styles. One infant is cheerful and happy much of the time; another baby seems to cry constantly. These tendencies reflect the concept of **temperament,** which is an individual's behavioral style and characteristic way of emotional response.

Describing and Classifying Temperament
How would you describe your temperament or the temperament of a friend? Researchers have described and classified the temperament of individuals in different ways. Here we will examine three ways of describing and classifying temperament.

Chess and Thomas' Classification   Psychiatrists Alexander Chess and Stella Thomas (Chess & Thomas, 1977; Thomas & Chess, 1991) identified three basic types, or clusters, of temperament:

- **Easy child.** This child is generally in a positive mood, quickly establishes regular routines in infancy, and adapts easily to new experiences.
- **Difficult child.** This child reacts negatively and cries frequently, engages in irregular daily routines, and is slow to accept change.
- **Slow-to-warm-up child.** This child has a low activity level, is somewhat negative, shows low adaptability, and displays a low intensity of mood.

In their longitudinal investigation, Chess and Thomas found that 40 percent of the children they studied could be classified as easy, 10 percent as difficult, and 15 percent as slow to warm up. Notice that 35 percent did not fit any of the three patterns. Researchers have found that these three basic clusters of temperament are moderately stable across the childhood years.

Kagan's Behavioral Inhibition   Another way of classifying temperament focuses on the differences between a shy, subdued, timid child and a sociable, extraverted, bold child. Jerome Kagan (1997, 2000, 2002, 2003; Kagan & Fox, 2006; Kagan & Snidman, 1991) regards shyness with strangers (peers or adults) as one feature of a broad temperament category called *inhibition to the unfamiliar*. Inhibited children react to many aspects of unfamiliarity with initial avoidance, distress, or subdued affect, especially beginning about 7 to 9 months of age.

Kagan has found that inhibition shows considerable stability from infancy through early childhood. One recent study classified toddlers into extremely inhibited, extremely uninhibited, and intermediate groups (Pfeifer & others, 2002). Follow-up assessments occurred at 4 and 7 years of age. Continuity was demonstrated for both inhibition and lack of inhibition, although a substantial number of the inhibited children moved into the intermediate groups at 7 years of age.

Rothbart and Bates' Classification   New classifications of temperament continue to be forged (Rothbart & Bates, 2006). Mary Rothbart (2004, p. 495) recently concluded that the following three broad dimensions best represent what researchers have found to characterize the structure of temperament

temperament An individual's behavioral style and characteristic way of emotional response.

easy child A child who is generally in a positive mood, who quickly establishes regular routines in infancy, and who adapts easily to new experiences.

difficult child A child who tends to react negatively and cry frequently, who engages in irregular daily routines, and who is slow to accept change.

slow-to-warm-up child A child who has a low activity level, is somewhat negative, shows low adaptability, and displays a low intensity of mood.

- *Extraversion/surgency* includes "positive anticipation, impulsivity, activity level, and sensation seeking." Kagan's uninhibited children fit into this category.
- *Negative affectivity* includes "fear, frustration, sadness, and discomfort."

These children are easily distressed; they may fret and cry often. Kagan's inhibited children fit this category.

- *Effortful control (self-regulation)* which includes "attentional focusing and shifting, inhibitory control, perceptual sensitivity, and low-intensity pleasure." Infants who are high on effortful control show an ability to keep their arousal from getting too high and have strategies for soothing themselves. Emily, 14 months old, is high on effortful control. She senses that some of her actions are not acceptable. For example, she may glance at her father as she reaches for his shiny reading glasses on the coffee table, or withdraw her hand at his firm "no." When Emily is offered one of her own toys instead of the desired object, she easily shifts her attention to the toy and begins to play with it.

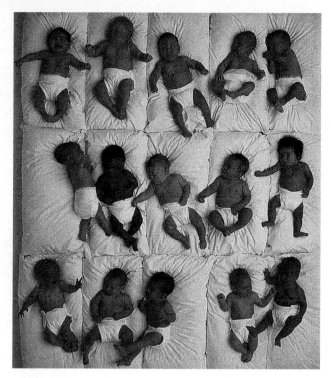

What are some ways that developmentalists have classified infants' temperaments? Which classification makes the most sense to you, based on your observations of infants?

In contrast, children low on effortful control, such as 20-month-old Matthew, are often unable to regulate their arousal; they become easily agitated and intensely emotional. When Matthew heads for the forbidden TV remote control, he may repeat his mother's "No touch" rule aloud, but because he has little effortful control, he hasn't yet learned to control the undesirable behavior. Matthew cries angrily when the remote is taken away from him and is difficult to soothe or redirect.

In Rothbart's (2004, p. 497) view, "early theoretical models of temperament stressed the way we are moved by our positive and negative emotions or level of arousal, with our actions driven by these tendencies." The more recent emphasis on effortful control, however, advocates that individuals can engage in a more cognitive, flexible approach to stressful circumstances.

Biological Foundations and Experience   Physiological characteristics are associated with different temperaments (Fox & others, 2004; Kagan & Fox, 2006; Rothbart & Bates, 1998, 2006). For example, the brain's limbic system is linked with positive affect and approach, especially through the neural circuits involved in reward. The amygdala in the brain plays an important role in fear and inhibition (Kagan, 2003; LeDoux, 1996, 2002). Inhibition also is associated with a unique physiological pattern that includes high and stable heart rate, high cortisol levels, and high activity in the right frontal lobe of the brain (Kagan, 2003; Kagan & Fox, 2006). Neurotransmitters also are linked to temperament. For example, low levels of the neurotransmitter serotonin may increase an individual's vulnerability to fear and frustration, which can contribute to negative affectivity (emotion), such as depression (Lowrey, 2002).

What is heredity's role in the biological foundations of temperament? Twin and adoption studies have found a heritability index for temperament in the range of .50 to .60, suggesting a moderate influence of heredity on temperament (Plomin & others, 1994). The contemporary view is that temperament is a biologically based but developmentally evolving feature of behavior. Further, the dimensions of temperament become increasingly more consistent over time as temperamental individuality emerges into the network of self-perceptions, behavioral preferences, and social experiences that together shape developing personality (Thompson & Goodvin, 2005).

Kagan (2002, 2003; Kagan & Fox, 2006) argues that children inherit a physiology that biases them to have a particular type of temperament. However, through experience they may learn to modify their temperament to some degree. For example,

An infant's temperament can vary across cultures. *What do parents need to know about a child's temperament?*

children may inherit a physiology that biases them to be fearful and inhibited, but they may learn to reduce their fear and inhibition.

Social contexts can influence temperament (Thompson & Goodvin, 2005). For example, gender and culture may shape the fate of temperament. Parents might react differently to a child's temperament, depending on whether the child is a boy or a girl (Kerr, 2001). For example, in one study, mothers were more responsive to the crying of irritable girls than to the crying of irritable boys (Crockenberg, 1986).

Similarly, the reaction to an infant's temperament may depend in part on culture (Austin & Chorpita, 2004). For example, an active temperament might be valued in some cultures (such as the United States) but not in other cultures (such as China). Indeed, children's temperament can vary across cultures (Putnam, Sanson, & Rothbart, 2002). Behavioral inhibition is more highly valued in China than in North America, and researchers have found that Chinese children are more inhibited than Canadian infants (Chen & others, 1998). The cultural differences in temperament were linked to parents' attitude and behaviors. Canadian mothers of inhibited 2-year-olds were less accepting of their infants' inhibited temperament while Chinese mothers were more accepting.

In short, many aspects of a child's environment can encourage or discourage the persistence of temperament characteristics. One useful way of thinking about these relationships applies the concept of goodness of fit, which we examine next.

Goodness of Fit
Goodness of fit refers to the match between a child's temperament and the environmental demands the child must cope with (Matheny & Phillips, 2001). Consider an active child who is made to sit still for long periods of time or a slow-to-warm-up child who is abruptly pushed into new situations on a regular basis. Both children face a lack of fit between their temperament and environmental demands. Lack of fit can produce adjustment problems for the child (Rothbart & Bates, 2006).

Some temperament characteristics pose more parenting challenges than others, at least in modern Western societies (Thompson & Goodvin, 2005). Children's proneness to distress, as exhibited by frequent crying and irritability, can contribute to the emergence of avoidant or coercive parental responses. In one research study, though, extra support and training for mothers of distress-prone infants improved the quality of mother-infant interaction (van den Boom, 1989). Also, in a recent longitudinal study, researchers found that a high level of fearlessness on the part of infants, when combined with harsh parenting, was linked with persistent conduct problems at age 8 (Shaw & others, 2003).

Parenting and the Child's Temperament
Many parents don't become believers in temperament's importance until the birth of their second child. Many parents view the first child's behavior as being solely a result of how they socialized the child. However, management strategies that worked with the first child might not be as effective with the second child. Problems experienced with the first child (such as those involved in feeding, sleeping, and coping with strangers) might not exist with the second child, but new problems might arise. Such experiences strongly suggest that children differ from each other very early in life, and that these differences have important implications for parent-child interaction (Kochanska & others, 2004; Rothbart & Putnam, 2002).

What are the implications of temperamental variations for parenting? Although answers to this question necessarily are speculative because of the incompleteness of the research literature, these conclusions were reached by temperament experts Ann Sanson and Mary Rothbart (1995):

- *Attention to and respect for individuality.* Parents need to be sensitive and flexible to the infant's signals and needs. One implication is that it is difficult to generate general prescriptions for "good parenting." A goal might be accomplished in one

goodness of fit The match between a child's temperament and the environmental demands the child must cope with.

way with one child and in another way with another child, depending on the child's temperament.

- *Structuring the child's environment.* Crowded, noisy environments can pose greater problems for some children (such as a "difficult child") than others (such as an "easygoing" child). We might also expect that a fearful, withdrawing child would benefit from slower entry into new contexts.
- *The "difficult child" and packaged parenting programs.* Programs for parents often focus on dealing with children who have "difficult" temperaments. Acknowledgment that some children are harder to parent is often helpful, and advice on how to handle particular difficult characteristics can also be useful. However, whether a particular characteristic is difficult depends on its fit with the environment. To label a child "difficult" has the danger of becoming a self-fulfilling prophecy. If a child is identified as "difficult," the labeling may maintain that categorization.

Some critics argue that too often we are prone to pigeon-holing children into categories without examining the context in which temperament occurs (Rothbart & Bates, 1998; Wachs, 2000). Nonetheless, children's temperament needs to be taken into account when considering caregiving behavior. Research does not yet allow for many highly specific recommendations, but in general caregivers should (1) be sensitive to the individual characteristics of the child, (2) be flexible in responding to these characteristics, and (3) avoid negative labeling of the child.

Personality Development

We have explored some important aspects of emotional development and temperament, which reveal individual variations in infants. Let's now examine the characteristics that often are thought of as central to the infant's personality development: trust and the development of self and independence.

Trust   Recall from chapter 2 that Erik Erikson (1968) proposed that people go through eight stages of development in the life span. In Erikson's (1968) first stage, **trust versus mistrust,** which occurs in the first year of life, infants experience the world as either secure and comfortable or insecure and uncomfortable. Following a life of regularity, warmth, and protection in the mother's womb, the infant faces a world that is less secure. Erikson believes that infants learn trust when they are cared for in a consistent, warm manner. If the infant is not well fed and kept warm on a consistent basis, a sense of mistrust is likely to develop.

Trust versus mistrust is not resolved once and for all in the first year of life. It arises again at each successive stage of development, which can have positive or negative outcomes. For example, children who enter school with a sense of mistrust may trust a particular teacher who has taken the time to make herself trustworthy. With this second chance, children overcome their early mistrust. By contrast, children who leave infancy with a sense of trust can still have their sense of mistrust activated at a later stage, perhaps if their parents are separated or divorced under conflicting circumstances.

Developing a Sense of Self and Independence   Individuals carry with them a sense of who they are and what makes them different from everyone else. They cling to this identity and begin to feel secure in the knowledge that their identity is becoming more stable. Real or imagined, the sense of self is a strong motivating force in life. When does the individual begin to sense a separate existence from others?

The Self   Infants are not "given" a self by their parents or the culture. Rather, they find and construct selves. Infants cannot verbally express their views and cannot

trust versus mistrust Erikson's first stage of development, occurring in the first year of life, in which infants experience the world as either secure and comfortable or insecure and uncomfortable.

FIGURE 8.4 **The Development of Self-Recognition in Infancy** The graph shows the findings of two studies in which infants less than 1 year of age did not recognize themselves in the mirror. A slight increase in the percentage of infant self-recognition occurred around 15 to 18 months of age and then by 2 years of age, a majority of children recognized themselves.

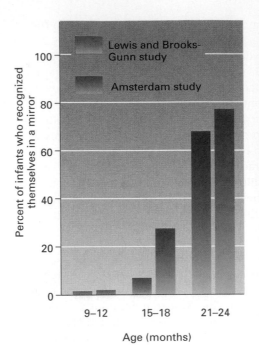

understand the complex instructions. Given these restrictions, how can researchers study infants' self-understanding? They test infants' *visual self-recognition* by presenting them with images of themselves.

For example, let's examine how the mirror technique works. An infant's mother puts a dot of rouge on the infant's nose. An observer watches to see how often the infant touches its nose. Next, the infant is placed in front of a mirror, and observers detect whether nose touching increases. The idea is that when the infant looks in the mirror and tries to touch or rub off the rouge, this violates the infant's self schema. The infant realizes that it is the self in the mirror but that something is not right since the real self does not have a dot of rouge on it. In two investigations, infants recognized their own images in the mirror in the second half of the second year of life (Amsterdam, 1968; Lewis & Brooks-Gunn, 1979) (see figure 8.4). In sum, human infants initially develop a sense of rudimentary self-understanding called *self-recognition* at approximately 18 months of age.

One recent study involved assessments of toddlers biweekly from 15 months to 23 months of age (Courage, Edison, & Howe, 2004) Self-recognition emerged gradually over this time, first appearing in the form of mirror recognition, followed by personal pronoun use and photo recognition.

Late in the second year and early in the third year, toddlers show other emerging forms of self-awareness (Thompson, 2006). These forms include verbal self-references, such as "me big," verbal labeling of internal experiences such as emotions, self-monitoring as when a toddler says "do it myself," and statements of ownership (Bates, 1990; Bretherton & others, 1986; Bullock & Lutkenhaus, 1990; Fasig, 2000).

Independence   Not only does the infant develop a sense of self in the second year of life, but independence also becomes a more central theme in the infant's life. The theories of Margaret Mahler and Erik Erikson have important implications for both self-development and independence. Mahler (1979) believes that the child goes through a separation and then an individuation process. Separation involves the infant's movement away from the mother. Individuation involves the development of self.

Erikson (1968), like Mahler, believed that independence is an important issue for toddlers. Erikson describes the second stage of development as **autonomy versus shame and doubt,** occurring from approximately 1 to 3 years of age. It is a time in

autonomy versus shame and doubt
Erikson's second stage, occurring from approximately 1 to 3 years of age, in which the child either develops self-determination and pride or is overcontrolled and experiences shame and doubt.

which the child either develops self-determination and a sense of pride or is overcontrolled and experiences shame and doubt. Autonomy builds on the infant's developing mental and motor abilities. At this point in development, not only can infants walk, but they can also climb, open and close, drop, push and pull, and hold and let go. Infants feel pride in these new accomplishments and want to do everything themselves, whether it is flushing a toilet, pulling the wrapping off a package, or deciding what to eat. It is important for parents to recognize the motivation of toddlers to do what they are capable of doing at their own pace. Then they can learn to control their muscles and their impulses themselves. But when caregivers are impatient and do for toddlers what they are capable of doing themselves, shame and doubt develop. Every parent has rushed a child from time to time. It is only when parents consistently overprotect toddlers or criticize accidents (wetting, soiling, spilling, or breaking, for example) that children develop an excessive sense of shame and doubt about their ability to control themselves and their world.

Erikson also believed that the stage of autonomy versus shame and doubt has important implications for the development of independence and identity during adolescence. The development of autonomy during the toddler years gives adolescents the courage to be independent individuals who can choose and guide their own future.

Erikson believed that autonomy versus shame and doubt is the key developmental theme of the toddler years. *What are some good strategies for parents to use with their toddlers?*

Review and Reflect • LEARNING GOAL 1

 Discuss emotional and personality development in infancy.

Review
- What are emotions? What is the nature of an infant's emotions and how do they change?
- What is temperament and how does it develop in infancy?
- What are some important aspects of personality in infancy and how do they develop?

Reflect
- How would you describe your temperament? Does it fit one of Chess and Thomas' three styles: easy, slow-to-warm up, or difficult? If you have siblings, is your temperament similar to or different from theirs?

2 HOW DOES ATTACHMENT DEVELOP IN INFANCY?

Theories of Attachment	The Significance of Attachment

Individual Differences and the Strange Situation	Caregiving Styles and Attachment Classification

So far, we have discussed emotions and their importance in infant development. We have also examined the role of emotional style; in effect, we have seen how emotions set the tone of our experiences in life. But emotions also write the lyrics because they are at the core of our relationships with others. Foremost among these relationships is attachment. **Attachment** is a close emotional bond between two people.

A small curly-haired girl named Danielle, age 11 months, begins to whimper. After a few seconds, she begins to wail. Soon her mother comes into the room, and Danielle's crying ceases. Quickly, Danielle crawls over to where her mother is seated and reaches out to be held. Danielle has just demonstrated attachment to her mother.

attachment A close emotional bond between two people.

FIGURE 8.5 Contact Time with Wire and Cloth Surrogate Mothers Regardless of whether the infant monkeys were fed by a wire or a cloth mother, they overwhelmingly preferred to spend contact time with the cloth mother.

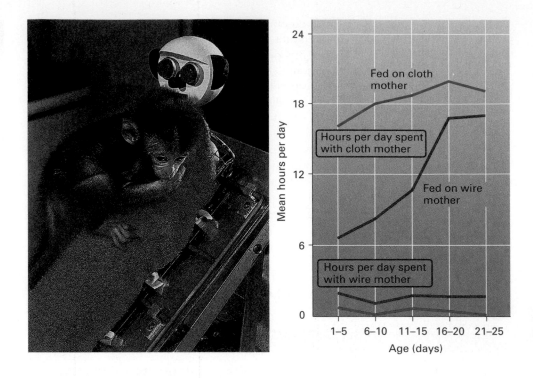

Attachment Theory and Research

Theories of Attachment

There is no shortage of theories about infant attachment. Three theorists—Freud, Erikson, and Bowlby—proposed influential views.

Freud argued that infants become attached to the person or object that provides oral satisfaction. For most infants, this is the mother, since she is most likely to feed the infant. Is feeding as important as Freud thought? A classic study by Harry Harlow (1958) reveals that the answer is no (see figure 8.5). Infant monkeys were removed from their mothers at birth; for six months they were reared by surrogate (substitute) "mothers." One surrogate mother was made of wire, the other of cloth. Half of the infant monkeys were fed by the wire mother, half by the cloth mother. Periodically, the amount of time the infant monkeys spent with either the wire or the cloth mother was computed. Regardless of which mother fed them, the infant monkeys spent far more time with the cloth mother. This study clearly demonstrated that feeding is not the crucial element in the attachment process and that contact comfort is important.

Erik Erikson (1968) stressed that the first year of life is the key time for the development of attachment. Recall his proposal (discussed in chapter 1) that the first year of life represents the stage of trust versus mistrust. A sense of trust requires a feeling of physical comfort and minimal fear or apprehension about the future. Trust in infancy sets the stage for a lifelong expectation that the world will be a good and pleasant place to be. Erikson also argued that responsive, sensitive parenting contributes to an infant's sense of trust.

The ethological perspective of British psychiatrist John Bowlby (1969, 1989) also stresses the importance of attachment in the first year of life and the responsiveness of the caregiver. Bowlby believes that an infant and its primary caregiver form an attachment. He argues that the newborn is biologically equipped to elicit attachment behavior (Weizmann, 2000). The baby cries, clings, coos, and smiles. Later, the infant crawls, walks, and follows the mother. The immediate result is to keep the primary caregiver nearby; the long-term effect is to increase the infant's chances of survival (Thompson, 2006).

Attachment does not emerge suddenly but rather develops in a series of phases, moving from a baby's general preference for human beings to a partnership with primary caregivers. Here are four such phases based on Bowlby's conceptualization of attachment (Schaffer, 1996):

- *Phase 1: from birth to 2 months.* Infants instinctively direct their attachment to human figures. Strangers, siblings, and parents are equally likely to elicit smiling or crying from the infant.
- *Phase 2: from 2 to 7 months.* Attachment becomes focused on one figure, usually the primary caregiver, as the baby gradually learns to distinguish familiar from unfamiliar people.
- *Phase 3: from 7 to 24 months.* Specific attachments develop. With increased locomotor skills, babies actively seek contact with regular caregivers, such as the mother or father.
- *Phase 4: from 24 months on.* Children become aware of others' feelings, goals, and plans and begin to take these into account in forming their own actions.

In sum, attachment emerges from the social cognitive advances that allow infants to develop expectations for the partner's behavior and determine the affective quality of their relationship (Thompson, 2006). These social cognitive advances include recognizing the partner's face, voice, and other features and expectations for the partner's behavior especially in terms of relief from distress and pleasure in social interaction, that increase the infant's preference for the person.

As children develop, they can cognitively represent the attachment relationship in more complex ways (Thompson, 2006). For example, in early childhood, children increasingly develop images of their attachment partner's characteristics. This cognitive representation of attachment especially appears in the form of the caregiver's physical and psychological accessibility when the child experiences stress.

Individual Differences and the Strange Situation

Although attachment to a caregiver intensifies midway through the first year, isn't it likely that some babies have a more positive attachment experience than others? Mary Ainsworth (1979) thinks so. Ainsworth created the **Strange Situation**, an observational measure of infant attachment in which the infant experiences a series of introductions, separations, and reunions with the caregiver and an adult stranger in a prescribed order. In using the Strange Situation, researchers hope that their observations will provide information about the infant's motivation to be near the caregiver and the degree to which the caregiver's presence provides the infant with security and confidence.

Based on how babies respond in the Strange Situation, they are described as being securely or insecurely attached (there are three types of insecure attachment) to the caregiver:

- **Securely attached babies** use the caregiver as a secure base from which to explore the environment. When in the presence of their caregiver, securely attached infants explore the room and examine toys that have been placed in it. When the caregiver departs, securely attached infants might mildly protest, and when the caregiver returns these infants reestablish positive interaction with her, perhaps by smiling or climbing on her lap. Subsequently, they often resume playing with the toys in the room.
- **Insecure avoidant babies** show insecurity by avoiding the mother. In the Strange Situation, these babies engage in little interaction with the caregiver, display little distress when she leaves the room, usually do not reestablish contact with her on her return, and may even turn their back on her at this point. If contact is established, the infant usually leans away or looks away.
- **Insecure resistant babies** often cling to the caregiver and then resist her by fighting against the closeness, perhaps by kicking or pushing away. In the Strange Situation, these babies often cling anxiously to the caregiver and don't explore the playroom. When the caregiver leaves, they often cry loudly and push away if she tries to comfort them on her return.

Strange Situation Ainsworth's observational measure of infant attachment to a caregiver that requires the infant to move through a series of introductions, separations, and reunions with the caregiver and an adult stranger in a prescribed order.

securely attached babies Babies who use the caregiver as a secure base from which to explore the environment.

insecure avoidant babies Babies who show insecurity by avoiding the mother.

insecure resistant babies Babies who might cling to the caregiver, then resist her by fighting against the closeness, perhaps by kicking or pushing away.

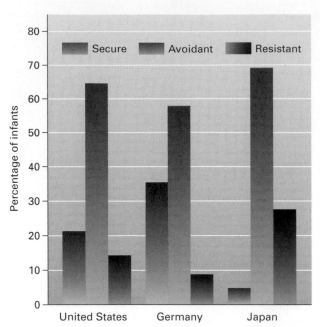

FIGURE 8.6 Cross-Cultural Comparison of Attachment
In one study, infant attachment in three countries—the United States, Germany, and Japan—was measured in the Ainsworth Strange Situation (van IJzendoorn & Kroonenberg, 1988). The dominant attachment pattern in all three countries was secure attachment. However, German infants were more avoidant and Japanese infants were less a avoidant and more resistant than U.S. infants.

- **Insecure disorganized babies** are disorganized and disoriented. In the Strange Situation, these babies might appear dazed, confused, and fearful. To be classified as disorganized, strong patterns of avoidance and resistance must be shown or certain select behaviors, such as extreme fearfulness around the caregiver, must be present.

Some critics believe that behavior in the Strange Situation—like other laboratory assessments—might not indicate what infants would do in a natural environment. Furthermore, as a measure of attachment it may be culturally biased. For example, German and Japanese babies often show different patterns of attachment than American infants. As shown in figure 8.6, German infants are more likely to show an avoidant attachment pattern and Japanese infants are less likely to show this pattern than U.S. infants (van IJzendoorn & Kroonenberg, 1988). The avoidant pattern in German babies likely occurs because their caregivers encourage them to be more independent (Grossmann & others, 1985). Also as shown in figure 8.7, Japanese babies are more likely than American babies to be categorized as resistant. This may have more to do with the Strange Situation as a measure of attachment than with attachment insecurity itself. Japanese mothers rarely let anyone unfamiliar with their babies care for them. Thus, the Strange Situation might create considerably more stress for Japanese infants than for American infants, who are more accustomed to separation from their mothers (Takahashi, 1990).

Even though there are cultural variations in attachment classification, the most frequent classification in every culture studied so far is secure attachment (Thompson, 2006; van IJzendoorn & Kroonenberg, 1988). Further, researchers have found that infants' behaviors in the Strange Situation are closely related to how they behave at home in response to separation and reunion with their mothers (Pederson & Moran, 1996). Thus, many infant researchers argue the Strange Situation continues to show merit as a measure of infant attachment.

The Significance of Attachment

Do individual differences in attachment matter? Ainsworth stresses that secure attachment in the first year of life provides an important foundation for psychological development later in life. The securely attached infant moves freely away from the mother but keeps track of where she is through periodic glances. The securely attached infant responds positively to being picked up by others and, when put back down, freely moves away to play. An insecurely attached infant, by contrast, avoids the mother or is ambivalent toward her, fears strangers, and is upset by minor, everyday separations.

If early attachment to a caregiver is important, it should relate to a child's social behavior later in development. For some children, early attachments seem to foreshadow later functioning (Carlson, Sroufe, & Egeland, 2004; Egeland & Carlson, 2004; Sroufe, Egeland, & Carlson, 1999, 2004; Sroufe & others, 2005, a, b; Waters, Corcoran, & Anafarta, 2005). In the extensive longitudinal study conducted by Alan Sroufe and his colleagues (2005 a, b), early secure attachment (assessed by the Strange Situation at 12 and 18 months) was linked to positive emotional health, high self-esteem, self-confidence, and socially competent interaction with peers, teachers, camp counselors, and romantic partners through adolescence. Another recent study found that infants who were securely attached at 15months of age were more cognitively and socioemotionally competent at four-years-of age than their counterparts who were insecurely attached at 15 months of age (Fish, 2004).

insecure disorganized babies Babies who show insecurity by being disorganized and disoriented.

For other children, there is little continuity (Thompson & Goodvin, 2005). Not all research reveals the power of infant attachment to predict subsequent development. In one longitudinal study, attachment classification in infancy did not predict attachment classification at 18 years of age (Lewis, 1997). In this study, the best predictor of an insecure attachment classification at 18 was the occurrence of parental divorce in intervening years. Consistently positive caregiving over a number of years is likely an important factor in connecting early attachment and the child's functioning later in development. Indeed, researchers have found that early secure attachment *and* subsequent experiences, especially maternal care and life stresses, are linked with children's later behavior and adjustment (Belsky & Pasco Fearon, 2002a, b; Thompson, 2006).

Not all developmentalists believe that attachment in infancy is the only path to competence in life. Indeed, some developmentalists believe that too much emphasis has been placed on the attachment bond in infancy. Jerome Kagan (1987, 2000), for example, believes that infants are highly resilient and adaptive; he argues that they are evolutionarily equipped to stay on a positive developmental course, even in the face of wide variations in parenting. Kagan and others stress that genetic and temperament characteristics play more important roles in a child's social competence than the attachment theorists, such as Bowlby and Ainsworth are willing to acknowledge (Bakermans-Kranenburg & others, 2004; Chaudhuri & Williams, 1999). For example, infants may have inherited a low tolerance for stress. This, rather than an insecure attachment bond, may be responsible for their inability to get along with peers.

In the Hausa culture, siblings and grandmothers provide a significant amount of care for infants. *How might these variations in care affect attachment?*

Another criticism of attachment theory is that it ignores the diversity of socializing agents and contexts in an infant's world (Lamb, 2005; Lewis, 2005; Thompson, 2005, 2006). In some cultures, infants show attachments to many people. Among the Nigerian Hausa both grandmothers and siblings provide a significant amount of care for infants (Harkness & Super, 1995). Infants in agricultural societies tend to form attachments to older siblings, who are assigned a major responsibility for younger siblings' care.

Researchers recognize the importance of competent, nurturant caregivers in an infant's development (Maccoby, 1999; McHale & others, 2001; Parke & Buriel 2006). At issue, though, is whether or not early secure attachment, especially to a single caregiver, by itself is the critical factor in whether children develop in a positive manner over the course of childhood and adolescence. It is likely, though, that early secure attachment has a positive influence on the child's future development but this influence works in concert with other positive experiences with parents and others across the course of childhood and adolescence (Thompson, 2006).

Caregiving Styles and Attachment Classification

Is the style of caregiving linked with the quality of the infant's attachment? Securely attached babies have consistently available caregivers who are sensitive to the infants' signals and respond to their needs (Gao, Elliot, & Waters, 1999; Main, 2000). These caregivers often let their babies have an active part in determining the onset and pacing of interaction in the first year of life. One recent study found that maternal sensitivity in parenting was linked with secure attachment in infants in two different cultures: the United States and Colombia (Carbonell & others, 2002).

How do the caregivers of insecurely attached babies interact with them? Caregivers of avoidant babies tend to be unavailable or rejecting (Berlin & Cassidy, 2000). They often don't respond to their babies' signals and have little physical contact with them. When they do interact with their babies, they may behave in an angry and irritable way. Caregivers of resistant babies tend to be inconsistent; sometimes they respond to their babies' needs, and sometimes they don't. In general, they tend not to be very affectionate with their babies and show little synchrony when interacting with them. Caregivers of disorganized babies often neglect or physically abuse them (Barnett, Ganiban, & Cicchetti, 1999). In some cases, these caregivers are depressed.

What is the nature of secure and insecure attachment? How are caregiving styles related to attachment classification?

Describe how attachment develops in infancy.

Review
- How can attachment be defined? What are some prominent theories of attachment?
- What are some individual differences in attachment? What is the Strange Situation?
- What is the significance of attachment?
- How are attachment categories linked with caregiving styles?

Reflect
- How might the infant's temperament be related to the way in which attachment is classified? Look at the temperament categories we described and reflect on how these might be more likely to occur in infants in some attachment categories rather than in others.

3 HOW DO SOCIAL CONTEXTS INFLUENCE SOCIOEMOTIONAL DEVELOPMENT IN INFANCY?

| The Family | | Child Care |

Now that we have explored the infant's emotional and personality development and attachment, let's examine the social contexts in which these occur. We will begin by studying a number of aspects of the family and then turn to a social context in which infants increasingly spend time—child care by people other than parents.

The Family

Most of us began our lives in families and spent thousands of hours during our childhood interacting with our parents. Some of you are already parents; others of you may become parents.

The Transition to Parenthood   What is the transition to parenting like? When people become parents through pregnancy, adoption, or stepparenting, they face disequilibrium and must adapt (Heincke, 2002; Lorensen, Wilson, & White, 2004). Parents want to develop a strong attachment with their infant, but they still want to maintain strong attachments to their spouse and friends, and possibly continue their careers. Parents ask themselves how this new being will change their lives. A baby places new restrictions on partners; no longer will they be able to rush out to a movie on a moment's notice, and money may not be readily available for vacations and other luxuries. Dual-career parents ask, "Will it harm the baby to place her in child care? Will we be able to find responsible baby-sitters?"

In a longitudinal investigation of couples from late pregnancy until 3½ years after the baby was born, couples enjoyed more positive marital relations before the baby was born than after (Cowan & Cowan, 2000, 2002). Still, almost one-third showed an increase in marital satisfaction. Some couples said that the baby had both brought them closer together *and* moved them farther apart. They commented that being parents enhanced their sense of themselves and gave them a new, more stable identity as a couple. Having a baby raised concerns for men about intimate relationships.

The demands of juggling work and family roles stimulated women to manage family tasks more efficiently and pay attention to their own personal growth.

One recent study examined the transition to parenting in young African American and Latino couples from 14 to 24 years of age (Florsheim & others, 2003). Fathers and mothers who had positive relationships with their own parents were more likely to show more positive adjustment to parenting than their counterparts who had negative relationships with their parents. At some point during the early years of the child's life, parents face the difficult task of juggling their roles as parents and as self-actualizing adults. Until recently in our culture, nurturing our children and having a career were thought to be incompatible. Fortunately, we have come to recognize that the balance between caring and achieving, nurturing and working—although difficult to manage—can be accomplished (Hoffman & Youngblade, 1999).

Reciprocal Socialization

Socialization between parents and children historically was viewed as a one-way process: Children were considered to be the products of their parents' socialization techniques. Today, however, we view parent-child interaction as reciprocal (Hartup & Laursen, 1999; Parke, 2004). **Reciprocal socialization** is bidirectional socialization. That is, children socialize parents just as parents socialize children. For example, the interaction of mothers and their infants is symbolized as a dance or a dialogue in which successive actions of the partners are closely coordinated. This coordinated dance or dialogue can assume the form of mutual synchrony in which each person's behavior depends on the partner's previous behavior (Feldman, Greenbaum, & Yirmiya, 1999). Or it can be reciprocal in the sense that actions of the partners are matched, as when one partner imitates the other or when there is mutual smiling.

When reciprocal socialization has been studied in infancy, mutual gaze, or eye contact, plays an important role in early social interaction. In one investigation, the mother and infant engaged in a variety of behaviors while they looked at each other. By contrast, when they looked away from each other, the rate of such behaviors dropped considerably (Stern & others, 1977). In sum, the behaviors of mothers and infants involve substantial interconnection, mutual regulation, and synchronization.

An important form of reciprocal socialization is **scaffolding,** in which parents time interactions in such a way that the infant experiences turn-taking with the parents. Scaffolding involves parental behavior that supports children's efforts, allowing them to be more skillful than they would be if they were to rely only on their own abilities. In using scaffolding, caregivers provide a positive, reciprocal framework in which they and their children interact. For example, in the game peek-a-boo, the mother initially covers the baby. Then she removes the cover and registers "surprise" at the infant's reappearance. As infants become more skilled at peek-a-boo, pat-a-cake, and "so big," there are other caregiver games that exemplify scaffolding and turn-taking sequences. In one study, infants who had more extensive scaffolding experiences with their parents (especially in the form of turn-taking) were more likely to engage in turn-taking when they interacted with their peers (Vandell & Wilson, 1988). Scaffolding is not confined to parent-infant interaction but can be used by parents to support children's achievement-related efforts in school by adjusting and modifying the amount and type of support that best suits the child's level of development.

The Family as a System

As a social system, the family can be thought of as a constellation of subsystems defined in terms of generation, gender, and role (Kreppner, 2002; Minuchin, 2002; Parke, 2004). Divisions of labor among family members define particular subunits, and attachments define others. Each family member is a participant in several subsystems. Some family systems are *dyadic* (involving two people), others are *polyadic* (involving more than two people). The father and child represent one dyadic subsystem, the mother and father another. The mother-father-child represent one polyadic subsystem, the mother and two siblings another.

reciprocal socialization Bidirectional socialization; children socialize parents, just as parents socialize children.

scaffolding Parental behavior that supports children's efforts, allowing them to be more skillful than they would if they relied only on their own abilities; parents time interactions so the infant experiences turn-taking with the parents.

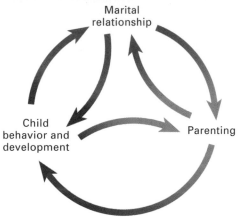

FIGURE 8.7 Interaction Between Children and Their Parents: Direct and Indirect Effects

Family Resources
Maternal Resources

Jay Belsky (1981) proposed an organizational scheme that highlights the reciprocal influences of family members and family subsystems (see figure 8.7). Belsky believes that marital relations, parenting, and infant behavior and development can have both direct and indirect effects on each other. An example of a direct effect is the influence of the parents' behavior on the child. An example of an indirect effect is how the relationship between the spouses mediates the way a parent acts toward the child (McHale, Lauretti, & Kuersten-Hogan, 1999). For example, marital conflict might reduce the efficiency of parenting, in which case marital conflict would have an indirect effect on the child's behavior.

Maternal and Paternal Infant Caregiving   Can fathers take care of infants as competently as mothers? Observations of fathers and their infants suggest that fathers have the ability to act as sensitively and responsively as mothers with their infants (Parke, 1995, 2000, 2002, 2004; Parke & Buriel, 2006). Perhaps the caregiving behavior of male humans resembles that of other male primates, who show notoriously low interest in their offspring. However, when forced to live with infants whose female caregivers are absent, the males can competently rear the infants. Remember, however, that although fathers can be active, nurturant, involved caregivers with their infants, many do not choose to follow this pattern (Chuang, Lamb, & Hwang, 2004; Day & Lamb, 2004; Lamb & Lewis, 2005; Marsiglio, 2004).

Do fathers behave differently toward infants than mothers do? Maternal interactions usually center on child-care activities—feeding, changing diapers, bathing. Paternal interactions are more likely to include play (Marsiglio & others, 2000). Fathers engage in more rough-and-tumble play. They bounce infants, throw them up in the air, tickle them, and so on (Lamb, 1986, 2000). Mothers do play with infants, but their play is less physical and arousing than that of fathers.

In one study, fathers were interviewed about their caregiving responsibilities when their children were 6, 15, 24, and 36 months of age (NICHD Early Child Care Research Network, 2000). Some of the fathers were videotaped while playing with their children at 6 and 36 months. Fathers were more involved in caregiving—bathing, feeding, dressing the child, taking the child to child care, and so on—when they worked fewer hours and mothers worked more hours, when mothers and fathers were younger, when mothers reported greater marital intimacy, and when the children were boys.

Child Care

Whether or not to put a baby in child care is a decision more parents than ever are facing. For example, graduate students Gordon and Tanisha have begun to look at child-care options for Robert, their 12-week-old son. But will care by others reduce Robert's emotional attachment to them? Harm his cognitive development? Will caregivers fail to teach Robert how to control his anger and allow him to be unduly influenced by his peers as he gets older?

Gordon and Tanisha are not alone in their concerns. Many parents worry whether care of their child by other people will adversely affect their children. How justified are their concerns and the concerns of other parents like them? How extensive is child care by people other than parents? How hard is it to find high-quality child care?

If you now have a child or plan to have children, these are questions you may need to deal with. Today far more young children are in child care in the United States than at any other time in history. Approximately 2 million children currently receive formal, licensed child care and uncounted millions of children are cared for by unlicensed baby-sitters.

Because the United States does not have a policy of paid leave for child care, child care in the United States has become a major national concern (Cohen, 2004; Vandell, 2004). In Sweden, mothers or fathers are given paid maternity or paternity leave for up to one year. For this reason, child care for Swedish infants under 1 year of age is usually not a major concern. Sweden and many other European countries have well-developed child-care policies. To learn about these policies, see the Caring for Children interlude.

CARING FOR CHILDREN

Child-Care Policy Around the World

Child care policies vary widely in countries around the world (Friedman, Randolph, & Kochanoff, 2004). Sheila Kammerman (1989, 2000a, b) has conducted extensive examinations of parental leave policies in different countries. Parental leaves were first enacted as maternity policies more than a century ago to protect the physical health of working women at the time of childbirth. More recently, child-rearing, parental, and paternity leaves were created in response not only to the needs of working women (and parents), but also because of concern for the child's well-being. The European Union (EU) mandated a paid 14-week maternity leave in 1992 and a three-month parental leave in 1998.

Across cultures, policies vary in eligibility criteria, leave duration, benefit level, and the extent to which parents take advantage of these policies. The European policies just mentioned lead the way in creating new standards of parental leave. The United States is alone among advanced industrialized countries in the briefness of parental leave granted and among the few countries with unpaid leave (Australia and New Zealand are the others).

There are five different types of parental leave from employment:

- *Maternity leave.* In some countries the prebirth leave is compulsory as is a 6- to 10-week leave following birth.
- *Paternity leave.* This is usually much briefer than maternity leave. It especially may be important when a second child is born and the first child requires care.
- *Parental leave.* This is a gender-neutral leave that usually follows a maternity leave and allows either women or men to take advantage of the leave policy and share it or choose which of them will use it.
- *Child-rearing leave.* In some countries, this is a supplement to a maternity leave or a variation on a parental leave. A child-rearing leave is usually longer than a maternity leave and is typically paid at a much lower level.
- *Family leave.* This covers reasons other than the birth of a new baby and can allow time off from employment to care for an ill child or other family members, time to accompany a child to school for the first time, or time to visit a child's school.

Sweden has one of the most extensive leave policies. Paid for by the government at 80 percent of wages, one year of parental leave is allowed (including maternity leave). Maternity leave may begin 60 days prior to expected birth of the baby and ends six weeks after birth. Another six months of parental leave can be used until the child's eighth birthday (Kammerman, 2000a). Virtually all eligible mothers take advantage of the leave policy and approximately 75 percent of eligible fathers take at least some part of the leave they are allowed. In addition, employed grandparents now also have the right to take time off to care for an ill grandchild.

Spain is an example of a relatively poor country that still provides substantial parental leave. Spain allows a 16-week paid maternity leave (paid at 100 percent of wages) at childbirth with up to 6 weeks prior to childbirth allowed. Fathers are permitted two days of leave.

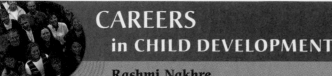

CAREERS in CHILD DEVELOPMENT

Rashmi Nakhre
Child-Care Director

Rashmi, Nakhre has two master's degrees—one in psychology, the other in child development—and is director of the Hattie Daniels Day Care Center in Wilson, North Carolina. At a recent ceremony, "Celebrating a Century of Women," Rashmi received the Distinguished Women of North Carolina Award for 1999–2000.

Nakhre first worked at the child-care center soon after she arrived in the United States 25 years ago. She says that she took the job initially because she needed the money but "ended up falling love with my job." Nakhre has turned the Wilson, North Carolina, child-care center into a model for other centers. The center almost closed several years after Nakhre began working there because of financial difficulties. Nakhre played a major role in raising funds not only to keep it open but to improve it. The center provides quality child care for the children of many Latino migrant workers.

Rashmi Nakhre, working with young children at her child-care center in Wilson, North Carolina.

National Child Care Information Center
NICHD Study of Early Child Care

The types of child care that young children receive vary extensively (Lamb & Ahmert, 2006; Marshall, 2004; Randolph & Kochanoff, 2004; Vandell, 2004). Many child-care centers house large groups of children and have elaborate facilities. Some are commercial operations; others are nonprofit centers run by churches, civic groups, and employers. Child care is frequently provided in private homes, at times by child-care professionals, at others by mothers who want to earn extra money. Researchers have found that children show more stress when they spend long hours in center-based care than in other types of care (Sagi & others, 2002). Further, children who have a fearful or easily frustrated temperament style are often the most negatively influenced by spending long hours in center care (Crockenberg & Leerkes, 2005).

There is increasing interest in the role of child care in ethnic minority families (Johnson & others, 2003). Child-care patterns vary by ethnicity. For example, Latino families fall far below non-Latino White and African American families in using center care (11 percent, 20 percent, and 21 percent, respectively, in one recent study; Smith, 2002). Despite indicating a preference for center-based care, African American and Latino families often rely on family-based care, especially by grandmothers. However, there has been a substantial increase in center-based care by African American mothers.

Researchers also have a special interest in the role of poverty in quality of child care (McLearn, 2004; Zaslow, 2004). In one study, child-care centers that served high-income children delivered better-quality care than did centers that served middle- and low-income children (Phillips & others, 1994). The indices of quality (such as teacher-child ratios) in subsidized centers for the poor were fairly good, but the quality of observed teacher-child interaction was lower than in high-income centers. A recent study found that extensive child care did not appear to be harmful to low-income children's development except when the care was of low quality (Votrub-Drzal & others, 2004). In this study, high-quality care, even when more than 45 hours a week, was related to lower incidences of internalizing (anxiety, for example) and externalizing problems (aggressive and destructive behaviors, for example). To read about one individual who provides quality child care to children from impoverished backgrounds, see the Careers in Child Development profile.

What constitutes a high-quality child-care program for infants? In a demonstration program at Harvard University, the child-care center included a pediatrician, a nonteaching director, and an infant-teacher ratio of 3 to 1 (Kagan, Kearsley, & Zelazo, 1978). Teachers' aides assisted at the center. The teachers and aides were trained to smile frequently, to talk with the infants, and to provide them with a safe environment, which included many stimulating toys. No adverse effects of child care were observed in this project. To read further about high-quality child care, see figure 8.8.

Aware of the growing use of child care, the National Institute of Child Health and Human Development (NICHD) developed a comprehensive, longitudinal study of child-care experiences. The study began in 1991, and data were collected on a diverse

1. The adult caregivers

- The adults should enjoy and understand how infants and young children grow.

- There should be enough adults to work with a group and to care for the individual needs of children. The recommended ratios of adult caregivers to children of different ages are:

Age of children	Adult to children ratio
0 to 1 Year	1:3
1 to 2 Years	1:5
2 to 3 Years	1:6
3 to 4 Years	1:8
4 to 5 Years	1:10

- Caregivers should observe and record each child's progress and development.

2. The program activities and equipment

- The environment should foster the growth and development of young children working and playing together.

- A good center should provide appropriate and sufficient equipment and play materials and make them readily available.

- Infants and children should be helped to increase their language skills and to expand their understanding of the world.

3. The relation of staff to families and the community

- A good program should consider and support the needs of the entire family. Parents should be welcome to observe, discuss policies, make suggestions, and work in the activities of the center.

- The staff in a good center should be aware of and contribute to community resources. The staff should share information about community recreational and learning opportunities with families.

4. The design of the facility and the program to meet the varied demands of infants and young children, their families, and the staff

- The health of children, staff, and parents should be protected and promoted. The staff should be alert to the health of each child.

- The facility should be safe for children and adults.

- The environment should be spacious enough to accommodate a variety of activities and equipment. More specifically, there should be a minimum of 35 square feet of usable playroom floor space indoors per child and 75 square feet of play space outdoors per child.

FIGURE 8.8 **What Is High-Quality Child Care?** What constitutes quality child care? These recommendations were made by the National Association for the Education of Young Children. They are based on a consensus arrived at by experts in early childhood education and child development. It is especially important for parents to meet the adults who will care for their child. Caregivers are responsible for every aspect of the program's operation.

sample of almost 1,400 children and their families at 10 locations across the United States over a period of seven years. Researchers are using multiple methods (trained observers, interviews, questionnaires, and testing) and measuring many facets of children's development, including physical health, cognitive development, and socioemotional development. Here are some of the results of this extensive study to date (NICHD Early Child Care Research Network, 2001, 2002, 2003).

- *Patterns of use.* There was high reliance on infant care, rapid entry into care postbirth, and considerable instability in care. By 4 months of age, nearly three-fourths of the infants had entered some form of nonmaternal child care. Almost half of the infants were cared for by a relative when they first entered care and only 12 percent were enrolled in child-care centers. Socioeconomic factors were linked to the amount and type of care. For example, mothers with higher incomes and families that were more dependent on the mother's income placed their infants in child care at an earlier age. Low-income families were more likely than affluent families to use child care. In the preschool years, mothers who were single, those with more education, and families with higher incomes used more hours of center care than other families. Minority families and mothers with less education used more hours of care by relatives.

- *Quality of care.* Quality of care was based on such characteristics as group size, child–adult ratio, physical environment, caregiver characteristics (such as formal education, specialized training, and child-care experience), and caregiver behavior (such as sensitivity to children). Infants from low-income families experienced lower quality of child care than infants from higher-income families. When quality of caregivers' care was high, children performed better on cognitive and language tasks, were more cooperative with their mothers during play, showed more positive and skilled interaction with peers, and had fewer behavior problems. Support was found for policies that improve state regulations for caregiver training and child-staff ratios, which were linked with higher cognitive and social competence at 54 months of age via positive caregiving by the child-care providers.

  Higher-quality child care was related to higher-quality mother-child interaction among the families that used nonmaternal care. Further, poor-quality care was related to an increase of infant insecure attachment to the mother at 15 months of age, but only when the mother was low in sensitivity and responsiveness. However, child-care quality was not linked to attachment security at 36 months of age.

- *Amount of child care.* The quantity of child care predicted some child outcomes. When children spend extensive amounts of time in child care beginning in infancy, they experience less sensitive interactions with their mother, show more behavior problems, and have higher rates of illness (Vandell, 2004). Many of these comparisons involved children in child care for less than 30 hours a week versus those in child care for more than 45 hours a week.

- *Family and parenting influences.* The results of this large national study indicated that the influence of families and parenting is not weakened by extensive child care. Parents played a significant role in helping children to regulate their emotions, which was related to positive cognitive and social outcomes through the first grade.

In sum, concerns continue about some aspects of child care in the United States. Experts increasingly recognize that child care may harm some children more than others (Langlois & Liben, 2003). Difficult children and those with poor self-control may be especially at risk in child care (Maccoby & Lewis, 2003). Thus, one intervention may involve teaching child-care providers how to foster self-regulatory skills in children (Fabes, Hanish, & Martin, 2003). Another intervention might involve more effort being invested in building attachment to the child-care center or school. For example, one study revealed that when children experienced their group, class, or school as a caring community, they showed increased concern for others, better conflict resolution skills, and a decrease in problem behaviors (Solomon & others, 2000).

What are some strategies parents can follow in regard to child care? Child-care expert Kathleen McCartney (2003, p. 4) offered this advice:

- *Recognize that the quality of your parenting is a key factor in your child's development.*
- *Make decisions that will improve the likelihood you will be good parents.* "For some this will mean working full-time"—for personal fulfillment, income, or both. "For others, this will mean working part-time or not working outside the home."
- *Monitor your child's development.* "Parents should observe for themselves whether their children seem to be having behavior problems." They need to talk with child-care providers and their pediatrician about their child's behavior
- *Take some time to find the best child care.* Observe different child-care facilities and be certain that you like what you see. "Quality child care costs money, and not all parents can afford the child care they want. However, state subsidies, and other programs like Head Start, are available for families in need."

Review and Reflect • LEARNING GOAL 3

3 Explain how social contexts influence the infant's socioemotional development.

Review
- What are some important family processes in infant development?
- How does child care influence infant development?

Reflect
- Imagine that a friend of yours is getting ready to put her baby in child care. What advice would you give to her? Do you think she should stay home with the baby? Why or why not? What type of child care would you recommend?

- Caregivers of secure babies are sensitive to the babies' signals and are consistently available to meet their needs. Caregivers of avoidant babies tend to be unavailable or rejecting. Caregivers of resistant babies tend to be inconsistently available to their babies and usually are not very affectionate. Caregivers of disorganized babies often neglect or physically abuse their babies.

 Explain how social contexts influence the infant's socioemotional development.

- The transition to parenthood requires considerable adaptation and adjustment on the part of parents. Children socialize parents just as parents socialize children. Mutual regulation and scaffolding are important aspects of reciprocal socialization. Belsky's model describes direct and indirect effects. The mother's primary role when interacting with the infant is caregiving; the father's is playful interaction.

- Child care has become a basic need of the American family. More children are now in child care in the United States than at any earlier point in history. The quality of child care is uneven, and child care remains a controversial topic. Quality child care can be achieved and seems to have few adverse affects on children. In the NICHD child-care study, infants from low-income families were found to receive the lowest quality of care. Also, higher quality of child care was linked with better performance on cognitive tasks and fewer child problems.

KEY TERMS

emotion 243
primary emotions 244
self-conscious emotions 244
basic cry 244
anger cry 244
pain cry 244
reflexive smile 246
social smile 246

stranger anxiety 246
separation protest 247
social referencing 247
emotional regulation 247
temperament 248
easy child 248
difficult child 248
slow-to-warm-up child 248

goodness of fit 250
trust versus mistrust 251
autonomy versus shame and doubt 252
attachment 253
Strange Situation 255
securely attached babies 255
insecure avoidant babies 255

insecure resistant babies 255
insecure disorganized babies 256
reciprocal socialization 259
scaffolding 259

KEY PEOPLE

John Watson 245
Jacob Gewirtz 245
Mary Ainsworth 245
John Bowlby 245

Alexander Chess and Stella Thomas 248
Jerome Kagan 248
Mary Rothbart 248

Erik Erikson 251
Margaret Mahler 252
Harry Harlow 254
Jay Belsky 260

Kathleen McCartney 264

MAKING A DIFFERENCE

Nurturing the Infant's Socioemotional Development

What are the best ways to help the infant develop socioemotional competencies?

- *Develop a secure attachment with the infant.* Infants need the warmth and support of one or more caregivers. The caregiver(s) should be sensitive to the infant's signals and respond nurturantly.
- *Be sure that both the mother and the father nurture the infant.* Infants develop best when both the mother and the father provide warm, nurturant support. Fathers need to seri-

ously evaluate their responsibility in rearing a competent infant.

- *Select competent child care.* If the infant will be placed in child care, spend time evaluating different options. Be sure the infant–caregiver ratio is low. Also assess whether the adults enjoy and are knowledgeable about interacting with infants. Determine if the facility is safe and provides stimulating activities.
- *Understand and respect the infant's temperament.* Be sensitive to the characteristics of each child. It may be necessary to provide extra support for distress-prone infants, for example. Avoid negative labeling of the infant.

- *Adapt to developmental changes in the infant.* An 18-month-old toddler is very different from a 6-month-old infant. Be knowledgeable about how infants develop and adapt to the changing infant. Let toddlers explore a wider but safe environment.
- *Be physically and mentally healthy.* Infants' socioemotional development benefits when their caregivers are physically and mentally healthy. For example, a depressed parent may not sensitively respond to the infant's signals.
- *Read a good book on infant development.* Any of T. Berry Brazelton's books are a good start. One is *Touchpoints*. Two other good books by other authors are *Infancy* by Tiffany Field and *Baby Steps* by Claire Kopp.

CHILDREN RESOURCES

Daycare (1993, rev. ed.)

by Alison Clarke-Stewart
Cambridge, MA: Harvard University Press

This book draws on extensive research to survey the social, political, and economic contexts of child care. The author discusses options and consequences to help parents make informed choices.

The Happiest Baby on the Block (2002)

by Harvey Karp
New York: Bantam.

An outstanding book on ways to calm a crying baby.

Touchpoints (1992)

by T. Berry Brazelton
Reading, MA: Addison-Wesley

Covering the period from pregnancy through first grade, Brazelton focuses on the concerns and questions parents have about the child's feelings, behavior, and development.

E-LEARNING TOOLS

Connect to **www.mhhe.com/santrockc9** to research the answers to complete these exercises. In addition, you'll find a number of other resources and valuable study tools for chapter 8, "Socioemotional Development in Infancy," on this website.

Taking It to the Net

1. Catherine is conducting a class for new parents at a local clinic. What advice should Catherine give the parents about how parenting practices can affect a child's inborn temperament?
2. Peter and Rachel are adopting a 3-month-old infant. What are some practical things they can do to help ensure that their child develops a healthy attachment bond with them, in spite of not being with them in the first few months of life?
3. Veronica is anxious about choosing the best child-care center for her child. What are the main things she should consider as she visits the facilities on her list?

Health and Well-Being, Parenting, and Education

Build your decision-making skills by trying your hand at the health and well-being, parenting, and education exercises.

Video Clips

The Online Learning Center includes the following videos for this chapter.

1. *Sex-Typed Play at Age 1—2*
   A 1-year-old girl is shown in a room surrounded by an assortment of toys. She only shows interest in the Barbie dolls, which she examines carefully from every angle.
2. *Attachment Theory—300*
   Renowned attachment researcher L. Alan Sroufe defines attachment theory and how it relates to children's social and emotional development. He states that attachment theory led to a revolution in developmental psychology. He uses examples from his own research to illustrate the significance of attachment relationships.
3. *Philosophy of Preschool Teaching—1018*
   A head teacher of a 4-year-old classroom describes her "whole child" philosophy to teaching young children.
4. *Daycare Environment at 3 Years—225*
   In this clip, we see 3-year-old Josh outside during preschool. With the guidance of his teacher he is making a necklace out of cereal, which they discuss as he works.

The bodies of 5-year-olds and 2-year-olds are different. Notice that the 5-year-old not only is taller and weights more, but also has a longer trunk and legs than the 2-year-old. *Can you think of some other physical differences between 2- and 5-year-olds?*

www.mhhe.com/santrock9

Preschool Growth and Development

growth hormone deficiency The absence or deficiency of growth hormone produced by the pituitary gland to stimulate the body to grow.

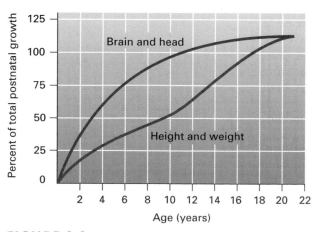

FIGURE 9.2 Growth Curves for the Head and Brain and for Height and Weight The more rapid growth of the brain and head can easily be seen. Height and weight advance more gradually over the first two decades of life.

Jason, and Jennifer are telling us they want to know more about the body's machinery. Two recommended books to help answer some of children's curious questions about their bodies are *The Body Book* by Claire Raynor and *Blood and Guts* by Linda Allison.

Growth patterns vary individually. Think back to your preschool years. This was probably the first time you noticed that some children were taller than you, some shorter; some were fatter, some thinner; some were stronger, some weaker. Much of the variation is due to heredity, but environmental experiences are involved to some extent. A review of the height and weight of children around the world concluded that the two most important contributors to height differences are ethnic origin and nutrition (Meredith, 1978). The urban, middle-socioeconomic-status, and firstborn children were taller than rural, lower-socioeconomic status, and later-born children. The children whose mothers smoked during pregnancy were half an inch shorter than the children whose mothers did not smoke during pregnancy. In the United States, African American children are taller than non-Latino White children.

Why are some children unusually short? The culprits are congenital factors (genetic or prenatal problems), growth hormone deficiency, a physical problem that develops in childhood, maternal smoking during pregnancy, or an emotional difficulty. A recent research review found that although children with short stature on average score lower than children of normal or tall stature on tests of motor skills, intelligence, and achievement, few short children score outside the normal range for these skills (Wheeler & others, 2004).

Growth hormone deficiency is the absence or deficiency of growth hormone produced by the pituitary gland to stimulate the body to grow. Growth hormone deficiency may occur during infancy or later in childhood (Awan, Sattar, & Khattak, 2005; Gandrud & Wilson, 2004; Mehta & others, 2005). As many as 10,000 to 15,000 U.S. children may have growth hormone deficiency (Stanford University Medical Center, 2005). Without treatment, most children with growth hormone deficiency will not reach a height of five feet. Treatment involves regular injections of growth hormone and usually lasts several years (Chernausek, 2004; Minczykowski & others, 2005; Radcliffe & others, 2004; Rosilio & others, 2005). Some children receive daily injections, others several times a week.

Chronically sick children are shorter than their rarely sick counterparts. Children who have been physically abused or neglected may not secrete adequate growth hormone, which can restrict their physical growth.

The Brain

One of the most important physical developments during early childhood is the continuing development of the brain and nervous system (Nelson, Thomas, & de Haan, 2006). Although the brain continues to grow in early childhood, it does not grow as rapidly as in infancy. By the time children reach 3 years of age, the brain is three-quarters of its adult size. By age 5, the brain has reached about nine-tenths of its adult size.

The brain and the head grow more rapidly than any other part of the body. The top parts of the head, the eyes, and the brain grow faster than the lower portions, such as the jaw. Figure 9.2 reveals how the growth curve for the head and brain advances more rapidly than the growth curve for height and weight. At 5 years of age, when the brain has attained approximately 90 percent of its adult weight, the 5-year-old's total body weight is only about one-third of what it will be when the child reaches adulthood.

Neuronal Changes Changes in neurons in early childhood involve connections between neurons and myelination. Communication in the brain is characterized by the transmission of information between neurons, or nerve cells. Some of the brain's increase in size during early childhood is due to the increase in the number and size of nerve endings and receptors, which allows more effective communication to occur.

Neurons communicate with each other through *neurotransmitters* (chemical substances) that carry information across gaps (called *synapses*) between the neurons. One neurotransmitter that has been shown to increase substantially in the 3- to 6-year age period is *dopamine* (Diamond, 2001). We will return to a discussion of dopamine shortly.

Some of the brain's increase in size also is due to the increase in **myelination,** in which nerve cells are covered and insulated with a layer of fat cells. This has the effect of increasing the speed of information traveling through the nervous system (Meier & others, 2004). Some developmentalists argue myelination is important in the maturation of a number of children's abilities (Nagy, Westerberg, & Klingberg, 2004). For example, myelination in the areas of the brain related to hand-eye coordination is not complete until about 4 years of age. One recent fMRI study of children (mean age: 4-years) found that children with developmental delay of motor and cognitive milestones had significantly reduced levels of myelination (Pujol & others, 2004). Myelination in the areas of the brain related to focusing attention is not complete until the end of the middle or late childhood.

Structural Changes   Until recently, scientists lacked adequate technology to detect sensitive changes and view detailed maps of the developing human brain. However, sophisticated brain-scanning techniques, such as magnetic resonance imaging (MRI), now allow us to better detect these changes (Blumenthal & others, 1999). With high-resolution MRI, scientists recently have evolved spatially complex, four-dimensional growth pattern maps of the developing brain, allowing the brain to be mapped with greater sensitivity than ever before. Using these techniques, scientists have discovered that children's brains undergo dramatic anatomical changes between the ages of 3 and 15 (Thompson & others, 2000). By repeatedly obtaining brain scans of the same children for up to four years, they found that the children's brains experience rapid, distinct spurts of growth. The amount of brain material in some areas can nearly double within as little as a year, followed by a drastic loss of tissue as unneeded cells are purged and the brain continues to reorganize itself. The scientists found that the overall size of the brain did not show dramatic growth in the 3- to 15-year age range. However, what did dramatically change were local patterns within the brain.

Researchers have found that from 3 to 6 years of age the most rapid growth takes place in the frontal lobe areas involved in planning and organizing new actions, and in maintaining attention to tasks. They have discovered that from age 6 through puberty, the most growth takes place in the temporal and parietal lobes, especially areas that play major roles in language and spatial relations.

The Brain and Cognitive Development   The increasing maturation of the brain, combined with opportunities to experience a widening world, contribute to children's emerging cognitive abilities (Cornish, 2004). Consider a child who is learning to read and is asked by a teacher to read aloud to the class. Input from the child's eyes is transmitted to the child's brain, then passed through many brain systems, which translate (process) the patterns of black and white into codes for letters, words, and associations. The output occurs in the form of messages to the child's lips and tongue. The child's own gift of speech is possible because brain systems are organized in ways that permit language processing.

The brain is organized according to many neural circuits, which are neural networks composed of many neurons with certain functions. One neural circuit is thought to have an important function in the development of attention and working memory (a type of short-term memory that is like a mental workbench in

myelination The process in which the nerve cells are covered and insulated with a layer of fat cells, which increases the speed at which information travels through the nervous system.

37 to 48 Months	49 to 60 Months	61 to 72 Months
Approximates a circle in drawing	Strings and laces shoelace	Folds paper into halves and quarters
Cuts paper	Cuts following a line	Traces around hand
Pastes using pointer finger	Strings 10 beads	Draws rectangle, circle, square, and triangle
Builds three-block bridge	Copies figure X	Cuts interior piece from paper
Builds eight-block tower	Opens and places clothespins (one-handed)	Uses crayons appropriately
Draws 0 and +	Builds a five-block bridge	Makes clay object with two small parts
Dresses and undresses doll	Pours from various containers	Reproduces letters
Pours from pitcher without spilling	Prints first name	Copies two short words

Note: The skills are listed in the approximate order of difficulty within each age period.

FIGURE 9.5 The Development of Fine Motor Skills in Early Childhood

"You moved."

placement stage Kellogg's term for 2- to 3-year-olds' drawings that are drawn in placement patterns.

shape stage Kellogg's term for 3-year-olds' drawings consisting of diagrams in different shapes.

design stage Kellogg's term for 3- to 4-year-olds' drawings that mix two basic shapes into more complex designs.

pictorial stage Kellogg's term for 4- to 5-year-olds' drawings depicting objects that adults can recognize.

developmental delay in children from birth through 6 years of age. The test is individually administered and includes separate assessments of gross and fine motor skills, as well as language and personal-social ability (Brachlow, Jordan, & Tervo, 2001). Among the gross motor skills this test measures are the child's ability to sit, walk, long jump, pedal a tricycle, throw a ball overhand, catch a bounced ball, hop on one foot, and balance on one foot. Fine motor skills measured by the test include the child's ability to stack cubes, reach for objects, and draw a person.

Young Children's Artistic Drawings

In the story that opened the chapter, you read about Teresa Amabile's artistic skills and interest in kindergarten, but how these were restricted once she went to elementary school. Indeed, many young children show a special interest in drawing.

Children's art emphasizes the flatness of the drawing or painting. Their art has simple lines and irregular contours that create disproportionate figures with bright, unmixed colors. The drawings come across as unrefined, unfinished products that clearly do not replicate reality. The unintended irregularities of children's drawings suggest spontaneity, freedom, and directness.

Young children often use the same formula for drawing different things. Though modified in small ways, one basic form can cover a range of objects. When children begin to draw animals, they portray them in the same way they portray humans: standing upright with a smiling face, legs, and arms. Pointed ears may be the only clue adults have as to the nature of the particular beast. As children become more aware of the nature of a cat, their drawings acquire more catlike features, and they show the cat on all four paws, tail in the air.

Not all children embrace art with equal enthusiasm, and the same child may want to draw one day but have no interest in it the next day. For most children, however, art is an important vehicle for conveying feelings and ideas that are not easily expressed in words. Drawing and constructing also provide children with a hands-on opportunity to use their problem-solving skills to develop creative ways to represent scale, space, and motion. Parents can provide a context for artistic exploration by giving children a work space where they are not overly concerned about messiness or damage. They can make supplies available, have a bulletin board display space for the child's art, and support and encourage the child's art activity.

Developmental Changes and Stages   The development of fine motor skills in the preschool years allows children to become budding artists. There are dramatic changes in how children depict what they see. Art provides unique insights into children's perceptual worlds—what they are attending to, how space and distance are

FIGURE 9.6 The Stages of Young Children's Artistic Drawings

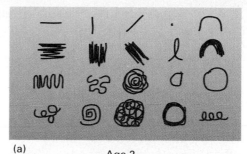

viewed, how they experience patterns and forms (Dorn, Madeja, & Sabol, 2004). Rhoda Kellogg is a creative teacher of preschool children who has observed and guided young children's artistic efforts for many decades. She has assembled an impressive array of tens of thousands of drawings produced by more than 2,000 preschool children. Adults who are unfamiliar with young children's art often view the productions of this age group as meaningless scribbles. However, Kellogg (1970) documented that young children's artistic productions are orderly, meaningful, and structured.

By their second birthday, children can scribble. Scribbles represent the earliest form of drawing. Every form of graphic art, no matter how complex, contains the lines found in children's artwork, which Kellogg calls the 20 basic scribbles. These include vertical, horizontal, diagonal, circular, curving, waving or zigzag lines and dots. As young children progress from scribbling to picture making, they go through four distinguishable stages: placement, shape, design, and pictorial (see figure 9.6).

Following young children's scribbles is the **placement stage,** Kellogg's term for 2- to 3-year-olds' drawings, drawn on a page in placement patterns. One example of these patterns is the spaced border pattern shown in figure 9.6*b.* The **shape stage** is Kellogg's term for 3-year-olds' drawings consisting of diagrams in different shapes (figure 9.6*c*). Young children draw six basic shapes: circles, squares or rectangles, triangles, crosses, Xs, and forms. The **design stage** is Kellogg's term for 3- to 4-year-olds' drawings in which young children mix two basic shapes into a more complex design (figure 9.6*d*). This stage occurs rather quickly after the shape stage. The **pictorial stage** is Kellogg's term for 4- to 5-year-olds' drawings that consist of objects that adults can recognize (figure 9.6*e*).

(b)   Age 2 to 3
Placement stage

Child Art in Context
The title of this section, "Child Art in Context," is also the title of a recent book by Claire Golomb (2002), who has studied and conducted research on children's art for a number of decades. Golomb especially criticizes views of young children's art that describe it as primitive and a reflection of conceptual immaturity. She argues that children, like all novices, tend to use forms economically and their comments indicate that their simplified version works. Rather than reflecting conceptual immaturity, Golomb views children's art as inventive problem solving.

Golomb believes that developmental changes in the way children draw are not strictly age-related but also depend on talent, motivation, familial support, and cultural values. Thus, her view contrasts with Kellogg's stage approach, which we just discussed. In Golomb's view, child art flourishes in sociocultural contexts where tools are made available and where this activity is valued. In chapter 10, we will look further at young children's art, paying special attention to the role of cognitive development in their art.

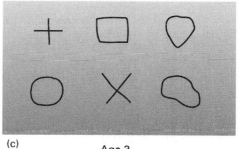

(c)   Age 3
Shape stage

Handedness

For centuries, left-handers have suffered unfair discrimination in a world designed for right-handers. Even the devil himself has been portrayed as a left-hander. For many years, teachers forced all children to write with their right hand, even if they had a left-hand tendency. Fortunately, today most teachers let children write with the hand they favor (Wenze & Wenze, 2004).

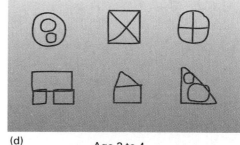

(d)   Age 3 to 4
Design stage

Origin and Development of Handedness
What is the origin of hand preference? Genetic inheritance likely is strong (Geschwind & others, 2002; Shibazaki, Shimizu, & Kuroda, 2004). In one study, the handedness of adopted children was not related to the handedness of their adoptive parents but was related to the handedness of their biological parents (Carter-Saltzman, 1980).

Right-handedness is dominant in all cultures (it appears approximately in a ratio of 90 percent right-handers and 10 percent left-handers) and it appears before the

(e)   Age 4 to 5
Pictorial stage

Today, most teachers let children write with the hand they favor. *What are the main reasons children become left- or right-handed?*

Handedness

impact of culture. For example, in one study ultrasound observations of fetal thumb sucking showed that 9 of 10 fetuses were more likely to be sucking their right hand's thumb (Hepper, Shahidullah, & White, 1990).

Thus, although adults often don't notice a child's hand preference until the toddler or early childhood years, researchers have found that hand preference occurs earlier, possibly even in the womb as we just saw (Stroganova & others, 2004). Newborns also show a preference for one side of their body over the other. In one study, 65 percent of the infants turned their head to the right when they were lying on their back in the crib (Michel, 1981). Fifteen percent preferred to face toward the left. These preferences for the right or left were linked with handedness later in development.

At about 7 months of age, infants prefer grabbing with one hand or the other and this is related to later handedness (Ramsay, 1980). By 2 years of age, about 10 percent of children prefer to use their left hand. Many preschool children, though, use both hands, with a clear hand preference not completely distinguished until later in development.

Handedness, the Brain, and Language   A contemporary interest is the role of the brain in handedness (Basic & others, 2004; Tang & Reeb, 2004; Tremblay, Monetta, & Joanette, 2004). Approximately 95 percent of right-handed individuals process speech primarily in the brain's left hemisphere (Springer & Deutsch, 1985). However, left-handed individuals show more variation. More than half of left-handers process speech in their left hemisphere, just like right-handers. However, about one-fourth of left-handers process speech in their right hemisphere and another one-fourth process speech equally in both hemispheres (Knecht & others, 2000).

Are there differences in the language development of left- and right-handers? The most consistent finding is that left-handers are more likely to have reading problems (Geschwind & Behan, 1984; Natsopoulos & others, 1998).

Handedness and Other Abilities   Although there is a tendency for left-handers to have more reading problems than right-handers, left-handers are more common among mathematicians, musicians, architects, and artists (Michaelangelo, Leonardo da Vinci, and Picasso were all lefties) (Schacter & Ransil, 1996). Architects and artists who are left-handed benefit from the tendency of left-handers to have unusually good visuospatial skills and be able to imagine spatial layouts (Holtzen, 2000). Also, in one study of more than 100,000 students taking the Scholastic Aptitude Test (SAT), 20 percent of the top-scoring group was left-handed, twice the rate of left-handedness found in the general population (10 percent) (Bower, 1985).

Review and Reflect ● LEARNING GOAL 2

2 **Describe changes in motor development in early childhood.**

Review
- How do gross and fine motor skills change in early childhood?
- How can young children's artistic drawings be characterized?
- What is the nature of handedness?

Reflect
- Assume that you are the director of a preschool program and the parents ask you to develop a program to teach the children how to participate in sports. Think through how you would explain to parents why most 3-year-olds are not ready for participation in sports programs. Include in your answer information about 3-year-olds' limited motor skills, as well as the importance of learning basic motor skills first and having unrealistic expectations for young children's development of sports skills.

So far we have discussed young children's body growth and change, as well as their development of motor skills. In this section, we will explore another aspect of young children's physical development—health. To learn more about young children's health we will focus on their sleep, nutrition, safety, and illness.

Sleep and Sleep Problems

Most young children sleep through the night and have one daytime nap (Davis, Parker, & Montgomery, 2004). Sometimes, though, it is difficult to get young children to go to sleep as they drag out their bedtime routine (Hoban, 2004). Helping the child slow down before bedtime often contributes to less resistance in going to bed. Reading the child a story, playing quietly with the child in the bath, or letting the child sit on the caregiver's lap while listening to music are quieting activities (Burke, Kuhn, & Peterson, 2004).

Transitional Objects

Many young children want to take a soft, cuddly object, such as a favorite blanket, teddy bear, or other stuffed animal, to bed with them. **Transitional objects** are those that children repeatedly use as bedtime companions. They usually are soft and cuddly, and most developmentalists view them as representing a transition from being a dependent person to being a more independent one. Therefore, using transitional objects at bedtime is normal behavior for young children (Steer & Lehman, 2000; Tabin, 1992). In one study, children who relied on transitional objects at age 4 showed the same level of emotional adjustment at ages 11 and 16 as children who had not relied on transitional objects (Newson, Newson, & Mahalski, 1982).

Sleep Problems

Children can experience a number of sleep problems (Givan, 2004; Glaze, 2004; Jenni & O'Connor, 2005; Owens, 2005; Sheldon, 2004). One recent estimate indicates that more than 40 percent of children experience a sleep problem at some point in their development (Boyle & Cropley, 2004). In one recent study, there was a connection between children's behavioral problems and sleep problems (Smedje, Broman, & Hetta, 2001):

- Children who were hyperactive during the day also were likely to toss and turn a lot during their sleep. They also were more likely to sleep walk than children who were not hyperactive.
- Children with conduct problems (for example, fighting) were more likely to resist going to bed at night.
- Children with emotional problems were more likely to have night terrors and difficulty falling asleep.
- Children with peer problems had a shorter sleep time.

Also, a longitudinal study obtained parental ratings of the sleep and behavioral problems of 490 children from 4 to 15 years of age (Gregory & O'Conner, 2002). Sleep problems in children were associated with depression and anxiety (Ivanenko, Crabtree, & Gozal, 2004).

Let's now explore these sleep problems in children: nightmares, night terrors, sleep walking, and sleep talking. **Nightmares** are frightening dreams that awaken the sleeper, more often toward the morning than just after the child has gone to bed at night. Caregivers should not worry about young children having occasional nightmares because almost every child has them. If children have nightmares persistently,

transitional objects Objects that children repeatedly use as bedtime companions. These usually are soft and cuddly and probably mark the child's transition from being dependent to being more independent.

nightmares Frightening dreams that awaken the sleeper.

FIGURE 9.7 Recommended Energy Intakes for Children Ages 1 Through 10

Age	Weight (kg)	Height (cm)	Energy needs (calories)	Calorie ranges
1 to 3	13	90	1,300	900 to 1,800
4 to 6	20	112	1,700	1,300 to 2,300
7 to 10	28	132	2,400	1,650 to 3,300

it may indicate that they are feeling too much stress during their waking hours. One recent study found that children who experience nightmares have higher levels of anxiety than those who do not have nightmares (Mindell & Barrett, 2002).

Night terrors are characterized by a sudden arousal from sleep and an intense fear, usually accompanied by a number of physiological reactions, such as rapid heart rate and breathing, loud screams, heavy perspiration, and physical movement. In most instances, the child has little or no memory of what happened during the night terror. Night terrors are less common than nightmares and occur more often in deep sleep than do nightmares. Many children who experience night terrors return to sleep rather quickly after the night terror. Caregivers tend to be especially worried when children have night terrors, although they are usually not a serious problem (Thiedke, 2001).

Children usually outgrow night terrors. Although benzodiazepines (diazepam, for example) occasionally may be prescribed to be given to children at bedtime to help reduce night terrors, medication usually is not recommended (National Institutes of Health, 2005). In most cases, reassuring and comforting the child is the only treatment needed.

Somnambulism (sleep walking) occurs during the deepest stage of sleep. Approximately 15 percent of children sleep walk at least once, and from 1 to 5 percent do it regularly. Most children outgrow the problem without professional intervention (Laberge & others, 2000). Except for the danger of accidents while walking around asleep in the dark, there is nothing abnormal about sleep walking. It is safe to awaken sleep-walking children, and it is a good idea to do so because they might harm themselves. If children sleep walk regularly, parents need to make the bedroom and house as safe from harm as possible (Remulla & Guilleminault, 2004).

Sleep talkers are soundly asleep as they speak, although occasionally they make fairly coherent statements for a brief period of time. Most of the time, though, you can't understand what children are saying during sleep talking. There is nothing abnormal about sleep talking, and there is no reason to try to stop it from occurring.

Nutrition

Four-year-old Bobby is on a steady diet of double cheeseburgers, french fries, and chocolate milkshakes. Between meals, he gobbles up candy bars and marshmallows. He hates green vegetables. Bobby, a preschooler, already has developed poor nutritional habits. What are a preschool child's energy needs? What is a preschooler's eating behavior like?

Energy Needs   Feeding and eating habits are important aspects of development during early childhood (Bruss & others, 2005; Morgan, 2005; Rhea & others, 2005). What children eat affects their skeletal growth, body shape, and susceptibility to disease (Leavitt, Tonniges, & Rogers, 2003). An average preschool child requires up to 1,800 calories per day. Figure 9.7 shows the increasing energy needs of children as they move from infancy through the childhood years. Energy requirements for individual children are determined by the **basal metabolism rate (BMR),** which is the minimum amount of energy a person uses in a resting state. Energy needs of

night terrors Sudden arousal from sleep, characterized by intense fear and usually accompanied by physiological reactions, such as rapid heart rate and breathing, loud screams, heavy perspiration, and physical movement.

somnambulism Sleep walking; occurs in the deepest stage of sleep.

basal metabolism rate (BMR) The minimum amount of energy a person uses in a resting state.

individual children of the same age, sex, and size vary. Reasons for these differences remain unexplained. Differences in physical activity, basal metabolism, and the efficiency with which children use energy are among the candidates for explanation.

Diet and Eating Behavior

One recent national study found that from the late 1970s through the late 1990s, key dietary shifts took place in U.S. children: greater away-from-home consumption, large increases in total energy from salty snacks, soft drinks, and pizza; and large decreases in energy from low- and medium-fat milk and medium- and high-fat beef and pork (Nielsen, Siega-Riz, & Popkin, 2002). In this study, children's total energy intake increased from the late 1970s to late 1990s. These dietary changes occurred for children as young as 2 years of age through the adult years.

Another recent national assessment found that most children's diets are poor or in need of improvement (Federal Interagency Forum on Child and Family Statistics, 2002). In this assessment, only 27 percent of 2- to 5-year-old children were categorized as having good diets. Their diets worsened as they became older—only 13 percent of 6- to 9-year-old children had healthy diets.

A special difficulty that many parents encounter is getting their young children to eat vegetables. One recent study randomly assigned 156 parents with 2- to 6-year-old children to one of three conditions: (1) exposure (parents gave their child a taste of a previously disliked vegetable for 14 days), (2) information (parents were given nutritional advice and left a leaflet to read), and (3) control (no intervention) (Wardle & others, 2003). After 14 days, only children in the exposure group reported an increased liking for the previously disliked vegetable. Thus, some persistence on the part of parents in exposing children to vegetables may lead to positive results.

Fat and Sugar Consumption

Caregivers' special concerns involve the appropriate amount of fat and sugar in young children's diets (Briefel & others, 2004; Brom, 2005; Sizer & Whitney, 2006; Skinner & others, 2004; Troiano & Flegal, 1998). Although some health-conscious parents may be providing too little fat in their infants' and children's diets, other parents are raising their children on diets in which the percentage of fat is far too high. Our changing lifestyles, in which we often eat on the run and pick up fast-food meals, contribute to the increased fat levels in children's diets. Most fast-food meals are high in protein, especially meat and dairy products. But the average American child does not need to be concerned about getting enough protein. What must be of concern is the vast number of young children who are being weaned on fast foods that are not only high in protein but also high in fat. Eating habits become ingrained very early in life; unfortunately, it is during the preschool years that many people get their first taste of fast food (Poulton & Sexton, 1996). The American Heart Association recommends that the daily limit for calories from fat should be approximately 35 percent. Compare this percentage with the numbers in figure 9.8. Clearly, many fast-food meals contribute to excess fat intake by children.

One recent study examined maternal and child characteristics involved in the mother's child-feeding style with 5-year-old, non-Latino White daughters (Francis, Hofer, & Birch, 2002). Mothers reported using more restricted feeding practices when their daughters were overweight and reported using more pressure in child feeding when their daughters were thinner.

The concern is not only about excessive fat in children's diets but also about excessive sugar (Briefel & others, 2004). Consider Robert, age 3, who loves chocolate. His mother lets him have three chocolate candy bars a day. He also drinks an average of four cans of caffeinated cola a day, and he eats sugar-coated cereal each morning at breakfast. The average American child consumes almost 2 pounds of sugar per week (Riddle & Prinz, 1984). One recent study found that children from low-income families were more likely to have added sugar consumption than their counterparts from higher-income families (Kranz & Siega-Riz, 2002).

Spinach: Divide into little piles. Re-arrange again into new piles. After five or six maneuvers, sit back and say you are full.
—DELIA EPHRON
American Writer and Humorist, 20th Century

This would be a better world for children if parents had to eat the spinach.
—GROUCHO MARX
American Comedian, 20th Century

FIGURE 9.8 The Fat and Calorie Content
of Selected Fast Foods

Food	Calories	% of calories from fat
Burger King Whopper, fries, vanilla shake	1,250	43
Big Mac, fries, chocolate shake	1,100	41
McDonald's Quarter-Pounder with cheese	418	52
McDonald's Happy Meal with cheeseburger, small french fries, 1% low-fat chocolate milk jug	710	47
Pizza Hut 10-inch pizza with sausage, mushrooms, pepperoni, and green pepper	1,035	35
Arby's roast beef sandwich, two potato patties, coleslaw, chocolate shake	1,200	30
Kentucky Fried Chicken dinner (three pieces chicken, mashed potatoes and gravy, coleslaw, roll)	830	50
Typical restaurant "diet plate" (hamburger patty, cottage cheese, etc.)	638	63

How does sugar consumption influence the health and behavior of young children? The association of sugar consumption with children's health problems—dental cavities and obesity, for example, has been widely documented (Hale, 2003; Lorah, 2002).

In sum, although there is individual variation in appropriate nutrition for children, their diets should be well-balanced and should include fats, carbohydrates, protein, vitamins, and minerals (Dietz & Robinson, 2005; Fox & others, 2004; Wardlaw, 2006). An occasional candy bar does not hurt, but a steady diet of hamburgers, french fries, milkshakes, and candy bars should be avoided.

"Fussy Eaters," Sweets, and Snacks   Many young children get labeled as "fussy" or "difficult eaters" when they are only trying to exercise the same rights to personal taste and appetite adults take for granted. Allow for the child's developing tastes in food. However, when young children eat too many sweets— candy bars, cola, and sweetened cereals, for example—they can spoil their appetite and then not want to eat more nutritious foods at mealtime. Thus, caregivers need to be firm in limiting the amount of sweets young children eat.

Most preschool children need to eat more often than the adults in the family because preschool children use up so much energy. It is a long time from breakfast to lunch and from lunch to dinner for the active young child. Thus, a mid-morning and mid-afternoon snack are recommended. A good strategy is to avoid giving sweets to young children during these snack times (Skinner & others, 2004). Better choices include whole-grain bagels spread with creamy peanut butter, pureed fruit shakes, or tortillas with refried beans. As mentioned in chapter 6, keep in mind that some foods are known choking hazards—avoid giving young children snack foods such as hard candy, nuts, any hard raw vegetable, or whole grapes.

Obesity in Young Children   Being overweight can be a serious problem in early childhood (Borra & others, 2003; Douglas, 2002; Regan & Alderson, 2003). Consider Ramn, an overweight 4-year-old kindergartner. His teachers noticed that Ramn never joined the running games the small superheroes played as they propelled themselves around the playground. Instead, Ramn always begged to stay inside to help during recess.

Should Ramn's parents put him on a restrictive very-low-calorie diet? The answer is no. Except for extreme cases of obesity, overweight preschool children are usually not encouraged to lose a great deal of weight. Instead, they need to slow their rate of weight gain so that they will attain a more normal weight for their height by thinning out as they grow taller.

The percentage of obese children in the United States has increased dramatically in recent decades and the percentage is likely to grow unless changes occur in children's lifestyles (Freeman-Fobbs, 2003). One recent comparison of 34 countries revealed that the United States had the second highest rate of child obesity (Janssen & others, 2005). Childhood obesity contributes to a number of health problems (Maher, 2004). For example, physicians are now seeing type II (adult-onset) diabetes (a condition directly linked with obesity and a low level of fitness) in children as young as 5 years of age (Datar & Sturm, 2004).

Is being overweight associated with lower self-esteem in young children? In one recent study, the relation between weight status and self-esteem in 5-year-old girls was examined (Davison & Birth, 2001). The girls who were overweight had lower body self-esteem than those who were not overweight. Thus, as early as 5 years of age, being overweight is linked with lower self-esteem.

Prevention of obesity in children includes helping children and parents see food as a way to satisfy hunger and nutritional needs, not as proof of love or as a reward for good behavior (Borra & others, 2003). Snack foods should be low in fat, simple sugars, and salt, as well as high in fiber. Routine physical activity should be a daily occurrence (Biddle, Gorely, & Stensel, 2004; Pate & others, 2004).

The child's life should be centered around activities, not meals (Rothstein, 2001). One recent study of 281 children examined the activity level of 3- to 5-year-olds (Pate & others, 2004). The preschool children wore accelerometers, a small activity monitor, for four to five hours a day and the researchers also observed the children's behavior. The young children engaged in an average of 7.7 minutes per hour of moderate to vigorous activity, usually in a block of time when they were outside. Boys were more likely to engage in moderate or vigorous physical activity than girls. The researchers concluded that young children need more vigorous play and organized activities. We will have much more to say about children's obesity in chapter 12, "Physical Development in Middle and Late Childhood."

Helping an Overweight Child

Malnutrition in Young Children from Low-Income Families   One of the most common nutritional problems in early childhood is iron deficiency anemia, which results in chronic fatigue (Carly, 2003). This problem results from the failure to eat adequate amounts of quality meats and dark green vegetables. Young children from low-income families are most likely to develop iron deficiency anemia (Majumdar & others, 2003).

Poor nutrition is a special concern in the lives of young children from low-income families (Drewnowski & Specter, 2004; Ghosh & Shah, 2004; Richter, 2003). Many of these children do not get essential amounts of iron, vitamins, or protein. In part, to address this problem in the United States, the Special Supplemental Nutrition Program for Women, Infants, and Children (WIC) serves approximately 7,500,000 participants in the United States. Positive influences on young children's nutrition and health have been found for participants in WIC (Black & others, 2004). For example, one recent study found that participating in WIC was linked with a lower risk for being overweight in young Mexican American children (Melgar-Quinonez & Kaiser, 2004). In another study, participation in WIC was related to improved nutrition in preschool children, including higher intake of fruit and lower intake of added sugar from snacks (Siega-Riz & others, 2004).

Some researchers argue that malnutrition is directly linked to cognitive deficits because of negative effects on brain development (Liu & others, 2003). However, an increasing number of researchers argue that the links between child undernutrition, physical growth, and cognitive development are more complex (Marcon, 2003). For example, nutritional influences can be viewed in the context of socioemotional factors that often coincide with undernutrition. Thus, children who vary considerably from the norm in physical growth also differ on other biological and socioemotional factors that might influence cognitive development. For example, children who are underfed

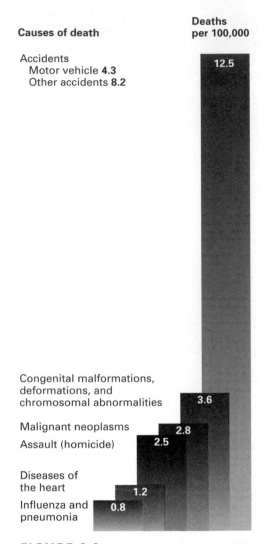

Causes of death	Deaths per 100,000

Accidents
  Motor vehicle **4.3**
  Other accidents **8.2**

12.5

Congenital malformations,
deformations, and
chromosomal abnormalities — 3.6

Malignant neoplasms — 2.8

Assault (homicide) — 2.5

Diseases of
the heart — 1.2

Influenza and
pneumonia — 0.8

FIGURE 9.9 Main Causes of Death in Children 1 through 4 Years of Age These figures are based on the number of deaths per 100,000 children 1 through 4 years of age in the United States in 1999 (National Vital Statistics Report, 2001).

often are also less supervised, less stimulated, and less educated than children who are well nourished (Wachs, 1995). As we saw earlier, poverty is an especially strong risk factor that interacts with children's nutritional status to affect physical and cognitive development (Marcon, 2003).

Malnutrition may be linked to other aspects of development in addition to cognitive deficits. One longitudinal study found that U.S. children who were malnourished at 3 years of age showed more aggressive and hyperactive behavior at age 8, had more externalizing problems at age 11, and evidenced more excessive motor behavior at age 17 (Liu & others, 2004).

Health, Safety, and Illness

The story of children's health in the past 50 years is a shift away from fighting infectious diseases toward prevention and outpatient care (Baraket, Kunin-Batson, & Kazak, 2003; Monsen, 2005; Sundelin, Magnusson, & Lagerberg, 2005). In recent decades, vaccines have nearly eradicated disabling bacterial meningitis and have greatly reduced the incidence of measles, rubella, mumps, and chicken pox. In the effort to make a child's world safer, one of the main strategies is to prevent childhood injuries (Dougherty & Simpson, 2004; Waibel & Misra, 2003).

Preventing Childhood Injuries
Young children's active and exploratory nature, coupled with being unaware of danger in many instances, often puts them in situations in which they are at risk for injuries (Sleet & Mercy, 2003). Most of young children's cuts, bumps, and bruises are minor, but some accidental injuries can produce serious injuries or even death.

As shown in figure 9.9, accidents are the leading cause of death in children 1 through 4 years of age in the United States (National Vital Statistics Reports, 2001). Motor vehicle accidents are at the top of the list of accidents that lead to death in young children. Drowning is the second most frequent cause of accidental death in young children. Falls and poisoning also can lead to death in young children.

Notice in figure 9.9 that the fourth leading cause of death in young children in the United States is assault (homicide). In one cross-cultural comparison, the rate of firearm-related death among children less than 15 years of age in 26 industrialized countries was by far the highest in the United States (American Academy of Pediatrics, 2001). Among those industrialized countries with no firearm-related deaths in children were Kuwait, Japan, Singapore, and the Netherlands.

Many of young children's injuries can be prevented (Greene & others, 2002; Rivara, 2002). Among the ways this can be accomplished are regularly restraining children in automobiles, reducing access to firearms, and making homes and playgrounds safer (Coyne-Beasley & others, 2005; Dunn, Burns, & Sattler, 2003; Langlois, Rutland-Brown, & Thomas, 2005; Sherker & others, 2005).

Influences on children's safety include the acquisition and practice of individual skills and safety behaviors, family and home influences, school and peer influences, and the community's actions. Notice that these influences reflect Bronfenbrenner's ecological model of development that we described in chapter 2, "The Science of Child Development." Figure 9.10 shows how these ecological contexts can influence children's safety, security, and injury prevention (Sleet & Mercy, 2003). We will have more to say about contextual influences on young children's health shortly.

Reducing access to firearms is a wise strategy (Jackman & others, 2001; Schaechter & others, 2003). In 12 states that passed laws requiring that firearms be made inaccessible to children, unintentional shooting deaths of children fell almost 25 percent.

Deaths in young children due to automobile accidents have declined considerably in the United States since the invention of the seat belt. All U.S. states and the District of Columbia have laws that require young children to be restrained in cars, either in specially designed seats or by seat belts. In many instances, when young children are killed today in automobile accidents, they are unrestrained (Chen & others, 2005; Morrison, Pettigrew, & Thomson, 2003).

Most fatal non-vehicle-related deaths in young children occur in or around the home. Young children have drowned in bathtubs and swimming pools, been burned in fires and explosions, experienced falls from heights, and drunk or eaten poisonous substances (Delgado & others, 2002; Schnake, Peterson, & Corden, 2005).

Playgrounds also can be a source of children's injuries (Powell, Ambardekar, & Sheehan, 2005). One of the major problems is that playground equipment is often not constructed over impact-absorbing surfaces, such as wood chips or sand.

Contexts of Young Children's Health

Among the contexts involved in young children's health are poverty, home and child care, environmental tobacco smoke, and exposure to lead (Gulotta & Phinney, 2000). In addition, we will discuss the state of illness and health in the world's children.

Poverty and Ethnicity A special concern focuses on the health of young children living in poverty (Ramey, Ramey, & Lanzi, 2006). Low income is linked with poor health in young children (Howell, Pettit, & Kingsley, 2005; Kendrick & Marsh, 2001; Malat, Oh, & Hamilton, 2005; Wagstaff & others, 2004). Many health problems of young children in poverty begin before birth when their mothers do not receive adequate health care, which can produce a low birth weight child and other complications that can still affect the child years later (Dubay & others, 2001). Children living in poverty may experience unsanitary conditions, live in crowded housing, and be inadequately supervised (Neumann, Gewa, & Bwibo, 2004). Children in poverty are more likely to be exposed to lead poisoning than children growing up in higher socioeconomic conditions (Morrissey-Ross, 2000). The families of many children in poverty do not have adequate medical insurance, and thus the children often receive less adequate medical care compared with children living in higher socioeconomic conditions (Children's Defense Fund, 2001; Olson, Tang, & Newacheck, 2005).

Ethnicity is also linked to children's health (Alio & Salihu, 2005; Andrulis, 2005; Malat, Oh, & Hamilton, 2005; Schneider, Freeman, & McGarvey, 2005). One recent study found that even when socioeconomic status was controlled, Latino, African American, and Asian American children were less likely to have a usual health care source, health professional, doctor visit, and dental visit in the past year (Shi & Stevens, 2005). Another recent study revealed that children whose parents had limited English proficiency were three times more likely to have fair or poor health status than their English proficiency counterparts (Flores, Abreu, & Tomany-Korman, 2005).

Safety at Home and in Child Care Caregivers, whether parents at home or teachers and supervisors in child care, play an important role in the health of young children (Bishay & others, 2003; Freedman & others, 2005; Gomel, Hanson, & Tinsley, 1999; Sleet & Mercy, 2003; Tolmie & others, 2005). For example, by controlling the speed of the vehicles they drive, by decreasing or eliminating their drinking—especially before driving —and by not smoking around children, caregivers enhance the likelihood that children will be healthy (Tinsley, 2003).

Young children may lack the intellectual skills—including reading ability—to discriminate between safe and unsafe household substances.

Individual

Development of social skills and ability to regulate emotions

Involvement in activities that promote positive attachment and prosocial skills

Acquisition of early academic skills and knowledge

Impulse control (such as not darting out into a street to retrieve a ball)

Frequent use of personal protection (such as bike helmets and safety seats)

Family/Home

High awareness and knowledge of child management and parenting skills

Caregiver participation in the child's education and social activities

Frequent parent protective behaviors (such as use of child safety seats)

Presence of home safety equipment (such as smoke alarms and cabinet locks)

School/Peers

Promotion of home/school partnerships

Availability of enrichment programs, especially for low-income families

Absence of playground hazards

Management support for safety and injury prevention

Injury prevention and safety promotion policies and programs

Community

Availability of positive activities for children and their parents

Active surveillance of environmental hazards

Effective prevention policies in place (such as pool fencing)

Commitment to emergency medical services for children and trauma care

Emphasis on safety themes

FIGURE 9.10 Contexts and Young Children's Safety, Security, and Injury Prevention

And they may lack the impulse control to keep from running out into a busy street while chasing a ball. In these and many other situations, competent adult supervision and monitoring of young children is important to prevent injuries (Sleet, Schieber, & Gilchrest, 2003).

In communicating with young children, caregivers need to make the information they give to children cognitively simple (Morrongiello, Midgett, & Shields, 2001). And an important strategy is for parents to guide children in learning how to control and regulate their own health behavior (Tinsley & others, 2002).

Young children need to be encouraged to identify feelings of wellness and illness and specify them to adults. In one study, young adults with fewer illness symptoms remembered their parents as concerned with teaching self-care and the promotion of positive health behaviors (Mechanic, 1979). When they were young children, their mothers were positively oriented toward health rather than concerned with seeking medical attention and making a big deal out of minor illnesses.

Parents also influence how children cope with medical treatment (Tinsley & others, 2002). Much of this research focuses on how parents influence children's fear and coping during inpatient and outpatient pediatric medical visits (Melamed, Roth, & Fogel, 2001). Researchers have found that parents who use distraction, are less agitated, and are more reassuring have children who display lower levels of distress in these medical settings (Stephens, Barkey, & Hall, 1999).

A special concern involves the selection of the best parenting strategies with a chronically ill child. Health researcher Barbara Melamed (2002, p. 341) recently provided these recommendations:

- *"Balance the illness with other family needs."*
- *"Maintain clear family boundaries."* During an illness crisis, extended family members may help with chores or caring for healthy children in the family.
- *"Develop communication competence."* Think about the best ways to talk to the physicians involved and communicate effectively about the illness to others.
- *"Attribute positive meanings to the situation."* Demonstrate how the family can be resilient in this difficult circumstance.
- *"Engage in active coping efforts."* Seek positive problem-solving solutions in dealing with stressful aspects of the child's illness.

Parents also should invest effort in finding a competent health-care provider for their children (Hickson & Clayton, 2002, p. 456). This "includes consulting sources of information and asking questions likely to provide useful information about practice characteristics that may affect the parent-doctor relationship. Parents, for example, might seek information concerning a physician's willingness to answer questions and involve parents in decision making or at least to outline options. Parents might also inquire about the physician's style of practice and philosophies about treatment, behavior management, nutrition, and other general health maintenance practices." To read about Barbara Deloin, a pediatric nurse who promotes positive parent-child experiences and positive links of families to the health-care system, see the Careers in Child Development profile.

Environmental Tobacco Smoke Estimates indicate that approximately 22 percent of children and adolescents in the United States are exposed to tobacco smoke in the home. An increasing number of studies reach the conclusion that children are at risk for health problems when they live in homes in which a parent smokes (Arshad, 2005; Gehrman & Hovell, 2003; Janson, 2004; Lloyd & Wise, 2004; Sheahan & Free, 2005). If the mother smoked, her children were twice as likely to develop respiratory problems (Etzel, 1988). In a recent study, young children whose fathers smoked at home were more likely to have upper respiratory tract infections than those whose fathers did not smoke at home (Shiva & others, 2004). Children exposed to tobacco smoke in the home are more likely to develop wheezing symptoms and asthma than children in nonsmoking homes (Arshad, 2005; Berman & others, 2003; Cabana & others, 2004).

Environmental tobacco smoke also affects the amount of vitamin C in children and adolescents. In a recent study, when parents smoked at home their 4- to 18-year-old children and adolescents had significantly lower levels of vitamin C in their blood than their counterparts in nonsmoking homes (Luria, Smith, & Chapman, 2000; Strauss, 2001). The more parents smoked, the less vitamin C the children and adolescents had. Children exposed to environmental smoke should be encouraged to eat foods rich in vitamin C or be given this vitamin as a supplement (Preston & others, 2003).

Exposure to Lead   There is a special concern about lead poisoning in young children. Approximately 3 million children under 6 years of age are estimated to be at risk for lead poisoning, which might harm their development (Ahamed & others, 2005; Breysse & others, 2004; Brittle & Zint, 2003; Jin & others, 2005, in press; Zierold & Anderson, 2004). As we mentioned earlier, children in poverty are at greater risk for lead poisoning than children living in higher socioeconomic conditions (Moralez, Gutierrez, & Escarce, 2005). Lead can get into children's bloodstreams through food or water that is contaminated by lead, from putting lead-contaminated fingers in their mouths, or from inhaling dust from lead-based paint (Gulson & others, 2004; McLaughlin & others, 2004).

The negative effects of high lead levels in children's blood include lower intelligence, lower achievement, attention deficient hyperactivity disorder, and elevated blood pressure (Canfield & others, 2003; Gump & others, 2005, in press). One recent study found that 5-year-old children exposed to lead performed more poorly on tests of memory and problem solving (Canfield, Gendle, & Cory-Slechta, 2004). Because of such negative outcomes, the Centers for Disease Control and Prevention recommends that children be screened for the presence of lead contamination in their blood.

CAREERS in CHILD DEVELOPMENT

Barbara Deloin
Pediatric Nurse

Barbara Deloin is a pediatric nurse in Denver, Colorado. She practices nursing in the Pediatric Oral Feeding Clinic and is involved in research as part of an irritable infant study for the Children's Hospital in Denver. She also is on the faculty of nursing at the Colorado Health Sciences Center. Deloin previously worked in San Diego where she was coordinator of the Child Health Program for the County of San Diego.

Her research interests focus on children with special health-care needs, especially high-risk infants and children, and promoting positive parent-child experiences. She recently was elected president of the National Association of Pediatric Nurse Associates and Practitioners for the 2000–2001 term.

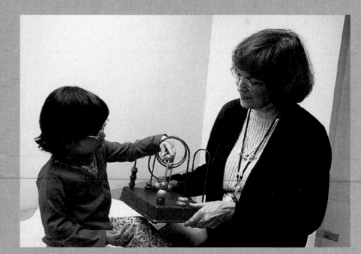

Barbara Deloin, conducting a pediatric evaluation.

The State of Illness and Health in the World's Children   Each year UNICEF produces a report entitled *The State of the World's Children*. In a recent report, UNICEF (2003) emphasized the importance of information about the under-5 mortality rate of a nation. UNICEF concluded that the under-5 mortality rate is the result of a wide range of factors, including the nutritional health and health knowledge of mothers, the level of immunization, dehydration, availability of maternal and child health services, income and food availability in the family, availability of clean water and safe sanitation, and the overall safety of the child's environment.

UNICEF reports annual data on the rank of nations under-5 mortality rate and recently described the percentage annual increase or decrease in these rates since 1960. Figure 9.11 shows these rates for a number of nations, including the United States (UNICEF, 2003). In 2001, there were 35 nations that had a lower under-5 mortality rate than the United States with Sweden having the lowest rate of all nations. The relatively high under-5 mortality rate of the United States compared with other developed nations is due to such factors as poverty and inadequate health care. The devastating effects on the health of young children occur in countries where poverty

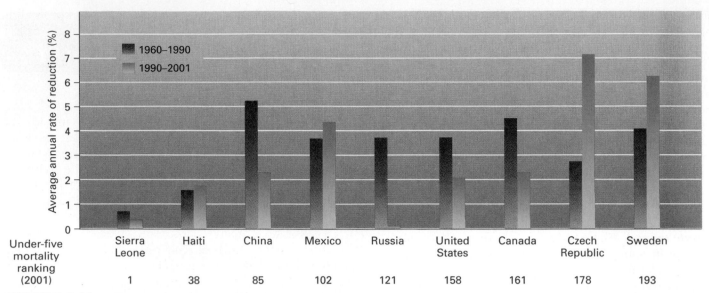

FIGURE 9.11 Under-Five Mortality Rankings and Average Annual Percent Reduction in Under-Five Mortality from 1960 to 2001 In 2001, Sierra Leone, an African nation, had the highest under-5 mortality ranking in the world and Sweden had the lowest (note that in the rankings, higher rankings refer to a lower mortality rate, lower rankings a higher rate). Notice the impressive improvement in the annual percentage reduction in the under-5 mortality rate for the Czech Republic since 1990. Also, even though Sweden had a very low under-5 mortality rate in 1990, note the substantial improvement in reducing death in infants and young children since 1990.

rates are high (UNICEF, 2004; Wagstaff & others, 2004). The poor are the majority in nearly one of every five nations in the world (UNICEF, 2003). They often experience lives of hunger, malnutrition, illness, inadequate access to health care, unsafe water, and a lack of protection from harm (Bahl & others, 2005; Bhutta & others, 2005; Neumann, Gewa, & Bwibo, 2004; Potera, 2004).

A leading cause of childhood death in impoverished countries is dehydration caused by diarrhea. In 1980, diarrhea was responsible for over 4.6 million childhood deaths. Oral rehydration therapy (ORT) was introduced in 1979 and quickly became the foundation for controlling diarrheal diseases. ORT now is given to the majority of children in impoverished countries suffering with diarrhea. Globally, the yearly number of deaths from diarrheal diseases for children under age 5 has fallen from its 1980 level to about 1.5 million in 1999 (Victora & others, 2000). Although increased immunization programs in the last several decades have led to a reduction in deaths from many diseases, measles, tetanus, and whooping cough still cause the deaths of many children around the world. In 1970, less than 10 percent of the world's children were immunized against diseases. In the beginning of the twenty-first century, approximately 75 percent of the world's children are now immunized against diseases such as tuberculosis, tetanus, and polio (Foege, 2000).

Acute respiratory infections, such as pneumonia, also have killed many children under the age of 5. Many of these children's lives could have been saved with antibiotics administered by a community health worker. Undernutrition also is a contributing factor to many deaths of children under the age of 5 in impoverished countries.

In the last decade, there has been a dramatic increase in the number of young children who have died because of HIV/AIDS transmitted to them by their parents (Atinmo & Oyewole, 2004; UNICEF, 2003). Deaths in young children due to HIV/AIDS especially occur in countries with high rates of poverty and low levels of education (Cohen, d'Adesky, & Anastos, 2005; Kalichman & others, 2005). For example, the uneducated are four times more likely to believe that there is no way to avoid AIDS and three times more likely to be unaware that the virus can be transmitted from mother to child (UNICEF, 2003).

Many of the deaths of young children around the world can be prevented by a reduction in poverty and improvements in nutrition, sanitation, education, and health services (Bhutta & others, 2005).

Many children in impoverished countries die before reaching the age of 5 from dehydration and malnutrition brought about by diarrhea. *What are some of the other main causes of death in young children around the world?*

Review and Reflect • LEARNING GOAL 3

3 **Characterize the health of young children.**

Review

- What is the nature of sleep and sleep problems in young children?
- What are young children's energy needs? What characterizes young children's eating behavior?
- How can the nature of children's injuries be summarized? How do contexts influence children's health? What is the state of illness and health in the world's children?

Reflect

- If you become a parent of a young child, what precautions will you take to improve your child's health?

REACH YOUR LEARNING GOALS

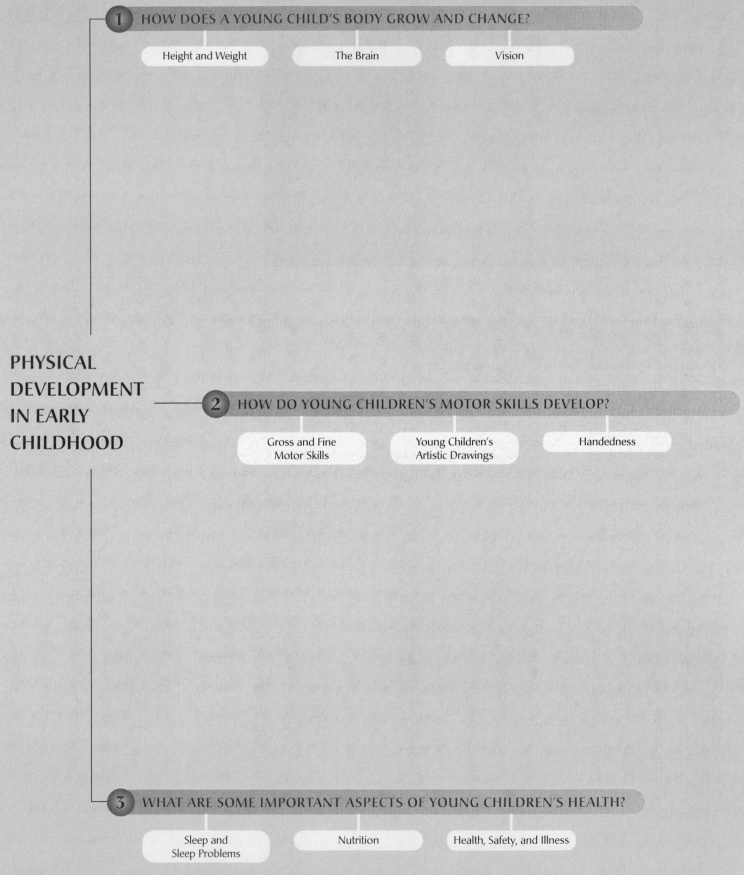

PHYSICAL
DEVELOPMENT
IN EARLY
CHILDHOOD

1 HOW DOES A YOUNG CHILD'S BODY GROW AND CHANGE?

Height and Weight   The Brain   Vision

2 HOW DO YOUNG CHILDREN'S MOTOR SKILLS DEVELOP?

Gross and Fine   Young Children's   Handedness
Motor Skills   Artistic Drawings

3 WHAT ARE SOME IMPORTANT ASPECTS OF YOUNG CHILDREN'S HEALTH?

Sleep and   Nutrition   Health, Safety, and Illness
Sleep Problems

SUMMARY

1 **Discuss body growth and change in early childhood.**

- The average child grows 2½ inches in height and gains between 5 and 7 pounds a year during early childhood. Growth patterns vary individually, though. Some children are unusually short because of congenital factors, a physical problem that develops in childhood, or an emotional difficulty.
- By age 5, the brain has reached nine-tenths of its adult size. Some of the increase is due to increases in the number and size of nerve endings and receptors. One neurotransmitter that increases in concentration from 3 to 6 years of age is dopamine. Recently, researchers have found that changes in local patterns in the brain occur from 3 to 15 years of age. From 3 to 6 years of age, the most rapid growth occurs in the frontal lobes. From age 6 through puberty, the most substantial growth takes place in the temporal and parietal lobes. Increasing brain maturation contributes to changes in cognitive abilities. One link involves the prefrontal cortex, dopamine, and improved attention and working memory.
- Visual maturity increases in early childhood. Some children develop vision problems such as functional amblyopia ("lazy eye") and strabismus, a misalignment of the eyes in which they do not point at the same object together.

2 **Describe changes in motor development in early childhood.**

- Gross motor skills increase dramatically in early childhood. Children become increasingly adventuresome as their gross motor skills improve. Rough-and-tumble play often occurs, especially in boys. It is important for early childhood educators to design and implement developmentally appropriate activities for young children's gross motor skills. Three types of these activities are fundamental movement, daily fitness, and perceptual-motor. Fine motor skills also improve substantially during early childhood. The Denver Developmental Screening Test is a simple, inexpensive method of diagnosing developmental delay and includes separate assessments of gross and fine motor skills.
- The development of fine motor skills allows young children to become budding artists. Scribbling begins at 2 years of age, followed by four stages of drawing, culminating in the pictorial stage at 4 to 5 years of age. Golomb believes that it is important to explore the sociocultural contexts of children's art and that such factors as talent, motivation, familial support, and cultural values influence the development of children's art.

- In today's world, the strategy is to let children use the hand they favor. Handedness likely has a strong genetic link. About 90 percent of children are right-handed and 10 percent left-handed. Left-handers are more likely to process speech in the right hemisphere of the brain than right-handers, and left-handers tend to have more reading problems. Left-handers often show up in higher than expected numbers as mathematicians, musicians, architects, and artists. Left-handers tend to have unusually good visuospatial skills.

3 **Characterize the health of young children.**

- Most young children sleep through the night and have one daytime nap. Helping the young child slow down before bedtime often leads to less resistance in going to bed. Many young children take transitional objects to bed with them; these objects represent a bridge between dependence and independence. Among the sleep problems that can develop in young children are nightmares, night terrors, and somnambulism (sleep walking), and sleep talking.
- Energy needs increase as children go through the early childhood years. Energy requirements vary according to basal metabolism rate, rate of growth, and level of activity. National assessments indicate that a large majority of young children in the United States do not have a healthy diet and that over the last two decades their eating habits have worsened. Too many parents are rearing young children on diets that are high in fat and sugar. Children's diets should contain well-balanced proportions of fats, carbohydrates, protein, vitamins, and minerals. Parents should keep children's eating completely separate from discipline. A special concern is the poor nutrition of young children from impoverished families.
- Injuries are the leading cause of death in children. Motor vehicle accidents are the injuries that cause the most deaths in children followed by drowning. Firearm deaths are especially high in children in the United States in comparison to other countries. Among the strategies for preventing childhood injuries are restraining children in automobiles, reducing access to firearms, and making the home and playground safer. Among the contexts involved in children's health are poverty, ethnicity, home and child care, environmental tobacco smoke, and exposure to lead. The most devastating effects on the health of young children occur in countries with high poverty rates. Among the problems that low-income families face in these countries around the world are hunger, malnutrition, illness, inadequate access to health care, unsafe water, and a lack of protection from harm. In recent decades, the trend in children's illness and health is

Chapter 10

COGNITIVE DEVELOPMENT IN EARLY CHILDHOOD

The mind is an enchanting thing.

—Marianne Moore
American Poet, 20th Century

CHAPTER OUTLINE

LEARNING GOALS

WHAT COGNITIVE CHANGES OCCUR IN EARLY CHILDHOOD?

1 Discuss the cognitive changes that occur in early childhood.

Piaget's Preoperational Stage

Vygotsky's Theory of Development

Evaluating and Comparing Piaget's and Vygotsky's Theories

Information Processing

The Young Child's Theory of Mind

HOW DO YOUNG CHILDREN DEVELOP LANGUAGE?

2 Describe language development in early childhood.

Understanding Phonology and Morphology

Understanding Syntax

Advances in Semantics

Advances in Pragmatics

WHAT ARE SOME IMPORTANT FEATURES OF EARLY CHILDHOOD EDUCATION?

3 Characterize early childhood education.

The Child-Centered Kindergarten

Developmentally Appropriate Practice

Literacy and Early Childhood Education

Early Childhood Education for Children from Low-Income Families

Issues in Early Childhood Education

CARING FOR CHILDREN: Parents and Schools as Partners in the Young Child's Education

Images of Children
The Story of Reggio Emilia's Children

The Reggio Emilia approach is an educational program for young children that was developed in the northern Italian city of Reggio Emilia. Children of single parents and children with disabilities have priority in admission; other children are admitted according to a scale of needs. Parents pay on a sliding scale based on income.

The children are encouraged to learn by investigating and exploring topics that interest them. A wide range of stimulating media and materials is available for children to use as they learn music, movement, drawing, painting, and sculpting, and work with collages, puppets and disguises, and photography, for example.

In this program, children often explore topics in a group, which fosters a sense of community, respect for diversity, and a collaborative approach to problem solving. Two co-teachers are present to serve as guides for children (Edwards, 2002). The Reggio Emilia teachers consider a project as an adventure, which can start from an adult's suggestion, from a child's idea, or from an event, such as a snowfall or something else unexpected. Every project is based on what the children say and do. The teachers allow children enough time to think and craft a project.

At the core of the Reggio Emilia approach is the image of children who are competent and have rights, especially the right to outstanding care and education. Parent participation is considered essential, and cooperation is a major theme in the schools. Many early childhood education experts believe the Reggio Emilia approach provides a supportive, stimulating context in which children are motivated to explore their world in a competent and confident manner (Saab, 2004; Stegelin, 2003).

A Reggio Emilia classroom in which young children explore topics that interest them.

PREVIEW

Children make a number of significant cognitive advances in early childhood. In the opening section, we will explore the cognitive changes described by the major cognitive theories. Then we will examine the dramatic changes in young children's language, and conclude by discussing a wide range of topics on early childhood education.

1 WHAT COGNITIVE CHANGES OCCUR IN EARLY CHILDHOOD?

Piaget's Preoperational Stage

Evaluating and Comparing Piaget's and Vygotsky's Theories

The Young Child's Theory of Mind

Vygotsky's Theory of Development

Information Processing

How do young children's minds change as they grow through early childhood? Piaget had some thoughts about these changes, as did Lev Vygotsky. First, we will explore Piaget's ideas about the preoperational stage. Next, we will examine Vygotsky's theory of development. Then we will discuss how young children process information, and the young child's theory of mind (awareness of mental processes).

Piaget's Preoperational Stage

Remember from chapter 7 that during Piaget's sensorimotor stage of development, the infant progresses in the ability to organize and coordinate sensations and perceptions with physical movements and actions. The next stage of development, according to Piaget, is the preoperational stage, a time when stable concepts are formed, mental reasoning emerges, egocentrism begins strongly and then weakens, and magical beliefs are constructed. Preoperational thought is anything but a convenient waiting period for concrete operational thought. However, the label *preoperational* emphasizes that the child at this stage does not yet think in an operational way.

Exploring What "Preoperational" Means

What are operations? **Operations** are internalized sets of actions that allow children to do mentally what before they did physically. Operations are highly organized and conform to certain rules and principles of logic.

An operation is much like a sensorimotor scheme (which we discussed in chapter 7) in that it involves some type of action—operating on the world to understand it. However, a major difference between a sensorimotor scheme and a concrete operation is that the concrete operation involves an *internal* action, whereas the sensorimotor scheme always consists of an *overt* action, such as reaching or grasping.

An example of a lack of operational thought in young children involves thinking simultaneously about part of a whole and the whole. If 5-year-olds are presented with six green candies and three red candies and asked, "Are there more green candies or more candies?" they are likely to say, "More green candies?" Piaget believed this reply indicated that young children cannot engage in the mental operation of reasoning about parts and wholes at the same time.

Thought in the preoperational stage is flawed and not well organized. Preoperational thought is the beginning of the ability to reconstruct at the level of thought what has been established in behavior. Preoperational thought also involves a transition from primitive to more sophisticated use of symbols. Preoperational thought can be divided into two substages: the symbolic function substage and the intuitive thought substage.

Symbolic Function Substage

The **symbolic function substage** is the first substage of preoperational thought, occurring roughly between the ages of 2 and 4. In this substage, the young child gains the ability to mentally represent an object that is not present. This vastly expands the child's mental world. Young children use scribbled designs to represent people, houses, cars, clouds, and so on. Other examples of symbolism in early childhood are language and the prevalence of pretend play (DeLoache, 2001).

Possibly because young children are not very concerned about reality, their drawings are fanciful and inventive. Suns are blue, skies are yellow, and cars float on clouds in their symbolic, imaginative world. One 3½-year-old looked at a scribble he had just drawn and described it as a pelican kissing a seal (see figure 10.1a). In the elementary school years, a child's drawings become more realistic, neat, and precise (see figure 10.1b). Suns are yellow, skies are blue, and cars travel on roads (Winner, 1986).

Although young children make distinct progress during this substage, their thought still has several important limitations. Two of these limitations are egocentrism and animism.

Egocentrism, the inability to distinguish between one's own perspective and someone else's perspective, characterizes preoperational thought. This telephone conversation between 4-year-old Mary, who is at home, and her father, who is at work, typifies Mary's egocentric thought:

> **Father:** Mary, is Mommy there?
> **Mary:** (Silently nods)
> **Father:** Mary, may I speak to Mommy?
> **Mary:** (Nods again silently)

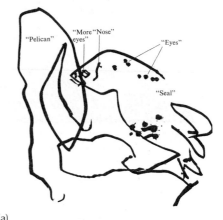

(a)

(b)

FIGURE 10.1 **The Symbolic Drawings of Young Children** (*a*) A 3½-year-old's symbolic drawing. Halfway into his drawing, the 3½-year-old artist said it was a "pelican kissing a seal." (*b*) This 11-year-old's drawing is neater and more realistic but also less inventive.

operations In Piaget's theory, an internalized set of actions that allows children to do mentally what they formerly did physically.

symbolic function substage Piaget's first substage of preoperational thought, in which the child gains the ability to mentally represent an object that is not present (between 2 and 4 years of age).

egocentrism The inability to distinguish between one's own perspective and someone else's (salient feature of the first substage of preoperational thought).

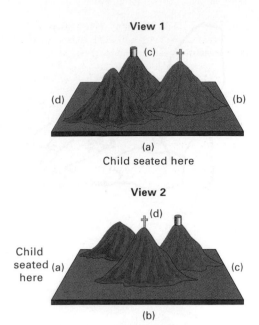

View 1

(c)

(d)   (b)

(a)
Child seated here

View 2

(d)

Child
seated (a)   (c)
here

(b)

FIGURE 10.2 **The Three Mountains Task**
View 1 shows the child's perspective from where
he or she is sitting. View 2 is an example of the
photograph the child would be shown, mixed in
with others from different perspectives. To correctly identify this view, the child has to take the
perspective of the person sitting at spot (b). Invari-
ably, a preschool child who thinks in a preoperational way cannot perform this task. When asked
what a view of the mountains looks like from position (b), the child selects a photograph taken from
location (a), the child's view at the time.

animism The belief that inanimate objects
have "lifelike" qualities and are capable of
action.

intuitive thought substage Piaget's second
substage of preoperational thought, in which
children begin to use primitive reasoning and
want to know the answers to all sorts of questions (between 4 and 7 years of age).

centration The focusing of attention on one
characteristic to the exclusion of all others.

conservation The concept that certain
physical characteristics of an object stay the
same even though their appearance has been
altered.

Mary's response is egocentric in that she fails to consider her father's perspective before replying. A nonegocentric thinker would have responded verbally.

Jean Piaget and Barbel Inhelder (1969) initially studied young children's egocentrism by devising the three mountains task (see figure 10.2). The child walks around
the model of the mountains and becomes familiar with what the mountains look like
from different perspectives, and they can see that there are different objects on the
mountains. The child is then seated on one side of the table on which the mountains
are placed. The experimenter moves a doll to different locations around the table, at
each location asking the child to select, from a series of photos, the one photo that
most accurately reflects the view the doll is seeing. Children in the preoperational
stage often pick their view from where they are sitting, rather than the doll's view.
Perspective-taking does not develop uniformly in preschool children, who frequently
show perspective skills on some tasks but not others.

Animism, the belief that inanimate objects have "lifelike" qualities and are capable of action, is another limitation of preoperational thought. A young child might
show animism by saying, "That tree pushed the leaf off, and it fell down," or "The
sidewalk made me mad; it made me fall down." A young child who uses animism fails
to distinguish the appropriate occasions for using human and nonhuman perspectives
(Gelman & Opfer, 2002).

Intuitive Thought Substage
Tommy is 4 years old. Although he is starting
to develop his own ideas about the world he lives in, his ideas are still simple, and he
is not very good at thinking things out. He has difficulty understanding events he
knows are taking place but which he cannot see. His fantasized thoughts bear little resemblance to reality. He cannot yet answer the question "What if . . .?" in any reliable
way. For example, he has only a vague idea of what would happen if a car were to hit
him. He also has difficulty negotiating traffic because he cannot do the mental calcu-
lations necessary to estimate whether an approaching car will hit him when he crosses
the road.

The **intuitive thought substage,** in which children begin to use primitive reasoning and want to know the answers to all sorts of questions, is the second substage
of preoperational thought, occurring approximately from 4 to 7 years of age. Piaget
called this time period *intuitive* because, on the one hand, young children seem so sure
about their knowledge and understanding, yet they are so unaware of how they know
what they know. That is, they say they know something but know it without the use
of rational thinking.

An important characteristic of preoperational thought is **centration**—the focusing, or centering, of attention on one characteristic to the exclusion of all others.
Centration is most clearly evidenced in young children's lack of **conservation**—
awareness that altering an object's or a substance's appearance does not change
its quantitative properties. To adults, it is obvious that a certain amount of liquid stays
the same, regardless of a container's shape but this is not at all obvious to young
children. Instead, they are struck by the height of the liquid in the container. In the
conservation task—Piaget's most famous test—a child is presented with two identical
beakers, each filled to the same level with liquid (see figure 10.3). The child is asked
if these beakers have the same amount of liquid, and she usually says yes. Then
the liquid from one beaker is poured into a third beaker, which is taller and thinner
than the first two. The child is then asked if the amount of liquid in the tall, thin
beaker is equal to that which remains in one of the original beakers. Children who are
less than 7 or 8 years old usually say no and justify their answers in terms of the differing height or width of the beakers. Older children usually answer yes and justify
their answers appropriately ("If you poured the milk back, the amount would still be
the same").

In Piaget's theory, failing the conservation of liquid task is a sign that children are
at the preoperational stage of cognitive development. Passing this test is a sign that
they are at the concrete operational stage. In Piaget's view, the preoperational child

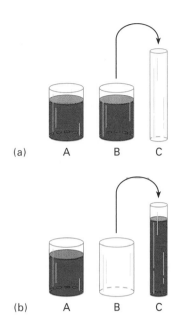

FIGURE 10.3 Piaget's Conservation Task
The beaker test is a well-known Piagetian test to determine whether a child can think operationally— that is, can mentally reverse actions and show conservation of the substance. (*a*) Two identical beakers are presented to the child. Then, the experimenter pours the liquid from B into C, which is taller and thinner than A or B. (*b*) The child is asked if these beakers (A and C) have the same amount of liquid. The preoperational child says no. When asked to point to the beaker that has more liquid, the preoperational child points to the tall, thin beaker.

fails to show conservation not only of liquid but also of number, matter, and length (see figure 10.4).

The child's inability to mentally reverse actions is an important characteristic of preoperational thought. For example, in the conservation of matter shown in figure 10.4, preoperational children say that the longer shape has more clay because they assume that "longer is more." Preoperational children cannot mentally reverse the clay-rolling process to see that the amount of clay is the same in both the shorter ball shape and the longer stick shape.

Some developmentalists do not believe Piaget was entirely correct in his estimate of when children's conservation skills emerge (Gelman & Williams, 1998). For example, Rochel Gelman (1969) showed that, when the child's attention to relevant aspects of the conservation task is improved, the child is more likely to conserve. Gelman has also demonstrated that attentional training on one dimension, such as number, improves the preschool child's performance on another dimension, such as mass. Thus, Gelman argues that conservation appears earlier than Piaget thought and that attention is especially important in explaining conservation.

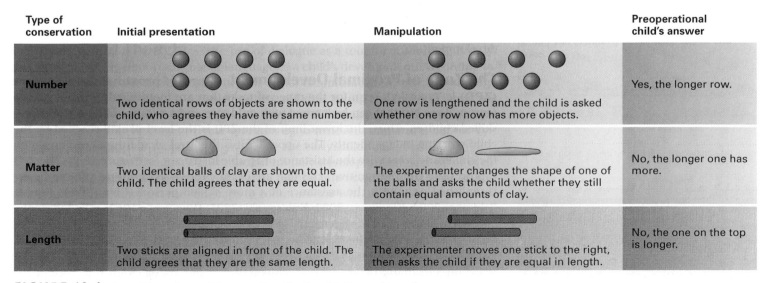

Type of conservation	Initial presentation	Manipulation	Preoperational child's answer
Number	Two identical rows of objects are shown to the child, who agrees they have the same number.	One row is lengthened and the child is asked whether one row now has more objects.	Yes, the longer row.
Matter	Two identical balls of clay are shown to the child. The child agrees that they are equal.	The experimenter changes the shape of one of the balls and asks the child whether they still contain equal amounts of clay.	No, the longer one has more.
Length	Two sticks are aligned in front of the child. The child agrees that they are the same length.	The experimenter moves one stick to the right, then asks the child if they are equal in length.	No, the one on the top is longer.

FIGURE 10.4 Some Dimensions of Conservation: Number, Matter, and Length

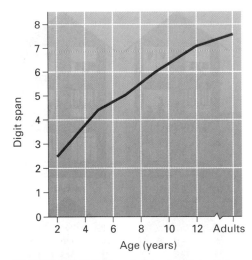

FIGURE 10.8 Developmental Changes in Memory Span In one study, memory span increased about 3 digits from 2 years of age to 5 digits at 7 years of age (Dempster, 1981). By 12 years of age, memory span had increased on average another 1½ digits to 7 digits.

Four-year-old Jennifer Royal was the only eyewitness to one of her playmates being shot to death. She was allowed to testify in open court and the clarity of her statements helped to convict the gunman. *What are some issues involved in whether young children should be allowed to testify in court?*

www.mhhe.com/santrockc9

Children's Eyewitness Testimony

Why are there differences in memory span at different ages? Rehearsal of information is important; older children rehearse the digits more than younger children. Speed and efficiency of processing information are important, too, especially the speed with which memory items can be identified. For example, in one study, children were tested on their speed at repeating words presented orally (Case, Kurland, & Goldberg, 1982). Speed of repetition was a powerful predictor of memory span. Indeed, when the speed of repetition was controlled, the 6-year-olds' memory spans were equal to those of young adults.

The speed-of-processing explanation highlights an important point in the information-processing perspective. That is, the speed with which a child processes information is an important part of the child's cognitive abilities. In one recent study, faster processing speed on a memory-span task was linked with reading and math achievement (Hitch, Towse, & Hutton, 2001).

How Accurate Are Children's Long-Term Memories? *Long-term memory,* as we will discuss in chapter 13, is a relatively permanent type of memory that holds huge amounts of information for a long period of time. In chapter 7, we saw that most of infants' memories are fragile and short-lived, except for their memory of perceptual-motor actions, which can be substantial (Mandler, 2000). Does their long-term memory become more accurate in the early childhood years? Yes, it does. Young children can remember a great deal of information if they are given appropriate cues and prompts (Howe, 1997). Sometimes the memories of preschoolers seem to be erratic but these memory inconsistencies may be due to the inadequacy of prompts and cues.

A current controversy focuses on whether young children should be allowed to testify in court. Increasingly, young children are being allowed to testify, especially if they are the only witnesses to abuse, a crime, and so forth. One recent study found that young children were less likely than older children to reject the occurrence of false events (Ghetti & Alexander, 2004). However, as we see next, a number of factors can affect the accuracy of a young child's memory.

These conclusions have been reached about children as eyewitnesses (Bruck & Ceci, 1999):

- *Age differences in children's susceptibility to suggestion.* Preschoolers are more suggestible than older children and adults (Koriat, Goldsmith, & Pansky, 2000). Young children can be led, under certain circumstances, to incorporate false suggestions into their accounts of even intimate body touching by adults (Hyman & Loftus, 2001). Despite their greater resistance to suggestibility, there is concern, too, about the effects of suggestive interviews on older children.
- *Individual differences in susceptibility.* Some preschoolers are highly resistant to interviewers' suggestions, whereas others immediately succumb to the slightest suggestion (Crossman, Scullin, & Melnyk, 2004; Gilstrap & Ceci, 2005). One recent study found that children with more advanced verbal abilities and self-control were more likely to resist interviewers' suggestive questions (Clarke-Stewart, Malloy, & Allhusen, 2004). A recent research review found that the following noncognitive factors were linked to being at risk for suggestibility: low self-concept, low support from parents, and mothers' insecure attachment in romantic relationships (Bruck & Melnyk, 2004).
- *Young children's accuracy as eyewitnesses.* Despite the evidence that many young children's responses can be influenced by suggestive interviews, they are capable of recalling much that is relevant about an event (Howe, 1997). Children are more likely to accurately recall an event when the interviewer has a neutral tone, does not use misleading questions, and they are not motivated to make a false report (Bruck & Ceci, 1999).

In sum, whether or not a young child's eyewitness testimony is accurate may depend on a number of factors such as the type, number, and intensity of the suggestive techniques the child has experienced (Bruck & Ceci, 2004; Pipe & others, 2004). The reliability of young children's reports may have as much or more to do with the skills and motivation of the interviewer as with any natural limitations on young children's memory. Because of the possibility that they can be led into saying something falsely, young children should be interviewed by a neutral professional (Hyman & Loftus, 2001).

Scripts   *Scripts* are cognitive frameworks or schemas for events—that is, memory for what occurs in a particular situation. For example, a child knows the events that take place on a picnic, such as mom packs lunch, we drive to the park, and then eat lunch on the grass. Scripts include the expected order in which things occur and how people behave in that event or situation. Children might have different scripts for what they do on a weekday, on Saturday, or on Sunday. They might have a script for what takes place when they go to kindergarten, a restaurant, or a birthday party (Farrar & Goodman, 1992; Fivush, Kuebli, & Clubb, 1992).

When do children first develop scripts? Researchers have found that even 1- and 2-year-olds have simple scripts for a sequence of two things that happen in a situation (such as "Put teddy bear in tub") (Bauer & Dow, 1994; Bauer & others, 2000). Although children this young cannot verbally report their memories, they can act out what they remember with toys. In early childhood, children's scripts become more elaborate. For example, a 3-year-old's script for a birthday party might be something like "You eat cake, open presents and play, and come home." The more extensive birthday party script of a 5-year-old might be: "Your mom buys balloons, bakes a cake, and puts candles on it. You get dressed up. Your friends come and bring presents. You play games, eat cake, and open presents. Then kids go home." Scripts can help children to remember. In one study, kindergarten children visited a museum. When questioned six weeks and one year later, they not only remembered a general museum script but also details of their personal script at the museum (Fivush, Hudson, & Nelson, 1984).

Strategies   In chapter 2, we mentioned that strategies are an integral part of information-processing theory. What are strategies? They consist of using deliberate mental activities to improve the processing of information (Siegler, 2004; Siegler & Alibali, 2005). For example, rehearsing information and organizing it are two typical strategies that older children and adults use to remember more effectively. Do young children use rehearsal and organization to remember? For the most part, they do not (Miller & Seier, 1994).

Do young children use any strategies at all? Problem-solving strategies in young children were the focus of research by Zhe Chen and Robert Siegler (2000). They placed young children at a table where an attractive toy was placed too far away for the children to reach (they were not allowed to crawl on the table). On the table, between the child and the toy, were six potential tools (see figure 10.9). Only one of them was likely to be useful in obtaining the toy. After initially assessing the young children's attempts to obtain the toy on their own, the experimenters either modeled how to obtain the toy (using the appropriate tool) or gave the child a hint (telling the child to use the particular tool). These 2-year-olds learned the strategy and subsequently mapped the strategy onto new problems. Admittedly, this is a rather simple problem-solving strategy—selecting the best tool to use to obtain a desired toy—but it does document that children as young as 2 years of age can learn a strategy.

During early childhood, the relatively stimulus-driven toddler is transformed into a child capable of flexible, goal-directed problem solving (Zelazo & Muller, 2004; Zelazo & others, 2003). For example, 3- to 4-year-olds are somewhat cognitively inflexible because of lack of understanding of the concept of perspectives and, thus, cannot understand that a single stimulus can be redescribed in a different, incompatible way from two different perspectives (Perner & others, 2002). Consider a problem in which children must sort stimuli using the rule of *color*. In the course of the color sorting, a child may describe a red rabbit as a *red one* to solve the problem. However, in a subsequent task, the child may need to discover a rule that describes the rabbit as just a *rabbit* to solve the problem. If 3- to 4-year-olds fail to understand that it is possible to provide multiple descriptions of the same stimulus, they persist in describing the stimulus a red rabbit. Researchers have found that at about 4-years-of-age, children acquire the

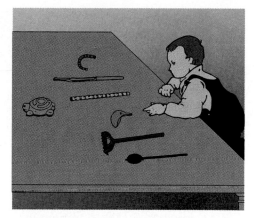

FIGURE 10.9   **The Toy-Retrieval Task in the Study of Young Children's Problem-Solving Strategies** The child needed to choose the target tool (in this illustration, the toy rake) to pull in the toy (in this case, the turtle).

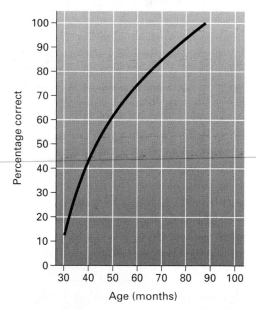

FIGURE 10.10   **Developmental Changes in False-Belief Performance** False-belief performance dramatically increases from 2½ years of age through the middle of the elementary school years. In a summary of the results of many studies, 2½-year-olds gave incorrect responses about 80 percent of the time (Wellman, Cross, & Watson, 2001). At 3 years, 8 months, they were correct about 50 percent of the time, and after that, gave increasingly correct responses.

CAREERS in CHILD DEVELOPMENT

Helen Schwe
Developmental Psychologist and Toy Designer

Helen Schwe obtained a Ph.D. from Stanford University in developmental psychology but she now spends her days talking with computer engineers and designing "smart" toys for children. Smart toys are designed to improve children's problem-solving and symbolic thinking skills.

When she was a graduate student, Schwe worked part-time for Hasbro toys, testing its children's software on preschoolers. Her first job after graduate school was with Zowie entertainment, which was subsequently bought by LEGO. According to Helen, "Even in a toy's most primitive stage of development, . . . you see children's creativity in responding to challenges, their satisfaction when a problem is solved or simply their delight when they are having fun" (p. 50). In addition to conducting experiments and focus groups at different stages of a toy's development, Schwe also assesses the age-appropriateness of a toy. Most of her current work focuses on 3-to-5 year old children. (Source: Schlegel, 2000, pp. 50–51).

Helen Schwe, a developmental psychologist, with some of the "smart" toys she designed.

concept of perspectives, which allows them to appreciate that a single description can be described in two different ways (Frye, 1999).

The Young Child's Theory of Mind

How aware are young children of the mental processes they and others use? This is called **theory of mind.** Even young children are curious about the nature of the human mind, and developmentalists have shown a flurry of interest in children's thoughts about what the human mind is like (Flavell, 1999; Wellman, 1997, 2000, 2004). Children's theory of mind changes as they go through the childhood years (Flavell, Miller, & Miller, 2002):

- *2 to 3 Years of Age.* Children begin to understand three mental states:

  Perceptions. Children realize that another person sees what is in front of their eyes and not necessarily what is in front of the children's eyes.

  Desires. Children understand that if someone wants something, he or she will try to get it. A child might say, "I want my mommy."

  Emotions. Children can distinguish between positive (for example, "happy") and negative (for example, "sad") emotions. A child might say, "Tommy feels bad." Despite these advances, at 2 to 3 years of age, children have only a minimal understanding of how mental life can be linked to behavior. They think that people are at the mercy of their desires and don't understand how beliefs influence behavior.

- *4 to 5 Years of Age.* Children begin to understand that the mind can represent objects and events accurately or inaccurately. The realization that people have *false beliefs*—beliefs that are not true—develops in a majority of children by the time they are 5 years old (Wellman, Cross, & Watson, 2001) (see figure 10.10). One study of false beliefs involved showing young children a Band-Aids box and asking them what was inside (Jenkins & Astington, 1996). To the children's surprise, the box actually contained pencils. When asked what a child who had never seen the box would think was inside, 3-year-olds typically responded "pencils." However, the 4- and 5-year-olds, grinning at the anticipation of other children's false-belief beliefs who had not seen what was inside the box, were more likely to say "Band-Aids."

- *6 Years of Age and Older.* Beyond the preschool years children have a deepening appreciation of the mind itself rather than just an understanding of mental states (Wellman, 2004). Not until middle and late childhood do children see the mind as an active constructor of knowledge or processing center (Flavell, 2004; Flavell, Green, & Flavell, 1995). In middle and late childhood, children move from understanding that beliefs can be false to an understanding of beliefs and mind as "interpretive," exemplified in an awareness that the same event can be open to multiple interpretations (Carpendale & Chandler, 1996).

theory of mind A concept that refers to awareness of one's own mental processes and the mental processes of others.

Some developmental psychologists use their training in areas such as cognitive development to pursue careers in applied areas. To read about the work of Helen Schwe, an individual who followed this path, see the Careers in Child Development profile.

Review and Reflect • LEARNING GOAL 1

1 Discuss the cognitive changes that occur in early childhood.

Review
- How can Piaget's preoperational stage be characterized?
- How can Vygotsky's theory of development be summarized?
- What are the similarities and differences in the theories of Piaget and Vygotsky?
- What changes take place in information processing during early childhood?
- What is meant by the concept of theory of mind? How does a child's theory of mind change developmentally?

Reflect
- Imagine that you have taken a job as a teacher in an early childhood education program. Do you think Piaget's theory or Vygotsky's theory would be more helpful to you in your new teaching job? Explain.

2 HOW DO YOUNG CHILDREN DEVELOP LANGUAGE?

Understanding Phonology and Morphology

Advances in Semantics

Understanding Syntax

Advances in Pragmatics

As children leave the two-word stage, they move rather quickly into three-, four-, and five-word combinations. The transition from simple sentences expressing a single proposition to complex sentences begins between 2 and 3 years of age and continues into the elementary school years (Bloom, 1998).

Young children's understanding sometimes gets way ahead of their speech. One 3-year-old, laughing with delight as an abrupt summer breeze stirred his hair and tickled his skin, commented, "I got breezed!" Many of the oddities of young children's language sound like mistakes to adult listeners. However, from the children's point of view, they are not mistakes. They represent the way young children perceive and understand their world at that point in their development. As children go through their early childhood years, their grasp of the rule systems that govern language increases.

Understanding Phonology and Morphology

During the preschool years, most children gradually become sensitive to the sounds of spoken words (National Research Council, 1999). They notice rhymes, enjoy poems, make up silly names for things by substituting one sound for another (such as *bubblegum, bubblebum, bubbleyum*), and clap along with each syllable in a phrase.

As they move beyond two-word utterances, there is clear evidence that children know morphological rules. Children begin using the plural and possessive forms of nouns (*dogs* and *dog's*); putting appropriate endings on verbs (*-s* when the subject is third-person singular, *-ed* for the past tense, and *-ing* for the present progressive tense); and using prepositions (*in* and *on*), articles (*a* and *the*), and various forms of the verb *to be* ("I was *going* to the store"). In fact, they *overgeneralize* these rules, applying them to words that do not follow the rules. For example, a preschool child might say "foots" instead of "feet" or "goed" instead of "went."

This is a wug.

Now there is another one.
There are two of them.
There are two _____.

FIGURE 10.11 **Stimuli in Berko's Study of Young Children's Understanding of Morphological Rules** In Jean Berko's (1958) study, young children were presented cards, such as this one with a "wug" on it. Then the children were asked to supply the missing word; in supplying the missing word, they had to say it correctly too. "Wugs" is the correct response here.

Children's understanding of morphological rules was the subject of a classic experiment by children's language researcher Jean Berko (1958). Berko presented preschool and first-grade children with cards such as the one shown in figure 10.11. Children were asked to look at the card while the experimenter read the words on it aloud. Then the children were asked to supply the missing word. This might sound easy, but Berko was interested not just in the children's ability to recall the right word but also in their ability to say it "correctly" with the ending that was dictated by morphological rules. *Wugs* is the correct response for the card in figure 10.11. Although the children were not perfectly accurate, they were much better than chance would dictate. Moreover, they demonstrated their knowledge of morphological rules not only with the plural forms of nouns ("There are two wugs") but also with the possessive forms of nouns and with the third-person singular and past-tense forms of verbs.

Berko's study demonstrated not only that the children relied on rules, but also that they had *abstracted* the rules from what they had heard and could apply them to novel situations. What makes Berko's study impressive is that all of the words were *fictional;* they were created especially for the experiment. Thus, the children could not base their responses on remembering past instances of hearing the words. Instead, they were forced to rely on *rules*. Their performance suggested that they did so successfully.

Understanding Syntax

Preschool children also learn and apply rules of syntax (Budwig, 1993). After advancing beyond two-word utterances, the child shows a growing mastery of complex rules for how words should be ordered. Consider the case of *wh-* questions, such as "Where is Daddy going?" or "What is that boy doing?" To ask these questions properly, the child must know two important differences between *wh-* questions and affirmative

How do children's language abilities develop during early childhood?

statements (for instance, "Daddy is going to work" and "That boy is waiting on the school bus"). First, a *wh-* word must be added at the beginning of the sentence. Second, the auxiliary verb must be inverted—that is, exchanged with the subject of the sentence. Young children learn quite early where to put the *wh-* word, but they take much longer to learn the auxiliary-inversion rule. Thus, it is common to hear preschool children asking such questions as "Where Daddy is going?" and "What that boy is doing?"

As children move into the elementary school years, they become skilled at using syntactical rules to construct lengthy and complex sentences. Utterances such as "The man who fixed the house went home" and "I don't want you to use my bike" are impressive demonstrations of how the child can use syntax to combine ideas into a single sentence. Just how young children master such complex rules while at the same time they may be struggling with relatively simple arithmetic rules is a mystery.

Advances in Semantics

As children move beyond the two-word stage, their knowledge of meanings also rapidly advances (Bloom, 2002). The speaking vocabulary of a 6-year-old child ranges from 8,000 to 14,000 words (Carey, 1977; Clark, 2000). Assuming that word learning began when the child was 12 months old, this translates into a rate of learning five to eight new word meanings a day between the ages of 1 and 6. The 6-year-old child does not slow down. According to some estimates, the average 6-year-old is moving along at the awe-inspiring rate of learning 22 words a day (Miller, 1981). How would you fare if you were given the task of learning 22 new words every day?

Advances in Pragmatics

Changes in pragmatics also characterize young children's language development. A 6-year-old is simply a much better conversationalist than a 2-year-old is. What are some of the improvements in pragmatics that are made in the preschool years?

At about 3 years of age, children improve their ability to talk about things that are not physically present—that is, they improve their command of an aspect of language known as *displacement*. Displacement is revealed in games of pretend. Although a 2-year-old might know the word *table,* he is unlikely to use this word to refer to an imaginary table that he pretends is standing in front of him. A child over 3 years of age is more likely to do so. There are large individual differences in preschoolers' talk about imaginary people and things.

At about 4 years of age, children develop a remarkable sensitivity to the needs of others in conversation. One way in which they show such sensitivity is their use of the articles *the* and *an* (or *a*). When adults tell a story or describe an event, they generally use *an* (or *a*) when they first refer to an animal or an object, and then use *the* when referring to it later. (For example, "Two boys were walking through the jungle when *a* fierce lion appeared. *The* lion lunged at one boy while the other ran for cover.") Even 3-year-olds follow part of this rule; they consistently use the word *the* when referring to previously mentioned things. However, the use of the word *a* when something is initially mentioned develops more slowly. Although 5-year-old children follow this rule on some occasions, they fail to follow it on others.

Around 4 to 5 years of age children learn to change their speech style to suit the situation. For example, even 4-year-old children speak differently to a 2-year-old than to a same-aged peer; they use shorter sentences with the 2-year-old. They also speak differently to an adult than to a same-aged peer, using more polite and formal language with the adult (Shatz & Gelman, 1973).

www.mhhe.com/santrockc9

Pragmatic Language

3   WHAT ARE SOME IMPORTANT FEATURES OF EARLY CHILDHOOD EDUCATION?

The Child-Centered Kindergarten	Literacy and Early Childhood Education	Issues in Early Childhood Education

Developmentally Appropriate Practice	Early Childhood Education for Children from Low-Income Families

There are many variations in the way young children are educated (Henninger, 2005; Hyson, Copple, & Jones, 2006; Morrison, 2006). In the story that opened this chapter, you read about the Reggio Emilia program in northern Italy, a promising strategy that is receiving increased attention. Another program that originated in Italy is patterned after the educational philosophy of Maria Montessori, an Italian physician-turned-educator, who crafted a revolutionary approach to young children's education at the beginning of the twentieth century (Edwards, 2002). Her work began in Rome with a group of children who were mentally retarded. She was successful in teaching them to read, write, and pass examinations designed for normal children. Some time later, she turned her attention to poor children from the slums of Rome and had similar success in teaching them. Her approach has since been adopted extensively in private nursery schools in the United States.

The **Montessori approach** is a philosophy of education in which children are given considerable freedom and spontaneity in choosing activities. They are allowed to move from one activity to another as they desire. The teacher acts as a facilitator rather than a director of learning. The teacher shows the child how to perform intellectual activities, demonstrates interesting ways to explore curriculum materials, and offers help when the child requests it.

Some developmentalists favor the Montessori approach, but others believe that it neglects children's social development (Chattin-McNichols, 1992). For example, while Montessori fosters independence and the development of cognitive skills, it deemphasizes verbal interaction between the teacher and child and peer interaction. Montessori's critics also argue that it restricts imaginative play.

The Child-Centered Kindergarten

Montessori approach   An educational philosophy in which children are given considerable freedom and spontaneity in choosing activities and are allowed to move from one activity to another as they desire.

In the 1840s, Friedrich Froebel's concern for quality education for young children led to the founding of the kindergarten—literally, "a garden for children." Froebel understood that, like growing plants, children require careful nurturing.

Closely aligned with many of Froebel's ideals, the **child-centered kindergarten** involves the whole child and includes concern for the child's physical, cognitive, and socioemotional development (Hendrick & Weissman, 2006). Instruction is organized around the child's needs, interests, and learning styles. The process of learning, rather than what is learned, is emphasized (Feeney, Christensen, & Moravcik, 2006; White & Coleman, 2000).

Play is extremely important in the child's total development (Youngquist & Pataray-Ching, 2004). *Experimenting, exploring, discovering, trying out, restructuring, speaking,* and *listening* are all words that describe excellent kindergarten programs. Such programs are closely attuned to the developmental status of 4- and 5-year-old children. They are based on a state of being, not on a state of becoming.

Today's kindergarten programs vary a great deal (Hyson, Copple, & Jones, 2006; Wardle, 2003). Some approaches place more emphasis on young children's social development, while others, such as the Montessori approach, emphasize their cognitive development (Estes, 2004). Each child follows a unique developmental pattern, and young children learn best through firsthand experiences with people and materials. Unfortunately, too many of today's kindergartens have forgotten the importance of careful nurturing for our nation's young children (Krogh & Slentz, 2001; Slentz & Krogh, 2001).

Some experts on early childhood education argue that the curriculum of many kindergarten and preschool programs place too much emphasis on achievement and success, putting pressure on young children too early in their development (Elkind, 1988). Placing such heavy focus on success is not what kindergartens were originally intended to do. Keeping in mind Froebel's "garden for children" as a guide can produce a wholesome atmosphere for kindergarten children, in which they can build skills and knowledge and reach their individual potentials.

Developmentally Appropriate Practice

Many educators and psychologists believe that preschool and young elementary school children learn best through active, hands-on teaching methods such as games and dramatic play (Youngquist & Pataray-Ching, 2004). They know that children develop at varying rates and that schools need to allow for these individual differences (Henninger, 1999; Jalongo & Isenberg, 2000; Miranda, 2004). They also believe that schools should focus on improving children's socioemotional development, as well as their cognitive development (Hyson, Copple, & Jones, 2006). Educators refer to this type of schooling as **developmentally appropriate practice,** which is based on knowledge of the typical development of children within an age span (age appropriateness) as well as the uniqueness of the child (individual appropriateness). Developmentally appropriate practice contrasts with developmentally inappropriate practice, which ignores the concrete, hands-on approach to learning (McDaniel & others, 2005; Neuman & Roskos, 2005). Direct teaching largely through abstract paper-and-pencil activities presented to large groups of children is believed to be developmentally inappropriate.

The most comprehensive documents that address the issue of developmentally appropriate practice in early childhood programs is the position statement by the National Association for the Education of Young Children (NAEYC) (Bredekamp, 1987, 1997; NAEYC, 1986). This document represents the expertise of many of the foremost experts in the field of early childhood education. Figure 10.12 describes some of the NAEYC recommendations for developmentally appropriate and inappropriate practice.

One recent study compared 182 children from five developmentally appropriate classrooms (hands-on activities and integrated curriculum tailored to meet age group, cultural, and individual learning styles) and five developmentally inappropriate kindergarten classrooms (academic, direct instruction emphasis with extensive use of workbooks/worksheets, seat work, and rote drill/practice activities) in a Louisiana school system (Hart & others, 2003). Children from the two types of classrooms did not differ in pre-kindergarten readiness and the classrooms were balanced in terms of sex and socioeconomic status. Teacher ratings of child behavior and scores on the California

www.mhhe.com/santrockc9

Early Childhood Education
Early Childhood Education Resources

child-centered kindergarten Education that involves the whole child by considering both the child's physical, cognitive, and social development and the child's needs, interests, and learning styles.

developmentally appropriate practice Education that focuses on the typical developmental patterns of children (age appropriateness) and the uniqueness of each child (individual appropriateness). Such practice contrasts with *developmentally inappropriate practice*, which ignores the concrete, hands-on approach to learning. Direct teaching largely through abstract paper-and-pencil activities presented to large groups of young children is believed to be developmentally inappropriate.

Component	Appropriate Practice	Inappropriate Practice
Curriculum goals	Experiences are provided in all developmental areas—physical, cognitive, social, and emotional.	Experiences are narrowly focused on cognitive development without recognition that all areas of the child's development are interrelated.
	Individual differences are expected, accepted, and used to design appropriate activities.	Children are evaluated only against group norms, and all are expected to perform the same tasks and achieve the same narrowly defined skills.
	Interactions and activities are designed to develop children's self-esteem and positive feelings toward learning.	Children's worth is measured by how well they conform to rigid expectations and perform on standardized tests.
Teaching strategies	Teachers prepare the environment for children to learn through active exploration and interaction with adults, other children, and materials.	Teachers use highly structured, teacher-directed lessons almost exclusively.
	Children select many of their own activities from among a variety the teacher prepares.	The teacher directs all activity, deciding what children will do and when.
	Children are expected to be mentally and physically active.	Children are expected to sit down, be quiet, and listen or do paper-and-pencil tasks for long periods of time. A major portion of time is spent passively sitting, watching, and listening.
Guidance of socioemotional development	Teachers enhance children's self-control by using positive guidance techniques, such as modeling and encouraging expected behavior, redirecting children to a more acceptable activity, and setting clear limits.	Teachers spend considerable time enforcing rules, punishing unacceptable behavior, demeaning children who misbehave, making children sit and be quiet, and refereeing disagreements.
	Children are provided many opportunities to develop social skills, such as cooperating, helping, negotiating, and talking with the person involved to solve interpersonal problems.	Children work individually at desks and tables most of the time and listen to the teacher's directions to the whole group.

FIGURE 10.12 NAEYC Recommendations for Developmentally Appropriate and Inappropriate Education

Achievement Test were obtained through the third grade. Children who were in developmentally inappropriate classrooms had slower growth in vocabulary, math application, and math computation. In another recent study, the academic achievement of mostly African American and Latino children who were attending Head Start was assessed in terms of whether they were in schools emphasizing developmentally appropriate or inappropriate practices (Huffman & Speer, 2000). The young children in the developmentally appropriate classrooms were more advanced in letter/word identification and showed better performance in applying problems over time.

A special worry of early childhood educators is that the back-to-basics movement that has recently characterized educational reform is filtering down to kindergarten. Another worry is that many parents want their children to go to school earlier than kindergarten for the purpose of getting a "head start" in achievement.

How common are programs that use developmentally appropriate practice? Unfortunately, as few as one-third to one-fifth of all early childhood programs follow this educational strategy. Even fewer elementary schools do. Child-initiated activities, divergent questioning, and small-group instruction are the exception rather than the rule (Dunn & Kontos, 1997).

Literacy and Early Childhood Education

An important emphasis in early childhood education programs is to help children develop a foundation for reading, writing, and math skills (Perez & others, 2004). Let's first examine reading and writing skills.

Reading and Writing   The concern about the ability of U.S. children to read and write has led to a careful examination of preschool and kindergarten children's experiences, with the hope that a positive orientation toward reading and writing can be developed early in life (Antonacci & O'Callaghan, 2006; Morrow, 2005; Saracho & Shirakawa, 2004; Vacca & others, 2006). What should a literacy program for preschool children be like? Instruction should be built on what children already know about oral language, reading, and writing. Further, early precursors of literacy and academic success include language skills, phonological and syntactic knowledge, letter identification, and conceptual knowledge about print and its conventions and functions (Arnold & Doctoroff, 2003; McWhorter, 2006; Rubin, 2006; Smith & Read, 2005). A longitudinal study found that phonological awareness, letter name and sound knowledge, and naming speed in kindergarten were linked to reading success in the first and second grade (Schattschneider & others, 2004). In another longitudinal study, the number of letters children knew in kindergarten was highly correlated (.52) with their reading achievement in high school (Stevenson & Newman, 1986).

All young children should experience feelings of success and pride in their early reading and writing exercises (Beatty, 2005; Edwards, 2004; Gunning, 2006; NAEYC, 1998; Ruddell, 2006). Teachers need to help them perceive themselves as people who can enjoy exploring oral and written language. Reading should be integrated into the broad communication process, which includes speaking, listening, and writing, as well as other communication systems, such as art, math, and music (Combs, 2006; May, 2006; Neuman & Roskos, 1993). Children's early writing attempts should be encouraged without concern for the proper formation of letters or correct conventional spelling. Children should be encouraged to take risks in reading and writing, and errors should be viewed as a natural part of the child's growth (Olson, 2001; Spandel, 2004; Tompkins, 2006). Teachers and parents should take time to regularly read to children from a wide variety of poetry, fiction, and nonfiction (Temple & others, 2005). Teachers and parents should present models for young children to emulate by using language appropriately, listening and responding to children's talk, and engaging in their own reading and writing. And children should be encouraged to be active participants in the learning process, rather than passive recipients of knowledge. This can be accomplished by using activities that stimulate experimentation with talking, listening, writing, and reading (Barone, Hardman, & Taylor, 2006).

Content area	Examples of typical knowledge and skills From age 3 ——————————————→ Age 6		Sample teaching strategies
Number and operations	Counts a collection of 1 to 4 items and begins to understand that the last counting word tells "how many"	Counts and produces (counts out) collections up to 100 using groups of 10	Models counting of small collections and guides children's counting in everyday situations, emphasizing that we use one counting word for each object: ♡　　♡　　♡ "One. . . two. . . three. . . " Models counting by 10s while making groups of 10s (for example, 10, 20, 30. . . or 14, 24, 34. . .)
Geometry and spatial sense	Begins to match and name 2-D and 3-D shapes, first only with same size and orientation, then shapes that differ in size and orientation (such as a large triangle sitting on its point versus a small one sitting on its side)	Recognizes and names a variety of 2-D and 3-D shapes (such as quadrilaterals, trapezoids, rhombi, hexagons, spheres, cubes) in any orientation Describes basic features of shapes (such as number of sides or angles)	Introduces and labels a wide variety of shapes (such as skinny triangles, fat rectangles, prisms) that are in a variety of positions (such as a square or a triangle standing on a corner, a cylinder "standing up" or horizontal) Involves children in constructing shapes and talking about their features
Measurement	Recognizes and labels measurable attributes of objects (such as: I need a long string; Is this heavy?)	Tries out various processes and units for measurement and begins to notice different results of one method or another (such as what happens when we *don't* use a standard unit)	Uses comparing words to model and discuss measuring (such as: This book feels heavier than that block. I wonder if this block tower is taller than the desk.)
Displaying and analyzing data	Sorts objects and counts and compares the groups formed	Organizes and displays data through simple numerical representations such as bar graphs and counts the number in each group	Invites children to sort and organize collected materials by color, size, shape, etc. Asks them to compare groups to find which group has the most

FIGURE 10.13 **Learning Paths and Teaching Strategies in Early Mathematics** Note: These lists of content areas and descriptions are not exhaustive but rather presented as examples of some of the important math skills that children can learn in early childhood education and the teaching strategies that can be used.

Math　Early childhood education has focused more on the development of reading skills than math skills. A quality early childhood education program guides young children in developing both reading and math skills. Early childhood educators need to introduce mathematical concepts, methods, and language through a range of appropriate experiences and teaching strategies (Burris, 2005; Ginsburg & Golbeck, 2004; Smith, 2006; Van de Walle & Lovin, 2006). Young children especially benefit when they can explore and manipulate mathematical ideas while they are engaging in play. There is a special concern about the math skills of young children from low-socioeconomic-status families with researchers finding that they receive less support for the development of their math skills than their higher SES counterparts (Starkey, Klein, & Wakeley, 2004).

Although there is developmental variation in math learning by young children, they tend to follow certain sequences or learning paths as they develop. Figure 10.13 describes some skills that many children know and use early and late in the 3- to 6-year range. These are simply two points along the learning path and may have many steps in between. The learning paths described in figure 10.13 were developed as a joint project by the National Association for the Education of Young Children and the National Council of Teachers of Mathematics (NAEYC, 2003).

Early Childhood Education for Children from Low-Income Families

For many years, children from low-income families did not receive any education before they entered the first grade. In the 1960s, an effort was made to try to break the cycle of poverty and poor education for young children in the United States through compensatory education. **Project Head Start** is a compensatory education program designed to provide children from low-income families the opportunity to acquire skills and experiences important for success in school. Project Head Start began in the summer of 1965, funded by the Economic Opportunity Act, and it continues to serve disadvantaged children today.

Initially, Project Head Start consisted of many different types of preschool programs in different parts of the country. Little effort was made to find out whether some programs worked better than others, but it eventually became apparent that some programs did work better than others. **Project Follow Through** was implemented in 1967 as an adjunct to Project Head Start. In Project Follow Through, different types of educational programs were tried to determine which were the most effective. In the Follow Through programs, the enriched programs were carried through the first several years of elementary school.

Were some Follow Through programs more effective than others? Many of the variations were able to produce the desired effects in children. For example, children in academically oriented, direct-instruction approaches did better on achievement tests and were more persistent on tasks than were children in the other approaches. Children in schools emphasizing socioemotional approaches (self-esteem, interpersonal relations) were absent from school less often and showed more independence than children in other approaches. Thus, Project Follow Through was important in demonstrating that variation in early childhood education does have significant effects in a wide range of social and cognitive areas (Stallings, 1975). Yolanda Garcia works as a director of children's services involving Project Head Start. To read about her work, see the Careers in Child Development profile.

The effects of early childhood compensatory education continue to be studied, and recent evaluations support the positive influence on both the cognitive and social worlds of disadvantaged young children (Castro & others, 2004; Reynolds, 1999). Of special interest are the long-term effects such intervention might produce. Model preschool programs lead to lower rates of placement in special education, dropping out of school, grade retention, delinquency, and use of welfare programs. Such programs might also lead to higher rates of high school graduation and employment. For every dollar invested in high-quality, model preschool programs, taxpayers receive about $1.50 in return by the time the participants reach the age of 20. The benefits include savings on public school education (such as special education services), tax payments on additional earnings, reduced welfare payments, and savings in juvenile justice system costs. Predicted benefits over a lifetime are much greater to the taxpayer, a return of $5.73 on every dollar invested.

One long-term investigation of early childhood education was conducted by Irving Lazar, Richard Darlington, and their colleagues (1982). They pooled their resources into what they called a "consortium for longitudinal studies," developed to share information about the long-term effects of preschool programs, so that better designs and methods could be created. When the data from the 11 different early education studies were analyzed, the children ranged in age from 9 to 19 years. The early education models varied substantially, but all were carefully planned and executed by experts in early childhood education. Outcome measures included indicators of school competence (such as special education and grade retention), abilities (as measured by standardized intelligence and achievement tests), attitudes and values, and impact on the family. The results indicated substantial benefits of competent preschool education with low-income children on all four dimensions investigated. In sum, ample evidence indicates that well-designed and well-implemented early

Project Head Start Compensatory education designed to provide children from low-income families the opportunity to acquire the skills and experiences important for school success.

Project Follow Through An adjunct to Project Head Start, in which the enrichment programs are carried through the first few years of elementary school.

CAREERS in CHILD DEVELOPMENT

Yolanda Garcia
Director of Children's Services/Head Start

Yolanda Garcia has worked in the field of early childhood education and family support for three decades. She has been the Director of the Children's Services Department for the Santa Clara, California, County Office of Education since 1980. As director, she is responsible for managing child development programs for 2,500 3- to 5-year-old children in 127 classrooms. Her training includes two master's degrees, one in public policy and child welfare from the University of Chicago and another in educational administration from San Jose State University.

Garcia has served on many national advisory committees that have resulted in improvements in the staffing of Head Start programs. Most notably, she served on the Head Start Quality Committee that recommended the development of Early Head Start and revised performance standards for Head Start programs. Garcia currently is a member of the American Academy of Science Committee on the Integration of Science and Early Childhood Education.

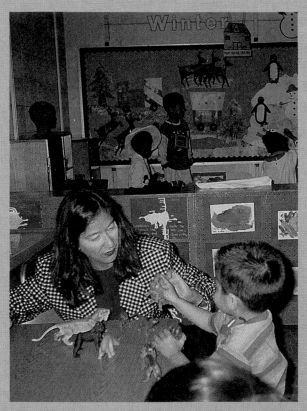

Yolanda Garcia, Director of Children's Services/Head Start, working with some Head Start children in Santa Clara, California.

childhood education programs with low-income children are successful.

Although educational intervention in impoverished children's lives is important, programs are not all created equal. One estimate is that 40 percent of the 1,400 Head Start programs are of questionable quality (Zigler & Styfco, 1994). More attention needs to be given to developing consistently high-quality Head Start programs (Bronfenbrenner, 1995). One emphasis currently being considered by the U.S. Congress is to infuse Head Start programs with a stronger academic focus. Although early childhood experts clearly hope that the overall quality of Head Start programs will improve, some worry that the emphasis on academic skills will come at the expense of reduced health services and decreased emphasis on socioemotional skills (Stipek, 2004).

One high-quality early childhood education program (although not a Head Start program) is the Perry Preschool program in Ypsilanti, Michigan, designed by David Weikart (1982). The Perry Preschool program is a two-year preschool program that includes weekly home visits from program personnel. In an analysis of the long-term effects of the program, as young adults the Perry Preschool children have higher high school graduation rates, more are in the workforce, fewer need welfare, crime rates are lower among them, and there are fewer teen pregnancies than in a control group from the same background who did not get the enriched early childhood education experience (Weikart, 1993). When the Perry preschoolers were 40 years old, they had significantly higher incomes and were less likely to have been arrested than the control group children (High/Scope Resource, 2005).

Too many young children go to substandard early childhood programs (Hyson, Copple, & Jones, 2006; Morrison, 2000). In a report by the Carnegie Corporation (1996), four out of five early childhood programs did not meet quality standards. Early childhood education should encourage adequate preparation for learning, varied learning activities, trusting relationships between adults and children, and increased parental involvement (Hillebrand, Phenice, & Hines, 2000).

In one recent well-designed study, the benefits of early educational and health enrichment were studied on the island of Mauritius, which is located in the Indian Ocean between Africa and India (Raine, 2000; Raine & others, 2001). One hundred 3- to 5-year-old children were given enriched early childhood education, nutrition education and nutritional meals, physical exercise, health screening and referral, remediation of behavioral and learning problems, and home visits to the family. Parents were educated about the importance of their positive involvement in their children's development. As such, it contained many of the components that are traditionally present in excellent Head Start programs. These 100 children were carefully matched to a control group of 100 3- to 5-year-old children who received a standard child-care type of schooling. When the two groups of children were 11 years old, their arousal and attention were assessed with physiological measures. The enriched group had less slow brain-wave activity, an indication of better mental maturity and alertness. It is not clear which of the specific aspects of the enriched program were responsible for the brain changes, such as exercise or cognitive stimulation.

Issues in Early Childhood Education

A number of issues characterize early childhood education (Driscoll & Nagel, 2005; Hyson, Copple, & Jones, 2006; Morrison, 2006). These include what the curriculum should be, whether preschool matters, and what constitutes school readiness.

Curriculum Controversy

Currently, there is controversy about what the curriculum for U.S. early childhood education should be (Cress, 2004; McDaniels & others, 2005). On one side are those who advocate a child-centered, constructivist approach much like that emphasized by the National Association of Education for Young Children along the lines of developmentally appropriate practice. On the other side are those who advocate an academic, instructivist approach. From the academic, instructivist perspective, the child is viewed as "dependent on adults' instruction in the academic knowledge and skills necessary for a good start for later academic achievement" (Katz, 1999, p. 1). The academic approach involves teachers directly instructing young children to learn basic academic skills, especially in reading and math.

The academic approach's emphasis on accountability and high standards for education has filtered down the preschool level. Thirty-six states now have standards that specify what young children "should know and be able to do before they enter kindergarten" (Jacobson, 2004). It is expected that 45 states will soon have early learning standards. Some critics argue that the standards focus too strongly on language and cognition, not giving adequate attention to physical, motor, and socioemotional skills (Kagan & Scott-Little, 2004).

Early childhood education expert Lilian Katz (1999, 2003) argues that both sides in this argument may be overlooking and undervaluing a third option—curriculum and teaching methods that emphasize children's *intellectual development*. Both academic and constructivist approaches endorse early childhood programs that promote young children's intellectual development. Katz' observations of large numbers of early childhood programs indicate that many of these include both academic and constructivist approaches in their effort to develop young children's intellectual competence. What many experts, such as Katz, do not advocate are academic early childhood programs that pressure young children to achieve, do not provide them with opportunities to actively construct their learning, at least in part of the curriculum, and do not emphasize the development of socioemotional skills.

NAEYC (2002) recently addressed the dramatic increase in the use of standards regarding desired results, outcomes, or learning expectations for U.S. children. NAEYC states that these standards can be a valuable part of early education but only if early learning standards (1) emphasize significant, developmentally appropriate content and outcomes; (2) are developed through inclusive, informed processes (in all instances, experts in early childhood education should be involved in creating the standards); (3) use implementation and assessment strategies that are ethical and appropriate for young children (assessment and accountability should be used to improve practices and services and should not be used to rank, sort, or penalize young children); and (4) are accompanied by strong supports for early childhood programs, professionals, and families.

Does Preschool Matter?

According to child developmentalist David Elkind (1988), parents who are exceptionally competent and dedicated, and who have both the time and the energy, can provide the basic ingredients of early childhood education in their home. If parents have the competence and resources to provide young

Head Start Resources
Early Childhood Care and Education

In most Japanese preschools, surprisingly little emphasis is put on academic instruction. In one study, 300 Japanese and 210 American preschool teachers, child development specialists, and parents were asked about various aspects of early childhood education (Tobin, Wu, & Davidson, 1989). Only 2 percent of the Japanese respondents listed "to give children a good start academically" as one of their top three reasons for a society to have preschools. In contrast, over half the American respondents chose this as one of their top three choices. To prepare children for successful careers in first grade and beyond, Japanese schools do not teach reading, writing, and mathematics but, rather, such skills as persistence, concentration, and the ability to function as a member of a group. The vast majority of young Japanese children are taught to read at home by their parents. *Are many American preschools becoming too academically oriented?*

What is the curriculum controversy in early childhood education?

children with a variety of learning experiences and exposure to other children and adults (possibly through neighborhood play groups), along with opportunities for extensive play, then home schooling may sufficiently educate young children. However, if parents do not have the commitment, the time, the energy, and the resources to provide young children with an environment that approximates a good early childhood program, then it *does* matter whether a child attends preschool. In this case, the issue is not whether preschool is important but whether home schooling can closely duplicate what a competent preschool program can offer.

We should always keep in mind the unfortunate idea of early childhood education as an early start to ensure that the participants will finish early or on top in an educational race. Elkind (1988) points out that perhaps the choice of the phrase *head start* for the education of disadvantaged children was a mistake. "Head Start program" does not imply a race. Not surprisingly, when middle-socioeconomic-status parents heard that low-income children were getting a "head start," they wanted a head start for their own young children. In some instances, starting children in formal academic training too early can produce more harm than good. In Denmark, where reading instruction follows a language experience approach and formal instruction is delayed until the age of 7, illiteracy is virtually nonexistent. By contrast, in France, where state-mandated formal instruction in reading begins at age 5, 30 percent of the children have reading problems. Education should not be stressful for young children. Early childhood education should not be solely an academic prep school.

Preschool is rapidly becoming a norm in early childhood education. In 2004, forty states provided state-funded preschool education. Although preschool attendance is increasing, only 10 percent of U.S. 3- and 4-year-old children attended a state-funded preschool in 2003.

The increase in public preschools underscores the growing belief that early childhood education should be a legitimate component of public education. There are dangers, though. According to Elkind (1988), early childhood education is often not well understood at higher levels of education. The danger is that public preschool education for 4-year-old children will become little more than a downward extension of traditional elementary education. This is already occurring in preschool programs in which testing, workbooks, and group drills are imposed on 4- and 5-year-old children.

Elkind believes that early childhood education should become a part of public education, but on its own terms. Early childhood should have its own curriculum, its own methods of evaluation and classroom management, and its own teacher-training programs. Although there may be some overlap with the curriculum, evaluation, classroom management, and teacher training at the upper levels of schooling, they certainly should not be identical.

Researchers have documented the stress that increased academic pressure can bring to young children (Hart & others, 1998). In one study, Diane Burts and her colleagues (1989) compared the frequencies of stress-related behaviors observed in young children in classrooms with developmentally appropriate instructional practices with those of children in classrooms with developmentally inappropriate instructional practices. They found that the children in the developmentally inappropriate classrooms exhibited more stress-related behaviors than the children in the developmentally appropriate classrooms. In another study, children in a highly academically oriented early childhood education program were compared with children in a low academically oriented early childhood education program (Hirsch-Pasek & others, 1989). No benefits appeared for children in the highly academically oriented early childhood education program, but some possible harmful effects were noted. Higher test anxiety, less creativity, and a less positive attitude toward school characterized more of the children who attended the highly academic program than who attended the low academic program.

Parents play an important role in young children's education. To learn more about parents and schools as partners in young children's education, see the Caring for Children interlude.

CARING FOR CHILDREN

Parents and Schools as Partners in the Young Child's Education

Mothers and fathers play important roles in the development of young children's positive attitudes toward learning and education (Morrow & Malin, 2004; Strickland, 2004). In one study, mothers and their preschool children were evaluated, and then the children's academic competence was assessed when they were in sixth grade (Hess & others, 1984). Maternal behavior in the preschool years was related to the children's academic competence in sixth grade. The best predictors of academic competence in sixth grade were the following maternal behaviors shown during the preschool years: effective communication with the child, a warm relationship with the child, positive expectations for achievement, use of rule-based rather than authority-based discipline, and not believing that success in school was based on luck.

The father's involvement with the child can also help build positive attitudes toward school and learning. Competent fathers of preschool children set aside regular time to be with the child, listen to the child and respond to questions, become involved in the child's play, and show an interest in the child's preschool and kindergarten activities. Fathers can help with the young child's schooling in these ways:

- Supporting their children's efforts in school and their children's unique characteristics
- Helping children with their problems when the children seek advice
- Communicating regularly with teachers
- Participating in school functions

The relationship between the school and the parents of young children is an important aspect of preschool and kindergarten education. Schools and parents can cooperate to provide young children with the best possible preschool and kindergarten experience, as well as a positive orientation toward learning (Grande & Downing, 2004). In one study, the most important factor contributing to the success of the preschool program was the positive involvement of the parents in their young children's learning and education (Lally, Mangione, & Honig, 1987).

School Readiness   Educational reform has prompted considerable concern about children's readiness to enter kindergarten and first grade (Crompton, 2005; Fiorentino & Howell, 2004; Lin, Lawrence, & Gorrell, 2003; Spooner, 2004; Webster-Stratton & Reid, 2004; Wesley & Buysse, 2003). National studies suggest that 40 percent of kindergartners are not ready for first grade (Kaufmann Early Education Exchange, 2002).

The National Association for the Education of Young Children (NAEYC, 1990) stresses that government officials and educators who promote universal school readiness should commit to:

- Addressing the inequities in early life experiences, such as poverty, so that all children have access to the opportunities that promote success in school
- Recognizing and supporting individual differences in children
- Establishing reasonable and appropriate expectations for children's capabilities on school entry

Inadequate health care and economic difficulties place many children at risk for academic failure before they enter school (Naude, Pretorius, & Vijoen, 2003). Thus, it is important to provide families with access to the services and support necessary to prepare children to succeed in school. These services include basic health care, economic support, basic nutrition, adequate housing, family support services, and high-quality early childhood education programs.

Craig and Sharon Ramey (1999, 2004) recently reviewed scientific research on school readiness and concluded that the following seven caregiver activities are necessary in the infant and early childhood years to ensure that children are ready for elementary school (Ramey & Ramey, 1999, p. 145):

1. Encourage exploration
2. Mentor in basic skills
3. Celebrate developmental advances
4. Research and extend new skills
5. Protect from inappropriate disapproval, teasing, and punishment
6. Guide and limit behavior

An increasing number of U.S. parents are delaying the entry of their children into the first grade with the hope that the additional year will provide their child with a competitive advantage. Borrowing the term from college athletics (in which an athlete is held out of competition for a year in hope that greater maturity and experience will produce improved performance), this strategy has been referred to as "academic redshirting." On the whole, the evidence about the short-term and long-term effects of redshirting are inconclusive (ERIC/EECE, 2002; West, Denton, & Germino-Hausken, 2000; Zill, Loomis, & West, 1997). When benefits of redshirting appear, they typically are short-lived and may in the long term be disadvantageous (Graue & DiPerna, 2000; Spitzer, Cupp, & Parke, 1995).

A related issue involves whether a child who is not doing well in kindergarten should be held back for a second year of kindergarten rather than entering the first grade. Researchers have found that this is generally not a good strategy, resulting in lower academic achievement and self-esteem (Carlton & Winsler, 1999; Dennebaum & Kulberg, 1994).

Characterize early childhood education.

Review

- What are some variations in early childhood education? What is child-centered kindergarten?

- How can developmentally appropriate practice be distinguished from developmentally inappropriate practice?

- What should early childhood education programs emphasize in developing young children's literacy and math skills?

- What is the nature of early childhood education for children from low-income families?

- What are some issues in early childhood education?

Reflect

- Imagine that you are an early childhood education consultant. What kind of advice would you give parents for selecting a good preschool or early childhood education program?

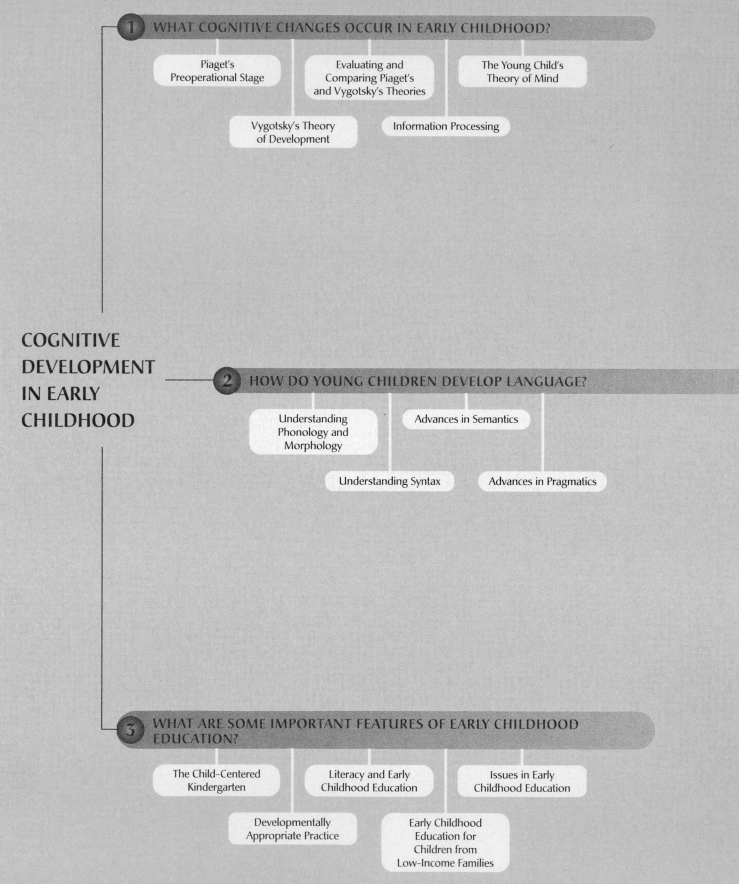

COGNITIVE DEVELOPMENT IN EARLY CHILDHOOD

1 WHAT COGNITIVE CHANGES OCCUR IN EARLY CHILDHOOD?

Piaget's Preoperational Stage

Evaluating and Comparing Piaget's and Vygotsky's Theories

The Young Child's Theory of Mind

Vygotsky's Theory of Development

Information Processing

2 HOW DO YOUNG CHILDREN DEVELOP LANGUAGE?

Understanding Phonology and Morphology

Advances in Semantics

Understanding Syntax

Advances in Pragmatics

3 WHAT ARE SOME IMPORTANT FEATURES OF EARLY CHILDHOOD EDUCATION?

The Child-Centered Kindergarten

Literacy and Early Childhood Education

Issues in Early Childhood Education

Developmentally Appropriate Practice

Early Childhood Education for Children from Low-Income Families

SUMMARY

1 Discuss the cognitive changes that occur in early childhood.

- In Piaget's theory, preoperational thought is the beginning of the ability to reconstruct at the level of thought what has been established in behavior, and a transition from primitive to more sophisticated use of symbols. The child at this stage does not yet think in an operational way. The symbolic function substage occurs roughly between 2 and 4 years of age and is characterized by symbolic thought, egocentrism, and animism. The intuitive thought substage stretches from about 4 to 7 years of age. It is called "intuitive" because on the one hand children seem so sure about their knowledge yet on the other hand are so unaware of how they k___ what they know. The preoperational child is char_____ centration, lacks conservation, and asks a ___ _____ions.

- Vygotsky described the zon_ _____ment (ZPD) as the difference _____ _an achieve independently _____ _ the guidance and as_____ed children. Scaffolding_____ __ the course of a teaching s_____ ___ed person adjusting guidance to _____ _t performance level. Dialogue is an im_____ _ __ scaffolding. Vygotsky believed that language p____ y role in guiding cognition. He said language and t__ __ght initially develop independently, but then children internalize their egocentric speech in the form of inner speech, which becomes their thoughts. This transition occurs at about 3 to 7 years of age. This view contrasts with Piaget's view that young children's inner speech is egocentric and immature. Teaching strategies based on Vygotsky's theory focus on the zone of proximal development, using scaffolding and more-skilled peers as teachers, monitoring and encouraging children's use of private speech, assessing the child's ZPD rather than IQ, and transforming the classroom with Vygotskian ideas.

- Vygotsky's theory gives more emphasis to the sociocultural context than Piaget's theory. Both theories are constructivist, but Vygotsky's is social constructivist, Piaget's cognitive constructivist. Vygotsky's theory does not include stages; Piaget's does. Vygotsky gives the more-skilled individual a stronger teaching role than does Piaget. Vygotsky says that language has a more important role in development than Piaget. Education plays a central role in Vygotsky's theory, less so in Piaget's theory. Both Vygotsky and Piaget view the teacher as a guide and facilitator rather than a director.

- The child's attentional control improves considerably during early childhood but still has a number of deficits. Much of the interest in attention focuses on selective attention. Younger children focus more on the salient than the relevant dimensions of a task; older children are more planful in their attentional strategies and adjust their attention better to demands of the task. Preschool children are less likely than elementary school children to know that they need to intensely focus their attention to remember something. Significant improvements in short-term memory take place in early childhood. With good probes and prompts, young children's long-term memory can be accurate, although they can be led to develop false memories. Currently, there is considerable interest in children's eyewitness testimony. Preschoolers are more suggestible than older children, there are individual differences in susceptibility, and interviewing techniques can produce distortions in children's reports. From 3 to 5 years of age, young children's scripts become more elaborate and these scripts improve their memory for events. Young children usually don't use strategies to remember, but they can learn rather simple problem-solving strategies. In early childhood, children engage in more flexible problem solving compared with the relatively stimulus-driven toddler.

- Theory of mind refers to awareness of one's own mental processes and the mental processes of others. Children's theory of mind changes as they go through the early childhood years. At 2 to 3 years of age, children begin to understand perceptions, desires, and emotions. At 4 to 5 years of age, children begin to understand that the mind can represent objects and events accurately or inaccurately. The realization that people have false beliefs develops in a majority of children by the time they are 5 years old. Further changes in theory of mind occur in middle and late childhood.

2 Describe language development in early childhood.

- Young children gradually become sensitive to the sounds of spoken words. They show this phonological awareness in many ways, such as noticing rhymes, enjoying poems, and making up silly names for things. In early childhood, children start using the plural and possessive forms of nouns, put appropriate endings on verbs, and use prepositions. Some of the best evidence for their improvement in morphology is their overgeneralization of rules, which was exemplified in Berko's (1958) classic "wugs" study.

- After advancing beyond two-word utterances, young children speak word sequences that show a growing mastery of complex rules for how words should be ordered. Young children's mastery of meanings rapidly advances.

- Vocabulary growth is substantial in the early childhood years.
- Changes in pragmatics characterize young children's development. Six-year-olds are much better conversationalists than 2-year-olds are. Children improve in their ability to talk about things that are not physically present. At about 4 years of age, children develop a sensitivity to the needs of others in conversation. At about 5 years of age, children develop the ability to modify their speech style according to context.

3 Characterize early childhood education.

- There is considerable variation in early childhood education. One variation is the Montessori approach, which emphasizes children's spontaneity and freedom in choosing activities. Child-centered kindergarten involves education of the whole child with emphases on individual variation, the process of learning, and play.
- Developmentally appropriate practice is age and individual appropriate; developmentally inappropriate practice is not.
- There has been increased interest in young children's literacy. Young children need to develop positive images of reading and writing skills through a supportive environment. Children should be active participants and be immersed in a wide range of interesting and enjoyable listening, talking, writing, and reading experiences. A quality early childhood education program also helps young children build a foundation for the development of their mathematical skills. From 3 to 6 years of age, young children develop mathematical skills in these areas: number and operations, geometry and spatial relations, measurement, and displaying and analyzing data.
- Head Start and Project Follow Through have been instituted to provide improved early education for young children from low-income backgrounds. Researchers have found that high-quality early childhood education programs improve the competence of young children from low-income backgrounds.
- Controversy characterizes early childhood education curricula. On the one side are the child-centered constructivist advocates, on the other those who advocate an instructivist, academic approach. Some parents can educate young children as effectively as a school does; however, most parents do not have the skills, time, and commitment to do so. A special concern is the increasing number of high-intensity, academically oriented preschools. School readiness guidelines should take into account inequities in young children's experiences, such as poverty, consider individual variation, and involve reasonable and appropriate expectations.

KEY TERMS

operations 303
symbolic function
  substage 303
egocentrism 303
animism 304

intuitive thought
  substage 304
centration 304
conservation 304
zone of proximal development
  (ZPD) 306

scaffolding 307
social constructivist
  approach 309
short-term memory 311
theory of mind 314
Montessori approach 318

child-centered
  kindergarten 319
developmentally appropriate
  practice 319
Project Head Start 323
Project Follow Through 323

KEY PEOPLE

MAKING A DIFFERENCE

Nourish the Young Child's Cognitive Development

What are some good strategies for helping young children develop their cognitive competencies?

- *Provide opportunities for the young child's development of symbolic thought.* Give the child ample opportunities to scribble and draw. Provide the child opportunities to engage in make-believe play. Don't criticize the young child's art and play. Let the child's imagination flourish.
- *Encourage exploration.* Let the child select many of the activities he or she wants to explore. Don't have the child do rigid paper-and-pencil exercises that involve rote learning. The young child should not be spending lots of time passively sitting, watching, and listening.
- *Be an active language partner with the young child.* Encourage the young child to speak in entire sentences instead of using single words. Be a good listener. Ask the child lots of questions. Don't spend time correcting the child's grammar; simply model correct grammar yourself when you talk with the child. Don't correct the young child's writing. Spend time selecting age-appropriate books for the young child. Read books with the young child.
- *Become sensitive to the child's zone of proximal development.* Monitor the child's level of cognitive functioning. Know what tasks the child can competently perform alone and those that are too difficult, even with your help. Guide and assist the child in the proper performance of skills and use of tools in the child's zone of proximal development. Warmly support the young child's practice of these skills.
- *Evaluate the quality of the child's early childhood education program.* Make sure the early childhood program the child attends involves developmentally appropriate education. The program should be age appropriate and individual appropriate for the child. It should not be a high-intensity, academic-at-all-costs program. Don't pressure the child to achieve at this age.

CHILDREN RESOURCES

National Association for the Education of Young Children (NAEYC)

1834 Connecticut Avenue, NW
Washington, DC 20009
202–232–8777
800–424–2460
http://www.naeyc.com

NAEYC is an important advocacy group for young children and has developed guidelines for a number of dimensions of early childhood education. It publishes the excellent journal *Young Children*.

Motivated Minds: Raising Children to Love Learning (2001)

by Deborah Stipek and Kathy Seal
Hudson, OH: Owl Books

An excellent book for parents who want to guide their children's learning effectively.

E-LEARNING TOOLS

Connect to **www.mhhe.com/santrockc9** to research the answers to complete the following exercises. In addition, you'll find a number of other resources and valuable study tools for chapter 10, "Cognitive Development in Early Childhood," on the Student CD-ROM that came with this book.

Taking It to the Net

1. Judith and Louis have a three-year-old son, Mitchell. Many of their friends are enrolling their children in preschool. Judith and Louis do not think they can afford to enroll Mitchell in a preschool program, although both of them think that the benefits of preschool might justify the cost. Are there significant benefits associated with preschool programs? Are there particular types of preschools that seem more beneficial for children?

2. Todd is working in a child-care center after school. He notices that there is a wide range in the children's use of language, even within age groups. Are there any guidelines that Todd can obtain that could help determine if a child is delayed in language development?

3. You are visiting a number of preschools to help your friend determine which program might be most appropriate for her 4-year-old child. You have heard that the National Association for the Education of Young Children is a great resource for both educators and parents. What kinds of tools can you find on the NAEYC website to assist you and your friend as you search the programs in your area?

Health and Well-Being, Parenting, and Education

Build your decision-making skills by trying your hand at the health and well-being, parenting, and education exercises.

Video Clips

The Online Learning Center includes the following videos for this chapter:

1. *Categorizing Animals and Food at Age 3*
   Here we watch a 3-year-old demonstrate his ability to categorize animals and food. In the second demonstration, when presented with pictures of a zebra, turtle, bird, and kite, he makes a distinction between animals and birds.

2. *Categorizing Pictures at Age 4*
   A 4-year-old is presented with pictures of a lion, bear, zebra, and wagon and asked which one is different from the others. He insists, "They're all different!" The interviewer probes him but he is more interested in adding and subtracting pictures, which he does very well. Another set of pictures is presented to him and again he says that all are different.

3. *Understanding Conservation (Liquid) at Age 4*
   A girl proves she has an understanding of the concept of conservation when presented with Piaget's classic liquid test. This clip provides a good example of the age variation in the emergence of conservation.

4. *Memory Ability at Age 4*
   Here a 4-year-old girl is presented with a sequence of numbers and asked to repeat them back. She recalls the numbers successfully and then smiles at her accomplishment.

FIGURE 11.1 A Young Child Expressing the Emotion of Shame

from others through many different physical and material attributes. Says 4-year-old Sandra, "I'm different from Jennifer because I have brown hair and she has blond hair." Says 4-year-old Ralph, "I am different from Hank because I am taller, and I am different from my sister because I have a bicycle."

Researchers stress that the *active dimension* is a central component of the self in early childhood (Keller, Ford, & Meacham, 1978). If we define the category *physical* broadly enough, we can include physical actions as well as body image and material possessions. For example, preschool children often describe themselves in terms of activities such as play. In sum, in early childhood, children frequently think of themselves in terms of a physical self or an active self.

Emotional Development

Young children, like adults, experience many emotions during the course of a day. At times, children also try to make sense of other people's emotional reactions and feelings.

Self–Conscious Emotions Recall our discussion (in chapter 8) of *self-conscious emotions,* which require that children be able to refer to themselves and be aware of themselves as distinct from others (Lewis, 1995, 2002). We indicated that self-conscious evaluative emotions—pride, shame, and guilt—first appear at about 2½ years of age. Expression of these emotions indicates that children are beginning to acquire and are able to use societal standards and rules to evaluate their behavior.

Pride is expressed when children feel joy as a result of the successful outcome of a particular action (Lewis, 2002). Pride is often associated with achieving a particular goal.

Shame emerges when children perceive they have not met standards or goals (Lewis, 2002). Children who experience shame often wish they could hide or disappear. Shame typically involves an attack on the entire self and can produce confusion in thought and an inability to speak. The bodies of shamed children seem to shrink as if to disappear from the view of others (see figure 11.1). Shame is not produced by any specific situation but rather by an individual's interpretation of an event.

In one study, girls showed more shame and pride than boys (Stipek, Recchia, & McClintic, 1992). This gender difference is interesting because girls are more at risk for internalizing disorders, such as anxiety and depression, in which feelings of shame and self-criticism are often evident (Cummings, Braungart-Rieker, & DuRocher-Schudlich, 2003).

Guilt feelings emerge when children judge their behavior to be a failure (Lewis, 2002). Guilt and shame have different physical characteristics. When children experience shame, they often try to shrink their bodies in an effort to disappear, but when they experience guilt, they typically move in space as if they are trying to correct their failure.

The development of evaluative, self-conscious emotions is especially influenced by parents' responses to children's behavior. For example, a young child may experience a twinge of guilt when a parent says, "You should feel bad about biting your sister."

Young Children's Emotion Language and Understanding of Emotion Among the most important changes in emotional development in early childhood are an increased ability to talk their own and others' emotions and an increased understanding of emotion (Kuebli, 1994). Between 2 and 3 years of age, children considerably increase the number of terms they use to describe emotions (Ridgeway, Waters, & Kuzaj, 1985). They also are learning about the causes and consequences of feelings (Denham, 1998).

When they are 4 to 5 years of age, children show an increased ability to reflect on emotions. In this developmental time frame, they also begin to understand that the

Moral Behavior

The study of moral behavior has been influenced by behavioral and social cognitive theories (Grusec, 2005). The processes of reinforcement, punishment, and imitation are used to explain children's moral behavior. When children are rewarded for behavior that is consistent with laws and social conventions, they are likely to repeat that behavior. When models who behave morally are provided, children are likely to adopt their actions. And, when children are punished for immoral behavior, those behaviors are likely to be reduced or eliminated. However, because punishment may have adverse side effects, it needs to be used judiciously and cautiously.

Another important point needs to be made about the social cognitive view of moral development. Moral behavior is influenced extensively by the situation. What children do in one situation is often only weakly related to what they do in other situations. A child might cheat in math class but not in English class; a child might steal a piece of candy when others are not present but not steal it when they are present. More than half a century ago, morality's situational nature was observed in a comprehensive study of thousands of children in many different situations—at home, at school, and at church, for example. The totally honest child was virtually nonexistent; so was the child who cheated in all situations (Hartshorne & May, 1928–1930).

Social cognitive theorists also believe that the ability to resist temptation is closely tied to the development of self-control. Children must overcome their impulses toward something they want that is prohibited. To achieve this self-control, they must learn to be patient and to delay gratification. Social cognitive theorists believe that cognitive factors are important in the child's development of self-control.

Moral Feelings

In chapter 2, we discussed Sigmund Freud's psychoanalytic theory. It describes the *superego* as one of the three main structures of personality—the id and ego being the other two. In Freud's classical psychoanalytic theory, the child's superego—the moral branch of personality—develops as the child resolves the Oedipus conflict and identifies with the same-sex parent in the early childhood years. Among the reasons children resolve the Oedipus conflict is the fear of losing their parents' love and of being punished for their unacceptable sexual wishes toward the opposite-sex parent. To reduce anxiety, avoid punishment, and maintain parental affection, children form a superego by identifying with the same-sex parent. Through their identification with the same-sex parent, children internalize the parents' standards of right and wrong that reflect societal prohibitions. And the child turns inward the hostility that was previously aimed externally at the same-sex parent. This inwardly directed hostility is now felt self-punitively as guilt, which is experienced unconsciously (beyond the child's awareness). In the psychoanalytic account of moral development, the self-punitiveness of guilt is responsible for keeping the child from committing transgressions. That is, children conform to societal standards to avoid guilt.

One recent study found a link between attachment in infancy and the young child's conscience (Kochanska & others, 2004). Children's secure attachment to their mothers at 14 months of age was related to the mother's adaptive parenting and promotion of conscience during early childhood.

Positive feelings, such as empathy, contribute to the child's moral development (Eisenberg, 2005; Hoffman, 2002). *Empathy* is reacting to another's feelings with an emotional response that is similar to the other's feelings. Although empathy is experienced as an emotional state, it often has a cognitive component. The cognitive component of empathy is the ability to discern another's inner psychological states, or what is called "perspective taking." Young infants have the capacity for some purely empathic responses, but for effective moral action children need to learn how to identify a wide range of emotional states in others. They also need to learn to anticipate what kinds of action will improve another person's emotional state.

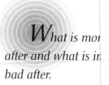

Approximate age of child	Description
2 to 3 years	Increase emotion vocabulary most rapidly
	Correctly label simple emotions in self and others and talk about past, present, and future emotions
	Talk about the causes and consequences of some emotions and identify emotions associated with certain situations
	Use emotion language in pretend play
4 to 5 years	Show increased capacity to reflect verbally on emotions and to consider more complex relations between emotions and situations
	Understand that the same event may call forth different feelings in different people and that feelings sometimes persist long after the events that caused them
	Demonstrate growing awareness about controlling and managing emotions in accord with social standards

same event can elicit different feelings in different people. Moreover, they show a growing awareness that they need to manage their emotions to meet social standards (Bruce, Olen, & Jensen, 1999). Figure 11.2 summarizes the characteristics of young children's talk about emotion and their understanding of it.

Emotion-Coaching and Emotion-Dismissing Parents

In chapter 8, we described the importance of self-regulation of emotion in infancy. The self-regulation of emotion continues to be an important aspect of socioemotional development in the childhood years, and parents can play an important role in helping young children regulate their emotions (Havighurst, Harley, & Prior, 2004; Thompson, 2006; Thompson & Lagattuta, 2005). Depending on how they talk with their children about emotion, parents can be described as taking an *emotion-coaching* or an *emotion-dismissing* approach (Katz, 1999). *Emotion-coaching parents* monitor their children's emotions, view their children's negative emotions as opportunities for teaching, assist them in labeling emotions, and coach them in how to deal effectively with emotions. In contrast, *emotion-dismissing parents* view their role as to deny, ignore, or change negative emotions. Researchers have found that when interacting with their children, emotion-coaching parents are less rejecting, use more scaffolding and praise, and are more nurturant than are emotion-dismissing parents (Gottman & DeClaire, 1997). The children of emotion-coaching parents were better at soothing themselves when they got upset, more effective in regulating their negative emotions, focused their attention better, and had fewer behavior problems than the children of emotion-dismissing parents.

Emotions and Peer Relations

Emotions play a strong role in whether a child's peer relationships are successful or not. Moody and emotionally negative children experience greater rejection by their peers, whereas emotionally positive children are more popular (Stocker & Dunn, 1990).

Emotional regulation is an important aspect of getting along with peers. In one study conducted in the natural context of young children's everyday peer interactions, self-regulation of emotion enhanced children's social competence (Fabes & others, 1999). Children who made an effort to control their emotional responses were more likely to respond in socially competent ways in an emotionally provocative peer situation (as when a peer made a hostile comment or took something

Children experience many emotions every day. An important aspect of child development is for children to understand and control their feelings. *What are some strategies that adults can adopt to encourage children to talk about their emotions?*

away from the child). In sum, the ability to modulate one's
skill that benefits children in their relationships with peers.

Moral Development

Moral development refers to rules and regulations about
their interactions with other people. Moral development inc
thoughts, feelings, and behaviors. We begin our exploration
children by focusing on a cognitive view of moral developm

Piaget's Theory
Interest in how children think about
lated by Piaget (1932), who extensively observed and inter
ages of 4 through 12. Piaget watched children play marble
and thought about the game's rules. He also asked children a
lies, punishment, and justice, for example. Piaget concluded
two distinct stages in how they think about morality.

- From 4 to 7 years of age, children display **heteronomo**
  stage of moral development in Piaget's theory. Children
  rules as unchangeable properties of the world, removed
  people.
- From 7 to 10 years of age, children are in a transition sh
  of the first stage of moral reasoning and some stages of t
  autonomous morality.
- From about 10 years of age and older, children show **au**
  the second stage of moral development. They become av
  are created by people, and in judging an action, they con
  tions as well as the consequences.

A heteronomous thinker judges the rightness or goodne
ering the consequences of the behavior, not the intentions o
the heteronomous thinker says that breaking twelve cups a
breaking one cup intentionally. For the moral autonomist,
sume paramount importance. The heteronomous thinker al
unchangeable and are handed down by all-powerful autho
gested to young children that they use new rules in a game
By contrast, older children—moral autonomists—accept ch
rules are merely convenient conventions, subject to change.

The heteronomous thinker also believes in **immanent**
that if a rule is broken, punishment will be meted out imme
believes that a violation is connected automatically to its pr
children often look around worriedly after committing a tra
evitable punishment. Immanent justice also implies that if
happens to someone, the person must have transgressed ear
are moral autonomists, recognize that punishment occurs or
the wrongdoing and that, even then, punishment is not inev

Piaget argued that, as children develop, they become mor
ing about social matters, especially about the possibilities an
tion. Piaget stressed that this social understanding comes ab
give-and-take of peer relations. In the peer group, where oth
tus similar to the child's, plans are negotiated and coordinate
reasoned about and eventually settled. Parent-child relation
the power and children do not, are less likely to advance m
rules are often handed down in an authoritarian way. Later, ir
cuss another highly influential cognitive view of moral devel
Kohlberg.

moral development Development regarding
rules and conventions about what people
should do in their interactions with other
people.

heteronomous morality The first stage of
moral development in Piaget's theory, occurring at 4 to 7 years of age. Justice and rules are
conceived of as unchangeable properties of the
world, removed from the control of people.

autonomous morality The second stage
of moral development in Piaget's theory,
displayed by older children (about 10 years of
age and older). The child becomes aware that
rules and laws are created by people and that,
in judging an action, one should consider the
actor's intentions as well as the consequences.

immanent justice Piaget's concept that if a
rule is broken, punishment will be meted out
immediately.

Gender Resources

gender The social and psychological dimension of being female or male.

gender role A set of expectations that
prescribe how females or males should think,
act, or feel.

gender typing The process by which children
acquire the thoughts, feelings, and behaviors
that are considered appropriate for their
gender in their culture.

estrogens A main class of sex hormones that
primarily influence the development of female
sexual characteristics and help regulate the
menstrual cycle. Estradiol is an important
estrogen.

androgens A main class of sex hormones that
primarily promote the development of male
genitals and secondary sex characteristics.
Testosterone is an important androgen.

Gender

What exactly do we mean by gender? **Gender** refers to the social and psychological
dimensions of being female or male (*sex* designates the biological aspects of being female or male). A **gender role** is a set of expectations that prescribe how females and
males should act, think, and feel. **Gender typing** is the process by which children acquire the thoughts, feelings, and behaviors that are considered appropriate for their
gender in a particular culture. To understand how gender develops in our lives, we
need to learn about biological, social, and cognitive influences on gender.

Biological Influences
It was not until the 1920s that researchers confirmed
the existence of human sex chromosomes, the genetic material that determines our
sex. As we discussed in chapter 3, "Biological Beginnings," humans normally have 46
chromosomes, arranged in pairs. A 23rd pair with two X-shaped chromosomes produces a female. A 23rd pair with an X chromosome and a Y chromosome produces a
male.

Hormones   Two classes of sex hormones have the most influence on gender: estrogens and androgens. Both estrogens and androgens occur in both females and males,
but in very different concentrations.

Estrogens primarily influence the development of female physical sex characteristics and help regulate the menstrual cycle. Estrogens are a general class of hormones.
An example of an important estrogen is estradiol. Estrogens are produced mainly by
the ovaries.

Androgens primarily promote the development of male genitals and secondary
sex characteristics. One important androgen is testosterone. Androgens are produced
by the adrenal glands in males and females, and by the testes in males.

Let's now further examine the early biological development of the sexes. In the
first few weeks of gestation, female and male embryos look alike. Male sex organs start
to differ from female sex organs when a gene on the Y chromosome directs a small
piece of tissue in the embryo to turn into testes. In females, there is no Y chromosome
so the tissue turns into ovaries. Once the tissue has turned into testes, they begin to
secrete testosterone.

To explore biological influences on gender, researchers have studied individuals
who are exposed to unusual levels of sex hormones early in development (Reiner &
Gearhart, 2004). Here are four examples of the problems that may occur as a result
(Lippa, 2005, pp. 122–124, 136–137):

- *Congenital adrenal hyperplasia (CAH).* Some girls have this condition, which is
  caused by a genetic defect. Their adrenal glands enlarge, resulting in abnormally
  high levels of androgens. CAH girls, although they are XX females, vary in how
  much their genitals look like male or female genitals. Often their genitals are
  surgically altered to look more like those of a typical female. Although CAH girls
  usually grow up to think of themselves as girls and women, they are less content
  with being a female and show a stronger interest in being a male than non-CAH
  girls (Berenbaum & Bailey, 2003; Ehrhardt, 1987; Hall & others, 2004; Slijper,
  1984). "They like rough-and-tumble activities, sports, and playing with boys and
  boys' toys. . . . CAH girls often dislike girl-typical activities such as playing with
  dolls and wearing makeup, jewelry, and frilly clothes" (p. 173).
- *Androgen-insensitive males.* "There are a small number of genetic XY males, who,
  because of a genetic error, do not have androgen receptors in their cells. . . . The
  effects of complete androgen insensitivity are dramatic. Affected XY individuals
  develop as females, in the sense that their bodies look completely female . . . ,
  and they develop a female gender identity. . . . Such individuals are generally
  romantically and sexually attracted to males (Wisniewski & others, 2000)"
  (pp. 104–105).

- *Pelvic field defect.* A small number of newborns have a disorder called pelvic field defect, which in boys involves a missing penis. For many years, doctors usually recommended that these genetic boys be raised as girls and undergo castration, which was required because they were born with testicles but not a penis. "Thus these XY boys were exposed to normal male amounts of testosterone prenatally but were castrated soon after birth and reared as females" (p. 114). According to one study, despite the efforts by parents to rear them as girls, most of the XY children insisted that they were boys (Reiner, 2001). Apparently, normal exposure to androgens prenatally had a stronger influence on their gender identity than being castrated and raised as girls.

- *Genital loss and sex assignment.* In another intriguing case, one of two identical twin boys lost his penis due to an errant circumcision. The twin who lost his penis was surgically reassigned to be a girl and to be reared as a girl. "Bruce (the real name of the boy) became Brenda. Although early reports suggested the sex reassignment had been successful (Money, 1975), later evidence revealed that Brenda was never really comfortable as a girl (Diamond & Sigmundson, 1997). In early adulthood, Brenda became Bruce once again, and now lived as a man with a wife and adopted children" (Colapinto, 2000). Tragically, in 2004 Bruce "committed suicide at the age of 38."

Although sex hormones alone, of course, do not determine behavior, researchers have found links between sex hormone levels and certain behaviors. The most established effects of testosterone on humans involve aggressive behavior and sexual behavior (Hyde, 2003). Levels of testosterone are correlated with sexual behavior in boys during puberty (Udry & others, 1985). Violent male criminals have above-average levels of testosterone (Dabbs & others, 1987), and professional football players have higher levels of testosterone than ministers do (Dabbs & Morris, 1990).

In sum, research suggests that biological factors, especially early hormonal production, play important roles in gender development (Lippa, 2005; Reiner & Gearhart, 2004).

The Evolutionary Psychology View In chapter 3 we described the approach of evolutionary psychology, which emphasizes that adaptation during the evolution of humans produced psychological differences between males and females (Buss, 1995, 2000, 2004). Evolutionary psychologists argue that primarily because of their differing roles in reproduction, males and females faced different pressures in primeval environments when the human species was evolving. In particular, because having multiple sexual liaisons improves the likelihood that males will pass on their genes, natural selection favored males who adopted short-term mating strategies. These males competed with other males to acquire more resources in order to access females. Therefore, say evolutionary psychologists, males evolved dispositions that favor violence, competition, and risk taking.

In contrast, according to evolutionary psychologists, females' contributions to the gene pool was improved by securing resources for their offspring, which was promoted by obtaining long-term mates who could support a family (Buss, 2004). As a consequence, natural selection favored females who devoted effort to parenting and chose mates who could provide their offspring with resources and protection. Females developed preferences for successful, ambitious men who could provide these resources.

This evolutionary unfolding, according to some evolutionary psychologists, explains key gender differences in sexual attitudes and sexual behavior. For example, in one study, men said that ideally they would like to have more than 18 sexual partners in their lifetime, whereas women stated that ideally they would like to have only 4 or 5 (Buss & Schmidt, 1993). In another study, 75 percent of the men but none of the women approached by an attractive stranger of the opposite sex consented to a request for sex (Clark & Hatfield, 1989).

FIGURE 11.3 A Comparison of the Psychoanalytic and Social Cognitive Views of Gender Development Parents influence their children's development by action and example.

Theory	Processes	Outcomes
Freud's psychoanalytic theory	Sexual attraction to opposite-sex parent at 3 to 5 years of age; anxiety about sexual attraction and subsequent identification with same-sex parent at 5 to 6 years of age	Gender behavior similar to that of same-sex parent
Social cognitive theory	Rewards and punishments of gender-appropriate and -inappropriate behavior by adults and peers; observation and initiation of models' masculine and feminine behavior	Gender-typed behavior

Such gender differences, says David Buss (1995, 2000, 2004) are exactly the type predicted by evolutionary psychology. Buss argues that men and women differ psychologically in those domains in which they have faced different adaptive problems during evolutionary history. In all other domains, predicts Buss, the sexes will be psychologically similar.

Critics of evolutionary psychology argue that its hypotheses are backed by speculations about prehistory, not evidence, and that in any event people are not locked into behavior that was adaptive in the evolutionary past. Critics also claim that the evolutionary view pays little attention to cultural and individual variations in gender differences.

Social Influences Many social scientists do not locate the cause of psychological gender differences in biological dispositions. Rather, they argue that these differences are due to social experiences such as parental, peer, school, and media influences. Three theories have been influential in this regard: social role theory, the psychoanalytic theory of gender, and the social cognitive theory of gender.

Social Role Theory Alice Eagly (2000, 2001; Eagly & Diekman, 2003) proposed **social role theory,** which states that gender differences result from the contrasting roles of women and men. In most cultures around the world, women have less power and status than men have and they control fewer resources. Compared with men, women perform more domestic work, spend fewer hours in paid employment, receive lower pay, and are more thinly represented in the highest levels of organizations. In Eagly's view, as women adapted to roles with less power and less status in society, they showed more cooperative, less dominant profiles than men. Thus, the social hierarchy and division of labor are important causes of gender differences in power, assertiveness, and nurture (Eagly & Diekman, 2003).

Psychoanalytic Theory of Gender The **psychoanalytic theory of gender** stems from Freud's view that the preschool child develops a sexual attraction to the opposite-sex parent. At 5 or 6 years of age, the child renounces this attraction because of anxious feelings. Subsequently, the child identifies with the same-sex parent, unconsciously adopting the same-sex parent's characteristics. However, developmentalists do not believe gender development proceeds as Freud proposed (Callan, 2001). Children become gender-typed much earlier than 5 or 6 years of age, and they become masculine or feminine even when the same-sex parent is not present in the family.

Social Cognitive Theory of Gender The social cognitive approach discussed in chapter 2 provides an alternative explanation of how children develop gender-typed behavior (see figure 11.3). According to the **social cognitive theory of gender,** children's gender development occurs through observation and imitation, and through the rewards and punishments children experience for gender-appropriate and gender-inappropriate behavior (Bussey & Bandura, 1999). Parents often use rewards and punishments to teach their daughters to be feminine ("Karen, you are being a good girl

social role theory Eagly's theory that psychological gender differences are caused by the contrasting social roles of women and men.

psychoanalytic theory of gender Stems from Freud's view that preschool children develop a sexual attraction to the opposite-sex parent, then, at 5 to 6 years of age, renounce the attraction because of anxious feelings, subsequently identifying with the same-sex parent and unconsciously adopting the same-sex parent's characteristics.

social cognitive theory of gender The idea that children's gender of development occurs through observation and imitation of gender behavior, as well as through the rewards and punishment children experience for behaviors believed to be appropriate or inappropriate for their gender.

when you play gently with your doll") and their sons to be masculine ("Keith, a boy as big as you is not supposed to cry"). Children also learn about gender from observing other adults in the neighborhood and on television (Fagot, Rodgers, & Leinbach, 2000).

Parental Influences   Once the label *girl* or *boy* is assigned by the obstetrician, virtually everyone, from parents to siblings to strangers, begins treating the infant differently. In one study, an infant girl, Avery, was dressed in a neutral outfit of overalls and a T-shirt (Brooks-Gunn & Matthews, 1979). People responded to her differently if they thought she was a girl rather than a boy. People who thought she was a girl made comments like "Isn't she cute. What a sweet little, innocent thing." By contrast, people who thought the baby was a boy made remarks like "I bet he is a tough little customer. He will be running around all over the place and causing trouble in no time."

In general, parents even hope that their offspring will be a boy. In one investigation in the 1970s, 90 percent of the men and 92 percent of the women wanted their firstborn child to be a boy (Peterson & Peterson, 1973). In a more recent study, parents still preferred a boy as the firstborn child—75 percent of the men and 79 percent of the women had that preference (Hamilton, 1991).

In some countries, a male child is so preferred over a female child that many mothers will abort a female fetus after fetal testing procedures, such as amniocentesis and sonograms, that reveal the fetus' sex. For example, in South Korea, where fetal testing to determine sex is common, male births exceed female births by 14 percent, in contrast to a worldwide average of 5 percent.

Both mothers and fathers are psychologically important in children's gender development. Mothers are more consistently given responsibility for nurturance and physical care; fathers are more likely to engage in playful interaction and be given responsibility for ensuring that boys and girls conform to existing cultural norms. And whether or not they have more influence on them, fathers are more involved in socializing their sons than in socializing their daughters (Lamb, 1986). Fathers seem to play an especially important part in gender-role development—they are more likely to act differently toward sons and daughters than mothers are, and thus contribute more to distinctions between the genders (Huston, 1983).

Many parents encourage boys and girls to engage in different types of play and activities (Fagot, 1995; Fisher-Thompson & others, 1993). Girls are more likely to be given dolls to play with during childhood and, when old enough, are more likely to be assigned baby-sitting duties. Girls are encouraged to be more nurturant and emotional than boys, and their fathers are more likely to engage in aggressive play with their sons than with their daughters. As adolescents increase in age, parents permit boys more freedom than girls, allowing them to be away from home and stay out later without supervision. When parents place severe restrictions on their adolescent sons, it has been found to be especially disruptive to the sons' development (Baumrind, 1989).

In recent years, the idea that parents are the critical socializing agents in gender-role development has come under fire (Huston, 1983). Parents are only one of many sources through which the individual learns gender roles. Culture, schools, peers, the media, and other family members are others. Yet it is important to guard against swinging too far in this direction because—especially in the early years of development—parents are important influences on gender development (Maccoby, 2002a).

Peer Influences   Parents provide the earliest discrimination of gender roles in development, but before long, peers join the societal process of responding to and modeling masculine and feminine behavior. There is increasing evidence that gender plays an important role in peer relations. This evidence involves the gender composition of children's groups, group size, and interaction in same-sex groups (Maccoby, 2002b):

- *Gender composition of children's groups.* Around the age of 3, children already show a preference to spend time with same-sex playmates. From 4 to 12 years of age,

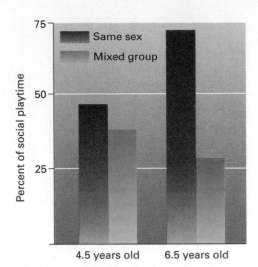

FIGURE 11.4 Developmental Changes in Percentage of Time Spent in Same-Sex and Mixed-Group Settings Observations of children show that they are more likely to play in same-sex than mixed-sex groups. This tendency increases between 4 and 6 years of age.

this preference for playing in same-sex groups increases and during the elementary school years children spend a large majority of their free time with children of their own sex (see figure 11.4).

• *Group size.* From about 5 years of age onward boys are more likely to participate in peer relations in larger clusters than girls. Boys are more likely to participate in organized group games than girls are. In one study, same-sex groups of six children were permitted to use play materials in any way they wished (Benenson, Apostolaris, & Parnass, 1997). Girls were more likely than boys to play in dyads or triads, whereas boys were more likely to interact in larger groups and seek to attain a group goal.

• *Interaction in same-sex groups.* Boys are more likely than girls to engage in rough-and-tumble play, competition, conflict, ego displays, and risk taking and to seek dominance. By contrast, girls are more likely to engage in "collaborative discourse," in which they talk and act in a more reciprocal manner.

School and Teacher Influences   There are concerns that schools and teachers have gender biases against both boys and girls. What evidence is there that the classroom is biased against boys? Here are some factors to consider (DeZolt & Hull, 2001):

• Compliance, following rules, and being neat and orderly are valued and reinforced in many classrooms. These are behaviors that usually characterize girls more than boys.

• A large majority of teachers are females, especially in the elementary school. This may make it more difficult for boys than girls to identify with their teachers and model their teachers' behavior.

• Boys are more likely than girls to have learning problems.

• Boys are more likely than girls to be criticized.

• School personnel tend to ignore that many boys are clearly having academic problems, especially in the language arts.

• School personnel tend to stereotype boys' behavior as problematic.

What evidence is there that the classroom is biased against girls? Consider the views of Myra and David Sadker (2000):

• In a typical classroom, girls are more compliant, boys more rambunctious. Boys demand more attention, girls are more likely to quietly wait their turn. Teachers are more likely to scold and reprimand boys, as well as send boys to school authorities for disciplinary action. Educators worry that girls' tendency to be compliant and quiet comes at a cost: diminished assertiveness.

• In many classrooms, teachers spend more time watching and interacting with boys while girls work and play quietly on their own. Most teachers don't intentionally favor boys by spending more time with them, yet somehow the classroom frequently ends up with this type of gendered profile.

• Boys get more instruction than girls and more help when they have trouble with a question. Teachers often give boys more time to answer a question, more hints at the correct answer, and further tries if they give the wrong answer.

• Boys are more likely than girls to get lower grades and to be grade repeaters, yet girls are less likely to believe that they will be successful in college work.

• Girls and boys enter first grade with roughly equal levels of self-esteem. Yet by the middle school years, girls' self-esteem is lower than boys'.

• When elementary school children are asked to list what they want to do when they grow up, boys describe more career options than girls do.

Thus, there is evidence of gender bias against both males and females in schools (DeZolt & Hull, 2001). Many school personnel are not aware of their gender-biased attitudes. These attitudes are deeply entrenched in and supported by the general culture. Increasing awareness of gender bias in schools is clearly an important strategy in reducing such bias.

Media Influences   Children encounter masculine and feminine roles in their everyday interactions with parents, peers, and teachers. The messages carried by the media about what is appropriate or inappropriate for males and for females are important influences on gender development as well (Roberts, Henrikson, & Foehr, 2004; Ward & Caruthers, 2001).

A special concern is the way females are pictured on television (Pacheco & Murtado, 2002). In the 1970s, it became apparent that television was portraying females as less competent than males. For example, about 70 percent of the prime-time characters were males, men were more likely to be shown in the workforce, women were more likely to be shown as homemakers and in romantic roles, men were more likely to appear in higher-status jobs and in a greater diversity of occupations, and men were presented as more aggressive and constructive (Sternglanz & Serbin, 1974).

In the 1980s and 1990s, television networks became more sensitive to how males and females were portrayed on television shows. Consequently, many programs now focus on divorced families, cohabitation, and women in high-status roles. Even with the onset of this type of programming, researchers continue to find that television portrays males as more competent than females (Durkin, 1985). In one investigation, young adolescent girls indicated that television occupations are more extensively stereotyped than real-life occupations (Wroblewski & Huston, 1987).

Gender stereotyping also appears in the print media. In magazine advertising, females are shown more often in advertisements for beauty products, cleaning products, and home appliances. Males are shown more often in advertisements for cars, liquor, and travel. As with television programs, females are now being portrayed as more competent in advertisements than in the past, but advertisers have not yet given them *equal* status with males.

Cognitive Influences   Observation, imitation, rewards, and punishment—these are the mechanisms by which gender develops according to social cognitive theory. Interactions between the child and the social environment are the main keys to gender development in this view. Some critics argue that this explanation pays too little attention to the child's own mind and understanding, and portrays the child as passively acquiring gender roles (Martin & Dinella, 2001; Martin & Ruble, 2004). Two cognitive theories—cognitive developmental theory and gender schema theory—stress that individuals actively construct their gender world:

- The **cognitive developmental theory of gender** states that children's gender typing occurs *after* children think of themselves as boys and girls. Once they consistently conceive of themselves as male or female, children prefer activities, objects, and attitudes consistent with this label.
- **Gender schema theory** states that gender typing emerges as children gradually develop gender schemas of what is gender-appropriate and gender-inappropriate in their culture. A *schema* is a cognitive structure, a network of associations that guides an individual's perceptions. A *gender schema* organizes the world in terms of female and male. Children are internally motivated to perceive the world and to act in accordance with their developing schemas.

Initially proposed by Lawrence Kohlberg (1966), the cognitive developmental theory of gender holds that gender development depends on cognition, and it applies the ideas of Piaget that we discussed in chapter 10. As young children develop the conservation and categorization skills described by Piaget, said Kohlberg, they develop a concept of gender. What's more, they come to see that they will always be male or female. As a result, they begin to select models of their own sex to imitate. The little girl acts as if she is thinking, "I'm a girl, so I want to do girl things. Therefore, the opportunity to do girl things is rewarding."

Notice that in this view gender-typed behavior occurs only after children develop *gender constancy,* which is the understanding that sex remains the same, even though activities, clothing, and hair style might change (Ruble, 2000; Ruble, Martin,

cognitive developmental theory of gender
The theory that children's gender typing occurs after they think of themselves as boys and girls. Once they consistently conceive of themselves as male or female, children prefer activities, objects, and attitudes that are consistent with this label.

gender schema theory   The theory that gender typing emerges as children gradually develop gender schemas of what is gender-appropriate and gender-inappropriate in their culture.

FIGURE 11.5 The Development of Gender Behavior According to the Cognitive Developmental and Gender Schema Theories of Gender Development

Theory	Processes	Emphasis
Cognitive developmental theory	Development of gender constancy, especially around 6 to 7 years of age, when conservation skills develop; after children develop ability to consistently conceive of themselves as male or female, children often organize their world on the basis of gender, such as selecting same-sex models to imitate	Cognitive readiness facilitates gender identity
Gender schema theory	Sociocultural emphasis on gender-based standards and stereotypes; children's attention and behavior are guided by an internal motivation to conform to these gender-based standards and stereotypes, allowing children to interpret the world through a network of gender-organized thoughts	Gender schemas reinforce gender behavior

& Berenbaum, 2006). However, researchers have found that children do not develop gender constancy until they are about 6 or 7 years old. Before this time, most little girls prefer girlish toys and clothes and games, and most little boys prefer boyish toys and games. Thus, contrary to Kohlberg's description of cognitive developmental theory, gender typing does not appear to depend on gender constancy.

Unlike cognitive developmental theory, gender schema theory does not require children to perceive gender constancy before they begin gender typing (see figure 11.5). Instead, gender schema theory states that gender typing occurs when children are ready to encode and organize information along the lines of what is considered appropriate for females and males in their society (Martin & Dinella, 2001; Martin & Halverson, 1981; Martin & Ruble, 2004; Ruble, Martin, & Berenbaum, 2006). Bit by bit, children pick up what is gender-appropriate and gender-inappropriate in their culture, and develop gender schemas that shape how they perceive the world and what they remember. Children are motivated to act in ways that conform with these gender schemas. Thus, gender schemas fuel gender typing.

In sum, cognitive factors contribute to the way children think and act as males and females (Gelman, Taylor, & Nguyen, 2004; Martin & Ruble, 2004; Ruble, Martin, & Berenbaum, 2006). Through biological, social, and cognitive processes, children develop their gender attitudes and behaviors.

Review and Reflect ● LEARNING GOAL 1

 Discuss emotional and personality development in young children.

Review
- What are changes in the self during early childhood?
- What changes take place in emotional development in early childhood?
- What is moral development? What are some key aspects of moral development in young children?
- How can gender, gender role, and gender typing be defined? What are some important gender theories? What are some important biological, social, and cognitive influences on gender development?

Reflect
- Which theory of gender development do you like best? What might an eclectic theoretical view of gender development be like? (You might want to review the discussion of an eclectic theoretical orientation in chapter 2.)

2 WHAT ROLES DO FAMILIES PLAY IN YOUNG CHILDREN'S DEVELOPMENT?

| Parenting | Sibling Relationships and Birth Order | The Changing Family in a Changing Society |

In chapter 8, we learned that attachment is an important aspect of family relationships during infancy. Remember that some experts believe attachment to a caregiver during the first several years of life is the key ingredient in the child's socioemotional development. We also learned that other experts believe secure attachment has been overemphasized and that the child's temperament, other social agents and contexts, and the complexity of the child's social world are also important in determining the child's social competence and well-being. Some developmentalists also emphasize that the infant years have been overdramatized as determinants of life-span development. They argue that social experiences in the early childhood years and later deserve more attention than they have sometimes been given.

In this chapter, we will discuss early childhood experiences beyond attachment. We will explore parenting styles, sibling relationships, and the ways in which children are now experiencing socialization in a greater variety of family structures than at any other point in history.

Parenting

Parenting plays an important role in children's development. Especially important are the parenting styles parents use when they interact with their children.

Parenting Styles
Especially widespread is the view of Diana Baumrind (1971). She believes parents should be neither punitive nor aloof. Rather, they should develop rules for their children and be affectionate with them. She emphasizes four types of parenting styles:

- **Authoritarian parenting** is a restrictive, punitive style in which parents exhort the child to follow their directions and respect their work and effort. The authoritarian parent places firm limits and controls on the child and allows little verbal exchange. For example, an authoritarian parent might say, "You do it my way or else." Authoritarian parents also might spank the child frequently, enforce rules rigidly but not explain them, and show rage toward the child. Children of authoritarian parents are often unhappy, fearful, and anxious about comparing themselves with others, fail to initiate activity, and have weak communication skills.

authoritarian parenting A restrictive punitive style in which parents exhort the child to follow their directions and to respect work and effort. The authoritarian parent places firm limits and controls on the child and allows little verbal exchange. Authoritarian parenting is associated with children's social incompetence.

Calvin and Hobbes

WHAT ASSURANCE DO I HAVE THAT YOUR PARENTING ISN'T SCREWING ME UP?

© 1993 Watterson/Distributed by Universal Press Syndicate

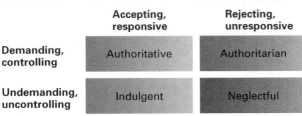

FIGURE 11.6   Classification of Parenting Styles The four types of parenting styles (authoritative, authoritarian, indulgent, and neglectful) involve the dimensions of acceptance and responsiveness, on the one hand, and demand and control on the other. For example, authoritative parenting involves being both accepting/responsive and demanding/controlling.

authoritative parenting A parenting style in which parents encourage their children to be independent but still place limits and controls on their actions. Extensive verbal give-and-take is allowed, and parents are warm and nurturant toward the child. Authoritative parenting is associated with children's social competence.

neglectful parenting A style of parenting in which the parent is very uninvolved in the child's life; it is associated with children's social incompetence, especially a lack of self-control.

indulgent parenting A style of parenting in which parents are highly involved with their children but place few demands or controls on them. Indulgent parenting is associated with children's social incompetence, especially a lack of self-control.

- **Authoritative parenting** encourages children to be independent but still places limits and controls on their actions. Extensive verbal give-and-take is allowed, and parents are warm and nurturant toward the child. An authoritative parent might put his arm around the child in a comforting way and say, "You know you should not have done that. Let's talk about how you can handle the situation better next time." Authoritative parents show pleasure and support of children's constructive behavior. They also expect mature, independent, and age-appropriate behavior of children. Children whose parents are authoritative are often cheerful, self-controlled and self-reliant, achievement-oriented, maintain friendly relations with peers, cooperate with adults, and cope well with stress.
- **Neglectful parenting** is a style in which the parent is very uninvolved in the child's life. Children whose parents are neglectful develop the sense that other aspects of the parents' lives are more important than they are. These children tend to be socially incompetent. Many have poor self-control and don't handle independence well. They frequently have low self-esteem, are immature, and may be alienated from the family. In adolescence, they may show patterns of truancy and delinquency.
- **Indulgent parenting** is a style of parenting in which parents are highly involved with their children but place few demands or controls on them. Such parents let their children do what they want. The result is that the children never learn to control their own behavior and always expect to get their way. Some parents deliberately rear their children in this way because they believe the combination of warm involvement and few restraints will produce a creative, confident child. However, children whose parents are indulgent rarely learn respect for others and have difficulty controlling their behavior. They might be domineering, egocentric, and noncompliant and have difficulties in peer relations.

These four styles of parenting involve combinations of acceptance and responsiveness on the one hand and demand and control on the other. How these dimensions combine to produce authoritarian, authoritative, neglectful, and indulgent parenting is shown in figure 11.6. Research studies continue to document more positive links between authoritative parenting and the well-being of children and adolescents than for the other three types (Slicker & Thornberry, 2003). Why is authoritative parenting likely to be the most effective style? These reasons have been given (Steinberg & Silk, 2002):

1. Authoritative parents establish an appropriate balance between control and autonomy, giving children opportunities to be self-initiative while providing the standards, limits, and guidance that children need (Rueter & Conger, 1995).
2. Authoritative parents are more likely to engage children in verbal give-and-take and allow children to express their views (Kuczynski & Lollis, 2002). This type of family discussion is likely to help children to understand social relationships and what is required for being a socially competent person.
3. The warmth and parental involvement provided by authoritative parents make children more receptive to parental influence (Sim, 2000).

Parenting Styles and Ethnicity   Do the benefits of authoritative parenting transcend the boundaries of ethnicity, socioeconomic status, and household composition? Although occasional exceptions to patterns have been found, the evidence linking authoritative parenting with competence on the part of the child has been found in research across a wide range of ethnic groups, social strata, cultures, and family structures (Steinberg & Silk, 2002).

Nonetheless, researchers have found that in some ethnic groups, aspects of the authoritarian style may be associated with more positive child outcomes than Baumrind predicts (Parke & Buriel, 2006). Aspects of traditional Asian childrearing practices are often continued by Asian American families. In some cases, these practices have been described as authoritarian. However, Ruth Chao (2001, 2005; Chao & Tseng, 2002) argues that the style of parenting used by many Asian American parents is best conceptualized as a type of training in which parents are concerned and involved in their children's lives rather than reflecting strict or authoritarian control. Thus, the parenting style Chao describes, *training,* is based on a type of parental control that is distinct from the more "domineering" control reflected in the authoritarian parenting style. The positive outcomes of the training parenting style in Asian American families occurs in the high academic achievement of Asian American children (Stevenson & Zusho, 2002).

Latino child-rearing practices encourage the development of a self and identity that is embedded in the family and requires respect and obedience (Harwood & others, 2002). As in African American families, there is a high level of cross-generational and coresidence arrangements and assistance (Zinn & Well, 2000).

Researchers have found that African American parents are more likely than non-Latino White parents to use physical punishment (Deater-Deckard & Dodge, 1997). A recent review found that when nonabusive physical punishment was used by African American parents, it was linked with beneficial or neutral outcomes for their children (Horn, Joseph, & Cheng, 2004). One explanation of this finding is the need for African American parents to enforce rules in the dangerous environments in which they are more likely to live (Harrison-Hale, McLoyd, & Smedley, 2004). In this context, requiring obedience to parental authority may be an adaptive strategy to keep children from engaging in antisocial behavior that can have serious consequences for the victim or the perpetrator. As we see next, though, overall, there are concerns about the use of physical punishment in disciplining children.

Punishment and Discipline

For centuries, corporal (physical) punishment, such as spanking, has been considered a necessary and even desirable method of disciplining children (Greven, 1991). Use of corporal punishment is legal in every state in America, and it is estimated that 70 to 90 percent of American parents have spanked their children (Straus, 1991). A recent national survey of U.S. parents with 3- and 4-year-old children found that 26 percent of parents reported spanking their children frequently and 67 percent of the parents reported yelling at their children frequently (Regaldo & others, 2004). A recent cross-cultural comparison found that individuals in the United States and Canada were among the most favorable toward corporal punishment and remembered it being used by their parents (Curran & others, 2001) (see figure 11.7).

Despite the widespread use of corporal punishment, there have been surprisingly few research studies on physical punishment, and those that have been conducted are correlational (Baumrind, Larzelere, & Cowan, 2002; Benjet & Kazdin, 2003; Kazdin & Benjet, 2003). Clearly, it would be highly unethical to randomly assign parents to either spank or not spank their children in an experimental study. Recall that cause and effect cannot be determined in a correlational study. In one correlational study, spanking by parents was linked with children's antisocial behavior, including cheating, telling lies, being mean to others, bullying, getting into fights, and being disobedient (Strauss, Sugarman, & Giles-Sims, 1997). In a recent study of White, African American, and Latino families, spanking by parents predicted an increase in children's problems over time in all three groups (McLoyd & Smith, 2002). However, when parents showed strong emotional support of the child, the link between spanking and child problems was reduced.

A recent research review concluded that corporal punishment by parents is associated with children's higher levels of immediate compliance and aggression among children, and lower levels of moral internalization and mental health (Gershoff,

Parenting is a very important profession, but no test of fitness for it is ever imposed in the interest of children.

—George Bernard Shaw
Irish Playwright, 20th Century

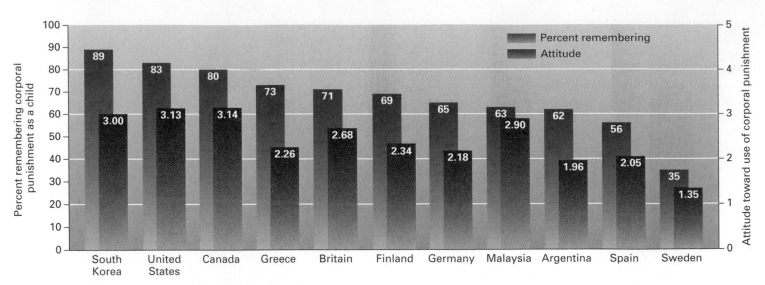

FIGURE 11.7 **Corporal Punishment in Different Countries** A 5-point scale was used to assess attitudes toward corporal punishment with scores closer to 1 indicating an attitude against its use and scores closer to 5 suggesting an attitude for its use.

2002). A longitudinal study found that spanking before age two was related to behavioral problems in middle and late childhood (Slade & Wissow, 2004). Some critics, though, argue that the research evidence is not yet sound enough to warrant a blanket injunction against corporal punishment, especially mild corporal punishment (Baumrind, Larzelere, & Cowan, 2002; Kazdin & Benjet, 2003).

What are some reasons for avoiding spanking or similar punishments? The reasons include:

- When adults yell, scream, or spank, they are presenting children with out-of-control models for handling stressful situations. Children may imitate this aggressive, out-of-control behavior (Sim & Ong, 2005).
- Punishment can instill fear, rage, or avoidance. For example, spanking the child may cause the child to avoid being around the parent and fear the parent.
- Punishment tells children what not to do rather than what to do. Children should be given feedback, such as "Why don't you try this?"
- Punishment can be abusive. When parents discipline their children, they might not intend to be abusive but become so aroused when they are punishing the child that they become abusive (Ateah, 2005; Baumrind, Larzelere, & Cowan, 2002).

Because of reasons such as these, Sweden passed a law in 1979 forbidding parents to physically punish (spank or slap, for example) children. Since the law was enacted, youth rates of delinquency, alcohol abuse, rape, and suicide have dropped in Sweden (Durrant, 2000). These improvements may have occurred for other reasons, such as changing attitudes and opportunities for youth. Nonetheless, the Swedish experience suggests that physical punishment of children may be unnecessary. Other countries that have passed antispanking laws include Finland (1984), Denmark (1986), Norway (1987), Austria (1989), Cyprus (1994), Latvia (1998), Croatia (1999), Germany (2000), and Israel (2000).

Most child psychologists recommend reasoning with the child, especially explaining the consequences of the child's actions for others, as the best way to handle children's misbehaviors. Time out, in which the child is removed from a setting where the child experiences positive reinforcement, can also be effective. For example, when the child has misbehaved, a parent might take away TV viewing for a specified period of time.

Child Abuse   Unfortunately, punishment sometimes leads to the abuse of infants and children (Sabol, Coulton, & Polousky, 2004). In 2002, approximately 896,000 U.S. children were found to be victims of child abuse (U.S. Department of Health and Human Services, 2004). Eighty-four percent of these children were abused by a parent or parents. Laws in many states now require doctors and teachers to report suspected cases of child abuse.

Many of us have difficulty understanding parents who abuse or neglect their children. Our response is often outrage and anger at the parent. This outrage focuses attention on parents as bad, sick, monstrous, sadistic individuals who cause their children to suffer. Experts on child abuse believe that this view is too simple and deflects attention away from the social context of the abuse and the parents' coping skills. Child abuse is a diverse condition, is usually mild to moderate in severity, and it is only partially caused by the parent's personality characteristics (Azar, 2002; Field, 2000). Most often, the abuser is not a raging, uncontrolled physical abuser but an overwhelmed single mother in poverty who neglects the child.

Whereas the public and many professionals use the term *child abuse* to refer to both abuse and neglect, developmentalists increasingly use the term *child maltreatment* (Cicchetti & Blender, 2004; Cicchetti & Toth, 2005, 2006; Kotch, 2003). This term does not have quite the emotional impact of the term *abuse* and acknowledges that maltreatment includes diverse conditions.

> *C*hild maltreatment involves grossly inadequate and destructive aspects of parenting.
>
> —Dante Cicchetti
> *Contemporary Developmental Psychologist, University of Rochester*

Types of Child Maltreatment   The four main types of child maltreatment are physical abuse, child neglect, sexual abuse, and emotional abuse (National Clearinghouse on Child Abuse and Neglect, 2002, 2004):

- *Physical abuse* is characterized by the infliction of physical injury as a result of punching, beating, kicking, biting, burning, shaking, or otherwise harming a child. The parent or other person may not have intended to hurt the child; the injury may have resulted from excessive physical punishment (Hornor, 2005; Maguire & others, 2005).
- *Child neglect* is characterized by failure to provide for the child's basic needs (Dubowitz, Pitts, & Black, 2004; Golden & others, 2003). Neglect can be physical, educational, or emotional:
  Physical neglect includes refusal of, or delay in, seeking health care; abandonment; expulsion from the home or refusal to allow a runaway to return home; and inadequate supervision.
  Educational neglect involves the allowance of chronic truancy, failure to enroll a child of mandatory school age in school, and failure to attend to a special education need.
  Emotional neglect includes such actions as marked inattention to the child's needs for affection; refusal of or failure to provide necessary psychological care; spouse abuse in the child's presence; and permission of drug or alcohol use by the child.
- *Sexual abuse* includes fondling a child's genitals, intercourse, incest, rape, sodomy, exhibitionism, and commercial exploitation through prostitution or the production of pornographic materials. Many experts believe that sexual abuse is the most underreported type of child maltreatment because of the secrecy or "conspiracy of silence" that so often characterizes sexual abuse cases (Hobbins, 2004; Jones & Worthington, 2005; London, Bruck, & Ceci, 2005).
- *Emotional abuse (psychological/verbal abuse/mental injury)* includes acts or omissions by parents or other caregivers that have caused, or could cause, serious behavioral, cognitive, or emotional problems (Gelles & Cavanaugh, 2005). In some cases of emotional abuse that warrant intervention, the child's behavior and condition do not reveal that the child has been harmed. For example, parents or others may use unusual types of punishment, such as confining a child in a dark closet. Less severe acts, such as frequent belittling and rejection of the child, are

www.mhhe.com/santrockc9

National Clearinghouse on Child Abuse Prevention Network

often difficult to prove and make it difficult for child protective services to intervene.

Although any of these forms of child maltreatment may be found separately, they often occur in combination. Emotional abuse is almost always present when other forms are identified.

Warning Signs for Abuse   As previously mentioned, many states now mandate that certain professionals, such as physicians, therapists, teachers, and child-care workers, must report suspected child abuse to social services or to various law enforcement agencies. The following signs may indicate a child is being abused (National Clearinghouse on Child Abuse and Neglect, 2005):

- A pattern of injuries with questionable and/or inconsistent explanations, numerous bruises or welts, fear of going home
- Age-inappropriate sexual knowledge, age-inappropriate sexual play with toys or with other children
- Poor hygiene, food hoarding, or stealing
- Behavioral extremes from overly aggressive to overly passive

Keeping children safe from child abuse is a shared responsibility. Becoming familiar with these warning signs is an important first step in getting help for maltreated children and their families.

The Context of Abuse   Researchers have found that no single factor causes child maltreatment (Cicchetti & Toth, 2005, 2006). A combination of factors, including the culture, family, and development, likely contribute to child maltreatment.

The extensive violence that takes place in American culture is reflected in the occurrence of violence in the family (Azar, 2002). A regular diet of violence appears on television screens, and parents often resort to power assertion as a disciplinary technique. In China, where physical punishment is rarely used to discipline children, the incidence of child abuse is reported to be very low.

Other aspects of the culture may be linked to abuse. In the United States, many abusing parents report that they do not have sufficient resources or help from others. This may be a realistic evaluation of the situation of many low-income families.

The family itself is obviously a key part of the context of abuse. The interactions of all family members need to be considered, regardless of who performs the violent acts against the child (Kim & Cicchetti, 2004; Margolin, 1994). For example, even though the father may be the one who physically abuses the child, contributions by the mother, the child, and siblings also should be evaluated.

The parents' personal history and beliefs have also been linked to abuse. Many parents who abuse their children come from families in which physical punishment was used. These parents view physical punishment as a legitimate way of controlling the child's behavior.

Were parents who abuse children abused by their own parents? About one-third of parents who were abused themselves when they were young abuse their own children (Cicchetti & Toth, 2005, 2006). Thus, some, but not a majority, of parents are locked into an intergenerational transmission of abuse (Dixon, Browne, & Hamilton-Giachritsis, 2005; Leifer & others, 2004). Mothers who break out of the intergenerational transmission of abuse often have at least one warm, caring adult in their background; have a close, positive marital relationship; and have received therapy (Egeland, Jacobvitz, & Sroufe, 1988).

Developmental Consequences of Abuse   Among the developmental consequences of child maltreatment are poor emotion regulation, attachment problems, problems in peer relations, difficulty in adapting to school, and other psychological problems (Azar, 2002; Cicchetti & Toth, 2005, 2006). Maltreated infants may show excessive negative affect (such as irritability and crying) or they may display blunted positive affect (rarely smiling or laughing). When younger children are maltreated they often show insecure attachment patterns in their social relationships later in development (Cicchetti & Toth, 2005). Maltreated children appear to be poorly equipped to develop successful peer relations. They tend to be overly aggressive with peers or avoid interacting with peers (Bolger & Patterson, 2001). Abused and neglected children are at risk for academic problems (Cicchetti & Toth, 2005, 2006).

Being physically abused has been linked with children's anxiety, personality problems, depression, suicide attempts, conduct disorder, and delinquency (Danielson & others, 2005; Malmgren & Meisel, 2004; Zielinski & others, 2003). Later, during the adult years, maltreated children often have difficulty in establishing and maintaining healthy intimate relationships (Colman & Widom, 2004). As adults, maltreated children also show increased violence toward other adults, dating partners, and marital partners, as well as increased substance abuse, anxiety, and depression (Sachs-Ericsson & others, 2005; Shea & others, 2005). In sum, maltreated children are at risk for developing a wide range of problems and disorders (Arias, 2004; Haugaard & Hazan, 2004).

An important strategy is to prevent child maltreatment (Cicchetti & Toth, 2005, 2006; Lyons, Henly, & Schuerman, 2005). In one recent study of maltreating mothers and their 1-year-olds, two treatments were effective in reducing child maltreatment: (1) home visitation that emphasized improved parenting, coping with stress, and increasing support for the mother, and (2) parent-infant psychotherapy that focused on improving maternal-infant attachment (Cicchetti, Toth, & Rogosch, 2005).

Coparenting

A dramatic increase in research on *coparenting* has occurred in the last two decades. The theme of this research is that poor coordination between parents, undermining of the other parent, lack of cooperation and warmth, and disconnection by one parent are conditions that place children at risk for problems (McHale, Kuersten-Hogan, & Rao, 2004; McHale & others, 2002; van Egeren & Hawkins, 2004). By contrast, parental cooperation and warmth are linked with children's prosocial behavior and competence in peer relations. For example, in one study, 4-year-old children from families characterized by low levels of mutuality and support in coparenting were more likely than their classmates to show difficulties in social adjustment on the playground (McHale, Johnson, & Sinclair, 1999).

Good Parenting Takes Time and Effort

In U.S. society today, an unfortunate theme is that parenting can be done quickly, with little or no inconvenience (Bornstein, 2006; Bradley & Corwyn, 2004; Kalil & DeLeire, 2004; Powell, 2006; Sroufe, 2000). One example is the practice of playing Mozart CDs in the hope that they will enrich infants' and young children's brains. One-minute bedtime stories are being marketed successfully for parents to read to their children (Walsh, 2000). Most of these are brief summaries of longer stories. There are one-minute bedtime bear books, puppy books, and so on. These parents know it is good to read to their children, but they don't want to spend a lot of time doing it.

Judith Harris' (1998) book *The Nurture Assumption* (which states that heredity and peer relations are the key factors in children's development) fits into this theme that parents don't need to spend much time with their children. Why did it become so popular? Perhaps in part because it made people who don't spend much time with their children feel less guilty.

What is wrong with these quick-fix approaches to parenting? Good parenting takes a lot of time and a lot of effort (Hoghugi & Long, 2004; Powell, 2005; Waldfogel, 2004). You can't do it in a minute here and a minute there. You can't do it with CDs. Parents who do not spend enough time with their children or who have problems in child rearing can benefit from counseling and therapy. To read about the work of marriage and family counselor Darla Botkin, see the Careers in Child Development profile.

www.mhhe.com/santrockc9

Parenting

CAREERS in CHILD DEVELOPMENT

Darla Botkin
Marriage and Family Therapist

Darla Botkin is a marriage and family therapist who teaches, conducts research, and engages in therapy in the area of marriage and family therapy. She is on the faculty of the University of Kentucky. She obtained a bachelor's degree in elementary education with a concentration in special education and then went on to receive a master's degree in early childhood education. She spent the next six years working with children and their families in a variety of settings, including child care, elementary school, and Head Start. These experiences led Botkin to recognize the interdependence of the developmental settings that children and their parents experience (such as home, school, and work). She returned to graduate school and obtained a Ph.D. in family studies from the University of Tennessee. She then became a faculty member in the Family Studies program at the University of Kentucky. Completing further coursework and clinical training in marriage and family therapy, she became licensed as a marriage and family therapist in the state of Kentucky and an Approved Supervisor with the American Association for Marriage and Family Therapy.

Botkin's current interests include (1) working with young children in family therapy and (2) the use of play in clinical, educational, and business settings.

Darla Botkin (*left*), conducting a family therapy session.

Sibling Relationships and Birth Order

What are sibling relationships like? How extensively does birth order influence behavior?

Sibling Relationships Any of you who have grown up with siblings probably have a rich memory of aggressive, hostile interchanges. But sibling relationships also have many pleasant, caring moments (Zukow-Goldring, 2002). Children's sibling relationships include helping, sharing, teaching, fighting, and playing. Children can act as emotional supports, rivals, and communication partners (Carlson, 1995). More than 80 percent of American children have one or more siblings (brothers or sisters). By virtue of having a sibling, children may be treated differently by their parents (Brody, 2004). Extensive sibling conflict is linked to poor adjustment outcomes (Bank, Burraston, & Snyder, 2004).

However, because there are so many possible sibling combinations, it is difficult to generalize about many aspects of sibling influences. Among the factors to consider are the number of siblings, the ages of siblings, birth order, age spacing, the sex of siblings, and whether sibling relationships are different from parent-child relationships (Teti, 2002).

Birth Order Birth order is a special interest of sibling researchers. When differences in birth order are found, they usually are explained by variations in interactions with parents and siblings associated with the unique experiences of being in a particular position in the family. This is especially true in the case of the firstborn child (Teti & others, 1993). Parents have higher expectations for firstborn children than for later-born children. They put more pressure on them for achievement and responsibility. They also interfere more with their activities (Rothbart, 1971).

Given the differences in family dynamics involved in birth order, it is not surprising that firstborns and later-borns have different characteristics (Rodgers, 2000; Zajonc, 2001). Firstborn children are more adult-oriented, helpful, conforming, anxious, and self-controlled than their siblings. Parents give more attention to firstborns and this is related to firstborns' nurturant behavior (Stanhope & Corter, 1993). Parental demands and high standards established for firstborns result in these children's excelling in academic and professional endeavors. Firstborns are overrepresented in *Who's Who* and among Rhodes scholars, for example. However, some of the same pressures placed on firstborns for high achievement may be the reason they also have more guilt, anxiety, and difficulty in coping with stressful situations, as well as higher admission to child guidance clinics.

What is the only child like? The popular conception is that the only child is a "spoiled brat," with such undesirable characteristics as dependency, lack of self-control, and self-centered behavior. But researchers present a more positive portrayal of the only child, who often is achievement-oriented and displays a desirable personality, especially in comparison with later-borns and children from large families (Falbo & Poston, 1993; Jiao, Ji, & Jing, 1996).

Keep in mind, though, that birth order by itself often is not a good predictor of behavior. When factors such as age spacing, sex of the siblings, heredity, temperament, parenting styles, peer influences, school influences, sociocultural factors, and so forth are taken into account, they often are more important in determining a child's behavior than birth order.

The Changing Family in a Changing Society

More children than ever before are growing up in diverse family structures. Many mothers spend the greatest part of their day away from their children, even their infants. More than one of every two mothers with a child under the age of 5 is in the labor force; more than two of every three with a child from 6 to 17 years of age is. And the increasing number of children growing up in single-parent families is staggering. As shown in figure 11.8, the United States has the highest percentage of single-parent families, compared with virtually all other countries.

The one-child family is becoming much more common in China because of the strong motivation to limit the population growth in the People's Republic of China. *In general, what have researchers found the only child to be like?*

Working Parents   Because household operations have become more efficient and family size has decreased in America, it is not certain that when both parents work outside the home, children receive less attention than children in the past whose mothers were not employed. Outside employment—at least for parents with school-age children—might simply be filling time previously taken up by added household burdens and more children. We also cannot assume that, if the mother did not work, the child would benefit from the time freed up by streamlined household operations and smaller families. Mothering does not always have a positive effect on the child. The educated, nonworking mother may overinvest her energies in her children. This can foster an excess of worry and discourage the child's independence. In such situations, the mother may give more parenting than the child can profitably handle.

As Lois Hoffman (1989) commented, maternal employment is a part of modern life. It is not an aberrant aspect of it but a response to other social changes. The growing child's needs require the mother to loosen her hold on the child. This task may be easier for the working woman, whose job is an additional source of identity and self-esteem.

A number of researchers have found no detrimental effects of maternal employment on children's development (Gottfried, Gottfried, & Bathurst, 2002; Hoffman & Youngblade, 1999). However, in specific circumstances, work can produce positive or negative effects on parenting (Crouter & McHale, 2005). In some families, work-related stress can spill over and harm parenting. In others, a greater sense of overall well-being produced by work can lead to more positive parenting.

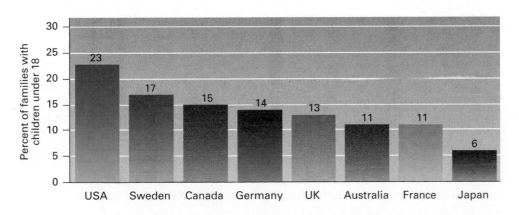

FIGURE 11.8 Single-Parent Families in Different Countries

Further, researchers are consistently finding when a child's mother works in the first year of life it can have a negative effect on the child's later development (Belsky & Eggebeen, 1991; Hill & others, 2001). For example, a recent major longitudinal study found that the 3-year-old children of mothers who went to work before the children were 9 months old had poorer cognitive outcomes than 3-year-old children who had stayed at home with their mothers in the first nine months of the child's life (Brooks-Gunn, Han, & Waldfogel, 2002). The negative effects of working mothers were less pronounced when the mothers worked less than 30 hours a week, the mothers were more sensitive (responsive and comforting) in their caregiving, and the child care the children received outside the home was higher in quality. Thus, when mothers do go back to work in the infant's first year of life, it clearly is important that they consider how many hours they are going to work, be sensitive in their caregiving, and get the best child care they can afford.

Divorced Families   The U.S. divorce rate increased dramatically in the 1960s and 1970s but has declined since the 1980s (Amato, 2005). Many other countries around the world have also experienced significant changes in their divorce rate. For example, Japan's divorce rate increased in the 1990s (Ministry of Health, Education, and Welfare, 2002). However, the U.S. divorce rate is still much higher than Japan's and higher than in most other countries as well. It is estimated that 40 percent of children born to married parents will experience their parents' divorce (Hetherington & Stanley-Hagan, 2002).

Let's explore some questions regarding children's development in divorced families (Hetherington, 2000; Hetherington & Kelly, 2002; Hetherington & Stanley-Hagan, 2002).

- ***Are children better adjusted in intact, never-divorced families than in divorced families?*** Most researchers agree that children from divorced families show poorer adjustment than their counterparts in nondivorced families (Amato & Keith, 1991; Hetherington & Stanley-Hagan, 2002; Wallerstein & Johnson-Reitz, 2004) (see figure 11.9). Those that have experienced multiple divorces are at greater risk. Children and adolescents in divorced families are more likely than those from nondivorced families to have academic problems, to show externalized problems (such as acting out and delinquency) and internalized problems (such as anxiety and depression), to be less socially responsible, to have less-competent intimate relationships, to drop out of school, to become sexually active at an earlier age, to take drugs, to associate with antisocial peers, and to have lower self-esteem (Conger & Chao, 1996). Nonetheless, the majority of children in divorced families do not have these problems. The weight of the research evidence underscores that most children competently cope with their parents' divorce.

- ***Should parents stay together for the sake of the children?*** Whether parents should stay in an unhappy or conflicted marriage for the sake of their children is one of the most commonly asked questions about divorce (Harvey & Fine, 2004; Hetherington, 2000; Hetherington & Kelly, 2002). The stresses and disruptions in family relationships associated with an unhappy, conflicted marriage might erode the well-being of the children; if these negative effects can be reduced by the move to a divorced single-parent family, divorce might be advantageous. However, if the diminished resources and increased risks associated with divorce also are accompanied by inept parenting and sustained or increased conflict, not only between the divorced couple but also between parents and the children and siblings, the best choice for the children might be for an unhappy marriage to be retained. These are "ifs," and it is difficult to determine how these will play out when parents either remain together in an acrimonious marriage or become divorced. Note that a high degree of conflict is detrimental to the child's development in both intact and divorced families (Cummings, Braungart-Rieker, DuRocher-Schudlich, 2003; Cummings & Davies, 2002).

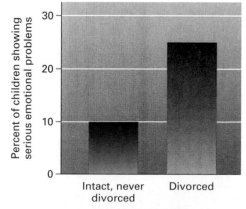

FIGURE 11.9   Divorce and Children's Emotional Problems In Hetherington's analysis, 25 percent of children from divorced families showed serious emotional problems compared with only 10 percent of children from intact, never-divorced families. However, keep in mind that a substantial majority (75 percent) of the children from divorced families did not show serious emotional problems.

- **How much do family processes matter in divorced families?** Family processes matter a great deal in divorced families (Fine & Harvey, 2005). When the divorced parents have a harmonious relationship and use authoritative parenting, children's adjustment improves (Hetherington, 2000; Hetherington, Bridges, & Insabella, 1998; Hetherington & Stanley-Hagan, 2002). Research has shown that a disequilibrium, including diminished parenting skills, occurs in the year following the divorce but that by two years after the divorce restabilization has occurred and parenting skills have improved (Hetherington, 1989). About one-fourth to one-third of children in divorced families, compared with 10 percent in nondivorced families, become disengaged from their families, spending as little time as possible at home and in interaction with family members (Hetherington & Jodl, 1994). This disengagement is higher for boys than for girls. However, if there is a caring adult outside the home, such as a mentor, the disengagement can be a positive solution to a disrupted, conflicted family circumstance. A secure attachment also matters. One recent study found that experiencing a divorce in childhood was associated with insecure attachment in early adulthood (Brockmeyer, Treboux, & Crowall, 2005).
- **What factors are involved in the child's individual risk vulnerability in a divorced family?** Among these factors are the child's adjustment prior to the divorce, personality and temperament, developmental status, gender, custody, and relocation. Children whose parents later divorce show poorer adjustment before the breakup (Amato & Booth, 1996).

  Personality and temperament also play a role in children's adjustment in divorced families. Socially mature and responsible children who show few behavioral problems and have an easy temperament are better able to cope with their parents' divorce. Children with a difficult temperament often have problems coping with their parents' divorce (Hetherington & Stanley-Hagan, 2002).

  Focusing on the child's developmental status involves taking into account the age of onset of the divorce and the time when the child's adjustment is assessed. In most studies, these factors are confounded with length of time since the divorce occurred. Some researchers have found that preschool children whose parents divorce are at greater risk for long-term problems than are older children (Zill, Morrison, & Coiro, 1993). The explanation for this focuses on their inability to realistically appraise the causes and consequences of divorce, their anxiety about the possibility of abandonment, their self-blame for the divorce, and their inability to use extra-familial protective resources. However, problems in adjustment can emerge or increase during adolescence, even if the divorce occurred much earlier.

  Earlier studies reported gender differences in response to divorce, with divorce being more negative for boys than for girls in mother-custody families. However, more recent studies have shown that gender differences are less pronounced and consistent than was previously believed. Some of the inconsistency could be due to the increase in father-custody and joint-custody families and increased involvement of noncustodial fathers, especially in their sons' lives. Female adolescents in divorced families are more likely to drop out of high school and college than are their male counterparts. Male and female adolescents from divorced families are similarly affected in the likelihood of becoming teenage parents, but single parenthood affects girls more adversely (McLanahan & Sandefur, 1994).

  In recent decades, an increasing number of children have lived in father-custody and joint-custody families. What is their adjustment like, compared with the adjustment of children and adolescents in mother-custody families? Although there have been few thorough studies of the topic, a recent review of studies concluded that children benefit from joint custody because it facilitates ongoing positive involvement with both parents (Bauserman, 2003). Some studies have shown that boys adjust better in father-custody families and that girls

As marriage has become a more optional, less permanent institution in contemporary America, children and adolescents are encountering stresses and adaptive challenges associated with their parents' marital transitions.

—E. Mavis Hetherington
Contemporary Psychologist, University of Virginia

Divorce Resources

adjust better in mother-custody families, but other studies have not. In one study, adolescents in father-custody families had higher rates of delinquency, believed to be due to less-competent monitoring by the fathers (Buchanan, Maccoby, & Dornbusch, 1992).

Another factor involved in a child's adjustment in a divorced family is relocation (Kelly & Lamb, 2003). One recent study found that when children whose parents have divorced experience a move away of either of their parents, they show less effective adjustment (Braver, Ellman, & Fabricus, 2003).

- *What role does socioeconomic status play in the lives of children in divorced families?* On the average, custodial mothers lose about 25 to 50 percent of their pre-divorce income, in comparison to an income loss of only 10 percent for custodial fathers (Emery, 1999). This income loss for divorced mothers is typically accompanied by increased workloads, high rates of job instability, and residential moves to less desirable neighborhoods with inferior schools.

We have discussed many aspects of children's development in divorced families. In the Caring for Children interlude, you can read about some strategies for effectively communicating with children about divorce.

CARING FOR CHILDREN

Communicating with Children About Divorce

Ellen Galinsky and Judy David (1988) developed a number of guidelines for communicating with young children about divorce.

Explaining the Separation

As soon as the daily activities in the home make it obvious that one parent is leaving, tell the children. If possible, both parents should be present when the children are made aware of the coming separation. The reasons for the separation are very difficult for young children to understand. No matter what parents tell children, children can find reasons to argue against the separation. A child may say something like "If you don't love each other anymore, you need to start trying harder." One set of parents told their 4-year-old, "We both love you. We will both always love you and take care of you, but we aren't going to live in the same house anymore. Daddy is moving to an apartment near the stores where we shop." It is extremely important for parents to tell the children who will take care of them and to describe the specific arrangements for seeing the other parent.

Explaining That the Separation Is Not the Child's Fault

Young children often believe their parents' separation or divorce is their own fault. Therefore, it is important to tell children that they are not the cause of the separation. Parents need to repeat this a number of times.

Explaining That It May Take Time to Feel Better

It is helpful to tell young children that it's normal to not feel good about what is happening, and that lots of other children feel this way when their parents separate. It is also okay for divorced parents to share some of their emotions with children, by saying something like "I'm having a hard time since the separation, just like you, but I know it's going to get better after a while." Such statements are best kept brief and should not criticize the other parent.

Keeping the Door Open for Further Discussion

Tell your children that, anytime they want to talk about the separation, to come to you. It is healthy for children to get out their pent-up emotions in discussions with their parents and to learn that the parents are willing to listen to their feelings and fears.

Providing as Much Continuity as Possible

The less children's worlds are disrupted by the separation, the easier their transition to a single-parent family will be. This means maintaining as much as possible the rules already in place. Children need parents who care enough to not only give them warmth and nurturance but also set reasonable limits. If the custodial parent has to move to a new home, it is important to preserve as much of what is familiar to the child as possible. In one family, the child helped arrange her new room exactly as it had been prior to the divorce. If children must leave friends behind, parents should help the children stay in touch by phone or by letter. Keeping children busy and involved in the new setting can also keep their minds off the stressful thoughts about the separation.

Providing Support for Your Children and Yourself

After a divorce or separation, parents are as important to children as before the divorce or separation. Divorced parents need to provide children with as much support as possible. Parents function best when other people are available to give them support as adults and as parents. They can find people who provide practical help and with whom they can talk about their problems. Too often, divorced parents criticize themselves and say they feel that they don't deserve help. One divorced mother commented, "I've made a mess of my life. I don't deserve anybody's help." However, seeking out others for support and feedback about problems can make the transition to a single-parent family more bearable.

Cultural, Ethnic, and Socioeconomic Variations in Families   Parenting can be influenced by culture, ethnicity, and socioeconomic status. In Bronfenbrenner's theory, these influences are described as part of the macrosystem.

Cross-Cultural Studies   Cultures vary on a number of issues involving families, such as what the father's role in the family should be, the extent to which support systems are available to families, and the ways in which children should be disciplined (Harkness & Super, 2002). Although there are cross-cultural variations in parenting (Whiting & Edwards, 1988), in one study of parenting behavior in 186 cultures around the world, the most common pattern was a warm and controlling style, one that was neither permissive nor restrictive (Rohner & Rohner, 1981). The investigators commented that the majority of cultures have discovered, over many centuries, a "truth" that only recently emerged in the Western world—namely, that children's healthy social development is most effectively promoted by love and at least some moderate parental control.

Nonetheless, in some countries, authoritarian parenting continues to be widely practiced. In the Arab world, families today are still very authoritarian and dominated by the father's rule (Booth, 2002). In Arab countries, children are taught strict codes of conduct and family loyalty.

In many countries, there are trends toward greater family mobility, migration to urban areas, family members working in distant cities or countries, smaller families, fewer extended-family households, and increases in the mother's employment (Brown & Larson, 2002; Larson, Brown, & Mortimer, 2003). These trends can change the resources available to children. For example, in the future there may be fewer extended-family members available and decreased support and guidance for children. Also, smaller families may produce more openness and communication between parents and children.

Ethnicity   What are some variations in the families of ethnic groups in the United States? How does acculturation affect family influences on children's development?

Families within different ethnic groups in the United States differ in their size, structure, composition, reliance on kinships networks, and levels of income and

What are some characteristics of families within different ethnic groups?

Family Diversity

education (Leyendecker & others, 2005; Parke, 2004; Parke & Buriel, 2006). Large and extended families are more common among minority groups than among the White majority. For example, 19 percent of Latino families have three or more children, compared with 14 percent of African American and 10 percent of White families. African American and Latino children interact more with grandparents, aunts, uncles, cousins, and more-distant relatives than do White children.

Single-parent families are more common among African Americans and Latinos than among White Americans (Weinraub, Horvath, & Gringlas, 2002). In comparison with two-parent households, single parents often have more limited resources of time, money, and energy (Gyamfi, Brooks-Gunn, & Jackson, 2001). Ethnic minority parents also are less educated and more likely to live in low-income circumstances than their White counterparts. Still, many impoverished ethnic minority families manage to find ways to raise competent children (Coll & Pachter, 2002).

Some aspects of home life can help protect ethnic minority children from injustice. The community and the family can filter out destructive racist messages, and parents can present alternative frames of reference to those presented by the majority. The extended family also can serve as an important buffer to stress (McAdoo, 2002).

Socioeconomic Status In America and most Western cultures, differences have been found in child rearing among different socioeconomic-status (SES) groups (Hoff, Laursen, & Tardif, 2002, p. 246):

- "Lower-SES parents (1) are more concerned that their children conform to society's expectations, (2) create a home atmosphere in which it is clear that parents have authority over children," (3) use physical punishment more in disciplining their children, and (4) are more directive and less conversational with their children.
- "Higher-SES parents (1) are more concerned with developing children's initiative" and delay of gratification, (2) "create a home atmosphere in which children are more nearly equal participants and in which rules are discussed as opposed to being laid down" in an authoritarian manner, (3) are less likely to use physical punishment, and (4) "are less directive and more conversational" with their children.

There also are socioeconomic differences in the way that parents think about education (Hoff, Laursen, & Tardif, 2002; Magnuson & Duncan, 2002). Middle- and upper-income parents more often think of education as something that should be mutually encouraged by parents and teachers. By contrast, low-income parents are more likely to view education as the teacher's job. Thus, increased school-family linkages especially can benefit students from low-income families.

Review and Reflect • LEARNING GOAL 2

 Explain how families can influence young children's development.

Review
- What aspects of parenting are linked with young children's development?
- How are sibling relationships and birth order related to young children's development?
- How is children's development affected when both parents work or when they become divorced? How are cultural, ethnic, and socioeconomic variations in families linked with young children's development?

Reflect
- Which style of parenting did your mother and father use in rearing you? What effects do you think their parenting styles had on your development?

3) HOW ARE PEER RELATIONS, PLAY, AND TELEVISION INVOLVED IN YOUNG CHILDREN'S DEVELOPMENT?

Peer Relations	Play	Television

The family is an important social context for children's development. However, children's development also is strongly influenced by what goes on in other social contexts, such as peer relations, play, and television.

Peer Relations

Peers are individuals of about the same age or maturity level. Same-age peer interaction fills a unique role in our culture (Hartup, 1983). Even if schools were not graded by age and children were left alone to determine the composition of their own societies, they would form peer groups. Peer groups provide a source of information and comparison about the world outside the family. Children receive feedback about their abilities from their peer group. Children evaluate what they do in terms of whether it is better than, as good as, or worse than what other children do. It is hard to do this at home because siblings are usually older or younger.

Are peers necessary for development? When peer monkeys who have been reared together are separated, they become depressed and regress socially (Suomi, Harlow, & Domek, 1970). The human development literature contains a classic example of the importance of peers in social development. Anna Freud (Freud & Dann, 1951) studied six children from different families who banded together after their parents were killed in World War II. Intensive peer attachment was observed; the children formed a tightly knit group, dependent on one another and aloof with outsiders. Even though deprived of parental care, they became neither delinquent nor psychotic.

Both Jean Piaget (1932) and Harry Stack Sullivan (1953) stressed that children learn reciprocity through interaction with their peers. Children explore the meanings of fairness and justice by working through disagreements with peers. They also learn to be keen observers of peers' interests and perspectives in order to smoothly integrate themselves into ongoing peer activities.

Of course, peer influences can be negative as well as positive (Brown, 2004; Bukowski & Adams, 2005; Ladd, 2006; McHale, Dariotis, & Kawh, 2003; Rubin, Bukowski, & Parker, 2006). Being rejected or overlooked by peers leads some children to feel lonely or hostile. Further, rejection and neglect by peers are related to an individual's subsequent mental health and criminal problems. Withdrawn children who are rejected by peers or victimized and lonely are at risk for depression. Children who are aggressive with their peers are at risk for developing a number of problems, including delinquency and dropping out of school. Peers can also undermine parental values and control (Masten, 2005).

What are some developmental aspects of peer relations in early childhood? Around the age of 3, children already prefer to spend time with same-sex rather than opposite-sex playmates, and this preference increases in early childhood. During these same years the frequency of peer interaction, both positive and negative, picks up considerably (Hartup, 1983). Although aggressive interaction and rough-and-tumble play increase, the proportion of aggressive exchanges, compared to friendly exchanges, decreases. Many preschool children spend considerable time in peer interaction just conversing with playmates about such matters as "negotiating roles and rules in play, arguing, and agreeing" (Rubin, Bukowski, & Parker, 2006).

Keep in mind that the influences of peer experiences vary according to the way peer experience is measured, the outcomes specified, and the developmental

peers Individuals of about the same age or maturity level.

trajectories traversed (Hartup, 1999). For example, "peer group" might refer to acquaintances, clique, neighborhood associates, a friendship network, or an activity group (Brown, 1999). We will have much more to say about peer relations in chapter 14, "Socioemotional Development in Middle and Late Childhood."

Play

An extensive amount of peer interaction during childhood involves play; however, social play is but one type of play. **Play** is a pleasurable activity that is engaged in for its own sake.

Functions of Play
Play is essential to a young child's health. Play increases affiliation with peers, releases tension, advances cognitive development, and increases exploration. Play increases the probability that children will converse and interact with each other. During this interaction, children practice the roles they will assume later in life.

Many theorists have emphasized various functions of play. According to Freud and Erikson, play helps children master anxieties and conflicts. In play, children work off excess physical energy and release pent-up tensions. They may feel less threatened and be more likely to express their feelings during play. Thus, therapists use **play therapy** as a means of letting children work off frustrations while analyzing their conflicts and coping methods (Drewes, Carey, & Schaefer, 2003).

According to Piaget (1962), play reflects children's cognitive development but also advances that development. During play, children practice their competencies and skills in a relaxed, pleasurable way. For example, children who have just learned to add or multiply begin to play with numbers in different ways as they perfect these operations, laughing as they do so.

Vygotsky (1962) also believed that play is an excellent setting for cognitive development. He was especially interested in the symbolic and make-believe aspects of play, as when a child rides a stick as if it were a horse. For young children, the imaginary situation is real. Parents should encourage such imaginary play, which advances the child's cognitive development, especially creative thought.

Daniel Berlyne (1960) described play as exciting and pleasurable because it satisfies the exploratory drive. This drive involves curiosity and a desire for information about something new or unusual. Through play, children can safely explore and seek out new information. Play encourages exploratory behavior by offering the possibilities of novelty, complexity, uncertainty, surprise, and incongruity.

Parten's Classic Study of Play
Many years ago, Mildred Parten (1932) developed an elaborate classification of children's play. Based on observations of children in free play at nursery school, Parten arrived at these play categories:

- **Unoccupied play** is not play as it is commonly understood. The child may stand in one spot or perform random movements that do not seem to have a goal. In most nursery schools, unoccupied play is less frequent than other forms of play.
- **Solitary play** happens when the child plays alone, independently of others. The child seems engrossed in the activity. Two- and 3-year-olds engage more frequently in solitary play than older preschoolers do.
- **Onlooker play** takes place when the child watches other children play. The child may talk with other children and ask questions but does not play with them. The child's active interest in other children's play distinguishes onlooker play from unoccupied play.
- **Parallel play** occurs when the child plays separately from others but with toys like those the others are using or in a manner that mimics their play. The older children are, the less frequently they engage in parallel play. However, even older preschool children engage in parallel play quite often.

And that park grew up with me; that small world widened as I learned its secrets and boundaries, as I discovered new refuges in the woods and jungles: hidden homes and lairs for the multitudes of imagination, for cowboys and Indians.... I used to dawdle on half holidays along the bent and Devon-facing seashore, hoping for gold watches or the skull of a sheep or a message in a bottle to be washed up with the tide.

—Dylan Thomas
Welsh Poet, 20th Century

---

play A pleasurable activity that is engaged in for its own sake.

play therapy Therapy that lets children work off frustrations while therapists analyze their conflicts and coping methods.

unoccupied play Play in which the child is not engaging in play as it is commonly understood and might stand in one spot or perform random movements that do not seem to have a goal.

solitary play Play in which the child plays alone, independently of others.

onlooker play Play in which the child watches other children play.

parallel play Play in which the child plays separately from others, but with toys like those the others are using or in a manner that mimics their play.

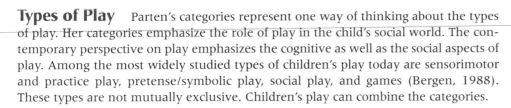

Mildred Parten classified play into six categories. *Study this photograph. Which of Parten's categories are reflected in the behavior of the children?*

- **Associative play** involves social interaction with little or no organization. During associative play, children seem more interested in each other than in what they are doing.
- **Cooperative play** consists of social interaction in a group with a sense of group identity and organized activity. Formal games, competitions, and groups formed by the teacher for doing things together are examples of cooperative play. Cooperative play is the prototype for the games of middle childhood. Little cooperative play is seen during the preschool years.

www.mhhe.com/santrockc9

Play

Types of Play   Parten's categories represent one way of thinking about the types of play. Her categories emphasize the role of play in the child's social world. The contemporary perspective on play emphasizes the cognitive as well as the social aspects of play. Among the most widely studied types of children's play today are sensorimotor and practice play, pretense/symbolic play, social play, and games (Bergen, 1988). These types are not mutually exclusive. Children's play can combine the categories.

Sensorimotor and Practice Play   **Sensorimotor play** is behavior by infants to derive pleasure from exercising their sensorimotor schemes. It develops along with sensorimotor thought, which we discussed in chapter 6. Infants initially engage in sensorimotor play in the second quarter of the first year of life. At 9 months of age, infants begin to select novel objects for exploration and play, especially those that respond, such as toys that make noise or bounce. At 12 months of age, infants enjoy making things work and exploring cause and effect.

    Practice play involves the repetition of behavior when new skills are being learned or when mastery and coordination of skills are required for games or sports. Sensorimotor play, which often involves practice play, is primarily confined to infancy, whereas practice play occurs throughout life. During the preschool years, children often engage in play that involves practicing various skills. Although practice play declines in the elementary school years, practice play activities such as running, jumping, sliding, twirling, and throwing balls or other objects are still frequent.

Pretense/Symbolic Play   **Pretense/symbolic play** occurs when the child transforms the physical environment into a symbol. Between 9 and 30 months of age, children increase their use of objects in symbolic play. They transform objects—substituting them for other objects and acting toward them as if they were these other objects. For example, a preschool child treats a table as if it were a car and says, "I'm fixing the car," as he grabs a leg of the table.

associative play Play that involves social interaction with little or no organization.

cooperative play Play that involves social interaction in a group with a sense of group identity and organized activity.

sensorimotor play Behavior by infants to derive pleasure from exercising their sensorimotor schemes.

practice play Play that involves repetition of behavior when new skills are being learned or when mastery and coordination of skills are required for games or sports. Sensorimotor play, which often involves practice play, is primarily confined to infancy, whereas practice play occurs throughout life.

pretense/symbolic play Play that occurs when a child transforms the physical environment into a symbol.

A preschool "superhero" at play. *Which category/type of play does "superhero" play belong?*

Many experts on play consider the preschool years the "golden age" of symbolic/pretense play that is dramatic or sociodramatic (Fein, 1986). This type of make-believe play often appears at about 18 months of age and reaches a peak at 4 to 5 years of age, then gradually declines.

Social Play   **Social play** is play that involves interaction with peers. Parten's categories, described earlier, are oriented toward social play. Social play increases dramatically during the preschool years.

Games   **Games** are activities that are engaged in for pleasure and include rules. They often involve competition. During the preschool years, children may begin to participate in social game play that involves simple rules of reciprocity and turn taking. However, games take on a much stronger role in the lives of elementary school children. In one study, the highest incidence of game playing occurred between 10 and 12 years of age (Eiferman, 1971). After age 12, games decline in popularity (Bergin, 1988).

Television

Few developments in society in the second half of the twentieth century had a greater impact on children than television (Kubey, 2004; Murray, 2000; Roberts, Henriksen, & Foehr, 2004). Many children spend more time in front of the television set than they do with their parents. Although it is only one of the many mass media that affect children's behavior, television is the most influential. The persuasive capabilities of television are staggering (Kotler, Wright, & Huston, 2001). The 20,000 hours of television watched by the time the average American adolescent graduates from high school are greater than the number of hours spent in the classroom.

Television can have a negative influence by taking children away from homework, making them passive learners, teaching them stereotypes, providing them with violent models of aggression, and presenting them with unrealistic views of the world. However, television can have a positive influence on children's development by presenting motivating educational programs, increasing their information about the world beyond their immediate environment, and providing models of prosocial behavior (Clifford, Gunter, & McAleer, 1995; Fisch, 2004).

Just how much television do young children watch? They watch a lot. In the 1990s, children watched an average of 26 hours of television each week, which is more than any other activity except sleep (National Center for Children Exposed to Violence, 2001). As shown in figure 11.10, considerably more children in the United States than their counterparts in other developed countries watch television for long periods. For example, seven times as many 9-year-olds in the United States as their counterparts in Switzerland watch television more than 5 hours a day.

A special concern is the extent to which children are exposed to violence and aggression on television. Up to 80 percent of the prime-time shows include violent acts, including beatings, shootings, and stabbings. The frequency of violence increases on the Saturday morning cartoon shows, which average more than 25 violent acts per hour.

Television, Prosocial Behavior, and Aggression   Television can teach children that it is better to behave in positive, prosocial ways than in negative, antisocial ways (Dorr, Rabin, & Irlin, 2002; Wilson, 2001). Aimee Leifer (1973) demonstrated that television is associated with prosocial behavior in young children. She selected a number of episodes from the television show *Sesame Street* that reflected positive social interchanges. She was especially interested in situations that taught children how to use their social skills. For example, in one interchange, two men were fighting over the amount of space available to them. They gradually began to cooperate and to share the space. Children who watched these episodes copied these behaviors, and in later social situations they applied the prosocial lessons they had learned.

www.mhhe.com/santrock9

Sesame Street

social play Play that involves social interactions with peers.

games Activities engaged in for pleasure, and include rules.

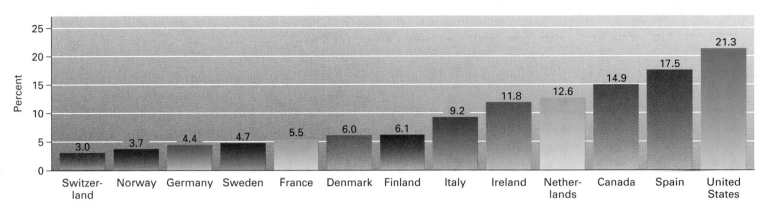

FIGURE 11.10 Percentage of 9-Year-Old Children Who Report Watching More Than Five Hours of Television per Weekday

Unfortunately, there are far fewer prosocial programs on commercial television than programs featuring violence. Attention-grabbing violence attempts to secure the widest possible TV audience and raises a number of questions. For example, what are the effects of TV violence on children's aggression? Does television merely stimulate a child to buy a Star Wars ray gun, or can it trigger an attack on a playmate? When children grow up, can television violence increase the likelihood they will violently attack someone?

In one longitudinal study, the amount of violence viewed on television at age 8 was significantly related to the seriousness of criminal acts performed as an adult (Huesmann, 1986). In another study, exposure to media violence at 6 to 10 years of age was linked with young adult aggressive behavior for both males and females (Huesmann & others, 2003). In yet another study, long-term exposure to television violence was significantly related to the likelihood of aggression in 1,565 12- to 17-year-old boys (Belson, 1978). Boys who watched the most aggression on television were the most likely to commit a violent crime, swear, be aggressive in sports, threaten violence toward another boy, write slogans on walls, or break windows. These studies are *correlational,* so we cannot conclude from them that television violence is *associated with* aggressive behavior. In one experiment, children were randomly assigned to one of two groups: One group watched television shows taken directly from violent Saturday morning cartoon offerings on 11 different days; the second group watched television cartoon shows with all of the violence removed (Steur, Applefield, & Smith, 1971). The children were then observed during play at their preschool. The preschool children who saw the TV cartoon shows with violence kicked, choked, and pushed their playmates more than did the preschool children who watched nonviolent TV cartoon shows. Because the children were randomly assigned to the two conditions (TV cartoons with violence versus nonviolent TV cartoons), we can conclude that exposure to TV violence *caused* the increased aggression in the children in this investigation.

In addition to television violence, there is increased concern about children who play violent video games, especially those that are highly realistic (Vastag, 2004). Electronic games share some characteristics with other forms of audiovisual violence but differ from them in several important ways (Roberts, Henrikson, & Foehr, 2004). One difference is the electronic games' ability to immerse children so deeply that they experience an altered state of consciousness in which rational thought is suspended and arousing aggressive scripts are learned. Another difference is the direct rewards that game players receive ("winning points") for their actions.

Correlational studies indicate that children who extensively play violent electronic games are more aggressive than their counterparts who spend less time playing the games or do not play them at all (Cohen, 1995). Surveys have found that adolescents who frequently play violent electronic games are more likely to engage in delinquent behavior and are rated as more aggressive by their teachers than adolescents who are infrequent players (Anderson & Dill, 2000; Fling & others, 1992). Experiments have not yet been conducted to demonstrate increased aggression subsequent to playing violent videogames, although a recent analysis of research studies concluded that playing violent videogames is linked to aggression in both males and females (Anderson & Bushman, 2001).

A recent panel of leading experts concluded that media violence can have harmful short-term and long-term effects on children (Anderson & others, 2003). The effects are clearest for television but point in the same negative direction for video games. The experts outlined several explanations of how media violence may influence children:

- Children learn social behavior by observation, even though they are often unaware that learning has occurred. And they may imitate what they see.
- Frequent exposure to violence may make aggressive thoughts or social "scripts" more readily available in the child's mind, making it easier to summon aggression-related emotions or behaviors in a given situation.
- Media violence can produce physiological arousal, which may amplify an existing aggressive mood or tendency.
- Repeated exposure to media violence may desensitize a viewer, diminishing the unpleasant physical effects of seeing or thinking about violence.

Some critics have argued that research results do not warrant the conclusion that TV violence causes aggression (Freedman, 1984). But many experts insist that TV violence can cause aggressive or antisocial behavior in children (Anderson & Bushman, 2002; Bushman & Huesmann, 2001; Perse, 2001). Of course, television violence is not the *only* cause of aggression. There is no *one* cause of any social behavior. Aggression, like all other social behaviors, has multiple determinants (Donnerstein, 2001). The link between TV violence and aggression in children is influenced by children's aggressive tendencies and by their attitudes toward violence and monitoring of children's exposure to it.

Television, Cognitive Development, and Achievement

Children bring various cognitive skills and abilities to their television viewing experience (Rabin & Dorr, 1995). Several important cognitive shifts take place between early childhood and middle and late childhood (Wilson, 2001). Preschool children often focus on the most striking perceptual features of a TV program and are likely to have difficulty in distinguishing reality from fantasy in the portrayals. As children enter elementary school, they are better able to link scenes together and draw causal conclusions from narratives. Judgments of reality also become more accurate in older children.

How does television influence children's creativity and mental ability? In general, television has not been shown to influence children's creativity but is negative related to their mental ability (Comstock & Scharrer, 2006). Exposure to aural and printed media does more than television to enhance children's verbal skills, especially expressive language (Beagles-Roos & Gat, 1983; Williams, 1986).

"Mrs. Horton, could you stop by school today?"
© Martha F. Campbell. Reprinted with permission.

The more children watch TV the lower their school achievement is (Comstock & Scharrer, 2006). Why might TV watching be negatively linked to children's achievement? Three possibilities involve interference, displacement, and self-defeating tastes/preferences (Comstock & Scharrer, 2006). In terms of interference, having a television on while doing homework can distract children while they are doing cognitive tasks, such as homework. In terms of displacement, television can take away time and attention from engaging in achievement-related tasks, such as homework, reading, writing, and mathematics. Researchers have found that children's reading achievement is negatively linked with the amount of time they watch TV (Comstock & Scharrer, 2006). In terms of self-defeating tastes and preferences, television attracts children to entertainment, sports, commercials, and other activities that capture their interest more than school achievement. Children who are heavy TV watchers tend to view books as dull and boring (Comstock & Scharrer, 2006).

However, some types of television content—such as educational programming for young children—may enhance achievement. In one longitudinal study, viewing educational programs, such as *Sesame Street* and *Mr. Rogers' Neighborhood*, as preschoolers was related to a number of positive outcomes through high school, including higher grades, reading more books, and enhanced creativity (Anderson & others, 2001) (see figure 11.11). Newer technologies, especially interactive television, hold promise for motivating children to learn and become more exploratory in solving problems (Singer, 1993).

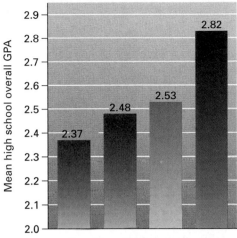

FIGURE 11.11 Educational TV Viewing and High School Grade Point Average for Boys When boys watched more educational television (especially *Sesame Street*) as preschoolers, they had higher grade point averages in high school (Anderson & others, 2001). The graph displays the boys' early TV viewing patterns in quartiles and the means of their grade point averages. The bar on the left is for the lowest 25 percent of boys who viewed educational TV programs, the next bar the next 25 percent, and so on, with the bar on the right for the 25 percent of the boys who watched the most educational TV shows as preschoolers.

Review and Reflect • LEARNING GOAL 3

3 **Describe the role of peers, play, and television in young children's development.**

Review
- How do peers affect young children's development?
- What are some functions, theories, and types of play?
- How does television influence children's development?

Reflect
- What guidelines would you recommend to parents to make television a more positive influence on their children's development? Consider such factors as the child's age, the child's activities other than TV, the parents' patterns of interaction with the children, and types of TV shows.

FIGURE 12.2 Changes in Motor Skills During Middle and Late Childhood

Age in years	Motor skills
6	Children can skip. Children can throw with proper weight shift and step. Girls can throw a small ball 19 feet, boys 34 feet. Girls and boys can vertically jump 7 inches. Girls can perform a standing long jump 33 inches, boys 36 inches. Children are more aware of their hands as tools. Children like to draw, paint, and color. Children can cut, paste paper toys, and sew crudely if needle is threaded. Children enjoy making simple figures in clay. Children can use a knife to spread butter or jam on bread.
7	Children balance on one foot without looking. Children can walk 2-inch-wide balance beams. Children can hop and jump accurately into small squares. Children can participate in jumping-jack exercise. Girls can throw a ball 25 feet, boys 45 feet. Girls can vertically jump 8 inches, boys 9 inches. Girls can perform standing long jump 41 inches, boys 43 inches. Children are able to maintain posture for a longer period of time. Children repeat physical performances to master them. Children brush and comb their hair, usually in an acceptable manner. Children use a table knife for cutting meat.
8	Children can engage in alternate rhythmic hopping in different patterns. Girls can throw a ball 34 feet, boys 59 feet. Girls can vertically jump 9 inches, boys 10 inches. Girls can perform standing long jump 50 inches, boys 55 inches. Grip strength increases. Children can use common tools, such as a hammer. Children can help with routine household tasks, such as dusting and sweeping.
9	Girls can throw a ball 41 feet, boys 71 feet. Girls can vertically jump 10 inches, boys 11 inches. Girls can perform standing long jump 53 inches, boys 57 inches. Perceptual-motor coordination becomes smoother.
10 to 11	Children can judge and intercept pathways of small balls thrown from distance. Girls can throw a small ball 49 feet, boys 94 feet at age 10; girls 58 feet and boys 106 feet at age 11. Girls can vertically jump 10 inches, boys 11 inches at age 10; girls 11 inches and boys 12 inches at age 11. Girls can perform standing long jump 57 inches, boys 61 inches at age 10; girls 62 inches and boys 66 inches at age 11. Children can make useful articles and do easy repair work. Children can cook and sew in small ways. Children can wash and dry their own hair.

colorless sticky film formed from bacteria. Conscientious brushing and flossing significantly reduce the risk of periodontal disease. Many children need orthodontic care for teeth that are not properly aligned. Malocclusion occurs when the teeth of the upper and lower dental arches do not fit together properly when the jaws are closed. Orthodontic treatment for malocclusion, as well as uneven, crowded, or overlapping teeth, is usually most successful when begun toward the end of middle and late childhood or in early adolescence.

Motor Development

During middle and late childhood, children's motor development becomes much smoother and more coordinated than it was in early childhood. For example, only one child in a thousand can hit a tennis ball over the net at the age of 3, yet by the age of 10 or 11 most children can learn to play the sport. Running, climbing, skipping rope, swimming, bicycle riding, and skating are just a few of the many physical skills elementary school children can master. And, when mastered, these skills are a source of great pleasure and accomplishment for children. In gross motor skills involving large muscle activity, boys usually outperform girls.

As children move through the elementary school years, they gain greater control over their bodies and can sit and attend for longer periods of time. However, elementary school children are far from being physically mature, and they need to be active. Elementary school children become more fatigued by long periods of sitting than by running, jumping, or bicycling. Physical action is essential for children to refine their developing skills, such as batting a ball, skipping rope, or balancing on a beam. An important principle of practice for elementary school children, therefore, is that they should be engaged in *active,* rather than passive, activities.

Increased myelination of the central nervous system is reflected in the improvement of fine motor skills during middle and late childhood. Children's hands are used more adroitly as tools. Six-year-olds can hammer, paste, tie shoes, and fasten clothes. By 7 years of age, children's hands have become steadier. At this age, children prefer a pencil to a crayon for printing, reversal of letters is less common, and printing becomes smaller. At 8 to 10 years of age, the hands can be used independently with more ease and precision. Fine motor coordination develops to the point at which children use cursive rather than print words. Letter size becomes smaller and more even. At 10 to 12 years of age, children begin to show manipulative skills similar to the abilities of adults. The complex, intricate, and rapid movements needed to produce fine-quality crafts or to play a difficult piece on a musical instrument can be mastered. Girls usually outperform boys in fine motor skills. A summary of changes in motor skills in middle and late childhood appears in figure 12.2.

Review and Reflect • LEARNING GOAL 1

 Discuss changes in body growth and motor development in middle and late childhood.

Review
- How do skeletal and muscular systems change in middle and late childhood?
- What characterizes tooth development and dental care in middle and late childhood?
- How do children's gross and fine motor skills change in middle and late childhood?

Reflect
- Look at figure 12.2. On which of the motor skills were you especially competent? Not competent? Do you think your motor skills as a child were primarily influenced by your heredity or your environment? Explain.

2 WHAT ARE THE CENTRAL ISSUES IN CHILDREN'S HEALTH?

| Nutrition | | Obesity | | Accidents and Injuries |

| | Exercise and Sports | | Diseases | |

Although we have become a health-conscious nation, many children as well as adults do not practice good health habits. Too much junk food and too much couch-potato behavior describes all too many children. We begin our exploration of children's

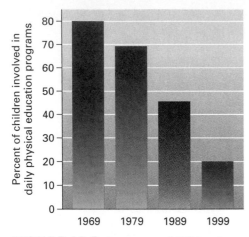

FIGURE 12.3 **Percentage of Children Involved in Daily Physical Education Programs in the United States from 1969 to 1999** There has been a dramatic drop in the percentage of children participating in daily physical education programs in the United States from 80 percent in 1969 to only 20 percent in 1999.

health with nutrition and exercise, then turn to a number of health problems that can emerge.

Nutrition

In the middle and late childhood years, children's average body weight doubles. Children exert considerable energy as they engage in many different motor activities. To support their growth and active lives, children need to consume more food than they did in early childhood. From 1 to 3 years of age, infants and toddlers need to consume 1,300 calories per day on the average. At 4 to 6 years of age, young children need to take in 1,700 calories per day on the average. From 7 to 10 years of age, children need to consume 2,400 calories per day on the average; however, depending on the child's size, the range of recommended calories for 7- to 10-year-olds is 1,650 to 3,300 per day.

Within these calorie ranges, it is important to impress on children the value of a balanced diet to promote their growth. Children usually eat as their families eat, so the quality of their diet often depends largely on their family's pattern of eating. Most children acquire a taste for an increasing variety of food in middle and late childhood. However, with the increased availability of fast-food restaurants and media inducements, too many children fill up on food that has "empty calories" that do not promote effective growth (Giammattei & others, 2003). Many of these empty-calorie foods have a high content of sugar, starch, and excess fat (Slyper, 2004).

Both parents and teachers can help children learn to eat better. In this vein, they can help children learn about the Food Guide Pyramid and what a healthy diet entails.

Children should begin their day by eating a healthy breakfast; according to nutritionists, breakfast should make up about one-fourth of the day's calories. A nutritious breakfast helps children have more energy and be more alert in the morning hours of school. In one study of low-income elementary-school-age children, those who participated in a school breakfast program improved their standardized achievement test scores more and had fewer absences than the children who qualified for the program but did not participate (Meyers & others, 1989).

Exercise and Sports

How much exercise do children get? What are children's sports like?

Exercise   Children are not getting enough exercise (Fitzgibbon & others, 2005; Morgan, 2005). In a 1997 national poll, only 22 percent of children in grades 4 through 12 were physically active for 30 minutes every day of the week (Harris, 1997). Their parents said their children were too busy watching TV, spending time on the computer, or playing video games to exercise much. Boys were more physically active at all ages than girls. In one historical comparison, the percentage of children involved in daily P.E. programs in schools decreased from 80 percent in 1969 to 20 percent in 1999 (Health Management Resources, 2001) (see figure 12.3).

Here are some ways to get children to exercise more:

- Offer more physical activity programs run by volunteers at school facilities.
- Improve physical fitness activities in schools.
- Have children plan community and school activities that really interest them.
- Encourage families to increase their participation in physical activities and encourage parents to help children to exercise more (in the national poll more than 50 percent of the parents engaged in no rigorous physical activities on a regular basis).

Television watching is linked with low activity and obesity in children (Fox, 2004; Graf & others, 2004). A related concern is the dramatic increase in computer use by children. Recent reviews of research have concluded that the total time that children spend in front of a television or computer screen places them at risk for reduced activity and possible weight gain (Caroli & others, 2004; Jordan, 2004). A longitudinal study found that a higher incidence of watching TV in childhood and adolescence was linked with being overweight, being less physically fit, and having higher cholesterol levels at 26 years of age (Hancox, Milne, & Poulton, 2004).

Thus, the more children watch television, the more they are likely to be overweight. No one is quite sure whether this is because children spend their leisure time in front of the television set instead of chasing each other around the neighborhood or because they tend to eat a lot of junk food they see advertised on television.

Some of the blame also falls on the nation's schools, many of which fail to provide daily physical education classes (Sallis & others, 2001). In the 1985 School Fitness Survey, 37 percent of the children in the first through fourth grades took gym classes only once or twice a week. The investigation also revealed that parents are poor role models when it comes to physical fitness. Less than 30 percent of the parents of the children in grades 1 through 4 exercised three days a week. Roughly half said they never get any vigorous exercise. In another study, observations of children's behavior in physical education classes at four elementary schools revealed how little vigorous exercise is done in these classes (Parcel & others, 1987). Children moved through space only 50 percent of the time they were in the class, and they moved continuously an average of only 2.2 minutes. In summary, not only do children's school weeks not include adequate physical education classes, but the majority of children do not exercise vigorously, even when they are in such classes (Kristjansdottir & Vilhjalmsson, 2001). Furthermore, most children's parents are poor role models for vigorous physical exercise (Lou, Ganley, & Flynn, 2002).

Does it make a difference if children are pushed to exercise more vigorously in elementary school? One study says yes (Tuckman & Hinkle, 1988). One hundred fifty-four elementary school children were randomly assigned either to three 30-minute running programs per week or to regular attendance in physical education classes. Although the results sometimes varied according to sex, for the most part, the cardiovascular health as well as the creativity of children in the running program were enhanced. For example, the boys in this program had less body fat, and the girls had more creative involvement in their classrooms. In a recent study, the influence of instruction time in physical education on children's weight was explored (Datar & Sturm, 2004). One more hour of physical education in the first grade was linked to girls being less likely to be overweight.

In addition to the school, the family plays an important role in a child's exercise program (McGarvey & others, 2004). A wise strategy is for the family to take up activities involving vigorous physical exercise that parents and children can enjoy together. Running, swimming, cycling, and hiking are especially recommended. In encouraging children to exercise more, parents should not push children beyond their physical limits or expose them to competitive pressures that take the fun out of sports and exercise (Demorest & Landry, 2004). For example, long-distance running may be too strenuous for young children and could result in bone injuries. Recently, there has been an increase in the number of children competing in strenuous athletic events, such as marathons and triathlons. Doctors are beginning to see some injuries in children that they previously saw only in adults. Some injuries, such as stress fractures and tendonitis, stem from the overuse of young, still-growing bodies. It is recommended that parents downplay cutthroat competition and encourage healthy sports that children can enjoy.

Sports   It is not surprising that more and more children become involved in sports every year. Both in public schools and in community agencies, children's sports programs that involve baseball, soccer, football, basketball, swimming, gymnastics, and other activities have changed the shape of many children's lives.

We are underexercised as a nation. We look instead of play. We ride instead of walk. Our existence deprives us of the minimum of physical activity essential for healthy living.
—JOHN F. KENNEDY
American President, 20th Century

What are some of the possible positive and negative aspects of children's participation in sports?

Participation in sports can have both positive and negative consequences for children (Cary, 2004). Sports can provide exercise, opportunities to learn how to compete, self-esteem, and a setting for developing peer relations and friendships. One recent study revealed that participation in sports for three hours per week or more beyond regular physical education classes was related to increased physical fitness and lower fat mass in 9-year-old boys (Ara & others, 2004).

However, sports also can have negative outcomes for children: the pressure to achieve and win, physical injuries, a distraction from academic work, and unrealistic expectations for success as an athlete (Adickes & Stuart, 2004; Demorest & Landry, 2003, 2004; Emery, 2003). Few people challenge the value of sports for children when conducted as part of a school physical education or intramural program. However, some critics question the appropriateness of highly competitive, win-oriented sports teams in schools and communities, intense participation in sports at an early age, and the physical strain placed on children's bodies that can result in overuse injuries (Baquet, van Praagh, & Berthoin, 2004; Lord & Winell, 2004). It is important to keep in mind that learning the basic skills of a sport, as opposed to a narrow focus on winning, develops a child's self-confidence, coordination, and strength.

There is a special concern for children in high-pressure sports settings involving championship play with accompanying media publicity (Cary, 2004). Some clinicians and child developmentalists argue such activities not only put undue stress on the participants but also teach children the wrong values—namely, a win-at-all-costs philosophy (Pratt, Patel, & Greydanus, 2003). The possibility of exploiting children through highly organized, win-oriented sports programs is an ever-present danger. Overly ambitious parents, coaches, and community boosters can unintentionally create a highly stressful atmosphere in children's sports. When parental, agency, or community prestige becomes the central focus of the child's participation in sports, the danger of exploitation is clearly present. Programs oriented toward such purposes often require long and arduous training sessions over many months and years, frequently leading to sports specialization at too early an age. In such circumstances, adults often transmit a distorted view of the role of the sport in the child's life, communicating to the child that the sport is the most important aspect of the child's existence. In the Caring for Children interlude that follows, you can read about some positive strategies for parents to follow regarding their children's sports participation.

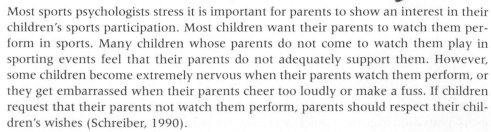

CARING FOR CHILDREN

Parents and Children's Sports

Most sports psychologists stress it is important for parents to show an interest in their children's sports participation. Most children want their parents to watch them perform in sports. Many children whose parents do not come to watch them play in sporting events feel that their parents do not adequately support them. However, some children become extremely nervous when their parents watch them perform, or they get embarrassed when their parents cheer too loudly or make a fuss. If children request that their parents not watch them perform, parents should respect their children's wishes (Schreiber, 1990).

Parents should compliment their children for their sports performance. In the course of a game, there are dozens of circumstances when the child has done something positive—parents should stress a child's good performance, even if the child has limited abilities. Parents can tell their children how much the children hustled in the game and how enthusiastically they played. Even if the child strikes out in a baseball game, a parent can say, "That was a nice swing."

One of the hardest things for parents to do is to watch their children practicing or performing at a sport without helping them, to let their children make mistakes without interfering. Former Olympic swimmer Donna de Varona commented that the best way parents can help children in sports is to let them get to know themselves, and the only way they can do this is by having experiences in life. Naturally, parents want to provide their children with support and encouragement, but there is a point at which parental involvement becomes overinvolvement.

I (your author) have coached a number of young tennis players and have seen many parents who handled their roles as a nurturant, considerate parent well, but I have observed others who became overinvolved in their children's sport. Some parents were aware of their tendency to become overinvolved and backed off from pushing their children too intensely. However, some were not aware of their overintrusiveness and did not back off. The worst parent had a daughter who, at the age of 9, was already nationally ranked and showed great promise. Her father went to every lesson, every practice session, every tournament. Her tennis began to consume his life. At one tournament, he stormed onto the court during one of her matches and accused his daughter's 10-year-old opponent of cheating, embarrassing his daughter and himself. I called him the next day, told him I no longer could coach his daughter because of his behavior, and recommended that he seek counseling or not go to any more of her matches.

If parents do not become overinvolved, they can help their children build their physical skills and help them emotionally—discussing with them how to deal with a difficult coach, how to cope with a tough loss, and how to put in perspective a poorly played game. Parents need to carefully monitor their children as they participate in sports for signs of developing stress. If the problems appear to be beyond the intuitive skills of a volunteer coach or parent, a consultation with a counselor or clinician may be needed. Also, the parent needs to be sensitive to whether the sport in which the child is participating is the best one for the child and whether the child can handle its competitive pressures.

Some guidelines provided by the Women's Sports Foundation in its booklet *Parents' Guide to Girls' Sports* can benefit both parents and coaches of all children in sports:

The Dos
- Make sports fun; the more children enjoy sports, the more they will want to play.
- Remember that it is okay for children to make mistakes; it means they are trying.
- Allow children to ask questions about the sport and discuss the sport in a calm, supportive manner.
- Show respect for the child's sports participation.
- Be positive and convince the child that he or she is making a good effort.
- Be a positive role model for the child in sports.

The Don'ts
- Yell or scream at the child
- Condemn the child for poor play or continue to bring up failures long after they happen
- Point out the child's errors in front of others
- Expect the child to learn something immediately
- Expect the child to become a pro
- Ridicule or make fun of the child
- Compare the child to siblings or to more talented children
- Make sports all work and no fun

Now let's turn our attention to additional children's health issues. For most children, middle and late childhood is a time of excellent health. Disease and death are less prevalent in this period than in other periods of childhood and adolescence. However, some children do have health problems, such as obesity, cancer, diabetes, cardiovascular disease, asthma, and injuries due to accidents.

Obesity

Childhood obesity is an increasing health problem (Brown, 2005; Dietz & Robinson, 2005; Sizer & Whitney, 2006). When is a child classified as obese? Defining when someone is obese is not a simple task. Weight for height is the most commonly used measure because it can be computed using a standard growth chart. If an individual is 20 percent over the expected weight for height, the individual is considered to be obese. In adults, body mass index (BMI) is currently in wide use, but for children this requires the development of age- and gender-based reference graphs. New BMI reference charts for children have been created (Centers for Disease Control and Prevention, 2005). One problem in accurately measuring obesity is that variation in body fat in normal-weight individuals can range from 12 to 30 percent. When body mass index is used to define obesity in children, 22 percent of 6- to 19-year-olds are considered to be overweight; approximately half of these individuals, slightly more than 10 percent, are obese (Wolfe & others, 1994). This represents a 15 percent increase in obesity from just a decade earlier. Also, in one recent analysis, the prevalence of being overweight from 6 to 11 years of age in the United States increased 325 percent from 1974 to 1999 (NHANES, 2001).

Girls are more likely than boys to be obese (Flegal, Ogden, & Carroll, 2004). Obesity is less common in African American than in White children during childhood, but during adolescence this reverses. Researchers have found that being obese as a child is a risk factor for being obese as an adult (Guo & others, 2002). For example, obesity at 6 years of age results in approximately a 25 percent probability that the child will be obese as an adult; obesity at age 12 results in approximately a 75 percent chance that the adolescent will be obese as an adult.

Overweight Children

What Factors Are Linked with Obesity?   These factors are related to obesity: heredity, blood chemistry, and environmental contexts. Obese parents tend to have obese children, even if they are not living in the same household (Salbe & others, 2002; Speakman, 2004; Wardlaw, 2006). A recent study found that the greatest risk factor for being overweight at 9 years of age was a parent being overweight (Agras & others, 2004). Characteristics such as body type, height, body fat composition, and metabolism are inherited from parents.

Blood chemistry also is involved in obesity. Especially important in this regard are *leptin* and *insulin*. Leptin is a protein that is released by fat cells. Leptin decreases food intake and increases energy expenditure. The importance of leptin was discovered with a strain of genetically obese mice (Campfield & others, 1995). The *ob mouse* (the label for this strain of mice) has a low metabolism, overeats, and gets extremely fat. A particular gene called *ob* produces leptin. However, because of a genetic mutation, the fat cells of *ob* mice cannot produce leptin. Leptin has a strong influence on metabolism and eating, acting as an antiobesity hormone (Appukutty & others, 2004; Clements, Boutin, & Froguel, 2002). If *ob* mice are given daily injections of leptin, their metabolic rate increases, they become more active, and they eat less. Consequently, their weight returns to normal (see figure 12.4). Scientists hope that at some point in the future some form of "leptin therapy" might be able to help obese individuals lose weight (Benini & others, 2001). However, this is unlikely to completely solve the current problem of childhood obesity—exercise and nutrition are still very important (Fox, 2004).

A child's insulin (a hormone that controls blood glucose) level is another important factor in eating behavior and obesity. What children eat influences their insulin levels (Rodin, 1984; Treuth & others, 2003). When children eat complex carbohydrates, such as cereals, bread, and pasta, insulin levels go up and fall off gradually. When children consume simple sugars, such as candy bars and soft drinks, insulin levels rise and then fall sharply—producing the sugar low with which many of us are all too familiar. Glucose levels in the blood are affected by these complex carbohydrates and simple sugars. Children are more likely to eat within the next several hours after eating simple sugars than after eating complex carbohydrates. And the food children eat at one meal influences what they will eat at the next meal. Thus, consuming doughnuts and candy bars, in addition to providing minimal nutritional value, sets up an ongoing sequence of what and how much children crave the next time they eat.

Environmental factors in obesity include the greater availability of food (especially food high in fat content), energy-saving devices, declining physical activity, heavy TV watching, and the context in which a child eats (Bell & Swinburn, 2004; Moore & others, 2003). The American culture provides ample encouragement of overeating in children. Food is everywhere children go and easily accessed—in vending machines, fast-food restaurants, and so on. Also, the size and proportions that children eat in meals in the United States has grown. Fast-food restaurants capitalize on this by providing families with the opportunity to "super size" their meals at a relatively lower cost for the extra food.

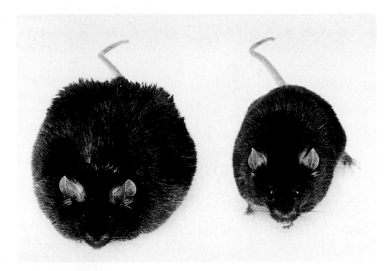

FIGURE 12.4 **Leptin and Obesity** The *ob* mouse on the left is untreated; the one on the right has been given injections of leptin.

In one recent study of fourth- through sixth-grade children, the context in which children ate was linked with what they ate and their tendency to be overweight (Cullen, 2001). Children who ate with their families were more likely to eat lower-fat foods (such as low-fat milk and salad dressing and lean meats), more vegetables, and drank fewer sodas than children who ate alone. Overweight children ate 50 percent of their meals in front of a TV, compared with only 35 percent of normal-weight children.

Television watching is linked with low activity and obesity in children (Ariza & others, 2004; Giammattei & others, 2003; Fox, 2004; Graf & others, 2004). A related concern is the dramatic increase in computer use by children. Recent reviews of research have concluded that the total time that children spend in front of a television or computer screen places them at risk for reduced activity and possible weight gain (Caroli & others, 2004; Jordan, 2004). A longitudinal study found that higher incidence of watching TV in childhood and adolescence was linked with being overweight, lower physical fitness, and higher cholesterol levels at 26 years of age (Hancox, Milne, & Poulton, 2004).

Consequences of Obesity in Children   We already have mentioned an important consequence of obesity in children: 25 percent of obese children become obese adults, and 75 percent of obese young adolescents become obese adults. Obesity also is a risk factor for many medical and psychological problems (Hodges, 2003). Obese children can develop pulmonary problems, such as sleep apnea (which we discussed in chapter 6, involving upper airway obstruction). Hip problems also are common in obese children. Obese children are more likely than nonobese children to develop diabetes (Botero & Wolfsdorf, 2005; Molnar, 2004). Obese children also are prone to have high blood pressure and elevated blood cholesterol levels (Burke & others, 2004; Clinton Smith, 2004). Once considered rare, hypertension in children has become increasingly common in association with obesity (Daniels, 2005; Hayman & others, 2004; Sorof & Daniels, 2002). Obese children are three times more likely to develop hypertension than nonobese children (Sorof & Daniels, 2002). Social and psychological consequences of obesity include low self-esteem, depression, and some exclusion of obese children from peer groups (Datar & Sturm, 2004; Lumeng & others, 2003).

One recent study found that overweight and obese children were more likely than normal weight children to be both the victims and perpetrators of bullying (Janssen & others, 2004).

Treatment of Obesity Many experts on childhood obesity recommend a treatment that involves a combination of diet, exercise, and behavior modification (Caballero, 2004; Eliakim & others, 2004; Fowler-Brown & Kahwati, 2004; Holcomb, 2004; Insel & Roth, 2006). One recent study found that obese children spent 51 percent more time in sedentary activity than nonobese children (Yu & others, 2002). Thus, exercise is an extremely important component of a successful weight-loss program for overweight children (Carrel & Bernhardt, 2004; Kirk, Scott, & Daniels, 2005; Magnusson, 2005; Sothern, 2004). Exercise increases the child's lean body mass, which increases the child's resting metabolic rate (Woo & others, 2004). This results in more calories being burned in the resting state.

A child's activity level is not only influenced by heredity but also by a child's motivation to engage in energetic activities and caregivers who model an active lifestyle or provide children with opportunities to be active (Borra & others, 2003; Golan & Crow, 2004). In a typical behavior modification program, children are taught to monitor their own behavior, keeping a food diary while attempting to lose weight (Moon & others, 2004; Wisotsky & Swencionis, 2003). The diary should record not only the type and amount of food eaten but also when, with whom, and where it was eaten. That is, do children eat in front of the TV, by themselves, or because they are angry or depressed? A diary identifies behaviors that need to be changed.

In keeping a diary, children can calculate and keep track of the number of calories consumed. Moderate-calorie diets are more successful over the long term than are those involving extreme deprivation of calories. Educating children to modify their eating habits and learn to make wise food choices can help in weight control. For example, a year-long school-based education program was successful in reducing the consumption of carbonated drinks, which was related to a reduction in the number of overweight children (James & others, 2004).

Diseases

Four childhood diseases can especially be harmful to children's development: (1) cancer, (2) diabetes, (3) cardiovascular disease, and (4) asthma.

Cancer Cancer is the second leading cause of death (with injuries the leading cause) in children 5 to 14 years of age in the United States. Three percent of all children's deaths in this age period are due to cancer. In the 15 to 24 age group, cancer accounts for 13 percent of all deaths. Currently, 1 in every 330 children in the United States develops cancer before the age of 19. Moreover, the incidence of cancer in children is increasing. Approximately 25 percent of children with cancer die because of the disease during the childhood years (Hurwitz, Duncan, & Wolfe, 2004).

Child cancers have a different profile than adult cancers. Adult cancers attack mainly the lungs, colon, breast, prostate, and pancreas. Child cancers are mainly those of the white blood cells (leukemia), brain, bone, lymph system, muscles, kidneys, and nervous system (Pickard, Topfer, & Feeny, 2004; Savell & others, 2004). All are characterized by an uncontrolled proliferation of abnormal cells.

As indicated in figure 12.5, the most common cancer in children is leukemia, a cancer of the tissues that make blood cells. In leukemia, the bone marrow makes an abundance of white blood cells that don't function properly. They invade the marrow and crowd out normal cells, making the child susceptible to bruising and infection. Lymphomas arise in the lymph system. Childhood lymphomas spread to the central nervous system and bone marrow. Treatments have been developed that can cure many children with lymphoma.

www.mhhe.com/santrockc9

Cancer in Children

When cancer strikes children, it behaves differently than it does when it attacks adults. Children frequently have a more advanced stage of cancer when they are first diagnosed. When cancer is first diagnosed in adults, it has spread to distant parts of the body in only about 20 percent of the cases; however, that figure rises to 80 percent in children. Most adult cancers result from lifestyle factors, such as smoking, diet, occupation, and exposure to other cancer-causing agents. By contrast, little is known about the causes of childhood cancers (National Childhood Cancer Foundation, 1998; Wakefield, 2001). Researchers are searching for possible genetic links to childhood cancers (Dong & Hemminki, 2001).

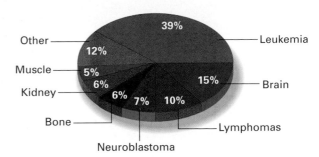

FIGURE 12.5 Types of Cancer in Children

Most adult cancer patients are treated in their local community by their family physician, consulting surgeon, or cancer specialist. Children with cancer are rarely treated by family physicians or pediatricians. They typically are treated by teams of physicians in children's hospitals, university medical centers, or cancer centers.

Many children with cancer and other potentially terminal illnesses may survive for a long period of time and experience problems associated with chronic illness or physical disability (Boman, Lindahl, & Bjork, 2003). Families initially may react with shock or denial when they find out that their child has cancer or any other type of terminal illness. Adjustment gradually follows and is usually characterized by an open admission that the illness exists. Most families move on to have realistic expectations for the child. A common pattern in parents of seriously ill children is chronic sorrow, in which acceptance of the child's illness is interspersed with periods of intense sorrow. Families with a terminally ill child benefit from the support of professionals and other families who have coped successfully with similar experiences (Friedman, Hilden, & Powaski, 2004; Hurwitz, Duncan, & Wolfe, 2004).

Diabetes   Diabetes is one of the most common chronic diseases in children and adolescents. In type I diabetes, the body produces little or no insulin (the hormone that regulates the body's blood sugar level). Type I diabetes is an autoimmune disease in which the body's immune system destroys insulin-producing cells.

In type II diabetes, the most common type of diabetes, the body is able to produce insulin but it may not be enough or the body cells may be unable to use it. Risk factors for type II diabetes include being overweight and/or physically inactive, having relatives with this disease, or belonging to certain ethnic groups. Native Americans, African Americans, Latinos, and Asian Americans are at greater risk for developing diabetes.

Cardiovascular Disease   Cardiovascular disease is uncommon in children. Children with heart problems usually have one of the following, which often can be corrected by surgery: holes in the heart, abnormal connections of heart vessels, abnormally narrow heart vessels, or abnormal heart valves. Unlike in adulthood, in which cardiovascular disease commonly arises from environmental experiences and behavior, such as smoking, most cases of cardiovascular disease in children are unrelated to environmental experiences and behavior. Rather, they are due to congenital factors (O'Callahan, Andrews, & Krantz, 2003).

Nonetheless, recent research has documented a number of risk factors in childhood that are linked to cardiovascular disease in adulthood. The precursors of cardiovascular disease often appear at a young age, with many elementary-school-age children already possessing one or more of the risk factors, such as hypertension and obesity (Cohen, 2004; Hanevold & others, 2004; Katzmarzyk & others, 2004; Sorof & others, 2004). Ethnic differences in blood pressure also are present. A recent study of more than 5,000 children revealed that high blood pressure was most likely to present in Latino (25 percent) and least characteristic of Asian American (14 percent) children (Sorof & others, 2004).

A recent study examined the role of diet and exercise on cardiovascular functioning in 82 overweight 9- to 12-year-old children (Woo & others, 2004). Children were randomly assigned to either a dietary only or a dietary plus supervised exercise program for six weeks and subsequently for one year. After six weeks, both treatments were linked with a decrease in waist-hip ratio, lower cholesterol, and improved functioning of arteries. After one year, the carotid wall of the children was thinner and body fat content was lower in the children in the dietary/exercise group.

One large-scale investigation designed to improve children's cardiovascular health is the Bogalusa Heart Study, also called "Heart Smart." It involves an ongoing evaluation of 8,000 boys and girls in Bogalusa, Louisiana (Berenson & others, 2005; Chen & others, 2005; Freedman & others, 2004, 2005; Katzmarzyk & others, 2004; Li & others, 2004; Nicklas & others, 2003, 2004 a,b; Rajeshwari & others, 2005). The school is the focus of the Heart Smart intervention. Since 95 percent of children and adolescents aged 5 to 18 are in school, schools are an efficient context in which to educate individuals about health. Special attention is given to teachers, who serve as role models. Teachers who value the role of health in life and who engage in health-enhancing behavior present children and adolescents with positive models for health. Teacher in-service education is conducted by an interdisciplinary team of specialists, including physicians, psychologists, nutritionists, physical educators, and exercise physiologists. The school's staff is introduced to heart health education, the nature of cardiovascular disease, and risk factors for heart disease. Coping behavior, exercise behavior, and eating behavior are discussed with the staff, and a Heart Smart curriculum is explained. For example, the Heart Smart curriculum for grade 5 includes the content areas of cardiovascular health (such as risk factors associated with heart disease), behavior skills (for example, self-assessment and monitoring), eating behavior (for example, the effects of food on health), and exercise behavior (for example, the effects of exercise on the heart).

The physical education component of Heart Smart involves two to four class periods each week to incorporate a "Superkids-Superfit" exercise program. The physical education instructor teaches skills required by the school system plus aerobic activities aimed at cardiovascular conditioning, including jogging, racewalking, interval workouts, rope skipping, circuit training, aerobic dance, and games. Classes begin and end with 5 minutes of walking and stretching.

The school lunch program serves as an intervention site, where sodium, fat, and sugar levels are decreased. Children and adolescents are given reasons they should eat healthy foods, such as a tuna sandwich, and why they should not eat unhealthy foods, such as a hot dog with chili. The school lunch program includes a salad bar, where children and adolescents can serve themselves. The amount and type of snack foods sold on the school premises are monitored.

High-risk children—those with elevated blood pressure, cholesterol, and weight—are identified as part of Heart Smart (Srinivasan & others, 2003). A multidisciplinary team of physicians, nutritionists, nurses, and behavioral counselors work with the high-risk boys and girls and their parents through group-oriented activities and individual-based family counseling. High-risk boys and girls and their parents receive diet, exercise, and relaxation prescriptions in an intensive 12-session program, followed by long-term monthly evaluations.

Extensive assessment is a part of this ongoing program. Short-term and long-term changes in children's knowledge about cardiovascular disease and changes in their behavior are assessed (Frontini & others, 2001).

Following are some results from the Bogalusa Heart Study:

- More than half of the children exceeded the recommended intake of salt, fat, cholesterol, and sugar (Nicklas & others, 1995).
- Consumption of sweetened beverages, sweets (desserts, candy), and total consumption of low-quality food were associated with being overweight in childhood (Nicklas & others, 2003).

Heart Smart
Child Health
Child Health Guide

- Adiposity (having excess body weight) beginning in childhood was related to cardiovascular problems in adulthood (Li & others, 2004).
- Higher body mass index (BMI) in childhood was linked to the likelihood of developing metabolic syndrome (a cluster of characteristics that include excessive fat around the abdomen, high blood pressure, and diabetes) in adulthood (Freedman & others, 2005).

Asthma   Asthma is a chronic lung disease that involves episodes of airflow obstruction. Symptoms of an asthma attack include shortness of breath, wheezing, or tightness in the chest. The incidence of asthma has risen steadily in recent decades, possibly because of increased air pollution (Neidell, 2004). Asthma is the most common chronic disease in U.S. children, being present in 7 to 12 percent of them (Liu, 2002). Asthma is the primary reason for absences from school, and is responsible for a number of pediatric admissions to emergency rooms and hospitals (Schmaling & others, 2003).

The exact causes of asthma are not known, but it is believed that the disease results from hypersensitivity to environmental substances, which trigger an allergic reaction (Stone, 2004; Wong & others, 2004). A recent research review concluded that the following are asthma risk factors: being male, having one or both parents with asthma, allergy sensitivity, stress early in life, infections, obesity, and exposure to environmental tobacco smoke, indoor allergens, and outdoor pollutants (King, Mannino, & Holguin, 2004).

Corticosteroids, which generally are inhaled, are the most effective anti-inflammatory drugs for treating asthmatic children (Mintz, 2004; Waikart & Blaiss, 2004). Often, parents have kept asthmatic children from exercising because they fear exercise will provoke an asthma attack. However, today it is believed that children with asthma should be encouraged to exercise, provided their asthma is under control, and participation should be evaluated on an individual basis (Welsh, Roberts, & Kemp, 2004). Some asthmatic children lose their symptoms in adolescence and adulthood (Vonk & others, 2004).

One individual who helps children cope with their health-care experiences is child life specialist Sharon McLeod. To read about her work see the Careers in Child Development profile.

Accidents and Injuries

The most common cause of severe injury and death in middle and late childhood is motor vehicle accidents, either as a pedestrian or as a passenger (Wong & others, 2003). Using safety-belt restraints is important in reducing the severity of motor vehicle injuries. The school-age child's motivation to ride a bicycle increases the risk of accidents. Other serious injuries involve skateboards, roller skates, and other sports equipment.

CAREERS in CHILD DEVELOPMENT

Sharon McLeod
Child Life Specialist

Sharon McLeod is a child life specialist who is clinical director of the Child Life and Recreational Therapy Department at the Children's Hospital Medical Center in Cincinnati.

Under McLeod's direction, the goals of the Child Life Department are to promote children's optimal growth and development, reduce the stress of health-care experiences, and provide support to child patients and their families. These goals are accomplished through therapeutic play and developmentally appropriate activities, educating and psychologically preparing children for medical procedures, and serving as a resource for parents and other professionals regarding children's development and health-care issues.

McLeod says that human growth and development provides the foundation for her profession of child life specialist. She also describes her best times as a student when she conducted fieldwork, had an internship, and experienced hands-on theories and concepts she learned in her courses.

Sharon McLeod, child life specialist, working with a child at Children's Hospital Medical Center in Cincinnati.

Vinckenbosch, R
learning disabiliti
problems in inte
in brain structur
bility is that som
opment or delive
prevalent in low

Many inter
(Berninger 2006
the kindergarten
reached the first

Unfortunate
ing problems hav
reading disability
dard interventio
tensive instructi
deficient reading

Children wi
recognition skills
moderate readin
designed reading

Improving o
and generally ha
outcomes (Berni
gram has proven
others, 1996).

Attention De

hyperactivity dis
ing to the teache
a few minutes a
very fidgety.

Attention
children consiste
(1) inattention,
have difficulty f
few minutes. Ch
most always see
curbing their rea
on the character
ADHD with prec
impulsivity, or
(Whalen, 2001).

The U.S. Off
in figure 12.6 in
learning disabili
children who re
rate in school th
with ADHD have
drop out of scho

Diagnosis and D
treated for ADH
(Damico, Tetnov
disorder occurs
others, 2004). T

Lear
Learning D

Autism

the cerebellum and cerebral cortex (frontal and temporal lobes), and neurotransmitters, including serotonin and dopamine (Akshoomoff, Pierce, & Courchesne, 2002; Courchesne, Redcay, & Kennedy, 2004; Herbert, 2004). There is some evidence that genetic factors play a role in the development of the autism spectrum disorders (Baron-Cohen, 2004; Korvatska & others, 2004; Muhle, Trentacoste, & Rapin, 2004). There is no evidence that family socialization causes autism (Rutter & Schopler, 1987). Mental retardation is present in some children with autism, while others show average or above-average intelligence.

Children with autism benefit from a well-structured classroom, individualized instruction, and small-group instruction (Pueschel & others, 1995). As with children who are mentally retarded, behavior modification sometimes has been effective in helping autistic children learn (Alberto & Troutman, 1999; Volkmar & others, 2004).

Educational Issues

The legal requirement that schools serve all children with a disability is fairly recent. Beginning in the mid-1960s to mid-1970s, legislatures, the federal courts, and the U.S. Congress laid down special educational rights for children with disabilities. Prior to that time, most children with a disability were either refused enrollment or inadequately served by schools. In 1975, **Public Law 94-142,** the Education for All Handicapped Children Act, required that all students with disabilities be given a free, appropriate public education and be provided the funding to help implement this education.

In 1990, Public Law 94-142 was recast as the **Individuals with Disabilities Education Act (IDEA).** IDEA was amended in 1997 and then reauthorized in 2004 and renamed the Individuals with Disabilities Education Improvement Act. IDEA spells out broad mandates for services to all children with disabilities (Friend, 2006; Hallahan & Kauffman, 2006; Hardman, Drew, & Egan, 2006; Smith, 2006). These include evaluation and eligibility determination, appropriate education and an individualized education plan (IEP), and education in the least restrictive environment (LRE).

A major aspect of the 2004 reauthorization of IDEA involved aligning it with the government's No Child Left Behind (NCLB) legislation that was designed to improve the educational achievement of all students, including those with disabilities. Both IDEA and NCLB mandate that most students with disabilities be included in general assessments of educational progress. This alignment includes requiring most students with disabilities "to take standard tests of academic achievement and to achieve at a level equal to that of students without disabilities. Whether this expectation is reasonable is an open question" (Hallahan & Kauffman, 2006, pp. 28–29). Alternate assessments for students with disabilities and funding to help states improve instruction, assessment, and accountability for educating students with disabilities are included in the 2004 reauthorization of IDEA.

Evaluation and Eligibility Determination
Children who are thought to have a disability are evaluated to determine their eligibility for services under IDEA. Schools are prohibited from planning special education programs in advance and offering them on a space-available basis.

Children must be evaluated before a school can begin providing special services (Smith, 2004). Parents should be involved in the evaluation process. Reevaluation is required at least every three years (sometimes every year), when requested by parents, or when conditions suggest a reevaluation is needed. A parent who disagrees with the school's evaluation can obtain an independent evaluation, which the school is required to consider in providing special education services. If the evaluation finds that the child has a disability and requires special services, the school must provide them to the child.

The IDEA has many specific provisions that relate to the parents of a child with a disability (Wardle, 2003). These include requirements that schools send notices to

dyslexia A catego
involving a severe
read and spell.

dyscalculia Also
arithmetic disorde
involves difficulty

Public Law 94-142 The Education for All Handicapped Children Act, created in 1975, which requires that all children with disabilities be given a free, appropriate public education and which provides the funding to help with the costs of implementing this education.

Individuals with Disabilities Education Act (IDEA) The IDEA spells out broad mandates for services to all children with disabilities (IDEA is a renaming of Public Law 94-142); these include evaluation and eligibility determination, appropriate education and the individualized education plan (IEP), and the least restrictive environment (LRE).

parents of proposed actions, of attendance at meetings regarding the child's placement or individualized education plan, and of the right to appeal school decisions to an impartial evaluator.

The IDEA, including its 1997 amendments, requires that technology devices and services be provided to students with disabilities if they are necessary to ensure a free, appropriate education. Two types of technology that can be used to improve the education of students with disabilities are instructional technology and assistive technology:

Education of Exceptional Children

- **Instructional technology** includes various types of hardware and software, combined with innovative teaching methods, to accommodate students' needs in the classroom. This technology includes videotapes, computer-assisted instruction, and complex hypermedia programs in which computers are used to control the display of audio and visual images stored on videodisc. The use of telecommunication systems, especially the Internet and its World Wide Web, hold considerable promise for improving the education of students with a disability.
- **Assistive technology** consists of various services and devices to help students with disabilities function within their environment. Examples include communication aids, alternative computer keyboards, and adaptive switches. To locate such services, educators can use computer databases, such as the Device Locator System.

Appropriate Education and the Individualized Education Plan

(IEP) The IDEA requires that students with disabilities have an **individualized education plan (IEP),** a written statement that spells out a program tailored specifically for the student with a disability (Dalton, 2002). In general, the IEP should be (1) related to the child's learning capacity, (2) specially constructed to meet the child's individual needs and not merely a copy of what is offered to other children, and (3) designed to provide educational benefits.

Amendments were made to the IDEA in 1997. Two of these involve positive behavioral support and functional behavioral assessment (U.S. Office of Education, 2000). *Positive behavioral support* focuses on culturally appropriate interventions to attain important behavioral changes in children. *Functional behavioral assessment* involves determining the consequences (what purpose the behavior serves), antecedents (what triggers the behavior), and setting events (in which contexts the behavior occurs).

Under the IDEA, a child with a disability must be educated in the **least restrictive environment (LRE).** This means a setting that is as similar as possible to the one in which children who do not have a disability are educated. This provision of the IDEA has given a legal basis to making an effort to educate children with a disability in the regular classroom (Crockett & Kauffman, 1999). The term used to describe the education of children with a disability in the regular classroom used to be *mainstreaming.* However, that term has been replaced by the term **inclusion,** which means educating a child with special education needs full-time in the general school program.

Not long ago, it was considered appropriate to educate children with disabilities outside the regular classroom. However, today, schools must make every effort to provide inclusion for children with disabilities (Friend & Bursuck, 2002; Smith, 2004; Smith & others, 2006; Wood, 2006). These efforts can be very costly financially and very time consuming in terms of faculty effort.

The principle of least restrictive environment compels schools to examine possible modifications of the regular classroom before moving the child with a disability to a more restrictive placement (Hallahan & Kauffman, 2006). Also, regular classroom teachers often need specialized training to help some children with a disability, and state educational agencies are required to provide such training (Dettmer, Dyck, & Thurston, 2002; Wardle, 2003).

Many legal changes regarding children with disabilities have been extremely positive. Compared with several decades ago, far more children today are receiving

instructional technology Various types of hardware and software, combined with innovative teaching methods, to accommodate students' learning needs in the classroom.

assistive technology Various services and devices to help children with disabilities function in their environment.

individualized education plan (IEP) A written statement that spells out a program tailored to a child with a disability. The plan should be (1) related to the child's learning capacity, (2) specially constructed to meet the child's individual needs and not merely a copy of what is offered to other children, and (3) designed to provide educational benefits.

least restrictive environment (LRE) The concept that a child with a disability must be educated in a setting that is as similar as possible to the one in which children who do not have a disability are educated.

inclusion Educating a child with special education needs full-time in the regular classroom.

Increasingly, children with disabilities are being taught in the regular classroom, as is this child with mild mental retardation.

competent, specialized services. For many children, inclusion in the regular classroom, with modifications or supplemental services, is appropriate (Friend, 2005; Kochhar, West, & Taymans, 2000). However, some leading experts on special education argue that the effort to use inclusion to educate children with disabilities has become too extreme in some cases. For example, James Kauffman and his colleagues (Kauffman & Hallahan, 2005; Kauffman, McGee, and Brigham, 2004) state that inclusion too often has meant making accommodations in the regular classroom that do not always benefit children with disabilities. They advocate a more individualized approach that does not always involve full inclusion but rather options such as special education outside the regular classroom. Kauffman and his colleagues (2004, p. 620) acknowledge that children with disabilities "*do* need the services of specially trained professionals to achieve their full potential. They *do* sometimes need altered curricula or adaptations to make their learning possible." However, "we sell students with disabilities short when we pretend that they are not different from typical students. We make the same error when we pretend that they must *not* be expected to put forth extra effort if they are to learn to do some things—or learn to do something in a different way." Like general education, an important aspect of special education should be to challenge students with disabilities "to become all they can be."

Review and Reflect • LEARNING GOAL 3

 Summarize information about children with disabilities.

Review
- Who are children with disabilities?
- What are some characteristics of the range of children's disabilities?
- What are some important issues in the education of children with disabilities?

Reflect
- Think back to your own schooling and how students with learning disabilities were or were not diagnosed. Were you aware of such individuals in your classes? Were they given special attention by teachers and/or specialists? You may know one or more individuals with a learning disability. Interview them about their school experiences. Ask them what they think could have been done better to help them with their disability.

REACH YOUR LEARNING GOALS

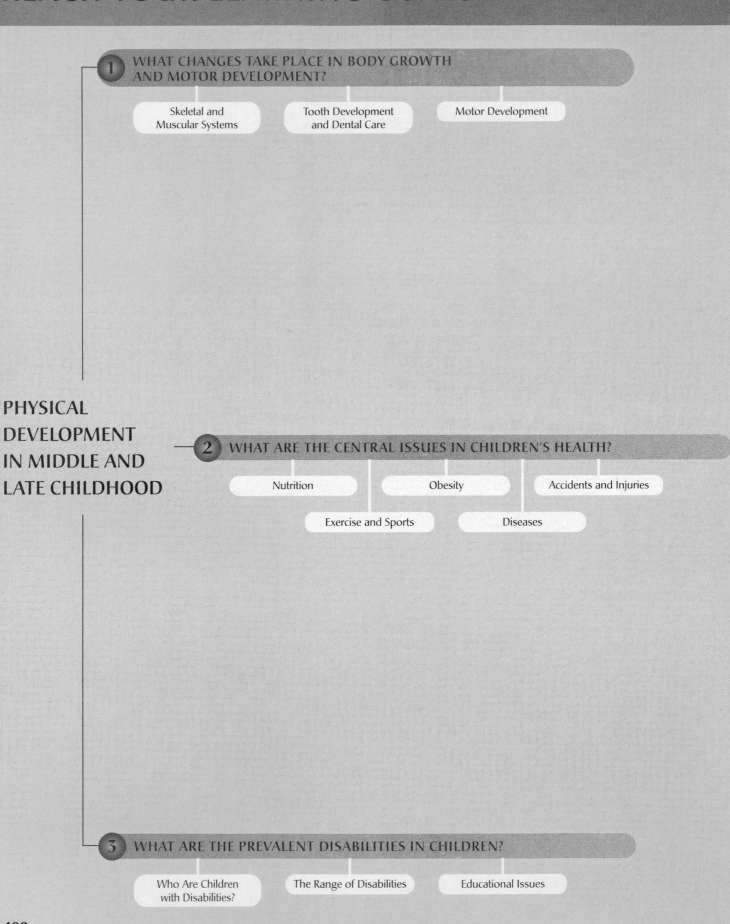

PHYSICAL DEVELOPMENT IN MIDDLE AND LATE CHILDHOOD

1 WHAT CHANGES TAKE PLACE IN BODY GROWTH AND MOTOR DEVELOPMENT?

Skeletal and Muscular Systems

Tooth Development and Dental Care

Motor Development

2 WHAT ARE THE CENTRAL ISSUES IN CHILDREN'S HEALTH?

Nutrition

Obesity

Accidents and Injuries

Exercise and Sports

Diseases

3 WHAT ARE THE PREVALENT DISABILITIES IN CHILDREN?

Who Are Children with Disabilities?

The Range of Disabilities

Educational Issues

SUMMARY

1 Discuss changes in body growth and motor development in middle and late childhood.

- The period of middle and late childhood involves slow, consistent growth. During this period, children grow an average of 2 to 3 inches a year. Muscle mass and strength gradually increase. Among the most pronounced changes are decreases in head circumference, waist circumference, and leg length in relation to body height.

- Most of the teeth we have as adults begin to come in during middle and late childhood. First permanent teeth erupt at about 6 years of age and appear at the rate of approximately four teeth per year for the next five years. Good dental hygiene is important during this period.

- During the middle and late childhood years, motor development becomes much smoother and more coordinated. Children gain greater control over their bodies and can sit and attend for longer periods of time. However, their lives should be activity-oriented and very active. Gross motor skills are expanded and children refine such skills as hitting a tennis ball, skipping rope, or balancing on a beam. Increased myelination of the central nervous system is reflected in improved fine motor skills such as handwriting development and playing a difficult piece on a musical instrument. Boys are usually better at gross motor skills, girls at fine motor skills.

2 Characterize children's health in middle and late childhood.

- In the middle and late childhood years, weight doubles and considerable energy is expended in motor activities. To support their growth, children need to consume more calories than when they were younger. A balanced diet is important. A special concern is that too many children fill up on "empty calories" that are high in sugar, starch, and excess fat. A healthy breakfast promotes higher energy and better alertness in school.

- Every indication suggests that children in the United States are not getting enough exercise. Television viewing, parents being poor role models for exercise, and inadequate physical education classes in schools are among the culprits. Children's participation in sports can have positive or negative consequences.

- Slightly more than one-fifth of U.S. children are overweight and 10 percent are obese. Factors linked with obesity include heredity, blood chemistry, and environmental contexts. Obesity in childhood is related to a number of problems. Diet, exercise, and behavior modification are recommended in the treatment of childhood obesity.

- Cancer is the second leading cause of death in children (after accidents). Child cancers have a different profile than adult cancers. Diabetes is also a common disease in childhood. Cardiovascular disease is uncommon in children but the precursors to adult cardiovascular disease are often already apparent in children. Asthma is the most common chronic disease in children.

- The most common cause of severe injury and death in childhood is motor vehicle accidents.

3 Summarize information about children with disabilities.

- An estimated 10 percent of U.S. children receive special education services. Slightly more than 50 percent of these children are classified as having a learning disability. Substantial percentages also are represented by children who are mentally retarded, children with speech and language disorders, and children with serious emotional disturbance. The term "children with disabilities" is now recommended rather than handicapped children. This is intended to focus the emphasis more on the child than the disability.

- Children's disabilities cover a wide range and include learning disabilities, ADHD, speech disorders, sensory disorders, physical disorders, emotional and behavioral disorders, and autism spectrum disorders. A learning disability includes three components: (1) a minimum IQ level; (2) a significant difficulty in a school-related area (especially reading or mathematics); and (3) exclusion of only severe emotional disorders, second-language background, sensory disabilities, and/or specific neurological deficits. Dyslexia is a category of learning disabilities involving a severe impairment in the ability to read and spell. Dyscalculia, also known as developmental arithmetic disorder, is a learning disability that involves difficulty in math computation. Diagnosing whether a child has a learning disability is often difficult. Various causes of learning disabilities have been proposed. Interventions with children who have a learning disability often focus on improving reading skills. Attention deficit hyperactivity disorder (ADHD) is a disability in which children consistently show problems in one or more of these areas: inattention, hyperactivity, and impulsivity. Speech disorders include articulation disorders, voice disorders, and fluency disorders. Sensory disorders include visual and hearing impairments. Physical disorders that children may have include orthopedic impairments and cerebral palsy. Emotional and behavioral disorders consist of serious, persistent problems that involve relationships, aggression, depression, fears associated with personal or school matters, as well as other inappropriate socioemotional characteristics. Autism is a severe disorder with an onset in the first three years of life and it involves abnormalities in social relationships and communications. It also is characterized by repetitive behaviors. The current consensus is that autism involves an organic brain dysfunction. Autism spectrum disorders (ASD) is an increasingly popular term that refers to a broad range of autism disorders including the classical, severe form of autism, as well as Asperger syndrome.

- Beginning in the 1960s and 1970s, the educational rights for children with disabilities were laid down. In 1975, Public Law 94-142 required all children to be given a free, appropriate public education. In 1990, Public Law 94-142 was renamed and called the Individuals with Disabilities Education Act (IDEA). Children who are thought to have a disability are evaluated to determine their eligibility for services. An individualized educational plan (IEP) is a written plan that spells out a program tailored to the child with a disability. The concept of a least restrictive environment (LRE) is contained in the IDEA. The term inclusion means educating children with disabilities full-time in the regular classroom. The trend is toward using inclusion more.

KEY TERMS

learning disability 397
dyslexia 398
dyscalculia 398
attention deficit hyperactivity
    disorder (ADHD) 399
articulation disorders 401
voice disorders 401
fluency disorders 401

low vision 402
educationally blind 402
oral approaches 402
manual approaches 402
orthopedic impairments 402
cerebral palsy 403
emotional and behavioral
    disorders 403

autism spectrum disorders
    (ASD) 403
autistic disorder 403
Asperger syndrome 403
Public Law 94-142 404
Individuals with Disabilities
    Education Act (IDEA) 404
instructional technology 405

assistive technology 405
individualized education plan
    (IEP) 405
least restrictive environment
    (LRE) 405
inclusion 405

KEY PEOPLE

Linda Siegel 397   James Kauffman 405

MAKING A DIFFERENCE

Nurturing Children's Physical Development and Health

What are some good strategies for supporting children's physical development and health in the middle and late childhood years?

- *Elementary school children should participate mainly in active rather than passive activities.* This especially means reducing TV watching and increasing participation in such activities as swimming, skating, and bicycling.
- *Parents should monitor children's eating behavior.* Children need more calories now than when they were younger. However, a special concern is the increasing number of obese children. They need to have a medical checkup, to revise their diet, and to participate in a regular exercise program.

- *Elementary schools need to develop more and better physical education programs.* Only about one of every three elementary school children participates in a physical education program. Many of those who do aren't exercising much during the program.
- *Parents need to engage in physical activities that they can enjoy together with their children.* These activities include running, bicycling, hiking, and swimming.
- *Parents should try to make their children's experience in sports positive.* This means not stressing a win-at-all-costs philosophy.
- *Parents should help children avoid accidents and injuries.* Educate children about the hazards of risk taking and the improper use of equipment.

CHILDREN RESOURCES

Children's HeartLink

5075 Arcadia Avenue
Minneapolis, MN 55436
952–928–4860

This organization provides treatment for needy children with heart disease and support for rheumatic fever prevention programs. It also supports the education of foreign medical professionals and provides technical advice and medical equipment and supplies.

The Council for Exceptional Children (CEC)

1110 North Glebe Road
Suite 300
Arlington, VA 22201
703–620–3660

The CEC maintains an information center on the education of children and adolescents with disabilities and publishes materials on a wide variety of topics.

Learning Disabilities Association of America (LDA)

4156 Library Road
Pittsburgh, PA 15234
412–341–1515

The LDA provides education and support for parents of children with learning disabilities, interested professionals, and others. More than 500 chapters are in operation nationwide, offering information services, pamphlets, and book recommendations.

E-LEARNING TOOLS

Connect to **www.mhhe.com/santrockc9** to research the answers to complete these exercises. In addition, you'll find a number of other resources and valuable study tools for chapter 12, "Physical Development in Middle and Late Childhood," on this website.

Taking It to the Net

1. Christina's daughter, Carmella, is having a difficult time in school. Her teacher says Carmella is unable to stay focused on her schoolwork, and she often gets into trouble for speaking out of turn and for getting out of her seat. The teacher recommends to Christina that her daughter be tested for ADHD. Christina has some reservations; she recently saw a television show about the overdiagnosis of ADHD. Is ADHD overdiagnosed in children? What are some of the controversies surrounding the ADHD diagnosis? What signs and symptoms characterize ADHD?

2. Morgan, a first-grader, has not been doing well in school. His father, John, doesn't think his poor performance has to do with his intelligence, because Morgan seems to be a fast learner. He does, however, suspect that Morgan might have problems with his vision. What kinds of visual impairments are common among school-age children? What accommodations can be made to improve Morgan's school performance?

3. Monika is a first-year physical education teacher at an elementary school. When she began her job, she was dismayed when she saw how sedentary most of her students were. Are her observations common? What levels of physical fitness do we commonly see in school-age children? How can children benefit from engaging in a physical fitness program?

Health and Well-Being, Parenting, and Education

Build your decision-making skills by trying your hand at the health and well-being, parenting, and education exercises.

Video Clips

The Online Learning Center includes the following videos for this chapter:

1. *Copying Shapes at Age 7—1125*
   More advanced fine motor skills in middle childhood are demonstrated by this 7-year-old. With careful attention he copies a square, a triangle, and a circle.
2. *Obesity—1714*
   Rebecca Roach, Registered Dietician, discusses reasons for the high rate of obesity in children today.
3. *Social Worker's View on Children's Abuse and Neglect—2000*
   An elementary school social worker describes the prevalence of abuse and neglect among children and how, unfortunately, it is difficult to identify until it is too late.

Images of Children
The Story of Jessica Dubroff, Child Pilot

Many parents want their children to be gifted and provide them with many opportunities to achieve this status. Child psychologists believe that some parents go too far and push their children too much, especially when they try to get their children to be a child star in a particular area, like figure skating, gymnastics, tennis, or music. To think further about parents' efforts to get their children to achieve lofty accomplishments, let's examine the tragic story of Jessica Dubroff.

In 1996, 55-pound, 4-foot, 2-inch Jessica Dubroff took off on a rainy day in a small airplane and died when the plane nose-dived into a highway. Only 7 years old, she was flying the airplane that rainy day in quest of being the youngest person ever to fly across the U.S. continent.

Jessica's parents seemed determined to make their daughter independent early in her life. Growing up, Jessica had no dolls, only tools. Instead of studying grammar at school, she was home schooled and did chores.

Jessica became interested in flying after her parents gave her an airplane ride for her sixth birthday, only 23 months before her fatal crash. Her father admitted the cross-country flight was his idea. The father became her press agent and contacted TV networks and newspapers to publicize her flight.

Did her parents endanger her? Did Jessica grow up too soon? Did her parents push her too much to achieve in a single activity? Should they instead have encouraged her to have a more well-rounded life and one more typical for her age? Were her parents living vicariously through her?

Some critics argue that Jessica Dubroff was not allowed to be a child. Was she given too much freedom and choice? Did her parents act irresponsibly?

PREVIEW

Achievement became an important theme in Jessica Dubroff's life. Later in the chapter, we will explore many aspects of achievement. First, though we will examine three main aspects of cognitive changes—Piaget's cognitive developmental theory, information process-ing, and intelligence—that characterize middle and late childhood. Then, following our coverage of achievement, we will explore changes in language during middle and late childhood.

1 WHAT IS PIAGET'S THEORY OF COGNITIVE DEVELOPMENT IN MIDDLE AND LATE CHILDHOOD?

| Concrete Operational Thought | Piaget and Education | Evaluating Piaget's Theory |

Piaget viewed the stage of concrete operational thought as a major benchmark in cognitive development. We will explore the main characteristics of concrete operational thought, how Paiget's ideas can be applied to educating children, and the contributions and criticisms of his work.

Concrete Operational Thought

According to Piaget (1952), the preschool child's thought is preoperational. Preoperational thought involves the formation of stable concepts, the emergence of mental reasoning, the prominence of egocentrism, and the construction of magical belief systems. Thought during the preschool years is not well organized and is still flawed about such concrete operational skills as conservation and classification. Piaget believed that concrete operational thought does not appear until about the age of 7, but, as we learned in chapter 10, Piaget may have underestimated some of the cognitive skills of preschool children. For example, by carefully and cleverly designing experiments on understanding the concept of number, Rochel Gelman (1972) demonstrated that some preschool children show conservation, a concrete operational skill.

Remember that, according to Piaget, concrete operational thought is made up of operations—mental actions that allow children to do mentally what they had done physically before. Concrete operations are also mental actions that are reversible. In the well-known test of reversibility of thought involving conservation of matter, the child is presented with two identical balls of clay. The experimenter rolls one ball into a long, thin shape; the other remains in its original ball shape. The child is then asked if there is more clay in the ball or in the long, thin piece of clay. By the time children reach the age of 7 or 8, most answer that the amount of clay is the same. To answer this problem correctly, children have to imagine that the clay ball is rolled out into a long, thin strip and then returned to its original round shape. This type of imagination involves a reversible mental action. Thus, a concrete operation is a reversible mental action on real, concrete objects.

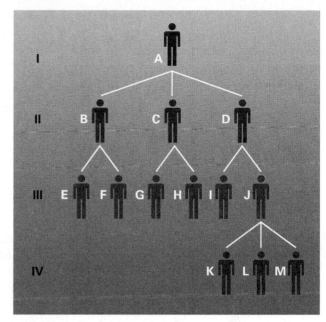

FIGURE 13.1 **Classification: An Important Ability in Concrete Operational Thought** A family tree of four generations (*I to IV*): The preoperational child has trouble classifying the members of the four generations; the concrete operational child can classify the members vertically, horizontally, and obliquely (up and down and across). For example, the concrete operational child understands that a family member can be a son, a brother, and a father, all at the same time.

Concrete operations allow the child to coordinate several characteristics rather than focus on a single property of an object. In the clay example, the preoperational child is likely to focus on height *or* width. The concrete operational child coordinates information about both dimensions.

Many of the concrete operations Piaget identified focus on the way children reason about the properties of objects. One important skill that characterizes the concrete operational child is the ability to classify or divide things into different sets or subsets and to consider their interrelationships. An example of the concrete operational child's classification skills involves a family tree of four generations (see figure 13.1) (Furth & Wachs, 1975). This family tree suggests that the grandfather (A) has three children (B, C, and D), each of whom has two children (E through J), and that one of these children (J) has three children (K, L, and M). A child who comprehends the classification system can move up and down a level (vertically), across a level (horizontally), and up and down and across (obliquely) within the system. The concrete operational child understands that person J can at the same time be father, brother, and grandson, for example.

Some Piagetian tasks require children to reason about relations between classes. One such task is **seriation,** the concrete operation that involves ordering stimuli along a quantitative dimension (such as length). To see if students can serialize, a teacher might haphazardly place eight sticks of different lengths on a table. The teacher then asks the students to order the sticks by length. Many young children end up with two or three small groups of "big" sticks or "little" sticks, rather than a correct ordering of all eight sticks. Another mistaken strategy they use is to evenly line up the tops of the sticks but ignore the bottoms. The concrete operational thinker simultaneously understands that each stick must be longer than the one that precedes it and shorter than the one that follows it.

Another aspect of reasoning about the relations between classes is **transitivity.** This involves the ability to logically combine relations to understand certain conclusions.

seriation The concrete operation that involves ordering stimuli along a quantitative dimension (such as length).

transitivity In concrete operational thought, a mental concept that underlies the ability to logically combine relations to understand certain conclusions. It focuses on reasoning about the relations between classes.

In this case, consider three sticks (A, B, and C) of differing lengths. A is the longest, B is intermediate in length, and C is the shortest. Does the child understand that, if A > B and B > C, then A > C? In Piaget's theory, concrete operational thinkers do; preoperational thinkers do not.

Piaget and Education

Piaget was not an educator and never pretended to be. However, he provided a sound conceptual framework from which to view learning and education. Earlier, we examined some specific suggestions for classroom activities based on Piaget's stages. Here are some more general principles in Piaget's theory that can be applied to teaching (Elkind, 1976; Heuwinkel, 1996):

1. *Take a constructivist approach.* In a constructivist vein, Piaget emphasized that children learn best when they are active and seek solutions for themselves. Piaget opposed teaching methods implying children are passive receptacles. The educational implication of Piaget's view is that, in all subjects, students learn best by making discoveries, reflecting on them, and discussing them, rather than blindly imitating the teacher or doing things by rote.

2. *Facilitate rather than direct learning.* Effective teachers design situations that allow students to learn by doing. These situations promote students' thinking and discovery. Teachers listen, watch, and question students to help them gain better understanding. Don't just examine *what* students think and the product of their learning. Rather, carefully observe them as they find out *how* they think. Ask relevant questions to stimulate their thinking and ask them to explain their answers.

3. *Consider the child's knowledge and level of thinking.* Students do not come to class with empty heads. They have many ideas about the physical and natural world. They have concepts of space, time, quantity, and causality. These ideas differ from the adults' ideas. Teachers need to interpret what a student says and respond in a way that is not too far from the student's level.

4. *Use ongoing assessment.* Individually constructed meanings cannot be measured by standardized tests. Student progress can be evaluated with math and language portfolios (which contain work in progress as well as finished products), individual conferences in which students discuss their thinking strategies, and students' written and verbal explanations of their reasoning.

5. *Promote the student's intellectual health.* When Piaget lectured in the United States, he was asked, "What can I do to get my child to a higher cognitive stage sooner?" He was asked this question so often here compared with other countries that he called it the American question. For Piaget, children's learning should occur naturally. Children should not be pushed and pressured into achieving too much too early in their development, before they are maturationally ready. Some parents spend long hours every day holding up large flash cards with words on them to improve their baby's vocabulary. In the Piagetian view, this is not the best way for infants to learn. It places too much emphasis on speeding up intellectual development, involves passive learning, and will not work.

6. *Turn the classroom into a setting of exploration and discovery.* What do actual classrooms look like when the teachers adopt Piaget's views? Several first- and second-grade math classrooms provide some good examples (Kamii, 1985, 1989). The teachers emphasize students' own exploration and discovery. The classrooms are less structured than what we think of as a typical classroom. Workbooks and predetermined assignments are not used. Rather, the teachers observe the students' interests and natural participation in activities to determine the course of learning. For example, a math lesson might be constructed around counting the day's lunch money or dividing supplies among students.

Often, games are used to stimulate mathematical thinking. For example, a version of dominoes teaches children about even-numbered combinations. A variation on tic-tac-toe involves replacing *X*s and *O*s with numbers. Teachers encourage peer interaction during the lessons and games because students' different viewpoints can contribute to advances in thinking.

Evaluating Piaget's Theory

What were Piaget's main contributions? Has his theory withstood the test of time?

Contributions   Piaget was a giant in the field of developmental psychology, the founder of the present field of children's cognitive development. Psychologists owe him a long list of masterful concepts of enduring power and fascination: assimilation, accommodation, object permanence, egocentrism, conservation, and others. Psychologists also owe him the current vision of children as active, constructive thinkers (Vidal, 2000). And they have a debt to him for creating a theory that generated a huge volume of research on children's cognitive development.

Piaget also was a genius when it came to observing children. His careful observations showed us inventive ways to discover how children act on and adapt to their world. Piaget showed us some important things to look for in cognitive development, such as the shift from preoperational to concrete operational thinking. He also showed us how children need to make their experiences fit their schemes (cognitive frameworks) yet simultaneously adapt their schemes to experience. Piaget also revealed how cognitive change is likely to occur if the context is structured to allow gradual movement to the next higher level. Concepts do not emerge suddenly, full-blown, but instead develop through a series of partial accomplishments that lead to increasingly comprehensive understanding (Haith & Benson, 1998).

Criticisms   Piaget's theory has not gone unchallenged (Byrnes, 2003; Feldman, 2003; Smith, 2004b). Questions are raised about estimates of children's competence at different developmental levels, stages, the training of children to reason at higher levels, and culture and education.

- *Estimates of children's competence.* Some cognitive abilities emerge earlier than Piaget thought (Bauer, 2006; Bjorklund, 2005; Bornstein, Arterberry, & Mash, 2005; Cohen & Cashon, 2006; Mandler, 2004). For example, as previously noted, some aspects of object permanence emerge earlier than he believed. Even 2-year-olds are nonegocentric in some contexts. When they realize that another person will not see an object, they investigate whether the person is blindfolded or looking in a different direction. Some understanding of the conservation of number has been demonstrated as early as age 3, although Piaget did not think it emerged until 7. Young children are not as uniformly "pre" this and "pre" that (precausal, preoperational) as Piaget thought.

  Other cognitive abilities also can emerge later than Piaget thought. Many adolescents still think in concrete operational ways or are just beginning to master formal operations. Even many adults are not formal operational thinkers. In sum, recent theoretical revisions highlight more cognitive competencies of infants and young children and more cognitive shortcomings of adolescents and adults (Cohen & Cashon, 2006; Keating, 2004; Kuhn & Franklin, 2006; Thomas, 2005).

- *Stages.* Piaget conceived of stages as unitary structures of thought. Thus, his theory assumes developmental synchrony—that is, various aspects of a stage should emerge at the same time. However, some concrete operational concepts do not appear in synchrony. For example, children do not learn to conserve at the same time they learn to cross-classify. Thus, most contemporary developmentalists agree that children's cognitive development is not as stage-like as

Piaget with his wife and three children; he often used his observations of his children to provide examples of his theory.

We owe to Piaget the present field of cognitive development with its image of the developing child, who through its own active and creative commerce with its environment, builds an orderly succession of cognitive structures enroute to intellectual maturity.

—JOHN FLAVELL
Contemporary Developmental Psychologist. Stanford University

Challenges to Piaget

minimum initially scaffold students' science learning, extensively monitor their progress, and ensure that they are learning science content. Thus, in pursuing science investigations, students need to "learn inquiry skills *and* science content" (Lehrer & Schauble, 2006).

Metacognition

Metacognition is cognition about cognition or knowing about knowing (Flavell, 1999, 2004). One expert on children's thinking, Deanna Kuhn (1999), believes that metacognition should be a stronger focus in efforts to help children become better critical thinkers. She distinguishes between first-order cognitive skills that enable children to know about the world (which has been the main focus of critical-thinking programs) and second-order cognitive skills—*meta-knowing skills*—that involve learning about one's own (and others') knowing.

Most "metacognitive" developmental studies have focused on metamemory, or knowledge about memory. This includes general knowledge about memory, such as knowing that recognition tests are easier than recall tests. It also encompasses knowledge about one's own memory, such as a student's ability to monitor whether she has studied enough for an upcoming test.

By 5 to 6 years of age, children usually know that unfamiliar items are harder to learn than familiar ones, that short lists are easier than long ones, that recognition is easier than recall, and that forgetting is more likely to occur over time (Lyon & Flavell, 1993). However, in other ways young children's metamemory is limited. They don't understand that related items are easier to remember than unrelated ones and that remembering the gist of a story is easier than remembering information verbatim (Kreutzer, Leonard, & Flavell, 1975). By the fifth grade students understand that gist recall is easier than verbatim recall. Young children also have an inflated opinion of their memory abilities. For example, in one study, a majority of young children predicted that they would be able to recall all 10 items of a list of 10 items. When tested for this, none of the young children managed this feat (Flavell, Friedrichs, & Hoyt, 1970). As they move through the elementary school years, children give more realistic evaluations of their memory skills (Schneider & Pressley, 1997).

In Michael Pressley's (2003; Presley & Hilden, 2006; McCormick & Pressley, 1997) view, the key to education is helping students learn a rich repertoire of strategies that result in solutions of problems. Good thinkers routinely use strategies and effective planning to solve problems. Good thinkers also know when and where to use strategies (metacognitive knowledge about strategies). Understanding when and where to use strategies often results from the learner's monitoring of the learning situation. In reading, summarizing, and getting the gist of what an author is saying are important strategies. In writing, the processes of planning, organizing, rereading, and writing multiple drafts are good strategies (McCormick, 2003).

Pressley and his colleagues (Pressley & Hilden, 2006; Pressley & others, 2001, 2003, 2004) have spent considerable time in recent years observing the use of strategy instruction by teachers and strategy use by students in elementary and secondary school classrooms. They conclude that teachers' use of strategy instruction is far less complete and intense than what is needed for students to learn how to use strategies effectively. They argue that education needs to be restructured so that students are provided with more opportunities to become competent strategic learners.

A final point about strategies is that many strategies depend on prior knowledge (Pressley & Hilden, 2006). For example, students can't apply organizational strategies to a list of items unless they know the correct categories into which the items fall. The point about the importance of prior knowledge in strategy use coincides with the emphasis in our discussion earlier in the chapter of how experts use more effective strategies than novices.

metacognition Cognition about cognition or knowing about knowing.

Review and Reflect • LEARNING GOAL 2

2 Describe changes in information processing in middle and late childhood.

Review

- What characterizes children's memory in middle and late childhood?
- What is involved in thinking critically, thinking creatively, and thinking scientifically?
- What is metacognition?

Reflect

- When you were in elementary school, did classroom instruction prepare you adequately for critical-thinking tasks? If you were a parent of an 8-year-old, what would you do to guide the child to think more critically and creatively?

3 HOW CAN CHILDREN'S INTELLIGENCE BE DESCRIBED?

What Is Intelligence?

Controversies and Issues in Intelligence

Multiple Intelligences

The Extremes of Intelligence

Twentieth-century English novelist Aldous Huxley said that children are remarkable for their curiosity and intelligence. What did Huxley mean when he used the word *intelligence?*

What Is Intelligence?

Intelligence is one of our most prized possessions, yet it is a concept that even the most intelligent people have not been able to agree on. Unlike such characteristics as height, weight, and age, intelligence cannot be directly measured. You can't peel back a student's scalp and observe the intelligence going on inside. You can evaluate students' intelligence only *indirectly,* by studying the intelligent acts they generate. For the most part, intelligence tests have been relied on to provide an estimate of a student's intelligence (Kail & Pelligrino, 1985).

Some experts describe intelligence as the possession of verbal ability and problem-solving skills. Others describe it as the ability to adapt to and learn from life's everyday experiences. Combining these ideas, we can arrive at a definition of **intelligence** as problem-solving skills and the ability to adapt to and learn from life's everyday experiences.

Interest in intelligence has often focused on individual differences and assessment. *Individual differences* are the stable, consistent ways in which people are different from each other. We can talk about individual differences in personality or any other domain, but it is in the domain of intelligence that the most attention has been directed at individual differences. For example, an intelligence test purports to inform us about whether a student can reason better than others who have taken the test.

intelligence Problem-solving skills and the ability to learn from and adapt to the experiences of everyday life.

"You're wise, but you lack tree smarts."

that he has what Sternberg calls *practical intelligence*. Practical intelligence includes the ability to get out of trouble and a knack for getting along with people. Sternberg describes practical intelligence as all of the important information about getting along in the world that you are not taught in school.

Triarchic Theory in the Classroom Sternberg (1997) says that students with different triarchic patterns look different in school. Students with high analytic ability tend to be favored in conventional schools. They often do well in classes in which the teacher lectures and gives objective tests. These students often are considered smart, typically get good grades, do well on traditional IQ tests and the SAT, and later gain admission to competitive colleges.

Students high in creative intelligence often are not in the top rung of their class. Creatively intelligent students might not conform to teachers' expectations about how assignments should be done. They give unique answers, for which they might get reprimanded or marked down.

Like students high in creative intelligence, students who are practically intelligent often do not relate well to the demands of school. However, these students frequently do well outside the classroom's walls. Their social skills and common sense may allow them to become successful managers, entrepreneurs, or politicians, despite undistinguished school records.

Sternberg (1999) believes that few tasks are purely analytic, creative, or practical. Most tasks require some combination of these skills. For example, when students write a book report, they might (1) analyze the book's main themes, (2) generate new ideas about how the book could have been written better, and (3) think about how the book's themes can be applied to people's lives. Sternberg argues that it is important for classroom instruction to give students opportunities to learn through all three types of intelligence.

Emotional Intelligence

Both Gardner's and Sternberg's theories include one or more categories related to social intelligence. In Gardner's theory, the categories are interpersonal intelligence and intrapersonal intelligence; in Sternberg's theory, practical intelligence. Another theory that emphasizes interpersonal, intrapersonal, and practical aspects of intelligence is called **emotional intelligence,** which has been popularized by Daniel Goleman (1995) in his book *Emotional Intelligence*. The concept of emotional intelligence was initially developed by Peter Salovey and John Mayer (1990), who define it as the ability to perceive and express emotion accurately and adaptively (such as taking the perspective of others), to understand emotion and emotional knowledge (such as understanding the roles that emotions play in friendship and marriage), to use feelings to facilitate thought (such as having a positive mood, which is linked to creative thinking), and to manage emotions in oneself and others (such as being able to control one's anger). There continues to be considerable interest in the concept of emotional intelligence today (Lopes, 2004; Mayer, Salovey, & Caruso, 2004; Van Rooy & Viswesvaran, 2004). Critics argue that emotional intelligence broadens the concept of intelligence too far and has not been adequately assessed and studied (Matthews, Roberts, & Zeidner, 2004; Schulte, Ree, & Carretta, 2004).

emotional intelligence The ability to perceive and express emotions accurately and adaptively, to understand emotion and emotional knowledge, to use feelings to facilitate thought, and to manage emotions in oneself and others.

Do People Have One Intelligence or Many Intelligences?

Figure 13.7 provides a comparison of Gardner's, Sternberg's, and Salovey/Mayer/Goleman's views. Notice that Gardner includes a number of types of intelligence that are not addressed by the other views and that Sternberg is unique in emphasizing creative intelligence. These theories of multiple intelligence have much to offer. They have stimulated us to think more broadly about what makes up people's intelligence and competence (Kornhaber, Fierros, & Veeneba, 2005; Moran & Gardner, 2006; Weber, 2005). And they have motivated educators to develop programs that instruct students in different domains.

Theories of multiple intelligences also have many critics. Many argue that the research base to support these theories has not yet developed. In particular, some critics say that Gardner's classification seems arbitrary. For example, if musical skills represent a type of intelligence, why don't we also refer to chess intelligence, prizefighter intelligence, and so on?

A number of psychologists still support Spearman's concept of *g* (general intelligence) (Johnson & others, 2004). For example, one expert on intelligence, Nathan Brody (2000) argues that people who excel at one type of intellectual task are likely to excel in other intellectual tasks. Thus, individuals who do well at memorizing lists of digits are also likely to be good at solving verbal problems and spatial layout problems. This general intelligence includes abstract reasoning or thinking, the capacity to acquire knowledge, and problem-solving ability (Brody, 2000; Carroll, 1993).

Some experts who argue for the existence of general intelligence believe that individuals also have specific intellectual abilities (Brody, 2000). In one study, John Carroll (1993) conducted an extensive examination of intellectual abilities and concluded that all intellectual abilities are related to each other, which supports the concept of general intelligence, but that there are many specialized abilities as well. Some of these specialized abilities, such as spatial abilities and mechanical abilities, are not adequately reflected in the curriculum of most schools. In sum, controversy still characterizes whether it is more accurate to conceptualize intelligence as a general ability or as a number of specific abilities (Birney & others, 2005).

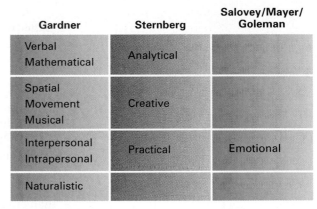

Gardner	Sternberg	Salovey/Mayer/Goleman
Verbal Mathematical	Analytical	
Spatial Movement Musical	Creative	
Interpersonal Intrapersonal	Practical	Emotional
Naturalistic		

FIGURE 13.7 Comparing Gardner's, Sternberg's, and Salovey/Mayer/Goleman's Intelligences

Controversies and Issues in Intelligence

The field of intelligence has its controversies and issues. We will examine the extent to which intelligence is due to heredity or environment, the role of ethnicity and culture in intelligence, and the use and misuse of intelligence tests.

The Influence of Heredity and Environment
One of the hottest areas in the study of intelligence centers on the extent to which intelligence is influenced by genetics and the extent to which it is influenced by environment. In chapter 2, we indicated how difficult it is to tease apart these influences, but that has not kept psychologists from trying to unravel them.

Genetic Influences on Intelligence The issue with respect to genetics and intelligence is the degree to which our genes make us smart. At one end of the debate, Arthur Jensen (1969) argued that intelligence is primarily inherited and that environment plays only a minimal role in intelligence. Jensen reviewed the research on intelligence, much of which involved comparisons of identical and fraternal twins, and which also used IQ as the indicator of intelligence. Identical twins have exactly the same genetic makeup; if intelligence is genetically determined, Jensen reasoned, identical twins' IQs should be more similar than the intelligence of fraternal twins.

The studies on intelligence in identical twins that Jensen examined showed an average correlation of .82, a very high positive association. Investigations of fraternal twins, however, produced an average correlation of .50, a moderately high positive correlation. A difference of .32 is substantial. However, a more recent research multistudy review conducted since Jensen's original review found that the difference in intelligence between identical and fraternal twins was .15, substantially less than what Jensen found (Grigorenko, 2000). See figure 13.8.

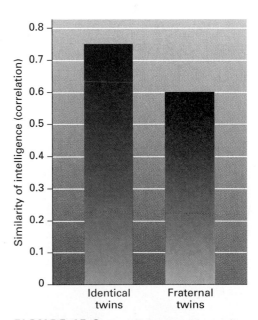

FIGURE 13.8 Correlation Between Intelligence Test Scores and Twin Status The graph represents a summary of research findings that have compared the intelligence test scores of identical and fraternal twins. An approximate .15 difference has been found, with a higher correlation (.75) for identical twins and a lower correlation (.60) for fraternal twins.

Jensen also compared the correlation of IQ scores for identical twins reared together with those reared apart. The correlation for those reared together was .89, and for those reared apart was .78, a difference of .11. Jensen argued that if environmental factors were more important than genetic factors, the difference should have been greater.

Adoption studies have been inconclusive about the relative importance of heredity in intelligence. In most *adoption studies,* researchers determine whether the behavior of adopted children is more like that of their biological parents or their adopted parents. In one study, the educational levels attained by biological parents were better predictors of children's IQ scores than were the IQ's of the children's adoptive parents (Scarr & Weinberg, 1983). Because of the stronger genetic link between the adopted children and their biological parents, the implication is that heredity is more important than environment. Environmental effects also have been found in studies of adoption. For example, moving children into an adoptive family with a better environment than the child had in the past increased the children's IQs by an average of 12 points (Lucurto, 1990).

How strong is the effect of heredity on intelligence? The concept of heritability attempts to tease apart the effects of heredity and environment in a population. **Heritability** is the fraction of the variance in a population that is attributed to genetics. The heritability index is computed using correlational techniques. Thus, the highest degree of heritability is 1.00 and correlations of .70 and above suggest a strong genetic influence. A committee of respected researchers convened by the American Psychological Association concluded that by late adolescence, the heritability of intelligence is about .75, which reflects a strong genetic influence (Neisser & others, 1996).

An important point to keep in mind about heritability is that it refers to a specific group (population), *not* to individuals. Researchers use the concept of heritability to try to describe why people differ. Heritability says nothing about why a single individual, like yourself, has a certain intelligence; nor does it say anything about differences *between* groups.

Most research on heredity and environment does not include environments that differ radically. Thus, it is not surprising that many genetic studies show environment to be a fairly weak influence on intelligence (Fraser, 1995).

The heritability index has several flaws. It is only as good as data entered into its analysis and interpretations made from it (Sternberg, Grigorenko, & Kidd, 2005). The data are virtually all from traditional IQ tests, which some experts believe are not always the best indicator of intelligence (Gardner, 2002; Sternberg, 2003). Also, the heritability index assumes that we can treat genetic and environmental influences as factors that can be separated, with each part contributing a distinct amount of influence. As we discussed in chapter 3, genes and the environment always work together. Genes always exist in an environment and the environment shapes their activity.

Environmental Influences on Intelligence Today, most researchers agree that heredity does not determine intelligence to the extent Jensen claimed (Gottlieb, Wahlsten, & Lickliter, 2006; Ramey, Ramey, & Lanzi, 2006; Sternberg & Grigorenko, 2004). For most people, this means modifications in environment can change their IQ scores considerably. Although genetic endowment may always influence a person's intellectual ability, the environmental influences and opportunities we provide children and adults do make a difference (Ramey, Ramey, & Lanzi, 2006).

In one study (discussed initially in chapter 7), researchers went into homes and observed how extensively parents from welfare and middle-income professional families talked and communicated with their young children (Hart & Risley, 1995). They found that the middle-income professional parents were much more likely to communicate with their young children than the welfare parents were. And how much the parents communicated with their children in the first three years of their lives was correlated with the children's Stanford-Binet IQ scores at age 3. The more parents communicated with their children, the higher the children's IQs were.

heritability The fraction of variance in IQ in a population that is attributed to genetics.

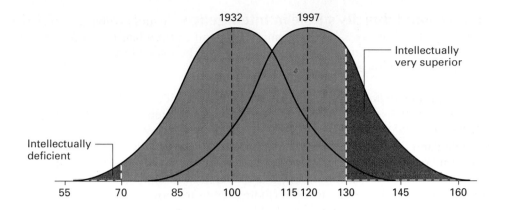

FIGURE 13.9 Increasing IQ Scores from 1932 to 1997 As measured by the Stanford-Binet intelligence test, American children seem to be getting smarter. Scores of a group tested in 1932 fell along a bell-shaped curve with half below 100 and half above. Studies show that if children took that same test today, half would score above 120 on the 1932 scale. Very few of them would score in the "intellectually deficient" end, on the left side, and about one-fourth would rank in the "very superior" range.

Schooling also influences intelligence (Ceci & Gilstrap, 2000; Christian, Bachnan, & Morrison, 2001). The biggest effects have been found when large groups of children have been deprived of formal education for an extended period, resulting in lower intelligence. One study examined the intellectual functioning of Indian children in South Africa whose schooling was delayed for four years because of the unavailability of teachers (Ramphal, 1962). Compared with children in nearby villages who had teachers, the Indian children whose entry into school was delayed by four years experienced a decrement of 5 IQ points for every year of delay.

Another possible effect of education can be seen in rapidly increasing IQ test scores around the world (Flynn, 1999). IQ scores have been increasing so fast that a high percentage of people regarded as having average intelligence at the turn of the century would be considered below average in intelligence today (Howard, 2001) (see figure 13.9). If a representative sample of people today took the Stanford-Binet test used in 1932, about one-fourth would be defined as having very superior intelligence, a label usually accorded to fewer than 3 percent of the population (Horton, 2001). Because the increase has taken place in a relatively short time, it can't be due to heredity, but rather may be due to increasing levels of education attained by a much greater percentage of the world's population or to other environmental factors such as the explosion of information to which people are exposed. The worldwide increase in intelligence test scores that has occurred over a short time frame has been called the *Flynn effect,* after the researcher who discovered it—James Flynn.

Keep in mind that environmental influences are complex (Greenfield, Suzuki, & Rothstein-Fisch, 2006; Neisser & others, 1996; Sternberg, 2001). Growing up with all the "advantages," for example, does not guarantee success. Children from wealthy families may have easy access to excellent schools, books, travel, and tutoring, but they may take such opportunities for granted and fail to develop the motivation to learn and to achieve. In the same way, "poor" or "disadvantaged" does not automatically equal "doomed."

Researchers increasingly are interested in manipulating the early environment of children at risk for impoverished intelligence (Ramey, Ramey, & Lanzi, 2001; Sternberg & Grigorenko, 2001). The emphasis is on prevention rather than remediation. Many low-income parents have difficulty providing an intellectually stimulating environment for their children. Programs that educate parents to be more sensitive caregivers and better teachers, as well as support services such as quality child-care programs, can make a difference in a child's intellectual development.

A recent review of the research on early interventions concluded that (1) high-quality center-based interventions improve children's intelligence and school achievement; (2) the effects are strongest for poor children and for children whose parents have little education; (3) the positive benefits continue into the late middle and late childhood, and adolescence, although the effects are smaller than in early childhood or the beginning of elementary school; and (4) the programs that are continued into elementary school have the most sustained long-term effects (Brooks-Gunn, 2003).

"You can't build a hut, you don't know how to find edible roots and you know nothing about predicting the weather. In other words, you do terribly on our I.Q. test."

ScienceCartoonsPlus.com.

Culture and Ethnicity's Role in Intelligence

Issues involving culture and intelligence focus on cross-cultural comparisons and cultural bias in testing. In addition, we will also examine ethnic comparisons and the issue of stereotype threat on intelligence test performance.

Cross-Cultural Comparisons   Cultures vary in the way they describe what it means to be intelligent (Benson, 2003; Greenfield, Suzuki, & Rothstein-Fisch, 2006; Sternberg & Grigorenko, 2004). People in Western cultures tend to view intelligence in terms of reasoning and thinking skills, whereas people in Eastern cultures see intelligence as a way for members of a community to successfully engage in social roles (Nisbett, 2003). One study found that Taiwanese-Chinese conceptions of intelligence emphasize understanding and relating to others, including when to show and when not to show one's intelligence (Yang & Sternberg, 1997).

Robert Serpell (1974, 2000) has studied concepts of intelligence in rural African communities since the 1970s. He has found that people in rural African communities, especially those in which Western schooling is not common, tend to blur the distinction between being intelligent and being socially competent. In rural Zambia, for example, the concept of intelligence involves being both clever and responsible. Elena Grigorenko and her colleagues (2001) have also studied the concept of intelligence among rural Africans. They found that people in the Luo culture of rural Kenya view intelligence as consisting of four domains: (1) academic intelligence; (2) social qualities such as respect, responsibility, and consideration; (3) practical thinking; and (4) comprehension. In another study in the same culture, children who scored highly on a test of knowledge about medicinal herbs—a measure of practical intelligence—tended to score poorly on tests of academic intelligence (Sternberg & others, 2001). These results indicated that practical and academic intelligence can develop independently and may even conflict with each other. They also suggest that the values of a culture may influence the direction in which a child develops. In a cross-cultural context, then, intelligence depends a great deal on environment (Greenfield, Suzuki, & Rothstein-Fisch, 2006).

Cultural Bias in Testing   Many of the early intelligence tests were culturally biased, favoring people who were from urban rather than rural environments, middle socioeconomic status rather than low socioeconomic status, and White rather than African American (Miller-Jones, 1989; Provenzo, 2002; Watras, 2002). For example, one question on an early test asked what you should do if you find a 3-year-old child in the street. The correct answer was "call the police." But children from inner-city families who perceive the police as adversaries are unlikely to choose this answer. Similarly, children from rural areas might not choose this answer if there is no police force nearby. Such questions clearly do not measure the knowledge necessary to adapt to one's environment or to be "intelligent" in an inner-city neighborhood or in rural America (Scarr, 1984). Also, members of minority groups who do not speak English or who speak nonstandard English are at a disadvantage in trying to understand questions framed in standard English.

A specific case illustrating how cultural bias in intelligence tests can affect people is that of Gregory Ochoa. When Gregory was a high school student, he and his classmates took an IQ test. Gregory understood only a few words on the test because he did not speak English very well and spoke Spanish at home. Several weeks later, Gregory was placed in a special class for mentally retarded students. Many of the students in the class, it turns out, had last names such as Ramirez and Gonzales. Gregory lost interest in school, dropped out, and eventually joined the Navy. In the Navy, Gregory took high school courses and earned enough credits to attend college later. He graduated from San Jose City College as an honor student, continued his education, and became a professor of social work at the University of Washington in Seattle.

As a result of cases like Gregory Ochoa's, researchers have developed **culture-fair tests**, which are intelligence tests intended not to be culturally biased. Two types of

culture-fair tests Intelligence tests that are intended to not be culturally biased.

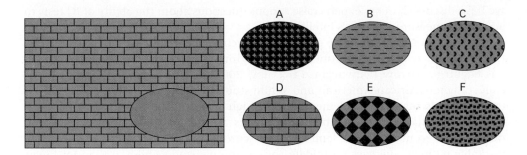

FIGURE 13.10 Sample Item from the **Raven Progressive Matrices Test** Individuals are presented with a matrix arrangement of symbols, such as the one at the top of this figure, and must then complete the matrix by selecting the appropriate missing symbol from a group of symbols.

culture-fair tests have been developed. The first includes questions familiar to people from all socioeconomic and ethnic backgrounds. For example, a child might be asked how a bird and a dog are different, on the assumption that virtually all children are familiar with birds and dogs. The second type of culture-fair test contains no verbal questions. Figure 13.10 shows a sample question from the Raven Progressive Matrices Test. Even though tests such as the Raven Progressive Matrices are designed to be culture-fair, people with more education still score higher than those with less education do (Greenfield, 2003).

Why is it so hard to create culture-fair tests? Most tests tend to reflect what the dominant culture thinks is important (Greenfield, Suzuki, & Rothstein-Fisch, 2006; Greenfield & others, 2003; Merenda, 2004). If tests have time limits, that will bias the test against groups not concerned with time. If languages differ, the same words might have different meanings for different language groups. Even pictures can produce bias because some cultures have less experience with drawings and photographs (Anastasi & Urbina, 1996). Within the same culture, different groups could have different attitudes, values, and motivation, and this could affect their performance on intelligence tests. Items that ask why buildings should be made of brick are biased against children who have little or no experience with brick houses. Questions about railroads, furnaces, seasons of the year, distances between cities, and so on can be biased against groups with less experience than others with these contexts.

Ethnic Comparisons   In the United States, children from African American and Latino families score below children from White families on standardized intelligence tests. On the average, African American schoolchildren score 10 to 15 points lower on standardized intelligence tests than White American schoolchildren do (Brody, 2000; Lynn, 1996). These are *average scores*, however. About 15 to 25 percent of African American schoolchildren score higher than half of White schoolchildren do, and many Whites score lower than most African Americans. The reason is that the distribution of scores for African Americans and Whites overlaps.

A controversy erupted in response to the book *The Bell Curve: Intelligence and Class Structure in American Life* (1994) by Richard Herrnstein and Charles Murray. Recall that the bell curve is the shape of a normal distribution graph, which represents large numbers of people who are sorted according to some shared characteristic, such as weight, taste in clothes, or IQ. Herrnstein and Murray note that predictions about any individual based exclusively on the person's IQ are virtually useless. Weak correlations between IQ and job success have predictive value only when they are applied to large groups of people. But within large groups, say Herrnstein and Murray, the pervasive influence of IQ on human society becomes apparent. The authors argued that America is developing a huge underclass of intellectually deprived individuals whose cognitive abilities will never match the future needs of most employers. They believe that this underclass, a large proportion of which is African American, may be doomed by their shortcomings to welfare dependency, poverty, and crime.

Significant criticisms have been leveled at *The Bell Curve*. The average score of African Americans is lower than the average score of Whites on IQ tests. However, as we have discussed, many experts raise serious questions about the ability of IQ tests to accurately measure a person's intelligence.

As African Americans have gained social, economic, and educational opportunities, the gap between African Americans and Whites on standardized intelligence tests has begun to narrow (Onwuegbuzi & Daley, 2001). This gap especially narrows in college, where African American and White students often experience more similar environments than in the elementary and high school years. Also, when children from disadvantaged African American families are adopted into more-advantaged middle-socioeconomic-status families, their scores on intelligence tests more closely resemble national averages for middle-socioeconomic-status children than for lower socioeconomic-status children (Scarr & Weinberg, 1983).

One potential influence on intelligence test performance is *stereotype threat*, the anxiety that one's behavior might confirm a negative stereotype about one's group. For example, when African Americans take an intelligence test, they may experience anxiety about confirming the old stereotype that Blacks are "intellectually inferior." In one study, the verbal part of the Graduate Record Exam (GRE) was given individually to African American and White students at Stanford University (Steele & Aronson, 1995). Half the students of each ethnic group were told that the researchers were interested in assessing their intellectual ability. The other half were told that the researchers were trying to develop a test and that it might not be reliable and valid (therefore, it would not mean anything in relation to their intellectual ability). The White students did equally well on the test in both conditions. However, the African American students did more poorly when they thought the test was assessing their intellectual ability; when they thought the test was just in the development stage and might not be reliable or valid, they performed as well as the White students.

Other studies have confirmed the existence of stereotype threat (Chen & Sherman, 2005; Helms, 2005; Good, Anderson, & Inzlicht, 2003; Steele & Marcus, 2003). African American students do more poorly on standardized tests if they believe they are being evaluated. If they believe the test doesn't count, they perform as well as White students (Aronson, 2002; Aronson & others, 1999; Aronson, Fried, & Good, 2002). However, some critics believe the extent to which stereotype threat explains the testing gap has been exaggerated (Cullen, Hardison, & Sackett, 2004; Sackett, Hardison, & Cullen, 2004).

The Use and Misuse of Intelligence Tests

Psychological tests are tools. Like all tools, their effectiveness depends on the knowledge, skill, and integrity of the user. A hammer can be used to build a beautiful kitchen cabinet, or it can be used as a weapon of assault. Like a hammer, psychological tests can be used for positive purposes, or they can be badly abused. Here are some cautions about IQ that can help you avoid the pitfalls of using information about a child's intelligence in negative ways:

- *Avoid stereotyping and expectations.* A special concern is that the scores on an IQ test easily can lead to stereotypes and expectations about students. Sweeping generalizations are too often made on the basis of an IQ score. An IQ test should always be considered a measure of current performance. It is not a measure of fixed potential. Maturational changes and enriched environmental experiences can advance a student's intelligence.
- *Note that IQ is not a sole indicator of competence.* Another concern about IQ tests occurs when they are used as the main or sole characteristic of competence. A high IQ is not the ultimate human value. As we have seen in this chapter, it is important to consider not only students' intellectual competence in such areas as verbal skills but also their creative and practical skills.
- *Use caution in interpreting an overall IQ score.* In evaluating a child's intelligence, it is wiser to think of intelligence as consisting of a number of domains. Keep in mind the different types of intelligence described by Sternberg and Gardner.

Remember that, by considering the different domains of intelligence, you can find that every child has at least one or more strengths.

The Extremes of Intelligence

Intelligence tests have been used to discover indications of mental retardation or intellectual giftedness, the extremes of intelligence. At times, intelligence tests have been misused for this purpose. Keeping in mind the theme that an intelligence test should not be used as the sole indicator of mental retardation or giftedness, we will explore the nature of these intellectual extremes.

Mental Retardation

Mental retardation is a condition of limited mental ability in which an individual has a low IQ, usually below 70 on a traditional intelligence test, and has difficulty adapting to everyday life. About 5 million Americans fit this definition of mental retardation.

There are several classifications of mental retardation. About 89 percent of the mentally retarded fall into the mild category, with IQs of 55 to 70. About 6 percent are classified as moderately retarded, with IQs of 40 to 54; these people can attain a second-grade level of skills and may be able to support themselves as adults through some types of labor. About 3.5 percent of the mentally retarded are in the severe category, with IQs of 25 to 39; these individuals learn to talk and engage in very simple tasks but require extensive supervision. Less than 1 percent have IQs below 25; they fall into the profoundly mentally retarded classification and need constant supervision (Zigler, 2002).

Mental retardation can have an organic cause, or it can be social and cultural in origin:

A child with Down Syndrome. *What causes a child to develop Down Syndrome?*

- **Organic retardation** is mental retardation that is caused by a genetic disorder or by brain damage; the word *organic* refers to the tissues or organs of the body, so there is some physical damage in organic retardation. Down syndrome, one form of mental retardation, occurs when an extra chromosome is present in an individual's genetic makeup. It is not known why the extra chromosome is present, but it may involve the health or age of the female ovum or male sperm. Most people who suffer from organic retardation have IQs that range between 0 and 50.
- **Cultural-familial retardation** is a mental deficit in which no evidence of organic brain damage can be found; individuals' IQs range from 50 to 70. Psychologists suspect that such mental deficits result from the normal variation that distributes people along the range of intelligence scores above 50, combined with growing up in a below-average intellectual environment.

Giftedness

There have always been people whose abilities and accomplishments outshine others': the whiz kid in class, the star athlete, the natural musician. People who are **gifted** have above-average intelligence (an IQ of 130 or higher) and/or superior talent for something. When it comes to programs for the gifted, most school systems select children who have intellectual superiority and academic aptitude. Children talented in the visual and performing arts (arts, drama, dance), athletics, or other special aptitudes tend to be overlooked. There has been speculation that giftedness is linked with having a mental disorder.

However, no relation between giftedness and mental disorder has been found. Recent studies support the conclusion that gifted people tend to be more mature, have fewer emotional problems than others, and grow up in a positive family climate (Davidson, 2000; Feldman, 2001).

What are the characteristics of children who are gifted? Lewis Terman (1925) conducted an extensive study of 1,500 children whose Stanford-Binet IQs averaged 150. A popular myth is that gifted children are maladjusted, but Terman found in his study that

mental retardation A condition of limited mental ability in which an individual has a low IQ, usually below 70 on a traditional test of intelligence, and has difficulty adapting to everyday life.

organic retardation Mental retardation caused by a genetic disorder or brain damage in which an individual usually has an IQ between 0 and 50.

cultural-familial retardation Retardation that is characterized by no evidence of organic brain damage, but the individual's IQ is between 50 and 70.

gifted Having above-average intelligence, usually an IQ of 130 or higher, and a superior talent for something.

At 2 years of age, art prodigy Alexandra Nechita colored in coloring books for hours and also took up pen and ink. She had no interest in dolls or friends. By age 5 she was using watercolors. Once she started school, she would start painting as soon as she got home. At the age of 8, in 1994, she saw the first public exhibit of her work. In succeeding years, working quickly and impulsively on canvases as large as 5 feet by 9 feet, she has completed hundreds of paintings, some of which sell for close to $100,000 apiece. As a teenager, she continues to paint—relentlessly and passionately. It is, she says, what she loves to do. *What are some characteristics of children who are gifted?*

www.mhhe.com/santrockc9

Gifted Education
National Association of Gifted Children

they were not only academically gifted but also socially well adjusted. Many of these gifted children went on to become successful doctors, lawyers, professors, and scientists.

Ellen Winner (1996) described three criteria that characterize gifted children, whether in art, music, or academic domains:

1. *Precocity.* Gifted children are precocious. They begin to master an area earlier than their peers. Learning in their domain is more effortless for them than for ordinary children. In most instances, these gifted children are precocious because they have an inborn high ability in a particular domain or domains.
2. *Marching to their own drummer.* Gifted children learn in a qualitatively different way than ordinary children. One way that they march to a different drummer is that they need minimal help, or scaffolding, from adults to learn. In many instances, they resist any kind of explicit instruction. They also often make discoveries on their own and solve problems in unique ways.
3. *A passion to master.* Gifted children are driven to understand the domain in which they have high ability. They display an intense, obsessive interest and an ability to focus. They are not children who need to be pushed by their parents. They motivate themselves, says Winner.

Is giftedness a product of heredity or environment? Likely both. Experts who study giftedness point out that individuals recall that they had signs of high ability in a particular area at a very young age, prior to or at the beginning of formal training (Howe & others, 1995; Olszewski-Kublilius, 2003). This suggests the importance of innate ability in giftedness. However, researchers also have found that the individuals of worldclass status in the arts, mathematics, science, and sports all report strong family support and years of training and practice (Bloom, 1985). Deliberate practice is an important characteristic of individuals who become gifted in a particular domain. For example, in one study, the best musicians engaged in twice as much deliberate practice over their lives as the least successful ones did (Ericsson, Krampe, & Tesch-Romer, 1993).

One career opportunity in child development involves working with children who are gifted as a teacher or supervisor. To read about the work of a supervisor of gifted and talented education, see the Careers in Child Development profile. Also, the following Caring for Children interlude provides strategies for improving the education of children who are gifted.

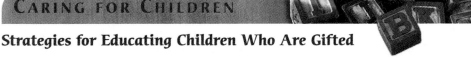

CARING FOR CHILDREN

Strategies for Educating Children Who Are Gifted

An increasing number of experts argue that the education of children who are gifted in the United States requires a significant overhaul, as reflected in the titles of recent books and reports: *Genius Denied: How to Stop Wasting Our Brightest Young Minds* (Davidson & Davidson, 2004) and *A Nation Deceived: How Schools Hold Back America's Brightest Students* (Colangelo, Assouline, & Gross, 2004).

Underchallenged gifted children can become disruptive, skip classes, and lose interest in achieving. Sometimes these children just disappear into the woodwork, becoming passive and apathetic toward school (Rosselli, 1996). It is extremely important for teachers to challenge children who are gifted to reach high expectations (Hargrove, 2005; Tassell-Baska & Stambaugh, 2006; Winner, 2006).

An *enrichment program* provides children with opportunities for learning that are usually not present in the curriculum. Enrichment opportunities can be made available in the regular classroom, through "pullout" to a special class; through a gifted education resource teacher who consults with the regular classroom teacher; through independent study, in after-school, Saturday, or summer sessions, and in apprenticeship and mentoring programs; and through work/study arrangements.

The Schoolwide Enrichment Model (SEM), developed by Joseph Renzulli (1998), is a program for educating children who are gifted that focuses on total school improvement. Renzulli says that when enrichment has a schoolwide emphasis, positive outcomes are likely to occur, not only for children who are gifted but also for nongifted children and for classroom and resource teachers. When schoolwide enrichment is emphasized, "us" versus "them" barriers often decrease, and classroom teachers are more willing to use curriculum compacting with their most gifted children. Instead of feeling isolated, resource teachers begin to feel more like members of a team, especially when they work with regular classroom teachers on enriching the entire classroom. Thus, important goals of SEM are to improve outcomes for both students who are gifted and those who are not gifted and to improve the contributions and relationships of classroom and resource teachers.

Here are some recommended strategies for working with children who are gifted (Colangelo, Assouline, & Gross, 2004, pp. 49–50):

1. *Recognize that the child is academically advanced.*
2. *Guide the child to new challenges and ensure that school is a positive experience.*
3. *Monitor the accurate evaluation of the child's readiness to be accelerated.*
4. *Discuss with parents ways to appropriately challenge the child.*
5. *Learn about and use resources for children who are gifted.* Among these are the National Research Center on Gifted and Talented Education at the University of Connecticut and the Belin-Blank Center at the University of Iowa; *Gifted Child Quarterly* and *Gifted Child Today* journals; and books on children who are gifted (such as *Genius Denied* by Davidson & Davidson (2004), *A Nation Deceived* by Colangelo and colleagues (2004), and *Handbook of Gifted Education* (3rd ed.) by Colangelo & Davis (2003).

CAREERS in CHILD DEVELOPMENT

Sterling Jones
Supervisor of Gifted and Talented Education

Sterling Jones is program supervisor for gifted and talented children in the Detroit Public School System. Jones has been working for more than three decades with children who are gifted. He believes that students' mastery of skills mainly depends on the amount of time devoted to instruction and the length of time allowed for learning. Thus, he believes that many basic strategies for challenging children who are gifted to develop their skills can be applied to a wider range of students than once believed. He has rewritten several pamphlets for use by teachers and parents, including *How to Help Your Child Succeed* and *Gifted and Talented Education for Everyone.*

Jones has undergraduate and graduate degrees from Wayne State University and taught English for a number of years before becoming involved in the program for gifted children. He also has written materials on African Americans, such as *Voices from the Black Experience,* that are used in the Detroit schools.

Sterling Jones with some of the children in the gifted program in the Detroit Public School System.

Review and Reflect • LEARNING GOAL 3

3 **Characterize children's intelligence.**

Review
- What is intelligence? How can the Binet tests and Wechsler scales be characterized?
- What is factor analysis? What are some different views of multiple intelligences? How can the multiple intelligences approach be evaluated?
- What are three important controversies and issues in intelligence? Explain them.
- What is the nature of children's mental retardation? How can children's giftedness be described?

Reflect
- A CD-ROM, *Children's IQ and Achievement Test,* now lets parents test their child's IQ. What might be some problems with parents giving their own children an IQ test?

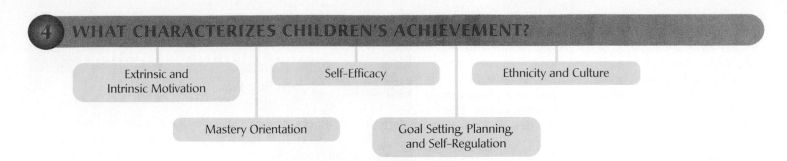

4   WHAT CHARACTERIZES CHILDREN'S ACHIEVEMENT?

Extrinsic and Intrinsic Motivation

Self-Efficacy

Ethnicity and Culture

Mastery Orientation

Goal Setting, Planning, and Self-Regulation

We are a species motivated to do well at what we attempt, to gain mastery over the world in which we live, to explore unknown environments with enthusiasm and curiosity, and to achieve the heights of success. What are some ways that children can effectively achieve their potential?

Extrinsic and Intrinsic Motivation

Extrinsic motivation involves external incentives such as rewards and punishments. The humanistic and cognitive approaches stress the importance of intrinsic motivation in achievement. **Intrinsic motivation** is based on internal factors such as self-determination, curiosity, challenge, and effort. Some individuals study hard because they want to make good grades or avoid parental disapproval (extrinsic motivation). Others study hard because they are internally motivated to achieve high standards in their work (intrinsic motivation).

One view of intrinsic motivation emphasizes self-determination (deCharms, 1984; Deci & Ryan, 1994; Ryan & Deci, 2001). In this view, children want to believe that they are doing something because of their own will, not because of external success or rewards.

Researchers have found that giving children some choice and providing opportunities for personal responsibility increases their internal motivation and intrinsic interest in school tasks (Blumenfeld, Krajik, & Kempler, 2006; Lepper & Henderlong, 2001; Pintrich, 2003; Stipek, 2002; Wiafield & others, 2006). For example, one study found that high school science students who were encouraged to organize their own experiments demonstrated more care and interest in laboratory work than their counterparts who were given detailed instructions and directions (Rainey, 1965). In another study, which included mainly African American students from low-income backgrounds, teachers were encouraged to give the students more responsibility for their school program (deCharms, 1984). This consisted of opportunities to set their own goals, plan how to reach the goals, and monitor their progress toward the goals. Students were given some choice of activities to engage in and when they would do them. They also were encouraged to take personal responsibility for their behavior,

extrinsic motivation External incentives such as rewards and punishments.

intrinsic motivation Internal factors such as self-determination, curiosity, challenge, and effort.

Calvin and Hobbes   **by Bill Watterson**

including reaching the goals that they had set. Compared with a control group, students in the intrinsic motivation/self-determination group had higher achievement gains and were more likely to graduate from high school.

Phyllis Blumenfeld and her colleagues (2006) have proposed another variation on intrinsic motivation that emphasizes the importance of creating learning environments that encourage students to become cognitively engaged and take responsibility for their learning. The goal is to get students to become motivated to expend the effort to persist and master ideas rather than simply doing enough work to just get by and make passing grades. Especially important in encouraging students to become cognitively engaged and responsible for their learning is to embed subject matter content and skills learning within meaningful contexts, especially real-world situations that mesh with students' interests.

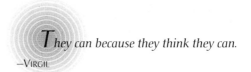

They can because they think they can.
—VIRGIL
Roman Poet, 1st Century B.C.

Mastery Orientation

Developmental psychologists Valanne Henderson and Carol Dweck (1990) have found that children show two distinct responses to difficult or challenging circumstances. Individuals with a **mastery orientation** are task-oriented; instead of focusing on their ability, they concentrate on learning strategies and the process of achievement rather than the outcome. Those with a **helpless orientation** seem trapped by the experience of difficulty and they attribute their difficulty to lack of ability. They frequently say such things as "I'm not very good at this," even though they might earlier have demonstrated their ability through many successes. And, once they view their behavior as failure, they often feel anxious, and their performance worsens even further. In contrast, mastery-oriented children often instruct themselves to pay attention, to think carefully, and to remember strategies that have worked for them in previous situations. They frequently report feeling challenged and excited by difficult tasks, rather than being threatened by them (Anderman, Maehr, & Midgley, 1996; Dweck, Mangels, & Good, 2004). One recent study of elementary school students found that a higher level of mastery motivation was linked to higher math and reading grades (Broussard & Garrison, 2004).

Another issue in motivation involves whether to adopt a mastery or a performance orientation. Children with a **performance orientation** are focused on winning, rather than on achievement outcome, and believe that happiness results from winning. Does this mean that mastery-oriented individuals do not like to win and that performance-oriented individuals are not motivated to experience the self-efficacy that comes from being able to take credit for one's accomplishments? No. A matter of emphasis or degree is involved, though. For mastery-oriented individuals, winning isn't everything; for performance-oriented individuals, skill development and self-efficacy take a back seat to winning.

www.mhhe.com/santrockc9

Exploring Self-Efficacy

Self-Efficacy

Self-efficacy is the belief that one can master a situation and produce favorable outcomes. Albert Bandura (1997, 2001, 2004), whose social cognitive theory we described in chapter 2, emphasizes that self-efficacy is a critical factor in whether or not students achieve. Self-efficacy has much in common with mastery motivation and intrinsic motivation. Self-efficacy is the belief that "I can"; helplessness is the belief that "I cannot" (Stipek, 2002). Students with high self-efficacy endorse such statements as "I know that I will be able to learn the material in this class" and "I expect to be able to do well at this activity."

Dale Schunk (2004; Zimmerman & Schunk, 2004) has applied the concept of self-efficacy to many aspects of students' achievement. In his view, self-efficacy influences a student's choice of activities. Students with low self-efficacy for learning may avoid many learning tasks, especially those that are challenging. By contrast,

mastery orientation An orientation in which one is task-oriented and, instead of focusing on one's ability, is concerned with learning strategies.

helpless orientation An orientation in which one seems trapped by the experience of difficulty and attributes one's difficulty to a lack of ability.

performance orientation An orientation in which one focuses on achievement outcomes; winning is what matters most, and happiness is thought to result from winning.

self-efficacy The belief that one can master a situation and produce favorable outcomes.

high-self-efficacy counterparts eagerly work at learning tasks. High-self-efficacy students are more likely to expend effort and persist longer at a learning task than low-self-efficacy students.

Goal Setting, Planning, and Self-Regulation

Researchers have found that self-efficacy and achievement improve when individuals set goals that are specific, proximal, and challenging (Bandura, 2001). A nonspecific, fuzzy goal is "I want to be successful." A more concrete, specific goal is "I want to make the honor roll by the end of the semester."

Individuals can set both long-term (distal) and short-term (proximal) goals. It is okay for individuals to set some long-term goals, such as "I want to graduate from high school" or "I want to go to college," but they also need to create short-term goals, which are steps along the way. "Getting an A on the next math test" is an example of a short-term, proximal goal. So is "Doing all of my homework by 4 P.M. Sunday." David McNally (1990), author of *Even Eagles Need a Push*, advises that when individuals set goals and plan, they should be reminded to live their lives one day at a time. Have them make their commitments in bite-size chunks. A house is built one brick at a time, a cathedral one stone at a time. The artist paints one stroke at a time. The student should also work in small increments.

Another good strategy is for individuals to set challenging goals (Theobold, 2005; Wolters, 2004). A challenging goal is a commitment to self-improvement. Strong interest and involvement in activities are sparked by challenges. Goals that are easy to reach generate little interest or effort. However, goals should be optimally matched to the individual's skill level. If goals are unrealistically high, the result will be repeated failures that lower the individual's self-efficacy.

It is not enough just to get individuals to set goals. It also is important to encourage them to plan how they will reach their goals. Being a good planner means managing time effectively, setting priorities, and being organized.

Individuals not only should plan their next week's activities but also monitor how well they are sticking to their plan. Once engaged in a task, they need to monitor their progress, judge how well they are doing on the task, and evaluate the outcomes to regulate what they do in the future. Researchers have found that high-achieving adolescents often are self-regulatory learners (Boekarts, 2006; Schunk & Zimmerman, 2003; Wigfield & others, 2006). For example, high-achieving children self-monitor their learning more and systematically evaluate their progress toward a goal more than low-achieving children do (Pintrich, 2003). Encouraging children to self-monitor their learning conveys the message that children are responsible for their own behavior and that learning requires active dedicated participation by the child (Sansone & Smith, 2001).

Ethnicity and Culture

What is the nature of achievement in ethnic minority children? How does culture influence children's achievement?

Ethnicity   The diversity that exists among ethnic minority children is evident in their achievement. For example, many Asian American students have a strong academic achievement orientation, but some do not.

In addition to recognizing the diversity that exists within every cultural group in terms of their achievement, it also is important to distinguish between difference and deficiency (Banks, 2006; Cushner, 2006). Too often, the achievement of ethnic minority students—especially African Americans, Latinos, and Native Americans—have been interpreted as *deficits* by middle-socioeconomic-status White standards, when they simply are *culturally different and distinct* (Jones, 1994).

Asian grade schools intersperse studying with frequent periods of activities. This approach helps children maintain their attention and likely makes learning more enjoyable. Shown here are Japanese fourth-graders making wearable masks. *What are some differences in the way children in many Asian countries are taught compared with children in the United States?*

At the same time, many investigations overlook the socioeconomic status of ethnic minority students. In many instances, when ethnicity *and* socioeconomic status are investigated in a study, socioeconomic status predicts achievement better than ethnicity does. Students from middle- and upper-income families fare better than their counterparts from low-income backgrounds in a host of achievement situations—for example, expectations for success, achievement aspirations, and recognition of the importance of effort (Gibbs, 1989).

Sandra Graham (1986, 1990) has conducted a number of studies that reveal not only stronger socioeconomic-status than ethnic differences in achievement but also the importance of studying ethnic minority student motivation in the context of general motivational theory. Her inquiries fall within the framework of attribution theory and focus on the causes that African American students give for their achievement orientation, such as why they succeed or fail. She is struck by how consistently middle-income African American students do not fit the stereotype of being unmotivated. Like their White middle-income counterparts, they have high achievement expectations and understand that failure is usually due to a lack of effort, rather than bad luck.

A special challenge for many ethnic minority students, especially those living in poverty, is dealing with racial prejudice, conflict between the values of their group and those of the majority group, and a lack of high-achieving adults in their cultural group who can serve as positive role models.

It also is important to consider the nature of the schools that primarily serve ethnic minority students (Blumenfeld & others, 2005; Garcia Coll & others, 2005; Ogbu, 2003). More than one-third of all African American and almost one-third of all Latino students attend schools in the 47 largest city school districts in the United States, compared with only 5 percent of all White and 22 percent of all Asian American students. Many of these ethnic minority students come from low-income families (more than half are eligible for free or reduced-cost lunches). These inner-city schools are less likely than other schools to serve more-advantaged populations or to offer high-quality academic support services, advanced courses, and courses that challenge students' active thinking skills. Even students who are motivated to learn and achieve may find it difficult to perform effectively in such contexts.

Culture   In the past two decades, the poor performance of American children in math and science has become well publicized. For example, in one cross-national comparison of the math and science achievement of 9- to 13-year-old students, the United States finished 13th (out of 15) in science and 15th (out of 16) in math

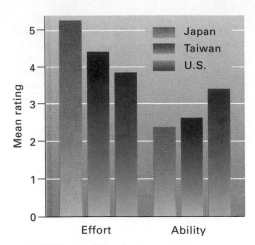

FIGURE 13.11 Mothers' Beliefs About the Factors Responsible for Children's Math Achievement in Three Countries In one study, mothers in Japan and Taiwan were more likely to believe that their children's math achievement was due to effort rather than innate ability, while U.S. mothers were more likely to believe their children's math achievement was due to innate ability (Stevenson, Lee, & Stigler, 1986). If parents believe that their children's math achievement is due to innate ability and their children are not doing well in math, the implication is that they are less likely to think their children will benefit from putting forth more effort.

We [the United States] accept performances in students that are nowhere near where they should be.

—HAROLD STEVENSON

Contemporary Psychologist, University of Michigan

achievement (Educational Testing Service, 1992). In this study, Korean and Taiwanese students placed first and second, respectively.

Harold Stevenson's (1995, 2000; Stevenson, Hofer, & Randel, 1999; Stevenson & others, 1990) research explores reasons for the poor performance of American students. Stevenson and his colleagues have completed five cross-cultural comparisons of students in the United States, China, Taiwan, and Japan. In these studies, Asian students consistently outperform American students. And, the longer the students are in school, the wider the gap becomes between Asian and American students—the lowest difference is in the first grade, the highest in the eleventh grade (the highest grade studied).

To learn more about the reasons for these large cross-cultural differences, Stevenson and his colleagues spent thousands of hours observing in classrooms, as well as interviewing and surveying teachers, students, and parents. They found that the Asian teachers spent more of their time teaching math than did the American teachers. For example, more than one-fourth of total classroom time in the first grade was spent on math instruction in Japan, compared with only one-tenth of the time in the U.S. first-grade classrooms. Also, the Asian students were in school an average of 240 days a year, compared with 178 days in the United States.

In addition to the substantially greater time spent on math instruction in the Asian schools than the American schools, differences were found between the Asian and American parents. The American parents had much lower expectations for their children's education and achievement than did the Asian parents. Also, the American parents were more likely to believe that their children's math achievement was due to innate ability; the Asian parents were more likely to say that their children's math achievement was the consequence of effort and training (see figure 13.11). The Asian students were more likely to do math homework than were the American students, and the Asian parents were far more likely to help their children with their math homework than were the American parents (Chen & Stevenson, 1989).

Critics of the cross-national comparisons argue that, in many comparisons, virtually all U.S. children are being compared with a "select" group of children from other countries, especially in the secondary school comparisons. Therefore, they conclude, it is no wonder that American students don't fare so well. That criticism holds for some international comparisons. However, even when the top 25 percent of students in different countries were recently compared, U.S. students did move up some, but not a lot (Mullis & others, 1998).

Review and Reflect • LEARNING GOAL 4

4 **Explain the development of achievement in children.**

Review
- How does extrinsic motivation differ from intrinsic motivation? What role do rewards play in extrinsic and intrinsic motivation?
- How can mastery, helpless, and performance orientations be differentiated?
- What is self-efficacy and how is it involved in achievement?
- What functions do goal setting, planning, and self-monitoring play in achievement?
- How is achievement related to ethnicity and culture?

Reflect
- Think about several of your own past schoolmates who showed low motivation in school. Why do you think they behaved that way? What teaching strategies may have helped them?

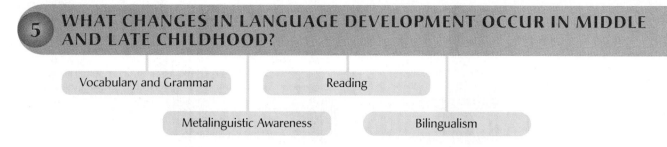

During middle and late childhood, children make advances in their vocabulary and grammar (Dale & Goodman, 2005; Ely, 2005). As children enter elementary school, they gain skills that make it possible for them to read and write. Reading and writing assume a prominent role in their language world.

Vocabulary and Grammar

How children think about words changes during middle and late childhood. They become less tied to the actions and perceptions associated with words, and they become more analytical in their approach to words.

This analytical approach is apparent if children are asked to say the first thing that comes to mind when they hear a word. Preschool children typically respond with a word that often follows the stimulus word in a sentence. For example, when asked to respond to "dog," the young child may say "barks"; to the word "eat, "lunch." But at about 7 years of age, children may begin to respond with a word that is the same part of speech as the stimulus word. For example, a child may now respond to the word "dog" with "cat" or "horse." To "eat," the 7-year-old might say "drink." This is evidence that children have begun to categorize their vocabulary by parts of speech (Berko Gleason, 2002).

During the elementary school years, children become increasingly able to understand and use complex grammar—for example, stating sentences such as *The boy who kissed his mother who wore a hat*. They also learn to use language in a more connected way. Now they can produce connected discourse, relating sentences to one another and producing descriptions, definitions, and narratives that hang together and make sense. Children must be able to do these things orally before they can be expected to do them in written assignments.

Metalinguistic Awareness

Metalinguistic awareness refers to knowledge of language, which allows children "to think about their language, understand what words are, and even define them," (Berko Gleason, 2005, p. 4). Recall from earlier in the chapter that metacognition is cognition about cognition, or knowing about knowing. Metalinguistic awareness is essentially cognition about language.

Metalinguistic awareness improves considerably during the elementary school years. Defining words becomes a regular part of classroom discourse and children increase their knowledge of syntax as they study and talk about the components of sentences such as subjects and verbs (Ely, 2005). Children also make progress in understanding how to use language in culturally appropriate ways—pragmatics. By the time they enter adolescence, most children know the rules for the use of language in everyday contexts, that is, what is appropriate to say and what is inappropriate to say.

Reading

One model describes the development of reading skills as occurring in five stages (Chall, 1979) (see figure 13.12). The age boundaries are approximate and do not apply

FIGURE 13.12 A Model of Developmental Stages in Reading

Stage	Age range/ grade level	Description
0	Birth to first grade	Children master several prerequisites for reading. Many learn the left-to-right progression and order of reading, how to identify the letters of the alphabet, and how to write their names. Some learn to read words that appear on signs. As a result of TV shows like *Sesame Street* and attending preschool and kindergarten programs, many young children today develop greater knowledge about reading earlier than in the past.
1	First and second grades	Many children learn to read at this time. In doing so, they acquire the ability to sound out words (that is, translate letters into sounds and blend sounds into words). They also complete their learning of letter names and sounds.
2	Second and third grades	Children become more fluent at retrieving individual words and other reading skills. However, at this stage reading is still not used much for learning. The demands of reading are so taxing for children at this stage that they have few resources left over to process the content.
3	Fourth through eighth grades	In fourth through eighth grades, children become increasingly able to obtain new information from print. In other words, they read to learn. They still have difficulty understanding information presented from multiple perspectives within the same story. When children don't learn to read, a downward spiral unfolds that leads to serious difficulties in many academic subjects.
4	High school	Many students become fully competent readers. They develop the ability to understand material told from many perspectives. This allows them to engage in sometimes more sophisticated discussions of literature, history, economics, and politics.

to every child, but the stages convey a sense of the developmental changes involved in learning to read.

Before learning to read, children learn to use language to talk about things that are not present; they learn what a word is; and they learn how to recognize and talk about sounds (Berko Gleason, 2002). They also learn the *alphabetic principle*—that letters represent sounds in the language. How should children be taught to read? Currently, debate focuses on the whole-language approach versus the basic-skill-and-phonetics approach (May, 2006; Ruddell, 2006; Smith, 2004a; Vacca & others, 2006).

The **whole-language approach** stresses that reading instruction should parallel children's natural language learning. Reading materials should be whole and meaningful. That is, children should be given material in its complete form, such as stories and poems, so that they learn to understand language's communicative function. Reading should be connected with listening and writing skills. Although there are variations in whole-language programs, most share the premise that reading should be integrated with other skills and subjects, such as science and social studies, and that it should focus on real-world material. Thus, a class might read newspapers, magazines, or books, and then write about and discuss them.

In contrast, the **basic-skills-and-phonetics approach** emphasizes that reading instruction should teach phonetics and its basic rules for translating written symbols into sounds. Early reading instruction should involve simplified materials. Only after they have learned phonological rules should children be given complex reading materials, such as books and poems.

Which approach is better? Children can benefit from both approaches. Researchers have found strong evidence that the basic-skills-and-phonetics approach should be used in teaching children to read but that students also benefit from the

whole-language approach An approach to reading instruction based on the idea that instruction should parallel children's natural language learning. Reading materials should be whole and meaningful.

basic-skills-and-phonetics approach An approach to reading instruction that stresses phonetics and basic rules for translating symbols into sounds. Early reading instruction should involve simplified materials.

whole-language approach (Fox & Hull, 2002; Heilman, Blair, & Rupley, 2002). These were the conclusions of the National Reading Panel (2000), which conducted a comprehensive review of research on reading. In addition, researchers have found that training for phonological awareness is best when it is integrated with reading and writing, is simple, and is conducted in small groups rather than with a whole class (Stahl, 2002).

Other conclusions reached by the National Reading Panel (2000) suggest that children benefit from *guided oral* reading—that is, from reading aloud with guidance and feedback. Learning strategies for reading comprehension—such as monitoring one's own reading progress and summarizing—also helps children (Pressley, 2003; Pressley & Hilden, 2006).

Having a good vocabulary helps readers to access word meaning effortlessly and researchers have found that vocabulary development is an important aspect of reading (Berninger, 2006; Snow & Kang, 2006). For example, a recent study found that a good vocabulary was linked to reading comprehension in second grade students (Berninger & Abbott, 2005). Other research studies have also found that vocabulary plays an important role in reading comprehension (Paris & Paris, 2006; Snow & Kang, 2006).

Reading, like other important skills, takes time and effort (McWhorter, 2005). In a national assessment, children in the fourth grade had higher scores on a national reading test when they read 11 or more pages daily for school and homework (National Assessment of Educational Progress, 2000) (see figure 13.13). Teachers who required students to read a great deal on a daily basis had students who were more proficient at reading than teachers who required little reading by their students.

In the cognitive approach, researchers have focused not so much on whether one teaching approach, such as whole language, is better than another, such as phonics. Rather, they have searched for the underlying cognitive processes that explain reading. The search has led to an interest in strategies, especially the strategies of expert readers compared with novice readers (Pressley, 2003). Researchers have found that monitoring one's reading is an important strategy. Summarizing is also another important reading strategy.

Bilingualism

Learning a second language is more readily accomplished by children than by adolescents or adults. Adults make faster initial progress, but their eventual success in the second language is not as great as children's. For example, in one study, Chinese and Korean adults who immigrated to the United States at different ages were given a test of grammatical knowledge (Johnston & Newport, 1991). Those who began learning English when they were 3 to 7 years old scored as well as native speakers on the test, but those who arrived in the United States (and started learning English) in later childhood or adolescence had lower test scores (see figure 13.14). Children's ability to pronounce a second language with the correct accent also decreases with age, with an especially sharp drop occurring after the age of about 10 to 12 (Asher & Garcia, 1969). In sum, researchers have found that early bilingual exposure is optimal and ensures the least amount of damage to the home language and to the new language (Petitto, Kovelman, & Harasymowycz, 2003).

Students in the United States are far behind their counterparts in many developed countries in learning a second language. For example, in Russia, schools have 10 grades, called *forms,* which roughly correspond to the 12 grades in American schools. Children begin school at age 7 in Russia and begin learning English in the third form. Because of this emphasis on teaching English, most Russian citizens under the age of 40 today are able to speak at least some English.

U.S. students may be missing more than the chance to acquire a skill by not learning to speak a second language. *Bilingualism*—the ability to speak two languages—has a positive effect on children's cognitive development. Children who are fluent in two

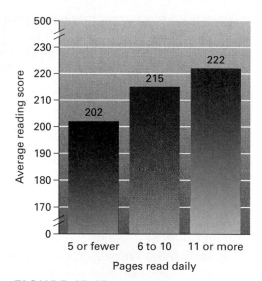

FIGURE 13.13 **The Relation of Reading Achievement to Number of Pages Read Daily** In the recent analysis of reading in the fourth grade in the National Assessment of Educational Progress (2000), reading more pages daily in school and as part of homework assignments was related to higher scores on a reading test in which scores ranged from 0 to 500.

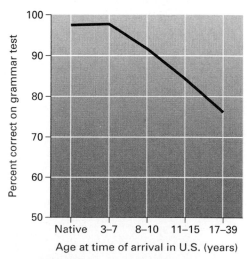

FIGURE 13.14 **Grammar Proficiency and Age at Arrival in the United States** In one study, ten years after arriving in the United States, individuals from China and Korea took a grammar test (Johnson & Newport, 1991). People who arrived before the age of 8 had a better grasp of grammar than those who arrived later.

CAREERS in CHILD DEVELOPMENT

Salvador Tamayo
Bilingual Education Teacher

Salvador Tamayo teaches bilingual education in the fifth grade at Turner Elementary School in West Chicago. He recently was given a national educator award by the Milken Family Foundation for his work in bilingual education. Tamayo especially is adept at integrating technology into his bilingual education classes. He and his students have created several award-winning websites about the West Chicago City Museum, the local Latino community, and the history of west Chicago. His students also developed an "I Want to Be an American Citizen" website to assist family and community members in preparing for the U.S. Citizenship Test. Tamayo also teaches a bilingual education class at Wheaton College.

Salvador Tamayo working with students on technology in his bilingual education fifth-grade class.

languages perform better than their single-language counterparts on tests of control of attention, concept formation, analytical reasoning, cognitive flexibility, and cognitive complexity (Bialystok, 1999, 2001). They also are more conscious of the structure of spoken and written language and better at noticing errors of grammar and meaning, skills that benefit their reading ability (Bialystok, 1993, 1997).

As many as 10 million children in the United States come from homes in which English is not the primary language. What is the best way to teach these children?

For the last two decades, the preferred strategy has been *bilingual education,* which teaches academic subjects to immigrant children in their native language while slowly teaching English (Adamson, 2004; Arisa, 2005; Brisk, 2005; Diaz-Rico & Weed, 2006; Gottlieb, 2006; Leslow-Hurley, 2005; Ouando, Combs, & Collier, 2006). Advocates of bilingual education programs argue that if children who do not know English are taught only in English, they will fall behind in academic subjects. How, they ask, can 7-year-olds learn arithmetic or history taught only in English when they do not speak the language?

Critics who oppose bilingual education argue that as a result of these programs, the children of immigrants are not learning English, which puts them at a permanent disadvantage in U.S. society. California, Arizona, and Massachusetts have significantly reduced access to bilingual education programs. Some states continue to endorse bilingual education, but the emphasis that test scores be reported separately for English Language Learners (students whose main language is not English) in the No Child Left Behind state assessments has shifted attention to literacy in English (Rivera & Collum, 2006; Snow & Yang, 2006).

What have researchers found regarding outcomes of bilingual education programs? Drawing general conclusions about the effectiveness of bilingual education is difficult because of variations across programs in the number of years they are in effect, type of instruction, qualities of schooling other than bilingual education, teachers, children, and other factors. Further, no effectively conducted experiments that compare bilingual to English-only education in the United States have been conducted (Snow & Kang, 2006). Some experts have concluded that the quality of instruction is more important in determining outcomes that the language in which it is delivered (Lesaux & Siegel, 2003).

Research supports bilingual education in that (1) children have difficulty learning a subject when it is taught in a language they do not understand and (2) when both languages are integrated in the classroom, children learn the second language more readily and participate more actively (Gonzalez, Yawkey, & Minaya-Rowe, 2006; Hakuta, 2000, 2001, 2005; Pérez & others, 2004; Soltero, 2004). However, many of the research results report only modest rather than strong support for bilingual education and some supporters of bilingual education now acknowledge that competent English-only instruction can produce positive outcomes for English Language Learners (Lesaux & Siegel, 2003).

Some critics of current programs argue that too often it is thought that immigrant children need only one year of bilingual education. However, researchers have found that in general it takes immigrant children approximately three to five years to develop speaking proficiency and seven years to develop reading proficiency in English (Hakuta, Butler, & Witt, 2001). Also, it is important to recognize that immigrant children vary in their ability to learn English (Diaz-Rico & Weed, 2006; Haley & Austin, 2004; Herrera & Murray, 2005; Lessow-Hurley, 2005). Children who come from lower socioeconomic backgrounds have more difficulty than those from higher socioeconomic backgrounds (Hakuta, 2001). Thus, especially for immigrant children from low socioeconomic backgrounds, more years of bilingual education may be needed than they currently are receiving. To read about the work of Salvador Tamayo, bilingual education teacher, see the Careers in Child Development profile.

Multilingual Multicultural Research

Review and Reflect • LEARNING GOAL 5

 5 **Summarize language development in middle and late childhood.**

Review
- What are some changes in vocabulary and grammar in the middle and late childhood years?
- What characterizes metalinguistic awareness and how does it improve in middle and late childhood?
- What is the main controversy in teaching children to read?
- What is bilingualism? What issues are involved in bilingual education?

Reflect
- What would be some of the key considerations in a balanced approach to teaching reading?

also called *self-worth* or *self-image,* refers to *global evaluations of* the self—in other words, how the child *feels* about herself. For example, a child may perceive that she is not merely a person but is a *good* person. **Self-concept** refers to *domain-specific evaluations* of the self—in other words, the child's mental image of who he is in specific areas (domains) such as athletics, attributes, appearance, and so on. For example, 10-year-old Fazir's self-concept might include being a student ("I'm doing well in school"), and being a friend ("I am somebody my friends can depend on"), and being athletic ("I'm not doing so good on my soccer team").

Investigators have not always made clear distinctions between self-esteem and self-concept, sometimes using the terms interchangeably or not precisely defining them. The distinction between self-esteem as global self-evaluation and self-concept as domain-specific self-evaluation should help you keep the terms straight.

Self-esteem reflects a perception that does not always match reality (Baumeister & others, 2003). A child's self-esteem might reflect a belief about whether she is intelligent and attractive, for example, but that belief is not necessarily accurate. Thus, high self-esteem may refer to accurate, justified perceptions of one's self-worth as a person and one's successes and accomplishments but it also can refer to an arrogant, grandiose, unwarranted sense of superiority over others. In the same manner, low self-esteem may reflect either an accurate perception of one's shortcomings or a distorted, even pathological insecurity and inferiority.

Variations in self-esteem have been linked with many aspects of children's development. However, much of the research is *correlational* rather than *experimental.* Recall from chapter 2 that correlation does not equal causation. Thus, if a correlational study finds an association between children's low self-esteem and low academic achievement, low academic achievement could cause the low self-esteem just as much as low self-esteem causes low academic achievement (Bowles, 1999).

In fact, there are only modest correlations between school performance and self-esteem, and these correlations do not suggest that high self-esteem produces better school performance (Baumeister & others, 2003). Efforts to increase students' self-esteem have not always led to improved school performance (Davies & Brember, 1999). Children with high self-esteem have greater initiative but this can produce positive or negative outcomes (Baumeister & others, 2003). High self-esteem children are prone to both prosocial and antisocial actions.

A current concern is that too many of today's children and adolescents grow up receiving empty praise and as a consequence have inflated self-esteem (Graham, 2005; Stipek, 2005). Too often they are given praise for performance that is mediocre or even poor. They may have difficulty handling competition and criticism. The title of a book, *Dumbing Down Our Kids: Why America's Children Feel Good about Themselves but Can't Read, Write, or Add* (Sykes, 1995) vividly captures the theme that many U.S. children's, adolescents', and college students' academic problems stem from unmerited praise as part of an effort to prop up their self-esteem. But it is possible to raise children's self-esteem by (1) identifying the domains of competence important to the child, (2) providing emotional support and social approval, (3) helping their achievement, and (4) encouraging coping (Bednar, Wells, & Peterson, 1995; Harter, 1999):

- *Identify the causes of low self-esteem.* Intervention should target the causes of low-esteem. Children have the highest self-esteem when they perform competently in domains that are important to them. Therefore, children should be encouraged to identify and value areas of competence. These areas might include academic skills, athletic skills, physical attractiveness, and social acceptance.
- *Provide emotional support and social approval.* Some children with low self-esteem come from conflicted families or conditions in which they experienced abuse or neglect—situations in which support was not available. In some cases, alternative sources of support can be implemented either informally through the encouragement of a teacher, a coach, or another significant adult, or more formally, through programs such as Big Brothers and Big Sisters.

self-concept Domain-specific evaluations of the self.

- *Help children to achieve.* Achievement also can improve children's self-esteem. For example, the straightforward teaching of real skills to children often results in increased achievement and, thus, in enhanced self-esteem. Children develop higher self-esteem because they know the important tasks to achieve goals, and they have experienced performing them or similar behaviors.
- *Encourage coping skills.* Self-esteem is often increased when children face a problem and try to cope with it, rather than avoid it. If coping rather than avoidance prevails, children often face problems realistically, honestly, and nondefensively. This produces favorable self-evaluative thoughts, which lead to the self-generated approval that raises self-esteem.

Industry Versus Inferiority In chapter 2, we described Erik Erikson's (1968) eight stages of human development. His fourth stage, **industry versus inferiority,** appears during middle and late childhood. At this stage, children attempt to master many skills and develop either a sense of competence or incompetence. The term *industry* expresses a dominant theme of this period: Children become interested in how things are made and how they work. It is the Robinson Crusoe age, in that the enthusiasm and minute detail Crusoe uses to describe his activities appeal to the child's budding sense of industry. When children are encouraged in their efforts to make, build, and work—whether building a model airplane, constructing a tree house, fixing a bicycle, solving an addition problem, or cooking—their sense of industry increases. However, parents who see their children's efforts at making things as "mischief" or "making a mess" encourage children's development of a sense of inferiority.

Children's social worlds beyond their families also contribute to a sense of industry. School becomes especially important in this regard. Consider children who are slightly below average in intelligence. They are too bright to be in special classes but not bright enough to be in gifted classes. They fail frequently in their academic efforts, developing a sense of inferiority. By contrast, consider children whose sense of industry is derogated at home. A series of sensitive and committed teachers may revitalize their sense of industry (Elkind, 1970).

Emotional Development

In chapter 11, we saw that preschoolers become more adept at talking about their own and others' emotions. They also show a growing awareness about controlling and managing emotions to meet social standards. Further developmental changes characterize emotion in middle and late childhood.

Developmental Changes There are some important developmental changes in emotions during the elementary school years (Kuebli, 1994; Wintre & Vallance, 1994):

- An increased ability to understand complex emotions such as pride and shame. These emotions become more internalized and integrated with a sense of personal responsibility
- Increased understanding that more than one emotion can be experienced in a particular situation
- An increased tendency to more fully take into account the events leading to emotional reactions
- Marked improvements in the ability to suppress or conceal negative emotional reactions
- The use of self-initiated strategies for redirecting feelings

Thus, "by middle childhood, children have become more reflective and strategic in their emotional lives. Emotions can be more effectively managed through cognitive means (such as using distracting thoughts) as well as behavioral strategies, and emotions

Industry versus inferiority Erikson's fourth developmental stage, occurring during middle and late childhood, in which children attempt to master many skills and either develop a sense of competence or incompetence.

What are some effective strategies to help children cope with traumatic events, such as the terrorist attacks on the United States on 9/11/2001?

are often intentionally hidden through display rules that dissemble genuine feelings. But children of this age are also capable of genuine empathy and greater emotional understanding than ever before" (Thompson & Goodvin, 2005, pp. 401–402).

Coping with Stress   An important aspect of children's lives is learning how to cope with stress (Bridges, 2002). As children get older, they are able to more accurately appraise a stressful situation and determine how much control they have over it. Older children generate more coping alternatives to stressful conditions and use more cognitive coping strategies (Compas & others, 2001; Saarni, 1999). They are better at intentionally shifting their thoughts to something that is less stressful than are younger children and are better at reframing (changing one's perception of a stressful situation). For example, younger children may be very disappointed that their teacher did not say hello to them when they arrived at school. Older children may reframe this type of situation and think, "She might have been busy with other things and just forgot to say hello."

By 10 years of age, most children are able to use these cognitive strategies to cope with stress (Saarni, 1999). However, in families that have not been supportive and are characterized by turmoil or trauma, children may be so overwhelmed by stress that they do not use such strategies.

Caring adults can not only help children facing personal difficulties, such as parental divorce, but also can help with their understanding of overwhelming events. For example, the terrorist attacks on the World Trade Center in New York City and the Pentagon in Washington, D.C., on September 11, 2001, raised special concerns about how to help children cope with such stressful events (La Greca & others, 2002). Children who have a number of coping techniques have the best chance of adapting and functioning competently in the face of such traumatic events. Here are some recommendations for helping children cope with the stress of these types of events (Gurwitch & others, 2001, pp. 4–11):

- *Reassure children of their safety and security.* This may need to be done numerous times.
- *Allow children to retell events and be patient in listening to them.*
- *Encourage children to talk about any disturbing or confusing feelings.* Tell them that these are normal feelings after a stressful event.
- *Help children make sense of what happened.* Children may misunderstand what took place. For example, young children "may blame themselves, believe things happened that did not happen, believe that terrorists are in the school, etc. Gently help children develop a realistic understanding of the event" (p. 10).
- *Protect children from re-exposure to frightening situations and reminders of the trauma.* This includes limiting conversations about the event in front of the children.

Traumatic events may cause individuals to think about the moral aspects of life. Hopelessness and despair may short-circuit moral development when a child is confronted by the violence of war zones and impoverished inner cities (Garbarino & others, 1992; Nadar, 2001). Let's further explore children's moral development.

Moral Development

Remember from chapter 11 our description of Piaget's view of moral development. Piaget believed that younger children are characterized by heteronomous morality but that, by 10 years of age, they have moved into a higher stage called "autonomous" morality. According to Piaget, older children consider the intentions of the individual, believe that rules are subject to change, and are aware that punishment does not always follow a wrongdoing.

A second major perspective on moral development was proposed by Lawrence Kohlberg. Kohlberg acknowledged that Piaget's cognitive stages of development (especially preoperational, concrete operational, and formal operational) serve as the underpinnings for his theory. However, Kohlberg believed there was more to moral development than Piaget's stages. Kohlberg especially emphasized the importance of opportunities to take the perspective of others and experiencing conflict between one's current stage of moral thinking and the reasoning of someone at a higher stage.

Kohlberg's Theory of Moral Development   Kohlberg stressed that moral development is based primarily on moral reasoning and unfolds in stages (Kohlberg, 1958, 1976, 1986). Kohlberg arrived at his view after 20 years of using a unique interview with children. In the interview, children are presented with a series of stories in which characters face moral dilemmas. Here is the most well-known Kohlberg dilemma:

> In Europe a woman was near death from a special kind of cancer. There was one drug that the doctors thought might save her. It was a form of radium that a druggist in the same town had recently discovered. The drug was expensive to make, but the druggist was charging ten times what the drug cost him to make. He paid $200 for the radium and charged $2,000 for a small dose of the drug. The sick woman's husband, Heinz, went to everyone he knew to borrow the money, but he could only get together $1,000 which is half of what it cost. He told the druggist that his wife was dying and asked him to sell it cheaper or let him pay later. But the druggist said, "No, I discovered the drug, and I am going to make money from it." So Heinz got desperate and broke into the man's store to steal the drug for his wife. (Kohlberg, 1969, p. 379)

This story is one of eleven that Kohlberg devised to investigate the nature of moral thought. After reading the story, the interviewee answers a series of questions about the moral dilemma. Should Heinz have stolen the drug? Was stealing it right or wrong? Why? Is it a husband's duty to steal the drug for his wife if he can get it no other way? Would a good husband steal? Did the druggist have the right to charge that much when there was no law setting a limit on the price? Why or why not? It is important to note that whether the individual says to steal the drug or not is not important in identifying the person's moral stage. What is important is the individual's moral reasoning behind the decision.

From the answers interviewees gave for this and other moral dilemmas, Kohlberg hypothesized three levels of moral development, each of which is characterized by two stages. A key concept in understanding moral development is **internalization,** the developmental change from behavior that is externally controlled to behavior controlled by internal standards and principles. As children and adolescents develop, their moral thoughts become more internalized. Let's look further at Kohlberg's three levels of moral development (see figure 14.1).

Level 1: Preconventional Reasoning
Preconventional reasoning is the lowest level in Kohlberg's theory of moral development. At this level, the individual shows no internalization of moral values—moral reasoning is controlled by external rewards and punishments.

- Stage 1. *Heteronomous morality.* Moral thinking is often tied to punishment. For example, children and adolescents obey adults because adults tell them to obey.
- Stage 2. *Individualism, instrumental purpose, and exchange.* Individuals pursue their own interests but also let others do the same. Thus, what is right involves an equal exchange. People are nice to others so that they will be nice to them in return.

Level 2: Conventional Reasoning
Conventional reasoning is the second, or intermediate, level in Kohlberg's theory of moral development. At this level, internalization is intermediate. Individuals abide by certain standards (internal), but they are the standards of others (external), such as parents or the laws of society.

Lawrence Kohlberg, the architect of a provocative cognitive developmental theory of moral development. *What is the nature of his theory?*

www.mhhe.com/santrockc9

Kohlberg's Theory of Moral Development
Kohlberg's Moral Dilemmas

internalization The developmental change from behavior that is externally controlled to behavior controlled by internal standards and principles.

preconventional reasoning The lowest level in Kohlberg's theory of moral development. The individual shows no internalization of moral values; moral reasoning is controlled by external rewards and punishment.

conventional reasoning The second, or intermediate, level in Kohlberg's theory of moral development. Internalization is intermediate. Individuals abide by certain standards (internal), but they are the standards of others (external), such as parents or the laws of society.

Level 1 Preconventional level no internalization	Level 2 Conventional level intermediate internalization	Level 3 Postconventional level full internalization
Stage 1 Heteronomous morality *Children obey because adults tell them to obey. People base their moral decisions on fear of punishment.* **Stage 2** Individualism, purpose, and exchange *Individuals pursue their own interests but let others do the same. What is right involves equal exchange.*	**Stage 3** Mutual interpersonal expectations, relationships, and interpersonal conformity *Individuals value trust, caring, and loyalty to others as a basis for moral judgments.* **Stage 4** Social systems morality *Moral judgments are based on understanding of the social order, law, justice, and duty.*	**Stage 5** Social contract or utility and individual rights *Individuals reason that values, rights, and principles undergird or transcend the law.* **Stage 6** Universal ethical principles *The person has developed moral judgments that are based on universal human rights. When faced with a dilemma between law and conscience, a personal, individualized conscience is followed.*

FIGURE 14.1 Kohlberg's Three Levels and Six Stages of Moral Development

- Stage 3. *Mutual interpersonal expectations, relationships, and interpersonal conformity.* Individuals value trust, caring, and loyalty to others as a basis of moral judgments. Children and adolescents often adopt their parents' moral standards at this stage, seeking to be thought of by their parents as a "good girl" or a "good boy."
- Stage 4. *Social systems morality.* Moral judgments are based on understanding the social order, law, justice, and duty. For example, adolescents may say that, for a community to work effectively, it needs to be protected by laws that are adhered to by its members.

Level 3: Postconventional Reasoning   **Postconventional reasoning** is the highest level in Kohlberg's theory of moral development. At this level, morality is completely internalized and is not based on others' standards. The individual recognizes alternative moral courses, explores the options, and then decides on a personal moral code.

- Stage 5. *Social contract or utility and individual rights.* Individuals reason that values, rights, and principles undergird or transcend the law. A person evaluates the validity of actual laws, and social systems can be examined in terms of the degree to which they preserve and protect fundamental human rights and values.
- Stage 6. *Universal ethical principles.* The person has developed a moral standard based on universal human rights. When faced with a conflict between law and conscience, the person will follow conscience, even though the decision might involve personal risk.

Figure 14.2 provides examples of responses to the "Heinz and the Druggist" story at each of the six Kohlberg stages.

Kohlberg believed that the levels and stages occur in a sequence and are age related: Before age 9, most children reason about moral dilemmas in a preconventional way; by early adolescence, they reason in more conventional ways. Most adolescents reason at stage 3, with some signs of stages 2 and 4. By early adulthood, a small number of individuals reason in postconventional ways. Figure 14.3 shows the results of a longitudinal investigation of Kohlberg's stages (Colby & others, 1983). A review of

postconventional reasoning The highest level in Kohlberg's theory of moral development. Morality is completely internalized.

Stage description	Examples of moral reasoning that support Heinz's theft of the drug	Examples of moral reasoning that indicate that Heinz should not steal the drug
Preconventional reasoning		
Stage 1: Heteronomous morality	Heinz should not let his wife die; if he does, he will be in big trouble.	Heinz might get caught and sent to jail.
Stage 2: Individualism, purpose, and exchange	If Heinz gets caught, he could give the drug back and maybe they would not give him a long jail sentence.	The druggist is a businessman and needs to make money.
Conventional reasoning		
Stage 3: Mutual interpersonal expectations, relationships, and interpersonal conformity	Heinz was only doing something that a good husband would do; it shows how much he loves his wife.	If his wife dies, he can't be blamed for it; it is the druggist's fault. The druggist is the selfish one.
Stage 4: Social systems morality	It isn't morally wrong for Heinz to steal the drug in this case because the law is not designed to take into account every particular case or anticipate every circumstance.	Heinz should obey the law because laws serve to protect the productive and orderly functioning of society.
Postconventional reasoning		
Stage 5: Social contract or utility and individual rights	Heinz was justified in stealing the drug because a human life was at stake and that transcends any right the druggist had to the drug.	It is important to obey the law because laws represent a necessary structure of common agreement if individuals are to live together in society.
Stage 6: Universal ethical principles	Human life is sacred because of the universal principle of respect for the individual and it takes precedence over other values.	Heinz needs to decide whether or not to consider the other people who need the drug as badly as his wife does. He ought not to act based on his particular feelings for his wife, but consider the value of all the lives involved.

FIGURE 14.2 Moral Reasoning at Kohlberg's Stages in Response to the "Heinz and the Druggist" Story

data from 45 studies in 27 diverse world cultures provided support for the universality of Kohlberg's first four stages, although there was more cultural diversity at stages 5 and 6 (Snarey, 1987).

Kohlberg's Critics
Kohlberg's provocative theory of moral development has not gone unchallenged (Lapsley, 2005; Nucci, 2004; Smetana, 2005; Walker, 2005). The criticisms involve the link between moral thought and moral behavior, inadequate consideration of culture's role and the family's role in moral development, and underestimation of the care perspective.

Moral Thought and Moral Behavior Kohlberg's theory has been criticized for placing too much emphasis on moral thought and not enough emphasis on moral behavior (Walker & Hennig, 2004). Moral reasons can sometimes be a shelter for immoral behavior. Bank embezzlers and presidents endorse the loftiest of moral virtues when commenting about moral dilemmas, but their own behavior may be immoral. We don't have to look further than the recent scandals involving Enron and WorldCom executives to find evidence for the presence of lofty moral thoughts and immoral behaviors. No one wants a nation of cheaters and thieves who can reason at the postconventional level. The cheaters and thieves may know what is right yet still do what is wrong. Heinous actions can be cloaked in a mantle of moral virtue.

The mantle of virtue is not necessarily a ruse; it is often taken on sincerely. Social cognitive theorist Albert Bandura (2002) argues that people usually do not engage in harmful conduct until they have justified the morality of their actions to themselves.

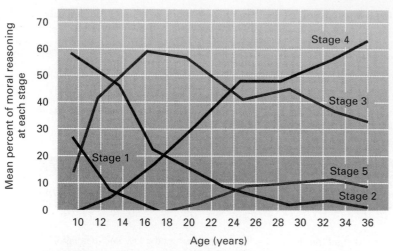

FIGURE 14.3 Age and the Percentage of Individuals at Each Kohlberg Stage In one longitudinal study of males from 10 to 36 years of age, at age 10 most moral reasoning was at stage 2 (Colby & others, 1983). At 16 to 18 years of age, stage 3 became the most frequent type of moral reasoning, and it was not until the mid-twenties that stage 4 became the most frequent. Stage 5 did not appear until 20 to 22 years of age and it never characterized more than 10 percent of the individuals. In this study, the moral stages appeared somewhat later than Kohlberg envisioned and stage 6 was absent.

Immoral conduct is made personally and socially acceptable by portraying it as serving socially worthy or moral purposes or even as doing God's will. Bandura provides the example of Islamic extremists who mount jihad (holy war) as self-defense against tyrannical, decadent people who they see as seeking to enslave the Islamic world.

Culture and Moral Development Yet another criticism of Kohlberg's view is that it is culturally biased (Miller, 2005; Tappan, 2005; Wainryb, 2005). A review of research on moral development in 27 countries concluded that moral reasoning is more culture-specific than Kohlberg envisioned and that Kohlberg's scoring system does not recognize higher-level moral reasoning in certain cultural groups (Snarey, 1987). Examples of higher-level moral reasoning that would not be scored as such by Kohlberg's system are values related to communal equity and collective happiness in Israel, the unity and sacredness of all life-forms in India, and the relation of the individual to the community in New Guinea. These examples of moral reasoning would not be scored at the highest level in Kohlberg's system because they do not emphasize the individual's rights and abstract principles of justice.

Family Processes and Moral Development Kohlberg believed that family processes are essentially unimportant in children's moral development. He argued that parent-child relationships are usually power-oriented and provide children with little opportunity for mutual give and take or perspective taking. Rather, Kohlberg said that such opportunities are more likely to be provided by children's peer relations (Brabeck, 2000).

Kohlberg likely underestimated the contribution of family relationships to moral development (White & Matawie, 2004). Inductive discipline, which involves the use of reasoning and focuses children's attention on the consequences of their actions for others, positively influences moral development (Hoffman, 1970). Parents' moral values influence children's developing moral thoughts (Gibbs, 2003).

Gender and the Care Perspective Carol Gilligan (1982, 1992, 1996) believes that Kohlberg's theory of moral development does not adequately reflect relationships and concern for others. The **justice perspective** is a moral perspective that is built on the rights of the individual; individuals stand alone and make moral decisions independently. Kohlberg's theory is a justice perspective. By contrast, the **care perspective** is a moral perspective that views people in terms of their connectedness with others and emphasizes interpersonal communication, relationships with others, and concern for others. Gilligan's theory is a care perspective.

According to Gilligan, Kohlberg greatly underplayed the care perspective in moral development. She believes that this may have happened because he was a male, because most of his research was with males rather than females, and because he used male responses as a model for his theory.

Gilligan believes that girls reach a critical juncture in their development when they reach adolescence. Usually around 11 to 12 years of age, girls become aware that their intense interest in intimacy is not prized by the male-dominated culture, even though society values women as caring and altruistic. The dilemma is that girls are presented with a choice that makes them look either selfish or selfless. Gilligan believes that, as adolescent girls experience this dilemma, they increasingly silence their "distinctive voice."

www.mhhe.com/santrockc9

Gilligan's Care Perspective

justice perspective A moral perspective that focuses on the rights of the individual; individuals independently make moral decisions. Kohlberg's theory is a justice perspective.

care perspective The moral perspective that views people in terms of their connectedness with others and emphasizes interpersonal communication, relationships with others, and concern for others. Carol Gilligan's perspective is a care perspective.

A recent meta-analysis (a statistical analysis that combines the results of many different studies) cast doubt on Gilligan's claim of substantial gender differences in moral judgment (Jaffee & Hyde, 2000). In this study, no substantial overall differences in moral orientation were found between males and females. When differences occurred, they were better explained by the nature of the dilemma than by gender (for example, both males and females tended to use care reasoning to deal with interpersonal dilemmas and justice reasoning to handle societal dilemmas).

Researchers, however, have found that females consider care-oriented, relational moral dilemmas to be more salient or moral than males do (Eisenberg & Morris, 2004). In support of this idea, one study found that females rated prosocial dilemmas as more significant than males did (Wark & Krebs, 1996). Another recent study revealed that young adolescent girls used more care-based reasoning about dating dilemmas than boys (Weisz & Black, 2002).

Prosocial Behavior and Altruism   Children's moral behavior can involve negative, antisocial acts—such as lying, cheating, and stealing—or it can involve their *prosocial behavior*—the positive aspects of moral behavior, such as showing empathy to someone or behaving altruistically (Carolo, 2005; Hoffman, 2002). While Kohlberg's and Gilligan's theories have focused primarily on the cognitive, thinking aspects of moral development, the study of prosocial moral behavior has placed more emphasis on its behavioral aspects.

As children get older, they are more likely to engage in prosocial behavior (Eisenberg, 2002; Eisenberg, Fabes, & Spinrad, 2006; Eisenberg & Wang, 2003). Among the factors that likely contribute to this age-related increase in prosocial behavior are advances in perspective-taking skills, moral judgment, and self-regulation (Eisenberg & Morris, 2004).

Altruism is an unselfish interest in helping someone else. Human acts of altruism are plentiful—the hardworking laborer who places five dollars in a Salvation Army kettle; rock concerts to feed the hungry, help farmers, and fund AIDS research; the child who takes in a wounded cat and cares for it, and so on.

William Damon (1988) described a developmental sequence of children's altruism, especially of sharing. Most sharing during the first three years of life is done not for empathy reasons, but for the fun of the social play ritual or out of mere imitation. Then, at about 4 years of age, a combination of empathic awareness and adult encouragement produces a sense of obligation on the part of the child to share with others. This obligation forces the child to share, even though the child may not perceive this as the best way to have fun. Most 4-year-olds are not selfless saints, however. Children believe they have an obligation to share but do not necessarily think they should be as generous to others as they are to themselves.

By the start of the elementary school years, children genuinely begin to express more objective ideas about fairness (Eisenberg, Fabes, & Spinrad, 2006). It is common to hear 6-year-old children use the word *fair* as synonymous with *equal* or *same*. By the mid to late elementary school years, children also believe that equity means special treatment for those who deserve it.

Missing from the factors that guide children's altruism is one that many adults might expect to be the most influential of all: the motivation to obey adult authority figures. Surprisingly, a number of studies have shown that adult authority has only a small influence on children's sharing (Eisenberg, 1982). Parental advice and prodding certainly foster standards of sharing, but the give-and-take of peer requests and arguments provides the most immediate stimulation of sharing.

Moral Exemplars   In chapter 10 and here in chapter 14, we have studied moral thought, behavior, and emotion. Thought, behavior, and emotion can all be involved in an individual's personality, character, and virtue. A new approach—the **moral exemplar approach**—emphasizes the development of personality, character, and virtue in terms of moral excellence. A leading advocate of this approach, Lawrence

Carol Gilligan is shown with some of the students she has interviewed about the importance of relationships in a female's development. *What is Gilligan's view of moral development?*

altruism Unselfish interest in helping another person.

moral exemplar approach Emphasizes the development of personality, character, and virtue in terms of moral excellence.

Walker (2002; Matsuba & Walker, 2004; Walker & Henning, 2004) stresses the importance of studying both individuals' conceptions of moral excellence and the psychological functioning of moral exemplars, people who have been identified as leading lives of moral virtue, integrity, and commitment.

In one study, three different exemplars of morality were examined—brave, caring, and just (Walker & Hennig, 2004). Different personality profiles emerged for the three exemplars. The brave exemplar was characterized by being dominant and extraverted, the caring exemplar by being nurturant and agreeable, and the just exemplar by being conscientious and open to experience. However, a number of traits characterized all three moral exemplars, considered by the researchers to reflect a possible core of moral functioning. This core included being honest and dependable.

Another recent study examined the personality of exemplary young adults to determine what characterized their moral excellence (Matsuba & Walker, 2004). Forty young adults were nominated by executive directors of a variety of social organizations (such as Big Brothers, AIDS Society, and Ronald MacDonald House) as moral exemplars based on their extraordinary moral commitment to these social organizations. They were compared with 40 young adults matched in age, education, and other variables who were attending a university. The participants were given a personality test and questionnaires, and were interviewed regarding their faith and moral reasoning. The moral exemplars "were more agreeable, more advanced in their faith and moral reasoning development, further along in forming an adult identity, and more willing to enter into close relationships" (Matsuba & Walker, 2004, p. 413).

Gender

In chapter 11, we discussed the biological, cognitive, and social influences on gender development. Gender is such a pervasive aspect of a individual's identity that we will further consider its role in children's development here. Among the gender-related topics we will examine are gender stereotypes, similarities, and differences; and gender-role classification.

Gender Stereotyping

Gender stereotypes are general impressions and beliefs about females and males. For example, men are powerful; women are weak. Men make good mechanics; women make good nurses. Men are good with numbers; women are good with words. Women are emotional; men are not. All of these are stereotypes. They are generalizations about a group that reflect widely held beliefs.

Traditional Masculinity and Femininity   A classic study in the early 1970s assessed which traits and behaviors college students believed were characteristic of females and which they believed were characteristic of males (Broverman & others, 1972). The traits associated with males were labeled *instrumental*—they included characteristics such as being independent, aggressive, and power-oriented. The traits associated with females were labeled *expressive*—they included characteristics such as being warm and sensitive.

Thus, the instrumental traits associated with males suited them for the traditional masculine role of going out into the world as the breadwinner. The expressive traits associated with females paralleled the traditional feminine role of being the sensitive, nurturing caregiver in the home.

These roles and traits, however, are not just different; they also are unequal in terms of social status and power. The traditional feminine characteristics are childlike, suitable for someone who is dependent and subordinate to others. The traditional masculine characteristics suit one to deal competently with the wider world and to wield authority.

Stereotyping and Culture   How widespread is gender stereotyping? In a far-ranging study of college students in 30 countries, stereotyping of females and males was

*W*hat *are little boys made of?*
Frogs and snails
And puppy dogs' tails.
What are little girls made of?
Sugar and spice
And all that's nice

—J. O. HALLIWELL
English Author, 19th Century

gender stereotypes Broad categories that reflect our impressions and beliefs about females and males.

pervasive (Williams & Best, 1982). Males were widely believed to be dominant, independent, aggressive, achievement-oriented, and enduring. Females were widely believed to be nurturant, affiliative, less esteemed, and more helpful in times of distress.

Of course, in the decades since this study was conducted, traditional gender stereotypes and gender roles have been challenged in many societies, and social inequalities between men and women have diminished. Do gender stereotypes change when the relationship between men and women changes? In a subsequent study, women and men who lived in relatively wealthy, industrialized countries perceived themselves as more similar than did women and men who lived in less developed countries (Williams & Best, 1989). In the more developed countries, the women were more likely to attend college and be gainfully employed. Thus, as sexual equality increases, gender stereotypes may diminish. However, recent research continues to find that gender stereotyping is pervasive (Best, 2001; Kite, 2001; Liben, Bigler, & Krogh, 2001).

Gender Similarities and Differences

What is the reality behind gender stereotypes? Let's now examine some of the differences between the sexes, keeping in mind that

- The differences are average and do not apply to all females or all males.
- Even when gender differences occur, there often is considerable overlap between males and females.
- The differences may be due primarily to biological factors, sociocultural factors, or both.

First, we will examine physical differences, and then we will turn to cognitive and socioemotional differences.

Physical Similarities and Differences We could devote pages to describing physical differences between the average man and woman. For example, women have about twice the body fat of men, most concentrated around breasts and hips. In males, fat is more likely to go to the abdomen. On the average, males grow to be 10 percent taller than females. Androgens (the "male" hormones) promote the growth of long bones; estrogens (the "female" hormones) stop such growth at puberty.

Many physical differences between men and women are tied to health. From conception on, females have a longer life expectancy than males, and females are less likely than males to develop physical or mental disorders. Females are more resistant to infection and their blood vessels are more elastic than males'. Males have higher levels of stress hormones, which cause faster clotting and higher blood pressure.

Does gender matter when it comes to brain structure and activity? Human brains are much alike, whether the brain belongs to a male or a female (Halpern, 2001; Hwang & others, 2004). However, researchers have found some differences (Goldstein & others, 2001; Kimura, 2000). Among the differences that have been discovered are:

- Female brains are smaller than male brains but female brains have more folds; the larger folds (called convolutions) allow more surface brain tissue within the skulls of females than males (Luders & others, 2004).
- One part of the hypothalamus involved in sexual behavior tends to be larger in men than in women (Swaab & others, 2001).
- An area of the parietal lobe that functions in visuospatial skills tends to be larger in males than in females (Frederikse & others, 2000).
- The areas of the brain involved in emotional expression tend to show more metabolic activity in females than in males (Gur & others, 1995).

Similarities and differences in the brains of males and females could be due to evolution and heredity, as well as social experiences.

Cognitive Similarities and Differences Many years ago, Eleanor Maccoby and Carol Jacklin (1974) concluded that males have better math and visuospatial skills (the

"So according to the stereotype, you can put two and two together, but I can read the handwriting on the wall."

Copyright © 1994 Joel Pett. All Rights Reserved.

There is more difference within the sexes than between them.

—IVY COMPTON-BURNETT
English Novelist, 20th Century

www.mhhe.com/santrockc9

Gender and Communication

kinds of skills an architect needs to design a building's angles and dimensions) than females, whereas females have better verbal abilities than males. Subsequently, Maccoby (1987) concluded that the verbal differences between females and males had virtually disappeared but that the math and visuospatial differences persisted. Today, some experts in gender, such as Janet Shibley Hyde (1993, 2004; Hyde & Mezulis, 2001), believe that the cognitive differences between females and males have been exaggerated. For example, Hyde points out that there is considerable overlap in the distributions of female and male scores on math and visuospatial tasks. However, some researchers have found that males have better visual-spatial skills than females (Blakemore, Berenbaum, & Liben, 2005; Ruble, Martin, & Berenbaum, 2006). Despite equal participation in the National Geography Bee, in most years all 10 finalists are boys (Liben, 1995).

When researchers examine how children perform in school or on standardized tests, some differences between U.S. boys and girls persist. In a national study by the U.S. Office of Education (2000), boys did slightly better than girls at math and science. Overall, though, girls were far superior students, and they were significantly better than boys in reading. In another recent national study, females had higher reading achievement and better writing skills than males in grades 4, 8, and 12 with the gap widening as students progressed through school (Coley, 2001).

Keep in mind, though, that measures of achievement in school or scores on standardized tests may reflect many factors besides cognitive ability. For example, some test scores may reflect stereotype threat (as discussed in chapter 13). Performance in school may in part reflect attempts to conform to gender roles or differences in motivation, self-regulation, or other socioemotional characteristics (Koch, 2003).

Socioemotional Similarities and Differences   Are "men from Mars" and "women from Venus"? Perhaps the gender differences that most fascinate people are those in how males and females relate to each other as people. For just about every imaginable socioemotional characteristic, researchers have examined whether there are differences between males and females. Here we will examine just four: communication, aggression, self-regulation, and prosocial behavior.

One aspect of relationships is how people communicate. Sociolinguist Deborah Tannen (1990) distinguishes between rapport talk and report talk:

- **Rapport talk** is the language of conversation and a way of establishing connections and negotiating relationships. Females enjoy private rapport talk and conversation that is relationship oriented more than do males.
- **Report talk** is talk that gives information. Public speaking is an example of report talk. Males hold center stage through report talk with such verbal performances as story telling, joking, and lecturing with information.

Tannen says that boys and girls grow up in different worlds of talk—parents, siblings, peers, teachers, and others talk to boys and girls differently. The play of boys and girls is also different. Boys tend to play in large groups that are hierarchically structured, and their groups usually have a leader who tells the others what to do and how to do it. Boys' games have winners and losers and often are the subject of arguments. And boys often boast of their skill and argue about who is best at what. In contrast, girls are more likely to play in small groups or pairs, and at the center of a girl's world is often a best friend. In girls' friendships and peer groups, intimacy is pervasive. Turn taking is more characteristic of girls' games than of boys' games. And much of the time, girls simply like to sit and talk with each other, concerned more about being liked by others than jockeying for status in some obvious way.

In sum, Tannen concludes that females are more relationship oriented than males—and that this relationship orientation should be prized as a skill in our culture more than it currently is. Note, however, that some researchers criticize Tannen's ideas as being overly simplified and that communication between males and females is more complex than Tannen indicates (Edwards & Hamilton, 2004). Further, some

rapport talk   Talk that provides information.

report talk   The language of conversation and a way of establishing connections and negotiating relationships; preferred by females.

researchers have found similarities in males' and females' relationship communication strategies. In one recent study, in their talk men and women described and responded to problems in ways that were more similar than different (MacGeorge & others, 2004).

Further modification of Tannen's view is suggested by a recent *meta-analytic* review of gender differences in talkativeness (general communicative competence), affiliative speech (language used to establish or maintain connections with others, such as showing support or expanding on a person's prior remarks), and self-assertive speech (language used to influence others, such as directive statements or disagreements) (Leaper & Smith, 2004). A *meta-analysis* is a statistical analysis that combines the results of many different studies. This recent review confirms the criticism that Tannen overemphasizes the size of the gender difference in communication. Gender differences did occur but they were small, with girls only slightly more talkative and engaging in more affiliative speech than boys, and boys being more likely to use self-assertive speech. Perhaps the most important message from this review is that gender differences in communication often depended on the context:

- *Group size.* The gender difference in talkativeness (girls being more competent in communicating) occurred more in large groups than in dyads.
- *Speaking with peers or adults.* No average differences in talk with peers occurred but girls talked more with adults than boys.
- *Familiarity.* The gender difference in self-assertive speech (boys using it more) was more likely to occur when talking with strangers than with familiar individuals.
- *Age.* The gender difference in affiliative speech was largest in adolescence. This may be due to adolescent girls' increased interest in socioemotional behavior traditionally prescribed for females.

One of the most consistent gender differences is that boys are more physically aggressive than girls. The difference occurs in all cultures and appears very early in children's development (White, 2001). The difference in physical aggression is especially pronounced when children are provoked.

Although boys are consistently more physically aggressive than girls, might girls show as much or more verbal aggression, such as yelling, than boys? When verbal aggression is examined, gender differences typically either disappear or are sometimes even more pronounced in girls (Eagly & Steffen, 1986). Also, girls are more likely to engage in *relational aggression,* which involves such behaviors as trying to make others dislike a certain child by spreading malicious rumors about the child or ignoring another child when angry at him or her, than physical aggression (Crick & others, 2004; Crick, 2005; Underwood, 2003, 2004). However, it is not clear whether girls engage in relational aggression more than boys do (Underwood & others, 2004).

Beginning in the elementary school years, boys are more likely to hide their negative emotions, such as sadness, and girls are less likely to express emotions such as disappointment that might hurt others' feelings (Eisenberg, Martin, & Fabes, 1996). Beginning in early adolescence, girls say they experience more sadness, shame, and guilt, and report more intense emotions, while boys are more likely to deny that they experience these emotions (Ruble, Martin, & Berenbaum, 2006).

An important skill is to be able to regulate and control one's emotions and behavior. Boys usually show less self-regulation than girls (Eisenberg, Spinrad, & Smith, 2004). This low self-control can translate into behavior problems. In one study, children's low self-regulation was linked with greater aggression, teasing of others, overreaction to frustration, low cooperation, and inability to delay gratification (Block & Block, 1980).

Are there gender differences in prosocial behavior? Females view themselves as more prosocial and empathic, and also engage in more prosocial behavior than males (Eisenberg & Morris, 2004). For example, reviews of research have found that across childhood and adolescence, females engage in more prosocial behavior (Eisenberg &

In China, females and males are usually socialized to behave, feel, and think differently. The old patriarchal traditions of male supremacy have not been completely uprooted. Chinese women still make considerably less money than Chinese men do, and, in rural China (such as here in the Lixian Village of Sichuan) male supremacy still governs many women's lives.

Fabes, 1998; Eisenberg, Fabes, & Spinrad, 2006). The biggest gender difference occurred for kind and considerate behavior with a smaller difference in sharing.

Gender Controversy   Controversy continues about the extent of gender differences and what might cause them. As we saw earlier, evolutionary psychologists such as David Buss (2004) argue that gender differences are extensive and caused by the adaptive problems they have faced across their evolutionary history. Alice Eagly (2001) also concludes that gender differences are substantial but reaches a very different conclusion about their cause. She emphasizes that gender differences are due to social conditions that have resulted in women having less power and controlling fewer resources than men.

By contrast, Janet Shibley Hyde (1986, 2005 in press) concludes that gender differences have been greatly exaggerated, especially fueled by popular books such as John Gray's (1992) *Men Are from Mars, Women Are from Venus* and Deborah Tannen's (1990) *You Just Don't Understand!* She argues that the research shows that females and males are similar on most psychological factors. In a recent review, Hyde (2005 in press) summarized the results of 44 meta-analyses of gender differences and similarities. In most areas, gender differences either were nonexistent or small, including math ability, communication, and aggression. The largest difference occurred on motor skills (favoring males), followed by sexuality (males masturbate more and are more likely to endorse sex in a casual, uncommitted relationship), and physical aggression (males are more physically aggressive than females).

Hyde's recent summary of meta-analyses is still not likely to quiet the controversy about gender differences and similarities, but further research should continue to provide a basis for more accurate judgments about this controversy.

Gender in Context   In thinking about gender, it is important to consider the context of behavior (Fischer, 1999; Galambos, 2004). Gender behavior often varies across contexts. Consider helping behavior. Males are more likely to help in contexts in which a perceived danger is present and they feel competent to help (Eagly & Crowley, 1986). For example, males are more likely than females to help a person who is stranded by the roadside with a flat tire; automobile problems are an area about which many males feel competent. In contrast, when the context involves volunteering time to help a child with a personal problem, females are more likely to help than males are, because there is little danger present and females feel more competent at nurturing. In many cultures, girls show more caregiving behavior than boys do. However, in the few cultures where they both care for younger siblings on a regular basis, girls and boys are similar in their tendencies to nurture (Whiting, 1989).

Context is also relevant to gender differences in the display of emotions (Shields, 1991, 1998). Consider anger. Males are more likely to show anger toward strangers, especially other males, when they think they have been challenged. Males also are more likely than females to turn their anger into aggressive action, especially when the culture endorses such action (Tavris & Wade, 1984).

We find contextual variations regarding gender in specific situations, not only within a particular culture, but also across cultures (Denmark, Rabinowitz, & Sechzer, 2005; Nadien & Denmark, 1999). In many cultures around the world, traditional gender roles guide the behavior of males and females. In China and Iran, for instance, it is still widely accepted for males to engage in dominant behavior and females to behave in subordinate ways. Many Western cultures, such as the United States, have become more flexible about gender behavior.

Sociocultural contexts determine what is considered to be gender-appropriate and gender-inappropriate socioemotional behavior. Not too long ago it was accepted that boys are made of "snips and snails and puppy dogs' tails" and that girls are made of "sugar and spice and all that's nice." The well-adjusted female was expected to display expressive traits, such as being dependent, nurturant, and uninterested in power. The well-adjusted male was expected to show instrumental traits, such as being independent, aggressive, and power-oriented.

The following items are from the Bem Sex-Role Inventory. When taking the BSRI, a person is asked to indicate on a 7-point scale how well each of the 60 characteristics describes herself or himself. The scale ranges from 1 (never or almost never true) to 7 (always or almost always true).

Examples of masculine items	Examples of feminine items
Defends open beliefs	Does not use harsh language
Forceful	Affectionate
Willing to take risks	Loves children
Dominant	Understanding
Aggressive	Gentle

Scoring: The items are scored on independent dimensions of masculinity and femininity as well as androgyny and undifferentiate classifications.

FIGURE 14.4 The Bem Sex-Role Inventory. Reproduced by special permission of the Publisher, Mind Garden, Inc., 1690 Woodside Road #202, Redwood City, CA 94061 USA www.mindgarden.com from the *Bem Sex-Role Inventory* by Sandra Bem. Copyright © 1978 by Consulting Psychologists Press. All rights reserved. Further reproduction is prohibited without the Publisher's written consent.

Today, our culture allows for more diversity (Bannon, 2005; Galambos, 2004). Although a girl's father might promote traditional femininity, her friends might engage in many traditionally masculine activities, and her teachers might encourage her to be assertive. One recent study found that societal changes are leading females to have more instrumental traits (Spence & Buckner, 2000).

Masculinity, Femininity, and Androgyny

In the 1970s, as both males and females became dissatisfied with the burdens imposed by their stereotyped roles, alternatives to "masculinity" and "femininity" were explored. Instead of thinking of masculinity and femininity as a continuum, with more of one meaning less of the other, it was proposed that individuals could show both expressive and instrumental traits. This thinking led to the development of the concept of **androgyny**, the presence of a high degree of masculine and feminine characteristics in the same individual (Bem, 1977; Spence & Helmreich, 1978). The androgynous individual might be a male who is assertive (masculine) and sensitive to others' feelings (feminine), or a female who is dominant (masculine) and caring (feminine). Measures have been developed to assess androgyny. One of the most widely used gender measures, the *Bem Sex-Role Inventory (BSRI)*, was constructed by a leading early proponent of androgyny, Sandra Bem (1977) (see figure 14.4). Based on their to the items in the Bem Sex-Role Inventory, individuals are classified as having one of four gender-role orientations: masculine, feminine, androgynous, or undifferentiated (see figure 14.5):

- The androgynous individual is simply a female or a male who has a high degree of both feminine (expressive) and masculine (instrumental) traits. No new characteristics are used to describe the androgynous individual.
- A feminine individual is high on feminine (expressive) traits and low on masculine (instrumental) traits.
- A masculine individual is high on instrumental traits and low on expressive traits.
- An undifferentiated person is low on both feminine and masculine traits.

Gender experts, such as Sandra Bem, argue that androgynous individuals are more flexible, competent, and mentally healthy than their masculine or feminine counterparts. To some degree, though, deciding on which gender-role classification is best depends on the context involved. For example, in close relationships, feminine and androgynous orientations might be more desirable because of the expressive nature of close relationships. However, masculine and androgynous orientations might be more desirable in traditional academic and work settings because of the achievement demands in these contexts. For example, a recent study found that masculine and androgynous individuals had higher expectations for being able to control the outcomes of their academic efforts than feminine or undifferentiated individuals

androgyny The presence of a high degree of masculine and feminine characteristics in the same individual.

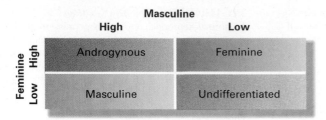

FIGURE 14.5 Gender-Role Classification

Androgyny
Gender and Culture

(Choi, 2004). And the culture in which individuals live also plays an important role in determining what is adaptive. On the one hand, increasing numbers of children in the United States and other modernized countries such as Sweden are being raised to behave in androgynous ways. But traditional gender roles continue to dominate the cultures of many countries around the world.

Concern about the ways boys have been brought up in traditional masculine ways has been called a "national crisis of boyhood" by William Pollack (1999) in his book *Real Boys*. Pollack says that although there has been considerable talk about the "sensitive male," little has been done to change what he calls the "boy code." He says that this code tells boys they should show little if any emotion as they are growing up. Too often boys are socialized to not show their feelings and act tough, says Pollack. Boys learn the boy code in many different contexts—sandboxes, playgrounds, schoolrooms, camps, hangouts—and are taught the code by parents, peers, coaches, teachers, and other adults. Pollack, as well as many others, believes that boys would benefit from being socialized to express their anxieties and concerns rather than keep them bottled up as well as to learn how to better regulate their aggression.

There also is a special concern about boys who adopt a strong masculine role in adolescence, because this is increasingly being found to be associated with problem behaviors. Joseph Pleck (1995) believes that what defines traditional masculinity in many Western cultures includes behaviors that do not have social approval but nonetheless validate the adolescent boy's masculinity. That is, in the male adolescent culture, male adolescents perceive that they will be thought of as more masculine if they engage in premarital sex, drink alcohol and take drugs, and participate in illegal delinquent activities.

Some critics of androgyny say enough is enough and that there is too much talk about gender. An alternative to androgyny is **gender-role transcendence,** the view that when an individual's competence is at issue, it should be conceptualized on a person basis rather than on the basis of masculinity, femininity, or androgyny (Pleck, 1983). That is, we should think about ourselves as people, not as masculine, feminine, or androgynous. Parents should rear their children to be competent individuals, not masculine, feminine, or androgynous, say the gender-role critics. They believe such gender-role classification leads to too much stereotyping.

Review and Reflect • LEARNING GOAL 1

① Discuss emotional and personality development in middle and late childhood.

Review

- What changes take place in the self in middle and late childhood? How can self-esteem be encouraged?

- How does emotion change in middle and late childhood?

- What is Kohlberg's theory of moral development and how has it been criticized? What are prosocial behavior and altruism and how do they develop in middle and late childhood? What is the moral exemplar approach?

- What are some important aspects of gender in middle and late childhood?

Reflect

- What do you think about the following circumstance? A man who had been sentenced to serve 10 years for selling a small amount of marijuana walked away from a prison camp six months after he was there. He is now in his fifties and has been a model citizen. Should he be sent back to prison? Why or why not? At which Kohlberg stage should your response be placed?

gender-role transcendence The view that people should be evaluated as persons, not in terms of femininity, masculinity, or androgyny.

2 WHAT ARE SOME PARENT-CHILD ISSUES AND SOCIETAL CHANGES IN FAMILIES?

Parent-Child Issues   Societal Changes in Families

As children move into the middle and late childhood years, parents spend considerably less time with them. In one study, parents spent less than half as much time with their children aged 5 to 12 in caregiving, instruction, reading, talking, and playing as when the children were younger (Hill & Stafford, 1980). This drop in parent-child interaction may be even more extensive in families with little parental education. Although parents spend less time with their children in middle and late childhood than in early childhood, parents continue to be extremely important socializing agents in their children's lives. What are some of the most important parent-child issues in middle and late childhood?

Parent-Child Issues

Parent-child interactions during early childhood focus on such matters as modesty, bedtime regularities, control of temper, fighting with siblings and peers, eating behavior and manners, autonomy in dressing, and attention seeking. While some of these issues—fighting and reaction to discipline, for example—were already occurring in early childhood, they continue through the elementary school years. Many new issues have appeared by the age of 7 (Maccoby, 1984). These include whether children should be made to perform chores and, if so, whether they should be paid for them; how to help children learn to entertain themselves, rather than relying on parents for everything; and how to monitor children's lives outside the family in school and peer settings.

School-related matters are especially important for families during middle and late childhood (Cowan & others, 2005). School-related difficulties are the number one reason that children in this age group are referred for clinical help. Children must learn to relate to adults outside the family on a regular basis—adults who interact with the child much differently than parents. During middle and late childhood, interactions with adults outside the family involve more formal control and achievement orientation.

Discipline during middle and late childhood is often easier for parents than it was during early childhood; it may also be easier than during adolescence. In middle and late childhood, children's cognitive development has matured to the point where it is possible for parents to reason with them about resisting deviation and controlling their behavior. By adolescence, children's reasoning has become more sophisticated, and they may be less likely to accept parental discipline. Adolescents also push more strongly for independence, which contributes to parenting difficulties. Parents of elementary school children use less physical discipline than do parents of preschool children. By contrast, parents of elementary school children are more likely to use deprivation of privileges, appeals directed at the child's self-esteem, comments designed to increase the child's sense of guilt, and statements indicating to the child that he or she is responsible for his or her actions.

During middle and late childhood, some control is transferred from parent to child, although the process is gradual and involves *coregulation* rather than control by either the child or the parent alone. The major shift to autonomy does not occur until about the age of 12 or later. During middle and late childhood, parents continue to exercise general supervision and exert control, while children are allowed to engage in moment-to-moment self-regulation. This coregulation process is a transition period between the strong parental control of early childhood and the increased relinquishment of general supervision of adolescence.

How does living in a stepfamily influence a child's development?

School-Family Linkages
Stepfamilies
Stepfamily Resources
Stepfamily Support

Societal Changes in Families

As we discussed in chapter 11, increasing numbers of children are growing up in divorced families and families in which both parents work outside the home. But there are several other major shifts in the composition of family life that especially affect children in middle and late childhood. Parents are divorcing in greater numbers than ever before and are also getting remarried more (Dunn & others, 2001; Stewart, 2005). It takes time for parents to marry, have children, get divorced, and then remarry. Consequently, there are far more elementary and secondary school children than infant or preschool children living in stepfamilies.

Stepfamilies   The number of remarriages involving children has grown steadily in recent years (Ganong, Coleman, & Haas, 2005). Also, divorces occur at a 10 percent higher rate in remarriages than in first marriages (Cherlin & Furstenberg, 1994). As a result of their parents' successive marital transitions, about half of all children whose parents divorce will have a stepparent within four years of parental separation.

In some cases, the creation of a stepfamily may have been preceded by the death of a spouse. However, the formation of most stepfamilies is preceded by divorce rather than death (Pasley & Moorefield, 2004).

Three common types of stepfamily structure are (1) stepfather, (2) stepmother, and (3) blended or complex. In stepfather families, the mother typically had custody of the children and remarried, introducing a stepfather into her children's lives. In stepmother families, the father usually had custody and remarried, introducing a stepmother into his children's lives. In a blended or complex stepfamily, both parents bring children from previous marriages to live in the newly formed stepfamily.

Researchers have found that children's relationships with custodial parents (mothers in stepfather families, fathers in stepmother families) are often better than with stepparents (Santrock, Sitterle, & Warshak, 1988). Also, children in simple families (stepmother, stepfather) often show better adjustment than their counterparts in complex (blended) families (Anderson & others, 1999; Hetherington & Kelly, 2002).

As in divorced families, children in stepfamilies show more adjustment problems than children in nondivorced families (Hetherington, Bridges, & Isabella, 1998). The adjustment problems are similar to those in divorced children—academic problems and lower self-esteem, for example (Anderson & others, 1999). However, as with divorced children, it is important to recognize that a majority of children in stepfamilies do not have problems. In one recent study, 20 percent of children from stepfamilies showed adjustment problems compared with 10 percent in intact, never-divorced families (Hetherington & Kelly, 2002; Hetherington & Stanley-Hagan, 2002).

In terms of the age of the child, researchers have found that early adolescence is an especially difficult time for the formation of a stepfamily (Anderson & others, 1999). This may occur because the stepfamily circumstances exacerbate normal adolescent concerns about identity, sexuality, and autonomy. In the Caring for Children interlude that follows, you can read further about parenting and stepfamilies.

CARING FOR CHILDREN

Parenting and Children in Stepfamilies

What are some problems frequently encountered by stepfamilies? What are some ways to build a strong, positive stepfamily? The following guidelines address these questions (O'Neil & Brown, 2005, pp. 12, 15).

Frequently Encountered Problems in Stepfamilies

- "Adapting to multiple viewpoints, attitudes, and personalities

- Arranging to comply with the visitation and other custodial rights granted by a court to the absent natural parent (holidays and vacations can pose special problems)
- Conflicting ideas concerning discipline expectations of the children
- Continuing legal battles over child custody issues
- Disagreements over expenses and how family finances are to be used
- Feelings of anger, hurt, mistrust, or guilt regarding ex-spouses that may be unduly transferred to the new mate
- Financial constraints related to feeding, clothing, housing, health care, and providing for the many economic needs and desires of children
- Interference by in-laws (especially grandparents) who may have an interest in the children
- Reduced space, privacy, and personal time
- Refusal of the children to follow the rules and wishes of the stepparent
- Reluctance of the children to accept the stepparent, with outright rejection a possibility
- Rivalry between children for attention and affection, especially when two sets of children are involved
- Unresolved emotional problems of the children arising from the great changes in their lives
- Unresolved personal problems of the parents, which may accompany individuals into the new union (alcoholism, drug use, psychological or behavioral problems) . . .

Strategies for Building a Strong, Positive Stepfamily

- "Agree upon and follow set rules of conduct.
- Attempt to develop and maintain a cooperative relationship with the absent natural parent who still has legal rights to the children.
- Create and maintain a stable home environment in which all family members feel physically and emotionally safe and secure.
- Develop good communication between family members and communicate clearly.
- Give the children age-appropriate responsibilities.
- Make a commitment to talk about and resolve disagreements based on mutual respect and kindness.
- Master those personal problems that may adversely affect the family.
- Openly express love and affection.
- Plan at least one sit-down meal per day that includes all family members.
- Plan family group entertainment and recreation.
- Respect individual privacy rights.
- Support one anothers' member's interests, hobbies, and goals.
- Talk with and listen to one another.
- Try not to react defensively to criticism; instead put it to constructive use.
- When family conflicts seem irreconcilable, or if the behavior of a child poses serious problems, seek professional help."

Self-Care/Latchkey Children   We concluded in chapter 9 that when both parents work outside the home it does not necessarily have negative outcomes for their children. However, a certain subset of children from dual-earner families deserves further scrutiny. These children typically do not see their parents from the time they leave for school in the morning until about 6 or 7 P.M. They are sometimes called "latchkey" children because they are given the key to their home, take the key to school, and then use it to let themselves into the home while their parents are still at work. Latchkey children are largely unsupervised for two to four hours a day during each school week. During the summer months, they might be unsupervised for entire days, five days a week.

In one recent study of 819 10- to 14-year-olds, out-of-home care, whether supervised or unsupervised, was linked to delinquency, drug and alcohol use, and school problems (Coley, Morris, & Hernandez, 2004). In another study, researchers interviewed more than 1,500 latchkey children (Long & Long, 1983). They concluded that a slight majority of these children had had negative latchkey experiences. Some latchkey children may grow up too fast, hurried by the responsibilities placed on them. How do latchkey children handle the lack of limits and structure during the latchkey hours? Without limits and parental supervision, latchkey children find their way into trouble more easily, possibly stealing, vandalizing, or abusing a sibling. Ninety percent of the juvenile delinquents in Montgomery County, Maryland, are latchkey children. Joan Lipsitz (1983), in testifying before the Select Committee on Children, Youth, and Families, called the lack of adult supervision of children in the after-school hours a major problem. Lipsitz called it the "three-to-six o'clock problem" because it was during this time that the Center for Early Adolescence in North Carolina, when Lipsitz was director, experienced a peak of referrals for clinical help. And, in a 1987 national poll, teachers rated the latchkey children phenomenon the number one reason that children have problems in school (Harris, 1987).

Although latchkey children may be vulnerable to problems, their experiences vary enormously, as do the experiences of all children with working parents (Belle, 1999). Parents need to give special attention to how their children's lives can be effectively monitored. Variations in latchkey experiences suggest that parental monitoring and authoritative parenting help the child cope more effectively, especially in resisting peer pressure (Galambos & Maggs, 1989; Steinberg, 1986). In one study, attending a formal after-school program that included academic, recreational, and remedial activities was associated with better academic achievement and social adjustment, in comparison with other types of after-school care (such as informal adult supervision or self-care) (Posner & Vandell, 1994). Practitioners and policymakers recommend that after-school programs have warm and supportive staff, a flexible and relaxed schedule, multiple activities, and opportunities for positive interactions with staff and peers (Pierce, Hamm, & Vandell, 1997).

Participation in five types of out-of-school care (before- and after-school programs, extracurricular activities, father care, and nonadult care—usually an older sibling) were examined in one recent study to determine their possible link with children's academic achievement toward the end of the first grade (NICHD Early Child Care Research Network, 2004). "Children who consistently participated in extracurricular activities during kindergarten and first grade obtained higher standardized math test scores than children who did not consistently participate in these activities. . . . Participation in other types of out-of-school care was not related to child functioning in the first grade" (p. 280). Parents who enroll their children in extracurricular activities may be more achievement-oriented and have higher achievement expectations for their children than parents who don't place their children in these activities.

Gay and Lesbian Parents   Increasingly, gay and lesbian couples are creating families that include children. This is controversial to many heterosexual individuals who view a gay or lesbian family as damaging to the development of a child. Researchers, however, have found few differences in children growing up with lesbian mothers or gay fathers and children growing up with heterosexual parents (Patterson, 2002). For example, children growing up in gay or lesbian families are just as popular with their peers, and there are no differences in the adjustment and mental health of children living in these families when they are compared with children in heterosexual families (Hyde & DeLamater, 2005). Also, the overwhelming majority of children growing up in a gay or lesbian family have a heterosexual orientation (Tasker & Golombok, 1997).

What are the research findings regarding the development and psychological well-being of children raised by gay and lesbian couples?

Approximately 20 percent of lesbians and 10 percent of gay men are parents, most of whom have children from a heterosexual marriage that ended in a divorce (Patterson, 2002). There may be more than 1 million gay and lesbian parents in the United States today. Gay and lesbian parents may be single or they may have same-gender partners. In addition, lesbians and gay men are increasingly choosing parenthood through donor insemination and surrogates.

An important aspect of lesbian and gay families with children is the sexual identity of parents at the time of a child's birth or adoption (Patterson, 2002). The largest group of children with lesbian and gay parents are likely those who were born in the context of heterosexual relationships with one or both parents only later identifying themselves as gay or lesbian.

Another issue focuses on custody arrangements for children (Peplau & Beals, 2004). Many lesbian mothers and gay fathers have lost custody of their children to heterosexual spouses following divorce. For this reason, many lesbian mothers and gay fathers are noncustodial parents.

Review and Reflect • LEARNING GOAL 2

2 **Describe parent-child issues and societal changes in families.**

Review
- What are some important parent-child issues in middle and late childhood?
- What are some societal changes in families that influence children's development?

Reflect
- What was your relationship with your parents like when you were in elementary school?
- How do you think it influenced your development?

---

3 **WHAT CHANGES CHARACTERIZE PEER RELATIONSHIPS IN MIDDLE AND LATE CHILDHOOD?**

| Friends | Peer Statuses | Bullying |

| Developmental Changes in Peer Relations | Social Cognition |

During middle and late childhood, children spend an increasing amount of time with their peers. First, we will explore children's friendships and then turn to other aspects of peer relations.

Friends

The world of peers is one of varying acquaintances; we interact with some people we barely know, and with others we know well, every day. It is to the latter type—friends—that we now turn.

Friendships serve six functions (Gottman & Parker, 1987):

1. *Companionship.* Friendship provides a familiar partner, someone who is willing to engage in collaborative activities.

What are the functions of children's friendships?

2. *Stimulation.* Friends provide interesting information, excitement, and amusement.
3. *Physical support.* Friendship provides resources and assistance.
4. *Ego support.* Friendship provides the expectation of support, encouragement, and feedback that helps individuals maintain an impression of themselves as competent, attractive, and worthwhile.
5. *Social comparison.* Friends provide information about where individuals stand.
6. *Intimacy/affection.* Friendship provides a warm, close, trusting relationship with another individual, a relationship that involves self-disclosure.

Willard Hartup (1996, 2000), who has studied peer relations across four decades, has concluded that many children use friends as cognitive and social resources on a regular basis. Hartup also commented that transitions, such as moving from elementary to middle school, are negotiated more competently by children who have friends than by those who don't.

The importance of friendship was recently underscored in a two-year longitudinal study (Wentzel, Bary, & Caldwell, 2004). Sixth-grade students who did not have a friend engaged in less prosocial behavior (cooperation, sharing, helping others), had lower grades, and were more emotionally distressed (depression, low well-being) than their counterparts who had one or more friends. Two years later, in the eighth grade, the students who did not have a friend in the sixth grade were still more emotionally distressed.

Although friendships serve important functions, such as companionship, its important to note that not all friendships and not all friends are equal. The quality of friendship is important to consider. Supportive friendships between socially skilled individuals are developmentally advantageous, whereas coercive and conflict-ridden friendships are not (Berndt, 2002; Hartup & Abecassis, 2002; Rubin, Bukowski, & Parker, 2006). Friendship and its developmental significance can vary from one child to another. Children's characteristics, such as temperament ("easy" versus "difficult" for example), likely influence the nature of their friendships.

Developmental Changes in Peer Relations

As children enter the elementary school years, reciprocity becomes especially important in peer interchanges. Children play games, function in groups, and cultivate friendships. Until about 12 years of age, their preference for same-sex groups increases. The amount of time children spend in peer interaction also rises during middle and late childhood and adolescence. Researchers estimate that the percentage of time spent in social interaction with peers increases from approximately 10 percent at 2 years of age to more than 30 percent in middle and late childhood (Rubin, Bukowski, & Parker, 2006). In one early study, children interacted with peers 10 percent of their day at age 2, 20 percent at age 4, and more than 40 percent between the ages of 7 and 11. A typical school day included 299 episodes with peers (Barker & Wright, 1951). Other changes in peer relations as children move through middle and late childhood involve an increase in the size of their peer group and peer interaction that is less closely supervised by adults (Rubin, Bukowski, & Parker, 2006).

Peer Statuses

The term *sociometric status* is used to describe the extent to which children are liked or disliked by their peer group. Sociometric status is typically assessed by asking children to rate how much they like or dislike each of their classmates. Or it may be assessed by asking children to nominate the children they like the most and those they like the least. Developmentalists have distinguished five types of peer statuses (Wentzel & Asher, 1995):

popular children Children who are frequently nominated as a best friend and are rarely disliked by their peers.

- **Popular children** are frequently nominated as a best friend and are rarely disliked by their peers.

- **Average children** receive an average number of both positive and negative nominations from their peers.
- **Neglected children** are infrequently nominated as a best friend but are not disliked by their peers.
- **Rejected children** are infrequently nominated as someone's best friend and are actively disliked by their peers.
- **Controversial children** are frequently nominated both as someone's best friend and as being disliked.

Popular children have a number of social skills that contribute to their being well liked (Ladd, 2006). Researchers have found that popular children give out reinforcements, listen carefully, maintain open lines of communication with peers, are happy, control their negative emotions, act like themselves, show enthusiasm and concern for others, and are self-confident without being conceited (Rubin, Bukowski, & Parker, 1998, 2006).

Neglected children engage in low rates of interaction with their peers and are often described as shy by peers. Rejected children often have more serious adjustment problems than those who are neglected (Parker & Asher, 1987). For example, one recent study found that in kindergarten, rejected children were less likely to engage in classroom participation, more likely to express a desire to avoid school, and more likely to report being lonely (Buhs & Ladd, 2002). In another study, 112 fifth-grade boys were evaluated over a period of seven years until the end of high school (Kupersmidt & Coie, 1990). The best predictor of whether rejected children would engage in delinquent behavior or drop out of school later during adolescence was aggression toward peers in elementary school. Another recent study found that when third-grade boys were highly aggressive and rejected by their peers, they showed markedly higher levels of delinquency as adolescents and young adults (Miller-Johnson, Coie, & Malone, 2003).

A recent analysis by John Coie (2004, pp. 252–253) provided three reasons why aggressive peer rejected boys have problems in social relationships:

- "First, the rejected, aggressive boys are more impulsive and have problems sustaining attention. As a result, they are more likely to be disruptive of ongoing activities in the classroom and in focused group play.
- Second, rejected, aggressive boys are more emotionally reactive. They are aroused to anger more easily and probably have more difficulty calming down once aroused. Because of this they are more prone to become angry at peers and attack them verbally and physically. . . .
- Third, rejected children have fewer social skills in making friends and maintaining positive relationships with peers."

Not all rejected children are aggressive (Bierman, 2004; Hymel, McDougall, & Renshaw, 2004; Ladd, 2006; Rubin, Bukowski, & Parker, 2006). Although aggression and its related characteristics of impulsiveness and disruptiveness underlie rejection about half the time, approximately 10 to 20 percent of rejected children are shy.

How can neglected children and rejected children be trained to interact more effectively with their peers? The goal of many training programs for neglected children is to help them attract attention from their peers in positive ways and to hold their attention by asking questions, by listening in a warm and friendly way, and by saying things about themselves that relate to the peers' interests. They also are taught to enter groups more effectively. Rejected children may be taught to more accurately assess whether the intentions of their peers are negative. Rejected children also may be asked to engage in role playing or to discuss hypothetical situations involving negative encounters with peers, such as when a peer cuts into a line ahead of them. In some programs, children are shown videotapes of appropriate peer interaction; then they are asked to comment on them and to draw lessons from what they have seen (Ladd, Buhs, & Troop, 2004).

average children Children who receive an average number of both positive and negative nominations from their peers.

neglected children Children who are infrequently nominated as a best friend but are not disliked by their peers.

rejected children Children who are infrequently nominated as a best friend and are actively disliked by their peers.

controversial children Children who are frequently nominated both as someone's best friend and as being disliked.

One recent social-skills intervention program was successful in increasing social acceptance and self-esteem and decreasing depression and anxiety in peer-rejected children (DeRosier, & Marcus, 2005). Students participated in the program once a week (50 to 60 minutes) for eight weeks. The program included instruction in how to manage emotions, how to improve prosocial skills, how to become better communicators, and how to compromise and negotiate.

Social Cognition

Social Cognition

Social cognitions involve thoughts about social matters (Gifford-Smith & Rabiner, 2004; Lewis & Carpendale, 2004). Children's social cognitions about their peers become increasingly important for understanding peer relationships in middle and late childhood (Rubin & others, 2005). Of special interest are the ways in which children process information about peer relations and their social knowledge (Dodge, 2000).

A boy accidentally trips and knocks a peer's soft drink out of his hand. The peer misinterprets the encounter as hostile, which leads him to retaliate aggressively against the boy. Through repeated encounters of this kind, other peers come to perceive the aggressive boy as habitually acting in inappropriate ways. Kenneth Dodge (1983) argues that children go through five steps in processing information about their social world. They decode social cues, interpret, search for a response, select an optimal response, and enact. Dodge has found that aggressive boys are more likely to perceive another child's actions as hostile when the child's intention is ambiguous. And, when aggressive boys search for cues to determine a peer's intention, they respond more rapidly, less efficiently, and less reflectively than do nonaggressive children. These are among the social cognitive factors believed to be involved in the nature of children's conflicts.

Social knowledge is also involved in children's ability to get along with peers. Social relationship goals, such as how to initiate and maintain a social bond, are also important. Children need to know what scripts to follow to get other children to be their friends. For example, as part of the script for getting friends, it helps to know that saying nice things, regardless of what the peer does or says, will make the peer like the child more.

Bullying

Significant numbers of students are victimized by bullies (Espelage & Swearer, 2004; Evertson & Weinstein, 2006; Hanish & Guerra, 2004; Rigby, 2004; Roberts, 2005; Snell & Hirschstein, 2005). In one recent national survey of more than 15,000 sixth-through tenth-grade students, nearly one of every three students said that they had experienced occasional or frequent involvement as a victim or perpetrator in bullying (Nansel & others, 2001). In this study, bullying was defined as verbal or physical behavior intended to disturb someone less powerful. Boys and younger middle-school students were most likely to be affected. As shown in figure 14.6, being belittled about looks or speech was the most frequent type of bullying. Children who said they were bullied reported more loneliness and difficulty in making friends, while those who did the bullying were more likely to have low grades and to smoke and drink alcohol. A recent study of 9- to 12-year-old children in the Netherlands found that the victims of bullies had a much higher incidence of headaches, sleeping problems, abdominal pain, feeling tired, and depression than children not involved in bullying behavior (Fekkes, Pijpers, & Verloove-Vanhorick, 2004). A study of U.S. sixth-grade students examined there groups: bullies, victims, and those who were both bullies and victims (Juvonen, Graham, & Schuster, 2003). Bully-victims were the most troubled group, displaying the highest level of conduct, school, and relationship problems. Despite increased conduct problems, bullies enjoyed the highest standing of the three groups among their classmates.

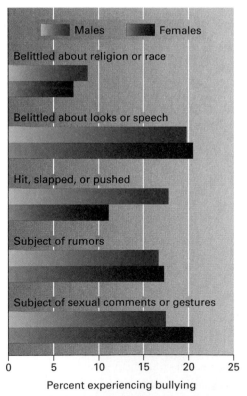

FIGURE 14.6 Bullying Behaviors Among U.S. Youth This graph shows the type of bullying most often experienced by U.S. youth. The percentages reflect the extent to which bullied students said that they had experienced a particular type of bullying. In terms of gender, note that when they were bullied, boys were more likely to be hit, slapped, or pushed than girls were.

To reduce bullying, schools can (Cohn & Canter, 2003; Hyman & others, 2006; Limber, 1997, 2004):

- Get older peers to serve as monitors for bullying and intervene when they see it taking place.
- Develop schoolwide rules and sanctions against bullying and post them throughout the school.
- Form friendship groups for adolescents who are regularly bullied by peers.
- Incorporate the message of the antibullying program into places of worship, school, and other community activities where adolescents are involved.
- Encourage parents to reinforce their children's positive behaviors and model appropriate interpersonal interactions.
- Identify bullies and victims early and use social skills training to improve their behavior.

To reduce bullying, parents can (Cohn & Canter, 2003):

- Contact the school's psychologist, counselor, or social worker and ask for help with their child's bullying or victimization concerns.
- Become involved in school programs to counteract bullying.
- Reinforce their children's positive behaviors and model interactions that do not include bullying or aggression.

Review and Reflect • LEARNING GOAL 3

 Identify changes in peer relationships in middle and late childhood.

Review
- What are children's friendships like?
- What are some developmental changes in peer relations during middle and late childhood?
- How do children's peer statuses influence their development?
- How is social cognition involved in children's peer relations?
- What is the nature of bullying?

Reflect
- If you were a school principal, what would you do to reduce bullying in your school?

---

4 WHAT ARE SOME IMPORTANT ASPECTS OF SCHOOLS?

Contemporary Approaches to Student Learning and Assessment	The Transition to Elementary School	Socioeconomic Status and Ethnicity

It is justifiable to be concerned about the impact of schools on children: By the time students graduate from high school, they have spent 10,000 hours in the classroom. Children spend many years in schools as members of a small society in which there are tasks to be accomplished, people to be socialized and socialized by, and rules that define and limit behavior, feelings, and attitudes.

Contemporary Approaches to Student Learning and Assessment

Controversy swirls about the best way for children to learn in school. Is direct instruction better for children or do they fare better with constructivist approaches to learning? How effectively are schools educating children?

Direct Instruction and Constructivist Approaches   The back-to-basics movement has many advocates who believe that schools should use a **direct instruction approach,** a teacher-centered approach that is characterized by teacher direction and control, mastery of academic skills, high expectations for students, and maximum time spent on learning tasks.

In the 1990s, interest in school reform focused on constructivist approaches (Santrock, 2006). **Cognitive constructivist approaches** emphasize the child's active, cognitive construction of knowledge and understanding. The teacher's role is to provide support for students to explore their world and develop understanding. Piaget's theory, which we discussed in chapter 6, is the main developmental theory that is linked with cognitive constructivist approaches. **Social constructivist approaches** focus on importance of collaboration with others to produce knowledge and understanding (John-Steiner & Mahn, 2003). The implication is that teachers should create many opportunities for students to learn with the teacher and with peers in coconstructing understanding. Vygotsky's theory, which we also discussed in chapter 6, is the main developmental theory that has served as the foundation for social constructivist approaches.

In short, constructivist approaches place the learner, not the teacher, at the center of the education process; they apply *learner-center principles* (Duffy & Kirkley, 2004; McCombs, 2003). Figure 14.7 summarizes 14 learner-centered principles. These principles were constructed by a prestigious group of scientists and educators from a wide range of disciplines and published by the American Psychological Association in *Learner-Centered Principles: A Framework for School Reform and Redesign* (Learner-Centered Principles Work Group, 1997).

Advocates of the cognitive and social constructivist and learner-centered approaches argue that the direct instruction approach turns children into passive learners and does not adequately challenge them to think in critical and creative ways. The direct instruction enthusiasts say that the constructivist approaches do not give enough attention to the content of a discipline, such as history or science. They also believe that the constructivist approaches are too relativistic and vague.

Accountability   As the public and government have demanded increased accountability of how effectively schools are educating children, state-mandated tests have taken on a more powerful role (Hambleton, 2002; Houston, 2005). Most states have or are in the process of identifying objectives that every student in the state is expected to achieve. Teachers are strongly encouraged to incorporate these objectives into their classroom planning and instruction.

A number of policymakers argue that state-mandated testing will have a number of positive effects. These include improved student performance; more time teaching the subjects tests; high expectations for all students; identification of poorly performing schools, teachers, and administrators; and improved confidence in schools as test scores increase.

The most visible aspect of state-mandated testing involves the No Child Left Behind (NCLB) act, the federal legislation that was signed into law in 2002. NCLB is the U.S. government's effort to hold schools and school districts accountable for the success or failure of their students (Kubrick & McLaughlin, 2005). The legislation shifts the responsibility to the states, with states being required to create their own standards for students' achievement in mathematics, English/language arts, and science. By 2005–2006, states are required to give all students annual tests in grades 3 through 8.

www.mhhe.com/santrock9

National Education Research Centers
Pathways to School Improvement
APA's Education Directorate
Phi Delta Kappan

direct instruction approach A teacher-centered approach characterized by teacher direction and control, mastery of academic skills, high expectations for students, and maximum time spent on learning tasks.

cognitive constructivist approach An approach that emphasizes the child's active, cognitive construction of knowledge and understanding; Piaget's theory is an example of this approach.

social constructivist approach An approach that focuses on collaboration with others to produce knowledge and understanding; Vygotsky's theory is an example of this approach.

FIGURE 14.7 Learner-Centered Psychological Principles

Cognitive and Metacognitive Factors

1. Nature of the Learning Process
   The learning of complex subject matter is most effective when it is an intentional process of constructing meaning and experience.

2. Goals of the Learning Process
   Successful learners, over time and with support and instructional guidance, can create meaningful, coherent representations of knowledge.

3. Construction of Knowledge
   Successful learners can link new information with existing knowledge in meaningful ways.

4. Strategic Thinking
   Successful learners can create a repertoire of thinking and reasoning strategies to achieve complex goals.

5. Thinking About Thinking
   Higher-order strategies for selecting and monitoring mental operations facilitate creative and critical thinking.

6. Context of Learning
   Learning is influenced by environmental factors, including culture, technology, and instructional practices.

Motivational and Instructional Factors

7. Motivational and Emotional Influences on Learning
   What and how much is learned is influenced by the learner's motivation. Motivation to learn, in turn, is influenced by the learner's emotional states, beliefs, interests, goals, and habits of thinking.

8. Intrinsic Motivation to Learn
   The learner's creativity, higher-order thinking, and natural curiosity all contribute to motivation to learn. Intrinsic (internal, self-generated) motivation is stimulated by tasks of optimal novelty and difficulty, tasks that are relevant to personal interests, and when learners are provided personal choice and control.

9. Effects of Motivation on Effort
   Acquiring complex knowledge and skills requires extended learner effort and guided practice. Without learners' motivation to learn, the willingness to exert this effort is unlikely without coercion.

Developmental and Social Factors

10. Developmental Influences on Learning
    As individuals develop, there are different opportunities and constraints for learning. Learning is most effective when development within and across physical, cognitive, and socioemotional domains is taken into account.

11. Social Influences on Learning
    Learning is influenced by social interactions, interpersonal relations, and communication with others.

Individual Difference Factors

12. Individual Differences in Learning
    Learners have different strategies, approaches, and capabilities for learning that are a function of prior experience and heredity.

13. Learning and Diversity
    Learning is most effective when differences in learners' linguistic, cultural, and social backgrounds are considered.

14. Standards and Assessment
    Setting appropriately high and challenging standards and assessing the learner as well as learning progress are integral aspects of the learning experience.

A number of criticisms of No Child Left Behind have been made. Critics argue that the NCLB legislation will do more harm than good (Ambrosio, 2004; Fair Test, 2004; Goldberg, 2005; Lewis, 2005; Neill, 2003). One criticism stresses that using a single score from a single test as the sole indicator of students' progress and competence represents a very narrow aspect of students' skills. This criticism is similar to the one leveled at IQ tests, which we described in Chapter 13. To more accurately assess student progress and achievement, many psychologists and educators emphasize that a number of measures should be used, including tests, quizzes, projects, portfolios, classroom observations, and so on, rather than a single score on a single test. Also, the tests schools are using to assess achievement and progress as part of NCLB don't measure such important skills as creativity, motivation, persistence, flexible thinking, and social skills (Droege, 2004). Critics point out that teachers are spending far too much class time "teaching to the test" by drilling students and having them memorize isolated facts at the expense of more student-centered constructivist teaching that focuses on higher level thinking skills, which students need for success in life.

Despite such criticisms, the U.S. Department of Education is committed to implementing No Child Left Behind and schools are making accommodations to meet the requirements of this law. Indeed, most educators support the importance of high expectations and high standards of excellence for students (Revelle, 2004). At issue, however, is whether the tests and procedures mandated by NCLB are the best ones for achieving these high standards.

The Transition to Elementary School

For most children, entering the first grade signals a change from being a "homechild" to being a "schoolchild"—a situation in which new roles and obligations are experienced. Children take up a new role (being a student), interact and develop relationships with new significant others, adopt new reference groups, and develop new standards by which to judge themselves. School provides children with a rich source of new ideas to shape their sense of self.

A special concern about children's early school experiences is that too often they involve negative feedback. For example, children's self-esteem in the latter part of elementary school is lower than it is in the earlier part, and older children rate themselves as less smart, less good, and less hardworking than do younger ones (Blumenfeld & others, 1981).

Children should be given opportunities to actively construct their learning. To illustrate, let's examine two elementary school classrooms (Katz & Chard, 1989). In one, children spent an entire morning making identical pictures of traffic lights. The teacher made no attempt to get the children to relate the pictures to anything else the class was doing. In the other class, the children were investigating a school bus. They wrote to the district's school superintendent and asked if they could have a bus parked at their school for a few days. They studied the bus, discovered the functions of its parts, and discussed traffic rules. Then, in the classroom, they built their own bus out of cardboard. The children had fun, but they also practiced writing, problem solving, and even some arithmetic. When the class had their parents' night, the teacher was ready with reports on how each child was doing. However, all that the parents wanted to see was the bus because their children had been talking about it at home for weeks. Many contemporary education experts believe that this is the kind of education all children deserve. That is, they believe that children should be active, constructivist learners and taught through concrete, hands-on experience.

Socioeconomic Status and Ethnicity

Children from low-income, ethnic minority backgrounds have more difficulties in school than do their middle-socioeconomic-status, White counterparts. Why? Critics argue that schools have not done a good job of educating low-income, ethnic minority students (Books, 2004; Scott-Jones, 1995). Let's further explore the roles of socioeconomic status and ethnicity in schools.

The Education of Students from Low-Socioeconomic Backgrounds Many children in poverty face problems at home that present barriers to their learning (Bradley & Corwyn, 2002). They might have parents who don't set high educational standards for them, who are incapable of reading to them, and who don't have enough money to pay for educational materials and experiences, such as books and trips to zoos and museums. They might be malnourished and live in areas where crime and violence are a way of life.

Children from a low-SES background face another obstacle: their schools (Bradley & Corwyn, 2002; Cooter, 2004). Compared with schools in higher-income areas, schools in low-income areas are more likely to have more students with low achievement test scores, low graduation rates, and small percentages of students going to college; they are more likely to have young teachers with less experience; and they are more likely to encourage rote learning (Spring, 2005). Too few schools in low-income neighborhoods provide students with environments that are conducive to learning. Many of the schools' buildings and classrooms are old and crumbling.

Jonathan Kozol (1991) vividly described some of the problems that children of poverty face in their neighborhood and at school in *Savage Inequalities*. Following are some of his observations in one inner-city area, East St. Louis, Illinois, which has no obstetric services, no regular trash collection, and few jobs. Nearly one-third of the families live on less than $7,500 a year, and 75 percent of its population lives on welfare of some form. Blocks upon blocks of housing consist of dilapidated, skeletal buildings. Residents breathe the chemical pollution of nearby Monsanto Chemical Company. Raw sewage repeatedly backs up into homes. Lead from nearby smelters poisons the soil. Child malnutrition and fear of violence are common. The problems of the streets spill over into the schools, where sewage also backs up from time to time. Classrooms and hallways are old and unattractive, athletic facilities inadequate. Teachers run out of chalk and paper, the science labs are 30 to 50 years out of date, and the school's heating system has never worked correctly. A history teacher has 110 students but only 26 books. Anyone who visits places like East St. Louis, says Kozol, comes away profoundly shaken.

Ethnicity in Schools East St. Louis is 98 percent African American. Kozol's interest was in describing what life is like in the nation's inner-city neighborhoods and schools, which are predominantly African American and Latino. More than one-third of all African American and almost one-third of all Latino students attend schools in the 47 largest city school districts in the United States, compared with only 5 percent of all White and 22 percent of all Asian American students. Many of these inner-city schools are still segregated, are grossly underfunded, and do not provide adequate opportunities for children to learn effectively. Thus, the effects of SES and the effects of ethnicity are often intertwined.

In his book *Savage Inequalities*, Jonathan Kozol (*above*) vividly portrayed the problems that children of poverty face in their neighborhood and at school. *What are some of these problems?*

www.mhhe.com/santrockc9

Interview with Jonathan Kozol
Diversity and Education

What are some positive strategies for improving interethnic relations among students in schools?

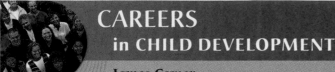

CAREERS in CHILD DEVELOPMENT

James Comer
Child Psychiatrist

James Comer grew up in a low-income neighborhood in East Chicago, Indiana, and credits his parents with leaving no doubt about the importance of education. He obtained a BA degree from Indiana University. He went on to obtain a medical degree from Howard University College of Medicine, a Master of Public Health degree from the University of Michigan School of Public Health, and psychiatry training at the Yale University School of Medicine's Child Study Center. He currently is the Maurice Falk Professor of Child Psychiatry at the Yale University Child Study Center and an associate dean at the Yale University Medical School. During his years at Yale, Comer has concentrated his career on promoting a focus on child development as a way of improving schools. His efforts in support of healthy development of young people are known internationally.

Dr. Comer, perhaps, is best known for the founding of the School Development Program in 1968, which promotes the collaboration of parents, educators, and community to improve social, emotional, and academic outcomes for children. His concept of teamwork is currently improving the educational environment in more than 500 schools throughout America.

James Comer (*left*) is shown with some of the inner-city African American children who attend a school that became a better learning environment because of Comer's intervention. Comer is convinced that a strong, familylike atmosphere is a key to improving the quality of inner-city schools.

School segregation is still a factor in U.S. education (Spring, 2005; Tozer, Senese, & Violas, 2005). Almost one-third of all African American and Latino students attend schools in which 90 percent or more of the students are from minority groups (Banks, 2002, 2003, 2006).

The school experiences of students from different ethnic groups vary considerably (Diaz, Pelletier, & Provenzo, 2006; Pang, 2005; Powell & Caseau, 2004; Spencer, 2006). African American and Latino students are much less likely than non-Latino White or Asian American students to be enrolled in academic, college preparatory programs and are much more likely to be enrolled in remedial and special education programs. Asian American students are far more likely than other ethnic minority groups to take advanced math and science courses in high school. African American students are twice as likely as Latinos, Native Americans, or Whites to be suspended from school. In one study of middle schools in predominantly Latino areas of Miami, Latino and White teachers rated African American students as having more behavioral problems than African American teachers rated the same students as having (Zimmerman & others, 1995).

Some experts say that a form of institutional racism permeates many American schools by which teachers accept a low level of performance from children of color (Ogbu, 2003; Ogbu & Stern, 2001). American anthropologist John Ogbu (1989) proposed the view that ethnic minority students are placed in a position of subordination and exploitation in the American educational system. He believes that students of color, especially African Americans and Latinos, have inferior educational opportunities, are exposed to teachers and school administrators who have low academic expectations for them, and encounter negative stereotypes (Ogbu & Stern, 2001).

Here are some strategies for improving relationships among ethnically diverse students (Santrock, 2006):

- *Turn the class into a jigsaw classroom.* When Eliot Aronson was a professor at the University of Texas at Austin, the school system contacted him for ideas on how to reduce the increasing racial tension in classrooms. Aronson (1986) developed the concept of "jigsaw classroom," in which students from different cultural backgrounds are placed in a cooperative group in which they have to construct different parts of a project to reach a common goal. Aronson used the term *jigsaw* because he saw the technique as much like a group of students cooperating to put different pieces together to complete a jigsaw puzzle. How might this work? Team sports, drama productions, and music performances are examples of contexts in which students cooperatively participate to reach a common goal.
- *Use technology to foster cooperation with students from around the world.*

- *Encourage students to have positive personal contact with diverse other students.* Contact alone does not do the job of improving relationships with diverse others. For example, busing ethnic minority students to predominantly White schools, or vice versa, has not reduced prejudice or improved interethnic relations (Minuchin & Shapiro, 1983). What matters is what happens after children get to school. Especially beneficial in improving interethnic relations is sharing one's worries, successes, failures, coping strategies, interests, and other personal information with people of other ethnicities. When this happens, people are seen more as individuals than as a heterogeneous cultural group.

- *Encourage students to engage in perspective taking.* Exercises and activities that help students see others' perspectives can improve interethnic relations. This helps students "step into the shoes" of peers who are culturally different and feel what it is like to be treated in fair or unfair ways.

- *Help students think critically and be emotionally intelligent when cultural issues are involved.* Students who learn to think critically and deeply about interethnic relations are likely to decrease their prejudice. Becoming more emotionally intelligent includes understanding the causes of one's feelings, managing anger, listening to what others are saying, and being motivated to share and cooperate.

- *Reduce bias.* Teachers can reduce bias by displaying images of children from diverse ethnic and cultural groups, selecting play materials and classroom activities that encourage cultural understanding, helping students resist stereotyping, and working with parents.

- *View the school and community as a team to help support teaching efforts.* James Comer (1988, 2004; Comer & others, 1996) believes that a community, team approach is the best way to educate children. Three important aspects of the Comer Project for Change are (1) a governance and management team that develops a comprehensive school plan, assessment strategy, and staff development plan; (2) a mental health or school support team; and (3) a parents' program. Comer believes that the entire school community should have a cooperative rather than an adversarial attitude. The Comer program is currently operating in more than 600 schools in 26 states. To read further about James Comer and his work, see the Careers in Child Development profile.

- *Be a competent cultural mediator.* Teachers can play a powerful role as a cultural mediator by being sensitive to racist content in materials and classroom interactions, learning more about different ethnic groups, being sensitive to children's ethnic attitudes, viewing students of color positively, and thinking of positive ways to get parents of color more involved as partners with teachers in educating children (Jones & Fuller, 2003).

 ***Review and Reflect* • LEARNING GOAL 4**

4 Characterize some important aspects of elementary school education.

Review
- What are some contemporary approaches to student learning and assessment?
- What is the transition to elementary school like?
- How do socioeconomic status and ethnicity influence schooling?

Reflect
- What do think about the No Child Left Behind legislation? What are some potential strengths and weaknesses of the legislation?

Growing up has never been easy. However, adolescence is not best viewed as a time of rebellion, crisis, pathology, and deviance. A far more accurate vision of adolescence describes it as a time of evaluation, of decision making, of commitment, and of carving out a place in the world. Most of the problems of today's youth are not with the youth themselves. What adolescents need is access to a range of legitimate opportunities and to long-term support from adults who deeply care about them. *What might be some examples of such support and caring?*

Practical Resources and Research
Profile of America's Youth
American Youth Policy Forum

are time-honored ways in which adolescents move toward accepting, rather than rejecting, parental values.

Although the majority of adolescents experience the transition from childhood to adulthood more positively than is portrayed by many adults and the media, too many adolescents today are not provided with adequate opportunities and support to become competent adults (Leventhal & Brooks-Gunn, 2004; Santrock, 2005). In many ways, today's adolescents are presented with a less stable environment than adolescents of a decade or two ago. High divorce rates, high adolescent pregnancy rates, and increased geographic mobility of families contribute to this lack of stability in adolescents' lives. Today's adolescents are exposed to a complex menu of lifestyle options through the media, and although the adolescent drug use rate is beginning to show signs of decline, the rate of adolescent drug use in the United States is higher than that of any other country in the industrialized Western world. Many of today's adolescents face these temptations, as well as sexual activity, at increasingly younger ages.

Our discussion underscores an important point about adolescents: They do not make up a homogeneous group (Larson & Wilson, 2004). Most adolescents negotiate the lengthy path to adult maturity successfully, but too large a group does not (Perkins & Borden, 2003; Youniss & Silbereisen, 2003). Ethnic, cultural, gender, socioeconomic, age, and lifestyle differences influence the actual life trajectory of every adolescent. Different portrayals of adolescence emerge, depending on the particular group of adolescents being described (Leventhal & Brooks-Gunn, 2004; Mortimer & Larson, 2002).

Review and Reflect ● LEARNING GOAL 1

 Discuss the foundations of adolescence and today's youth.

Review
- What are today's youth like?

Reflect
- You likely experienced some instances of stereotyping as an adolescent. What are some examples of the circumstances in which you feel that you were stereotyped as an adolescent?

2 WHAT ARE THE PHYSICAL AND PSYCHOLOGICAL ASPECTS OF PUBERTY?

Determinants of Puberty	Sexual Maturation	Psychological Dimensions	Early and Late Maturation

Growth Spurt	Secular Trends in Puberty	The Brain

One father joked that the problem with his teenage son was not that he grew, but that he did not know when to stop growing. As we will see, there is considerable variation in the timing of the adolescent growth spurt.

Determinants of Puberty

Puberty is a period of rapid physical maturation involving hormonal and bodily changes that occur primarily during early adolescence. Puberty is often thought of as a marker for the beginning of adolescence. However, for most individuals adolescence continues beyond puberty. Among the most important factors that contribute to the onset of puberty are heredity, hormones, and weight and body fat.

Heredity   Puberty is not an environmental accident. Programmed into the genes of every human being is a timing for the emergence of puberty (Adair, 2001; Eaves & others, 2004; Mustanski & others, 2005). Puberty does not take place at 2 or 3 years of age and it does not occur in the twenties. In the future, we are likely to see molecular genetic studies that identify specific genes linked to the onset and progression of puberty. Nonetheless, as you will see in our further discussion of puberty, within the boundaries of about 9 to 16 years of age, environmental factors can influence the onset and duration of puberty.

Hormones   Behind the first whisker in boys and the widening of hips in girls is a flood of hormones. Let's explore the nature of these hormonal changes.

Hormones are powerful chemical substances that are secreted by the endocrine glands and carried through the body by the bloodstream. The endocrine system's role in puberty involves the interaction of the hypothalamus, the pituitary gland, and the gonads (sex glands) (see figure 15.1). The *hypothalamus* is a structure in the higher portion of the brain that monitors eating, drinking, and sex. The *pituitary gland* is an important endocrine gland that controls growth and regulates other glands. The *gonads* are the sex glands—the testes in males, the ovaries in females.

How does this hormonal system work? The pituitary gland sends a signal via gonadotropins (hormones that stimulate the testes or ovaries) to the appropriate gland to manufacture the hormone. Then the pituitary gland, through interaction with the hypothalamus, detects when the optimal level of hormones is reached and responds by maintaining gonadotropin secretion.

As you read in chapter 11, two classes of hormones have significantly different concentrations in males and females: *Androgens* are the main class of male sex hormones and *estrogens* are the main class of female hormones.

Testosterone is an androgen that plays an important role in male pubertal development. Throughout puberty, increasing testosterone levels are associated with a number of physical changes in boys—the development of external genitals, an increase in height, and voice changes. *Estradiol* is an estrogen that plays an important role in female pubertal development. As the estradiol level rises, breast development, uterine development, and skeletal changes occur. In one study, testosterone levels increased 18-fold in boys but only twofold in girls across the pubertal period; estradiol levels increased eight-fold in girls but only twofold in boys during puberty (Nottleman & others, 1987).

puberty A period of rapid physical maturation involving hormonal and bodily changes that occur primarily in early adolescence.

hormones Powerful chemicals secreted by the endocrine glands and carried through the body by the bloodstream.

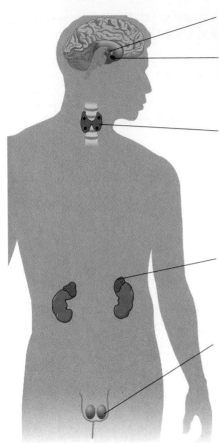

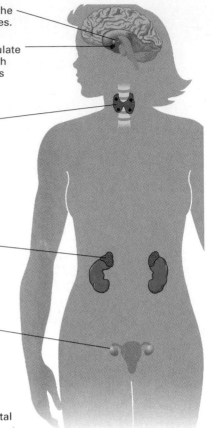

Hypothalamus: A structure in the brain that interacts with the pituitary gland to monitor the bodily regulation of hormones.

Pituitary: This master gland produces hormones that stimulate other glands. It also influences growth by producing growth hormones; it sends gonadotropins to the testes and ovaries and a thyroid-stimulating hormone to the thyroid gland. It sends a hormone to the adrenal gland as well.

Thyroid gland: It interacts with the pituitary gland to influence growth.

Adrenal gland: It interacts with the pituitary gland and likely plays a role in pubertal development, but less is known about its function than about sex glands. Recent research, however, suggests it may be involved in adolescent behavior, particularly for boys.

The gonads, or sex glands: These consist of the testes in males and the ovaries in females. The sex glands are strongly involved in the appearance of secondary sex characteristics, such as facial hair in males and breast development in females. The general class of hormones called estrogens is dominant in females, while androgens are dominant in males. More specifically, testosterone in males and estradiol in females are key hormones in pubertal development.

FIGURE 15.1   The Major Endocrine Glands Involved in Pubertal Change

www.mhhe.com/santrockc9

Biological Changes

menarche A girl's first menstrual period.

spermarche A boy's first ejaculation of semen.

Are there links between concentrations of hormones and adolescent behavior? Hormonal factors are thought to account for at least part of the increase in negative and variable emotions that characterize adolescents (Susman & Rogol, 2004). Researchers have found that higher levels of androgens are associated with violence and acting-out problems in boys (van Goozen & others, 1998). Few studies have focused on estrogens; however, there is some indication that increased levels of estrogen are linked with depression in adolescent girls (Angold, Costello, & Worthman, 1998).

It is important to understand that hormonal factors alone are not responsible for adolescent behavior. For example, in one study, social factors accounted for two to four times as much variance as hormonal factors in young adolescent girls' depression and anger (Brooks-Gunn & Warren, 1989). Stress, eating patterns, sexual activity, and depression can activate or suppress various aspects of the hormone system.

Puberty has two phases that are linked with hormonal changes: adrenarche and gonadarche (Susman, Dorn, & Schiefelbein, 2003; Susman & Rogol, 2004). *Adrenarche* involves hormonal changes in the adrenal glands, which are located just above the kidneys. These changes occur surprisingly early, from about 6 to 9 years of age and before what we generally consider to be the beginning of puberty.

Gonadarche is what most people think of as puberty and it follows adrenarche by approximately two years (Archibald, Graber, & Brooks-Gunn, 2003). Gonadarche involves sexual maturation and the development of reproductive maturity. Gonadarche begins at approximately 9 to 10 years of age in non-Latino White girls, and 8 to 9 years of age in African American girls in the United States. Gonadarche begins at about 10 to 11 years of age in boys. The culmination of gonadarche in girls is **menarche,** a girl's first menstrual period, and in boys is **spermarche,** a boy's first ejaculation of semen.

From *Penguin Dreams and Stranger Things* by Berkeley Breathed. Copyright © 1985 by The Washington Post Company. By permission of Little, Brown and Co., Inc. and International Creative Management, Inc.

Weight and Body Fat   One view is that a critical body mass must be attained before puberty, especially menarche, is attained (Friesch, 1984; Styne, 2004). A body weight of approximately 106 ± 3 pounds can trigger menarche and the end of the pubertal growth spurt. For menarche to begin and continue, fat must make up approximately 17 percent of the girl's body weight. Both anorexic adolescents whose weight drops dramatically and females in certain sports (such as gymnastics) may become amenorrheic (having an absence or suppression of menstrual discharge) (Swenne, 2004). Undernutrition also may delay puberty in boys (Susman, Dorn, & Schiefelbein, 2003).

The hormone *leptin,* which we discussed in chapter 12, has been proposed as a possible signal of the beginning and progression of puberty (Grasemann & others, 2004; Li & others, 2005; Plant & Barker-Glbb, 2004). Leptin may be one of the messengers that signals the adequacy of fat stores for reproduction and maintenance of pregnancy at puberty. Leptin concentrations are higher in girls than in boys. They also are related to the amount of fat in girls and androgen concentrations in boys (Apter, 2003; Celi & others, 2004).

In sum, the determinants of puberty include heredity, hormones, weight, body fat, and possibly leptin. Next, we will turn our attention to the growth spurt that characterizes puberty.

Growth Spurt

Growth slows throughout childhood and puberty ushers in the most rapid increases in growth since infancy. As indicated in figure 15.2, the growth spurt associated with puberty occurs approximately two years earlier for girls than for boys. The mean beginning of the growth spurt is 9 years of age for girls and 11 years of age for boys. The peak of pubertal change occurs at 11½ years for girls and 13½ years for boys. During their growth spurt, girls increase in height about 3½ inches per year, boys about 4 inches.

Boys and girls who are shorter or taller than their peers before adolescence are likely to remain so during adolescence. In our society, there is a stigma attached to being a short boy. At the beginning of adolescence, girls tend to be as tall or taller than boys their age, but by the end of the middle school years most boys have caught up, or in many cases even surpassed, girls in height. And even though height in elementary school is a good predictor of height later in adolescence, as much as 30 percent of the height of individuals in late adolescence is unexplained by height in the elementary school years.

The rate at which adolescents gain weight follows approximately the same developmental timetable as the rate at which they gain height. Marked weight gains

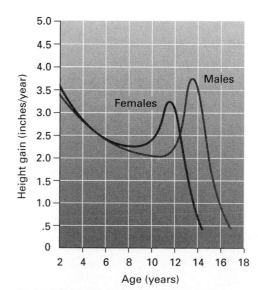

FIGURE 15.2 Pubertal Growth Spurt On the average, the peak of the growth spurt that characterizes pubertal change occurs two years earlier for girls (11½) than for boys (13½).

What are some of the differences in the ways girls and boys experience pubertal growth?

coincide with the onset of puberty. Fifty percent of adult body weight is gained during adolescence (Rogol, Roemmich, & Clark, 1998). At the peak of weight gain during puberty, girls gain an average of 18 pounds in one year at about 12 years of age (approximately six months after their peak height increase). Boys' peak weight gain per year (20 pounds in one year) occurs at about the same time as their peak increase in height (about 13 to 14 years of age). During early adolescence, girls tend to outweigh boys, but just as with height, by about age 14 boys begin to surpass girls in weight.

In addition to increases in height and weight, changes in hip and shoulder width occur. Adolescent girls experience a spurt in hip width, while boys undergo an increase in shoulder width. Increased hip width is linked with an increase in estrogens in girls. Increased shoulder width in boys is associated with an increase in testosterone in boys.

The later growth spurt of boys also produces greater leg length in boys than is experienced by girls. Also, in many cases, the facial structure of boys becomes more angular during puberty while that of girls becomes more round and soft.

Sexual Maturation

Think back to the onset of your puberty. Of the striking changes that were taking place in your body, what was the first change that occurred? Researchers have found that male pubertal characteristics develop in this order: increase in penis and testicle size, appearance of straight pubic hair, minor voice change, first ejaculation (spermarche—usually occurs through masturbation or a wet dream), appearance of kinky pubic hair, onset of maximum growth, growth of hair in armpits, more detectable voice changes, and growth of facial hair. Three of the most noticeable areas of sexual maturation in boys are penis elongation, testes development, and growth of pubic hair. The normal range and average age of development for these sexual characteristics, along with height spurt, are shown in figure 15.3.

What is the order of appearance of physical changes in females? First, either the breasts enlarge or pubic hair appears. Later, hair appears in the armpits. As these changes occur, the female grows in height, and her hips become wider than her shoulders. Her first menstruation (menarche) comes rather late in the pubertal cycle. Initially, her menstrual cycles may be highly irregular. For the first several years, she might not ovulate during every menstrual cycle. Some girls do not become fertile until two years after the period begins. No voice changes comparable to those in pubertal males occur in pubertal females. By the end of puberty, the female's breasts have become more fully rounded. Two of the most noticeable aspects of female pubertal change are pubic hair and breast development. Figure 15.3 shows the normal range and average development of these sexual characteristics and also provides information about menarche and height gain.

It is important to understand that there may be wide individual variations in the onset and progression of puberty. The pubertal sequence may begin as early as 10 years of age or as late as 13½ for boys. It may end as early as 13 years or as late as 17. The normal range is wide enough that, given two boys of the same chronological age, one might complete the pubertal sequence before the other one has begun it. For girls, the age range of menarche is even wider. It is considered within a normal range when it occurs between 9 and 15 years of age.

Secular Trends in Puberty

Imagine a toddler displaying all the features of puberty—a 3-year-old girl with fully developed breasts or a boy just slightly older with a deep male voice. That is what we would see by the year 2250 if the age at which puberty arrives would be getting younger at the same rate at which it was occurring for much of the twentieth century.

The term *secular trends* refers to patterns over time, especially across generations. For example, in Norway menarche now occurs at just over 13 years of age compared with 17 years of age in the 1840s (de Munich Keizer & Mul, 2001; Petersen, 1979). In the United States—where children physically mature up to a year earlier than in European countries—the average age of menarche declined an average of two to four months per decade for much of the twentieth century (see figure 15.4). In the United States, menarche occurred at an average of 15 years of age in the late nineteenth century compared with about 12½ years today.

The earlier onset of puberty in the twentieth century was likely due to improved health and nutrition. Fortunately, we are unlikely to see pubescent toddlers in the future, because in the last decade a slowdown in earlier onset of puberty has been occurring (Delemarre-van de Waal, 2005; Lee, Kulin, & Guo, 2001).

Psychological Dimensions

A host of psychological changes accompany an adolescent's pubertal development (Sarigiani & Peterson, 2000). Try to remember when you were beginning puberty. Not only did you probably think of yourself differently, but your parents and peers also probably began acting differently toward you. Maybe you were proud of your changing body, even though you were perplexed about what was happening. Perhaps your parents no longer perceived you as someone they could sit in bed with to watch television or someone who should be kissed good night.

There has been far less research on the psychosocial aspects of male pubertal transitions than on those of females, possibly because of the difficulty in defining when the male transitions occur. Wet dreams are one such marker, yet there has been little research on this topic (Susman & others, 1995).

Body Image   One psychological aspect of physical change in puberty is certain: Adolescents are preoccupied with their bodies and develop individual images of what their bodies are like. Perhaps you looked in the mirror on a daily and sometimes even hourly basis to see if you could detect anything different about your changing body. Preoccupation with one's body image is strong throughout adolescence, but it is especially acute during puberty, a time when adolescents are more dissatisfied with their bodies than in late adolescence (Wright, 1989).

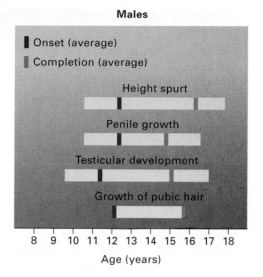

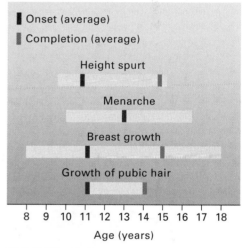

FIGURE 15.3 Normal Range and Average Development of Sexual Characteristics in Males and Females

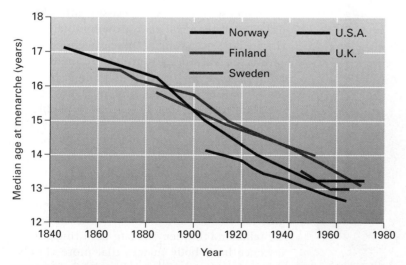

FIGURE 15.4 Median Ages at Menarche in Selected Northern European Countries and the United States from 1845 to 1969 Notice the steep decline in the age at which girls experienced menarche in five different countries. Recently the age at which girls experience menarche has been leveling off.

CAREERS in CHILD DEVELOPMENT

Anne Petersen
Researcher and Administrator

Anne Petersen has had a distinguished career as a researcher and administrator with a main focus on adolescent development. Petersen obtained three degrees (B.A., M.A., and Ph.D.) from the University of Chicago in math and statistics. Her first job after she obtained her Ph.D. was as a research associate/professor involving statistical consultation, and it was on this job that she was introduced to the field of adolescent development, which became the focus of her subsequent work

Petersen moved from the University of Chicago to Pennsylvania State University, where she became a leading researcher in adolescent development. Her research included a focus on puberty and gender. Petersen also held numerous administrative positions. In the mid-1990s, she became Deputy Director of the National Science Foundation and since 1996 has been Senior Vice President for programs at the W. K. Kellogg Foundation.

Petersen says that what inspired her to enter the field of adolescent development and take her current position at the Kellogg Foundation was her desire to make a difference for people, especially youth. In her position at Kellogg, Petersen is responsible for all programming and services provided by the foundation for adolescents. Her goal is to make a difference for youth in this country and around the world. She believes that too often adolescents have been neglected.

Anne Petersen interacting with adolescents.

There are gender differences in adolescents' perceptions of their bodies. In general, girls are less happy with their bodies and have more negative body images, compared with boys, throughout puberty (Brooks-Gunn & Paikoff, 1993). Also, as pubertal change proceeds, girls often become more dissatisfied with their bodies, probably because their body fat increases, while boys become more satisfied as they move through puberty, probably because their muscle mass increases.

Early and Late Maturation

Adolescents who mature earlier or later than their peers perceive themselves differently (Pinyerd & Zipf, 2005). In the Berkeley Longitudinal Study some years ago, early-maturing boys perceived themselves more positively and had more successful peer relations than did their late-maturing counterparts (Jones, 1965). The findings for early-maturing girls were similar but not as strong as for boys. When the late-maturing boys were studied in their thirties, however, they had developed a stronger sense of identity than the early-maturing boys (Peskin, 1967). Late-maturing boys may have had more time to explore a wide variety of options. They may have focused on career development and achievement that would serve them better in life than their early-maturing counterparts' emphasis on physical status. More recent research confirms, though, that at least during adolescence it is advantageous to be an early-maturing rather than a late-maturing boy (Petersen, 1987). Roberta Simmons and Dale Blyth (1987) studied more than 450 individuals for five years, beginning in the sixth grade and continuing through the tenth grade, in Milwaukee, Wisconsin. Students were individually interviewed, and achievement test scores and grade point averages were obtained. The presence or absence of menstruation and the relative onset of menses were used to classify girls as early, middle, or late maturers. The peak growth in height was used to classify boys according to these categories.

In the Milwaukee study, more mixed and complex findings emerged for girls (Simmons & Blyth, 1987). Early-maturing girls had more problems in school, were more independent, and were more popular with boys than late-maturing girls were. The time at which maturation was assessed also was a factor. In the sixth grade, early-maturing girls were more satisfied with their body image than late-maturing girls were, but by the tenth grade, late-maturing girls were more satisfied (see figure 15.5). Why? Because by late adolescence, early-maturing girls are shorter and stockier, while late-maturing girls are taller and thinner. The late-maturing girls in late adolescence have body images that more closely approximate the current American ideal of feminine beauty—tall and thin.

In the last decade an increasing number of researchers have found that early maturation increases girls' vulnerability to a number of problems (Brooks-Gunn & Paikoff, 1993; McCabe & Ricciardelli, 2004; Sarigiani & Petersen, 2000; Stattin & Magnusson,

1990; Waylen & Wolke, 2004). Early-maturing girls are more likely to smoke, drink, be depressed, have an eating disorder, request earlier independence from their parents, and have older friends; and their bodies are likely to elicit responses from males that lead to earlier dating and earlier sexual experiences. In one study, the early-maturing girls had lower educational and occupational attainment in adulthood (Stattin & Magnusson, 1990). In a recent study, early-maturing females had a higher incidence of mental disorders than late-maturing females (Graber & others, 2004). Apparently as a result of their social and cognitive immaturity, combined with early physical development, early-maturing girls are easily lured into problem behaviors, not recognizing the possible long-term effects of these on their development.

One individual who has made substantial contributions to our understanding of puberty is Anne Petersen. To read about her work, see the Careers in Child Development profile.

The Brain

Until recently, little research has been conducted on developmental changes in the brain during adolescence. Although research in this area is still in its infancy, an increasing number of studies are under way (Walker, 2002). Scientists now believe that the adolescent's brain is different from the child's brain, and that in adolescence the brain is still growing (Giedd, 2004; Keating, 2004, Kuhn & Franklin, 2006; Steinberg, 2005; White, 2005).

In one study, researchers used MRIs to discover if brain activity during the processing of emotional information differed in adolescents (10 to 18 years of age) and adults (20 to 40 years of age) (Baird & others, 1999). In this study, participants were asked to view pictures of faces displaying fearful expressions while they underwent an MRI. When adolescents (especially younger ones) processed the emotional information, their brain activity was more pronounced in the amygdala than in the frontal lobe (see figure 15.6). The reverse occurred in the adults. The amygdala is involved in processing information about emotion, whereas the frontal lobes are involved in higher-level reasoning and thinking. The researchers interpreted their findings to mean that adolescents tend to respond with "gut" reactions to emotional stimuli and adults are more likely to respond in rational, reasoned ways. The researchers also concluded that these changes are linked to growth in the frontal lobe of the brain from adolescence to adulthood. However, more research is needed to clarify these findings on possible developmental changes in brain activity during the processing of emotional stimuli (Dahl, 2001; De Bellis & others, 2001; Spear, 2000, 2004). Other researchers have found that the amygdala and hippocampus, both limbic system structures involved in emotion, increase in volume during adolescence (Giedd & others, 1999; Sowell & Jernigan, 1998).

Leading researcher Charles Nelson (2003) points out that while adolescents are capable of very strong emotions their prefrontal cortex hasn't adequately developed to the point at which they can control these passions. It is as if their brain doesn't have the brakes to slow down their emotions. Or consider this interpretation of the development of emotion and cognition in adolescents: "early activation of strong 'turbocharged' feelings with a relatively unskilled set of 'driving skills' or cognitive abilities to modulate strong emotions and motivations" (Dahl, 2004, p. 18).

Laurence Steinberg (2004, 2005) emphasizes that the reward and pleasure aspects of the limbic system may also be involved in adolescents' difficulty in controlling their behavior. The argument is that changes in the limbic system during puberty lead adolescents to seek novelty and need higher levels of stimulation to experience pleasure (Spear, 2000, 2004). However, the relatively slow development of the prefrontal cortex, which continues to mature into emerging adulthood, means that adolescents may lack the cognitive skills to effectively control their pleasure seeking. This developmental disjunction may account for an increase in risk taking and other problems in adolescence. Steinberg (2004, p. 56) concludes that a helpful strategy may be to limit

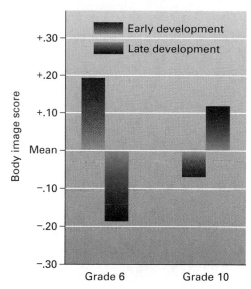

FIGURE 15.5 Early- and Late-Maturing Adolescent Girls' Perceptions of Body Image in Early and Late Adolescence

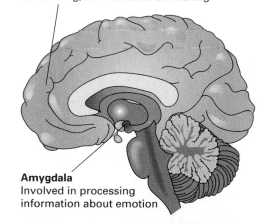

Prefrontal cortex
Involved in higher-order cognitive functioning, such as decision making

Amygdala
Involved in processing information about emotion

FIGURE 15.6 Developmental Changes in the Brain during Adolescence The amygdala, which is responsible for processing information about emotion, matures earlier than the prefrontal cortex, which is responsible for making decisions and other higher-order cognitive functions. *What are some possible implications of these developmental changes in the brain for adolescents' behavior?*

adolescents "opportunities for immature judgment to have harmful consequences. . . . Thus, strategies such as raising the price of cigarettes, more vigilantly enforcing laws governing the sale of alcohol, expanding access to mental health and contraceptive services, and raising the driving age would likely be more effective in limiting adolescent smoking, substance abuse, suicide, pregnancy, and automobile fatalities than strategies aimed at making adolescents wiser, less impulsive, or less shortsighted. Some things just take time to develop and mature judgment is probably one of them."

> ### Review and Reflect ● LEARNING GOAL 2
>
> **2   Describe puberty's determinants, developmental changes, and psychological dimensions.**
>
> **Review**
> * What is puberty? What are the determinants of puberty?
> * How can the adolescent growth spurt be described?
> * What characterizes sexual maturation in adolescence?
> * What are some secular trends in puberty?
> * What are the psychological dimensions of puberty?
> * What developmental changes occur in the brain during adolescence?
>
> **Reflect**
> * Did you experience puberty early, late, or on time? How do you think the timing of your puberty influenced your development?

3   WHAT ARE THE DIMENSIONS OF ADOLESCENT SEXUALITY?

Developing a Sexual Identity and Sexual Activity

Sexually Transmitted Infections

Contraceptive Use

Adolescent Pregnancy

Adolescence is a time of sexual exploration and experimentation, sexual fantasies and sexual realities, and the incorporation of sexuality into one's identity. Adolescents have an almost insatiable curiosity about sexuality. They think about whether they are sexually attractive, how to perform sexually, and what the future holds for their sexual lives. The majority of adolescents eventually manage to develop a mature sexual identity, but for most there are times of vulnerability and confusion along life's sexual journey.

Adolescence is a bridge between the asexual child and the sexual adult (Feldman, 1999). In every society, there is some attention to adolescent sexuality. In some societies, adults clamp down and protect adolescent females from males by chaperoning them. Other societies promote very early marriage. Yet other societies, such as the United States, allow some sexual experimentation, although there is controversy about just how far sexual experimentation should be allowed to go. And yet other countries—such as Sweden and the Netherlands—have a very permissive attitude about sexuality.

Many Americans are ambivalent about sex. Advertisers use sex to sell just about everything, from cars to detergents. Sex is explicitly portrayed in movies, TV shows, videos, lyrics of popular music, MTV, and Internet websites (Pettit, 2003; Roberts,

Sex is virtually everywhere in the American culture and is used to sell just about everything. *Is it surprising, then, that adolescents are so curious about sex and tempted to experiment with sex?*

Henrikson, & Foehr, 2004; Ward, 2003). A recent study of 1,762 12- to 17-year-olds found that those who watched more sexually explicit TV shows were more likely than their counterparts who watched these shows less to initiate sexual intercourse in the next 12 months (Collins & others, 2004). Adolescents in the highest 10 percent of viewing sexually explicit TV shows were twice as likely to engage in sexual intercourse as those in the lowest 10 percent. The results held regardless of whether the exposure to explicit sex involved sexual behavior or just talk about sex. A recent research review found that frequent watching of soap operas and music videos were linked with greater acceptance of casual attitudes about sex and higher expectations of engaging in sexual activity (Ward, 2003).

An important thing to keep in mind as you read about adolescent sexuality is that sexual development and interest are normal aspects of adolescent development and that the majority of adolescents have healthy sexual attitudes and engage in sexual practices that will not compromise their development (Crockett, Raffaelli, & Moilanen, 2003; Feldman, 1999). In our discussion of adolescent sexuality, we will focus on developing a sexual identity, the progression of adolescent sexual behaviors, contraceptive use, sexually transmitted infections, and adolescent pregnancy.

Sexual arousal emerges as a new phenomenon in adolescence and it is important to view sexuality as a normal aspect of adolescent development.

—SHIRLEY FELDMAN
Contemporary Psychologist, Stanford University

Developing a Sexual Identity and Sexual Activity

Mastering emerging sexual feelings and forming a sense of sexual identity is multifaceted. This lengthy process involves learning to manage sexual feelings, such as sexual arousal and attraction, developing new forms of intimacy, and learning the skills to regulate sexual behavior to avoid undesirable consequences. Developing a sexual identity also involves more than just sexual behavior. It includes interfaces with other developing identities. Sexual identities emerge in the context of physical factors, social factors, and cultural factors with most societies placing constraints on the sexual behavior of adolescents.

An adolescent's sexual identity involves an indication of sexual orientation (whether an individual has same-sex or other-sex attractions) and it involves activities, interests, and styles of behavior (Buzwell & Rosenthal, 1996). For example, some adolescents have a high anxiety level about sex, others a low level. Some adolescents are strongly aroused sexually, others less so. Some adolescents are very active sexually, others are virgins. Some adolescents are sexually inactive because of a strong religious

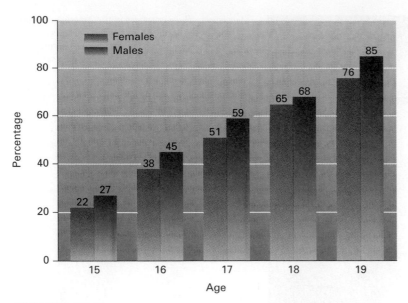

FIGURE 15.7 Percentage of Youth Who Say They Have Had Sexual Intercourse at Various Ages

upbringing, others go to church regularly and it does not inhibit their sexual activity (Thornton & Camburn, 1989).

Heterosexuality
In what order do adolescents engage in various sexual behaviors? When do they first have sexual intercourse on average? What are some risk factors for developing sexual problems in adolescence?

Timing of Sexual Activity Adolescents engage in a rather consistent progression of sexual behaviors (DeLamater & MacCorquodale, 1979). Necking usually comes first, followed by petting. Next comes intercourse, or, in some cases, oral sex, which has increased substantially in adolescents. More adolescents today are choosing oral sex as an alternative to sexual intercourse. They perceive oral sex as safer than vaginal intercourse and as being more acceptable to their peers. In a recent study, 20 percent of ninth-graders reported having had oral sex compared with 13 percent who reported having had sexual intercourse (Halpern-Felsher & others, 2005). Reasons given for why oral sex was chosen included the misconception that it would not transmit STIs such as herpes, AIDS, or chlamydia, and was less likely to produce guilt or a bad reputation. In an investigation of tenth- through twelfth-graders, 25 percent of the males and 15 percent of the females who reported not having had intercourse reported having had oral sex (Newcomer & Udry, 1985). In another study 452 individuals 18 to 25 years of age were asked about their own past sexual experiences (Feldman, Turner, & Araujo, 1999). The following progression of sexual behaviors occurred: kissing preceded petting, which preceded sexual intercourse and oral sex.

What is the current profile of the sexual activity of adolescents? Based on a national survey of adolescents, sexual intercourse is uncommon in early adolescence but becomes more common in the high school and college years (see figure 15.7) (Alan Guttmacher Institute, 1995, 1998). These are some of the findings:

- Eight in ten girls and seven in ten boys are virgins at age 15.
- The probability that adolescents will have sexual intercourse increases steadily with age, but one in five individuals has not yet had sexual intercourse by age 19.
- Initial sexual intercourse occurs in the mid- to late-adolescent years for most teenagers, about eight years before they marry; more than half of 17-year-olds have had sexual intercourse.
- Most adolescent females' first voluntary sexual partners are either younger, the same age, or no more than two years older; 27 percent are three to four years older; 12 percent are five or more years older.

Researchers are finding that adolescents are waiting until they are older to have sexual intercourse (Sonenstein, 2004). A study of more than 30,000 15- to 17-year-old girls found a decrease from 51 percent in 1991 to 43 percent in 2001 in ever having had sexual intercourse (Santelli & others, 2004a). The decrease for non-Latino White girls went from 47 to 41 percent and for African American girls from 75 percent to 54 percent. The percentage for Latino 15- to 17-year-old girls remained the same from 1991 to 2001: 45 percent.

Most studies find that adolescent males are more likely than adolescent females to report that they have had sexual intercourse and are sexually active (Feldman, Turner, & Araujo, 1999; Hayes, 1987). Adolescent males also are more likely than their female counterparts to report that sexual intercourse is an enjoyable experience. And African

Americans are more likely to have a less restrictive timetable for sexual behaviors than other groups, whereas Asian Americans are more likely to have a more restrictive one (Feldman, Turner, & Araujo, 1999).

In some areas of the United States, the percentages of sexually active young adolescents may be even greater. In an inner-city area of Baltimore, 81 percent of the males at age 14 said that they already had engaged in sexual intercourse. Other surveys in inner-city, low-SES areas also reveal a high incidence of early sexual intercourse (Clark, Zabin, & Hardy, 1984).

By age 19, a substantial majority of individuals have had sexual intercourse. Male, African American, and inner-city adolescents report being the most sexually active. Though sexual intercourse can be a meaningful experience for older, mature adolescents, many adolescents are not emotionally prepared to handle sexual experiences, especially in early adolescence. In one study, the earlier in adolescence the boys and girls engaged in sexual intercourse, the more likely they were to show adjustment problems (Bingham & Crockett, 1996).

The timing of teenage sexual initiation varies widely by country and gender. In one recent study, among females, the proportion having first intercourse by age 17 ranged from 72 percent in Mali to 47 percent in the United States and 45 percent in Tanzania (Singh & others, 2000). The proportion of males who had their first intercourse by age 17 ranged from 76 percent in Jamaica to 64 percent in the United States and 63 percent in Brazil.

Sexual activity patterns for 15- to 19-year-olds follow very different patterns for males and females in almost every geographic region of the world (Singh & others, 2000). The vast majority of sexually experienced males in this age group are unmarried, while two-thirds or more of the sexually experienced females at these ages are married.

Risk Factors, Youth Assets, and Sexual Problems   Most adolescents become sexually active at some point during adolescence, but many adolescents are at risk for sexual problems and other problems when they have sexual intercourse or oral sex before 16 years of age. Adolescents who have sex before they are 16 years old are often ineffective users of contraceptives, which puts them at risk for adolescent pregnancy and sexually transmitted infections. One recent study found that use of alcohol and other drugs, as well as low academic achievement, were linked with the initiation of sexual intercourse in early adolescence (Santelli & others, 2004b).

Early maturation is also linked with early initiation of sexual activity. One recent study found that early maturation was related to early sexual activity in non-Latino White and Latino White girls (Cavanaugh, 2004). In this study, these early-maturing girls had more older friends, although the nature of the older friendship varied by ethnic group. Non-Latino White early-maturing girls were more likely to have older friends who engaged in problem behavior than their late-maturing counterparts, while the Latino early-maturing girls were more likely to have older boys in their friendship circle than their late-maturing counterparts.

Risk factors for sexual problems in adolescence also include contextual factors such as socioeconomic status (SES) and family/parenting circumstances (Huebner & Howell, 2003). In one recent review, living in a dangerous and/or a low-income neighborhood were at-risk factors for adolescent pregnancy (Miller, Benson, & Galbraith, 2001). Also in this review, these aspects of parenting were linked with reduced risk of adolescent pregnancy: parent/adolescent closeness or connectedness, parental supervision or regulation of adolescents' activities, and parental values against intercourse or unprotected intercourse in adolescence (Miller, Benson, and Galbraith, 2001). Other researchers have found that an attachment style in which adolescents and parents avoid each other is associated with early sexual activity (Williams & Schmidt, 2003). Further, having older sexually active siblings or pregnant/parenting teenage sisters places adolescents at an elevated risk of adolescent pregnancy (Miller, Benson, & Galbraith, 2001).

What are some risk factors for developing sexual problems in adolescence?

Another important factor in sexual risk-taking is *self-regulation*—the ability to regulate one's emotions and behavior. One longitudinal study found that a lower level of self-regulation at 12 to 13 years of age was linked with a higher level of sexual risk taking four years later (Rafaelli & Crockett, 2003). Other researchers have also found a relation between low self-regulation and high sexual risk taking (Kahn & others, 2002).

One recent study examined the potential protective influence of youth assets on sexual risk-taking behavior in adolescence (Vesely & others, 2004). In-home interviews were conducted with 1,253 inner-city African American adolescents (average age = 15 years) and their parents. Adolescents who had not yet had sexual intercourse were more likely than those who had to have positive non-parental adult role models and peer role models, be involved in religion, and have positive future aspirations.

Sexual Minority Attitudes and Behavior   On the surface it might seem that heterosexual behavior and sexual-minority behavior are distinct patterns that can be easily defined. In fact, however, preference for a sexual partner of the same or other sex is not always a fixed decision, made once in life and adhered to forever. For example, it is not unusual for an individual, especially a male, to engage in same-sex experimentation in adolescence, but not engage in same-sex behavior as an adult. For others, the opposite progression applies.

Until the middle of the twentieth century, it was generally believed that people were either heterosexual or homosexual. However, there recently has been a move away from using the term "homosexual" because the term has negative historical connotations. Also, recent research indicates that the use of the term "homosexual" as clear-cut sexual type is often oversimplified. For example, many more individuals report having same-sex attractions and behavior than ever identify with being a *sexual minority*—someone who identifies with being lesbian, gay, or bisexual. The term *bisexual* refers to someone who is attracted to people of both sexes. Researchers have gravitated toward more descriptive and limited terms than "homosexual," preferring such terms as "individuals with same-sex attractions," or "individuals who have engaged in same-sex behavior."

National surveys reveal that 2.3 to 2.7 percent of U.S. individuals identify with being a gay male and 1.1 to 1.3 percent identify with being a lesbian (Alan Guttmacher Institute, 1995; Michael & others, 1994).

Why do some people have same-sex attractions and identify with being a gay male or a lesbian? Speculation about this question has been extensive, but no firm answers are available. Heterosexual and sexual minority males and females have similar physiological responses during sexual arousal and seem to be aroused by the same types of tactile stimulation. Investigators find no differences between heterosexuals and sexual minority individuals for a wide range of attitudes, behaviors, and adjustments (Bell, Weinberg, & Mammersmith, 1981; Savin-Williams, 1995). In the 1970s, both the American Psychiatric Association and the American Psychological Association recognized that being attracted to someone of the same sex is not a form of mental illness and discontinued classification of this category as a disorder.

Recently researchers have explored the possible biological basis of same-sex attractions (D'Augelli, 2000; Herek, 2000; Swaab & others, 2002). In this regard, we will evaluate hormone, brain, and twin studies regarding same-sex attraction. The results of hormone studies have been inconsistent. Indeed, if sexual-minority males are given male sexual hormones (androgens), their sexual orientation does not change; their sexual desire merely increases. A very early critical period might influence sexual orientation. In the second to fifth months after conception, exposure of the fetus to hormone levels characteristic of females might cause the individual (female or male) to become attracted to males (Ellis & Ames, 1987). If this critical-period hypothesis turns out to be correct, it would explain why clinicians have found that sexual orientation is difficult, if not impossible, to modify (Meyer-Bahlburg & others, 1995).

Although research suggests there may be a genetic contribution to sexual attraction in some individuals, we are far from understanding the mechanisms involved

What developmental pathways characterize attraction to same-sex individuals?

(Diamond, 2004). Most experts believe that no one factor alone causes same-sex attraction and that the relative weight of each factor may vary from one individual to the next. An individual's sexual attraction is most likely determined by a combination of genetic, hormonal, cognitive, and environmental factors (Mustanski, Chivers, & Bailey, 2003; Strickland, 1995). In effect, no one knows exactly what causes an individual to be attracted to individuals of the same sex. Having investigated and rejected a variety of hypotheses, scientists have a clearer picture of what does *not* cause same-sex attraction. For example, children raised by gay or lesbian parents or couples are no more likely to be homosexual than are children raised by heterosexual parents (Patterson, 2002). There also is no evidence to support the once popular theories that being a gay male is caused by a dominant mother or a weak father, or that being a lesbian is caused by girls' choosing male role models.

It is commonly believed that most gay males and lesbians quietly struggle with same-sex attractions in childhood, do not engage in heterosexual dating, and gradually recognize that they are gay or lesbian in mid to late adolescence (Diamond, 2003; Savin-Williams & Diamond, 2004). Many youths do follow this developmental pathway, but others do not. For example, many youths have no recollection of same-sex attractions and experience a more abrupt sense of their same-sex attraction in late adolescence (Savin-Williams, 2001). Researchers also have found that the majority of adolescents with same-sex attractions also experience some degree of other-sex attractions (Garofalo & others, 1999). And although some adolescents who are attracted to same-sex individuals fall in love with these individuals, others claim that their same-sex attractions are purely physical (Savin-Williams, 2001).

Unfortunately, many individuals who have same-sex attractions experience discrimination. Having irrational negative feelings against individuals who have same-sex attractions is called *homophobia*. In its more extreme forms, homophobia can lead individuals to ridicule, physically assault, or even murder people they believe to have same-sex attractions. More typically homophobia is associated with avoidance of same-sex individuals, faulty beliefs about sexual minority lifestyles (such as believing the falsehood that most child molesters have same-sex attractions), and subtle or overt discrimination in housing, employment, and other areas of life (Meyer, 2003).

Contraceptive Use

Sexual activity carries with it considerable risks if appropriate safeguards are not taken (Hyde & Delamater, 2005). There are two kinds of risk that youth encounter:

unintended and unwanted pregnancy and sexually transmitted infections. Both of these risks can be reduced significantly if contraception is used.

The good news is that adolescents are increasing their use of contraceptives (Child Trends, 2000; Santelli & others, 2004a). Adolescent girls' contraceptive use at first intercourse rose from 48 percent to 65 percent during the 1980s (Forrest & Singh, 1990). By 1995, use at first intercourse reached 78 percent, with two-thirds of that figure involving condom use. A recent analysis revealed that from 1991 to 2001 there was a decline from 20 percent to 13 percent in use of withdrawal as a contraceptive strategy and an increase in condom use from 40 percent to 51 percent in U.S. 15- to 17-year-olds (Santelli & others, 2004b).

Although adolescent contraceptive use is increasing, many sexually active adolescents still do not use contraceptives, or they use them inconsistently (Ford, Sohn, & Lepkowski, 2001). Sexually active younger adolescents (under age 16) are less likely to take contraceptive precautions than older adolescents. Younger adolescents are more likely to use a condom or withdrawal, while older adolescents are more likely to use the pill or a diaphragm. Thus, these younger adolescents are at higher risk for sexually transmitted infections and unwanted pregnancies.

Sexually Transmitted Infections

Tammy, age 15, has just finished listening to a lecture in her health class. We overhear her talking to one of her girlfriends as she walks down the school corridor: "That was a disgusting lecture. I can't believe all the diseases you can get by having sex. I think she was probably trying to scare us. She spent a lot of time talking about AIDS, which I've heard that normal people don't get. Right? I've heard that only homosexuals and drug addicts get AIDS. And I've also heard that gonorrhea and most other sexual diseases can be cured, so what's the big deal if you get something like that?" Tammy's view of sexually transmitted infections—that they always happen to someone else, that they can be easily cured without any harm done, that they are too disgusting for a nice young person to hear about, let alone get—is common among adolescents. Tammy's view is wrong. Adolescents who are having sex run the risk of getting sexually transmitted infections.

Sexually transmitted infections (STIs) are diseases that are contracted primarily through sexual contact. This contact is not limited to vaginal intercourse but includes oral-genital and anal-genital contact as well. STIs are an increasing health problem. Approximately 25 percent of sexually active adolescents are estimated to become infected with an STI each year (Alan Guttmacher Institute, 1998).

Among the main STIs adolescents can get are bacterial infections (such as gonorrhea syphilis, and chlamydia), and STIs caused by viruses—genital herpes, genital warts, and AIDS (acquired immune deficiency syndrome). Figure 15.8 describes these sexually transmitted infections.

No single STI has had a greater impact on sexual behavior, or created more fear, in the last two decades than **AIDS,** a sexually transmitted infection that is caused by a virus, the human immunodeficiency virus (HIV), which destroys the body's immune system. Following exposure to HIV, an individual is vulnerable to germs that a normal immune system could destroy.

Through December 2001, there were 4,428 cases of AIDS in 13- to 19-year-olds in the United States (Centers for Disease Control and Prevention, 2002). Among those 20 to 24 years of age, more than 28,665 AIDS cases had been reported. Because of its long incubation period between infection with the HIV virus and AIDS diagnosis, most of the 20- to 24-year-olds were infected during adolescence.

Worldwide, the greatest concern about AIDS is in sub-Saharan Africa, where it has reached epidemic proportions (Singh, Darroch, & Bankole, 2004; UNICEF, 2003). Adolescent girls in many African countries are especially vulnerable to infection with the HIV virus by adult men. Approximately six times as many adolescent girls as boys have AIDS in these countries. In Kenya, 25 percent of the 15- to 19-year-old girls are

sexually transmitted infections (STIs) Diseases that are contracted primarily through sexual contact. This contact is not limited to vaginal intercourse but includes oral-genital contact and anal-genital contact as well.

AIDS A sexually transmitted disease that is caused by a virus, the human immunodeficiency virus (HIV), which destroys the body's immune system.

STI	Description/cause	Incidence	Treatment
Gonorrhea	Commonly called the "drip" or "clap." Caused by the bacterium *Neisseria gonorrhoeae*. Spread by contact between infected moist membranes (genital, oral-genital, or anal-genital) of two individuals. Characterized by discharge from penis or vagina and painful urination. Can lead to infertility.	500,000 cases annually in U.S.	Penicillin, other antibiotics
Syphilis	Caused by the bacterium *Treponema palladium*. Characterized by the appearance of a sore where syphilis entered the body. The sore can be on the external genitals, vagina, or anus. Later, a skin rash breaks out on palms of hands and bottom of feet. If not treated, can eventually lead to paralysis or even death.	100,000 cases annually in U.S.	Penicillin
Chlamydia	A common STI named for the bacterium *Chlamydia trachomatis*, an organism that spreads by sexual contact and infects the genital organs of both sexes. A special concern is that females with chlamydia may become infertile. It is recommended that adolescent and young adult females have an annual screening for this STI.	About 3 million people in U.S. annually; estimates are that 10 percent of adolescent girls have this STI.	Antibiotics
Genital herpes	Caused by a family of viruses with different strains. Involves an eruption of sores and blisters. Spread by sexual contact.	One of five U.S. adolescents and adults	No known cure but antiviral medications can shorten outbreaks
AIDS	Caused by a virus, the human immunodeficiency virus (HIV) that destroys the body's immune system. Semen and blood are the main vehicles of transmission. Common symptoms include fevers, night sweats, weight loss, chronic fatigue, and swollen lymph nodes.	4,000 13- to 19-year-olds in the U.S.; epidemic incidence in sub-Saharan adolescent girls	New treatments have slowed the progression from HIV to AIDS; no cure
Genital warts	Caused by the human papillomavirus, which does not always produce symptoms. Usually appear as small, hard painless bumps in the vaginal area, or around the anus. Very contagious. Certain high-risk types of this virus cause cervical cancer and other genital cancers. May recur despite treatment.	About 5.5 million new cases annually; considered the most common STI in the U.S.	A topical drug, freezing, or surgery.

FIGURE 15.8 Sexually Transmitted Infections

HIV positive, compared with only 4 percent of this age group of boys. In Botswana, more than 30 percent of the adolescent girls who are pregnant are infected with the HIV virus. In some sub-Saharan countries, less than 20 percent of women and 40 percent of 15- to 19-year-olds reported that they used a condom the last time they had sexual intercourse (Singh, Darroch, & Bankole, 2004).

There continues to be great concern about AIDS in many parts of the world, not just sub-Saharan Africa. In the United States, prevention is especially targeted at groups that show the highest incidence of AIDS. These include drug users, individuals with other STIs, young homosexual males, individuals living in low-income circumstances, Latinos, and African Americans (Centers for Disease Control and Prevention, 2002). Also, in recent years, there has been increased heterosexual transmission of the HIV virus in the United States.

Adolescent Pregnancy

Another problem associated with adolescent sexuality is pregnancy. Angela is 15 years old and pregnant. She reflects, "I'm three months pregnant. This could ruin my whole life. I've made all of these plans for the future, and now they are down the drain. I don't have anybody to talk with about my problem. I can't talk to my parents. There is no way they can understand." Pregnant adolescents were once virtually invisible and unmentionable. But yesterday's secret has become today's national dilemma. Our exploration of adolescent pregnancy focuses on its incidence and nature, its consequences, cognitive factors that may be involved, adolescents as parents, and ways adolescent pregnancy rates can be reduced.

www.mhhe.com/santrockc9

American Social Health Association
Preventing STIs in Adolescents
HIV InfoWeb

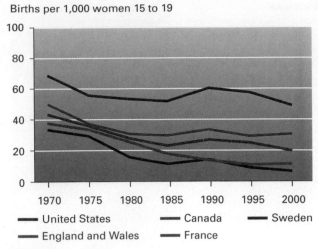

Births per 1,000 women 15 to 19

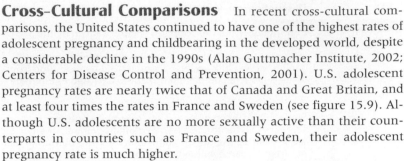

FIGURE 15.9 Cross-Cultural Comparisons of Adolescent Pregnancy Rates

The Alan Guttmacher Institute
Adolescent Pregnancy

Cross-Cultural Comparisons   In recent cross-cultural comparisons, the United States continued to have one of the highest rates of adolescent pregnancy and childbearing in the developed world, despite a considerable decline in the 1990s (Alan Guttmacher Institute, 2002; Centers for Disease Control and Prevention, 2001). U.S. adolescent pregnancy rates are nearly twice that of Canada and Great Britain, and at least four times the rates in France and Sweden (see figure 15.9). Although U.S. adolescents are no more sexually active than their counterparts in countries such as France and Sweden, their adolescent pregnancy rate is much higher.

Why are U.S. adolescent pregnancy rates so high? Three reasons based on cross-cultural studies are as follows (Boonstra, 2002, pp. 9–10):

- *"Childbearing regarded as adult activity."* European countries, as well as Canada, give a strong consensus that childbearing belongs in adulthood "when young people have completed their education, have become employed and independent from their parents and are living in stable relationships. . . . In the United States, this attitude is much less strong and much more variable across groups and areas of the country."
- *"Clear messages about sexual behavior.* While adults in other countries strongly encourage teens to wait until they have established themselves before having children, they are generally more accepting than American adults of teens having sex. In France and Sweden, in particular, teen sexual expression is seen as normal and positive, but there is also widespread expectation that sexual intercourse will take place within committed relationships. (In fact, relationships among U.S. teens tend to be more sporadic and of shorter duration.) Equally strong is the expectation that young people who are having sex will take actions to protect themselves and their partners from pregnancy and sexually transmitted infections," which is much stronger in Europe than in the United States. "In keeping with this view, . . . schools in Great Britain, France, Sweden, and most of Canada" have sex education programs that provide more comprehensive information about prevention than U.S. schools. In addition, these countries use the media more often in "government-sponsored campaigns for promoting responsible sexual behavior."
- *"Access to family planning services.* In countries that are more accepting of teenage sexual relationships, teenagers also have easier access to reproductive health services."

"In Canada, France, Great Britain, and Sweden, contraceptive services are integrated into other types of primary health care and are available free or at low cost for all teenagers. Generally, teens (in these countries) know where to obtain information and services and receive confidential and nonjudgmental care. . . . In the United States, where attitudes about teenage sexual relationships are more conflicted, teens have a harder time obtaining contraceptive services. Many do not have health insurance or cannot get birth control as part of their basic health care."

Decreasing U.S. Adolescent Pregnancy Rates   Despite the negative comparisons of the United States with many other developed countries, there are encouraging trends in U.S. adolescent pregnancy rates (Alan Guttmacher Institute, 2003). In 2002, births to adolescent girls fell to a record low (Centers for Disease Control and Prevention, 2003). For every 1,000 girls 15 to 19 years of age, there were 43 births—the lowest rate in the six decades this statistic has been kept. The rate of births to adolescent girls has dropped 30 percent since 1991. The rate for the youngest adolescents—10 to 14 years of age—declined to .7 per 1,000 girls, 50 percent of the rate reported in 1994. Reasons for these declines include increased contraceptive use and fear of sexually transmitted infections such as AIDS.

The greatest drop in the U.S. adolescent pregnancy rate in the 1990s was for 15- to 17-year-old African American girls. Fear of sexually transmitted infections, especially AIDS; school/community health classes; and a greater hope for the future are the likely reasons for the decrease in U.S. adolescent pregnancy rates in the 1990s. Latino adolescents are more likely than African American and non-Latino White adolescents to become pregnant (Child Trends, 2001). Latino and African American adolescent girls who have a child are more likely to have a second child than are non-Latino White adolescent girls.

Even though adolescent childbearing overall has declined steeply over the last half century, the proportion of nonmarital adolescent births has increased in equally dramatic fashion, from 13 percent in 1950 to 79 percent in 2000. Two factors are responsible for this trend. First, marriage in adolescence has now become quite rare (the average age of first marriage in the United States is now 26 for women and 28 for men). Second, this trend has extended to pregnant adolescents as well. In contrast to the days of the "shotgun marriage" (when a male was forced to marry an adolescent girl if she became pregnant), very few adolescents who become pregnant now marry before their baby is born.

Consequences of Adolescent Pregnancy   The consequences of America's high adolescent pregnancy rate are cause for great concern (Kalil & Konz, 2000). Adolescent pregnancy creates health risks for both the offspring and the mother. Infants born to adolescent mothers are more likely to have low birth weights—a prominent factor in infant mortality—as well as neurological problems and childhood illness (Dryfoos, 1990). Adolescent mothers often drop out of school. Although many adolescent mothers resume their education later in life, they generally do not catch up with women who postpone childbearing. In the National Longitudinal Survey of Work Experience of Youth, it was found that only half of the 20- to 26-year-old women who first gave birth at age 17 had completed high school by their twenties (the percentage was even lower for those who gave birth at a younger age) (Mott & Marsiglio, 1985). By contrast, among young females who waited until age 20 to have a baby, more than 90 percent had obtained a high school education (Kenney, 1987). Among the younger adolescent mothers, almost half had obtained a general equivalency diploma (GED), which does not often open up good employment opportunities.

These educational deficits have negative consequences for the young women and for their children (Kenney, 1987). Adolescent parents are more likely than those who delay childbearing to have low-paying, low-status jobs, or to be unemployed. The mean family income of White females who give birth before age 17 is approximately half that of families in which the mother delays birth until her middle or late twenties. One longitudinal study found that the children of women who had their first birth during their teens had lower achievement test scores and more behavioral problems than did children whose mothers had their first birth as adults (Hofferth & Reid, 2002).

Though the consequences of America's high adolescent pregnancy rate are cause for great concern, it often is not pregnancy alone that leads to negative consequences for an adolescent mother and her offspring (Brooks-Gunn & Paikoff, 1997). Adolescent mothers are more likely to come from low-SES backgrounds (Hoffman, Foster, & Furstenberg, 1993). Many adolescent mothers also were not good students before they became pregnant. Also keep in mind that not every adolescent female who bears a child lives a life of poverty and low achievement. Thus, although adolescent pregnancy is a high-risk circumstance and in general adolescents who do not become pregnant fare better than those who do, some adolescent mothers do well in school and have positive outcomes (Ahn, 1994; Leadbetter & Way, 2000).

Reducing Adolescent Pregnancy   Serious, extensive efforts are needed to help pregnant adolescents and young mothers enhance their educational and occupational opportunities. Adolescent mothers also need extensive help in obtaining

CAREERS in CHILD DEVELOPMENT

Lynn Blankenship
Family and Consumer Science Educator

Lynn Blankenship is a family and consumer science educator. She has an undergraduate degree in this area from University of Arizona. She has taught for more than 20 years, the last 14 at Tucson High Magnet School.

Blankenship was awarded the Tucson Federation of Teachers Educator of the Year Award for 1999–2000 and the Arizona Teacher of the Year in 1999.

Blankenship especially enjoys teaching life skills to adolescents. One of her favorite activities is having students care for an automated baby that imitates the needs of real babies. She says that this program has a profound impact on students because the baby must be cared for around the clock for the duration of the assignment. Blankenship also coordinates real-world work experiences and training for students in several child-care facilities in the Tucson area.

Lynn Blankenship (center), teaching life skills to students.

competent child care and in planning for the future. John Conger (1988) offered the following four recommendations for attacking the high rate of adolescent pregnancy: (1) sex education and family planning, (2) access to contraceptive methods, (3) positive life options, and (4) broad community involvement and support, each of which we consider in turn.

Age-appropriate family-life education benefits adolescents. In addition to age-appropriate family-life and sex education, sexually active adolescents need access to contraceptive methods. These needs often can be handled through adolescent clinics that provide comprehensive, high-quality health services. In one analysis, at four of the nation's oldest adolescent clinics, in St. Paul, Minnesota, the overall annual rate of first-time pregnancies has dropped from 80 per 1,000 to 29 per 1,000 (Schorr, 1989). These clinics offer everything from immunizations to sports physicals to treatment for sexually transmitted infections. Significantly, they also advise adolescents on contraception and dispense prescriptions for birth control (provided parents have agreed beforehand to allow their adolescents to visit the clinic). An important aspect of the clinics is the presence of individuals trained to understand the special needs and confusions of the adolescent age group.

Better sex education, family planning, and access to contraceptive methods alone will not remedy the adolescent pregnancy crisis, especially for high-risk adolescents. Adolescents have to become *motivated* to reduce their pregnancy risk. This motivation will come only when adolescents look to the future and see that they have an opportunity to become self-sufficient and successful. Adolescents need opportunities to improve their academic and career-related skills, job opportunities, life-planning consultation, and extensive mental health services.

Finally, for adolescent pregnancy prevention to ultimately succeed, we need broad community involvement and support (Duckett, 1997). This support is a major reason for the success of pregnancy prevention efforts in other developed nations where rates of adolescent pregnancy, abortion, and childbearing are much lower than in America despite similar levels of sexual activity. In Holland, as well as other European countries such as Sweden, sex does not carry the mystery and conflict it does in American society. Holland does not have a mandated sex education program, but adolescents can obtain contraceptive counseling at government-sponsored clinics for a small fee. The Dutch media also have played an important role in educating the public about sex through frequent broadcasts focused on birth control, abortion, and related matters. Dutch adolescents do not consider having sex without contraception.

So far, we have discussed four ways to reduce adolescent pregnancy: sex education and family planning, access to contraceptive methods, life options, and broad community involvement and support. A fifth consideration, which is especially important for young adolescents, is abstinence. Abstinence is increasingly being included as a theme in sex education classes (Darroch, Landry, & Singh, 2000). Lynn Blankenship is a family and consumer science educator who teaches life skills to adolescents, including what is required for competently caring for babies and the difficulties of being an adolescent mother. To read about her work, see the Careers in Child Development profile.

Review and Reflect • LEARNING GOAL 3

3 **Characterize adolescent sexuality.**

Review

- How do adolescents develop a sexual identity? How can adolescents' other-sex and same-sex attraction be summarized?
- How effectively do adolescents use contraceptives?
- What are sexually transmitted infections (STIs)? What are some common STIs in adolescence?
- How high is the adolescent pregnancy rate in the United States? What are the consequences of adolescent pregnancy? How can the adolescent pregnancy rate in the United States be reduced?

Reflect

- Caroline contracted genital herpes from her boyfriend, whom she had been dating for the last three years. After breaking off the relationship and spending more time on her own, she began dating Blake. Should Caroline tell Blake about her sexually transmitted infection? If so, how and when?

4   HOW CAN ADOLESCENT PROBLEMS AND HEALTH BE CHARACTERIZED?

Risk Factors and Assets		Substance Use		Adolescent Health
	Risk-Taking Behavior		Eating Disorders	

Initially, we will examine risk factors and assets as factors in adolescent problems. Then we will discuss several adolescent problems.

Risk Factors and Assets

Many studies have shown that factors such as poverty, ineffective parenting, and mental disorder in parents *predict* adolescent problems (Compas & others, 2001). Predictors of problems are called *risk factors*. Risk factor means that there is an elevated probability of a problem outcome in groups of people who have that factor. Children with many risk factors are said to have a "high risk" for problems in childhood and adolescence, but not every one of these children will develop problems (Spencer, 2001).

The Search Institute in Minneapolis has described 40 developmental assets that they believe adolescents need to achieve positive outcomes in their lives (Benson, 1997). Half of these assets are external, half internal. The 20 *external* assets include support (such as family and neighborhood), empowerment (such as adults in the community valuing youth and youth being given useful community roles), boundaries and expectations (such as the family setting clear rules and consequences and monitoring the adolescent's whereabouts as well as positive peer influence), and constructive use of time (such as engaging in creative activities three or more times a week and participating three or more hours a week in organized youth programs). The 20 *internal* assets include commitment to learning (such as motivation to achieve in school and doing at least one hour of homework on school days), positive values (values helping others and demonstrating integrity), social competencies (such as knowing how to plan and make decisions, and having interpersonal competencies like empathy and friendship skills), and positive identity (such as having a sense of control

Developmental Assets
Monitoring the Future Study

over life and high self-esteem). In research conducted by the Search Institute, adolescents with more assets reported engaging in fewer risk-taking behaviors, such as alcohol and tobacco use, sexual intercourse, and violence. For example, in one survey of more than 12,000 ninth- to twelfth-graders, 53 percent of the students with 0 to 10 assets reported using alcohol three or more times in the past month or getting drunk more than once in the past two weeks, compared with only 16 percent of the students with 21 to 30 assets or 4 percent of the students with 31 to 40 assets.

Risk-Taking Behavior

One type of health-compromising behavior that increases in adolescence is risk taking. For example, beginning in early adolescence, individuals "*seek* experiences that create high intensity feelings. . . . Adolescents *like* intensity, excitement, and arousal. They are drawn to music videos that shock and bombard the senses. Teenagers flock to horror and slasher movies. They dominate queues waiting to ride the high-adrenaline rides at amusement parks. Adolescence is a time when sex, drugs, *very* loud music, and other high-stimulation experiences take on great appeal. It is a developmental period when an appetite for adventure, a predilection for risks, and a desire for novelty and thrills seem to reach naturally high levels. While these patterns of emotional changes are evident to some degree in most adolescents, it is important to acknowledge the wide range of individual differences during this period of development" (Dahl, 2004, p. 6).

As we discussed earlier in the chapter, the self-regulatory skills necessary to inhibit risk-taking behavior often don't develop until later in adolescence or emerging adulthood. We also indicated that this gap between the increase in risk-taking behavior and the delay in self-regulation is linked to brain development with the limbic system (involved in pleasure-seeking and emotion) developing earlier than the frontal lobes (involved in self-regulation) (Steinberg, 2004; Spear, 2004).

What can be done to help protect adolescents from engaging in risk-taking behavior? As Laurence Steinberg (2004, p. 58) argues, one strategy is to limit "opportunities for immature judgment to have harmful consequences. . . . Thus, strategies such as raising the price of cigarettes, more vigilantly enforcing laws governing the sale of alcohol, expanding access to mental health and contraceptive services, and raising the driving age would likely be more effective in limiting adolescent smoking, substance abuse, suicide, pregnancy, and automobile fatalities than strategies aimed at making adolescents wiser, less impulsive, and less-short-sighted." It also is important for parents, teachers, mentors, and other responsible adults to effectively monitor adolescents' behavior (Dahl, 2004). In many cases, adults decrease their monitoring of adolescents too early, leaving them to cope with tempting situations alone or with friends and peers (Masten, 2004). When adolescents are in tempting and dangerous situations with minimal adult supervision, their inclination to engage in risk-taking behavior combined with their lack of self-regulatory skills can make them vulnerable to a host of negative outcomes.

Among the problems that can develop in adolescence are substance use and abuse, and eating disorders. We will discuss these problems here, then, in chapter 17, explore the adolescent problems of juvenile delinquency, as well as depression and suicide.

Substance Use

Beside exercising, another important healthy practice is to avoid using substances such as alcohol, cigarettes, and other psychoactive drugs (Hales, 2006; Ksir, Hart, & Ray, 2006). In Chapter 4, we described the negative effects on the fetus and developing child that can result from drug use by the pregnant mother. Here we will examine how drug use affects adolescents.

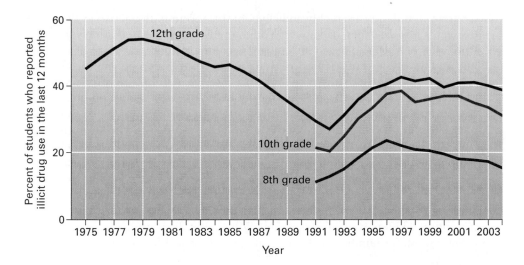

FIGURE 15.10 Trends in Drug Use by U.S. Eighth-, Tenth-, and Twelfth-Grade Students This graph shows the percentage of U.S. eighth-, tenth-, and twelfth-grade students who reported having taken an elicit drug in the last 12 months from 1991 to 2004 for eighth- and tenth-graders, and from 1975 to 2004 for twelfth-graders (Johnston & others, 2005).

Cigarette smoking begins primarily in childhood and adolescence, and many alcoholics established their drinking habits during secondary school or college (Wood, Vinson, & Sher, 2001). In fact, most adolescents use drugs at some point, whether limited to alcohol, caffeine, and cigarettes or extended to marijuana, cocaine, and other so-called "hard" drugs. However, drug use poses a special hazard to development when adolescents use drugs as a way of coping with stress. This practice can interfere with the development of coping skills and responsible decision making (Perkins & Borden, 2003). Drug use in childhood or early adolescence has more detrimental long-term effects on the development of responsible, competent behavior than drug use in late adolescence (Newcomb & Bentler, 1988).

Trends in Drug Use   Each year since 1975, Lloyd Johnston, and his colleagues at the University of Michigan have carefully monitored the drug use of America's high school seniors in a wide range of public and private high schools. Since 1991, they also have surveyed drug use by eighth- and tenth-graders. The University of Michigan study is called the Monitoring the Future Study. In 2004, the study surveyed approximately 50,000 students in nearly 400 secondary schools.

According to this study, the use of drugs among U.S. secondary school students declined in the 1980s but began to increase in the early 1990s (Johnston & others, 2005). In the late 1990s and the first several years of the twenty-first century, the proportions of tenth- and twelfth-grade students' use of any illicit drug have been gradually declining (Johnston & others, 2005). In 2004, the proportion of students reporting the use of any illicit drug in the past 30 days declined at all three grade levels. Figure 15.10 shows the trends in illegal drug use by U.S. high school seniors since 1975 and by U.S. eighth- and tenth-graders since 1991.

Nonetheless, even with the recent leveling off in use, the United States still has the highest rate of adolescent drug use of any industrialized nation. Also, the University of Michigan survey likely underestimates the percentage of adolescents who take drugs because it does not include high school dropouts, who have a higher rate of drug use than do students who are still in school. Johnston, O'Malley, and Bachman (2003) believe that "generational forgetting" contributed to the rise of adolescent drug use in the 1990s, with adolescents' beliefs about the dangers of drugs eroding considerably. The recent downturn in drug use by U.S. adolescents has been attributed to such factors as an increase in the perceived dangers of drug use and a sobering effect from the terrorist attacks of 9/11/01.

An alarming trend has recently emerged in adolescents' use of prescription painkillers. A 2004 survey revealed that 18 percent of U.S. adolescents had used Vicodin at some point in their lifetime while 10 percent had ever used Oxycontin (Partnership for a Drug-Free America, 2005) These drugs fall into the general class of drugs called narcotics and they are highly addictive. In this recent national survey, 9 percent of adolescents also said they had abused cough medications to intentionally get high. The University of Michigan began including Oxycontin in its survey of twelfth-graders in 2002, and the adolescents' reports of using it increased from 4 percent to 5 percent from 2002 to 2004 for use at any time in the previous year (Johnston & others, 2005).

In the Partnership for a Drug Free America (2005) survey, almost one-half of the adolescents said that using prescription medications to get high was much safer than using street drugs. About one-third of the adolescents erroneously believed that prescription painkillers are not addictive. The adolescents cited the medicine cabinets of their parents or of friends' parents as the main source for their prescription painkillers.

A recent analysis of data from the National Survey on Drug Use and Health revealed that abuse of prescription painkillers by U.S. adolescents may become an epidemic (Sung & others, 2005). In this survey, adolescents especially at risk for abusing prescription painkillers were likely to already be using illicit drugs, came from low-socioeconomic-status families, had detached parents, or had friends who used drugs.

Alcohol How extensive is alcohol use by U.S. adolescents? Sizeable declines have occurred in recent years (Johnston & others, 2005). The percentage of U.S. eighth-graders saying that they had any alcohol to drink in the past 30 days has fallen from a 1996 high of 26 percent to 19 percent in 2004. From 2001 to 2004, 30-day prevalence among tenth-graders fell from 39 to 35 percent. Monthly prevalence among high school seniors was 72 percent in 1980 but had declined to 48 percent in 2004.

Binge drinking (defined in the University of Michigan surveys as having five or more drinks in a row in the last two weeks) by high school seniors declined from 41 percent in 1980 to 30 percent in 2002 but increased slightly to 33 percent in 2004. Binge drinking by eighth- and tenth-graders also has dropped in recent years. A consistent sex difference occurs in binge drinking, with males engaging in this more than females. In 1997, 39 percent of male high school seniors said they had been drunk in the last two weeks, compared with 29 percent of their female counterparts.

Cigarette Smoking Cigarette smoking is also decreasing among adolescents. Cigarette smoking peaked in 1996 and 1997 and then gradually declined. In the national survey by the Institute of Social Research, the percentage of U.S. adolescents who are current cigarette smokers has continued to decline in the early twenty-first century (Johnston & others, 2005). Following peak use in 1996, smoking rates for U.S. eighth-graders have fallen by 50 percent. In 2004, the percentage of adolescents who said they smoked cigarettes in the last 30 days were 25 percent (twelfth grade), 16 percent (tenth grade), and 9 percent (eighth grade) (figure 15.11).

There are a number of explanations for the decline in cigarette use by U.S. youth (Kinney, 2006). These include increasing prices, less tobacco advertising reaching adolescents, more antismoking advertisements, and an increase in negative publicity about the tobacco industry. Since the mid-1990s, an increasing percentage of adolescents have reported that they perceive cigarette smoking as dangerous, that they disapprove of it, that they are less accepting of being around smokers, and that they prefer to date non-smokers (Johnston, O'Malley, & Bachman, 2003).

The devastating effects of early smoking were brought home in a research study that found that smoking in the adolescent years causes permanent genetic changes in the lungs and forever increases the risk of lung cancer, even if the smoker quits (Weincke & others, 1999). The damage was much less likely among smokers in the study who started in their twenties. One of the remarkable findings in the study was that the early age of onset of smoking was more important in predicting genetic damage than how much the individuals smoked.

The Roles of Development, Parents, and Peers Most adolescents experiment with drugs at some point in their development, whether their use is limited to alcohol, caffeine, and cigarettes, or extended to marijuana, cocaine, and hard drugs. A

www.mhhe.com/santrockc9

National Institute of Alcohol Abuse and Alcohol
Effective Prevention Programs for Tobacco Use

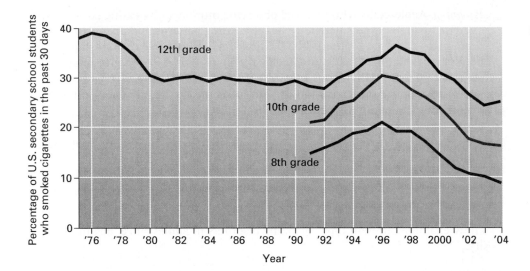

FIGURE 15.11 Trends in Cigarette Smoking by U.S. Secondary School Students

special concern involves adolescents who begin to use drugs early in adolescence or even in childhood. There also is a concern about adolescents who use drugs as a way of coping with stress, which can interfere with the development of competent coping skills and responsible decision making. Researchers have found that drug use in childhood or early adolescence has more detrimental long-term effects on the development of responsible, competent behavior than drug use that occurs in late adolescence (Newcomb & Bentler, 1988). One longitudinal study of individuals from 8 to 42 years of age found that early onset of drinking was linked to increased risk of heavy drinking in middle age (Pitkanen, Lyyra, & Pulkkinen, 2005). When they use drugs to cope with stress, young adolescents often enter adult roles of marriage and work prematurely without adequate socioemotional growth and thus experience greater failure in adult roles.

Parents and peers play important roles in preventing adolescent drug use (Callas, Flynn, & Worden, 2004; Eitle, 2005; Engels & others, 2005, Nash, McQueen, & Bray, 2005; Windle & Windle, 2003). One recent study revealed that parental control and monitoring were linked with lower drug use by adolescents (Fletcher, Steinberg, & Williams-Wheeler, 2004). In another study, low parental involvement, peer pressure, and associating with problem-behaving friends were linked with higher use of drugs by adolescents (Simons-Morton & others, 2001). Also, in a recent national survey, parents who were more involved in setting limits (such as where adolescents went after school and what they were exposed to on TV and the Internet) were more likely to have adolescents who did not use drugs (National Center for Addiction and Substance Abuse, 2001). Further, one longitudinal study linked the early onset of substance abuse with early childhood predictors (Kaplow & others, 2002). Risk factors at kindergarten for substance use at 10 to 12 years of age included being male, having a parent who abused substances, a low level of verbal reasoning by parents, and low social-problem-solving skills.

Substance abuse is a serious problem in adolescence. As we see next, eating disorders also can become serious problems in adolescents, especially for females.

Eating Disorders

Eating disorders have become increasing problems in adolescence (Dietz & Robinson, 2005; Lowrey & others, 2005). Here are some research findings regarding adolescent eating disorders:

- *Body image.* Girls who felt negatively about their bodies in early adolescence were more likely to develop eating disorders two years later than their counterparts who did not feel negatively about their bodies (Attie & Brooks-Gunn, 1989).

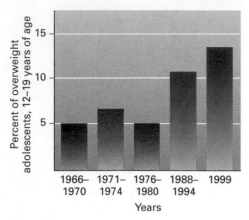

FIGURE 15.12 **The Increase in Being Overweight in Adolescence from 1968 to 1999 in the United States** In this study, being overweight was determined by body mass index (BMI), which is computed by a formula that takes into account height and weight (National Center for Health Statistics, 2000). Only adolescents above the 95th percentile in the overweight category were included in the study. There was a substantial increase in the percentage of adolescents who were overweight from 1968 to 1999.

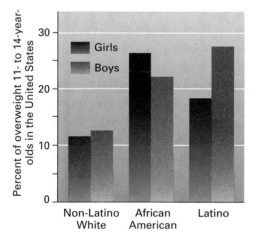

FIGURE 15.13 **Percentage of Overweight U.S. Adolescent Boys and Girls in Different Ethnic Groups**

- *Parenting.* Adolescents who reported observing more healthy eating patterns and exercise by their parents had more healthy eating patterns and exercised more themselves (Pakpreo & others, 2004). Girls who had positive relationships with both parents had healthier eating habits than girls who had negative relationships with one or both parents (Swarr & Richards, 1996). Negative parent-adolescent relationships were linked with increased dieting in adolescent girls over a one-year period (Archibald, Graber, & Brooks-Gunn, 1999).
- *Sexual activity.* Girls who were both sexually active with their boyfriends and in pubertal transition were the most likely to be dieting or engaging in disordered eating patterns (Caufmann, 1994).
- *Role models.* Girls who were making a lot of effort to look like same-sex figures in the media were more likely than their peers to become very concerned with their weight (Field & others, 2001).

Let's now examine different types of eating disorders in adolescence, beginning with obesity.

Obesity   We presented extensive information about obesity earlier in chapter 9, "Physical Development in Early Childhood," and chapter 12, "Physical Development in Middle and Late Childhood." Here we focus on information about obesity in adolescence. In a national survey, 14 percent of 12- to 19-year-olds in the United States were overweight (National Center for Health Statistics, 2000). Only adolescents at or above the 95th percentile of body mass index (BMI) were included in the overweight category. This represents a significant increase in obesity over past years (see figure 15.12). Other research indicates increases in being overweight during adolescence in European countries (Irwin, 2004; Lissau & others, 2004).

Are there ethnic variations in being overweight during adolescence in the United States? A recent survey by the National Center for Health Statistics (2002) found that African American girls and Latino boys have especially high risks of being overweight during adolescence (see figure 15.13). Another recent study of 2,379 girls from 9 to 19 years of age found that the prevalence of being overweight was considerably higher for African American girls than non-Latino White girls (Kimm & others, 2002). Another study revealed that the higher obesity rate for African American females is linked with a diet higher in calories and fat, as well as sedentary behavior (Sanchez-Johnsen & others, 2004).

There have been few cross-cultural comparisons of obesity in childhood and adolescence. However, in one study, U.S. children and adolescents (6 to 18 years of age) were four times more likely to be classified as obese than their counterparts in China and almost three times as likely to be classified as obese than their counterparts in Russia (Wang, 2000).

One recent study examined the extent to which adolescents in the United States, China, Brazil, and Russia have been overweight in the last two to three decades (Wang, Monteiro, & Popkin, 2002): adolescent overweight increased 7.7 percent in China, 13.9 percent in Brazil, and 25.6 percent in the United States.

Eating patterns established in childhood and adolescence are highly associated with obesity in adulthood (Caballero, 2004; Holcomb, 2004; Williams, 2005). For example, 80 percent of obese adolescents become obese adults.

In a recent U.S. study, adolescents with an overweight mother or father were more likely to be overweight than their counterparts without an overweight parent (Dowda & others, 2001). Also in this study, adolescent girls who watched four or more hours of television a day were more likely to be overweight than those who watched less than four hours a day. Adolescent boys who participated in sports team and exercise programs were less likely to be overweight than those who did not participate in these programs.

What types of interventions have been successful in reducing overweight in adolescents? A recent review indicated that clinical approaches that focus on the individual adolescent and include a combination of caloric restriction, exercise (walking or biking to school, participating in a regular exercise program), reduction of sedentary activity (watching TV, playing videogames), and behavioral therapy (such as keeping weight loss diaries and rewards for meeting goals) have been moderately effective in helping overweight adolescents lose weight (Fowler-Brown & Kahwati, 2004). In general, school-based approaches (such as instituting a school-wide program to improve eating habits) have been less effective than the clinically based individual approaches (Lytle & others, 2004).

Anorexia Nervosa and Bulimia Nervosa
Two eating disorders that may appear in adolescence are anorexia nervosa and bulimia nervosa. Both can become life threatening and affect an increasing number of adolescents, primarily girls.

Anorexia Nervosa **Anorexia nervosa** is an eating disorder that involves the relentless pursuit of thinness through starvation. Anorexia nervosa is a serious disorder that can lead to death. Three main characteristics of anorexia nervosa are:

Anorexia nervosa has become an increasing problem for adolescent girls and young adult women. *What are some possible causes of anorexia nervosa?*

- Weighing less than 85 percent of what is considered normal for their age and height.
- Having an intense fear of gaining weight. The fear does not decrease with weight loss.
- Having a distorted image of their body shape (Polivy & others, 2003; Stice, 2002; Wiseman, Sunday, & Becker, 2005). Even when they are extremely thin, they see themselves as too fat. They never think they are thin enough, especially in the abdomen, buttocks, and thighs. They usually weigh themselves frequently, often take their body measurements, and gaze critically at themselves in mirrors (Muris & others, 2005; Seidenfeld, Sosin, & Rickert, 2004).

Anorexia nervosa typically begins in the early to middle teenage years, often following an episode of dieting and some type of life stress (Lee & others, 2005). It is about 10 times more likely to characterize females than males. Although most U.S. adolescent girls have been on a diet at some point, slightly less than 1 percent ever develop anorexia nervosa (Walters & Kendler, 1994). When anorexia nervosa does occur in males, the symptoms and other characteristics (such as a distorted body image or family conflict) are usually similar to those reported by females with the disorder (Ariceli & others, 2005; Olivardia & others, 1995).

Most anorexics are White adolescent or young adult females from well-educated, middle- and upper-income families that are competitive and high-achieving (Schmidt, 2003). They set high standards, become stressed about not being able to reach the standards, and are intensely concerned about how others perceive them (Striegel-Moore, Silberstein, & Rodin, 1993). Unable to meet these high expectations, they turn to something they can control: their weight.

The fashion image in the American culture emphasizing that "thin is beautiful" contributes to the incidence of anorexia nervosa (Polivy & others, 2003). This image is reflected in the saying, "You never can be too rich or too thin." The media portrays thin as beautiful in their choice of fashion models, which many adolescent girls want to emulate (Wiseman, Sunday, & Becker, 2005).

Bulimia Nervosa Although anorexics control their eating by restricting it, most bulimics cannot (Mitchell & Mazzeo, 2004). **Bulimia nervosa** is an eating disorder in which the individual consistently follows a binge-and-purge eating pattern. The bulimic goes on an eating binge and then purges by self-inducing vomiting or using a laxative. Although many people binge and purge occasionally and some experiment with it, a person is considered to have a serious bulimic disorder only if the episodes must occur at least twice a week for three months.

As with anorexics, most bulimics are preoccupied with food, have a strong fear of becoming overweight, and are depressed or anxious (Garcia-Alba, 2004; Quadflieg &

www.mhhe.com/santrockc9

Anorexia Nervosa

anorexia nervosa An eating disorder that involves the relentless pursuit of thinness through starvation.

bulimia nervosa An eating disorder in which the individual consistently follows a binge-and-purge eating pattern.

Fichter, 2003; Ramacciotti & others, 2005; Speranza & others, 2005). Unlike anorexics, people who binge and purge typically fall within a normal weight range, which makes bulimia more difficult to detect (Orbanic, 2001).

Bulimia nervosa typically begins in late adolescence or early adulthood. About 90 percent of the bulimics are women. Approximately 1 to 2 percent of women are estimated to develop bulimia nervosa (Gotesdam & Agras, 1995). Many women who develop bulimia nervosa were somewhat overweight before the onset of the disorder and the binge eating often began during an episode of dieting. One recent study of adolescent girls found that increased dieting, pressure to be thin, exaggerated importance of appearance, body dissatisfaction, depression symptoms, low self-esteem, and low social support predicted binge eating two years later (Stice, Presnell, & Spangler, 2002). As with anorexia nervosa, about 70 percent of individuals who develop bulimia nervosa eventually recover from the disorder (Agras & others, 2004; Keel & others, 1999).

Adolescent Health
**Adolescent Health Attitudes
and Behavior**
**National Longitudinal Study
of Adolescent Health**
Health Risks for Adolescents

Adolescent Health

Adolescence is a critical juncture in the adoption of behaviors relevant to health (Blum & Nelson-Mmari, 2004; Roth & Brooks-Gunn, 2000). Many of the factors linked to poor health habits and early death in the adult years begin during adolescence.

The early formation of healthy behavioral patterns, such as eating foods low in fat and cholesterol and engaging in regular exercise, not only has immediate health benefits but contributes to the delay or prevention of major causes of premature disability and mortality in adulthood—heart disease, stroke, diabetes, and cancer (Barakat, Kunin-Batson, & Kaszak, 2003; Phillips, 2003; Payne, Hahn, & Mauer, 2005).

In one recent study, activity habits of more than 1,000 African American and more than 1,000 non-Latino White girls were examined annually from 9 to 10 years of age to 18 to 19 years of age (Kimm & others, 2002). The study did not examine boys because it was designed to determine why more African American women than non-Latino White women become obese. At 9 to 10 years of age, most girls reported that they were engaging in some physical activity outside of school. However, by 16 to 17 years of age, 56 percent of African American girls and 31 percent of non-Latino White girls were not engaging in any regular physical activity in their spare time. By 18 to 19 years of age, the figures were 70 percent and 29 percent, respectively. In sum, substantial declines in physical activity occur during adolescence in girls and are greater in African American than non-Latino White girls (Kimm & Obarzanek, 2002).

In a recent comparison of adolescent health behavior in 28 countries, U.S. adolescents exercised less and ate more junk food than their counterparts in most countries (World Health Organization, 2000b). Just two-thirds of U.S. adolescents exercised at least twice a week compared with 80 percent or more adolescents in Ireland, Austria, Germany, and the Slovak Republic. U.S. adolescents were more likely to eat fried food and less likely to eat fruits and vegetables than adolescents in most other countries studied. U.S. adolescents' eating choices were similar to those of adolescents in England. Eleven-year-olds in the United States were as likely as European 11-year-olds to smoke but by age 15, U.S. adolescents were less likely to smoke.

Many health experts believe that improving health involves far more than trips to a doctor's office when sick. The health experts increasingly recognize that whether adolescents will develop a health problem or be healthy is primarily based on their behavior (Phillips, 2003). The goals are to (1) reduce adolescents' *health-compromising behaviors,* such as drug abuse, violence, unprotected sexual intercourse, and dangerous driving; and (2) increase *health-enhancing behaviors,* such as eating nutritiously, exercising, and wearing seat belts.

Sleep   Recently there has been a surge of interest in adolescent sleep patterns (Gau & Merikangas, 2004; Hansen & others, 2005; Pollack & Bright, 2003; Voelker, 2004;

Yang & others, 2005). This interest focuses on the belief that many adolescents are not getting enough sleep and that their desire to stay up later at night and sleep longer in the morning has physiological underpinnings. These findings have implications for the hours during which adolescents learn most effectively in school (Dahl & Lewin, 2002).

Mary Carskadon and her colleagues (Carskadon, 2004; 2005; Carskadon, Acebo, & Jenni, 2004; Carskadon, Acebo, & Seifer, 2001; Carskadon & others, 1998) have conducted a number of research studies on adolescent sleep patterns. They found that when given the opportunity adolescents will sleep an average of nine hours and 25 minutes a night. Most get considerably less than nine hours of sleep, especially during the week. This shortfall creates a sleep deficit, which adolescents often attempt to make up on the weekend. The researchers also found that older adolescents tend to be more sleepy during the day than younger adolescents. They theorized that this sleepiness was not due to academic work or social pressures. Rather, their research suggests that adolescents' biological clocks undergo a shift as they get older, delaying their period of wakefulness by about one hour. A delay in the nightly release of the sleep-inducing hormone melatonin, which is produced in the brain's pineal gland, seems to underlie this shift. Melatonin is secreted at about 9:30 P.M. in younger adolescents and approximately an hour later in older adolescents.

Carskadon has suggested that early school starting times may cause grogginess, inattention in class, and poor performance on tests. Based on her research, school officials in Edina, Minnesota, decided to start classes at 8:30 A.M. rather than the usual 7:25 A.M. Since then, there have been fewer referrals for discipline problems and the number of students who report being ill or depressed has decreased. The school system reports that test scores have improved for high school students, but not for middle school students. This finding supports Carskadon's suspicion that early start times are likely to be more stressful for older than for younger adolescents.

How might changing sleep patterns in adolescents affect their school performance?

Health Services   Though adolescents have a greater number of acute health conditions than adults do, they use private physician services at a lower rate than any other age group does (Edelman, 1996). And adolescents often underutilize other health-care systems as well (Drotar, 2000; Marcell & Halpern-Felsher, 2005; Millstein, 1993). Health services are especially unlikely to meet the health needs of younger adolescents, ethnic minority adolescents, and adolescents living in poverty.

In the National Longitudinal Study of Adolescent Health, more than 12,000 adolescents were interviewed about the extent to which they needed health care but did not obtain it (Ford, Bearman, & Moody, 1999). Approximately 19 percent of the adolescents reported forgoing health care in the preceding year. Among the adolescents who especially needed health care but did not seek it were those who smoked cigarettes on a daily basis, frequently drank alcohol, and engaged in sexual intercourse.

A special concern is the decrease in use of health services by older adolescent males (Wilson, Pritchard, & Revalee, 2005). One recent national study in the United States found that 16- to 20-year-old males significantly reduce their contacts with health-care services compared with 11- to 15-year-old males, while 16- to 20-year-old females show an increase in the use of health-care services compared with their younger female counterparts (Marcell & others, 2002). In one recent study, parents of urban adolescents reported that they want health-care providers to talk with their adolescents about sensitive health issues such as sexually transmitted infections, contraception, drug use, depression, nutrition, and stress (Cohall & others, 2004). However, the health-care providers rarely communicated with adolescents about these issues.

Among the chief barriers to better health services for adolescents are cost, poor organization, and availability of health services, as well as confidentiality of care. Also, few health-care providers receive any special training for working with adolescents. Many say that they feel unprepared to provide services such as contraceptive counseling and accurate evaluation of what constitutes abnormal behavior in adolescence (Irwin, 1993). Health-care providers might transmit to their patients their discomfort in discussing such topics as sexuality, which can lead to adolescents' unwillingness to discuss sensitive issues with them.

An increasing number of schools are adopting a life sciences curriculum and/or full health services that focus on reducing health-compromising behaviors and increasing health-enhancing behaviors. The Caring for Children interlude that follows describes the life sciences curriculum and full-service schools.

CARING FOR CHILDREN

Life Science and Life Skills Education

Early adolescence is a time when many health-compromising behaviors—drug abuse, unprotected sex, poor dietary habits, and lack of exercise, for example—either occur for the first time or intensify. As children move through puberty and often develop a feeling that they should be able to engage in adult-like behaviors, they essentially ask, "How should I use my body?" According to David Hamburg and his colleagues (1993), any responsible education must answer that basic question with a substantial life science curriculum that provides adolescents with accurate information about their own bodies, including what the consequences are for engaging in health-compromising behaviors.

Most adolescent health experts believe that a life science education program should be an important part of the curriculum in all middle schools (Hamburg, 1990, 1997; Kolbe, Collins, & Cortese, 1997). This education involves providing adolescents with a better understanding of adolescent development, including puberty (its biological and social ramifications), the reproductive system, sexual behavior, sexually transmitted infections, nutrition, diet, and exercise. In addition, young adolescents should have readily accessible health services, nutritious food in the cafeteria, a smoke-free and physically safe environment, and appropriate physical fitness activities.

Many adolescent health experts also believe that life skills training should be part of the life science curriculum (Hamburg, 1990; Hamburg & others, 1993). Life skills training programs teach young adolescents how to make informed, deliberate, and constructive decisions that will reduce their health-compromising behaviors. Life skills training programs also can improve the interpersonal skills of young adolescents, helping them relate better with others and solve interpersonal problems more effectively.

One school-based model for enhancing the life opportunities of adolescents is the full-service school, which encompasses school-based primary health clinics, youth service programs, and other innovative services to improve access to health and social services. These programs have in common the use of school facilities for delivering services through partnerships with community agencies, a shared vision of youth development, and financial support from sources outside of school systems, especially states and foundations. Organizing a full-service school requires careful planning to involve school personnel, community agencies, parents, and students. Evaluation of the full-service school's effectiveness is still scattered, although some recent results are encouraging with regard to adolescents' health and mental health care, dropout rates, substance abuse, pregnancy prevention, and improved attendance (Dryfoos, 1990).

It is also important to remember that health promotion in adolescence should not be solely the responsibility of schools. Adolescent health can benefit from the cooperation and integration of a number of societal institutions: the family, schools, the health-care system, the media, and community organizations (Hamburg & others, 1993).

Peter Benson and his colleagues (2004) argue that the United States has a fragmented social policy for youth that too often has focused only on the negative developmental deficits of adolescents, especially health-compromising behaviors such as drug use and delinquency, and not enough on positive strength-based approaches. According to Benson and his colleagues (2004, p. 783), a strength-based approach to social policy for youth "adopts more of a wellness perspective, places particular emphasis on the existence of healthy conditions, and expanded the concept of health to include the skills, prosocial behaviors, and competencies needed to succeed in employment, education, and life. It moves beyond the eradication of risk and deliberately argues for the promotion of well-being." In their view, what the United States needs is a *developmentally attentive youth policy,* which would emphasize "the family, neighborhood, school, youth organization, places of work, and congregations as policy intervention points. Transforming schools into more developmentally rich settings, building linkages across multiple socializing institutions, launching community-wide initiatives organized around a shared vision of strength building, and expanding funding for quality out-of-school programs" would reflect this policy (Benson & others, 2004, p. 798).

Leading Causes of Death in Adolescence

Medical improvements have increased the life expectancy of today's adolescents compared with their counterparts who lived early in the twentieth century. Still, life-threatening factors continue to exist in adolescents' lives.

The three leading causes of death in adolescence are accidents, homicides, and suicides (National Center for Health Statistics, 2000) (see figure 15.14). More than half of all deaths in adolescents and emerging adults from 15 to 24 years of age are due to accidents, and approximately three-fourths of these involve motor vehicles. Risky driving habits, such as speeding, tailgating, and driving under the influence of alcohol or other drugs, might be more important causes of these accidents than lack of driving experience. In about 50 percent of the motor vehicle fatalities involving an adolescent, the driver has a blood alcohol level of 0.10 percent, twice the level needed to be "under the influence" in some states. A high rate of intoxication is also often present in adolescents who die as pedestrians or while using recreational vehicles.

Homicide also is a leading cause of death in adolescence. Homicide is especially high among African American male adolescents. They are three times more likely to be killed by guns than by natural causes (Simons, Finlay, & Yang, 1991).

Suicide is the third leading cause of death in adolescence (Rueter & Kwon, 2005). Since the 1950s, the adolescent suicide rate has tripled. We will discuss suicide further in chapter 17.

FIGURE 15.14 Leading Causes of Death in Adolescents and Emerging Adults

---

Review and Reflect • LEARNING GOAL 4

4 Summarize adolescent problems and health.

Review

- What are some important risk factors and assets that are linked with whether or not adolescents develop problems?
- What steps can be taken to help protect adolescents from engaging in risk-taking behaviors?
- What characterizes trends in adolescent substance use?
- How can these three eating disorders be described in adolescence: obesity, anorexia nervosa, and bulimia nervosa?
- What are some important aspects of health in adolescence?

Reflect

- To what extent did you engage in good health habits in adolescence? If you engaged in any bad health habits in adolescence, have you changed those habits now that you are in college? Explain.

Images of Children
Kim-Chi and Thuy

Kim-Chi Trinh was only 9 years old in Vietnam when her father used his savings to buy passage for her on a fishing boat. It was a costly and risky sacrifice for the family, who placed Kim-Chi on the small boat, among strangers, in the hope that she eventually would reach the United States, where she would get a good education and enjoy a better life.

Kim made it to the United States and coped with a succession of three foster families. When she graduated from high school in San Diego in 1988, she had a straight-A average and a number of college scholarship offers. When asked why she excels in school, Kim-Chi says that she has to do well because she owes it to her parents, who are still in Vietnam.

Kim-Chi is one of a wave of bright, highly motivated Asians who are immigrating to America. Asian Americans are the fastest-growing ethnic minority group in the United States—two out of five immigrants are now Asian. Although Asian Americans make up only 2.4 percent of the U.S. population, they constitute 17 percent of the undergraduates at Harvard, 18 percent at MIT, 27 percent at the University of California at Berkeley, and a staggering 35 percent at the University of California at Irvine.

Not all Asian American youth do this well, however. Poorly educated Vietnamese, Cambodian, and Hmong refugee youth are especially at risk for school-related problems. Many refugee children's histories are replete with losses and trauma. Thuy, a 12-year-old Vietnamese girl, has been in the United States for two years and resides with her father in a small apartment with a cousin's family of five in the inner city of a West Coast metropolitan area (Huang, 1989). While trying to escape from Saigon, "the family became separated, and the wife and two younger children remained in Vietnam. . . . Thuy's father has had an especially difficult time adjusting to the United States. He struggles with English classes and has been unable to maintain several jobs as a waiter" (Huang, 1989, p. 307). When Thuy received a letter from her mother saying that her 5-year-old brother had died, Thuy's schoolwork began to deteriorate, and she showed marked signs of depression—lack of energy, loss of appetite, withdrawal from peer relations, and a general feeling of hopelessness. At the insistence of the school, she and her father went to the child and adolescent unit of a community mental health center. It took the therapist a long time to establish credibility with Thuy and her father, but eventually they began to trust the therapist who was a good listener who gave them competent advice about how to handle different experiences in the new country. The therapist also contacted Thuy's teacher, who said that Thuy had been involved in several interethnic skirmishes at school. With the assistance of the mental health clinic, the school initiated interethnic student panels to address cultural differences and discuss reasons for ethnic hostility. Thuy was selected to participate in these panels. Her father became involved in the community mutual assistance association, and Thuy's academic performance began to improve.

PREVIEW

When people think of the changes that characterize adolescents, they often focus on puberty and adolescent problems. However, there are some impressive cognitive changes that occur during adolescence. We begin this chapter by focusing on these cognitive changes and then turn our attention to adolescents' values, moral education, and religion. Next, we will study what schools for adolescents are like and conclude the chapter by examining career development and work in adolescence.

1 HOW DO ADOLESCENTS THINK AND PROCESS INFORMATION?

| Piaget's Theory | Adolescent Egocentrism | Information Processing |

Adolescents' developing power of thought opens up new cognitive and social horizons. Let's examine what their developing power of thought is like, beginning with Piaget's theory.

Piaget's Theory

We discussed Piaget's infant and child stages in chapters 7, 10, and 13. What is the nature of Jean Piaget's (1952) ideas about cognitive development in adolescence? To answer this question, we will study Piaget's stage of formal operational thought, which he believed first appears at 11 to 15 years of age.

Most significantly, formal operational thought is more *abstract* than concrete operational thought. Adolescents are no longer limited to actual, concrete experiences as anchors for thought. They can conjure up make-believe situations, events that are purely hypothetical possibilities or strictly abstract propositions, and can try to reason logically about them.

The abstract quality of the adolescent's thought at the formal operational level is evident in the adolescent's verbal problem-solving ability. Whereas the concrete operational thinker needs to see the concrete elements A, B, and C to be able to make the logical inference that, if A > B and B > C, then A > C, the formal operational thinker can solve this problem merely through verbal presentation.

Another indication of the abstract quality of adolescents' thought is their increased tendency to think about thought itself. One adolescent commented, "I began thinking about why I was thinking what I was. Then I began thinking about why I was thinking about what I was thinking about what I was." If this sounds abstract, it is, and it characterizes the adolescent's enhanced focus on thought and its abstract qualities.

Accompanying the abstract nature of formal operational thought in adolescence is thought full of idealism and possibilities. While children frequently think in concrete ways, or in terms of what is real and limited, adolescents begin to engage in extended speculation about ideal characteristics—qualities they desire in themselves and in others. Such thoughts often lead adolescents to compare themselves with others in regard to such ideal standards. And, during adolescence, the thoughts of individuals are often fantasy flights into future possibilities. It is not unusual for the adolescent to become impatient with these newfound ideal standards and to become perplexed over which of many ideal standards to adopt.

At the same time that adolescents think more abstractly and idealistically, they also think more logically. Adolescents begin to think more as a scientist thinks, devising plans to solve problems and systematically testing solutions. This type of problem solving has an imposing name. **Hypothetical-deductive reasoning** is Piaget's formal operational concept that adolescents have the cognitive ability to develop hypotheses, or best guesses, about ways to solve problems, such as algebraic equations. Then they systematically deduce, or conclude, which is the best path to follow in solving the equation. By contrast, children are more likely to solve problems in a trial-and-error fashion.

One example of hypothetical-deductive reasoning involves a modification of the familiar game Twenty Questions. Individuals are shown a set of 42 color pictures, displayed in a rectangular array (six rows of seven pictures each) and are asked to determine which picture the experimenter has in mind (that is, which is "correct"). The subjects are allowed to ask only questions to which the experimenter can answer yes

hypothetical-deductive reasoning Piaget's formal operational concept that adolescents have the cognitive ability to develop hypotheses, or best guesses, about ways to solve problems, such as an algebraic equation.

Might adolescents' ability to reason hypothetically and to evaluate what is ideal versus what is real lead them to engage in demonstrations, such as this protest related to better ethnic relations? What other causes might be attractive to adolescents' newfound cognitive abilities of hypothetical-deductive reasoning and idealistic thinking?

or no. The object of the game is to select the correct picture by asking as few questions as possible. Adolescents who are deductive hypothesis testers formulate a plan and test a series of hypotheses, which considerably narrows the field of choices. The most effective plan is a "halving" strategy (*Q:* Is the picture in the right half of the array? *A:* No. *Q:* OK. Is it in the top half? And so on.). A correct halving strategy guarantees the answer in seven questions or less. By contrast, concrete operational thinkers may persist with questions that continue to test some of the same possibilities that previous questions could have eliminated. For example, they may ask whether the correct picture is in row 1 and are told that it is not. Later, they ask whether the picture is *x*, which is in row 1.

Thus, formal operational thinkers test their hypotheses with judiciously chosen questions and tests. By contrast, concrete operational thinkers often fail to understand the relation between a hypothesis and a well-chosen test of it, stubbornly clinging to ideas that already have been discounted.

Piaget argued that formal operational thought is the best description of how adolescents think. As we will see next, though, formal operational thought is not a homogeneous stage of development.

Some of Piaget's ideas on formal operational thought are being challenged (Byrnes, 2003; Keating, 2004). There is much more individual variation in formal operational thought than Piaget envisioned. Only about one in three young adolescents is a formal operational thinker. Many American adults never become formal operational thinkers, and neither do many adults in other cultures. Consider this conversation between a researcher and an illiterate Kpelle farmer in the West African country of Liberia (Scribner, 1977):

> **Researcher:** All Kpelle men are rice farmers. Mr. Smith is not a rice farmer. Is he a Kpelle man?
> **Kpelle farmer:** I don't know the man. I have not laid eyes on the man myself.

Members of the Kpelle culture who had gone through formal schooling answered the researcher in a logical way. As with our discussion of concrete operational thought in chapter 10, we find that cultural experiences influence whether individuals reach a Piagetian stage of thought. Education in the logic of science and mathematics is an important cultural experience that promotes the development of formal operational thinking.

Also, for adolescents who become formal operational thinkers, as-similation (incorporating new information into existing knowledge) dominates the initial development of formal operational thought, and the world is perceived subjectively and idealistically. Later in adolescence, as intellectual balance is restored, these individuals accommodate (adjust to new information) to the cognitive upheaval that has occurred.

In addition to thinking more logically, abstractly, and idealistically, which characterize Piaget's formal operational thought stage, in what other ways does adolescent cognition change? One important way involves adolescent egocentrism.

Adolescent Egocentrism

"Oh, my gosh! I can't believe it. Help! I can't stand it!" Tracy desperately yells. "What is wrong? What is the matter?" her mother asks. Tracy responds, "Everyone in here is looking at me." The mother queries, "Why?" Tracy says, "Look, this one hair just won't stay in place," as she rushes to the restroom of the restaurant. Five minutes later, she returns to the table in the restaurant after she has depleted an entire can of hairspray.

During a conversation between two 14-year-old girls, the one named Margaret says, "Are you kidding, I won't get pregnant." And 13-year-old Adam describes himself, "No one understands me, particularly my parents. They have no idea of what I am feeling."

Adolescent egocentrism is the heightened self-consciousness of adolescents, which is reflected in their belief that others are as interested in them as they themselves are, and in their sense of personal uniqueness and invulnerability.

David Elkind (1976) believes that adolescent egocentrism can be dissected into two types of social thinking—imaginary audience and personal fable:

- **Imaginary audience** refers to the heightened self-consciousness of adolescents that others are as interested in them as they themselves are. The imaginary audience involves attention-getting behavior—the attempt to be noticed, visible, and "on stage." Tracy's comments and behavior, in the first paragraph of this section, reflect the imaginary audience. Another adolescent might think that others are as aware of a small spot on his trousers as he is, possibly knowing that he has masturbated. Another adolescent, an eighth-grade girl, walks into her classroom and thinks that all eyes are riveted on her complexion. Adolescents especially sense that they are "on stage" in early adolescence, believing they are the main actors and all others are the audience.

- **Personal fable** is the aspect of adolescent egocentrism that involves an adolescent's sense of uniqueness and invulnerability. The comments of Margaret and Adam, mentioned earlier, reflect the personal fable. Adolescents' sense of personal uniqueness makes them feel that no one can understand how they really feel. For example, an adolescent girl thinks that her mother cannot possibly sense the hurt she feels because her boyfriend has broken up with her. As part of their effort to retain a sense of personal uniqueness, adolescents might craft a story about the self that is filled with fantasy, immersing themselves in a world that is far removed from reality. Personal fables frequently show up in adolescent diaries.

Developmentalists have increasingly studied adolescent egocentrism in recent years. The research interest focuses on what the components of egocentrism really are, the nature of self-other relationships, the reasons egocentric thought emerges in adolescence, and the role of egocentrism in adolescent problems. For example, David Elkind (1985) argues that adolescent egocentrism is brought about by formal

Many adolescent girls spend long hours in front of the mirror, depleting cans of hairspray, tubes of lipstick, and jars of cosmetics. *How might this behavior be related to changes in adolescent cognitive and physical development?*

adolescent egocentrism The heightened self-consciousness of adolescents that is reflected in their belief that others are as interested in them as they are in themselves, and in their sense of personal uniqueness and invulnerability.

imaginary audience Adolescents' heightened self-consciousness, reflected in their belief that others are as interested in them as they themselves are; attention-getting behavior motivated by a desire to be noticed, visible, and "on stage."

personal fable The part of adolescent egocentrism that involves an adolescent's sense of uniqueness and invulnerability.

operational thought. Others, however, stress that adolescent egocentrism is not entirely a cognitive phenomenon. Rather, they think the imaginary audience is due both to the ability to think hypothetically (formal operational thought) and to the ability to step outside oneself and anticipate the reactions of others in imaginative circumstances (perspective taking) (Lapsley & Murphy, 1985).

Information Processing

The ability to process information improves during adolescence (Byrnes, 2001, 2003, 2005; Keating, 2004; Siegler, 2006). Among the areas in which this improvement occurs are memory and executive functioning.

Memory   What are some aspects of memory that change during adolescence? They include short-term memory, working memory, and long-term memory.

Short-Term Memory   How might short-term memory be used in problem solving? In a series of experiments, Robert Sternberg (1977) and his colleagues (Sternberg & Nigro, 1980; Sternberg & Rifkin, 1979) attempted to answer this question by giving third-grade, sixth-grade, ninth-grade, and college students analogies to solve. The main differences occurred between the younger (third- and sixth-grade) and older (ninth-grade and college) students. The older students were more likely to complete the information processing required to solve the analogy task. The children, by contrast, often stopped their processing of information before they had considered all of the necessary steps required to solve the problems. Sternberg believes that incomplete information processing occurred because the children's short-term memory was overloaded. Solving problems, such as analogies, requires individuals to make continued comparisons between newly encoded information and previously encoded information. Sternberg argues that adolescents probably have more storage space in short-term memory, which results in fewer errors on such problems as analogies.

In addition to more storage space, are there other reasons adolescents perform better on memory span tasks and in solving analogies? Although many other factors may be involved, information-processing psychologists believe that changes in the speed and efficiency of information processing are important, especially the speed with which information can be identified.

Working Memory   An increasing number of psychologists believe that the way short-term memory has been historically described is too passive and does not do justice to the amount of cognitive work that is done over the short term in memory (Kail & Hall, 2001). They prefer the concept of working memory to describe how memory works on a short-term basis (Mayer, 2003). British psychologist Alan Baddeley (1992, 2000) proposed the concept of *working memory,* which is a kind of "mental workbench" where information is manipulated and assembled to help make decisions, solve problems, and comprehend written and spoken language.

In one study, the performances of individuals from 6 to 57 years of age were examined on both verbal and visuospatial working memory tasks (Swanson, 1999). The two verbal tasks were auditory digit sequence (the ability to remember numerical information embedded in a short sentence, such as "Now suppose somebody wanted to go to the supermarket at 8651 Elm Street") and semantic association (the ability to organize words into abstract categories) (Swanson, 1999, p. 988). In the semantic association task, the participant was presented with a series of words (such as shirt, saw, pants, hammer, shoes, and nails) and then asked to remember how they go together. The two visuospatial tasks involved mapping/directions and a visual matrix. In the mapping/directions task, the participant was shown a street map indicating the route a bicycle (child/young adolescent) or car (adult) would take through a city. After briefly looking at the map, participants were asked to redraw the route on a blank map. In the visual matrix task, participants were asked to study a matrix showing a

The error of youth is to believe that intelligence is a substitute for experience, while the error of age is to believe that experience is a substitute for intelligence.

—LYMAN BRYSON
American Author, 20th Century

series of dots. After looking at the matrix for five seconds, they were asked to answer questions about the location of the dots.

As shown in figure 16.1, working memory increased substantially from 8 through 24 years of age no matter what the task. Thus, the adolescent years are likely to be an important developmental period for improvement in working memory (Swanson, 2005). Note that working memory continues to improve through the transition to adulthood and beyond.

Long-Term Memory   Long-term memory increases substantially in the middle and late childhood years and likely continues to improve during adolescence, although this has not been well documented by researchers. If anything at all is known about long-term memory, it is that it depends on the learning activities engaged in when learning and remembering information (Pressley, 2003; Siegler & Alibali, 2005).

Executive Functioning   Attention and memory
are important dimensions of information processing, but other dimensions also are important. Once adolescents attend to information and retain it, they can use the information to engage in a number of higher-order cognitive activities, such as making decisions and thinking critically. These types of higher-order, complex cognitive processes are often called *executive functioning*. Alan Baddeley (1992, 2000) recognized the importance of these higher-order cognitive processes and actually called this aspect of his cognitive model the *executive*.

It is increasingly thought that executive functioning strengthens during adolescence (Kuhn, 2005, in press; Kuhn & Franklin, 2006). This executive functioning "assumes a role of monitoring and managing the deployment of cognitive resources as a function of a task demands. As a result, cognitive development and learning itself, become more effective. . . . Emergence and strengthening of this executive (functioning) is arguably the single most important and consequential intellectual development to occur in the second decade of life" (Kuhn & Franklin, 2006). An example of how executive functioning increases in adolescence is its role in determining how attention will be allocated. We begin our examination of executive functioning by focusing on decision making.

Decision Making   Adolescence is a time of increased decision making—which friends to choose, which person to date, whether to have sex, buy a car, go to college, and so on (Byrnes, 1998, 2003, 2005; Galotti & Kozberg, 1996; Jacobs & Klaczynski, 2005; Klaczynski, 2005, in press; Parker & Fischoff, 2002; Reyna & others, 2005). How competent are adolescents at making decisions? In some reviews, older adolescents are described as more competent than younger adolescents, who in turn are more competent than children (Keating, 1990). Compared with children, young adolescents are more likely to generate different options, examine a situation from a variety of perspectives, to anticipate the consequences of decisions, and consider the credibility of sources.

One study documents that older adolescents are better at decision making than younger adolescents are (Lewis, 1981). Eighth-, tenth-, and twelfth-grade students were presented with dilemmas involving the choice of a medical procedure. The oldest students were most likely to spontaneously mention a variety of risks, to recommend consultation with an outside specialist, and to anticipate future consequences.

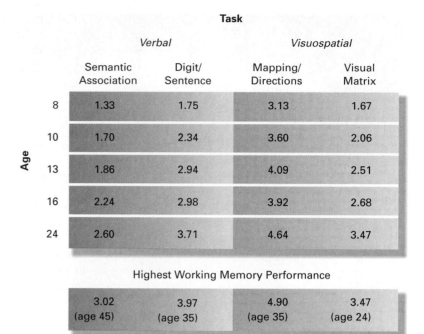

| | Task | | | |
| | *Verbal* | | *Visuospatial* | |
Age	Semantic Association	Digit/ Sentence	Mapping/ Directions	Visual Matrix
8	1.33	1.75	3.13	1.67
10	1.70	2.34	3.60	2.06
13	1.86	2.94	4.09	2.51
16	2.24	2.98	3.92	2.68
24	2.60	3.71	4.64	3.47

Highest Working Memory Performance

3.02 (age 45)	3.97 (age 35)	4.90 (age 35)	3.47 (age 24)

FIGURE 16.1 Developmental Changes in Working Memory Note: The scores shown here are the means for each age group and the age also represents a mean age. Higher scores reflect superior working memory performance.

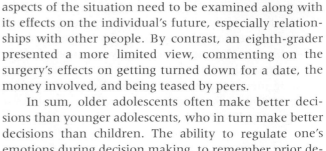

CAREERS in CHILD DEVELOPMENT

Laura Bickford
Secondary School Teacher

Laura Bickford teaches English and journalism in grades 9 to 12 and she is Chair of the English Department at Nordhoff High School in Ojai, California.

Bickford especially believes it is important to encourage students to think. Indeed, she says that "the call to teach is the call to teach students how to think." She believes teachers need in show students the value in asking their own questions, in having discussions, and in engaging in stimulating intellectual conversations. Bickford says that she also encourages students to engage in metacognitive strategies (knowing about knowing). For example, she asks students to comment on their learning after particular pieces of projects have been completed. She requires students to keep reading logs so they can observe their own thinking as it happens.

Laura Bickford, working with students writing papers.

For example, when asked a question about whether to have cosmetic surgery, a twelfth-grader said that different aspects of the situation need to be examined along with its effects on the individual's future, especially relationships with other people. By contrast, an eighth-grader presented a more limited view, commenting on the surgery's effects on getting turned down for a date, the money involved, and being teased by peers.

In sum, older adolescents often make better decisions than younger adolescents, who in turn make better decisions than children. The ability to regulate one's emotions during decision making, to remember prior decisions and their consequences, and to adapt subsequent decision making on the basis of those consequences appear to improve with age at least through the early adulthood years (Byrnes, 2005).

However, older adolescents' decision-making skills are far from perfect, as are adults' (Jacobs & Klaczynski, 2002; Keating, 2004; Klaczynski, 2005, in press). Indeed, some researchers have found that adolescents and adults do not differ in their decision-making skills (Quadrel, Fischoff, & Davis, 1993). Furthermore, researchers have found that adolescent decision making is linked to some personality traits. Adolescents who are impulsive and seek sensation are often not very effective decision makers, for example (Byrnes, 1998).

Being able to make competent decisions does not guarantee that one will make them in everyday life, where breadth of experience often comes into play (Jacobs & Klaczynski, 2005; Keating, 1990, 2004). For example, driver-training courses improve adolescents' cognitive and motor skills to levels equal to, or sometimes superior to, those of adults. However, driver training has not been effective in reducing adolescents' high rate of traffic accidents (Potvin, Champagne, & Laberge-Nadeau, 1988). An important research agenda is to study the ways adolescents make decisions in practical situations (Fantino & Stolarz-Fantino, 2005).

Most people make better decisions when they are calm rather than emotionally aroused. That may especially be true for adolescents. Recall from our discussion of brain development in chapter 15 that adolescents have a tendency to be emotionally intense. Thus, the same adolescent who makes a wise decision when calm may make an unwise decision when emotionally aroused (Dahl, 2004). In the heat of the moment, then, adolescents' emotions may especially overwhelm their decision-making ability.

Adolescents need more opportunities to practice and discuss realistic decision making (Jones, Rasmussen, & Moffitt, 1997). Many real-world decisions on matters such as sex, drugs, and daredevil driving occur in an atmosphere of stress that includes time constraints and emotional involvement. One strategy for improving adolescent decision making in such circumstances is to provide more opportunities for them to engage in role-playing and group problem solving.

Another strategy is for parents to involve adolescents in appropriate decision-making activities. In one study of more than 900 young adolescents and a subsample of their parents, adolescents were more likely to participate in family decision making when they perceived themselves as in control of what happens to them and if they thought that their input would have some bearing on the outcome of the decision-making process (Liprie, 1993).

www.mhhe.com/santrockc9

Critical Thinking

Critical Thinking　Making competent decisions and reasoning logically are closely related to critical thinking, currently a buzzword in education and psychology (Black, 2004; Case, 2005; Gong, 2005; Van Gelder, 2005). *Critical thinking* is thinking reflectively and productively and evaluating evidence. In one study of fifth-, eighth-, and eleventh-graders, critical thinking increased with age, but still occurred only in 43 percent of eleventh-graders (Klaczynski & Narasimham, 1998). Many adolescents showed self-serving biases in their reasoning that included:

- Greater breadth of content knowledge in a variety of domains
- Increased ability to construct new combinations of knowledge
- A greater range and more spontaneous use of strategies and procedures for obtaining and applying knowledge, such as planning, considering the alternatives, and cognitive monitoring

Although adolescence is an important period in the development of critical-thinking skills, if an individual has not developed a solid basis of fundamental skills (such as literacy and math skills) during childhood, critical-thinking skills are unlikely to mature in adolescence. For the subset of adolescents who lack such fundamental skills, potential gains in adolescent thinking are not likely.

Laura Bickford is a secondary school teacher who encourages her students to think critically. To read about her work, see the Careers in Child Development profile.

Although driver-training courses can improve adolescents' cognitive and motor skills related to driving, these courses have not been effective in reducing adolescents' high rate of traffic accidents. *Why might this be so?*

Review and Reflect ● LEARNING GOAL 1

1 **Discuss different approaches to adolescent cognition.**

Review
- What is Piaget's view on adolescent cognitive development?
- What is adolescent egocentrism?
- How does information processing change during adolescence?

Reflect
- Suppose an 8-year-old and a 16-year-old are watching a political convention on television. In view of where they are likely to be in terms of Piaget's stages of cognitive development, how would their perceptions of the proceedings likely differ?

---

2 **WHAT CHARACTERIZES ADOLESCENTS' VALUES, MORAL EDUCATION, AND RELIGION?**

| Values | Moral Education | Religion |

What are adolescents' values like today? How can moral education be characterized? How powerful is religion in adolescents' lives?

Values

Adolescents carry with them a set of values that influences their thoughts, feelings, and actions. **Values** are beliefs and attitudes about the way things should be. They involve what is important to us. We attach values to all sorts of things: politics, religion, money, sex, education, helping others, family, friends, career, cheating, self-respect, and so on.

values Beliefs and attitudes about the way things should be.

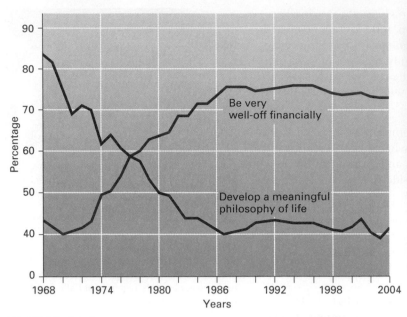

FIGURE 16.2 Changing Freshmen Life Goals, 1968–2004 In the last three decades, a significant change has occurred in freshmen students' life goals. A far greater percentage of today's college freshmen state that a "very important" life goal is to be well-off financially, and far fewer state that developing a meaningful philosophy of life is a "very important" life goal.

Changing Values Over the past two decades, adolescents have shown an increased concern for personal well-being and a decreased concern for the well-being of others, especially for the disadvantaged (Sax & others, 2004). As shown in figure 16.2, today's college freshmen are more strongly motivated to be well off financially and less motivated to develop a meaningful philosophy of life than were their counterparts of 20 years ago. Student commitment to becoming very well off financially as a "very important" reason for attending college was at a high level in the 2004 survey (74 percent), compared with the 1970s (50 percent in 1971).

Two aspects of values that increased during the 1960s, though, continue to characterize many of today's youth: self-fulfillment and self-expression (Conger, 1981, 1988). As part of their motivation for self-fulfillment, many adolescents show great interest in their physical health and well-being. Greater self-fulfillment and self-expression can be laudable goals, but if they become the only goals, self-destruction, loneliness, or alienation may result. Young people also need to develop a corresponding sense of commitment to others' welfare. Encouraging adolescents to have a strong commitment to others, in concert with an interest in self-fulfillment, is an important task for America at the beginning of the twenty-first century.

However, there are some signs that today's college students are shifting toward a stronger interest in the welfare of our society. For example, between 1986 and 2004, there was a small increase in the percentage of college freshmen who said that they were strongly interested in participating in community action programs (21.5 percent in 2004 compared with 18 percent in 1986) and helping promote racial understanding (30 percent in 2004 compared with 27 percent in 1986) (Sax & others, 2004). For successful adjustment in life, it is important to seek self-fulfillment *and* have a strong commitment to others.

Research on adolescents in seven different countries revealed that family values of compassion and social responsibility were the values that were most consistently linked with adolescent participation in community service, commitment to serving their country, and empathy for disenfranchised groups (Bowes & Flanagan, 2000; Flanagan & others, 1998). Other research on values has found that adolescents who are involved in groups that connect themselves to others in school, their communities, or faith-based institutions, report higher levels of social trust, altruism, commitments to the common good of people, and endorsements of the rights of immigrants for full inclusion in society (Flanagan, 2004; Flanagan & Faison, 2001). In this research, adolescents who were uninvolved in such groups were more likely to endorse self-interest and materialistic values.

One recent study of 459 students from 20 different high school classrooms participated in focus group discussions about the most important values they perceived that youth could possess. The students especially endorsed the character strengths of "leadership, practical intelligence, wisdom, love of learning, spirituality, and the capacity to love and be loved" (Steen, Kachorek, & Peterson, 2003, p. 5). Students reasoned that the strengths are mainly learned rather than innate and that they develop through ongoing real-world experiences rather than through formal instruction.

Service Learning

Service learning is a form of education that promotes social responsibility and service to the community. In service learning, adolescents engage in activities such as tutoring, helping older adults, working in a hospital, assisting at a child-care center, or cleaning up a vacant lot to make a play area. An important goal of service learning is for adolescents to become less self-centered and more strongly motivated to help others (Benson & others, 2006; Hart, 2005; Metz & Youniss, 2005; Pritchard & Whitehead, 2004)

Service learning takes education out into the community (Flanagan, 2004; Hart, 2005; Youniss & others, 2003). One eleventh-grade student worked as a reading tutor for students from low-income backgrounds with reading skills well below their grade levels. She commented that until she did the tutoring, she did not realize how many students had not experienced the same opportunities that she had when she was growing up. An especially rewarding moment was when one young girl told her, "I want to learn to read like you so I can go to college when I grow up." Thus, a key feature of service learning is that it not only benefits adolescents but also the recipients of their help.

"Adolescent volunteers tend to share certain characteristics, such as extraversion, a commitment to others, and a high degree of self-understanding" (Eisenberg & Morris, 2004, p. 174). Also, adolescent girls are more likely to volunteer to engage in service learning than adolescent boys (Eisenberg & Morris, 2004).

Researchers have found that service learning benefits adolescents in a number of ways:

- Their grades improve, they become more motivated, and they set more goals (Johnson & others, 1998; Search Institute, 1995; Serow, Ciechalski, & Daye, 1990).
- Their self-esteem improves (Hamburg, 1997; Johnson & others, 1998).
- They have an improved sense of being able to make a difference for others (Search Institute, 1995).
- They become less alienated (Calabrase & Schumer, 1986).
- They increasingly reflect on society's political organization and moral order (Yates, 1995).

Recent figures suggest that 26 percent of U.S. public high schools require students to participate in service learning (Metz & Youniss, 2005). One recent study found that participating in the required 40 hours of community service improved the civic attitudes and behaviors of twelfth-grade students who had never participated in a service learning program (Metz & Youniss, 2005). The benefits of service learning, both for the volunteer and the recipient, suggest that more adolescents should be required to participate in such programs.

Moral Education

Moral education is hotly debated in educational circles (Lapsley & Narvaez, 2006; Nucci, 2005). We will study one of the earliest analyses of moral education, then turn to some contemporary views.

www.mhhe.com/santrockc9

Values of American College Freshmen
National Service Learning Clearinghouse
Give Five Volunteering Matching Online

service learning A form of education that promotes social responsibility and service to the community.

The Hidden Curriculum

More than 60 years ago, educator John Dewey (1933) recognized that, even when schools do not have specific programs in moral education, they provide moral education through a "hidden curriculum." The **hidden curriculum** is conveyed by the moral atmosphere that is a part of every school. The moral atmosphere is created by school and classroom rules, the moral orientation of teachers and school administrators, and text materials. Teachers serve as models of ethical or unethical behavior. Classroom rules and peer relations at school transmit attitudes about cheating, lying, stealing, and consideration of others. And, through its rules and regulations, the school administration infuses the school with a value system.

Character Education

Character education is a direct education approach that involves teaching students a basic moral literacy to prevent them from engaging in immoral behavior and doing harm to themselves or others. The argument is that such behaviors as lying, stealing, and cheating are wrong, and students should be taught this throughout their education. Every school should have an explicit moral code that is clearly communicated to students. Any violations of the code should be met with sanctions (Bennett, 1993). Instruction in specified moral concepts, such as cheating, can take the form of example and definition, class discussions and role playing, or rewarding students for proper behavior.

Some character education movements are the Character Education Partnership, the Character Education Network, the Aspen Declaration on Character Education, and the publicity campaign "Character Counts." Among the books that promote character education are William Bennett's (1993) *The Book of Virtues* and William Damon's (1995) *Greater Expectations.*

Values Clarification

Values clarification means helping people to clarify what is important to them, what is worth working for, and what purpose their lives are to serve. In this approach, students are encouraged to define their own values and understand the values of others (Williams & others, 2003). Values clarification differs from character education in that it does not tell students what their values should be.

In values clarification exercises, there are no right or wrong answers. The clarification of values is left up to the individual student. Advocates of values clarification say it is value-free. However, critics argue that its controversial content offends community standards. They also say that because of its relativistic nature, values clarification undermines accepted values and fails to stress distinctions between right and wrong behavior.

Cognitive Moral Education

Cognitive moral education is a concept based on the belief that students should learn to value such aspects of life as democracy and justice as their moral reasoning develops. Kohlberg's theory, which we discussed in chapter 14, has been the basis for a number of cognitive moral education programs. In a typical program, high school students meet in a semester-long course to discuss a number of moral issues. The instructor acts as a facilitator, rather than as a director, of the class. The hope is that students will develop more advanced notions of concepts such as cooperation, trust, responsibility, and community. Toward the end of his career, Kohlberg (1986) recognized that the moral atmosphere of the school is more important than he initially envisioned. For example, in one study, a semester-long moral education class based on Kohlberg's theory was successful in advancing moral thinking in three democratic schools, but not in three authoritarian schools (Higgins, Power, & Kohlberg, 1983).

Recall from chapter 14 that Carol Gilligan (1982, 1996) believes that moral development should focus more on social relationships than Kohlberg does. Thus, applying Gilligan's view to moral education, emphasis should be placed on such topics as caring, sensitivity to others' feelings, and relationships. In her view, schools should better recognize the importance of relationships in the development of adolescent girls.

www.mhhe.com/santrockc9

Moral Development and Education

hidden curriculum Dewey's concept that every school has a pervasive moral atmosphere, even if it doesn't have a program of moral education.

character education A direct education approach to moral education that involves teaching students a basic moral literacy to prevent them from engaging in immoral behavior and doing harm to themselves and others.

values clarification An approach to moral education that emphasizes helping people clarify what their lives are for and what's worth working for. Students are encouraged to define their own values and to understand the values of others.

cognitive moral education An approach to moral education based on the belief that students should develop such values as democracy and justice as their moral reasoning develops; Kohlberg's theory has been the basis of a number of cognitive moral education programs.

Religion

Religious issues are important to adolescents (Benson, 2004; Dowling & others, 2004; Oser, Scarlett, & Bucher, 2006). In one survey, 95 percent of 13- to 18-year-olds said that they believe in God or a universal spirit (Gallup & Bezilla, 1992). Almost three-fourths of adolescents said that they pray, and about one-half indicated that they had attended religious services within the past week. Almost one-half of the youth said that it is very important for a young person to learn religious faith.

In a recent survey of college students, a belief in God was still strong but a more complex perspective on religion and spirituality emerged. In the national study of American freshmen described earlier in the chapter in our discussion of values, in 2004, 79 percent of the students said they believe in God and 69 percent said they pray (Sax & others, 2004). However, 69 percent said they are still searching for purpose or meaning and less than 50 percent reported that they don't feel secure about their current spiritual and religious views and life. It is common to hear college students say that they are spiritual but not necessarily religious or that they don't identify with a particular religious denomination.

The Positive Role of Religion in Adolescents' Lives
Researchers have found that various aspects of religion are linked with positive outcomes for adolescents (King & Benson, 2005; Oser, Scarlett, & Bucher, 2006). For example, in one recent study of 9,700 adolescents, going to church was linked with better grades for students from low-income backgrounds (Regnerus, 2002). Churchgoing may benefit students because religious communities encourage socially acceptable behavior, which includes doing well in school. Churchgoing may also benefit students because churches often offer positive role models for students. Another recent study revealed that adolescents' religious development was positively related to participation in civic and extracurricular activities and negatively related to alcohol and drug use (Keretes, Youniss, & Metz, 2004).

Many religious adolescents also internalize their religion's message about caring and concern for others (Ream & Savin-Williams, 2003). For example, in one survey, religious youth were almost three times as likely to engage in community service as nonreligious youth (Youniss, McLellan, & Yates, 1999).

Religion is often an asset to the communities in which adolescents live (Ream & Savin-Williams, 2003). In some instances, religious institutions are the only organization that initiates efforts to work with adolescents in inner cities. For inner-city youth, as well as other youth, religion offers possible answers to questions about meaning, purpose, and direction in life (Trulear, 2000).

> *Religion enlightens, terrifies, subdues; it gives faith, inflicts remorse, inspires resolutions, and inflames devotion.*
>
> —HENRY NEWMAN
> *English Churchman and Writer, 19th Century*

Developmental Changes
Adolescence can be an important juncture in religious development (Oser, Scarlett, & Bucher, 2006; Scarlett, 2005; Walker & Reimer, 2005). Even if children have been indoctrinated into a religion by their parents, because of advances in their cognitive development they may begin to question what their own religious beliefs truly are.

Erikson's Theory and Identity During adolescence, especially in late adolescence and the college years, identity development becomes a central focus. In Erik Erikson's (1968) theory, adolescents want to know answers to questions like these: "Who am I?" "What am I all about as a person?" "What kind of life do I want to lead?" As part of their search for identity, adolescents begin to grapple in more sophisticated, logical ways with such questions as "Why am I on this planet?" "Is there really a God or higher spiritual being, or have I just been believing what my parents and the church imprinted in my mind?" "What really are my religious views?"

Piaget's Theory and Religious Development The cognitive developmental theory of famous Swiss psychologist Jean Piaget (1952) provides a theoretical backdrop for understanding religious development in children and adolescents. For example, in one study children were asked about their understanding of certain religious pictures and Bible stories (Goldman, 1964). The children's responses fell into three stages closely related to Piaget's theory.

In the first stage (up until 7 or 8 years of age)—*preoperational intuitive religious thought*—children's religious thoughts were unsystematic and fragmented. The children often either did not fully understand the material in the stories or did not consider all of the evidence. For example, one child's response to the question "Why was Moses afraid to look at God?" (Exodus 3:6) was "Because God had a funny face!"

In the second stage (occurring from 7 or 8 to 13 or 14 years of age)—*concrete operational religious thought*—children focused on particular details of pictures and stories. For example, in response to the question about why Moses was afraid to look at God, one child said, "Because it was a ball of fire. He thought He might burn him." Another child voiced, "It was a bright light and to look at it might blind him."

In the third stage (age 14 through the remainder of adolescence)—*formal operational religious thought*—adolescents revealed a more abstract, hypothetical religious understanding. For example, one adolescent said that Moses was afraid to look at God because "God is holy and the world is sinful." Another youth responded, "The awesomeness and almightiness of God would make Moses feel like a worm in comparison."

Other researchers have found similar developmental changes in children and adolescents. For example, in one study, at about 17 or 18 years of age, adolescents increasingly commented about freedom, meaning, and hope—abstract concepts—when making religious judgments (Oser & Gmnder, 1991).

Religious Beliefs and Parenting

Religious institutions created by adults are designed to introduce certain beliefs to children and thereby ensure that they will carry on a religious tradition. Various societies utilize Sunday schools, parochial education, tribal transmission of religious traditions, and parental teaching of children at home to further this aim.

Does this socialization work? In many cases it does (Paloutzian, 2000). In general, adults tend to adopt the religious teachings of their upbringing. For instance, individuals who are Catholics by the time they are 25 years of age, and who were raised as Catholics, likely will continue to be Catholics throughout their adult years. If a religious change or reawakening occurs, it is most likely to take place during adolescence.

However, when examining religious beliefs and adolescence, it is important to consider the quality of the parent-adolescent relationship (Ream & Savin-Williams, 2003; Regenerus, Smith, & Smith, 2004). Adolescents who have a positive relationship with their parents or are securely attached to them are likely to adopt their parents' religious affiliation. But when conflict or insecure attachment characterizes parent-adolescent relationships, adolescents may seek religious affiliation that is different from their parents (Streib, 1999).

Religiousness and Sexuality in Adolescence

One area of religion's influence on adolescent development involves sexual activity. Although variability and change in church teachings make it difficult to generalize about religious doctrines, most churches discourage premarital sex. Thus, the degree of adolescent participation in religious organizations may be more important than affiliation with a particular religion as a determinant of premarital sexual attitudes and behavior. Adolescents who frequently attend religious services are likely to hear messages about abstaining from sex. Involvement of adolescents in religious organizations also enhances the probability that they will become friends with adolescents who have restrictive attitudes toward premarital sex.

One recent national study of 3,356 adolescent girls (mean age =16 years) focused on four aspects of religiousness: (1) attendance at religious events ("In the past 12 months, how often did you attend religious services?" and "Many churches,

Exploring the Psychology of Religion
Psychology of Religion Resources

Many children and adolescents show an interest in religion, and many religious institutions created by adults (such as this Muslim school in Malaysia) are designed to introduce them to religious benefits and ensure that they will carry on a religious tradition.

synagogues, and other places of worship have special activities for teenagers, such as youth groups, Bible classes, or choir. In the past 12 months, how often did you attend such youth activities?"), (2) personal conservatism ("Do you agree or disagree that the sacred scriptures of your religion are the word of God and are completely without any mistakes?" and "Do you think of yourself as a born-again Christian?"), (3) personal devotion ("How often do you pray?" and "How important is religion to you?"), and (4) religious denomination (Miller & Gur, 2002, p. 402). In this study, there was a link between engaging in personal devotion and having fewer sexual partners outside a romantic relationship. Frequent attendance at religious events was related to fear of contracting HIV or pregnancy from unprotected intercourse and planned use of birth control. Having a personal conservative orientation was linked with unprotected sex. Another study similarly found links between religion and sexuality (Fehring & others, 1998). In college students, guilt, prayer, organized religious activity, and religious well-being were associated with fewer sexual encounters.

Review and Reflect ● LEARNING GOAL 2

2 **Describe changes in values and religion in adolescence.**

Review
- What characterizes adolescents' values? What is service learning?
- What are some variations in moral education?
- What are adolescents' religious views and experiences?

Reflect
- What are your values? What is really important to you in life? Does the way you spend your time reflect the values that are most important to you?

The impressive changes in adolescents' cognition lead us to examine the nature of schools for adolescents. In chapter 14, we discussed different ideas about the effects of schools on children's development. Here, we will focus more exclusively on the nature of secondary schools.

The American Middle School

One worry of educators and psychologists is that middle schools (most often consisting of grades 6 through 8) are simply watered-down versions of high schools, mimicking their curricular and extracurricular schedules. The critics argue that unique curricular and extracurricular activities reflecting a wide range of individual differences in biological and psychological development in early adolescence should be incorporated into our junior high and middle schools. The critics also stress that many high schools foster passivity rather than autonomy and that schools should create a variety of pathways for students to achieve an identity.

The transition to middle school from elementary school interests developmentalists because, even though it is a normative experience for virtually all children, the transition can be stressful (Eccles, 2004; Seidman, 2000). Why? The transition takes place at a time when many changes—in the individual, in the family, and in school—are occurring simultaneously. These changes include puberty and related concerns about body image; the emergence of at least some aspects of formal operational thought, including accompanying changes in social cognition; increased responsibility and independence in association with decreased dependency on parents; change from a small, contained classroom structure to a larger, more impersonal school structure; change from one teacher to many teachers and from a small, homogeneous set of peers to a larger, more heterogeneous set of peers; and an increased focus on achievement and performance and their assessment. This list includes a number of negative, stressful features, but there can be positive aspects to the transition. Students are more likely to feel grown up, have more subjects from which to select, have more opportunities to spend time with peers and to locate compatible friends, and enjoy increased independence from direct parental monitoring, and they may be more challenged intellectually by academic work.

When students make the transition from elementary school to middle or junior high school, they experience the **top-dog phenomenon,** the circumstance of moving from the top position (in elementary school, being the oldest, biggest, and most powerful students in the school) to the lowest position (in middle or junior high school, being the youngest, smallest, and least powerful students in the school). Researchers who have charted the transition from elementary to middle school find that the first year of middle school can be difficult for many students (Hawkins & Berndt, 1985).

How effective are the middle schools U.S. students attend? In 1989 the Carnegie Council on Adolescent Development issued an extremely negative evaluation of U.S. middle schools. In the report—*Turning Points: Preparing American Youth for the Twenty-First Century*—the conclusion was reached that most young adolescents attend massive, impersonal schools; learn from seemingly irrelevant curricula; trust few adults in school; and lack access to health care and counseling. The Carnegie report recommended:

- Developing smaller "communities" or "houses" to lessen the impersonal nature of large middle schools
- Lowering student-to-counselor ratios from several hundred-to-1 to 10-to-1
- Involving parents and community leaders in schools
- Developing curricula that produce students who are literate, understand the sciences, and have a sense of health, ethics, and citizenship

www.mhhe.com/santrockc9

Schools for Adolescents
National Center for Education Statistics
United States Department of Education

top-dog phenomenon The circumstance of moving from the top position (in elementary school, the oldest, biggest, and most powerful students) to the lowest position (in middle or junior high school, the youngest, smallest, and least powerful).

The transition from elementary to middle or junior high school occurs at the same time as a number of other developmental changes. *What are some of these other developmental changes?*

- Having teachers team-teach in more flexibly designed curriculum blocks that integrate several disciplines, instead of presenting students with disconnected, rigidly separated 50-minute segments
- Boosting students' health and fitness with more in-school programs and helping students who need public health care to get it

Turning Points 2000 (Jackson & Davis, 2000) continued to endorse the recommendations set forth in *Turning Points 1989*. One new recommendation in the 2000 report stated that it is important to teach a curriculum grounded in rigorous academic standards for what students should and be able to know. A second new recommendation was to engage in instruction to achieve higher standards and become life-long learners. These new recommendations reflect the increasing emphasis on challenging students to meet higher standards.

The American High School

Many high school graduates not only are poorly prepared for college, they also are poorly prepared for the demands of the modern, high-performance workplace. In a review of hiring practices at major companies, it was concluded that many companies now have sets of basic skills they want the individuals they hire to have. These include the ability to read at relatively high levels, do at least elementary algebra, use personal computers for straightforward tasks such as word processing, solve semistructured problems in which hypotheses must be formed and tested, communicate effectively (orally and in writing), and work effectively in groups with persons of various backgrounds (Hemmings, 2004; Murnane & Levy, 1996).

An increasing number of educators believe that the nation's high schools need a new mission for the twenty-first century, which addresses these problems (National Commission on the High School Senior Year, 2001):

1. More support is needed to enable all students to graduate from high school with the knowledge and skills needed to succeed in postsecondary education and careers. Many parents and students, especially those in low-income and minority communities, are unaware of the knowledge and level of skills required to succeed in postsecondary education.

2. High schools need to have higher expectations for student achievement. A special concern is the senior year of high school, which has become too much of a party time rather than a time to prepare for one of life's most important transitions. Some students who have been accepted to college routinely ignore the academic demands of their senior year. Low academic expectations harm students from all backgrounds.

3. U.S. high school students spend too much time working in low-level service jobs. Researchers have found that when tenth-graders work more than 14 hours a week their grades drop, and when eleventh-graders work 20 or more hours a week their grades drop (Greenberger & Steinberg, 1986). At the same time, shorter, higher-quality work experiences, including community service and internships, have been shown to benefit high school students.

High School Dropouts

Dropping out of high school has been viewed as a serious educational and societal problem for many decades. By leaving high school before graduating, adolescents approach adult life with educational deficiencies that severely curtail their economic and social well-being. In this section, we study the scope of the problem, the causes of dropping out, and ways to reduce dropout rates.

Reducing the Dropout Rate

High School Dropout Rates   In the last half of the twentieth century and continuing through the first several years of the twenty-first century, high school dropout rates declined overall (National Center for Education Statistics, 2002). For example, in the 1940s, more than half of 15- to 24-year-olds had dropped out of school, but in 2001 this figure had decreased to 10.7 percent. Figure 16.3 shows the trends in high school dropout rates from 1972 through 2001. Notice that the dropout rate of Latino adolescents remains precariously high (27 percent of 16- to 24-year old Latino adolescents had dropped out of school in 2001). Although statistics on Native American youth have not been adequately obtained, some estimates indicate that they likely have highest dropout rate in the United States with only about 50 to 70 percent completing their high school education.

Gender differences characterize U.S. dropout rates with males more likely to drop out than females (12.2 versus 9.3 percent). The gender gap in dropout rates is especially large for Latino adolescents (31.6 versus 22.1 percent) and African American adolescents (13.0 versus 9.0 percent) (data for 2001).

The Causes of Dropping Out of School   Students drop out of school for school-related, economic, family-related, peer-related, and personal reasons. School-related problems are consistently associated with dropping out of school (Christensen

FIGURE 16.3 **Trends in High School Dropout Rates** From 1972 through 2001, the school dropout rate for Latinos remained very high (27 percent of 16- to 24-year-olds in 2001). The African American dropout rate was still higher (10.9 percent) than the White non–Latino rate (7.3 percent in 2001). The overall dropout rate declined considerably from the 1940s through the 1960s but has declined only slightly since 1972.

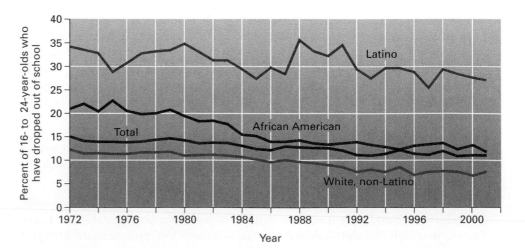

The juku, or "cramming school," is available to Japanese children and adolescents in the summertime and after school. It provides coaching to help them improve their grades and their entrance exam scores for high schools and universities. The Japanese practice of requiring an entrance exam for high school is a rarity among the nations of the world.

& Thurlow, 2004; Ianni & Orr, 1996; Sewell, 2000). In one investigation, almost 50 percent of the dropouts cited school-related reasons for leaving school, such as not liking school, being suspended, or being expelled (Rumberger, 1983). Twenty percent of the dropouts (but 40 percent of the Latino students) cited economic reasons for dropping out. Many of these students quit school and go to work to help support their families. Students from low–income families are more likely to drop out than those from middle-income families. Many school dropouts have friends who also are school dropouts. Approximately one-third of the girls who drop out of school do so for personal reasons, such as pregnancy or marriage.

Reducing the Dropout Rate   A recent review of school-based dropout programs found that the most effective programs provided early reading programs, tutoring, counseling, and mentoring (Lehr & others, 2003). They also emphasized the importance of creating caring environments and relationships and offered community-service opportunities.

Clearly, then, early detection of children's school-related difficulties and getting children engaged with school in positive ways are important strategies for reducing the dropout rate. One program that has been very effective in reducing school dropout rates is described in the following Caring for Children interlude:

CARING FOR CHILDREN

The I Have a Dream Program

"I Have a Dream" (IHAD) is an innovative comprehensive, long-term dropout prevention program administered by the National "I Have a Dream" Foundation in New York. Since the National IHAD Foundation was created in 1986, it has grown to number over 180 projects in 64 cities and 27 states, serving more than 12,000 children ("I Have a Dream" Foundation, 2005). Local IHAD projects around the country "adopt" entire grades (usually the third or fourth) from public elementary schools, or corresponding age cohorts from public housing developments. These children— "Dreamers"—are then provided with a program of academic, social, cultural, and recreational activities throughout their elementary, middle school, and high school years. An important part of this program is that it is personal rather than institutional: IHAD sponsors and staff develop close long-term relationships with the children. When participants complete high school, IHAD provides the tuition assistance necessary for them to attend a state or local college or vocational school.

The IHAD Program was created in 1981, when philanthropist Eugene Lang made an impromptu offer of college tuition to a class of graduating sixth-graders at P.S. 121 in East Harlem. Statistically, 75 percent of the students should have dropped out of school; instead, 90 percent graduated and 60 percent went on to college. Other evaluations of IHAD programs have found dramatic improvements in grades, test scores, and school attendance, as well as a reduction of behavioral problems of Dreamers. For example, in Portland, Oregon, twice as many Dreamers as control group students had reached a math standard, and the Dreamers were less likely to be referred to the juvenile justice system (Davis, Hyatt, & Arrasmith, 1998).

These adolescents participate in the "I Have a Dream" (IHAD) Program, a comprehensive, long-term dropout prevention program that has been very successful. The IHAD program was created in 1981, when philanthropist Eugene Lang made an impromptu offer of college tuition to a class of graduating sixth-graders at P.S. 121 in East Harlem. Statistically, 75 percent of the students should have dropped out of school; instead, 90 percent graduated and 60 percent went on to college. Since the National IHAD Foundation was created in 1986, it has grown to number over 150 Projects in 57 cities and 28 states, serving some 12,000 children. *What are some other strategies for reducing high school dropout rates?*

Review and Reflect • LEARNING GOAL 3

3 **Characterize schools for adolescents.**

Review
- What is the transition from elementary to middle school like? What are some criticisms of, and recommendations for improving, U.S. middle schools?
- How can the American high school be improved so that students are better prepared for the demands of the modern workplace?
- What is the nature of high school dropouts?

Reflect
- What was your own middle school like? How did it measure up to the Turning Points recommendations?

4 **HOW DO ADOLESCENTS EXPERIENCE CAREER DEVELOPMENT AND WORK?**

Career Development   Work

What characterizes career development in adolescence? Does working part-time while going to school have a positive or negative effect on adolescent development?

Career Development

What theories have been developed to direct our understanding of adolescents' career choices? What roles do exploration, decision making, and planning play in career development? How do sociocultural factors affect career development?

Theories of Career Development   Three main theories describe the manner in which adolescents make choices about career development: Ginzberg's developmental theory, Super's self-concept theory, and Holland's personality-type theory.

Ginzberg's Developmental Theory   **Developmental career choice theory** is Eli Ginzberg's theory that children and adolescents go through three career choice stages: fantasy, tentative, and realistic. When asked what they want to be when they grow up, young children might answer "a doctor," "a superhero," "a teacher," "a movie star," "a sports star," or any number of other occupations. In childhood, the future seems to hold almost unlimited opportunities. Ginzberg argues that, until about the age of 11, children are in the *fantasy stage* of career choice. From the ages of 11 to 17, adolescents are in the *tentative stage* of career development, a transition from the fantasy stage of childhood to the realistic decision making of young adulthood. Ginzberg stresses that adolescents progress from evaluating their interests (11 to 12 years of age) to evaluating their capacities (13 to 14 years of age) to evaluating their values (15 to 16 years of age). Thinking shifts from less subjective to more realistic career choices at 17 to 18 years of age. Ginzberg calls the period from 17 to 18 years of age through the early twenties the *realistic stage* of career choice. During this time, the individual extensively explores available careers, then focuses on a particular career, and finally selects a specific job within the career (such as family practitioner or orthopedic surgeon, within the career of doctor).

Critics have attacked Ginzberg's theory on a number of grounds. For one, the initial data were collected from middle-socioeconomic-status youth, who probably had

developmental career choice theory
Ginzberg's theory that children and adolescents go through three career choice stages—fantasy, tentative, and realistic.

"Your son has made a career choice, Mildred. He's going to win the lottery and travel a lot."
Copyright © 2004. Reprinted courtesy of Bunny Hoest and Parade Magazine.

FIGURE 16.4 **Holland's Model of Personality Types and Career Choices** Reproduced by special permission of the Publisher, Psychological Assessment Resources, Inc., from Making Vocational Choices, Third Edition. Copyright © 1973, 1985, 1992, 1997 by Psychological Assessment Resources, Inc. All rights reserved.

career self-concept theory Super's theory that individuals' self-concepts play central roles in their career choices.

personality-type theory Holland's theory that an effort should be made to match an individual's career choice with his personality.

more career options open to them. And, as with other developmental theories (such as Piaget's), the time frames are too rigid. Moreover, Ginzberg's theory does not take into account individual differences—some adolescents make mature decisions about careers (and stick with them) at much earlier ages than specified by Ginzberg. Not all children engage in career fantasies, either. In a revision of his theory, Ginzberg (1972) conceded that lower-class individuals do not have as many options available as middle-class individuals do. Ginzberg's general point—that at some point during late adolescence or early adulthood more realistic career choices are made—probably is correct.

Super's Self-Concept Theory **Career self-concept theory** is Donald Super's theory that individuals' self-concepts play central roles in their career choices. Super argues that it is during adolescence that individuals first construct a career self-concept (Super, 1976). He emphasizes that career development consists of five phases. First, at about 14 to 18 years of age, adolescents develop ideas about work that mesh with their already existing global self-concept—this phase is called *crystallization*. Between 18 and 22 years of age, they narrow their career choices and initiate behavior that enables them to enter some type of career—the *specification* phase. Between 21 and 24 years of age, young adults complete their education or training and enter the world of work—the *implementation* phase. The decision on a specific, appropriate career is made between 25 and 35 years of age—the *stabilization* phase. Finally, after the age of 35, individuals seek to advance their careers and reach higher-status positions—the *consolidation* phase. The age ranges should be thought of as approximate rather than rigid. Super emphasizes that career exploration in adolescence is a key ingredient of the adolescent's career self-concept. He constructed the Career Development Inventory to assist counselors in promoting adolescents' career exploration.

Holland's Personality-Type Theory **Personality-type theory** is John Holland's theory that an effort should be made to match an individual's career choice with his personality (Holland, 1987). Once individuals find a career that fits with their personality, they are more likely to enjoy that career and stay in a job for a longer period of time than are individuals who work at jobs unsuitable for their personality. Holland believes six basic personality types are to be considered when matching the individual's psychological makeup with a career (see figure 16.4):

- *Realistic.* These individuals show characteristically "masculine" traits. They are physically strong, deal in practical ways with problems, and have very little social know-how. They are best oriented toward practical careers, such as labor, farming, truck driving, and construction.
- *Intellectual.* These individuals are conceptually and theoretically oriented. They are thinkers, rather than doers. Often, they avoid interpersonal relations and are best suited to careers in math and science.
- *Social.* These individuals often show characteristically "feminine" traits, especially those associated with verbal skills and interpersonal relations. They are likely to be best equipped to enter "people" professions, such as teaching, social work, and counseling.
- *Conventional.* These youth show a distaste for unstructured activities. They are best suited for jobs as subordinates, such as bank tellers, secretaries, and file clerks.
- *Enterprising.* These individuals energize their verbal abilities toward leading others, dominating individuals, and selling people on issues or products. They are best counseled to enter careers such as sales, politics, and management.
- *Artistic.* These youth prefer to interact with their world through artistic expression, avoiding conventional and interpersonal situations in many instances, and should be oriented toward careers such as art and writing.

If all individuals were to fall conveniently into Holland's personality types, career counselors would have an easy job. But individuals are more varied and complex than

Holland's theory suggests. Even Holland now admits that most individuals are not pure types. Still, the basic idea of matching individuals' abilities to particular careers is an important contribution to the career field (Brown, 1987; Lent & others, 2003). Holland's personality types are incorporated into the Strong-Campbell Vocational Interest Inventory, a widely used measure in career guidance.

Exploration, Decision Making, and Planning

Exploration, decision making, and planning play important roles in adolescents' career choices (Germeijs & De Boeck, 2003; Miller & Shevlin, 2003). In countries where equal employment opportunities have emerged—such as the United States, Canada, Great Britain, and France—the exploration of various career paths is critical in the adolescent's career development. Adolescents often approach career exploration and decision making with considerable ambiguity, uncertainty, and stress. Their career decisions often involve floundering and unplanned changes. Many adolescents not only do not know *what* information to seek about careers but also do not know *how* to seek it.

Sociocultural Influences

Not every individual born into the world can grow up to become a nuclear physicist or a doctor—there is a genetic limitation that keeps some adolescents from performing at the high intellectual levels necessary to enter such careers. Similarly, there are genetic limitations that restrict some adolescents from becoming professional football players or professional golfers. But there usually are many careers available to each of us, careers that provide a reasonable match with our abilities. Our sociocultural experiences exert strong influences on our career choices from among the wide range available. Among the important sociocultural factors that influence career development are parents and peers, schools, socioeconomic status, ethnicity, and gender.

Parents can play an important role in the adolescent's achievement and career development. It is important for parents to neither pressure the adolescent too much nor challenge the adolescent too little.

Parents and Peers Parents and peers are strong influences on adolescents' career choices (Vondracek & Porfelli, 2003). David Elkind (1981) argues that today's parents are pressuring their adolescents to achieve too much too soon. In some cases, though, adolescents do not get challenged enough by their parents. Consider a 25-year-old woman who vividly describes the details of her adolescence that later prevented her from seeking a competent career. From early in adolescence, both of her parents encouraged her to finish high school, but at the same time they emphasized that she needed to get a job to help them pay the family's bills. She was never told that she could not go to college, but both parents encouraged her to find someone to marry who could support her financially. This very bright girl is now divorced and feels intellectually cheated by her parents, who socialized her in the direction of marriage and away from a college education.

From an early age, children see and hear about what jobs their parents have. In some cases, parents even take their children to work with them on jobs. When we (your author and his wife) were building our house, the bricklayer brought his two sons to help with the work. They were only 14 years old, yet were already engaging in apprenticeship work with their father.

Unfortunately, some want to live vicariously through their son's or daughter's career achievements. The mother who did not get into medical school and the father who did not make it as a professional athlete may pressure their youth to achieve a career status that is beyond the youth's talents.

Many factors influence the parent's role in the adolescent's career development (Hargrove, Creak, & Burgess, 2002). For one, mothers who work regularly outside the home and show effort and pride in their work probably have strong influences on their adolescents' career development. A reasonable conclusion is that, when both parents work and enjoy their work, adolescents learn work values from both parents. Peers also can influence the adolescent's career development. In one study, when adolescents had friends and parents with high career standards, they were more likely to seek higher-career-status jobs, even if they came from low-income families (Simpson, 1962).

www.mhhe.com/santrockc9

School-to-Work Transitions
Career Planning
Career Development Quarterly
Occupational Outlook Handbook

CAREERS
in CHILD DEVELOPMENT

Armando Ronquillo
High School Counselor/College Advisor

Armando Ronquillo is a high school counselor and college advisor at Pueblo High School, which is in a low-socioeconomic-status area in Tucson, Arizona. More than 85 percent of the students have a Latino background. Ronquillo was named top high school counselor in the state of Arizona for the year 2000. He has especially helped to increase the number of Pueblo High School students who go to college.

Ronquillo has an undergraduate degree in elementary and special education, and a master's degree in counseling. He counsels the students on the merits of staying in school and on the lifelong opportunities provided by a college education. Ronquillo guides students in obtaining the academic preparation that will enable them to go to college, including how to apply for financial aid and scholarships. He also works with parents to help them understand that "their child going to college is not only doable but also affordable."

Ronquillo works with students on setting goals and planning. He has students plan for the future in terms of 1-year (short-term), 5-year (midrange), and 10-plus-year (long-term) time periods. Ronquillo says he does this "to help students visualize how the educational plans and decisions they make today will affect them in the future." He also organizes a number of college campus visitations for students from Pueblo High School each year.

Armando Ronquillo, counseling a Latina high school student about college.

School Influences   Schools, teachers, and counselors can exert a powerful influence on adolescents' career development (Heppner & Heppner, 2003). School is the primary setting where individuals first encounter the world of work. School provides an atmosphere for continuing self-development in relation to achievement and work. And school is the only institution in society that is presently capable of providing the delivery systems necessary for career education—instruction, guidance, placement, and community connections.

However, many adolescents receive little direction from school guidance counselors and do not adequately explore careers on their own. On the average, high school students spend less than three hours per year with guidance counselors, and in some schools the average is even less. School counseling has been criticized heavily, both inside and outside the educational establishment. Insiders complain about the large number of students per school counselor and the weight of noncounseling administrative duties. Outsiders complain that school counseling is ineffective, biased, and a waste of money. Short of a new profession, several options are possible (William T. Grant Foundation Commission on Work, Family, and Citizenship, 1988). First, twice the number of counselors are needed to meet all students' needs. Second, there could be a redefinition of teachers' roles, accompanied by retraining and a reduction in teaching loads, so that classroom teachers could assume a stronger role in handling the counseling needs of adolescents. The professional counselor's role in this plan would be to train and assist teachers in their counseling and to provide direct counseling in situations the teacher could not handle. Third, the whole idea of school counselors would be abandoned, and counselors would be located elsewhere—in neighborhood social service centers or labor offices, for example. (Germany forbids teachers to give career counseling, reserving this task for officials in well-developed networks of labor offices.)

Armando Ronquillo is one high school counselor who made a difference in the lives of many students. To read about his work helping youth to plot the course to college, see the Careers in Child Development profile.

Socioeconomic Status   The channels of upward mobility open to lower-SES youth are largely educational in nature. The school hierarchy from grade school through high school, as well as through college and graduate school, is programmed to orient individuals toward some type of career. Less than 100 years ago, it was believed that only eight years of education were necessary for vocational competence, and anything beyond that qualified the individual for advanced placement in higher-status occupations. By the middle of the twentieth century, the high school diploma had already lost ground as a ticket to career success, and in today's workplace college is a prerequisite for entering a higher-status occupation.

Many of the ideas that have guided career development theory were based on experiences in middle-income and well-educated contexts. Underlying this theory is the concept that individuals have a wide range of career choices from which they can select and pursue. However, youth in low-income circumstances may have more limited career choices. Barriers such as low-quality schools, violence, and lack of access to jobs, can restrict low-income inner-city youths' access to desirable careers (Chaves & others, 2004).

Ethnicity   To improve the career development of ethnic minority youth, counselors need to increase their knowledge of communication styles, values regarding the importance of the family, the impact of language fluency, and achievement expectations in various ethnic minority groups. Counselors need to be aware of and respect the cultural values of ethnic minority youth, but such values need to be discussed within the context of the realities of the educational and occupational world (Leong, 1995). For example, assertiveness training might be called for when Asian youth are following a cultural tradition of nonassertiveness.

The educational achievement and orientation of parents is also important in the career development of ethnic minority youth. In one recent study, African American adolescents were more likely to have U.S.-born, college-educated parents, whereas Latino adolescents were more likely to have immigrant parents with a high school education or less (Cooper, Cooper, & Chavira, 2001). In this study, resources and challenges across social worlds (parents' and teachers' help and siblings' challenges) were positively linked with adolescents' higher grade point average, eligibility, and admission to more prestigious colleges.

In another recent study, it was concluded that U.S. schools are especially doing a poor job of meeting the needs of America's fastest-growing minority population—Latinas (Ginorio & Huston, 2001). The study indicates that many high school counselors view success as "going away to college," yet some Latinas, because of family responsibilities, think it is important to stay close to home. The high school graduation rate for Latinas lags behind that for girls of any other ethnic minority group. Latinas also are less likely to take the SAT exam than other non-Latino White and other ethnic group females. Thus, a better effort needs to be made at encouraging Latinas' academic success and involving the Latina's family more in the process of college preparation.

Gender   Not only Latinas, but many girls from other backgrounds have also not been adequately exposed to career possibilities. As growing numbers of females pursue careers, they are faced with questions involving career and family: Should they delay marriage and childbearing and establish their career first? Or should they combine their career, marriage, and childbearing in their twenties? Some females in the last decade have embraced the domestic patterns of an earlier historical period. They have married, borne children, and committed themselves to full-time mothering. These "traditional" females have worked outside the home only intermittently, if at all, and have subordinated the work role to the family role.

Many other females, though, increasingly postpone motherhood. They develop committed, permanent ties to the workplace that resemble the pattern once reserved only for males. When they have had children, they have strived to combine a career and motherhood. Although there have always been "career" women, today their numbers are growing at an unprecedented rate.

Work

One of the greatest changes in adolescents' lives in recent years has been the increased number of adolescents who work part-time and still attend school on a regular basis. Our discussion of adolescents and work includes information about the sociohistorical context of adolescent work, as well as the advantages and disadvantages of part-time work.

The Sociocultural Context of Work   Over the past century, the percentage of youth who worked full-time as opposed to those who were in school has decreased dramatically. In the late 1800s, fewer than 1 of every 20 high-school-age adolescents was in school. Today, more than 9 of every 10 adolescents receive high school diplomas. In the nineteenth century, many adolescents learned a trade from their father or another adult member of the community.

Even though prolonged education has kept many contemporary youth from holding full-time jobs, it has not prevented them from working on a part-time basis while going to school. Most high school seniors have had some work experience. In a national survey of 17,000 high school seniors, three of four reported some job income during the average school week (Bachman, 1982). For 41 percent of the males and 30 percent of the females, this income exceeded $50 a week. The typical part-time job for high school seniors involves 16 to 20 hours of work per week, although 10 percent work 30 hours a week or more.

In 1940, only 1 of 25 tenth-grade males attended school and simultaneously worked part-time. In the 1970s, the number increased to more than 1 of every 4. And, in the 1980s, as just indicated, 3 of 4 combined school and part-time work. Adolescents also are working longer hours now than in the past. For example, the number of 14- to 15-year-olds who work more than 14 hours per week has increased substantially in the past three decades. A similar picture emerges for 16-year-olds. In 1960, 44 percent of 16-year-old males who attended school worked more than 14 hours a week, but, by the 1980s, the figure had increased to more than 60 percent.

What kinds of jobs are adolescents working at today? About 17 percent who work do so in restaurants, such as McDonald's and Burger King, waiting on customers and cleaning up. Other adolescents work in retail stores as cashiers or salespeople (about 20 percent), in offices as clerical assistants (about 10 percent), or as unskilled laborers (about 10 percent). In one study, boys reported higher self-esteem and well-being when they perceived that their jobs were providing skills that would be useful to them in the future (Mortimer & others, 1992).

Do male and female adolescents take the same types of jobs, and are they paid equally? Some jobs are held almost exclusively by male adolescents—busboy, gardener, manual laborer, and newspaper carrier—while other jobs are held almost exclusively by female adolescents—baby-sitter and maid. Male adolescents work longer hours and are paid more per hour than female adolescents (Helson, Elliot, & Leigh, 1989).

The Advantages and Disadvantages of Part-Time Work   Does the increase in work have benefits for adolescents? In some cases, yes; in others, no. Ellen Greenberger and Laurence Steinberg (1981, 1986) examined the work experiences of students in four California high schools. Their findings disproved some common myths. For example, generally it is assumed that adolescents get extensive on-the-job training when they are hired for work. The reality is that they got little training at all. Also, it is assumed that youth—through work experiences—learn to get along better with adults. However, adolescents reported that they rarely felt close to the adults with whom they worked. The work experiences of the adolescent did help them understand how the business world works, how to get and keep a job, and how to manage money. Working also helped adolescents learn to budget their time, take pride in their accomplishments, and to evaluate their goals. But working adolescents often have to give up sports, social affairs with peers, and sometimes sleep. And they have to balance the demands of work, school, family, and peers.

Greenberger and Steinberg asked students about their grade point averages, school attendance, and satisfaction from school, as well as the number of hours spent studying and participating in extracurricular activities since they began working. They found that the working adolescents had lower grade point averages than nonworking adolescents. More than one of four students reported that their grades dropped when they began working; only one of nine said their grades improved. But it was not just working that affected adolescents' grades—more important, it was *how long* they worked. Tenth-graders who worked more than 14 hours a week suffered a drop in grades. Eleventh-graders worked up to 20 hours a week before their grades dropped. When adolescents spend more than 20 hours per week working, there is little time to study for tests and to complete homework assignments.

In addition to the work affecting grades, the working adolescents felt less involved in school, were absent more, and said they did not enjoy school as much as their nonworking counterparts did. The adolescents who worked also spent less time with their families—but just as much time with their peers—as their nonworking counterparts. The adolescents who worked long hours also were more frequent users of alcohol and marijuana. More recent research confirms the link between part-time work during adolescence and problem behaviors (Hansen, 1996).

Although working too many hours may be detrimental to adolescent development, work may especially benefit adolescents in low-income, urban contexts by providing them with economic benefits and adult monitoring. This may increase school engagement and decrease delinquency. In one recent study, low-income, urban adolescents who never worked had more school-related difficulties than those who did work (Leventhal, Graber, & Brooks-Gunn, 2001). Stable work increased the likelihood that the adolescent males in low-income, urban contexts would go to college more than the adolescent females.

Work Profiles of Adolescents Around the World

In many developing countries where it is common for adolescents to not attend school on a regular basis, boys often spend more time in income-generating labor than girls do, whereas girls spend more time in unpaid labor than boys (Larson & Verma, 1999). By early adolescence, total labor exceeds eight hours a day in many nonindustrial, unschooled populations. In literate societies, total labor "averages less than one hour per day across childhood and adolescence, with U.S. adolescents being the exception," p. 708. For example, U.S. adolescents are far more likely to participate in paid labor than European and East Asian adolescents. As we saw earlier, many U.S. high school students work 10 or even 20 hours or more per week. One study found that U.S. high school students spent an average of 50 minutes per day working at a job, whereas North European adolescents spent an average of only 15 minutes per day working at a job (Alsaker & Flammer, 1999). In this study, employment of adolescents was virtually nonexistent in France and Russia. In another study, 80 percent of Minneapolis eleventh-graders had part-time jobs compared with only 27 percent of Japanese eleventh-graders and 26 percent of Taiwanese eleventh-graders (Fuligni & Stevenson, 1995).

Overall, the weight of the evidence suggests that spending large amounts of time in paid labor has limited developmental benefits for youth, and for some it is associated with risk behavior and costs to physical health (Larson & Verma, 1999). Some youth, though, are engaged in challenging work activities, are provided constructive supervision by adults, and experience favorable work conditions. However, in general, given the repetitive nature of most labor carried out by adolescents around the world, it is difficult to argue that working 15 to 25 hours per week in such labor provides developmental gains (Larson & Verma, 1999).

When are the efforts of working and going to school on adolescents' grades and integration into school activities?

www.mhhe.com/santrock9

The Working Adolescent
Girls and Careers

Review and Reflect • LEARNING GOAL 4

④ Summarize career development and work in adolescence.

Review
- What are three theories of career development? What characterizes career development in adolescence?
- What are adolescents' work experiences like?

Reflect
- Did you work during high school? What were some of the pluses and minuses of the experience if you did work? Are you working part-time or full-time now while you are going to college? If so, what effect does the work experience have on your academic success?

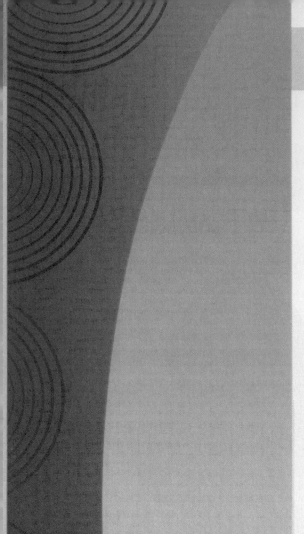

Images of Children
A 15-Year-Old Girl's Self-Description

How do adolescents describe themselves? How would you have described yourself when you were 15 years old? What features would you have emphasized? The following is a self-portrait of one 15-year-old girl:

> What am I like as a person? Complicated! I'm sensitive, friendly, outgoing, popular, and tolerant, though I can also be shy, self-conscious, and even obnoxious. Obnoxious! I'd like to be friendly and tolerant all of the time. That's the kind of person I *want* to be, and I'm disappointed when I'm not. I'm responsible, even studious now and then, but on the other hand, I'm a goof-off, too, because if you're too studious, you won't be popular. I don't usually do that well at school. I'm a pretty cheerful person, especially with my friends, where I can even get rowdy. At home I'm more likely to be anxious around my parents. They expect me to get all A's. It's not fair! I worry about how I probably *should* get better grades. But I'd be mortified in the eyes of my friends. So I'm usually pretty stressed-out at home, or sarcastic, since my parents are always on my case. But I really don't understand how I can switch so fast. I mean, how can I be cheerful one minute, anxious the next, and then be sarcastic? Which one is the *real* me? Sometimes, I feel phony, especially around boys. Say I think some guy might be interested in asking me out. I try to act different, like Madonna. I'll be flirtatious and fun-loving. And then everybody, I mean *everybody* else is looking at me like they think I'm totally weird. Then I get self-conscious and embarrassed and become radically introverted, and I don't know who I really am! Am I just trying to impress them or what? But I don't really care what they think anyway. I don't *want* to care, that is. I just want to know what my close friends think. I can be my true self with my close friends. I can't be my real self with my parents. They don't understand me. What do *they* know about what it's like to be a teenager? They still treat me like I'm still a kid. At least at school people treat you more like you're an adult. That gets confusing, though. I mean, which am I, a kid or an adult? It's scary, too, because I don't have any idea what I want to be when I grow up. I mean, I have lots of *ideas.* My friend Sheryl and I talk about whether we'll be flight attendants, or teachers, or nurses, veterinarians, maybe mothers, or actresses. I know I *don't* want to be a waitress or a secretary. But how do you decide all of this? I really don't know. I mean, I think about it a lot, but I can't resolve it. There are days when I wish I could just become immune to myself. (Harter, 1990, pp. 352–353)

PREVIEW

Increased self-understanding, identity exploration, and emotional changes are among the hallmarks of adolescent development. Far more than as children, adolescents seek to know who they are, what they are all about, and where they are going in life. In this chapter, we initially will explore adolescents' emotional and personality development, then turn to adolescents' experiences in three important social contexts—families, peers, and culture. We will conclude the chapter by examining some adolescent problems.

1 **WHAT CHARACTERIZES EMOTIONAL DEVELOPMENT AND SELF-DEVELOPMENT IN ADOLESCENCE?**

Emotional Development   Identity

Self-Esteem

Among the changes in socioemotional development during adolescence are those involving emotions, self-esteem, identity, and personality. In our coverage of emotional development, we will explore adolescents' moods.

Emotional Development

Adolescence has long been described as a time of emotional turmoil (Hall, 1904). In its extreme form, this view is too stereotypical because adolescents are not constantly in a state of "storm and stress." Nonetheless, early adolescence is a time when emotional highs and lows increase (Rosenblum & Lewis, 2003). Young adolescents can be on top of the world one moment and down in the dumps the next. In many instances, the intensity of their emotions seems out of proportion to the events that elicit them (Steinberg & Levine, 1997). Young adolescents might sulk a lot, not knowing how to adequately express their feelings. With little or no provocation, they might blow up at their parents or siblings, which could involve using the defense mechanism of displacing their feelings onto another person.

Reed Larson and Maryse Richards (1994) found that adolescents reported more extreme emotions and more fleeting emotions than their parents did. For example, adolescents were far more likely to report being "very happy" and "very sad" than their parents (see figure 17.1). These findings lend support to the perception of adolescents as moody and changeable (Rosenblum & Lewis, 2003).

Researchers have also found that from the fifth through the ninth grades, both boys and girls experience a 50 percent decrease in being "very happy" (Larson & Lampman-Petraitis, 1989). In this same study, adolescents were more likely than preadolescents to report mildly negative mood states.

It is important for adults to recognize that moodiness is a *normal* aspect of early adolescence and most adolescents make it through these moody times to become competent adults. Nonetheless, for some adolescents, such emotions can reflect serious problems (Scarmella & Conger, 2004). For example, rates of depressed moods become more elevated for girls during adolescence (Nolen-Hoeksema, 2004). We will have much more to say about depression later in the chapter.

As we saw in chapter 15, "Physical Development in Adolescence," significant hormonal changes characterize puberty. Emotional fluctuations in early adolescence may be related to the variability of hormones during this time period. Moods become less extreme as adolescents move into adulthood, and this decrease in emotional fluctuation may be due to adaptation to hormone levels over time (Rosenbaum & Lewis, 2003).

Researchers have discovered that pubertal change is associated with an increase in negative emotions (Archibald, Graber, & Brooks-Gunn, 2003; Brooks-Gunn, Graber, & Paikoff, 1994; Dorn, Williamson, & Ryan, 2002). However, most researchers conclude that hormonal influences are small and that when they occur they usually are associated with other factors, such as stress, eating patterns, sexual activity, and social relationships (Rosenbaum & Lewis, 2003; Susman, Dorn, & Schiefelbein, 2003).

Indeed, environmental experiences may contribute more to the emotions of adolescence than hormonal changes. Recall from chapter 15 that in one study, social factors accounted for two to four times as much variance as hormonal factors in young

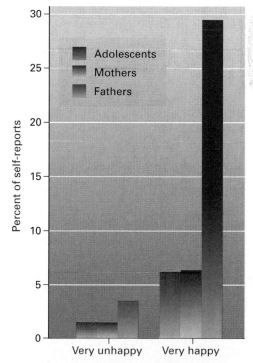

FIGURE 17.1 **Self-Reported Extremes of Emotion by Adolescents, Mothers, and Fathers Using the Experience Sampling Method** In the study by Reed Larson and Maryse Richards (1994), adolescents and their mothers and fathers were beeped at random times by researchers using the experience sampling method. The researchers found that adolescents were more likely to report more emotional extremes than their parents.

FIGURE 17.2 Self-Esteem Across the Life Span One large-scale study asked more than 300,000 individuals to rate the extent to which they have high self-esteem on a 5-point scale, 5 being "Strongly Agree" and 1 being "Strongly Disagree." Self-esteem dropped in adolescence and late adulthood. Self-esteem of females was lower than self-esteem of males through most of the life span.

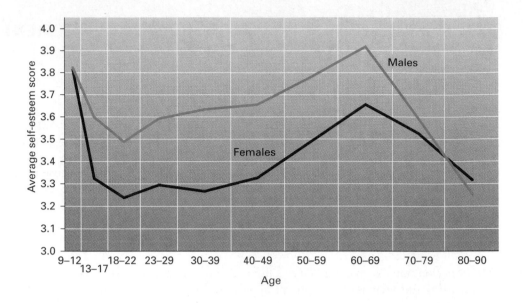

adolescent girls' depression and anger (Brooks-Gunn & Warren, 1989). In sum, both hormonal changes and environmental experiences are involved in the changing emotional landscape of adolescence.

Self-Esteem

Recall from chapter 14 that *self-esteem* is the overall way we evaluate ourselves—in other words, how we *feel* about ourselves—and that self-esteem also is referred to as self-image or self-worth. The extent to which self-esteem changes during adolescence, and the question of whether there are gender differences in adolescent self-esteem, are still the subject of controversy.

Researchers have found that self-esteem often decreases when children make the transition from elementary school to middle or junior high school (Harter, 2006; Hawkins & Berndt, 1985; Simmons & Blyth, 1987; Twenge & Campbell, 2001). Indeed, during and just after many life transitions, individuals' self-esteem often decreases. This decrease in self-esteem may occur during the transition from middle or junior high school to high school, and from high school to college.

Self-esteem does seem to fluctuate across the lifespan. One recent cross-sectional study assessed the self-esteem of a very large, diverse sample of 326,641 individuals from 9 to 90 years of age (Robins & others, 2002). About two-thirds of the participants were from the United States. The individuals were asked to respond to the item, "I have high self-esteem" on a 5-point scale in which 1 stood for "strongly agree" and 5 stood for "strongly disagree." Self-esteem decreased in adolescence, increased in the twenties, leveled off in the thirties, rose in the fifties and sixties, and then dropped in the seventies and eighties (see figure 17.2). At most ages, males reported higher self-esteem than females.

Some researchers argue that while there may be a decrease in self-esteem during adolescence, the drop is actually very slight and not nearly as pronounced as presented in the media (Harter, 2002; Kling & others, 1999). Also note in figure 17.2 that despite the drop in self-esteem among adolescent girls, their average score (3.3) was still slightly higher than the neutral point on the scale (3.0).

One explanation for the decline in the self-esteem among females during early adolescence focuses on girls' more negative body images during pubertal change compared with boys. Another explanation involves the greater interest young adolescent girls take in social relationships and society's failure to reward that interest.

Identity

By far the most comprehensive and provocative story of identity development has been told by Erik Erikson. As you may remember from chapter 2, identity versus identity confusion is the fifth stage in Erikson's eight stages of the life span, occurring at about the same time as adolescence. It is a time of being interested in finding out who one is, what one is all about, and where one is headed in life.

During adolescence, worldviews become important to the individual, who enters what Erikson (1968) calls a "psychological moratorium," a gap between the security of childhood and the autonomy of adulthood. Adolescents experiment with the numerous roles and identities they draw from the surrounding culture. Youth who successfully cope with these conflicting identities during adolescence emerge with a new sense of self that is both refreshing and acceptable (Moshman, 1999). Adolescents who do not successfully resolve this identity crisis are confused, suffering what Erikson calls "identity confusion." This confusion takes one of two courses: The individuals withdraw, isolating themselves from peers and family, or they lose their identity in the crowd.

Identity is a self-portrait composed of many pieces. These pieces include:

- The career and work path a person wants to follow (vocational/career identity)
- Whether a person is conservative, liberal, or a middle-of-the roader (political identity)
- A person's spiritual beliefs (religious identity)
- Whether a person is single, married, divorced, and so on (relationship identity)
- The extent to which a person is motivated to achieve and is intellectual (achievement, intellectual identity)
- Whether a person is heterosexual, homosexual, or bisexual (sexual identity)
- Which part of the world or country a person is from and how intensely the person identifies with her cultural heritage (cultural/ethnic identity)
- The kind of things a person likes to do, which can include sports, music, hobbies, and so on (interest)
- An individual's personality characteristics (such as being introverted or extraverted, anxious or calm, friendly or hostile, and so on) (personality)
- An individual's body image (physical identity)

Contemporary Views of Identity Contemporary views of identity development suggest several important considerations. First, identity development is a lengthy process; in many instances, it is a more gradual, less cataclysmic transition than Erikson's term *crisis* implies. Second, identity development is extraordinarily complex.

Identity formation neither begins nor ends with adolescence. It begins with the appearance of attachment, the development of a sense of self, and the emergence of independence in infancy, and it reaches its final phase with a life review and integration in old age. What is important about identity in adolescence, especially late adolescence, is that for the first time physical development, cognitive development, and social development advance to the point at which the individual can sort through and synthesize childhood identities and identifications to construct a viable pathway toward adult maturity. Resolution of the identity issue at adolescence does not mean that identity will be stable through the remainder of one's life. A person who develops a healthy identity is flexible, adaptive, and open to changes in society, in relationships, and in careers. This openness assures numerous reorganizations of identity features throughout the life of the person who has achieved identity.

Identity formation does not happen neatly, and it usually does not happen cataclysmically (Kroger, 2003). At the bare minimum, it involves commitment to a vocational direction, an ideological stance, and a sexual orientation. Synthesizing the identity components can be a long, drawn-out process, with many negations and

*A*s long as one keeps searching, the answers come.

—JOAN BAEZ
American Folk Singer, 20th Century

Identity Development

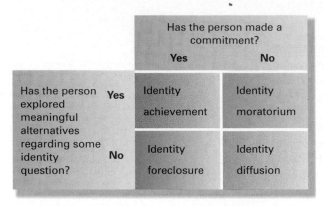

FIGURE 17.3 Marcia's Four Statuses of Identity

affirmations of various roles and faces (Marcia, 1996; Marcia & Carpendale, 2004). Identities are developed in bits and pieces. Decisions are not made once and for all but have to be made again and again. And the decisions may seem trivial at the time: whom to date, whether or not to break up, whether or not to have intercourse, whether or not to take drugs, whether to go to college after high school or get a job, which major to choose, whether to study or whether to play, whether or not to be politically active, and so on. Over the years of adolescence, the decisions begin to form a core of what the individual is all about as a person—what is called "identity."

Identity Statuses and Development

Canadian psychologist James Marcia (1980, 1994) analyzed Erikson's theory of identity development and concluded that it is important to distinguish between crisis and commitment in identity development.

Crisis is a period of identity development during which the adolescent is choosing among meaningful alternatives. Most researchers now use the term *exploration* rather than *crisis*, although, in the spirit of Marcia's original formulation, we will use the term *crisis*. **Commitment** is defined as the part of identity development in which adolescents show a personal investment in what they are going to do.

The extent of an individual's crisis and commitment is used to classify him according to one of four identity statuses (see figure 17.3).

- **Identity diffusion** occurs when individuals have not yet experienced a crisis (that is, they have not yet explored meaningful alternatives) or made any commitments. Not only are they undecided about occupational and ideological choices, but they are also likely to show little interest in such matters.
- **Identity foreclosure** occurs when individuals have made a commitment but have not yet experienced a crisis. This occurs most often when parents hand down commitments to their adolescents, more often than not in an authoritarian manner. In these circumstances, adolescents have not had adequate opportunities to explore different approaches, ideologies, and vocations on their own.
- **Identity moratorium** occurs when individuals are in the midst of a crisis but their commitments are either absent or only vaguely defined.
- **Identity achievement** occurs when individuals have undergone a crisis and have made a commitment.

Let's explore some examples of Marcia's identity statuses. A 13-year-old adolescent has neither begun to explore her identity in any meaningful way nor made an identity commitment, so she is *identity diffused*. An 18-year-old boy's parents want him to be a medical doctor so he is planning on majoring in premedicine in college and really has not adequately explored any other options, so he is *identity foreclosed*. Nineteen-year-old Sasha is not quite sure what life paths she wants to follow, but she recently went to the counseling center at her college to find out about different careers, so she is in *identity moratorium* status. Twenty-one-year-old Marcelo extensively explored a number of different career options in college, eventually getting his degree in science education, and is looking forward to his first year of teaching high school students, so he is *identity achieved*. Our examples of identity statuses have focused on the career dimension, but remember that the whole of identity is made up of a number of dimensions.

Young adolescents are primarily in Marcia's identity diffusion, foreclosure, or moratorium status. At least three aspects of the young adolescent's development are important in identity formation: Young adolescents must establish confidence in parental support, develop a sense of industry, and gain a self-reflective perspective on their future. Some researchers believe the most important identity changes take place in the college years, rather than earlier in adolescence. For example, Alan Waterman (1992) has found that, from the years preceding high school through the last few

crisis Marcia's term for a period of identity development during which the adolescent is choosing from among meaningful alternatives.

commitment Marcia's term for the part of identity development in which adolescents show a personal investment in what they are going to do.

identity diffusion Marcia's term for adolescents who have not yet experienced a crisis (explored meaningful alternatives) or made any commitments.

identity foreclosure Marcia's term for adolescents who have made a commitment but have not experienced a crisis.

identity moratorium Marcia's term for adolescents who are in the midst of a crisis, but their commitments are either absent or vaguely defined.

identity achievement Marcia's term for adolescents who have undergone a crisis and have made a commitment.

years of college, the number of individuals who are identity achieved increases, along with a decrease in those who are identity diffused. College upperclassmen are more likely than college freshmen or high school students to be identity achieved. Many young adolescents are identity diffused. These developmental changes are especially true in regard to vocational choice. For religious beliefs and political ideology, fewer college students have reached the identity achieved status, with a substantial number characterized by foreclosure and diffusion. Thus, the timing of identity may depend on the particular role involved, and many college students are still wrestling with ideological commitments.

Many identity status researchers believe that a common pattern of individuals who develop positive identities is to follow what are called "MAMA" cycles of *m*oratorium-*a*chievement-*m*oratorium-*a*chievement. These cycles may be repeated throughout life. Personal, family, and societal changes are inevitable, and as they occur, the flexibility and skill required to explore new alternatives and develop new commitments are likely to facilitate an individual's coping skills.

Do you have any idea who I am?

Family Influences on Identity   Parents are important figures in the adolescent's development of identity. One recent study found that poor communication between mothers and adolescents and persistent conflicts with friends were linked to less positive identity development (Reis & Youniss, 2004). The presence of a family atmosphere that promotes both individuality and connectedness is important in the adolescent's identity development (Cooper & Grotevant, 1989):

- **Individuality** consists of two dimensions: self-assertion, the ability to have and communicate a point of view, and separateness, the use of communication patterns to express how one is different from others.
- **Connectedness** consists of these two dimensions: mutuality, sensitivity to, and respect for others' views, and permeability—openness to others' views.

In general, research findings reveal that identity formation is enhanced by family relationships that are both individuated, which encourages adolescents to develop their own point of view, and connected, which provides a secure base from which to explore the widening social worlds of adolescence.

Cultural and Ethnic Aspects of Identity   Erikson was especially sensitive to the role of culture in identity development. He points out that, throughout the world, ethnic minority groups have struggled to maintain their cultural identities while blending into the dominant culture (Erikson, 1968). Erikson said that this struggle for an inclusive identity, or identity within the larger culture, has been the driving force in the founding of churches, empires, and revolutions throughout history.

For ethnic minority individuals, adolescence is often a special juncture in their development (Phinney, 2000; Spencer & others, 2001). Although children are aware of some ethnic and cultural differences, most ethnic minority individuals consciously confront their ethnicity for the first time in adolescence. In contrast to children, adolescents have the ability to interpret ethnic and cultural information, to reflect on the past, and to speculate about the future.

Jean Phinney (1996) defined **ethnic identity** as an enduring, basic aspect of the self that includes a sense of membership in an ethnic group and the attitudes and feelings related to that membership. Thus, for adolescents from ethnic minority groups, the process of identity formation has an added dimension due to exposure to alternative sources of identification—their own ethnic group and the mainstream or dominant culture. Researchers have found that ethnic identity increases with age and that higher levels of ethnic identity are linked with more positive attitudes not only toward one's own ethnic group but toward members of other ethnic groups as well (Phinney, Ferguson, & Tate, 1997). Many ethnic minority adolescents have bicultural

individuality According to Cooper and her colleagues, individuality consists of two dimensions: self-assertion (the ability to have and communicate a point of view) and separateness (the use of communication patterns to express how one is different from others).

connectedness According to Cooper and her colleagues, connectedness consists of two dimensions: mutuality (sensitivity to and respect for others' views) and permeability (openness to others' views).

ethnic identity An enduring, basic aspect of the self that includes a sense of membership in an ethnic group and the attitudes and feelings related to that membership.

Michelle Chin, age 16: "Parents do not understand that teenagers need to find out who they are, which means a lot of experimenting, a lot of mood swings, a lot of emotions and awkwardness. Like any teenager, I am facing an identity crisis. I am still trying to figure out if I am a Chinese American or an American with Asian eyes."

www.mhhe.com/santrockc9

Cultural Identity in Canada
Exploring Ethnic Identities

Researcher Margaret Beale Spencer, shown here talking with adolescents, believes that adolescence is often a critical juncture in the identity development of ethnic minority individuals. Most ethnic minority individuals consciously confront their ethnicity for the first time in adolescence.

identities—identifying in some ways with their ethnic minority group, in other ways with the majority culture (Comas-Díaz, 2001; Phinney & Devich-Navarro, 1997).

The ease or difficulty with which ethnic minority adolescents achieve healthy identities depends on a number of factors (Ferrer-Wreder & others, 2002). Many ethnic minority adolescents have to confront issues of prejudice and discrimination, and barriers to the fulfillment of their goals and aspirations (Comas-Díaz, 2001).

In one investigation, ethnic identity exploration was higher among ethnic minority than among White American college students (Phinney & Alipuria, 1990). In this same investigation, ethnic minority college students who had thought about and resolved issues involving their ethnicity had higher self-esteem than did their ethnic minority counterparts who had not. In another investigation, the ethnic identity development of Asian American, African American, Latino, and White American tenth-grade students in Los Angeles was studied (Phinney, 1989). Adolescents from each of the three ethnic minority groups faced a similar need to deal with their ethnic-group identification in a predominantly White American culture. In some instances, the adolescents from the three ethnic minority groups perceived different issues to be important in their resolution of ethnic identity. For Asian American adolescents, pressures to achieve academically and concerns about quotas that make it difficult to get into good colleges were salient issues. Many African American adolescent females discussed their realization that White American standards of beauty (especially hair and skin color) did not apply to them; African American adolescent males were concerned with possible job discrimination and the need to distinguish themselves from a negative societal image of African American male adolescents. For Latino adolescents, prejudice was a recurrent theme, as was the conflict in values between their Latino culture heritage and the majority culture.

The contexts in which ethnic minority youth live influence their identity development (Spencer, 1999). Many ethnic minority youth in the United States live in low-income urban settings where support for developing a positive identity is absent. Many of these youth live in pockets of poverty, are exposed to drugs, gangs, and criminal activities, and interact with other youth and adults who have dropped out of school and/or are unemployed. In such settings, effective organizations and programs for youth can make important contributions to developing a positive identity.

The indicators of identity change are often different for each succeeding generation (Phinney, 2003). The identity of the first generation of immigrants is likely to be secure and unlikely to change considerably. They may or may not develop an "American" identity. The degree to which they begin to feel American appears to be related to learning English, developing social networks beyond their group, and becoming culturally competent in the new context. For the second generation of immigrants, an "American" identity is more secure possibly because citizenship is granted with birth. Their ethnic identity is likely to be linked to retention of their ethnic language and social networks. For the third and later generations, the issues become more complex. Various historical, contextual, and political factors unrelated to acculturation may affect the extent to which their ethnic identity is retained (Bryant & LaFromboise, 2005; Cuéllar, Siles, & Bracamontes, 2004; Newman, 2005; Ramirez, 2004). For non-European ethnic groups, racism and discrimination influence whether ethnic identity is retained.

Researchers are also increasingly finding that a positive ethnic identity is related to positive outcomes for ethnic minority adolescents (Fridrich & Flannery, 1995; Lee, 2005; Riekmann, Wadsworth, & Deyhle, 2004; Umana-Taylor, 2004; Yasui, Dorham, & Dishion, 2004; Zarate, Bhimji, & Reese, 2005). For example, one recent study revealed that ethnic identity was linked with higher school engagement and lower aggression (Van Buren & Graham, 2003). Another recent study indicated that a stronger ethnic identity was linked to higher self-esteem in African American, Latino, and Asian American youth (Bracey, Bamaca, & Umana-Taylor, 2004). And yet another study with ninth-grade students found that the strength of adolescents' ethnic identification was a better predictor of their academic success than the specific ethnic labels they used to describe themselves (Fuligni, Witkow, & Garcia, 2005). In this study, the ethnic groups most likely to incorporate more of their families' national origin and cultural background into their ethnic identifications were Mexican and Chinese immigrant adolescents.

---

2 WHAT IS THE NATURE OF PARENT-ADOLESCENT RELATIONSHIPS?

Autonomy and Attachment   Parent-Adolescent Conflict

In chapter 14, we discussed how, during middle and late childhood, parents spend less time with their children than in early childhood, that discipline involves an increased use of reasoning and deprivation of privileges, and that there is a gradual transfer of control from parents to children but still within the boundary of coregulation. Among the most important aspects of family relationships in adolescence are those that involve autonomy and attachment, and parent-adolescent conflict.

Autonomy and Attachment

The adolescent's push for autonomy and responsibility puzzles and angers many parents. Parents see their teenager slipping from their grasp. They may have an urge to take stronger control as the adolescent seeks autonomy and responsibility. Heated emotional exchanges may ensue, with either side calling names, making threats, and doing whatever seems necessary to gain control. Parents may seem frustrated because they *expect* their teenager to heed their advice, to want to spend time with the family, and to grow up to do what is right. Most parents anticipate that their teenager will have some difficulty adjusting to the changes that adolescence brings, but few parents can imagine and predict just how strong an adolescent's desires will be to spend time with peers or how much adolescents will want to show that it is they—not their parents—who are responsible for their successes and failures.

The ability to attain autonomy and gain control over one's behavior in adolescence is acquired through appropriate adult reactions to the adolescent's desire for control (Collins & Steinberg, 2006; Zimmer-Gembeck & Collins, 2003). At the onset of adolescence, the average individual does not have the knowledge to make appropriate or mature decisions in all areas of life. As the adolescent pushes for autonomy, the wise

It is not enough for parents to understand children. They must accord children the privilege of understanding them.

—Milton Saperstein
American Psychiatrist, 20th Century

Research on Gender and Identity
Parent-Adolescent Relationships
Joseph Allen's Research

adult relinquishes control in those areas in which the adolescent can make reasonable decisions but continues to guide the adolescent to make reasonable decisions in areas in which the adolescent's knowledge is more limited. Gradually, adolescents acquire the ability to make mature decisions on their own.

Gender differences characterize autonomy-granting in adolescence with boys being given more independence than girls. In one recent study, this was especially true in U.S. families with a traditional gender-role orientation (Bumpus, Crouter, & McHale, 2001).

Cultural differences also characterize adolescent autonomy. In one study, U.S. adolescents sought autonomy earlier than Japanese adolescents (Rothbaum & others, 2000). In the transition to adulthood, Japanese youth are less likely to live outside the home than Americans (Hendry, 1999).

Recall from chapter 8 that one of the most widely discussed aspects of socioemotional development in infancy is secure attachment to caregivers. In the past decade, researchers have explored whether secure attachment also might be an important concept in adolescents' relationships with their parents (Carlson, Sroufe, & Egeland, 2004; Collins & Steinberg, 2006; Sroufe & others, 2005). For example, Joseph Allen and his colleagues (Allen, Hauser, & Borman-Spurrell, 1996; Allen & Kuperminc, 1995; Allen, Kuperminc, & Moore, 2005; Allen & others, 2005) found that securely attached adolescents were less likely than those who were insecurely attached to engage in problem behaviors, such as juvenile delinquency and drug abuse. In other research, securely attached adolescents had better peer relations than their insecurely attached counterparts (Laible, Carlo, & Raffaeli, 2000).

However, whereas adolescent-parent attachments are correlated with adolescent outcomes, the correlations are moderate, indicating that the success or failure of parent-adolescent attachments does not necessarily guarantee success or failure in peer relationships (Buhrmester, 2003). Clearly, secure attachment with parents can be an asset for the adolescent, fostering the trust to engage in close relationships with others and lay down the foundation for close relationship skills. But a significant minority of adolescents from strong, supportive families, nonetheless, struggle in peer relations for a variety of reasons, such as being physically unattractive, maturing late, and experiencing cultural and SES discrepancies. On the other hand, some adolescents from troubled families find a positive, fresh start with peer relations that can compensate for their problematic family backgrounds.

Parent-Adolescent Conflict

Although attachment to parents remains strong during adolescence, the connectedness is not always smooth. Early adolescence is a time when conflict with parents escalates beyond childhood levels. This increase may be due to a number of factors: the biological changes of puberty, cognitive changes involving increased idealism and logical reasoning, social changes focused on independence and identity, maturational changes in parents, and expectations that are violated by parents and adolescents. The adolescent compares her parents to an ideal standard and then criticizes their flaws. A 13-year-old girl tells her mother, "That is the tackiest-looking dress I have ever seen. Nobody would be caught dead wearing that." The adolescent demands logical explanations for comments and discipline. A 14-year-old boy tells his mother, "What do you mean I have to be home at 10 P.M. because it's the way we do things around here? Why do we do things around here that way? It doesn't make sense to me."

Many parents see their adolescent changing from a compliant child to someone who is noncompliant, oppositional, and resistant to parental standards. When this happens, parents tend to clamp down and put more pressure on the adolescent to conform to parental standards. Parents often expect their adolescents to become mature adults overnight, instead of understanding that the journey takes 10 to 15 years. Parents who recognize that this transition takes time handle their youth more competently and calmly than those who demand immediate conformity to adult standards. The opposite tactic—letting adolescents do as they please without supervision—is also unwise.

Old model	New model
Autonomy, detachment from parents; parent and peer worlds are isolated	Attachment and autonomy; parents are important support systems and attachment figures; adolescent-parent and adolescent-peer worlds have some important connections
Intense, stressful conflict throughout adolescence; parent-adolescent relationships are filled with storm and stress on virtually a daily basis	Moderate parent-adolescent conflict common and can serve a positive developmental function; conflict greater in early adolescence, especially during the apex of puberty

FIGURE 17.4 Old and New Models of Parent-Adolescent Relationships

Conflict with parents increases in early adolescence, but it does not reach the tumultuous proportions G. Stanley Hall envisioned at the beginning of the twentieth century (Collins & Laursen, 2004; Collins & Steinberg, 2006; Steinberg & Silk, 2002). Rather, much of the conflict involves the everyday events of family life, such as keeping a bedroom clean, dressing neatly, getting home by a certain time, and not talking forever on the phone. The conflicts rarely involve major dilemmas, such as drugs and delinquency.

It is not unusual to hear parents of young adolescents ask, "Is it ever going to get better?" Things usually do get better as adolescents move from early to late adolescence. Conflict with parents often escalates during early adolescence, remains somewhat stable during the high school years, and then lessens as the adolescent reaches 17 to 20 years of age. Parent-adolescent relationships become more positive if adolescents go away to college than if they stay at home and go to college (Sullivan & Sullivan, 1980).

The everyday conflicts that characterize parent-adolescent relationships may actually serve a positive developmental function. These minor disputes and negotiations facilitate the adolescent's transition from being dependent on parents to becoming an autonomous individual. For example, in one study, adolescents who expressed disagreement with their parents explored identity development more actively than did adolescents who did not express disagreement with their parents (Cooper & others, 1982). As previously mentioned, one way for parents to cope with the adolescent's push for independence and identity is to recognize that adolescence is a 10- to 15-year transitional period in the journey to adulthood, rather than an overnight accomplishment. Recognizing that conflict and negotiation can serve a positive developmental function can tone down parental hostility too. Understanding parent-adolescent conflict, though, is not simple (Conger & Ge, 1999).

In sum, the old model of parent-adolescent relationships suggested that as adolescents mature, they detach themselves from parents and move into a world of autonomy apart from parents. The old model also suggested that parent-adolescent conflict is intense and stressful throughout adolescence. The new model emphasizes that parents serve as important attachment figures and support systems as adolescents explore a wider, more complex social world. The new model also emphasizes that, in most families, parent-adolescent conflict is moderate rather than severe and that the everyday negotiations and minor disputes are normal and can serve the positive developmental function of helping the adolescent make the transition from childhood dependency to adult independence (see figure 17.4).

Still, a high degree of conflict characterizes some parent-adolescent relationships. One estimate of the proportion of parents and adolescents who engage in prolonged, intense, repeated, unhealthy conflict is about one in five families (Montemayor, 1982). Although this figure represents a minority of adolescents, it indicates that 4 to 5 million

CAREERS
in CHILD DEVELOPMENT

Martha Chan
Marriage and Family Therapist

Martha Chan is a marriage and family therapist who works for Adolescent Counseling Services in Palo Alto, California. She has been the program director of Adolescent Counseling Services for more than a decade.

Among her activities, Chan counsels parents and adolescents about family issues, conducts workshops for parents at middle schools, and writes a monthly column that addresses such topics as "I'm a single mom: How do I talk with my son about sex?", "My daughter wants to dye her hair purple," and "My son is being bullied."

American families encounter serious, highly stressful parent-adolescent conflict. And this prolonged, intense conflict is associated with a number of adolescent problems—movement out of the home, juvenile delinquency, school dropout, pregnancy and early marriage, membership in religious cults, and drug abuse (Brook & others, 1990). To read about the work of Martha Chan, a therapist who provides guidance for families in which there is a high degree of conflict between parents and adolescents, see the Careers in Child Development profile.

It should be pointed out that in some cultures there is less parent-adolescent conflict than in others. American psychologist Reed Larson (1999) spent six months in India studying middle-socioeconomic-status adolescents and their families. He observed that in India there seems to be little parent-adolescent conflict and that many families likely would be described as "authoritarian" in Baumrind's categorization. Larson also observed that in India adolescents do not go through a process of breaking away from their parents and that parents choose their youths' marital partners. Researchers have also found considerably less conflict between parents and adolescents in Japan than in the United States (Rothbaum & others, 2000).

We have seen that parents play very important roles in adolescent development. Although adolescents are moving toward independence, they still need to stay connected with families (Roth & Brooks-Gunn, 2000). In the National Longitudinal Study on Adolescent Health (Council of Economic Advisors, 2000) of more than 12,000 adolescents, those who did not eat dinner with a parent five or more days a week had dramatically higher rates of smoking, drinking, marijuana use, getting into fights, and initiation of sexual activity. In another recent study, parents who played an active role in monitoring and guiding their adolescents' development were more likely to have adolescents with positive peer relations and lower drug use than parents who had a less active role (Mounts, 2002).

Competent adolescent development is most likely to happen when adolescents have parents who (Small, 1990):

- Show them warmth and mutual respect
- Demonstrate sustained interest in their lives
- Recognize and adapt to their cognitive and socioemotional development
- Communicate expectations for high standards of conduct and achievement
- Display constructive ways of dealing with problems and conflict

These ideas coincide with Diana Baumrind's (1971, 1991) authoritative parenting style, which we discussed in chapter 11, "Socioemotional Development in Early Childhood."

Review and Reflect • LEARNING GOAL 2

 Describe changes in adolescents' relationships with their parents.

Review
- How do autonomy and attachment develop in adolescence?
- What is the nature of parent-adolescent conflict?

Reflect
- How much autonomy did your parents give you in adolescence? Too much? Too little? How intense was your conflict with your parents during adolescence? What were the conflicts mainly about? Would you behave differently toward your own adolescents than your parents did with you? If so, how?

3 WHAT ASPECTS OF PEER RELATIONSHIPS ARE IMPORTANT IN ADOLESCENCE?

Friendships

Peer Groups

Peers and Culture

Dating and Romantic Relationships

In chapter 14, we discussed how children spend more time with their peers in middle and late childhood than in early childhood. We also found that friendships become more important in middle and late childhood and that popularity with peers is a strong motivation for most children. Advances in cognitive development during middle and late childhood also allow children to take the perspective of their peers and friends more readily, and their social knowledge of how to make and keep friends increases.

Friendships

Harry Stack Sullivan (1953) was the most influential theorist to discuss the importance of adolescent friendships, and his ideas have withstood the test of time. He argued that there is a dramatic increase in the psychological importance and intimacy of close friends during early adolescence. In contrast to other psychoanalytic theorists' narrow emphasis on the importance of parent-child relationships, Sullivan contended that friends also play important roles in shaping children's and adolescents' well-being and development. In terms of well-being, he argued that all people have a number of basic social needs, including the need for tenderness (secure attachment), playful companionship, social acceptance, intimacy, and sexual relations. Whether or not these needs are fulfilled largely determines our emotional well-being. For example, if the need for playful companionship goes unmet, then we become bored and depressed; if the need for social acceptance is not met, we suffer a lowered sense of self-worth.

Developmentally, friends become increasingly depended on to satisfy these needs during adolescence; thus, the ups-and-downs of experiences with friends increasingly shape adolescents' state of well-being. In particular, Sullivan believed that the need for intimacy intensifies during early adolescence, motivating teenagers to seek out close friends. He felt that, if adolescents fail to forge such close friendships, they experience painful feelings of loneliness, coupled with a reduced sense of self-worth.

Research findings support many of Sullivan's ideas. For example, adolescents report disclosing intimate and personal information to their friends more often than do younger children (Buhrmester, 1998; Buhrmester & Furman, 1987) (see figure 17.5). Adolescents also say they depend more on friends than on parents to satisfy their needs for companionship, reassurance of worth, and intimacy (Furman & Buhrmester, 1992). In another study, friendship in early adolescence was a significant predictor of self-worth in early adulthood (Bagwell, Newcomb, & Bukowski, 1994).

Not only does the quality of friendships have important influences on adolescents, but the friend's character, interests, and attitudes also matter (Brown, 2004). For example, researchers have found that delinquent adolescents often have delinquent friends, and they reinforce each other's delinquent behavior (Dishion, Andrews, & Crosby, 1995). Other research has indicated that nonsmoking adolescents who become friends with smoking adolescents are more likely to start smoking themselves (Urberg, 1992). By the same token, having friends who are into school, sports, or religion is likely to have a positive influence on the adolescent.

Are the friendships of adolescent girls more intimate than the friendships of adolescent boys? When asked to describe their best friends, girls refer to intimate

What changes take place in friendship during the adolescent years?

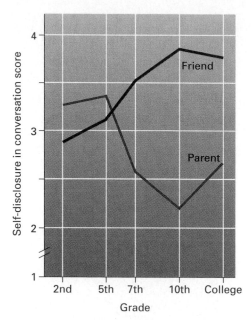

FIGURE 17.5 Developmental Changes in Self-Disclosing Conversations Self-disclosing conversations with friends increased dramatically in adolescence while declining in an equally dramatic fashion with parents. However, self-disclosing conversations with parents began to pick up somewhat during the college years. The measure of self-disclosure involved a 5-point rating scale completed by the children and youth with a higher score representing greater self-disclosure. The data shown represent the means for each age group.

Peer Pressure Youth Connections

---

cliques Small groups that range from 2 to about 12 individuals, averaging about 5 to 6 individuals. Members usually are the same age, same sex, and often engage in similar activities.

crowds A larger group structure than cliques, crowds are usually formed based on reputation and members may or may not spend much time together.

---

conversations and faithfulness more than boys do (Collins & Steinberg, 2006; Ruble, Martin, & Berenbaum, 2006). For example, girls, are more likely to describe their best friend as "sensitive just like me" or "trustworthy just like me" (Duck, 1975). When conflict is present, girls place a higher priority on relationship goals such as being patient until the relationship improves, while boys are more likely to seek control over a friend (Rose & Asher, 1999; Ruble, Martin, & Berenbaum, 2006). While girls' friendships in adolescence are more likely to focus on intimacy, boys' friendships tend to emphasize power and excitement (Rose, 2002; Ruble, Martin, & Berenbaum, 2006). Boys may discourage one another from openly disclosing their problems because self-disclosure is not masculine (Maccoby, 1996). Boys make themselves vulnerable to being called "wimps" if they can't handle their own problems and insecurities. These gender differences are generally assumed to reflect a greater orientation toward interpersonal relationships among girls than boys.

Although most adolescents develop friendships with individuals who are close to their own age, some adolescents become best friends with younger or older individuals. A common fear, especially among parents, is that adolescents who have older friends will be encouraged to engage in delinquent behavior or early sexual behavior. Researchers have found that adolescents who interact with older youth do engage in these behaviors more frequently, but it is not known whether the older youth guide younger adolescents toward deviant behavior or whether the younger adolescents were already prone to deviant behavior before they developed the friendship with the older youth (Billy, Rodgers, & Udry, 1984).

Peer Groups

Conforming to peers' behaviors and attitudes is common in adolescence, although adolescents' peer relations can vary across cultures. In addition, membership in cliques and crowds becomes more important in adolescence than in childhood.

Conformity to Peers   Conformity to peer pressure in adolescence can be positive or negative. Teenagers engage in all sorts of negative conformity behavior—use seedy language, steal, vandalize, and make fun of parents and teachers. However, a great deal of peer conformity is not negative and consists of the desire to be involved in the peer world, such as dressing like friends and wanting to spend large amounts of time with groups of friends who share similar interests. Such circumstances may involve prosocial activities as well, as when clubs raise money for worthy causes.

Young adolescents conform more to peer standards than children do. Investigators have found that, around the eighth and ninth grades, conformity to peers—especially to their antisocial standards—peaks (Leventhal, 1994). At this point, adolescents are most likely to go along with a peer to steal hubcaps off a car, draw graffiti on a wall, or steal cosmetics from a store counter. However, researchers have found that U.S. adolescents are more likely to put pressure on their peers to resist parental influence than Japanese adolescents are (Rothbaum & others, 2000).

Cliques and Crowds   Cliques and crowds assume more important roles in the lives of adolescents than children (Brown, 2004). **Cliques** are small groups that range from 2 to about 12 individuals and average about 5 to 6 individuals. The clique members are usually of the same sex and about the same age. Cliques can form because adolescents engage in similar activities, such as being in a club or on a sports team (Ennett & Bauman, 1996). What do adolescents do in cliques? They share ideas, hang out together, and often develop an in-group identity in which they believe that their clique is better than other cliques.

Crowds are a larger group structure than cliques. Adolescents are usually members of a crowd based on reputation and may or may not spend much time together. Crowds are less personal than cliques. Many crowds are defined by the activities adolescents engage in (such as "jocks" who are good at sports or "druggies" who take drugs). Reputation-based crowds often appear for the first time in early adolescence and usually become less prominent in late adolescence (Collins & Steinberg, 2006).

In one study, crowd membership was associated with adolescent self-esteem (Brown & Lohr, 1987). The crowds included jocks (athletically oriented), populars (well-known students who led social activities), normals (middle-of-the-road students who made up the masses), druggies or toughs (known for illicit drug use or other delinquent activities), and nobodies (low in social skills or intellectual abilities). The self-esteem of the jocks and the populars was highest, whereas that of the nobodies was lowest. One group of adolescents not in a crowd had self-esteem equivalent to that of the jocks and the populars; this group was the independents, who indicated that crowd membership was not important to them. Keep in mind that these data are correlational; self-esteem could increase an adolescent's probability of becoming a crowd member, just as crowd membership could increase the adolescent's self-esteem.

Peers and Culture

In some countries, adults restrict adolescents' access to peers. For example, in many areas of rural India and in Arab countries, opportunities for peer relations in adolescence are severely restricted, especially for girls (Brown & Larson, 2002). If girls attend school in these regions of the world, it is usually in sex-segregated schools. In these countries, interaction with the other sex or opportunities for romantic relationships are restricted (Booth, 2002).

Street youth in Rio De Janeiro. *What are some examples of cross-cultural variations in peer relations?*

Earlier in the chapter, we indicated that Japanese adolescents seek autonomy from their parents later and have less conflict with them than American adolescents do. In a recent cross-cultural analysis, the peer group was more important to U.S. adolescents than to Japanese adolescents (Rothbaum & others, 2000). Japanese adolescents spend less time outside the home, have less recreational leisure time, and engage in fewer extracurricular activities with peers than U.S. adolescents (White, 1993). Also, U.S. adolescents are more likely to put pressure on their peers to resist parental influence than Japanese adolescents are (Rothbaum & others, 2000).

A trend, though, is that in societies in which adolescents' access to peers has been restricted, adolescents are engaging in more peer interaction during school and in shared leisure activities, especially in middle-SES contexts (Brown & Larson, 2002). For example, in Southeast Asia and some Arab regions, adolescents are starting to rely more on peers for advice and share interests with them (Booth, 2002; Santa Maria, 2002).

In many countries and regions, though, peers play more prominent roles in adolescents' lives (Brown & Larson, 2002). For example, in sub-Saharan Africa, the peer group is a pervasive aspect of adolescents' lives (Nsamenang, 2002); similar results have been observed throughout Europe and North America (Arnett, 2002).

Dating and Romantic Relationships

Adolescents spend considerable time either dating or thinking about dating, which has gone far beyond its original courtship function to become a form of recreation, a source of status and achievement, and a setting for learning about close relationships. One function of dating, though, continues to be mate selection. One recent study of 14- to 19-year-olds found that adolescents who were not involved in a romantic relationship had more social anxiety than their counterparts who were dating or romantically involved (La Greca & Harrison, 2005).

Types of Dating and Developmental Changes   There are a number of dating variations and developmental changes that characterize dating and romantic relationships (Bouchey & Furman, 2003; Collins & Steinberg, 2006; Florsheim, 2003). First, we will examine heterosexual romantic relationships and then turn to romantic relationships in sexual minority youth.

FIGURE 17.6 **Age of Onset of Romantic Activity** In this study, announcing that "I like someone" occurred earliest, followed by going out with the same person three or more times, having an exclusive relationship for over two months, and finally planning an engagement or marriage (which characterized only a very small percentage of participants by the twelfth grade) (Buhrmester, 2001).

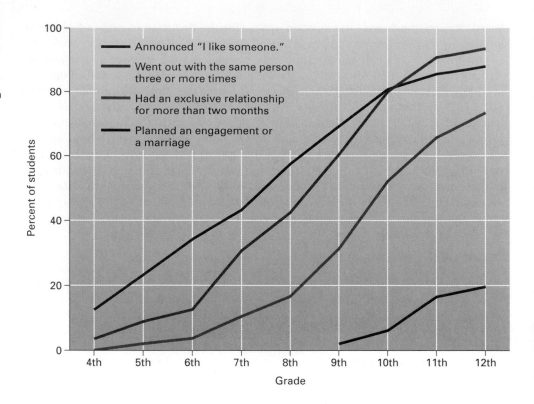

Heterosexual Romantic Relationships In one recent study, announcing that "I like someone" occurred by the sixth grade for 40 percent of the individuals sampled (Buhrmester, 2001) (see figure 17.6). However, it was not until the tenth grade that 50 percent of the adolescents had a sustained romantic relationship that lasted two months or longer. By their senior year, 25 percent still had not engaged in this type of sustained romantic relationship. Also, in this study, girls' early romantic involvement was linked with lower grades, less active participation in class discussion, and school-related problems. A rather large portion of adolescents in dating relationships say that their relationships have persisted 11 months or longer: 20 percent of adolescents 14 or younger, 35 percent of 15- to 16-year-olds, and almost 60 percent of 17- and 18-year-olds (Carver, Joyner, & Udry, 2003). A special concern is early dating and "going with" someone, which is associated with adolescent pregnancy and problems at home and school (Florsheim, 2003; Florsheim, Moore, & Edgington, 2003).

In their early exploration of romantic relationships, today's adolescents often find comfort in numbers and begin hanging out together in heterosexual groups. Sometimes they just hang out at someone's house or get organized enough to get someone to drive them to a mall or a movie. Indeed, peers play an important role in adolescent romantic relationships. In one study, adolescents who were part of mixed-sex peer groups moved more readily into romantic relationships than their counterparts whose mixed-sex peer groups were more limited (Connolly, Furman, & Konarksi, 2000). And a recent study also found that young adolescents increase their participation in mixed-gender peer groups (Connolly & others, 2004). This participation was "not explicitly focused on dating but rather brought boys and girls together in settings in which heterosocial interaction might occur but is not obligatory . . . We speculate that mixed-gender groups are important because they are easily available to young adolescents who can take part at their own comfort level" (p. 201).

One study had fifth- to eighth-grade adolescents carry electronic pagers for one week and complete self-report forms in response to signals sent to them at random times (Richards & others, 1998). Four years later, the participants underwent the same procedure. Time with, and thoughts about, the opposite sex occupied more of the adolescents' week in high school than in fifth and sixth grades. Fifth- and sixth-grade girls spent approximately one hour a week in the presence of a boy, and their male counterparts spent even less time in the presence of a girl. Although more time was spent thinking about an individual of the opposite sex, it still added up to less than two hours a week for girls, and less than one hour per week for boys, in fifth and sixth grades. By eleventh and twelfth grades, girls were spending about 10 hours a week with a boy, boys about half that time with a girl. Frequency of thoughts had increased as well. The high school girls spent about eight hours a week thinking about a boy, the high school boys about five or six hours thinking about a girl.

What are some developmental changes in dating and romantic relationships in adolescence?

Romantic Relationships in Sexual Minority Youth   Most research on romantic relationships in adolescence has focused on heterosexual relationships. Recently, researchers have begun to study romantic relationships in gay, lesbian, and bisexual youth (Diamond & Savin-Williams, 2003; Savin-Williams & Diamond, 2004).

The average age of the initial same-sex activity for females ranges from 14 to 18 years of age and for males from 13 to 15 (Savin-Williams & Diamond, 2004). The most common initial same-sex partner is a close friend. More lesbian adolescent girls have sexual encounters with boys before same-sex activity, whereas gay adolescent boys are more likely to show the opposite sequence (Savin-Williams & Diamond, 2004).

Most sexual minority youth have same-sex sexual experience, but relatively few have same-sex romantic relationships because of limited opportunities and the social disapproval such relationships may generate from families or heterosexual peers (Diamond, 2003; Diamond, Savin-Williams, & Dube, 1999). The importance of romance to sexual minority youth was underscored in a study that found that they rated the breakup of a current romance as their second most stressful problem, second only to disclosure of their sexual orientation to their parents (D'Augelli, 1991).

The romantic possibilities of sexual minority youth are complex (Diamond, 2003; Savin-Williams & Diamond, 2004). To adequately address the relational interests of sexual minority youth, we can't simply generalize from heterosexual youth and simply switch the labels. Instead, the full range of variation in sexual minority youths' sexual desires and romantic relationships for same- and other-sex partners need to be considered.

Dating and Romantic Relationships
Teen Chat

Emotion, Adjustment, and Romantic Relationships

Romantic emotions can envelop adolescents' lives (Barber & Eccles, 2003; Harper, Welsh, & Woody, 2002). A 14-year-old reports feeling in love and can't think about anything else. A 15-year-old is distressed that "everyone else has a boyfriend but me." As we just saw, adolescents spend a lot of time thinking about romantic involvement. Some of this thought can involve positive emotions of compassion and joy, but it also can include negative emotions such as worry, disappointment, and jealousy.

Romantic relationships often are involved in an adolescent's emotional experiences (Larson, Clore, & Wood, 1999). In one study of ninth- to twelfth-graders, girls gave real and fantasized heterosexual relationships as the explanation for more than one-third of their strong emotions, and boys gave this reason for 25 percent of their strong emotions (Wilson-Shockley, 1995). Strong emotions were attached far less to school (13 percent), family (9 percent), and same-sex peer relations (8 percent). The majority of the emotions were reported as positive, but a substantial minority (42 percent), were reported as negative, including feelings of anxiety, anger, jealousy, and depression.

In one recent study of more than 8,000 adolescents, those in love had a higher risk for depression than their counterparts who did not get romantically involved (Joyner & Udry, 2000). Young adolescent girls who were in love were especially at risk for depression. Other researchers have also found that depression may result, especially in girls, following a romantic breakup (Welsh, Grello, & Harper, 2003).

In a recent study of the links between adjustment and dating in tenth-grade adolescents, mixed outcomes occurred (Furman, Ho, & Low, 2005). Adolescents who dated had more externalized problems (such as delinquency), and engaged in

How is emotion involved in adolescent romantic relationships?

substance use and genital sexual behavior more than their counterparts who did not date. However, adolescents who dated were more likely to be accepted by their peers and be perceived as more physically attractive.

Sociocultural Contexts and Dating   The sociocultural context exerts a powerful influence on adolescent dating patterns and on mate selection (Booth, 2002; Stevenson & Zusho, 2002). Values and religious beliefs of people in various cultures often dictate the age at which dating begins, how much freedom in dating is allowed, whether dates must be chaperoned by adults or parents, and the roles of males and females in dating. In the Arab world, Asian countries, and South America, adults are typically highly restrictive of adolescent girls' romantic relationships.

Immigrants to the United States have brought these restrictive standards with them. For example, in the United States, Latino and Asian American cultures have more conservative standards regarding adolescent dating than the Anglo-American culture. Dating can be a source of cultural conflict for many immigrants and their families who have come from cultures in which dating begins at a late age, little freedom in dating is allowed, dates are chaperoned, and adolescent girls' dating is especially restricted.

In one recent study, Latino young adults living in the Midwestern region of the United States reflected on their socialization for dating and sexuality (Raffaelli & Ontai, 2001). Because U.S.-style dating was viewed as a violation of traditional courtship styles by most of their parents, the parents placed strict boundaries on their romantic involvement. As a result many of the Latinos described their adolescent dating experiences as filled with tension and conflict. The average age at which the girls began dating was 15.7 years with early dating experiences usually occurring without parental knowledge or permission. Over half of the girls engaged in "sneak dating."

Review and Reflect • LEARNING GOAL 3

 Characterize the changes that occur in peer relations during adolescence.

Review
- What changes take place in friendship during adolescence according to Sullivan?
- What are adolescents' peer groups like?
- What role does culture play in peer relations?
- What is the nature of adolescent dating and romantic relationships?

Reflect
- What were your peer relationships like during adolescence? What peer groups were you involved in? How did they influence your development? What were your dating and romantic relationships like in adolescence? If you could change anything about the way you experienced peer relations in adolescence, what would it be?

4 WHY IS CULTURE AN IMPORTANT CONTEXT FOR ADOLESCENT DEVELOPMENT?

| Cross-Cultural Comparisons | Ethnicity |

We live in an increasingly diverse world, one in which there is increasing contact between adolescents from different cultures and ethnic groups. How do adolescents vary cross-culturally? What rites of passage do adolescents experience? What is the nature of ethnic minority adolescents and their development?

Cross-Cultural Comparisons

Ideas about the nature of adolescents and orientation toward adolescents may vary from culture to culture and within the same culture over different time periods (Cole, 2006; Shweder & others, 2006; Whiting, 1989). For example, some cultures (such as the Mangaian culture in the South Sea islands) have more permissive attitudes toward adolescent sexuality than the American culture, and some cultures (the Ines Beag culture off the coast of Ireland, for example) have more conservative attitudes toward adolescent sexuality than the American culture. Over the course of the twentieth century, attitudes toward sexuality —especially for females—have become more permissive in the American culture.

Early in the last century, overgeneralizations about the universal aspects of adolescents were made based on data and experience in a single culture—the middle-class culture of the United States. For example, it was believed that adolescents everywhere went through a period of "storm and stress," characterized by self-doubt and conflict. However, when Margaret Mead visited the island of Samoa, she found that the adolescents of the Samoan culture were not experiencing much stress.

As we discovered in chapter 1, *cross-cultural studies* involve the comparison of a culture with one or more other cultures, which provides information about the degree to which development is similar, or universal, across cultures, or the degree to which it is culture-specific. The study of adolescence has emerged in the context of Western industrialized society with the practical needs and social norms of this culture dominating thinking about adolescents. Consequently, the development of adolescents in Western cultures has evolved as the norm for all adolescents of the human species, regardless of economic and cultural circumstances. This narrow viewpoint can produce erroneous conclusions about the nature of adolescents. One variation in the experiences of adolescents in different cultures is whether the adolescents go through a rite of passage, which we will discuss later in the chapter.

How Adolescents Around the World Spend Their Time
Do adolescents around the world spend their time in ways similar to U.S. adolescents? Reed Larson and Suman Verma (Larson, 2001; Larson & Verma, 1999) examined how adolescents spend their time in work, play, and developmental activities such as school. As we saw in chapter 16, U.S. adolescents spend more time in paid work than their counterparts in most developed countries. We also saw that adolescent males in developing countries often spend more time in paid work than adolescent females, who spend more time in unpaid household labor.

Figure 17.7 summarizes the average daily time use by adolescents in different regions of the world (Larson & Verma, 1999). U.S. adolescents spend about 60 percent as much time on schoolwork as East Asian adolescents do, which is mainly due to U.S. adolescents doing less homework.

U.S. adolescents have more discretionary time than adolescents in other industrialized countries. About 40 to 50 percent of U.S. adolescents' waking hours (not counting

Activity	Nonindustrial, unschooled populations	Postindustrial, schooled populations		
		United States	Europe	East Asia
Household labor	5 to 9 hours	20 to 40 minutes	20 to 40 minutes	10 to 20 minutes
Paid labor	0.5 to 8 hours	40 to 60 minutes	10 to 20 minutes	0 to 10 minutes
Schoolwork	—	3.0 to 4.5 hours	4.0 to 5.5 hours	5.5 to 7.5 hours
Total work time	6 to 9 hours	4 to 6 hours	4.5 to 6.5 hours	6 to 8 hours
TV viewing	Insufficient data	1.5 to 2.5 hours	1.5 to 2.5 hours	1.5 to 2.5 hours
Talking	Insufficient data	2 to 3 hours	Insufficient data	45 to 60 minutes
Sports	Insufficient data	30 to 60 minutes	20 to 80 minutes	0 to 20 minutes
Structured voluntary activities	Insufficient data	10 to 20 minutes	1.0 to 20 minutes	0 to 10 minutes
Total free time	4 to 7 hours	6.5 to 8.0 hours	5.5 to 7.5 hours	4.0 to 5.5 hours

Note. The estimates in the table are averaged across a 7-day week, including weekdays and weekends. Time spent in maintenance activities like eating, personal care, and sleeping is not included. The data for nonindustrial, unschooled populations come primarily from rural peasant populations in developing countries.

FIGURE 17.7 Average Daily Time Use of Adolescents in Different Regions of the World

summer vacations) is spent in discretionary activities, compared with 25 to 35 percent in East Asia and 35 to 45 percent in Europe. Whether this additional discretionary time is a liability or an asset for U.S. adolescents, of course, depends on how they use it.

The largest amounts of U.S. adolescents' free time is spent using the media and engaging in unstructured leisure activities, often with friends. We will further explore adolescents' media use later in the chapter. U.S. adolescents spent more time in voluntary structured activities—such as sports, hobbies, and organizations—than East Asian adolescents.

According to Reed Larson (2001), U.S. adolescents may have too much unstructured time for optimal development. When adolescents are allowed to choose what they do with their time, they typically engage in unchallenging activities such as hanging out and watching TV. Although relaxation and social interaction are important aspects of adolescence, it seems unlikely that spending large numbers of hours per week in unchallenging activities fosters development. Structured voluntary activities may provide more promise for adolescent development than unstructured time, especially if adults give responsibility to adolescents, challenge them, and provide competent guidance in these activities (Larson, 2001; Larson & Wilson, 2004).

Rites of Passage Some societies have elaborate ceremonies that signal the adolescent's move to maturity and achievement of adult status (Kottak, 2002). A **rite of passage** is a ceremony or ritual that marks an individual's transition from one status to another. Most rites of passage focus on the transition to adult status. In many primitive cultures, rites of passage are the avenue through which adolescents gain access to sacred adult practices, to knowledge, and to sexuality. These rites often involve dramatic practices intended to facilitate the adolescent's separation from the immediate family, especially the mother. The transformation is usually characterized by some form of ritual death and rebirth, or by means of contact with the spiritual world. Bonds are forged between the adolescent and the adult instructors through shared rituals, hazards, and secrets to allow the adolescent to enter the adult world. This kind of ritual provides a forceful and discontinuous entry into the adult world at a time when the adolescent is perceived to be ready for the change.

Africa has been the location of many rites of passage for adolescents, especially sub-Saharan Africa. Under the influence of Western culture, many of the rites are

rite of passage A ceremony or ritual that marks an individual's transition from one status to another. Most rites of passage focus on the transition to adult status.

disappearing today, although some vestiges remain. In locations where formal education is not readily available, rites of passage are still prevalent.

Do we have such rites of passage for American adolescents? We certainly do not have universal formal ceremonies that mark the passage from adolescence to adulthood. Certain religious and social groups do have initiation ceremonies that indicate that an advance in maturity has been reached—the Jewish bar mitzvah and bat mitzvah, the Catholic confirmation, and social debuts, for example. School graduation ceremonies come the closest to being culturewide rites of passage in the United States. The high school graduation ceremony has become nearly universal for middle-class adolescents and increasing numbers of adolescents from low-income backgrounds. Nonetheless, high school graduation does not result in universal changes; many high school graduates continue to live with their parents, continue to be economically dependent on them, and continue to be undecided about career and lifestyle matters. Another rite of passage for increasing numbers of American adolescents is sexual intercourse (Halonen & Santrock, 1999). By 19 years of age, four out of five American adolescents have had sexual intercourse.

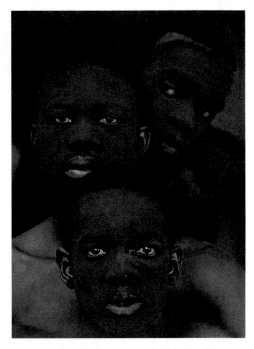

These Congolese Kota boys painted their faces as part of a rite of passage to adulthood. *What rites of passage do American adolescents have?*

Ethnicity

Earlier in this chapter, we explored the identity development of ethnic minority adolescents. Here we will examine other aspects of ethnicity, beginning with difficulty of separating ethnicity and socioeconomic influences. Next we will examine differences and diversity among ethnic groups and discuss aspects of value conflicts, assimilation, and pluralism.

Ethnicity and Socioeconomic Status

Much of the research on ethnic minority adolescents has failed to tease apart the influences of ethnicity and socioeconomic status. Ethnicity and socioeconomic status can interact in ways that exaggerate the influence of ethnicity because ethnic minority individuals are overrepresented in the lower socioeconomic levels of American society. Consequently, researchers too often have given ethnic explanations of adolescent development that were largely due to socioeconomic status rather than ethnicity. For example, decades of research on group differences in self-esteem failed to consider the socioeconomic status of African American and White children and adolescents. When African American adolescents from low-income backgrounds are compared with White adolescents from middle-income backgrounds, the differences are often large but not informative because of the confounding of ethnicity and socioeconomic status (Scott-Jones, 1995).

Although some ethnic minority youth are from middle-income backgrounds, economic advantage does not entirely enable them to escape their ethnic minority status (Díaz, Pelletier, & Provenzo, 2006; Harrison-Hale, McLoyd, & Smedley, 2004; McLoyd, 2005; Spencer, 2006; Spencer & Dornbusch, 1990). Middle-income ethnic minority youth still encounter much of the prejudice, discrimination, and bias associated with being a member of an ethnic minority group. Often characterized as a "model minority" because of their strong achievement orientation and family cohesiveness, Japanese Americans still experience stress associated with ethnic minority status (Sue, 1990). Even though middle-income ethnic minority adolescents have more resources available to counter the destructive influences of prejudice and discrimination, they still cannot completely avoid the pervasive influence of negative stereotypes about ethnic minority groups.

Not all ethnic minority families are poor. However, poverty contributes to the stressful life experiences of many ethnic minority adolescents (Stevens, 2005). Thus, many ethnic minority adolescents experience a double disadvantage: (1) prejudice, discrimination, and bias because of their ethnic minority status; and (2) the stressful effects of poverty.

These adolescents participate in the Brooklyn, New York's, El Puente program, located in a predominantly low-income Latino neighborhood. The El Puente program stresses five areas of youth development: health, education, achievement, personal growth, and social growth.

were entering the ninth grade at a high school with high rates of poverty, were minorities, and came from families that received public assistance. Each day for four years, mentors provided sustained support, guidance, and concrete assistance to their students.

The Quantum program required students to participate in (1) academic-related activities outside school hours, including reading, writing, math, science, and social studies, peer tutoring, and computer skills training; (2) community service projects, including tutoring elementary school students, cleaning up the neighborhood, and volunteering in hospitals, nursing homes, and libraries; and (3) cultural enrichment and personal development activities, including life skills training, and college and job planning. In exchange for their commitment to the program, students were offered financial incentives that encouraged participation, completion, and long-range planning. A stipend of $1.33 was given to students for each hour they participated in these activities. For every 100 hours of education, service, or development activities, students received a bonus of $100. The average cost per participant was $10,600 for the four years, which is one half the cost of one year in prison.

An evaluation of the Quantum project compared the mentored students with a non-mentored control group. Sixty-three percent of the mentored students graduated from high school but only 42 percent of the control group did; 42 percent of the mentored students are currently enrolled in college but only 16 percent of the control group are. Furthermore, control-group students were twice as likely as the mentored students to receive food stamps or welfare, and they had more arrests. Such programs clearly have the potential to overcome the intergenerational transmission of poverty and its negative outcomes.

Another effort to improve the lives of adolescents living in poverty is the El Puente program. Primarily aimed at Latino adolescents living in low-SES areas, El Puente ("the bridge") was founded in New York City in 1982 by Luis Garden Acosta and community activists in response to a 1981 wave of violence in which 48 young people were killed in Brooklyn's Williamsburg neighborhood. Other factors contributing to the establishment of the program were community dissatisfaction with the health, education, and social services youth were receiving (Simons, Finlay, & Yang, 1991). El Puente emphasizes five areas of youth development: health, education, achievement, personal growth, and social growth. The program endeavors to build positive interactions among cultures, races, and economic classes and works for racial healing and human rights.

El Puente is located in a former Roman Catholic church on the south side of Williamsburg in Brooklyn, a neighborhood made up primarily of low-income Latino families, many of which are far below the poverty line. Sixty-five percent of the residents receive some form of public assistance. The neighborhood has the highest school dropout rate for Latinos in New York City and the highest felony rate for adolescents in Brooklyn.

When the youth, aged 11 through 25, first enroll in El Puente, they meet with counselors and develop a four-month plan that includes the programs they are interested in joining, and meeting with peers and adult mentors. At the end of four months, youth and staff develop a plan for continued participation. Twenty-six bilingual classes are offered in such subjects as music, theater, photography, and dance. In addition, a medical and fitness center, GED night school, and mental health and social services centers are also a part of El Puente. The success of El Puente has resulted in the opening of new centers—three in New York, one in San Diego, and two in Massachusetts—replicating the El Puente model.

Review and Reflect • LEARNING GOAL 4

4 Explain how culture influences adolescent development.

Review

• What are some comparisons of adolescents in different cultures? What are rites of passage?

• How does ethnicity influence adolescent development?

Reflect

• What is your ethnicity? Have you ever been stereotyped because of your ethnicity? How diverse is your ethnicity?

---

5 WHAT ARE SOME SOCIOEMOTIONAL PROBLEMS IN ADOLESCENCE?

| Juvenile Delinquency | Depression and Suicide | Successful Prevention/ Intervention Programs |

In chapter 15, we described these adolescent problems: substance abuse, sexually transmitted infections, and eating disorders. Here, we will examine the problems of juvenile delinquency, depression, and suicide.

Juvenile Delinquency

The label **juvenile delinquent** is applied to an adolescent who breaks the law or engages in behavior that is considered illegal. Like other categories of disorders, juvenile delinquency is a broad concept; legal infractions range from littering to murder (Farrington, 2004). Because the adolescent technically becomes a juvenile delinquent only after being judged guilty of a crime by a court of law, official records do not accurately reflect the number of illegal acts juvenile delinquents commit. Estimates of the number of juvenile delinquents in the United States are sketchy, but FBI statistics indicate that at least 2 percent of all youth are involved in juvenile court cases.

U.S. government statistics reveal that 8 of 10 cases of juvenile delinquency involve males (Snyder & Sickmund, 1999). Although males are still far more likely to engage in juvenile delinquency, in the last two decades there has been a greater increase in female delinquency than male delinquency (Snyder & Sickmund, 1999). For both male and female delinquents, rates for property offenses are higher than for other rates of offenses (such as toward persons, drug offenses, and public order offenses). Arrests of adolescent males for delinquency still are much higher than for adolescent females. However, the juvenile delinquency rate of females has increased substantially in the last several decades (Office of Juvenile Justice and Prevention, 1998). This is especially true for adolescent females committing violent crimes.

Delinquency rates among African Americans, other minority groups, and lower-socioeconomic-status youth are especially high in proportion to the overall population of these groups. However, such groups have less influence over the judicial decision-making process in the United States and, therefore, may be judged delinquent more readily than their White, middle-socioeconomic-status counterparts.

One issue in juvenile justice is whether an adolescent who commits a crime should be tried as an adult (Steinberg & Cauffman, 2001). In one study, trying adolescent offenders as adults increased rather than reduced their crime rate (Myers, 1999).

juvenile delinquent An adolescent who breaks the law or engages in behavior that is considered illegal.

Office of Juvenile Justice and
Delinquency Prevention
Justice Information Center

The study evaluated more than 500 violent youth in Pennsylvania, which has adopted a "get tough" policy. Although these 500 offenders had been given harsher punishment than a comparison group retained in juvenile court, they were more likely to be rearrested—and rearrested more quickly—for new offenses once they were returned to the community. This suggests that the price of short-term public safety attained by prosecuting juveniles as adults might increase the number of criminal offenses over the long run.

Antecedents of Delinquency   Predictors of delinquency include conflict with authority, minor covert acts followed by property damage and other more serious acts, minor aggression followed by fighting and violence, identity (negative identity), self-control (low degree), age (early initiation), sex (male), expectations for education (low expectations, little commitment), school grades (low achievement in early grades), peer influence (heavy influence, low resistance), socioeconomic status (low), parental role (lack of monitoring, low support, and ineffective discipline), siblings (having an older sibling who is a delinquent), and neighborhood quality (urban, high crime, high mobility).

In the Pittsburgh Youth Study, a longitudinal study, three developmental pathways to delinquency were found (Loeber & Farrington, 2001; Loeber & others, 1998; Stoutheimer-Loeber & others, 2002):

- *Authority conflict.* Youth on this pathway showed stubbornness prior to age 12, then moved on to defiance and avoidance of authority.
- *Covert.* This pathway included minor covert acts, such as lying, followed by property damage and moderately serious delinquency, then serious delinquency.
- *Overt.* This pathway included minor aggression followed by fighting and violence.

Let's look in more detail at several other factors that are related to delinquency. Erik Erikson (1968) argues that adolescents whose development has restricted their access to acceptable social roles, or made them feel that they cannot measure up to the demands placed on them, may choose a negative identity. Adolescents with a negative identity may find support for their delinquent image among peers, reinforcing the negative identity. For Erikson, delinquency is an attempt to establish an identity, although it is a negative identity.

Although delinquency is less exclusively a lower-SES phenomenon than it was in the past, some characteristics of lower-SES culture can promote delinquency. The norms of many low-SES peer groups and gangs are antisocial, or counterproductive, to the goals and norms of society at large. Getting into and staying out of trouble are prominent features of life for some adolescents in low-income neighborhoods. Adolescents from low-income backgrounds may sense that they can gain attention and status by performing antisocial actions. Being "tough" and "masculine" are high-status traits for low-SES boys, and these traits are often measured by the adolescent's success in performing and getting away with delinquent acts. A community with a high crime rate also lets the adolescent observe many models who engage in criminal activities. These communities may be characterized by poverty, unemployment, and feelings of alienation toward higher-SES individuals. Quality schooling, educational funding, and organized neighborhood activities may be lacking in these communities.

Family support systems are also associated with delinquency (Capaldi & Shortt, 2003; Dodge, Coie, & Lynam, 2006; Quincey & others, 2004). Parents of delinquents are less skilled in discouraging antisocial behavior and in encouraging skilled behavior than are parents of nondelinquents. Parental monitoring of adolescents is especially important in determining whether an adolescent becomes a delinquent (Patterson, DeBaryshe, & Ramsey, 1989). One recent longitudinal study found that the less parents knew about their adolescents' whereabouts, activities, and peers, the more likely they were to engage in delinquent behavior (Laird & others, 2003). Family discord and inconsistent and inappropriate discipline are also associated with delinquency (Capaldi & Shortt, 2003). Another recent study revealed that father absence, assessed when youth were 14 to 17 years of age, was linked with a higher risk of incarceration in males, assessed at 15 to 30 years of age (Harper & McLanahan, 2004). An increasing number of studies have found that siblings can have a strong influence on delinquency (Bank, Burraston, & Snyder, 2004; Conger & Reuter, 1996). In one recent study, high levels of hostile sibling relationships and older sibling delinquency were linked with younger sibling delinquency in both brother pairs and sister pairs (Slomkowski & others, 2001).

Peer relations also play an important role in delinquency (Dodge, Coie, & Lynam, 2006; Lauber, Marshall, & Meyers, 2005). Having delinquent peers increases the risk of becoming delinquent (Henry, Tolan, & Gorman-Smith, 2001). Two recent studies found that the link between associating with delinquent peers and engaging in delinquency held for both boys and girls (Heinze, Toro, & Urberg, 2004; Laird & others, 2005).

Youth Violence
Youth violence is a special concern in the United States today (Barton, 2005; Rappaport & Thomas, 2004; Richards & others, 2004; Robinson & Clay, 2005). In one study, 17 percent of U.S. high school students reported carrying a gun or other weapon during the past 30 days (National Center for Health Statistics, 2000). In this same study, a smaller percentage (7 percent) reported bringing a gun or other weapon onto school property. Not all violence-related behaviors involve weapons. In this study, 44 percent of male and 27 percent of female high school students said they had been involved in one or more fights.

In the late 1990s, a series of school shootings gained national attention. In April 1999, in Littleton, Colorado, two Columbine High School students—18-year-old Eric Harris and 17-year-old Dylan Klebold—shot and killed 12 students and a teacher, wounded 23 others, and then killed themselves. In May 1998, slightly built Kip Kinkel strode into a cafeteria at Thurston High School in Springfield, Oregon, and opened fire on his fellow students, murdering two and injuring many others. Later that day, police went to Kip's home and found his parents lying dead on the floor, also victims of Kip's violence.

In 2001, 15-year-old Charles "Andy" Williams fired shots at Santana High School in Southern California that killed two classmates and injured 13 others. According to students at the school, Andy was a victim of bullying and had joked the previous weekend of his violent plans, but no one took him seriously after he later said he was just kidding.

Is there any way psychologists can predict whether a youth will turn violent? It's a complex task, but researchers have pieced together some clues (Cowley, 1998). Violent youth are overwhelmingly male, and many are driven by feelings of powerlessness. Violence seems to infuse these youth with a sense of power. In one study based on data collected in the National Longitudinal Study of Adolescent Health, secure attachment to parents, living in an intact family, and attending church services with parents were linked with lower incidences of violent behavior in seventh- through twelfth-graders (Franke, 2000).

Small-town shooting sprees attract attention, but youth violence is far greater in poverty-infested areas of inner cities. Urban poverty fosters powerlessness and rage, and many inner-city neighborhoods provide almost daily opportunities to observe violence. Many urban youth who live in poverty also lack adequate parent involvement and supervision (Tolan, 2001).

James Garbarino (1999, 2001) says there is a lot of ignoring that goes on in these kinds of situations. Parents often don't want to acknowledge what might be a very upsetting reality. Harris and Klebold were members of the "Trenchcoat Mafia" clique of Columbine outcasts. The two even had made a video for a school video class the previous fall that depicted them walking down the halls at the school shooting other students. Allegations were made that a year earlier the sheriff's department had been given information that Harris had bragged openly on the Internet that he and Klebold had built four bombs. Kip Kinkel had an obsession with guns and explosives, a history of abusing animals, and a nasty temper when crossed. When police examined his room, they found two pipe bombs, three larger bombs, and bomb-making recipes Kip had downloaded from the Internet. Clearly, some signs were present in these students' lives to suggest that they had some serious problems, but it is still very difficult to

www.mhhe.com/santrockc9

Violence and Gangs
Prevention of Youth Violence
Lost Boys

"Andy" Williams, escorted by police after being arrested for killing two classmates and injuring 13 others at Santana High School. *What factors might contribute to youth murders?*

Youth who kill often have a distorted perspective on what is right and wrong. This distorted perspective can become a self-justifying rationale for violence.

—James Garbarino
Contemporary Developmental Psychologist, Cornell University

predict whether youth like these will act on their anger and sense of powerlessness to commit murder.

Garbarino (1999, 2001) has interviewed a number of youth killers. He concludes that nobody really knows precisely why a tiny minority of youth kill but that it might be a lack of a spiritual center. In the youth killers he interviewed, Garbarino often found a spiritual or emotional emptiness in which the youth sought meaning in the dark side of life. Some interventions can reduce or prevent youth violence (Carnegie Council on Adolescent Development, 1995). Efforts at prevention should include developmentally appropriate schools, supportive families, and youth and community organizations.

At a more specific level, one promising strategy for preventing youth violence is the teaching of conflict management as part of health education in elementary and middle schools. To build resources for such programs, the Carnegie Foundation is supporting a national network of violence prevention practitioners based at the United States Department of Education, linked with a national research center on youth violence at the University of Colorado.

These are some of the Oregon Social Learning Center's recommendations for reducing youth violence (Walker, 1998):

- *Recommit to raising children safely and effectively.* This includes engaging in parenting practices that have been shown to produce healthy, well-adjusted children. Such practices include consistent, fair discipline that is not harsh or severely punitive, careful monitoring and supervision, positive family management techniques, involvement in the child's daily life, daily debriefings about the child's experiences, and teaching problem-solving strategies.
- *Make prevention a reality.* Too often lip service is given to prevention strategies without investing in them at the necessary levels to make them effective.
- *Give more support to schools, which are struggling to educate a population that includes many at-risk children.*
- *Forge effective partnerships among families, schools, social service systems, churches, and other agencies to create the socializing experiences that will provide all youth with the opportunity to develop in positive ways.*

One individual whose goal is to reduce violence in adolescence and help at-risk adolescents cope more effectively with their lives is Rodney Hammond. To read about his work, see the Careers in Child Development profile.

Depression and Suicide

What is the nature of depression in adolescence? What causes an adolescent to commit suicide?

Depression   Depression is more likely to occur in adolescence than in childhood. Also, adolescent girls consistently have higher rates of depression than adolescent boys (Graber, 2004; Nolen-Hocksema, 2004). Among the reasons for this sex difference are that

- Females tend to ruminate in their depressed mood and amplify it.
- Females' self-images, especially their body images, are more negative than males'.
- Females face more discrimination than males do.
- Puberty occurs earlier for girls than for boys, and as a result girls experience a piling up of changes and life experiences in the middle school years, which can increase depression.

Certain family factors place adolescents at risk for developing depression. These include having a depressed parent, emotionally unavailable parents, parents with high marital conflict, and parents with financial problems.

Poor peer relationships also are associated with adolescent depression (Kistner, 2006). Not having a close relationship with a best friend, having less contact with friends, and experiencing peer rejection all increase depressive tendencies in adolescents. Problems in adolescent romantic relationships can also trigger depression (Davila & Steinberg, 2006).

The experience of difficult changes or challenges also is associated with depressive symptoms in adolescence (Compas & Grant, 1993; Lewinsohn & others, 2006), and parental divorce increases depressive symptoms in adolescents. Also, when adolescents go through puberty at the same time as they move from elementary school to middle or junior high school, they report being depressed more than do adolescents who go through puberty after the school transition.

Suicide

Depression is linked to an increase in suicidal ideation and suicide attempts in adolescence (Werth, 2004). A recent study also found that the psychological factors of being overly self-critical and having a sense of hopelessness were also related to suicidal ideation and behavior (Cox, Enns, & Clara, 2004).

Suicidal behavior is rare in childhood but escalates in adolescence (Judge & Billick, 2004). Suicide is the third-leading cause of death in 10- to 19-year-olds today in the United States (National Center for Health Statistics, 2002). Although the incidence of suicide in adolescence has increased in recent years, suicide rates in adolescence have declined in recent years (Gould & others, 2003). In 2000, 1,921 U.S. individuals from 10 to 19 years of age committed suicide (National Center for Health Statistics, 2002).

Although a suicide threat should always be taken seriously, far more adolescents contemplate or attempt it unsuccessfully than actually commit it (Borowsky, Ireland, & Resnick, 2001; Holmes & Holmes, 2005; Mazza, 2005; Seroczynski, Jacquez, & Cole, 2003). In a national study, 19 percent of U.S. high school students said that they had seriously considered or attempted suicide in the last 12 months (National Center for Health Statistics, 2002). Less than 3 percent reported a suicide attempt that resulted in an injury, poisoning, or drug overdose that had been treated by a doctor. Females were more likely to attempt suicide than males, but males were more likely to succeed in committing suicide. Males use more lethal means, such as guns, in their suicide attempts, whereas adolescent females are more likely to cut their wrists or take an overdose of sleeping pills—methods less likely to result in death. A recent study indicated that during adolescence suicide ideation peaked at age 15 (Rueter & Kwon, 2005). In this study, adolescents who thought about committing suicide often had parents who had engaged in suicide ideation. Another recent study also revealed that suicidal behavior in their families placed adolescents at risk for engaging in suicidal ideation and attempts themselves (Cerel & Roberts, 2005). A recent study revealed that for both male and female adolescents, illegal drug use was associated with an increase in suicidal ideation and suicide attempts (Hallfors & others, 2004).

Some researchers argue that homosexual adolescents may be vulnerable to suicide. For example, in one study of 12,000 adolescents, approximately 15 percent of gay and lesbian youth said that they had attempted suicide compared with 7 percent

CAREERS in CHILD DEVELOPMENT

Rodney Hammond
Health Psychologist

Rodney Hammond described his college experiences, "When I started as an undergraduate at the University of Illinois, Champaign-Urbana, I hadn't decided on my major. But to help finance my education, I took a part-time job in a child development research program sponsored by the psychology department. There, I observed inner-city children in settings designed to enhance their learning. I saw first-hand the contribution psychology can make, and I knew I wanted to be a psychologist" (American Psychological Association, 2003, p. 26).

Rodney Hammond went on to obtain a doctorate in school and community college with a focus on children's development. For a number of years, he trained clinical psychologists at Wright State University in Ohio and directed a program to reduce violence in ethnic minority youth. There, he and his associates taught at-risk youth how to use social skills to effectively manage conflict and to recognize situations that could lead to violence. Today, Hammond is Director of Violence Prevention at the Centers for Disease Control and Prevention in Atlanta. Hammond says that if you are interested in people and problem solving, psychology is a wonderful way to put these together. (Source: American Psychological Association, 2003, pp. 26–27)

Rodney Hammond, counseling an adolescent girl about the risks of adolescence and how to effectively cope with them.

Depression is more likely to occur in adolescence than in childhood and female adolescents are more likely than male adolescents to be depressed.

Adolescent Depression
Suicide

of heterosexual youth (Russell & Joyner, 2001). However, in another study, gay and lesbian adolescents were only slightly more likely than heterosexual adolescents to attempt suicide (Savin-Williams, 2001). According to a leading researcher on gay youth, Richard Savin-Williams (2001), the earlier studies likely exaggerated the suicide rates for gay adolescents because they surveyed only the most disturbed youth who were attending support groups or hanging out at shelters for gay youth.

Distal, or earlier, experiences often are involved in suicide attempts as well (Gould, 2003). The adolescent might have a long-standing history of family instability and unhappiness. Just as a lack of affection and emotional support, high control, and pressure for achievement by parents during childhood are related to adolescent depression, such combinations of family experiences are also likely to show up as distal factors in suicide attempts. The adolescent might also lack supportive friendships.

Just as genetic factors are associated with depression, they are also associated with suicide. The closer a person's genetic relationship to someone who has committed suicide, the more likely that person is to also commit suicide. Another factor is previous attempts, with the risk of actual suicide increasing with each prior attempt.

What is the psychological profile of the suicidal adolescent? Suicidal adolescents often have depressive symptoms (American Academy of Pediatrics, 2000). Although not all depressed adolescents are suicidal, depression is the most frequently cited factor associated with adolescent suicide. A sense of hopelessness, low self-esteem, and high self-blame are also associated with adolescent suicide (Harter & Marold, 1992; Seroczynski, Jacquez, & Cole, 2003).

In some instances, suicides in adolescence occur in clusters. That is, when one adolescent commits suicide, other adolescents who find out about this also commit suicide. Such "copycat" suicides raise the issue of whether or not suicides should be reported in the media; a news report might plant the idea of committing suicide in other adolescents' minds.

A recent concern related to adolescent suicide is a link between the use of antidepressants and suicidal thoughts. In October 2004, the Federal Drug Administration issued a report based on its review of a number of research studies; the report concluded that 2 to 3 percent of adolescents taking antidepressants experience an increase in suicidal thoughts. It is estimated that antidepressants are prescribed for approximately one million U.S. children and adolescents.

Successful Prevention/Intervention Programs

We have described some of the major adolescent problems in this chapter and chapters 15 and 16: substance abuse; juvenile delinquency; school-related problems, such as dropping out of school; adolescent pregnancy and sexually transmitted infections; depression; and suicide.

The most at-risk adolescents have more than one problem. Researchers are increasingly finding that problem behaviors in adolescence are interrelated (Tubman & Windle, 1995). For example, heavy substance abuse is related to early sexual activity, lower grades, dropping out of school, and delinquency. Early initiation of sexual activity is associated with the use of cigarettes and alcohol, the use of marijuana and other illicit drugs, lower grades, dropping out of school, and delinquency. Delinquency is related to early sexual activity, early pregnancy, substance abuse, and dropping out of school. As many as 10 percent of all adolescents in the United States have serious multiple-problem behaviors (for example, adolescents who have dropped out of school, are behind in their grade level, are users of heavy drugs, regularly use cigarettes and marijuana, and are sexually active but do not use contraception). Many, but not all, of these very high-risk youth "do it all." Another 15 percent of adolescents participate in many of these behaviors but with slightly lower frequency and less deleterious consequences. These high-risk youth often engage in two- or three-problem behaviors (Dryfoos, 1990, 1997).

In addition to understanding that many adolescents engage in multiple-problem behaviors, it also is important to develop programs that reduce adolescent problems

(Compas, 2004). In a review of the programs that have been successful in preventing or reducing adolescent problems, adolescence researcher Joy Dryfoos (1990) described the common components of these successful programs:

1. *Intensive individualized attention.* In successful programs, high-risk children are attached to a responsible adult, who gives the child attention and deals with the child's specific needs. This theme occurs in a number of programs. In a successful substance-abuse program, a student assistance counselor is available full-time for individual counseling and referral for treatment.

2. *Community-wide multiagency collaborative approaches.* The basic philosophy of community-wide programs is that a number of different programs and services have to be in place. In one successful substance-abuse program, a community wide health promotion campaign has been implemented that uses local media and community education, in concert with a substance-abuse curriculum in the schools.

3. *Early identification and intervention.* Reaching children and their families before children develop problems, or at the beginning of their problems, is a successful strategy (Pianta, 2005). One preschool program serves as an excellent model for the prevention of delinquency, pregnancy, substance abuse, and dropping out of school. Operated by the High/Scope Foundation in Ypsilanti, Michigan, the Perry Preschool has had a long-term positive impact on its students. This enrichment program, directed by David Weikart, serves disadvantaged African American children. They attend a high-quality two-year preschool program and receive weekly home visits from program personnel. Based on official police records, by age 19, individuals who had attended the Perry Preschool program were less likely to have been arrested and reported fewer adult offenses than a control group. The Perry Preschool students also were less likely to drop out of school, and teachers rated their social behavior as more competent than that of a control group who had not received the enriched preschool experience.

One current program that seeks to prevent adolescent problems is called Fast Track (Dodge, 2001; The Conduct Problems Prevention Research Group, 2002). High-risk children who show conduct problems at home and at kindergarten were identified. Then, during the elementary school years, the at-risk children and their families are given support and training in parenting, problem-solving and coping skills, peer relations, classroom atmosphere and curriculum, academic achievement, and home-school relations. Ten project interventionists work with the children, their families, and schools to increase the protective factors and decrease the risk factors in these areas. Thus far, results show that the intervention effectively improved parenting practices and children's problem-solving and coping skills, peer relations, reading achievement, and problem behavior at home and school during the elementary school years compared with a control of high-risk children who did not experience the intervention.

Review and Reflect • LEARNING GOAL 5

5 **Identify adolescent problems in socioemotional development and strategies for helping adolescents with problems.**

Review
- What is juvenile delinquency? What causes it?
- What is the nature of depression and suicide in adolescence?
- How are adolescent problems interrelated? What are some components of successful prevention/intervention programs for adolescents?

Reflect
- Are the consequences of choosing a course of risk taking in adolescence today more serious than in the past? If so, why?

E-LEARNING TOOLS

Connect to **www.mhhe.com/santrockc9** to research the answers to complete these exercises. In addition, you'll find a number of other resources and valuable study tools for chapter 17, "Socioemotional Development in Adolescence," on the website.

Taking It to the Net

1. Marissa is 12 years old, and she has already begun puberty. She is much taller than her classmates, and she has well-developed breasts and other secondary sex characteristics. Marissa is embarrassed about the sudden physical changes in her body, and she feels very insecure. Moreover, Marissa, who has always done very well in school, is learning very quickly that the "brains" in school are not very popular. What factors may be contributing to Marissa's struggles? What can family members and teachers do to support adolescent girls during the early stages of development?

2. Shawn just learned that a classmate of his, Glenn, was hospitalized for depression and suicidality. Shawn was very surprised when he heard this; he saw Glenn as very popular and never would have guessed that he was depressed. How common is it for adolescents to be depressed? How commonly does adolescent suicide occur? How can friends, family members, and teachers determine whether someone is depressed and/or suicidal? What can they do to support the depressed/suicidal adolescent?

3. Shelley's mother is Euro-American, and her father is Japanese. Many people who do not know her have a hard time identifying her ethnic background, and she is constantly asked, "What are you?" There are a couple of other students of color at her school, although few of them openly identify as biracial or multiracial. Shelley is now in the process of figuring out who she is. What are some of the challenges biracial or multiracial adolescents face? How might the process of identity development progress?

Health and Well-Being, Parenting, and Education Exercises

Build your decision-making skills by trying your hand at the health and well-being, parenting, and education exercises.

Video Clips

The Online Learning Center includes the following videos for this chapter:

1. *Relationships with Parents at Age 16—1982*
   In this clip, three adolescent friends describe their relationships with their parents. They describe "normal" fights and they discuss differences between their relationships with their mothers versus fathers.

2. *Ethnic and Racial Identity in Adolescence—2259*
   Two African American girls discuss candidly their feelings about being Black. One describes being Black as being a mixture of many cultures. The other says it's hard to be African American because there is no distinct culture for Blacks.

3. *Talking about Ethnic Identity in Adolescence—1994*
   They view the diversity among them, as well as among their peers, very positively. They admit that they are different from one another because of their ethnic backgrounds but they each benefit from one another because of these differences.

A

A̅B̅ error The Piagetian object-permanence concept in which an infant progressing into substage 4 makes frequent mistakes, selecting the familiar hiding place (A) rather than the new hiding place (B̅). 214

accommodation Occurs when children adjust their knowledge to fit new information and experience. 46

accommodation Piagetian concept of adjusting schemes to fit new information and experiences. 209

active (niche-picking) genotype-environment correlations Correlations that exist when children seek out environments they find compatible and stimulating. 98

adolescence The developmental period of transition from childhood to early adulthood, entered at approximately 10 to 12 years of age and ending at 18 to 22 years of age. 19

adolescent egocentrism The heightened self-consciousness of adolescents that is reflected in their belief that others are as interested in them as they are in themselves, and in their sense of personal uniqueness and invulnerability. 541

adoption study A study in which investigators seek to discover whether, in behavior and psychological characteristics, adopted children are more like their adoptive parents, who provided a home environment, or more like their biological parents, who contributed their heredity. Another form of the adoption study is to compare adoptive and biological siblings. 98

affordances Opportunities for interaction offered by objects that fit within our capabilities to perform activities. 191

afterbirth The third stage of birth, when the placenta, umbilical cord, and other membranes are detached and expelled. 141

AIDS A sexually transmitted disease that is caused by a virus, the human immunodeficiency virus (HIV), which destroys the body's immune system. 514

altruism Unselfish interest in helping another person. 467

amnion The life-support system that is a thin bag or envelope that contains a clear fluid in which the developing embryo floats. 110

analgesia Drugs used to alleviate pain, such as tranquilizers, barbiturates, and narcotics. 144

androgens A main class of sex hormones that primarily promote the development of male genitals and secondary sex characteristics. Testosterone is an important androgen. 344

androgyny The presence of a high degree of masculine and feminine characteristics in the same individual. 473

anesthesia Drugs used in late first-stage labor and during expulsion of the baby to block sensation in an area of the body or to block consciousness. 144

anger cry A cry similar to the basic cry, with more excess air forced through the vocal chords. 244

animism The belief that inanimate objects have "lifelike" qualities and are capable of action. 304

anorexia nervosa An eating disorder that involves the relentless pursuit of thinness through starvation. 525

anoxia The insufficient availability of oxygen to the fetus/newborn. 141

Apgar Scale A widely used method to assess the health of newborns at one and five minutes after birth. The Apgar Scale evaluates infants' heart rate, respiratory effort, muscle tone, body color, and reflex irritability. 152

aphasia A language disorder resulting from brain damage that involves a loss of the ability to use words. 230

articulation disorders Problems in pronouncing sounds correctly. 401

Asperger syndrome A relatively mild autism spectrum disorder in which the child has relatively good verbal language, milder nonverbal language problems, and a restricted range of interests and relationships. 403

assimilation Occurs when children incorporate new information into their existing knowledge. 46

assimilation Piagetian concept of the incorporation of new information into existing knowledge (schemes). 209

assimilation The absorption of ethnic minority groups into the dominant group, which often involves the loss of some or virtually all of the behavior and values of the ethnic minority group. 591

assistive technology Various services and devices to help children with disabilities function in their environment. 405

associative play Play that involves social interaction with little or no organization. 367

attachment A close emotional bond between two people. 253

attention The focusing of mental resources. 216

attention deficit hyperactivity disorder (ADHD) A disability in which children consistently show one or more of the following characteristics: (1) inattention, (2) hyperactivity, and (3) impulsivity. 399

authoritarian parenting A restrictive punitive style in which parents exhort the child to follow their directions and to respect work and effort. The authoritarian parent places firm limits and controls on the child and allows little verbal exchange. Authoritarian parenting is associated with children's social incompetence. 351

authoritative parenting A parenting style in which parents encourage their children to be independent but still place limits and controls on their actions. Extensive verbal give-and-take is allowed, and parents are warm and nurturant toward the child. Authoritative parenting is associated with children's social competence. 352

autism spectrum disorders (ASD) Also called pervasive developmental disorders, they range from the severe disorder labeled autistic disorder to the milder disorder called Asperger syndrome. Children with these disorders are characterized by problems in social interaction, verbal and nonverbal communication, and repetitive behaviors. 403

autistic disorder A severe autism spectrum disorder that has its onset in the first three years of life and includes deficiencies in social relationships, abnormalities in communication, and restricted, repetitive, and stereotyped patterns of behavior. 403

autonomous morality The second stage of moral development in Piaget's theory, displayed by older children (about 10 years of age and older). The child becomes aware that rules and laws are created by people and that, in judging an action, one should consider the actor's intentions as well as the consequences. 342

autonomy versus shame and doubt Erikson's second stage, occurring from approximately 1 to 3 years of age, in which the child either develops self-determination and pride or is overcontrolled and experiences shame and doubt. 252

average children Children who receive an average number of both positive and negative nominations from their peers. 481

B

basal metabolism rate (BMR) The minimum amount of energy a person uses in a resting state. 286

basic cry A rhythmic pattern usually consisting of a cry, a briefer silence, a shorter inspiratory whistle that is higher pitched than the main cry, and then a brief rest before the next cry. 244

basic-skills-and-phonetics approach An approach to reading instruction that stresses phonetics and basic rules for translating symbols into sounds. Early reading instruction should involve simplified materials. 446

Bayley Scales of Infant Development Scales developed by Nancy Bayley, which are widely used in the assessment of infant development. The current version has three components: a mental scale, a motor scale, and an infant behavior profile. 219

behavior genetics The field that seeks to discover the influence of heredity and environment on individual differences in human traits and development. 97

biological processes Changes in an individual's body. 18

blastocyst The inner layer of cells that develops during the germinal period. These cells later develop into the embryo. 109

bonding A close connection, especially a physical bond between parents and their newborn in the period shortly after birth. 157

Brazelton Neonatal Behavioral Assessment Scale (NBAS) A test performed within 24 to 36 hours after birth to assess newborns' neurological development, reflexes, and reactions to people. 153

breech position The baby's position in the uterus that causes the buttocks to be the first part to emerge from the vagina. 145

Broca's area An area of the brain's left frontal lobe that directs the muscle movements involved in speech production. 230

bulimia nervosa An eating disorder in which the individual consistently follows a binge-and-purge eating pattern. 525

C

care perspective The moral perspective that views people in terms of their connectedness with others and emphasizes interpersonal communication, relationships with others, and concern for others. Carol Gilligan's perspective is a care perspective. 466

career self-concept theory Super's theory that individuals' self-concepts play central roles in their career choices. 558

case study An in-depth look at a single individual. 59

centration The focusing of attention on one characteristic to the exclusion of all others. 304

cephalocaudal pattern The sequence in which the greatest growth occurs at the top—the head—with physical growth in size, weight, and feature differentiation gradually working from top to bottom. 169

cerebral palsy A disorder that involves a lack of muscular coordination, shaking, and unclear speech. 403

cesarean delivery The baby is removed from the mother's uterus through an incision made in her abdomen. This also is sometimes referred to as cesarean section. 145

character education A direct education approach to moral education that involves teaching students a basic moral literacy to prevent them from engaging in immoral behavior and doing harm to themselves and others. 548

child-centered kindergarten Education that involves the whole child by considering both the child's physical, cognitive, and social de- velopment and the child's needs, interests, and learning styles. 319

child-directed speech Language spoken in a higher pitch than normal with simple words and sentences. 232

chromosomes Threadlike structures that come in 23 pairs, one member of each pair coming from each parent. Chromosomes contain the genetic substance DNA. 84

cliques Small groups that range from 2 to about 12 individuals, averaging about 5 to 6 individuals. Members usually are the same age, same sex, and often engage in similar activities. 582

cognitive constructivist approach An approach that emphasizes the child's active, cognitive construction of knowledge and understanding; Piaget's theory is an example of this approach. 484

cognitive developmental theory of gender The theory that children's gender typing occurs after they think of themselves as boys and girls. Once they consistently conceive of themselves as male or female, children prefer activities, objects, and attitudes that are consistent with this label. 349

cognitive moral education An approach to moral education based on the belief that students should develop such values as democracy and justice as their moral reasoning develops; Kohlberg's theory has been the basis of a number of cognitive moral education programs. 548

cognitive processes Changes in an individual's thought, intelligence, and language. 19

commitment Marcia's term for the part of identity development in which adolescents show a personal investment in what they are going to do. 574

concepts Categories that group objects, events, and characteristics on the basis of common properties. 218

connectedness According to Cooper and her colleagues, connectedness consists of two dimensions: mutuality (sensitivity to and respect for others' views) and permeability (openness to others' views). 575

conservation The concept that certain physical characteristics of an object stay the same even though their appearance has been altered. 304

context The settings, influenced by historical, economic, social, and cultural factors, in which development occurs. 10

continuity-discontinuity issue The issue regarding whether development involves gradual, cumulative change (continuity) or distinct stages (discontinuity). 21

controversial children Children who are frequently nominated both as someone's best friend and as being disliked. 481

conventional reasoning The second, or intermediate, level in Kohlberg's theory of moral development. Internalization is intermediate. Individuals abide by certain standards (internal), but they are the standards of others (external), such as parents or the laws of society. 463

convergent thinking Thinking that produces one correct answer and is characteristic of the kind of thinking tested by standardized intelligence tests. 422

cooperative play Play that involves social interaction in a group with a sense of group identity and organized activity. 367

coordination of secondary circular reactions Piaget's fourth sensorimotor substage, which develops between 8 and 12 months of age. In this substage, several significant changes take place involving the coordination of schemes and intentionality. 212

correlation coefficient A number based on a statistical analysis that is used to describe the degree of association between two variables. 60

correlational research Research in which the goal is to describe the strength of the relation between two or more events or characteristics. 60

creativity The ability to think in novel and unusual ways and to come up with unique solutions to problems. 422

crisis Marcia's term for a period of identity development during which the adolescent is choosing from among meaningful alternatives. 574

critical thinking Thinking that involves grasping the deeper meaning of ideas, keeping an open mind about different approaches and perspectives, and deciding for oneself what to believe or do. 421

cross-cultural studies Comparisons of one culture with one or more other cultures. These provide information about the degree to which children's development is similar, or universal, across cultures, and to the degree to which it is culture-specific. 10

cross-sectional approach A research strategy in which individuals of different ages are compared at one time. 62

crowds A larger group structure than cliques, crowds are usually formed based on reputa-

tion and members may or may not spend much time together. 582

cultural-familial retardation Retardation that is characterized by no evidence of organic brain damage, but the individual's IQ is between 50 and 70. 437

culture The behavior patterns, beliefs, and all other products of a group that are passed on from generation to generation. 10

culture-fair tests Intelligence tests that are intended to not be culturally biased. 434

D

deferred imitation Imitation that occurs after a time delay of hours or days. 217

Denver Developmental Screening Test A test used to diagnose developmental delay in children from birth to 6 years of age; includes separate assessments of gross and fine motor skills, language, and personal-social ability. 281

descriptive research Research that aims to observe and record behavior. 60

design stage Kellogg's term for 3- to 4-year-olds' drawings that mix two basic shapes into more complex designs. 282

development The pattern of movement or change that begins at conception and continues through the human life span. 7

developmental career choice theory Ginzberg's theory that children and adolescents go through three career choice stages—fantasy, tentative, and realistic. 557

developmental quotient (DQ) An overall developmental score that combines subscores in motor, language, adaptive, and personal-social domains in the Gesell assessment of infants. 219

developmentally appropriate practice Education that focuses on the typical developmental patterns of children (age appropriateness) and the uniqueness of each child (individual appropriateness). Such practice contrasts with *developmentally inappropriate practice*, which ignores the concrete, hands-on approach to learning. Direct teaching largely through abstract paper-and-pencil activities presented to large groups of young children is believed to be developmentally inappropriate. 319

difficult child A child who tends to react negatively and cry frequently, who engages in irregular daily routines, and who is slow to accept change. 248

direct instruction approach A teacher-centered approach characterized by teacher

direction and control, mastery of academic skills, high expectations for students, and maximum time spent on learning tasks. 484

dishabituation The recovery of a habituated response after a change in stimulation. 193

divergent thinking Thinking that produces many answers to the same question and is characteristic of creativity. 422

DNA A complex molecule that contains genetic information. 84

doula A professional trained in childbirth who provides continuous physical, emotional, and educational support to the mother before, during, and just after childbirth. 143

Down syndrome A chromosomally transmitted form of mental retardation, caused by the presence of an extra copy of chromosome 21. 88

dynamic systems theory A theory, proposed by Esther Thelen, that seeks to explain how motor behaviors are assembled for perceiving and acting. 183

dyscalculia Also known as developmental arithmetic disorder, this learning disability involves difficulty in math computation. 398

dyslexia A category of learning disabilities involving a severe impairment in the ability to read and spell. 398

E

early childhood The developmental period that extends from the end of infancy to about 5 to 6 years, sometimes called the preschool years. 19

early-later experience issue The issue of the degree to which early experiences (especially infancy) or later experiences are the key determinants of the child's development. 22

easy child A child who is generally in a positive mood, who quickly establishes regular routines in infancy, and who adapts easily to new experiences. 248

eclectic theoretical orientation An orientation that does follow any one theoretical approach, but rather, selects from each theory whatever is considered the best in it. 56

ecological theory Bronfenbrenner's environmental systems theory that focuses on five environmental systems: microsystem, mesosystem, exosystem, macrosystem, and chronosystem. 52

ecological view The view, proposed by the Gibsons, that people directly perceive information in the world around them. Perception brings people in contact with the environment in order to interact with it and adapt to it. 191

ectoderm The outermost layer of cells, which becomes the nervous system, sensory receptors (ears, nose, and eyes, for example), and skin parts (hair and nails, for example). 109

educationally blind Unable to use one's vision in learning. It implies a need to use hearing and touch to learn. 402

egocentrism The inability to distinguish between one's own perspective and someone else's (salient feature of the first substage of preoperational thought). 303

elaboration Engaging in more extensive processing of information. 420

embryonic period The period of prenatal development that occurs two to eight weeks after conception. During the embryonic period, the rate of cell differentiation intensifies, support systems for the cells form, and organs appear. 109

emotion Feeling, or affect, that occurs when people are in a state or interaction important to them, especially to their well-being. Can be positive, such as joy, or negative, such as anger. 243

emotional and behavioral disorders These consist of serious, persistent problems that involve relationships, aggression, depression, fears associated with personal and school matters, as well as other inappropriate socioemotional characteristics. 403

emotional intelligence The ability to perceive and express emotions accurately and adaptively, to understand emotion and emotional knowledge, to use feelings to facilitate thought, and to manage emotions in oneself and others. 430

emotional regulation Effectively managing arousal to adapt and reach a goal. 247

endoderm The inner layer of cells, which develops into digestive and respiratory systems. 109

epigenetic view Emphasizes that development is the result of an ongoing, bidirectional interchange between heredity and environment. 100

Erikson's theory Includes eight stages of human development. Each stage consists of a unique developmental task that confronts individuals with a crisis that must be faced. 44

estrogens A main class of sex hormones that primarily influence the development of female sexual characteristics and help regulate the menstrual cycle. Estradiol is an important estrogen. 344

ethnic gloss Using an ethnic label such as African American or Latino is a superficial way that portrays an ethnic group as being more homogeneous than it really is. 68

ethnic identity A sense of membership in an ethnic group, based on shared language, religion, customs, values, history, and race. 10

ethnic identity An enduring, basic aspect of the self that includes a sense of membership in an ethnic group and the attitudes and feelings related to that membership. 575

ethnicity A characteristic based on cultural heritage, nationality, race, religion, and language. 10

ethological theory of development Stresses that behavior is strongly influenced by biology, is tied to evolution, and is characterized by critical or sensitive periods. 50

evocative genotype-environment correlations Correlations that exist when the child's genotype elicits certain types of physical and social environments. 98

evolutionary psychology Emphasizes the importance of adaptation, reproduction, and "survival of the fittest" in shaping behavior. 82

expanding Restating, in a linguistically sophisticated form, what a child has said. 233

experiment A carefully regulated procedure in which one or more of the factors believed to influence the behavior being studied is manipulated and all other factors are held constant. 61

extrinsic motivation External incentives such as rewards and punishments. 440

F

factor analysis A statistical procedure that correlates test scores to identify underlying clusters, or factors. 428

fertilization A stage in reproduction whereby an egg and a sperm fuse to create a single cell, called a zygote. 86

fetal alcohol syndrome (FAS) A cluster of abnormalities that appears in the offspring of mothers who drink alcohol heavily during pregnancy. 124

fetal period The prenatal period of development that begins two months after conception and lasts for seven months, on the average. 111

fine motor skills Motor skills that involve more finely tuned movements, such as finger dexterity. 189

first habits and primary circular reactions Piaget's second sensorimotor substage, which develops between 1 and 4 months of age. In this substage, infants' reflexes evolve into adaptive schemes that are more refined and coordinated. 210

fluency disorders Various disorders that involve what is commonly called "stuttering." 401

fragile X syndrome A genetic disorder involving an abnormality in the X chromosome, which becomes constricted and often breaks. 89

functional amblyopia An eye defect that results from not using one eye enough to avoid the discomfort of double vision produced by imbalanced eye muscles: "lazy eye." 278

fuzzy trace theory Memory is best understood by considering verbatim memory and gist. 419

G

games Activities engaged in for pleasure, and include rules. 368

gender The psychological and sociocultural dimension of being female or male. 12

gender The social and psychological dimension of being female or male. 344

gender role A set of expectations that prescribe how females or males should think, act, or feel. 344

gender-role transcendence The view that people should be evaluated as persons, not in terms of femininity, masculinity, or androgyny. 474

gender schema theory The theory that gender typing emerges as children gradually develop gender schemas of what is gender-appropriate and gender-inappropriate in their culture. 349

gender stereotypes Broad categories that reflect our impressions and beliefs about females and males. 468

gender typing The process by which children acquire the thoughts, feelings, and behaviors that are considered appropriate for their gender in their culture. 344

genes Units of hereditary information composed of DNA. Genes direct cells to reproduce themselves and manufacture the proteins that maintain life. 84

genetic epistemology The study of how children's knowledge changes over the course of their development. 17

genotype A person's genetic heritage; the actual genetic material. 86

germinal period The period of prenatal development that takes place in the first two weeks after conception. It includes the creation of the zygote, continued cell division, and the attachment of the zygote to the uterine wall. 109

gifted Having above-average intelligence, usually an IQ of 130 or higher, and a superior talent for something. 437

goodness of fit The match between a child's temperament and the environmental demands the child must cope with. 250

grasping reflex A neonatal reflex that occurs when something touches the infant's palms. The infant responds by grasping tightly. 184

gross motor skills Motor skills that involve large-muscle activities, such as walking. 185

growth hormone deficiency The absence or deficiency of growth hormone produced by the pituitary gland to stimulate the body to grow. 276

H

habituation Decreased responsiveness to a stimulus after repeated presentations of the stimulus. 192

helpless orientation An orientation in which one seems trapped by the experience of difficulty and attributes one's difficulty to a lack of ability. 441

heritability The fraction of variance in IQ in a population that is attributed to genetics. 432

heteronomous morality The first stage of moral development in Piaget's theory, occurring at 4 to 7 years of age. Justice and rules are conceived of as unchangeable properties of the world, removed from the control of people. 342

hidden curriculum Dewey's concept that every school has a pervasive moral atmosphere, even if it doesn't have a program of moral education. 548

hormones Powerful chemicals secreted by the endocrine glands and carried through the body by the bloodstream. 501

hypothesis Specific assumption and prediction that can be tested to determine accuracy. 40

hypothetical–deductive reasoning Piaget's formal operational concept that adolescents have the cognitive ability to develop hypotheses, or best guesses, about ways to solve problems, such as an algebraic equation. 539

I

identity achievement Marcia's term for adolescents who have undergone a crisis and have made a commitment. 574

identity diffusion Marcia's term for adolescents who have not yet experienced a crisis (explored meaningful alternatives) or made any commitments. 574

identity foreclosure Marcia's term for adolescents who have made a commitment but have not experienced a crisis. 574

identity moratorium Marcia's term for adolescents who are in the midst of a crisis, but their commitments are either absent or vaguely defined. 574

imaginary audience Adolescents' heightened self-consciousness, reflected in their belief that others are as interested in them as they themselves are; attention-getting behavior motivated by a desire to be noticed, visible, and "on stage." 541

immanent justice Piaget's concept that if a rule is broken, punishment will be meted out immediately. 342

inclusion Educating a child with special education needs full-time in the regular classroom. 405

individuality According to Cooper and her colleagues, individuality consists of two dimensions: self-assertion (the ability to have and communicate a point of view) and separateness (the use of communication patterns to express how one is different from others). 575

individualized education plan (IEP) A written statement that spells out a program tailored to a child with a disability. The plan should be (1) related to the child's learning capacity, (2) specially constructed to meet the child's individual needs and not merely a copy of what is offered to other children, and (3) designed to provide educational benefits. 405

Individuals with Disabilities Education Act (IDEA) The IDEA spells out broad mandates for services to all children with disabilities (IDEA is a renaming of Public Law 94-142); these include evaluation and eligibility determination, appropriate education and the individualized education plan (IEP), and the least restrictive environment (LRE). 404

indulgent parenting A style of parenting in which parents are highly involved with their children but place few demands or controls on them. Indulgent parenting is associated with children's social incompetence, especially a lack of self-control. 352

Industry versus inferiority Erikson's fourth developmental stage, occurring during middle and late childhood, in which children attempt to master many skills and either develop a sense of competence or incompetence. 461

infancy The developmental period that extends from birth to 18 to 24 months. 19

infinite generativity The ability to produce an endless number of meaningful sentences using a finite set of words and rules. 224

information-processing theory A theory that emphasizes that individuals manipulate information, monitor it, and strategize about it. The processes of memory and thinking are central. 48

initiative versus guilt In this third of Erikson's eight stages, which occurs in early childhood, young children enthusiastically begin new activities but feel guilt when their effort results in failure or criticism. 339

innate goodness view The idea, presented by Swiss-born French philosopher Jean-Jacques Rousseau, that children are inherently good. 15

insecure avoidant babies Babies who show insecurity by avoiding the mother. 255

insecure disorganized babies Babies who show insecurity by being disorganized and disoriented. 256

insecure resistant babies Babies who might cling to the caregiver, then resist her by fighting against the closeness, perhaps by kicking or pushing away. 255

instructional technology Various types of hardware and software, combined with innovative teaching methods, to accommodate students' learning needs in the classroom. 405

intelligence Problem-solving skills and the ability to learn from and adapt to the experiences of everyday life. 425

intelligence quotient (IQ) A person's mental age divided by chronological age, multiplied by 100. 426

intermodal perception The ability to relate and integrate information about two or more sensory modalities, such as vision and hearing. 199

internalization The developmental change from behavior that is externally controlled to behavior controlled by internal standards and principles. 463

internalization of schemes Piaget's sixth and final sensorimotor substage, which develops between 18 and 24 months of age. In this substage, the infant's mental functioning shifts from a purely sensorimotor plane to a symbolic plane, and the infant develops the ability to use primitive symbols. 212

intrinsic motivation Internal factors such as self-determination, curiosity, challenge, and effort. 440

intuitive thought substage Piaget's second substage of preoperational thought, in which children begin to use primitive reasoning and want to know the answers to all sorts of questions (between 4 and 7 years of age). 304

involution The process by which the uterus returns to its prepregnant size. 155

J

justice perspective A moral perspective that focuses on the rights of the individual; individuals independently make moral decisions. Kohlberg's theory is a justice perspective. 466

juvenile delinquent An adolescent who breaks the law or engages in behavior that is considered illegal. 593

K

kangaroo care A way of holding an infant so that there is skin-to-skin contact. 152

Klinefelter syndrome A chromosomal disorder in which males have an extra X chromosome, making them XXY instead of XY. 89

kwashiorkor A condition caused by a deficiency in protein in which the child's abdomen and feet become swollen with water. 179

L

labeling Identifying the names of objects. 233

laboratory A controlled setting in which many of the complex factors of the "real world" are removed. 57

language A form of communication, whether spoken, written, or signed, that is based on a system of symbols. 224

language acquisition device (LAD) Chomsky's term that describes a biological endowment that enables the child to detect the features and rules of language, including phonology, syntax, and semantics. 230

lateralization Specialization of function in one hemisphere of the cerebral cortex or the other. 173

learning disability Includes three components: (1) a minimum IQ level, (2) a significant difficulty in a school-related area (especially reading or mathematics), and (3) exclusion of only severe emotional disorders, second-language background, sensory disabilities, and/or specific neurological deficits. 397

least restrictive environment (LRE) The concept that a child with a disability must be educated in a setting that is as similar as possible to the one in which children who do not have a disability are educated. 405

longitudinal approach A research strategy in which the same individuals are studied over a period of time, usually several years or more. 62

long-term memory A relatively permanent type of memory that holds huge amounts of information for a long period of time. 419

low birth weight infant Weighs less than 5½ pounds at birth. 148

low vision Visual acuity between 20/70 and 20/2000. 402

M

manual approaches Educational approaches to help hearing-impaired children; they include sign language and finger spelling. 402

marasmus A wasting away of body tissues in the infant's first year, caused by severe protein-calorie deficiency. 179

mastery orientation An orientation in which one is task-oriented and, instead of focusing on one's ability, is concerned with learning strategies. 441

meiosis A specialized form of cell division that occurs to form eggs and sperm (or gametes). 86

memory A central feature of cognitive development, pertaining to all situations in which an individual retains information over time. 217

menarche A girl's first menstrual period. 502

mental age (MA) Binet's measure of an individual's level of mental development, compared with that of others. 426

mental retardation A condition of limited mental ability in which an individual has a low IQ, usually below 70 on a traditional test of intelligence, and has difficulty adapting to everyday life. 437

mesoderm The middle layer of cells, which becomes the circulatory system, bones, mus-

cles, excretory system, and reproductive system. 109

metacognition Cognition about cognition or knowing about knowing. 424

middle and late childhood The developmental period that extends from about 6 to 11 years of age, sometimes called the elementary school years. 19

mitosis Cellular reproduction in which the cell's nucleus duplicates itself with two new cells being formed, each containing the same DNA as the parent cell, arranged in the same 23 pairs of chromosomes. 86

Montessori approach An educational philosophy in which children are given considerable freedom and spontaneity in choosing activities and are allowed to move from one activity to another as they desire. 318

moral development Development regarding rules and conventions about what people should do in their interactions with other people. 342

moral exemplar approach Emphasizes the development of personality, character, and virtue in terms of moral excellence. 467

Moro reflex A neonatal startle response that occurs in reaction to a sudden, intense noise or movement. When startled, the newborn arches its back, throws its head back, and flings out its arms and legs. Then the newborn rapidly closes its arms and legs to the center of the body. 184

morphology Units of meaning involved in word formation. 225

multiple-factor theory L. L. Thurstone's theory that intelligence consists of seven primary mental abilities: verbal comprehension, number ability, word fluency, spatial visualization, associative memory, reasoning, and perceptual speed. 428

myelination The process in which the nerve cells are covered and insulated with a layer of fat cells, which increases the speed at which information travels through the nervous system. 277

N

natural childbirth Developed in 1914 by Dick-Read, it attempts to reduce the mother's pain by decreasing her fear through education about childbirth and relaxation techniques during delivery. 145

naturalistic observation Observing behavior in real-world settings. 58

nature–nurture issue Nature refers to an organism's biological inheritance, nurture to environmental influences. The "nature" proponents claim biological inheritance is the most important influence on development; the "nurture" proponents claim that environmental experiences are the most important. 21

neglected children Children who are infrequently nominated as a best friend but are not disliked by their peers. 481

neglectful parenting A style of parenting in which the parent is very uninvolved in the child's life; it is associated with children's social incompetence, especially a lack of self-control. 352

Neonatal Intensive Care Unit Network Neurobehavioral Scale (NNNS) An "offspring" of the NBAS, the NNNS provides a more comprehensive analysis of the newborn's behavior, neurological and stress responses, and regulatory capacities. 154

neo-Piagetians They argue that Piaget got some things right but reinterpret Piaget's theory from an information-processing perspective. 418

neuron Nerve cell that handles information processing at the cellular level. 171

night terrors Sudden arousal from sleep, characterized by intense fear and usually accompanied by physiological reactions, such as rapid heart rate and breathing, loud screams, heavy perspiration, and physical movement. 286

nightmares Frightening dreams that awaken the sleeper. 285

nonshared environmental experiences The child's own unique experiences, both within the family and outside the family, that are not shared by another sibling. Thus, experiences occurring within the family can be part of the "nonshared environment." 99

normal distribution A distribution that is symmetrical, with most cases falling in the middle of the possible range of scores and a few scores appearing toward the extremes of the range. 426

O

object permanence The Piagetian term for one of an infant's most important accomplishments: understanding that objects and events continue to exist even when they cannot directly be seen, heard, or touched. 212

onlooker play Play in which the child watches other children play. 366

operations In Piaget's theory, an internalized set of actions that allows children to do mentally what they formerly did physically. 303

oral approaches Educational approaches to help hearing-impaired children; they include lip reading, speech reading, and whatever hearing the child has. 402

organic retardation Mental retardation caused by a genetic disorder or brain damage in which an individual usually has an IQ between 0 and 50. 437

organogenesis Organ formation that takes place during the first two months of prenatal development. 110

original sin view Advocated during the Middle Ages, the belief that children were born into the world as evil beings and were basically bad. 15

orthopedic impairments Restrictions in movement abilities due to muscle, bone, or joint problems. 402

oxytocics Drugs that are synthetic hormones designed to stimulate contractions. 144

P

pain cry A sudden appearance of an initial loud cry without preliminary moaning followed by an extended period of breath holding. 244

parallel play Play in which the child plays separately from others, but with toys like those the others are using or in a manner that mimics their play. 366

passive genotype-environment correlations Correlations that exist when the biological parents, who are genetically related to the child, provide a rearing environment for the child. 98

peers Individuals of about the same age or maturity level. 365

perception The interpretation of sensation. 191

performance orientation An orientation in which one focuses on achievement outcomes; winning is what matters most, and happiness is thought to result from winning. 441

personal fable The part of adolescent egocentrism that involves an adolescent's sense of uniqueness and invulnerability. 541

personality-type theory Holland's theory that an effort should be made to match an individual's career choice with his personality. 558

phenotype The way an individual's genotype is expressed in observed and measurable characteristics. 86

phenylketonuria (PKU) A genetic disorder in which an individual cannot properly metabolize phenylalanine, an amino acid. PKU is now easily detected but, if left untreated, results in mental retardation and hyperactivity. 90

phonology Rules regarding how sounds are perceived as different and which sound sequences may occur in the language. 224

Piaget's theory States that children actively construct their understanding of the world and go through four stages of cognitive development. 45

pictorial stage Kellogg's term for 4- to 5-year-olds' drawings depicting objects that adults can recognize. 282

placement stage Kellogg's term for 2- to 3-year-olds' drawings that are drawn in placement patterns. 282

play A pleasurable activity that is engaged in for its own sake. 366

play therapy Therapy that lets children work off frustrations while therapists analyze their conflicts and coping methods. 366

pluralism The coexistence of distinct ethnic and cultural groups in the same society. Individuals with a pluralistic stance usually advocate that cultural differences be maintained and appreciated. 591

popular children Children who are frequently nominated as a best friend and are rarely disliked by their peers. 480

postconventional reasoning The highest level in Kohlberg's theory of moral development. Morality is completely internalized. 464

postpartum depression Strong feelings of sadness, anxiety, or despair in new mothers that make it difficult for them to carry out daily tasks. 156

postpartum period The period after childbirth when the mother adjusts, both physically and psychologically, to the process of childbearing. This period lasts for about six weeks, or until her body has completed its adjustment and has returned to a near-prepregnant state. 155

practice play Play that involves repetition of behavior when new skills are being learned or when mastery and coordination of skills are required for games or sports. Sensorimotor play, which often involves practice play, is primarily confined to infancy, whereas practice play occurs throughout life. 367

pragmatics The appropriate use of language in context. 226

preconventional reasoning The lowest level in Kohlberg's theory of moral development. The individual shows no internalization of moral values; moral reasoning is controlled by external rewards and punishment. 463

prenatal period The time from conception to birth. 19

prepared childbirth Developed by French obstetrician Ferdinand Lamaze, this childbirth strategy is similar to natural childbirth but includes a special breathing technique to control pushing in the final stages of labor and a more detailed anatomy and physiology course. 145

pretense/symbolic play Play that occurs when a child transforms the physical environment into a symbol. 367

preterm infants Babies born three weeks or more before the pregnancy has reached its full term. 148

primary circular reaction A scheme based on the infant's attempt to reproduce an interesting or a pleasurable event that initially occurred by chance. 211

primary emotions Emotions present in humans and animals, including surprise, joy, anger, sadness, fear, and disgust; appear in first six months of life. 244

Project Follow Through An adjunct to Project Head Start, in which the enrichment programs are carried through the first few years of elementary school. 323

Project Head Start Compensatory education designed to provide children from low-income families the opportunity to acquire the skills and experiences important for school success. 323

proximodistal pattern The sequence in which growth starts at the center of the body and moves toward the extremities. 170

psychoanalytic theories Describe development as primarily unconscious and heavily colored by emotion. Behavior is merely a surface characteristic and the symbolic workings of the mind have to be analyzed to understand behavior. Early experiences with parents are emphasized. 42

psychoanalytic theory of gender Stems from Freud's view that preschool children develop a sexual attraction to the opposite-sex parent, then, at 5 to 6 years of age, renounce the attraction because of anxious feelings, subsequently identifying with the same-sex parent and unconsciously adopting the same-sex parent's characteristics. 346

puberty A period of rapid physical maturation involving hormonal and bodily changes that occur primarily in early adolescence. 501

Public Law 94–142 The Education for All Handicapped Children Act, created in 1975, which requires that all children with disabilities be given a free, appropriate public education and which provides the funding to help with the costs of implementing this education. 404

 R

rapport talk Talk that provides information. 470

recasting Rephrasing a statement that a child has said, perhaps turning it into a question or restating the child's utterance in the form of a fully grammatical sentence. 232

reciprocal socialization Bidirectional socialization; children socialize parents, just as parents socialize children. 259

reflexive smile A smile that does not occur in response to external stimuli. It happens during the month after birth, usually during sleep. 246

rejected children Children who are infrequently nominated as a best friend and are actively disliked by their peers. 481

report talk The language of conversation and a way of establishing connections and negotiating relationships; preferred by females. 470

rite of passage A ceremony or ritual that marks an individual's transition from one status to another. Most rites of passage focus on the transition to adult status. 588

rooting reflex A newborn's built-in reaction that occurs when the infant's cheek is stroked or the side of the mouth is touched. In response, the infant turns its head toward the side that was touched, in an apparent effort to find something to suck. 184

 S

scaffolding In cognitive development, Vygotsky used this term to describe the changing support over the course of a teaching session, with the more-skilled person adjusting guidance to fit the child's current performance level. 307

scaffolding Parental behavior that supports children's efforts, allowing them to be more skillful than they would be if they relied only on their own abilities; parents time interactions so the infant experiences turn-taking with the parents. 259

schema theory People mold memories to fit information that already exists in their mind. 419

schemas Mental frameworks that organize concepts and information. 419

schemes In Piaget's theory, actions or mental representations that organize knowledge. 209

scientific method An approach that can be used to obtain accurate information. It includes these steps: (1) conceptualize the problem, (2) collect data, (3) draw conclusions, and (4) revise research conclusions and theory. 39

secondary circular reactions Piaget's third sensorimotor substage, which develops between 4 and 8 months of age. In this substage, the infant becomes more object-oriented, or focused on the world, moving beyond preoccupation with the self in sensorimotor interactions. 212

securely attached babies Babies who use the caregiver as a secure base from which to explore the environment. 255

self-concept Domain-specific evaluations of the self. 460

self-conscious emotions Sometimes referred to as "secondary emotions," they require self-awareness; they include empathy, jealousy, embarrassment, pride, shame, and guilt and appear for the first time from the middle of the second year through the middle of the third year of life. 244

self-efficacy The belief that one can master a situation and produce favorable outcomes. 441

self-esteem The global evaluative dimension of the self. Self-esteem is also referred to as self-worth or self-image. 459

self-understanding The child's cognitive representation of self, the substance and content of the child's self-conceptions. 339

semantics The meanings of words and sentences. 226

sensation Reaction that occurs when information contacts sensory receptors—the eyes, ears, tongue, nostrils, and skin. 191

sensorimotor play Behavior by infants to derive pleasure from exercising their sensorimotor schemes. 367

sensorimotor stage The first of Piaget's stages, which lasts from birth to about 2 years of age and is nonsymbolic throughout; infants construct an understanding of the world by coordinating sensory experiences (such as seeing and hearing) with motoric actions. 210

separation protest Infants' distress to being separated from their caregivers. 247

seriation The concrete operation that involves ordering stimuli along a quantitative dimension (such as length). 415

service learning A form of education that promotes social responsibility and service to the community. 547

sexually transmitted infections (STIs) Diseases that are contracted primarily through sexual contact. This contact is not limited to vaginal intercourse but includes oral-genital contact and anal-genital contact as well. 514

shape constancy Recognition that an object remains the same even though its orientation to us changes. 196

shape stage Kellogg's term for 3-year-olds' drawings consisting of diagrams in different shapes. 282

shared environmental experiences Siblings' common environmental experiences, such as their parents' personalities and intellectual orientation, the family's socioeconomic status, and the neighborhood in which they live. 98

short-term memory The memory component in which individuals retain information for up to 15 to 30 seconds, assuming there is no rehearsal. 311

sickle-cell anemia A genetic disorder that affects the red blood cells and occurs most often in people of African descent. 91

simple reflexes Piaget's first sensorimotor substage, which corresponds to the first month after birth. In this substage, the basic means of coordinating sensation and action is through reflexive behaviors, such as rooting and sucking, which the infant has at birth. 210

size constancy Recognition that an object remains the same even though the retinal image of the object changes. 195

slow-to-warm-up child A child who has a low activity level, is somewhat negative, shows low adaptability, and displays a low intensity of mood. 248

small for date (small for gestational age) infants Babies whose birth weight is below normal when the length of pregnancy is considered. 148

social cognitive theory The view of psychologists who emphasize that behavior, environment, and person/cognition are the key factors in development. 49

social cognitive theory of gender The idea that children's gender of development occurs through observation and imitation of gender behavior, as well as through the rewards and punishment children experience for behaviors believed to be appropriate or inappropriate for their gender. 346

social constructivist approach An approach that emphasizes the social contexts of learning and the fact that knowledge is mutually built and constructed; Vygotsky's theory is a social constructivist approach. 309

social constructivist approach An approach that focuses on collaboration with others to produce knowledge and understanding; Vygotsky's theory is an example of this approach. 484

social play Play that involves social interactions with peers. 368

social policy The laws, regulations, and government programs that influence the welfare of its citizens. 12

social referencing "Reading" emotional cues in others to help determine how to act in a particular situation. 247

social role theory Eagly's theory that psychological gender differences are caused by the contrasting social roles of women and men. 346

social smile A smile in response to an external stimulus, which, early in development, typically is in response to a face. 246

socioeconomic status (SES) The grouping of people with similar occupational, educational, and economic characteristics. 10

socioemotional processes Changes in an individual's relationships with other people, emotions, and personality. 19

solitary play Play in which the child plays alone, independently of others. 366

somnambulism Sleep walking; occurs in the deepest stage of sleep. 286

spermarche A boy's first ejaculation of semen. 502

standardized test A test with uniform procedures for administration and scoring. Many standardized tests allow a person's performance to be compared with the performance of other individuals. 58

strabismus A misalignment of the eyes in which they do not point at the same object together; crossed eyes are one type of strabismus. 278

Strange Situation Ainsworth's observational measure of infant attachment to a caregiver that requires the infant to move through a series of introductions, separations, and reunions with the caregiver and an adult stranger in a prescribed order. 255

stranger anxiety An infant's fear and wariness of strangers that typically appears in the second half of the first year of life. 246

sucking reflex A newborn's built-in reaction of automatically sucking an object placed in its mouth. The sucking reflex enables the infant to get nourishment before it has associated a nipple with food. 184

sudden infant death syndrome (SIDS) Occurs when an infant stops breathing, usually during the night, and suddenly dies without an apparent cause; also called crib death. 176

symbolic function substage Piaget's first substage of preoperational thought, in which the child gains the ability to mentally represent an object that is not present (between 2 and 4 years of age). 303

syntax The ways words are combined to form acceptable phrases and sentences. 225

tabula rasa view The idea, proposed by John Locke, that children are like a "blank tablet." 15

telegraphic speech The use of short and precise words without grammatical markers such as articles, auxiliary verbs, and other connectives. 229

temperament An individual's behavioral style and characteristic way of emotional response. 248

teratogen From the Greek word *tera*, meaning "monster," any agent that causes a birth defect. The field of study that investigates the causes of birth defects is called teratology. 122

tertiary circular reactions, novelty, and curiosity Piaget's fifth sensorimotor substage, which develops between 12 and 18 months of age. In this substage, infants become intrigued by the variety of properties that objects possess and by the multiplicity of things they can make happen to objects. 212

theory An interrelated, coherent set of ideas that helps to explain and to make predictions. 40

theory of mind A concept that refers to awareness of one's own mental processes and the mental processes of others. 314

top-dog phenomenon The circumstance of moving from the top position (in elementary school, the oldest, biggest, and most powerful students) to the lowest position (in middle or junior high school, the youngest, smallest, and least powerful). 552

transitional objects Objects that children repeatedly use as bedtime companions. These usually are soft and cuddly and probably mark the child's transition from being dependent to being more independent. 285

transitivity In concrete operational thought, a mental concept that underlies the ability to logically combine relations to understand certain conclusions. It focuses on reasoning about the relations between classes. 415

triarchic theory of intelligence Sternberg's theory proposing that there are three main types of intelligence: analytical, creative, and practical. 429

trophoblast The outer layer of cells that develops in the germinal period. These cells provide nutrition and support for the embryo. 109

trust versus mistrust Erikson's first stage of development, occurring in the first year of life, in which infants experience the world as either secure and comfortable or insecure and uncomfortable. 251

Turner syndrome A chromosome disorder in females in which either an X chromosome is missing, making the person XO instead of XX, or the second X chromosome is partially deleted. 89

twin study A study in which the behavioral similarity of identical twins is compared with the behavioral similarity of fraternal twins. 97

two-factor theory Spearman's theory that individuals have both general intelligence, which he called g, and a number of specific intelligences, referred to as s. 427

unoccupied play Play in which the child is not engaging in play as it is commonly understood and might stand in one spot or perform random movements that do not seem to have a goal. 366

values Beliefs and attitudes about the way things should be. 545

values clarification An approach to moral education that emphasizes helping people clarify what their lives are for and what's worth working for. Students are encouraged to define their own values and to understand the values of others. 548

visual preference method A method developed by Fantz to determine whether infants can distinguish one stimulus from another by measuring the length of time they attend to different stimuli. 192

voice disorders Disorders reflected in speech that is hoarse, harsh, too loud, too high-pitched, or too low-pitched. 401

Vygotsky's theory A sociocultural cognitive theory that emphasizes how culture and social interaction guide cognitive development. 47

Wernicke's area An area of the brain's left hemisphere that is involved in language comprehension. 230

whole-language approach An approach to reading instruction based on the idea that instruction should parallel children's natural language learning. Reading materials should be whole and meaningful. 446

XYY syndrome A chromosomal disorder in which males have an extra Y chromosome. 89

zone of proximal development (ZPD) Vygotsky's term for the difference between what children can achieve independently and what they can achieve with the guidance and assistance of adults or more-skilled children. 306

zygote A single cell formed through fertilization. 86

A

Aboud, F., & Skerry, S. (1983). Self and ethnic concepts in relation to ethnic constancy. *Canadian Journal of Behavioral Science, 15,* 3–34.

Abruscato, J. (2004). *Teaching children science* (2nd ed.). Boston: Allyn & Bacon.

Adair, L. S. (2001). Size at birth predicts age at menarche. *Pediatrics, 107,* E59.

Adams, R. J. (1989). Newborns' discrimination among mid- and long-wavelength stimuli. *Journal of Experimental Child Psychology, 47,* 130–141.

Adamson, H. D. (2004). *Language minority students in America.* Mahwah, NJ: Erlbaum.

Adickes, M. S., & Stuart, M. J. (2004). Youth football injuries. *Sports Medicine, 34,* 201–207.

Adler, S. A., & Haith, M. M. (2003). The nature of infants' visual expectations for event content. *Infancy, 4,* 389–411.

Adler, T. (1991, January). Seeing double? Controversial twins study is widely reported, debated. *APA Monitor, 22,* (No. 1), 8.

Adolph, K. E. (1997). Learning in the development of infant locomotion. *Monographs of the Society for Research in Child Development, 62* (3, Serial No. 251).

Adolph, K. E. (2002). Learning to keep balance. In R. Kail (Ed.), *Advances in child development and behavior.* San Diego: Academic Press.

Adolph, K. E., & Avolio, A. M. (2000). Walking infants adapt locomotion to changing body dimensions. *Journal of Experimental Psychology: Human Perception and Performance, 26,* 1148–1166.

Adolph, K. E., & Berger, S. E. (2005). Physical and motor development. In M. H. Bornstein & M. E. Lamb (Eds.), *Developmental psychology* (5th ed.). Mahwah, NJ: Erlbaum.

Adolph, K. E., & Berger, S. E. (2006). Motor development. In W. Damon & R. Lerner (Eds.), *Handbook of child psychology* (6th ed.). New York: Wiley.

Adolph, K. E., Vereijkeni, B., & Shrout, P. E. (2003). What changes in infant walking and why? *Child Development, 74,* 475–497.

Agran, P. F., Anderson, C. L., & Winn, D. G. (2004). Violators of a child passenger safety law. *Pediatrics, 114,* 109–115.

Agras, W. S., & others. (2004). Report of the National Institutes of Health workshop on overcoming barriers to treatment research in anorexia nervosa. *International Journal of Eating Disorders, 35,* 509–521.

Agras, W. S., Hammer, L. D., McNicholas, F., & Kraemer, H. C. (2004). Risk factors for childhood overweight: A prospective study from birth to 9.5 years. *Journal of Pediatrics, 145,* 20–25.

Aguiar, A., & Baillargeon, R. (2002). Developments in young infants' reasoning about occluded objects. *Cognitive Psychology, 45,* 267–336.

Ahamed, M., Verma, S., Kumar, A., & Siddiqui, M. K. (2005). Environmental exposure to lead and its correlation with biochemical indices in children. *Science of the Total Environment, 346,* 48–55.

Ahluwalia, I. B., Tessaro, I., Grumer-Strawn, L. M., MacGowan, C., & Benton-Davis, S. (2000). Georgia's breastfeeding promotion program for low-income women. *Pediatrics, 105,* E-85–E-87.

Ahn, H. (1994). Teenage childbearing and high school completion: Accounting for individual heterogeneity. *Family Planning Perspectives, 26,* 17–21.

Aiken, L. R. (2003). *Psychological testing and assessment* (11th ed.). Boston: Allyn & Bacon.

Ainsworth, M. D. S. (1979). Infant-mother attachment. *American Psychologist, 34,* 932–937.

Akshoomoff, N., Pierce, K., & Courchesne, E. (2002). The neurobiological basis of autism from a developmental perspective. *Development and Psychopathology, 14,* 613–634.

Alan Guttmacher Institute. (1995). *National survey of the American male's sexual habits.* New York: Author.

Alan Guttmacher Institute. (1998). *Teen sex and pregnancy.* New York: Author.

Alan Guttmacher Institute. (2002). Teen pregnancy: Trends and lessons learned. In *Policy analysis: Issues in brief.* New York: Author.

Alan Guttmacher Institute. (2003). *U.S. teenage pregnancy statistics.* New York: Author.

Alberto, P. A., & Troutman, A. C. (1999). *Applied behavior analysis for teachers* (5th ed.). Englewood Cliffs, NJ: Merrill.

Alexander, G. R., Kogan, M. D., & Nabukera, S. (2002). Racial differences in prenatal care in the United States: Are disparities decreasing? *American Journal of Public Health, 92,* 1970–1975.

Alexander, R. T., & Radisch, D. (2005). Sudden infant death syndrome risk factors with regards to sleep position, sleep surface, and co-sleeping. *Journal of Forensic Science, 50,* 147–151.

Alfirevic, Z., & Neilson, J. P. (2004). Antenatal screening for Down syndrome. *British Medical Journal, 329,* 811–812.

Alio, A. P., & Salihu, H. M. (2005). Maternal determinants of pediatric preventive care utilization among blacks and whites. *Journal of the National Medical Association, 97,* 792–797.

Aliyu, M. H., Salihu, H. M., Blankson, M. L., Alexander, G. R., & Keith, L. (2004). Risks in triplet pregnancy: Advanced maternal age, premature rupture of membranes, and risk of mortality. *Journal of Reproductive Medicine, 49,* 721–726.

Allen, J. P., & Kuperminc, G. P. (1995, March). *Adolescent attachment, social competence, and problematic behavior.* Paper presented at the meeting of the Society for Research in Child Development, Indianapolis.

Allen, J. P., Hauser, S. T., & Borman-Spurrell, E. (1996). Attachment security and related sequelae of severe adolescent psychopathology: An eleven-year follow-up study. *Journal of Consulting and Clinical Psychology, 64,* 254–263.

Allen, J. P., Kuperminc, G. P., & Moore, C. (2005, April). *Stability and predictors of change in attachment security across adolescence.* Paper presented at the meeting of the Society for Research in Child Development, Atlanta.

Allen, J. P., McElhaney, K. B., Kuperminc, G. P., & Jodl, K. M. (2004). Stability and change in attachment security across adolescence. *Child Development, 75,* 1792–1805.

Allen, M., Brown, P., & Finlay, B. (1992). *Helping children by strengthening families.* Washington, DC: Children's Defense Fund.

Allen, R., McGeorge, P., Paearson, D., & Milne, A. B. (2004). Attention and expertise in multiple target tracking. *Applied Cognitive Psychology, 18,* 337–347.

Als, H., Duffy, F. H., McAnulty, G. B., Rivkin, M. J., Vajapeyam, S., Mulkern, R. V., Warfield, S. K., Huppi, P. S., Butler, S. C., Conneman, N., Fischer, C., & Eichenwald,

E. C. (2004). Early experience alters brain function and structure. *Pediatrics, 113,* 846–857.

Alsaker, F. D., & Flammer, A. (1999). *The adolescent experience: European and American adolescents in the 1990s.* Mahwah, NJ: Erlbaum.

Alvarez, M. (2004). Caregiving and early infant crying in a Danish community. *Journal of Developmental and Behavioral Pediatrics, 25,* 91–98.

Amabile, T. (1993). Commentary. In D. Goleman, P. Kaufman, & M. Ray. *The Creative Spirit,* New York: Plume.

Amabile, T. M., & Hennesey, B. A. (1992). The motivation for creativity in children. In A. K. Boggiano & T. S. Pittman (Eds.), *Achievement and motivation.* New York: Cambridge.

Amato, P. (2005). Historical trends in divorce and dissolution in the United States. In M. A. Fine & J. H. Harvey (Eds.), *Handbook of divorce and relationship dissolution.* Mahwah, NJ: Erlbaum.

Amato, P. R., & Booth, A. (1996). A prospective study of divorce and parent-child relationships. *Journal of Marriage and the Family, 58,* 356–365.

Amato, P. R., & Keith, B. (1991). Parental divorce and the weening of children: A meta-analysis. *Psychological Bulletin, 110,* 26–46.

Ambrose, D. (2004). Creativity in teaching. In J. C. Kaufman & J. Baer (Eds.), *Creativity across domains.* Mahwah, NJ: Erlbaum.

Ambrosio, J. (2004). No child left behind. *Phi Delta Kappan, 85,* 709–711.

American Academy of Pediatrics Task Force on Infant Positioning and SIDS. (2000). Changing concepts of sudden infant death syndrome. *Pediatrics, 105,* 650–656.

American Academy of Pediatrics. (2000). Suicide and suicide attempts in adolescence. *Pediatrics, 105,* 871–874.

American Academy of Pediatrics. (2001). Falls from heights: Windows, roofs, and balconies. *Pediatrics, 107,* 1188–1191.

American Academy of Pediatrics. (2001). *Toilet training.* Available on the World Wide Web at: http://www.aap.org/family/toil.htm

American Academy of Pediatrics. (2004). Recommended childhood and adolescent immunization schedule—United States, January-June 2004. *Pediatrics, 113,* 142–143.

American Academy of Pediatrics (AAP) Work Group on Breastfeeding. (1997). Breastfeeding and the use of human milk. *Pediatrics, 100,* 1035–1039.

American Pregnancy Association. (2004). Using narcotics for pain relief during pregnancy. Available on the Internet at: www.americanpregnancy.org/labornbirth/narcotics.html

American Psychological Association. (2003). *Psychology: Scientific problem solvers.* Washington, DC: American Psychological Association.

Amsterdam, B. K. (1968). *Mirror behavior in children under two years of age.* Unpublished doctoral dissertation. University of North Carolina, Chapel Hill.

Ananth, C. V., Joseph, K. S., Oyelese, Y., Demissie, K., & Vintzileos, A. M. (2005). Trends in preterm birth and perinatal mortality among singletons: United States, 1989 through 2000. *Obstetrics and Gynecology, 105,* 1084–1091.

Anastasi, A., & Urbina, S. (1996). *Psychological testing* (7th ed.). Upper Saddle River, NJ: Prentice Hall.

Anderman, E. M., Maehr, M. L., & Midgley, C. (1996). *Declining motivation after the transition to middle school: Schools can make a difference.* Unpublished manuscript, University of Kentucky, Lexington.

Anderson, C. A., & Bushman, B. J. (2001). Effects of violent video games on aggressive behavior, aggressive cognition, aggressive affect, physiological arousal, and prosocial behavior: A meta-analytic review of the scientific literature. *Psychological Science, 12,* 353–359.

Anderson, C. A., & Bushman, B. J. (2002). Human aggression. *Annual Review of Psychology* (Vol. 53). Palo Alto, CA: Annual Reviews.

Anderson, C. A., & Dill, K. E. (2000). Video games and aggressive thoughts, feelings, and behavior in the laboratory and in life. *Journal of Personality and Social Psychology, 78,* 772–790.

Anderson, D. R., Huston, A. C., Schmitt, K., Linebarger, D. L., & Wright, J. C. (2001). Early childhood viewing and adolescent behavior: The recontact study. *Monographs of the Society for Research in Child Development, 66* (1, Serial No. 264).

Anderson, D. R., Lorch, E. P., Field, D. E., Collins, P. A., & Nathan, J. G. (1985, April). *Television viewing at home: Age trends in visual attention and time with TV.* Paper presented at the biennial meeting of the Society for Research in Child Development, Toronto.

Anderson, E., Greene, S. M., Hetherington, E. M., & Clingempeel, W. G. (1999). The dynamics of parental remarriage. In E. M. Hetherington (Ed.), *Coping with divorce, single parenting, and remarriage.* Mahwah, NJ: Erlbaum.

Anderson, J. L., Waller, D. K., Canfield, M. A., Shaw, G. M., Watkins, M. L., & Werler, M. M. (2005). Maternal obesity, gestational diabetes, and central nervous system birth defects. *Epidemiology, 16,* 87–92.

Anderson, L. M., Shinn, C., Pullilove, M. T., Serimshaw, S. C., Fielding, J. E., Normand, J., & Carande-Kulis, V. G. (2003). The effectiveness of early childhood development programs: A systematic review. *American Journal of Preventive Medicine, 24* (Suppl. 3), 32–46.

Andrade, S. E., Gurwitz, J. H., Davis, R. L., Chan, K. A., Finkelstein, J. A., Fortman, K., McPhillips, H., Raebel, M. A., Roblin, D., Smith, D. H., Yood, M. U., Morse, A. N., & Platt, R. (2004). Prescription drug use in pregnancy. *American Journal of Obstetrics and Gynecology, 191,* 398–407.

Andreasen, K. R., Anderson, M. L., & Schantz, A. L. (2004). Obesity and pregnancy. *Acta Obstetrics and Gynecology Scandanavia, 83,* 1022–1029.

Andrulis, D. P. (2005). Moving beyond the status quo in reducing racial and ethnic disparities in children's health. *Public Health Reports, 120,* 370–377.

Angold, A., Costello, E. J., & Worthman, C. M. (1998). Puberty and depression: The roles of age, pubertal status and pubertal timing. *Psychological Medicine, 28,* 51–61.

Antonacci, P. A. P., & O'Callaghan, C. M. (2006). *A handbook for literacy instructional and assessment strategies, K-8.* Boston: Allyn & Bacon.

Antonarakis, S. E., Lyle, R., Dermitzakis, E. T., Reymond, A., & Deutsch, S. (2004). Chromosome 21 and Down syndrome: From genomics to pathophysiology. *Nature Review: Genetics, 5,* 725–738.

Appelman, Z., & Furman, B. (2005). Invasive genetic diagnosis in multiple pregnancies. *Obstetrics and Gynecological Clinics of North America, 32,* 97–103.

Appukutty, M., Anuar, S., Nagoor, M., Fatimah, F., Norliza, A., Zarida, H., & Rizam. M. (2004). The relationship of plasma leptin to anthropoetrical and biochemical markers of overweight primary school students. *Asia Pacific Journal of Clinical Nutrition, 13* (Suppl.), S137.

Apter, D. (2003). The role of leptin in female adolescence. *Annals of the New York Academy of Science, 997,* 64–76.

Ara, I., Vicente-Rodriguez, G., Jimenez-Ramirez, J., Dorado, C., Serrano-Sanchez, J. A., & Calber, J. A. (2004). Regular participation in sports is associated with enhanced physical fitness and lower fat mass in prepubertal boys. *International Journal of Obesity and Related Metabolic Disorders, 28,* 1585–1593.

Archibald, A. B., Graber, J. A., & Brooks-Gunn, J. (1999). Associations among parent-adolescent relationships, pubertal growth, dieting, and body image in young adolescent girls: A short-term longitudinal study. *Journal of Research on Adolescence, 9,* 395–415.

Archibald, A. B., Graber, J. A., & Brooks-Gunn, J. (2003). Pubertal processes and physical growth in adolescence. In G. R. Adams & M. Berzonsky (Eds.), *Handbook on adolescence.* Malden, MA: Blackwell.

Archibald, S. L., Fennema-Notetine, C., Gamst, A., Riley, E. P., Mattson, S. N., & Jernigan, T. L. (2001). Brain dysmorphology in individuals with severe prenatal alcohol exposure. *Developmental Medicine and Child Neurology, 43,* 148–154.

Arendt, R., Angelopouos, J., Salvator, A., & Singer, L. (1999). Motor development of cocaine-exposed children at age two years. *Pediatrics, 103,* 86–92.

Arendt, R. E., Short, E. J., Singer, L. T., Minnes, S., Hewitt, J., Flynn, S., Carlson, L., Min, M. O., Klein, N., & Flannery, D. (2004). Children prenatally exposed to cocaine: Developmental outcomes and environmental risks at seven years of age. *Journal of Developmental and Behavioral Pediatrics, 25,* 83–90.

Arés, P. (1962). *Centuries of childhood* (R. Baldrick, Trans.). New York: Knopf.

Arias, I. (2004). The legacy of child maltreatment: Long-term health consequences for women. *Journal of Women's Health, 13,* 468–473.

Ariceli, G., Castro, J., Cesena, J., & Toro, J. (2005). Anorexia nervosa in male adolescents: Body image, eating attitudes, and psychological traits. *Journal of Adolescent Health, 36,* 221–226.

Arisa, E. N. W. (2005). *Not for ESOL Teachers: What every classroom teacher needs to know about the linguistically, culturally, and ethnically diverse student.* Boston: Allyn & Bacon.

Ariza, A. J., Chen, E. H., Binns, H. J., & Christoffel, K. K. (2004). Risk factors for overweight in five- to six-year-old Hispanic-American children: A pilot study. *Journal of Urban Health, 81,* 150–161.

Armstrong, J., Boada, M., Rey, M. J., Vidal, N., Ferrer, I. (2004). Familizal Alzheimer disease associated with A713T mutation in App. *Neuroscience Letters, 370,* 241–243.

Arnett, J. J. (2002). Adolescents in Western countries in the 21st century: Vast opportunities—for all? In B. B. Brown, R. W. Larson, & T. S. Saraswathi (Eds.), *The world's youth.* New York: Cambridge University Press.

Arnold, D. H., & Doctoroff, G. I. (2003). The early education of socioeconomically disadvantaged children. *Annual Review of Psychology* (Vol. 54). Palo Alto, CA: Annual Reviews.

Aronson, E. (1986, August). *Teaching students things they think they already know about: The case of prejudice and desegregation.* Paper presented at the meeting of the American Psychological Association, Washington, DC.

Aronson, J. (2002). Stereotype threat: Contending and coping with unnerving expectation. In *Improving academic achievement.* San Diego: Academic Press.

Aronson, J., Fried, C. B., & Good. C. (2002). Reducing the effects of stereotype threat on African American college students by shaping theories of intelligence. *Journal of Experimental Social Psychology, 38,* 113–125.

Aronson, J. M., Lustina, M. J., Good, C., Keough, K., Steele, C. M., & Brown, J. (1999). When white men can't do math: Necessary and sufficient factors in stereotype threat. *Journal of Experimental Social Psychology, 35,* 29–46.

Arshad, S. H. (2005). Primary prevention of asthma and allergy. *Journal of Allergy and Clinical Immunology, 116,* 3–14.

Ashdown-Lambert, J. R. (2005). A review of low birth weight: predictors, precursors, and morbidity outcomes. *Journal of Research in Society and Health, 125,* 76–83.

Asher, J., & Garcia, R. (1969). The optimal age to learn a foreign language. *Modern Language Journal, 53,* 334–341.

Aslin, R. (1987). Visual and auditory development in infancy. In J. Osofsky (Ed.), *Handbook of infant development* (2nd ed.). New York: Wiley.

Aslin, R. N., Jusczyk, P. W., & Pisoni, D. B. (1998). Speech and auditory processing during infancy: Constraints on and precursors to language. In W. Damon (Ed.), *Handbook of child psychology* (5th ed., Vol. 2). New York: Wiley.

Assaf, A. V., Meneghim, M. C., Zanin, L., Mialhe, F. L., Pereira, A. C., & Ambrosano, G. M. (2004). Assessment of different methods for diagnosing dental caries in epidemiological surveys. *Community Dentistry and Oral Epidemiology, 32,* 418–425.

Ateah, C. A. (2005). Maternal use of physical punishment in response to child misbehavior: Implications for child abuse prevention. *Child Abuse and Neglect, 29,* 169–185.

Atinmo, T., & Oyewole, D. (2004). Finding solutions to the nutritional dilemmas in Africa for child health: HIV/AIDS orphans, poverty, and hunger. *Asian Pacific Journal of Clinical Nutrition, 13* (Suppl.), S6.

Ativeh, G. N., & El-Mohandes, A. (2005) Preventive healthcare of infants in a region of Lebanon: Parental beliefs, attitudes, and behaviors. *Maternal and Child Health Journal 9,* 83–90.

Atkinson, A. P., & Wheeler, M. (2004). The grain of domains: The evolutionary-psychological case against domain-general cognition. *Mind and Language, 19,* 147–176.

Atkinson, L., & Goldberg, S. (Eds.). (2004). *Attachment issues in psychopathology and intervention.* Mahwah, NJ: Erlbaum.

Attie, I., Brooks-Gunn, J. (1989). Development of eating problems in adolescent girls: A longitudinal study. *Developmental Psychology, 25,* 70–79.

Austin, A. A., & Chorpita, B. F. (2004). Temperament, anxiety, and depression: Comparisons across five ethnic groups of children. *Journal of Clinical Child and Adolescent Psychology, 33,* 216–226.

Awan, T. M., Sattar, A., & Khattak, E. G. (2005). Frequency of growth hormone deficiency in short statured children. *Journal of the College Physicians and Surgeons Pakistan, 15,* 295–298.

Axelsson, S., & others. (2004). Effects of combined caries-preventive methods: A systematic review of controlled clinical trials. *Acta Odontologica Scandinavica, 62,* 163–169.

Azar, S. T. (2002). Parenting and child maltreatment. In M. H. Bornstein (Ed.), *Handbook of parenting* (2nd ed., Vol. 4). Mahwah, NJ: Erlbaum.

B

Babbie, E. R. (2005). *The basics of social research* (3rd ed.). Belmont, CA: Wadsworth.

Bacak, S. J., Baptiste-Roberts, K., Amon, E., Ireland, B., & Leet, T. (2005). Risk factors for neonatal mortality among extremely-low-birth-weight infants. *American Journal of Obstetrics and Gynecology, 192,* 862–867.

Bachman, J. G. (1982, June 28). *The American high school student: A profile based on national survey data.* Paper presented at a conference entitled "The American High School Today and Tomorrow", Berkeley, CA.

Baddeley, A. (1992). Working memory. *Science, 255,* 556–560.

Baddeley, A. (2000). Short-term and working memory. In E. Tulving & F. I. M. Craik (Eds.), *The Oxford handbook of memory.* New York: Oxford University Press.

Bagwell, C. L., Newcomb, A. F., & Bukowski, W. M. (1994, February). *Early adolescent friendship as a predictor of adult adjustment: A twelve-year follow-up investigation.* Paper presented at the biennial meeting of the Society for Research on Adolescence, San Diego.

Bahl, R., Frost, C., Kirkwood, B. R., Edmond, K., Martines, J., Bhandari, N., & Arthur, P. (2005). Infant feeding patterns and risk of death and hospitalization in the first half of infancy: Multicentre cohort study. *Bulletin of the World Health Organization, 83,* 418–426.

Bailey, B. N., Delaney-Black, V., Covington, C. Y., Ager, J., Janisse, J., Hannigan, J. H., & Sokol, R. J. (2004). Prenatal exposure to binge drinking and cognitive and behavioral outcomes at age 7 years. *American Journal of Obstetrics and Gynecology, 191,* 1037–1043.

Bailey, L. B., & Berry, R. J. (2005). Folic acid supplementation and the occurrence of congenital heart defects, orofacial clefts, multiple births, and miscarriage. *American Journal of Clinical Nutrition, 81,* l213S-1217S.

Baillargeon, R. (1995). The object concept revisited: New directions in the investigation of infants' physical knowledge. In C.E. Granrud (Ed.), *Visual perception and cognition in infancy.* Hillsdale, NJ: Erlbaum.

Baillargeon, R. (2002). The acquisition of physical knowledge in infancy: A summary in eight lessons. In U. Goswami (Ed.), *Handbook of childhood cognitive development.* Malden, MA: Blackwell.

Baillargeon, R. (2004). Infants' physical world. *Current Directions in Psychological Science, 13,* 89–95.

Baillargeon, R., & DeVos, J. (1991). Object permanence in young children: Further evidence. *Child Development, 62,* 1227–1246.

Baird, A. A., Gruber, S. A., Cohen, B. M., Renshaw, R. J., & Yureglun-Todd, D. A. (1999). FMRI of the amygdala in children and adolescents. *American Academy of Child and Adolescent Psychiatry, 38,* 195–199.

Bakeman, R., & Brown, J. V. (1980). Early interaction: Consequences for social and mental development at three years. *Child Development, 51,* 437–447.

Bakermans-Kranenburg, M. J., van Uzendoorn, M. H., Bokhorst, C. L., & Schuengel, C. (2004). The importance of shared environment in infant-father attachment: A behavioral genetic study of the attachment q-sort. *Journal of Family Psychology, 18,* 545–549.

Bakheit, A. M., Bower, E., Cosgrove, A., Fox, M., Morton, R., Phillips, S., Scrutton, D., Shrubb, V., & Yude, C. (2001). Opinion statement on the minimal acceptable standards of health care in cerebral palsy. *Disabilities Rehabilitation, 13,* 578–582.

Bakker, E., Van Gool, J. D., Van Sprundel, M., Van Der Auwerea, C., & Wyndaele, J. J. (2002). Results of a questionnaire evaluating the effects of different methods of toilet training on achieving bladder control. *BJU International, 90,* 456–461.

Balkany, T. J., Hodges, A, Miyamoto, R. T., Gibbin, K., & Odabasi, O. (2001). Cochlear implants in children. *Otolaryngology Clinics of North America, 34,* 445–467.

Ballem, K. D., & Plunkett, K. (2005). Phonological specificity in children at 1; 2. *Journal of Child Language, 32,* 159–173.

Baltes, P. B. (2003). On the incomplete architecture of human ontogeny: Selection, optimization, and compensation as foundation of developmental theory. In U. M. Staudinger & U. Lindenberger (Eds.), *Understanding human development.* Boston: Kluwer.

Baltes, P. B., Lindenberger, U., & Staudinger, U. (2006). Life span theory in developmental psychology. In W. Damon & R. Lerner (Eds.), *Handbook of child psychology* (6th ed.). New York: Wiley.

Bandstra, E. S., Morrow, C. E., Anthony, J. C., Haynes, V. L., Johnson, A. L., Xue, L., & Audrey, Y. (2000, May). *Effects of prenatal cocaine exposure on attentional processing in children through five years of age.* Paper presented at the joint meetings of the Pediatric Academic Societies and the American Academy of Pediatrics, Boston.

Bandstra, E. S., Vogel, A. L., Morrow, C. E., Xue, L., & Anthony, J. C. (2004). Severity of prenatal cocaine exposure and child language functioning through age seven years: A longitudinal latent growth curve analysis. *Substance Use and Misuse, 39,* 25–59.

Bandura, A. (2002). Selective moral disengagements in the exercise of moral agency. *Journal of Moral Education, 31,* 101–119.

Bandura, A. (1986). *Social foundations of thought and action: A social cognitive theory.* Englewood Cliffs, NJ: Prentice Hall.

Bandura, A. (1997). *Self-efficacy.* New York: W. H. Freeman.

Bandura, A. (1998, August). *Swimming against the mainstream: Accentuating the positive aspects of humanity.* Paper presented at the meeting of the American Psychological Association, San Francisco.

Bandura, A. (2001). Social cognitive theory. *Annual Review of Psychology* (Vol. 52). Palo Alto, CA: Annual Reviews.

Bandura, A. (2004, May). *Toward a psychology of human agency.* Paper presented at the meeting of the American Psychological Society, Chicago.

Bank, L., Burraston, B., & Snyder, J. (2004). Sibling conflict and ineffective parenting as predictors of adolescent boys' antisocial behavior and peer difficulties: Additive and interactional effects. *Journal of Research on Adolescence, 14,* 99–125.

Banks, J. A. (2002). *Introduction to multicultural education* (3rd ed.). Boston: Allyn & Bacon.

Banks, J. A. (2003). *Teaching strategies for ethnic studies* (7th ed.). Boston: Allyn & Bacon.

Banks, J. A. (2006). *Cultural diversity and education* (5th ed.). Boston: Allyn & Bacon.

Banks, M. S., & Salapatek, P. (1983). Infant visual perception. In P. H. Mussen (Ed.), *Handbook of child psychology* (4th ed., Vol. 2). New York: Wiley.

Bannon, L. (2005). *Gender: Psychological perspectives* (4th ed.). Boston: Allyn & Bacon.

Baquet, G., van Praagh, E., & Berthoin, S. (2004). Endurance training and aerobic fitness in young people. *Sports Medicine, 33,* 1127–1143.

Baraket, L. P., Kunin-Batson, A., & Kazak, A. E. (2003). Child health psychology. In I. B. Weiner (Ed.), *Handbook of psychology* (Vol. 9). New York: McGraw-Hill.

Barber, B., & Eccles, J. (2003). The joy of romance: Healthy adolescent relationships as an educational agenda. In P. Florsheim (Ed.), *Adolescent romantic relations and sexual behavior.* Mahwah, NJ: Erlbaum.

Bardenheir, B. H., Yusuf, H. R., Rosenthal, J., Santoli, J. M., Shefer, A. M., Rickert, D. L., & Chu, S. Y. (2004). Factors associated with underimmunization at 3 months of age in four medically underserved areas. *Public Health Reports, 119,* 479–485.

Barker, R., & Wright, H. F. (1951). *One boy's day.* New York: Harper & Row.

Barnett, D., Ganiban, J., & Cicchetti, D. (1999). Maltreatment, negative expressivity, and the development of type D attachments from 12 to 24 months of age. In J. I. Vondra & D. Barnett (Eds.), *Monograph of the Society for Research in Child Development, 64* (3, Serial No. 258, 97–118).

Barnett, S. B., & Maulik, D. (2001). Guidelines and recommendations for safe use of Doppler ultrasound in perinatal applications. *Journal of Maternal and Fetal Medicine, 10,* 75–84.

Barnhill, L. J. (2004). Evolutionary perspective on adolescent sexuality. *Journal of the American Academy of Child and Adolescent Psychiatry, 43,* 925–926.

Baron, N. S. (1992). *Growing up with language.* Reading, MA: Addison-Wesley.

Baron-Cohen, S. (2004). Autism: Research into causes and intervention. *Pediatric Rehabilitation, 7,* 73–78.

Barone, D., Hardman, D., & Taylor, J. (2006). *Reading first in the classroom.* Boston: Allyn & Bacon.

Bar-Oz, B., Levicheck, Z., Moretti, M. E., Mah, C., Andreou, S., & Koren, G. (2004). Pregnancy outcome following rubella vaccination: A prospective study. *American Journal of Medical Genetics, 130A,* 52–54.

Barr, H. M., & Streissguth, A. P. (2001). Identifying maternal self-reported alcohol use associated with fetal alcohol disorders. *Alcoholism: Clinical and Experimental Research, 25,* 283–287.

Barrett, D. E., Radke-Yarrow, M., & Klein, R. E. (1982). Chronic malnutrition and child behavior: Effects of calorie supplementation on social and emotional functioning at school age. *Developmental Psychology, 18,* 541–556.

Barton, W. H. (2005). Juvenile justice policies and programs. In J. M. Jenson & M. W. Fraser (Eds.), *Social policy for children and families.* Thousand Oaks, CA: Sage.

Basic, S., Hajnsek, S., Poljakovic, Z., Basic, M., Culic, V., & Zadro, L. (2004). Determination of cortical language dominance using functional transcranial Doppler sonography on left-handers. *Clinical Neurophysiology, 115,* 154–160.

Bassett, K., Lee, P. M., Green, C. J., Mitchell, L., & Kazanjian, A. (2004). Improving population health or the population itself? Health technology assessment and our genetic future. *International Journal of Technology Assessment in Health Care, 20,* 106–114.

Bates, A. S., Fitzgerald, J. F., Dittus, R. S., & Wollinsky, F. D. (1994). Risk factors for underimmunization in poor urban infants. *Journal of the American Medical Association, 272,* 1105–1109.

Bates, E. (1990). Language about me and you: Pronomial reference and the emerging concept of self. In D. Cicchetti & M. Beeghly (Eds.), *The self in transition: Infancy to childhood* (pp. 165–182). Chicago: University of Chicago Press.

Bauer, P. J. (2004). Getting explicit memory off the ground: Steps toward construction of a neuro-developmental account of changes in the first two years of life. *Developmental Review, 24,* 347–373.

Bauer, P. J. (2005). Developments in declarative memory. *Psychological Science, 16,* 41–47.

Bauer, P. J. (2006). Event memory. In W. Damon & R. Lerner (Eds.), *Handbook of child psychology* (6th ed.). New York: Wiley.

Bauer, P. J., & Dow, G. A. (1994). Episodic memory in 16- and 20-month-old children: Specifics are generalized but not forgotten. *Developmental Psychology, 30,* 403–417.

Bauer, P. J., Wenner, J. A., Dropik, P. I., & Wewerka, S. S. (2000). Parameters of remembering and forgetting in the transition from infancy to early childhood. *Monographs of the Society for Research in Child Development, 65* (4, Serial No. 263).

Bauer, P. J., Wiebe, S.A., Carver, L. J., Waters, J. M., & Nelson, C. A. (2003). Developments in long-term explicit memory late in the first year of life: Behavioral and electrophysiological indices. *Psychological Science, 14,* 629–635.

Baumeister, R. F., Campbell, J. D., Krueger, J. I., & Vohs, K. D. (2003). Does high self-esteem cause better performance, interpersonal success, happiness, or healthier lifestyles? *Psychological Science in the Public Interest, 4* (No. 1), 1–44.

Baumrind, D. (1971). Current patterns of parental authority. *Developmental Psychology Monographs, 4* (1. Pt. 2).

Baumrind, D. (1989, April). *Sex-differentiated socialization effects in childhood and adolescence.* Paper presented at the biennial meeting of the Society for Research in Child Development, Kansas City.

Baumrind, D. (1991). Effective parenting during the early adolescent transition. In P. A. Cowan & E. M. Hetherington (Eds.), *Advances in family research* (Vol. 2). Hillsdale, NJ: Erlbaum.

Baumrind, D. (1999, November). Unpublished review of J. W. Santrock's *Child Development,* 9th ed. (New York: McGraw-Hill).

Baumrind, D., Larzelere, R. E., & Cowan, P. A. (2002). Ordinary physical punishment: Is it harmful? Comment on Gershoff (2002). *Psychological Bulletin, 128,* 590–595.

Bauserman, R. (2003). Child adjustment in joint-custody versus sole-custody arrangements: A meta-analytic review. *Journal of Family Psychology, 16,* 91–102.

Bayley, N. (1969). *Manual for the Bayley Scales of Infant Development.* New York: Psychological Corporation.

Bayley, N. (1970). Development of mental abilities. In P. H. Mussen (Ed.), *Manual of child psychology* (3rd ed., Vol. 1). New York: Wiley.

BBC News World Edition. (2003, November 10). Premature babies. Available on the Internet at: http://news.bbc.co.uk/2/hi/health/medical_notes/3256615.stm.

Beachy, J. M. (2003). Premature infant massage in the NICU. *Neonatal Networking, 22,* 39–45.

Beagles-Roos, J., & Gat, J. (1983). Specific impact of radio and television on children's story comprehension. *Journal of Educational Psychology, 75,* 128–137.

Bearison, D. J., & Dorval, B. (2002). *Collaborative cognition.* Wesport, CT: Ablex.

Beaty, J. J. (2005). *50 early childhood literacy strategies.* Upper Saddle River, NJ: Prentice Hall.

Beaudet, A. L. (2004). Complex imprinting. *Nature Genetics, 36,* 793–795.

Bechtold, A. G., Bushnell, E. W., & Salapatek, P. (1979, April). *Infants' visual localization of visual and auditory targets.* Paper presented at the meeting of the Society for Research in Child Development, San Francisco.

Beck, C. T. (2002). Theoretical perspectives of postpartum depression and their treatment implications. *American Journal of Maternal/Child Nursing, 27,* 282–287.

Becker, A. B. (2005). Primary prevention of allergy and asthma is possible *Clinical Review of Allergy and Immunology, 28,* 5–16.

Becker-Blease, K. A., Deater-Deckard, K., Eley, T., Freyd, J. J., Stevenson, J., & Plomin, R. (2004). A genetic analysis of individual differences in dissociative behaviors in childhood and adolescence. *Journal of Child Psychology and Psychiatry, 45,* 522–532.

Bednar, R. L, Wells, M. G., & Peterson, S. R. (1995). *Self-esteem* (2nd ed.). Washington, DC: American Psychological Association.

Beeber, L. (2002). The pinks and the blues: Symptoms of chronic depression in mothers during their children's first year. *American Journal of Nursing, 102,* 91–98.

Begley, S. (1997). How to build a baby's brain. *Newsweek Special Issue.* Spring/Summer, 28–32.

Beins, B. (2004). *Research methods.* Boston: Allyn & Bacon.

Bell, A. C., & Swinburn, B. A. (2004), What are the key food groups to target for preventing obesity and improving nutrition in schools? *European Journal of Clinical Nutrition, 58,* 258–263.

Bell, A. P., Weinberg, M. S., & Mammersmith, S. K. (1981). *Sexual preference: Its development in men and women.* New York: Simon & Schuster.

Bell, M. A., & Fox, N. A. (1992). The relations between frontal brain electrical activity and cognitive development during infancy. *Child Development, 63,* 1142–1163.

Bell, S. M., & Ainsworth, M. D. S. (1972). Infant crying and maternal responsiveness. *Child Development, 42,* 1171–1190.

Belle, D. (1999). *The after school lives of children.* Mahwah, NJ: Erlbaum.

Bellinger, D. C. (2005). Teratogen update: Lead and pregnancy. *Birth Defects Research, 73,* 409–420.

Bellinger, D. C., Leviton, A., Waternaux, C., Needleman, H., & Rabinowitz, M. (1987). Longitudinal analysis of prenatal and postnatal lead exposure and early cognitive development. *New England Journal of Medicine, 316,* 1037–1043.

Belsky, J. (1981). Early human experience: A family perspective. *Developmental Psychology, 17,* 3–23.

Belsky, J., & Eggebeen, D. (1991). Early and extensive maternal employment/child care and

4–6-year-olds socioemotional development: Children of the National Longitudinal Survey of Youth. *Journal of Marriage and the Family, 53,* 1083–1099.

Belsky, J., & Pasco Fearon, R. (2002a). Early attachment security, subsequent maternal sensitivity, and later child development: Does continuity in development depend upon continuity of caregiving? *Attachment & Human Development, 4,* 361–387.

Belsky, J., & Pasco Fearon, R. (2002b). Infant-mother attachment security, contextual risk, and early development: A moderational analysis. *Development and Psychopathology, 14,* 293–310.

Belson, W. (1978). *Television violence and the adolescent boy.* London: Saxon House.

Bendersky, M., & Sullivan, M. W. (2002). Basic methods in infant research. In A. Slater & M. Lewis (Eds.), *Infant development.* New York: Oxford University Press.

Benenson, J. F., Apostolaris, N. H., & Parnass, J. (1997). Age and sex differences in dyadic and group interaction. *Developmental Psychology. 33,* 538–543.

Benfey, P. (2005). *Essentials of genomics.* Upper Saddle River, NJ: Prentice Hall.

Benini, A. L., Camilloni, M. A., Scordato, C., Lezzi, G., Savia, G., Oriani, G., Bertoli, S., Balzola, F., Liuzzi, A., & Petroni, M. L. (2001). Contribution of weight cycling to serum leptin in human obesity. *International Journal of Obesity and Related Metabolic Disorders, 25,* 721–726.

Benjet, C., & Kazdin, A. E. (2003). Spanking children: The controversies, findings, and new directions. *Clinical Psychology Review, 23,* 197–224.

Ben-Meir, A., Schenker, J. G., & Ezra, Y. (2005). Cesarean section upon request: Is it appropriate for everybody? *Journal of Perinatal Medicine, 33,* 106–111.

Benn, P. A., Fang, M., & Egan, J. F. (2005). Trends in the use of second trimester maternal serum screening from 1991 to 2003. *Genetics in Medicine, 7,* 328–331.

Bennett, W. (1993). *The book of virtues.* New York: Simon & Schuster.

Benson, E. (2003, February). Intelligence across cultures. *Monitor on Psychology, 34* (No. 2), 56–58.

Benson, P. L. (1997). *All kids are our kids: What communities must do to raise caring and responsible children and adolescents.* Minneapolis: Search Institute.

Benson, P. L. (2004). Emerging themes in research on adolescent spiritual and religious development. *Applied Developmental Science, 8,* 47–50.

Benson, P. L., Mannes, M., Pittman, K., & Ferber, T. (2004). Youth development: Developmental assets and public policy. In R. Lerner & L. Steinberg (Eds.), *Handbook of adolescent psychology* (2nd Ed.). New York: Wiley.

Benson, P. L., Scales, P. C., Hamilton, S. F., & Sesma, A. (2006). Positive youth development: Theory, research, and applications. In W. Damon & R. Lerner (Eds.), *Handbook of child psychology* (6th ed.). New York: Wiley.

Benz, E. J. (2004). Genotypes and phenotypes—another lesson from the hemoglobinpathies. *New England Journal of Medicine, 351,* 1532–1538.

Berenbaum, S. A., & Bailey, J. M. (2003). Effects on gender identity of prenatal androgens and genital appearance: Evidence from girls with congenital adrenal hyperplasia. *Journal of Clinical Endocrinology and Metabolism, 88,* 1102–1106.

Berensen, G. S., Srinivasan, S. R., & the Bogalusa Heart Study Group. (2005). Cardiovascular risk factors in youth with implications for aging: The Bogalusa Heart Study. *Neurobiology of Aging, 26,* 303–307.

Bergen, D. (1988). Stages of play development. In D. Bergen (Ed.), *Play as a medium for learning and development.* Portsmouth, NH: Heinemann.

Berk, L. F. (1994). Why children talk to themselves. *Scientific American, 271* (No. 5), 78–83.

Berk, L. F., & Spuhl, S. T. (1995). Maternal interaction, private speech, and task performance in preschool children. *Early Childhood Research Quarterly, 10,* 145–169.

Berko, J. (1958). The child's learning of English morphology. *Word, 4,* 150–177.

Berko, Gleason, J. (2002). Unpublished review of Santrock *Life-span Development* (9th ed.). New York: McGraw-Hill.

Berko, Gleason, J. (2005). *The development of language* (6th ed.). Boston: Allyn & Bacon.

Berkowitz, C. D. (2004). Cosleeping: Benefits, risks, and cautions. *Advances in Pediatrics, 51,* 329–349.

Berlin, L., & Cassidy, J. (2000). Understanding parenting: Contributions of attachment theory and research . In J. D. Osofsky & H. E. Fitzgerald (Eds.), *WAIMH handbook of infant mental health* (Vol. 3). New York: Wiley.

Berlyne, D. E. (1960). *Conflict, arousal, and curiosity.* New York: McGraw-Hill.

Berman, B. A., Wong, G. C., Bastani, R., Hoang, T., Jones, C., Goldstein, D. R., Bernert, J. T., Hammond, K. S., Tashkin, D., & Lewis, M. A. (2003). Household smoking behavior and ETS exposure among children with asthma in low-income, minority households. *Addictive Behaviors, 28,* 111–128.

Bern, S. L. (1977). On the utility of alternative procedures for assessing psychological androgyny. *Journal of Consulting and Clinical Psychology, 45,* 196–205.

Berndt, T. J. (2002). Friendship Quality and social development. *Current Directions in Psychological Science, 11,* 7–10.

Berninger, V. W. (2006). Learning disabilities. In W. Damon & R. Lerner (Eds.), *Handbook of child psychology* (6th ed.). New York: Wiley.

Berninger, V. W., & Abbott, R. (2005). *Paths leading to reading comprehension in at-risk and normally development second-grade readers.* Paper presented at the meeting of the Society of Research in Child Development, Atlanta.

Berninger, V. W., Dunn, A., Shin-Ju, C. L., & Shimada, S. (2004). School evolution: Scientist-practiener educators creating optimal learning environments for all students. *Journal of Learning Disabilities, 37,* 500–508.

Bernstein, J. (2004). The low-wage labor market: Trends and policy implications. In A. C. Crouter & A. Booth (Eds.), *Work-family challenges for low-income families and their children.* Mahwah, NJ: Erlbaum.

Best, D. (2001). Cross-cultural gender roles. In J. Worell (Ed.), *Encyclopedia of women and gender.* San Diego: Academic Press.

Best, J. W., & Kahn, J. V. (2003). *Research in education* (9th ed.). Boston: Allyn & Bacon.

Best, J. W., & Kahn, J. V. (2006). *Research in education* (10th ed.). Boston: Allyn & Bacon.

Bhutta, Z. A., Darmstadt, G. L., Hasan, B. S., & Haws, R. A. (2005). Community-based interventions for improving perinatal and neonatal health outcomes in developing countries: A review of the evidence. *Pediatrics, 115,* 519–6l6.

Bialystok, E. (1993). Metalinguistic awareness: The development of children's representations in language. In C. Pratt & A. Garton (Eds.), *Systems of representation in children.* London: Wiley.

Bialystok, E. (1997). Effects of bilingualism and biliteracy on children's emerging concepts of print. *Developmental Psychology, 33,* 429–440.

Bialystok, E. (1999). Cognitive complexity and attentional control in the bilingual mind. *Child Development, 70,* 537–804.

Bialystok, E. (2001). *Bilingualism in development: Language, literacy, and cognition.* New York: Cambridge University Press.

Biddle, S. J., Gorely, T., & Stensel, D. J. (2004). Health-enhancing physical activity and sedentary behavior in children and adolescents. *Journal of Sports Science, 22,* 679–701.

Biderman, J., & Faraone, S. V. (2003). Current concepts on the neurobiology of attention-deficit/hyperactivity disorder. *Journal of Attention Disorders 6* (Suppl. 1), S7–S16.

Bierman, K. L. (2004). *Peer rejection.* New York: Guilford.

Billman, J. (2003). *Observation and participation in early childhood settings: A practicum guide* (2nd ed.). Boston: Allyn & Bacon.

Billson, F. A., Fitzgerald, B. A., & Provis, J. M. (1985). Visual deprivation in infancy and childhood: Clinical aspects. *Australian and New Zealand Journal of Ophthalmology, 13,* 279–286.

Billy, J. O. G., Rodgers, J. L., & Udry, J. R. (1984). Adolescent sexual behavior and friendship choice. *Social Forces, 62,* 653–678.

Bingham, C. R., & Crockett, L. J. (1996). Longitudinal adjustment patterns of boys and girls experiencing early, middle, and late sexual intercourse. *Developmental Psychology, 32,* 647–658.

Birney, D. P., Citron-Pusty, J. H., Lutz, D. J., & Sternberg, R. J. (2005). The development of cognitive and intellectual abilities. In M. H. Bornstein & M. E. Lamb (Eds.), *Developmental psychology* (5th ed.). Mahwah, NJ: Erlbaum.

Bishay, D., Mahoney, P., DeFrancsco, S., Guyer, B., & Carlson, G. A. (2003). How willing are parents to improve pedestrian safety in their community? *Journal of Epidemiology and Community Health, 57,* 951–955.

Bjorklund, D. F. (2005). *Children's thinking* (4th ed.). Belmont, CA: Wadsworth.

Bjorklund, D. F., & Pellegrini, A. D. (2002). *The origins of human nature.* New York: Oxford University Press.

Blachman, B. A., Ball, E., Black, R., & Tangel, D. (1994). Kindergarten teachers develop phoneme awareness in low-income inner-city classrooms: Does it make a difference? In B. A. Blachman (Ed.), *Reading and writing.* Mahwah, NJ: Erlbaum.

Black, J. E. (2001, April). *Complex and interactive effects of enriched experiences on brain development.* Paper presented at the meeting of the Society for Research in Child Development, Minneapolis.

Black, L. L., Suarez, E. C., & Medina, S. (2004). Helping students help themselves: Strategies for successful mentoring relationships. *Counselor Education and Supervision, 44,* 44–55.

Black, M. M., & others. (2004). Special Supplemental Nutrition Program for Women, Infants, and Children participation and infants' growth and health: A multisite surveillance study. *Pediatrics, 114,* 169–176.

Black, R. A., & Hill, D. A. (2003). Over-the-counter medications in pregnancy. *American Family Physician, 67,* 2517–2524.

Black, S. (2004). Teaching students to think critically. *American School Board Journal, 191,* 52–54.

Blakemore, J. E. O., Berenbaum, S. A., & Liben, L. S. (2005). *Gender development.* Mahwah, NJ: Erlbaum, in preparation.

Bloch, M., Rotenberg, N., Koren, D., & Klein, E. (2005). Risk factors associated with the development of postpartum mood disorders. *Journal of Affective Disorders,* in press.

Block, J. H., & Block, J. (1980). The role of ego-control and ego-resiliency in the organization of behavior. In W. A. Collins (Ed.), *Minnesota symposium on child psychology* (Vol. 13). Minneapolis: University of Minnesota Press.

Bloom, B. S. (Ed.). (1985). *Developing talent in young people.* New York: Ballantine.

Bloom, K. C., Bednarzyk, M. S., Devitt, D. L., Renault, R. A., Teaman, V., & Van Loock, D. M. (2004). Barriers to prenatal care for homeless pregnant women. *Journal of Obstetrics, Gynecologic, and Neonatal Nursing, 33,* 428–435.

Bloom, L. (1998). Language acquisition in its developmental context. In W. Damon (Ed.), *Handbook of child psychology* (5th ed., Vol. 2). New York: Wiley.

Bloom, L., Lifter, K., & Broughton, J. (1985). The convergence of early cognition and language in the second year of life: Problems in conceptualization and measurement. In M. Barrett (Ed.), *Single word speech.* London: Wiley.

Bloom, P. (2002). *How children learn the meaning of words.* Cambridge, MA: MIT Press.

Blum, J. W., Beaudoin, C. M., & Caton-Lemos, L. (2005). Physical activity patterns and maternal well-being in postpartum women. *Maternal and Child Health Journal, 8,* 163–169.

Blum, N. J., Taubman, B., & Nemeth, N. (2004). Why is toilet training occurring at older ages? A study of factors associated with later training. *Journal of Pediatrics, 145,* 107–111.

Blum, R., & Nelson-Mmari, K. (2004). Adolescent health from an international perspective. In R. Lerner & L. Steinberg (Eds.), *Handbook of adolescent psychology.* New York: Wiley.

Blumenfeld, P. C., Pintrich, P. R., Wessles, K., & Meece, J. (1981, April). *Age and sex differences in the impact of classroom experiences on self-perceptions.* Paper presented at the biennial meeting of the Society of Research in Child Development, Boston.

Blumenfeld, P., Krajik, J., & Kempler, T. (2006). Motivation in the classroom. In W. Damon & R. Lerner (Eds.), *Handbook of child psychology* (6th ed.). New York: Wiley.

Blumenfeld, P., Modell, J., Bartko, T., Secada, W., Fredricks, J., Friedel, J., & Paris, A. (2005). School engagement of inner city students during middle childhood. In C. R. Cooper, C. T. Garcia Coll, W. T. Bartko, H. M. Davis, & C. Chatman (Eds.), *Developmental pathways through middle childhood.* Mahwah, NJ: Erlbaum.

Blumenthal, J., Jeffries, N. O., Castellanos, F. X., Liu, H., Zidjdenbos, A., Paus, T., Evans, A. C., Rapoport, J. L., & Giedd, J. N. (1999). Brain development during childhood and adolescence: A longitudinal MRI study. *Nature Neuroscience, 10,* 861–863.

Boblin, G., & Hagekull, B. (1993). Stranger wariness and sociability in the early years. *Infants Behavior and Development, 16,* 53–67.

Bodnar, R. L., Wells, M. G., & Peterson, S. R. (1995). *Self-esteem* (2nd ed.), Washington, DC: American Psychological Association.

Bodrova, E., & Leong, D. J. (2003). Learning and development of preschool children from Vygotskian perspective. In A. Kozulin, R. Gindis, V. S. Ageyev, & S. M. Miller (Eds.), *Vygotsky's educational theory in cultural context.* New York: Cambridge University Press.

Boekaerts, M. (2006). Self-regulation and effort investment. In W. Damon & R. Lerner (Eds.). *Handbook of child psychology* (6th ed.). New York: Wiley.

Bolger, K. E., & Patterson, C. J. (2001). Developmental pathways from child maltreatment to peer rejection. *Child Development, 72,* 339–351.

Boman, K., Lindahl, A., & Bjork, O. (2003). Disease-related distress in parents of children with cancer at various stages after the time of diagnosis. *Acta Oncology, 42,* 137–146.

Bonari, L., Bennett, H., Einarson, A., & Koren, G. (2004). Risk of untreated depression during pregnancy. *Journal of Family Health Care, 13,* 144–145.

Bonvillian, J. (2005). Unpublished review of Santrock, *Topical life-span development* (3rd ed.). New York: McGraw-Hill.

Books, S. (2004). *Poverty and schooling in the U.S.* Mahwah, NJ: Erlbaum.

Boonstra, H. (2002, February). Teen pregnancy: Trends and lessons learned. *The Guttmacher Report on Public Policy,* pp. 7–10.

Booth, M. (2002). Arab adolescents facing the future: Enduring ideals and pressures to change. In B. B. Brown, R. W. Larson, & T. S. Saraswathi (Eds.), *The world's youth.* New York: Cambridge University Press.

Bornstein, M. H. (2006). Parenting science and education. In W. Damon & R. Lerner (Eds.), *Handbook of child psychology* (6th ed.). New York: Wiley.

Bornstein, M. H., & Sigman, M. D. (1986). Continuity in mental development from infancy. *Child Development, 57,* 251–274.

Bornstein, M. H., Arterberry, M. E., & Mash, C. (2005). Perceptual development. In M. H. Bornstein & M. E. Lamb (Eds.), *Developmental psychology* (5th ed.). Mahwah, NJ: Erlbaum.

Borowsky, I. W., Ireland, M., & Resnick, M. D. (2001). Adolescent suicide attempts: Risks and protectors. *Pediatrics, 107,* 485–493.

Borra, S. T., Kelly, L., Shirreffs, M. B., Neville, K., & Geiger, C. J. (2003). Developing health messages. *Journal of the American Dietary Association, 103,* 721–728.

Bost, C. S., & Vaughn, S. (2002). *Strategies for teaching students with learning and behavioral problems* (5th ed.). Boston: Allyn & Bacon.

Botero, D., & Wolfsdorf, J. I. (2005). Diabetes mellitus in children and adolescents. *Archives of Medical Research, 36,* 281–290.

Bouchard, T. J. (1995, August). *Heritability of intelligence.* Paper presented at the meeting of the American Psychological Association, New York, NY.

Bouchard, T. J. (2004). Genetic influence on human psychological traits. *Current Directions in Psychological Science, 13,* 148–151.

Bouchard, T. J., Lykken, D. T., McGue, M., Segal, N. L., & Tellegen, A. (1990). Source of human psychological differences. The Minnesota Study of Twins Reared Apart. *Science, 250,* 223–228.

Bouchey, H. A., & Furman, W. (2003). Dating and romantic relationships in adolescence. In G. Adams & M. Berzonsky (Eds.), *Blackwell handbook of adolescence.* Malden, MA: Blackwell.

Boukydis, C. F. Z., Bigsby, R., & Lester, B. M. (2004). Clinical use of the Neonatal Intensive Care Unit Network Neurobehavioral Scale. *Pediatrics, 113* (Supplement), S679–S689.

Bower, B. (1985). The left hand of math and verbal talent. *Science News, 127,* 263.

Bower, T. G. R. (1966). Slant perception and shape constancy in infants. *Science, 151,* 832–834.

Bower, T. G. R. (2002). Space and objects. In A. Slater & M. Lewis (Eds.), *Introduction to infant development.* New York: Oxford University Press.

Bowes, J., & Flanagan, C. A. (2000, July). *The relationship of empathy, sympathy, and altruism in adolescence: International comparisons.* Paper presented at the meeting of the international Society for the Study of Behavioral Development, Beijing, China.

Bowlby, J. (1969). *Attachment and loss* (Vol. 1). London: Hogarth Press.

Bowlby, J. (1989). *Secure and insecure attachment.* New York: Basic Books.

Bowles, T. (1999). Focusing on time orientation to explain adolescent self concept and academic achievement: Part II. Testing a model. *Journal of Applied Health Behavior, 1,* 1–8.

Boyer, K., & Diamond, A. (1992). Development of memory for temporal order in infants and young children. In A. Diamond (Ed.), *Development and neural bases of higher cognitive function.* New York: New York Academy of Sciences.

Boyle, J., & Cropley, M. (2004). Children's sleep: Problems and solutions. *Journal of Family Health Care, 14,* 61–63.

Boyles, N. S., & Contadino, D. (1997). *The learning differences sourcebook.* Los Angeles: Lowell House.

Brabeck, M. M. (2000). Kohlberg, Lawrence. In A Kazdin (Ed.), *Encyclopedia of psychology.* Washington, DC, & New York: American Psychological Association and Oxford University Press.

Bracey, J. R., Bamaca, M. Y., & Umana-Taylor, A. J. (2004). Examining ethnic identity among biracial and mororacial adolescents. *Journal of Youth and Adolescence, 33,* 123–132.

Brachlow, A., Jordan, A. E., & Tervo, R. (2001). Developmental screenings in rural settings: A comparison of the child developmental review and the Denver II Developmental Screening Test. *Journal of Rural Health, 17,* 156–159.

Bradley, R. H., & Corwyn, R. F. (2002). Socioeconomic status and child development. *Annual Review of Psychology* (Vol. 53). Palo Alto, CA: Annual Reviews.

Bradley, R. H., & Corwyn, R. F. (2004). "Family process" investments that matter for child well-being. In A. Kalil & T. DeLeire (Eds.), *Family investments in children's potential*. Mahwah, NJ: Erlbaum.

Bradley, R. H., Corwyn, R. F., McAdoo, H. P., & Coll, C. G. (2001). The home environments of children in the United States Part I: Variations by age, ethnicity, and poverty status. *Child Development 72*, 1844–1867.

Brainerd, C. J., & Reyna, V. F. (1993). Domains of fuzzy-trace theory. In M. L. Howe & R. Pasnak (Eds.), *Emerging themes in cognitive development*. New York: Springer.

Brainerd, C. J., & Reyna, V. F. (2004). fuzzy-trace theory and memory development. *Developmental Review, 24*, 396–439.

Bransford, J. D., & Donovan, M. S. (2005). Scientific inquiry and *How people learn*. In M. S. Donovan & J. D. Bransford (Eds.), *How students learn*. Washington, DC: National Academic Press.

Braver, S. L., Ellman, I. M., & Fabricus, W. V. (2003). Relocation of children after divorce and children's best interests: New evidence and legal considerations. *Journal of Family Psychology, 17*, 206–219.

Brazelton, T. B. (1956). Sucking in infancy. *Pediatrics, 17*, 400–404.

Brazelton, T. B. (2004). Preface: The Neonatal Intensive Care Unit Network Neurobehavioral Scale. *Pediatrics, 113* (Supplement), S632–S633.

Brazelton, T. B., Nugent, J. K., & Lester, B. M. (1987). Neonatal behavioral assessment scale. In J. D. Osofsky (Ed.), *Handbook of infant development* (2nd ed.). New York: Wiley.

Bredekamp, S. (1987). *Developmentally appropriate practice in early childhood programs serving children from birth through age 8*. Washington, DC: National Association for the Education of Young Children.

Bredekamp, S. (1997). NAEYC issues revised position statement on developmentally appropriate practice in early childhood programs. *Young Children, 52*, 34–40.

Bremner, G. (2004). Cognitive development: Knowledge of the physical world. In A. Fogel & G. Bremner (Eds.), *Blackwell handbook of infant development*. London: Blackwell.

Brent, R. L. (2004). Environmental causes of human congenital malformations. *Pediatrics, 113* (No. 4, Supplement), 957–968.

Breslau, N., Paneth, N. S., & Lucia, V. C. (2004). The lingering academic deficits of low birth weight children. *Pediatrics, 114*, 1035–1040.

Bretherton, I., Fritz, J., Zahn-Waxler, C., & Ridgeway, D. (1986). Learning to talk about emotions: A functionalist perspective. *Child Development, 57*, 529–548.

Bretherton, L., Stolberg, U., & Kreye, M. (1981). Engaging strangers in proximal interaction: Infants' social initiative. *Developmental Psychology, 17*, 746–755.

Breysse, P., Farr, N., Galke, W., Lanphear, B., Morely, R., & Bergofsky, L. (2004). The relationship between housing and health: Children at risk. *Environmental Health Perspectives, 112*, 1583–1588.

Bridges, L. J. (2002). Coping as an element of developmental well-being. In M. H. Bornstein, L. Davidson, C. L. M. Keyes, & K. A. Moore (Eds.), *Well-being*. Mahwah, NJ: Erlbaum.

Briefel, R. R., Redy, K., Karwe, V., Jankowski, L., & Hendricks, K. (2004). Toddler's transition to table foods: Impact on nutrient intakes and food patterns. *Journal of the American Dietic Association, 104*, 38–44.

Briem, V., Radeborg, K., Salo, I., & Bengstsson, H. (2004). Developmental aspects of children's behavior and safety while cycling. *Journal of Pediatric Psychology, 29*, 369–377.

Bril, B. (1999). Dires sur l'enfant selon les cultures. Etat des lieux et perspectives. In B. Brill, P. R. Dasen, C. Sabatier, & B. Krewer (Eds.), *Propos sur l'enfant et l'adolescent. Quels enfants pour quelles cultures?* Paris: L'Harmattan.

Brisk, M. E. (2005). *Bilingual education*. Mahwah, NJ: Erlbaum.

Brittle, C., & Zint, M. (2003). Do newspapers lead with lead? A content analysis of how lead health risks to children are covered. *Journal of Environmental Health, 65*, 17–22, 30, 34.

Brockmeyer, S., Treboux, D., & Crowell, J. A. (2005, April). *Parental divorce and adult children's attachment status and marital relationships*. Paper presented at the meeting of the Society for Research in Child Development, Atlanta.

Brodeur, D. A., & Pond, M. (2001). The development of selective attention in children with attention deficit hyperactivity disorder. *Journal of Abnormal Child Psychology, 29*, 229–239.

Brody, G. (2004). Siblings' direct and indirect contributions to child development. *Current Directions in Psychological Science, 13*, 124–126.

Brody, J. E. (1994, April 6). The value of breast milk. *New York Times*, p. C11.

Brody, N. (2000). Intelligence. In A. Kazdin (Ed.), *Encyclopedia of psychology*. Washington, DC, & New York: American Psychological Association and Oxford University Press.

Brodzinsky, D. M., & Pinderhughes, E. (2002). Parenting and child development in adoptive families. In M. H. Bornstein (Ed.), *Handbook of parenting* (Vol. 1). Mahwah, NJ: Erlbaum.

Brodzinsky, D. M., Lang, R., & Smith, D. W. (1995). Parenting adopted children. In M. H. Bornstein (Ed.), *Handbook of parenting* (Vol. 3). Hillsdale, NJ: Erlbaum.

Brodzinsky, D. M., Schechter, D. E., Braff, A. M., & Singer, L. M. (1984). Psychological and academic adjustment in adopted children. *Journal of Consulting and Clinical Psychology, 52*, 582–590.

Brom, B. (2005). *Nutrition Now* (4th ed.). Belmont, CA: Wadsworth.

Bronfenbrenner, U. (1986). Ecology of the family as a context for human development: Research perspectives. *Developmental Psychology, 72*, 723–742.

Bronfenbrenner, U. (1995). Developmental ecology through space and time: A future perspective. In P. Moen, G. H. Elder, & K. Lüscher (Eds.), *Examining lives in context*. Washington, DC: American Psychological Association.

Bronfenbrenner, U. (1995, March). *The role research has played in Head Start*. Paper presented at the meeting of the Society for Research in Child Development, Indianapolis.

Bronfenbrenner, U. (2000). Ecological theory. In A. Kazdin (Ed.), *Encyclopedia of psychology*. Washington, DC, & New York: American Psychological Association and Oxford University Press.

Bronfenbrenner, U. (2004). *Making human beings human*. Thousand Oaks, CA: Sage.

Bronfenbrenner, U., & Morris, P. (1998). The ecology of developmental processes. In W. Damon (Ed.), *Handbook of child psychology* (5th ed., Vol. 1). New York: Wiley.

Bronfenbrenner, U., & Morris, P. A. (2006). The ecology of developmental processes. In W. Damon & R. Lerner (Eds.), *Handbook of child psychology* (6th ed.). New York: Wiley.

Brook, J. S., Brook, D. W., Gordon, A. S., Whiteman, M., & Cohen, P. (1990). The psychological etiology of adolescent drug use: A family interactional approach. *Genetic Psychology Monographs, 116*, no. 2.

Brook, J. S., Whiteman, M., Balka, E. B., Win, P. T., & Gursen, M. D. (1998). Drug use among Puerto Ricans: Ethnic identity as a protective factor. *Hispanic Journal of Behavioral Sciences, 20*, 241–254.

Brooker, R. J. (2005). *Genetics* (2nd ed.). New York: McGraw-Hill.

Brooks, J. G., & Brooks, M. G. (1993). *The case for constructivist classrooms*. Alexandria, VA: Association for Supervision and Curriculum.

Brooks, J. G., & Brooks, M. G. (2001). *The case for constructivist classrooms*. Upper Saddle River, NJ: Erlbaum.

Brooks-Gunn, J. (2003). Do you believe in magic?: What we can expect from early childhood programs. *Social Policy Report, Society for Research in Child Development, XVII* No. 1, 1–13.

Brooks-Gunn, J., & Matthews, W. S. (1979). *He and she: How children develop their sex role identity*. Englewood Cliffs, NJ: Prentice Hall.

Brooks-Gunn, J., & Paikoff, R. (1993). "Sex is a gamble, kissing is a game": Adolescent sexuality and health promotion. In S. P. Millstein, A. C. Petersen, & E. O. Nightingale (Eds.), *Promoting the health behavior of adolescents*. New York: Oxford University Press.

Brooks-Gunn, J., & Paikoff, R. L. (1997). Sexuality and developmental transitions during adolescence. In J. Schulenberg, J. Maggs, & K. Hurrelmann (Eds.), *Health risks and developmental transitions during adolescence.* New York: Cambridge University Press.

Brooks-Gunn, J., & Warren, M. P. (1989). The psychological significance of secondary sexual characteristics in 9- to 11-year-old girls. *Child Development 59,* 161–169.

Brooks-Gunn, J., Currie, J., Emde, R. E., & Zigler, E. (2003). Do you believe in magic? What we can expect from early childhood intervention programs. *SRCD Social Policy Report, 17* (No. 1), 3–15.

Brooks-Gunn, J., Graber, J. A., & Paikoff, R. L. (1994). Studying links between hormones and negative affect: Models and measures. *Journal of Research on Adolescence, 4,* 469–486.

Brooks-Gunn, J., Han, W. J., & Waldfogel, J. (2002). Maternal employment and child cognitive outcomes in the first three years of life: The NICHD Study of Early Child Care. *Child Development, 73,* 1052–1072.

Broussard, S. C., & Garrison, M. E. B. (2004). The relationship between classroom motivation and academic achievement in elementary-school-aged children. *Family and Consumer Sciences, Research Journal, 33* 106–120.

Broverman, I., Vogel, S., Broverman, D., Clarkson, F., & Rosenkranz, P. (1972). Sex-role stereotypes: A current appraisal. *Journal of Social Issues, 28,* 59–78.

Brown, B. (2006). *Nutrition Now* (4th ed.). Belmont, CA: Wadsworth.

Brown, B. B. (1999). Measuring the peer environment of American adolescents. In S. L. Friedman & T. D. Wachs (Eds.), *Measuring environment across the life span.* Washington, DC: American Psychological Association.

Brown, B. B. (2004). Adolescent relationships with peers. In R. Lerner & L. Steinberg (Eds.), *Handbook of adolescent psychology* (2nd ed.). New York: Wiley.

Brown, B. B., & Larson, R. W. (2002). The kaleidoscope of adolescence: Experiences of the world's youth at the beginning of the 21st century. In B. B. Brown, R. W. Larson, & T. S. Saraswathi (Eds.), *The world's youth.* New York: Cambridge University Press.

Brown, B. B., & Lohr, M. J. (1987). Peer-group affiliation and adolescent self-esteem: An integration of ego-identity and symbolic-interaction theories. *Journal of Personality and Social Psychology, 52,* 47–55.

Brown, D. (1987). The status of Holland's theory of vocational choice. *Career Development Quarterly, 36,* 13–24.

Brown, R. (1973). *A first language: The early stages.* Cambridge, MA: Harvard University Press.

Brown, R. (1986). *Social psychology* (2nd ed.). New York: Free Press.

Browne-Krimsley, V. (2004). Lessons learned: Providing culturally-competent care in a nurse-managed center. *ABNF Journal, 15,* 71–73.

Brownlee, S. (1998, June 15). Baby talk. *U.S. News & World Report,* pp. 48–54.

Bruck, M., & Ceci, S. (2004). Forensic developmental psychology. *Current Directions in Psychological Science, 13,* 229–232.

Bruck, M., & Ceci, S. J. (1999). The suggestibility of children's memory. *Annual Review of Psychology, 50,* 419–439.

Bruck, M., & Melnyk, L. (2004). Individual differences in children's suggestibility: A review and a synthesis. *Applied Cognitive Psychology, 18,* 947–996.

Brumm, V. L., Azen, C., Moats, R. A., Stern, A. M., Broomand, C., Nelson, M. D., & Koch, R. (2004). Neuropsychological outcome of subjects participating in mild phenylketonuria mutations. *Journal of Inherited Metabolic Disease, 27,* 549–566.

Bruner, J. S. (1983). *Child talk.* New York: W. W. Norton.

Bruner, J. S. (1996). *The culture of education.* Cambridge, MA: Harvard University Press.

Bruss, M. B., Morris, J. R., Dannison, L. L., Orbe, M. P., Quituga, J. A., & Palacios, R. T. (2005). Food, culture, and family: Exploring the coordinated management of meaning regarding childhood obesity. *Health Communication, 18,* 155–175.

Bryant, A., & LaFromboise, T. D. (2005). The racial identity and cultural orientation of Lumbee American Indian high school students. *Cultural Diversity and Ethnic Minority Psychology, 11,* 82–89.

Bryant, J. B. (2005). Language in social contexts: The development of communicative competence. In J. Berko Gleason, *The development of language* (6th ed.). Boston: Allyn & Bacon.

Buchanan, C. M., Maccoby, E. E., & Dornbusch, S. (1992). Adolescents and their families after divorce: Three residential arrangements compared. *Journal of Research on Adolescence, 2,* 261–291.

Budwig, N. (1993). *A developmental functionalist approach to child language.* Hillsdale, NJ: Erlbaum.

Bugental, D. B., & Grusec, J. E. (2006). Socialization processes. In W. Damon & R. Lerner (Eds.), *Handbook of child psychology* (6th ed.). New York Wiley.

Buhrmester, D. (1998). Need fulfillment, interpersonal competence, and the development contexts of early adolescent friendship. In W. M. Bukowski & A. F. Newcomb (Eds.), *The company they keep: Friendship in childhood and adolescence.* New York: Cambridge University Press.

Buhrmester, D. (2001, April). *Does age at which romantic involvement start matter?* Paper presented at the meeting of the Society for Research in Child Development, Minneapolis.

Buhrmester, D. (2003). Unpublished review of Santrock, J. W., *Adolescence, 10th Ed.* New York: McGraw-Hill.

Buhrmester, D., & Furman, W. (1987). The development of companionship and intimacy. *Child Development, 58,* 1101–1113.

Buhs, E. S., & Ladd, G. W. (2002). Peer rejections as antecedent of young children's school adjustment: An examination of ineditating processes. *Developmental Psychology, 37,* 550–560.

Bukowski, R., Burgett, A. D., Gei, A., Saade, G. R., & Hankins, G. D. (2003). Impairments of fetal growth potential and neonatal encephalopathy. *American Journal of Obstetrics and Gynecology, 188,* 1011–1015.

Bukowski, W. M., & Adams, R. (2005). Peer relationships and psychopathology. *Journal of Clinical Child and Adolescent Psychology, 34,* 3–10.

Bullock, M., & Lutkenhaus, P. (1990). Who am I? Self-understanding in toddlers. *Merrill-Palmer Quarterly, 36,* 217–238.

Bumpas, M. F., Crouter, A. C., & McHale, M. (2001). Parental autonomy granting during adolescence: Exploring gender differences in context. *Developmental Psychology, 37,* 163–173.

Burden, M. J., Jacobson, S. W., Sokol, R. J., & Jacobson, J. L. (2005). Effects of prenatal alcohol exposure on attention and working memory at 7.5 years of age. *Alcoholism: Clinical and Experimental Research, 29,* 443–452.

Burke, R. V., Kuhn, B. R., & Peterson, J. L. (2004). Brief report: A "storybook" ending to children's bedtime problems—the use of a rewarding social story to reduce bedtime resistance and frequent nighttime waking. *Journal of Pediatric Psychology, 29,* 389–396.

Burke, V., Beilin, L. J., Dunbar, D., & Kevan, M. (2004). Associations between blood pressure and overweight defined by new standards for body mass index in childhood. *Preventive Medicine, 38,* 558–564.

Burnes, Bolton, S. L., Giger, J. N., & Georges, C. A. (2004). Structural and racial barriers to health care. *Annual Review of Nursing Research, 22,* 39–58.

Burris, A. C. (2005). *Understanding the math you teach.* Upper Saddle River, NJ: Prentice Hall.

Burrow, A. L., Tubman, J. G., & Finley, G. E. (2004). Adolescent adjustment in a nationally collected sample: Identifying group differences by adoption status adoption subtype, and developmental stage and gender. *Journal of Adolescence, 27,* 267–282.

Burts, D. C., Hart, C. H., Charlesworth, R., Hernandez, S., Kirk, L., & Mosley, J. (1989, March). *A comparison of the frequencies of stress behaviors observed in kindergarten children in classrooms with developmentally appropriate and developmentally inappropriate instructional practices.* Paper presented at the meeting of the American Educational Research Association, San Francisco.

Bush, P. G., Mayhew, T. M., Abramovich, D. R., Aggett, P. J., Burke, M. D., Page, K. R. (2001). Maternal cigarette smoking and oxygen diffusion across the placenta. *Placenta, 21,* 824–833.

Bushman, B. J., & Huesmann, L. R. (2001). Effects of televised violence on aggression. In D. Singer & J. Singer (Eds.), *Handbook of children and the media.* Thousand Oaks, CA: Sage.

Buss, D. M. (1995). Psychological sex differences: Origins through sexual selection. *American Psychologist, 50,* 164–168.

Buss, D. M. (2000). Evolutionary psychology. In A. Kazdin (Ed.), *Encyclopedia of psychology.* Washington, DC, & New York: American Psychological Association and Oxford University Press.

Buss, D. M. (2004). *Evolutionary psychology: The new science of the mind* (2nd ed.). Boston: Allyn & Bacon.

Buss, D. M., & Schmitt, D. P. (1993). Sexual strategies theory: An evolutionary perspective on human mating. *Psychological Review, 100,* 204–232.

Bussey, K., & Bandura, A. (1999). Social cognitive theory of gender development and differentiation. *Psychological Review, 106,* 676–713.

Buzwell, S., & Rosenthal, D. (1996). Constructing a sexual self: Adolescents' sexual self-perceptions and sexual risk-taking. *Journal of Research on Adolescence, 6,* 489–513.

Bybee, J. (Ed.). (1999). *Guilt and children.* San Diego: Academic Press.

Byrnes, J. P. (1998). *The nature and development of decision making and self-regulation.* Mahwah, NJ: Erlbaum.

Byrnes, J. P. (2001). *Minds, brains, and learning.* New York: Guilford.

Byrnes, J. P. (2003). Cognitive development during adolescence. In G. Adams & M. Berzonsky (Eds.). *Blackwell handbook of adolescence.* Malden, Ma: Blackwell.

Byrnes, J. P. (2005). The development of regulated decision making. In J. E. Jacobs & P. A. Klaczynski (Eds.), *The development of judgment and decision making in children and adolescents.* Mahwah, NJ: Erlbaum.

C

Caballero, B. (2004). Obesity prevention in children: Opportunities and challenges. *International Journal of Obesity and Related Metabolic Disorders, 28* (Suppl. 3), S90–S95.

Cabana, M. D., Rand, C., Slish, K., Nan, B., Davis, M. M., & Clark, N. (2004). Pediatrician self-efficacy for counseling parents of asthmatic children to quit smoking. *Pediatrics, 111,* 78–81.

Cairns, R. B. (1983). The emergence of developmental psychology. In P. H. Mussen (Ed.), *Handbook of child psychology* (4th ed., Vol. 1). New York: Wiley.

Cairns, R. B. (2006). The making of developmental psychology. In W. Damon & R. Lerner (Eds.), *Handbook of child psychology* (6th ed.). New York: Wiley.

Calabrese, R. L., & Schumer, H. (1986). The effects of service activities on adolescent alienation. *Adolescence, 21,* 675–687.

Caley, L. M., Kramer, C., & Robinson, L. K. (2005). Fetal alcohol spectrum disorder. *Journal of School Nursing, 21,* 139–146.

Callaghan, W. M., & Berg, C. J. (2003). Pregnancy-related mortality among women aged 35 years and older, United States 1991–1997. *Obstetrics and Gynecology, 102,* 1015–1021.

Callan, J. E. (2001). Gender development: Psychoanalytic perspectives. In J. Worrell (Ed.), *Encyclopedia of women and gender.* San Diego: Academic Press.

Callas, P. W., Flynn, B. S., & Worden, J. K. (2004). Potentially modifiable psychosocial factors associated with alcohol use during early adolescence. *Addictive Behavior, 29,* 1503–1515.

Callender, E. S., Rickard, L., Rinsky-Eng, J. (2001). Knowledge and use of folic acid supplementation: A study of Colorado women whose pregnancies were affected by a fetal neural tube defect. *Clinical Investigations in Medicine, 24,* 124–128.

Camaioni, L. (2004). The transition from communication to language. In A. Fogel & G. Bremner (Eds.), *Blackwell handbook of infant development.* Malden, MA: Blackwell.

Camilleri, B. (2005). Dynamic assessment and intervention: Improving children's narrative abilities. *International Journal of Language & Communication Disorders, 40,* 240–242.

Campbell, L., Campbell, B., & Dickinson, D. (2004). *Teaching and learning through multiple intelligences* (3rd ed.). Boston: Allyn & Bacon.

Campbell, M. K., & Mottola, M. F. (2001). Recreational exercise and occupational safety during pregnancy and birth weight: A case-control study. *American Journal of Obstetrics and Gynecology, 184,* 403–408.

Campfield, L. A., Smith, F. J., Gulsez, Y., Devos, R., & Burn, P. (1995). Mouse OB protein: Evidence for a peripheral signal linking adiposity and central neural networks. *Science, 269,* 546–549.

Campos, J. (1994, spring). The new functionalism in emotions. *SRCD Newsletter,* pp. 1, 7, 9–11, 14.

Campos, J. (2003, April). *The strengths and weaknesses of the dynamic systems and functionalist approaches to emotion are not one and the same.* Paper presented at the meeting of the Society for Research in Child Development, Tampa.

Campos, J. J. (2004). Unpublished review of Santrock, J. W., *Life-span development* (10th ed.). New York: McGraw-Hill.

Campos, J. J., Langer, A., & Krowtiz, A. (1970). Cardiac responses on the visual cliff in prelocomotor human infants. *Science, 170,* 196–197.

Canfield, R. L., & Haith, M. M. (1991). Young infants' visual expectations for symmetric and asymmetric stimulus sequences. *Developmental Psychology, 27,* 198–208.

Canfield, R. L., Gendle, M. H., Cory-Slechta, D. A. (2004). Impaired neuropsychological functioning in lead-exposed children. *Developmental Neuropsychology, 26,* 513–540.

Canfield, R. L., Henderson, C. R., Cory-Slechta, D. A., Cox, C., Jusko, T. A., & Lamphear, B. P. (2003). Intellectual impairment in children with blood lead concentrations below 10 microg per deciliter. *New England Journal of Medicine, 348,* 1517–1526.

Canterino, J. C., Ananth, C. V., Smulian, J., Harrigan, J. T., & Vintzileos, A. M. (2004). Maternal age and risk of fetal death in Singleton gestations: United States, 1995–2000. *Obstetrics and Gynecology Survey, 59,* 649–650.

Capaldi, D. M., & Shortt, J. W. (2003). Understanding conduct problems in adolescence from a life-span perspective. In G. Adams & M. Berzonsky (Eds.), *Blackwell handbook of adolescence.* Malden, MA: Blackwell.

Carbonell, O. A., Alzte, G., Bustamante, M. R., & Quiceno, J. (2002). Maternal caregiving and infant security in two cultures. *Developmental Psychology, 38,* 67–78.

Carey, S. (1977). The child as word learner. In M. Halle, J. Bresman, & G. Miller (Eds.), *Linguistic theory and psychological reality.* Cambridge, MA: MIT Press.

Carkskadon, M. A., Acebo, C., & Jenni, O. G. (2004). Regulation of adolescent sleep: Implications for behavior. *Annals of the New York Academy of Sciences, 102,* 276–291.

Carley, A. (2003). Anemia: When is it iron deficiency? *Pediatric Nursing 29,* 127–133.

Carlson, E. A., Sroufe, L. A., & Egeland, B. (2004). The construction of experience: A longitudinal study of representation and behavior. *Child Development, 75,* 66–83.

Carlson, K. S. (1995, March). *Attachment in sibling relationships during adolescence: Links to other familial and peer relationships.* Paper presented at the meeting of the Society for Research in Child Development, Indianapolis.

Carlton, M. P., & Winsler, A. (1999). School readiness: The need for a paradigm shift. *School Psychology Review, 28,* 338–352.

Carmichael, S. L., Shaw, G. M., & Nelson, V. (2002). Timing of prenatal care initiation and risk of congenital malformations. *Teratology, 66,* 326–330.

Carnegie Corporation. (1989). *Turning points: Preparing youth for the 21st century.* New York: Author.

Carnegie Corporation. (1996). *Report on education for children 3–10 years of age.* New York: The Carnegie Foundation.

Carnegie Council on Adolescent Development. (1995). *Great transitions.* New York: The Carnegie Corporation.

Caroli, M., Argentieri, L., Cardone, M., & Masi, A. (2004). Role of television in childhood obesity prevention. *International Journal of Obesity and Related Metabolic Disorders, 28* (Suppl. 3), S104–S108.

Carolo, G. (2005). Care and altruism. In M. Killen & J. Smetana (Eds.), *Handbook of moral development.* Mahwah, NJ: Erlbaum.

Carpendale, J. I., & Chandler, M. J. (1996). On the distinction between false belief understanding and subscribing to an interpretive theory of mind. *Child Development, 67,* 1686–1706.

Carrell, A. L., & Bernhardt, D. T. (2004). Exercise prescription for the prevention of obesity in adolescents. *Current Sports Medicine Reports, 3,* 330–336.

Carroll, J. (1993). *Human cognitive abilities.* Cambridge: Cambridge University Press.

Carskadon, M. A. (2004). Sleep difficulties in young people. *Archives of Pediatric and Adolescent Medicine, 158,* 597–598.

Carskadon, M. A. (2005). Sleep and circadian rhythms in children and adolescents: Relevance for athletic performance of young people. *Clinical Sports Medicine, 24,* 319–328.

Carskadon, M. A., Acebo, C., & Seifer, R. (2001). Extended nights, sleep loss, and recovery sleep in adolescence. *Archives of Italian Biology, 139,* 301–312.

Carskadon, M.A., Wolfson, A. R., Acebo, C., Tzischinsky, O., & Seifer, R. (1998). Adolescent sleep patterns, circadian timing, and sleepiness at a transition to early school days. *Sleep, 21,* 873–884.

Carter-Saltzman, L. (1980). Biological and sociocultural effects on handedness: Comparison between biological and adaptive families. *Science, 209,* 1263–1265.

Carver, K., Joyner, K., & Udry, J. R. (2003). National estimates of romantic relationships. In P. Florsheim (Ed.), *Adolescent romantic relations and sexual behavior.* Mahwah, NJ: Erlbaum.

Carver, L. J., & Bauer, P. J. (1999). When the event is more than the sum of its parts: Nine-month-olds' long-term ordered recall. *Memory, 7,* 147–174.

Carver, L. J., & Bauer, P. J. (2001). The dawning of a past: The emergence of long-term explicit memory in infancy. *Journal of Experimental Psychology: General, 130*(4), 726–745.

Cary, P. (2004). Fixing kids' sports. *U.S. News and World Report, 136,* 44–48, 50, 52–53.

Case, R. (1999). Conceptual development in the child and the field: A personal view of the Piagetian legacy. In E. K. Skolnick, K. Nelson, S. A. Gelman, & P. H. Miller (Eds.), *Conceptual development.* Mahwah, NJ: Erlbaum.

Case, R. (2005). Bring critical thinking to the main stage. *Education Canada, 45,* 45–48.

Case, R., & Mueller, M. P. (2001). Differentiation, integration, and covariance mapping as fundamental processes in cognitive and neurological growth. In J. L. McClelland & R. S. Siegler (Eds.), *Mechanisms of cognitive development.* Mahwah, NJ: Erlbaum.

Case, R., Kurland, D. M., & Goldberg, J. (1982). Operational efficiency and the growth of short-term memory span. *Journal of Experimental Child Psychology, 33,* 386–404.

Casey, B. J., Durston, S., & Fossella, J. A. (2001). Evidence for a mechanistic model of cognitive control. *Clinical Neuroscience Research, 1,* 267–282.

Casey, B. M., McIntire, D. D., Leveno, K. J. (2001). The continuing value of the Apgar score for the assessment of newborn infants. *New England Journal of Medicine, 344,* 467–471.

Caspi, A. (2006). Personality development. In W. Damon & R. Lerner (Eds.), *Handbook of child psychology* (6th ed.). New York: Wiley.

Casterline, A. (2004). Caries prevention. *Journal of the American Dental Association, 135,* 1224–1226.

Castoldi, A. F., Coccini, T., & Manzo, L. (2003). Neurotoxic and molecular effects of methylmercury in humans. *Review of Environmental Health, 18,* 19–31.

Castro, D. C., Bryant, D. M., Peisner-Feinberg, E. S., & Skinner, M. L. (2004). Parent involvement in Head Start programs: The role of the parent, teacher, and classroom characteristics. *Early Childhood Research Quarterly, 19,* 413–430.

Castro, L. C., & Avina, R. L. (2002). Maternal obesity and pregnancy outcomes. *Current Opinions in Obstetrics and Gynecology, 14,* 601–606.

Cauffman, B. E. (1994, February). *The effects of puberty, dating, and sexual involvement on dieting and disordered eating in young adolescent girls.* Paper presented at the meeting of the Society for Research on Adolescence, San Diego.

Cavanaugh, S. E. (2004). The sexual debut of girls in adolescence: The intersection of race, pubertal timing, and friendship group characteristics. *Journal of Research on Adolescence, 14,* 285–312.

Ceci, S. J. (2000). Bronfenbrenner, Urie. In A. Kazdin (Ed.), *Encyclopedia of psychology.* Washington, DC, & New York: American Psychological Association and Oxford University Press.

Ceci, S. J., & Gilstrap, L. L. (2000). Determinants of intelligence: Schooling and intelligence. In A. Kazdin (Ed.), *Encyclopedia of psychology.* Washington, DC, & New York: American Psychological Association and Oxford University Press.

Celi, F., Bini, V., Papi, F., Contessa, G., Santilli, F., & Falorni, A. (2004). Leptin serum levels are involved in the relapse after weight excess reduction in obese children and adolescents. *Diabetes Nutrition and Metabolism, 16,* 306–311.

Centers for Disease Control and Prevention. (2000). *CDC growth charts: United States.* Atlanta: Author.

Centers for Disease Control and Prevention. (2000). *Reproductive health.* Atlanta: Author.

Centers for Disease Control and Prevention. (2001). *Data and statistics: Adolescent pregnancy.* Atlanta: Author.

Centers for Disease Control and Prevention. (2002). *Sexually transmitted diseases.* Atlanta: Author.

Centers for Disease Control and Prevention. (2003). Births: Final data for 2002. *National Vital Statistics Reports, 52* (No. 10), 1–5.

Centers for Disease Control and Prevention. (2004, October 8). Smoking during pregnancy—United States, 1990–2002. *MMWR Morbidity and Mortality Report, 53,* 911–915.

Centers for Disease Control and Prevention. (2005). BMI—Body mass index: BMI for children and teens. Available on World Wide Web at www.cdc.gov/nccdphp/dnpa/bmi/bmi-for-age.htm.

Cerel, J., & Roberts, T. A. (2005). Suicidal behavior in the family and adolescent risk behavior. *Journal of Adolescent Health, 36,* e8–e14.

Chall, J. S. (1979). The great debate: Ten years later with a modest proposal for reading stages. In I. B. Resnick & P. A. Weaver (Eds.), *Theory and practice of early reading.* Hillsdale, NJ: Erlbaum.

Challis, J. R., Lye, S. J., Gibb, W., Whittle, W., Patel, F., & Alfaidy, N. (2001). Understanding preterm labor. *Annals of the New York Academy of Science, 943,* 225–234.

Chama, C. M., Audu, B. M., & Kyari, O. (2004). Prevention of mother-to-child transmission of HIV at Maiduguri, Nigeria. *Journal of Obstetrics and Gynecology, 24,* 266–269.

Chan, W. S. (1963). *A source book in Chinese philosophy.* Princeton, NJ: Princeton University Press.

Chang, L., Smith, L. M., LoPresti, C., Yonekura, M. L., Kuo, J., Walot, I., & Ernst, T. (2004). Smaller subcortical volumes and cognitive deficits in children with prenatal methamphetamine exposure. *Psychiatry Research, 132,* 95–106.

Chang, S. C., O'Brien, K. O., Nathanson, M. S., Mancini, J., & Witter, F. R. (2003). Characteristics and risk factors for adverse birth outcomes in pregnant black adolescents. *Journal of Obstetrics and Gynecology Canada, 25,* 751–759.

Channon, S., German, E., Cassina, C., & Lee, P. (2004). Executive functioning, memory, and learning in phenylketonuria. *Neuropsychology, 18*, 613–620.

Chan-Yeung, M., & Dimich-Ward, H. (2003). Respiratory health effects of exposure to environmental tobacco smoke. *Respirology, 8*, 131–139.

Chao, R. (2001). Extending research on the consequences of parenting style for Chinese Americans and European Americans. *Child Development, 72*, 1832–1843.

Chao, R., & Tseng, V. (2002). Parenting of Asians. In M. H. Bornstein, *Handbook of parenting* (2nd ed., Vol. 4). Mahwah, NJ: Erlbaum.

Chao, R. K. (2005, April). *The importance of Guan in describing control of immigrant Chinese.* Paper presented at the meeting of the Society for Research in Child Development, Atlanta.

Chapman, D. J., Damio, G., Young, S., & Perez-Escamilla, R. (2004). Effectiveness of breastfeeding peer counseling in a low-income, predominantly Latina population: A randomized controlled trial. *Archives of Pediatric and Adolescent Medicine, 158*, 897–902.

Chattin-McNichols, J. (1992). *The Montessori controversy.* Albany, NY: Delmar.

Chaudhry, V., Comblath, D. R., Corse, A., Freimer, M., Simmons-O'Brien, E., & Vogelsang, G. (2002). Thalidomide-induced neuropathy. *Neurology, 59*, 1872–1875.

Chaudhuri, J. H., & Williams, P. H. (1999, April). *The contribution of infant temperament and parent emotional availability to toddler attachment.* Paper presented at the meeting of the Society for Research in Child Development. Albuquerque.

Chaves, A. P., Diemer, M. A., Blustein, D. L., Gallagher, L. A., DeVoy, J. E., Casares, M. T., & Perry, J. C. (2004). Conceptions of work: The view from urban youth. *Journal of Counseling Psychology, 51*, 257–286.

Chavkin, W. (2001). Cocaine and pregnancy—time to look at the evidence. *Journal of the American Medical Association, 285*, 1626–1628.

Chen, C., & Stevenson, H. W. (1989). Homework: A cross-cultural comparison. *Child Development, 60*, 551–561.

Chen, I. G., Durbin, D. R., Elliott, M. R., Kallan, M. J., & Winston, F. K. (2005). Trip characteristics of vehicle crashes involving child passengers. *Injury Prevention, 11*, 219–224.

Chen, W., Srinivasan, S. R., Li, S., Xu, J., & Berensen, G. S. (2005). Metabolic syndrome variables at low levels in childhood are beneficially associated with adulthood cardiovascular risk: The Bogalusa Heart Study. *Diabetes Care, 28*, 126–131.

Chen, X., Hastings, P. D., Rubin, K. H., Chen, H., Cen, G., & Stewart, S. L. (1998). Childrearing attitudes and behavioral inhibition in Chinese and Canadian toddlers: A cross-cultural study. *Developmental Psychology, 34*, 677–686.

Chen, X., Striano, T., & Rakoczy, H. (2004). Auditory-oral matching behaviors in newborns. *Developmental Science, 7*, 42–47.

Chen, Z., & Siegler, R. S. (2000). Across the great divide: Bridging the gap between understanding of toddler's and older children's thinking. *Monograph of the Society for Research in Child Development, 65* (No. 2).

Cherlin, A. J., & Furstenberg, F. F. (1994). Stepfamilies in the United States: A reconsideration. In J. Blake & J. Hagen (Eds.), *Annual review of sociology.* Palo Alto, CA: Annual Reviews.

Chernausek, S. D. (2004). Growth hormone treatment of short children born small for gestational age: A U.S. perspective. *Hormone Research, 62* (Suppl. 3), S124–S127.

Chess, S., & Thomas, A. (1977). Temperamental individuality from childhood to adolescence. *Journal of Child Psychiatry, 16*, 218–226.

Chi, M. T. (1978). Knowledge structures and memory development. In R. S. Siegler (Ed.), *Children's thinking: What develops?* Hillsdale, NJ: Erlbaum.

Chiappetta, E. L., & Koballa, T. R. (2006). *Science instruction in the middle and secondary schools* (6th ed.). Upper Saddle River, NJ: Prentice Hall.

Child Trends. (2000). Trends in sexual activity and contraceptive use among teens. *Child trends research brief.* Washington, DC: Author.

Child Trends. (2001). *Trends among Hispanic children, youth, and families.* Washington, DC: Author.

Children's Defense Fund. (2001). *The state of America's children yearbook.* Washington, DC: Author.

Children's Defense Fund. (2004). *Leave no child behind.* Washington, DC: Children's Defense Fund.

Chisholm, J. S. (1989). Biology, culture, and the development of temperament: A Navajo example. In J. K. Nugent, B. Lester, & T. B. Brazelton (Eds.), *The cultural context of infancy: Vol. 1: Biology, culture, and infant development* (pp. 341–364). Norwood, NJ: Ablex.

Chiurazzi, P., Neri, G., & Oostra, B. A. (2003). Understanding the biological underpinnings of fragile X syndrome. *Current Opinions in Pediatrics, 15*, 559–566.

Choi, N. (2004). Sex role group differences in specific, academic, and general self-efficacy. *Journal of Psychology, 138*, 149–159.

Chomsky, N. (1957). *Syntactic structures.* The Hague: Mouton.

Christensen, L. B. (2004). *Experimental methodology* (9th ed.). Boston: Allyn & Bacon.

Christenson, S. L., & Thurlow, M. L. (2004). School dropouts: Prevention considerations, interventions, and challenges. *Current Directions in Psychological Science, 13*, 36–39.

Christian, K., Bachnan, H. J., & Morrison, F. J. (2001). Schooling and cognitive development. In R. J. Sternberg & E. L. Grigorenko (Eds.), *Environmental effects on cognitive development.* Mahwah, NJ: Erlbaum.

Chronis, A. M., Chacko, A., Fabiano, G. A., Wymbs, B. T., & Pelham, W. E. (2004). Enhancements to the behavioral parent training paradigm for families of children with ADHD: Review and future directions. *Clinical Child and Family Psychology Review, 7*, 1–27.

Chuang, M. E., Lamb, C. P., & Hwang, C. P. (2004). Internal reliability, temporal stability, and correlates of individual differences in paternal involvement: A 15-year longitudinal study in Sweden. In R. D. Day & M. E. Lamb (Eds.), *Conceptualizing and measuring father involvement.* Mahwah, NJ: Erlbaum.

Cicchetti, D. (2001). How a child builds a brain. In W. W. Hartup & R. A. Weinberg (Eds.), *Child psychology in retrospect and prospect.* Mahwah, NJ: Erlbaum.

Cicchetti, D., & Blender, J. A. (2004, December 14). A multiple-levels-of-analysis approach to the study of developmental processes in maltreated children. *Proceedings of the National Academy of Science USA, 101*, 17325–17326.

Cicchetti, D., & Toth, S. L. (1998). Perspectives on research and practice in developmental psychology. In W. Damon (Ed.), *Handbook of child psychology* (Vol. 4). New York: Wiley.

Cicchetti, D., & Toth, S. L. (2005). Child maltreatment. *Annual Review of Clinical Psychology, Vol. 1.* Palo Alto, CA: Annual Reviews.

Cicchetti, D., & Toth, S. L. (2006). A developmental pathways perspective on preventive interventions with high risk children and families. In W. Damon & R. Lerner (Eds.), *Handbook of child psychology* (6th ed.). New York: Wiley.

Cicchetti, D., Toth, S. L., & Rogosch, F. A. (2005). *A prevention program for child maltreatment.* Unpublished manuscript, University of Rochester, Rochester, NY.

Cioffi, J. (2004). Caring for women from culturally diverse backgrounds: Midwives' experiences. *Journal of Midwifery and Women's Health, 49*, 437–442.

Clampet-Lundquist, S., Edin, K., London, A., Scott, E., & Hunter, V. (2004). "Making a way out of no way": How mothers meet the basic family needs while moving from welfare to work. In A. C. Crouter & A. Booth (Eds.), *Work-family challenges for low-income families and their children.* Mahwah, NJ: Erlbaum.

Clapp, J. F., Kim, H., Burtclu, B., & Lopez, B. (2000). Beginning regular exercise in early pregnancy: Effect on fetoplacental growth. *American Journal of Obstetrics and Gynecology, 183*, 1484–1488.

Clark, E. (2000). Language acquisition. In A. Kazdin (Ed.), *Encyclopedia of psychology.* Washington, DC, & New York: American Psychological Association and Oxford University Press.

Clark, R. D., & Hatfield, E. (1989). Gender differences in receptivity to sexual offers. *Journal of Psychology and Human Sexuality, 2,* 39–55.

Clark, S. D., Zabin, L. S., & Hardy, J. B. (1984). Sex, contraception, and parenthood: Experience and attitudes among urban black young men. *Family Planning Perspectives, 16,* 77–82.

Clarke-Stewart, K. A., Malloy, L. C., & Allhusen, V. D. (2004). Verbal ability, self-control, and close relationships with parents protect children against misleading suggestions. *Applied Cognitive Psychology, 18,* 1037–1058.

Clay, E. C., & Seehusen, D. A. (2004). A review of postpartum depression for the primary care physician. *Southern Medical Journal, 97,* 157–162.

Cleary-Goldman, J., & others. (2005). Impact of maternal age on obstetric outcome. *Obstetrics and Gynecology, 105,* 983–990.

Clements, K., Boutin, P., & Froguel, P. (2002). Genetics of obesity. *American Journal of Pharmacogenomics, 2,* 177–187.

Clifford, B. R., Gunter, B., & McAleer, J. L. (1995). *Television and children.* Hillsdale, NJ: Erlbaum.

Clifton, R. K., Morrongiello, B. A., Kulig, J. W., & Dowd, J. M. (1981). Developmental changes in auditory localization in infancy. In R. N. Aslin, J. R. Alberts, & M. R. Petersen (Eds.), *Development of perception* (Vol. 1). Orlando, FL: Academic Press.

Clifton, R. K., Muir, D. W., Ashmead, D. H., & Clarkson, M. G. (1993). Is visually guided reaching in early infancy a myth? *Child Development, 64,* 1099–1110.

Clinton Smith, J. (2004). The current epidemic of childhood obesity and its implications for future coronary heart disease. *Pediatric Clinics of North America, 51,* 1679–1695.

Cnattinugius, S., Bergstrom, R., Lipworth, L., & Kramer, M. S. (1998). Prepregnancy weight and the risk of adverse pregnancy outcomes. *New England Journal of Medicine, 338,* 147–152.

Cogswell, M. E., Perry, G. S., Schieve, L. A., & Dietz, W. H. (2001). Obesity in women of childbearing age: Risks, prevention, and treatment. *Primary Care Update in Obstetrics and Gynecology, 8,* 89–105.

Cohall, A. T., Cohall, R., Ellis, J. A., Vaughan, R. D., Northridge, M. E., Watkins-Bryant, G., & Butcher, J. (2004). More than heights and weights: What parents of urban adolescents want from health care providers. *Journal of Adolescent Health, 34,* 258–261.

Cohen, G. J. (2000). *American Academy of Pediatrics guide to your child's sleep: Birth through adolescence.* New York: Villard Books.

Cohen, G. L., & Sherman, D. K. (2005). Stereotype threat and the social and scientific contexts of the race achievement gap. *American Psychologist, 60,* 270–271.

Cohen, L. B. (1995). Violent video games: Aggression, arousal, and desensitization in young adolescent boys. Doctoral dissertation, University of Southern California, (1995). *Dissertation Abstracts International, 57* (2-B), 1463. University Microfilms No. 9616947.

Cohen, L. B., & Cashon, C. H. (2006). Infant cognition. In W. Damon & R. Lerner (Eds.), *Handbook of child psychology* (6th ed.). New York: Wiley.

Cohen, M. H., d'Adesky, A. C., & Anastos, K. (2005). Women in Rowanda: Another world is possible. *JAMA, 294,* 613–615.

Cohen, M. S. (2004). Fetal and childhood onset of adult cardiovascular diseases. *Pediatric Clinics of North America, 51,* 1697–1719.

Cohen, S. S. (2004). Child care: A crucial legislative issue. *Journal of Pediatric Health Care, 18,* 312–314.

Cohn, A., & Canter, A. (2003). *Bullying: Facts for schools and parents.* Washington, DC: National Association of School Psychologists Center.

Coie, J. D. (2004). The impact of negative social experiences on the development of antisocial behavior. In J. B. Kupersmidt & K. A. Dodge (Eds.), *Children's peer relations: From development to intervention.* Washington, DC: American Psychological Association.

Colangelo, N. C., Assouline, S. G., & Gross, M. U. M. (2004). *A nation deceived: How schools hold back America's brightest students.* Available on the World Wide Web at http://nationdeceived.org/

Colangelo, N. C., Davis, G. A. (2003). *Handbook of gifted education* (3rd ed.). Boston: Allyn & Bacon.

Colapinto, J. (2000). *As nature made him.* New York: Simon & Schuster.

Colby, A., Kohlberg, L., Gibbs, J., & Lieberman, M. (1983). A longitudinal study of moral judgment. *Monographs of the Society for Research in Child Development* (Serial No. 201).

Cole, M. (2005). Culture in child development. In M. H. Bornstein & M. E. Lamb (Eds.), *Developmental psychology* (5th ed.). Mahwah, NJ: Erlbaum.

Cole, M. (2006). Culture and cognitive development in phylogenetic, historical, and ontogenetic perspective. In W. Damon & R. Lerner (Eds.), *Handbook of child psychology* (6th ed.). New York: Wiley.

Coleman, V. H., Erickson, K., Schulkin, J., Zinberg, S., & Sachs, B. P. (2005). Vaginal birth after cesarean delivery: Practice patterns of obstetricians-gynecologists. *Journal of Reproductive Medicine, 50,* 261–266.

Coles, R. (1970). *Erik H. Erikson: The growth of his work.* Boston: Little, Brown.

Coley, R. (2001). *Differences in the gender gap: Comparisons across racial/ethnic groups in education and work.* Princeton: Educational Testing Service.

Coley, R. L., Morris, J. E., & Hernandez, D. (2004). Out-of-school care and problem behavior trajectories among low-income adolescents: Individual, family, and neighborhood characteristics as added risks. *Child Development, 75,* 948–965.

Coll, C. G., Bearer, E. L., & Lerner, R. M. (Eds.). (2004). *Nature and nurture.* Mahwah, NJ: Erlbaum.

Coll, C. T. G., & Pachter, L. M. (2002). Ethnic and minority parenting. In M. H. Bornstein (Ed.), *Handbook of parenting* (2nd ed., Vol. 4). Mahwah, NJ: Erlbaum.

Coll, C. T. G., Meyer, E. C., & Brillion, L. (1995). Ethnic and minority parenting. In M. H. Bornstein (Ed.), *Children and parenting* (Vol. 2). Hillsdale, NJ: Erlbaum.

Collins, R. L., Elliott, M. N., Berry, S. H., Kanocouse, D. E., Kunkel, D., Hunter, S. B., & Miu, A. (2004). Watching sex on television predicts adolescent initiation of sexual behavior. *Pediatrics, 114,* e280–e289.

Collins, W. A., & Laursen, B. (2004). Parent-adolescent relationships and influences. In R. Lerner & L. Steinberg (Eds.), *Handbook of adolescent psychology.* New York: Wiley.

Collins, W. A., & Steinberg, L. (2006). Adolescent development in interpersonal context. In W. Damon & R. Lerner (Eds.), *Handbook of child psychology* (6th ed.). New York: Wiley.

Collins, W. A., Maccoby, E. E., Steinberg, L., Hetherington, E. M., & Bornstein, M. H. (2000). Contemporary research on parenting: The case for nature and nurture. *American Psychologist, 55,* 218–223.

Collins, W. A., Maccoby, E. E., Steinberg, L., Hetherington, E. M., & Bornstein, M. H. (2001). Toward nature WITH nurture. *American Psychologist, 56,* 171–173.

Colman, R. A., & Widom, C. S. (2004). Childhood abuse and neglect and adult intimate relationships: A prospective study. *Child Abuse and Neglect, 28,* 1133–1151.

Colombo, J., Shaddy, J. D., Richman, A. W., Malkranz, J. M., & Blaga, O. M. (2004). The developmental course of habituation in infancy and preschool outcome. *Infancy, 5,* 1–38.

Comas-Diaz, L. (2001). Hispanics, Latinos, or Americanos: The evolution of identity. *Cultural Diversity and Ethnic Minority Psychology, 7,* 115–120.

Combs, M. (2006). *Readers and writers in the primary grades* (3rd ed.). Upper Saddle River, NJ: Prentice Hall.

Comer, J. (2004). *Leave no child behind.* New Haven, CT: Yale University Press.

Comer, J. P. (1988). Educating poor minority children. *Scientific American, 259,* 42–48.

Comer, J. P., Haynes, N. M., Joyner, E. T., & Ben-Avie, M. (1996). *Rallying the whole village: The Comer process for reforming urban education.* New York: Teachers College Press.

Committee on Substance Abuse. (2000). Fetal alcohol syndrome an alcohol-related neurodevelopmental disorders. *Pediatrics, 106,* 258–261.

Commoner, B. (2002). Unraveling the DNA myth: The spurious foundation of genetic engineering. *Harper's Magazine, 304,* 39–47.

Compas, B. (2004). Processes of risk and resilience during adolescence: Linking contexts and individuals. In R. Lerner & L. Steinberg (Eds.), *Handbook of adolescent psychology* (2nd ed.). New York: Wiley.

Compas, B. E., Connor-Smith, J. K., Saltzman, H., Thomsen, A. H., & Wadsworth, M. E. (2001). Coping with stress during childhood and adolescence: Problems, progress, and potential in theory and research. *Psychological Bulletin, 127,* 87–127.

Compas, B. E., & Grant, K. E. (1993, March). *Stress and adolescent depressive symptoms: Underlying mechanisms and processes.* Paper presented at the biennial meeting of the Society for Research in Child Development, New Orleans.

Comstock, G., & Scharrer, E. (2006). Media and popular culture. In W. Damon & R. Lerner (Eds.), *Handbook of child psychology* (6th ed.). New York: Wiley.

Coney, J. (2004). World frequency and the lateralization of lexical processes. *Neuropsychologia, 43,* 142–148.

Conger, J. J. (1981). Freedom and commitment: Families, youth, and social change. *American Psychologist, 36,* 1475–1484.

Conger, J. J. (1988). Hostages to the future: Youth, values, and the public interest. *American Psychologist, 43,* 291–300.

Conger, R. D., & Chao, W. (1996). Adolescent depressed mood. In R. L. Simons (Ed.), *Understanding differences between divorced and intact families: Stress, interaction, and child outcome.* Thousand Oaks, CA: Sage.

Conger, R. D., & Ge, X. (1999). Conflict and cohesion to parent-adolescent relations: Changes in emotional expression. In M. J. Cox & J. Brooks-Gunn (Eds.), *Conflict and cohesion in families.* Mahwah, NJ: Erlbaum.

Conger, R., & Reuter, M. (1996). Siblings, parents, and peers: A longitudinal study of social influences in adolescent risk for alcohol use and abuse. In G. H. Brody (Ed.), *Sibling relationships: Their causes and consequences.* Norwood, NJ: Ablex.

Connolly, J., Craig, W., Goldberg, A., & Pepler, D. (2004). Mixed-gender groups, dating, and romantic relationships in early adolescence. *Journal of Research on Adolescence, 14,* 815–207.

Connolly, J., Furman, W., & Konarski, R. (2000). The role of parents in the emergence of heterosexual romantic relationships in adolescence. *Child Development, 71,* 1395–1408.

Connor, C. M., & Zwolan, T. A. (2004). Examining multiple sources of influence on the reading comprehension skills of children who use cochlear implants. *Journal of Speech, Language, and Hearing Research, 47,* 509–526.

Cook, M., & Birch, R. (1984). Infant perception of the shapes of tilted plane forms. *Infant Behavior and Development, 7,* 389–402.

Cooper, C. R., & Grotevant, H. D. (1989, April). *Individuality and connectedness in the family and adolescent's self and relational competence.* Paper presented at the meeting of the Society for Research in Child Development, Kansas City.

Cooper, C. R., Cooper, R. G., & Chavira, G. (2001). *Bridging multiple worlds: How African American and Latino youth in academic outreach programs navigate math pathways to college.* Unpublished manuscript, University of California at Santa Cruz.

Cooper, C. R., Garcia Coll, C. T., Bartko, W. T., Davis, H. M., & Chatman, C. (Eds.). (2005). *Developmental pathways through middle childhood.* Mahwah, NJ: Erlbaum.

Cooper, C. R., Grotevant, H. D., Moore, M. S., & Condon, S. M. (1982, August). *Family support and conflict: Both foster adolescent identity and role taking.* Paper presented at the meeting of the American Psychological Association, Washington, DC.

Cooper, P. J., Murray, L., Wilson, A., & Romaniuk, H. (2003). Controlled trial of the short-term and long-term effect of psychological treatment of postpartum depression I. Impact on maternal mood. *British Journal of Psychiatry, 182,* 412–419.

Cooter, R. B. (Ed.). (2004). *Perspectives on rescuing urban literacy education.* Mahwah, NJ: Erlbaum.

Cornish, K. (2004). The role of cognitive neuroscience in understanding atypical developmental pathways. *Journal of Cognitive Neuroscience, 16,* 4–5.

Corrigan, R. (1981). The effects of task and practice on search for invisibly displaced objects. *Developmental Review, 1,* 1–17.

Cortesi, F., Giannotti, F., Sebastiani, T., & Vagnoni, C. (2004). Cosleeping and sleep behavior in Italian school-aged children. *Journal of Developmental and Behavioral Pediatrics, 25,* 28–33.

Cosey, E. J., & Bechtel, G. A. (2001). Family support and prenatal care among unmarried African American teenage primiparas. *Journal of Community Health and Nursing, 18,* 107–114.

Cosmides, L., Tooby, J., Cronin, H., & Curry, O. (Eds.). (2003). *What is evolutionary psychology? Explaining the new science of the mind.* Hew Haven, CT: Yale University Press.

Council of Economic Advisors. (2000). *Teens and their parents in the 21st century: An examination of trends in teen behavior and the role of parent involvement.* Washington, DC: Author.

Courage, M. L., Howe, M. L., & Squires, S. E. (2004). Individual differences in 3.5 month olds' visual attention: What do they predict at 1 year? *Infant Behavior and Development, 127,* 19–30.

Courchesne, E., Redcay, E., & Kennedy, D. P. (2004). The autistic brain: Birth through adulthood. *Current Opinions in Neurology, 17,* 489–496.

Cowan, C. P., & Cowan, P. A. (2000). *When partners become parents.* Mahwah, NJ: Erlbaum.

Cowan, P. A., & Cowan, C. P. (2002). What an intervention design reveals about how parents affect their children's academic behavior and behavior problems. In J. G. Borkowski, S. L. Ramey, & M. Bristol-Power (Eds.), *Parenting and the child's world.* Mahwah, NJ: Erlbaum.

Cowan, P. A, Cowan, C. P., Ablow, J. C., Johnson, V. K., & Measelle, J. R. (Eds.). (2005). *The family context in children's adaptation to elementary school.* Mahwah, NJ: Erlbaum.

Cowan, P. A., Cowan, C. P., Ablow, J. C., Johnson, V. K., & Measelle, J. R. (Eds.). (2005). *The family context of parenting in children's adaptation to elementary school.* Mahwah, NJ: Erlbaum.

Cowley, G. (1998, April 6). Why children turn violent. *Newsweek,* pp. 24–25.

Cox, B. J., Enns, M. W., & Clara, I. P. (2004). Psychological dimensions associated with suicidal ideation and attempts in the National Comorbidity Study. *Suicide and Life-Threatening Behavior, 34,* 209–219.

Cox, J. L., Holden, J. M., & Sagovsky, R. (1987). Detection of postnatal depression: Development of the 10-items Edinburgh Postnatal Depression Scale. *British Journaling of Psychiatry, 150,* 782–786.

Coyne-Beasley, T., Baccaglini, L., Johnson, R. M., Webster, B., & Wiebe, D. J. (2005). Do partners with children know about firearms in their home? Evidence of a gender gap and implications for practitioners. *Pediatrics, 115,* e662–e667.

Crano, W., & Brewer, M. (2002). *Principles and methods of social research* (2nd ed.). Mahwah, NJ: Erlbaum.

Crespo, C. J., Smit, E., Troiano, R. P., Bartlett, S. J., Macera, C. A., & Anderson, B. E. (2001). Television watching, energy intake, and obesity in U.S. children. *Archives of Pediatric and Adolescent Medicine, 155,* 360–365.

Cress, S. W. (2004). Assessing standards in the "real" kindergarten classroom. *Early Childhood Education Journal, 32,* 95–99.

Crick, N. R. (2005, April). *Gender and psychopathology.* Paper presented at the meeting of the Society for Research in Child Development, Atlanta.

Crocetti, M., Dudas, A. R., & Krugman, S. (2004). Parental beliefs and practices regarding early introduction of solid foods to their children. *Clinical Pediatrics, 43,* 541–547.

Crockenberg, S. B. (1986). Are temperamental differences in babies associated with predictable differences in caregiving? In J. V. Lerner & R. M. Lerner (Eds.), *Temperament and social interaction during infancy and childhood.* San Francisco: Jossey-Bass.

Crockenberg, S. C., & Leerkes, E. M. (2005). Infant temperament moderates associations between childcare type and quantity and externalizing and internalizing behaviors at 2 years. *Infant Behavior and Development, 28,* 20–35.

Crockett, J. B., & Kauffman, J. M. (1999). *The least restrictive environment.* Mahwah, NJ: Erlbaum.

Crockett, L. J., Raffaelli, M., & Moilanen, K. (2003). Adolescent sexuality: Behavior and meaning. In G. R. Adams & M. Berzonsky (Eds.), *Blackwell handbook of adolescence.* Malden, MA: Blackwell.

Crompton, D. (2005). Building bridges with early childhood education. *Young Children, 60,* (no. 2), 6.

Crossman, A. M., Scullin, M. H., & Melnyk, L. (2004). Individual and developmental differences in suggestibility. *Applied Cognitive Psychology, 18,* 941–945.

Crouter, A. C., & Booth, A. (Eds.). (2004). *Work-family challenges for low-income parents and their children.* Mahwah, NJ: Erlbaum.

Crouter, A. C., & McHale, S. (2005). The long arm of the job revisited: Parenting in dual-earner families. In T. Luster & L. Okagaki (Eds.), *Parenting.* Mahwah, NJ: Erlbaum.

Crowley, A. A., Rains, R. M., & Pellico, L. H. (2005). A model preschool vision and hearing screening program: Students and faculty serve a community. *American Journal of Nursing, 105,* 52–55.

Crowley, K., Callahan, M. A., Tenenbaum, H. R., & Allen, E. (2001). Parents explain more to boys than to girls during shared scientific thinking. *Psychological Science, 12,* 258–261.

Csikszentmihalyi, M. (2000). Creativity: An overview. In A. Kazdin (Ed.), *Encyclopedia of psychology.* Washington, DC, and New York: American Psychological Association and Oxford University Press.

Cuéllar, I., Siles, R. I., & Bracamontes, E. (2004). Acculturation: A psychological construct of continued relevance for Chicana/o psychology. In R. J. Velasquet, B. W. McNeil, & L. M. Arellano (Eds.), *The handbook of Chicano psychology and mental health.* Mahwah, NJ: Erlbaum.

Cuevas, K. D., Silver, D. R., Brooten, D., Youngblut, J. M., & Bobo, C. M. (2005). The cost of prematurity: Hospital charges at birth and frequency of rehospitalization and acute care visits over the first year of life: A comparison by gestational age and birth weight. *American Journal of Nursing, 105,* 56–64.

Cullen, K. (2001). *Context and eating behavior in children.* Unpublished research, Children's Nutrition Research Center, Baylor School of Medicine, Houston.

Cullen, M. J., Hardison, C. M., & Sackett, P. R. (2004). Using SAT-grade and ability-job performance relationships to test predictions derived from stereotype threat theory. *Journal of Applied Psychology, 89,* 220–230.

Cummings, E. M. (1987). Coping with background anger in early childhood. *Child Development, 58,* 976–984.

Cummings, E. M., & Davies, P. T. (2002). Effects of marital conflict on children: Recent advances and emerging themes in process-oriented research. *Journal of Child Psychology and Psychiatry, 43,* 31–63.

Cummings, E. M., Braungart-Rieker, J. M., & DuRocher-Schudlich, T. (2003). Emotion and personality development. In I. B. Weiner (Ed.), *Handbook of psychology* (Vol. 6). New York: Wiley.

Cummings, M. (2006). *Human heredity* (7th ed.). Pacific Grove, CA: Brooks Cole.

Curley, J. P., Barton, S., Surani, A., & Keverne, E. B. (2004). Coadaptation of mother and infant regulated by a paternally expressed imprinted gene. *Proceedings of the Royal Society of London: Biological Sciences, 27,* 1303–1309.

Curran, K., DuCette, J., Eisenstein, J., & Hyman, I. A. (2001, August). *Statistical analysis of the cross-cultural data: The third year.* Paper presented at the meeting of the American Psychological Association, San Francisco, CA.

Currie, J., & Hotz, V. J. (2004). Accidents will happen? Unintentional childhood injuries and the effects of child care regulations. *Journal of Health Economics, 23,* 25–59.

Curtiss, S. (1977). *Genie.* New York: Academic Press.

Cushner, K. H. (2003). *Human diversity in action: Developing multicultural competencies for the classroom.* New York: McGraw-Hill.

Cushner, K. H. (2006). *Human diversity* (3rd ed.). New York: McGraw-Hill.

Cushner, K. H. (2006). *Human diversity in action* (4th ed.). Boston: McGraw-Hill.

Czeizel, A. E., & Puho, E. (2005). Maternal use of nutritional supplements during the first month of pregnancy and decreased risk of Down's syndrome: Case-control study. *Nutrition, 21,* 698–704.

D

Dabbs, J. M., Jr., & Morris, R. (1990). Testosterone, social class, and antisocial behavior in a sample of 4,462 men. *Psychological Science, 1,* 209–211.

Dabbs, J. M., Jr., Frady, R. I., Carr, T. S., & Besch, M. F. (1987). Saliva, testosterone, and criminal violence in young adult prison inmates. *Psychosomatic Medicine, 49,* 174–182.

Dahl, R. E. (2001). Affect regulation, brain development, and behavioral/emotional health in adolescence. *CNS Spectrums, 6,* 60–72.

Dahl, R. E. (2004). Adolescent brain development: A period of vulnerabilities and opportunities. *Annals of the New York Academy of Sciences, 1021,* 1–22.

Dahl, R. E., & Lewin, D. S. (2002). Pathways to adolescent sleep regulation and behavior. *Journal of Adolescent Health, 31* (Suppl. 6), 175–184.

Dale, P., & Goodman, J. (2005). Commonality and individual differences in vocabulary development. In M. Tomasello & D. I. Slobin (Eds.), *Beyond nature-nurture.* Mahwah, NJ: Erlbaum.

Dalton, M. A. (2002). Education rights and the special needs child. *Child and Adolescent Psychiatric Clinics of North America, 11,* 859–868.

Damico, J. S., Tetenowski, J. A., & Nettleton, S. K. (2004). Emerging issues and trends in attention deficit hyperactivity disorder: An update for the speech-language pathologist. *Seminars and Speech and Language, 25,* 207–213.

Damon, W. (1988). *The moral child.* New York: Free Press.

Damon, W. (1995). *Greater expectations.* New York: Free Press.

Damon, W., & Hart, D. (1992). Self-understanding and its role in social and moral development. In M. H. Bornstein & M. E. Lamb (Eds.), *Developmental psychology: An advanced textbook* (3rd ed.). Hillsdale, NJ: Erlbaum.

Daniels, S. R. (2005). What is the best method to identify cardiovascular risk related to obesity? *Journal of Pediatrics, 146,* A3.

Danielson, C. K., De Arellano, M. A., Kilpatrick, D. G., Saunders, B. E., & Resnick, H. S. (2005). Child maltreatment in depressed adolescents: Differences in symptomatology based on history of abuse. *Child Maltreatment, 10,* 37–48.

Darroch, J. E., Landry, D. J., & Singh, S. (2000). Changing emphases in sexuality education in U.S. public secondary schools, 1988–1999. *Family Planning Perspectives, 32,* 204–211, 265.

Darwin, C. (1859). *On the origin of species.* London: John Murray.

Datar, A., & Sturm, R. (2004). Physical education in elementary school and body mass index: Evidence from the early childhood longitudinal study. *American Journal of Public Health, 94,* 1501–1506.

Datar, A., & Sturm, R. (2004). Childhood overweight and parent- and teacher-reported behavior problems: Evidence from a prospective study of kindergartners. *Archives of Pediatric and Adolescent Medicine, 158,* 804–810.

Dattilio, F. M. (Ed.) (2001). *Case studies in couple and family therapy.* New York: Guilford.

D'Augelli, A. R. (1991). Gay men in college: Identity processes and adaptations. *Journal of College Student Development, 32,* 140–146.

D'Augelli, A. R. (2000). Sexual orientation. In A. Kazdin (Ed.), *Encyclopedia of psychology.* Washington, DC, & New York: American Psychological Association and Oxford University Press.

Davidson, J. (2000). Giftedness. In A. Kazdin (Ed.), *Encyclopedia of psychology.* Washington, DC, & New York: American Psychological Association and Oxford University Press.

Davidson, J., & Davidson, B. (2004). *Genius denied: How to stop wasting our brightest young minds.* New York: Simon & Schuster.

Davies, J., & Brember, L. (1999). Reading and mathematics attainments and self-esteem in years 2 and 6—an eight-year cross-sectional study. *Educational Studies, 25,* 145–157.

Davila, J., & Steinberg, S. J. (2006). Depression and romantic dysfunction during adolescence. In T. E. Joiner, J. S. Brown, & J. Kistner (Eds.), *The interpersonal, cognitive, and social nature of depression.* Mahwah, NJ: Erlbaum.

Davis, A. F., Hyatt, G., & Arrasmith, D. (1998, February). "I Have a Dream" program. *Class One Evaluation Report.* Portland, OR: Northwest Regional Education Laboratory.

Davis, B. E., Moon, R. Y., Sachs, M. C., & Ottolini, M. C. (1998). Effects of sleep position on infant motor development. *Pediatrics, 102,* 1135–1140.

Davis, D. K. (2005). Leading the midwifery renaissance. *RCM Midwives, 8,* 264–268.

Davis, K. F., Parker, K. P., & Montgomery, G. L. (2004). Sleep in infants and young children: Part one: Normal sleep. *Journal of Pediatric Health Care, 18,* 65–71.

Davison, K. K., & Birch, L. L. (2001). Weight status, parent reaction, and self-concept in five-year-old girls. *Pediatrics, 107,* 46–53.

Daws, D. (2000). *Through the night.* San Francisco: Free Association Books.

Day, M. C. (1975). Developmental trends in visual scanning. In H. W. Reese (Ed.), *Advances in child development and behavior* (Vol. 10). New York: Academic Press.

Day, N. L., Leech, S. L., Richardson, G. A., Cornelius, M. D., Robles, N., & Larkby, C. (2002). Prenatal alcohol exposure predicts continued deficits in offspring size at 14 years of age. *Alcohol: Clinical and Experimental Research, 26,* 1584–1591.

Day, R. D., & Lamb, M. E. (2004). Conceptualizing and measuring father involvement: Pathways, problems, and progress. In R. D. Day & M. E. Lamb (Eds.), *Conceptualizing and measuring father involvement.* Mahwah, NJ: Erlbaum.

Day, R. H., & McKenzie, B. E. (1973). Perceptual shape constancy in early infancy. *Perception, 2,* 315–320.

Day-Stirk, F. (2005). The big push for normal birth. *RCM Midwives, 8,* 18–20.

De Bellis, M. D., Keshavan, M. S., Beers, S. R., Hall, J., Frustaci, K., Masalehdan, A., Noll, J., & Boring, A. M. (2001). Sex differences in brain maturation during childhood and adolescence. *Cerebral Cortex, 11,* 552–557.

de Jong, J. (2004). Grammatical impairment. In L. Verhoeven & H. Van Balkom (Eds.), *The classification of language disorders.* Mahwah, NJ: Erlbaum.

de la Rocheborchard, E., & Thonneau, P. (2002). Paternal age and maternal age are risk factors for miscarriage: Results of a multicentre European study. *Human Reproduction, 17,* 1649–1656.

de Montigny, F., & Lacharite, C. (2004). Fathers' perceptions of the immediate postpartal period. *Journal of Obstetric, Gynecologic, and Neonatal Nursing, 33,* 328–329.

de Munich Keizer, S. M., & Mul, D. (2001). Trends in pubertal development in Europe. *Human Reproduction Update, 7,* 287–291.

de Vries, P. (2005). Lessons from home: Scaffolding vocal improvisation and song acquisition in a 2-year-old. *Early Childhood Education Journal, 32,* 307–312.

De, D. (2005). Sickle cell anemia. *British Journal of Nursing, 14,* 447–450.

Deater-Deckard, K., & Dodge, K. (1997). Externalizing behavior problems and discipline revisited: Non-linear effects and variation by culture, context and gender. *Psychological Inquiry, 8,* 161–175.

DeCasper, A. J., & Spence, M. J. (1986). Prenatal maternal speech influences newborn's perception of speech sounds. *Infant Behavior and Development, 9,* 133–150.

Decca, L., Daldoss, C., Fratelli, N., Lojacono, A., Slompo, M., Stegher, C., Valcamonico, A., & Frusca, T. (2004). Labor course and delivery in epidural amnesia: A case-control study. *Journal of Maternal-Fetal and Neonatal Medicine, 16,* 115–118.

deCharms, R. (1984). Motivation enhancement in educational settings. In R. Ames & C. Ames (Eds.), *Research on motivation in education* (Vol. 1). Orlando, FL: Academic Press.

Deci, R., & Ryan, R. (1994). Promoting self-determined education. *Scandinavian Journal of Educational Research, 38,* 3–14.

DeLamater, J., & MacCorquodale, P. (1979). *Premarital sexuality.* Madison: University of Wisconsin Press.

Delemarre-van de Waal, H. A. (2005). Secular trend of timing puberty. *Endocrine Development, 8,* 1–14.

Delgado, J., Ramirez-Cardich, M. E., Gilman, R. H., Lavarello, R., Dahodwala, N., Bazan, A., Rodriquez, V., Cama, R. I., Tovar, M., & Lescano, A. (2002). Risk factors for burns in children: Crowding, poverty, and poor maternal education. *Injury Prevention, 8,* 38–41.

Delmore-Ko, P., Pancer, S. M., Hunsberger, B., & Partt, M. (2000). Becoming a parent: The relation between prenatal expectations and postnatal experience. *Journal of Family Psychology, 14,* 625–640.

DeLoache, J. (2001). The symbol-mindedness of young children. In W. W. Hartup & R. A. Weinberg (Eds.), *Child psychology in retrospect and prospect.* Mahwah, NJ: Erlbaum.

Demetrious, A. (2001, April). *Towards a comprehensive theory of intellectual development: Integrating psychometric and post-Piagetian theories.* Paper presented at the meeting of the Society for Research in Child Development. Minneapolis.

Demorest, R. A., & Landry, A. G. (2003). Prevention of pediatric sports injuries. *Current Sports Medicine Reports, 2,* 337–343.

Demorest, R. A., & Landry, G. L. (2004). Training issues in elite young athletes. *Current Sports Medicine Reports, 3,* 167–172.

Dempster, F. N. (1981). Memory span: Sources of individual and developmental differences. *Psychological Bulletin, 80,* 63–100.

Denham, S. A. (1998). *Emotional development in young children.* New York: Guilford.

Denmark, F. L., Rabinowitz, V. C., & Seehzer, J. A. (2005). *Engendering psychology: Women and gender revisited* (2nd ed.). Boston: Allyn & Bacon.

Denmark, F. L., Russo, N. F., Frieze, I. H., & Eschuzur, J. (1988). Guidelines for avoiding sexism in psychological research: A report of the ad hoc committee on nonsexist research. *American Psychologist, 43,* 582–585.

Dennebaum, J. M., & Kulberg, J. M. (1994). Kindergarten retention and transition classrooms: Their relationship to achievement. *Psychology in the Schools, 31,* 5–12.

Dennis, C. L. (2004). Can we identify mothers at risk for postpartum depression in the immediate postpartum period using the Edinburgh Postnatal Depression Scale? *Journal of Affective Disorders, 78,* 163–169.

Dennis, C. L., & Stewart, D. E. (2004). Treatment of postpartum depression, part I: A critical review of biological interventions. *Journal of Clinical Psychiatry, 65,* 1242–1251.

Denny, C. B. (2001). Stimulant effects in attention deficit hyperactivity disorder. *Journal of Clinical Child Psychology, 30,* 98–109.

Denschlag, D., Tempfer, C., Kunze, M., Wolff, G., & Keck, C. (2004). Assisted reproductive techniques in patients with Klinefelter syndrome: A critical review. *Fertility and Sterility, 82,* 775–779.

DeRosier, M. E., & Marcus, S. R. (2005). Building friendships and combating bullying: Effectiveness of S. S. Grin at one-year follow-up. *Journal of Clinical Child and Adolescent Psychology, 34,* 140–150.

Dettmer, P., Dyck, N., & Thurston, L. P. (2002). *Consultation, collaboration, and teamwork for students with special needs* (4th ed.). Boston: Allyn & Bacon.

Dewey, J. (1933). *How we think.* Lexington, MA: D. C. Heath.

Dewey, K. G. (2003). Is breastfeeding protective against childhood obesity? *Journal of Human Lactation, 19,* 9–18.

DeZolt, D. M., & Hull, S. H. (2001). Classroom and school climate. In J. Worell (Ed.), *Encyclopedia of women and gender.* San Diego: Academic Press.

Diamond, A. (2001). A model system for studying the role of dopamine in the prefrontal cortex during early development in humans: Early and continuously treated phenylketonuria. In C. Nelson & M. Luciana (Eds.), *Handbook of developmental cognitive neuroscience.* Cambridge, MA: MIT Press.

Diamond, A. D. (1985). Development of the ability to use recall to guide action as indicated by infants' performance on AB. *Child Development, 56,* 868–883.

Diamond, L. M. (2003). Love matters: Romantic relationships among sexual-minority adolescents. In P. Florsheim (Ed.), *Adolescent romantic relationships and sexual behavior.* Mahwah, NJ: Erlbaum.

Diamond, L. M. (2004). Unpublished review of Santrock, *Adolescence* (11th ed.). New York: McGraw-Hill.

Diamond, L. M., & Savin-Williams, R. C. (2003). The intimate relationships of sexual-minority youths. In G. Adams & M. Berzonsky (Eds.), *Blackwell handbook of adolescence.* Malden, MA: Blackwell.

Diamond, L., Savin-Williams, R. C., & Dube, E. M. (1999). Sex, dating, passionate friendships, and romance: Intimate peer relations among lesbian, gay, and bisexual adolescents. In W. Furman & B. Brown & C. Feiring (Eds.), *The development of relationships during adolescence.* New York: Cambridge University Press.

Diamond, M., & Sigmundson, H. K. (1997). Sex reassignment at birth: Long-term review and clinical implications. *Archives of Pediatric and Adolescent Medicine, 151,* 298–304.

Diaz, C. (2003). *Multicultural education in the 21st century.* Boston: Allyn & Bacon.

Diaz, C. F., Pelletier, C. M., & Provenzo, E. F. (2006). *Touch the future . . . teach!* Boston: Allyn & Bacon.

Diaz-Rico, L. T., & Weed, K. Z. (2006). *Cross-cultural language and academic development handbook* (3rd ed.). Boston: Allyn & Bacon.

Dick, F., Dronkers, N. F., Pizzamiglio, L., Saygin, A. P., Small, S. L. & Wilson, S. (2005). Language and the brain. In M. Tomasello & D.A. Slobin (Eds.), *Beyond nature-nurture.* Mahwah, NJ: Erlbaum.

Dietl, J. (2005). Maternal obesity and complications during pregnancy. *Journal of Perinatal Medicine, 33,* 100–105.

Dietz, W. H., & Robinson, T. N. (2005). Clinical practice: Overweight children and adolescents. *New England Journal of Medicine, 352,* 2100–2109.

DiGiorgio, L. F. (2005). Promoting breastfeeding to mothers in the Special Supplemental Nutrition Program for Women, Infants, and Children. *Journal of the American Diet Association, 105,* 716–717.

Dishlon, T. J., Andrews, D. W., & Crosby, L. (1995). Antisocial boys and their friends in early adolescence: Relationship characteristics, quality, and interactional process. *Child Development, 66,* 139–151.

Dixon, L., Browne, K., & Hamilton-Giachritsis, C. (2005). Risk factors of parents abused as children: A mediational analysis of the intergenerational continuity of child maltreatment (Part I). *Journal of Child Psychology and Psychiatry and Allied Disciplines, 46,* 47–57.

Dodd, V. L. (2005). Implications of kangaroo care for growth and development in preterm infants. *Journal of Obstetrical, Gynecological, and Neonatal Nursing, 34,* 218–222.

Dodge, K. A. (2001). The science of youth violence prevention: Progressing from developmental psychopathology to efficacy to effectiveness in public policy. *American Journal of Preventive Medicine, 20,* 63–70.

Dodge, K. A. (1983). Behavioral antecedents of peer social status. *Child Development, 54,* 1386–1399.

Dodge, K. A. (2000). Developmental psychology. In M. H. Ebert, P. T. Loosen, & B. Nurcombe (Eds.), *Current diagnosis and treatment in psychiatry.* East Norwalk, CT: Appleton & Lange.

Dodge, K. A., Coie, J. D., & Lynam, D. R. (2006). Aggression and antisocial behavior in youth. In W. Damon & R. Lerner (Eds.), *Handbook of child psychology* (6th ed.). New York: Wiley.

Dong, C., & Hemminki, K. (2001). Modification of cancer risks in offspring by sibling and parental cancers from 2,112,616 nuclear families. *International Journal of Cancer, 92,* 144–150.

Donnerstein, E. (2001). Media violence. In J. Worrell (Ed.), *Encyclopedia of gender and women.* San Diego: Academic Press.

Donovan, C. A., & Smolkin, L. B. (2002). Children's genre knowledge: An examination of K-5 students' performance on multiple tasks providing different levels of scaffolding. *Reading Research Quarterly, 17,* 428–465.

Dopp, J., & Block, T. (2004). Peer mentoring that works! *Teaching Exceptional Children, 37,* 56–62.

Dorn, C. M., Madeja, S. S., & Sabol, F. R. (2004). *Assessing expressive learning.* Mahwah, NJ: Erlbaum.

Dorn, L. D., Williamson, D. E., & Ryan, N. D. (2002, April). *Maturational hormone differences in adolescents with depression and risk for depression.* Paper presented at the meeting of the Society for Research on Adolescence, New Orleans.

Dorr, A., Rabin, B. E., & Irlen, S. (2002). Parents, children, and the media. In M. H. Bornstein (Ed.), *Handbook of parenting* (2nd ed., Vol. 5). Mahwah, NJ: Erlbaum.

Dosreis, S., Zito, J. M., Safer, D. J., Soeken, K. L., Mitchell, J. W., Ellwood, L. C. (2003). Parental perceptions and satisfaction with stimulant medication for attention deficit hyperactivity disorder. *Journal of Developmental and Behavioral Pediatrics, 24,* 155–162.

Dougherty, D., & Simpson, L. A. (2004). Measuring the quality of children's health care: A prerequisite to action. *Pediatrics, 113,* 185–198.

Douglas, G., Grimley, M., McLinden, M., & Watson, L. (2004). Reading errors made by children with low vision. *Ophthalmic and Physiological Optics, 24,* 319–322.

Douglas, J. (2002). Eating problems in young children. *Hospital Medicine, 63,* 140–143.

Dowda, M., Ainsworth, B. E., Addy, C. L., Saunders, R., & Riner, W. (2001). Environmental influences, physical activity, and weight status in 8- to 16-year-olds. *Archives of Pediatric and Adolescent Medicine, 155,* 711–717.

Dowling, E. M., Gestsdottir, S., Anderson, P. M., Eye, A. V., Almerigi, J., & Lerner, R. M. (2004). Structural relations among spirituality, religiosity, and thriving in adolescence. *Applied Developmental Science, 8,* 7–16.

Drake, A. J., & Walker, B. R. (2004). The intergenerational effects of fetal programming: Non-genomic mechanisms for the inheritance of low birth weight and cardiovascular risk. *Journal of Endocrinology, 180,* 1–16.

Draper, J. (2003). Men's passage to fatherhood: An analysis of the contemporary relevance of transition theory. *Nursing Inquiry, 10,* 66–77.

Drewes, A. A., Carey, L. J., & Schaefer, C. E. (Eds.). (2003). *School-based play therapy.* New York: Wiley.

Drewnowski, A., & Specter, S. E. (2004). Poverty and obesity: The role of energy density and energy costs. *American Journal of Clinical Nutrition, 79,* 6–16.

Driscoll, A., & Nagel, N. G. (2005). *Early childhood education, birth-8* (3rd ed.). Boston: Allyn & Bacon.

Driscoll, M. P. (2005). *Psychology of learning for instruction* (3rd ed.). Boston: Allyn & Bacon.

Droege, K. L. (2004). Turning accountability on its head. *Phi Delta Kappan, 85,* 610–612.

Drotar, D. (2000). *Promoting adherence to medical treatment in chronic childhood illness.* Mahwah, NJ: Erlbaum.

Dryfoos, J. G. (1990). *Adolescents at risk: Prevalence or prevention.* New York: Oxford University Press.

Dryfoos, J. G. (1997). The prevalence of problem behaviors: Implications for programs. In R. P. Weissberg, T. P. Gullotta, R. L. Hampton, B. A. Ryan, & G. R. Adams (Eds.), *Healthy children 2010: Enhancing children's wellness.* Thousand Oaks, CA: Sage.

Dubay, L., Joyce, T., Kaestner, R., & Kenney, G. M. (2001). Changes in prenatal care timing and low birth weight by race and socioeconomic status: Implications for the Medicaid expansions for pregnant women. *Health Services Research, 36,* 373–398.

Dubowitz, H., Pitts, S. C., & Black, M. M. (2004). Measurement of three subtypes of child neglect. *Child Maltreatment, 9,* 344–356.

Duck, S. W. (1975). Personality similarity and friendship choices by adolescents. *European Journal of Social Psychology, 5,* 351–365.

Duckett, R. H. (1997, July). *Strengthening families/building communities.* Paper presented at the conference on Working with America's Youth, Pittsburgh.

Duffy, T. M., & Kirkley, J. R. (Eds.). (2004). *Learner-centered theory and practice in distance education.* Mahwah, NJ: Erlbaum.

Duggan, A., Fuddy, L., Burrell, L., Higman, S. M., McFarlane, E., Windham, A., & Sia, C. (2004). Randomized trial of statewide home visiting program to prevent child abuse: Impact in reducing parental risk factors. *Child Abuse and Neglect, 28,* 623–643.

Dunkel-Schetter, C. (1998). Maternal stress and preterm delivery. *Prenatal and Neonatal Medicine, 3,* 39–42.

Dunkel-Schetter, C., Gurung, R. A. R., Lobel, M., & Wadhwa, P. D. (2001). Stress processes in pregnancy and birth. In A. Baum, T. A. Revenson, & J. E. Singer (Eds.), *Handbook of health psychology.* Mahwah, NJ: Erlbaum.

Dunn, A. M., Burns, C., & Sattler, B. (2003). Environmental health of children. *Environmental Health of Children, 17,* 223–231.

Dunn, J., Davies, L. C., O'Connor, T. G., & Sturgess, W. (2001). Family lives and friendships: The perspectives of children in step-, singe-parent, and nonstep families. *Journal of Family Psychology, 15,* 272–287.

Dunn, L., & Kontos, S. (1997). What have we learned about developmentally appropriate education? *Young Children, 52* (No. 2), 4–13.

Dunson, D. B., Baird, D. D., & Columbo, B. (2004). Increased fertility with age in men and women. *Obstetrics and Gynecology, 103,* 51–56.

Durkin, K. (1985). Television and sex-role acquisition: I. Content. *British Journal of Social Psychology, 24,* 101–113.

Durodola, A., Kuti, O., Orji, E. O., & Ogunniyi, S. O. (2005). Rate of increase in oxytocin dose on the outcome of labor induction. *International Journal of Gynecology and Obstetrics,* in press.

Durrant, J. E. (2000). Trends in youth crime and well-being since the abolition of corporal punishment in Sweden. *Youth and Society, 3,* 437–455.

Dutton, G. N. (2003). Cognitive vision, its disorders and differential diagnosis in adults and children: Knowing where and what things are. *Eye, 17,* 289–304.

Dweck, C. S., Mangels, J. A., & Good, C. (2004). Motivational effects on attention, cognition, and performance. In D. Yun Dai & R. J. Sternberg (Eds.), *Motivation, emotion, and cognition.* Mahwah, NJ: Erlbaum.

E

Eagle, M. (2000). Psychoanalytic theory: History of the field. In A. Kazdin (Ed.), *Encyclopedia of psychology.* Washington, DC, & New York: American Psychological Association and Oxford University Press.

Eagly, A. H. (1996). Differences between women and men. *American Psychologist, 51,* 158–159.

Eagly, A. H. (2000). Gender roles. In A. Kazdin (Ed.), *Encyclopedia of psychology.* Washington, DC, & New York: American Psychological Association and Oxford University Press.

Eagly, A. H. (2001). Social role theory of sex differences and similarities. In J. Worrell (Ed.), *Encyclopedia of women and gender.* San Diego: Academic Press.

Eagly, A. H., & Crowley, M. (1986). Gender and helping behavior: A meta-analytic review of the social psychological literature. *Psychological Bulletin, 100,* 283–308.

Eagly, A. H., & Diekman, A. B. (2003). The malleability of sex differences in response to social roles. In L. G. Aspinwall & V. M. Standinger (Eds.), *A psychology of human strengths.* Washington, DC: American Psychological Association.

Eagly, A. H., & Steffen, V. J. (1986). Gender and aggressive behavior: A meta-analytic review of the social psychological literature. *Psychological Bulletin, 100,* 309–330.

Eaves, L., Silberg, J., Foley, D., Bulik, C., Maes, H., Erkanli, A., Angold, A., Costello, E. J., & Worthman, C. (2004). Genetic and environmental influences on the relative timing of pubertal change. *Twin Research, 7,* 471–481.

Eccles, J. (2004). Schools, academic motivation, and stage-environment fit. In R. Lerner & L. Steinberg (Eds.), *Handbook of adolescent psychology* (2nd ed.). New York: Wiley.

Eccles, J. S., & Roeser, R. W. (2005). School and community influences on human development. In M. H. Bornstein & M. E. Lamb (Eds.), *Developmental psychology* (5th ed.). Mahwah, NJ: Erlbaum.

Edelman, M. W. (1992). *The measure of our success.* Boston: Beacon Press.

Edelman, M. W. (1996). *The state of America's children.* Washington, DC: Children's Defense Fund.

Edelman, M. W. (2000). Commentary in *The state of America's children.* Washington, DC: Children's Defense Fund.

Edelman, M. W. (2004, October 28). *Interfaith service for justice for children and the poor.* Presentation, Children's Defense Fund, Washington, DC.

Educational Testing Service. (1992, February). *Cross-national comparisons of 9-13 year olds' science and math achievement.* Princeton, NJ: Educational Testing Service.

Edwards, C. P. (2002). Three approaches from Europe: Waldorf, Montessori, and Reggio Emilia. *Early Childhood Practice and Research, 4,* 36–40.

Edwards, P. A. (2004). *Children's literacy development.* Boston: Allyn & Bacon.

Edwards, R., & Hamilton, M. A. (2004). You need to understand my gender role: An empirical test of Tannen's model of gender and communication. *Sex Roles, 50,* 491–504.

Edwards, S. L., & Sarwark, J. F. (2005). Infant and child motor development. *Clinical and Orthopedic Related Research, 434,* 33–39.

Egan, J. F., Benn, P. A., Zelop, C. M., Bolnick, A., Gianferrari, E., & Borgida, A. F. (2004). Down syndrome births in the United States from 1989 to 2001. *American Journal of Obstetrics and Gynecology, 191,* 1044–1048.

Egeland, B., & Carlson, B. (2004). Attachment and psychopathology. In L. Atkinson & S. Goldberg (Eds.), *Attachment issues in psychopathology and intervention.* Mahwah, NJ: Erlbaum.

Egeland, B., Jacobvitz, D., & Sroufe, L. A. (1988). Breaking the cycle of abuse. *New Directions for Child Development, 11,* 77–92.

Ehrhardt, A. A. (1987). A transactional perspective on the development of gender differences. In J. M. Reinisch, L. A. Rosenblum, & S. A. Sanders (Eds.), *Masculinity/femininity: Basic perspectives.* New York: Oxford University Press.

Eidelman, A. I., & Feldman, R. (2004). Positive effect of human milk on neurobehavioral and cognitive development of premature infants. *Advances in Experimental Medicine and Biology, 554,* 359–364.

Eiferman, R. R. (1971). Social play in childhood. In R. Herron & B. Sutton-Smith (Eds.), *Child's play.* New York: Wiley.

Eiger, M. S., & Olds, S. W. (1999). *The complete book of breastfeeding* (3rd ed.). New York: Bantam.

Eigsti, I. M., & Cicchetti, D. (2004). The impact of child maltreatment on expressive syntax at 60 months. *Developmental Science, 7,* 88–102.

Eisenberg, A., Murkoff, H., & Hathaway, S. (2002). *What to expect when you're expecting* (3rd ed.). New York: Workman.

Eisenberg, N. (Ed.). (1982). *The development of prosocial behavior.* New York: Wiley.

Eisenberg, N. (2001). Emotion-regulated regulation and its relation to quality of social functioning. In W. W. Hartup & R. A. Weinberg (Eds.), *Child psychology in retrospect and prospect.* Mahwah, NJ: Erlbaum.

Eisenberg, N. (2002). Prosocial behavior, empathy, and sympathy. In M. H. Bornstein, L. Davidson, C. L. M. Keyes, & K. A. Moore (Eds.), *Well-being.* Mahwah, NJ: Erlbaum.

Eisenberg, N. (2005). Empathy-related responding in children. In M. Killen & J. G. Smetana (Eds.), *Handbook of moral development.* Mahwah, NJ: Erlbaum.

Eisenberg, N., & Fabes, R. A. (1998). Prosocial development. In N. Eisenberg (Ed.), *Handbook of child psychology* (5th ed., Vol. 3). New York: Wiley.

Eisenberg, N., & Morris, A. S. (2004). Moral cognitions and prosocial responding in adolescence. In R. Lerner & L. Steinberg (Eds.), *Handbook of adolescent psychology* (2nd ed.). New York: Wiley.

Eisenberg, N., & Wang, V. O. (2003). Toward a positive psychology: Social developmental and cultural contributions. In L. G. Aspinwall & U. M. Staudinger (Eds.), *A psychology of human strengths.* Washington, DC: American Psychological Association.

Eisenberg, N., Fabes, R. A., & Spinrad, T. L. (2006). Prosocial development. In W. Damon & R. Lerner (Eds.), *Handbook of child psychology* (6th ed.). New York: Wiley.

Eisenberg, N., Fabes, R. A., Guthrie, I. K., & Reiser, M. (2002). The role of emotionality and regulation in children's social competence and adjustment. In L. Pulkkinen & A. Caspi (Eds.), *Paths to successful development.* New York: Cambridge University Press.

Eisenberg, N., Guthrie, I. K., Fabes, R. A., Shepard, S., Losoya, S., Murphy, B. C., & others. (2000). Prediction of elementary school children's externalizing problem behaviors from attentional and behavioral regulation and negative emotionality. *Child Development, 71,* 1367–1382.

Eisenberg, N., Martin, C. L., & Fabes, R. A. (1996). Gender development and gender effects. In D. C. Berliner & R. C. Calfee (Eds.), *Handbook of educational psychology.* New York: Macmillan.

Eisenberg, N., Spinrad, T. L., & Smith, C. L. (2004). Emotion-related regulation: Its conceptualization, relations to social functioning, and socialization. In P. Philippot & R. S. Feldman (Eds.), *The regulation of emotion.* Mahwah, NJ: Erlbaum.

Eisinger, F., & Burke, W. (2003). Breast cancer and breastfeeding. *Lancet, 361,* 176–177.

Eitle, D. (2005). The moderating effects of peer substance abuse on the family structure-adolescent substance use association: Quantity versus quality of parenting. *Addictive Behaviors, 30,* 963–980.

Ekwo, E. E., & Moawad, A. (2000). Maternal age and preterm births in a black population. *Pediatric Perinatal Epidemiology, 2,* 145–151.

Elder, G. H., & Shanahan, M. J. (2006). The life course and human development. In W. Damon & R. Lerner (Eds.), *Handbook of child psychology* (6th ed.). New York: Wiley.

Eliakim, A., Frieland, O., Kowen, G., Wolach, B., & Nemet, D. (2004). Parental obesity and higher pre-intervention BMI reduce the likelihood of a multidisciplinary childhood obesity program to succeed—A clinical observation. *Journal of Pediatric Endocrinology and Metabolism, 17,* 1055–1071.

Elkind, D. (1970, April 5). Erik Erikson's eight ages of man. *New York Times Magazine.*

Elkind, D. (1976). *Child development and education: A Piagetian perspective.* New York: Oxford University Press.

Elkind, D. (1981). *The hurried child.* Reading, MA: Addison-Wesley.

Elkind, D. (1985). Reply to D. Lapsley and M. Murphy's *Developmental Review* paper. *Developmental Review, 5,* 218–226.

Elkind, D. (1988, January). Educating the very young: A call for clear thinking. *NEA Today,* pp. 2–27.

Elkind, D. (2004). Vygotsky's educational theory in cultural context. *Bulletin of the Menninger Clinic, 68,* 352–353.

Elliott, V. S. (2004). Methamphetamine use increasing. Available on the Internet at:www.ama-assn.org/amednews/2004/07/26/hlsc0726.htm

Ellis, L., & Ames, M. A. (1987). Neurohormonal functioning and sexual orientation: A theory of homosexuality-heterosexuality. *Psychological Bulletin, 101,* 233–258.

Elwig, K. (2005). Fetal nutrition and adult disease. *Journal of Human Nutrition and Diet, 18,* 224–225.

Ely, R. (2005). Language development in the school years. In J. Berko Gleason (Ed.), *The development of language* (6th ed.). Boston: Allyn & Bacon.

Emde, R. N., Gaensbauer, T. G., & Harmon, R. J. (1976). Emotional expression in infancy: A biobehavioral study. *Psychological Issues: Monograph Series, 10* (37).

Emery, C. A. (2003). Risk factors for injury in child and adolescent sport: A systematic review of the literature. *Clinical Journal of Sport Medicine, 13,* 256–268.

Emery, R. E. (1999). *Renegotiating family relationships* (2nd ed.). New York: Guilford Press.

Engels, R. C., Vermulst, A. A., Dubas, J. S., Bot, S. M., & Gerris, J. (2005). Long-term effects of family functioning and child characteristics on problem drinking in young adulthood. *European Addiction Research, 11,* 32–37.

England, L. J., Kendrick, J. S., Gargiullo, P. M., Zhniser, S. C., & Hannon, W. H. (2001). Measures of maternal tobacco exposure and infant birth weight at term. *American Journal of Epidemiology, 153,* 954–960.

Engler, A. J., Ludington-Hoe, S. M., Cusson, R. M., Adams, R., Bahnsen, M., Brumbaugh, E., Coates, P., Grief, J., McHargue, L., Ryan, D. L., Settle, M., & Williams, D. (2002). Kangaroo care: National survey of practice, knowledge, barriers, and perceptions. *American Journal of Maternal/Child Nursing, 27,* 146–153.

Ennett, S., & Bauman, K. (1996). Adolescent social networks: School, demographic, and longitudinal considerations. *Journal of Adolescent Research, 11,* 194–215.

Enoch, M. A., & Goldman, D. (2002). Problem drinking and alcoholism: Diagnosis and treatment. *American Family Physician, 65,* 441–448.

Epstein, J. A., Botvin, G. J., & Diaz, T. (1998). Linguistic acculturation and gender effects on smoking among Hispanic youth. *Preventive Medicine, 27,* 538–589.

Epstein, J. L. (2001). *School, family, and community partnerships.* Boulder, CO: Westview Press.

Epstein, J. L., & Sanders, M. G. (2002). Family, schools, and community partnerships. In M. H. Bornstein (Ed.), *Handbook of parenting* (2nd ed.). Mahwah, NJ: Erlbaum.

Epstein, J. L., Sanders, M. G., Salinas, K. C., Simon, B. S., Jansorn, N. R., & Van Voorhis, F. L. (2002). *School, family, and community partnerships* (2nd ed.). Thousand Oaks, CA: Corwin Press.

ERIC/EECE. (2002). Academic redshirting. *ERIC Clearinghouse on Elementary and Early Childhood Education,* pp. 1–15.

Ericsson, K. A., Krampe, R., & Tesch-Romer, C. (1993). The role of deliberate practice in the acquisition of expert performance. *Psychological Review, 100,* 363–406.

Erikson, E. H. (1950). *Childhood and society.* New York: W. W. Norton.

Erikson, E. H. (1968). *Identity: Youth and crisis.* New York: W. W. Norton.

Erikson, E. H. (1969). Ghandi's truth. New York: Norton.

Eskenazi, B., Stapleton, A. L., Kharrazi, M., & Chee, W. Y. (1999). Associations between maternal decaffeinated and caffeinated coffee consumption and fetal growth and gestational duration. *Epidemiology, 10,* 242–249.

Eslinger, P. J., Flaherty-Craig, C. V., & Benton, A. L. (2004). Developmental outcomes after early prefrontal cortex damage. *Brain and Cognition, 55,* 84–103.

Espelage, D. L., & Swearer, S. M. (Eds.). (2004). *Bullying in American schools.* Mahwah, NJ: Erlbaum.

Espy, K. A., McDiarmid, M. M., Cwik, M. F., Stalets, M. M., Hamby, A., & Senn, T. E. (2004). The contribution of executive functions to emergent mathematic skills in preschool children. *Developmental Neuropsychology, 26,* 465–486.

Estelles, J., Rodriquez-Arias, M., Maldonado, C., Aguilar, M.A., & Minarro, J. (2005). Prenatal cocaine exposure alters spontaneous and cocaine-induced motor and social behaviors. *Neurotoxicology and Teratology, 27,* 449–457.

Estes, L. S. (2004). *Essentials of child care and early education.* Boston: Allyn & Bacon.

Etzel, R. (1988, October). *Children of smokers.* Paper presented at the American Academy of Pediatrics meeting, New Orleans.

Evans, G. W. (2004). The environment of childhood poverty. *American Psychologist, 59,* 77–92.

Evertson, C. M., & Weinstein, C. S. (Eds.). (2006). *Handbook of classroom management.* Mahwah, NJ: Erlbaum.

Ezmerli, N. M. (2000). Exercise in pregnancy. *Primary Care Update in Obstetrics and Gynecology, 7,* 260–265.

F

Fabes, R. A., Eisenberg, N., Jones, S., Smith, M., Gutherie, I., Poulin, R., Shepard, S., & Friedman, J. (1999). Regulation, emotionality, and preschoolers' socially competent peer interactions. *Child Development, 70,* 432–442.

Fabes, R. A., Hanish, L. D., & Martin, C. L. (2003). Children at play: The role of peers in understanding the effects of child care. *Child Development, 74,* 1039–1043.

Fagan, J. F. (1992). Intelligence: A theoretical viewpoint. *Current Directions in Psychological Science, 1,* 82–86.

Fagot, B. I. (1995). Parenting boys and girls. In M. H. Bornstein (Ed.), *Handbook of parenting* (Vol. 1). Hillsdale, NJ: Erlbaum.

Fagot, B. I., Rodgers, C. S., & Leinbach, M. D. (2000). Theories of gender socialization. In T. Eckes & H. M. Trautner (Eds.), *The developmental social psychology of gender.* Mahwah, NJ: Erlbaum.

Fair Test. (2004). "No child left behind" after two years: A track record of failure. Retrieved online at http://www.fairtest.org

Falbo, T., & Poston, D. L. (1993). The academic, personality, and physical outcomes of only children in China. *Child Development, 64,* 18–35.

Famy, C., Streissguth, A. P., & Unis, A. S. (1998). Mental illness in adults with fetal alcohol syndrome or fetal alcohol effects. *American Journal of Psychiatry, 155,* 552–554.

Fantino, E., & Stolarz-Fantino, S. (2005). Decision-making: Context matters. *Behavioural Processes, 69,* 165–171.

Fantz, R. L. (1963). Pattern vision in newborn infants. *Science, 140,* 286–297.

Farr, M. (2005). *Latino language and literacy in ethnolinguistic Chicago.* Mahwah, NJ: Erlbaum.

Farrar, M. J., & Goodman, G. S. (1992). Developmental changes in event memory. *Child Development, 63,* 173–187.

Farrington, D. (2004). Conduct disorder, aggression, and delinquency. In R. Lerner & L. Steinberg, (Eds.), *Handbook of adolescent psychology* (2nd ed.). New York: Wiley.

Fasig, L. (2000). Toddlers' understanding of ownership: Implications for self-concept development. *Social Development, 9,* 370–382.

Federal Interagency Forum on Child and Family Statistics. (2002). *American children: Key national indicators of well-being.* Washington, DC: U.S. Government Printing Office.

Federal Register. (2005). *The 2005 HHS poverty guidelines.* Washington, DC: U.S. Department of Health and Human Services.

Federenko, I. S., & Wadhwa, P. D. (2004). Women's mental health during pregnancy influences fetal and infant developmental and health outcomes. *CNS Spectrum, 9,* 198–206.

Feeny, S., Christensen, D., & Moravcik, E. (2006). *Who am I in the lives of children?* (7th ed.). Upper Saddle River, NJ: Prentice Hall.

Fehring, R. J., Cheever, K. H., German, K., & Philpot, C. (1998). Religiosity and sexual activity among older adolescents. *Journal of Religion and Health, 37,* 229–239.

Fein, G. G. (1986). Pretend play. In D. Gorlitz & J. F. Wohlwill (Eds.), *Curiosity, imagination, and play.* Hillsdale, NJ: Erlbaum.

Feinberg, M., & Hetherington, E. M. (2001). Differential parenting as a within-family variable. *Journal of Family Psychology, 15,* 22–37.

Fekkes, M., Pijpers, F. I., & Verloove-Vanhorick, S. P. (2004). Bullying behavior and associations with psychosomatic complaints and depression in victims. *Journal of Pediatrics, 144,* 17–22.

Feldman, D. H. (2003). Cognitive development in childhood. In I. B. Weiner (Ed.), *Handbook of psychology* Vol. 6. New York: Wiley.

Feldman, H. D. (2001, April). *Contemporary developmental theories and the concept of talent.* Paper presented at the meeting of the Society for Research in Child Development, Minneapolis.

Feldman, R., & Eidelman, A. I. (2003). Skin-to-skin (kangaroo care) accelerates autonomic and neurobehavioral maturation in preterm infants. *Developmental Medicine and Child Neurology, 45,* 274–281.

Feldman, R., Greenbaum, C. W., & Yirmiya, N. (1999). Mother-infant affect synchrony as an antecedent of the emergence of self-control. *Developmental Psychology, 35,* 223–231.

Feldman, R., Weller, A., Sirota, L., & Eidelman, A. I. (2002). Skin-to-skin contact (Kangaroo care) promotes self-regulation in premature infants: Sleep-wake cyclicity, arousal modulation, and sustained exploration. *Developmental Psychology, 38,* 194–207.

Feldman, R., Weller, A., Sirota, L., & Eidelman, A. I. (2003). Testing a family intervention hypothesis: The contribution of mother-infant skin-to-skin contact (kangaroo care) to family intervention, proximity, and touch. *Journal of Family Psychology, 17,* 94–107.

Feldman, S. S. (1999). Unpublished review of J. W. Santrock's *Adolescence,* 8th ed. New York: McGraw-Hill.

Feldman, S. S., & Elliott, G. R. (1990). Progress and promise of research on normal adolescent development. In S. S. Feldman & G. Elliott (Eds.), *At the threshold: The developing adolescent.* Cambridge, MA: Harvard University Press.

Feldman, S. S., Turner, R., & Araujo, K. (1999). Interpersonal context as an influence on sexual timetables of youths: Gender and ethnic effects. *Journal of Research on Adolescence, 9,* 25–52.

Felkner, M., Suarez, L., Hendricks, K., & Larsen, R. (2005). Implementation and outcomes of recommended folic acid supplementation in Mexican-American women with prior neural tube defect-affected pregnancies. *Preventive Medicine, 40,* 867–87l.

Ferber, S. G., & Makhoul, J. R. (2004). The effect of skin-to-skin (kangaroo care) shortly after birth on the neurobehavioral responses of the term newborn. *Pediatrics, 113,* 858–865.

Ferguson, D. M., Harwood, L. J., & Shannon, F. T. (1987). Breastfeeding and subsequent social adjustment in 6- to 8-year-old children. *Journal of Child Psychology and Psychiatry, 28,* 378–386.

Fernandes, O., Sabharwal, M., Smiley, T., Pastuszak, A., Koren, G., & Einarson, T. (1998). Moderate to heavy caffeine consumption during pregnancy and relationship to spontaneous abortion and abnormal fetal growth: A meta-analysis. *Reproductive Toxicology, 12,* 435–444.

Ferrer-Wreder, L., Lorene, C. C., Kurtines, W., Briones, E., Bussell, J., Berman, S., & Arrufat, O. (2002). Promoting identity development in marginalized youth. *Journal of Adolescent Research, 17,* 168–187.

Fidalgo, Z., & Pereira, F. (2005). Sociocultural differences and the adjustment of mothers' speech to their children's cognitive and language comprehension skills. *Learning & Instruction, 15,* 1–21.

Field, A. E., Cambargo, C. A., Taylor, C. B., Berkey, C. S., Roberts, S. B., & Colditz, G. A. (2001). Peer, parent, and media influences on the development of weight concerns and frequent dieting among preadolescent and adolescent girls and boys. *Pediatrics, 107,* 54–60.

Field, T. M. (1992, September). Stroking babies helps growth, reduces stress. *Brown University Child and Adolescent Behavior Letter,* pp. 1, 6.

Field, T. M. (1998). Massage therapy effects. *American Psychologist, 53,* 1270–1281.

Field, T. M. (2000). Child abuse. In A. Kazdin (Ed.), *Encyclopedia of psychology.* Washington, DC, & New York: American Psychological Association and Oxford University Press.

Field, T. M. (2001). Massage therapy facilitates weight gain in preterm infants. *Current Directions in Psychological Science, 10,* 51–55.

Field, T. M. (2002). Infants' need for touch. *Human Development, 45,* 100–103.

Field, T. M. (2003). Stimulation of preterm infants. *Pediatrics Review, 24,* 4–11.

Field, T. M., Diego, M., Hernandez-Reif, M., Schanberg, S., Kuhn, C., Ynado, R., & Bendell, D. (2003). Pregnancy anxiety and comormid depression and anger: Effects on the fetus and neonate. *Depression and Anxiety, 17,* 140–151.

Field, T. M., Grizzle, N., Scafidi, F., & Schanberg, S. (1996). Massage and relaxation therapies' effects on depressed adolescent mothers. *Adolescence, 31,* 903–911.

Field, T. M., Henteleff, T., Hernandez-Reif, M., Martines, E., Mavunda, K., Kuhn, C., & Schanberg, S. (1998). Children with asthma have improved pulmonary functions after massage therapy. *Journal of Pediatrics, 132,* 854–858.

Field, T. M., Hernandez-Reif, M., & Freedman, J. (2004). Stimulation programs for preterm infants. *Social Policy Report, Society for Research in Child Development,* XVIII (No. 1), 1–19.

Field, T. M., Hernandez-Reif, M., Seligman, S., Krasnegor, J., & Sunshine, W. (1997). Juvenile rheumatoid arthritis: Benefits from massage therapy. *Journal of Pediatric Psychology, 22,* 607–617.

Field, T. M., Hernandez-Reif, M., Taylor, S., Quinitino, O., & Burman, I. (1997). Labor pain is reduced by massage therapy. *Journal of Psychosomatic Obstetrics and Gynecology, 18,* 286–291.

Field, T. M., Lasko, D., Mundy, P., Henteleff, T., Kabat, S., Talpins, S., & Dowling, M. (1997). Brief report: Autistic children's attentiveness and responsivity improve after touch therapy. *Journal of Autism and Developmental Disorders, 27,* 333–338.

Field, T. M., Quintino, O., Hernandez-Reif, M., & Koslosky, G. (1998). Adolescents with attention deficit hyperactivity disorder benefit from massage therapy. *Adolescence, 33,* 103–108.

Field, T. M., Schanberg, S. M., Scafidi, F., Bauer, C. R., Vega-Lahr, N., Garcia, R., Nystrom, J., & Kuhn, C. M. (1986). Tactile/kines-

thetic stimulation effects on preterm neonates. *Pediatrics, 77,* 654–658.

Filkins, K., & Koos, B. J. (2005). Ultrasound and fetal diagnosis. *Current Opinions in Obstetrics and Gynecology, 17,* 185–195.

Fine, M. A., & Harvey, J. H. (2005). Divorce and its relationship dissolution in the 21st century. In M. A. Fine & J. H. Harvey (Eds.), *Handbook of divorce and relationship dissolution.* Mahwah, NJ: Erlbaum.

Fiorentino, L., & Howe, N. (2004). Language competence, narrative ability, and school readiness in low-income preschool children. *Canadian Journal of Behavioral Science, 36,* 280–294.

Fisch, S. M. (2004). *Children's learning from educational television.* Mahwah, NJ: Erlbaum.

Fischer, A. H. (Ed.). (1999). *Gender and emotion.* New York: Cambridge University Press.

Fischer, K. W., & Bidell, T. R. (1998). Dynamic development of psychological structures in action and thought. In W. Damon (Ed.), *Handbook of child psychology* (Vol. 1). New York: Wiley.

Fischer, K. W., & Rose, S. P. (1995, Fall). Concurrent cycles in the dynamic development of brain and behavior. *SRCD Newsletter,* pp. 3–4, 15–16.

Fish, M. (2004). Attachment in infancy and preschool in low socioeconomic status rural Appalachian children: Stability and change and relations to preschool and kindergarten competence. *Developmental Psychopathology, 16,* 293–312.

Fisher-Thompson, D., Polinski, L., Eaton, M., & Hefferman, K. (1993, March). *Sex-role orientation of children and their parents: Relationship to the sex-typing of Christmas toys.* Paper presented at the biennial meeting of the Society for Research in Child Development, New Orleans.

Fitzgerald, E. F., Hwang, S. A., Lannguth, K., Cayo, M., Yang, B. Z., Bush, S., Worswick, P., & Lauzon, T. (2004). Fish consumption and other environmental exposures and their associations with serum PCB concentrations among Mohawk women at Akwesasne. *Environmental Research, 94,* 160–170.

Fitzgibbon, M. L., Stolley, M. R., Schiffer, L., Van Horn, L., KauferChristoffel, K., & Dyer, A. (2005). Two-year follow-up results for Hip-Hop to Health Jr.: A randomized controlled trial for overweight prevention in preschool minority children. *Journal of Pediatrics, 146,* 618–625.

Fivush, R., Hudson, J., & Nelson, K. (1984). Children's long-term memory for a novel event: An exploratory study. *Merrill-Palmer Quarterly, 30,* 303–316.

Fivush, R., Kuebli, J., & Clubb, P. A. (1992). The structure of events and event representations: A developmental analysis. *Child Development, 63,* 188–201.

Flanagan, C. (2004). Volunteerism, leadership, political socialization, and civic engagement. In

R. Lerner & L. Steinberg (Eds.), *Handbook of adolescent psychology* (2nd ed.). New York: Wiley.

Flanagan, C. A., Bowes, J., Jonsson, B., Csapo, B., & Sheblanova, E. (1998). The ties that bind: Correlates of male and female adolescents' civic commitments in seven countries. *Journal of Social Issues, 54,* 457–476.

Flanagan, C., & Fiason, N. (2001). Youth civic development: Implications of research for social policy and programs. *SRCD Social Policy Report, XV* (No. 1), 1–14.

Flavell, J. H. (1999). Cognitive development: Children's knowledge about the mind. *Annual Review of Psychology* (Vol. 50). Palo Alto, CA: Annual Reviews.

Flavell, J. H. (2004). Theory-of-mind development: Retrospect and prospect. *Merrill-Palmer Quarterly, 50,* 274–290.

Flavell, J. H., Friedrichs, A., & Hoyt, J. (1970). Developmental changes in memorization processes. *Cognitive Psychology, 1,* 324–340.

Flavell, J. H., Green, F. L., & Flavell, E. R. (1995). Young children's knowledge about thinking. *Monographs of the Society for Research in Child Development, 60* (1, Serial No. 243).

Flavell, J. H., Miller, P. H., & Miller, S. A. (2002). *Cognitive development* (4th ed.), Upper Saddle River, NJ: Prentice Hall.

Flegal, K. M., Ogden, C. L., & Carroll, M. D. (2004). Prevalence and trends in Mexican-American adults and children. *Nutrition Review, 62,* S144–S148.

Fletcher, A. C., Steinberg, L., & Williams-Wheeler, M. (2004). Parental influences on adolescent problem behavior: Revisiting Stattin and Kerr. *Child Development, 75,* 781–796.

Flick, L., White, D. K., Vemulapalli, C., Stulac, B. B., & Kemp, J. S. (2001). Sleep position and the use of soft bedding during bed sharing among African American infants at increased risk for sudden infant death syndrome. *Journal of Pediatrics, 138,* 338–343.

Fling, S., Smith, L., Rodriguez, T., Thornton, D., Atkins, E., & Nixon, K. (1992). Videogames, aggression, and self-esteem: A survey. *Social Behavior and Personality, 20,* 39–46.

Flohr, J. W., Atkins, D. H., Bower, T. G. R., & Aldridge, M. A. (2001, April). *Infant music preferences.* Paper presented at the meeting of the Society for Research in Child Development, Minneapolis.

Flores, D. L., & Hendrick, V. C. (2002). Etiology and treatment of postpartum depression. *Current Psychiatry Reports, 4,* 461–466.

Flores, G., Abreu, M., & Tomany-Korman, S. C. (2005). Limited English proficiency, primary language at home, and disparities in children's health care: How language barriers are measured matters. *Public Health Reports, 120,* 418–420.

Florsheim, P., Moore, D., & Edgington, C. (2003). Romantic relationships among pregnant and parenting adolescents. In P. Florsheim (Ed.), *Adolescent romantic relations and sexual behavior.* Mahwah, NJ: Erlbaum.

Florsheim, P., Sumida, E., McCann, C., Winstanley, M., Fukui, R., Seefeldt, T., & Moore, D. (2003). The transition to parenthood among young African American and Latino couples: Relational predictors of risk for parental dysfunction. *Journal of Family Psychology, 17,* 65–79.

Florsheim, P. (Ed.). (2003). *Adolescent romantic relations and sexual behavior.* Mahwah, NJ: Erlbaum.

Flynn, J. R. (1999). Searching for justice: The discovery of IQ gains over time. *American Psychologist. 54,* 5–20.

Foege, W. (2000). The power of immunization. *The progress of nations.* New York: UNICEF.

Ford, C. A., Bearman, P. S., & Moody, J. (1999). Foregone health care among adolescents. *Journal of the American Medical Association, 282* (No. 23), 2227–2234.

Ford, K., Sohn, W., & Lepkowski, J. (2001). Characteristics of adolescents' sexual partners and their association with use of condoms and other contraceptive methods. *Family Planning Perspectives, 33,* 100–105, 132.

Forrest, J. D., & Singh, S. (1990). The sexual and reproductive behavior of American women, 1982–1988. *Family Planning Perspectives, 22,* 206–214.

Fowler-Brown, A., & Kahwati, L. C. (2004). Prevention and treatment of overweight in children and adolescents. *American Family Physician, 69,* 2591–2598.

Fox, B., & Hull, M. (2002). *Phonics for the teacher of reading* (8th ed.). Upper Saddle River, NJ: Merrill.

Fox, K. R. (2004). Childhood obesity and the role of physical activity. *Journal of Research in Social Health, 124,* 34–39.

Fox, M. K., Pac, S., Devaney, B., & Jankowski, L. (2004). Feeding infants and toddlers study: What foods are infants and toddlers eating? *Journal of the American Diet Association. 104,* 22–30.

Fox, N. A., Henderson, H. A., & Marshall, P. J., Nichols, K. E., & Ghera, M. M. (2004). Behavioral inhibition: Linking biology and behavior within a developmental framework. *Annual Review of Psychology, 55,* Palo Alto, CA: Annual Reviews.

Fraenkel, J. R., & Wallen, N. E. (2006). *How to design and evaluate research in education* (6th ed.). New York: McGraw-Hill.

Fraiberg, S. (1959). *The magic years.* New York: Scribner's.

Francis, L. A., Hofer, S. M., & Birch, L. L. (2002). Predictors of maternal child-feeding style: Maternal and child characteristics. *Appetite, 37,* 231–243.

Franke, T. M. (2000, Winter). The role of attachment as a protective factor in adolescent vi-

olent behavior. *Adolescent & Family Health, 1,* 29–39.

Fraser, S. (Ed.). (1995). *The bell curve wars: Race, intelligence, and the future of America.* New York: Basic Books.

Freda, M. C. (2004). Issues in patient education. *Journal of Midwifery and Women's Health, 49,* 203–209.

Frede, E. C. (1995). The role of program quality in producing early childhood program benefits. *The Future of Children* (Vol. 5, No. 3), 115–132.

Frederikse, M., Lu, A., Aylward, E., Barta, P., Sharma, T., & Pearlson, G. (2000). Sex differences in inferior lobule volume in schizophrenia. *American Journal of Psychiatry, 157,* 422–427.

Fredrickson, D. D. (1993). Breastfeeding research priorities, opportunities, and study criteria: What we learned from the smoking trail. *Journal of Human Lactation, 3,* 147–150.

Freedman, D. S., Khan, L. K., Serdula, M. K., Dietz, W. H., Srinivasan, S. R., & Berensen, G. S. (2004). Inter-relationships among childhood BMI, childhood height, and adult obesity: The Bogalusa Heart Study. *International Journal of Obesity and Related Metabolic Disorders, 28,* 10–16.

Freedman, D. S., Khan, L. K., Serdula, M. K., Dietz, W. H., Srinivasan, S. R., & Berensen, G. S. (2005). The relation of childhood BMI to adult adiposity: The Bogalusa Heart Study. *Pediatrics, 115,* 22–27.

Freedman, J. L. (1984). Effects of television violence on aggressiveness. *Psychological Bulletin, 96,* 227–246.

Freedman, L. P., Waldman, R. J., de Pinho, H., Wirth, M. E., Chowdhury, A. M., & Rosenfield, A. (2005). Transforming health systems to improve the lives of women and children. *Lancet, 365,* 997–1000.

Freeman-Fobbs, P. (2003). Feeding our children to death: The tragedy of childhood obesity in America. *Journal of the National Medical Association, 95,* 119.

Freud, A., & Dann, S. (1951). Instinctual anxiety during puberty. In A. Freud (Ed.), *The ego and its mechanisms of defense.* New York: International Universities Press.

Freud, S. (1917). *A general introduction to psychoanalysis.* New York: Washington Square Press.

Frias, J. L., & Davenport, M. L. (2003). Health supervision for children with Turner syndrome. *Pediatrics, 111,* 692–702.

Fridrich, A. H., & Flannery, D. J. (1995). The effects of ethnicity and acculturation on early adolescent delinquency. *Journal of Child & Family Studies, 4* (No. 1), 69–87.

Fried, P. A., & Smith, A. M. (2001). A literature review of the consequences of prenatal marijuana exposure. An emerging theme of a deficiency in executive function. *Neurotoxicology and Teratology, 23,* 1–11.

Fried, P. A., & Watkinson, B. (1990). 36- and 48-month neurobehavioral follow-up of children prenatally exposed to marijuana, cigarettes, and alcohol. *Developmental and Behavioral Pediatrics, 11,* 49–58.

Friedman, D. L., Hilden, J. M., & Pulaski, K. (2004). Issues and challenges in palliative care for children with cancer. *Current Oncology Reports, 6,* 431–437.

Friedman, N. J., & Zeiger, R. S. (2005). The role of breast-feeding in the development of allergies and asthma. *Journal of Allergy and Clinical Immunology, 115,* 1238–1248.

Friedman, S. L., Randolph, S., & Kochanoff, A. (2004). Child care research. In J. G. Bremner & A. Fogel (Eds.). *Blackwell handbook of infant development.* Malden, MA: Blackwell.

Friend, M. (2005). *Special education.* Boston: Allyn & Bacon.

Friend, M. (2006). *Special education* (IDEA 2004 Updated ed.). Boston: Allyn & Bacon.

Friend, M., & Bursuck, W. D. (2002). *Including students with special needs* (3rd ed.). Boston: Allyn & Bacon.

Friesch, R. E. (1984). Body fat, puberty and fertility. *Biological Review, 59,* 161–188.

Frontini, M. G., Bao, W., Elkasbany, A., Srinivasan, S. R., & Berensen, G. S. (2001). Comparison of weight-for-height indices as a measure of adiposity and cardiovascular risk from childhood to young adulthood: The Bogalusa Heart Study. *Journal of Clinical Epidemiology, 54,* 817–822.

Frost, J. L., Thorton, C., Brown, J., Sutterby, J. A., & Therrell, J. (2001). *The developmental benefits and use patterns of overhead equipment on playgrounds.* Research commissioned by Game Time, A Playcore company, Fort Payne, AL.

Frye, D. (1999). Development of intention: The relation of executive function to theory of mind. In P. D. Zelazo, J. W. Astingron, & D. R. Olson (Eds.), *Developing theories of intention: Social understanding and self-control.* Mahwah, NJ: Erlbaum.

Frye, D., Zelazo, P. D., Brooks, P. J., & Samuels, M. C. (1996). Inference and action in early causal reasoning. *Developmental Psychology, 32,* 120–131.

Fuchs, D., Mock, D., Morgan, P. L., & Young, C. L. (2003). Responsiveness-to-intervention: Definitions, evidence, and implications for the learning disabilities construct. *Learning Disabilities Research & Practice, 18,* 157–171.

Fulgini, A., & Stevenson, H. W. (1995). Time use and mathematics achievement among American, Chinese, and Japanese high school students. *Child Development, 66,* 830–842.

Fulgini, A. J., & Hardway, C. (2004). Preparing diverse adolescents for the transition to adulthood. *Future of Children, 14,* 99–119.

Fulgini, A. J., Witkow, M., & Garcia, C. (2005, April). *Ethnic identity and the academic adjustment of adolescents from Mexican, Chinese, and*

European backgrounds. Paper presented at the meeting of the Society for Research in Child Development, Atlanta.

Fullerton, J. T., Nelson, C., Shannon, R., & Bader, J. (2004). Prenatal care in the Pasco del Norte border region. *Journal of Perinatology, 24,* 62–71.

Fulton, J. E., McGuire, M. T., Caspersen, C. J., & Dietz, W. H. (2001). Interventions for weight loss and weight gain prevention among youth: Current issues. *Sports Medicine, 31,* 153–165.

Furman, W., & Buhrmester D. (1992). Age and sex differences in perceptions of networks of personal relationships. *Child Development, 63,* 103–115.

Furman, W., Ho, M., & Low, S. (2005, April). *Adolescent dating experiences and adjustment.* Paper presented at the meeting of the Society for Research in Child Development, Atlanta.

Furnival, R. A., Street, K. A., & Schunk, J. E. (1999). Too many pediatric trampoline injuries. *Pediatrics, 103,* e57.

Furth, H. G., & Wachs, H. (1975). *Thinking goes to school.* New York: Oxford University Press.

G

Galambos, N. L. (2004). Gender and gender role development in adolescence. In R. Lerner & L. Steinberg (Eds.), *Handbook of adolescence* (2nd ed.). New York: Wiley.

Galambos, N. L., & Maggs, J. L. (1989, April). *The afterschool ecology of young adolescents and self-reported behavior.* Paper presented at the biennial meeting of the Society for Research in Child Development, Kansas City.

Gale, C. R., & Martin, C. N. (2004). Birth weight and later risk of depression in a national cohort. *British Journal of Psychiatry, 184,* 28–33.

Galinsky, E., & David, J. (1988). *The preschool years: Family strategies that work—from experts and parents.* New York: Times Books.

Gall, J. P., Gall, M. D., & Borg, W. R. (2005). *Applying educational research* (5th ed.). Boston: Allyn & Bacon.

Galloway, J. C., & Thelen, E. (2004). Feet first: Object exploration in young infants. *Infant Behavior and Development, 27,* 107–112.

Gallup, G. W., & Bezilla, R. (1992). *The religious life of young Americans.* Princeton, NJ: Gallup Institute.

Galtier-Dereure, F., & Bringer, J. (2002). Obesity and pregnancy. *Annals of Endocrinology, 63,* 470–475.

Gandrud, L. M., & Wilson, D. M. (2004). Is growth hormone stimulation testing in children still appropriate? *Growth Hormone IGF Research, 14,* 185–194.

Ganong, L., Coleman, M., & Haas, J. (2005). Divorce as prelude to stepfamily living and the consequences of re-divorce. In M. A. Fine & J. H. Harvey (Eds.), *Handbook of divorce and relationship dissolution.* Mahwah, NJ: Erlbaum.

Gao, Y., Elliot, M. E., & Waters, E. (1999, April). *Maternal attachment representations and support for three-year-olds' secure base behavior.* Paper presented at the meeting of the Society for Research in Child Development, Albuquerque.

Garbarino, J. (1999). *Lost boys: Why our sons turn violent and how we can save them.* New York: Free Press.

Garbarino, J. (2001). Violent children. *Archives of Pediatrics & Adolescent Medicine, 55,* 1–2.

Garbarino, J., Bradshaw, C. P., & Kostelny, K. (2005). Neighborhood and community influences on parenting. In T. Luster & L. Okaghi (Eds.), *Parenting: An ecological perspective.* Mahwah, NJ: Erlbaum.

Garbarino, J., Dubrow, N., Kostelny, K., & Pardo, C. (1992). *Children in danger.* San Francisco: Jossey-Bass.

Garcia Coll, C. T., Szalacha, L. A., & Palacios, N. (2005). Children of Dominican, Portuguese, and Cambodian immigrant families: Academic attitudes and pathways during middle childhood. In C. R. Cooper, C. T. Garcia Coll, W. T. Bartko, H. M. Davis, & C. Chatman (Eds.), *Developmental pathways through middle childhood.* Mahwah, NJ: Erlbaum.

Garcia-Alba, C. (2004). Anorexia and depression. *Spanish Journal of Psychology, 7,* 40–52.

Gard, J. W., Alexander, J. M., Bawdon, R. E., & Albrecht, J. T. (2002). Oxytocin preparation stability in several common intravenous solutions. *American Journal of Obstetrics and Gynecology, 186,* 496–498.

Gardner, H. (1983). *Frames of mind.* New York: Basic Books.

Gardner, H. (1993). *Multiple intelligences.* New York: Basic Books.

Gardner, H. (2002). The pursuit of excellence through education. In M. Ferrari (Ed.), *Learning from extraordinary minds.* Mahwah. NJ: Erlbaum.

Garmezy, N. (1993). Children in poverty: Resilience despite risk. *Psychiatry, 56,* 127–136.

Garofalo, R., Wolf, R. C., Wissow, L. S., Woods, E. R., & Goodman, E. (1999). Sexual orientation and risk of suicide attempts among a representative sample of youth. *Archives of Pediatrics and Adolescent Medicine, 153,* 487–493.

Gau, S. S., & Merikangas, K. R. (2004). Similarities and differences in sleep-wake patterns among adults and their children. *Sleep, 27,* 299–304.

Gaylor, A. S., & Condren, M. E. (2004). Type 2 diabetes mellitus in the pediatric population. *Pharmacotherapy, 24,* 871–888.

Gazzaniga, M. J., Ivry, R. B., & Mangum, G. R. (2002). *Cognitive neuroscience* (2nd ed.). New York: N. W. Norton.

Gazzaniga, M. S. (1986). *The social brain.* New York: Plenum.

Gehrman, C., & Hovell, M. (2003). Protecting children from environmental tobacco smoke (ETS) exposure: A critical review. *Nicotine and Tobacco Research, 5,* 289–301.

Gelles, R. J., & Cavanaugh, M. M. (2005). Violence, abuse, and neglect in families and intimate relationships. In P. C. McKenry & S. J. Price (Eds.), *Families and change* (3rd ed.). Thousand Oaks, CA: Sage.

Gelman, R. (1969). Conservation acquisition: A problem of learning to attend to relevant attributes. *Journal of Experimental Child Psychology, 7,* 67–87.

Gelman, R. (1972). Logical capacity of very young children: Number invariance rules. *Child Development, 43,* 75–90.

Gelman, R., & Williams, E. M. (1998). Enabling constraints for cognitive development and learning. In W. Damon (Ed.), *Handbook of child psychology* (5th ed., Vol. 4). New York: Wiley.

Gelman, S. A., & Opfer, J. E. (2002). Development of the animate-inanimate distinction. In U. Goswami (Ed.), *Blackwell handbook of childhood cognitive development.* Malden, MA: Blackwell.

Gelman, S. A., Taylor, M. G., & Nguyen, S. P. (2004). Mother-child conversations about gender. *Monographs of the Society for Research in Child Development, 69* (No. 1, Serial No. 275).

Gennetian, L. A., & Miller, C. (2002). Children and welfare reform: A view from an experimental welfare reform program in Minnesota. *Child Development, 73,* 601–620.

Germeijs, V., & De Boeck, P. (2003). Career indecision: Three factors from decision theory. *Journal of Vocational Behavior, 62,* 11–25.

Gershoff, E. T. (2002). Corporal punishment by parents and associated child behaviors and experiences: A meta-analysis and theoretical review. *Psychological Bulletin, 128,* 539–579.

Geschwind, D. H., Miller, B. L., DeCarli, C., & Carmelli, D. (2002). Heritability of lobar brain volumes in twins supports genetic models of cerebral laterality and handedness. *Proceedings of the National Academic of Science U.S.A. 99,* 3176–3181.

Geschwind, N., & Behan, P. O. (1984). Laterality, hormones, and immunity. In N. Geschwind & A. M. Galaburda (Eds.), *Cerebral dominance: The biological foundations.* Cambridge, MA: Harvard University Press.

Gesell, A. (1934). *An atlas of infant behavior.* New Haven, CT: Yale University Press.

Gesell, A. L. (1929). *Infancy and human growth.* New York: Macmillan.

Gesell, A. L. (1937). *Infancy and human growth.* New York: Macmillan.

Getahun, D., Demissie, K., Lu, S. E., & Rhoads, G. G. (2004). Sudden infant death syndrome among twin births: United States, 1995–1998. *Journal of Perinatology, 24,* 544–551.

Gewirtz, J. (1977). Maternal responding and the conditioning of infant crying: Directions of influence within the attachment-acquisition process. In B. C. Etzel, J. M. LeBlanc, & D. M. Baer (Eds.), *New developments in behavioral research*. Hillsdale, NJ: Erlbaum.

Ghetti, S., & Alexander, K. W. (2004). "If it happened, I would remember it": Strategic use of event memorability in the rejection of false autobiographical events. *Child Development, 75*, 542–561.

Ghosh, S., & Shah, D. (2004). Nutritional problems in urban slum children. *Indian Pediatrics, 41*, 682–696.

Giammattei, J., Blix, G., Marshak, H. H., Wollitzer, A. O., & Pettitt, D. J. (2003). Television watching and soft drink consumption: Associations with obesity in 11- to 13-year-old schoolchildren. *Archives of Pediatric and Adolescent Medicine, 157*, 882–886.

Gibbs, J. C. (2003). *Moral development & reality*. Thousand Oaks, CA: Sage.

Gibbs, J. T. (1989). Black American adolescents. In J. T. Gibbs & L. N. Huang (Eds.), *Children of color*. San Francisco: Jossey-Bass.

Gibson, E. J. (1969). *Principles of perceptual learning and development*. New York: Appleton-Century-Crofts.

Gibson, E. J. (1989). Exploratory behavior in the development of perceiving, acting, and the acquiring of knowledge. *Annual Review of Psychology* (Vol. 39). Palo Alto, CA: Annual Reviews.

Gibson, E. J. (2001). *Perceiving the affordances*. Mahwah, NJ: Erlbaum.

Gibson, E. J., & Walk, R. D. (1960). The "visual cliff." *Scientific American, 202*, 64–71.

Gibson, E. J., Riccio, G., Schmuckler, M. A., Stoffregen, T. A., Rosenberg, D., & Taormina, J. (1987). Detection of the traversability of surfaces by crawling and walking infants. *Journal of Experimental Psychology: Human Perception and Performance, 13*, 533–544.

Gibson, J. H., Harries, M., Mitchell, A., Godfrey, R., Lunt, M., & Reeve, J. (2000). Determinants of bone density and prevalence of osteopenia among female runners in their second to seventh decades of age. *Bone, 26*, 591–598.

Gibson, J. J. (1966). *The senses considered as perceptual systems*. Boston: Houghton Mifflin.

Gibson, J. J. (1979). *The ecological approach to visual perception*. Boston: Houghton Mifflin.

Giedd, J. N. (2004). Structural magnetic resonance imaging of the adolescent brain. *Annals of the New York Academy of Sciences, 1021*, 77–85.

Giedd, J., Jeffries, N., Blumenthal, J., Castellanos, F., Vaituzis, A., Fernandez, T., Hamburger, S., Liu, H., Nelson, J., Bedwell, J., Tran, L., Lenane, M., Nicolson, R., & Rapoport, J. (1999). Childhood-onset schizophrenia: Progressive brain changes during adolescence. *Biological Psychiatry, 46*, 892–898.

Gifford-Smith, M. E., & Rabiner, D. L. (2004). The relation between social information processing and children's adjustment. In J. B. Kupersmidt & K. A. Dodge (Eds.), *Children's peer relations: From development to intervention*. Washington, DC: American Psychological Association.

Gilliam, F. D., & Bales, S. N. (2001). Strategic frame analysis: Reframing America's youth. *Social Policy Report of the Society for Research in Child Development, XV* (No. 3), 1–14.

Gilligan, C. (1982). *In a different voice*. Cambridge, MA: Harvard University Press.

Gilligan, C. (1992, May). *Joining the resistance: Girls' development in adolescence*. Paper presented at the symposium on development and vulnerability in close relationships, Montreal, Quebec.

Gilligan, C. (1996). The centrality of relationships in psychological development: A puzzle, some evidence, and a theory. In G. G. Noam & K. W. Fischer, (Eds.), *Development and vulnerability in close relationships*. Hillsdale, NJ: Erlbaum.

Gilstrap, L. L., & Ceci, S. J. (2005). Reconceptualizing children's suggestibility: Bidirectional and temporal properties. *Child Development, 76*, 40–53.

Ginorio, A. B., & Huston, M. (2001). *Sil Puede! Yes, we can: Latinas in school*. Washington, DC: AAUW.

Ginsburg, H. P., & Golbeck, S. L. (2004). Thoughts on the future of research on mathematics and science learning and education. *Early Childhood Research Quarterly, 19*, 190–200.

Ginzberg, E. (1972). Toward a theory of occupational choice: A restatement. *Vocational Guidance Quarterly, 20*, 169–176.

Givan, D. C. (2004). The sleepy child. *Pediatric Clinics of North America, 5*, 15–31.

Glantz, J. C. (2005). Elective induction vs. spontaneous labor associations and outcomes. *Journal of Reproductive Medicine, 50*, 235–240.

Glaze, D. G. (2004). Childhood insomnia: Why Chris can't sleep. *Pediatric Clinics of North America, 5*, 33–50.

Godding, V., Bonnier, C., Fiasse, L., Michel, M., Longueville, E., Lebecque, P., Robert, A., & Galanti, L. (2004). Does in utero exposure to heavy maternal smoking induce nicotine withdrawal symptoms in neonates? *Pediatric Research, 55*, 645–651.

Gojnic, M., Pervulov, M., Petkovic, S., Mostic, T., & Jeremic, K. (2004). Acceleration of fetal maturation by oxytocin-produced uterine contraction in pregnancies complicated with gestational diabetes mellitus: A preliminary report. *Journal of Maternal-Fetal and Neonatal Medicine, 16*, 111–114.

Golan, M., & Crow, S. (2004). Parents are key players in the prevention and treatment of weight-related problems. *Nutrition Review, 62*, 39–50.

Goldberg, M. (2005, January). Test mess 2: Are we doing any better a year later? *Phi Delta Kappan*, 389–395.

Golden, M. H., Samuels, M. P., & Southall, D. P. (2003). How to distinguish between neglect and deprivational abuse. *Archives of Diseases in Childhood, 88*, 105–107.

Goldman, R. (1964). *Religious thinking from childhood to adolescence*. London: Routledge & Kegan Paul.

Goldstein, J. M., Seidman, L. J., Horton, N. J., Makris, N., Kennedy, D. N., Caviness, V. S., Faraone, S. V., & Tsuang, M. T. (2001). Normal sexual dimorphism of the adult human brain assessed by in vivo magnetic resonance imaging. *Cerebral Cortex, 11*, 490–497.

Goldstein-Ferber, S. (1997, April). *Massage in preterm infants*. Paper presented at the Child Development Conference, Bar-Ilan, Israel.

Goldwater, P. N. (2001). SIDS: More facts and controversies. *Medical Journal of Australia, 174*, 302–304.

Goleman, D. (1995). *Emotional intelligence*. New York: Basic Books.

Goleman, D., Kaufman, P., & Ray, M. (2003). *The creative spirit*. New York: Plume.

Golomb, C. (2002). *Child art in context*. Washington, DC: American Psychological Association.

Golombok, S., MacCallum, F., & Goodman, E. (2001). The "test-tube" generation: Parent-child relationships and the psychological well-being of in vitro fertilization children at adolescence. *Child Development, 72*, 599–608.

Gomel, J. N., Hanson, T. L., & Tinsley, B. J. (1999, April). *Cultural influences on parents' beliefs about the relations between health and eating: A domain analysis*. Paper presented at the meeting of the Society for Research in Child Development, Albuquerque, NM.

Gong, R. (2005). The essence of critical thinking. *Journal of Developmental Education, 28*, 40–42.

Gonzales, N. A., Knight, G. P., Morgan Lopez, A., Saenz, D., & Sirolli, A. (2002). Acculturation and the mental health of Latino youths: An integration and critique of the literature. In J. M. Contreras, K. A. Kerns, & A. M. Neal-Barnett (Eds.), *Latino children and families in the United States*. Westport, CT: Greenwood.

Gonzales, V., Yawkey, T. D., & Minaya-Rowe, L. (2006). *English-as-a-second language (ESL) teaching and learning*. Boston: Allyn & Bacon.

Gonzalez-Barranco, J., & Rios-Torres, J. M. (2004). Early malnutrition and metabolic abnormalities later in life. *Nutrition Review, 62*, S134–S139.

Gonzalez-del Angel, A. A., Vidal, S., Saldan, Y., del Castillo, V., Angel, M., Macias, M., Luna, P., & Orozco, L. (2000). Molecular diagnosis of the fragile X and FRAXE syndromes in patients with mental retardation of unknown cause in Mexico. *Annals of Genetics, 43*, 29–34.

Good, C., Aronson, J., & Inzlicht, M. (2003). Improving adolescents' standardized test performance: An intervention to reduce the effects of stereotype threat. *Journal of Applied Developmental Psychology, 24,* 645–662.

Goodman, J. H. (2004). Paternal postpartum depression, its relationship to maternal postpartum depression, and implications for family health. *Journal of Advanced Nursing, 45,* 26–35.

Goodway, J. D., & Branta, C. F. (2003). Influence of a motor skill intervention on fundamental motor skill development of disadvantaged preschool children. *Research Quarterly for Exercise and Sport, 74,* 36–46.

Goos, M. (2004). Learning mathematics in a classroom community of inquiry. *Journal for Research in Mathematics Education, 35,* 258–291.

Gotesdam, K. G., & Agras, W. S. (1995). General population-based epidemiological survey of eating disorders in Norway. *International Journal of Eating Disorders, 18,* 119–126.

Gottfried, A. E., Gottfried, A. W., & Bathurst, K. (2002). Maternal and dual-earner employment status and parenting. In M. H. Bornstein (Ed.), *Handbook of parenting* (2nd ed., Vol. 2). Mahwah, NJ: Erlbaum.

Gottlieb, G. (1998). Normally occurring environmental and behavioral influences on gene activity: From central dogma to probabilistic epigenesis. *Psychological Review, 105,* 792–802.

Gottlieb, G. (2003). *Developmental behavior genetics and the statistical concept of interaction.* Unpublished manuscript, Department of Psychology, University of North Carolina, Chapel Hill.

Gottlieb, G. (2004). Normally occurring environmental and behavioral influences on gene activity. In C. G. Coll, E. L. Bearer, & R. M. Lerner (Eds.), *Nature and nurture.* Mahwah, NJ: Erlbaum.

Gottlieb, G., Wahlsten, D., & Lickliter, R. (1998). The significance of biology for human development: A developmental psychobiological systems view. In W. Damon (Ed.), *Handbook of child psychology* (5th ed., Vol. 1). New York: Wiley.

Gottleib, G., Wahlsten, D., & Lickliter, R. (2006). The significance of biology for human development: A developmental psychobiological systems view. In W. Damon & R. Lerner (Eds.), *Handbook of child psychology* (6th ed.). New York: Wiley.

Gottlieb, M. (2006). *Assessing English language learners.* Thousand Oaks, CA: Sage.

Gottman, J. M., & DeClaire, J. (1997). *The heart of parenting: Raising an emotionally intelligent child.* New York: Simon & Schuster.

Gottman, J. M., & Parker, J. G. (Eds.). (1987). *Conversations of friends.* New York: Cambridge University Press.

Gould, M. (2003). Suicide risk among adolescents. In D. Romer (Ed.), *Reducing adolescent risk.* Thousand Oaks, CA: Sage.

Gould, M. S., Greenberg, T., Velting, D. M., & Shaffer, D. (2003). Youth suicide risk and preventive interventions: A review of the past 10 years. *Journal of the American Academy of Child and Adolescent Psychiatry, 42,* 386–405.

Gould, S. J. (1981). *The mismeasure of man.* New York: W. W. Norton.

Graber, J. A. (2004). Internalizing problems during adolescence. In R. Lerner & L. Steinberg (Eds.), *Handbook of adolescent psychology* (2nd ed.). New York: Wiley.

Graber, J. A., Seeley, J. R., Brooks-Gunn, J., & Lewinsohn, P. M. (2004). Is pubertal timing associated with psychopathology in young adulthood? *Journal of the American Academy of Child and Adolescent Psychiatry, 43,* 718–726.

Grady, M. A., & Bloom, K. C. (2004). Pregnancy outcomes of adolescents enrolled in a Centering Pregnancy program. *Journal of Midwifery and Women's Health, 49,* 419–420.

Graf, C., Koch, B. Dordl, S., Schindler-Marlow, S., Icks, A., Schuller, A., Bjarnason-Wehrens, B., Tokarski, W., & Predel, H. G. (2004). Physical activity, leisure activities, and obesity in first-grade children. *European Journal of Cardiovascular and Preventive Rehabilitation, 11,* 284–290.

Graham, S. (1986, August). *Can attribution theory tell us something about motivation in blacks?* Paper presented at the meeting of the American Psychological Association, Washington, DC.

Graham, S. (1990). Motivation in Afro-Americans. In G. L. Berry & J. K. Asamen (Eds.), *Black students: Psychosocial issues and academic achievement.* Newbury Park, CA: Sage.

Graham, S. (1992). Most of the subjects were white and middle class. *American Psychologist, 47,* 629–637.

Graham, S. (2005, February 16). Commentary in *USA TODAY,* p. 2D.

Grande, M., & Downing, J. A. (2004). Increasing parent participation and knowledge using home literacy bags. *Intervention in School and Clinic, 40,* 120–126.

Grant, J. (1997). *State of the world's children.* New York: UNICEF and Oxford University Press.

Grant, J. P. (1996). *The state of the world's children.* New York: UNICEF and Oxford University Press.

Grantham-McGregor, C., Ani, C., & Fernald, L. (2001). The role of nutrition in intellectual development. In R. J. Sternberg & E. L. Girogorenko (Eds.), *Environmental effects on cognitive abilities.* Mahwah, NJ: Erlbaum.

Grasemann, C., Wessels, H. T., Knauer-Fischer, S., Richter-Unruh, A., & Hauffa, B. P. (2004). Increase of serum leptin after short-term pulsatile GnRH administration in children with delayed puberty. *European Journal of Endocrinology, 150,* 691–698.

Graue, M. E., & DiPerna, J. (2000). Redshirting and early retention: Who gets the "gift of time" and what are its outcomes? *American Educational Research Journal, 37,* 509–534.

Graven, S. N. (2004). Early neurosensory visual development of the fetus and newborn. *Clinical Perinatology, 31,* 199–216.

Gray, J. (1992). *Men are from Mars, women are from Venus.* New York: HarperCollins.

Gray, J. R., & Kagan J. (2000). The challenge of determining which children with attention deficit hyperactivity disorder will respond positively to methylphenidate. *Journal of Applied Developmental Psychology, 21,* 471–489.

Gray, P., & Feldman, J. (2004). Playing in the zone of proximal development: Qualities of self-directed age mixing between adolescents and young children at a democratic school. *American Journal of Education, 110,* 108–143.

Greenberger, E., & Steinberg, L. (1981). *Project for the study of adolescent work: Final report.* Report prepared for the National Institute of Education, U.S. Department of Education, Washington, DC.

Greenberger, E., & Steinberg, L. (1986). *When teenagers work: The psychological social costs of adolescent employment.* New York: Basic Books.

Greene, A., Barnett, P., Crossen, J., Sexton, G., Ruzicka, P., & Neuwelt, E. (2002). Evaluation of THINK FIRST For KIDS injury prevention curriculum for primary students. *Injury Prevention, 8,* 257–258.

Greene, R. W., Biederman, J., Faraone, S. V., Monuteaux, M. C., Mick, E., DuPre, E. P., Fine, C. S., & Goring, J. C. (2001). Social impairment in girls with ADHD. *Journal of the American Academy of Child and Adolescent Psychiatry, 40,* 704–710.

Greenfield, P. M. (2000). Culture and development. In A. Kazdin (Ed.), *Encyclopedia of psychology.* Washington, DC, & New York: American Psychological Association and Oxford University Press.

Greenfield, P. M. (2003, February). Commentary. *Monitor on Psychology, 34,* No. 2, p. 58.

Greenfield. P. M., Keller, H., Fulgini, A., & Maynard, A. (2003). Cultural pathways through universal development. *Annual Review of Psychology, 54,* 461–490.

Greenfield, P. M., Suzuki, L. K., & Rothstein-Fisch, C. (2006). Cultural pathways through human development. In W. Damon & R. Lerner (Eds.), *Handbook of child psychology* (6th ed.). New York: Wiley.

Greenough, W. T. (1997, April 21). Commentary in article, "Politics of biology." *U.S. News & World Report,* p. 79.

Greenough, W. T. (1999, April). *Experience, brain development, and links to mental retardation.*

Paper presented at the meeting of the Society for Research in Child Development, Albuquerque.

Greenough, W. T. (2000). Brain development. In A. Kazdin (Ed.), *Encyclopedia of psychology.* Washington, DC, & New York: American Psychological Association and Oxford U. Press.

Greenough, W. T. (2001, April). *Nature and nurture in the brain development process.* Paper presented at the meeting of the Society for Research in Child Development, Minneapolis.

Greenough, W. T., Klintsova, A. Y., Irvan, S. A., Galvez, R., Bates, K. E., & Weiler, I. J. (2001). Synaptic regulation of protein synthesis and the fragile X protein. *Proceedings of the National Academy of Science USA, 98,* 7101–7106.

Gregory, A. M., & O'Connor, T. G. (2002). Sleep problems in childhood: A longitudinal study of developmental change and association with behavioral problems. *Journal of the American Academy of Child and Adolescent Psychiatry, 41,* 964–971.

Gregory, R. L. (2004). *Psychological testing* (4th ed.). Boston: Allyn & Bacon.

Greven, P. (1991). *Spare the child: The religious roots of punishment and the psychological impact of physical abuse.* New York: Knopf.

Grigorenko, E. (2000). Heritability and intelligence. In R. J. Sternberg (Ed.), *Handbook of intelligence.* New York: Cambridge U. Press.

Grigorenko, E. L. (2001). The invisible danger: The impact of ionizing radiation on cognitive development and functioning. In R. J. Sternberg & E. L. Grigorenko (Eds.), *Environmental effects on cognitive abilities.* Mahwah, NJ: Erlbaum.

Grigorenko, E. L., Geissler, P., Prince, R., Okatcha, F., Nokes, C., Kenney, D. A., Bundy, D. A., & Sternberg, R. J. (2001). The organization of Luo conceptions of intelligence: A study of implicit theories in a Kenyan village. *International Journal of Behavioral Development, 25,* 367–378.

Grigoriadis, S., & Kennedy, S. H. (2002). Role of estrogen in the treatment of depression. *American Journal of Therapy, 9,* 503–509.

Groark, C. J., & McCall, R. B. (2005). Integrating developmental scholarship into practice and policy. In M. H. Bornstein & M. E. Lamb (Eds.), *Developmental psychology* (5th ed.). Mahwah, NJ: Erlbaum.

Grodzinsky, Y. (2001). The neurology of syntax: Language use without Broca's area. *Behavior and Brain Sciences, 23,* 1–21.

Grolnick, W. S., Bridges, L. J., & Connell, J. P. (1996). Emotion regulation in two-year-olds: Strategies and emotional expression in four contexts. *Child Development, 67,* 928–941.

Gronlund, N. W. (2006). *Assessment of student achievement* (8th ed.). Boston: Allyn & Bacon.

Grossmann, K., Grossmann, K. E., Spangler, G., Suess, G, & Unzner, L. (1985). Maternal sensitivity and newborns' orientation responses as related to quality of attachment in Northern Germany. In I. Bretherton & E. Waters (Eds.), *Growing points of attachment theory and research. Monographs of the Society for Research in Child Development, 50* (1–2, Serial No. 209).

Grotevant, H. D., & McRoy, R. G. (1990). Adopted adolescents in residential treatment: The role of the family. In D. M. Brodzinsky & M. D. Schechter (Eds.), *The psychology of adoption.* New York: Oxford University Press.

Grummer-Strawn, L. M., & Mei, Z. (2004). Does breastfeeding protect against pediatric overweight? Analysis of longitudinal data from the Centers for Disease Control and Prevention pediatric nutrition surveillance system. *Pediatrics, 113,* e81–e86.

Grusec, J. (2005). Development of moral behavior and conscience. In M. Killen & J. G. Smetana (Eds.), *Handbook of moral development.* Mahwah, NJ: Erlbaum.

Guilford, J. P. (1967). *The structure of intellect.* New York: McGraw-Hill.

Gulotta, C. S., & Phinney, J. W. (2000). Intervention models for mothers and children at risk for injuries. *Clinical, Child, and Family Psychology Review, 3,* 25–36.

Gulson, B. L., Mizon, K. J., Davis, J. D., Palmer, J. M., & Vimpani, G. (2004). Identification of sources of lead in children in a primary zinc-lead smelter environment. *Environmental Health Perspectives, 112,* 52–60.

Gump, B. B., Stewart, P., Reihman, J., Lonky, E., Darvill, T., Matthews, K. A., & Parsons, P. J. (2005, in press). Prenatal and early childhood blood lead levels and cardiovascular functioning in 9($\frac{1}{2}$) year old children. *Neurotoxicology and Teratology.*

Gunnar, M. R. (2000). Early adversity and the development of stress reactivity and regulation. In C. A. Nelson (Ed.), *The effects of early adversity on neurobehavioral development. The Minnesota Symposia on Child Psychology* (Vol. 31, pp. 163–200). Mahwah, NJ: Erlbaum.

Gunnar, M. R., & David, E. P. (2003). Stress and emotion in early childhood. In I. B. Weiner (Ed.), *Handbook of psychology* (Vol. 6). New York: Wiley.

Gunnar, M. R., Malone, S., & Fisch, R. O. (1987). The psychobiology of stress and coping in the human neonate: Studies of the adrenocortical activity in response to stress in the first week of life. In T. Field, P. McCabe, & N. Scheiderman (Eds.), *Stress and coping.* Hillsdale, NJ: Erlbaum.

Gunning, T. G. (2006). *Closing the literacy gap.* Boston: Allyn & Bacon.

Guo, S. S., Wun, W., Chumlea, W. C., & Roche, A. F. (2002). Predicting overweight and obesity in adulthood from body mass index in childhood and adolescence. *American Journal of Clinical Nutrition, 76,* 653–658.

Gur, R. C., Mozley, L. H., Mozley, P. D., Resnick, S. M., Karp, J. S., Alavi, A., Arnold, S. E., & Gur, R. E. (1995). Sex differences in regional cerebral glucose metabolism during a resting state. *Science, 267,* 528–531.

Gurwitch, R. H., Silovsky, J. F., Schultz, S., Kees, M., & Burlingame, B. A. (2001). Reactions and guidelines for children following trauma/disaster. *APA Online.* Washington, DC: American Psychological Association.

Gustafsson, P. A., Duchen, K., Birberg, U., & Karlsson, T. (2004). Breastfeeding, very long polyunsaturated fatty acids (PUFA), and IQ at 6½ years of age. *Acta Pediatrics, 93,* 1280–1287.

Gutherie, G. M., Masangkay, Z., & Gutherie, H. A. (1976). Behavior, malnutrition, and mental development. *Journal of Cross-Cultural Psychology, 7,* 169–180.

Gyamfi, P., Brooks-Gunn, J., & Jackson, A. P. (2001). Associations between employment and financial and parental stress in low-income single Black mothers. In M. C. Lennon (Ed.), *Welfare, work, and well-being.* New York: Haworth Press.

H

Haertsch, M., Campbell, E., & Sanson-Fisher, R. (1999). What is recommended for healthy women during pregnancy? *Birth, 26,* 24–30.

Hahn, C. S., & DiPietro, J. A. (2001). In vitro fertilization and the family: Quality of parenting, family functioning, and child psychosocial adjustment. *Developmental Psychology, 37,* 37–48.

Hahn, D. B., Payne, W. A., & Mauer, E. B. (2005). *Focus on health* (7th ed.). New York: McGraw-Hill.

Hahn, W. K. (1987). Cerebral lateralization of function: From infancy through childhood. *Psychological Bulletin, 101,* 376–392.

Haig, D. (2003). Behavioral genetics: Family matters. *Nature, 421,* 491–492.

Haith, M. M., & Benson, J. B. (1998). Infant cognition. In W. Damon (Ed.), *Handbook of child psychology* (5th ed., Vol. 2). New York: Wiley.

Haith, M. M., Hazen, C., & Goodman, G. S. (1988). Expectation and anticipation of dynamic visual events by 3.5 month-old babies. *Child Development, 59,* 467–479.

Hakuta, K. (2001, April 5). *Key policy milestones and directions in the education of English language learners.* Paper prepared for the Rockefeller Foundation Symposium, Leveraging change: Are emerging framework for educational equity. Washington, DC.

Hakuta, K. (2000). Bilingualism. In A. Kazdin (ed.), *Encyclopedia of psychology.* Washington, DC, & New York: American Psychological Association and Oxford University Press.

Hakuta, K. (2005, April). *Bilingualism at the intersection of research and public policy.* Paper presented at the meeting of the Society for Research in Child Development, Atlanta.

Hakuta, K., Bialystok, E., & Wiley, E. (2003). Critical evidence: A test of the critical-period hypothesis for second-language acquisition. *Psychological Science, 14,* 31–38.

Hakuta, K., Butler, Y. G., & Witt, D. (2000). *How long does it take English learners to attain proficiency?* Berkeley, CA: The University of California Linguistic Minority Research Institute Policy Report 2000–1.

Hale, K. J. (2003). Oral health risk assessment timing and establishment of the dental home. *Pediatrics, 111,* 1113–1116.

Hales, D. (2006). *An invitation to health* (4th ed., Brief). Belmont CA: Wadsworth.

Haley, M. H., & Austin, T. Y. (2004). *Content-based second language teaching and learning.* Boston: Allyn & Bacon.

Hall, C. M., Jones, J. A., Meyer-Bahlburg, H. F., Dolezal, C., Coleman, M., Foster, P., Price, D. A., & Clayton, P. E. (2004). Behavioral and physical masculinization are related to genotype in girls with congenital adrenal hyperplasia. *Journal of Clinical Endocrinology and Metabolism, 89,* 419–424.

Hall, G. S. (1904). *Adolescence* (Vols. 1 & 2). Englewood Cliffs, NJ: Prentice Hall.

Hall, J. (2005). Postnatal emotional wellbeing. *Practicing Midwife, 8,* 35–40.

Hallahan, D. P., & Kauffman, J. M. (2006). *Exceptional learners* (10th ed.). Boston: Allyn & Bacon.

Hallemans, A., Aerts, P., Otten, B., De Deyn, P. O., & De Clercq, D. (2005). Mechanical energy in toddler gait: A trade-off between economy and stability. *Journal of Experimental Biology, 207,* 2417–2431.

Hallfors, D. D., Waller, M. W., Ford, C. A., Halpern, C. T., Brodish, P. H., & Iritani, B. (2004). Adolescent depression and suicide risk: Association with sex and drug behavior. *American Journal of Preventive Medicine, 27,* 224–231.

Halonen, J., & Santrock, J. W. (1999). *Psychology: Contexts and applications.* Boston: McGraw-Hill.

Halpern, D. (2001). Sex difference research: Cognitive abilities. In J. Worrell (Ed.), *Handbook of women and gender.* San Diego: Academic Press.

Halpern-Felsher, B. L., Cornell, J. L., Kropp, R. Y., & Tschann, J. M. (2005). Oral versus vaginal sex among adolescents: Perceptions, attitudes, and behavior. *Pediatrics, 115,* 845–851.

Hambelton, R. K. (2002). How can we make NAEP and state test score reporting scales and reports more understandable? In R. W. Lissitz & W. D. Schafer (Eds.), *Assessment in educational reform: Both means and ends.* Boston: Allyn & Bacon.

Hamburg, B. A. (1990). *Life skills training: Preventive interventions for adolescents.* Washington, DC: Carnegie Council on Adolescent Development.

Hamburg, D. A. (1997). Meeting the essential requirements for healthy adolescent development in a transforming world. In R. Takanishi & D. Hamburg (Eds.), *Preparing adolescents for the 21st century.* New York: Cambridge University Press.

Hamburg, D. A., Millstein, S. G., Mortimer, A. M., Nightingale, E. O., & Petersen, A. C. (1993). Adolescent health promotion in the twenty-first century: Current frontiers and future directions. In S. G. Millstein, A. C. Petersen, & E. O. Nightingale (Eds.), *Promoting the health of adolescents.* New York: Oxford University Press.

Hamilton, M. C. (1991). *Preference for sons or daughters and the sex role characteristics of potential parents.* Paper presented at the meeting of the Association for Women in Psychology, Hartford, CT.

Hamilton, S. F., & Hamilton, M. A. (2004). Contexts for mentoring: Adolescent-adult relationships in workplaces and communities. In R. Lerner & L. Steinberg (Eds.), *Handbook of adolescent psychology* (2nd ed.). New York: Wiley.

Hancox, R. J., Milne, B. J., & Poulton, R. (2004). Association between child and adolescent television viewing and adult health: A longitudinal birth cohort study. *Lancet, 364,* 257–262.

Hanevold, C., Waller, J., Daniels, S., Portman, R., & Sorol, J. (2004). The effects of obesity, gender, and ethnic group on left ventricular hypertrophy and geometry in hypertensive children: A collaborative study of the International Pediatric Hypertension Association. *Pediatrics, 113,* 328–333.

Hannah, W. J. (2005). Avoiding asphyxia during vaginal breech delivery. *British Journal of Gynecology, 112,* 846.

Hannish, L. D., & Guerra, N. G. (2004). Aggressive victims, passive victims, and bullies: Developmental continuity or developmental change? *Merrill-Palmer Quarterly, 50,* 17–38.

Hansen, D. (1996, M). *Adolescent employment and psychosocial outcomes: A comparison of two employment contexts.* Paper presented at the meeting of the Society for Research on Adolescence, Boston.

Hansen, M., Janssen, I., Schiff, A., Zee, P. C., & Dubocovich, M. L. (2005). The impact of school daily schedule on adolescent sleep. *Pediatrics, 115,* 1555–1561.

Hanson, L. A., Korotkova, M., Haversen, L., Mattsby-Baltzer, I., Hahn-Zoric, M., Silferdal, S. A., Strandvik, B., & Telemo, E. (2002). Breastfeeding, a complex support system for the offspring. *Pediatrics International, 44,* 347–352.

Harding, B., Risdon, R. A., & Krous, H. F. (2004). Shaken baby syndrome. *British Medical Journal, 328,* 719–720.

Hardman, M. L., Drew, C. J., Egan, M. W. (2006). *Human exceptionality* (8th ed., updated). Boston: Allyn & Bacon.

Hargrove, B. K., Creak, M. G., & Burgess, B. L. (2002). Family interaction patterns as predictors of vocational identity and career decision-making self-efficacy. *Journal of Vocational Behavior, 61,* 185–201.

Hargrove, K. (2005). What makes a "good" teacher "great"? *Gifted Child Today, 28,* 30–31.

Harkness, S., & Super, C. M. (2002). Culture and parenting. In M. H. Bornstein (Ed.), *Handbook of parenting* (2nd ed., Vol. 2). Mahwah, NJ: Erlbaum.

Harkness, S., & Super, E. M. (1995). Culture and parenting. In M. H. Bornstein (Ed.), *Handbook of parenting* (Vol. 3). Hillsdale, NJ: Erlbaum.

Harlow, H. F. (1958). The nature of love. *American Psychologist, 13,* 673–685.

Harper, B. (2000). Waterbirth basics. *Midwifery today with International Midwife, 54,* 9–15, 68.

Harper, C. C., & McLanahan, S. S. (2004). Father absence and youth incarceration. *Journal of Research on Adolescence, 14,* 369–397.

Harper, M. S., Welsch, D., & Woody, T. (2002, April). *Silencing the self: Depressive symptoms and loss of self in adolescent romantic relationships.* Paper presented at the meeting of the Society for Research on Adolescence, New Orleans.

Harris, G., Thomas, A., & Booth, D. A. (1990). Development of salt taste in infancy. *Developmental Psychology, 26,* 534–538.

Harris, J. R. (1998). *The nurture assumption: Why children turn out the way they do. Parents matter less than you think and peers matter more.* New York: Free Press.

Harris, L. (1987, September 3). The latchkey child phenomena. *Dallas Morning News,* pp. 1A, 10A.

Harris, L. (1997). *A national poll of children and exercise.* Washington, DC: Lou Harris & Associates.

Harrison-Hale, A. O., McLoyd, V. C., & Smedley, B. (2004). Racial and ethnic status: Risk and protective processes among African-American families. In K. I. Meston, C. J. Schellenbach, B. J. Leadbeater, & A. L. Solarz (Eds.), *Investing in children, youth, families, and communities.* Mahwah, NJ: Erlbaum.

Harrison-Hale, A. O., McLoyd, V. C., & Smedley, B. (2004). Racial and ethnic status: Risk and protective processes among African-American families. In K. L. Maton, C. J. Schellenbach, B. J. Leadbetter, & A. L. Solarz (Eds.), *Investing in children, families, and communities.* Washington, DC: American Psychological Association.

Hart, B., & Risley, T. R. (1995). *Meaningful differences.* Baltimore, MD: Paul Brookes.

Hart, B., & Risley, T. R. (1995). *Meaningful differences in the everyday experience of young Americans.* Baltimore: Paul H. Brookes.

Hart, C. H., Burts, D. C., Durland, M. A., Charlesworth, R., DeWolf, M., & Fleege, P. O. (1998). Stress behaviors and activity type participation of preschoolers in more and less developmentally appropriate classrooms: SES and sex differences. *Journal Research in Childhood Education, 12,* 176–196.

Hart, C. H., Yang, C., Charlesworth, R., & Burts, D. C. (2003, April). *Early childhood teachers' curriculum beliefs, classroom practices, and children's outcomes: What are the connections?* Paper presented at the biennial meeting of the Society for Research in Child Development, Tampa, FL.

Hart, D. (2005). Service commitment and care exemplars. In M. Killen & J. G. Smetana (Eds.), *Handbook of moral development.* Mahwah, NJ: Erlbaum.

Harter, S. (1990). Processes underlying adolescent self-concept formation. In R. Montemayor, G. R. Adams, & R. P. Gulotta (Eds.), *From childhood to adolescence: A transitional period?* Newbury Park, CA: Sage.

Harter, S. (1999). *The construction of the self.* New York: Guilford.

Harter, S. (2002). Unpublished review of Santrock *Child Development* (10th ed.). New York: McGraw-Hill.

Harter, S. (2006). The self. In W. Damon & R. Lerner (Eds.), *Handbook of child psychology* (6th ed.). New York: Wiley.

Harter, S., & Marold, D. B. (1992). Psychosocial risk factors contributing to adolescent suicide ideation. In G. Noam & S. Borst (Eds.), *Child and adolescent suicide.* San Francisco: Jossey-Bass.

Hartmann, D. P., & Pelzel, K. E. (2005). Design, measurement, and analysis in developmental research. In M. H. Bornstein & M. E. Lamb (Eds.), *Developmental psychology* (5th ed.). Mahwah, NJ: Erlbaum.

Hartshorne, H., & May, M. S. (1928–1930). *Moral studies in the nature of character: Studies in the nature of character.* New York: Macmillan.

Hartup, W. W. (1983). Peer relations. In P. H. Mussen (Ed.), *Handbook of child psychology* (4th ed., Vol. 4). New York: Wiley.

Hartup, W. W. (1996). The company they keep: Friendships and their development significance. *Child Development, 67,* 1–13.

Hartup, W. W. (1999, April). *Peer relations and the growth of the individual child.* Paper presented at the meeting of the Society for Research in Child Development, Albuquerque.

Hartup, W. W. (2000). Middle childhood: Socialization and social context. In A. Kazdin (Ed.), *Encyclopedia of psychology.* Washington, DC, & New York: American Psychological Association and Oxford University Press.

Hartup, W. W., & Abecassis, M. (2002). Friends and enemies. In P. K. Smith & C. H. Hart (Eds.), *Blackwell handbook of childhood social development.* Malden, MA: Blackwell.

Hartup, W. W., & Laursen, B. (1999). Relationships as developmental contexts: Retrospective themes and contemporary issues. In W. Andrew Collins & B. Laursen (Eds.), *Relation-ships as developmental contexts.* Mahwah, NJ: Erlbaum.

Hartwell, L., Hood, L., Goldberg, M. L., Silver, L. M., Veres, R. C., & Reynolds, A. (2004). *Genetics* (2nd ed.). New York: McGraw-Hill.

Harty-Golder, B. (2005). The plus and minus sides of Rh transfusions. *MLO Medical Laboratory Observer, 37,* 36.

Harvald, B., Hauge, G., Kyvik, K. O., Christensen, K., Skytthe, A., & Holm, V. V. (2004). The Danish twin registry: Past and present. *Twin Research, 7,* 318–335.

Harvey, J. A. (2004). Cocaine effects on the developing brain: Current status. *Neuroscience and Biobehavior Review, 27,* 751–764.

Harvey, J. H., & Fine, M. A. (2004). *Children of divorce.* Mahwah, NJ: Erlbaum.

Harwood, R., Leyendecker, B., Carlson, V., Asencio, M., & Miller, A. (2002). Parenting among Latino families in the U.S. In M. H. Bornstein (Ed.), *Handbook of parenting* (2nd ed.). Mahwah, NJ: Erlbaum.

Hauck, F. R., Moore, C. M., Herman, S. M., Donovan, M., Kalelkar, M., Christoffel, K. K., Hoffman, H. J., & Rowley, D. (2002). The contribution of prone sleeping position to the racial disparity in sudden infant death syndrome: The Chicago Infant Mortality Study. *Pediatrics, 110,* 772–780.

Haugaard, J. J., & Hazan, C. (2004). Adoption as a natural experiment. *Developmental Psychopathology, 15,* 909–926.

Haugaard, J. J., & Hazan, C. (2004). Recognizing and treating uncommon behavioral and emotional disorders in children and adolescents who have been severely maltreated: Reactive attachment disorder. *Child Maltreatment, 9,* 154–160.

Hauth, J. C., & Cunningham, F. G. (2002). Vaginal breech delivery is still justified. *Obstetrics and Gynecology, 99,* 1115–1116.

Havighurst, S. S., Harley, A., & Prior, M. (2004). Building preschool children's emotional competence. *Early Education and Development, 15,* 423–447.

Hawkins, D. N., & Whiteman, S. D. (2004). Balancing work and family: Problems and solutions with low-income families. In A. C. Crouter & A. Booth (Eds.), *Work-family challenges for low-income families and their children.* Mahwah, NJ: Erlbaum.

Hawkins, J. A., & Berndt, T. J. (1985, April). *Adjustment following the transition to junior high school.* Paper presented at the biennial meeting of the Society for Research in Child Development, Toronto.

Hayakawa, M., Okumura, A., Hayakawa, F., Kato, Y., Ohshiro, M., Tauchi, N., & Watanable, K. (2003). Nutritional state and growth and functional maturation of the brain in ex-tremely low birth weight infants. *Pediatrics, 111,* 991–995.

Hayman, L. L., Williams, C. L., Daniels, S. R., Steinberger, J., Paridon, S., Dennison, B. A., McCrindle, B. W., and the Committee on Atherosclerosis, Hypertension, and Obesity in Youth (AHOY) of the Council on Cardiovascular Disease in the Young, American Heart Association. (2004). Cardiovascular heart promotion in the schools. *Circulation, 110,* 2266–2275.

Hayes, C. (Ed.). (1987). *Risking the future: Adolescent sexuality, pregnancy, and childbearing* (Vol. 1). Washington, DC: National Academy Press.

Hayne, H. (2004). Infant memory development: Implications for infantile amnesia. *Developmental Review, 24,* 33–73.

Health Management Resources. (2001). *Child health and fitness,* Boston: Author.

Hedley, A. A., Ogden, C. L., Johnson, C. L., Carroll, M. D., Curtin, L. R., & Flegal, K. M. (2004). Prevalence of overweight and obesity among U. S. children, adolescents, and adults, 1999–2002. *Journal of the American Medical Association, 29,* 2847–2850.

Heilman, A. W., Blair, T. R., & Rupley, W. H. (2002). *Principles and practices of teaching reading* (10th ed.). Upper Saddle River, NJ: Merrill.

Heinicke, C. M. (2002). The transition to parenting. In M. H. Bornstein (Ed.), *Handbook of parenting* (2nd ed.). Mahwah, NJ: Erlbaum.

Heinze, H. J., Toro, P. A., & Urberg, K. A. (2004). Antisocial behavior and affiliation with deviant peers. *Journal of Clinical Child and Adolescent Psychology, 33,* 336–346.

Heiser, P., Friedel, S., Dempfile, A., Konrad, K., Smidt, J., Grabarkiewicz, J., Herpertz-Dahlann, B., Remschmidt, H., & Hebebrand, J. (2004). Molecular genetic aspects of attention deficit/hyperactivity disorder. *Neuroscience and Biobehavioral Reviews, 28,* 625–641.

Helms, J. E. (2005). Stereotype threat might explain the black-white test-score difference. *American Psychologist, 60,* 269–270.

Helson, R., Elliot, T., & Leigh, J. (1989). Adolescent antecedents of women's work patterns. In D. Stern & D. Eichorn (Eds.), *Adolescence and work.* Hillsdale, NJ: Erlbaum.

Hemmings, A. (2004). *Coming of age in U.S. high schools.* Mahwah, NJ: Erlbaum.

Henderson, A. T., & Mapp, K. L. (2002). *A new wave of evidence: The impact of school, family, and community connections on academic achievement.* Austin, TX: National Center for Family and Community Connections with Schools.

Henderson, P., Martines, J., & de Zoysa, I. (2004). Mortality associated with reasons for not breastfeeding. *AIDS, 18,* 361–362.

Henderson, V. L., & Dweck, C. S. (1990). Motivation and achievement. In S. S. Feldman & G. R. Elliott (Eds.), *At the threshold: The developing* *adolescent.* Cambridge, MA: Harvard University Press.

Hendrick, J., & Weissman, P. (2006). *The whole child* (8th ed.). Upper Saddle River, NJ: Prentice Hall.

Hendry, J. (1999). *Social anthropology.* New York: Macmillan.

Henninger, M. L. (1999). *Teaching young children.* Columbus, OH: Merrill.

Henninger, M. L. (2005). *Teaching young children* (3rd ed.). Boston: Allyn & Bacon.

Henriksen, T. B., Hjollund, N. H., Jensen, T. K., Bonde, J. P., Andersson, A. M., Kolstad, H., Ernst, E., Giwereman, A., Skakkebaek, N. E., & Olsen, J. (2004). Alcohol consumption at the time of conception and spontaneous abortion. *American Journal of Epidemiology, 160,* 661–667.

Henry, D. B., Tolan, P. H., & Gorman-Smith, D. (2001). Longitudinal family and peer group effects on violence and nonviolent delinquency. *Journal of Clinical Child Psychology, 30,* 172–186.

Hepper, P. G., Shahidullah, S., & White, R. (1990). Origins of fetal handedness. *Nature, 347,* 431.

Heppner, M. J., & Heppner, P. P. (2003). Identifying process variables in career counseling: A research agenda. *Journal of Vocational Behavior, 62,* 429–452.

Herbst, M. A., Mercer, B. M., Beasley, D., Meyer, N., & Carr, T. (2003). Relationship of prenatal care and perinatal morbidity in low-birth-weight infants. *American Journal of Obstetrics and Gynecology, 189,* 930–933.

Herek, G. (2000). Homosexuality. In A Kazdin (Ed.), *Encyclopedia of psychology.* Washington, DC, & New York: American Psychological Association and Oxford University Press.

Hermstein, R. J., & Murray, C. (1994). *The bell curve: Intelligence and class structure in American life.* New York: Macmillan.

Herrera, S. G., & Murry, K. G. (2005). *Mastering ESL and bilingual methods.* Boston: Allyn & Bacon.

Hess, R. D., Holloway, S. D., Dicson, W. P., & Price, G. G. (1984). Maternal variables as predictors of children's school readiness and later achievement in vocabulary and mathematics in the sixth grade. *Child Development, 55,* 1902–1912.

Hetherington, E. M. (1989). Coping with family transitions: Winners, losers, and survivors. *Child Development, 60,* 1–14.

Hetherington, E. M. (1993). An overview of the Virginia Longitudinal Study of Divorce and Remarriage with a focus on early adolescence. *Journal of Family Psychology, 7,* 39–56.

Hetherington, E. M. (2000). Divorce. In A. Kazdin (Ed.), *Encyclopedia of psychology.* Washington, DC, & New York: American Psychological Association and Oxford University Press.

Hetherington, E. M., & Jodl, K. M. (1994). Stepfamilies as settings for child development. In A. Booth & J. Dunn (Eds.), *Stepfamilies: Who benefits? Who does not?* Hillsdale, NJ: Erlbaum.

Hetherington, E. M. & Kelly, J. (2002). *For better or for worse: Divorce reconsidered.* New York: Norton.

Hetherington, E. M., & Stanley-Hagan, M. (2002). Parenting in divorced and remarried families. In M. H. Bornstein (Ed.), *Handbook of parenting* (2nd ed., Vol. 3). Mahwah, NJ: Erlbaum.

Hetherington, E. M., Bridges, M. & Insabella, G. M. (1998). What matters? What does not? Five perspectives on the association between marital transitions and children's adjustment. *American Psychologist, 53,* 167–184.

Hetherington, E. M., Reiss, D., & Plomin, R. (Eds.). (1994). *Separate social worlds of siblings: The impact of nonshared environment on development.* Hillsdale, NJ: Erlbaum.

Heuwinkel, M. K. (1996). New ways of learning (8th ed.). New ways of teaching. *Childhood Education, 72,* 27–31.

Hickson, G. B., & Clayton, E. W. (2002). Parents and children's doctors. In M. H. Bornstein (Ed.), *Handbook of parenting* (Vol. 5). Mahwah, NJ: Erlbaum.

Higgins, A., Power, C., & Kohlberg, L. (1983, April). *Moral atmosphere and moral judgment.* Paper presented at the biennial meeting of the Society for Research in Child Development, Detroit.

Higgins, D. J. (2004). The importance of degree versus type of maltreatment: a cluster analysis of child abuse types. *Journal of Psychology, 138,* 303–324.

High/Scope Resource. (2005, Spring). The High/Scope Perry Preschool Study and the man who began it. *High/Scope Resource,* p. 9. Ypsilanti, MI: High/Scope Press.

Hill, C. R., & Stafford, F. P. (1980). Parental care of children: Time diary estimate of quantity, predictability, and variety. *Journal of Human Resources, 15,* 219–239.

Hill, J., Waldfogel, J., Brooks-Gunn, J., & Han, W. (2001, November). *Towards a better estimate of causal links in child policy: The case of maternal employment and child outcomes.* Paper presented at the Association for Public Policy Analysis and Management Fall Research Conference, Washington, DC.

Hillebrand, V., Phenice, A., & Hines, R. P. (2000). *Knowing and serving diverse families.* Columbus, OH: Merrill.

Hinde, R. A. (1992). Developmental psychology in the context of other behavioral sciences. *Developmental Psychology, 28,* 1018–1029.

Hintz, S. R., Kendrick, D. E., Vohr, B. R., Poole, W. K., Higgins, R. D., and the National Institute of Child Health and Human Development Neonatal Research Network. (2005). Changes in neurodevelopment outcomes at 18 and 22 months' corrected age among infants of less than 25 weeks' gestational age born in 1993–1999. *Pediatrics, 115,* 1645–1651.

Hipwell, A. E., Murray, L., Ducournau, P., & Stein, A. (2005). The effects of maternal depression and parental conflict on children's peer play. *Child Care, Health, and Development, 31,* 11–23.

Hirsch-Pasek, K., Hyson, M., Rescorla, L., & Cone, J. (1989, April). *Hurrying children: How does it affect their academic, social, creative, and emotional development?* Paper presented at the Society for Research in Child Development meeting, Kansas City.

Hirsh, R. (2004). *Early childhood curriculum: Incorporating multiple intelligences developmentally appropriate practices, and play.* Boston: Allyn & Bacon.

Hiscock, H., & Jordan, B. (2004). Problem crying in infancy. *Medical Journal of Australia, 181,* 507–512.

Hitch, G. J., Towse, J. N., & Hutton, U. (2001). What limits children's working memory span? Theoretical accounts and applications for scholastic development. *Journal of Experimental Psychology: General, 130,* 184–198.

Hoban, T. F. (2004). Sleep and its disorders in children. *Seminars in Neurology, 24,* 327–340.

Hobbins, D. (2004). Survivors of childhood sexual abuse: Implications for perinatal nursing care. *Journal of Obstetric, Gynecologic, and Neonatal Nursing, 33,* 485–497.

Hobel, C. J., Dunkel-Schetter, C., Roesch, S. C., Castro, L. C., & Aurora, C. P. (1999). Maternal plasma corticotrophin-releasing hormone associated with stress at 20 weeks' gestation in pregnancies ending in preterm delivery. *American Journal of Obstetrics and Gynecology, 180,* S257–S263.

Hodges, E. A. (2003). A primer on early childhood obesity and parental influence. *Pediatric Nursing, 29,* 13–16.

Hoff, E., Laursen, B., & Tardiff, T. (2002). Socioeconomic status and parenting. In M. H. Bornstein (Ed.), *Handbook of parenting* (2nd ed., Vol. 2). Mahwah, NJ: Erlbaum.

Hofferth, S. L., & Reid, L. (2002). Early childbearing and children's achievement behavior over time. *Perspectives on Sexual and Reproductive Health, 34,* 41–49.

Hoffman, L. W. (1989). Effects of maternal employment in two-parent families. *American Psychologist, 44,* 283–293.

Hoffman, L. W., & Youngblade, L. M. (1999). *Mothers at work: Effects on children's well-being.* New York: Cambridge.

Hoffman, M. L. (1970). Moral development. In P. H. Mussen (Ed.), *Manual of child psychology* (3rd ed., Vol. 2). New York: Wiley.

Hoffman, M. L. (2002). *Empathy and moral development.* New York: Cambridge University Press.

Hoffman, S., Foster, E., & Furstenberg, F. (1993). Reevaluating the costs of teenage childbearing. *Demography, 30,* 1–13.

Hogan, D. M., & Tudge, J. (1999). Implications of Vygotsky's theory for peer learning. In A. M. O'Donnell & A. King (Eds.), *Cognitive perspectives on peer learning.* Mahwah, NJ: Erlbaum.

Hoghughi, M. S., & Long, N. (Eds.). (2004). *Handbook of parenting.* Newbury Park, CA: Sage.

Holcomb, S. S. (2004). Obesity in children and adolescents: Guidelines for prevention and management. *Nurse Practitioner, 29,* 14–15.

Holding, S. (2002). Current state of screening for Down syndrome. *Annals of Clinical Biochemistry, 39,* 1–11.

Holland, J. L. (1987). Current status of Holland's theory of careers: Another perspective. *Career Development Quarterly, 36,* 24–30.

Hollich, G., Newman, R. S., & Jusczyk, P. W. (2005). Infants' use of synchronized visual information to separate streams of speech. *Child Development, 76,* 598–613.

Hollier, L. M., Harstad, T. W., Sanchez, P. J., Twickler, D. M., & Wendel, G. D. (2001). Fetal syphilis: Clinical and laboratory characteristics. *Obstetrics and Gynecology, 97,* 947–953.

Holmes, R. M., & Holmes, S. T. (2005). *Suicide in the U.S.* Thousand Oaks, CA: Sage.

Holtzen, D. W. (2000). Handedness and professional tennis. *International Journal of Neuroscience, 105,* 101–119.

Honein, M. A., Paulozzi, L. J., Mathews, T. J., Erickson, J. D., & Wong, L. Y. (2001). Impact of folic acid fortification of the U.S. food supply on the occurrence of tube defects. *Journal of the American Medical Association, 285,* 2981–2986.

Hopkins, B. (1991). Facilitating early motor development: An intracultural study of West Indian mothers and their infants living in Britain. In J. K. Nugent, B. M. Lester, & T. B. Brazelton (Eds.), *The cultural context of infancy: Vol. 2. Multicultural and interdisciplinary approaches to parent-infant relations.* Norwood, NJ: Ablex.

Hopkins, B., & Westra, T. (1988). Maternal handling and motor development: An intracultural study. *Genetic Psychology Monographs, 14,* 377–420.

Hopkins, B., & Westra, T. (1990). Motor development, maternal expectations, and the role of handling. *Infant Behavior and Development, 13,* 117–122.

Hopkins, J. R. (2000). Erikson, E. H. (2000). In A. Kazdin (Ed.), *Encyclopedia of psychology.* Washington, DC, & New York: American Psychological Association and Oxford University Press.

Horgan, G. (2005). Healthier lifestyles series, 1. Exercise for children. *Journal of Family Health Care, 15,* 15–17.

Horn, I. B., Joseph, J. G., & Cheng, T. L. (2004). Nonabusive physical punishment and child behavior among African American children: A systematic review. *Journal of the National Medical Association, 96,* 1162–1168.

Horne, R. S., Franco, P., Adamson, T. M., Groswasser, J., & Kahn, A. (2002). Effects of body position on sleep and arousal characteristics in infants. *Early Human Development, 69,* 25–33.

Horne, R. S., Franco, P., Adamson, T. M., Groswasser, J., & Kahn, A. (2004). Influences of maternal cigarette smoking on infant arousability. *Early Human Development, 79,* 49–58.

Horne, R. S., Parslow, P. M., & Harding, R. (2004). Respiratory control and arousal in sleeping infants. *Pediatric Respiratory Reviews, 5,* 190–198.

Hornor, G. (2005). Physical abuse: Recognition and reporting. *Journal of Pediatric Health Care, 19,* 4–11.

Horowitz, F. D., & O'Brien, M. (1989). In the interest of the nation: A reflective essay on the state of knowledge and the challenges before us. *American Psychologist, 44,* 441–445.

Horowitz, J. A., & Goodman, J. H. (2005). Identifying and treating postpartum depression. *Journal of Obstetrics, Gynecology, and Neonatal Nursing, 34,* 264–273.

Horst, J. S., Oakes, L. M., & Madole, K. L. (2005). What does it look like and what can it do? Category structure influences how infants categorize. *Child Development, 76,* 614–631.

Horton, D. M. (2001). The disappearing bell curve. *Journal of Secondary Gifted Education, 12,* 185–188.

Hoskin, J., & Herman, R. (2001). The communication, speech, and gesture of a group of hearing impaired children. *International Journal of Language and Communication Disorders, 36* (Suppl.), 206–209.

Host, A., & Halken, S. (2005). Primary prevention of food allergy in infants who are at risk. *Current Opinions in Allergy and Clinical Immunology, 5,* 255–259.

Hotchner, T. (1997). *Pregnancy and childbirth.* New York: Avon.

Houston, P. D. (2005, February). NCLB: Dreams and nightmares. *Phi Delta Kappan,* 466–470.

Houston-Price, C., Plunkett, K., & Harris, P. (2005). Word-learning wizardry at 1; 6. *Journal of Child Language, 32,* 179–189.

Howard, R. W. (2001). Searching the real world for signs of rising population intelligence. *Personality & Individual Differences, 30,* 1039–1058.

Howe, M. J. A., Davidson, J. W., Moore, D. G., & Sloboda, J. A. (1995). Are there early childhood signs of musical ability? *Psychology of Music, 23,* 162–176.

Howe, M. L. (1997). Children's memory for traumatic experiences. *Learning and Individual Differences, 9,* 153–174.

Howell, C. J., Dean, T., Lucking, L., Dziedzic, K., Jones, P. W., & Johanson, R. B. (2002). Randomized study of long term outcome after epidural versus non-epidural analgesia during labor. *British Medical Journal, 352,* 357.

Howell, E. M. (2001). The impact of Medicaid expansions for pregnant women: A synthesis of the evidence. *Medical Care Research Review, 58,* 3–30.

Howell, E. M., Pettit, K. L., & Kingsley, G. T. (2005). Trends in maternal and infant health in poor urban neighborhoods: Good news from the 1990s, but challenges remain. *Public Health Reports, 120,* 409–417.

Howell, K. K., Lynch, M. E., Platzman, K. A., Smith, G. H., & Coles, C. D. (2005, in press). Prenatal alcohol exposure and ability, academic achievement, and school functioning in adolescence: A longitudinal follow-up. *Journal of Pediatric Psychology.*

Hoyle, R. H., & Judd, C. M. (2002). *Research methods in social psychology* (7th ed.). Belmont, CA: Wadsworth.

Hoza, B., Pelham, W. E., Waschbusch, D. A., Kipp, H., & Owens, J. S. (2001). Academic task persistence of normally achieving ADHD and control boys. *Journal of Consulting and Clinical Psychology, 69,* 271–283.

Hsu, H. (2004, May). *Separation anxiety in mothers of one-year-olds.* Paper presented at the International Conference on Infant Studies, Chicago.

Huang, C. M., Tung, W. S., Kuo, L. L., & Ying-Ju, C. (2004). Comparison of pain responses of premature infants to the heelstick between containment and swaddling. *Journal of Nursing Research, 12,* 31–40.

Huang, L. N. (1989). Southeast Asian refugee children and adolescents. In J. T. Gibbs & L. N. Huang (Eds.), *Children of color.* San Francisco: Jossey-Bass.

Huebner, A. J., & Howell, L.W. (2003). Examining the relationship between adolescent sexual risk-taking and perceptions of monitoring, communication, and parenting styles. *Journal of Adolescent Health, 33,* 71–438.

Huesmann, L. R. (1986). Psychological processes promoting the relation between exposure to media violence and aggressive behavior by the viewer. *Journal of Social Issues, 42,* 125–139.

Huesmann, L. R., Moise-Titus, J., Podolski, C., & Eron, L. D. (2003). Longitudinal relations between exposure to TV violence and their aggressive and violent behavior in young adulthood: 1977–1992. *Developmental Psychology, 39,* 201–221.

Huffman, L. R., & Speer, P. W. (2000). Academic performance among at-risk children: The role of developmentally appropriate practices. *Early Childhood Research Quarterly, 15,* 167–184.

Hulse, G. K., O'Neill, G., Pereira, C., & Brewer, C. (2001). Obstetric and neonatal outcomes associated with maternal naltrexone exposure. *Australian and New Zealand Journal of Obstetrics and Gynecology, 41,* 424–428.

Huncharek, M., Kupelnick, B., & Klassen, H. (2002). Paternal smoking during pregnancy and the risk of childhood brain tumors: Results of a meta-analysis. *In Vivo, 15,* 535–541.

Hunsley, M., & Thoman, E. B. (2002). The sleep of co-sleeping infants when they are not co-sleeping: Evidence that co-sleeping is stressful. *Developmental Psychobiology, 40,* 14–22.

Hunt, C. E., Leo, S. M., Vezina, R. M., McCoy, R., Corwin, J. J., Mandell, F., Willinger, M., Hoffma, H. J., & Mitchell, A. A. (2003). Infant sleep position and associated health outcome. *Archives of Pediatric and Adolescent Medicine, 157,* 469–474.

Hurlburt, R. T. (2006). *Comprehending behavioral statistics* (4th ed.). Belmont, CA: Wadsworth.

Hurt, H., Brodsky, N. L., Roth, H., Malmud, F., & Giannetta, J. M. (2005). School performance of children with gestational cocaine exposure. *Neurotoxicology and Teratology, 27,* 203–211.

Hurwitz, C. A., Duncan, J., & Wolfe, J. (2004). Caring for a child with cancer at the close of life: "There are people who make it, and I'm hoping I'm one of them." *Journal of the American Medical Association, 292,* 2141–2149.

Huston, A. C. (1983). Sex-typing. In P. H. Mussen (Ed.), *Handbook of child psychology* (4th ed., Vol. 4). New York: Wiley.

Huttenlocher, J., Haight, W., Bruk, A., Seltzer, M., & Lyons, T. (1991). Early vocabulary growth: Relation to language input and gender. *Developmental Psychology, 27,* 236–248.

Huttenlocher, J., Levine, S., & Vevea, J. (1998). Environmental input and cognitive growth: A study using time-period comparisons. *Child Development, 69,* 1012–1029.

Huttenlocher, P. R., & Dabholkar, A. S. (1997). Regional differences in synaptogenesis in human cerebral cortex. *Journal of Comparative Neurology, 37* (2), 167–178.

Hwang, S. J., Ji, E. K., Lee, K. K., Kim, Y. M., Shinn, Y., Cheon, Y. H., & Rhyu, I. J. (2004). Gender differences in the corpus callosum of neonates. *Neuroreport, 29,* 1029–1032.

Hyde, A., & Roche-Reid, B. (2004). Midwifery practice and the crisis of modernity. *Social Science Medicine, 58,* 2613–2623.

Hyde, J. S. (1986). Gender differences in aggression. In J. S. Hyde & M. C. Linn (Eds.), *The psychology of gender: Advances through meta-analysis.* Baltimore: Johns Hopkins University Press.

Hyde, J. S. (1993). Meta-analysis and the psychology of women. In F. L. Denmark & M. A.

Paludi (Eds.), *Handbook on the psychology of women.* Westport, CT: Greenwood.

Hyde, J. S. (2003). Unpublished review of Santrock, J. W., *Topical life-span development* (2nd ed.). New York: McGraw-Hill.

Hyde, J. S. (2004). *Half the human experience* (5th ed.), Boston: Houghton Mifflin.

Hyde, J. S. (2005 in press). The gender similarities hypothesis. *American Psychologist.*

Hyde, J. S., & DeLamater, J. (2005). *Human Sexuality* (8th ed., updated). New York: McGraw-Hill.

Hyde, J. S., & Delamater, J. D. (2005). *Understanding human sexuality* (8th ed. updated). New York: McGraw-Hill.

Hyde, J. S., & Mezulis, A. H. (2001). Gender differences research: Issues and critique. In J. Worrell (Ed.), *Encyclopedia of women and gender.* San Diego: Academic Press.

Hyman, E. E., & Loftus, E. F. (2001). In M. L. Eisen, J. A. Quas, & G. S. Goodman (Eds.), *Memory and suggestibility in the forensic interview.* Mahwah, NJ: Erlbaum.

Hyman, L., Kay, B., Tabori, A., Weber, M., Mahon, M., & Cohen, I. (2006). Bullying: Theory, research, and interventions with student victimization. In. C. M. Evertson & C. S. Weinstein (Eds.), *Handbook of classroom management.* Mahwah, NJ: Erlbaum.

Hymel, S., McDougall, P., & Renshaw, P. (2004). Peer acceptance/rejection. In P. K. Smith & C. H. Hart (Eds.), *Blackwell handbook of childhood social development.* Malden, MA: Blackwell.

Hyson, M. C., Copple, C., & Jones, J. (2006). Early childhood development and education. In W. Damon & R. Lerner (Eds.), *Handbook of child psychology* (6th ed.). New York: Wiley.

I

"I Have a Dream" Foundation. (2005). *About us.* Available on the World Wide Web at http://www.ihad.org.

Ianni, F. A. J., & Orr, M. T. (1996). Dropping out. In J. A. Graber, J. Brooks-Gunn, & A. C. Petersen (Eds.), *Transitions in adolescence.* Mahwah, NJ: Erlbaum.

Iannucci, L. (2000). *Birth defects.* New York: Enslow.

Ige, F., & Shelton, D. (2004). Reducing the risk of sudden infant death syndrome (SIDS) in African-American communities. *Journal of Pediatric Nursing, 19,* 290–292.

Iliyasu, Z., Kabir, M., Galadanci, H. S., Abubaker, I. S., & Aliyu, M. H. (2005). Awareness and attitude of antenatal clients toward HIV voluntary counseling and testing in Aminu Kano Teaching Hospital, Kano, Nigeria. *Nigerian Journal of Medicine, 14,* 27–32.

Insel, P. M., & Roth, W. T. (2006). *Core concepts in health* (10th ed.). New York: McGraw-Hill.

International Human Genome Sequencing Consortium. (2004). Finishing the euchromatic sequence of the human genome. *Nature, 431,* 931–945.

Irwin, C. E. (1993). The adolescent, health, and society: From the perspective of the physician. In S. G. Millstein, A. C. Petersen, & E. O. Nightingale (Eds.), *Promoting the health of adolescents.* New York: Oxford University Press.

Irwin, C. E. (2004). Eating and physical activity during adolescence: Does it make a difference in adult health status? *Journal of Adolescent Health, 34,* 459–460.

Irwin, S. A., Christmon, C. A., Grossman, A. W., Galvez, R., Kim, S. H., DeGrush, B. J., Weiler, I. J., & Greenough, W. T. (2005). Fragile X mental retardation protein levels increase following complex environment exposure in rat brain regions undergoing active synaptogenesis. *Neurobiology, Learning, and Memory, 83,* 180–187.

Isaacs, C. E. (2005). Human milk inactivates pathogens individually, additively, and synergistically. *Journal of Nutrition, 135,* 1286–1288.

Ito, M. (2004). "Nurturing the brain" as an emerging research field involving child neurology. *Brain Development, 26,* 429–433.

Ivanenko, A., Crabtree, V. M., & Gozal, D. (2004). Sleep in children with psychiatric disorders. *Pediatric Clinics of North America, 51,* 51–68.

Iverson, P., & Kuhl, P. K. (1996). Influences of phonetic identification and category goodness on American listeners' perception of /r/ and /l/. *Journal of the Acoustical Society of America, 99,* 1130–1140.

Iverson, P., Kuhl, P. K., Akahane-Yamada, R., Diesch, E., Tohkura, Y., Ketterman, A., & Siebert, C. (2003). A perceptual interference account of acquisition difficulties in non-native phonemes. *Cognition 87,* B47–57.

J

Jabbour, R. A., Hempel, A., Gates, J. R., Zhang, W., & Risse, G. L. (2005). Right hemisphere language mapping in patients with bilateral language. *Epilepsy & Behavior, 6,* 587–592.

Jackman, G. A., Farah, M. M., Kellerman, A. L., & Simon, H. K. (2001). Seeing is believing: What do boys do when they find a real gun? *Pediatrics, 107,* 1247–1250.

Jackson, A. W., & Davis, G. A. (2000). *Turning points 2000.* New York: Teachers College Press.

Jacobs, J. E., & Klaczynski, P. A. (2002). The development of judgment and decision making during childhood and adolescence. *Current Directions in Psychological Science, 11,* 145–149.

Jacobs, J., & Klaczynski, P. (Eds.) (2005). *The development of judgment and decision making in children and adolescents.* Mahwah, NJ: Erlbaum.

Jacobson, J. L., & Jacobson, S. W. (2002). Association of prenatal exposure to an environmental containment with intellectual function in childhood. *Journal of Toxicology—Clinical Toxicology, 40,* 467–475.

Jacobson, J. L., & Jacobson, S. W. (2003). Prenatal exposure to polychlorinated biphenyls and attention at school age. *Journal of Pediatrics, 143,* 780–788.

Jacobson, J. L., Jacobson, S. W., Fein, G. G., Schwartz, P. M., & Dowler, J. (1984). Prenatal exposure to an environmental toxin: A test of the multiple-effects model. *Developmental Psychology, 20,* 523–532.

Jacobson, L. (2004). Pre-K standards said to slight social, emotional skills. *Education Week, 23* (No. 42), 13–14.

Jaffee, S., & Hyde, J. S. (2000). Gender differences in moral orientation. *Psychological Bulletin, 126,* 703–726.

Jain, A. E., & Lacy, T. (2005). Psychotropic drugs in pregnancy and lactation. *Journal of Psychiatric Practice, 11,* 177–191.

Jalongo, M. R., & Isenberg, J. P. (2000). *Exploring your role: A practitioner introduction to early childhood education.* Columbus, OH: Merrill.

James, D. C., & Dobson, B. (2005). Position of the American Dietetic Association: Promoting and supporting breastfeeding. *Journal of the American Dietetic Association, 105,* 810–818.

James, J., Thomas, P., Cavan, D., & Kerr, D. (2004). Preventing childhood obesity by reducing consumption of carbonated drinks: Cluster randomized trial. *British Medical Journal, 328,* 1237.

James, W. (1890/1950). *The principles of psychology.* New York: Dover.

Jankov, R. P., Asztolos, E. V., & Skidmore, M. B. (2000). Favorable neurological outcomes following delivery room cardiopulmonary resuscitation of infants < or = 750 g at birth. *Journal of Pediatric and Child Health, 36,* 19–22.

Jansen, A., Floel, A., Deppe, M., Van Randenborgh, J., Drager, B., Kanowski, M., & Knecht, S. (2004). Determining the hemispheric dominance of spatial attention: A comparison between fTCD and fMRI. *Human Brain Mapping, 23,* 168.

Janson, C. (2004). The effects of passive smoking on respiratory health in children and adults. *International Journal of Tuberculosis and Lung Diseases, 8,* 510–516.

Janssen, I., Craig, W. M., Boyce, W. F., & Pickett, W. (2004). Associations between overweight and obesity with bullying behaviors in school-aged children. *Pediatrics, 113,* 1187–1194.

Janssen, I., Katzmarzyk, P. T., Boyce, W. F., Vereecken, C., Mulvihill, C., Roberts, C., Currie, C., & Pickett, W. (2005). Comparison of overweight and obesity prevalence in school-aged youth from 34 countries and their relationships with physical activity and dietary patterns. *Obesity Reviews, 6,* 123–132.

Jenkins, J. M., & Astington, J. W. (1996). Cognitive factors and family structure associated with theory of mind development in young children. *Developmental Psychology, 32,* 70–78.

Jenkins, T. M., Sciscione, A. C., Wapner, R. J., & Sarton, G. E. (2004). Training in chorionic villus sampling: Limited experience of U.S. fellows. *American Journal of Obstetrics and Gynecology, 191,* 1288–1290.

Jenni, O. G., & O'Connor, B. B. (2005). Children's sleep: An interplay between culture and sleep. *Pediatrics, 115,* 204–216.

Jensen, A. R. (1969). How much can we boost IQ and scholastic achievement? *Harvard Educational Review, 39,* 1–123.

Ji, B. T., Shu, X. O., Linet, M. S., Zheng, W., Wacholde, S., Gao, Y. T., Ying, D. M., & Jin, F. (1997). Paternal cigarette smoking and the risk of childhood cancer among offspring of nonsmoking mothers. *Journal of the National Cancer Institute, 89,* 238–244.

Jiao, S., Ji, G., & Jing, Q. (1996). Cognitive development of Chinese urban only children and children with siblings. *Child Development, 67,* 387–395.

Jimenez, V., Herniquez, M., Llanos, P., & Riquelme, G. (2004). Isolation and purification of human placental plasma membranes from normal and pre-eclamptic pregnancies: A comparative study. *Placenta, 25,* 422–437.

Jin, S. H., Kim, T. J., Han, D. S., Shin, S. K., & Kim, W. H. (2002). Thalidomide suppresses the interleukin 1 beta-induced NfkappaB signaling pathway in colon cancer cells. *Annals of the New York Academy of Science, 973,* 414–418.

Jin, Y., Liao, Y., Lu, C., Li, G., Yu, F., Zhi, X., Xu, J., Liu, S., Liu, M., & Yang, J. (2005, in press). Health effects in children aged 3–6 years induced by environmental lead exposure. *Ecotoxicology and Environmental Safety.*

Jinon, S. (1996). The effect of infant massage on growth of the preterm infant. In C. Yarbes-Almirante & M. De Luma (Eds.), *Increasing safe and successful pregnancy.* Amsterdam: Elsevier.

Johnson, A. N. (2005). Kangaroo holding beyond the NICU. *Pediatric Nursing, 31,* 53–56.

Johnson, D. J., Jaeger, E., Randolph, S. M., Cauce, A., Ward, J., & National Institute of Child Health and Human Development Early Child Care Research Network. (2003). Studying the effects of early child care experiences on the development of children of color in the United States: Toward a more inclusive research agenda. *Child Development, 74,* 1227–1244.

Johnson, G. B. (2005). *The living world* (4th ed.). New York: McGraw-Hill.

Johnson, G. B. (2006). *The living world* (4th ed.). New York: McGraw-Hill.

Johnson, J. S., & Newport, E. L. (1991). Critical period effects on universal properties of language: The status of subjacency in the acquisition of a second language. *Cognition, 39,* 215–258.

Johnson, K., Gerada, C., & Greenough, A. (2003). Substance misuse during pregnancy. *British Journal of Psychiatry, 183,* 187–189.

Johnson, M. H. (2000). Infancy: Biological processes. In A. Kazdin (Ed.), *Encyclopedia of psychology.* Washington, DC, & New York: American Psychological Association and Oxford University Press.

Johnson, M. H. (2001). Functional brain development during infancy. In A. Fogel & G. Bremner (Eds.), *Blackwell handbook of infant development.* London: Blackwell.

Johnson, M. H. (2005). Developmental neuroscience. In M. H. Bornstein & M. E. Lamb (Eds.), *Developmental psychology* (5th ed.). Mahwah, NJ: Erlbaum.

Johnson, M. K., Beebe, T., Mortimer, J. T., & Snyder, M. (1998). Volunteerism in adolescence: A process perspective. *Journal of Research on Adolescence, 8,* 309–332.

Johnson, M. P. (2002). The implications of unfulfilled expectations and perceived pressure to attend the birth on men's stress levels following birth attendance: A longitudinal study. *Journal of Psychosomatic Obstetrics and Gynecology, 23,* 173–182.

Johnson, M. P., & Baker, S. R. (2004). Implications of coping repertoire as predictors of mens' stress, anxiety, and depression following pregnancy, childbirth, and miscarriage: A longitudinal study. *Journal of Psychosomatic Obstetrics and Gynecology, 25,* 87–94.

Johnson, W., Bouchard, T. J., Krueger, R. F., McGue, M., & Gottesman, I. I. (2004). Just one g: Consistent results from three test batteries. *Intelligence, 32,* 95–107.

John-Steiner, V., & Mahn, H. (2003). Sociocultural contexts for teaching and learning. In I. B. Weiner (Ed.), *Handbook of psychology* (Vol. VII). New York: Wiley.

Johnston, L. D., O'Malley, P. M., & Bachman, J. G. (2003). *Monitoring the future national results on adolescent drug use: Overview of key findings, 2002.* Bethesda, MD: National Institute on Drug Abuse.

Johnston, L. D., O'Malley, P. M., Bachman, J. G., & Schulenberg, J. E. (2005). *Monitoring the future national results on adolescent drug use: Overview of key findings, 2004.* Bethesda, Md: National Institute on Drug Abuse.

Jones, B. F., Rasmussen, C. M., & Moffit, M. C. (1997). *Real-life problem solving.* Washington, DC: American Psychological Association.

Jones, J. G., & Worthington, T. (2005). Management of sexually abused children by non-forensic sexual abuse examiners. *Journal of the Arkansas Medical Society, 101,* 224–226.

Jones, J. M. (1994). The African American: A duality dilemma? In W. J. Lonner & R. Malpass

(Eds.), *Psychology and culture*. Needham Heights, MA: Allyn & Bacon.

Jones, M. C. (1965). Psychological correlates of somatic development. *Child Development, 36,* 899–911.

Jones, T. G., & Fuller, M. L. (2003). *Teaching Hispanic children*. Boston: Allyn & Bacon.

Jordan, A. (2004). The role of the media in children's development: An ecological perspective. *Journal of Developmental and Behavioral Pediatrics, 25,* 196–206.

Jordan, B. (1993). *Birth in four cultures*. Prospect Heights, IL: Waveland.

Jordan, I. M., Robert, A., Francart, J., Sann, L., & Putet, G. (2005). Growth in extremely low birth weight infants up to three years. *Biology of the Neonate, 88,* 57–65.

Joyner, K., & Udry, J. R. (2000). You don't bring me anything but down: Adolescent, romance and depression. *Journal of Health and Social Behavior, 41,* 369–391.

Jr., R. M., Lyman, R., Fatsis, J., Prystowiski, E., Nguyen, A., Wright, C., Kissinger, P., & Jr., J. M. (2004). Characteristics of women who deliver with no prenatal care. *Journal of Maternal, Fetal, and Neonatal Medicine, 16,* 45–50.

Judge, B., & Billick, S. B. (2004). Suicidality in adolescence: Review and legal considerations. *Behavioral Science and the Law, 22,* 681.

Jusczyk, P. W. (2000). *The discovery of spoken language*. Cambridge, MA: MIT Press.

Jusczyk, P. W. (2002). Language development: From speech perception to words. In A. Slater & M. Lewis (Eds.), *Introduction to infant development*. New York: Oxford University Press.

Jusczyk, P. W., & Hohne, E. A. (1997). Infants' memory for spoken words. *Science, 277,* 1984–1986.

Juvonen, J., Graham, S., & Schuster, M. A. (2003). Bullying among young adolescents. *Pediatrics, 112,* 1231–1237.

K

Kagan, J. (1987). Perspectives on infancy. In J. D. Osofsky (Ed.), *Handbook on infant development* (2nd ed.). New York: Wiley.

Kagan, J. (1992). Yesterday's promises, tomorrow's promises. *Developmental Psychology, 28,* 990–997.

Kagan, J. (1997). Temperament and the reactions to unfamiliarity. *Child Development, 68,* 139–143.

Kagan, J. (2000). Temperament. In A. Kazdin (Ed.), *Encyclopedia of psychology*. Washington, DC, & New York: American Psychological Association and Oxford University Press.

Kagan, J. (2002). Behavioral inhibition as a temperamental category. In R. J. Davidson, K. R. Scherer, & H. H. Goldsmith (Eds.), *Handbook of affective sciences*. New York: Oxford University Press.

Kagan, J. (2003). Biology, context and developmental inquiry. *Annual Review of Psychology, 54.* Palo Alto, CA: Annual Reviews.

Kagan, J., & Fox, N. A. (2006). Biology, culture, and temperamental biases. In W. Damon & R. Lerner (Eds.), *Handbook of child psychology* (6th ed.). New York: Wiley.

Kagan, J., & Herschkowitz, N. (2005). *A young mind in a growing brain*. Mahwah, NJ: Erlbaum.

Kagan, J., & Snidman, N. (1991). Infant predictors of inhibited and uninhibited behavioral profiles. *Psychological Science, 2,* 40–44.

Kagan, J. J., Kearsley, R. B., & Zelazo, P. R. (1978). *Infancy: Its place in human development*. Cambridge, MA: Harvard University Press.

Kagan, S. L., & Scott-Little, C. (2004). Early learning standards. *Phi Delta Kappan, 82,* 388–395.

Kahn, A., Gorswasser, J., Franco, P., Scaillet, S., Sawaguchi, T., Kelmanson, I., & Dan, B. (2004). Sudden infant deaths: Stress, arousal, and SIDS. *Pathophysiology, 10,* 241–252.

Kahn, J. A., Kaplowitz, R. A., Goodman, E., & Emans, J. (2002). The association between impulsiveness and sexual risk behaviors in adolescent and young adult women. *Journal of Adolescent Health, 30,* 229–232.

Kail, R., & Hall, L. K. (2001). Distinguishing short-term memory from working memory. *Memory and Cognition, 29,* 1–9.

Kail, R., & Pellegrino, J. W. (1985). *Human intelligence*. New York: W. H. Freeman.

Kaiser, L. L., & Allen, L. (2002). Position of the American Dietetic Association: Nutrition and lifestyle for a healthy pregnancy outcome. *Journal of the American Dietetic Association, 102,* 1479–1490.

Kalant, H. (2004). Adverse effects of cannabis on health: an update of the literature since 1996. *Progress in Neuropsychopharmacology and Biological Psychiatry, 28,* 849–863.

Kalichman, S. C., Simbayi, L. C., Jooste, S., Cherry, C., & Cain, D. (2005). Poverty-related stressors and HIV AIDS transmission risks in two South African communities. *Journal of Urban Health, 82,* 237–249.

Kalil, A., & DeLaire, T. (Eds.). (2004). *Family investments in children's potential*. Mahwah, NJ: Erlbaum.

Kalil, A., & Kunz, J. (2000, April). *Psychological outcomes of adolescent mothers in young adulthood*. Paper presented at the meeting of the Society for Research on Adolescence. Chicago.

Kamii, C. (1985). *Young children reinvent arithmetic: Implications of Piaget's theory*. New York: Teachers College Press.

Kamii, C. (1989). *Young children continue to reinvent arithmetic*. New York: Teachers College Press.

Kammerman, S. B. (1989). Child care, women, work, and the family: An international overview of child-care services and related policies. In J. S. Lande, S. Scarr, & N. Gunzenhauser (Eds.), *Caring for children: Challenge to America*. Hillsdale, NJ: Erlbaum.

Kammerman, S. B. (2000a). Parental leave policies. *Social Policy Report of the Society for Research in Child Development, XIV* (No. 2), pp. 1–15.

Kammerman, S. B. (2000b). From maternity to paternity child leave policies. *Journal of the Medical Women's Association, 55,* 98–99.

Kanazawa, S. (2004). General intelligence as a domain-specific adaptation. *Psychological Review, 111,* 512–523.

Kantrowitz, B. (1991, Summer). The good, the bad, and the difference. *Newsweek*, pp. 48–50.

Kantrowitz, B. H., Roediger, H. L., & Elmes, D. G. (2005). *Experimental psychology* (8th ed.). Belmont, CA: Wadsworth.

Kaplow, J. B., Curran, P. J., Dodge, K. A., & the Conduct Problems Prevention Research Group. (2002). Child, parent, and peer predictors of early-onset substance use: A multisite longitudinal study. *Journal of Abnormal Child Psychology, 30,* 199–216.

Karp, H. (2002). *The happiest baby on the block*. New York: Bantam.

Katz, L. (1999). Curriculum disputes in early childhood education. *ERIC Clearinghouse on Elementary and Early Childhood Education*. Document EDO-PS-99–13.

Katz, L. F. (1999, April). *Toward a family-based hypervigilance model of childhood aggression: The role of the mother's and the father's meta-emotion philosophy*. Paper presented at the meeting of the Society for Research in Child Development, Albuquerque.

Katz, L., & Chard, S. (1989). *Engaging the minds of young children: The project approach*. Norwood, NJ: Ablex.

Katz, L. G. (2003, May 23). State of the art of early childhood education—2003. *ERIC Documentation Service*, # ED 475–599.

Katz, P. A. (1987, August). *Children and social issues*. Paper presented at the meeting of the American Psychological Association, New York.

Katzmarzyk, P. T., Srinivasan, S. R., Chen, W., Malina, R. M., Bouchard, C., & Berensen, G. S. (2004). Body mass index, waist circumference, and clustering of cardiovascular disease risk factors in a biracial sample of children and adolescents. *Pediatrics, 114,* e198–e205.

Kauffman, J. M., & Hallahan, D. P. (2005). *Special education: What it is and why we need it*. Boston: Allyn & Bacon.

Kauffman, J. M., McGee, K., & Brigham, M. (2004). Enabling or disabling? Observations on changes in special education. *Phi Delta Kappan, 85,* 613–620.

Kauffmann Early Education Exchange. (2002). *Set for success: Building a strong foundation for school readiness based on the social-emotional development of young children* (No. 1). Kansas City: The Ewing Marian Kauffman Foundation.

Kaufman, J. C., & Baer, J. (Eds.). (2004). *Creativity across domains.* Mahwah, NJ: Erlbaum.

Kaufmann, L. (2003). More evidence for the role of the central executive in retrieving arithmetic facts—a case study of severe developmental dyscalculia. *Journal of Clinical and Experimental Neuropsychology, 24,* 302–310.

Kaugers, A. S., Russ, S. W., & Singer, L. T. (2000, May). *Self-regulation among cocaine-exposed four-year-old children.* Paper presented at the joint meetings of the Pediatric Academic Societies and the American Academy of Pediatrics, Boston.

Kavale, K. A., Holdnack, J. A., & Mostert, M. P. (2005). Responsiveness to intervention and the identification of specific learning disability: A critique and alternative proposal. *Learning Disability Quarterly, 28,* 2–16.

Kazdin, A. E., & Benjet, C. (2003). Spanking children: Evidence and issues. *Current Directions in Psychological Science, 12,* 99–103.

Keating, D. P. (1990). Adolescent thinking. In S. S. Feldman, & G. R. Elliott (Eds.), *At the threshold: The developing adolescent.* Cambridge, MA: Harvard University Press.

Keating, D. P. (2004). Cognitive and brain development. In R. Lerner & L. Steinberg (Eds.), *Handbook of adolescence* (2nd ed.). New York: Wiley.

Keel, P. K., Mitchell, J. E., Miller, K. B., Davis, T. L., & Crowe, S. J. (1999). Long-term outcome of bulimia nervosa. *Archives of General Psychiatry 56,* 63–69.

Keen, R. (2005). Unpublished review of Santrock *Topical Life-Span Development,* 3rd ed. New York: McGraw-Hill.

Keen, R. (2005b). Using perceptual representations to guide reaching and grasping. In J. J. Reiser, J. J. Lockman, & C. A. Nelson (Eds.), *The role of action in learning and development.* Mahwah, NJ: Erlbaum.

Keenan, K., Gunthorpe, D., & Young, D. (2002). Patterns of cortisol reactivity in African-American neonates from low-income environments. *Developmental Psychology, 41,* 265–276.

Keenan, K., Hipwell, A., Duax, J., Stouthamer-Loeber, M., & Lober, R. (2004). Phenomenology of depression in young girls. *Journal of the Academy of Child and Adolescent Psychiatry, 43,* 1098–1106.

Keller, A., Ford, L., & Meacham, J. (1978). Dimensions of self-concept in preschool children. *Developmental Psychology, 14,* 483–489.

Kellman, P. J., & Arterberry, M. E. (2006). Infant visual perception. In W. Damon & R. Lerner (Eds.), *Handbook of child psychology* (6th ed.) New York: Wiley.

Kellman, P. J., & Banks, M. S. (1998). Infant visual perception. In W. Damon (Ed.), *Handbook*

of child psychology (5th ed., Vol. 2). New York: Wiley.

Kellogg, R. (1970). *Understanding children's art: Readings in developmental psychology today.* Del Mar, CA: CRM.

Kelly, J. B., & Lamb, M. E. (2003). Developmental issues in relocation cases involving young children: When, whether, and how. *Journal of Family Psychology, 17,* 193–205.

Kendall, G., & Peebles, D. (2005). Acute fetal hypoxia: The modulating effect of infection. *Early Human Development, 81,* 27–34.

Kendrick, D., & Marsh, P. (2001). How useful are sociodemographic characteristics in identifying children at risk of unintentional injury? *Public Health, 115,* 103–107.

Kennedy, H. P., Beck, C. T., & Driscoll, J. W. (2002). A light in the fog: Caring for women with postpartum depression. *Journal of Midwifery & Women's Health, 47,* 318–330.

Kennell, J. H., & McGrath, S. K. (1999). Commentary: Practical and humanistic lessons from the third world for perinatal caregivers everywhere. *Birth, 26,* 9–10.

Kenney, A. M. (1987, June). Teen pregnancy: An issue for schools. *Phi Delta Kappan,* pp. 728–736.

Keretes, M., Youniss, J., & Metz, E. (2004). Longitudinal patterns of religious perspective and civic integration. *Applied Developmental Science, 8,* 39–46.

Kerr, M. (2001). Culture as a context for temperament. In T. D. Wachs & G. A. Kohnstamm (Eds.), *Temperament in context.* Mahwah, NJ: Erlbaum.

Kerr, P. (2005). Midwifery reborn: Opportunities for a new generation. *RCM Midwives, 8,* 260–263.

Kessen, W., Haith, M. M., & Salapatek, P. (1970). Human infancy. In P. H. Mussen (Ed.), *Manual of child psychology* (3rd ed., Vol. 1). New York: Wiley.

Khan, A. A., Whelton, H., & O'Mullane, D. (2004). Is the fluoride level in drinking water a gold standard for the control of dental caries? *International Dentistry Journal, 54,* 256–260.

Khan, R. U., & El-Refaey, H. (2003). Pharmakinetics and adverse-effect profile of rectally administered misprostol in the third stage of labor. *Obstetrics and Gynecology, 101,* 968–974.

Kiarie, J. N., Richardson, B. A., Mbori-Ngacha, B., Nduati, R. W., & John-Stewart, T. M. (2004). Infant feeding practices of women in a perinatal HIV-1 prevention study in Nairobi, Kenya. *Journal of Acquired Immune Deficiency Syndrome, 35,* 75–81.

Kilbride, H. W., Thorstad, K., & Daily, D. K. (2004). Preschool outcome of less than 801-gram preterm infants compared with full-term siblings. *Pediatrics, 113,* 742–747.

Kim, A. H., Chen, J., Ottar-Pfeifer, W., Holgado, S., Stager, D. R., Parks, M. M.,

Beauchamp, G. R., Scott, W., Marsh, M. J., & Tong, P. Y. (2005). Screening for amblyopia in preverbal children with photoscreening photographs: IV. *Binocular Vision and Strabismus Quarterly, 20,* 71–80.

Kim, J., & Cicchetti, D. (2004). A longitudinal study of child maltreatment, mother-child relationship quality and maladjustment: The role of self-esteem and social competence. *Journal of Abnormal Child Psychology, 32,* 341–354.

Kimm, S. Y., & Obarzanek, E. (2002). Childhood obesity: A new pandemic of the new millennium. *Pediatrics, 110,* 1003–1007.

Kimm, S. Y., Barton, B. A., Obarzanek, E., McMahon, R. P., Kronsberg, S. S., Waclawiw, M. A., Morrison, J. A., Schreiber, G. G., Sabry, Z. I., & Daniels, S. R. (2002). Obesity development during adolescence in a biracial cohort: The NHLBI Growth and Health Study. *Pediatrics, 110,* e54.

Kimura, D. (2000). *Sex and cognition.* Cambridge, MA: MIT Press.

King, M. F., Mannino, D. M., & Holguin, F. (2004). Risk factors for asthma incidence: A review of recent prospective evidence. *Panminerva Medicine, 46,* 97–110.

King, P. E., & Benson, P. L. (2005). Spiritual development and adolescent well-being and thriving. In E. C. Roehkepartain, P. E. King, L. Wagner, & P. L. Benson (Eds.), *Handbook of spiritual development in childhood and adolescence.* Thousand Oaks, CA: Sage.

Kinginger, C. (2002). Defining the zone of proximal development in U.S. foreign language education. *Applied Linguistics, 23,* 240–261.

Kinney, J. (2006). *Loosening the grip: A handbook of alcohol information* (8th ed.). New York: McGraw-Hill.

Kirk, S., Scott, B. J., & Daniels, S. R. (2005). Pediatric obesity epidemic: Treatment options. *Journal of the American Dietetic Association, 105* (5 Suppl. 1), S44–S51.

Kirkham, C., Harris, S., & Grzybowski, S. (2005). Evidence-based prenatal care II: Third-trimester care and prevention of infectious diseases. *American Family physician, 71,* 1555–1560.

Kirley, A., Hawi, Z., Daly, G., McCarron, M., Mullins, C., Millar, N. Waldman, I., Fitzgerald, M., & Gill, M. (2002). Dopaminergic system genes in ADHD: Toward a biological hypothesis. *Neuropsychopharmacology, 27,* 607–619.

Kisilevsky, B. S. (1995). The influence stimulus and subject variables on human fetal responses to sound and vibration. In J.-P. Lecaunet, W. P. Fifer, M. A. Krasnegor, & W. P. Smotherman (Eds.), *Fetal development.* Hillsdale, NJ: Erlbaum.

Kisilevsky, B. S., Hains, S. M. J., Lee, K., Xie, X., Huang, H., Ye, H. H., Zhang, K., & Wang, Z. (2003). Effects of experience on fetal voice recognition. *Psychological Science, 14,* 220–225.

Kisilevsky, S., Hains, S. M., Jacquet, A. Y., Granier-Deferre, C., & Lecanuet, J. P. (2005). Maturation of fetal responses to music. *Developmental Science, 7,* 550–559.

Kistner, J. (2006). Children's peer acceptance, perceived acceptance, and risk of depression. In T. E. Joiner, J. S. Brown, & J. Kistner (Eds.), *The interpersonal, cognitive, and social nature of depression.* Mahwah, NJ: Erlbaum.

Kite, M. (2001). Genders stereotypes. In J. Worrell (Ed.), *Encyclopedia of women and gender.* San Diego: Academic Press.

Klaczynski, P. (2005, in press). Metacognition and cognitive variability: A two-process model of decision making and its development. In J. Jacobs & P. Klaczynski (Eds.), *The development of decision making: Cognitive, sociocultural, and legal perspectives.* Mahwah, NJ: Erlbaum.

Klaczynski, P. A., & Narasimham, G. (1998). Development of scientific reasoning biases: Cognitive versus ego-protective explanations. *Developmental Psychology, 34,* 175–187.

Klaus, M., & Kennell, H. H. (1976). *Maternal-infant bonding.* St. Louis: Mosby.

Kleberg, A., Westrup, B., & Stjernqvist, K. (2000). Developmental outcome, child behavior, and mother-child interaction at 3 years of age following Newborn Individualized Care and Intervention Program (NIDCAP) intervention. *Early Human Development, 60,* 123–135.

Klesges, L. M., Johnson, K. C., Ward, K. D., & Barnard, M. (2001). Smoking cessation in pregnant women. *Obstetrics and Gynecological Clinics of North America, 28,* 269–282.

Kling, K. C., Hyde, J. S., Showers, C. J., & Buswell, B. N. (1999). Gender differences in self-esteem: A meta-analysis. *Psychological Bulletin, 125,* 470–600.

Klish, W. J. (1998, September). Childhood obesity. *Pediatrics in Review, 19,* 312–315.

Klonoff-Cohen, H. S., & Natarajan, L. (2004). The effect of advancing paternal age on pregnancy and live birth rates in couples undergoing in vitro fertilization or gamete intrafallopian transfer. *American Journal of Obstetrics and Gynecology, 191,* 507–514.

Klug, W. S., & Cummings, M. R. (2005). *Essentials of genetics* (5th ed.). Upper Saddle River, NJ: Prentice Hall.

Klug, W. S., Cummings, M. R., & Spencer, C. (2006). *Concepts of genetics* (8th ed.). Upper Saddle River, NJ: Prentice Hall.

Knafo, A., Iervolino, A. C., & Plomin, R. (2005). Masculine girls and feminine boys: Genetic and environmental contributions to atypical gender development in early childhood. *Journal of Personality and Social Psychology, 88,* 400–412.

Knecht, S., Drager, B., Deppe, M., Bobe, L., Lohmann, H., Floel, A., Ringelstein, E. B., & Henningsen, H. (2000). Handedness and hemispheric language dominance in healthy humans. *Brain, 135,* 2512–2518.

Kobayashi, K., Tajima, M., Toishi, S., Fujimori, K., Suzuki, Y., & Udagama, H. (2005). Fetal growth restriction associated with measles virus infection during pregnancy. *Journal of Perinatal Medicine, 33,* 67–68.

Koch, J. (2003). Gender issues in the classroom. In I. B. Weiner (Ed.), *Handbook of psychology* (Vol. 7). New York: Wiley.

Kochanska, G., Aksan, N., Knaack, A., & Rhines, H. M. (2004). Maternal parenting and children's conscience: Early security as moderator. In T. Luster & L. Okagaki (Eds.), *Parenting.* Mahwah, NJ: Erlbaum.

Kochanska, G., Friesenborg, A. E., Lange, L. A., Martel, M. M., & Kochanska, G. (2004). Parents' personality and infants' temperament as contributors to their emerging relationship. *Journal of Personality and Social Psychology, 86,* 744–759.

Kochhar, C. A., West, L., & Taymans, J. M. (2000). *Handbook for successful inclusion.* Columbus, OH: Merrill.

Kohlberg, L. (1958). *The development on modes of moral thinking and choice in the years 10 to 16.* Unpublished doctoral dissertation, University of Chicago.

Kohlberg, L. (1966). A cognitive-developmental analysis of children's sex-role concepts and attitudes. In E. E. Maccoby (Ed.), *The development of sex differences.* Palo Alto, CA: Stanford University Press.

Kohlberg, L. (1969). Stage and sequence: The cognitive-developmental approach to socialization. In D. A. Goslin (Ed.), *Handbook of socialization theory and research.* Chicago: Rand McNally.

Kohlberg, L. (1976). Moral stages and moralization: The cognitive-developmental approach. In T. Lickona (Ed.), *Moral development and behavior.* New York: Holt, Rinehart & Winston.

Kohlberg, L. (1986). A current statement of some theoretical issues. In S. Modgil & C. Modgil (Eds.), *Lawrence Kohlberg.* Philadelphia: Palmer.

Kolbe, L. J., Collins, J., & Cortese, P. (1997). Building the capacity of schools to improve the health of the nation. *American Psychologist, 52,* 256–265.

Kolliker, M. (2005). Ontogeny in the family. *Behavior Genetics, 35,* 7–18.

Komitova, M., Mattsson, B., Johansson, B. B., & Eriksson, P. S. (2005). Enriched environment increases neural stem/progenitor cell proliferation and neurogenesis in the subventricular zone of stroke-lesioned adult rats. *Stroke, 36,* 1278–1282.

Kopp, C. B. (1992, October). *Trends and directions in studies of developmental risk.* Paper presented at the 27th Minnesota Symposium on Child Psychology, University of Minnesota, Minneapolis.

Kopp, C. B., & Neufeld, S. J. (2002). Emotional development in infancy. In R. Davidson & K. Scherer (Eds.), *Handbook of affective sciences.* New York: Oxford University Press.

Koppelman, K. (2005). *Understanding human differences.* Upper Saddle River, NJ: Prentice Hall.

Koriat, A., Goldsmith, M., Pansky, A. (2000). Toward a psychology of memory accuracy. *Annual Review of Psychology* (Vol. 51). Palo Alto, CA: Annual Reviews.

Kornhaber, M., Fierros, E., & Veenema, S. (2005). *Multiple intelligence: Best ideas from research and practice:* Boston: Allyn & Bacon.

Korvatska, E., Van de Water, J., Anders, T. F., & Gershwin, M. E. (2004). Genetic and immunologic considerations in autism. *Neurobiology of Disease, 9,* 107–125.

Kotch, J. B. (2003). Psychological maltreatment. *Pediatrics, 111,* 444–445.

Kotler, J. A., Wright, J. C., & Huston, A. C. (2001). Television use in families with children. In J. Bryant & J. A. Bryant (Eds.), *Television and the American Family.* Mahwah, NJ: Erlbaum.

Kotovsky, L., & Baillargeon, R. (1994). Calibration-based reasoning about collision events in 11-month-old infants. *Cognition, 51,* 107–129.

Kottak, C. P. (2002). *Cultural anthropology* (9th ed.). New York: McGraw-Hill.

Kozol, J. (1991). *Savage inequalities.* New York: Crown.

Kozulin, A., Gindis, B., Ageyev, V. S., & Miller, S. M. (Eds.). (2003). *Vygotsky's educational theory in cultural context.* New York: Cambridge University Press.

Kranz, S., & Siega-Riz, A. M. (2002). Sociodemographic determinants of added sugar intake in preschoolers 2 to 5 years old. *Journal of Pediatrics, 140,* 667–672.

Krause, K. H., Dresel, S. H., Krause, J., la Fougere, C., & Ackenheil, M. (2003). The dopamine transporter and neuroimaging in attention deficit hyperactivity disorder. *Neuroscience and Biobehavior Review, 27,* 605–613.

Krebs, L., & Langhoff-Roos, J. (2003). Elective cesarean delivery for term breech. *Obstetrics and Gynecology, 101,* 690–696.

Kreppner, K. (2002). Retrospect and prospect in the study of families as systems. In J. P. McHale & W. S. Grolnick (Eds.), *Retrospect and prospect in the study of families.* Mahwah, NJ: Erlbaum.

Kreutzer, M., Leonard, C., & Flavell, J. H. (1975). An interview study of children's knowledge about memory. *Monographs of the Society for Research in Child Development, 40* (1, Serial No. 159).

Krimer, L. S., & Goldman-Rakic, P. S. (2001). Prefrontal microcircuits. *Journal of Neuroscience, 21,* 3788–3796.

Kristjansdottir, G., & Vilhjalmsson, R. (2001). Sociodemographic differences in patterns of sedentary and physically active behavior in older children and adolescents. *Acta Pediatrica, 90,* 429–435.

Kroger, J. (2003). Identity development in adolescence. In G. Adams & M. Berzonsky (Eds.), *Blackwell handbook of adolescence.* Malden, MA: Blackwell.

Krogh, D. (2005). *Biology* (3rd ed.). Upper Saddle River, NJ: Prentice Hall.

Krogh, K. L., & Slentz, S. L. (2001). *Teaching young children.* Mahwah, NJ: Erlbaum.

Ksir, C. J., Hart, C. L., & Ray, O. S. (2006). *Drugs, society, and human behavior* (11th ed.). New York: McGraw-Hill.

Kubey, R. (2004). *Creating television.* Mahwah, NJ: Erlbaum.

Kubrick, R. J., & McLaughlin, C. S. (2005). No Child Left Behind Act of 2001. In S. W. Lee (Ed.), *Encyclopedia of school psychology.* Thousand Oaks, CA: Sage.

Kuczynski, L., & Lollis, S. (2002). Four foundations for a dynamic model of parenting. In J. R. M. Gerris (Ed.), *Dynamics of parenting.* Hillsdale, NJ: Erlbaum.

Kuebli, J. (1994, March). Young children's understanding of everyday emotions. *Young Children,* pp. 36–48.

Kuhl, P. K. (1993). Infant speech perception: A window on psycholinguistic development. *International Journal of Psycholinguistics, 9,* 33–56.

Kuhl, P. K. (2000). A new view of language acquisition. *Proceedings of the National Academy of Science, 97*(22), 11850–11857.

Kuhn, D. (1998). Afterword to Volume 2: Cognition, perception, and language. In W. Damon (Ed.), *Handbook of child psychology* (5th ed., Vol. 2). New York: Wiley.

Kuhn, D. (1999). A developmental model of critical thinking. *Educational Researcher, 28,* 26–37.

Kuhn, D. (2000). Adolescence: Adolescent thought processes. In A. Kazdin (Ed.), *Encyclopedia of psychology.* Washington, DC, and New York: American Psychological Association and Oxford University Press.

Kuhn, D. (2004). What is scientific thinking, and how does it develop? In. U. Goswami (Ed.), *Blackwell handbook of childhood cognitive development.* Malden, MA: Blackwell.

Kuhn, D. (2005, in press). *Education for thinking.* Cambridge: Harvard University Press.

Kuhn, D., & Franklin, S. (2006). The second decade: What develops (and how)? In W. Damon & R. Lerner (Eds.), *Handbook of child psychology* (6th ed.). New York: Wiley.

Kuhn, D., Amsel, E., & O'Laughlin, M. (1988). *The development of scientific thinking skills.* Orlando, FL Academic Press.

Kuhn, D., Schauble, L., & Garcia-Mila, M. (1992). Cross-domain development of scientific reasoning. *Cognition and Instruction, 9,* 285–327.

Kuiper, S., Maas, T., Schayck, C. P., Muris, J. W., Schonberger, H. J., Dompeling, E., Gijsbers, B., Weel, C., Andre Knotterus, J., and the PREVASC Group (2005). *Pediatric Allergy and Immunology, 16,* 321–331.

Kulczewski, P. (2005). Vygotsky and the three bears. *Teaching Children Mathematics, 11,* 246–248.

Kumari, A. S. (2001). Pregnancy outcome in women with morbid obesity. *International Journal of Gynecology and Obstetrics, 73,* 101–107.

Kuo, P. H., Lin, C. C., Yang, H. J., Soong, W. T., & Chen, W. J. (2004). A twin study of competence and behavioral/emotional problems among adolescents in Taiwan. *Behavior Genetics, 34,* 63–74.

Kupersmidt, J. B., & Coie, J. D. (1990). Preadolescent peer status, aggression, and school adjustment as predictors of externalizing problems in adolescence. *Child Development, 61,* 1350–1363.

Kwan, M. L., Buffler, P. A., Abrams, B., & Kiley, V. A. (2004). Breastfeeding and the risk of childhood leukemia: A meta-analysis. *Public Health Reports, 119,* 521–535.

L

La Greca, A. M., & Harrison, H. M. (2005). Adolescent peer relations, friendships, and romantic relationships: Do they predict anxiety and depression? *Journal of Clinical Child & Adolescent Psychology, 34,* 49–61.

La Greca, A. M., Silverman, W. K., Vernberg, E. M., & Roberts, M. C. (Eds.). (2002). *Helping children cope with disasters and terrorism.* Washington, DC: American Psychological Association.

Laberge, L., Tremblay, R. E., Vitarao, E., & Montplaiser, J. (2000). Development of parasomnias from childhood to early adolescence. *Pediatrics, 106,* 67–74.

Ladd, G. W. (2006). *Peer relationships and social competence of children and adolescents.* New Haven, CT: Yale University Press.

Ladd, G., Buhs, E., & Troop, W. (2004). School adjustment and social skills training. In P. K. Smith & C. H. Hart (Eds.), *Blackwell handbook of childhood social development.* Malden, MA: Blackwell.

Laditka, S. B., Laditka, J. N., Bennett, K. J., & Probst, J. C. (2005). Delivery complications associated with prenatal care access for Medicaid-insured mothers in rural and urban hospitals. *Journal of Rural Health, 21,* 158–166.

Laible, D. J., Carlo, G., & Raffaeli, M. (2000). The differential relations of parent and peer attachment to adolescent adjustment. *Journal of Youth and Adolescence, 29,* 45–53.

Laird, R. D., Pettit, G. S., Bates, J. E., & Dodge, K. A. (2003). Parents' monitoring-relevant knowledge and adolescents' delinquent behavior: Evidence of correlated developmental changes and reciprocal influences. *Child Development, 74,* 752–768.

Laird, R. D., Pettit, G. S., Kodge, K. A., & Bates, J. E. (2005). Peer relationship antecedents of delinquent behavior in late adolescence: Is there evidence of demographic group differences in developmental processes? *Development and Psychopathology, 17,* 127–144.

Lally, J. R., Mangione, P., & Honig, S. (1987). *The Syracuse University family development research program.* Unpublished manuscript, Syracuse University, Syracuse, NY.

Lamb, M. E. (1986). *The father's role: Applied perspectives.* New York: Wiley.

Lamb, M. E. (1994). Infant care practices and the application of knowledge. In C. B. Fisher & R. M. Lerner (Eds.), *Applied developmental psychology.* New York: McGraw-Hill.

Lamb, M. E. (2000). The history of research on father involvement: An overview. *Marriage and Family Review, 29,* 23–42.

Lamb, M. E. (2005). Attachments, social networks, and developmental contexts. *Human Development, 48,* 108–112.

Lamb, M. E., & Ahnert, M. E. (2006). Nonparental child care. In W. Damon & R. Lerner (Eds.), *Handbook of child psychology* (6th ed.). New York: Wiley.

Lamb, M. E., & Lewis, C. (2005). The role of parent-child relationships in child development. In M. H. Bornstein & M. E. Lamb (Eds.), *Developmental psychology* (5th ed.). Mahwah, NJ: Erlbaum.

Lamb, M. E., & Sternberg, K. J. (1992). Sociocultural perspectives in nonparental child-care. In M. E. Lamb, K. J. Sternberg, C. Hwang, & A. G. Broberg, (Eds.), *Child care in context.* Hillsdale, NJ: Erlbaum.

Lamb, M. E., Bornstein, M. H., & Teti, D. (2001). *Development in infancy* (4th ed.). Mahwah, NJ: Erlbaum.

Lane, K. L., Greshman, F. M., & O'Shaughnessy, T. E. (2002). *Interventions for child with or at-risk for emotional and behavioral disorders.* Boston: Allyn & Bacon.

Langley-Evans, S. C., & Langley-Evans, A. J. (2002). Use of folic acid supplements in the first trimester of pregnancy. *Journal of the Royal Society of Health, 122,* 181–186.

Langlois, J. A., Rutland-Brown, W., & Thomas, K. E. (2005). The incidence of traumatic brain injury among children in the United States: Differences by race. *Journal of Head and Trauma Rehabilitation, 20,* 229–238.

Langlois, J. H., & Liben, L. S. (2003). Child care research. An editorial perspective. *Child Development, 74,* 969–1226.

Langston, W. (2002). *Research methods manual for psychology.* Belmont, CA: Wadsworth.

Lantz, P. M., Low, L. K., Varkey, S., & Watson, R. L. (2005). Doulas as childbirth professionals: Results from a national survey. *Womens Health Issues, 15,* 109–116.

Lapsley, D. (2005). Stage theories generated by Kohlberg. In M. Killen & J. Smetana (Eds.), *Handbook of moral development.* Mahwah, NJ: Erlbaum.

Lapsley, D. K. & Narvaez, D. (2006). Character education. In W. Damon & R. Lerner (Eds.), *Handbook of child psychology* (6th ed.). New York: Wiley.

Lapsley, D. K., & Murphy, M. N. (1985). Another look at the theoretical assumptions of adolescent egocentrism. *Developmental Review, 5,* 201–217.

Larson, R., & Lampman-Petraitis, C. (1989). Daily emotional states as reported by children and adolescents. *Child Development, 60,* 1250–1260.

Larson, R., & Richards, M. H. (1994). *Divergent realities.* New York: Basic Books.

Larson, R. W. (1999, September). Unpublished review of J. W. Santrock's *Adolescence* (8th ed.). New York: McGraw-Hill.

Larson, R. W. (2001). How U.S. children and adolescents spend their time: What it does (and doesn't) tell us about their development. *Current Directions in Psychological Science, 10,* 160–164.

Larson, R. W., & Varma, S. (1999). How children and adolescents spend time across the world: Work, play, and developmental opportunities. *Psychological Bulletin, 125,* 701–736.

Larson, R. W., & Wilson, S. (2004). Adolescence across place and time: Globalization and the changing pathways to adulthood. In R. Lerner & L. Steinberg (Eds.), *Handbook of adolescent psychology* (2nd ed.). New York: Wiley.

Larson, R. W., Brown, B. B., & Mortimer, J. (2003). Introduction: Globalization, societal change, and new technologies: What they mean for the future of adolescence. In R. W. Larson, B. B. Brown, & J. Mortimer (Eds.), *Adolescents' preparation for the future: Perils and promises.* Malden, MA: Blackwell.

Larson, R. W., Clore, G. L., & Wood, G. A. (1999). The emotions of romantic relationships. In W. Furman, B. B. Brown, & C. Feiring (Eds.), *Contemporary perspectives on romantic relationships.* New York: Cambridge University Press.

Larsson, J. O., Larsson, H., & Lichtenstein, P. (2004). Genetic and environmental contributions to stability and change of ADHD symptoms between 8 and 13 years of age: A longitudinal twin study. *Journal of the American Academy of Child and Adolescent Psychiatry, 43,* 1267–1275.

Lasiuk, G. C., & Ferguson, L. M. (2005). From practice to midrange theory and back again: Beck's theory of postpartum depression. *Advanced Nursing Science, 28,* 127–136.

Lasker, J. N., Coyle, B., Li, K., & Ortynsky, M. (2005). Assessment of risk factors for low birth weight deliveries. *Health Care for Women International, 26,* 262–280.

Lauber, M. O., Marshall, M. L., & Meyers, J. (2005). Gangs. In S. W. Lee (Ed.), *Encyclopedia of school psychology.* Thousand Oaks, CA: Sage.

Lazar, L., Darlington, R., & Collaborators. (1982). Lasting effects of early education: A report from the consortium for longitudinal studies. *Monographs of the Society for Research in Child Development, 47.*

Leach, P. (1990). *Your baby and child: From birth to age five.* New York: Knopf.

Leadbeater, B. J. R., & Way, N. (2000). *Growing up fast.* Mahwah, NJ: Erlbaum.

Leaper, C., & Smith, T. E. (2004). A meta-analytic review of gender variations in children's language use: Talkativeness, affiliative speech, and assertive speech. *Developmental Psychology, 40,* 993–1027.

Learner-Centered Principles Work Group. (1997). *Learner-centered psychological principles: A framework for school redesign and reform.* Washington, DC: American Psychological Association.

Leary, M. R. (2004). *Introduction to behavioral research methods* (4th ed.). Boston: Allyn & Bacon.

Leavitt, C. H., Tonniges, T. F., & Rogers, M. F. (2003). Good nutrition: The imperative for positive development. In M. H. Bornstein, L. Davidson, C. L. M. Keyes, & K. A. Moore (Eds.), *Well-being.* Mahwah, NJ: Erlbaum.

LeDoux, J. (2002). *The synaptic self.* New York: Viking.

LeDoux, J. E. (1996). *The emotional brain: The mysterious underpinnings of emotional life.* New York: Simon & Schuster.

Lee, H. Y., Lee, E. L., Pathy, P., & Chan, Y. H. (2005). Anorexia nervosa in Singapore: An eight-year retrospective study. *Singapore Medical Journal, 46,* 275–281.

Lee, J., & others. (2005). Maternal and infant characteristics associated with perinatal arterial stroke in the infant. *Obstetrical and Gynecological Survey, 60,* 430–431.

Lee, P. A., Kulin, H. E., & Guo, S. S. (2001). Age of puberty among girls and the diagnosis of precocious puberty. *Pediatrics, 107,* 1493.

Lee, R. M. (2005). Resilience against discrimination: Ethnic identity and other-group orientation as protective factors for Korean Americans. *Journal of Counseling Psychology, 52,* 36–44.

Lee, R., Rhee, G., An, S., Kim, S., Kwack, S., Seok, J., Chae, S., Park, C., Yoon, H., Cho, D., Kim, H., & Park, K. (2004). Differential gene profiles in developing embryo and fetus after in utero exposure to ethanol. *Journal of Toxicology and Environmental Health, 67,* 2073–2084.

Lehr, C. A., Hanson, A., Sinclair, M. F., & Christensen, S. L. (2003). Moving beyond dropout prevention towards school completion. *School Psychology Review, 32,* 342–364.

Lehrer, R., & Schauble, L. (2006). Scientific thinking and scientific literacy. In W. Damon & R. Lerner (Eds.), *Handbook of child psychology,* (6th ed.). New York: Wiley.

Lehtonen, L., & Martin, R. J. (2004). Ontogeny of sleep and awake states in relation to breathing in preterm infants. *Seminars in Neonatology, 9,* 229–238.

Leifer, A. D. (1973). *Television and the development of social behavior.* Paper presented at the meeting of the International Society for the Study of Behavioral Development, Ann Arbor, MI.

Leifer, M., Kilbane, T., Jacobsen, T., & Grossman, G. (2004). A three-generational study of transmission of risk for sexual abuse. *Journal of Clinical Child and Adolescent Psychology, 33,* 662–665.

Leitner, Y., Goez, H., Gull, I., Mesterman, R., Winer, E., Jaffa, A., & Harel, S. (2004). Antenatal diagnosis of central nervous system anomalies: Can we predict prognosis? *Journal of Child Neurology, 19,* 435–438.

Lenders, C. M., McElrath, T. F., & Scholl, T. O. (2000). Nutrition in pregnancy. *Current Opinions in Pediatrics, 12,* 291–296.

Lenneberg, E. (1967). *The biological foundations of language.* New York: Wiley.

Lenoir, C. P., Mallet, E., & Calenda, E. (2000). Siblings of sudden infant death syndrome and near miss in about 30 families: Is there a genetic link? *Medical Hypotheses, 54,* 408–411.

Lent, R. W., Brown, S. D., Nota, L., & Sorest, S. (2003). Testing social cognitive interest and choice hypotheses across Holland types in Italian high school students. *Journal of Vocational Behavior, 62,* 101–118.

Leong, F. T. L. (1995). Introduction and overview. In F. T. I. Leong (Ed.), *Career development and vocational behavior in racial and ethnic minorities.* Hillsdale, NJ: Erlbaum.

Leong, F. T. L. (2000). Cultural Pluralism. In A. Kazdin (Ed.), *Encyclopedia of psychology.* Washington, DC, & New York: American Psychological Association and Oxford University Press.

Lepper, M. R., & Henderlong, J. R. (2001). Turning "play" into "work." In C. Sansone & J. M. Harakiewicz (Eds.), *Intrinsic and extrinsic motivation.* San Diego: Academic Press.

Lerner, R. M., Theokas, C., & Bobek, D. L. (2005). Concepts and theories of human development: Historical and contemporary dimensions. In M. H. Bornstein & M. E. Lamb (Eds.), *Developmental Psychology* (5th ed.). Mahwah, NJ: Erlbaum.

Lesaux, N., & Siegel, L. (2003). The development of reading in children who speak English as a second language. *Developmental Psychology, 39,* 1005–1019.

Lessow-Hurley, J. (2005). *The foundations of dual language instruction (*4th ed.*).* Boston: Allyn & Bacon.

Lester, B. (2000). Unpublished review of J. W. Santrock's *Life-span development.* 8th ed. (New York: McGraw-Hill).

Lester, B. M., & Tronick, E. Z. (1990). Introduction. In B. M. Lester & E. Z. Tronick (Eds.), *Stimulation and the preterm infant: The limits of plasticity.* Philadelphia: W. B. Saunders.

Lester, B. M., Tronick, E. Z., & Brazelton, T. B. (2004). The Neonatal Intensive Care Unit Network Neurobehavioral Scale procedures. *Pediatrics, 113* (Supplement), S641–S667.

Lester, B. M., Tronick, E. Z., LaGasse, L., Seifer, R., Bauer, C. R., Shankaran, S., Bada, H. S., Wright, L. L., Smeriglio, V. L., Lu, J., Finnegan, L. P., & Maza, P. L. (2002). The maternal lifestyle study: Effects of substance exposure during pregnancy on neurodevelopmental outcome in 1-month-old infants. *Pediatrics, 110,* 1182–1192.

Leventhal, A. (1994, February). *Peer conformity during adolescence: An integration of developmental, situational, and individual characteristics.* Paper presented at the meeting of the Society for Research on Adolescence, San Diego.

Leventhal, T., & Brooks-Gunn, J. (2003). Children and youth in neighborhood contexts. *Current Directions in Psychological Science, 12,* 27–31.

Leventhal, T., & Brooks-Gunn, J. (2004). Diversity in developmental trajectories across adolescence: Neighborhood influences. In R. Lerner & L. Steinberg (Eds.), *Handbook of adolescent psychology* (2nd ed.). New York: Wiley.

Leventhal, T., Graber, J. A., & Brooks-Gunn, J. (2001). *Adolescent transitions into young adulthood.* Unpublished manuscript, Center for Children and Families, Columbia University.

Levesque, J., Joanette, Y., Mensour, B., Beaudoin, G., Leroux, J. M., Bourgouin, P., & Beauregard, M. (2004). Neural basis of emotional self-regulation in childhood. *Neuroscience, 129,* 361–369.

Levy, R., Chernomoretz, T., Appleman, Z., Levin, D., Or, Y., & Hagay, Z. I. (2005). Head pushing versus breech extraction in cases of impacted fetal head during cesarean section. *European Journal of Obstetrics, Gynecology, and Reproductive Biology, 121,* 24–26.

Lewallen, L. P. (2004). Healthy behaviors and sources of health information among low-income pregnant women. *Public Health Nursing, 21,* 200–206.

Lewin, B. (2006). *Essential genes.* Upper Saddle River, NJ: Prentice Hall.

Lewinsohn, P. M., Rohde, P., Seeley, J. R., Kline, D. N., & Gotlib, L. H. (2006). The psychosocial consequences of adolescent major depressive disorder on young adults. In T. E. Joiner, J. S. Brown, & J. Kistner (Eds.), *The interpersonal, cognitive, and social nature of depression.* Mahwah, NJ: Erlbaum.

Lewis, A. C. (2005, January). States feeling the crunch of NCLB. *Phi Delta Kappan,* 339–340.

Lewis, C., & Carpendale, J. (2004). Social cognition. In P. K. Smith & C. H. Hart (Eds.), *Blackwell handbook of childhood social development.* Malden, MA: Blackwell.

Lewis, C. G. (1981). How adolescents approach decisions: Changes over grades seven to twelve and policy implications. *Child Development, 52,* 538–554.

Lewis, M. (1995). Embarrassment. The emotion of self-exposure and evaluation. In J. Tangney & K. Fischer (Eds.), *Self-conscious emotions: The psychology of shame, guilt, embarrassment and price.* New York: Guilford Press.

Lewis, M. (1997). *Altering fate: Why the past does not predict the future.* New York: Guilford Press.

Lewis, M. (2002). Early emotional development. In A. Slater & M. Lewis (Eds.), *Infant development.* New York: Oxford University Press.

Lewis, M. (2005). The child and its family: The social networks model. *Human Development, 48,* 8–27.

Lewis, M., & Brooks-Gunn, J. (1979). *Social cognition and the acquisition of the self.* New York: Plenum.

Lewis, M., & Ramsay, D. S. (1999). Effect of maternal soothing and infant stress response. *Child Development, 70,* 11–20.

Lewis, M., Hitchcock, D. F., & Sullivan, M. W. (2004). Physiological and emotional reactivity to learning and frustration. *Infancy, 6,* 121–143.

Lewis, M. D., & Steiben, J. (2004). Emotion regulation in the brain. Conceptual issues and directions for developmental research. *Child Development, 75,* 371–376.

Lewis, M. W., Misra, S., Johnson, H. L., & Rosen, T. S. (2004). Neurological and developmental outcomes of prenatally cocaine-exposed offspring from 12 to 36 months. *American Journal of Drug and Alcohol Abuse, 30,* 299–320.

Lewis, R. (2005). *Human genetics* (6th ed.). New York: McGraw-Hill.

Lewis, R. (2007). *Human genetics* (7th ed.). New York: McGraw-Hill.

Leyendecker, B., Harwood, R. L., Comparini, L., & Yalcinkaya, A. (2005). Socioeconomic status, ethnicity, and parenting. In T. Luster & L. Okagaki (Eds.), *Parenting.* Mahwah, NJ: Erlbaum.

Leyendecker, R. L., Harwood, R. L., Comparini, L., & Yalcinkaya, A. (2005). Socioeconomic status, ethnicity, and parenting. In T. Luster & L. Okaghi (Eds.), *Parenting: An ecological perspective* (2nd ed.). Mahwah, NJ: Erlbaum.

Li, H. J., Ji, C. Y., Wang, W., & Hu, Y. H. (2005). A twin study for serum leptin, soluble leptin receptor, and free insulin-like growth factor-1 in pubertal females. *Journal of Clinical Endocrinology and Metabolism, 90,* 3659–3664.

Li, X., Li, S., Ulusovy, E., Chen, W., Srinivasan, S. R., & Berensen, G. S. (2004). Childhood adiposity as a predictor of cardiac mass in adulthood: The Bogalusa Heart Study. *Circulation, 110,* 3488–3492.

Liaw, J. J. (2000). Tactile stimulation and preterm infants. *Journal of Perinatal and Neonatal Nursing, 14,* 84–103.

Liben, L. S. (1995). Psychology meets geography: Exploring the gender gap on the national geography bee. *Psychological Science Agenda, 8,* 8–9.

Liben, L. S., Bigler, R. S., & Krogh, H. R. (2001). Pink and blue collar jobs: Children's judgments of job status and job aspiration in relation to sex of worker. *Journal of Experimental Child Psychology, 79,* 346–363.

Lickliter, R., & Bahrick, L. E. (2000). The development of infant intersensory perception: Advantages of a comparative convergent-operations approach. *Psychological Bulletin, 126,* 260–280.

Lidral, A. C., & Murray, J. C. (2005). Genetic approaches to identify disease genes for birth defects with cleft lip/palate as a model. *Birth Defects Research, 70,* 893–901.

Lie, E., & Newcombe, N. (1999). Elementary school children's explicit and implicit memory for faces of preschool classmates. *Developmental Psychology, 35,* 102–112.

Lieberman, E., Davidson, K., Lee-Parritz, A., & Shearer, E. (2005). Changes in fetal position during labor and their association with epidural analgesia. *Obstetrics and Gynecology, 105,* 974–982.

Liederman, J., Kantrowitz, L., & Flannery, K. (2005). Male vulnerability to reading disability is not likely to be a myth: A call for new data. *Journal of Learning Disabilities, 38,* 109–129.

Lifshitz, F., Pugliese, M. T., Moses, N., & Weyman-Daum, M. (1987). Parental health beliefs as a cause of nonorganic failure to thrive. *Pediatrics, 80,* 175–182.

Lightwood, J. M., Phibbs, C. S., & Glantz, S. A. (1999). Short-term health and economic benefits of smoking cessation. *Pediatrics, 104,* 1312–1320.

Limber, S. P. (1997). Preventing violence among school children. *Family Futures, 1,* 27–28.

Limber, S. P. (2004). Implementation of the Olweus Bullying Prevention Program in American schools: Lessons learned from the field. In D. L. Espelage & S. M. Swearer (Eds.), *Bullying in American schools.* Mahwah, NJ: Erlbaum.

Lin, H., Lawrence, F. R., & Gorrell, J. (2003). Kindergarten teachers' views of children's readiness for school. *Early Childhood Research Quarterly, 18,* 225–237.

Lingard, L., Hodges, B., MacRae, H., & Freeman, R. (2004). Expert and trainee determinations of rhetorical relevance in referral and consultation letters. *Medical Education, 38,* 168–176.

Linne, Y. (2004). Effects of obesity on women's reproduction and complications during pregnancy. *Obesity Review, 5,* 137–143.

Linver, M. R., Fuligni, A. S., Hernandez, M., & Brooks-Gunn, J. (2004). Poverty and child development: Promising interventions. In P. Allen-Meares & M. W. Fraser (Eds.), *Intervention with children & adolescents: An interdisciplinary perspective*. New York: Allyn & Bacon.

Liou, J. D., Chu, D. C., Cheng, P. J., Chang, S. D., Sun, C. F., Wu, Y. C., Liou, W. Y., & Chiu, D. T. (2004). Human chromosome 21-specific DNA markers are useful in prenatal detection of Down syndrome. *Annals of Clinical Laboratory Science, 34,* 319–323.

Lippa, R. A. (2002). *Gender, nature, and nurture.* Mahwah, NJ: Erlbaum.

Lippa, R. A. (2005). *Gender, nature, and nurture* (2nd ed.). Mahwah, NJ: Erlbaum.

Liprie, M. L. (1993). Adolescents' contribution to family decision making. In B. H. Settles, R. S. Hanks, & M. B. Sussman (Eds.), *American families and the future: Analysis of possible destinies.* New York: Haworth Press.

Lipsitz, J. (1983, October). *Making it the hard way: Adolescents in the 1980s.* Testimony presented at the Crisis Intervention Task Force. House Select Committee on Children. Youth. And Families, Washington, DC.

Lissau, I., Overpeck, M. D., Ruan, W. J., Due, P., Holstein, B. E., & Hediger, M. L. (2004). Body mass index and overweight in adolescents in 13 European countries, Israel, and the United States. *Archives of Pediatrics & Adolescent Medicine, 158,* 27–33.

Litovsky, R. Y., & Ashmead, D. H. (1977). Development of binaural and spatial hearing in infants and children. In R. H. Gilkey & T. R. Anderson (Eds.), *Binaural and spatial hearing in real and virtual environments,* Mahwah, NJ: Erlbaum.

Litt, J., Taylor, H. G., Klein, N., & Hack, M. (2005). Learning disabilities in very low birthweight: Prevalence, neuropsychological correlates, and educational interventions. *Journal of Learning Disabilities, 38,* 130–141.

Liu, A. H. (2002). Early intervention for asthma prevention in children. *Allergy and Asthma Processes, 23,* 289–293.

Liu, J., Raine, A., Venables, P. H., & Mednick, S. A. (2004). Malnutrition at 3 years and externalizing behavior problems at age 8, 11, and 17 years. *American Journal of Psychiatry, 161,* 2005–2013.

Liu, J., Raine, A., Venables, P. H., Dalais, C., & Mednick, S. A. (2003). Malnutrition at age 3 years and lower cognitive ability at age 11 years: Independence from psychosocial adversity, *Archives of Pediatric and Adolescent Medicine, 157,* 593–600.

Livealy, W., & Bromley, D. (1973). *Person perception in childhood and adolescence.* New York: Wiley.

Lloyd, K., & Wise, K. (2004). Protecting children from exposure to environmental tobacco. *Nursing Times, 100,* 36–38.

Lobel, M., Yali, A. M., Zhu, W., DeVincent, C. J., & Meyer, B. A. (2002). Beneficial associations between optimistic disposition and emotional distress in high-risk pregnancy. *Psychology and Health, 17,* 77–95.

Lock, A. (2004). Preverbal communication. In U. Goswami (Ed.), *Blackwell handbook of childhood cognitive development.* Malden, MA: Blackwell.

Lockman, J. J. (2000). A perception-action perspective on tool use development. *Child Development, 71,* 137–144.

Loebel, M., & Yali, A. M. (1999, August). *Effects of positive expectancies on adjustments to pregnancy.* Paper presented at the meeting of the American Psychological Association, Boston.

Loeber, R., & Farrington, D. P. (Eds.). (2001). *Child delinquents: Development, intervention and service needs.* Thousand Oaks, CA: Sage.

Loeber, R., Farrington, D. P., Stouthamer-Loeber, M., Moffitt, T., & Caspi, A. (1998). The development of male offending: Key findings from the first decade of the Pittsburgh Youth Study. *Studies in Crime and Crime Prevention, 7,* 141–172.

London, K., Bruck, M., & Ceci, S. J. (2005). Disclosure of child sexual abuse: What does the research tell us about the ways that children tell? *Psychology, Public Policy, and Law, 11,* 194–226.

Long, T., & Long, L. (1983). *Latchkey children.* New York: Penguin.

Loos, R. J., & Rankinen, T. (2005). Gene-diet interactions in body-weight changes. *Journal of the American Dietary Association, 105* (5, Pt 2), 29–34.

Lopes, P. N. (2004). Emotional intelligence and social interaction. *Personality and Social Psychology Bulletin, 30,* 1018–1034.

Lorah, C. (2002). New age, new meals, old problem. *Dentistry Today, 21,* 50–53.

Lord, J., & Winell, J. J. (2004). Overuse injuries in pediatric athletes. *Current Opinions in Pediatrics, 16,* 47–50.

Lorensen, M., Wilson, M. E., & White, M. A. (2004). Norwegian families: Transition to parenthood. *Health Care for Women International, 25,* 334–348.

Lorenz, K. Z. (1965). *Evolution and the modification of behavior.* Chicago: University of Chicago Press.

Lou, J. E., Ganley, T. J., & Flynn, A. J. (2002). Exercise and children's health. *Current Sports Medicine Reports, 1,* 349–353.

Louv, R. (1990). *Childhood's future.* Boston: Houghton Mifflin.

Lowrey, C. A. (2002). Functional subsets of serotonergic hevrons: Implications for control of the hypothalamic-pituitary-adrenal axis. *Journal of Neuroendocrinology, 11,* 911–923.

Lowry, R., Galuska, D. A., Fulton, J. E., Burgeson, C. R., & Kann, L. (2005). Weight management goals and use of exercise for weight control among U.S. high school students, 1991–2001. *Journal of Adolescent Health, 36,* 320–326.

Lucurto, C. (1990). The malleability of IQ as judged from adoption studies. *Intelligence, 14,* 275–292.

Luders, E., Narr, K. L., Thompson, P. M., Rex, D. E., Jancke, L., Steinmetz, H., & Toga, A. W. (2004). Gender differences in cortical complexity. *Nature Neuroscience, 1,* 799–800.

Ludington-Hoe, S., & Golant, S. K. (1993). *Kangaroo care: The best you can do to help your preterm baby.* New York: Bantam, Doubleday.

Ludington-Hoe, S. M., Anderson, G. C., Swinth, J. Y., Thompson, C., & Hadeed, A. J. (2004). Randomized controlled trial of kangaroo care: Cardiorespiratory and thermal effects on healthy preterm infants. *Neonatal Network, 23,* 39–48.

Lumeng, J. C., Gannon, K., Cabral, H. J., Frank, D. A., & Zuckerman, B. (2003). Association between clinically meaningful behavior problems and overweight in children. *Pediatrics, 112,* 1138–1145.

Luo, Y., & Baillargeon, R. (2005). When the ordinary seems unexpected: Evidence for incremental physical knowledge in infants. *Cognition, 95,* 297–328.

Luria, J. W., Smith, G. A., & Chapman, J. I. (2000). An evaluation of a safety education program for kindergarten and elementary school children. *Archives of Pediatric and Adolescent Medicine. 154,* 227–231.

Luster, T., & Okaghi, L. (Eds.). (2005). *Parenting: An ecological perspective* (2nd ed.). Mahwah, NJ: Erlbaum.

Lynn, R. (1996). Racial and ethnic differences in intelligence in the U.S. on the Differential Ability Scale. *Personality and Individual Differences, 26,* 271–273.

Lyon, G. R. (1996). Learning disabilities. *The Future of Children 6* (No. 1), 54–76.

Lyon, T. D., & Flavell, J. H. (1993). Young children's understanding of forgetting over time. *Child Development, 64,* 789–800.

Lyons, S. J., Henly, J. R., & Schuerman, J. R. (2005). Informal support in maltreating families: Its effects on parenting practices. *Children and Youth Services Review, 27,* 21–38.

Lytle, L. A., Murray, D. M., Perry, C. L., Story, M., Birnbaum, A. S., Kubik, M. Y., & Varnell, S. (2004). School-based approaches to affect adolescents' diets Results from the TEENS study. *Health Education and Behavior, 31,* 270–287.

M

Maccoby, E. E. (1984). Middle childhood in the context of the family. In *Development during middle childhood*. Washington, DC: National Academy Press.

Maccoby, E. E. (1987, November). Interview with Elizabeth Hall: All in the family. *Psychology Today*, pp. 54–60.

Maccoby, E. E. (1996). Peer conflict and intrafamily conflict: Are there conceptual bridges? *Merrill-Palmer Quarterly, 42,* 165–176.

Maccoby, E. E. (1999). The uniqueness of the parent-child relationship. In W. A. Collins & B. Laursen (Eds.), *Relationships as developmental contexts*. Mahwah, NJ: Erlbaum.

Maccoby, E. E. (2002). Parenting effects. In J. G. Borrows, S. L. Ramey, & M. Bristol-Power (Eds.), *Parenting and the child's world*. Mahwah, NJ: Erlbaum.

Maccoby, E. E. (2002a). Parenting effects. In J. G. Borkowski, S. L. Ramey, & M. Bristol-Power (Eds.), *Parenting and the child's world*. Mahwah, NJ: Erlbaum.

Maccoby, E. E. (2002b). Gender and group processes. *Current Directions in Psychological Science, 11,* 54–58.

Maccoby, E. E., & Jacklin, C. N. (1974). *The psychology of sex differences*. Palo Alto, CA: Stanford University Press.

Maccoby, E. E., & Lewis, C. C. (2003). Less daycare or better daycare? *Child Development, 74,* 1069–1073.

MacDorman, M. F., & Singh, G. K. (1998). Midwifery care, social and medical factors, and birth outcomes in the USA. *Journal of Epidemiology and Community Health, 52,* 310–317.

MacDorman, M. F., Minino, A. M., Strobino, D. M., & Guyer, B. (2002). Annual summary of vital statistics—2001. *Pediatrics, 110,* 1037–1052.

MacDorman, M. F., Minino, A. M., Strobino, D. M., & Guyer, B. (2002). Annual summary of vital statistics-2001. *Pediatrics, 110,* 1037–1052.

MacFarlane, J. A. (1975). Olfaction in the development of social preferences in the human neonate. In *Parent-infant interaction*. Ciba Foundation Symposium No. 33. Amsterdam: Elsevier.

MacGeorge, E. L., Graves, A. R., Feng, B., Gillihan, S. J., & Burleson, B. R. (2004). The myth of gender cultures: Similarities outweigh differences in men's and women's provisions of and responses to supportive communication. *Sex Roles, 50,* 143–175.

MacWhinney, B. (2005). Language development. In M. H. Bornstein & M. E. Lamb (Eds.), *Developmental psychology* (6th ed.). Mahwah, NJ: Erlbaum.

Mader, S. S. (2006). *Inquiry into life* (11th ed.). New York: McGraw-Hill.

Magnuson, K. A., & Duncan, G. J. (2002). Parents in poverty. In M. H. Bornstein (Ed.), *Handbook of parenting* (2nd ed., Vol. 4). Mahwah, NJ: Erlbaum.

Magnusson, J. (2005). Childhood obesity: Prevention, treatment, and recommendations for health. *Community Practice, 78,* 147–149.

Maguire, S., Mann, M. K., Sibert, J., & Kemp, A. (2005). Are there patterns of bruising in childhood which are diagnostic or suggestive of abuse? A systematic review. *Archives of Diseases in Childhood, 90,* 182–186.

Mahler, M. (1979). *Separation-individuation* (Vol. 2). London: Jason Aronson.

Mahoney, J. L., Larson, R. W., & Eccles, J. S. (Eds.). (2004). *Organized activities as contexts of development*. Mahwah, NJ: Erlbaum.

Main, M. (2000). Attachment theory. In A. Kazdin (Ed.), *Encyclopedia of psychology*. Washington, DC, & New York: American Psychological Association and Oxford University Press.

Maizels, M., Rosenbaum, D., & Keating, B. (1999). *Getting to dry: How to help your child overcome bedwetting*. Cambridge, MA: Harvard Common Press.

Majumdar, I., Paul, P., Talib, V. H., & Ranga, S. (2003). The effect of iron therapy on the growth of iron-replete and iron-deplete children. *Journal of Tropical Pediatrics, 49,* 84–88.

Makrides, M., Neumann, M., Simmer, K., Pater, J., & Gibson, R. (1995). Are long-chain polyunsaturated fatty acids essential nutrients in infancy? *Lancet, 345,* 1463–1468.

Malat, J., Oh, H. J., & Hamilton, M. A. (2005). Poverty, experience, race, and child health. *Public Health Reports, 120,* 442–447.

Malm, M., Martikainen, J., Klaukka, T., & Neuvonen, P. J. (2004). Prescription of hazardous drugs during pregnancy. *Drug Safety, 27,* 899–908.

Malmgren, K. W., & Meisel, S. M. (2004). Examining the link between child maltreatment and delinquency for youth with emotional and behavioral disorders. *Child Welfare, 83,* 175–188.

Mandler, J. M. (2000). Review of J. W. Santrock's *Life-span development*, 8th ed. New York: McGraw-Hill.

Mandler, J. M. (2003). Conceptual categorization. In D. Rakison & L. M. Oakes (Eds.), *Early category and concept development*. New York: Oxford University Press.

Mandler, J. M. (2004). *The foundations of the mind: Origins of conceptual thought*. New York: Oxford University Press.

Mandler, J. M. (2004). *The origins of mind*. New York: Oxford University Press.

Mandler, J. M. (2005). *Jean Mandler*. Available on the World Wide Web at: http://cogsci.ucsd.edu/~jean/

Mandler, J. M., & McDonough, L. (1993). Concept formation in infancy. *Cognitive Development, 8,* 291–318.

Mandler, J. M., & McDonough, L. (1995). Long-term recall in infancy. *Journal of Experimental Child Psychology, 59,* 457–474.

Mannessier, L., Alie-Daram, S., Roubinet, F., & Brossard, Y. (2000). Prevention of fetal hemolytic disease: It is time to take action. *Transfusions in Clinical Biology, 7,* 527–532.

Mansfield, A. (2005). Advancing midwifery practice. *Practicing Midwife, 8,* 4–5.

Many, J. E. (2002). An exhibition and analysis of verbal tapestries: Understanding how scaffolding is woven into the fabric of instructional conversations. *Reading Research Quarterly, 37,* 376–407.

Mao, R., McDonald, J., Cantwell, M., Tang, W., & Ward, K. (2005). The implication of novo 21-hydroxylase mutation in clinical and molecular diagnoses. *Genetic Testing, 9,* 121–125.

Marcell, A. V., & Halpern-Felsher, B. L. (2005). Adolescents' health beliefs are critical in their intentions to seek physician care. *Preventive Medicine, 41,* 118–125.

Marcell, A. V., Klein, J. D., Fischer, I., Allan, M. J., & Kokotailo, P. K. (2002). Male adolescent use of health care services: Where are the boys? *Journal of Adolescent Health Care, 30,* 35–43.

Marchman, V., & Thal, D. (2005). Words and grammar. In M. Tomasello & D. I. Slobin (Eds.), *Beyond nature-nurture*. Mahwah, NJ: Erlbaum.

Marcia, J. E. (1980). Ego identity development. In J. Adelson (Ed.), *Handbook of adolescent psychology*. New York: Wiley.

Marcia, J. E. (1994). The empirical study of ego identity. In H. A. Bosma, T. L. G. Graafsma, H. D. Grotevant, & D. J. De Levita (Eds.), *Identity and development*. Newbury Park, CA: Sage.

Marcia, J. E. (1996). Unpublished review of J. W. Santrock's *Adolescence* (7th ed. Dubuque, IA: Brown & Benchmark).

Marcia, J. E., & Carpendale, J. (2004). Identity: Does thinking make it so? In C. Lightfoot, C. Lalonde, & M. Chandler (Eds.), *Changing conceptions of psychological life*. Mahwah, NJ: Erlbaum.

Marcon, R. A. (2003). The physical side of development. *Young Children, 58* (No. 1), 80–87.

Marcovitch, H. (2004). Use of stimulants for attention deficit hyperactivity disorder: AGAINST. *British Medical Journal, 329,* 908–909.

Marcus, D. L., Mulrine, A., & Wong, K. (1999, September 13). How kids learn. *U.S. News & World Report*, pp. 44–50.

Margolin, L. (1994). Child sexual abuse by uncles. *Child Abuse and Neglect, 18,* 215–224.

Marild, S., Hansson, S., Jodal, U., Oden, A., & Svedberg, K. (2004). Protective effect of breastfeeding against urinary tract infection. *Acta Pediatrics, 93,* 164–168.

Markowitz, M. (2000). Lead poisoning. *Pediatrics in Review, 21,* 327–335.

Marks, M. N., Siddle, K., & Warwick, C. (2003). Can we prevent postnatal depression? A randomized controlled trial to assess the effect of continuity of midwifery care on rates of postnatal depression in high-risk women. *Journal of Maternal, Fetal, and Neonatal Medicine, 13,* 119–127.

Marshall, N. L. (2004). The quality of early child care and children's development. *Current Directions in Psychological Science, 13,* 165–168.

Marsiglio, W. (2004). Studying father trajectories. In R. D. Day & M. E. Lamb (Eds.), *Conceptualizing and measuring father Involvement.* Mahwah, NJ: Erlbaum.

Martin, C. L., & Dinella, L. (2001). Gender development: Gender schema theory. In J. Worrell (Ed.), *Encyclopedia of women and gender.* San Diego: Academic Press.

Martin, C. L., & Halverson, C. F. (1981). A schematic processing model of sex typing and stereotyping in children. *Child Development, 52,* 1119–1134.

Martin, D. W. (2004). *Doing psychology experiments* (6th ed.). Belmont, CA: Wadsworth.

Martin, G. L., & Ruble, D. (2004). Children's search for gender cues: Cognitive perspectives on gender development. *Current Directions in Psychological Science, 13,* 67–70.

Martin, J. A., Kochanek, K. D., Strobino, D. M., Guyer, B., & MacDorman, M. F. (2005). Annual summary of vital statistics—2003. *Pediatrics, 115,* 619–634.

Martin, R., Sexton, C., Franklin, T., & Gerlovich, J. (2005). *Teaching science for all children* (4th ed.). Boston: Allyn & Bacon.

Martinez-Frias, M. L., Frias, J. P., Bermejo, F., Rodriquez-Pinilla, E., Prieto, L., & Frias, J. L. (2005). Pre-gestational maternal body mass index predicts an increased risk of congenital malformations in infants of mothers with gestational diabetes. *Diabetic Medicine, 22,* 775–781.

Martinez-Pasarell, O., Nogues, C., Bosch, M., Egozcue, J., & Templado, C. (1999). Analysis of sex chromosome aneupolidy in sperm from fathers of Turner syndrome patients. *Human Genetics, 104,* 345–349.

Masten, A. S. (2001). Ordinary magic: Resilience processes in development. *American Psychologist, 56,* 227–238.

Masten, A. S. (2004). Regulatory processes, risk, and resilience in adolescent development. *Annals of the New York Academy of Science, 102,* 310–319.

Masten, A. S. (2005). Peer relationships and psychopathology in developmental perspective: Reflections on progress and promise. *Journal of Clinical Child and Adolescent Psychology, 34,* 87–92.

Masten, A. S., & Coatsworth, J. D. (1998). The development of competence in favorable and unfavorable environments. *American Psychologist, 53,* 205–220.

Masur, E. F., Flynn, V., & Eichorst, D. L. (2005). Maternal responsive and directive behaviors and utterances as predictors of children's lexical development. *Journal of Child Language, 32,* 63–91.

Matheny, A. P., & Phillips, K. (2001). Temperament and context: Correlates of home environment with temperament continuity and change. In T. D. Wachs & G. A. Kohnstamm (Eds.), *Temperament in context.* Mahwah, NJ: Erlbaum.

Mathews, T. J., Menacker, F., & MacDorman, M. F. (2003). Infant mortality statistics from the 2001 period linked birth/infant death data set. *National Vital Statistics Reports, 52,* 1–28.

Mathole, T., Lindmark, G., Majoko, F., & Ahlberg, B. M. (2004). A qualitative study of women's perspectives of antenatal care in rural areas of Zimbabwe. *Midwifery, 20,* 122–132.

Matias, A., Montenegro, N., & Blickstein, I. (2005). Down syndrome screening in multiple pregnancies. *Obstetrics and Gynecological Clinics of North America, 32,* 81–96.

Matsuba, M. K., & Walker, L. J. (2004). Extraordinary moral commitment: Young adults involved in social organizations. *Journal of Personality, 72,* 413–436.

Matsumoto, D. (2004). *Culture and psychology* (3rd ed.). Belmont, CA: Wadsworth.

Mattanah, J. (2005). Authoritative parenting and encouragement of children's autonomy. In P. A. Cowan, C. P. Cowan, J. C. Ablow, V. K. Johnson, & J. R. Measelle (Eds.), *The family context of parenting in children's adaptation to elementary school.* Mahwah, NJ: Erlbaum.

Matthews, F., Youngman, L., & Neil, A. (2004). Maternal circulating nutrient concentrations in pregnancy: Implications for birth and placental weights of term infants. *American Journal of Clinical Nutrition, 79,* 103–110.

Matthews, G., Roberts, R. D., & Zeidner, M. (2004). Seven myths about emotional intelligence. *Psychological Inquiry, 15,* 179–196.

Maulik, D. (2003). New directions in prenatal care. *Journal of Maternal, Fetal, and Neonatal Medicine, 13,* 361.

Maurer, D., & Salapatek, P. (1976). Developmental changes in the scanning of faces by young infants. *Child Development, 47,* 523–527.

Mauro, V. P., Wood, I. C., Krushel, L., Crossin, K. L., & Edelman, G. M. (1994). Cell adhesion alters gene transcription in chicken embryo brain cells and mouse embryonal carcinoma cells. *Proceedings of the National Academy of Sciences USA, 91,* 2868–2872.

May, F. B. (2006). *Teaching reading creatively: Reading and writing as communication* (7th ed.). Upper Saddler River, NJ: Prentice Hall.

Mayer, J. D., Salovey, P., & Caruso, D. R. (2004). Emotional intelligence: Theory, findings, and implications. *Psychological Inquiry, 15,* 197–215.

Mayer, R. E. (2003). Memory and information processes. In I. B. Weiner (Ed.), *Handbook of psychology* (Vol. 8). New York: Wiley.

Mayes, L. (2003). Unpublished review of J. W. Santrock's *Tropical life-span development,* 2nd ed. (New York: McGraw Hill).

Mayeux, R. (2005). Mapping the new frontier: Complex genetic disorders. *Journal of Clinical Investigations, 115,* 1404–1407.

Mazza, J. J. (2005). Suicide. In S. W. Lee (Ed.), *Encyclopedia of school psychology.* Thousand Oaks, CA: Sage.

McAdoo, H. P. (2002). African-American parenting. In M. H. Bornstein (Ed.), *Handbook of parenting* (2nd ed.). Mahwah, NJ: Erlbaum.

McCabe, M. P., & Ricciardelli, L. A. (2004). A longitudinal study of pubertal timing and extreme body change behaviors among adolescent boys and girls. *Adolescence, 39,* 145–166.

McCall, R. B., & Carriger, M. S. (1993). A meta-analysis of infant habituation and recognition memory performance as predictors of later IQ. *Child Development, 64,* 57–79.

McCartney, K. (2003, July 16). Interview with Kathleen McCartney in A. Bucuvalas, Child care and behavior. *HGSE News.* pp. 1–4. Cambridge, MA: Harvard Graduate School of Education.

McCarty, M. E., & Ashmead, D. H. (1999). Visual control of reaching and grasping in infants. *Developmental Psychology, 35,* 620–631.

McClearn, G. E. (2004). Nature and nurture: Interaction and coaction. *American Journal of Medical Genetics, 124B,* 124–130.

McCombs, B. L. (2003). Research to policy for guiding educational reform. In I. B. Weiner (Ed.), *Handbook of psychology* (Vol. VII). New York: Wiley.

McCormick, C. B. (2003). Metacognition and learning. In I. B. Weiner (Ed.), *Handbook of psychology* (Vol. 7). New York: Wiley.

McCormick, C. B., & Pressley, M. (1997). *Educational psychology.* New York: Longman.

McCormick, M. C. (2001). Prenatal care—necessary, but not sufficient. *Health Services Research, 36,* 399–403.

McCracken, L. (2000). Birthing free at the edge of the new millennium. *Midwifery Today with International Midwife, 53,* 40.

McCray, T. M. (2004). An issue of culture: The effects of daily activities on prenatal care utilization patterns in rural South Africa. *Social Science Medicine, 59,* 1843–1855.

McCrory, E. J., Mechelli, A., Frith, U., & Price, C. J. (2005). More than words: A common neural basis for reading and naming deficits in developmental dyslexia. *Brain, 128,* 261–267.

McDaniels, G., Issac, M., Brooks, H., & Hatch, A. (2005). Confronting K-3 challenges in an era of accountability. *Young Children, 60* (no. 2), 20–26.

McGarvey, E., Keller, A., Forrester, M., Williams, E., Seward, D., & Suttle, D. E. (2004). Feasability and benefits of a parent-focused preschool child obesity intervention. *American Journal of Public Health, 94*, 1490–1495.

McGechan, J., Shields, B. J., & Smith, G. A. (2004). Children should wear helmets while ice-skating: A comparison of skating-related injuries. *Pediatrics, 114*, 124–128.

McGough, J. J., & Barkley, R. A. (2004). Diagnostic controversies in adult attention deficit hyperactivity disorder. *American Journal of Psychiatry, 161*, 1948–1956.

McGrath, S., Kennell, J., Suresh, M., Moise, K., & Hinkley, C. (1999, May). *Doula support vs. epidural analgesia: Impact on cesarean rates*. Paper presented at the meeting of the Society for Pediatric Research, San Francisco.

McHale, J., Johnson, D., & Sinclair, R. (1999). Family dynamics, preschoolers' family representations, and preschool peer relationships. *Early Education and Development, 10*, 373–401.

McHale, J., Khazan, I., Erera, P., Rotman, T., DeCourcey, W., & McConnell, M. (2002). Coparenting in diverse family systems. In M. H. Bornstein (Ed.), *Handbook of parenting* (2nd ed., Vol. 3). Mahwah, NJ: Erlbaum.

McHale, J. P., Kuersten-Hogan, R., & Rao, N. (2004). Growing points for coparenting theory and research. *Journal of Adult Development, 11*, 221–234.

McHale, J. P., Lauretti, A. F., & Kuersten-Hogan, R. (1999, April). *Linking family-level patterns to father-child, mother-child, and marital relationship qualities*. Paper presented at the meeting of the Society for Research in Child Development. Albuquerque.

McHale, J. P., Luretti, A., Talbot, J., & Pouquette, C. (2001). Retrospect and prospect in the psychological study of marital and couple relationships. In J. P. McHale & W. S. Grolnick (Eds.), *Retrospect and prospect in the psychological study of families*. Mahwah, NJ: Erlbaum.

McHale, S., Dariotis, J., & Kauh, T. J. (2003). Social development and social relationships in middle childhood. In I. B. Weiner (Ed.), Handbook of psychology (Vol. 6). New York: Wiley.

McKee, J. K., Poirier, F. E., & McGraw, W. S. (2005). *Understanding human evolution* (5th ed.). Upper Saddle River, NJ: Prentice Hall.

McKenna, J. J., Mosko, S. S., & Richard, C. A. (1997). Bedsharing promotes breastfeeding. *Pediatrics, 100*, 214–219.

McKinney, P. A., Fear, N. T., Stockton, D., & UK Childhood Cancer Study Investigators. Parental occupation at periconception: Findings from the United Kingdom Childhood Cancer Study. *Occupational and Environmental Medicine, 60*, 901–909.

McLanahan, S., & Sandefur, G. (1994). *Growing up with a single parent: What hurts, what helps?* Cambridge, MA: Harvard University Press.

McLaughlin, T. J., Humphries, O., Nguyen, T., Muljanian, R., & McCormack, K. (2004). "Getting the lead out" in Hartford, Connecticut: A multifaceted lead-poisoning awareness campaign. *Environmental Health Perspectives, 112*, 1–5.

McLearn, K. T. (2004). Narrowing the income gaps in preventive care for young children: Families in healthy steps. *Journal of Urban Health, 81*, 556–567.

McLoyd, V. C. (1998). Children in poverty: Development, public policy, and practice. In W. Damon (Ed.), *Handbook of child psychology* (5th ed., Vol. 4). New York: Wiley.

McLoyd, V. C. (2000). Poverty. In A. Kazdin (Ed.), *Encyclopedia of psychology*. Washington, DC, & New York: American Psychological Association and Oxford University Press.

McLoyd, V. C. (2005). Pathways to academic achievement among children from immigrant families: A commentary. In C. R. Cooper, C. T. Garcia Call, W. T. Bartko, H. M. Davis, & C. Chatman (Eds.), *Developmental pathways through middle childhood*. Mahwah, NJ: Erlbaum.

McLoyd, V. C., & Smith, J. (2002). Physical discipline and behavior problems in African American, European American, and Hispanic children: Emotional support as a moderator. *Journal of Marriage and Family, 64*, 40–53.

McMillan, J. H. (2004). *Educational research* (4th ed). Boston: Allyn & Bacon.

McMillan, J. H., & Schumacher, S. (2006). *Research in education: Evidence based inquiry* (6th ed.). Boston: Allyn & Bacon.

McMillan, J. H., & Wergin, J. F. (2002). *Understanding and evaluating educational research* (2nd ed.). Upper Saddle River, NJ: Prentice Hall.

McNally, D. (1990). *Even eagles need a push*. New York: Dell.

McNamara, F., & Sullivan, C. E. (2000). Obstructive sleep apnea in infants. *Journal of Pediatrics, 136*, 318–323.

McVeigh, C. A., Baafi, M., & Williamson, M. (2002). Functional status after fatherhood: An Australian study. *Journal of Obstetrics, Gynecology, and Neonatal Nursing, 31*, 165–171.

McWhorter, K. (2005). *Efficient and flexible reading* (7th ed.). Boston: Allyn & Bacon.

McWhorter, K. T. (2006). *Vocabulary simplified* (2nd ed.). Upper Saddle River, NJ: Prentice Hall.

Mechanic, D. (1979). Correlates of physician utilization: Why do major multivariate studies of physician utilization find trivial psychosocial and organizational effects? *Journal of Health and Social Behavior, 20*, 389–396.

Medd, S. E. (2003). Children with ADHD need our advocacy. *Journal of Pediatric Health Care, 17*, 102–104.

Mehler, J., Jusczyk, P. W., Lambertz, G., Halsted, N., Bertoncini, J., & Amiel-Tison, C. (1988). A precursor of language acquisition in young infants. *Cognition, 29*, 132–178.

Mehta, A., Hindmarsh, P. C., Stanhope, R. G., Turton, J. P., Cole, T. J., Preece, M. A., & Dattani, M. T. (2005). The role of growth hormone in determining birth size and early postnatal growth, using congenital growth hormone deficiency (GHD) as a model. *Clinical Endocrinology, 63*, 223–231.

Meier, S., Brauer, A. U., Heimrich, B., Nitsch, R., & Savaskan, N. E. (2004). Myelination in the hippocampus during development and following lesion. *Cellular and Molecular Life Sciences, 61*, 1082–1094.

Meis, P. J. (2003, February 6). *Effects of progesterone on preterm births*. Paper presented at the meeting of the Society for Maternal-Fetal Medicine, San Francisco.

Melamed, B. G. (2002). Parenting the ill child. In M. H. Bornstein (Ed.), *Handbook of parenting* (Vol. 5). Mahwah, NJ: Erlbaum.

Melamed, B. G., Roth, B., & Fogel, J. (2001). Childhood health issues across the life span. In A. Baum, T. A. Revenson, & J. E. Singer (Eds.), *Handbook of health psychology*. Mahwah, NJ: Erlbaum.

Melgar-Quinonez, H. R., & Kaiser, L. L. (2004). Relationship of child-feeding practices to overweight in low-income Mexican-American preschool-aged children. *Journal of the American Dietetic Association, 104*, 1110–1119.

Meltzoff, A. N. (1988). Infant imitation and memory: Nine-month-old infants in immediate and deferred tests. *Child Development, 59*, 217–225.

Meltzoff, A. N. (2002). Elements of a developmental theory of imitation. In A. N. Meltzoff & W. Prinz (Eds.), *The imitative mind: Development, evolution, and brain bases*. Cambridge: Cambridge University Press.

Meltzoff, A. N., & Decety, J. (2003). What imitation tells us about social cognition: A rapproachement between developmental psychology and cognitive neuroscience. *Philosophical Transactions of the Royal Society of London, Series B, Biological Sciences, 38*, 491–500.

Meltzoff, A. N., & Gopnik, A. (1997). *Words, thoughts, and theories*. Cambridge, MA: MIT Press.

Meltzoff, A. N., & Moore, M. K. (1999). A new foundation for cognitive development in infancy: The birth of the representational infant. In E. K. Skolnick, K. Nelson, S. A. Gelman, & P. H. Miller (Eds.), *Conceptual development*. Mahwah, NJ: Erlbaum.

Menn, L., & Stoel-Gammon, C. R. (2005). Phonological development: Learning sounds and sound patterns. In J. Berko Glenson (Ed.), *The development of language* (6th ed.). Boston: Allyn & Bacon.

Ment, L. R., Vohr, B., Allan, W., Katz, K. H., Schneider, C., Westerveld, M., Duncan, C. C., & Makuch, R. W. (2003). Change in cognitive function over time in very low-birthweight infants. *Journal of the American Medical Association, 289*, 705–711.

Menyuk, P., Liebergott, J., & Schultz, M. (1995). *Early language development in full-term and premature infants.* Hillsdale, NJ: Erlbaum.

Mercer, C. D., & Pullen, P. C. (2005). *Students with learning disabilities* (6th ed.). Upper Saddle River, NJ: Prentice Hall.

Merchant, R. H., & Lala, M. M. (2005). Prevention of mother-to-child transmission of HIV—An overview. *Indian Journal of Medical Research, 121,* 489–501.

Meredith, N. V. (1978). Research between 1960 and 1970 on the standing height of young children in different parts of the world. In H. W. Reece & L. P. Lipsitt (Eds.), *Advances in child development and behavior* (Vol. 12). New York: Academic Press.

Merenda, P. (2004). Cross-cultural adaptation of educational and psychological testing. In R. K. Hambleton, P. F. Merenda, & C. D. Spielberger (Eds.), *Adapting educational and psychological tests for cross-cultural assessment.* Mahwah, NJ: Erlbaum.

Merrick, J., Aspler, S., & Schwartz, G. (2001). Should adults with phenylketonuria have diet treatment? *Mental Retardation, 39,* 215–217.

Mertler, C. A., & Charles, C. M. (2005). *Introduction to educational research* (5th ed.). Boston: Allyn & Bacon.

Metz, E. C., & Youniss, J. (2005). Longitudinal gains in civic development through school-based required service. *Political Psychology, 26,* 413–437.

Meyer, I. H. (2003). Prejudice, social stress, and mental health in gay, lesbian, and bisexual populations: Conceptual issues and research evidence. *Psychological Bulletin, 129,* 674–697.

Meyer-Bahlburg, H. F., Ehrhart, A. A., Rosen, L. R., Gruen, R. S., Veridiano, N. P., Vann, F. H., & Neuwalden, H. F. (1995). Prenatal estrogens and the development of homosexual orientation. *Developmental Psychology, 31,* 12–21.

Meyers, A. F., Sampson, A. E., Weitzman, M., Rogers, B. L., & Kayne, H. (1989). School breakfast program and school performance. *American Journal of Diseases of Children, 143,* 1234–1239.

Mezzacappa, E. (2004). Alerting, orienting, and executive attention: Developmental properties and socioeconomic correlates in an epidemiological sample of young, urban children. *Child Development, 75,* 1373–1386.

Mezzacappa, E. S. (2004). Breastfeeding and maternal stress response and health. *Nutrition Review, 62,* 261–268.

Michael, R. T., Gagnon, J. H., Laumann, E. O., & Kolata, G. (1994). *Sex in America.* Boston: Little, Brown.

Michel, G. L. (1981). Right-handedness: A consequence of infant supine head-orientation preference? *Science, 212,* 685–687.

Michel, R. S. (2000). Toilet training. *Pediatric Review, 20,* 240–245.

Millar, R., & Shevlin, M. (2003). Predicting career information-seeking behavior of school pupils using the theory of planned behavior. *Journal of Vocational Behavior, 62,* 26–42.

Miller, B. C., Benson, B., & Galbraith, K. A. (2001). Family relationships and adolescent pregnancy risk: A research synthesis. *Developmental Review, 21,* 1–38.

Miller, B. C., Fan, X., Christensen, M., Grotevant, H. D., & von Dulmen, M. (2000). Comparisons of adopted and nonadopted adolescents in a large, nationally representative sample. *Child Development, 71,* 1458–1473.

Miller, G. A. (1981). *Language and speech.* New York: W. H. Freeman.

Miller, J. (2005). Insights into moral development from cultural psychology. In M. Killen & J. Smetana (Eds.), *Handbook of moral development.* Mahwah, NJ: Erlbaum.

Miller, L., & Gur, M. (2002). Religiousness and sexual responsibility in adolescent girls. *Journal of Adolescent Health, 31,* 401–406.

Miller, N. M., Fisk, N. M., Modi, N., & Glover, V. (2005). Stress responses at birth: determinants of cord arterial cortisol and links with cortisol response in infancy. *British Journal of Gynecology, 112,* 921–926.

Miller, P. H., & Seier, W. L. (1994). Strategy utilization deficiencies in children: When, where, and why. In H. W. Reese (Ed.), *Advances in child development and behavior* (Vol. 24). New York: Academic Press.

Miller-Johnson, S., Coie, J., & Malone, P. S. (2003). *Do aggression and peer rejection in childhood predict early adult outcomes?* Paper presented at the meeting of the Society for Research in Child Development, Tampa.

Miller-Jones, D. (1989). Culture and testing. *American Psychologist, 44,* 360–366.

Miller-Loncar, C., Lester, B. M., Seifer, R., Lagasse, L. L., Bauer, C. R., Shankaran, S., Bada, H. S., Wright, L. L., Smeriglio, V. L., Bigsby, R., & Liu, J. (2005). Predictors of motor development in children prenatally exposed to cocaine. *Neurotoxicology and Teratology, 27,* 213–220.

Millstein, S. G. (1993). A view of health from the adolescent's perspective. In S. G. Millstein, A. C. Petersen, & E. O. Nightingale (Eds.), *Promoting the health of adolescents.* New York: Oxford University Press.

Minczykowski, A., Gryczynska, M., Ziemnicka, K., Sowinksi, J., & Wysocki, H. (2005). The influence of growth hormone therapy on ultrasound myocardial tissue characterization in patients with childhood onset GH deficiency. *International Journal of Cardiology, 101,* 257–263.

Mindell, J. A., & Barrett, K. M. (2002). Nightmares and anxiety in elementary-aged children: Is there a relationship? *Child Care: Health and Development, 28,* 317–322.

Ministry of Health, Education, and Welfare. (2002). *Divorce trends in Japan.* Tokyo: Ministry of Health, Education, and Welfare.

Minns, R. A., & Busuttil, A. (2004). Patterns of presentation of the shaken baby syndrome: four types of inflicted brain injury predominate. *British Medical Journal, 328,* 766.

Minstrell, J., & Kraus, P. (2005). Guided inquiry in the science classroom. In *How people learn.* Washington, DC: National Academies Press.

Mintz, M. (2004). Asthma update: Part II: Medical management. *American Family Physician, 70,* 1061–1066.

Minuchin, P. (2002). Looking toward the horizon: Present and future in the study of family systems. In J. P. McHale & W. S. Grolnick (Eds.), *Retrospect and prospect in the study of families.* Mahwah, NJ: Erlbaum.

Minuchin, P. O., & Shapiro, E. K. (1983). The school as a context for social development. In P. H. Mussen (Ed.), *Handbook of child psychology* (4th ed., Vol. 4). New York: Wiley.

Miranda, M. L. (2004). The implications of developmentally appropriate practices for the kindergarten general music classroom. *Journal of Research in Music Education, 52,* 43–53.

Mirowsky, J. (2005). Age at first birth, health, and mortality. *Journal of Health and Social Behavior, 46,* 32–50.

Mischel, W. (2004). Toward an integrative science of the person. *Annual Review of Psychology* (Vol. 55). Palo Alto, CA: Annual Reviews.

Mitchell, E. A., Stewart, A. W., Crampton, P., & Salmond, C. (2000). Deprivation and sudden infant death syndrome. *Social Science and Medicine, 51,* 147–150.

Mitchell, K. S., & Mazzeo, S. E. (2004). Binge eating and psychological distress in ethnically diverse college men and women. *Eating Behavior, 5,* 157–169.

Moats, L. (2004). Relevance of neuroscience to effective education for students with reading and other learning disabilities. *Journal of Child Neurology, 19,* 840–845.

Moely, B. E., Santilli, K. A., & Obach, M. S. (1995). Strategy instruction, metacognition, and motivation in the elementary school classroom. In F. E. Weinert & W. Schneider (Eds.), *Memory performance and competencies.* Mahwah, NJ: Erlbaum.

Mohlala, B. K., Tucker, T. J., Besser, M. J., Williamson, C., Yeats, J., Smit, L., Anthony, J., & Puren, A. (2005). Investigation of HIV in amniotic fluid from HIV-infected pregnant women at full term. *Journal of Infectious Diseases, 192,* 488–491.

Moise, K. J. (2005). Fetal RhD typing with free DNA I maternal plasma. *American Journal of Obstetrics and Gynecology, 192,* 663–665.

Molholm, S., Christodoulou, C., Ritter, W., & Cowan, N. (2001). *The development of auditory attention in children.* Unpublished manuscript, Department of Psychology, City College of the City University of New York.

Molnar, D. (2004). The prevalence of the metabolic syndrome and type 2 diabetes mellitus in children and adolescents. *International Journal of Obesity and Related Metabolic Disorders, 28* (Suppl. 3), S70–S74.

Monastirli, A., & others. (2005). Short stature, type E brachydactyly, gynecomastia, and cryptorchidism in a patient with 47, XYY/45, X/46, XY mosaicism. *American Journal of Medical Science, 329,* 208–210.

Money, J. (1975). Ablatio penis: Normal male infant sex-reassigned as a girl. *Archives of Sexual Behavior, 4,* 65–71.

Monsen, R. B. (2005). Improving child health. *Journal of Pediatric Nursing, 20,* 285–286.

Montemayor, R. (1982). The relationship between parent-adolescent conflict and the amount of time adolescent spends with parents, peers, and alone. *Child Development, 53,* 1512–1519.

Monuteaux, M. C., Faraone, S. V., Herzig, J., Navsaria, N., & Biederman, J. (2005). ADHD and dyscalculia: Evidence for independent familial transmission. *Journal of Learning Disabilities, 38,* 86–93.

Moon, R. Y., Oden, R. P., & Grady, K. C. (2004). Back to sleep: An educational intervention with women, infants, and children program clients. *Pediatrics, 113,* 542–547.

Moon, Y. I., Park, H. R., Koo, H. Y., & Kim, H. S. (2004). Effects of behavior modification on body image, depression, and body fat in obese Korean elementary school children. *Yonsei Medical Journal, 45,* 61–67.

Mooney, C. G. (2006). *Theories of childhood.* Upper Saddle River, NJ: Prentice Hall.

Moore, C., & Lemmon, K. (Eds.). (2001). *The self in time.* Mahwah, NJ: Erlbaum.

Moore, D. (2001). *The dependent gene.* New York: W. H. Freeman.

Moore, L. L., Gao, D., Bradlee, M. L., Cupples, L. A., Sundarajan-Ramamurti, A., Proctor, M. H., Hood, M. Y., Singer, M. R., & Ellison, R. C. (2003). Does early physical activity predict body fat change throughout childhood? *Preventive Medicine, 37,* 10–17.

Moore, V. M., & Davies, M. J. (2005). Diet during pregnancy, neonatal outcomes, and later health. *Reproduction, Fertility, and Development, 17,* 341–348.

Moralez, L. S., Gutierrez, P., & Escarce, J. J. (2005). Demographic and socioeconomic factors associated with blood levels among Mexican-American children and adolescents in the United States. *Public Health Reports, 120,* 448–454.

Moran, S., & Gardner, H. (2006). Extraordinary achievements. In W. Damon & R. Lerner (Eds.), *Handbook of child psychology* (6th ed.). New York: Wiley.

Morelli, G. A., Rogoff, B., Oppenheim, D., & Goldsmith, D. (1992). Cultural variation in infants' sleeping arrangements: Questions of independence. *Developmental Psychology, 28,* 604–613.

Morgan, J. (2005). Nutrition for toddlers: The foundation for good health—1. *Journal of Family Health Care, 15,* 56–59.

Morin, K. H. (2004). Current thoughts on healthy term infant nutrition: The first twelve months. *MCN American Journal of Child Nursing, 29,* 312–317.

Morrison, D. S., Pettigrew, M., & Thompson, H. (2003). What are the most effect ways of improving population health through transport interventions? Evidence from systematic reviews. *Journal of Epidemiology and Community Health, 57,* 327–333.

Morrison, G. S. (2000). *Fundamentals of early childhood education.* Columbus, OH: Merrill.

Morrison, G. S. (2006). *Fundamentals of early childhood education* (4th ed.). Upper Saddle River, NJ: Prentice Hall.

Morrissey-Ross, M. (2000). Lead poisoning and its elimination. *Public Health Nursing, 17,* 229–230.

Morrongiello, B. A., Fenwick, K. D., & Chance, G. (1990). Sound localization acuity in very young infants: An observer-based testing procedure. *Developmental Psychology, 26,* 75–84.

Morrongiello, B. A., Midgett, C., & Shields, R. (2001). Don't run with scissors: Young children's knowledge of home safety rules. *Journal of Pediatric Psychology, 26,* 105–115.

Morrow, A. L., & Rangel, J. M. (2004). Human milk protection against infectious diarrhea: Implications for prevention and clinical care. *Seminars in Pediatric Infectious Diseases, 15,* 221–228.

Morrow, C. E., Bandstra, E. S., Anthony, J. C., Ofir, A. Y., Xue, L., & Reyes, M. B. (2003). Influence of prenatal cocaine exposure on early language development: Longitudinal findings from four months to three years of age. *Journal of Developmental and Behavioral Pediatrics, 24,* 39–50.

Morrow, G., & Malin, N. (2004). Parents and professionals working together: Turning the rhetoric into reality. *Early Years: Journal of International Research and Development, 24,* 163–177.

Morrow, L. (2005). *Literacy development in the early years* (5th ed.). Boston: Allyn & Bacon.

Mortimer, J. T., & Larson, R. W. (2002). *The changing adolescent experience.* New York: Cambridge University Press.

Mortimer, J. T., Finch, M., Shanahan, M., & Ryu, S. (1992). Work experience, mental health, and behavioral adjustment in adolescence. *Journal of Research on Adolescence, 2,* 24–57.

Moscucci, O. (2003). Holistics obstetrics: The origins of "natural childbirth" in Britain. *Postgraduate Medicine Journal, 79,* 168–173.

Moshman, D. (1999). *Adolescent psychological development: Rationality, morality, and identity.* Mahwah, NJ: Erlbaum.

Mott, F. L., & Marsiglio, W. (1985, September/October). Early childbearing and completion of high school. *Family Planning Perspectives,* p. 234.

Mounts, N. S. (2002). Parental management of adolescent peer relationships in context: The role of parenting style. *Journal of Family Psychology, 16,* 58–69.

Mozingo, J. N., Davis, M. W., Droppleman, P. G., & Merideth, A. (2000). "It wasn't working" women's experiences with short-term breast feeding. *American Maternal Journal of Nursing, 25,* 120–126.

Muhle, R., Trentacoste, S. V., & Rapin, I. (2004). The genetics of autism. *Pediatrics, 113,* e472–e486.

Mullick, S., Beksinksa, M., & Msomi, S. (2005). Treatment for syphilis in antenatal care. *Sexually Transmitted Infections, 81,* 220–222.

Mullis, I. V. S., Martin, M. O., Beaton, A. E., Gonzales, E. J., Kelly, D. L., & Smith, T. A. (1998). *Mathematics and science achievement in the final year of secondary school.* Chestnut Hill, MA: Boston College, TIMSS International Study Center.

Mumme, D. L., Fernald, A., & Herrera, C. (1996). Infant's responses to facial & emotional signals in a social referencing paradigm. *Child Development, 67,* 3219–3237.

Munakata, Y. (2006). Information processing approaches to development. In W. Damon & R. Lerner (Eds.), *Handbook of child psychology* (6th ed.). New York: Wiley.

Muris, P., Meesters, C., van de Blom, W., & Mayer, B. (2005). Biological, psychological, and sociocultural correlates of body change strategies and eating problems in adolescent boys and girls. *Eating Behavior, 6,* 11–22.

Murnane, R. J., & Levy, F. (1996). *Teaching the new basic skills.* New York: Free Press.

Murphy, D. J., Fowlie, P. W., & McGuire, W. (2004). Obstetric issues and preterm birth. *British Medical Journal, 329,* 783–786.

Murray, J. P. (2000). Media effects. In A. Kazdin (Ed.), *Encyclopedia of psychology.* Washington, DC, & New York: American Psychological Association and Oxford University Press.

Mustanski, B. S., Chivers, M. L., & Bailey, J. M. (2003). A critical review of recent biological research on human sexual orientation. *Annual Review of Sex Research, 13,* 89–140.

Mustanski, B. S., Viken, R. J., Kaprio, J., Pulkkinen, L., & Rose, R. J. (2004). Genetic and environmental influences on pubertal development: Longitudinal data from Finnish twins at age 11 and 14. *Developmental Psychology, 40,* 1188–1198.

Myers, B. J., Dawson, K. S., Britt, G. C., Lodder, D. E., Meloy, L. D., Saunders, M. K., Meadows, S. L., & Elswick, R. K. (2003). Prenatal cocaine exposure and infant performance on the Brazelton Neonatal Behavioral Assessment Scale. *Substance Use and Misuse, 38,* 2065–2096.

Myers, D. L. (1999). *Excluding violent youths from juvenile court: The effectiveness of legislative waiver.* Doctoral dissertation, University of Maryland, College Park, MD.

N

Nader, K. (2001). Treatment methods for childhood trauma. In J. P. Wilson, M. J. Friedman, & J. Lindy (Eds.), *Treating psychological trauma and PTSD.* New York: Guilford Press.

Nadine, M. B., & Denmark, F. L. (Eds.). (1999). *Females and autonomy: A Life-span perspective.* Boston: Allyn & Bacon.

NAEYC. (1986). Position statement on developmentally appropriate practice in programs for 4– and 5-years-olds. *Young Children, 41,* 20–29.

NAEYC. (1990). NAEYC position statement on school readiness. *Young Children, 46,* 21–28.

NAEYC. (1998). *Overview of learning to read and write: Appropriate practices for young children.* Washington, DC: Author.

NAEYC. (2002). *Early learning standards: Creating the conditions for success.* Washington, DC: Author.

NAEYC. (2003). Learning paths and teaching strategies in early mathematics. *Young children, 58* (No. 1), 41–44.

Naglieri, J. (2000). Stanford-Binet Intelligence Scale. In A. Kazdin (Ed.), *Encyclopedia of psychology.* Washington, DC, & New York: American Psychological Association and Oxford University Press.

Nagy, Z., Westerberg, H., & Klingberg, T. (2004). Maturation of white matter is associated with the development of cognitive functions during childhood. *Journal of Cognitive Neuroscience, 16,* 1227–1233.

Nakai, K., & others (2004). The Tohoku Study of Child Development: A cohort study of effects of perinatal exposure to methylmercury and environmentally persistent organic pollutants on neurobehavioral development in Japanese children. *Tohoku Journal of Experimental Medicine, 202,* 227–237.

Nansel, T. R., Overpeck, M., Pilla, R., Ruan, W., Simons-Morton, B., & Scheidt, P. (2001). Bullying behaviors among U.S. youth. *Journal of the American Medical Association, 285,* 2094–2100.

Narang, A., & Jain, N. (2001). Haemolytic disease of newborn. *Indian Journal of Pediatrics, 68,* 167–172.

Nash, J. M. (1997, February 3). Fertile minds. *Time,* pp. 50–54.

Nash, S. G., McQueen, A., & Bray, J. H. (2005). Pathways to adolescent alcohol use: Family environment, peer influence, and parental expectations. *Journal of Adolescent Health, 37,* 19–28.

National Assessment of Educational Progress. (2000). *The nation's report card.* Washington, DC: National Center for Education Statistics.

National Center for Addiction and Substance Abuse. (2001). *2000 teen survey.* New York: Author.

National Center for Children Exposed to Violence. (2001). *Statistics.* New Haven, CT: Author.

National Center for Children in Poverty (2004). *Low-income children in the United States.* New York: National Center for Children in Poverty, Columbia University.

National Center for Education Statistics. (2002). *School dropouts, Table 108.* Washington DC: U.S. Department of Education.

National Center for Health Statistics. (2000). *Health United States, 2000, with adolescent health chartbook.* Bethesda, MD: U.S. Department of Health and Human Services.

National Center for Health Statistics. (2002). Prevalence of overweight among children and adolescents: United States 1999–2000 (Table 71). *Health United States, 2002.* Atlanta, GA: Centers for Disease Control and Prevention.

National Center for Health Statistics. (2002, June 6). *Births: Preliminary data for 2001.* Atlanta: Centers for Disease Control and Prevention.

National Center for Health Statistics. (2002, September 16). *Deaths, Tables 1 and 60 National Vital Statistics. Report, 50,* pp. 13, 194.

National Center for Health Statistics. (2004). *Birth Statistics.* Hyattsville, Md: U.S. Department of Health and Human Services.

National Center for Health Statistics. (2004). *Health United States.* Hyattsville, MD: U.S. Department of Health and Human Services.

National Center for Learning Disabilities. (2005). *Learning disabilities.* Available on the World Wide Web at http://www.ncid.org/.

National Childhood Cancer Foundation. (1998). *Cancer in children.* Washington, DC: Author.

National Clearinghouse on Child Abuse and Neglect. (2002). *What is child maltreatment?* Washington, DC: Administration for Children & Families.

National Clearinghouse on Child Abuse and Neglect. (2004). *What is child abuse and neglect?* Washington, DC: U.S. Department of Health and Human Services.

National Clearinghouse on Child Abuse and Neglect. (2005). Safe children and healthy families are a shared responsibility: 2005 community resource packet. Available on the World Wide Web at: http://nccanch.acf.hhs.gov/topics/prevention/childabuse_neglect/recognize.cfm.

National Commission on the High School Year. (2001). *Youth at the crossroads: Facing high school and beyond.* Washington, DC: The Education Trust.

National Institute of Drug Abuse. (2001). *Marijuana.* Washington, DC: National Institutes of Health.

National Institute of Mental Health. (2005). *Autism spectrum disorders (pervasive developmental disorders).* Available on the World Wide Web at: http://www.nimh.nih.gov/Publicat/autism.cfm.

National Institutes of Health. (1993). *Learning disabilities* (NIH publication No. 93–3611). Bethesda, MD: Author.

National Institutes of Health. (2005, January 19). Night terror. Available on the World Wide Web at: *http://www.nlm.nih.gov/medlineplus/ency/article/000809.htm.*

National Reading Panel. (2000). *Teaching children to read.* Washington, DC: National Institute of Child Health and Human Development.

National Research Council. (1999). *How people learn.* Washington, DC: National Academy Press.

National Vital Statistics Reports. (2001). Deaths and death rates for the 10 leading causes of death in specified age groups. *National Vital Statistics Reports, 48* (No. 11), Table 8.

Natsopoulos, D., Kiosseoglou, G., Xeroxmeritou, A., & Alevriadou, A. (1998). Do the hands talk on the mind's behalf? Differences in language between left- and right-handed children. *Brain and Language, 64,* 182–214.

Naude, H., Pretorius, E., & Vijoen, J. (2003). The impact of impoverished language development on preschoolers' readiness-to-learn during the foundation phase. *Early Child Development and Care, 173,* 271–291.

Needham, A., Barrett, T., & Peterman, K. (2002). A pick-me-up for infants' exploratory skills: Early simulated experiences reaching for objects using "sticky mittens" enhances young infants' object exploration skills. *Infant Behavior and Development, 25,* 279–295.

Neidell, M. J. (2004). Air pollution, health, and socioeconomic status: The effect of outdoor air quality on childhood asthma. *Journal of Health Economics, 23,* 1209–1236.

Neill, M. (2003). Leaving children behind. *Phi Delta Kappan, 84,* 225–228.

Neisser, U. (2004). Memory development: New questions and old. *Developmental Review, 24,* 154–158.

Neisser, U., Boodoo, G., Bouchard, T. J., Boykin, A. W., Brody, N., Ceci, S. J., Halpern, D. F., Loehlin, J. C., Perloff, R. J., Sternberg, R., & Urbina, S. (1996).

Intelligence: Knowns and unknowns. *American Psychologist, 51,* 77–101.

Nelson, C. (2003, April). *Gray matters: A neuro-constructivist perspective on cognitive development.* Paper presented at the meeting of the Society for Research in Child Development, Tampa.

Nelson, C. A. (2003). Neural development and lifelong plasticity. In R. M. Lerner, F. Jacobs, & D. Wertlieb (Eds.), *Handbook of applied developmental science* (Vol. 1). Thousand Oaks, CA: Sage.

Nelson, C. A., Thomas, K. M. S., de Haan, M. (2006). Neural basis of cognitive development. In W. Damon & R. Lerner (Eds.), *Handbook of child psychology* (6th ed.). New York: Wiley.

Nelson, C. A., Thomas, K. M., & de Haan, M. (2006). Neural bases of cognitive development. In W. Damon & R. Lerner (Eds.), *Handbook of child psychology* (6th ed.). New York: Wiley.

Nelson, K. (1999). Levels and modes of representation: Issues for the theory of conceptual change and development. In E. K. Skolnick, K. Nelson, S. A. Gelman, & P. H. Miller (Eds.), *Conceptual development.* Mahwah, NJ: Erlbaum.

Nelson, K. (2004). A welcome turn to meaning in infant development: Commentary on Mandler's *The foundation of the mind: Origins of conceptual thought. Developmental Science, 7,* 506–507.

Neuman, S. B., & Roskos, K. (1993). *Language and literacy learning in the early years.* Fort Worth, TX: Harcourt Brace.

Neuman, S. B., & Roskos, K. (2005). Whatever happened to developmentally appropriate practice in early literacy? *Young Children, 60* (no. 4), 22–27.

Neumann, C. G., Gewa, C., & Bwibo, N. B. (2004). Child nutrition in developing countries. *Pediatric Annals, 33,* 658–674.

Neville, H., & Bavelier, D. (2002). Human brain plasticity: Evidence from sensory deprivation and altered language experience. *Progress in Brain Research, 138,* 177–188.

Newcomb, M. D., & Bentler, P. M. (1988). Substance use and abuse among children and teenagers. *American Psychologist, 44,* 242–248.

Newcombe, N., & Fox, N. (1994). Infantile amnesia: Through a glass darkly. *Child Development, 65,* 31–40.

Newcombe, N. S., Drummey, A. B., Fox, N. A., Lile, E., & Ottinger-Alberts, W. (2000). Remembering early childhood: How much, how, and why (or why not). *Current Directions in Psychological Science, 9,* 55–58.

Newcomer, S. F. & Udry, J. R. (1985). Oral sex in an adolescent population. *Archives of Sexual Behavior, 14,* 41–46.

Newell, K., Scully, D. M., McDonald, P. V., & Baillargeon, R. (1989). Task constraints and infant grip configurations. *Developmental Psychobiology, 22,* 817–832.

Newman, D. L. (2005). Ego development and ethnic identity formation in rural American Indian adolescents. *Child Development, 76,* 734–746.

Newson, J., Newson, E., & Mahalski, P. A. (1982). Persistent infant comfort habits and their sequelae at 11 and 16 years. *Journal of Child Psychology and Psychiatry, 23,* 421–436.

Newton, A. W., & Vandeven, A. M. (2005). Update on child maltreatment with a special focus on shaken baby syndrome. *Current Opinions in Pediatrics, 17,* 246–251.

NHANES. (2001, March). *National Health and Nutrition Examination Surveys.* Washington, DC: U.S. Department of Health and Human Services.

NICHD Early Child Care Research Network. (2000). Factors associated with fathers' caregiving activities and sensitivity with young children. *Developmental Psychology, 14,* 200–219.

NICHD Early Child Care Research Network. (2001). Nonmaternal care and family factors in early development: An overview of the NICHD Study of Early Child Care. *Journal of Applied Developmental Psychology, 22,* 457–492.

NICHD Early Child Care Research Network. (2002). Structure ➔ Process ➔ Outcome: Direct and indirect effects of child care quality on young children's development. *Psychological Science, 13,* 199–206.

NICHD Early Child Care Research Network. (2003). Do children's attention processes mediate the link between family predictors and school readiness. *Developmental Psychology, 39,* 581–593.

NICHD Early Child Care Research Network. (2003). Does amount of time spent in child care predict socioemotional adjustment during the transition to kindergarten. *Child Development, 74,* 976–1005.

NICHD Early Child Care Research Network. (2004). Are child developmental outcomes related to before- and after-school care arrangement? *Child Development, 75,* 280–295.

NICHD Early Child Care Research Network. (2005). Duration and developmental timing of poverty and children's cognitive and social development from birth through third grade. *Child Development, 76,* 795–810.

NICHD Early Child Care Research Network. (2005). Predicting individual differences in attention, memory, and planning in first graders from experiences at home, child care, and school. *Developmental Psychology, 41,* 99–114.

Nichols, F. H., & Humenick, S. S. (2000). *Childbirth education* (2nd ed.). London: Harcourt International.

Nichols, S., & Good, T. L. (2004). *America's teenagers—myths and realities.* Mahwah, NJ: Erlbaum.

Nicklas, T. A., Demory-Luce, D., Yang, S. J., Baranowski, T., Zakeri, I., & Berensen, G. (2004b). Children's food consumption patterns have changed over two decades (1973–1994): The Bogalusa Heart Study. *Journal of the American Dietetic Association, 104,* 1127–1140.

Nicklas, T. A., Morales, M., Linares, A., Yang, S. J., Baranowski, T., De Moor, C., & Berensen, G. (2004a). Children's meal patterns have changed over a 21-year-period: The Bogalusa Heart Study. *Journal of the American Dietetic Association, 104,* 753–761.

Nicklas, T. A., Webber, L. S., Jonson, C. S., Srinivasan, S. R., & Berensen, G. S. (1995). Foundations for health promotion with youth: A review of observations from the Bogalusa Heart Study. *Journal of Health Education, 26,* S18–S26.

Nicklas, T. A., Yang, S. J., Baranowski, T., Zakeri, I., & Berensen, G. (2003). Eating patterns and obesity in children. The Bogalusa Heart Study. *American Journal of Preventive Medicine, 25,* 9–16.

Niederhofer, H., & Reiter, A. (2004). Prenatal maternal stress, prenatal fetal movements, and perinatal temperament factors influence behavior and school marks at the age of 6 years. *Fetal Diagnosis and Therapy, 19,* 160–162.

Nielsen, S. J., Siega-Riz, A. M., & Popkin, B. M. (2002). Trends in energy intake in U.S. between 1977 and 1996: Similar shifts seen across age groups. *Obesity Research, 10,* 370–378.

Nisbett, R. (2003). *The geography of thought.* New York: Free Press.

Nocenteni, U., Goulet, P., Roberts, P. M., & Joanette, Y. (2001). The effects of left- versus right-hemisphere lesions on the sensitivity to intra- and interconceptual semantic relationships. *Neuropsychologia, 39,* 443–451.

Nolan, K., Schell, L. M., Stark, A. D., & Gomez, M. I. (2002). Longitudinal study of energy and nutrient intakes for infants from low-income, urban families. *Public Health Nutrition, 5,* 405–412.

Noland, N. S., Singer, L. T., Short, E. J., Minnes, S., Arendt, R. E., Kirchner, H., & Bearer, C. (2005). Prenatal drug exposure and selective attention in preschoolers. *Neurotoxicology and Teratology, 27,* 429–438.

Nolen-Hoeksema, S. (2004). *Abnormal psychology* (3rd ed.). New York: McGraw-Hill.

Norremolle, A., Hasholt, L., Petersen, C. B., Eiberg, H., Hasselbalch, S. G., Gideon, P., Nielson, J. E., & Sorensen, S. A. (2004). Mosaicism of the CAG repeat sequence in the Huntington disease gene in a pair of monozygotic twins. *American Journal of Medical Genetics, 130A,* 154–159.

Nottelmann, E. D., Susman, E. J., Blue, J. H., Inoff-Germain, G., Dorn, L. D., Loriaux, D. L., Cutler, G. B., & Chrousos, G. P. (1987). Gonadal and adrenal hormone correlates of adjustment in early adolescence. In R. M. Lerner & T. T. Foch (Eds.), *Biological-psychological interactions in early adolescence,* Hillsdale, NJ: Erlbaum.

Nsamenang, A. B. (2002). Adolescence in sub-Saharan Africa: An image constructed from

Africa's triple heritage. In B. B. Brown, R. W. Larson, & T. S. Saraswathi (Eds.), *The world's youth*. New York: Cambridge University Press.

Nucci, L. (2005). Education in the moral domain. In M. Killen & J. G. Smetana (Eds.), *Handbook of moral development*. Mahwah, NJ: Erlbaum.

Nucci, L. P. (2004). The development of moral reasoning. In P. Smith & C. Hart (Eds.), *Blackwell handbook of cognitive development*. Malden, MA: Blackwell.

Nugent, K., & Brazelton, T. B. (2000). Preventive infant mental health: Uses of the Brazelton scale. In J. D. Osofsky & H. E. Fitzgerald (Eds.), *WAJMH handbook of infant mental health* (Vol. 2). New York: Wiley.

O

Oakes, L. M., Kannass, K. N., & Shaddy, D. J. (2002). Developmental changes in the endogenous control of attention: The role of target familiarity on infants' distraction latency. *Child Development, 73,* 1644–1655.

Obler, L. K. (1993). Language beyond childhood. In J. B. Gleason (Ed.), *The development of language* (3rd ed.). New York: Macmillan.

O'Callahan, M., Andrews, A. M., & Krantz, D. S. (2003). Coronary heart disease and hypertension. In I. B. Weiner (Ed.), *Handbook of psychology* (Vol. IX). New York: Wiley.

O'Dowd, A. (2004). Why are midwife numbers in crlsls? *Nursing Times, 100,* 12–13.

Offer, D., Ostrov E., Howard, K. I., & Atkinson, R. (1988). *The teenage world: Adolescents' self-image in ten countries*. New York: Plenum.

Office of Juvenile Justice and Prevention. (1998). *Arrests in the United States under age 18, 1997*. Washington, DC: Author.

Ogbu, J. U. (1989, April). *Academic socialization of Black children: An inoculation against future failure?* Paper presented at the meeting of the Society for Research in Child Development. Kansas City.

Ogbu, J. U. (2003). *Thinking and doing: The significance of minority status*. Paper presented at the meeting of the American Psychological Association, Toronto.

Ogbu, J. U., & Stern, P. (2001). Caste status and intellectual ability. In R. J. Sternberg & E. L. Grigorenko (Eds.), *Environmental effects on cognitive abilities*. Mahwah, NJ: Erlbaum.

Ogby, J. (2003, August). *Thinking and doing: The significance of minority status*. Paper presented at the meeting of the American Psychological Association, Toronto.

Ohgi, S., Akiyama, T., & Fukuda, M. (2005). Neurobehavioral profile of low-birthweight infants with cystic periventricular leukomalacia. *Developmental Medicine and Child Neurology, 47,* 221–228.

Ohgi, S., Akiyama, T., Arisawa, K., & Shigemori, K. (2004). Randomized controlled trial of swaddling versus massage in the management of excess crying in infants with cerebral injuries. *Archives of Disease in Childhood, 89,* 212–216.

Ohgi, S., Fukuda, M., Moriuchi, H., Kusumoto, T., Akiyama, T., Nugetn, J. K., Brazelton, T. B., Arisawa, K., Takahashi, T., & Saitoh, H. (2002). Comparison of kangaroo care and standard care: Behavioral organization, development, and temperament in healthy, low birth weight infants through 1 year. *Journal of Perinatology, 22,* 374–379.

Okah, F. A., Cai, J., & Hoff, G. L. (2005). Term-gestation low birth weight and health-compromising behaviors during pregnancy. *Obstetrics and Gynecology, 105,* 543–550.

O'Keefe, M., & Nolan, L. (2004). LASIK surgery in children. *British Journal of Ophthalmology, 88,* 19–21.

Olds, S. B., London, M. L., & Ladewig, P. W. (1988). *Maternal newborn nursing* (3rd ed.). Boston: Addison Wesley.

Olds, S. B., London, M. L., & Ladewig, P. W. (2001). *Maternal-newborn nursing: A family and community-based approach* (6th ed.). Upper Saddle River, NJ: Prentice Hall.

Olivardia, R., Pope, H. G., Mangweth, B., & Hudson, J. I. (1995). Eating disorders in college men. *American Journal of Psychiatry, 152,* 1279–1284.

Olson, D. (2001). What writing does to the mind. In J. Brynes & E. Amsel (Eds.), *Language, literacy, and cognitive development*. Mahwah, NJ: Erlbaum.

Olson, L. M., Tang, S. F., & Newacheck, P. W. (2005). Children in the United States with discontinuous health insurance coverage. *New England Journal of Medicine, 353,* 418–419.

Olszewski-Kubilius. P. (2003). Gifted education programs and procedures. In I. B. Weiner (Ed.), *Handbook of psychology* (Vol. VII). New York: Wiley.

O'Neil, C. F., & Brown, W. K. (2005). *Planning and building a stepfamily*. Huntington, NY: The William Gladden Foundation.

Ong, C. N., Shen, H. M., & Chia, S. B. (2002). Biomarkers for male reproductive health hazards: Are they available? *Toxicology Letters, 134,* 17–30.

Onwuegbuzi, A. J., & Daley, C. E. (2001). Racial differences in IQ revisited: A synthesis of nearly a century of research. *Journal of Black Psychology, 27,* 209–220.

Orbanic, S. (2001). Understanding bulimia. *American Journal of Nursing, 101,* 35–41.

Oser, F., & Gmunder, P. (1991). *Religious judgment: A developmental perspective*. Birmingham, AL: Religious Education Press.

Oser, F., Scarlett, W. G., & Bucher, A. (2006). Religious and spiritual development through the lifespan. In W. Damon & R. Lerner (Eds.), *Handbook of child psychology* (6th ed.). New York: Wiley.

Osterlind, S. J. (2006). *Modern measurement theory*. Upper Saddle River, NJ: Prentice Hall.

Ovando, C. J., Combs, M. C., & Collier, V. P. (2006). *Bilingual and ESL classrooms* (4th ed.). New York: McGraw-Hill.

Overton, T. (2000). *Assessment in special education* (3rd ed.). Upper Saddle River, NJ: Merrill.

Overton, W. F. (2004). Embodied development: Biology, person, and culture in a relational context. In C. G. Coll, E. L. Bearer, & R. M. Lerner (Eds.), *Nature and nurture*. Mahwah, NJ: Erlbaum.

Owen, C. G., Martin, R. M., Whincup, P. H., Smith, G. D., & Cook, D. B. (2005). Effect of infant feeding on the risk of obesity across the life course: A quantitative review of published evidence. *Pediatrics, 115,* 1367–1377.

Owens, J. A. (2005). Introduction: Culture and sleep in children. *Pediatrics, 115,* 201–203.

Oztop, E., Bradley, N. S., & Arbib, M. A. (2004). Infant grasp learning: A computational model. *Experimental Brain Research, 158,* 480–503.

P

Pacheco, S., & Murtado, A. (2002). Media stereotypes. In J. Worrell (Ed.), *Encyclopedia of women and gender*. San Diego: Academic Press.

Paisley, T. S., Joy, E. A., & Price, R. J. (2003). Exercise during pregnancy. *Current Sports Medicine Reports, 2,* 325–330.

Pakpreo, P., Ryan, S., Auinger, P., & Aten, M. (2004). The association between parental lifestyle behaviors and adolescent knowledge, attitudes, intentions, and nutritional and physical activity behaviors. *Journal of Adolescent Health, 34,* 129–130.

Paloutzian, R. F. (2000). *Invitation to the psychology of religion* (3rd ed.). Needham Heights, MA: Allyn & Bacon.

Paludi, M. A. (2002). *Psychology of women* (2nd ed.). Upper Saddle River, NJ: Prentice Hall.

Pan, B. A. (2005). Semantic development. In J. Berko Gleason, *The development of language* (6th ed.). Boston: Allyn & Bacon.

Pan, B. A., Rowe, M. L., Singer, J. D., & Snow, C. E. (2005). Maternal correlates of growth in toddler vocabulary production in low-income families. *Child Development, 76,* 763–782.

Pang, V. O. (2005). *Multicultural education* (2nd ed.). New York: McGraw-Hill.

Papp, C., & Papp, Z. (2003). Chorionic villus sampling and amniocentesis: What are the risks in current practice? *Current Opinions in Obstetrics and Gynecology, 15,* 159–165.

Parazzini, F., Chatenoud, L., Surace, M., Tozzi, L., Salerio, B., Bettoni, G., & Benzi, G. (2003). Moderate alcohol drinking and risk of preterm birth. *European Journal of Clinical Nutrition, 57,* 1345–1349.

Parcel, G. S., Simons-Morton, G. G., O'Hara, N. M., Baranowski, T., Kolbe, L. J., & Bee, D. E. (1987). School promotion of healthful diet and exercise behavior: An integration of organizational change and social learning theory interventions. *Journal of School Health, 57,* 150–156.

Paredes, I., Hidalgo, L., Chedraui, P., Palma, J., & Eugenio, J. (2005). Factors associated with inadequate prenatal care in Ecuadorian women. *International Journal of Gynecology and Obstetrics, 88,* l68–172.

Paris, S. G., & Paris, A. H. (2006). Assessments of early reading. In W. Damon & R. Lerner (Eds.), *Handbook of child psychology* (6th ed.). New York: Wiley.

Parke, R. D. (1995). Fathers and families. In M. H. Bornstein (Ed.), *Children and parenting* (Vol. 3). Hillsdale, NJ: Erlbaum.

Parke, R. D. (2000). Father involvement: A developmental psychology perspective. *Marriage and Family Review, 29,* 43–58.

Parke, R. D. (2001). Parenting in the new millenium. In J. P. McHale & W. S. Grolnick (Eds.), *Retrospect and prospect in the psychological study of families.* Mahwah, NJ: Erlbaum.

Parke, R. D. (2002). Fathering. In M. H. Bornstein (Ed.), *Handbook of parenting* (2nd ed.). Mahwah, NJ: Erlbaum.

Parke, R. D. (2004). Development in the family. *Annual Review of Psychology, 55,* Palo Alto, CA: Annual Reviews.

Parke, R. D., & Buriel, R. (2006). Socialization in the family: Ethnic and ecological perspectives. In W. Damon & R. Lerner (Eds.), *Handbook of child psychology* (6th ed.). New York: Wiley.

Parke, R. D., & Clarke-Stewart, K. A. (2003). Developmental psychology. In I. B. Weiner (Ed.), *Handbook of psychology* (Vol. 1). New York: Wiley.

Parke, R., Dennis, J., Flyr, M. L., Leidy, M. S., & Schofield, T. J. (2005). Fathers: Cultural and ecological perspectives. In T. Luster & L. Okaghi (Eds.), *Parenting: An ecological perspective* (2nd ed.). Mahwah, NJ: Erlbaum.

Parker, A., & Fischhoff, B. (2002, April). *Individual differences in decision-making competence.* Paper presented at the meeting of the Society for Research on Adolescence, New Orleans.

Parker, J. G., & Asher, S. R. (1987). Peer relations and later personal adjustment: Are low accepted children at risk? *Psychological Bulletin, 102,* 357–389.

Parmet, S., Lynn, C., & Glass, R. M. (2004). Prenatal care. *Journal of the American Medical Association, 291,* 146.

Parrillo, V. N. (2004). *Diversity in America* (2nd ed.). Thousand Oaks, CA: Sage.

Parten, M. (1932). Social play among preschool children. *Journal of Abnormal Social Psychology, 27,* 243–269.

Partnership for a Drug-Free America. (2005, April 21). Generation Rx: National study reveals new category of substance abuse emerging: Teens abusing Rx and OTC medications intentionally to get high. Available on the World Wide Web at: http://www.drugfree.org/Portal/DrugIssue/Research/Generation_Rx_National_Study_Reveals_New_Category/Teens_Abusing_Rx_and_OTC_Medications

Pascali-Bonaro, D. (2002). Pregnant and widowed on September 11: The birth community reaches out. *Birth, 29,* 62–64.

Pascali-Bonaro, D., & Kroeger, M. (2004). Continuous female companionship during childbirth: a crucial resource in times of stress or calm. *Journal of Midwifery and Women's Health, 49* (No. 4, Supplement 1), 19–27.

Pasley, K., & Moorefield, B. S. (2004). Stepfamilies. In M. Coleman & L. Ganong (Eds.), *Handbook of contemporary families.* Thousand Oaks, CA: Sage.

Pate, R. R., Pfeiffer, K. A., Trost, S. G., Ziegler, P., & Dowda, M. (2004). Physical activity among children attending preschools. *Pediatrics, 114,* 1258–1263.

Patterson, B., Ryan, J., & Dickey, J. H. (2004). The toxicology of mercury. *New England Journal of Medicine, 350,* 945–947.

Patterson, C. J. (2002). Lesbian and gay parenthood. In M. H. Bornstein (Ed.), *Handbook of parenting* (2nd ed., Vol. 3). Mahwah, NJ: Erlbaum.

Patterson, G. R., De Baryshe, B. D., & Ramsey, E. (1989). A developmental perspective on antisocial behavior. *American Psychologist, 44,* 329–355.

Patterson, K., & Wright, A. E. (1990, Winter). The speech, language, or hearing-impaired child: At-risk academically. *Childhood Education,* pp. 91–95.

Pavlov, L. P. (1927). In G. B. Anrep (Trans.), *Conditioned reflexes.* London: Oxford University Press.

Payne, W. A., Hahn, D. B., & Mauer, E. B. (2005). *Understanding your health* (7th ed.). New York: McGraw-Hill.

Pederson, D. R., & Moran, G. (1996). Expressions of the attachment relationship outside of the Strange Situation. *Child Development, 67,* 915–927.

Peplau, L. A., & Beals, K. P. (2004). Family lives of lesbians and gay men. In A. L. Vangelisti (Ed.), *Handbook of family communication.* Mahwah, NJ: Erlbaum.

Pérez, B., McCarty, T. L., Watahomigie, L. J., Torres-Guzman, M. E., Dien, T., Chang, J., Smith, H. L., Davila de Silva, A., & Norlander, A. (Eds.). (2004). *Sociocultural contexts of language and literacy.* Mahwah, NJ: Erlbaum.

Perkins, D. F., & Borden, L. M. (2003). Positive behaviors, problem behaviors, and resiliency in adolescence. In I. B. Weiner (Ed.), *Handbook of psychology,* (Vol. VI). New York: Wiley.

Perner, J., Stummer, S., Sprung, M., & Doherty, M. (2002). Theory of mind finds its Piagetian perspective: Why alternative naming comes with understanding belief. *Cognitive Development, 17,* 1451–1472.

Perry-Jenkins, M. (2004). The time and timing of work: Unique challenges facing low-income families. In A. C. Crouter & A. Booth (Eds.), *Work-family challenges for low-income families and their children.* Mahwah, NJ: Erlbaum.

Perse, E. M. (2001). *Media effects and society.* Mahwah, NJ: Erlbaum.

Persons, D. A., & Tisdale, J. F. (2004). Gene therapy for the hemoglobin disorders. *Seminars in Hematology, 41,* 279–286.

Peskin, H. (1967). Pubertal onset and ego functioning. *Journal of Abnormal Psychology, 72,* 1–15.

Peters, J. M., & Stout, D. L. (2006). *Concepts and inquiries for teaching elementary school science* (5th ed.). Upper Saddle River, NJ: Prentice Hall.

Petersen, A. C. (1979, January). Can puberty come any faster? *Psychology Today,* pp. 45–56.

Petersen, A. C. (1987, September). Those gangly years. *Psychology Today,* pp. 28–34.

Peterson, C. C., & Peterson, J. L. (1973). Preference for sex of offspring as a measure of change in sex attitudes. *Psychology, 10,* 3–5.

Petrill, S. A., & Deater-Deckard, K. (2004). Task orientation, parental warmth, and SES account for a significant portion of the shared environmental variance in general cognitive ability in early childhood: Evidence from a twin study. *Developmental Science, 7,* 25–32.

Petrini, J. (2004). *Preterm birth: A public health priority.* White Plains, NY: National March of Dimes.

Pettit, R. B. (2003). Sexual teens, sexual media: Investigating media's influence on adolescent sexuality. *Journal of Social and Personal Relationships, 20,* 262–263.

Pettito, L. A., Kovelman, I., & Harasymowycz, U. (2003, April). *Bilingual language development: Does learning the new damage the old.* Paper presented at the meeting of the Society for Research in Child Development. Tampa.

Pfeifer, M., Goldsmith, H. H., Davidson, R. J., & Rickman, M. (2002). Continuity and change in inhibited and uninhibited children. *Child Development, 73,* 1474–1485.

Phillips, D. A., Voran, K., Kisker, E., Howes, C., & Whitebook, M. (1994). Child care for children in poverty: Opportunity or inequity? *Child Development, 65,* 472–492.

Phillips, S. (2003). Adolescent health. In I. B. Weiner (Ed.), *Handbook of psychology* (Vol. 9). New York: Wiley.

Phinney, J. S. (1989). Stages of ethnic identity development in minority group adolescents. *Journal of Early Adolescence, 9,* 34–49.

Phinney, J. S. (1996). When we talk about American ethnic groups, what do we mean? *American Psychologist, 51,* 918–927.

Phinney, J. S. (2000). Ethnic identity. In A. Kazdin (Ed.), *Encyclopedia of psychology.* Washington, DC, & New York: American Psychological Association and Oxford University Press.

Phinney, J. S. (2003). Ethnic identity and acculturation. In K. M. Chun, P. B. Organista, & G. Marin (Eds.), *Acculturation.* Washington, DC: American Psychological Association.

Phinney, J. S. (2003). Identity and acculturation. In K. M. Chun, P. B. Organista, & G. Marin (Eds.), *Acculturation.* Washington, DC: American Psychological Association.

Phinney, J. S., & Alipura, L. L. (1990). Ethnic identity in college students from four ethnic groups. *Journal of Adolescence, 13,* 171–183.

Phinney, J. S., & Devich-Navarro, M. (1997). Variations in bicultural identification among African American and Mexican American adolescents. *Journal of Research on Adolescence, 7,* 3–32.

Phinney, J. S., Ferguson, D. L., & Tate, J. D. (1997). Intergroup attitudes among ethnic minority adolescents: A causal model. *Child Development, 68,* 955–969.

Phinney, J. S., Ong, A., & Madden, T. (2000). Cultural values and intergenerational discrepancies in immigrant and non-immigrant families. *Child Development, 71,* 528–539.

Piaget, J. (1932). *The moral judgment of the child.* New York: Harcourt Brace Jovanovich.

Piaget, J. (1952). *The origins of intelligence in children* (M. Cook, Trans.). New York: International Universities Press.

Piaget, J. (1952). *The origins of intelligence in children.* New York: International Universities Press.

Piaget, J. (1952a). Jean Piaget. In C. A. Murchison (Ed.). *A history of psychology in autobiography* (Vol. 4). Worcester, MA: Clark University Press.

Piaget, J. (1954). *The construction of reality in the child.* New York: Basic Books.

Piaget, J. (1962). *Play, dreams, and imitation.* New York: W. W. Norton.

Piaget, J., & Inhelder, B. (1969). *The child's conception of space* (F. J. Langdon & J. L. Lunger, Trans.). New York: W. W. Norton.

Pianta, R. C. (2005). Prevention. In H. W. Lee (Ed.), *Encyclopedia of school psychology.* Thousand Oaks, CA: Sage.

Pickard, A. S., Topfer, L. A., & Feeny, D. H. (2004). A structured review of studies on health-related quality of life and economic evaluation in pediatric acute lymphoblastic leukemia. *Journal of National Cancer Institute Monograph, 33,* 102–125.

Pierce, K. M., Hamm, J. V., & Vandell, D. L. (1997, April). *Experiences in after-school programs and children's adjustment at school and at home.*

Paper presented at the meeting of the Society for Research in Child Development, I. Washington, DC.

Pietz, J., Peter, J., Graf, R., Rauterberg-Ruland, I., Rupp, A., Southheimer, D., & Linderkamp, O. (2004). Physical growth and neurodevelopmental outcome of nonhandicapped low-risk children born preterm. *Early Human Development, 79,* 131–143.

Pinker, S. (1994). *The language instinct.* New York: HarperCollins.

Pintrich, P. R. (2003). Motivation and classroom learning. In I. B. Weiner (Ed.), *Handbook of psychology* (Vol. VII). New York: Wiley.

Pinyerd, B., & Zipf, W. B. (2005). Puberty—timing is everything! *Journal of Pediatric Nursing, 20,* 75–82.

Pipe, M.-E., Lamb, M. E., Orbach, Y., & Esplin, P. W. (2004). Recent research on children's testimony about experienced and witnessed events. *Developmental Review, 24,* 440–468.

Pitkanen, T., Lyyra, A. L., & Pulkkinen, L. (2005). Age of onset of drinking and the use of alcohol in adulthood: A follow-up study from age 8–42 for females and males. *Addiction, 100,* 652–661.

Pittman, J. F., & Lee, C. Y. (2004). Comparing different types of child abuse and spouse abuse offenders. *Journal of Violence and Victims, 19,* 137–156.

Piwoz, E. G., & Ross, J. S. (2005). Use of population-specific infant mortality rates to inform policy decisions regarding HIV and infant feeding. *Journal of Nutrition, 135,* 1113–1119.

Plant, T. M., & Barker-Gibb, M. L. (2004). Neurobiological mechanisms of puberty in higher primates. *Human Reproduction Update, 10,* 67–77.

Pleck, J. H. (1983). The theory of male sex identity. In M. Lewis (Ed.), *In the shadow of the past: Psychology portrays the sexes.* New York: Columbia University Press.

Pleck, J. H. (1995). The gender-role strain paradigm. In R. F. Levant & W. S. Pollack (Eds.), *A new psychology of men.* New York: Basic Books.

Plomin, R. (1993, March). *Human behavioral genetics and development: An overview and update.* Paper presented at the biennial meeting of the Society for Research in Child Development. New Orleans.

Plomin, R., Asbury, K., & Dunn, J. (2001). Why are children in the same family so different? Nonshared environment a decade later. *Canadian Journal of Psychiatry, 46,* 225–233.

Plomin, R., DeFries, J. C., McClearn, G. E., & McGuffin, P. (2001). *Behavioral genetics* (4th ed.). New York: Worth.

Plomin, R., Reiss, D., Hetherington, E. M., & Howe, G. W. (1994). Nature and nurture: Contributions to measures of the family environment. *Developmental Psychology, 30,* 32–43.

Poelmans, S. A. (Ed.) (2005). *Work and family.* Mahwah, NJ: Erlbaum.

Poest, C. A., Williams, J. R., Witt, D. D., & Atwood, M. E. (1990). Challenge me to move: Large muscle development in young children. *Young Children, 45,* 4–10.

Polaha, J., Warzak, W. J., & Dittmer-Memahon, K. (2002). Toilet training in primary care: Current practice and recommendations from behavioral pediatrics. *Journal of Developmental and Behavioral Pediatrics, 23,* 424–429.

Polivy, J., Herman, C. P., Mills, J., & Brock, H. (2003). Eating disorders in adolescence. In G. Adams & M. Berzonsky (Eds.), *Blackwell handbook of adolescence.* Malden, MA: Blackwell.

Pollack, W. (1999). *Real boys.* New York: Owl Books.

Pollak, C. P., & Bright, D. (2003). Caffeine consumption and weekly sleep patterns in U.S. seventh-, eight-, and ninth-graders. *Pediatrics, 111,* 42–46.

Pollitt, E. P., Gorman, K. S, Engle, P. L., Martorell, R., & Rivera, J. (1993). Early supplementary feeding and cognition, *Monographs of the Society for Research in Child Development, 58* (7, Serial No. 235).

Ponterotto, J. G., Casas, J. M., Suzuki, L. A., & Alexander, C. M. (Eds.). (2001). *Handbook of multicultural counseling.* Thousand Oaks, CA: Sage.

Porath, A. J., & Fried, P. A. (2005). Effects of prenatal cigarette and marijuana exposure on drug use among offspring. *Neurotoxicology and Teratology, 27,* 267–277.

Porges, S. W., Doussard-Roosevelt, J. A., & Maiti, A. K. (1994). Vagal tone and the physiological regulation of emotion. In N. A. Fox (Ed.), *Emotion regulation: Behavioral and biological considerations. Monographs of the Society for Research in Child Development, 59* (Serial No. 240), 167–196.

Posner, J. K., & Vandell, D. L. (1994). Low-income children's after-school care: Are there benefits of after-school programs? *Child Development, 65,* 440–456.

Potera, C. (2004). The opposite of obesity: Undernutrition overwhelms the world's children. *Environmental Health Perspectives, 11,* A802.

Potter, S. M., Zelazo, P. R., Stack, D. M., & Papageorgiou, A. N. (2000). Adverse effects of fetal cocaine exposure on neonatal auditory information processing. *Pediatrics, 105,* e40–e41.

Potvin, L., Champagne, F., & Laberge-Nadeau, C. (1988). Mandatory driver training and road safety: The Quebec experience. *American Journal of Public Health, 78,* 1206–1212.

Poulton, S., & Sexton, D. (1996). Feeding young children: Developmentally appropriate considerations for supplementing family care. *Childhood Education, 73,* 66–71.

Powell, C., Porooshani, H., Bohorquez, M., & Richardson, S. (2005, July 20). Screening for amblyopia in childhood. *Cochrane Database System Review, 20,* CD005020.

Powell, D. R. (2004). Early intervention and risk. In A. Fogel & G. Bremner (Eds.), *Blackwell handbook of infant development.* London: Blackwell.

Powell, D. R. (2005). Searches for what works in parenting interventions. In T. Luster & L. Okagaki (Eds.), *Parenting* (2nd ed.). Mahwah, NJ: Erlbaum.

Powell, D. R. (2006). Families and early childhood intervention. In W. Damon & R. Lerner (Eds.), *Handbook of child psychology* (6th ed.). New York: Wiley.

Powell, E. C., Ambardekar, E. J., & Sheehan, K. M. (2005, in press). Poor neighborhoods: Safe Playgrounds. *Journal of Urban Health.*

Powell, R. G., & Caseau, D. (2004). *Classroom communication and diversity.* Mahwah, NJ: Erlbaum.

Pratt, H. D., Patel, D. R., & Greydanus, D. E. (2003). Behavioral aspects of children's sports. *Pediatric Clinics of North America, 50,* 879–899.

Pressley, M. (2003). Psychology of literacy and literacy instruction. In I. B. Weiner (Ed.), *Handbook of psychology.* New York: Wiley.

Pressley, M., Allington, R., Wharton-McDonald, R., Block, C. C., & Morrow, L. M. 2001). *Learning to read: Lessons from exemplary first grades.* New York: Guilford.

Pressley, M., & Hilden, K. (2006). Cognitive strategies. In W. Damon & R. Lerner (Eds.), *Handbook of child psychology* (6th ed.). New York: Wiley.

Pressley, M., Cariligia-Bull, T., Deane, S., & Schneider, W. (1987). Short-term memory, verbal competence, and age as predictors of imagery instructional effectiveness. *Journal of Experimental Child Psychology, 43,* 194–211.

Pressley, M., Dolezal, S. E., Raphael, L. M., Welsh, L. M., Bogner, K., & Roehrig, A. D. (2003). *Motivating primary-grades teachers.* New York: Guilford.

Pressley, M., Levin, J. R., & McCormick, C. B. (1980). Young children's learning of a foreign language vocabulary: A sentence variation of the keyword. *Contemporary Educational Psychology, 5,* 22–29.

Pressley, M., Raphael, L., Gallagher, D., & DiBella, J. (2004). Providence-St. Mel School: How a school that works for African-American students works. *Journal of Educational Psychology, 96,* 216–235.

Pressley, M., Roehrig, A. D., Raphael, L., Dolezal, S., Bohn, C., Mohan, L., Wharton-McDonald, R., Bogner, K., & Hogna, K. (2003). Teaching processes in elementary and secondary education. In I. B. Weiner (Ed.), *Handbook of psychology* (Vol. 7). New York: Wiley.

Preston, A. M., Rodrigquez, C., Rivera, C. E., & Sahai, H. (2003). Influence of environmental tobacco smoke on vitamin C status in children. *American Journal of Clinical Nutrition, 77,* 167–172.

Pringle, P. J., Geary, M. P., Rodeck, C. H., Kingdom, J. C., Kayamba-Kays, S., & Hindmarsh, P. C. (2005). The influence of cigarette smoking on antenatal growth, birth size, and the insulin-like growth factor axis. *Journal of Clinical Endocrinology and Metabolism, 90,* 2556–2562.

Pritchard, F. F., & Whitehead, G. I. (2004). *Implementing and evaluating service learning in middle and high schools.* Mahwah, NJ: Erlbaum.

Provenzo, E. F. (2002). *Teaching, learning, and schooling in American culture: A critical perspective.* Boston: Allyn & Bacon.

Pueschel, S. M., Scola, P. S., Weidenman, L. E., & Bernier, J. C. (1995). *The special child.* Baltimore: Paul Brookes.

Pujol, J., Lopez-Sala, A., Sebastian-Galles, N., Deus, J., Cardoner, N., Soriano-Mas, C., Moreno, A., & Sans, A. (2004). Delayed myelination in children with developmental delay detected by volumetric MRI. *Neuroimage, 22,* 897–903.

Putnam, S. P., Sanson, A. V., & Rothbart, M. K. (2002). Child temperament and parenting. In M. H. Bornstein (Ed.), *Handbook of parenting* (2nd ed.). Mahwah, NJ: Erlbaum.

Q

Quadflieg, N., & Fichter, M. M. (2003). The course and outcome of bulimia nervosa. *European Child and Adolescent Psychiatry, 12* (Suppl. 1), 1199–1209.

Quadrel, M. J., Fischoff, B., & Davis, W. (1993). Adolescent (in) vulnerability. *American Psychologist, 48,* 102–116.

Quincey, V. L., Skilling, T. A., Lalumiére, M. L., & Craig, W. M. (2004). *Juvenile delinquency.* Washington, DC: American Psychological Association.

Quinn, P. C. (2004). Multiple sources of information and their integration, not dissociation, as an organizing framework for understanding infant concept formation. *Developmental Science, 7,* 511–513.

Quinn, P. C., & Eimas, P. D. (1996). Peceptual organization and categorization. In C. Rovee-Collier & L. P. Lipsitt (Eds.), *Advances in infancy research* (Vol. 10, pp. 1–36). Norwood, NJ: Ablex.

Quintana, S. M. (2004). Ethnic identity development in Chicana/o youth. In R. J. Velasquez, B. W. McNeil, & L. M. Arellano (Eds.), *The handbook of Chicano psychology and mental health.* Mahwah, NJ: Erlbaum.

Qutub, M., Klapper, P., Vallely, P., & Cleator, G. (2001). Genital herpes in pregnancy: Is screening cost effective? *International Journal of STD and AIDS, 12,* 14–16.

R

Rabin, B. E., & Dorr, A. (1995, March). *Children's understanding of emotional events on family television series.* Paper presented at the meeting of the Society for Research in Child Development, Indianapolis.

Radcliffe, D. J., Pliskin, J. S., Silvers, J. B., & Cuttler, L. (2004). Growth hormone therapy and quality of life in adults and children. *Pharmacoeconomics, 22,* 499–524.

Rafaelli, M., & Crockett, L. J. (2003). Sexual risk taking in adolescence: The role of self-regulation and attraction to risk. *Developmental Psychology, 39,* 1036–1046.

Rafaelli, M., & Ontai, L. (2001). "She's sixteen years old and there's boys calling over to the house": An exploratory study of sexual socialization in Latino families. *Culture, Health, and Sexuality, 3,* 295–310.

Raine, A. (2000, October). *Early educational and health attainment at age 3–5 years is associated with increased autonomic nervous system arousal and orienting at age 11 years: Evidence from the Mauritius Health Project.* Paper presented at the meeting of the Society for Psychophysiological Research, San Diego.

Raine, A., Venables, P. H., Dalils, C., Mellingen, K., Reynolds, C., & Mednick, S. A. (2001). Early educational and health attainment at age 3–5 years is associated with increased autonomic nervous system arousal and orientating at age 11 years: Evidence from the Mauritius Health Project. *Psychophysiology, 38,* 254–266.

Rainey, R. (1965). The effects of directed vs. nondirected laboratory work on high school chemistry achievement. *Journal of Research in Science Teaching, 3,* 286–292.

Rajeshwari, R., Yang, S. J., Niclas, T. A., & Berensen, G. S. (2005). Secular trends in children's sweetened-beverage consumption (1973 to 1994): The Bogalusa Heart Study. *Journal of the American Dietetic Association, 105,* 208–214.

Ramacciotti, C. E., Coli, E., Paoli, R., Gabriellini, G., Schulte, F., Castrogiovanni, S., Dell'Osso, L., & Garfinkel, P. E. (2005). The relationship between binge eating disorder and non-purging bulimia nervosa. *Eating and Weight Disorders, 10,* 8–12.

Ramakrishnan, U. (2004). Maternal circulating nutrient concentrations in pregnancy. *American Journal of Clinical Nutrition, 79,* 17–21.

Ramey, C. T., & Campbell, F. A. (1984). Preventive education for high-risk children: Cognitive consequences of the Carolina Abecedarian Project. *American Journal of Mental Deficiency, 88,* 515–523.

Ramey, C. T., & Ramey, S. L. (1998). Early prevention and early experience. *American Psychologist, 53,* 109–120.

Ramey, C. T., & Ramey, S. L. (2000). Intelligence and public policy. In R. J. Sternberg (Ed.), *Handbook of intelligence.* New York: Cambridge.

Ramey, C. T., & Ramey, S. L. (2004). Early learning and school readiness: Can early intervention make a difference? *Merrill-Palmer Quarterly, 50,* 471–491.

Ramey, C. T., Ramey, S. L., & Lanzi, R. G. (2001). Intelligence and experience. In R. J. Sternberg & E. L. Grigorenko (Eds.), *Environmental effects on cognitive abilities.* Mahwah, NJ: Erlbaum.

Ramey, C. T., Ramey, S. L., & Lanzi, R. G. (2006). Children's health and education. In W. Damon & R. Lerner (Eds.), *Handbook of child psychology* (6th ed.). New York: Wiley.

Ramey, S. L., & Ramey, C. T. (1999). *Going to school: How to help your child succeed.* New York: Goddard Press.

Ramey, S. L., & Ramey, C. T. (2000). Early childhood experiences and developmental competence. In S. Danzinger & J. Waldfogel (Eds.), *Securing the future: Investing in children from birth to college.* New York: Russell Sage Foundation.

Ramharter, M., Chai, S. K., Adegnika, A. A., Klopfer, A., Langin, M., Agnandji, S. T., Oyakhirome, S., Schwarz, N. G., Grobusch, M. P., Issifou, S., & Kremsner, P. G. (2004). Shared breastfeeding in Central Africa, *AIDS, 18,* 1847–1849.

Ramirez, M. (2004). Mestiza/o and Chicana/o: General issues. In R. J. Velasquez, B. W. McNeil., & L. M, Arellano (Eds.), *The handbook of Chicano psychology and mental health.* Mahwah, NJ: Erlbaum.

Rampage, C., Eovaldi, M., Ma, C., & Weigel-Foy, C. (2003). Adoptive families. In F. Walsh (Ed.), *Normal family processes: growing diversity and complexity* (3rd ed.). New York: Guilford Press.

Ramphal, C. (1962). *A study of three current problems in education.* Unpublished doctoral dissertation. University of Natal, India.

Ramsay, D. S. (1980). Onset of unimanual handedness in infants. *Infant Behavior and Development, 3,* 377–385.

Ramsey, P. S., Nuthalapaty, F. S., Lu, G., Ramin, S., Nuthalapaty, E. S., & Ramin, K. D. (2004). A survey of maternal-fetal medicine providers. *American Journal of Obstetrics and Gynecology, 191,* 1497–1502.

Ramus, F. (2004). Neurobiology of dyslexia: A reinterpretation of the data. *Trends in Neuroscience, 27,* 720–726.

Randolph, S., & Kochanoff, A. (2004). Child care research at the dawn of a new millennium. In J. G. Bremner & A. Fogel (Eds.), *Blackwell handbook of infant development.* Malden, MA: Blackwell.

Ransjo-Arvidson, A. B., Matthiesen, A. S., Nissen, L. G., Widstrom, A. M., & Uvnas-Moberg, K. (2001). Maternal analgesia during labor disturbs newborn behavior: Effects on breastfeeding, temperature, and crying. *Birth, 28,* 5–12.

Raphaelson, M. (2004). Stimulants and attention-deficit/hyperactivity disorder. *Journal of the American Medical Association, 292,* 2214.

Rappaport, N., & Thomas, C. (2004). Recent research findings on aggressive and violent behavior in youth: implications for clinical assessment and intervention. *Journal of Adolescent Health, 35,* 260–277.

Raudenbush, S. (2001). Longitudinal data analysis. *Annual Review of Psychology* (Vol. 52). Palo Alto, CA: Annual Reviews.

Raven, P. H., Johnson, G. B., Singer, S., & Losos, J. (2005). *Biology* (7th ed.). New York: McGraw-Hill.

Ravid, D., Levie, R., & Ben-Zvi, G. A. (2004). Morphological disorders. In L. Verhoeven & H. Van Balkom (Eds.), *The classification of language disorders.* Mahwah, NJ: Erlbaum.

Ream, G. L., & Savin-Williams, R. (2003). Religious development in adolescence. In G. Adams & M. Berzonsky (Eds.), *Blackwell handbook of adolescence.* Malden, MA: Blackwell.

Reeves, G., & Schweitzer, J. (2004). Pharmacological management of attention deficit hyperactivity disorder. *Expert Opinions in Pharmacotherapy, 5,* 1313–1320.

Regalado, M., Sareen, H., Inkelas, M., Wissow, L. S., & Halfon, N. (2004). Parents' discipline of young children: Results from the National Survey of Early Childhood Health. *Pediatrics, 113* (Suppl.), 1952–1958.

Regan, J., & Alderson, A. (2003). Obesity: A growing and serious epidemic for children and adolescents. *Tennessee Medicine, 96,* 229–230.

Regev, R. H., Lusky, A., Dolfin, T., Litmanovitz, I., Arnon, S., Reichman, B., & the Israel Neonatal Network. (2003). Excess mortality and morbidity among small-for-gestational-age premature infants: A population based study. *Journal of Pediatrics, 143,* 186–191.

Regnerus, M. D. (2002). *Making the grade: The influence of religion upon the academic performance of youth in disadvantaged communities.* Report 01–04, Center for Research on Religion and Urban Civil Society, University of Pennsylvania.

Regnerus, M. D., Smith, C., & Smith, B. (2004). Social context in the development of religiosity. *Applied Developmental Science, 8,* 27–38.

Reid, M. E. (2002). Molecular biology in transfusion medicine: Current applications and future practice. *Current Hematology Reports, 1,* 134–141.

Reid, P. T., & Zalk, S. R. (2001). Academic environments: Gender and ethnicity in U.S. higher education. In J. Worell (Ed.), *Encyclopedia of women and gender.* New York: Oxford University Press.

Reiner, W. G. (2001). Gender identity and sex reassignment. In L. King, B. Beltnan, & S. Kramer (Eds.), *Clinical Pediatric Urology* (3rd ed.). London: ISIS Medical.

Reiner, W. G., & Gearhart, J. P. (2004). Discordant sexual identity in some genetic males with cloacalexstrophy assigned to female sex at birth. *New England Journal of Medicine, 350,* 333–341.

Reis, O., & Youniss, J. (2004). Patterns of identity change and development in relationships with mothers and friends. *Journal of Adolescent Research, 19,* 31–44.

Remulla, A., & Guilleminault, C. (2004). Somnambulism (sleepwalking). *Expert Opinions in Pharmacotherapy, 5,* 2069–2074.

Renninger, K. A., & Sigel, I. E. (2006). Applying research to practice. In W. Damon & R. Lerner (Eds.), *Handbook of child psychology* (6th ed.). New York: Wiley.

Renzulli, J. S. (1998). A rising tide lifts all shifts: Developing the gifts and talents of all students. *Phi Delta Kappan, 80,* 1–15.

Reschly, D. J. (1996). Identification and assessment of students with disabilities. In *Special education for students with disabilities.* Los Altos, CA: The David and Lucile Packard Foundation.

Revelle, S. P. (2004). High standards + highstakes = high achievement in Massachusetts. *Phi Delta Kappan, 85,* 591–597.

Reyna, V. F. (2004). How people make decisions that involve risk: A dual-process approach. *Current Directions in Psychological Science, 13,* 60–66.

Reyna, V. F., & Brainerd, C. J. (1995). Fuzzytrace theory: An interim synthesis. *Learning and Individual Differences, 7,* 1–75.

Reyna, V. G., Adam, M. B., Walsk, M. E., LeCroy, C. W., Muller, K., & Brainerd, C. J. (2005). The development of judgment and decision making from childhood to adolescence. In J. E. Jacobs & P. A. Klaczynski (Eds.), *The development of judgment and decision making in children and adolescents.* Mahwah, NJ: Erlbaum.

Reynolds, A. J. (1999, April). *Pathways to longterm effects in the Chicago Child-Parent Center Programs.* Paper presented at the meeting of the Society for Research in Child Development, Albuquerque.

Reynolds, C. R., Livingston, R., & Wilson, V. (2006). *Measurement and assessment in education.* Boston: Allyn & Bacon.

Rhee, K. E., De Largo, C. W., Arscott-Mills, T., Mehta, S. D., & Davis, R. K. (2005). Factors associated with parental readiness to make changes for overweight children. *Pediatrics, 115,* e94–e101.

Rhodes, J. E., Grossman, J. B., & Resch, N. L. (2000). Agents of change: Pathways through which mentoring relationships influence adolescents' academic adjustment. *Child Development, 71,* 1662–1671.

Richards, M. H., Crowe, P. A., Larson, R., & Swarr, A. (1998). Developmental patterns and gender differences in the experience of peer companionship during adolescence. *Child Development, 69,* 154–163.

Richards, M. H., Larson, R., Miller, B. V., Luo, Z., Sims, B., Parrella, D. P., & McCauley, C. (2004). Risky and protective contexts and exposure to violence in urban African American young adolescents. *Journal of Clinical Child and Adolescent Psychology, 33,* 138–148.

Richardson, B. A., & Hughes, J. P. (2003). Modeling breastmilk infectivity in HIV-1 infected mothers. *Biometrics, 59,* 179–185.

Richardson, G. A., Ryan, C., Willford, J., Day, N. L., & Goldschmidt, L. (2002). Prenatal alcohol and marijuana exposure: Effects on neuropsychological outcomes at 10 years. *Neurotoxicology and Teratology, 24,* 309–320.

Richter, L. (2003). Poverty, underdevelopment, and infant mental health. *Journal of Pediatric and Child Health, 39,* 243–248.

Rickards, T., & deCock, C. (2003). Understanding organizational creativity: Toward a paradigmatic approach. In M. A. Runco (Ed.), *Creativity research handbook.* Cresskill, NJ: Hampton Press.

Riddle, D. B., & Prinz, R. (1984, August). *Sugar consumption in young children.* Paper presented at the meeting of the American Psychological Association, Toronto.

Ridgeway, D., Waters, E., & Kuczaj, S. A. (1985). Acquisition of emotion-descriptive language: Receptive and productive vocabulary norms for ages 18 months to 6 years. *Developmental Psychology, 21,* 901–908.

Rieckmann, T. R., Wadsworth, M. E., & Deyhle, D. (2004). Cultural identity, explanatory style, and depression in Navajo adolescents. *Cultural Diversity & Ethnic Minority Psychology, 10,* 365–382.

Rietveld, M. J., Dolan, C. V., van Baal, G. C., & Boomsma, D. I. (2003). A twin study of differentiation of cognitive abilities in childhood. *Behavior Genetics, 33,* 367–381.

Rigby, K. (2004). Bullying in childhood. In P. K. Smith & C. H. Hart (Eds.), *Blackwell handbook of childhood social development.* Malden, MA: Blackwell.

Righetti-Veltema, M., Conne-Perreard, E., Bousquest, A., & Manzano, J. (2002). Postpartum depression and mother-infant relationship at 3 months old. *Journal of Affective Disorders, 70,* 291–306.

Rilea, S. L., Roskos-Ewoldsen, B., & Boles, D. (2004). Sex differences in spatial ability: A lateralization of function approach. *Brain and Cognition, 56,* 332–343.

Rivara, F. P. (2002). Prevention of injuries to children and adolescents. *Injury Prevention, 8* (Suppl. 4), IV5–IV8.

Rivara, F. P. (2004). Modification of the home environment for the reduction of injuries. *Archives of Pediatric and Adolescent Medicine, 158,* 513.

Rivera, C., & Collum, E. (Eds.). *State assessment policy and practice for English Language Learners.* Mahwah, NJ: Erlbaum.

Rob, G. (2004). Attending to the execution of a complex sensorimotor skill: Expertise differences. *Journal of Experimental Psychology: Applied, 10,* 42–54.

Roberts, D. F., Henriksen, L., & Foehr, U. G. (2004). Adolescents and the media. In R. Lerner & L. Steinberg, (Eds.), *Handbook of adolescent psychology* (2nd ed.). New York: Wiley.

Roberts, W. B. (2005). *Bullying from both sides.* Thousand Oaks, CA: Sage.

Robins, R. W., Trzesniewski, K. H., Tracev, J. L., Potter, J., & Gosling, S. D. (2002). Age differences in self-esteem from age 9 to 90. *Psychology and Aging, 17,* 423–434.

Robinson, J. H., & Clay, D. L. (2005). Potential school violence: Relationship between teacher anxiety and warning-sign identification. *Psychology in the Schools, 42,* 623–635.

Robinson, W. P., McGillivrary, B., Lewis, M. E., Arbour, L., Barrett, I., & Kalousek, D. K. (2005). Prenatally detected trisomy 20 mosaicism. *Prenatal Diagnosis, 25,* 239–244.

Rode, S. S., Chang, P., Fisch, R. O., & Sroufe, L. A. (1981). Attachment patterns of infants separated at birth. *Developmental Psychology, 17,* 188–191.

Rodgers, J. L. (2000). Birth order. In A. Kazdin (Ed.), *Encyclopedia of psychology.* Washington, DC, & New York: American Psychological Association and Oxford University Press.

Rodier, P. M. (2004). Environmental causes of central nervous system maldevelopment. *Pediatrics, 113* (No. 4, Supplement), 1076–1083.

Rodin, J. (1984, December). Interview: A sense of control. *Psychology Today,* pp. 38–45.

Rogoff, B. (1990). *Apprenticeship in thinking.* New York: Oxford University Press.

Rogoff, B. (1998). Cognition as a collaborative process. In W. Damon (Ed.), *Handbook of child psychology* (5th ed., Vol. 2). New York: Wiley.

Rogoff, B. (2003). *The cultural nature of human development.* New York: Oxford University Press.

Rogoff, B., Paradise, R., Arauz, R. M., Correa-Chavez, M., & Angelillo, C. (2003). First hand learning through intent participation. *Annual Review of Psychology, 54,* Palo Alto, CA: Annual Reviews.

Rogol, A. D., Roemmich, J. N., & Clark P. A. (1998, September). *Growth at puberty.* Paper presented at a workshop, Physical Development, Health Futures of Youth II: Pathways to Adolescent health, Maternal and Child Health Bureau, Annapolis.

Rohner, R. P., & Rohner, E. C. (1981). Parental acceptance-rejection and parental control: Cross-cultural codes. *Ethnology, 20,* 245–260.

Roisman, G. I., Masten, A. S., Coatsworth, J. D., & Tellegen, A. (2004). Salient and emerging developmental tasks in the transition to adulthood. *Child Development, 75,* 123–133.

Roosa, M. W., Dumka, L. E., Gonzales, N. A., & Knight, G. P. (2002). Cultural/ethnic issues and the prevention scientist in the 21st century. *Prevention & Treatment, 5,* 1–13.

Rose, A. J. (2002). Co-rumination in the friendships of girls and boys. *Child Development, 73,* 1830–1843.

Rose, A. J., & Asher, S. R. (1999). Children's goals and strategies in response to conflicts within a friendship. *Developmental Psychology, 35,* 69–79.

Rose, L. C., & Gallup, A. M. (2000). The 32nd annual Phi Delta Kappa/Gallup Poll of the public's attitudes toward the public schools. *Phi Delta Kappan, 82* (No. 10), 41–58.

Rose, M. R., & Mueller, L. D. (2006). *Evolution and ecology of the organism.* Upper Saddle River, NJ: Prentice Hall.

Rose, S. A. (1990). Cross-modal transfer in human infants: What is being transferred? *Annals of the New York Academy of Sciences, 608,* 38–47.

Rosenblith, J. F. (1992). *In the beginning* (2nd ed.). Newbury Park, CA: Sage.

Rosenblum, G. D., & Lewis, M. (2003). Emotional development in adolescence. In G. Adams & Berzonsky (Eds.), *Blackwell handbook of adolescence.* Malden, MA: Blackwell.

Rosenstein, D., & Oster, H. (1988). Differential facial responses to four basic tastes in newborns. *Child Development, 59,* 1555–1568.

Rosenzweig, M. (2000). Ethology. In A. Kazdin (Ed.), *Encyclopedia of psychology.* Washington, DC, & New York: American Psychological Association and Oxford University Press.

Rosenzweig, M. R. (1969). Effects of heredity and environment on brain chemistry, brain anatomy, and learning ability in the rat. In M. Monosevitz, G. Lindzey, & D. D. Thiessen (Eds.), *Behavioral genetics.* New York: Appleton-Century-Crofts.

Rosilio, M., Carel, J. C., Ecosse, E., & Chaussainon, J. L. (2005). Adult height of prepubertal short children born small for gestational age treated with GH. *European Journal of Endocrinology, 152,* 835–843.

Rosnow, R. L. (1995). Teaching research ethics through role-playing and discussion. In M. E. Ware & D. E. Johnson (Eds.), *Demonstrations and activities in teaching psychology* (Vol. 1). Mahwah, NJ: Erlbaum.

Rosnow, R. L., & Rosenthal, R. (2005). *Beginning behavioral research* (5th ed.). Upper Saddle River, NJ: Prentice-Hall.

Rosselli, H. C. (1996, February/March). Gifted students. *National Association for Secondary School Principals,* pp. 12–17.

Roth, J., & Brooks-Gunn, J. (2000). What do adolescents need for healthy development? Implications for youth policy. *Social Policy Report, So-*

ciety for Research in Child Development, XIV, No. 1, 1–19.

Rothbart, M. K. (2004). Temperament and the pursuit of an integrated developmental psychology. *Merrill-Palmer Quarterly, 50,* 492–505.

Rothbart, M. K., & Bates, J. E. (1998). Temperament. In W. Damon (Ed.), *Handbook of child psychology* (5th ed., Vol. 3). New York: Wiley.

Rothbart, M. K., & Bates, J. E. (2006). Temperament. In W. Damon & R. Lerner (Eds.), *Handbook of child psychology* (6th ed.). New York: Wiley.

Rothbart, M. K., & Putnam, S. P. (2002). Temperament and socialization. In L. Pulkkinen & A. Caspi (Eds.), *Paths to successful development.* New York: Cambridge University Press.

Rothbart, M. L. K. (1971). Birth order and mother-child interaction. *Dissertation Abstracts, 27,* 45–57.

Rothbaum, F., Poll, M., Azuma, H., Miyake, K., & Weisz, J. (2000). The development of close relationships in Japan and the United States: Paths of symbiotic harmony and generative tension. *Child Development, 71,* 1121–1142.

Rothstein, D. (2001, January 7). Commentary. *Parade Magazine,* p. 12.

Rovee-Collier, C. (1987). Learning and memory in children. In J. D. Osofsky (Ed.), *Handbook of infant development* (2nd ed.). New York: Wiley.

Rovee-Collier, C. (2004). Infant learning and memory. In U. Goswami (Ed.), *Blackwell handbook of childhood cognitive development.* Malden, MA: Blackwell.

Rowe, S. M., & Wertsch, J. V. (2004). Vygotsky's model of cognitive development. In U. Goswami (Ed.), *Blackwell handbook of child development.* Malden, MA: Blackwell.

Rubenstein, D. (2004). Language games and natural resources. *Journal of the Theory of Social Behavior, 34,* 55–71.

Rubin, D. (2006). *Gaining word power* (7th ed.). Upper Saddle River, NJ: Prentice Hall.

Rubin, D. H., Krasilnikoff, P. A., Leventhal, J. M., Weile, B., & Berget, A. (1986, August 23). Effect of passive smoking on birthweight. *The Lancet, 2,* 415–417.

Rubin, K. H., Bukowski, W., & Parker, J. (2006). Peer interactions, relationships, and groups. In W. Damon & R. Lerner (Eds.), *Handbook of child psychology* (6th ed.). New York: Wiley.

Rubin, K. H., Bukowski, W., & Parker, J. G. (1998). Peer interactions, relationships, and groups. In N. Eisenberg, (Ed.), *Handbook of child psychology* (5th ed., Vol. 3). New York: Wiley.

Rubin, K. H., Coplan, R., Chen, X., Buskirk, A. A., & Wojslawowicz, J. C. (2005). Peer relationships in childhood. In M. H. Bornstein & M. E. Lamb (Eds.), *Developmental psychology* (5th ed.). Mahwah, NJ: Erlbaum.

Rubin, Z., & Mitchell, C. (1976). Couples research as couples counseling. *American Psychologist, 31,* 17–25.

Ruble, D. (1983). The development of social comparison processes and their role in achievement-related self-socialization. In E. Higgins, D. Ruble, & W. Hartup (Eds.), *Social cognitive development: A social-cultural perspective.* New York: Cambridge University Press.

Ruble, D. N. (2000). Gender constancy. In A. Kazdin (Ed.), *Encyclopedia of psychology.* Washington, DC, and New York: American Psychological Association and Oxford University Press.

Ruble, D. N., Martin, C. L., & Berenbaum, S. A. (2006). Gender development. In W. Damon & R. Lerner (Eds.), *Handbook of child psychology* (6th ed.). New York: Wiley.

Ruddell, R. B. (2006). *Teaching children to read and write* (4th ed.). Boston: Allyn & Bacon.

Rueter, M., & Conger, R. (1995). Antecedents of parent-adolescent disagreements. *Journal of Marriage and the Family, 57,* 435–448.

Rueter, M. A., & Kwon, H.-K. (2005). Developmental trends in adolescent suicide ideation. *Journal of Research on Adolescence, 15,* 205–222.

Ruff, H. A., & Capozzoli, M. C. (2003). Development of attention and distractibility in the first four years of life. *Developmental Psychology, 39,* 877–890.

Ruff, H. A., & Rothbart, M. K. (1996). *Attention in early development.* New York: Oxford University Press.

Rumberger, R. W. (1983). Dropping out of high school: The influence of race, sex, and family background. *American Educational Research Journal, 20,* 199–220.

Runco, M. A. (2004). Creativity. *Annual Review of Psychology* (Vol. 55). Palo Alto, CA: Annual Reviews.

Rupp, R., Rosenthal, S. L., & Stanberry, L. R. (2005). Pediatrics and herpes simple virus vaccines. *Seminars in Pediatric Infectious Diseases, 16,* 31–37.

Rusak, B., Robertson, H. A., Wisden, W., & Hunt, S. P. (1990). Light pulses that shift rhythms induce gene expression in the suprachiasmatic nucleus. *Science, 248,* 1237–1240.

Rusen, I. D., Liu, S., Sauve, R., Joseph, K. S., & Kramer, M. S. (2004). Sudden infant death syndrome in Canada: Trends in rates and risk factors, 1985–1998. *Chronic Diseases in Canada, 25,* 1–6.

Russell, S. T., & Joyner, K. (2001). Adolescent sexual orientation and suicide risk: Evidence from a national study. *American Journal of Public Health, 91,* 1276–1281.

Russman, B. S., & Ashwal, S. (2004). Evaluation of the child with cerebral palsy. *Seminars in Pediatric Neurology, 11,* 47–57.

Rutter, M., & Schopler, E. (1987). Autism and pervasive developmental disorders: Concepts and diagnostic issues. *Journal of Autism and Pervasive Developmental Disorders, 17,* 159–186.

Ryan, A. S. (1997). The resurgence of breastfeeding in the United States. *Pediatrics, 99,* E12.

Ryan, A. S., Wenjun, Z., & Acosta, A. (2002). Breastfeeding continues to increase into the new millennium. *Pediatrics, 110,* 1103–1109.

Ryan, R. M., & Deci, E. L. (2001). When rewards compete with nature. In C. Sansone & J. M. Harackiewicz (Eds.), *Intrinsic and extrinsic motivation.* San Diego: Academic Press.

Ryan-Finn, K. D., Cauce, A. M., & Grove, K. (1995, March). *Children and adolescents of color: Where are you? Selection, recruitment, and retention in developmental research.* Paper presented at the meeting of the Society for Research in Child Development, Indianapolis.

Rymer, R. (1992). *Genie.* New York: HarperCollins.

S

Saab, J. F. (2004). Bringing learning to life: The Reggio approach to early childhood education. *Childhood Education, 80,* 277–279.

Saarni, C. (1999). *The development of emotional competence.* New York: Guilford.

Saarni, C., Campos, J., Camras, L. A., & Witherington, D. (2006). Emotional development. In W. Damon & R. Lerner (Eds.), *Handbook of child psychology* (6th ed.). New York: Wiley.

Sabol, W., Coulton, C., & Polousky, E. (2004). Measuring child maltreatment risk in communities: A life table approach. *Child Abuse and Neglect, 28,* 967–983.

Sachs-Ericsson, N., Blazer, D., Plant, A. E., & Arnow, B. (2005). Childhood sexual and physical abuse and the 1-year prevalence of medical problems in the National Comorbidity Study. *Health Psychology, 24,* 32–40.

Sackett, P. R., Hardison, C. M., & Cullen, M. J. (2004). On interpreting stereotype threat as accounting for African-American White differences in cognitive tests. *American Psychologist, 59,* 7–13.

Sadker, D. M. P., & Sadker, D. M. (2000). *Teachers, schools, and society* (5th ed.). New York: McGraw-Hill.

Sadker, M. P., & Sadker, D. M. (2005). *Teachers, schools, and society* (7th ed.). New York: McGraw-Hill.

Saffran, J. R., Werker, J. F., & Werner, L. A. (2006). The infant's auditory world: Hearing, speech, and the beginnings of language. In W. Damon & R. Lerner (Eds.), *Handbook of child psychology* (6th ed.). New York: Wiley.

Sagan, C. (1977). *The dragons of Eden.* New York: Random House.

Sagi, A., Koren-Karie, N., Gini, M., Ziv, Y., & Joels, T. (2002). Shedding further light on the effects of various types and quality of early child care on infant-mother attachment relationship: The Haifa study of early child care. *Child Development, 73,* 1166–1186.

Said, T. M., Agarwal, A., Sharma, R. K., Mascha, E., Sikka, S. C., & Thomas, A. J. (2004). Human sperm superoxide anion generation and correlation with semen quality in patients with male infertility. *Fertility and Sterility, 82,* 871–877.

Saigal, S., den Ouden, L., Wolke, D., Hoult, L., Paneth, N., Streiner, D. L., Whitaker, A., & Pinto-Martin, J. (2003). School-age outcomes in children who were extremely low birth weight from four international population-based cohorts. *Pediatrics, 112,* 943–950.

Sakai, K. L., Tatsuno, Y., Suzuki, K., Kimura, H., & Ichida, Y. (2005). Sign and speech: Amodal commonality in left hemisphere dominance for comprehension of sentences. *Brain, 128,* 1407–1417.

Salbe, A. D., Weyer, C., Lindsay, R. S., Ravussin, E., & Tataranni, P. A. (2002). Assessing risk factors for obesity between adolescence: In birth weight, childhood adiposity, parental obesity, insulin, & leptin. *Pediatrics, 110,* 299–306.

Salkind, N. J. (2003). *Exploring research* (5th ed.). Upper Saddle River, NJ: Prentice Hall.

Sallis, J. F., Conway, T. L., Prochaska, J. T., McKenzie, T. L., Marshall, S. J., & Brown, M. (2001). The association of school environments with youth physical activity. *American Journal of Public Health, 91,* 618–620.

Salovey, P., & Mayer, J. D. (1990). Emotional intelligence. *Imagination, Cognition, and Personality, 9,* 185–211.

Samour, P. Q., Helm, K. K., & Lang, C. E. (Eds.). (2000). *Handbook of pediatric nutrition* (2nd ed.). Aspen, CO: Aspen.

Samuelsson, S., Lundberg, I., & Herkner, B. (2004). ADHD and reading disability in adults: Is there a connection? *Journal of Learning Disabilities, 37,* 155–168.

Sanchez-Johnsen, L. A., Fitzgibbon, M. L., Martinovich, Z., Stolley, M. R., Dyer, A. R., & Van Horn, L. (2004). Ethnic differences in correlates of obesity between Latin-American and black Women. *Obesity Research, 12,* 652–660.

Sanson, A., & Rothbart, M. K. (1995). Child temperament and parenting. In M. H. Bornstein (Ed.), *Handbook of parenting* (Vol. 4). Hillsdale, NJ: Erlbaum.

Sansone, C., & Smith, J. L. (2001). Interest and self-regulation. In C. Sansone & J. M. Harakiewlcz (Eds.), *Intrinsic and extrinsic motivation.* San Diego: Academic Press.

Santa Maria, M. (2002). Youth in Southeast Asia: Living within the continuity of tradition and the turbulence of change. In B. B. Brown, R. W. Larson, & T. S. Saraswathi (Eds.), *The world's youth.* New York: Cambridge University Press.

Santelli, J. S., Abma, V., Ventura, S., Llindberg, L., Morrow, B., Anderson, J. E., Lyss, S., & Hamilton, B. E. (2004b). Can changes in sexual behavior among high school students explain the decline in teen pregnancy rates in the 1990s? *Journal of Adolescent Health, 35,* 80–90.

Santelli, J. S., Kaiser, J., Hirsch, L., Radosh, A., Simkin, L., & Middlestadt, S. (2004a). Initiation of intercourse among middle school adolescents: The influence of social factors. *Journal of Adolescent Health, 34,* 200–208.

Santiago-Delefosse, M. J., & Delefosse, J. M. O. (2002). Three positions on child thought and language. *Theory and Psychology, 12,* 723–747.

Santrock, J. W. (2005). *Adolescence* (10th ed.). New York: McGraw-Hill.

Santrock, J. W. (2006). *Educational psychology* (2nd ed., updated). New York: McGraw-Hill.

Santrock, J. W. (2006). *Life-span development* (10th ed.). New York: McGraw-Hill.

Santrock, J. W., Sitterie, K. A., & Warshak, R. A. (1988). Parent-child relationships in stepfather families. In L. Bornstein & C. P. Cowan (Eds.), *Fatherhood today: Men's changing roles in the family.* New York: Wiley.

Saracho, O. N., & Shirakawa, Y. (2004). A comparison of the literacy development context of the United States and Japanese families. *Early Childhood Research Quarterly, 19,* 261–266.

Sarigiani, P. A., & Petersen, A. C. (2000). Adolescence: Puberty and biological maturation. In A. Kazdin (Ed.), *Encyclopedia of psychology.* Washington, DC, & New York: American Psychological Association and Oxford University Press.

Sarsam, S. E., Elliott, J. P., & Lam, G. K. (2005). Management of wound complications from cesarean delivery. *Obstetrical and Gynecological Survey, 60,* 462–473.

Sauls, D. J. (2002). Effects of labor support on mothers, babies, and birth outcomes. *Journal of Obstetric, Gynecologic, and Neonatal Nursing, 31,* 733–741.

Savell, V. H., Hughes, S. M., Bower, C., & Parham, D. M. (2004). Lymphocytie infiltration in pediatric thyroid carcinomas. *Pediatric and Developmental Pathology, 7,* 487–492.

Savin-Williams, R. C. (1995). An exploratory study of pubertal maturation timing and self-esteem among gay and bisexual male youths. *Developmental Psychology, 31,* 56–64.

Savin-Williams, R., & Diamond, L. (2004). Sex. In R. Lerner & L. Steinberg, (Eds.), *Handbook of adolescent psychology* (2nd ed.). New York: Wiley.

Savin-Williams, R. C. (2001). *Mom, dad, I'm gay.* Washington, DC: American Psychological Association.

Savin-Williams, R. C. (2001). A critique of research on sexual minority youths. *Journal of Adolescence, 24,* 5–13.

Savin-Williams, R. C., & Diamond, L. (2004). Sex. In R. Lerner & L. Steinberg (Eds.), *Handbook of adolescent psychology* (2nd ed.). New York: Wiley.

Sawnani, H., Jackson, T., Murphy, T., Beckerman, R., & Simakajornboom, N. (2004). The effect of maternal smoking on respiratory and arousal patterns in preterm infants during sleep. *American Journal of Respiratory and Critical Care Medicine, 169,* 733–738.

Sax, L. J., Hurtado, S., Lindholm, J. A., Astin, A. W., Korn, W. S., & Mahoney, K. M. (2004). *The American freshman: National norms for fall, 2004.* Los Angeles: Higher Education Research Institute, UCLA.

Scafidi, F., & Field, T. M. (1996). Massage therapy improves behavior in neonates born to HIV-positive mothers. *Journal of Pediatric Psychology, 21,* 889–897.

Scaramella, L. V., & Conger, R. D. (2004). Continuity versus discontinuity in parent and adolescent negative affect. In R. D. Conger, F. O. Lorenz, & K. A. S. Wickrama (Eds.), *Continuity and change in family relations.* Mahwah, NJ: Erlbaum.

Scarlett, W. G. (2005). Toward a developmental analysis of religious and spiritual development. In E. C. Roehkepartain, P. E. King, L. Wagner, & P. L. Benson (Eds.), *Handbook of spiritual development in childhood and adolescence.* Thousand Oaks, CA: Sage.

Scarr, S. (1984, May). Interview. *Psychology Today,* pp. 59–63.

Scarr, S. (1993). Biological and cultural diversity: The legacy of Darwin for development. *Child Development, 64,* 1333–1353.

Scarr, S., & Weinberg, R. A. (1983). The Minnesota adoption studies: Genetic differences and malleability. *Child Development, 54,* 182–259.

Schachter, S. C., & Ransil, B. J. (1996). Handedness distributions in nine professional groups. *Perceptual and Motor Skills, 82,* 51–63.

Schacter, D. L. (2001). *The seven deadly sins of memory.* Boston: Houghton Mifflin.

Schaechter, J., Duran, I., De Marchena, J., Lemard, G., & Villar, M. E. (2003). Are "accidental" gun deaths as rare as they seem? *Pediatrics, 111,* 741–744.

Schaffer, H. R. (1996). *Social development.* Cambridge, MA: Blackwell.

Schattschneider, C., Fletcher, J. M., Francis, D. J., Carlson, C. D., & Foorman, B. R. (2004). Kindergarten prediction of reading skills: A longitudinal comparative analysis. *Journal of Educational Psychology, 96,* 265–282.

Schauble, L. (1996). The development of scientific reasoning in knowledge-rich contexts. *Developmental Psychology, 32,* 102–119.

Schlegel, M. (2000). All work and play. *Monitor on Psychology 31* (No. 11), 50–51.

Schmaling, K. B., Lehrer, P. M., Giardino, N. D., & Feldman, J. M. (2003). Asthma. In

I. B. Weiner (Ed.), *Handbook of psychology* (Vol. IX). New York: Wiley.

Schmidt, P., & others. (2004). Comparison of preschool vision screening tests as administered by licensed eye care professionals in the Vision in Preschools Study. *Ophthalmology, 111,* 637–650.

Schmidt, U. (2003). Aetiology of eating disorders in the 21st century: New answers to old questions. *European Child and Adolescent Psychiatry, 12* (Suppl. 1), 1130–1137.

Schmitt, D. P., & Pilcher, J. J. (2004). Evaluating evidence of psychological adaptation: How do we know one when we see one? *Psychological Science. 15,* 643–649.

Schnake, E. M., Peterson, N. M., & Corden, T. E. (2005). Promoting water safety: The physician's role. *Wisconsin Journal of Medicine, 104,* 45–49.

Schneider, D., Freeman, N. C., & McGarvey, P. (2005). Asthma and respiratory dysfunction among urban, primarily Hispanic children. *Archives of Environmental Health, 59,* 4–13.

Schneider, W. (2004). Memory development in childhood. In P. Smith & C. Han (Eds.), *Blackwell handbook of childhood cognitive development.* Malden, MA: Blackwell.

Schneider, W., & Pressley, M. (1997). *Memory development from 2 to 20* (2nd ed.), Mahwah, NJ: Erlbaum.

Schnorr, T. M., & others. (1991). Video-display terminals and the risk of spontaneous abortion. *New England Journal of Medicine, 324,* 727–733.

Schorr, L. B. (1989, April). *Within out reach: Breaking the cycle of disadvantage.* Paper presented at the biennial meeting of the Society for Research in Child Development, Kansas City.

Schrag, S. G., & Dixon, R. L. (1985). Occupational exposure associated with male reproductive dysfunction. *Annual Review of Pharmacology and Toxicology, 25,* 467–592.

Schreiber, L. R. (1990). *The parents guide to kids' sports.* Boston: Little, Brown.

Schulte, M. J., Ree, M. J., & Carretta, T. R. (2004). Emotional intelligence: No much more than g and personality. *Personality and Individual Differences, 37,* 1059–1068.

Schultz, T. R., Fisher, G. W., Pratt, C. C., & Rulf, S. (1986). Selection of causal rules. *Child Development, 57,* 143–152.

Schum, T. R., McAuliffe, T. L., Simms, M. D., Walter, J. A., Lewis, M., & Pupp, R. (2001). Factors associated with toilet training in the 1990s. *Ambulatory Pediatrics, 1,* 79–86.

Schunk, D. H. (2004). *Learning theories* (4th ed.). Upper Saddle River, NJ: Prentice Hall.

Schunk, D. M., & Zimmerman, B. J. (2003). Self-regulation and learning. In I. B. Weiner (Ed.), *Handbook of Psychology* (Vol. VII). New York: Wiley.

Schunn, C., & Anderson, J. (2001). Acquiring expertise in science. In K. Crowley, C. Schunn, & T. Okada (Eds.), *Designing for science.* Mahwah, NJ: Erlbaum.

Scott, K. D., Klaus, P. H., & Klaus, M. H. (1999). The obstetrical and postpartum benefits of continuous support during childbirth. *Journal of Women's Health and Gender Based Medicine, 10,* 1257–1264.

Scott-Jones, D. (1995, March). *Incorporating ethnicity and socioeconomic status in research with children.* Paper presented at the meeting of the Society for Research in Child Development, Indianapolis.

Scourfield, J., Van den Bree, M., Martin, N., & McGuffin, P. (2004). Conduct problems in children and adolescents: A twin study. *Archives of General Psychiatry, 61,* 489–496.

Scribner, S. (1977). Modes of thinking and ways of speaking: Culture and logic reconsidered. In F. N. Johnson-Laird & P. C. Wason (Eds.), *Thinking: Readings in cognitive science.* New York: Cambridge University Press.

Search Institute. (1995). *Barriers to participation in youth programs.* Unpublished manuscript, the Search Institute, Minneapolis.

Secada, W. G. (2005). The mediation of contextual resources. In C. R. Cooper, C. T. Garcia Coll, W. T. Barko, H. M. Davis, & C. Chatham (Eds.), *Developmental pathways through middle childhood.* Mahwah, NJ: Erlbaum.

Seeds, J. W. (2004). Diagnostic mid trimester amniocentesis: How safe? *American Journal of Obstetrics and Gynecology, 191,* 542–545.

Seehusen, D. A., Baldwin, L. M., Runkle, G. P., & Clark, G. (2005). Are family physicians appropriately screening for postpartum depression? *Journal of the American Board of Family Practitioners, 18,* 104–112.

Seidenfeld, M. E., Sosin, E., & Rickert, V. I. (2004). Nutrition and eating disorders in adolescents. *Mt. Sinai Journal of Medicine, 71,* 155–161.

Seifer, R. (2001). Socioeconomic status, multiple risks, and development of intelligence. In R. J. Sternberg & E. L. Grigorenko (Eds.), *Environmental effects on cognitive abilities.* Mahwah, NJ: Erlbaum.

Seldman, E. (2000). School transitions. In A. Kazdin (Ed.), *Encyclopedia of psychology.* Washington, DC, and New York: American Psychological Association and Oxford University Press.

Selman, R. L., & Dray, A. J. (2006). Risk and prevention. In W. Damon & R. Lerner (Eds.), *Handbook of child psychology* (6th ed.). New York: Wiley.

Sepulveda, W., Dezerega, V., & Be, C. (2004). First-trimester sonographic diagnosis of holoprosencephaly: value of the "butterfly" sign. *Journal of Ultrasound Medicine, 23,* 761–765.

Seroczynski, A. D., Jacquez, F. M., & Cole, D. (2003). Depression and suicide in adolescence. In G. Adams & M. Berzonsky (Eds.), *Blackwell handbook of adolescence.* Malden, MA: Blackwell.

Serow, R. C., Ciechalski, J., & Daye, C. (1990). Students as volunteers. *Urban Education, 25,* 157–168.

Serpell, R. (1974). Aspects of intelligence in a developing country. *African Social Research, 17,* 576–596.

Serpell, R. (2000). Culture and intelligence. In A. Kazdin (Ed.), *Encyclopedia of psychology.* Washington, DC, & New York: American Psychological Association and Oxford University Press.

Sewell, T. E. (2000). School dropout. In A. Kazdin (Ed.), *Encyclopedia of psychology.* Washington, DC, & New York: American Psychological Association and Oxford University Press.

Shaddy, J. D., & Colombo, J. (2004). Developmental changes in infant attention to dynamic and static stimuli. *Infancy, 5,* 355–365.

Shalev, R. S. (2004). Developmental dysealculia. *Journal of Child Neurology, 19,* 765–771.

Shanker, A. V., Sastry, J., Erande, A., Joshi, A., Suryawanshi, N., Phadke, M. A., & Bollinger, R. C. (2005). Making the choice: the translation of global HIV and infant feeding policy to local practice among mothers in Pune, India. *Journal of Nutrition, 135,* 960–965.

Sharma, A. R., McGue, M. K., & Benson, P. L. (1996). The emotional and behavioral adjustment of adopted adolescents: Part I: Age at adoption. *Children and Youth Services Review, 18,* 101–114.

Sharma, A. R., McGue, M. K., & Benson, P. L. (1998). The psychological adjustment of United States adopted adolescents and their nonadopted siblings. *Child Development, 69,* 791–802.

Sharma, V. (2002). Pharmacotherapy of postpartum depression. *Expert Opinions on Pharmocotherapy, 3,* 1421–1431.

Shatz, M., & Gelman, R. (1973). The development of communication skills: Modifications in the speech of young children as a function of the listener. *Monographs of the Society for Research in Child Development, 18* (Serial No. 152).

Shaw, D. S., Gilliom, M., Ingoldsby, E. M., & Nagin, D. S. (2003). Trajectories leading to school-age conduct problems. *Developmental Psychology, 39* (2), 189–200.

Shaw, G. M. (2001). Adverse human reproductive outcomes and electromagnetic fields. *Bioelectromagnetics, 5* (Supplement), S5–S18.

Shea, A., Walsh, C., MacMillan, H., & Steiner, M. (2005). Child maltreatment and HPA axis dysregulation: Relationship to major depressive disorder and post traumatic stress disorder in females. *Psychoneuroendocrinology, 30,* 162–178.

Sheahan, S. L., & Free, T. A. (2005). Counseling parents to quit smoking. *Pediatric Nursing, 31,* 98–102, 105–109.

Sheets, R. H. (2005). *Diversity pedagogy.* Upper Saddle River, NJ: Prentice-Hall.

Sheiner, E., Levy, A., Katz, M., & Mazor, M. (2005). Short stature—an independent risk factor for cesarean delivery. *European Journal of Obstetrics, Gynecology, and Reproductive Medicine, 120,* 175–178.

Sheldon, S. H. (2004). Parasomnias in childhood. *Pediatric Clinics of North America, 51,* 69–88.

Sheppard, V. B., Zambrana, R. E., & O'Malley, A. S. (2004). Providing health care to low-income women: A matter of trust. *Family Practice, 21,* 484–491.

Sherker, S., Ozanne-Smith, J., Rechnitzer, G., & Grzebieta, R. (2005). Out on a limb: Risk factors for arm fracture in playground equipment falls. *Injury Prevention, 11,* 120–124.

Shi, L., & Stevens, G. D. (2005). Disparities in access to care and satisfaction among U.S. children: The roles of race/ethnicity and poverty status. *Public Health Report, 120,* 431–441.

Shibazaki, Y., Shimizu, M., & Kuroda, R. (2004). Body handedness is directed by genetically determined dynamics in the early embryo. *Current Biology, 24,* 1462–1467.

Shields, S. A. (1991). Gender in the psychology of emotion: A selective research review. In K. T. Strongman (Ed.), *International review of studies on emotion* (Vol. 1). New York: Wiley.

Shields, S. A. (1998, August). *What Jerry Maguire can tell us about gender and emotion.* Paper presented at the meeting of the International Society for Research on Emotions, Wurzburg, Germany.

Shiffrin, R. M. (1996). Laboratory experimentation on the genesis of expertise. In K. A. Ericsson (Ed.), *The road to excellence.* Mahwah, NJ: Erlbaum.

Shiono, P. H., & Behrman, R. E. (1995, spring). Low birth weight: Analysis and recommendations. *Future of Children, 5* (No. 1), 4–18.

Shiva, F., Nasiri, M., Sadeghi, B., & Padyab, M. (2004). Effects of passive smoking on common respiratory symptoms in young children. *Acta Pediatrics, 92,* 1394–1397.

Shweder, R., Goodnow, J., Hatano, G., Le Vine, R. A., Markus, H., & Miller, P. (2006). The cultural psychology of development: One mind, many mentalities. In W. Damon & R. Lerner (Eds.), *Handbook of child psychology* (6th ed.). New York: Wiley.

Siega-Riz, A. M., Kranz, S., Blanchette, D., Haines, P. S., Guilkey, D. K., & Popkin, B. M. (2004). The effect of participation in the WIC program on preschoolers' diets. *Journal of Pediatrics, 144,* 229–234.

Siegel, L. S. (1989, April). *Perceptual-motor, cognitive, and language skills as predictors of cognitive abilities at school age.* Paper presented at the biennial meeting of the Society for Research in Children, Kansas City.

Siegel, L. S. (2003). Learning disabilities. In I. B. Weiner (Ed.), *Handbook of psychology* (Vol. VII). New York: Wiley.

Siegler, R. S. (1998). *Children's thinking* (3rd ed.). Upper Saddle River, NJ: Prentice Hall.

Siegler, R. S. (2004). Learning about learning. *Merrill Palmer Quarterly, 50,* 353–368.

Siegler, R. S. (2006). Microgenetic analysis of learning. In W. Damon & R. Lerner (Eds.), *Handbook of child psychology* (6th ed.). New York: Wiley.

Siegler, R. S., & Alibali, M. W. (2005). *Children's thinking* (4th ed.). Upper Saddle River, NJ: Prentice Hall.

Signore, R. J. (2004). Bradley method offers option for natural childbirth. *American Family Physician, 70,* 650.

Sim, T. (2000). Adolescent psychosocial competence: The importance and role of regard for parents. *Journal of Research on Adolescence, 10,* 49–64.

Sim, T. N., & Ong, L. P. (2005). Parent punishment and child aggression in a Singapore Chinese preschool sample. *Journal of Marriage and the Family, 67,* 85–99.

Simkin, P., Whalley, J., & Keppler, A. (2001). *Pregnancy, childbirth, and the newborn* (revised and updated edition). New York: Meadowood Publishers.

Simmons, R. G., & Blyth, D. A. (1987). *Moving into adolescence.* Hawthorne, NY: Aldine.

Simons, J. M., Finlay, B., & Yang, A. (1991). *The adolescent and young adult fact book.* Washington, DC: Children's Defense Fund.

Simons-Morton, B., Haynie, D. L., Crump, A. D., Eitel, P., & Saylor, K. E. (2001). Peer and parent influences on smoking and drinking among early adolescents. *Health Education & Behavior, 28,* 95–107.

Simpson, R. L. (1962). Parental influence, anticipatory socialization, and social mobility. *American Sociological Review, 27,* 517–522.

Singer, D. G. (1993). Creativity of children in a changing world. In G. L. Berry & J. K. Asamen (Eds.), *Children and television: Images in a changing sociocultural world.* Newbury Park, CA: Sage.

Singer, L. T., Arendt, R., Fagan, J., Minnes, S., Salvator, A., Bolek, T., & Becker, M. (1999). Neonatal visual information processing in cocaine-exposed and non-exposed infants. *Infant Behavior and Development, 22,* 1–15.

Singh, S., Darroch, J. E., & Bankole, A. (2004). A. B. and C in Uganda: The roles of abstinence, monogramy, and condom use in HIV decline. *Reproductive Health Matters, 12,* 129–131.

Singh, S., Wulf, D., Samara, R., & Cuca, Y. P. (2000). Gender differences in the timing of first intercourse: Data from 14 countries. *International Family Planning Perspectives, 26,* 21–28, 43.

Sininger, Y. S., & Cone-Wesson, B. (2004). Asymmetric cochlear processing mimics hemispheric specialization. *Science, 305,* 1581.

Sirois, S., & Mareschal, D. (2004). An interacting systems model of infant habituation. *Journal of Cognitive Neuroscience, 16,* 1352–1362.

Sizer, F., & Whitney, E. (2006). *Nutrition* (10th ed.). Belmont, CA: Wadsworth.

Skinner, B. F. (1938). *The behavior of organisms: An experimental analysis.* New York: Appleton-Century-Crofts.

Skinner, B. F. (1957). *Verbal behavior.* New York: Appleton-Century-Crofts.

Skinner, J. D., Ziegler, P., Pac, S., & Devaney, B. (2004). Meal and snack patterns of infants and toddlers. *Journal of the American Dietetic Association, 104,* 65–70.

Slade, E. P., & Wissow, L. S. (2004). Spanking in early childhood and later behavior problems: A prospective study. *Pediatrics, 113,* 1321–1330.

Slama, R., Bouyer, J., Windham, G., Fenster, L., Werwatz, A., & Swan, S. H. (2005). Influence of paternal age on the risk of spontaneous abortion. *American Journal of Epidemiology, 161,* 816–823.

Slater, A. (2004). Visual perception, In A. Fogel & G. Bremner (Eds.), *Blackwell handbook of infant development.* London: Blackwell.

Slater, A., Field, T., & Hernandez-Reif, M. (2002). The development of the senses. In A. Slater & M. Lewis (Eds.), *Introduction to infant development.* New York: Oxford University Press.

Slater, A., Morison, V., & Somers, M. (1988). Orientation discrimination and cortical function in the human newborn. *Perception. 17,* 597–602.

Sleet, D. A., & Mercy, J. A. (2003). Promotion of safety, security, and well-being. In M. H. Bornstein, L. Davidson, C. L. M. Keyes, & K. A. Moore (Eds.), *Well-being.* Mahwah, NJ: Erlbaum.

Sleet, D. A., Schieber, R. A., & Gilchrist, J. (2003). Health promotion policy and politics: Lessons from childhood injury prevention. *Health Promotion and Practice, 4,* 103–108.

Slentz, K. L., & Krogh, S. L. (2001). *Early childhood and its variations.* Mahwah, NJ: Erlbaum.

Slicker, E. K., & Thornberry, I. (2003). Older adolescent well-being and authoritative parenting. *Adolescent & Family Health, 3,* 9–19.

Slijper, F. M. E. (1984). Androgens and gender role behavior in girls with congenital adrenal hyperplasia (CAH). *Progress in Brain Research, 61,* 417–422.

Slobin, D. (1972, July). Children and language: They learn the same way around the world. *Psychology Today,* pp. 71–76.

Slomkowski, C., Rende, R., Conger, K. J., Simons, R. L., & Conger, R. D. (2001). Sisters, brothers, and delinquency: Social influence during early and middle adolescence. *Child Development, 72,* 271–283.

Slyper, A. H. (2004). The pediatric obesity epidemic: Causes and controversies. *Journal of Clinical Endocrinology and Metabolism, 89,* 2540–2547.

Small, S. A. (1990). *Preventive programs that support families with adolescents.* Washington, DC: Carnegie Council on Adolescent Development.

Smedje, H., Broman, J. E., & Hetta, J. (2001). Associations between disturbed sleep and behavioral difficulties in 635 children aged six to eight years: A study based on parent's perceptions. *European Journal of Child and Adolescent Psychiatry, 10,* 1–9.

Smetana, J. (2005). Social domain theory. In M. Killen & J. Smetana (Eds.), *Handbook of moral development.* Mahwah, NJ: Erlbaum.

Smith, D. (2004). *Introduction to special education* (5th ed.). Boston: Allyn & Bacon.

Smith, D. D. (2006). *Introduction to special education* (5th ed., updated). Boston: Allyn & Bacon.

Smith, F. (2004a). *Understanding reading* (6th ed.). Mahwah, NJ: Erlbaum.

Smith, J. A., & Read, S. (2005). *Early literacy instruction.* Upper Saddle River, NJ: Prentice Hall.

Smith, K. (2002). Who's minding the kids? Child care arrangements: Spring 1977. *Current Population Reports,* P70–P86. Washington, DC: U.S. Census Bureau.

Smith, L. (2004b). Piaget's model. In P. Smith & C. Hart (Eds.), *Blackwell handbook of cognitive development.* Malden, MA: Blackwell.

Smith, L., Muir, D. W., & Kisilevsky, B. (2001, April). *Preterm infants' responses to auditory stimulation of varying intensity.* Paper presented at the meeting of the Society for Research in Child Development, Minneapolis.

Smith, L. M., Chang, L., Yonekura, M. L., Gilbride, K., Kuo, J., Poland, R. E., Walot, I., & Ernst, T. (2001). Brain proton magnetic resonance spectroscopy and imaging in children exposed to cocaine in utero. *Pediatrics, 107,* 227.

Smith, S. S. (2006). *Early childhood mathematics* (3rd ed.). Upper Saddle River, NJ: Prentice Hall.

Smith, T. E. C., Polloay, E. A., Patton, J. R., & Dowdy, C. A. (2006). *Teaching students with special needs in inclusive settings* (4th ed., updated). Boston: Allyn & Bacon.

Smulian, J. C., Ananath, C. V., Vintzileos, A. M., Scorza, W. E., & Knuppel, R. A. (2002). Fetal deaths in the United States: Influence of high-risk conditions and implications for management. *Obstetrics and Gynecology, 100,* 1183–1189.

Snarey, J. (1987, June), A question of morality. *Psychology Today,* pp. 6–8.

Snell, J. L., & Hirschstein, M. (2005). Bullying and victimization. In H. W. Lee (Ed.), *Encyclopedia of school psychology.* Thousand Oaks, CA: Sage.

Snow, C. E., & Kang, J. Y. (2006). Becoming bilingual, biliterate, and bicultural. In W. Damon & R. Lerner (Eds.), *Handbook of child psychology* (6th ed.). New York: Wiley.

Snow, C. E., & Yang, J. Y. (2006). Becoming bilingual, biliterate, and bicultural. In W. Damon & R. Lerner (Eds.), *Handbook of child psychology* (6th ed.). New York: Wiley.

Snyder, H. N., & Sickmund, M. (1999, October). *Juvenile offenders and victims: 1999 national report.* Washington, DC: National Center for Juvenile Justice.

Sobieszczyk, M. E., Talley, A. K., Wilkin, T., & Hammer, S. M. (2005). Advances in antiretroviral therapy. *Topics in HIV Medicine, 13,* 24–44.

Sokol, R. J., Delaney-Black, V., & Nordstrom, B. (2003). Fetal alcohol spectrum disorder. *Journal of the American Medical Association, 290,* 2996–2999.

Solomon, D., Battistich, V., Watson, M., Schaps, E., & Lewis, C. (2000). A six-district study of educational change: Direct and mediated effects of the Child Development Project. *Social Psychology of Education, 4,* 3–51.

Sonenstein, F. L. (2004). What teenagers are doing right: Changes in sexual behavior over the past decade. *Journal of Adolescent Health, 35,* 77–78.

Sophian, C. (1985). Perseveration and infants, search: A comparison of two- and three-location tasks. *Developmental Psychology, 21,* 187–194.

Sorof, J., & Daniels, S. (2002). Obesity hypertension: A problem of epidemic proportions. *Hypertension, 404,* 441–447.

Sorof, J. M., Lai, D., Turner, J., Poffenberger, T., & Portman, R. J. (2004). Overweight, ethnicity, and the prevalence of hypertension in school-aged children. *Pediatrics, 113,* 475–482.

Sothern, M. S. (2004). Obesity prevention in children: Physical activity and nutrition. *Nutrition, 20,* 704–708.

Souza-Dias, C., Scott, A. B., & Wang, A. H. (2005). Progressive restrictive strabismus acquired in infancy. *British Journal of Ophthalmology, 89,* 986–987.

Sowell, E., & Jernigan, T. (1998). Further MRI evidence of late brain maturation: Limbic volume increases and changing asymmetries during childhood and adolescence. *Developmental Neuropsychology, 14,* 599–617.

Sowter, B., Doyle, L. W., Morley, C. J., Altmann, A., & Halliday, J. (1999). Is sudden infant death syndrome still more common in very low birth weight infants in the 1990s? *Medical Journal of Australia, 171,* 411–413.

Spafford, C. S., & Grosser, G. S. (2005). *Dyslexia and reading difficulties* (2nd ed.). Boston: Allyn & Bacon.

Spandel, V. (2004). *Creating young writers.* Boston: Allyn & Bacon.

Spandorfer, S. D., Davis, O. K., Barmat, L. I., Chung, P. H., & Rosenwaks, Z. (2004). Relationship between maternal age and aneuploidy in in vitro fertilization pregnancy loss. *Obstetrics and Gynecology Survey, 59,* 773–774.

Speakman, J. R. (2004). Obesity: The integrated roles of environment and genetics. *Journal of Nutrition, 134* (Suppl. 8), 2090S-2105S.

Spear, L. P. (2004). Adolescent brain development and animal models. *Annals of the New York Academy of Sciences, 1021,* 23–26.

Spearman, C. E. (1927). *The abilities of man.* New York: Macmillan.

Spelke, E. S. (1979). Perceiving bimodally specified events in infancy. *Developmental Psychology, 5,* 626–636.

Spelke, E. S. (1991). Physical knowledge in infancy: Reflections on Piaget's theory. In S. Carey & R. Gelman (Eds.), *The epigenesis of mind: Essays on biology and cognition.* Hillsdale, NJ: Erlbaum.

Spelke, E. S. (2000). Core knowledge. *American Psychologist, 55,* 1233–1243.

Spelke, E. S., & Hespos, S. J. (2001). Continuity, competence, and the object concept. In E. Dupoux (Ed.), *Language, brain, and behavior.* Cambridge, MA: Bradford/MIT Press.

Spelke, E. S., & Newport, E. L. (1998). Nativism, empiricism, and the development of knowledge. In W. Damon (Ed.), *Handbook of child psychology* (5th ed., Vol. 2). New York: Wiley.

Spelke, E. S., & Owsley, C. J. (1979). Intermodal exploration and knowledge in infancy. *Infant Behavior and Development, 2,* 13–28.

Spelke, E. S., Breinlinger, K., Macomber, J., & Jacobson, K. (1992). Origins of knowledge. *Psychological Review, 99,* 605–632.

Spence, J. T., & Buckner, C. E. (2000). Instrumental and expressive traits, trait stereotypes, and sexist attitudes: What do they signify? *Psychology of Women Quarterly, 24,* 44–62.

Spence, J. T., & Helmreich, R. (1978). *Masculinity and feminity: Their psychological dimensions.* Austin: University of Texas Press.

Spence, M. J., & DeCasper, A. J. (1987). Prenatal experience with low-frequency maternal voice sounds influences neonatal perception of maternal voice samples. *Infant Behavior and Development, 10,* 133–142.

Spencer, J. P., Vereijken, B., Diedrich, F. J., & Thelen, E. (2000). Posture and the emergence of manual skills. *Developmental Science, 3,* 216–233.

Spencer, K. M. (2004). The primal touch of birth: Midwives, mothers, and massage. *Midwifery Today, 70,* 11–13.

Spencer, M. B. (1999). Social and cultural influences on school adjustment: The application of an identity-focused cultural ecological perspective. In K. Wentzel & T. Berndt (Eds.), *Social influences on school adjustment.* Mahwah, NJ: Erlbaum.

Spencer, M. B. (2001). Resiliency and fragility factors associated with the contextual experiences of low-resource urban African-American male youth and families. In A. Booth & A. C. Crouter (Eds.), *Does it take a village?* Mahwah, NJ: Erlbaum.

Spencer, M. B. (2006). Phenomendogy and ecological systems theory: Development of diverse groups. In W. Damon & R. Lerner (Eds.), *Handbook of child psychology* (6th ed.). New York: Wiley.

Spencer, M. B., & Dornbusch, S. M. (1990). Challenges in studying minority youth. In S. S. Feldman & G. R. Elliott (Eds.), *At the threshold: The developing adolescent.* Cambridge, MA: Harvard University Press.

Spencer, M. B., & Harpalani, V. (2004). Nature, nurture, and the question of "how?" In C. G. Coll, E. L. Bearer, & R. M. Lerner (Eds.), *Nature and nurture.* Mahwah, NJ: Erlbaum.

Spencer, M. B., Noll, E., Stoltzfuz, J., & Harpalani, V. (2001). Identity and school adjustment: Revisiting the "acting white" assumption. *Educational Psychologist, 36,* 21–30.

Speranza, M., Corcos, M., Loas, G., Stephan, P., Guilbaud, O., Perez-Diaz, F., Venisse, J. L., Bizouard, P., Halfon, O., Flament, M., & Jeammet, P. (2005). Depressive personality dimensions and alexithymia in eating disorders. *Psychiatry Research, 135,* 153–163.

Spitzer, A. R. (2005). Current controversies in the pathophysiology and prevention of sudden infant death syndrome. *Current Opinion in Pediatrics, 17,* 181–185.

Spitzer, S., Cupp, R., & Parke, R. D. (1995). School entrance age, social acceptance, and self-perceptions in kindergarten and the first grade. *Early Childhood Research Quarterly, 10,* 433–450.

Spooner, A. S. (2004). Preschoolers, computers, and school readiness: Are we onto something? *Pediatrics, 114,* 852.

Spring, J. (2005). *The American school* (6th ed.). New York: McGraw-Hill.

Spring, J. (2006). *American education* (12th ed.). New York: McGraw-Hill.

Springer, S. P., & Deutsch, G. (1985). *Left brain, right brain.* New York: W. H. Freeman.

Srinivasan, S. R., Frontini, M. G., Berensen, G. S., and the Bogalusa Heart Study Group. (2003). Longitudinal changes in risk variables of insulin resistance syndrome from childhood to young adulthood in offspring of parents with type 2 diabetes: The Bogalusa Heart Study. *Metabolism, 5,* 443–450.

Sroufe, L. A. (2000, Spring). The inside scoop on child development: Interview. *Cutting through the hype.* Minneapolis: College of Education and Human Development, University of Minnesota.

Sroufe, L. A., & Waters, E. (1976). The ontogenesis of smiling and laughter: A perspective on the organization of development in infancy. *Psychological Review, 83,* 173–198.

Sroufe, L. A., Egeland, B., & Carlson, E. A. (1999). One social world: The integrated development of parent-child and peer relationships. In W. A. Collins & B. Laursen (Eds.), *Minnesota symposium on child psychology* (Vol. 31). Mahwah, NJ: Erlbaum.

Sroufe, L. A., Egeland, B., Carlson, E., & Collins, W. A. (2005). The place of early attachment in developmental context. In K. E. Grossman, K. Krossman, & E. Waters (Eds.), *The power of longitudinal attachment research: From infancy and childhood to adulthood.* New York: Guilford Press.

Sroufe, L. A., Egeland, B., Carlson, E., & Collins, W. (2005b). *The development of the person: The Minnesota Study of Risk and Adaptation from birth to maturity.* New York: Guilford.

Sroufe, L. A., Waters, E., & Matas, L. (1974). Contextual determinants of infant affectional response. In M. Lewis & L. Rosenblum (Eds.), *Origins of fear.* New York: Wiley.

St. Sauver, J. L., Barbaresi, W. J., Katusie, S. K., Colligan, R. C., Weaver, A. L., & Jacobsen, S. J. (2004). Early life risk factors for attention-deficit/hyperactivity disorder: A population-based cohort study. *Mayo Clinic Proceedings, 79,* 1124–1131.

Stahl, S. (2002, January). *Effective reading instruction in the first grade.* Paper presented at the Michigan Reading Recovery conference, Dearborn, MI.

Stallings, J. (1975). Implementation and child effects of teaching practices in Follow Through classrooms. *Monographs of the Society for Research in Child Development, 40* (Serial No. 163).

Stanford University Medical Center. (2005). *Growth hormone deficiency.* Palo Alto, CA: Author.

Stanhope, L., & Corter, C. (1993, March). *The mother's role in the transition to siblinghood.* Paper presented at the biennial meeting of the Society for Research in Child Development. New Orleans.

Stanley, C., Murray, L., & Stein, A. (2004). The effect of postnatal depression on mother-infant interaction, infant response to the still-face perturbation and performance on the Instrumental Learning Task. *Developmental Psychopathology, 16,* 1–18.

Stanovich, K. E. (2004). *How to think straight about psychology* (7th ed.). Boston: Allyn & Bacon.

Stanwood, G. D., & Levitt, P. (2004). Drug exposure early in life: Functional repercussions of changing neuropharmacology during sensitive periods of brain development. *Current Opinions in Pharmacology, 4,* 65–71.

Starkey, P., Klein, A., & Wakeley, A. (2004). Enhancing young children's mathematical knowledge through a pre-kindergarten mathematics intervention. *Early Childhood Research Quarterly, 19,* 99–120.

Starr, C. (2005). *Biology today and tomorrow.* Pacific Grove, CA: Brooks Cole.

Starr, C. (2006). *Biology* (6th ed.). Pacific Grove, CA: Books Cole.

Stattin, H., & Magnusson, D. (1990). *Pubertal maturation in female development: Paths through life* (Vol. 2). Hillsdale, NJ: Erlbaum.

Steele, C., & Markus, H. R. (2003, November 14). *Stereotype threat and black college students.* Paper presented at the meeting of the Stanford Alumni Association, Palo Alto, CA.

Steele, C. M., & Aronson, J. A. (2004). Stereotype threat does not live by Steele and Aronson (1995) alone. *American Psychologist, 59,* 47–48.

Steen, T. A., Kachorek, L. V., & Peterson, C. (2003). Character strengths among youth. *Journal of Youth and Adolescence, 32,* 5–16.

Steer, A. J., & Lehman, E. B. (2000). Attachment to transitional objects. *American Journal of Orthopsychiatry, 70,* 340–350.

Stegelin, D. A. (2003). Application of Reggio Emilia approach to early childhood science curriculum. *Early Childhood Education Journal, 30,* 163–169.

Stein, M. T. (2004). ADHD: The diagnostic process from different perspectives. *Journal of Developmental and Behavioral Pediatrics, 25* (Suppl. 5), S54–S58.

Stein, M. T., & Perrin, J. M. (2003). Diagnosis and treatment of ADHD in school-age children in primary care settings: A synopsis of the AAP practice guidelines. *Pediatric Review, 24,* 92–98.

Stein, M. T., Kennell, J. H., & Fulcher, A. (2004). Benefits of a doula present at the birth of a child. *Journal of Developmental and Behavioral Pediatrics 25* (No. 5, Supplement), S89–S92.

Steinberg, L. (2004). Risk taking in adolescence: What changes, and why? *Annals of the New York Academy of Sciences, 1021,* 51–58.

Steinberg, L. (2005). Cognitive and affective development in adolescence. *Trends in Cognitive Science, 9,* 69–74.

Steinberg, L., & Caufman, E. (2001). Adolescents as adults in court. *Social Policy Report, SRC D, XV,* no. 4, 1–13.

Steinberg, L., & Silk, J. S. (2002). Parenting adolescents. In M. Bornstein (Ed.), *Handbook of parenting* (2nd ed., Vol. 1). Mahwah, NJ: Erlbaum.

Steinberg, L. D. (1986). Latchkey children and susceptibility to peer pressure: An ecological analysis. *Developmental Psychology, 22,* 433–439.

Steinberg, L. D., & Levine, A. (1997). *You and your adolescent* (2nd ed.). New York: Harper Perennial.

Steinberg, L. D., & Silk, J. S. (2002). Parenting adolescents. In M. Bornstein (Ed.), *Handbook of parenting* (2nd ed., Vol. 1). Mahwah, NJ: Erlbaum.

Steiner, J. E. (1979). Human facial expressions in response to taste and smell stimulation. In H. Reese & L. Lipsitt (Eds.), *Advances in child develop-*

ment and behavior (Vol. 13). New York: Academic Press.

Stepanuk, K. M., Tolosa, J. E., Lewis, D., Myers, V., Royds, C., Sabogal, J. C., & Librizzi, R. (2002). Folic acid supplementation use among women who contact a teratology information service. *American Journal of Obstetrics and Gynecology, 187,* 964–967.

Stephens, B. K., Barkey, M. E., & Hall, H. R. (1999). Techniques to comfort children during stressful procedures. *Advance in Mind-Body Medicine, 15,* 49–60.

Stephenson, J. (2004). FDA warns on mercury in tuna. *Journal of the American Medical Association, 291,* 171.

Steri, A. (1987). Tactile discrimination of shape and intermodal transfer in two- to three-month-old infants. *British Journal of Developmental Psychology, 5,* 213–220.

Stern, D. N., Beebe, B., Jaffe, J., & Bennett, S. L. (1977). The infant's stimulus world during social interaction: A study of caregiver behaviors with particular reference to repetition and timing. In H. R. Schaffer (Ed.), *Studies in mother-infant interaction.* London: Academic Press.

Sternberg, R. J. (1977). *Intelligence, information processing, and analogical reasoning: The componential analysis of human abilities.* Hillsdale, NJ: Erlbaum.

Sternberg, R. J. (1986). *Intelligence applied.* Ft. Worth, TX: Harcourt Brace.

Sternberg, R. J. (1997). Educating intelligence: Infusing the triarchic theory into instruction. In R. J. Sternberg & E. Grigorenko (Eds.), *Intelligence, heredity, and environment.* New York: Cambridge University Press.

Sternberg, R. J. (1999). Intelligence. In M. A. Runco & S. Pritzker (Eds.), *Encyclopedia of creativity.* San Diego: Academic Press.

Sternberg, R. J. (2001). Is there a heredity-environment paradox? In R. J. Sternberg & E. I. Grigorenko (Eds.), *Environmental effects on cognitive abilities.* Mahwah, NJ: Erlbaum.

Sternberg, R. J. (2003). Contemporary theories of intelligence. In I. B. Weiner (Ed.), *Handbook of psychology* (Vol. VII). New York: Wiley.

Sternberg, R. J. (2004). Individual differences in cognitive development. In P. Smith & C. Hart (Eds.), *Blackwell handbook of cognitive development.* Malden, MA: Blackwell.

Sternberg, R. J. (2006). *Cognitive psychology,* (4th ed.). Belmont, CA: Wadsworth.

Sternberg, R. J., & Ben-Zeev, T. (2001). *Complex cognitive processes.* New York: Oxford University Press.

Sternberg, R. J., & Grigorenko, E. I. (Eds.). (2001). *Environmental effects on cognitive abilities.* Mahwah, NJ: Erlbaum.

Sternberg, R. J., & Grigorenko, E. L. (Eds.). (2004). *Culture and competence.* Washington, DC: American Psychological Association.

Sternberg, R. J., & Nigro, C. (1980). Developmental patterns in the solution of verbal analogies. *Child Development 51,* 27–38.

Sternberg, R. J., & Rifkin, B. (1979). The development of analogical reasoning processes. *Journal of Experimental Child Psychology, 27,* 195–232.

Sternberg, R. J., Grigorenko, E. L., & Kidd, K. K. (2005). Intelligence, race, and genetics. *American Psychologist, 60,* 46–59.

Sternberg, R. J., Grigorenko, E. L., & Singer, J. L. (Eds.). (2004). *Creativity: From potential to realization.* Washington, DC: American Psychological Association.

Sternberg, R. J., Nokes, K., Geissler, P. W., Prince, R., Okatcha, F., Bundy, D. A., & Grigorenko, E. L. (2001). The relationship between academic and practical intelligence: A case study in Kenya. *Intelligence, 29,* 401–418.

Sternglanz, S. H., & Serbin, L. A. (1974). Sex-role stereotyping in children's television programming. *Developmental Psychology, 10,* 710–715.

Stetsenko, A., & Arievitch, I. M. (2004). The self in cultural-historical activity theory: Reclaiming the unity of social and individual dimensions of human development. *Theory and Psychology, 14,* 475–503.

Stetsenko, A., Little, T. D., Gordeeva, T., Grasshof, M., & Oettingen, G. (2000). Gender effects in children's beliefs about school performance. *Child Development, 71,* 517–527.

Steur, F. B., Applefield, J. M., & Smith, R. (1971). Televised aggression and interpersonal aggression of preschool children. *Journal of Experimental Child Psychology, 11,* 442–447.

Stevens, J. W. (2005). Lessons learned from poor urban African American youth. In M. Ungar (Ed.), *Handbook for working with children and youth.* Thousand Oaks, CA: Sage.

Stevenson, H. W. (1995). Mathematics achievement of American students: First in the world by the year 2000? In C. A. Nelson (Ed.), *Basic and applied perspectives on learning, cognition, and development.* Minneapolis: University of Minnesota Press.

Stevenson, H. W. (2000). Middle childhood: Education and schooling. In A. Kazadin (Ed.), *Encyclopedia of psychology.* Washington, DC, & New York: American Psychological Association and Oxford University Press.

Stevenson, H. W., & Newman, R. S. (1986). Long-term prediction of achievement and attitudes in mathematics and reading. *Child Development, 57,* 646–659.

Stevenson, H. W., & Zusho, A. (2002). Adolescence in China and Japan: Adapting to a changing environment. In B. B. Brown, R. W. Larson, & T. S. Saraswathi (Eds.), *The world's youth.* New York: Cambridge University Press.

Stevenson, H. W., Hofer, B. K., & Randel, B. (1999). *Middle childhood: Education and schooling.*

Unpublished manuscript, Department of Psychology, University of Michigan, Ann Arbor.

Stevenson, H. W., Lee, S., & Stigler, J. W. (1986). Mathematics achievement of Chinese, Japanese, and American children. *Science, 231,* 693–699.

Stevenson, H. W., Lee, S., Chen, C., Stigler, J. W., Hsu, C., & Kitamura, S. (1990). Contexts of achievement. *Monograph of the Society for Research in Child Development, 55* (Serial No. 221).

Stewart, C. F., Moseley, M. J., Stephens, D. A., & Fielder, A. R. (2004). Treatment-dose-response in amblyopia therapy: The Monitored Occlusion Treatment of Amblyopia Study. *Investigations in Ophthalmologic Vision Science, 45,* 3048–3054.

Stewart, S. D. (2005). How the birth of a child affects involvement with stepchildren. *Journal of Marriage and the Family, 67,* 461–473.

Stice, E. (2002). Risk and maintenance factors for eating pathology: A meta-analytic review. *Psychological Bulleting, 128,* 825–848.

Stice, E., Presnell, K., & Spangler, D. (2002). Risk factors for binge eating onset in adolescent girls: A 2-year prospective investigation. *Health Psychology, 21,* 131–138.

Stipek, D. (2002). *Motivation to learn* (4th ed.). Boston: Allyn & Bacon.

Stipek, D. (2004). Head Start: Can't we have our cake and eat it too. *Education Week, 23* (No. 34), 52–53.

Stipek, D. (2005, February 16), Commentary in *USA TODAY,* p. 1D.

Stipek, D., Recchia, S., & McClintic, S. (1992). Self-evaluation in young children. *Monographs of the Society for Research in Child Development, 57* (1, Serial No. 226).

Stocker, C., & Dunn, J. (1990). Sibling relationships in adolescence: Links with friendships and peer relationships. *British Journal of Developmental Psychology, 8,* 227–244.

Stolley, K. S. (1993). Statistics on adoption in the United States. *The Future of Children, 3,* 26–42.

Stone, K. D. (2004). Advances in pediatric allergy. *Current Opinions in Pediatrics, 16,* 571–578.

Stouthamer-Loeber, M., Loeber, R., Wei, E., Farrington, D. P., & Wikstrom, P. H. (2002). Risk and promotive effects: In the explanation of serious delinquency in boys. *Journal of Consulting and Clinical Psychology, 20,* 111–123.

Strathearn, L. (2003). Long-term cognitive function in very low birth weight infants. *Journal of the American Medical Association, 289,* 2209.

Strauss, M. A. (1991). Discipline and deviance: Physical punishment of children and violence and other crimes in adulthood. *Social Problems, 38,* 133–154.

Strauss, M. A., Sugarman, D. B., & Giles-Sims, J. (1997). Spanking by parents and subsequent anti-social behavior in children.

Archives of Pediatrics and Adolescent Medicine, 151, 761–767.

Strauss, R. S. (2001). Environmental tobacco smoke and serum vitamin C levels in children. *Pediatrics, 107,* 540–542.

Streib, H. (1999). Off-road religion? A narrative approach to fundamentalist and occult orientation of adolescents. *Journal of Adolescence, 22,* 255–267.

Streissguth, A. P., Martin, D. C., Sandman, B. M., Kirchner, G. L., & Darby, B. L. (1984). Intrauterine alcohol and nicotine exposure: Attention and reaction time in four-year-old children. *Developmental Psychology, 20,* 533–543.

Strickland, B. R. (1995). Research on sexual orientation and human development: A commentary. *Developmental Psychology, 31,* 137–140.

Strickland, D. S. (2004). Working with families as partners in literacy. *Reading Teacher, 58,* 86–88.

Striegel-Moore, R. H., Silberstein, L. R., & Rodin, J. (1993). The social self in bulimia nervosa: Public self-consciousness, social anxiety, and perceived fraudulence. *Journal of Abnormal Psychology, 102,* 297–303.

Stroganova, T. A., Pushina, N. P., Orekhova, E. V., Posikera, I. N., & Tsetlin, M. M. (2004). Functional brain asymmetry and individual differences in hand preference in early ontogeny, *Human Physiology, 30,* 20–30.

Styne, D. M. (2004). Puberty, obesity, and ethnicity. *Trends in Endocrinology and Metabolism, 15,* 472–478.

Sue, S. (1990, August). *Ethnicity and culture in psychological research and practice.* Paper presented at the meeting of the American Psychological Association, Boston.

Sugita, Y. (2004). Experience in early infancy is indispensable for color perception. *Current Biology, 14,* 1267–1271.

Sullivan, H. S. (1953). *The interpersonal theory of psychiatry.* New York: W. W. Norton.

Sullivan, J. L. (2003). Prevention of mother-to-child transmission of HIV—what next? *Journal of Acquired Immune Deficiency Syndrome, 34* (Supplement 1), S67–S72.

Sullivan, K., & Sullivan, A. (1980). Adolescent-parent separation. *Developmental Psychology, 16,* 93–99.

Summers, A. M., Farrell, S. A., Huang, T., Meier, C., & Wyatt, P. R. (2004). Maternal serum screening in Ontario using the triple marker test. *Journal of Medical Screening, 10,* 107–111.

Sundelin, C., Magnusson, M., & Lagerberg, D. (2005). Child health services in transition: Theories, methods, and launching. *Acta Pediatrica, 94,* 329–336.

Sung, H.-E., Richter, L., Vaughan, R., Johnson, P. B., & Thom, B. (2005). Nonmedical use of prescription opioids among teenagers in the United States: Trends and correlates. *Journal of Adolescent Health, 37,* 44–51.

Suomi, S. J., Harlow, H. F., & Domek, C. J. (1970). Effect of repetitive infant-infant separations of young monkeys. *Journal of Abnormal Psychology, 76,* 161–172.

Super, C., & Harkness, S. (1997). The cultural structuring of child development. In J. W. Berry, Y. H. Poortinga, & J. Pandey (Eds.), *Handbook of cross-cultural psychology: Vol. 2. Theory and method.* Boston: Allyn & Bacon.

Super, D. E. (1976). *Career education and the meanings of work.* Washington, DC: U.S. Office of Education.

Susman, E. J., & Rogol, A. (2004). Puberty and psychological development. In R. Lerner & L. Steinberg (Eds.), *Handbook of adolescent psychology.* New York: Wiley.

Susman, E. J., Dorn, L. D., & Schiefelbein, V. L. (2003). Puberty, sexuality, and health. In R. M. Lerner, M. A. Easterbrooks, & J. Mistry (Eds.), *Comprehensive handbook of psychology: Developmental psychology* (Vol. 6). New York: Wiley.

Susman, E. J., Murowchick, E., Worrall, B. K., & Murray, D. A. (1995, March). *Emotionality, adrenal hormones, and context interactions during puberty and pregnancy.* Paper presented at the meeting of the Society for Research in Child Development, Indianapolis.

Sutterby, J. A., & Frost, J. L. (2002). Making playgrounds fit for children and children fit for playgrounds. *Young Children, 57* (No. 3), 36–41.

Swaab, D. F., Chung, W. C., Kruijver, F. P., Hofman, M. A., & Ishunina, T. A. (2001). Structural and functional sex differences in the human hypothalamus. *Hormones and Behavior, 40,* 93–98.

Swaab, D. F., Chung, W. C., Kruijver, F. P., Hofman, M. A., & Ishunina, T. A. (2002). Sexual differentiation of the human hypothalamus. *Advances in Experimental Medicine and Biology, 511,* 75–100.

Swanson, H. L. (1999). What develops in working memory? A life-span perspective. *Developmental Psychology, 35,* 986–1000.

Swanson, H. L. (2005). Memory. In S. W. Lee (Ed.), *Encyclopedia of school psychology.* Thousand Oaks, CA: Sage.

Swanson, J. M., & others. (2001). Clinical relevance of the primary findings of MTA: Success rates based on severity of ADHD and ODD symptoms at the end of treatment. *Journal of the American Academy of Child and Adolescent Psychiatry, 40,* 168–179.

Swanson, J. M., & Volkow, N. D. (2002). Pharmacokinetic and pharmacodynamic properties of stimulants: Implications for the design of new treatments for ADHD. *Behavior and Brain Research, 130,* 73–80.

Swarr, A. E., & Richards, M. H. (1996). Longitudinal effects of adolescent girls' pubertal development, perceptions of pubertal timing, and parental relations. *Developmental Psychology, 32,* 636–646.

Swenne, I. (2004). Weight requirements for return of menstruations in teenage girls with eating disorders, weight loss, and secondary amenorrherea. *Acta Pediatrica, 93,* 1449–1455.

Swetlow, K. (2003, June). Children at clandestine methamphetamine labs: Helping meth's youngest victims. *OVC Bulletin.* Available on the Internet at: www.ojp.usdoj.gov/ovc/publications/bulletins/children/welcome.html

Sykes, C. J. (1995). *Dumbing down our kids: Why America's children feel good about themselves but can't read, write, or add.* New York: St. Martin's Press.

T

Tabin, J. K. (1992). Transitional objects as objectifiers of the self in toddlers and adolescents. *Bulletin of the Menninger Clinic, 56,* 209–220.

Tager-Flusberg, H. (2005). Morphology and syntax in the preschool years. In J. Berko Gleason, *The development of language* (6th ed.). Boston: Allyn & Bacon.

Takahashi, K. (1990). Are the key assumptions of the "Strange Situation" procedure universal? A view from Japanese research. *Human Development, 33,* 23–30.

Tang, A. C., & Reeb, B. C. (2004). Neonatal novelty exposure, dynamics of brain asymmetry, and social recognition memory. *Developmental Psychobiology, 44,* 84–93.

Tang, M. P., Chon, H. C., Tsao, K. I., & Hsich, W. S. (2004). Outcome of very low birth weight infants with sonographic enlarged occipital horn. *Pediatric Neurology, 30,* 42–45.

Tannen, D. (1990). *You just don't understand: Women and men in conversation.* New York: Ballamine.

Tappan, M. (2005). Sociocultural approaches to morality. In M. Killen & J. Smetana (Eds.), *Handbook of moral development.* Mahwah, NJ: Erlbaum.

Tappan, M. B. (1998). Sociocultural psychology and caring psychology: Exploring Vygotsky's "hidden curriculum." *Educational Psychologist, 33,* 23–33.

Tasker, F. L., & Golombok, S. (1997). *Growing up in a lesbian family: Effects on child development.* New York: Guilford.

Tassell-Baska, J., & Stambaugh, T. (2006). *Comprehensive curriculum for gifted learners* (3rd ed.). Boston: Allyn & Bacon.

Tavris, C., & Wade, C. (1984). *The longest war: Sex differences in perspective* (2nd ed.), San Diego: Harcourt Brace Jovanovich.

Taylor, H. G., Klein, N., & Hack, M. (1994). Academic functioning in <750 gm birthweight children who have normal cognitive abilities: Evidence for specific learning disabilities. *Pediatric Research, 35,* 289A.

Taylor, H. G., Klein, N., Minich, N. M., & Hack, M. (2000). Middle-school-age outcomes with very low birth weight. *Child Development, 71,* 1495–1511.

Temple, C. A., MaKinster, J. G., Buchmann, L. G., Logue, J., Mrvova, G., & Gearan, M. (2005). *Intervening for literacy.* Boston: Allyn & Bacon.

ten Tusscher, G. W., & Koppe, J. G. (2004). Perinatal dioxin exposure and later effects—a review. *Chemosphere, 54,* 1329–1336.

Terman, D. L., Larner, M. B., Stevenson, C. S., & Behrman, R. E. (1996). Special education for students with disabilities: Analysis and recommendations. *The Future of Children, 6* (No. 1), 4–24.

Terman, L. (1925). *Genetic studies of genius: Vol. 1. Mental and physical traits of a thousand gifted children.* Stanford, CA: Stanford University Press.

Terry, W. S. (2006). *Learning and memory* (3rd ed.). Boston: Allyn & Bacon.

Teti, D. M. (2002). Retrospect and prospects in the study of sibling relationships. In J. P. McHale & W. S. Grolnick (Eds.), *Retrospect and prospect in the psychological study of families.* Mahwah, NJ: Erlbaum.

Teti, D. M., Sakin, J., Kucera, E., Caballeros, M., & Corns, K. M. (1993, March). *Transitions to siblinghood and security of firstborn attachment: Psychosocial and psychiatric correlates of changes over time.* Paper presented at the biennial meeting of the Society for Research in Child Development, New Orleans.

Thapar, A., Fowler, T., Rice, F., Scourfield, J., Van Den Bree, M., Thomas, S., Harold, G., & Hay, D. (2003). Maternal smoking during pregnancy and attention deficit hyperactivity disorder symptoms in offspring. *American Journal of Psychiatry, 160,* 1985–1989.

Tharp, R. G. (1994). Intergroup difference among Native Americans in socialization and child cognition: An erthogenetic analysis. In P. M. Greenfield & R. Cocking (Eds.), *Cross-cultural roots of minority child development.* Mahwah, NJ: Erlbaum.

Tharp, R. G., & Gallimore, R. (1988). *Rousing minds to life: Teaching, learning, and schooling in social context.* New York: Cambridge University Press.

The Conduct Problems Prevention Research Group. (2002). Evaluation of the first 3 years of the Fast Track prevention trial with children at high risk for adolescent conduct problems. *Journal of Abnormal Child Psychology, 30,* 19–35.

Thelen, E. (1995). Motor development: A new synthesis. *American Psychologist, 50,* 79–95.

Thelen, E. (2000). Perception and motor development. In A. Kazdin (Ed.), *Encyclopedia of psychology.* Washington, DC, & New York: American Psychological Association and Oxford University Press.

Thelen, E. (2001). Dynamic mechanisms of change in early perceptual-motor development. In J. L. McClelland & R. S. Siegler (Eds.), *Mechanisms of cognitive development.* Mahwah, NJ: Erlbaum.

Thelen, E., & Smith, L. B. (1998). Dynamic systems theory. In W. Damon (Ed.), *Handbook of child psychology* (5th ed., Vol. 1). New York: Wiley.

Thelen, E., & Smith, L. B. (2006). Dynamic development of action and thought. In W. Damon & R. Lerner (Eds.), *Handbook of child psychology* (6th ed.). New York: Wiley.

Thelen, E., & Whitmeyer, V. (2005). Using dynamic systems theory to conceptualize the interface of perception, action, and cognition. In J. J. Reiser, J. J. Lockman, & C. A. Nelson (Eds.), *The role of action in learning and development.* Mahwah, NJ: Erlbaum.

Thelen, E., Corbetta, D., Kamm, K., Spencer, J. P., Schneider, K., & Zernicke, R. F. (1993). The transition to reaching: Mapping intention and intrinsic dynamics. *Child Development, 64,* 1058–1098.

Theobold, M. A. (2005). *Increasing student motivation.* Thousand Oaks, CA: Sage.

Thiedke, C. C. (2001). Sleep disorders and sleep problems in childhood. *American Family Physician, 63,* 277–284.

Thiessen, E. D., Hill, E. A., & Saffran, J. R. (2005). Infant-directed speech facilitates word segmentation. *Infancy, 7,* 53–71.

Tholin, S., Rasmussen, F., Tynelius, P., & Karlsson, J. (2005). Genetic and environmental influences on eating behavior: the Swedish Young Male Twins Study. *American Journal of Clinical Nutrition, 81,* 564–569.

Thomas, A., & Chess, S. (1991). Temperament in adolescence and its functional significance. In R. M. Lerner, A. C. Petersen, & J. Brooks-Gunn (Eds.), *Encyclopedia of adolescence* (Vol. 2). New York: Garland.

Thomas, R. M. (2005). *Comparing theories of child development* (6th ed.). Belmont, CA: Wadsworth.

Thompson, G. (2004). Common childhood eye problems. *Current Eye Research, 28,* 121–127.

Thompson, J. (2005). Breastfeeding: Benefits and implications. Part One. *Community Practice, 78,* 183–184.

Thompson, J. W., Ryan, K. W., Pindiya, S. D., & Bost, J. E. (2003). Quality of care for children in commercial and Medicaid managed care. *Journal of the American Medical Association, 290,* 1486–1493.

Thompson, P. M., Giedd, J. N., Woods, R. P., MacDonald, D., Evans, A. C., & Toga, A. W. (2000). Growth patterns in the developing brain detected by using continuum mechanical tensor maps. *Nature, 404,* 190–193.

Thompson, R. (2006). The development of the person. In W. Damon & R. Lerner (Eds.), *Handbook of child psychology* (6th ed.). New York: Wiley.

Thompson, R. A. (1994). Emotion regulation: A theme in search of a definition. *Monographs of the Society for Research in Child Development, 59* (Serial No. 240, 2–3).

Thompson, R. A. (2000). Early experience and socialization. In A. Kazdin (Ed.), *Encyclopedia of psychology.* Washington, DC, & New York: American Psychological Association and Oxford University Press.

Thompson, R. A. (2005). Multiple relationships multiply considered. *Human Development, 48,* 102–107.

Thompson, R. A. (2006). The development of the person. In W. Damon & R. Lerner (Eds.), *Handbook of child psychology* (6th ed.). New York: Wiley.

Thompson, R. A., & Goodvin, R. (2005). The individual child, temperament, emotion, self, and personality. In M. H. Bornstein & M. E. Lamb (Eds.), *Developmental science* (5th ed.). Mahwah, NJ: Erlbaum.

Thompson, R. A., & Lagattuta, K. H. (2005). Feeling and understanding: Early emotional development. In K. McCartney & D. Phillips (Eds.), *The Blackwell handbook of early childhood development.* Malden, MA: Blackwell.

Thompson, R. A., & Nelson, C. A. (2001). Developmental science and the media. *American Psychologist, 56,* 5–15.

Thompson, R. A., Easterbrooks, M. A., & Walker, L. (2003). Social and emotional development in infancy. In I. B. Weiner (Ed.), *Handbook of psychology* (Vol. 6). New York: Wiley.

Thoppil, J., Riutcel, T. L., & Nalesnik, S. W. (2005). Early intervention for perinatal depression. *American Journal of Obstetrics and Gynecology, 192,* 1446–1448.

Thorne, C., & Newell, M. L. (2003). Mother-to-child transmission of HIV infection and its prevention. *Current HIV Research, 4,* 447–462.

Thorne, C., & Newell, M. L. (2004). Prevention of mother-to-child transmission of HIV infection. *Current Opinions in Infectious Diseases, 17,* 247–252.

Thornton, A., & Camburn, D. (1989). Religious participation and sexual behavior and attitudes. *Journal of Marriage and the Family, 49,* 117–128.

Thung, S. F., & Grobman, W. A. (2005). The cost-effectiveness of routine antenatal screening for maternal herpes simplex virus-1 and -2 antibodies. *American Journal of Obstetrics and Gynecology, 192,* 483–488.

Thurstone, L. L. (1938). *Primary mental abilities.* Chicago: University of Chicago Press.

Tinsley, B. J. (2003). *How children learn to be healthy.* New York: Cambridge University Press.

Tinsley, B. J., Markey, C. N., Ericksen, A. J., Kwasman, A., & Ortiz, R. V. (2002). Health promotion for parents. In M. H. Bornstein (Ed.),

Handbook of parenting (Vol. 5). Mahwah, NJ: Erlbaum.

Tobin, A. J., & Dusheck, J. (2005). *Asking about life* (3rd ed.). Pacific Grove, CA: Brooks Cole.

Tobin, J. J., Wu, D. Y. H., & Davidson, D. H. (1989). *Preschool in three cultures.* New Haven, CT: Yale University Press.

Tolan, P. H. (2001). Emerging themes and challenges in understanding youth violence. *Journal of Clinical Child Psychology, 30,* 233–239.

Tolmie, A., Thomson, J. A., Foot, H. C., Whelen, K., Morrison, S., & McLaren, B. (2005). The effects of adult guidance and peer discussion on the development of children's representations: Evidence from the training of pedestrian skills. *British Journal of Psychology, 96,* 181–204.

Tomasello, M. (2006). Acquiring linguistic constructions. In W. Damon & R. Lerner (Eds.), *Handbook of child psychology* (6th ed.). New York: Wiley.

Tomasello, M., & Slobin, D. I. (Eds.). (2005). *Beyond nature-nurture.* Mahwah, NJ: Erlbaum.

Tompkins, G. E. (2006). *Literacy for the 21st century* (4th ed.). Upper Saddle River, NJ: Prentice Hall.

Tong, E. K., England, L., & Glantz, S. A. (2005). Changing conclusions on secondhand smoke in a sudden infant death syndrome review funded by the tobacco industry. *Pediatrics, 115,* e356–e366.

Torgesen, J. K. (1999). Reading disabilities. In R. Gallimore, L. P. Bernheimer, D. L. MacMillan, D. L. Speece, & S. Vaughn (Eds.), *Developmental perspectives on children with learning disabilities.* Mahwah, NJ: Erlbaum.

Tough, S. C., Newburn-Cook, C., Johnston, D. W., Svenson, L. W., Rose, S., & Belik, J. (2002). Delayed childbearing and its impact on population rate changes in lower birth weight, multiple birth, and preterm delivery. *Pediatrics, 109,* 399–403.

Tourangeau, R. (2004). Survey research and societal change. *Annual Review of Psychology* (Vol. 55). Palo Alto, CA: Annual Reviews.

Tozer, S. E., Senese, G., & Violas, P. C. (2005). *School and society* (5th ed.). New York: McGraw-Hill.

Trappe, R., Laccone, F., Cobilanschi, J., Meins, M., Huppke, P., Hanefeld, F., & Engel, W. (2001). MECP2 mutations in sporadic cases of Rett syndrome are almost exclusively of paternal origin. *American Journal of Human Genetics, 68,* 1093–1101.

Trasler, J. (2000). Paternal exposures: Altered sex ratios. *Teratology, 62,* 6–7.

Treffers, P. E., Eskes, M., Kleiverda, G., & van Alten, D. (1990). Home births and minimal medical interventions. *Journal of the American Medical Association, 246,* 2207–2208.

Trehub, S. E., Schneider, B. A., Thorpe, L. A., & Judge, P. (1991). Observational measures of auditory sensitivity in early infancy. *Developmental Psychology, 27,* 40–49.

Tremblay, T., Monetta, L., & Joanette, Y. (2004). Phonological processing of words in right- and left-handers. *Brain and Cognition, 55,* 427–432.

Treuth, M. S., Sunehag, A. L., Trautwein, L. M., Bier, D. M., Haywood, M. W., & Butte, N. F. (2003). Metabolic adaptation to high-fat and high-carbohydrate diets in children and adolescents. *American Journal of Clinical Nutrition, 77,* 479–489.

Trimble, J. E. (1989, August). *The enculturation of contemporary psychology.* Paper presented at the meeting of the American Psychological Association, New Orleans.

Tritten, J. (2004). Embracing midwives everywhere. *Practicing Midwife, 7,* 4–5.

Troiano, R. P., & Flegal, K. M. (1998). Overweight children and adolescents: Description, epidemiology, and demographics. *Pediatrics, 101,* 497–504.

Trulear, H. D. (2000). *Faith-based institutions and high-risk youth: First report to the field.* Philadelphia, PA: Public/Private Ventures.

Tsigos, C., & Chrousos, G. P. (2002). Hypothalamic-pituitary-adrenal axis, neuroendocrine factors, and stress. *Journal of Psychosomatic Research, 53,* 865–871.

Tsujimoto, S., Yamamoto, T., Kawaguchi, H., Koizumi, H., & Sawaguchi, T. (2004). Prefrontal cortex activation associated with working memory in adults and preschool children: An event-related optical topography study. *Cerebral Cortex, 14,* 703–712.

Tubman, J. G., & Windle, M. (1995). Continuity of difficult temperament in adolescence: Relations with depression, life events, family support, and substance abuse. *Journal of Youth and Adolescence, 24,* 133–152.

Tucker, L. A. (1987). Television, teenagers, and health. *Journal of Youth and Adolescence, 16,* 415–425.

Tuckman, B. W., & Hinkle, J. S. (1988). An experimental study of the physical and psychological effects of aerobic exercise on school children. In B. G. Melamed, K. A. Matthews, D. K. Routh, B. Stabler, & N. Schneiderman (Eds.), *Child health psychology.* Hillsdale, NJ: Erlbaum.

Tudge, J., & Scrimsher, S. (2003). Lev S. Vygotsky on education: A cultural-historical, interpersonal, and individual approach to development. In B. J. Zimmerman & D. H. Schunk (Eds.), *Educational psychology: A century of contributions.* Mahwah, NJ: Erlbaum.

Tuladhar, R., Harding, R., Cranage, S. M., Adamson, T. M., & Horne, R. S. (2003). Effects of sleep position, sleep state and age on heart rate responses following provoked arousal in term infants. *Early Human Development, 71,* 157–169.

Tutka, P., Wielosz, M., & Zatonski, W. (2003). Exposure to environmental tobacco smoke and children's health. *International Journal of Occupational, Medical, and Environmental Health, 15,* 325–335.

Twenge, J. M., & Campbell, W. K. (2001). Age and birth cohort differences in self-esteem: A cross-temporal meta-analysis. *Personality and Social Psychology Bulletin, 5,* 321–344.

Tyler, C., & Edman, J. C. (2004). Down syndrome, Turner syndrome, and Klinefelter syndrome: Primary care throughout the life span. *Primary Care, 31,* 627–648.

U

U.S. Bureau of the Census. (2002). *National population projections I. Summary files.* Washington, DC: U.S. Bureau of the Census.

U.S. Department of Education. (2001). *Number and disabilities of children and youth served under IDEA.* Washington, DC: Office of Special Education Programs. Data Analysis System.

U.S. Department of Energy. (2001). *The human genome project.* Washington, DC: Author.

U.S. Department of Health and Human Services (DHHS). (2004). Administration on Children, Youth, and Families (ACF). Child maltreatment 2002. Washington, DC: Government Printing Office; 2004. [cited 2005 Jan 1]. Available on the World Wide Web at: www.acf.hhs.gov/programs/cb/publications/cm02/index.htm.

U.S. Food and Drug Administration. (2004, March 19). *An important message for pregnant women and women of childbearing age who may become pregnant about the risk of mercury in fish.* Washington, DC: Author.

U.S. General Accounting Office. (1987, September). *Prenatal care: Medicaid recipients and uninsured women obtain insufficient care.* A report to the Congress of the United States, HRD-97-137. Washington, DC: GAO.

U.S. Office of Education. (2000). *The nation's report card: 2000.* Washington, DC: U.S. Office of Education.

U.S. Office of Education. (2000). *To assure a free and appropriate public education of all children with disabilities.* Washington, DC: Author.

U.S. Preventive Services Task Force. (2004). Screening for visual impairment in children younger than 5 years: Recommendation statement. *Annals of Family Medicine, 2,* 263–266.

Udry, J. R., & others. (1985). Serum androgenic hormones motivate sexual behavior in adolescent boys. *Fertility and Sterility, 43,* 90–94.

Umana-Taylor, A. J. (2004). Ethnic identity and self-esteem: Examining the role of social contexts. *Journal of Adolescence, 27,* 139–146.

Umana-Taylor, M., & Fine, M. A. (2004). Examining ethnic identity among Mexican-origin adolescents living in the United States. *Hispanic Journal of Behavioral Sciences, 26,* 36–59.

Underwood, M. K. (2003). *Social aggression among girls.* New York: Guilford.

Underwood, M. K. (2004). Gender and peer relations: Are the two cultures really all that different? In J. B. Kupersmidt & K. A. Dodge (Eds.), *Children's peer relations: From development to intervention.* Mahwah, NJ: Erlbaum.

Underwood, M. K., Scott, B. L., Galperin, M. B., Bjornstad, G. J., & Sexton, A. M. (2004). An observational study of social exclusion under varied conditions: Gender and developmental differences. *Child Development, 75,* 1538–1555.

Unger, B., Kemp, J. S., Wilins, D., Psara, R., Ledbetter, T., Graham, M., Case, M., & Thach, B. T. (2003). Racial disparity and modifiable risk factors among infants dying suddenly and unexpectedly. *Pediatrics, 111,* E127–E131.

UNICEF. (2001). *UNICEF statistics: Low birthweight.* Geneva: Author.

UNICEF (2003). *The state of the world's children: 2003.* Geneva, SWIT: UNICEF.

UNICEF. (2004). *Progress for children.* Geneva: World Health Organization.

UNICEF. (2004). *The state of the world's children 2004.* Geneva: Author.

Urbano, M. T., & Tait, D. M. (2004). Can the irradiated uterus sustain a pregnancy? *Clinical Oncology, 16,* 24–28.

Urberg, K. (1992). Locus of peer influence: Social crowd and best friend. *Journal of Youth and Adolescence, 21,* 439–450.

V

Vacca, J. A. L., Vacca, R. T., Gove, M. K., Burkey, L. C., Lenhart, L. A., & McKeon, C. A. (2006). *Reading and learning to read* (6th ed.). Boston: Allyn & Bacon.

Vaglenova, J., Birru, S., Pandiella, N. M., & Breese, C. R. (2004). An assessment of long-term developmental and behavioral teatogenicity of prenatal nicotine exposure. *Behavior and Brain Research, 150,* 159–170.

Vahratian, A., Siega-Riz, A. M., Savitz, D. A., & Throp, J. M. (2004). Mutivitamin use and risk of preterm birth. *American Journal Epidemiology, 160,* 886–892.

Valencia, R. R., & Suzuki, L. A. (2001). *Intelligence testing and minority students.* Thousand Oaks, CA: Sage.

Van Buren, E., & Graham, S. (2003). *Redefining ethnic identity: Its relationship to positive and negative school adjustment outcomes for minority youth.* Paper presented at the meeting of the Society for Research in Child Development, Tampa.

Van de Walle, J. A., & Lovin, L. A. (2005). *Teaching student-centered mathematics: Grades K-3.* Boston: Allyn & Bacon.

Van den Bergh, B. R., Mulder, E. J., Mennes, M., & Glover, V. (2005). Antenatal maternal anxiety and stress and the neurobehavioral development of the fetus and child. *Neuroscience and Biobehavioral Review, 29,* 237–258.

van den Boom, D. C. (1989). Neonatal irritability and the development of attachment. In G. A. Kohnstamm, J. E. Bates, & M. K. Rothbart (Eds.), *Temperament in childhood.* New York: Wiley.

Van Egeren, L. A., & Hawkins, D. P. (2004). Coming to terms with coparenting: Implications of definition and measurement. *Journal of Adult Development, 11,* 165–178.

Van Gelder, T. (2005). Teaching critical thinking. *College Teaching, 53,* 41–46.

Van Goozen, S. H. M., Matthys, W., Cohen-Kettenis, P. T., Thisjssen, J. H. H., & van Engeland, H. (1998). Adrenal androgens and aggression in conduct disorder prepubertal boys and normal control. *Biological Psychiatry, 43,* 156–158.

van IJzendoorn, M. H., & Kroonenberg, P. M. (1988). Cross-cultural patterns of attachment: A meta-analysis of the Strange Situation. *Child Development, 59,* 147–156.

Van Rooy, D. L., & Viswesvaran, C. (2004). Emotional intelligence: A meta-analytic Investigation of predictive validity and nomological net. *Journal of Vocational Behavior, 65,* 71–95.

VanBeveren, T. T. (2004, January). *Personal conversation.* Richardson, TX: Department of Psychology, U. of Texas at Dallas.

Vandell, D. L. (2004). Early child care: The known and unknown. *Merrill-Palmer Quarterly, 50,* 387–414.

Vandell, D. L., & Wilson, K. S. (1988). Infant's interactions with mother, sibling, and peer: Contrasts and relations between interaction systems. *Child Development, 48,* 176–186.

Vargas, L., & Koss-Chiono, J. (1999). *Working with Latino youth.* San Francisco. Jossey-Bass.

Vastag, B. (2004). Does video game violence sow aggression? *Journal of the American Medical Association, 291,* 1822–1824.

Ventura, S. J., Hamilton, B. E., Mathews, T. J., & Chandra, A. (2003). Trends and variations in smoking during pregnancy and low birth weight: Evidence from the birth certificate, 1990–2000. *Pediatrics, 111,* 1176–1180.

Ventura, S. J., Martin, J. A., Curtin, S. C., & Mathews, T. J. (1997, June 10). *Report of final natality statistics, 1995.* Washington, DC: National Center for Health Statistics.

Vesely, S. K., Wyatt, V. H., Oman, R. F., Aspy, C. B., Kegler, M. C., Rodine, S., Marshall, L., & McLeroy, K. R. (2004). The potential protective effects of youth assets from adolescent sexual risk behaviors. *Journal of Adolescent Health, 34,* 356–365.

Victora, G. C., Bryce, J., Fontaine, O., & Monasch, R. (2000). Reducing deaths from diarrhoea through oral rehydration therapy. *Bulletin of the World Health Organization, 78,* 1246–1255.

Vidaeff, A. C., & Mastrobattista, J. M. (2003). In utero cocaine exposure: A thorny mix of science and mythology. *American Journal of Perinatology, 20,* 165–172.

Vidal, F. (2000). Piaget's theory. In A. Kazdin (Ed.), *Encyclopedia of psychology.* Washington, DC, & New York: American Psychological Association and Oxford University Press.

Vidyasagar, T. R. (2004). Neural underpinnings of dyslexia as a disorder of visuo-spatial attention. *Clinical and Experimental Optometry, 87,* 4–10.

Villevielle, T., Mercier, F., Shannon, P. E., Auroy, Y., & Benhamou, D. (2003). Efficacy of epidural analgesia during labor and delivery: A comparison of singleton vertex presentation, breech presentation, and twin pregnancies. *European Journal of Anaesthesiology, 20,* 164–165.

Vinckenbosch, E., Robichon, F., & Eliez, S. (2005). Gray matter alteration in dyslexia: Converging evidence from volumetric and voxel-by-voxel MRI analyses. *Neuropsychologia 43,* 324–331.

Vintzileos, A. M., Ananath, C. V., Smulian, J. C., Scoraza, W. E., & Knuppel, R. A. (2002). The impact of prenatal care on post-neonatal deaths in the presence and absence of antenatal high-risk conditions. *American Journal of Obstetrics and Gynecology, 187,* 1258–1262.

Voelker, R. (2004). Stress, sleep loss, and substance abuse create potent recipe for college depression. *Journal of the American Medical Association, 291,* 2177–2179.

Voeller, K. K. (2004a). Dyslexia. *Journal of Child Neurology, 19,* 740–744.

Voeller, K. K. (2004b). Attention-deficit hyperactivity disorder. *Journal of Child Neurology, 19,* 798–814.

Volkmar, F. R., Lord, C., Bailey, A., Schultz, R. T., & Klin, A. (2004). Autism and pervasive developmental disorders. *Journal of Child Psychology and Psychiatry, 45,* 135–170.

Volterra, V., Caselli, M. C., Capirici, O., & Pizzuto, E. (2005). Gesture and the emergence and development of language. In M.Tomasello & D. I. Slobin (Eds.), *Beyond nature-nurture.* Mahwah, NJ: Erlbaum.

Vondracek, F. W., & Porfeli, E. J. (2003). The world of work and careers. In G. Adams & M. Berzonsky (Eds.), *Blackwell handbook of adolescence.* Malden, MA: Blackwell.

Vonk, J. M., Postma, D. S., Boezen, H. M., Grol, M. H., Schouten, J. P., Koeter, G. H., & Gerritsen, J. (2004). Childhood factors associated with asthma remission after year follow up. *Thorax, 59,* 925–929.

Votrub-Drzal, E., Coley, R. L., & Chase-Lansdale, P. L. (2004). Child care and low-income children's development: Direct and moderated effects. *Child Development, 75,* 296–312.

Vreugdenhil, H. J., Mulder, P. G., Emmen, H. H., & Weisglas-Kuperus, N. (2004). Effects of perinatal exposure to PCBs on neuropsychological functions in the Rotterdam cohort at 9 years of age. *Neuropsychology, 18,* 185–193.

Vurpillot, E. (1968). The development of scanning strategies and their relation to visual differentiation. *Journal of Experimental Child Psychology, 6,* 632–650.

Vygotsky, L. S. (1962). *Thought and language.* Cambridge, MA: MIT Press.

W

Wachs, T. D. (1995). Relation of mild-to-moderate malnutrition to human development: Correlational studies. *Journal of Nutrition Supplement, 125,* 2245s-2254s.

Wachs, T. D. (2000). *Necessary but not sufficient.* Washington, DC: American Psychological Association.

Wadhwa, P. D. (2005). Psychoneuroendocrine processes in human pregnancy influence fetal development and health. *Psychoneuroendocrinology, 30,* 724–743.

Wadsworth, S. J., Olson, R. K., Pennington, B. F., & DeFries, J. C. (2004). Differential genetic etiology of reading disability as a function of IQ. *Journal of Learning Disabilities, 33,* 192–199.

Wagstaff, A., Bustreo, F., Bryce, J., Claeson, M., and the WHO-World Bank Child Health and Poverty Working Group. (2004). Child health: Reaching the poor. *American Journal of Public Health, 94,* 726–736.

Waibel, R., & Misra, R. (2003). Injuries to preschool children and infection control practices in childcare programs. *Journal of School Health, 73,* 167–172.

Waikart, L., & Blaiss, M. S. (2004). Pharmacologic therapy for the treatment of asthma in children. *Minerva Pediatrics, 56,* 457–467.

Wainryb, C. (2005). Culture and morality. In M. Killen & J. Smetana (Eds.), *Handbook of moral development.* Mahwah, NJ: Erlbaum.

Wake, M., & Poulakis, Z. (2004). Slight and mild hearing loss in primary school children. *Journal of Pediatrics and Child Health, 40,* 11–13.

Wakefield, J. (2001). Toxic inheritance: Fathers' job may mean cancer for kids. *Environmental Health Perspectives, 109,* 193–196.

Walden, T. (1991). Infant social referencing. In J. Garber & K. Dodge (Eds.), *The development of emotional regulation and dysregulation.* New York: Cambridge University Press.

Waldfogel, J. (2004). A cross-national perspective on policies to promote investments in children. In A. Kalil & T. DeLeire (Eds.), *Family investments in children's potential.* Mahwah, NJ: Erlbaum.

Wales, C. (2003). Recognizing dyslexia. *British Journal of General Practice, 53,* 153–154.

Walker, E. F. (2002). Adolescent neurodevelopment and psychopathology. *Current Directions in Psychological Science, 1,* 24–28.

Walker, H. (1998, May 31). Youth violence: Society's problem. *Eugene Register Guard,* p. 1C.

Walker, L. (2005). Gender and morality. In M. Killen & J. Smetana (Eds.), *Handbook of moral development.* Mahwah, NJ: Erlbaum.

Walker, L. J. (2002). Moral exemplarity. In W. Damon (Ed.), *Bringing in a new era of character education.* Stanford, CA: Hoover Press.

Walker, L. J., & Hennig, K. H. (2004). Differing conceptions of moral exemplars: Just, brave, and caring. *Journal of Personality and Social Psychology, 86,* 629–647.

Walker, L. J., & Reimer, K. S. (2005). The relationship between moral and spiritual development. In E. C. Roehkepartain, P. E. King, L. Wagner, & P. L. Benson (Eds.), *Handbook of spiritual development in childhood and adolescence.* Thousand Oaks, CA: Sage.

Walker, S. O., Petrill, S. A., & Plomin, R. (2005). A genetically sensitive investigation of the effects of the school environment and socioeconomic status on academic achievement in seven-year-olds. *Educational Psychology, 25,* 55–63.

Wallerstein, J. S., & Johnson-Reitz, L. (2004). Communication in divorced and single parent families. In A. L. Vaneglisti (Ed.), *Handbook of family communication.* Mahwah, NJ: Erlbaum.

Walsh, L. A. (2000, Spring). The Inside scoop on child development: Interview. *Cutting through the hype.* Minneapolis: College of Education & Human Development, University of Minnesota.

Walsh, W. B., & Betz, N. E. (2001). *Tests and measurement* (4th ed.). Upper Saddle River, NJ: Prentice-Hall.

Walters, E., & Kendler, K. S. (1994). Anorexia nervosa and anorexia-like symptoms in a population based twin sample. *American Journal of Psychiatry, 152,* 62–71.

Waltman, P. A., Brewer, J. M., Rogers, B. P., & May, W. L. (2004). Building evidence for practice: A pilot study of newborn bulb suctioning at birth. *Journal of Midwifery and Women's Health, 49,* 32–38.

Wang, J. Q. (2000, November). *A comparison of two international standards to assess child and adolescent obesity in three populations.* Paper presented at the meeting of American Public Health Association, Boston.

Wang, S. H., Baillargeon, R., & Paterson, S. (2005). Detecting continuity violations in infancy: A new account and new evidence from covering and tube events. *Cognition, 95,* 129–173.

Wang, Y., Monteiro, C., & Popkin, B. M. (2002). Trends in obesity and underweight in older children and adolescents in the United States, Brazil, China, and Russia. *American Journal of Clinical Nutrition, 75,* 971–977.

Ward, L. M. (2003). Understanding the role of entertainment media in the sexual socialization of American youth: A review of empirical research. *Developmental Review, 23,* 347–388.

Ward, L. M., & Caruthers, A. (2001). Media influences. In J. Worrell (Ed.), *Encyclopedia of women and gender.* San Diego: Academic Press.

Wardlaw, G. M. (2006). *Contemporary nutrition* (6th ed.). New York: McGraw-Hill.

Wardle, F. (2003). *Introduction to early childhood education.* Boston: Allyn & Bacon.

Wardle, F. (2003). *Introduction to special education.* Boston: Allyn & Bacon.

Wardle, J., Cooke, E. J., Gibson, E. L., Sapochnik, M., Sheiham, A., & Lawson, M. (2003). Increasing children's acceptance of vegetables: A randomized trial of parent-led exposure. *Appetite, 40,* 155–162.

Wark, G. R., & Krebs, D. L. (1996). Gender and dilemma differences in real-life moral judgment. *Developmental Psychology, 32,* 220–230.

Warrick, P. (1992, March 1). The fantastic voyage of Tanner Roberts, *Los Angeles Times,* pp. E1, E11, E12.

Warshak, R. A. (2004, January). Personal communication, Department of Psychology, University of Texas at Dallas, Richardson.

Watemberg, N., Silver, S., Harel, S., & Lerman-Sagie, T. (2002). Significance of microcephaly among children with developmental abilities. *Journal of Child Neurology, 17,* 117–122.

Waterman, A. S. (1992). Identity as an aspect of optimal psychological functioning. In G. R. Adams, T. P. Gullotta, & R. Montemayor (Eds.), *Adolescent identity formation.* Newbury Park, CA: Sage.

Waters, E., Corcoran, D., & Anafara, M. (2005). Attachment, other relationships, and the theory that all good things go together. *Human Development, 48,* 85–88.

Watras, J. (2002). *The foundations of educational curriculum and diversity: 1565 to the present.* Boston: McGraw-Hill.

Watson, J. B. (1928). *Psychological care of infant and child.* New York: W. W. Norton.

Watson, J. B., & Rayner, R. (1920). Conditioned emotional reactions. *Journal of Experimental Psychology, 3,* 1–14.

Watson, M., Kash, K. M., Homewood, J., Ebbs, S., Murday, V., & Eeles, R. (2005). Does genetic counseling have any impact on management of breast cancer risk? *Genetic Testing, 9,* 167–174.

Waxman, S. R. (2004). Early word-learning and conceptual development. In U. Goswami (Ed.), *Blackwell handbook of infant development.* Malden, MA: Blackwell.

Waxman, S. R., & Lidz, J. L. (2006). Early word learning. In W. Damon & R. Lerner (Eds.), *Handbook of child psychology* (6th ed.). New York: Wiley.

Waylen, A., & Wolke, D. (2004). Sex 'n' rock 'n' roll: The meaning and social consequences of pubertal timing. *European Journal of Endocrinology, 151* (Suppl. 3), U151–159.

Weaver, A., & Dobson, P. (2004). Home and dry—Some toilet training tips to give parents. *Journal of Family Health Care, 14,* 64, 66.

Weber, E. (2005). *MI strategies in the classroom and beyond.* Boston: Allyn & Bacon.

Webster, W. S., & Freeman, J. A. (2003). Prescription drugs and pregnancy. *Expert Opinions in Pharmacotherapy, 4,* 949–961.

Webster-Stratton, C., & Reid, J. M. (2004). Strengthening social and emotional competence in children—The foundation for early school readiness and success. *Infants and Young Children, 17,* 96–115.

Wehrens, X. H., Offermans, J. P., Snijders, M., & Peeters, L. L. (2004). Fetal cardiovascular response to large placental chorionangiomas. *Journal of Perinatal Medicine, 32,* 107–112.

Weikart, D. P. (1982). Preschool education for disadvantaged children. In J. R. Travers & R. J. Light (Eds.), *Learning from experience: Evaluating early childhood demonstration programs.* Washington, DC: National Academy Press.

Weikart, D. P. (1993). *Long-term positive effects in the Perry Preschool Head Start Program.* Unpublished data. High Scope Foundation, Ypsilanti, MI.

Weikart, P. S. (1987). *Round the circle: Key experiences in movement for children ages 3 to 5.* Ypsilanti, MI: High/Scope Press.

Weincke, J. K., Thurston, S. W., Kelsey, K. T., Varkonyi, A., Wain, J. C., Mark, E. J., & Christiani, D. C. (1999). Early age at smoking initiation and tobacco carcinogen DNA damage in the lung. *Journal of the National Cancer Institute, 91,* 614–619.

Weinraub, M., Horuath, D. L., & Gringlas, M. B. (2002). Single parenthood. In M. H. Bornstein (Ed.), *Handbook of parenting* (2nd ed., Vol. 3). Mahwah, NJ: Erlbaum.

Weinstock, M. (2005). The potential influence of maternal stress hormones on development and mental health of the offspring. *Brain, Behavior, and Immunology, 19,* 296–308.

Weiss, A. H., & Kelly, J. P. (2004). Spatial-frequency-dependent changes in cortical activation before and after patching in amblyopic children. *Investigations in Ophthalmologic Vision Science, 45,* 3531–3537.

Weiss, R. E. (2001). *Pregnancy and birth: Rh factor in pregnancy.* Available on the Internet at: http://www.about.com.

Weisz, A. N., & Black, B. M. (2002). Gender and moral reasoning: African American youth respond to dating dilemmas. *Journal of Human Behavior in the Social Environment, 5,* 35–52.

Weizmann, F. (2000). Bowlby, John. In A. Kazdin (Ed.), *Encyclopedia of psychology.* Washington, DC, & New York: American Psychological Association and Oxford U. Press.

Wellman, H. M. (1997, April). *Ten years of theory of mind: Telling the story backwards.* Paper presented at the meeting of the Society for Research in Child Development. Washington, DC.

Wellman, H. M. (2000). Early Childhood. In A. Kazdin (Ed.), *Encyclopedia of psychology.* Washington, DC, & New York: American Psychological Association and Oxford University Press.

Wellman, H. M. (2004). Understanding the psychological world: Developing a theory of mind. In U. Goswami (Ed.), *Blackwell handbook of childhood cognitive development.* Malden, MA: Blackwell.

Wellman, H. M., Cross, D., & Watson, J. (2001). Meta-analysis of theory-of-mind development: The truth about false belief. *Child Development, 72,* 655–684.

Welsh, D. P., Grello, C. M., & Harper, M. S. (2003). When love hurts: Depression and adolescent romantic relations. In P. Florsheim (Ed.), *Adolescent romantic relations and sexual behavior.* Mahwah, NJ: Erlbaum.

Welsh, L., Roberts, R. G., & Kemp, J. G. (2004). Fitness and physical activity in children with asthma. *Sports Medicine, 34,* 861–870.

Wen, S.W., & Walker, M. (2005). An exploration of health effects of folic acid in pregnancy beyond reducing neural tube defects. *Journal of Obstetrics and Gynecology Canada, 27,* 13–19.

Wentzel, K. R., & Asher, S. R. (1995). The academic lives of neglected, rejected, popular, and controversial children. *Child Development, 66,* 754–763.

Wentzel, K. R., Barry, C. M., & Caldwell, K. A. (2004). Friendships in middle school: Influences on motivation and school adjustment. *Journal of Educational Psychology, 96,* 195–203.

Wenze, G. T., & Wenze, N. (2004). Helping left-handed children adapt to school expectations. *Childhood Education, 81,* 25–31.

Werth, J. L. (2004). The relationships among clinical depression, suicide, and other actions that may hasten death. *Behavioral Science and the Law, 22,* 627.

Wesley, P. W., & Buysse, V. (2003). Making meaning of school readiness in schools and communities. *Early Childhood Research Quarterly, 18,* 351–375.

West, J., Denton, K., & Germino-Hausken, E. (2000). *America's kindergartners.* Washington, DC: National Center for Education Statistics.

West, J. R., & Blake, C. A. (2005). Fetal alcohol syndrome: an assessment of the field. *Experimental Biology and Medicine, 230,* 354–356.

Whalen, C. K. (2001). ADHD treatment in the 21st century: Pushing the envelope. *Journal of Clinical Child Psychology, 30,* 136–140.

Wheeler, P. G., Bresnahan, K., Shephard, B. A., Lau, J., & Balk, E. M. (2004). Short stature and functional impairments: A systematic review. *Archives of Pediatric and Adolescent Medicine, 158,* 236–243.

White, A. M. (2005). The changing adolescent brain. *Education Canada, 45* (No. 2), 4–7.

White, B., Castle, P., & Held, R. (1964). Observations on the development of visually directed reaching. *Child Development, 35,* 349–364.

White, C. W., & Coleman, M. (2000). *Early childhood education.* Columbus, OH: Merrill.

White, F. A., & Matawic, K. M. (2004). Parental morality and family processes as predictors of morality. *Journal of Child and Family Studies, 13,* 219–233.

White, J. W. (2001). Aggression and gender. In J. Worell (Ed.), *Encyclopedia of gender and women.* San Diego: Academic Press.

White, M. (1993). *The material child: Coming of age in Japan and America.* New York: Free Press.

White, S. H. (1995, March). *The children's cause: Some early organizations.* Paper presented at the meeting of the Society for Research in Child Development, Indianapolis.

Whiting, B. B. (1989, April). *Culture and interpersonal behavior.* Paper presented at the biennial meeting of the Society for Research in Child Development. Kansas City.

Whiting, B. B., & Edwards, C. P. (1988). *Children of different worlds.* Cambridge, MA: Harvard University Press.

Whiting, J. (1981). Environmental constraint on infant care practices. In R. L. M. R. H. Munroe, & B. Whiting (Eds.), *Handbook of cross-cultural human development.* New York: Garland STPM Press.

Whitley, B. E. (2002). *Principles of research in behavioral science* (2nd ed.). New York: McGraw-Hill.

Wiersma, W. W., & Jurs, S. G. (2005). *Research methods in education* (8th ed.). Boston: Allyn & Bacon.

Wigfield, A., Eccles, J. S., Schiefele, U., Roeser, R., & Davis-Kean, P. (2006). Development of achievement motivation. In W. Damon & R. Lerner (Eds.), *Handbook of child psychology* (6th ed.). New York: Wiley.

Wilens, T. E., & Dodson, W. (2004). A clinical perspective on attention-deficit/hyperactivity disorder into adulthood. *Journal of Clinical Psychiatry, 65,* 1301–1313.

Willford, J. A., Richardson, G. A., Leech, S. L., & Day, N. L. (2004). Verbal and visuospatial learning and memory function in children with moderate prenatal alcohol exposure. *Alcoholism: Clinical and Experimental Research, 28,* 497–507.

William T. Grant Foundation Commission on Work, Family, and Citizenship. (1988). *The forgotten half: Non-college-bound youth in America.* New York: William T. Grant Foundation.

Williams, C. R. (1986). *The impact of television. A natural experiment in three communities.* New York: Academic Press.

Williams, D. D., Yancher, S. C., Jensen, L. C., & Lewis, C. (2003). Character education in a public high school: A multi-year inquiry into unified studies. *Journal of Moral Education, 32,* 3–33.

Williams, F., & Schmidt, M. (2003, April). *Parent and peer relationships predicting early adolescent sexual behavior.* Paper presented at the meeting of the Society for Research in Child Development, Tampa.

Williams, J. B., & Best, D. L. (1982). *Measuring sex stereotypes: A thirty-nation study.* Newbury Park. CA: Sage.

Williams, J. B., & Best, D. L. (1989). *Sex and psyche: Self-concept viewed cross-culturally.* Newbury Park, CA: Sage.

Williams, M. H. (2005). *Nutrition* (7th ed.). New York: McGraw-Hill.

Williams, W. M., Papierno, P. B., Makel, M. C., & Ceci, S. J. (2004). Thinking like a scientist about real-world problems: The Cornell Institute for Research on Children Science Education Program. *Applied Developmental Psychology, 25,* 107–126.

Willis, W. O., Eder, C. H., Lindsay, S. P., Chavez, G., & Shelton, S. T. (2004). Lower rates of low birth weight and preterm births in the California Black Infant Health Program. *Journal of the National Medical Association, 96,* 315–324.

Wills-Karp, M., Brandt, D., & Morrow, A. L. (2004). Understanding the origin of asthma and its relationship to breastfeeding. *Advances in Experimental Medicine and Biology, 554,* 171–191.

Wilson, B. (2001, April). *The role of television in children's emotional development and socialization.* Paper presented at the meeting of the Society for Research in Child Development, Minneapolis.

Wilson, G. S., Pritchard, M. E., & Revalee, B. (2005). Individual differences in adolescent health symptoms: The effects of gender and coping. *Journal of Adolescence, 28,* 369–379.

Wilson, M. N. (2000). Cultural diversity. In A. Kazdin (Ed.), *Encyclopedia of psychology.* Washington, DC, & New York: American Psychological Association and Oxford University Press.

Wilson-Shockley, S. (1995). *Gender differences in adolescent depression: The contribution of negative affect.* M. S. thesis, University of Illinois at Urbana-Champaign.

Windle, M., & Windle, R. C. (2003). Alcohol and other substance use and abuse. In G. Adams & M. Berzonsky (Eds.), *Blackwell handbook of adolescence.* Malden, MA: Blackwell.

Windle, W. F. (1940). *Physiology of the human fetus.* Philadelphia: Saunders.

Winn, I. J. (2004). The high cost of uncritical teaching. *Phi Delta Kappan, 85,* 496–497.

Winner, E. (1986, August). Where pelicans kiss seals. *Psychology Today,* pp. 24–35.

Winner, E. (1996). *Gifted children: Myths and realities.* New York: Basic Books.

Winner, E. (2006). Development in the arts. In W. Damon & R. Lerner (Eds.), *Handbook of child psychology* (6th ed.). New York: Wiley.

Winsler, A., Carlton, M. P., & Barry, M. J. (2000). Age-related changes in preschool children's systematic use of private speech in natural setting. *Journal of Child Language, 27,* 665–687.

Winsler, A., Caverly, S. I., Willson-Quayle, A., Carlton, M. P., & Howell, C. (2002). The social and behavioral ecology of mixed-age and same-age preschool classrooms: A natural experiment. *Journal of Applied Developmental Psychology, 23,* 305–330.

Winsler, A., Diaz, R. M., & Montero, I. (1997). The role of private speech in the transition from collaborative to independent task performance in young children. *Early Childhood Research Quarterly, 12,* 59–79.

Wintre, M. G., & Vallance, D. D. (1994). A developmental sequence in the comprehension of emotions: Intensity, multiple emotions, and valence. *Developmental Psychology, 30,* 509–514.

Wiseman, C. V., Sunday, S. R., & Becker, A. E. (2005). Impact of the media on adolescent body image. *Child and Adolescent Psychiatric Clinics of North America, 14,* 453–471.

Wisniewski, A. B., Migeon, C. J., Meyer-Bahlburg, H. F. L., Gearhart, J. P., Berkovitz, G. D., Brown, T. R., & Money, J. (2000). Complete androgen insensitivity syndrome: Long-term medical, surgical, and psychosexual outcome. *The Journal of Clinical Endocrinology and Metabolism, 85,* 2664–2669.

Wisotsky, W., & Swencionis, C. (2003). Cognitive-behavioral approaches to the management of obesity. *Adolescent Medicine, 14,* 37–48.

Witkin, H. A., Mednick, S. A., Schulsinger, R, Bakkestrom, E., Christiansen, K. O., Goodenbough, D. R., Hirchhorn, K., Lunsteen, C., Owen, D. R., Philip, J., Ruben, D. B., & Stocking, M. (1976). Criminality in XYY and XXY men. *Science, 192,* 547–555.

Wolfe, W. S., Campbell, C., Fongillo, E. A., Haas, J. D., & Melnick, T. A. (1994). Overweight school children in New York State: Prevalence and characteristics. *American Journal of Public Health, 84,* 807–813.

Wolff, P. (1969). The natural history of crying and other vocalizations in infants. In B. M. Foss (Ed.), *The competent infant: Research and commentary.* New York: Basic Books.

Wolters, C. A. (2004). Advancing achievement goal theory: Using goal structures and goal ori-

entations to predict students' motivation, cognition, and achievement. *Journal of Educational Psychology, 96,* 236–250.

Wong, A. H., Gottesman, I. I., & Petronis, A. (2005). Phenotypic differences in genetically different organisms: The epigenetic perspective. *Human Molecular Genetics, 14,* R11–18.

Wong, D. L., Hockenberry-Eaton, M., Wilson, D., Winkelsein, M. L., & Schwartz, P. (2001). *Wong's essentials of pediatric nursing* (6th ed.). St. Louis: Mosby.

Wong, D. L., Hockenberry, M. J., Wilson, D., Winkelstein, M. L., & Kline, N. E. (2003). *Whaley & Wong's nursing care of infants and children.* St. Louis: Mosby.

Wong, D. L., Perry, S. E., & Hockenberry, M. (2001). *Maternal child nursing care* (2nd ed.). St. Louis: Mosby.

Wong, K. (2004). Baby talk beginnings. *Scientific American, 291,* 30–31.

Wong, S. T., Korenbrot, C. C., & Stewart, A. L. (2004). Consumer assessment of the quality of prenatal care among ethnically diverse low-income women: Development of a new measure. *Women's Health Issues, 14,* 118–129.

Woo, K. S., Chook, P., Yu, C. W., Suung, R. Y., Qiao, M., Leung, S. S., Law, C. W., Metreweli, C., & Celermajer, D. S. (2004). Effects of diet and exercise on obesity-related vascular dysfunction in children. *Circulation, 109,* 1981–1986.

Wood, A. G., Harvey, A. S., Wellard, R. M., Abbott, D. F., Anderson, V., Kean, M., Saling, M. M., & Jackson, G. D. (2004). Language cortex activation in normal children. *Neurology, 63,* 1035–1044.

Wood, J. W. (2006). *Teaching students in inclusive settings* (5th ed.). Upper Saddle River, NJ: Prentice Hall.

Woodward, A. L., & Markman, E. M. (1998). Early word learning. In D. Kuhn & R. S. Siegler (Eds.), *Handbook of child psychology* (5th ed., Vol. 2). New York: Wiley.

Worku, B., & Kassie, A. (2005). Kangaroo mother care: A randomized controlled trial on effectiveness of early kangaroo care for low birthweight infants in Addis Ababa, Ethiopia. *Journal of Tropical Pediatrics, 51,* 93–97.

World Health Organization. (2000, February 2). *Adolescent health behavior in 28 countries.* Geneva: Author.

Worobey, J., & Belsky, J. (1982). Employing the Brazelton scale to influence mothering: An experimental comparison of three strategies. *Developmental Psychology, 18,* 736–743.

Wright, M. R. (1989). Body image satisfaction in adolescent girls and boys. *Journal of Youth and Adolescence, 18,* 71–84.

Wroblewski, R., & Huston, A. C. (1987). Televised occupational stereotypes and their effects on early adolescents: Are they changing? *Journal of Early Adolescence, 7,* 283–297.

Wyganski-Jaffe, T. (2005). The effect on pediatric ophthalmologists of the randomized trial of patching regimens for treatment of moderate amblyopia. *Journal of the American Optometric Association, 9,* 208–211.

Y

Yang, C. K., Kim, J. K., Patel, S. R., & Lee, J. H. (2005). Age-related changes in sleep/wake patterns among Korean teenagers. *Pediatrics, 115* (Suppl. 1), S250–S256.

Yang, S., & Sternberg, R. J. (1997). Taiwanese Chinese people's conceptions of intelligence. *Intelligence, 25,* 21–36.

Yang, Y., May, Y., Ni, L., Zhao, S., Li, L., Zhang, J., Fan, M., Liang, C., Cao, J., & Xu, L. (2003). Lead exposure through gestation-only caused long-term memory deficits in young adult offspring. *Experimental Neurology, 184,* 489–495.

Yasui, M., Dorham, C. L., & Dshion, T. J. (2004). Ethnic identity and psychological adjustment: A validity analysis for European American and African American adolescents. *Journal of Adolescent Research, 19,* 807–825.

Yates, M. (1995, March). *Political socialization as a function of volunteerism.* Paper presented at the meeting of the Society for Research in Child Development, Indianapolis.

Yeung, W. J., Linver, M. R., & Brooks-Gunn, J. (2002). How money matters for young children's development: Investment and family process. *Child Development, 73,* 1861–1879.

Ying, G. S., Kulp, M. T., Maguirre, M., Ciner, E., Cyert, L., Schmidt, P., & the Vision in Preschoolers Study Group. (2005). Sensitivity in screening tests for detecting vision in preschoolers—Targeted vision disorders when specificity is 94%. *Optometry and Vision Science, 82,* 432–438.

Young, K. T. (1990). American conceptions of infant development from 1955 to 1984: What the experts are telling parents. *Child Development, 61,* 17–28.

Youngquist, J., & Pataray-Ching, J. (2004). Revisiting "play": Analyzing and articulating acts of inquiry. *Early Childhood Education Journal, 31,* 171–178.

Youniss, J., & Silbereisen, V. (2003). Civic and community engagement of adolescents in the 21st century. In G. Adams & M. Berzonsky (Eds.), *Blackwell handbook of adolescence.* Malden, MA: Blackwell.

Youniss, J., McLellan, J. A., & Yates, M. (1999). Religion, community service, and identity in American youth. *Journal of Adolescence, 22,* 243–253.

Youniss, J., Silbereisen, R., Christmas-Best, V., Bales, S., Diversi, M., & McLaughlin, M. (2003). Civic and community engagement of adolescents in the 21st century. In R. Larson, B. Brown, & J. Mortimer (Eds.), *Adolescents' preparation for the future: Perils and promises.* Malden, MA: Blackwell.

Yu, C. W., Sung, R. Y., So, R., Lam, K., Nelson, E. A., Li, A. M., Yuan, Y., & Lam, P. K. (2002). Energy expenditure and physical activity of obese children: Cross-sectional study. *Hong Kong Medical Journal, 8,* 313–317.

Z

Zaffanello, M., Maffeis, C., & Zamboni, G. (2005). Multiple positive results during a neonatal screening program. *Journal of Perinatal Medicine, 33,* 246–251.

Zajonc, R. B. (2001). The family dynamics of intellectual development. *American Psychologist, 56,* 523–524.

Zarate, M. E., Bhimji, F., & Reese, L. (2005). Ethnic identity and academic achievement among Latino/a adolescents. *Journal of Latinos & Education, 4,* 95–104.

Zaslow, M. (2004). Childcare for low-income families: Challenges and prospects. In A. C. Crouter & A. Booth (Eds.), *Work-Family challenges for low-income parents and their children.* Mahwah, NJ: Erlbaum.

Zdravkovic, T., Genbacev, O., McMaster, M. T., & Fisher, S. J. (2005). The adverse effects of maternal smoking on the human placenta: A review. *Placenta, 26* (Suppl. A), S81–S86.

Zelazo, P. D., & Muller, U. (2004). Executive function in typical and atypical development. In U. Goswami (Ed.), *Blackwell handbook of cognitive development.* Malden, MA: Blackwell.

Zelazo, P. D., Muller, U., Frey, D., & Marcovitch, S. (2003). The development of executive function in early childhood. *Monographs of the Society for Research in Child Development, 68* (No. 3, Serial No. 274).

Zentall, S. S. (2006). *ADHD and education.* Upper Saddle River, NJ: Prentice Hall.

Zeskind, P. S., Klein, L., & Marshall, T. R. (1992). Adults' perceptions of experimental modifications of educations and expiratory sounds in infant crying. *Developmental Psychology, 28,* 1153–1162.

Zielinksi, D. S., Campa, M. I., & Eckenrode, J. J. (2003, April). *Child maltreatment and the early onset of problem behaviors: A follow-up at 19 years.* Paper presented at the meeting of the Society for Research in Child Development, Tampa.

Zierold, K. M., & Anderson, H. (2004). Trends in blood levels among children enrolled in the Special Supplemental Nutrition Program for Women, Infants, and Children from 1996 to 2000. *American Journal of Public Health, 94,* 1513–1515.

Zigler, E. F. (2002). Looking back 40 years and seeing the person with mental retardation as a whole person. In H. N. Switzky (Ed.), *Personality and motivational differences in persons with mental retardation.* Mahwah, NJ: Erlbaum.

Zigler, E. F., & Styfco, S. J. (1994). Head Start: Criticisms in a constructive context. *American Psychologist, 49,* 127–132.

Zill, N., Loomis, L., & West, J. (1997). *The elementary school performance and adjustment of children who enter kindergarten late or repeat kindergarten.* Washington, DC: National Center for Education Statistics.

Zill, N., Morrison, D. R., & Coiro, M. J. (1993). Long-term effects of parental divorce on parent-child relationships, adjustment, and achievement in young adulthood. *Journal of Family Psychology, 7,* 91–103.

Zimmer-Gembeck, M. J., & Collins, W. A. (2003). Autonomy development during adolescence. In G. Adams & M. Berzonsky (Eds.), *Blackwell handbook of adolescence.* Malden, MA: Blackwell.

Zimmerman, B. J., & Schunk, D. H. (2004). Self-regulating intellectual processes and outcomes: A social cognitive perspective. In D. Y. Dai & R. J. Sternberg (Eds.), *Motivation, emotion, and cognition.* Mahwah, NJ: Erlbaum.

Zimmerman, R. S., Khoury, E., Vega, W. A., Gil, A. G., & Warhelt, G. J. (1995). Teacher and student perceptions of behavior problems among a sample of African American, Hispanic, and non-Hispanic White students. *American Journal of Community Psychology, 23,* 181–197.

Zinn, M. B., & Well, B. (2000). Diversity within Latino families: New lessons for family social science. In D. M. Demo, K. R. Allen, & M. A. Fine (Eds.), *Handbook of family diversity.* New York: Oxford University Press.

Zukow-Goldring, P. (2002). Sibling caregiving. In M. H. Bornstein (Ed.), *Handbook of parenting* (Vol. 3). Mahwah, NJ: Erlbaum.

Photo Credits

Prologue © Bachmann/Photo Network/Grant Heilman

Section Openers

1: © Ariel Skelley/CORBIS; 2: © Petit Format/Nestle/Photo Researchers; 3: Courtesy of Northern Telecom; 4: © Aerial Skelley/CORBIS; 5: © Aerial Skelley/CORBIS; 6: © David Young-Wolff/Stone/Getty Images

Chapter 1

Opener: © Franciso Cruz/Superstock; **p. 6 (top):** © Sygma/CORBIS/; **p. 6 (bottom):** © AP/Wide World Photos; **p. 8:** Courtesy of Luis Vargas; **p. 9:** © National Association for the Education of Young Children/photo © Robert Maust/Photo Agora; **p. 11:** © Nancy Agostini; **p. 13:** Courtesy of Children's Defense Fund, Washington, DC; **1.2:** Photo © Erich Lessing/Art Resource, NY/Painting by A.I>G. Velasquez, *Infanta Margarita Teresa in white garb,* Kunsthistorisches Museum, Vienna, Austria; **p. 17:** © Archives of the History of American Psychology/Louise Bates Ames Gift; **1.5 (Prenatal):** © Dr. Landrum B. Shettles; (Infancy): Courtesy of John Santrock; (Early childhood): © Chromosohm Media/The Image Works; (middle childhood): © CORBIS website; (Adolescence): © James Shaffer; **p. 22:** © PhotoDisc website; **p. 25:** Courtesy of Valerie Pang; **p. 29:** Courtesy of Katherine Duchen Smith, Certified Pediatric Nurse Practicioner, Ft. Collins, Colorado

Chapter 2

Opener: © Ray Stott/The Image Works; **p. 42:** © Bettmann/CORBIS; **p. 45:** © Sarah Putnam/Index Stock; **p. 46:** © Yves DeBraine/Stock Photo; **p. 48:** © Courtesy of A.R. Lauria/Dr. Michael Cole/Laboratory of Human Cognition; **p. 49:** © Bettmann/CORBIS; **p. 50:** © Bettmann/CORBIS; **p. 51:** © Nina Leen/Time/Life Magazine/Getty News Service; **p. 53:** Courtesy of Urie Bronfenbrenner; **2.8 (Freud):** © Bettmann/CORBIS; (Pavlov): © CORBIS; (Piaget): © Yves deBraine/Stock Photo; (Vygotsky): © A.R. Lauria/Dr. Michael Cole, Laboratory of Human Cognition, University of California, San Diego; (Skinner): © Harvard University News Office; (Erikson): © UPI/Bettmann/CORBIS; (Bandura): © Bettmann/CORBIS; (Bronfenbrenner): Courtesy of Urie Bronfenbrenner; **p. 57:** © Richard Nowitz/Photo Researachers; **2.11:** © Sovereign/Phototake; **p. 60:** © Bettmann/CORBIS; **p. 64:** © McGraw-Hill Higher Education, John Thoeming photographer; **p. 67a:** © Kevin Fleming/CORBIS; **p. 67b:** © Ed Honowitz/Stone/Getty Images; **p. 68:** Courtesy of Pamela Trotman Reid

Chapter 3

Opener: © SuperStock; **p. 80:** © Enrico Ferorelli; **3.3:** © Sundstrom/Gamma; **3.4 (left & right):** © Custom Medical Stock Photo; **p. 89:** © Joel Gordon 1989; **p. 90:** © Andrew Eccles/Janet Botaish Group; **p. 91:** Courtesy of Holly Ishmael; **p. 93:** © Jacques Pavlosky/Sygma/CORBIS; **p. 95:** © Sonda Dawes/The Image Works; **p. 97:** © Myrleen Ferguson Cate/Photo Edit

Chapter 4

Opener: © Lennart Nilsson; **p. 108:** © Vol. 15/PhotoDisc; **p. 111 (all):** © Lennart Nilsson; **4.3a:** © Lennart Nilsson; **4.3b&c:** © Petit Format/Nestle/Photo Researchers; **p. 115:** © Charles Grupton/Stock Boston; **p. 116:** © David Young-Wolff/Photo Edit; **p. 119:** Courtesy of Elizabeth Noble; **p. 121:** © Vivianne Moos/CORBIS; **p. 124:** Courtesy of Ann Streissguth; **4.8:** © Will & Deni McIntyre/Photo Researchers **p. 127:** © R.I.A./Gamma; **p. 130:** © Betty Press/Woodfin Camp & Associates; **p. 131:** © Alon Reininger/Contact Press Images

Chapter 5

Opener: © SIU/Peter Arnold, Inc.; **p. 142:** © Charles Gupton; **p. 143:** Courtesy of Rachel Thompson; **p. 144:** M.Shostak/Anthro-Photo; **p. 145:** Courtesy of Linda Pugh; **p. 146:** © Roger Tully/Stone/Getty Images; **p. 147:** © Stephen McBrady/Photo Edit; **p. 149:** © Charles Gupton/Stock Boston; **p. 151:** © Dr. Tiffany Field; **p. 152:** Courtesy of Dr. Susan M. Ludington; **5.5:** © Stephen Marks, Inc./The Image Bank/Getty Images; **p. 155:** © Michael Newman/Photo Edit; **p. 158:** © James G. White

Chapter 6

Opener: © George Disario/The Stock Market/CORBIS; **6.5:** © 1990 Kenneth Jarecke/Contact Press Images; **6.7:** © A. Glauberman/Photo Researchers; **6.8a&b:** Courtesy of Dr. Harry T. Chugani, Children's Hospital of Michigan; **6.9a:** © David Grubin Productions Inc. Reprinted by permission; **6.9b:** Courtesy of Dana Boatman, Ph.D., Department of Neurology, John Hopkins University. Reprinted with permission from *The Secret Life of the Brain,* © 2001 by the National Academy of Sciences, the National Academies Press, Washington, D.C.; **p. 177:** © Tom Rosenthal/SuperStock; **p. 178:** © Vol. DV251 Digital Vision/Getty Images; **p. 179:** © Bob Dammrich/The Image Works; **p. 180:** Courtesy of Dr. T. Berry Brazelton; **p. 182:** Courtesy of The Hawaii Family Support/Healthy Start Program; **p. 183:** Courtesy of Esther Thelen; **6.13 (left):** © Elizabeth Crews/The Image Works; **6.13 (middle):** © James G. White; **6.13 (right):** © Petit Format/Photo Researchers; **6.14 (left & right):** © Karen Adolph, New York University; **p. 189 (top):** Michael Greenlar/The Image Works; **p. 189 (bottom):** © Frank Bailey Studio; **6.16:** Courtesy Amy Needham; **p. 192:** © James Kilkelly; **6.17:** Adapted from "The Origin of Form and Perception" by R.L. Fantz © 1961 by *Scientific American.* Photo © by David Linton; **6.19: (all):** Courtesy of Dr. Charles Nelson; **6.21:** © Enrico Ferorelli; **6.22a:** © Michael Siluk; **6.22b:** © Dr. Melanie J. Spence, University of Texas at Dallas; **6.23:** © Jean Guichard/Sygma/CORBIS; **6.24abc:** D. Rosenstein and R. Oster, "Differential Facial Response to Four Basic Tastes in Newborns" in *Child Development,* Volume 59, pp. 1561–1563. Reprinted with permission of the Society for Research in Child Development

Chapter 7

Opener: © Spencer Grant/Photo Edit; **7.2a&b:** © D. Goodman/Photo Researchers; **7.5:** Courtesy of Carolyn Rovee-Collier; **7.6:** © Enrico Ferorelli; **p. 220:** Courtesy of John Santrock; **p. 222:** © Peter Byron/Photo Researchers; **7.9:** © 2003 University of Washington, Institute for Learning and Brain Sciences (I-LABS); **p. 228:** © Anthony Bannister/Animals Animals/Earth Scenes; **p. 229:** © Tim Davis/CORBIS; **p. 231 (top):** © AFP/CORBIS; **p. 231 (bottom):** From Curtis, Genie:A Psycholinguistic Study of a Modern Day "Wild Child." © 1977 Academic Press reproduced by permission of the publisher; **p. 234:** © John Carter/Photo Researchers

Chapter 8

Opener: © Jamie Marcial/SuperStock; **p. 242:** © Andy Sacks/Stone/Getty Images; **8.2 (all):** © Michael Lewis, Institute for the Study of Child Development; **p. 246:** © Andy Cox/Stone/Getty Images; **p. 249:** © Michael Tcherevkoff/The Image Bank/Getty Images; **p. 250:** © Alan Oddie/Photo Edit; **8.4:** © Myrleen Fergusoncate/Photo Edit; **p. 253:** © Vol. 63 PhotoDisc/Getty Images; **8.5:** © Martin Rogers/Stock Boston; **p. 257 (top):** © Penny Tweedie/Stone/Getty Images; **p. 257 (bottom):** © David Young-Wolff/Photo Edit; **p. 260:** © Comstock, Inc.; **p. 262:** Courtesy of

Rashmi Nakhre, the Hattie Daniels Day Care Center

Chapter 9

Opener: © Tom & Dee Ann McCarthy/CORBIS; **p. 276:** © Bob Daemmrich/The Image Works; **p. 284:** © Eyewire Vol. EP078/Getty Images; **p. 293:** Courtesy of Barbara Deloian; **p. 295:** © AP/Wide World Photos

Chapter 10

Opener: © Ariel Skelley/The Stock Market/CORBIS; **p. 302:** From 'Open Window'; © 1994 Municipality of Reggio Emilia; Infant-toddler Centers and Preschools; Published by Reggio Children; **10.3:** © Paul Fusco/Magnum Photos; **p. 307 (top):** © James Wertsch/Washington University at St. Louis; **p. 307 (bottom):** Courtesy of Barbara Rogoff; **10.5:** © Bob Daemmrich/The Image Works; **10.6 (left):** © A.R. Lauria/Dr. Michael Cole, Laboratory of Human Cognition, University of California, San Diego; **10.6 (right):** © Bettmann/CORBIS; **p. 312:** © 1999 James Kamp; **p. 314:** © Nita Winter; **p. 316:** © Rosanne Olson/Stone/Getty Images; **10.12:** © Ken Fisher/Stone/Getty Images; **p. 324:** Courtesy of Yolanda Garcia; **p. 325:** © Robert Wallis/SIPA Press/Newsweek, April 17, 1989; **p. 327:** © Ronnie Kaufman/The Stock Market/CORBIS

Chapter 11

Opener: © R. Hermine Dreyfuss; **11.1:** © Michael Lewis, Institute for the Study of Child Development; **p. 341:** Copyright © 2002/Visionsof America.com; **11.6:** © Peter Correz/Stone/Getty Images; **p. 358:** D. Botkin (2000). Family play therapy: A creative approach to including young children in family therapy. *Journal of Systematic Therapies*, 19, 30-41; **p. 359:** © Christopher Arnesen/Stone/Getty Images; **p. 364:** © Karen Kasmauski/Woodfin Camp & Associates; **p. 367:** © Richard Hutchings/Photo Edit; **p. 368:** © Bryan F. Peterson

Chapter 12

Opener: © Michael Pole/The Stock Market/CORBIS; **p. 388:** © Ariel Skelley/The Stock Market/CORBIS; **12.4:** © AP/Wide World Photos; **p. 395:** Courtesy of Sharon McLeod; **p. 397:** © Will & Deni McIntyre/Photo Researchers; **p. 400:** © David Young-Wolff/Photo Edit; **p. 401:** Courtesy of Charla Peltier; **p. 403:** Used by permission of Don Johnston Inc. **p. 406:** © Richard Hutchings/Photo Researchers

Chapter 13

Opener: © Gabe Palmer/CORBIS; **p. 414:** © P. West/San Jose Mercury News/Sygma/CORBIS; **p. 417:** © Archives Jean Piaget, Universite De Geneve, Switzerland; **p. 418:** © M & E Bernheim/Woodfin Camp & Associates; **p. 423:** © Will Hart/Photo Edit; **p. 429:** © Joe McNally; **p. 437:** © Jill Cannefax; **p. 438:** © Koichi Kamashida/Getty News Service; **p. 439:** Courtesy of Sterling Jones; **p. 443:** © Eiji Miyazawa/Stock Photo; **p. 448:** Courtesy of Salvador Tamayo

Chapter 14

Opener: © Rolf Bruderer/CORBIS; **p. 462:** © AFP/CORBIS; **p. 467:** © Keith Carter; **p. 472:** © Catherine Gehm; **p. 476:** © Michael Newman/Photo Edit; **p. 478:** © S. Gazin/The Image Works; **p. 480:** © Jiang Jin/SuperStock website; **p. 487 (top):** © Lonnie Harp; **p. 487 (bottom):** © Bruce Ayres/Stone/Getty Images; **p. 488:** © John S. Abbott

Chapter 15

Opener: © Mug Shots/The Stock Market/CORBIS; **p. 500:** © M. Regine/The Image Bank/Getty Images; **p. 504:** © Mary Kate Denny/Photo Edit; **p. 506:** Courtesy of Anne Peterson, W.K. Kellogg Foundation; **p. 509:** © Joel Gordon 1995; **p. 512:** © Lawrence Migdale/Stock Boston; **p. 513:** © Marilyn Humphries; **p. 518:** © 1998 Frank Fournier; **p. 525:** © Tony Freeman/Photo Edit; **p. 527:** © Rob Lewine/The Stock Market/CORBIS

Chapter 16

Opener: © Vol. RFCD697/CORBIS; **p. 540:** © David Young-Wolff/Photo Edit; **p. 541:** © Stewart Cohen/Stone/Getty Images; **p. 544:** Courtesy of Laura Bickford; **p. 545:** © Susan Lapides 2003; **p. 546:** © Penny Tweedie/Stone/Getty Images; **p. 551:** © Stone/Getty Images; **p. 553:** © Marc Antman/The Image Works; **p. 555:** © Fujifots/The Image Works; **p. 556:** Courtesy of I Have a Dream-Houston, Houston, TX; **p. 559:** © Bill Stanton; **p. 561:** Courtesy of Dr. Armando Ronquillo; **p. 563:** © Richard Anderson

Chapter 17

Opener: © George Disario/The Stock Market/CORBIS; **p. 576 (top):** © USA Today Library, photo by Robert Deutsch; **p. 576 (bottom):** Courtesy of Margaret Beale Spencer; **17.4:** © Spencer Grant/Photo Edit; **p. 581:** © Tony Freeman/Photo Edit; **p. 583:** ©AP/Wide World Photos; **p. 585:** © Tessa Codrington/Stone /Getty Images; **p. 586:** © David DeLossy/The Image Bank/Getty Images; **p. 589:** © Daniel Laine; **p. 590:** © USA Today Library, photo by H. Darr Beiser; **p. 591:** Courtesy of Carola Suarez-Orozco and photographer Kris Snibble/Harvard News Office, © President and Fellows of Harvard College; **p. 592:** Courtesy of El Puente Academy; **p. 596:** © Charlie Neuman/SDUT/Zuma; **p. 597:** Courtesy of Rodney Hammond, National Center for Injury Prevention and Control, CDCP; **p. 598:** © Jim Smith/Photo Researchers

Text and Line Art Credits

Prologue, p. 3 "If I Had My Child to Raise Over Again," from the book *100 Ways to Build Self-Esteem and Teach Values*. Copyright © 1994, 2003 by Diane Loomans. Reprinted with permission of H. J. Kramer/New World Library, Novato, CA. www.newworldlibrary.com.

Chapter 2

Figure 2.7 From C. B. Kopp and J. B. Krakow, *The Child,* © 1982. Reprinted by permission of Pearson Education, Inc. **Figure 2.10:** From

Crowley, et al, 2002, "Parents Explains More to Boys than Girls During Shared Scientific Thinking," *Psychological Science,* Vol. 12, pp. 258–261. Reprinted with permission of Blackwell Publishing.

Chapter 3

Figure 3.1: From John T. Bonner, *The Evolution of Culture in Animals.* © 1980 Princeton University Press. Reprinted by permission of Princeton University Press. **Figure 3.8:** Centers for Disease Control and Prevention, 2000, Figure 26, CDC website, Reproductive Health: Assisted Reproductive Technology Success Rates. Atlanta. **Figure 3.9:** From Golombok et al., "The Test Tube Generation," *Child Development* 72, pp. 599–605. Reprinted with permission from the Society for Research in Child Development. **Text p. 96** Selections based on D. M. Brozkinsky and E. Pinderhughes (2002). "Parenting and Child Development in Adoptive Families." In M. Bornstein (ed.) *Handbook of Parenting* 2/e, Vol. 1, pp. 280–282 and pp. 288–292. Reprinted with permission of Lawrence Erlbaum Associates, Inc.

Chapter 4

Figure 4.1: From Charles Carroll and Dean Miller, *Health: The Science of Human Adaptation,* 5th edition. Copyright © The McGraw-Hill Companies. Reprinted by permission. **Figure 4.3:** Reprinted from *Pregnancy, Childbirth, and the Newborn* with permission from Meadowbrook Press. © 1984 by Childbirth Education Association of Seattle. **Figure 4.5:** Data from Food and Nutrition Board, "Recommended Nutrient Increases for Adult Pregnancy," National Academy of Sciences, Washington, D.C. **Text pp. 118–119** S. B. Olds, M. L. London, P. Ladewig. *Maternal Newborn Nursing,* 4th edition, © 1992. Adapted by permission of Pearson Education, Inc. Upper Saddle River, NJ. **Figure 4.6:** Adapted from data presented by MacDorman and others, 2002. Annual Summary of Vital Satistics-2001. *Pediatrics,* 10, pp. 1037–1052. **Figure 4.7:** Reprinted from *The Developing Human: Clinically Oriented Embryology* 4/e, K. L. Moore. Copyright © 1988 with permission from Elsevier. **Figure 4.8:** Art from Quennan and Quennan, *New Life: Pregnancy, Birth and Your Child's First Year.* Copyright © 1986 Marshall Cavendish, Ltd., London, England Reprinted by permission. **Figure 4.9:** National Institute on Drug Abuse.

Chapter 5

Text p. 140: From Pamela Warrick, "The Fantastic Voyage of Tanner Roberts," *Los Angeles Times,* March 1, 1992, pp. E1, E11, E12. Copyright © 1992 Tribune Media Services. Reprinted with permission. **Figure 5.2:** Data by the National Center for Health Statistics, 2004. **Figure 5.5:** From Virginia Apgar, 1975, "A Proposal for a New Method of Evaluation of a Newborn Infant," *Anesthesia and Analgesia,* Vol. 32, pp. 260–257. Reprinted with permission of Lippincott Williams & Wilkins. **Figure 5.6:** From *Cultural Perspectives on Child Development* by Daniel A. Wagner and Harold W. Stevenson.

Chapter 6

Figure 6.4: From Huttenlocher and Dabholkar, "Regional Differences in the Synaptogenesis in the Human Cerebral Cortex," *Journal of Comparative Neurology,* 387 (2), 1997, pp. 167–168. Copyright © 1997 John Wiley & Sons, Inc. Reprinted with permission of John Wiley & Sons, Inc. Electronic rights are with permission by Wiley-Liss, Inc. A Wiley company. **Figure 6.15:** Reprinted from *Journal of Pediatrics,* Vol. 71, W. K. Frankenburg and J. B. Dobbs, "The Denver Development Screening Test," pp. 181–191. Copyright © 1967, with permission from Elsevier. **Figure 6.17:** Art adapted from "The Origin of Form Perception" by R. L. Frantz. Copyright © 1961 by Scientific American, Inc. **Figure 6.18:** From A. Slater, V. Morison, and M. Somers, 1988, "Orientation Discrimination and Cortical Functions in the Human Newborn," *Perception,* Vol. 17. Reprinted with permission of Pion Limited, a UK Registered Company.

Chapter 7

Text p. 208: From Jean Piaget, *The Origins of Intelligence in the Child,* 1952. Extracts from pp. 27, 159, 225, 273, and 339. Used with permission by Taylor & Francis and International Universities Press. **Figure 7.3:** From R. Ballargeon and J. De-Vos, 1991, "Object Permanence in Young Children: Further Evidence," *Child Development,* 62, 1227–1246. Reprinted with permission from the Society for Research in Child Development. **Figure 7.4:** From Renee Ballargeon, 1994, "How Infants Learn About the Physical World," *Current Directions in Psychological Science,* Vol. 3, 133–139. With permission from Blackwell Publishing. **Figure 7.7:** From Craig T. Ramey, Frances A. Campbell and Clancy Blair, Figure 6.7, "Retained in Grade by Age Fifteen, Abecedarian Project. In *An American Dilemma Revisited: Race Relations in a Changing World.* © Russell Sage Foundation, 112 East 64th Street, New York, NY 10021. Reprinted with permission. **Figure 7.8:** From S.L. Haight, Language Overview, 2002. Reprinted with permission of Sherrel Lee Haight. **Figure 7.10:** From L. Bloom, Language Acquisition in Development Context, in W. Damon (ed.) *Handbook of Child Psychology,* 1998. Copyright © 1998 John Wiley & Sons, Inc. Reprinted with permission of John Wiley & Sons, Inc. **Figure 7.12:** From *Brain, Mind, and Behavior,* 3/e by Floyd Bloom, et al. © 1985, 1988, 2001 by Educational Broadcasting Corp. Used with permission of Worth Publishers. **Figure 7.13:** Adapted from J. Huttenlocher et al., "Early Vocabulary Growth: Relation to Language Input and Gender," *Developmental Psychology* 27, 1991, pp. 236–248. **Figure 7.14:** From B. Hart and T. R. Risley (1995). *Meaningful Differences in the Everyday Experience of Young American Children,* pp. 234–235. Baltimore: Paul H. Brookes Publishing Co. Reprinted by permission.

Chapter 8

Figure 8.6: From van IJzendoom and Kroonenberg, 1986, "Cross-Cultural Patterns of Attachment," *Child Development,* 59, 147–156. Reprinted with permission from the Society for Research in Child Development.

Chapter 9

Figure 9.1: CDC Growth Charts 2000, U.S. Government Center for Disease Control and Prevention, Atlanta, GA. **Figure 9.2:** Figure 10.6 from *Human Biology and Ecology* by Albert Damon. Copyright © 1977 by W. W. Norton & Company, Inc. Used by permission of W. W. Norton & Company, Inc. **Figure 9.4:** Data from C. J. Schiner (ed.), *Performance Objectives for Preschool Children,* Adapt Press, Sioux Falls, SD. 1974. **Figure 9.5:** Data from C. J. Schiner (ed.), *Performance Objectives for Preschool Children,* Adapt Press, Sioux Falls, SD. 1974. **Figure 9.7:** Food and Nutrition Board. **Figure 9.8:** From Virginia DeMoss, "Good, the Bad, and the Edible," *Runner's World,* June 1980. Copyright © Virginia DeMoss. Reprinted by permission. **Figure 9.9:** National Vital Statistics Report (2001). National Center for Health, Statistics, Center for Disease Control and Prevention. Atlanta. **Figure 9.10:** From Sleet and Mercy, "Promotion of Safety, Security and Well-Being." In M. H. Bornstein et al. (eds.), *Well-Being: Positive Development,* 2003. Reprinted with permission of Lawrence Erlbaum Associates, Inc. **Figure 9.11:** Data presented by UNICEF (2003). The State of the World's Children, Table 9.

Chapter 10

Figure 10.1: Courtesy of D. Wolf and J. Nove. **Figure 10.7:** Reprinted from *Journal of Experimental Child Psychology,* Vol. 6, E. Vorpillot, "The Development of Scanning Strategies," pp. 632–650. Copyright © 1968, with permission from Elsevier. **Figure 10.8:** From Dempster, "Memory Span," *Psychological Bulletin,* Vol. 80, pp. 63–100. Copyright © 1981 by the American Psychological Association. Adapted with permission. **Figure 10.9:** From John Santrock, *Life Span Development* 10th edition. Copyright © The McGraw-Hill Companies. Reprinted by permission of The McGraw-Hill Companies. **Figure 10.10:** From John Santrock, *Life Span Development* 10th edition. Copyright © The McGraw-Hill Companies. Reprinted by permission of The McGraw-Hill Companies. **Figure 10.11:** From J. Berko, "The Child's Learning of English Morphology," in *Word* 14:361. Copyright © 1958 International Linguistic Association, New York, NY. Reprinted by permission. **Figure 10.12:** Text from Position Statement on Developmentally Appropriate Practice in Programs for 4- and 5-year-olds. *Young Children,* 41: 23-27. Copyright © 1986 by the National Association for the Education of young Children. Reprinted by permission. www.naeyc.org/about/positions/pdf/PSDAP98.RDF. **Figure 10.13:** From National Association for the Education of young Children and National Council of Teachers of Mathematics, 2003 "Learning Paths and Teaching Strategies in Early Mathematics." From Early Childhood Mathematics: Promoting Good Beginnings: A Joint Position Statement, *Young Children* 58 (1), pp. 41–44. Reprinted with permission.

Chapter 11

Text pp. 344–345: Selection from R. A. Lippa (2002). *Gender, Nature and Nurture,* pp. 103–105. Reprinted with permission of Lawrence Erlbaum Associates, Inc. **Figure 11.7:** From K. Curran, J. DuCette, J. Eisenstein, and I. A. Hyman, "Statistical Analysis of the Cross-Cultural Data: The Third Year," paper presented at the meeting of the American Psychological Association, San Francisco, Calif., August 2001. Reprinted with permission of Joseph DuCette. **Figure 11.8:** Bureau of the Census. **Figure 11.10:** From D. Robitallie and R. Gardner, The IDEA Study of Mathematics II: Contexts and Outcomes of School Mathematics.

Chapter 12

Figure 12.1: Reprinted from *Nelson Textbook of Pediatrics,* R. E. Behman and V. C. Vaughan (eds.). Copyright © 1987, with permission from Elsevier. **Figure 12.2:** From B. J. Cratty, *Perceptual and Motor Development in Infants and Young Children.* Prentice Hall, Inc. Englewood Cliffs, NJ. Reprinted by permission of Pearson Education, Inc.; and from *Essentials of Pediatric Nursing,* 3/d, L. F. Whaley and D. L. Wong. Copyright © 1988, with permission from Elsevier. **Figure 12.3:** Data presented by Health Management Resources 2001. *Child Health and Times.* Boston: Health Management Resources. **Text p. 389** from Parents' *Guide to Girls' Sports.* Reprinted by permission from The Women's Sports Foundation. **Figure 12.6:** U.S. Department of Education, Office of Special Education Programs.

Chapter 13

Figure 13.1: From John Santrock, *Life Span Development,* 10th edition. Copyright © The McGraw-Hill Companies. Reprinted by permission of The McGraw-Hill Companies. **Figure 13.2:** From M. H. H. Chu, "Knowledge Structures and Memory Development," in R. S. Siegler (ed.), *Children's Thinking: What Develops?* 1978. Reprinted with permission of Lawrence Erlbaum Associates, Inc. and R. S. Siegler. **Figure 13.3:** Reprinted from *Contemporary Educational Psychology,* Vol. 4, Pressley, Levin & McCormick, "Young Children's Learning of a Foreign Language Vocabulary," pp. 22–29. Copyright © 1980 with permission from Elsevier. **Figure 13.4:** Reprinted from *Journal of Experimental Child Psychology,* Vol. 43, M. Pressley, T. Cariligia-Bull, S. Dean, & W. Schneider, "Short-Term Memory, Verbal Competence, and Age as Predictors of Imagery Instructional Effectiveness," pp. 194-211. Copyright © 1987, with permission from Elsevier. **Figure 13.8:** From *Handbook of Intelligence* by Robert J. Sternberg, ed., Cambridge University Press. Used with permission. **Figure**

SANTROCK

CHILDREN, Ninth Edition

STUDENT TEXTBOOK SURVEY

INSTRUCTIONS FOR SENDING IN YOUR RESPONSE BY MAIL:

Please fill out this survey, detach, affix stamp and drop in the mail. Your comments will help John Santrock and McGraw-Hill improve this textbook in future editions.

... OR, YOU MAY SEND IN YOUR SURVEY REPONSE _ONLINE_ AT: *www.mhhe.com/santrockc9*

Thank you for your participation!

← REMOVE TOP PORTION BEFORE SENDING →

SANTROCK

CHILDREN, Ninth Edition

STUDENT TEXTBOOK SURVEY

NAME: _____   SCHOOL: _____

COURSE TITLE: _____   TEXT(Author/Title): Santrock/Children, 9/e

1. How is the book assigned for use in this course?

   ❑ required primarily for reading material

   ❑ required primarily for homework

   ❑ required for both reading and homework

2. a) To what extent would you say using the text contributes to your getting a good grade in the course?

   ❑ little or no extent   ❑ moderate extent   ❑ high extent

   b) How extensively do you actually use your text?

   ❑ don't use   ❑ use only as assigned   ❑ use extensively, even more than what is assigned

3. What study aids have you found within textbooks to be particularly useful?

   _____
   _____
   _____

4. What comes to mind as being particularly good about your book?

   _____
   _____
   _____
   _____
   _____

5. Where do you feel improvements could be made?

   _____
   _____
   _____
   _____
   _____

6. Do you have any other comments?

   _____
   _____
   _____

7. May we quote you?   ❑ yes   ❑ no

TEAR OFF CARD ALONG PERFORATION

The McGraw-Hill Companies

McGraw-Hill Higher Education

1333 Burr Ridge Parkway

Burr Ridge, Illinois 60527

Attn: Melissa Caughlin